CAN

ULYSSES
TRAVEL PUBLICATIONS
Travel better... enjoy more

Editorial *Series Director:* Claude Morneau; *Project Supervisor:* Pascale Couture; *Editors:* Claude Morneau, Jennifer McMorran.

Research *Authors:* Atlantic Canada (Benoit Prieur), Québec (François Rémillard, Gabriel Audet, Caroline Béliveau, Daniel Desjardins, Stéphane G.-Marceau, Judith Lefebvre, Claude Morneau, Yves Ouellet, Joël Pomerleau, Yves Séguin), Ontario (Pascale Couture), Toronto (Jennifer McMorran, Alain Rondeau), Manitoba and Saskatchewan (Paul Karr), Alberta (Jennifer McMorran), Rocky Mountains (Lorette Pierson), British Columbia (Pierre Longnus, Paul-Éric Dumontier, François Rémillard), Yukon (François Brodeur, Pierre Longnus), Northwest Territories (Lorette Pierson), Portrait (François Brodeur, Benoit Prieur, JenniferMcMorran, Alain Rondeau); *Contributors*: Alain Legault, Francis Plourde, Pascale Tremblay, Virginie Bonneau, Christian Roy.

Production *Design:* Patrick Farei (Atoll Direction); *English Editing;* Jennifer McMorran, Tara Salman; *Translation:* Tracy Kendrick, Sarah Kresh, Danielle Gauthier, Emmy Pahmer, Tara Salman; *Cartography:* André Duchesne, Patrick Thivierge (Assistant); *Layout:* Tara Salman, Christian Roy, Stéphane Marceau, Isabelle Lalonde.

Illustrations *Cover Photo:* Steve Vidler (Superstock); *Interior Photos:* Tibor Bognar, Pierre Longnus, Roger Michel, Walter Bibikow, Sean O'Neill; *Chapter Headings:* Jennifer McMorran; *Drawings:* Lorette Pierson.

Thanks to SODEC and the Department of Canadian Heritage for their financial support.

Distributors

AUSTRALIA:
Little Hills Press
11/37-43 Alexander St.
Crows Nest NSW 2065
☎ (612) 437-6995
Fax: (612) 438-5762

BELGIUM AND LUXEMBOURG:
Vander
Vrijwilligerlaan 321
B-1150 Brussel
☎ (02) 762 98 04
Fax: (02) 762 06 62

CANADA:
Ulysses Books & Maps
4176 Saint-Denis
Montréal, Québec
H2W 2M5
☎ (514) 843-9882, ext.2232
or 1-800-748-9171
Fax: 514-843-9448
www.ulysse.ca

GERMANY AND AUSTRIA:
Brettschneider
Fernreisebedarf
Feldfirchner Strasse 2
D-85551 Heimstetten
München
☎ 89-99 02 03 30
Fax: 89-99 02 03 31

GREAT BRITAIN AND
IRELAND:
World Leisure Marketing
9 Downing Road
West Meadows, Derby
UK DE21 6HA
☎ 1 332 34 33 32
Fax: 1 332 34 04 64

ITALY:
Centro Cartografico del Riccio
Via di Soffiano 164/A
50143 Firenze
☎ (055) 71 33 33
Fax: (055) 71 63 50

NETHERLANDS:
Nilsson & Lamm
Pampuslaan 212-214
1380 AD Weesp (NL)
☎ 0294-465044
Fax: 0294-415054
E-mail: nilam@euronet.nl

PORTUGAL:
Dinapress
Lg. Dr. Antonio de Sousa de Macedo, 2
Lisboa 1200
☎ (1) 395 52 70
Fax: (1) 395 03 90

SCANDINAVIA:
Scanvik
Esplanaden 8B
1263 Copenhagen K
DK
☎ (45) 33.12.77.66
Fax: (45) 33.91.28.82

SPAIN:
Altaïr
Balmes 69
E-08007 Barcelona
☎ 454 29 66
Fax: 451 25 59
E-mail: altair@globalcom.es

SWITZERLAND:
OLF
P.O. Box 1061
CH-1701 Fribourg
☎ (026) 467.51.11
Fax: (026) 467.54.66

U.S.A.:
The Globe Pequot Press
6 Business Park Road
P.O. Box 833
Old Saybrook, CT 06475
☎ 1-800-243-0495
Fax: 1-800-820-2329
E-mail: sales@globe-pequot.com

Other countries, contact Ulysses Books & Maps (Montréal), Fax: (514) 843-9448

No part of this publication may be reproduced in any form or by any means, including photocopying, without the written permission of the publisher.

Canadian Cataloguing in Publication Data

Canadian Cataloguing in Publication
Main entry under title:
    Canada
    (Ulysses travel guides)
    Also issued in French under title: Canada
    Includes index.
    ISBN 2-89464-159-1
    1. Canada - Guidebooks. I. Series
FC38.C23 1998   917.104'648   C97-941454-7
F1009.C23 1998

© May 1998, Ulysses Travel Publications. All rights reserved
ISBN 2-89464-159-1
Printed in Canada

"In summer we staggered out of the boiling city; the landscape closed around us; we sank into it like peasants into a feather bed... And in winter the same valleys that had sucked us in tightened below our feet into fold upon fold of snow..."

Patrick Anderson, *Search Me*, 1957

TABLE OF CONTENTS

Help make Ulysses Travel Guides even better!

The information contained in this guide was correct at press time. However, mistakes can slip in, omissions are always possible, places can disappear, etc. The authors and publisher hereby disclaim any liability for loss or damage resulting from omissions or errors.

We value your comments, corrections and suggestions, as they allow us to keep each guide up to date. The best contributions will be rewarded with a free book from Ulysses Travel Publications. All you have to do is write us at the following address and indicate which title you would be interested in receiving (see the list at the end of guide).

Ulysses Travel Publications
4176 Rue Saint-Denis
Montréal, Québec
Canada H2W 2M5
www.ulysse.ca
E-mail: guiduly@ulysse.ca

LIST OF MAPS

Map Symbols

🛈	Tourist Information (Permanent)	▲	Mountain
?	Tourist Information (Seasonal)	△	Glacier
?	Tourist Information	◐	Beach
🚢	Car Ferry	🏌	Golf Course
🚤	Ferry	⛷	Downhill Ski Centre
🚌	Bus Station	🏝	Ulysses Travel Bookshop
🚉	Train Station	P	Parking Lot
✈	Airport	✝	Church
Ⓜ	Metro Station (Montréal)	H	Hospital

TABLE OF SYMBOLS

☎	Telephone number
⇄	Fax number
≡	Air conditioning
⊗	Ceiling fan
≈	Pool
ℜ	Restaurant
⊛	Whirlpool
ℝ	Refrigerator
K	Kitchenette
⌂	Sauna
#	Screen
☺	Exercise room
♿	Handicapped-accessible rooms
P	Parking
tv	Colour television
fb	Full-board (lodging + 3 meals)
½b	Half-board (lodging + 2 meals)
pb	Private bathroom
sb	Shared bathroom
ps	Private shower
hw	Hot water
½b	half-board (lodging + 2 meals)
bkfst	Breakfast

ATTRACTION CLASSIFICATION

★	Interesting
★★	Worth a visit
★★★	Not to be missed

HOTEL CLASSIFICATION

The prices in the guide are for one room in the high season, double occupancy, not including taxes.

RESTAURANT CLASSIFICATION

$	$10 or less
$$	$10 to $20
$$$	$20 to $30
$$$$	$30 or more

The prices in the guide are for a meal for one person, not including taxes, drinks or tip.

All prices in this guide are in Canadian dollars.

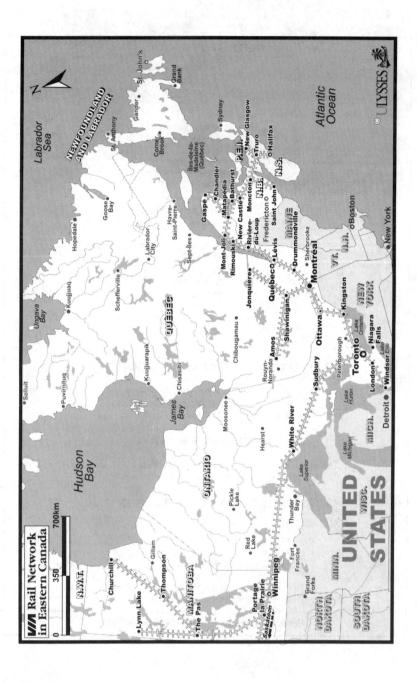

VIA Rail Network in Eastern Canada

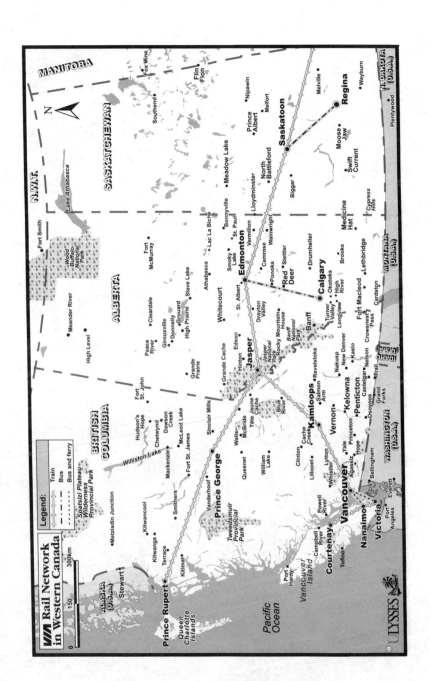

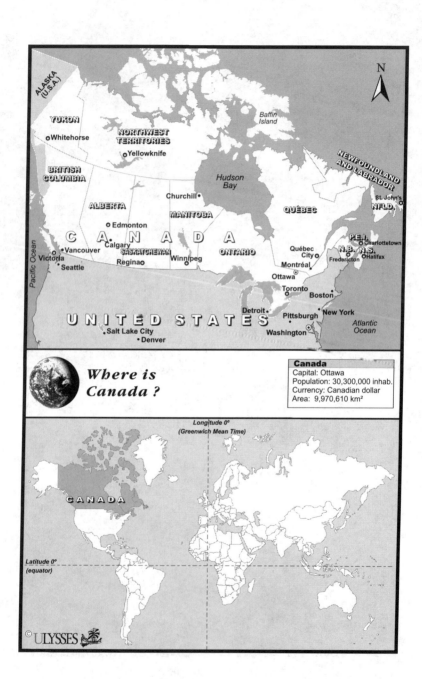

Where is Canada ?

Canada
Capital: Ottawa
Population: 30,300,000 inhab.
Currency: Canadian dollar
Area: 9,970,610 km²

© ULYSSES

PORTRAIT

How to describe Canada? It's simply too vast to be characterized by any one cliché, except maybe the one regarding winter. Canadians themselves subdivide their country in different ways. For some there are simply two large regions: Eastern Canada and Western Canada, or even French and English, while for others the question is much more complicated. There is Atlantic Canada, which includes the three maritime provinces (Nova Scotia, New Brunswick and Prince Edward Island) and the province of Newfoundland and Labrador; then Québec and Ontario, which stand alone, the latter occasionally being referred to (perhaps tongue-in-cheek) as the centre of Canada; next, Manitoba and Saskatchewan are called prairie provinces, despite the fact that fifty per cent of both provinces is forested; Alberta is also considered a prairie province, though from a touristic point of view, its mighty Rocky Mountains imply a stronger connection to its neighbour to the west, British Columbia, and these two provinces are often grouped together as Western Canada; finally, there are the Yukon and Northwest Territories, which occupy a vast northern region extending from east to west above the 60th parallel. To simply say there is an East and a West is to deny that each of these areas has its own history, economy and demographic composition. As for a common identity, some will argue there is no such thing, that Canada hasn't had time to develop one. The framework for the first Canadian constitution was only laid out in 1867 and the country's current borders have existed as such for less than 50 years ago. Perhaps this multiplicity is what defines and strengthens Canada.

It is not surprising that Canadians have difficulty defining themselves collectively. Most of the time they do it by differentiation. They'll tell you that they're not Americans, pointing out that they live in a society where the State plays an important social role, priding themselves with the fact that they are nicer, more polite and more considerate and that their country is safer. Also, the 'melting pot' concept promoted in the United States isn't used as a model here; multiculturalism has become one of the ideologies on which Canadian society is being built. But whether English-speaking or French-Speaking, Canadians work, construct and consume in much the same way as is done throughout North America.

Regardless of how Canadians respond to the questions of their existence, it's almost certain that they will continue to live in a free and peaceful democracy. And how could it be otherwise? The Canadian substratum is rich, the earth is fertile and the climate is just harsh enough to remind people that it is a waste of energy not to live in peace. On top of that, Canada has something precious that is missing elsewhere and that can give life to an idea, build a different future or simply be admired: space.

GEOGRAPHY

A bit bigger than the United States, Canada is thirteen times the size of France and the United Kingdom. It occupies the whole northern part of North America, with the exception of Alaska, and spans five and a half time zones. To the north the Arctic Ocean is the only boundary. Greenland lies to the northeast. To the east and west, the Atlantic Ocean and Pacific Ocean, respectively, put several thousand kilometres between Canada and its neighbours, except for the tiny French islands of St-Pierre and Miquelon located between Nova Scotia and Newfoundland. Finally the United States lie across all of Canada's land-based borders. This is actually the world's longest undefended border.

The most striking thing about Canada when looking at a map is that there's water everywhere. A large part of the world's fresh water supply flows across this land or is stored in the form of ice. Some huge bodies of water stand out, such as Great Slave Lake, Bear Lake, Lakes Superior, Erie, Huron and Ontario, and the reservoirs in the Quebec mid-north. Rivers are also abundant.

The country is a lot hillier in the western region where three mountain chains running north-south succeed each other. The highest peak in Canada, Mount Logan, whose summit reaches an altitude of 6,054 metres, is here. East of these mountains, great plains stretch across Alberta, Saskatchewan and Manitoba, as well as in the continental part of the Northwest Territories to the Canadian Shield. From north to south, these flatlands go from tundra to boreal forest to the prairies which are mainly consecrated to grain farming. The prairies have given Canada a reputation for being the world's bread basket.

Northern Ontario and Québec are part of the same geological formation, the Canadian Shield. This undulating terrain is the last vestige of what was, during the Precambrian period, an imposing mountain massif. There are major metal deposits here. This area is also dominated by tundra and boreal forest. The Québec peninsula becomes more hilly toward the Atlantic Ocean and the Gulf of St. Lawrence. The coast is a succession of, sometimes very impressive, fjords and cliffs. Southern Ontario borders the Great Lakes. This is the most highly populated region of Canada; it includes Toronto, the biggest city in Canada and the fourth biggest in North America by population.

The St. Lawrence River originates from the Great Lakes, quickly enters into Québec territory, surrounds the island of Montréal, and flows below the walls of Québec City before widening into the gulf. The St. Lawrence is one of the continent's main points of entry and remains the main focus of Québec's history, population and economy. In the late 1950s, channels and locks opened up the Great Lakes to ocean traffic, thousands of kilometres from the coast. Southern Ontario and the St. Lawrence Valley offer rich soil and a slightly milder climate favouring agriculture. Along the Atlantic coast, originating in the southern U.S., the Appalachians shape the landscape of southern Quebec. These mountains aren't very high, especially in western Québec.

To the east, beyond the Appalachians, New Brunswick, Prince Edward Island and Nova Scotia along with Newfoundland and Labrador make up the Atlantic provinces. Fishing, sea traffic, farming and forestry have characterized their economies for a long time. For centuries, the shallow waters of the Grand Banks have been an ideal habitat for bottom feeders, at least until overfishing decimated cod stocks and led to the collapse of the fishery in the early nineties. This is possibly the worst ecological disaster to have occurred in Canada and the country is still lost in conjectures about what became of the Grand Banks.

Finally, way in the north, large islands form a triangle-shaped archipegalo, a paradise for arctic explorers in search of a challenge. The magnetic North Pole is found here and, by logical conclusion so is Santa Claus. This distinguished guest has no neighbours except for the odd military base "occupying" the territory.

The Canadian climate gets more and more harsh the further you are from the temperate south. With respect to climate, the eastern part of the country is quite similar to Scandinavia except for the southernmost regions, where the climate resembles that of Poland or Slovakia. The Pacific coast enjoys the warmest temperatures, comparable to the weather in England, with just as much rain...

Climate is the primary factor in agriculture, which in turn affects how Canada is populated. So it's not surprising that the vast majority of

Canada's 30,300,000 inhabitants live less than 300 kilometres from the country's southern border. Microclimates, native settlement, the exploitation of natural resources and concerted efforts to colonize regions have nonetheless led to the creation of pockets of populated areas in the north.

The Provinces and Territories

Canada is a federation divided into 10 provinces not including the vast northern regions above the 60th parallel. The great Canadian North is divided into territories under the tutelage of the federal government. Presently there are two: Yukon and the Northwest Territories. Unfortunately, neither of these territories has an international airport which makes access more difficult.

The last province to enter into Canadian confederation was **Newfoundland and Labrador**. The majority of its 563,000 inhabitants live around the perimeter of a large island, called Newfoundland or "The Rock", in the Gulf of St. Lawrence. The capital, St. John's, overlooks the Atlantic. Labrador, the provincial territory extending from the Quebec peninsula, including the whole eastern border, was granted to Newfoundland after lengthy proceedings pitting the two British colonies against each other. Newfoundland has for a long time been the poorest of Canada's provinces, its main resources coming from the sea. Significant petroleum discoveries off its coast bring hopes of better days to come. In order to exploit these resources, a consortium has just started operating the biggest petroleum platform in the world, Hibernia.

The smallest Canadian province is an island in the Gulf of St. Lawrence, between Québec, New Brunswick and Nova Scotia. **Prince Edward Island** has only 137,000 residents. Charlottetown is its capital. The island has always relied on fishing, agriculture (primarily potatoes) and tourism, its beaches are among the most beautiful in Canada. Nineteen-ninety-seven was a memorable year for islanders: it is the year the Confederation Bridge, linking the island to the mainland, was opened.

Nova Scotia is linked to the continent by a narrow strip of land, the Chignecto Isthmus. Its shores are washed by waters from the Gulf of St. Lawrence, the Atlantic and the Bay of Fundy. North of the peninsula, Cape Breton Island completes the province's territory. This was the first place in North America settled by Europeans, namely the French, who baptised it Acadia. Acadians were later deported by the English who then settled the area and built Halifax, the provincial capital and one of Canada's busiest ports. Some Acadians stayed in Nova Scotia or returned; they remain a small minority in the overall population of 948,000. The sea is omnipresent in Nova Scotia. Other resources are agriculture, forestry and coal mining.

Over 762,000 people live in **New Brunswick**, Canada's only officially bilingual province. One third of the population is French-speaking, they are Acadians with their unique accent, their own flag and a history that is distinct from that of the French population in the rest of Canada. Fishing, farming and forestry have for a long time fed, however meagrely, the New Brunswick economy. It was one of the main beneficiaries, along with Newfoundland, of wealth redistribution programs instituted by the federal government. The situation is changing, however. New Brunswick's government resolved to improve public finances here long before this became common practice in the rest of Canada. The provincial government also conducted an aggressive campaign to attract leading businesses, especially in the telecommunications sector.

Québec is unique in Canada. It's vast territory is three times the size of France and yet it has a population of only 7,420,000. Its French-speaking majority distinguishes it not only from the rest of Canada but all of North America as well. The use of French has been legislated in order to counteract the assimilation that has led to the near extinction of francophone communities elsewhere in Canada. This protection of the French language also directs immigrants toward inclusion into the francophone majority. Anglophones, however, have been established here for a long time, particularly in southwestern Quebec and on the West Island of Montreal and obviously don't favour local language laws, and since Québec started seriously questioning its place in Canada many anglophones have left the province. Almost half of Québec's population and almost all new immigrants live in the Montréal area, the focus of the province's industrial and service sectors. Québec City is as the capital. As in Ontario, the substratum is rich in minerals. The St. Lawrence Valley is very well suited to agricultural activities, and forestry in the north has already made Québec the world's primary paper producer. The eastern part of the province, which is more reliant on natural resources, doesn't enjoy the same economic prosperity as the more industrialized regions. Sparsely populated northern Québec has seen a boom since the decision to exploit the hydro-electric potential of the many rivers leading to either James Bay or the Gulf of St. Lawrence estuary.

Ontario is geographically the second largest province in Canada but the most highly populated with 11,407,000 inhabitants. It's also the most prosperous province, as it is responsible for 40% of Canada's gross national product. Ontario is rich in natural resources with mineral deposits and vast forests. Heavy industry, notably the automobile manufacturing industry has chosen this province over others. Finally, Toronto, the capital of Ontario and Canada's biggest city, is home to most of Canada's major businesses. This huge cosmopolitan city rivals those in the United States. The proximity of the U.S. markets contributes to the province's wealth, the Canadian city of Windsor, for example, is just north of Detroit. The warm climate in this southern region permits fruit growing on the same scale as in southern British Columbia. Southern Ontario's white wines, particularly the ice wines, have acquired an international reputation.

Much of the Quebec-Ontario border follows the Ottawa River. The National Capital Region includes **Ottawa**, the capital, located on the Ontario side of the river, the city of Hull, on the Québec side, and the surrounding area. The wealth of museums, public buildings and other attractions have made the region a showcase for Canadian culture, politics and tourism. Civil service and high-technology industry are predominant here.

In **Manitoba**, you have to cover hundreds of kilometres before the landscape starts getting a bit hilly. The major city and capital of this province, Winnipeg, was built south of the lake of the same name, on the shores of the Red River. The local economy had for a long time been dominated by wheat farming, until progress in agricultural techniques made it possible to diversify. Nickel mining was one notable new activity. The whole northeast part of the province opens onto Hudson Bay, and from there, onto the Atlantic. Having to transport grain to the east necessitated the construction of the major sea port of Churchill. For many years, the province had a

francophone majority, until the arrival of new anglophones and the banning of the official use of French. It would take a court decision a few decades later to recognize the rights of what, in the meantime, had become a persistent yet very small community in the midst of a total population of 1,145,000.

The straight borders of **Saskatchewan** say a lot about it's a geography. It's a vast, flat terrain where grain farming has been favoured since its colonization, notably by a wave of Ukrainian immigrants. Farming is closely supervised by the federal government as is the sale and transport of the wheat harvest. Saskatchewan has a population of 1,023,000. The two main cities are Saskatoon, world potash capital, and Regina, the provincial capital. Saskatchewan was the first region to implement aspects of the social safety net, in particular, health insurance. In fact, the political landscape would very likely not be as it is today were it not for the spirit of initiative and cooperation that developed on the plains of Manitoba, Saskatchewan and Alberta. It was in Saskatchewan that the first ever North American socialist government was elected. This success wasn't to be repeated on the federal level but the political shock was enough to force other political parties to reconsider some of the ideas put forth by the socialists.

Saskatchewan's neighbour to the west is **Alberta**. Incidently, these are the only two provinces that are completely landlocked. Alberta's territory is divided into various zones: mountainous (the Rockies offer breathtaking views), boreal forests, wheat fields, pastures and even deserts. Edmonton is the provincial capital. Alberta is the domain of cowboys: pointy boots and cowboy hats are still a common sight in downtown Calgary, and the annual Calgary Stampede is indeed the greatest outdoor show on Earth. But the best thing in Alberta, economically speaking, is the oil that's pumped out of it. The prosperity brought by this black gold has caused the population to climb to 2,847,000, has brought about the restabilization of government finances and has made Calgary one of the country's most important business centres. In terms of politics, Alberta is also the most established seat of the Canadian right. In the last few years, it has led to some administrative reforms that would be considered unthinkable elsewhere in Canada.

British Columbia covers some 950,000 square kilometres. Its Pacific coastline stretches from Alaska to Washington State. The most striking thing about this province is its geography. Three quarters of the territory lies above 930 metres and a mountain chain reaching 3,000 metres stands between the coast and the horizon. The choppy coastline is dotted with hundreds of islands. The biggest one, Vancouver Island, which is the size of the Netherlands, is home to Victoria, the province's capital. Vancouver is also the name of the province's major city; it's on the mainland coast. The climate is much milder here in winter than in the rest of Canada. Nature is equally generous in providing fruit, fish and timber. Over 3,933,000 people live in British Columbia including a very vibrant Asian community.

The **Yukon** is located in the mountainous region between Alaska, Mount Mackenzie to the east and British Columbia to the south. Whitehorse is the administrative capital for the 31,500 inhabitants of the territory but the most famous spot in the Yukon remains Dawson. Not far from this small town, a little river called the Klondike is associated with the most famous goldrush in the west.

The land east of the Yukon forms the **Northwest Territories**. There are 67,500 people living here, mostly aboriginals. To accommodate the various native groups as well as anglophones and francophones, the government here functions in eight different languages. Yellowknife is the capital. Before the end of the millennium, this territory will be divided in two. The northeastern section and the Arctic islands will become Nunavut in response to the desire by the Inuit for self-government.

FLORA

Considering the climatic differences, the flora varies markedly from one region to another; in the north, it is either scraggly or non-existent and in the south it may be lush. Generally the vegetation is divided according to the four strata, from north to south: tundra, subarctic forest, boreal forest and mixed forest. The unusual climates in British Columbia and in the Rocky Mountains have given these areas unique vegetation.

Tundra is the northernmost type of vegetation. It exists where ice limits the growing season to a few weeks per year. Only the top layer of the ground is free of permafrost and the only things that grow are miniature trees, moss and lichen.

The subarctic forest, or transition forest, comes after the tundra. It has sparse vegetation; trees are small and grow extremely slowly. Spruce and larch in particular are present here.

The boreal forest is next. It's a very homogeneous forest region consisting of coniferous trees, mainly white spruce, black spruce, balsam, jackpine and larch. This area is exploited for paper pulp and timber.

The mixed forest is the southernmost forest in Canada. In particular, it's found in the St. Lawrence Valley and consists of both conifers and leafy trees. There are many species of trees including eastern white pine, red pine, hemlock spruce, spruce, wild cherry, maple, birch and aspen. Every year the landscape is ablaze with colour as maple trees turn from green to yellow to bright red.

Along the British Columbia coastline and on the neighbouring islands, 60% of the land is covered with such a lush forest that it has been called northern rain forest, a counterpart to tropical rain forest. Douglas firs, red cedars and giant sitka spruces reach impressive proportions. For example, a douglas fir lucky enough to survive the local lumber industry can reach 90 metres in height with a trunk 4.5 metres in diameter at the bottom.

There are also several unique ecosystems. This is the case from Alberta to Manitoba where the prairies regain the soil, confined in the north by bordering aspens. In the boreal forest parasitic invasions, forest fires and large-scale cutting often lead to the planting of a provisional forest that encourages regeneration of the original forest. And, of course, a country as humid as Canada has many wetlands and bogs that are among the richest and most interesting environments to observe.

FAUNA

With all this land, diverse geography and varied climates, it is no wonder that Canada's wildlife is one of its riches. A multitude of animals populate the vast forests, plains and northern regions, and the oceans, lake and rivers are teeming with fish and aquatic animals. Here are a few of the main mammals found in Canada.

PORTRAIT

Beaver. This tireless worker is a Canadian icon. The beaver-pelt trade was at the origin of the European colonization of the country. It can be recognized by its heavy body, its short, webbed hind feet, and its wide, flat, scaly tail that serves as a rudder when swimming. Its incisors are constantly growing and allow it to cut down the trees required to built its shelter on the water. It then builds a dam to create a pond that will submerge the entrance to its home. Finally, the beaver lays down small trees in this pond. In winter, the hut will be safe from predators and open to an underwater food-storage space which is protected by a layer of ice.

Beaver

The **white-tailed deer** is the smallest species of deer in eastern North America, attaining a maximum weight of about 150 kg. This graceful creature lives at the forest's edge and is one of the most commonly hunted animals in Québec. The male's antlers fall off each winter and grow back in the spring.

The **wolf** is a predator that lives in packs. It measures between 67 and 95 cm, and weighs no more than 50 kg. Wolves attack their prey (often deer) in packs, and their viciousness makes them rather unsympathetic creatures. Wolves keep their distance from humans.

The **skunk** is known mostly for its defence mechanism: it sprays its attackers with a foul-smelling liquid. The first European settlers called this mammal *bête puante* or stinking beast. The animal is common to eastern North America, even to some cities and, while it is attractive, it is a good idea to keep your distance.

The **moose** is the largest member of the deer family in the world; it can measure more than two metres in height and weigh up to 600 kg. The male is distinguished by its broad, flattened antlers, large head, rounded nose and by the hump on its back.

Most often found in forests, the **black bear** is the most common species of bear in eastern Canada, it is also found in the West. It can weigh up to 150 kg when fully grown, yet is the smallest type of bear in Canada. Be careful – the black bear is unpredictable and dangerous.

The **grizzly bear** is not only the biggest bear in existence, but also the biggest land predator. Grizzlies are found mostly in the mountains and on the coast in northwestern Canada. Extremely dangerous.

Polar bears are very large bear that lives in the far north. It's a powerful swimmer and a great seal hunter. This bear is just as deadly as the grizzly, perhaps because there's hardly ever a place to hide on the ice field...

Found in significant numbers in both deciduous and coniferous forests, the **porcupine** is famous for the way it defends itself. When threatened, the quills covering its body stand on end, turning the porcupine into a kind of unassailable pin cushion. Some aboriginals used it as an emergency food source, as the meat can be eaten raw.

Porcupine

Lynxes are members of the cat family, weighing about 11 kilograms. Their bob tails and pointed ears topped with little tufts of longer fur make them easy to identify. They are nocturnal and hard to spot.

The **raccoon** is a nocturnal and particularly crafty animal found in southeastern Canada. It has a reputation for cleanliness because of its habit of plunging its food underwater before eating it.

The **red fox** has striking auburn fur and is found throughout the forests of eastern Canada. A cunning creature, it keeps its distance from humans and is rarely spotted. It hunts small animals and also feeds on nuts and berries.

Beluga whales are white and measure about five metres in length. These marine mammals live mainly in polar waters, but can be found in the estuary of the St. Lawrence at the mouth of the Saguenay. This is the smallest species of whale in the St. Lawrence.

Countless **orcas** inhabit the waters around Vancouver Island and are commonly spotted from the ferries that link this island with the mainland. They are the only marine mammals that eat warm-blooded animals like seals, belugas and other smaller whales, which probably explains their more common appellation, killer whales.

Bigger than its European relative, the **bison (American buffalo)** was the high lord of the American plains for many years. Millions of them lived here and migrated over long distances. Their meat, leather and tendons fulfilled the essential needs of nomadic natives. Overhunted, it has come very close to extinction. It is now found on breeding farms and in national parks.

A bit smaller than an ox, the **musk ox** lives on the tundra and travels in herds. It's easy to recognize its long, woolly fleece, and big stumpy horns. When under attack, musk oxen will form a circle to collectively protect themselves.

HISTORY

This vast continent had already been home to a medley of indigenous peoples for several thousands of years when the Europeans discovered the New World. These native populations' ancestors, nomads originating from northern Asia, had crossed the Bering Strait toward the end of the ice age, over 12,000 years ago, slowly appropriating the entire continent. It was in the course of the following thousands of years, as the glaciers receded, that some of them began emigrating to more northern lands, notably those of Canada.

There is some doubt, however, as to whether or not native civilization on the West Coast originated with these same vast waves of immigration. According to one theory, the ancestors of the West Coast tribes came here more recently (around 3000 BC) from islands in the Pacific. Proponents of this hypothesis base their argument on the natives' art, traditions and spoken languages, which are not unlike those of the indigenous peoples of the Pacific islands.

Nevertheless, native were still moving about when the Europeans established themselves here. The bands of the Iroquois confederacy, for instance, were then on the run from powerful rivals who were constantly pushing them farther north, all the way to the St. Lawrence River. Farther west, the populating of the Prairies by the Cree, the Assiniboines and the Blackfoot would occur mainly in the mid 18th century. They came, for the most part, in pursuit of wild horses and buffaloes. In fact, only the Inuit, as those we erroneously refer to as Eskimos call themselves, were able to enjoy their hunting grounds in peace — but only just.

When the Europeans launched their first intensive explorations of North America, several native nations, often united in the bosom of linguistic families, shared or vied for a place in Canada. The Great North belonged to the Inuit, who speak Inuktitut. The island of Newfoundland was home to the Beothuk nations. The St. Lawrence Valley was occupied by the Iroquois, Huron-Wendat, Pétun and Neutral nations. Almost the entire Canadian Shield as well as the north and west of the Prairies accommodated the Algonquin nations. From east to west lived the Welustuk (Malecites), Mi'gmaq (Micmacs), Innu (Montagnais), Ottawa, Ojibwa, Noooheenoos (Cree), Blackfoot, Blood, Peigans and Gros Ventres. In Manitoba lived the Sioux communities. The Yukon and the southern part of the Northwest Territories were inhabited by communities belonging to the Athabaskan linguistic family. In the Rockies, to the south, were the Kootenai and the Salish. Finally, from north to south on the west coast, what was to become British Columbia, was occupied by Nootka, Coast Salish, Kwakiutl, Bella Coola, Tsimshian, Haida and Tlinkit. Tagish, Tahltan, Testsaut, Carrier, Chilcotin, Interior Salish, Nicola and Kootenays occupied the interior. Some of these nations would be exterminated or repelled by neighbouring communities before the continent was even explored by the Europeans. Moreover, the wars between

European colonies would lead to more shifts in indigenous populations.

Living in groups, aboriginal peoples in this vast country developed societies whose customs were distinctly different from one another. Nations in the St. Lawrence Valley, for example, lived mainly on produce from their vegetable gardens, supplementing this with fish and game, while the more northern and nomadic communities in the western plains essentially depended on hunting to survive. With the passing centuries, a communication network was woven over the entire continent. Many aboriginal peoples made ample use of the canoe and maintained very close commercial ties with neighbouring nations. From the 16th century on, these First Nations peoples, who were well adapted to the rigours and particularities of the land, were quickly marginalized by the coming of the Europeans.

First Contacts

The first Europeans came to Canada over the Atlantic Ocean, reaching the shores of what we know refer to as the Atlantic Provinces. The first to undertake this venture were the Vikings, circa AD 1000. They took advantage of a temporary warm spell to fish and attempt to settle on the island of Newfoundland, which they named Vinland. In 1497, Giovanni Caboto, rechristened John Cabot in English, left Bristol for Newfoundland. The navigator was seeking a direct route to China. Though he failed to find it, he did report back to England the existence of inestimable amounts of cod in the gulf and on the open sea. From that moment on, British, French, Spanish and Basque fishermen flocked to the Grand Banks and put into port on a regular basis to smoke or salt their catch.

In 1534, Francis I, who also keen on finding gold and the mythical route that would put the riches of the Orient within the grasp of French vessels, commissioned navigator Jacques Cartier, who made three voyages to the New World. These voyages marked an important stage as they constituted France's first official contacts with the peoples and land in this part of North America. During these expeditions, the Breton navigator travelled far up the St. Lawrence River, to the native villages of Stadacona (Québec City) and Hochelaga (the island of Montréal). Cartier's discoveries, however, received little consideration from the French authorities, who were solely interesting

in Asia. Following this failure, the French Crown ignored this inhospitable land for several decades.

Acadia

It was the growing fashion for fur hats and coats in Europe as well as the benefits this trade promised that later rekindled France's interest in North America. Because the fur trade required close and constant ties to local suppliers, a permanent presence soon became essential. Up to the end of the 16th century, several attempts were made to set up trading posts on the Atlantic coast or inland.

Finally, in 1604, in the reign of the good king Henry IV, the Frenchman Pierre du Gua, sieur de Monts, established the first colony. He did so with 80 men, on a small island in the Bay of Fundy, naming it "Acadie" (Acadia). It was an unfortunate choice, for winter completely cut the island off from the mainland, which provided them with wood, game and drinking water. Close to half of the new colonists would not survive the winter. In the spring, those that did moved to the other side of the bay and founded the Port Royal colony. The Micmac, who looked favourably on trade with the Europeans, welcomed them and came to the new colony's assistance. They would have cause to regret it, for the Europeans passed on diseases their immune systems were unable to fight. Nine-tenths of the Micmac population would perish as a result.

The Port Royal colony was later abandoned as Henry IV proved rather unimpressed by the trade results of the venture. It was nevertheless reopened in 1610 by a companion of de Monts', who pointed out to wealthy French Catholics the possibility of converting aboriginals to their faith. The Micmac actually acquiesced in good faith, without ever really renouncing their own beliefs.

Port Royal was not destined to know peace, however. Between 1613 and 1690, the British seized the colony on three occasions, occupying it for varying periods of time. The resolution of conflicts in Europe and the Saint-Germain-en-Laye, Breda and Ryswick treaties returned it to the French every time. Finally, in 1710, the British seized Acadia once more and did not surrender it again. They renamed it "Nova Scotia".

The seizure was hardly symbolic, though, as the French colonists, mainly Poitevins, succeeded in founding several other colonies and becoming self-sufficient, practising farming, fishing, hunting and trade.

Québec

Populating efforts by the French were not confined to Acadia. From 1608, Samuel de Champlain undertook the adventure, which he shared with the Sieur de Monts. He ventured up the St. Lawrence River and settled at the foot of a cliff facing a narrowing of the river, where he built a few fortified buildings. This was the "Abitation de Québec" (in Algonquin, "Québec" means "where the river narrows"). For the merchants financing the operation, the Quebec settlement was meant to secure and facilitate fur trade on the St. Lawrence. Their suppliers, the Innu (Montagnais), were in fact at war with the Iroquois, who fully intended monopolizing the sale of furs to the French. Champlain, for his part, wished to found a genuine populated colony.

Their first winter in Québec was an extremely hard one. Indeed, 20 of the 28 men died of scurvy and under-nourishment before the supply ships arrived in the spring of 1609. Be that as it may, this date marks the beginning of a permanent French presence in North America. When Samuel de Champlain died on Christmas day of 1635, New France already boasted about 300 pioneers, and the French recognized the entire St. Lawrence River and the Great Lakes region.

Between 1627 and 1663, the Compagnie des Cents Associés had the purchasing monopoly of furs and was slowly populating New France. Moreover, French religious circles began taking a growing interest in the colony. The Recollet priests were the first to arrive, in 1615. They would be replaced by the Jesuits from 1632 on. In 1642, it was first the will for evangelization that justified the creation of a small village, Ville-Marie, which would later become Montréal. The missionaries settled in Huronnie, where they were very likely tolerated because of trade agreements.

Five Jesuits perished in 1648-49 during the defeat of the Huron-Wendats at the hands of the Iroquois. This war was, in fact, part of a huge military campaign waged by the mighty Five Nations Iroquois confederacy, which annihilated all rival nations between 1645 and 1655. The Hurons-Wendat, Pétun, Neutral and Erie nations, each numbering at least 10,000, were almost entirely decimated in the space of a decade. The offensive even threatened the existence of the French colony. In 1660-61, Iroquois warriors struck throughout New France, bringing about the ruin of crops and the decline of the fur trade.

Louis XIV, king of France, thus decided to govern the colony himself. New France, comprising approximately 3,000 inhabitants, consequently became a French province. The royal government recruited farm workers and even sent a full regiment to put down the Iroquois. This proved effective, and the soldiers were encouraged to stay on as colonists. To make up for an insufficient female population, the king dowered close to 800 volunteers, who came here to enter into marriage. This period of New France's history is also that of the famed *coureurs des bois* (trappers) era. Forsaking their lands for the fur trade, these young intrepid men went far into the interior in order to trade directly with native trappers. Nevertheless, most of the colonists' main occupation remained the cultivation of the soil.

Society revolved around the seigneurial system; land in New France was divided into seigneuries, which were further subdivided into lands held by commoners. The land was partitioned into deep and narrow strips to allow everyone access to waterways. This system obliged eligible voters to pay an annual allowance and fulfil a series of duties for their seigneur. As there were few eligible voters and a certain rivalry between seigneurs, these voters benefitted from living conditions far superior to those of French peasants.

French territorial claims in North America grew rapidly at this time due to expeditions undertaken by trappers, the clergy and explorers, who were to discover virtually the entire North American continent. New France reached its peak at the dawn of the 18th century, when it monopolized the fur trade in North America, controlled the St. Lawrence River and undertook the development of Louisiana. These positions enabled it to keep the expansion of British colonies in check, despite the fact that these were far more populous between the Atlantic Ocean and the Appalachian Mountains. A new word referring to French colonists having opted for New France rather than their mother country thus emerged: these were Canadians. This designation would take on its current meaning considerably later, much like the word "Canada" would come to refer to a much larger territory than it had originally.

The West: A Source of Fur

In 1670, the territory now known as the prairies, made up of the provinces of Manitoba, Saskatchewan and Alberta, was ceded by the British Crown to the Hudson's Bay Company (HBC), which took over the economic and political administration of the region, called Rupert's Land.

The HBC controlled trade in Rupert's Land, which encompassed all land that drained into Hudson Bay, therefore covering much of present-day Canada. In 1691, Henry Kelsey, an employee of the company was the first to set sight on the eastern boundary of Alberta. HBC traders, however, had competition from French fur trappers, who headed inland to the source of the fur instead of waiting for the natives to bring the pelts to the trading posts. Ultimately it was Anthony Henday, an independent trader, who became the first white man to trade in Alberta in 1754-55. Encouraged by favourable reports, independent fur traders in Montreal formed the Northwest Company in 1787, and then founded the first trading post in Alberta, Fort Chipewyan, on Lake Athabasca.

The 18th century had seen an increase in exploration and colonization all over the world by European sea powers, but there was an immense area that still seemed inaccessible: the far-off and mysterious Pacific Ocean. Some of the many peoples inhabiting its shores were completely unknown to French, Spanish and English navigators. The Panama Canal had not yet been dug, and sailing ships had to cover incredible distances, their crews braving starvation, just to reach the largest of the Earth's oceans.

In 1792, English explorer James Cook's compatriot George Vancouver (1757-1798) took possession of the territory surrounding the city that now bears his name for the King of England, and by so doing put an end to any plans the Russians and Spaniards had of laying claim to the region. The former would have liked to extend their empire southward from Alaska, while the latter, firmly entrenched in California, were looking northward. Spanish explorers had even made a brief trip into Burrard Inlet in the 16th century. This far-flung region was not coveted enough to cause any bloody wars, however, and was left undeveloped for years to come.

The Vancouver region was hard to reach not only by sea, but also by land, with the virtually insurmountable obstacle of the Rocky Mountains blocking the way. Imagine setting out across the immense North American continent from Montreal, following the lakes and rivers of the Canadian Shield, and exhausting yourself crossing the endless Prairies, only to end up barred from the Pacific by a wall of rock several thousand metres high. In 1808, the fabulously wealthy fur merchant and adventurer Simon Fraser became the first person to reach the site of Vancouver from inland. This belated breakthrough had little impact on the region, though, since Fraser was unable to reach any trade agreements with the coastal tribes and quickly withdrew to his trading posts in the Rockies.

In 1818, Great Britain and the United States created the condominium of Oregon, a vast fur-trading zone along the Pacific bounded by California to the south and Alaska to the north. In so doing, these two countries excluded the Russians and the Spanish from this region once and for all. The employees of the North West Company, combed the valley of the Fraser River in search of furs.

The Decline of New France

Conquered in Europe, France agreed to hand control of Hudson Bay, Newfoundland and French Acadia over to England in accordance with the 1713 Treaty of Utrecht. With this treaty, New France lost much of its stake in the fur trade as well as its strategic military positions. Severely weakened, it was unable to resist for very long. Even the construction of an impressive fortress, Louisbourg, on the island of Cape Breton, would prove futile.

In 1749, 2,500 British colonists and two regiments founded Halifax, in proximity of the Acadian communities already in place. From 1755, the British colonel, Charles Lawrence, ordered what he believed to be a preventive measure: the deportation of Acadians he suspected had remained faithful to France. This great upheaval led to the exodus of at least 7,000 Acadians. Some would take years to come home, ultimately to find British colonists on their lands, which they had been clearing and farming for over a century. The Acadians therefore settled in New Brunswick, on the northwest coast of Nova Scotia, in Quebec and even in Newfoundland, taking the memory of Acadia with them. Other Acadians reached the French colony of Louisiana and became "Cadiens", or "Cajuns".

The showdown for the control of North America concluded a few years later with the final victory of British troops over the French. Montréal was the last to fall, in 1760, though the outcome had ultimately been settled since the capture of Québec City the previous year. General Wolfe's British troops, who arrived aboard a 200-ship fleet, conquered those of General Montcalm after a summer of siege. At the time of the British conquest, New France boasted approximately 60,000 inhabitants, 8,967 of whom lived in Québec City and 5,733 in Montréal.

The British Regime and Loyalist Settlement

In accordance with the 1763 Treaty of Paris, France officially ceded Canada, its possessions east of the Mississippi and what it had left of Acadia to England. The first years of British government were very trying for the former subjects of the French Crown. First, the provisions of the Royal Proclamation of 1763 instituted territorial divisions that deprived the colony of its most lucrative sector, the fur trade. Moreover, the setting up of British civil laws and the refusal to recognize papal authority meant the destruction of the two pillars on which colonial society had rested up to then: the seigneurial system and religious hierarchy. Finally, Catholics were excluded from administrative duties. A good many of the elite left the country for France, while British merchants gradually took control of trade.

England later agreed to rescind the Royal Proclamation, for it had to increase its hold over Canada and win over its population in order to better resist the upsurge of independence movements in its 13 Southern colonies. As such, from 1774, the Québec Act replaced the Royal Proclamation and inaugurated a more realistic policy toward this British colony, whose population was a predominantly Catholic and French-speaking one.

The Canadian population remained almost essentially of French stock until the end of the War of American Independence, which brought about a first wave of Anglo-Saxon colonists. American citizens wishing to remain faithful to the British Crown, the Loyalists migrated to Nova Scotia as well as other maritime territories in the region. Their arrival spawned the first real colonies in New Brunswick, Prince Edward Island and Cape Breton Island. Between 5,000 and 6,000 Loyalists also settled upriver from Canadians, mainly on the shores of to Lake Ontario and, though more seldomly, in the regions populated by the French. Aboriginal peoples who had supported the cause of the British against the American revolutionaries would also obtain territories in the region. In what would later become Upper Canada then Ontario, the Loyalists settled en masse in the open spaces. Though the French had recognized and explored the Great Lakes well before, their only settlements there were trading posts and forts, which controlled the roads, including the Fort Rouillé, later to become Toronto.

Wherever colonists chose to settle and whatever their ethnic group, their lives were very difficult, often amounting to a race against winter. Indeed, they had to be sufficiently set up to withstand the cold season. This compelled them to build rudimentary and uncomfortable shelters and clear the land, which they could then sow, as quickly as possible. And there was no plough that could lift soil in which stumps and stones remained...

It goes without saying that for Loyalists and British colonists who would later join their ranks, being part of the Empire was a major advantage. They looked upon French-speaking Canadians, who considered the pope to have higher authority than that of the king, with suspicion. The British authorities wished to allow the Loyalists to keep their customs, and in 1791, divided Canada into two provinces: Upper and Lower Canada. The former was situated west of the Ottawa River and mainly inhabited by Anglo-Saxons, with British civil laws henceforth in current use. The latter, which consisted mainly of French Canadians, remained governed according to the French tradition of common law, Moreover, the Constitution Act of 1791 introduced an initial parliamentary government in Canada by creating a House of Assembly in each of the two provinces. At the time, the term "Canada" did not yet encompass the British Atlantic colonies, which led a completely separate existence. The Act aimed to restrict the powers of the legislative assemblies elected by the people. Under the terms of this act, the executive functions of government were carried out by a governor appointed by the British government, who in turn would name the members of the Executive Council who were to assist him. The legislature took the form of an elected Legislative Assembly holding very little real power and subject to vetos by the governor and the Executive Council. Loyalists in Upper Canada first chose Newark (now Niagara-on-the-Lake) for a capital, but soon moved it to York (which would later become Toronto) in fear of an American invasion.

They had reason to be wary of their southern neighbours for in 1812 the United States took advantage of the Napoleonic wars to attempt an invasion of both Canadas... and in so doing set York ablaze. The American military was remarkably ineffectual, however, and none of the British colonies fell completely into their hands. The Americans even suffered stinging defeats, the British having managed to seize a part of Maine, set fire to the White House and burn Buffalo. At the end of the war, both sides assumed their former positions.

The British government came to the conclusion that the loss of 13 of its colonies (creating the United States) had been caused by the excessive freedom they had enjoyed. The governor's surrounded themselves with some of the colony's most powerful and influential men. Together they ruled, taking little account of the wishes of the people's elected representatives. This oligarchy became known in Upper Canada as the Family Compact and in Lower Canada as the *Clique du Château*.

Meanwhile, Napoleon's Continental System forced Britain to get its lumber from Canada. From an economic standpoint, this was good for the colony. The development of a new industry was especially timely, as the fur trade, the original reason for the existence of the colony, was in steady decline. In 1821, the take-over of the Montréal-based Northwest Company by the Hudson's Bay Company marked the end of Montréal as the centre of the North American fur trade. Meanwhile, rural Québec suffered through an agricultural crisis caused by the exhaustion of farmlands and rapid population growth resulting from high birth rates among French-Canadian families.

These economic difficulties and the struggle for power between francophones and anglophones

in largely French-speaking Lower Canada kindled the Patriotes Rebellions of 1837-38 . French-Canadians chose Louis-Joseph Papineau as spokesman. The period of political conflict which fuelled the rebellion was initiated by the 1834 publication of the *92 Résolutions*, a scathing indictment of British colonial policy. The authors of the resolutions, a group of parliamentarians led by Papineau, decided to hold back from voting on the budget until Britain addressed their demands. Britain's response came in 1837 in the form of the *10 Resolutions*, written by Lord Russell, which categorically refused any compromise with their opponents in Lower Canada. In the fall of 1837, Montréal was the scene of violent clashes between the Fils de la Liberté (Sons of Liberty), made up of young French Canadians, and the Doric Club, comprised of Loyalists. Further confrontations occurred in the Richelieu valley region and in the county of Deux-Montagnes, where small insurgent groups stood up to the British army before being crushed. The following year, a group of Patriotes met with the same fate in Napierville where they confronted 7,000 British troops. This time, however, colonial authorities sent a strong message to prospective rebels. In 1839, they hanged 12 Patriotes and deported many others.

Meanwhile, the farming and working classes of Upper Canada became convinced that the Family Compact was using its political monopoly to assure its economic monopoly. Two political parties emerged, the Conservatives, also known as Tories, who wanted to maintain the status quo, and the Reformists, whose aim was to make the government more democratic. Despite the absence of intense cultural conflicts, there was a call for reform in Upper Canada. The reformist leader was William Lyon Mackenzie, a Torontonian of Scottish descent who launched his first attacks against the government and the Family Compact in his newspaper, *The Colonial Advocate*. He was later elected to the Legislative Assembly, where he immediately attacked government finances. As time went on, Mackenzie's remarks became ever harsher regarding the protectionism and abusive powers of the Family Compact, which expelled him from the Assembly for defamation. In 1835, he was elected the first mayor of Toronto, but his increasingly extreme views worried some of his more moderate supporters, who ended up rejecting his program completely. The ideas put forth by Mackenzie were shared by a great number of those who expressed their discontent with the Family Compact, but many were unwilling to break ties with Britain.

A powerful new governor, quashed hopes for change through constitutional means with Mackenzie's more radical supporters. When Mackenzie learned of this, he decided to launch his revolutionary forces. Unfortunately, despite its leader's enthusiasm, this movement of workers and small farmers was very poorly organized, and its attempt to capture Toronto was put down quickly, with little violence. A vanquished Mackenzie would follow Papineau into exile in the United States, where they would try in vain to reassemble their troops and to win American support.

When hostilities first broke out, London had sent an emissary, Lord Durham, to study the colony's problems. Expecting to find a population in revolt against colonial authority, Durham found instead two peoples, one French and one British at odds. The solution he later proposed in his report, known as the Durham Report, was radical. He suggested to authorities in Britain that gradual efforts should be made to assimilate French Canadians.

The Union Act, laid down by the British government in 1840, was largely based on the conclusions of the Durham Report. A new parliamentary system was introduced giving the two former colonies the same number of delegates, despite the fact that Lower Canada had a much larger population than Upper Canada. Public finances were also consolidated, and, finally, English was made the sole official language. As armed insurrection had proven futile in the past, French Canada's political class sought to align itself with progressive anglophones in an attempt to resist these changes. Later the struggle for responsible government became the central goal of this coalition.

The agricultural crisis, intensified by the arrival of immigrants and the high birth rate resulted in a massive emigration of French Canadians to the United States. Between 1840 and 1850, 40,000 French Canadians left the country to seek employment in the factories of New England. To counteract this exodus, the Catholic Church and the government launched an extensive campaign to colonize outlying regions, such as Lac Saint-Jean. Nevertheless, the mass exodus from Québec did not stop until the beginning of the next century. It is estimated that about 750,000 French Canadians left the province between 1840 and 1930. From this point of view, the colonization campaign, which doubled the amount of farmland in Lower Canada, ended in failure. The swelling population of rural Québec was not effectively absorbed until several decades later with the start of industrialization.

The Canadian economy received a serious blow during this era when Britain abandoned its policy of mercantilism and preferential tariffs for its colonies. To counter the effects of this change in British policy, United Canada signed a treaty in 1854, making it possible for certain goods to enter the United States without import duties. The Canadian economy recovered, albeit timidly, until American industrialists lobbied to have the treaty revoked in 1866. Resolving these economic difficulties was the impetus behind Canadian confederation in 1867.

The Confederation and Expansion of Canada

In 1867, confederation gave what were formerly known as Upper and Lower Canada new shape as the provinces of Ontario and Québec, respectively. Two other provinces — Nova Scotia and New Brunswick — adhered to this pact, which would later unite a vast territory stretching from Atlantic to Pacific. For francophone Canadians, this new political system confirmed their minority status set up by the Union Act of 1840. A bilingual central government and provincial legislatures (bilingual in Quebec only) shared the various legislative powers. It was not until the latter half of the following century that New Brunswick became officially bilingual, thus recognizing the role of its significant Acadian minority. The province's obtained jurisdiction in the sensitive areas of education, culture and civil laws, while the central government was entrusted with wide powers of taxation and economic regulation. The pact that created modern-day Canada was markedly favourable to Ontario. This province's population did in fact top that of Québec's, with the result that the former's proportional representation gave it an advantage over the latter.

Though Canada, in 1867, did not extend beyond Ontario to the west, the British Empire did, including Canadian territory all the way to the Rockies in the west and to the north pole.

The fur trade being the principle activity of the HBC, the Company had done all it could to discourage colonization in the region, which explains why the population had only reached 12,000 by 1871.

The fur-trading companies offered nothing in the way of law enforcement. American whisky traders were thus drawn north to this lawless land. With dwindling buffalo herds, natives were exploited and generally taken advantage of by the Americans, not to mention the deleterious effect the whisky trade had on them. Uprisings, including the Cypress Hills Massacre, prompted the formation of the Northwest Mounted Police and the March West began. Starting from Fort Garry in Winnipeg, the police crossed the plains lead by James Macleod. Their presence got rid of the whisky traders at Fort Whoop-Up in 1874, and they then set about establishing four forts in southern Alberta including Fort Macleod and Fort Calgary.

This police corps, which would become the Royal Canadian Mounted Police (RCMP), had much more in common with the French police force than with the British. Offenders were arrested by privates and judged by their officers, which was altogether exceptional in British judicial tradition. The opening of Western territories to colonization was also preceded by treaties with First Nation peoples and by land surveying. This is probably what spared Canada from the serious wars between white and Native American communities the United States had experienced.

Following the United States' purchase of Alaska from Russia in 1867, and the 1868 resolution by Minnesota favouring the annexation of the Canadian prairies, leaders of the fledgling Canadian Confederation (1867) were forced into action. They negotiated with Great Britain and the Hudson's Bay Company to acquire the Northwest Territories (which at the time included present-day Alberta, Saskatchewan, Manitoba and the Northwest Territories) in 1868 without so much as consulting the people who had settled there, for the most part French-speaking Métis.

Land in Manitoba began to be surveyed, but the Métis had no intention of letting themselves be dispossessed. They resisted and prevented the governor appointed by Canada from taking power. Their leader, Louis Riel, attempted to obtain recognition of his people's rights. The Canadian government turned a deaf ear. Pressure from the Americans, who were just waiting for a reason to intervene, the

difficulty of taking military action against the well-organized Métis in a region so far from the central government, fear the First Nations would back the Métis and finally Québec support for the Métis forced the federal government to negotiate. Finally, the bilingual province of Manitoba was created in 1870 on a minuscule territory, smaller than Belgium, and granting it most of the powers that the other provinces enjoyed, except those related to natural resources and the development of the land.

Some fifteen years later, the Métis would recall their leader from exile to face a similar situation, in Saskatchewan this time. However, Ottawa was in a better position and had troops at its disposal that quashed the rebellion. Riel was accused of treason under an antiquated British law, then hung. His prosecution and execution deeply divided public opinion in Ontario and Québec, where he was considered a compatriot fallen victim to Ottawa's colonial policies.

By 1871, only the British possessions of Newfoundland, Prince Edward Island (which joined the country as of 1873), the far north and British Columbia, had yet to join Confederation. Unlike the prairies, which were simply annexed to the Canadian Confederation in 1868, British Columbia was already a British colony and was thus able to negotiate its entrance into confederation. Isolated on the Pacific coast, British Columbia's principal trading partner was California. As its population grew with the gold rush of the 1850s, certain residents even dreamed of creating an independent country. But these hopes were dashed at the end of this prosperous period, when in 1871, British Columbia's population was only 36,000. Great Britain had already joined its colony on Vancouver Island with British Columbia in anticipation of their eventual integration into the new Canadian Confederation.

But Canada remained far away. With a promise from Canada that a pan-Canadian railway would reach the coast by 1881, British Columbia accepted to join confederation in 1871. However, all sorts of problems delayed the construction of the railroad, and in 1873, as a severe recession gripped Canada, causing major delays in the railway, British Columbia threatened to separate. It wasn't until November 7, 1885 that the railway from Montréal to Vancouver was finally completed, four years late.

As the railway expanded, more and more farmers settled in the region known as the Northwest Territories, which had no responsible government on the provincial level. You will recall that Canada had annexed the territories (prairies) without giving them provincial status, except for a small parcel of land, which became the province of Manitoba. Inevitably, the federal government was compelled to expand Manitoba and create the provinces of Saskatchewan and Alberta in 1905.

Most settlers arrived in Alberta when the Canadian Pacific Railway reached Fort Calgary in 1883 and eight years later in 1891 when the Grand Trunk Railway's northern route reached Edmonton. Ranchers from the United States and Canada initially grabbed up huge tracts of land with grazing leases. Much of this open range land was eventually granted to homesteaders. To Easterners, the West was ranches, rodeos and cheap land, but the reality was more often a sod hut and loneliness. Though a homestead could be registered for $10, and own so many head of cattle. But the endless potential for a better future kept people coming from far and wide.

In 1895, London officially granted Canada the far north; the Yukon territory was officially ceded in 1898 to ensure Canadian jurisdiction over that area during the Klondike gold rush. Contacts between the Inuit and Europeans had been constant since the 16th century, when the Nordic waters first attracted whalers.

From an economic standpoint, Confederation failed initially to provide the expected results. It was not until three decades had passed, characterized by sharp fluctuations, that Canada really experienced its first great period of rapid economic growth. The foundations for this growth were laid several years after Confederation by Sir John A. Macdonald, the federal Conservative Prime Minister re-elected in 1878 after five years out of office. His electoral campaign had centred around his National Policy, a series of measures aimed at protecting and promoting Canada's nascent industries by means of protective tariffs, the creation of a big internal market unified by a transcontinental railway, and the growth of this internal market by a policy of populating the Prairies through massive immigration. At the same time, the arrival in Canada of the industrial revolution and the use of steam as a power source brought about enormous changes. Though Montreal and Toronto remained the undisputed hubs of this movement, numerous other smaller cities were also affected. The lumber industry, which had been one of the mainsprings of the economy during the 19th century, began exporting more cut wood than raw lumber, giving rise to a processing industry. The expansion of the railway, the hub of which was Montréal, led to the specialization in the production of rolling stock. The leather goods, clothing and food industries also enjoyed significant growth.

This wave of industrialization accelerated the pace of urbanization and created a large and poor working class. Factory neighbourhoods were terribly unhealthy, coal mines in Alberta and British Columbia were the most dangerous in the world. Strikes broke out, but were soon suppressed by the public authorities.

The Golden Age of Economic Liberalism

With the beginning of the 20th century, a period of prodigious economic growth in Canada started and lasted until the Great Depression of the 1930s. Sharing the optimism and euphoria of Canadians, Prime Minister Wilfrid Laurier predicted that the 20th century would be Canada's.

Manufacturers profited during this period of growth. Thanks to new technology and new markets, the abundance of natural resources was the principal catalyst of this second wave of industrialization. Central to the new era was the production of electrical power. With its numerous powerful rivers, Québec became a major producer of hydroelectric power in a matter of years. The pulp and paper industry found huge markets in the United States, due to the depletion of American forests and the rise of the popular press.

This new period of industrialization differed from the first one in several ways. Taking place largely outside the major cities, it led to an increase in urban growth in outlying regions. In some cases, cities sprang up in a matter of a few years. Unlike the manufacturing industries, the exploitation of natural resources required more qualified workers and a level of financing far beyond local means. Britain's stake in the economy, which up until now had been the largest, gave way to the triumphant rise of American capitalism. The Canadian population was then in full transformation. Half the citizenry became urban as of 1921.

When the First World War broke out in Europe in 1914, the Canadian government gave its full support to Britain without hesitation. A significant number of French Canadians voluntarily enrolled in the army, although the percentage of volunteers per capita was far lower than that in other provinces. This lack of enthusiasm can doubtless be attributed both to Québec's long severed ties with France and, what is more important, to francophones' somewhat ambivalent feelings toward Britain. Canada soon set a goal of inducting 500,000 men. Since there were not enough volunteers, the government voted, in 1917, to introduce conscription. Reaction to this in Québec was violent and marked by fights, bombings and riots. In the end, conscription failed to appreciably increase the number of French-Canadian recruits. Instead, it simply underlined out once again the ongoing friction between English and French Canada.

The two wars would at least have one positive result in Canada in that the departure of such a great number of able-bodied men was to oblige companies to replace them with women. These women were never to forget that they were entirely qualified to fulfill the same duties as their "menfolk". They would later demand and, after a concerted and lengthy struggle, obtain the right to vote.

Life in Western Canada was hard around the turn of the century. In British Columbia, a strike by 7,000 miners looking to improve their working conditions lasted two years, from 1912 to 1914, and finally had to be broken by the Canadian army. For the farmers who came here to grow wheat, the high cost of rail transport, lack of rail service, low wheat prices and bad harvests, along with duties too high to protect the fledgling industry in central Canada, all came together to make for miserable and desperate times. The First World War created a temporary boom, which lasted until 1920, causing a rise in the price of raw materials and wheat. The workers remained dissatisfied, though, and in 1919, the workers' unions of the West created their own central union, the One Big Union. As supporters of Russian Bolsheviks, the union's goal was to abolish capitalism. However, a general strike in Winnipeg, Manitoba quickly created a rift between the workers with respect to their objectives, and demonstrated Canada's determination not to let the country fall into the Marxist ideology. The 1920s again proved prosperous for the West, and Alberta, at the time an essentially agricultural province, was able finish clearing its territory.

The Great Depression

Between 1929 and 1945, two international-scale events, the Depression and Second World War, greatly disrupted the country's political, economic and social progress. The Great Depression of the 1930s, originally viewed as a cyclical, temporary crisis, lengthened into a decade-long nightmare and put an end to the country's rapid economic expansion. With Canada strongly dependent on foreign markets, the country as a whole was hard hit by the international stock market crash. Exporting industries were the hardest hit. The textile and food industries, which sold to the Canadian market, held up better during the first years of the Depression, before foundering as well. The trend towards urbanization slowed as people began to view the countryside as a refuge where they could grow their own food. Poverty became more and more widespread, and unemployment levels reached 27% in 1933. Governments were at a loss in the face of this crisis, which they had expected to be short-lived. Massive public works projects were introduced to provide jobs for the unemployed.

Western Canada was devastated, in particular the Prairie provinces, which saw their agricultural revenues drop by 94% between 1929 and 1931! And the fact that their farms specialized almost exclusively in wheat made the situation even worse. This period was marked by the evolution of two Western Canadian political movements, both of which remained almost exclusively local, the Social Credit and the Co-operative Commonwealth Federation (CCF). The doctrine of the Social Credit, which supported the small farmers' and workers' stand against the capitalist ascendancy by providing interest-free credit, reached its height under William Aberhart, who was elected premier of Alberta in 1935. His government dared to defy the capitalist system like no Canadian government ever had before (or has since).

The federal government was also compelled to question the merits of economic liberalism and to redefine the role of the state. Part of this trend included establishing the Bank of Canada in 1935, which permitted greater control over the monetary and financial system. However, it was not until the ensuing war years that a full-scale welfare state was created. In the meantime, the crisis that shook liberalism continued to engender ideologies. In Quebec, for example, traditional nationalism secured a place of choice, lauding traditional values typified by the rural world, the family, religion and language.

The Second World War

The Second World War began in 1939, and Canada became officially involved September 10th of that year. The Canadian economy received a much-needed boost as industry set out to modernize the country's military equipment and to meet the requirements of the Allies. Canada's close ties to Great Britain and the United States gave it an important diplomatic role, as indicated by the Québec conferences of 1943 and 1944. Early in the war, however, the problem of conscription surfaced again. While the federal government wanted to avoid the issue, mounting pressure from the country's anglophones forced a plebiscite on the issue. The results once again showed the division between francophones and anglophones: 80% of English Canadians voted in favour of conscription, while the same percentage of French Canadians were opposed to the idea. Mixed feelings toward Britain and France left French Canadians very reluctant to become involved in the fighting. However, they were forced to follow the will of the majority. In the end, 600,000 Canadians were recruited, 42,000 of whom died in action.

Canada was profoundly changed by the war. Its economy became much stronger and more diversified than before. The federal government's massive intervention during the war marked the beginning of its increased role in the economy and of the relative marginalization of provincial governments. In addition, the contact thousands of Canadians had with European life and the jobs women held in the factories modified people's expectations. The winds of change were blowing.

The Post-War Period

Canada's current borders have only existed as such since 1949, when Newfoundland chose to join confederation. A dire economic situation was the deciding factor in its becoming the tenth Canadian province.

The end of the Second World War signalled a period of considerable economic growth, during which consumer demands repressed by the economic crisis and wartime rationing could finally be satisfied. Despite a few fluctuations, the economy performed spectacularly until 1957.

It became increasingly evident that the real Canadian market was located south of the border. Trade proliferated to the point that Canada and the United States became the two most active mutual economic trading partners. Moreover, Canada was in need of capital to ensure its development and could no longer count on the support of British moneylenders. The Americans would take over, more often than not as majority shareholders in the growing heavy-industry sector.

The St. Lawrence Seaway was dug, opening the Great Lakes to Atlantic navigation. Montréal lost its place as the main transshipment port and maritime traffic in its port fell off. The city, which had been *the* Canadian metropolis since the British conquest, consequently yielded its place to Toronto.

This prosperity was not equally felt by the various social and ethnic groups. Francophone communities were increasingly lagging behind the anglophone majority. Economic development in Québec allowed Maurice Duplessis — a Premier at once conservative, capitalist and nationalist — to maintain control and prevent the emergence of modern and secular institutions. The Duplessis era can only be explained by the tacit co-operation of much of the traditional and business elite, both francophone and anglophone. Though seemingly in its finest hour, the church felt its authority weakening, which prompted it to support, and to encourage its followers to support, the Duplessis government in full measure.

Despite Duplessis's iron hand, opposing voices nonetheless emerged. The most organized opposition came from union leaders, journalists and the intellectual community. All these groups wanted modernization for Québec and endorsed the same neo-liberalist economic credo favouring a strong welfare system.

In 1960, the Québec Liberal Party under Jean Lesage was elected on a platform of change and stayed in power until 1966. This period,

PORTRAIT

referred to as the Révolution Tranquille, or Quiet Revolution, was indeed marked by a veritable race for modernism that put Québec "in line with the rest of the world". Religion lost its place at the centre of French-Canadian culture. Language would henceforth be the identity of francophones. The steps taken by the Quebec state would repeatedly gain widespread acceptance elsewhere in Canada, notably with regard to the powerful economic levers put into place.

Politics and the Constitutional Crisis

The lively nature of Québec society in the 1960s engendered a number of new ideological movements there, particularly on the left. The extreme was the Front de Libération du Québec (FLQ), a small group of radicals who launched a series of terrorist strikes in Montréal. In October 1970, the FLQ abducted James Cross, a British diplomat, and Jean Laporte, a Québec cabinet minister. The Canadian Prime Minister at the time, Pierre Elliot Trudeau, fearing a political uprising, called for the War Measures Act to be enforced. The Canadian army took to the streets of Montréal. Shortly afterward, Pierre Laporte was found dead. The crisis finally ended when the James Cross' kidnappers agreed to let him go in exchange for their safe conduct to Cuba.

The most significant political event in Canada between 1960 and 1980 was the rapid rise of moderate nationalism in Québec. Since the Quiet Revolution, successive Québec governments have all considered themselves the spokespeople of a distinct nation, demanding special status and increased powers for Québec to the detriment of the Canadian government. For nationalist Quebecers, Canada is the work of two founding peoples, one of which, francophones, resides mainly in Québec. They are therefore opposed to the present situation in which this population is simply a minority in an increasingly integrated Canadian whole.

Pierre Trudeau's federal government put up staunch resistance. At once anglophone and francophone, Trudeau was also an ardent nationalist. His allegiance was nonetheless to a strong and united Canadian state where there would be but one people. His vision of a multicultural Canada denied Québec nationalists their place as one of the two founding peoples. Trudeau's idealized policy of bilingualism was seen to deny Québec's desire to become the champion of the official linguistic minority. Trudeau's nationalism led him to cut certain symbolic ties uniting Canada to London. The goal was to repatriate the constitution and, with it, the power to amend the Canadian constitution. London proved willing, but the provinces' consent was required. Fearing an even more centralized Canada where it would not obtain desired recognition, Québec opposed all attempts to repatriate the constitution. It was not the only province to be concerned about Ottawa's plans.

Breaking with the traditionalism of the past, Québec nationalism championed a strong, open and modern Québec with increased powers for the provincial government, and, ultimately, political independence for the province. The nationalist forces rallied around René Lévesque, who eight years after founding the Parti Québécois surprised everyone with a stunning victory in the 1976 provincial election. With a mandate to negotiate sovereignty for Québec, the party called a referendum in 1980. From the beginning, the referendum campaign revived the division between Québec sovereigntists and federalists. The struggle was intense and mobilized the entire population right up until the vote. Finally after a campaign based on promises of a new style of federalism, the "No" (no to sovereignty association) side won out with 60% of the vote. Despite this loss, sovereigntists were consoled by how far their cause had come in only a few years. From a fringe movement in the 1960s, nationalism quickly proved itself to be a major political phenomenon.

The federal government finally unveiled its reworked constitutional plan. This consisted of repatriating the constitution by including the Canadian Charter of Rights and Freedoms and an amendment formula that would allow a change in the balance of powers without the consent of all provinces. Ottawa followed up on its plan with the consent of nine provinces and despite the unanimous opposition of Quebec's National Assembly, sovereigntists and federalists alike. By doing so, the federal government itself plunged Canada into a constitutional crisis, one which has been monopolizing Canadian politics ever since.

For many, the 1980s began with a post-referendum depression, accentuated by a period of economic crisis in Canada unmatched since the 1930s. Though the economy improved slightly over time, the unemployment rate remained very high and government spending resulted in a massive deficit. Like many other western governments, the provincial and federal governments had to reassess the policies of the past.

The 1980s and early 1990s were a time of streamlining and one that saw the creation of global markets and the consolidation of large economic blocks. Canada and the United States signed the Free-Trade Agreement in 1989. The 1994 North American Free Trade Agreement (NAFTA) brought Mexico into this market, creating the largest tariff-free market in the world.

In 1984, a new federal government was ushered in, that of the Conservative Brian Mulroney. As regards the constitution, he would take it upon himself, in 1982, to repair the damage done by his predecessor. The context was also right, particularly since Québec's separatist government itself had been replaced. All ten premiers got together at Meech Lake in 1987 and came to an agreement. Robert Bourassa, the premier of Québec at the time, was willing to let bygones be bygones if five conditions were met, including the recognition of Québec as a distinct society.

To become official, the Accord had to be ratified by the Legislative Assemblies of the ten provinces before June 24, 1990. This seemed simple enough. However, the situation turned into a monumental fiasco when certain provincial premiers were elected out of office and replaced by opponents of the deal, when the Premier of Newfoundland changed his mind on the matter, and when public opinion in English Canada turned against the agreement,

In an attempt to avert a major swing towards sovereignty, Premier Bourassa resolved to present the federal government with an ultimatum. He announced that a referendum would be held before October 26, 1992, either on an acceptable federalist offer or on the proposition of sovereignty for Québec. Until the last moment, Robert Bourassa truly believed the other provinces and the federal government would produce, for the first time in the recent history of the country, an agreement responding to the demands of a majority of Quebecers. The governments did consent to return to the negotiation table a little before the deadline. A general agreement, the Charlottetown Accord, was thrown together in

a few days. This was presented not only as a response to Québec's aspirations, but also to those of the other Canadian provinces and Canada's aboriginal peoples. October 26, 1992, the date originally planned for a provincial referendum on Québec's future, was kept as the date for this Canada-wide referendum. For Quebecers, the Accord was deemed an unacceptable setback with regard to the prior agreement. They therefore refused to endorse it. The rest of Canada also refused, considering the offer still too generous to Québec.

Worn out by the fruitless discourse around their place within Canada, many Quebecers, since the failure the "Meech Lake Accord", were impatiently awaiting the opportunity to express their desire for change. This opportunity would first present itself during the 1993 federal elections. For the first time, Quebecers had the option of voting for a well-structured sovereignist party, the Bloc Québécois, which would represent them within Canadian Parliament itself. The Bloc Québécois would ultimately walk off with more than two-thirds of the ridings at stake in Quebec and form the Official Opposition in Ottawa. The following year, the people of Quebec were destined to elect a new government to manage the province, the Parti Québécois, the main standard bearer of the Quebec separatist cause in the course of the last quarter century.

Fifteen years after the 1980 referendum, federalist and sovereignist forces embarked on a new referendum campaign. No one could then have predicted such a close final result. On the night of the referendum, the counting of the very last vote had to be made before the verdict could finally be determined. Quebecers voted 49,4% in favour (i.e.. "Yes") of the sovereignist plan, while 50,6% voted "No"! Only one percentage point divided the two options; Quebec was literally split in two. No one was therefore surprised to hear the big sovereignist names announce yet another referendum in the very near future. The day after the referendum, Jacques Parizeau nevertheless tendered his resignation as leader of the Parti Québécois and Premier of Quebec. He would be replaced by Lucien Bouchard, the leader of the Bloc Québécois in Ottawa up to that point, who enjoyed great popularity in Quebec.

PORTRAIT

Other Tensions

Federalists, who had always believed themselves immune to a potential majority vote of Quebecers in favour of sovereignty, were badly shaken up by the close results of the 1995 referendum. It was a brutal wake-up call. The federal government was fully resolved to prevent Quebec separatists from following up on their plan. The strategies put forth aimed to dissuade Quebec nationalists by threatening them with a potential division of their territory, by praising the merits of Canada and discussing the legality of potential secession.

In 1997, federal Prime Minister Jean Chrétien wished to take advantage of the favourable economic situation and launched early elections. The Liberal Party was re-elected, though with a smaller majority despite massive support from Ontario, the most populous Canadian province. The Reform Party was once again the big winner in the West, claiming even more seats than in the previous election. The Bloc Québécois's performance was not as strong as in 1993. They nevertheless won 45 of the 75 seats in Québec. As for the Progressive Conservatives and the New Democrats, they regained some of their former strengths thanks to voters in Atlantic Canada. The Canadian political map has never been so complex. The Liberal Party's inability to gain much support outside of Ontario, Reform's performance in the West and the large contingent of Bloc Québécois members of parliament certainly puts in question the idea of a Canadian consensus.

Quebec, in fact, has not been the only region to question its place within Canada. The 20th century has made governments into much more active participants than the fathers of Canadian confederation had anticipated. Ottawa has increasingly expanded its role, often by curtailing the legislative powers of the provinces. From a confederation, Canada has thus slowly become a much more centralized federation. This centralization is generally to the advantage of poorer or weaker provinces. These first get part of a redistribution of the national wealth (something the state of public finances allows less and less, however). Moreover, they need not assume all the obligations of a modern government. The system also favours Ontario, which takes advantage of its demographic strength to guide national policies.

A certain dissatisfaction arose elsewhere, too. The Albertan example of this is revealing. At the end of the seventies, the oil boom, combined with an economic slowdown in Ontario and Québec, gave Alberta almost total employment and made it the province with the highest revenue per capita. Though growth was phenomenal, it was not as marked as anticipated. Alberta's demands for larger control of its oil and gas widened the a split between the province and the federal government, and in the 1980 federal elections, the Liberal Party, the party ultimately brought to power, failed to elect any members of parliament from British Columbia or Alberta. The Liberals thus lead the country until 1984 without any representation from these two provinces. The National Energy Program tabled by the Trudeau government was the straw that broke the camel's back as far as Albertans were concerned. Under this program, the federal government was to claim a greater and greater share of the price of Canadian oil and natural gas, leaving only a very marginal amount of the profits generated by the explosion of the world markets for the provinces and producers. This appropriation by the federal government of natural resources that had been regulated and private since Confederation was strongly repudiated by Alberta and was one of the reasons for the federal Liberals' defeat in the 1984 election. The Conservative government's attempts to make amends to Québec further alienated Albertans, who finally turned to the Reform Party. In fact, in the early eighties, separatist movements in Alberta even succeeded in gaining the support of 20% of the population and in electing a member to the Alberta legislature in 1981.

Another bone of contention between the provinces and Ottawa stemmed from the fact that the federal government had unlimited powers of taxation at their disposal (which was not the case with the provinces) and the right to spend this money in whatever sphere they chose. The federal government used these powers to impose national standards in sectors clearly outside provincial jurisdiction. These standards had no legal merit, but any province neglecting to respect them could see itself deprived of major funding. The yoke was that much heavier for the provinces as the economic situation led the federal government to reduce the extent of what it paid out.

Are all these tensions cause for concern? Probably not. The political conflicts that have occupied Canada over the last 25 years are simply signs of the current restoration of balance. The issues at the heart of the dispute often date back to the British conquest. It is therefore virtually certain that they are not about to find a definitive answer. One of Canadian democracy's greatest strengths is nevertheless to tackle these issues peacefully, respecting democratic rules. And there is nothing to indicate that this is about to change.

DEMOGRAPHY

The population of Canada, much like that of the rest of Americas for that matter, springs from very diverse origins. In what would become Canada, were joined by French colonists, whose descendants now make up the most significant national minority, as early as the 16th century. And, in the course of the last two centuries, Canada has, by turns, grown richer with immigrants from the British Isles and the United States, then Europe and eventually from all over the world. This infusion of new blood will only intensify given that the Canadian population is aging.

Aboriginals

The first nations to conquer what is now known as Canadian territory, the Inuit and First Nations peoples, now represent, numerically speaking, no more than a marginal fraction of the total population. First Nations peoples are scattered throughout Canada and remain under the injudicious and scurrilous aegis of the federal government. Though some still have the use of hunting and fishing territories, their traditional way of life has, to a large extent, been annihilated.

Not conforming to modern society, suffering from loss of culture, aboriginals are currently face major social problems. For the last few decades, however, they have adopted more effective political structures to put forward their claims, and with results as it is henceforth impossible to disregard aboriginal dynamics when it comes to planning regional development or exploiting natural resources in Canada.

The aboriginal lobby remains a powerful moral lever on the Canadian government. These last few years, natives have also succeeded in attracting the attention of both the media and the general population. Interest has primarily focused on their political and territorial claims. Armed standoffs over land claims have made the news across the country. Most land claims, which result for hundred-year-old treaties, are far from being resolved. Nevertheless, important steps have been taken. Notably when the principle of autonomy for aboriginal governments was tackled during the 1992 constitutional talks. Native and Inuit claims now find very solid support throughout most of Canada.

Francophones

The francophone population forms the majority in Quebec and a significant minority in New Brunswick. Its endurance throughout the rest of Canada, however, can hardly be considered a success, despite its own efforts and the support of the federal government.

A large percentage of Québec's francophones are descendants of the original French colonists who arrived in the country between 1608 and 1759. These immigrants arrived gradually. By 1663 there were only 3,000 settlers in New France. With an increased number of immigrants starting to arrive and with settlers starting families, the population of Québec stood at about 60,000 at the time of the British conquest of 1759. The settlers were mostly farmers from western France.

Today, after just over two centuries, the descendants of these 60,000 French-Canadians number in the millions, seven million of whom still live in Canada. Some interesting comparisons have been made between Québec's sharp rate of population growth and the growth rates seen elsewhere between 1760 and 1960. For example, while the population of the world during this same two hundred year period grew three times, and the population of Europe grew five times, the population of francophone Canada grew 24 times. This statistic is particularly surprising given that immigration from France had dwindled to almost nothing and that there were very few marriages between British and French families (with the exception of a number of Irish-French unions). In addition, between 1840 and 1930, about 900,000 Quebecers, most of them francophone, left Canada for the United States. This phenomenal growth of Canada's French population resulted largely from a

PORTRAIT

remarkably high birth rate. Indeed, for a long time, French-Canadian women had an average of eight children. Families of 15 or 20 children were not unusual. This trend can be attributed to the influence of the Catholic church which sought to counterbalance the growth of the Protestant church in Canada. Interestingly, francophone Quebecers now have one of the lowest birth rates in the world, similar to that found in Germany and other western European countries.

The French majority in Québec had long been deprived of control over the economy of the province. In 1960, on average, francophones earned 66% of what anglophones did. With the Quiet Revolution, francophones began to take control of their economy. At the same time, they stopped thinking of themselves as French-Canadians and began to define themselves as Quebecers. Québec's total population, 82% of which is francophone, is characterized by an increasing number of immigrants. Unfortunately, French communities outside Quebec, particularly in the west, are increasingly declining.

Anglophones

The first anglophones, most of whom were merchants, to arrive in Canada only represented a minute portion of the population, even more than 20 years after the conquest of 1759. The British established various trading posts, notably in the west and on Hudson Bay. At the time, populated colonies were already prospering in the Maritime Provinces.

The American Revolution would provoke a veritable influx of British immigrants, who would populate the territories now grouped within Canada. Whether because they wished to seek new lands or to remain faithful to England, Loyalists left the United States for Canada between 1783 and the beginning of the 19th century. No matter where they settled, these Loyalists were anxious to show their attachment to the laws, customs and religions their ancestors had brought over from Great Britain. Generally farmers rather than merchants, they did not mix much with the established English communities that controlled business in Québec City and Montréal.

These colonists settled in the anglophone colonies of Nova Scotia, Prince Edward Island and New Brunswick. They soon became the majority in the latter colony. Farther west, in what constituted Canada at the time, they settled in the southwest of what is now Quebec territory and, most particularly, to the north of the Great Lakes, in what would become Ontario. They prospered and populated the plains stretching from Ontario to the Rockies, as the railway progressed and opened these territories up to colonization. Finally, on the other side of the mountains, two more British colonies established themselves, one on Vancouver Island, the other on the coast. They would later unite to create the province of British Columbia.

Later, others from the United Kingdom joined the loyalists, often through necessity rather than choice. Thus arrived the Scottish and Irish, many of latter were driven from their homelands by the potato famine. The decline of British immigration from the end of the 19th century was offset by the integration of newcomers of other nationalities.

Other Cultural Communities

Immigration from countries other than France, the United States or England only really began in the late 19th century. In the first part of the century, before the economic crisis of the 1930s and Second World War put a stop to immigration to Canada, most new arrivals were mainly of Central European Jews, Ukrainians and Italians. Post-war prosperity brought immigrants in even greater numbers than before. Most originated in Southern and Eastern Europe. Starting in the 1960s, Canada began to see the arrival of immigrants from every continent including many from Indochina and the West Indies and more recently Chinese nationals fleeing Hong Kong before its return to Beijing China.

Even though these new arrivals tended to preserve their own culture as much as possible, they eventually adopted either the English or the French language, and were then integrated into that particular community. For the most part, English was the chosen language as English is often one of the languages spoken in their native countries and perceived as the language of North America, indeed, as that which ensures greater success. This caused problems in Québec, where the use of French was quickly being supplanted by English. Strict language laws now oblige new immigrants to send their children to French schools.

PORTRAIT

THE ECONOMY

Canada emerged from the eighties with a colossal national debt, incurred by all its governments in order to sustain and generate economic activity. Only Alberta and New Brunswick managed to come out of it relatively unscathed. The former owes this to the wealth generated by its oil industry, the latter to clear-sightedness and heavy sacrifices. By 1990, a quarter or more of the State's tax revenues were used neither to finance its activities nor to reimburse the accumulated debt. This money only paid the interest due and payable on the accumulated debt. The governments were thus left with very little room for manoeuvre, obliging politicians to make battling the deficit a priority. Federal government spending cuts have since allowed the State to envisage budget surpluses.

Provincial deficits, however, were harder to fight because federal transfers melted away and every cutback directly affected voters. Certain more right-wing governments, notably those of Ontario and Alberta, made drastic cuts, notably in social programs, to get rid of their deficits. Other governments set cutback targets and gave themselves leeway to meet them. The whole country was nevertheless well on its way to getting out of the downward spiral begun in the seventies.

The globalization of markets and free trade with the United States seemed to have benefitted Canada, which was thus able to increase the volume of its exports. On the other hand, unemployment rates hovered steadily around 10%. The fact that employment has proved less and less directly linked to the volume of investments during the last few years is a disturbing phenomenon.

All this has resulted in a widening gap between the rich and poor in Canada, with the middl-class quality of life diminishing because they are more taxed and less well served. That said, the situation in Canada is hardly desperate. It remains one of the countries in which citizens enjoy a very high standard of living. The United Nations named Canada as the country with the highest standard of living. State-of-the-art Canadian industries, notably as regards transport, media, electronics, engineering, services and biotechnology, are the largest in their sector on the world market. New models have emerged to sustain entrepreneurship. Tax reliefs have even been obtained by unions to set up investment funds meant to support private enterprise.

POLITICS

The British North America Act of 1867 is the constitutional document on which Canadian Confederation is based. It creates a division of powers between the levels of government. In addition to a central government based in Ottawa, therefore, the ten Canadian provinces each has a government with the power to legislate in certain domains. The constitutional conflict between Québec and the Canadian government is largely a product of disagreements over precisely how these powers should be divided.

Canada is a constitutional monarchy. The Head of State is the Queen, Elizabeth II of England. Royal prerogatives are generally delegated to the Governor General, appointed for five years by the Queen upon the Prime Minister's recommendation. If the powers assigned to the Governor are in theory unlimited, it is because these are not exercised, British parliamentary tradition requiring the strictest reserve and co-operation with the people's elected representatives. In every province, a Lieutenant Governor fulfills duties analogous to those of the Governor General.

In Canada, as in all Western democracies, legislative, executive and judicial powers do not all rest in the same hands. Technically speaking, the most important of these is legislative power, which, in Ottawa, is exercised by Parliament, independent of the Government. This Parliament is divided into two Houses, according to the English model of Lower and Upper Chambers. The Senate is the Upper Chamber. Senators are appointed by the Governor General on the Prime Minister's recommendation, and their task is to examine and amend bills, which are ultimately passed by the House of Commons. Because they are not elected representatives, senators are not empowered to obstruct the wishes expressed by the votes of Members of Parliament. Elected Members of Parliament, who each represent a riding for a four to five year mandate, sit in the House of Commons, or Lower Chamber. Elections function according to the single ballot majority system This kind of system generally leaves room for only two major political parties. It also, however, has the advantage of ensuring great stability between each election, while making it possible to identify each member of Parliament with a particular riding.

Members of the same party generally all vote the same way after having adopted their position in caucus. The House of Commons passes laws, but also oversees the actions of the Government, which the Members can question on any matter. Moreover, the Auditor General, the Chief Electoral Officer and, in certain legislatures, the Public Protector are directly responsible to Parliament. In every province, a Legislative Assembly operates according to the same rules, with the exception that almost all have abolished their Senate.

The party leader who wins the largest number of seats is invited by the Governor General to become Prime Minister and select the Ministers who will form the Cabinet with him or her. By custom, almost all Cabinet Ministers must already be Members of the House of Commons, as they are responsible to Parliament for their official actions and those of their departments. Tradition dictates that the Cabinet resign if defeated by a majority in the House of Commons. This is very rare since the Prime Minister usually has a majority of Members of the Commons at his or her service. The Cabinet is responsible for most legislation, the administration of the Government and the establishment of its policy, as well as the Treasury Department. It is the real seat of power in Canada.

Finally, judicial power is exercised by judges. These are appointed by the federal Minister of Justice and Attorney General if pertaining to courts of law, and by provincial counterparts in other cases. Judges' independence and impartiality are guaranteed by the permanence of their appointment and by the fact that they are very generously remunerated for their services.

At the federal level, two parties, the Liberal Party and the Conservative Party, have each governed the country at various times since Confederation in 1867. The more left-wing New Democratic Party (NDP) was long the only third party worthy of the name in the Commons. In the last two general elections, however, two new regional parties have emerged, the Reform Party and the Bloc Québécois.

Diplomacy

Canada occupies an enviable place on the international scene. It sits at the table of the seven most industrialized countries (known as the G7) as well as on the Organization for Economic Cooperation and Development (OECD). It is a member of the United Nations Organization (UNO) and one of its fiercest supporters. It is, for that matter, to a Canadian Prime Minister, Lester B. Pearson, to whom we owe the creation of the United Nations peacekeeping force. Moreover, the Canadian armed forces have served as peacekeepers on numerous occasions, which is no simple task since no one ever really "wins" a peacekeeping mission. Because of Canada's position as a former colony and a current industrial power, it often finds itself in a diplomatic position. Canada has also recently distinguished itself by spearheading the campaign to ban the use of antipersonnel land mines.

Canada is both a member of the Commonwealth and the French-speaking world. On the trade level, it is a member of the World Trade Organization (WTO). What is more, its North American trade is governed by the North American Free Trade Agreement (NAFTA). Militarily, Canada is a member of the North Atlantic Treaty Organization (NATO). Moreover, Canada has forged a particular alliance with the United States to ensure continental defence. This alliance, the North American Aerospace Defence Command, is better known by the acronym NORAD.

THE ARTS

When it comes to the arts, it is impossible to avoid the influence of the United States. Many Canadians, particularly English-Canadians have ambiguous feelings towards their American neighbours. American popular culture is omnipresent in their everyday lives. It is fascinating, but also troubling, and much time and energy is invested in defining just what distinguishes Canadian culture from that found south of the border. Nevertheless, countless extremely talented artists of all kinds have gained international renown and have established cultural trends that are uniquely Canadian.

The aspirations and the concerns of a society are reflected in the work of its artists. For a long time, artistic expression in French Canada presented an image of a people constantly on the defensive, tormented by an unsatisfactory present situation and filled with doubt over the future. However, after World War II, and particularly after the Quiet Revolution, Québec culture evolved and became more affirming. Open to outside influences, and often very innovative, Québec culture is now remarkably vital.

Aboriginal Art

Unfortunately little remains of aboriginal art history. Aboriginal art has always been linked to native beliefs, which were consistently viewed with suspicion by European missionaries, who did all they could to convert the aboriginals. This ultimately led to a loss of interest in native art among natives themselves.

The first native works to be listed were "petroglyphs", which can notably be seen in Lake Superior and Petroglyph National Parks, in Ontario and in Writing-on-Stone Provincial Park in Southern Alberta. The Inuit have sculpted whale-bone and soapstone since time immemorial and such pieces are among the most prized by collectors. Perhaps the most spectacular form of native art comes from the Pacific coast. Totemic culture is surely on of the greatest legacy of Canada's First Nations. This culture reached its height at the middle of the last century, and it is easy to imagine the wonder that the sight of 30 to 40 totem poles along the rivers leading to each native village must have engendered in the first Europeans to settle in British Columbia. The totems were not revered like idols but featured elements relating to native beliefs.

Among the top contemporary visual artists are Benjamin Chee-Chee, of Ojibwa descent, who has produced works with abstract lines and geometric motifs, and Norval Morrisseau, who developed a style dubbed "pictographic", with themes drawn from native legends.

Painting

Québec

Visual art in Québec through most of the 19th century displayed a rather antiquated aesthetic. With the support of major art collectors in Montréal, Québec artists began to experiment somewhat towards the end of the 19th century and the beginning of the 20th century. Landscape artists, including Lucius R. O'Brien, achieved a certain success during this period. The Barbizon school, characterized by representations of rural life, was also influential. Inspired by the La Haye school, painters like Edmund Morris began to introduce a suggestion of subjectivism into their work.

The works of Ozias Leduc, which are attributed to the Symbolism trend, began to show a tendency towards the subjective interpretation of reality, as did the sculptures of Alfred Laliberté at the beginning of the 20th century. Some works completed around this time exhibit a certain receptiveness of European styles, among them the paintings of Suzor-Côté. It is however, in the work of James Wilson Morrice, who was inspired by Matisse, that the influence of the European School is most explicitly detectable. Morrice, who died in 1924, is considered by most as the forerunner of modern art in Québec . It would, however, take several years, marked notably by the work of Marc-Aurèle Fortin, landscape and urban artist, before the visual arts in Québec were in line with contemporary trends.

Québec modern art began to affirm itself during World War II thanks to the leaders of the group, Alfred Pellan and Paul-Émile Borduas. In the 1950s, two major trends developed in Québec's art community. The most significant of these involved non-figurative works, of which there were two general categories: abstract expressionism, as seen in the works of Marcelle Ferron, Marcel Barbeau, Pierre Gauvreau and Jean-Paul Riopelle, and geometric abstraction, represented by artists such as Jean-Paul Jérôme, Fernand Toupin, Louis Belzile and Redolphe de Repentigny. The other major trend in art was a new wave of figurative painting by artists including Jean Dallaire and Jean-Paul Lemieux.

Post-war trends continued into the 1960s. The emergence of new painters, such as Guido Molinari, Claude Tousignant and Yves Gaucher

PORTRAIT

brought increased attention to the geometric abstraction style. Engraving and print-making became more common mediums of expression, art "happenings" were frequent and artists began to be asked to provide work for public places. Styles and influences diversified greatly in the early 1970s, resulting in the eclectic art scene found in Québec today.

English Canada

It was not until the 19th century that it became possible to speak of Ontario art movements. At the turn of the 1840s, a few artists began to stand out, producing paintings that extolled the land, portraying the immensity of a scarcely inhabited territory, with pastoral scenes and typical landscapes. Encouraged by local collectors, a few artists began gradually to develop personal styles. This was true, for instance, of Cornelius Krieghoff, a painter of Dutch descent whose canvases evoke the rustic lives of the new settlers, and of Robert R. Whale, a landscape painter.

At the beginning of the 20th century, the creation of the Canadian Art Club set out to promote painting in Canada and to raise the profile of Canadian artists, some of whom had emigrated to Europe, through a series of exhibitions held between 1907 and 1915. Among Ontario-born painters who spent much of their lives in Europe, James Wilson Morrice is no doubt the most famous, creating works that show the mark of European masters, especially of the impressionists and of Matisse.

In the early years of the 20th century, some of the great Ontario landscape painters became known by creating genuinely Canadian art. Tom Thomson, whose paintings provide a distinctive portrayal of landscapes unique to the Canadian Shield, was an originator of this movement. He died prematurely in 1917 at the age of 40 though his work had an indisputable effect over one of the most notable groups of painters in Ontario, the Group of Seven, whose first exhibition was held in Toronto in 1920. These artists, Franklin Carmichael, Lawren S. Harris, Frank H. Johnson, Arthur Lismer, J.E.H. MacDonald, Alexander Young Jackson and Frederick Varley, were all landscape painters. Although they worked together closely, each developed his own pictorial language. They were distinguished by their use of bright colours in their portrayal of typical Canadian landscapes. Their influence over Canadian painting is substantial, and only a handful of

contemporary artists distinguished themselves from the movement, among them David Milne Brown, developed a technique inspired by Fauvism and impressionism.

Painters began gradually to put landscapes aside and to exploit social themes instead. This was true of Peraskeva Clark, whose canvasses evoke the difficult years of the Great Depression, and of Carl Schaefer, who chose to reproduce rural scenes from his home region of Hanover, Ontario, using them to portray the Depression's harsh consequences.

Abstract art, which flourished in Québec around the 1940s also had its disciples in Ontario, among them Lawren Harris, a former member of the Group of Seven, and also the Painters Eleven, Ontario's second great pictorial movement, created in 1954.

The stark landscape of the Canadian prairie with its cold winters and fields are typical of artist William Kurelek. Of Ukrainian descent Kurelek's has recreated scenes from across Canada.

It is impossible to cast a cursory glance at Canadian painting without treating the work of Emily Carr, which rendered all the splendour of British-Columbian landscapes in shades of green and blue and conveyed something of the Native American spirit. Jack Shadbolt and Gordon Smith would also convey the particular vision of the surrounding landscapes shared by those living on the West Coast.

At the other end of the country, in the white light of the Atlantic, Alex Coleville paints. His hyperrealist style, great technical mastery and the gaze of his characters are spellbinding.

Literature

Literature in English

Over the years, Canadian literature has sought to create its own space among English-language literatures. Although Britain and the United States have had a commanding influence in defining this identity, English-speaking Canadian authors have gradually given shape to a literary thinking they can call their own.

Although trading posts were set up at points across Ontario and there was a small

PORTRAIT

population of settlers in the 17th century, it was not until the end of the 18th century that colonization began in earnest, with towns and villages developing along the St. Lawrence and the Great Lakes. One cannot really speak of Canadian literature in English until the 1820s.

The first writers, mostly poets, set out to describe the geographic reality that surrounded them, with its wild, untamed nature. This movement can well be described as realist literature and is representative of the concerns of Canadian society of that era, with a vast space to occupy. Several works mark these early moments in English-Canadian literature, such as those of William Kirby and Alexander McLachlan. There gradually developed a desire to create a romantic literature with Canadian accents. In Eastern Canada, Lucy Maud Montgomery wrote her most famous work *Anne of Green Gables*. She is doubtless the most widely renowned of local writers and her book, perhaps the most famous Canadian novel. Literary works reflecting urban realities and their harmonization with nature also began to evolve, giving a foretaste of important urban developments in the 20th century and issuing warnings of their dangers. These themes are brought out in the works of Archibald Lampman, Duncan Campbell Scott and Isabella Valancy Crawford.

The beginning of the 20th century was marked by a tragic world event, the outbreak of the First World War with its profound influence on English-Canadian thinking. Some people began to feel a need to face up to the British Empire and seek a more equal position for Canada. Writers were hardly exempt from this movement, and the first demands for the development of Canadian culture began to be heard. Writers felt a need to break away from the omnipresent British cultural domination. In the United States, many authors had established themselves not merely as writers of English but as American writers. This emancipation drew envy from several English-speaking Canadian authors and spurred them to create a style of their own. But this movement was not unanimous in its support, and some authors, such as Mazo de la Roche in her chronicles, still called for solid links with the British Empire.

This movement would grow all the same, allowing modern Canadian literature in English to define itself more clearly. Hugh McLennan, in his novel *Two Solitudes*, speaks of relations between English- and French-speakers, creating a work with distinctly Canadian themes. The 20th century was also the era of industrialization and of the deep social upheavals that came in its wake, bringing on a more active social engagement and the denunciation of injustice and social evils. This led to a protest movement reflecting a need the build a more just Canadian society. Many voices were heard, including those of authors such as Morley Callaghan, who depicted the hard life of city-dwellers and promoted a stronger social engagement, Stephen Leacock, whose works offer humorous criticisms of Canadian society, and Raymond Souster, a Toronto writer known for his political engagement.

The theatre world has also blossomed thanks, among others, to the works of playwright and novelist and novelist Robertson Davies. His *Deptford Trilogy* and *Cornish Trilogy*, both set in Toronto, are analytical and thoughtful looks at the growth of the city from provincialism to sophistication. *The Cunning Man*, the last novel in the latter trilogy, is particularly noteworthy. Summer theatre festivals have become an important element in Ontario cultural life, in particular the Shakespeare festival held every year in Stratford since 1953, and the Shaw festival in Niagara-on-the-Lake.

Margaret Atwood, a feminist, satirist, nationalist, poet and novelist carried modernism into the seventies. Her literary and critical writings have contributed much to an attempt at defining Canadian culture and literature. The 1970s saw the appearance of modern movements such as Open Letter in Toronto, seeking to bring new contributions to old ideas. Several authors have also distinguished themselves, notably John Ralston Saul for his essay *Voltaire's Bastards*, Michael Ondaatje, the Sri Lankan-born Toronto author who won Britain's prestigious Booker Prize in 1993 for his novel *The English Patient*, and, more recently, Toronto writer Timothy Findley, upon whom the French government conferred the title of *chevalier des arts et lettres* for his body of work.

One of the earliest pieces of western-Canadian literature is *David Thompson's Narrative of his Explorations in Western North American 1784-1812*. Earle Birney was born in Alberta, and was brought up there and in British Columbia. His belief that geography links man to his history is evident in his poetry and its attempts to define the significance of place and time.

Born in 1920 in the Yukon, which was overrun by gold-diggers in the 19th century, to a father who participated in the Klondike gold rush, Pierre Berton lived in Vancouver for many years. He has written many accounts of the high points of Canadian history including *The Last Spike* which recounts the construction of the pan-Canadian railway across the Rockies all the way to Vancouver.

Renowned for her powerful paintings of Canada's Pacific coast, Emily Carr wrote her first book at the age of 70, just a few years before her death. The few books she wrote are autobiographical works, which vividly portray the atmosphere of British Columbia and exhibit her extensive knowledge of the customs and beliefs of the First Nations.

Robert Kroetch and Rudy Wiebe are two of Alberta's most well-respected writers. Kroetch is a storyteller above all, and his *Out West* trilogy offers an in-depth look at Alberta over four decades. *Alberta* is part travel guide, part wonderful collection of stories and essays, and captures the essence of the land and people of Alberta. *Seed Catalogue* is another of his excellent works. Rudy Wiebe is not a native Albertan but spent most of his life there. He was raised as a Mennonite, and the moral vision instilled in him by his religious background is the most important feature of his writing. *The Temptations of Big Bear*, for which he won the Governor General's Award, describes the disintegration of native culture caused by the growth of the Canadian nation.

The writings of Jane Rule, an American who has lived in British Columbia since 1956, reflect a mentality that is typical of both the American and Canadian west. However, she is better known for her efforts to bridge the gap between the homosexual and heterosexual communities. Other notable western writers include poets Patrick Lane from British Columbia and Sid Marty from Alberta. More recently, however, Vancouver can be proud of its native son Douglas Coupland, who in 1991 at the age of 30 published his first novel, *Generation X*. His work coined a new catchphrase that is now used by everyone from sociologists to ad agencies to describe this young, educated and underemployed generation. Coupland's novel *Microserfs*, is just as sociological, as he describes the world of young computer whizzes, making sweeping generalizations about American popular culture that are both ironic and admiring; interestingly paralleling English-Canadian sentiment about

the United States. More recently *Life After God* explores spirituality in a modern world and the impact of a generation raised without religion.

Vancouver playwrite George Ryga's play *Ecstasy of Rita Joe* marked a renewal for Canadian theatre in 1967. This work deals with the culture shock experienced by native communities, inherently turned towards nature yet existing in a dehumanized western society. Albertan Brad Fraser's powerful play *Unidentified Human Being Remains or the True Nature of Love* analyzes contemporary love in an urban setting. The play was adapted for the cinema by Denys Arcand under the title *Love and Human Remains*.

Literature in French

Literary output in Québec began with the writings of early explorers, like Jacques Cartier, and members of religious communities. These manuscripts were usually intended to describe the New World to authorities back in France. The lifestyles of the aboriginals, the geography of the region and the beginnings of colonization were the topics most often covered by authors of the period, such as Père Sagard (*Le Grand Voyage au Pays Hurons*, 1632) and Baron de La Hontan (*Nouveaux Voyages en Amérique Septentrionale*, 1703).

The oral tradition dominated literature during 18th century and the beginning of the 19th century. Most of the literary output of this period dealt with the theme of survival and reflected nationalist, religious and conservative values. The romanticization of life in the country, far from the temptations of the city, was a common element. Glorifying the past, particularly the period of French rule, was another common theme in the literature of the time. With the exception of certain works, most of the novels from this period are only of sociohistoric interest.

Traditionalism continued to profoundly influence literary creation until 1930, when certain new literary movements began to emerge. The École Littéraire de Montréal (Montréal Literary School), and particularly the works of the poet Émile Nelligan, who was inspired by Baudelaire, Rimbaud, Verlaine and Rodenbach, stood in contrast to the prevailing style of the time. Nelligan, who remains a mythical figure, wrote poetry at a very young age, before lapsing into mental illness. Rural life remained an important ingredient of Québec

PORTRAIT

fiction during this period, though certain authors began to put country life in a different light. Louis Hémon, in *Maria Chapdelaine* (1916), presented rural life more realistically, while Albert Laberge (*La Scouine*, 1918) presented the mediocrity of a country existence.

During the Great Depression and Second World War, Québec literature began to reflect modernism. Literature with a rural setting, which continued to dominate, gradually began to incorporate themes of alienation. Another major step was taken when cities, where most of Québec's population actually lived, began to be used as settings in francophone fiction, in books such as *Bonheur d'Occasion* (*The Tin Flute* 1945), by Franco-Manitoban Gabrielle Roy.

Modernism became a particularly strong literary force with the end of the war, despite Maurice Duplessis's repressive administration. Two genres of fiction dominated during this period. The urban novel, and the psychological novel. Québec poetry entered a golden era distinguished by the work of a multitude of writers such as Gaston Miron, Alain Grandbois, Anne Hébert, Rina Lasnier and Claude Gauvreau. This era essentially saw the birth of Québec theatre as well. With regard to essay writing, the *Refus Global* (1948), signed by a group of painters, was the most incisive of many diatribes critical of the Duplessis administration.

Québec writers gained greater prominence with the political and social vitality brought about by the Quiet Revolution in the 1960s. A great number of political essays, such as *Nègre Blanc d'Amérique* (1968), by Pierre Vallière reflected an era of reappraisal, conflict and cultural upheaval. Through the plays of Marcel Dubé and those of rising talents such as Michel Tremblay, Québec theatre truly came into its own during this period. The use by novelists, poets and dramatists of idiomatic French-Canadian speech, called *joual*, was an important literary breakthrough of the time.

Nancy Huston was born in Calgary and lived there for 15 years. More than 20 years ago, after a five-year stay in New York City, she decided to relocate to Paris, where she finished her doctoral studies in semiology under the tutelage of Roland Barthes. After winning the Governor General's Award in 1993 for her novel *Cantique des Plaines* (*Plainsong* in English) she became a major contributor to French-language literature. Since then she has published, among other things, *Tombeau de Romain Gary*, another brilliant work.

Contemporary literature is rich and diversified. New writers, such as Victor-Levy Beaulieu, Alice Parizeau, Roch Carrier, Jacques Poulin, Louis Caron, Yves Beauchemin and Christian Mistral, have joined the ranks of previously established authors.

Music

Music entered a modern era in Canada after The Second World War. World renowned symphony orchestras and operas make their homes in Canadian cities from east to west. Major music festivals including the Scotia Music Festival in Halifax, International Baroque Music Festival on Lameque Island in New Brunswick, the International Music Festival in the Québec's Lanaudière region, Montréal, Toronto and Vancouver's famous jazz festivals, Edmonton's Folk Music Festival, the list goes on and on.

The Canadian Radio-television and Telecommunications Commission (CRTC) supervises all types of broadcasting in Canada, ensuring among other things Canadian content. For example any non-Canadian songs are limited to 18 airplays per week. Though this may seem restrictive, it has gone a long way to promoting Canadian music and television in all its forms and languages, and to ensuring that Canadian artists get a fair chance in an area that is all too often dominated by the sleeping giant to the south.

With the Quiet Revolution, song writing in Québec entered a new and vital era. Singers like Claude Leveille, Jean-Pierre Ferland, Gilles Vigneault et Claude Gauthier won over crowds with nationalist and culturally significant lyrics. In 1968, Robert Charlebois made an important contribution to the Québec music scene by producing the first French-language rock album. Currently, established performers like Plume Latravarse, Michel Rivard, Diane Dufresne, Pauline Julien, Claude Dubois, Richard Seguin, Paul Piche are being joined by newcomers like Jean Leloup, Joe Bocan, Sylvie Bernard, Vilains Pingouins and Richard Desjardins.The most well known name these days is Celine Dion, who sings in both French and English. Her amazing voice has made her *the* pop diva around the world. There is also the particular achievement of songwriter Luc Plamondon and his participation in the production of *Starmania*. Québec also has its share of non-francophone artists, like singer and poet Leonard Cohen, eighties pop star Corey Hart and the Innu musical group Kashtin.

English-Canadian artists working in the greatest variety of genres have made their mark on the world music scene. In classical music, Toronto's Glen Gould stood out very quickly as an exceptionally gifted pupil who learned musical composition starting at age 5. His virtuosity was recognized unanimously and he is remembered on the world scene as one of the most talented musicians of his period.

Neil Young was born in Toronto but only spent part of his youth there before moving with his mother to Winnipeg, Manitoba. At first he was a member of various groups, including The Squires, Buffalo Springfield and, most notably, Crosby, Stills, Nash and Young. He began his solo career in 1969, and in 1972 he recorded *Harvest*, his most popular and best known album.

Bruce Cockburn was born in Ottawa. Widely recognized in the United States and Europe, especially in Britain, as well as in Canada, Cockburn sits atop many lists of pop music writers, composers and singers. His words, often poetic, sometimes present thoughts on rural life, as in his early albums, sometimes offer more mystical connotations, or sometimes display political and environmental commitment, as in his album *Humans*. Among his recordings, some that stand out are *High Winds, White Sky* (his second album), *Dancing in the Dragon's Jaws* (nominated for various awards), *Stealing Fire*, *Humans* and *Big Circumstance*. He also wrote musical scores for famous films such as *Goin' Down the Road*, which won him a BMI Award as well as a Juno Award for Canadian popular singer of the year.

Among other musicians who have become noted on the international scene are the hard-rock group Rush, the crooner Paul Anka and, lately, Barenaked Ladies, whose music moves between rock, jazz and folk. Alanis Morissette exploded onto the scene in 1996, Shania Twain contributed to country's move into the mainstream. Country music is most representative of Alberta music. Wilf Carter, from Calgary became famous in the United States as a yodelling cowboy. More recently k.d. lang, of Consort, Alberta became a Grammy-winning superstar. In her early days with the Reclines she was known for her outrageous outfits and honky-tonk style, but of late, her exceptional voice and blend of country and pop are her trademarks. A rarity in show business, she has always had the courage to be open about her homosexuality. Alberta also has its share of more mainstream stars, among them Jann Arden.

British Columbia, and more particularly cosmopolitan Vancouver prefers a little more variety and has produced some significant mainstream stars. Bryan Adams was actually born in Kingston, Ontario, but eventually settled in Vancouver. This grammy-nominated rock and roll performer is known the world over. Grammy-winner Sarah McLachlan, herself born in Halifax, Nova Scotia, now calls Vancouver home and has set up her own record label, Nettwerk, in the city.

In Atlantic Canada, the Celtic and Irish influences make for wonderfully melodious music that is very much a part of everyday life. The growing mainstream popularity of this kind of music is thanks in part to artists like the famous rock-fiddler Ashley McIsaac, the brother and sister group the Rankin Family, songstress Rita McNeil and Newfoundland group Great Big Sea.

Film

The weak sister of the arts scene, the Canadian film industry has developed only slowly, financially unable to match the big-budget films produced by the major American studios. As a result, it has not achieved much recognition among the Canadian public. During the 1950s, the creation of the National Film Board paved the way for the emergence of many documentaries and other quality films, as well as bringing fame to Canadian film-makers.

In French Canada, however, the film industry has been free to flourish. With documentaries and realistic films, directors focused primarily on a critique of Québec society. Later, the full-length feature film dominated with the success of certain directors like Claude Jutras (*Mon Oncle Antoine*), Jean-Claude Lord (*Les Colombes*), Gilles Carle (*La Vraie Nature de Bernadette*), Michel Brault (*Les Ordres*), Jean Beaudin (*J.A. Martin Photographe*) and Frank Mankiewicz (*Les Bons Débarras*). The NFB-ONF and other government agencies provided most of the funding for these largely uncommercial works.

Import feature films of recent years include those of Denys Arcand (*Le Déclin de l'Empire Américain,* and *Jésus de Montréal,* 1989, both available in English), Jean-Claude Lauzon (*Un Zoo la Nuit,* and *Léolo*) Léa Pool (*À Corps Perdu*) and Jean Beaudin (*Being at Home With Claude*).

The 1970s were important for the English-Canadian film industry, with the production of certain films that finally found favour with the public. Some producers, such as Don Shebib with his film *Goin' Down the Road,* even achieved commercial success.

Despite difficult beginnings, Canadian cinema has recently achieved greater recognition thanks to talented producers such as David Cronenberg, with his films *Rabid, The Fly, Naked Lunch, M. Butterfly,* and *Crash,* which won the jury prize at Cannes in 1996. Others include Robin Spry, with *Flowers on a One-Way Street* and *Obsessed,* and Atom Egoyan, with *The Adjuster, Family Viewing, Exotica* and *The Sweet Hereafter.* Several avant-garde film-makers have also stood out, notably Bruce MacDonald, with *Road Kill* and *Highway 61.* Sticking more to the mainstream, director James Cameron spent a lot of Hollywood dollars on blockbusters like *Terminator* and *Titanic.*

Animated films from the early days of the National Film Board achieved great success on the international scene. Norman McLaren, who developed various techniques that revolutionized this art such as painting directly onto the film, won an Oscar for his 1952 film *Neighbours.* Other contributions to this field include J. Hoedman with *Sand Castle* and John Weldon and Eunice Macaumay with *Special Delivery.* Director Frédérick Back won an Academy Award in 1988 for his superb animated film, *The Man who Planted Trees.*

PRACTICAL INFORMATION

I nformation in this chapter will help you to better plan your trip, not only well in advance, but once you've arrived in Canada. Important details on entrance formalities and other procedures, as well as general information, have been compiled for visitors from other countries. Finally, we explain how this guide works, which will not only fully benefit tourists from other countries, but also Canadians. We wish you happy travels in Canada!

ENTRANCE FORMALITIES

Passport

For a stay of less than three months in Canada, a valid passport is usually sufficient for most visitors and a visa is not required. American residents do not need passports, though these are the best form of identification. A three-month extension is possible, but a return ticket and proof of sufficient funds to cover this extension may be required.

Caution: some countries do not have an agreement with Canada concerning health and accident insurance, so it is advisable to have the appropriate coverage. For more information, see the section entitled, "Health", on page 57.

Canadian citizens who wish to enter the United States, to visit Alaska or Washington State for example, do not need visas, neither do citizens of the majority of Western European countries. A valid passport is sufficient for a stay of less than three months. A return ticket and proof of sufficient funds to cover your stay may be required.

Extended Visits

A visitor must submit a request to extend his or her visit **in writing, before** the expiration of his or her visa (the date is usually written in your passport) to an Immigration Canada office. To make a request you must have a valid passport, a return ticket, proof of sufficient funds to cover the stay, as well as the $65 non-refundable filing-fee. In some cases (work, study), however, the request must be made **before** arriving in Canada.

CUSTOMS

If you are bringing gifts into Canada, remember that certain restrictions apply. Smokers (minimum age is 16) can bring in a maximum of 200 cigarettes, 50 cigars, 400 grams of tobacco, or 400 tobacco sticks. For wine and alcohol the limit is 1.1 litres; in practice, however, two bottles per person are usually allowed. The limit for beer is twenty-four 355-ml size cans or bottles.

Plants, vegetation, and food: there are very strict rules regarding the importation of plants, flowers, and other vegetation; it is therefore not advisable to bring any of these types of products into the country. If it is absolutely necessary, contact the Customs-Agriculture service of the Canadian embassy **before** leaving your country.

Pets: if you are travelling with your pet, you will need a health certificate (available from your veterinarian) as well as a rabies vaccination certificate. It is important to remember that the vaccination must have been administered **at least 30 days before** your departure and should not be more than a year old.

Tax reimbursements for visitors: it is possible to be reimbursed for certain taxes paid on purchases made in Canada (see p 56).

EMBASSIES AND CONSULATES

Canadian Embassies and Consulates Abroad

Australia
Canadian Consulate General, Level 5, Quay West, 111 Harrington Road, Sydney, N.S.W., Australia 2000, ☎(612) 364-3000, ☛(612) 364-3098

Belgium
Canadian Embassy, 2 Avenue de Tervueren, 1040 Brussels, ☎(2) 735.60.40, ☛(2) 732.67.90

Denmark
Canadian Embassy, Kr. Bernikowsgade 1, DK = 1105 Copenhagen K, Denmark, ☎(45) 12.22.99, ☛(45) 14.05.85

Finland
Canadian Embassy, Pohjos Esplanadi 25 B, 00100 Helsinki, Finland, ☎(9) 171-141, ☛(9) 601-060

Germany
Canadian Consulate General, Internationales, Handelzentrum, Friedrichstrasse 95, 23rd Floor, 10117 Berlin, Germany, ☎(30) 261.11.61, ☛(30) 262.92.06

Great Britain
Canada High Commission, Macdonald House, One Grosvenor Square, London W1X 0AB, England, ☎(171) 258-6600, ☛(171) 258-6384

Italy
Canadian Embassy, Via G.B. de Rossi 27, 00161 Rome, ☎(6) 44.59.81, ☛(6) 44.59.87

Netherlands
Canadian Embassy, Parkstraat 25, 2514JD The Hague, Netherlands, ☎(70) 361-4111, ☛(70) 365-6283

Norway
Canadian Embassy, Oscars Gate 20, Oslo 3, Norway, ☎(47) 46.69.55, ☛(47) 69.34.67

Spain
Canadian Embassy, Edificio Goya, Calle Nunez de Balboa 35, 28001 Madrid, ☎(1) 431.43.00, ☛(1) 431.23.67

Sweden
Canadian Embassy, Tegelbacken 4, 7th floor, Stockholm, Sweden, ☎(8) 613-9900, ☛(8) 24.24.91

Switzerland
Canadian Embassy, Kirchenfeldstrasse 88, 3000 Berne 6, ☎(31) 532.63.81, ☛(31) 352.73.15

United States
Canadian Embassy, 501 Pennsylvania Avenue NW, Washington, DC, 20001, ☎(202) 682-1740, ☛(202) 682-7726

Canadian Consulate General, Suite 400 South Tower, One CNN Center, Atlanta, Georgia, 30303-2705, ☎(404) 577-6810 or 577-1512, ☛(404) 524-5046

Canadian Consulate General, Three Copley Place, Suite 400, Boston, Massachusetts, 02116, ☎(617) 262-3760, ☛(617) 262-3415

Canadian Consulate General, Two Prudential Plaza, 180 N. Stetson Avenue, Suite 2400, Chicago, Illinois, 60601, ☎(312) 616-1860, ☛(312) 616-1877

Canadian Consulate General, St. Paul Place, Suite 1700, 750 N. St. Paul Street, Dallas, Texas, 75201, ☎(214) 922-9806, ☛(214) 922-9815

Canadian Consulate General, 600 Renaissance Center, Suite 1100, Detroit, Michigan,

48234-1798, ☎(313) 567-2085, ✉(313) 567-2164

Canadian Consulate General, 300 South Grande Avenue, 10th Floor, California Plaza, Los Angeles, California, 90071, ☎(213) 687-7432, ✉(213) 620-8827

Canadian Consulate General, Suite 900, 701 Fourth Avenue South, Minneapolis, Minnesota, 55415-1899, ☎(612) 333-4641, ✉(612) 332-4061

Canadian Consulate General, 1251 Avenue of the Americas, New York, New York, 10020-1175, ☎(212) 596-1600, ✉(212) 596-1793

Canadian Consulate General, One Marine Midland Center, Suite 3000, Buffalo, New York, 14203-2884, ☎(716) 852-1247, ✉(716) 852-4340

Canadian Consulate General, 412 Plaza 600, Sixth and Stewart Streets, Seattle, Washington, 98101-1286, ☎(206) 442-1777, ✉(206) 443-1782

Foreign Embassies in Ottawa

Australia
Australian High Commission: 50 O'connor Street, Ottawa, Ontario, K1N 5R2, ☎(613) 236-0841, ✉(613) 236-4376.

Belgium
Embassy: 80 Elgin Street, 4th Floor, Ottawa, Ontario, K1P 1B7, ☎(613) 236-7267, ✉(613) 236-7882.

Denmark
Embassy: 47 Clarence, Ottawa, Ont., K1N 9K1, (613) 562-1811

Finland
Embassy: 55 Metcalfe, Suite 850, Ottawa, Ont., K1P 6L5, (613) 236-2389

Germany
Embassy: 1 Waverley, Ottawa, Ont., K2P 0T8, ☎(613) 232-1101, ✉(613) 594-9330.

Great Britain
Embassy: 80 Elgin, Ottawa, Ont., K1P 5K7, ☎(613) 237-1303, ✉(613) 237-6537.

Italy
Embassy: 275 Slater Street, 21st Floor, K1P 5H9, ☎(613) 232-2401, ✉(613) 233-1484.

Netherlands
Embassy: 350 Albert Street, Suite 2020, Ottawa, Ont., K1R 1A4, ☎(613) 237-5030, ✉(613) 237-6471.

Norway
Embassy: 90 Sparks, Ottawa, Ont., K1P 5B4, ☎(613) 238-6571.

Spain
Embassy: 74 Stanley Avenue, K1M 1P4, ☎(613) 747-2252, ✉(613) 744-1224.

Sweden
Embassy: 377 Dalhousie, Ottawa, Ont., K1N 9N8, ☎(613) 241-8553, ✉(613) 241-2277.

Switzerland
Swiss Embassy: 5 Malborough Avenue, K1N 8E6, ☎(613) 235-1837, ✉(613) 563-1394.

United States
Embassy: 100 Wellington, Ottawa, Ont., K1P 5T1, ☎(613) 238-5335, ✉(613) 238-5720.

Foreign Consulates in Toronto

Australia
Consulate General: 175 Bloor Street East, Toronto, Ont., M4W 3R8, ☎(416) 323-1155, ✉(416) 323-3910.

Belgium
Consulate General: 2 Bloor Street West, Suite 2006, Toronto, Ontario, N4W 3E2, ☎(416) 944-1422, ✉(416) 944-1421.

Denmark
Consulate General: 151 Bloor W, Suite 310,Toronto, Ont., M5S 1S4, (416) 962-5661, ✉(416) 962-3668.

Finland
Consulate General: 1200 Bay, Toronto, Ont., M5R 2A5, (416) 964-0066

Germany
Consulate General: 77 Admiral Road, Toronto, Ont., ☎(416) 925-2813, ✉(416) 925-2818.

PRACTICAL INFORMATION

Great Britain
Consulate General: 777 Bay Street, Suite 2800, Toronto, Ont., M5G 2G2, ☎(416) 593-1290, ⊷(416) 593-1229.

Italy
Consulate General: 136 Beverly Street, Toronto, Ont., M5T 1Y5, ☎(416) 977-1566, ⊷(416) 977-1119.

Netherlands
Consulate General: 1 Dundas Street West, Suite 2106, Toronto, Ont., M5G 1Z3, ☎(416) 598-2520, ⊷(416) 598-8064.

Norway
Honourary Consulate: 2600 South Sheridan Way, Clarkson, Ont., L5J 2M4, ☎(905) 822-2339, ⊷(905) 855-1450.

Norwegian Trade Council: 175 Bloor e, Suite 909, South Tower, Toronto, Ont., M4W 3R8, ☎(416) 920-0434, ⊷(416)920-5982.

Spain
Consulate General: Simcoe Place, 200 Front St. W., Suite 2401,Toronto, Ont., M5V 3K2, ☎(416) 977-1661, ⊷(416) 593-4949.

Sweden
Consulate General: 2 Bloor W, Suite 1504,Toronto, Ont., M4W 3E2, ☎(416) 963-8768

Switzerland
Consulate General: 154 University, Toronto, Ont., M5H 3Y9, ☎(416) 593-5371, ⊷(416) 593-5083.

United States
Consulate General: 360 University Avenue, Toronto, Ont., M5G 1S4, ☎(416) 595-1700, ⊷(416) 595-0051 or 595-5419.

Foreign Consulates in Montreal

Australia
Australian High Commission: (no office in Montréal), 50 O'Connor Street, Ottawa, Ontario, K1N 5R2, ☎(613) 236-0841, ⊷(613) 236-4376.

Belgium
Consulate General of Belgium: 999 Boulevard de Maisonneuve Ouest, suite 1250, Montréal, H3A 3C8, ☎(514) 849-7394, ⊷(514) 844-3170.

Denmark
Consulate General of Denmark: 1 Place-Ville-Marie, 35th Floor, Montréal, H3B 4M4, ☎(514) 871-8977.

Germany
Consulate General of Germany: Edifice Marathon, 1250 Boulevard René-Lévesque Ouest, Suite 4315, Montréal, H3B 4X1, ☎(514) 931-2277, ⊷(514) 931-7239..

Great Britain
British Consulate General: 1155 Rue University, Suite 901, Montréal, H3B 3A7, ☎(514) 866-5863.

Italy
Consulate General of Italy: 3489 Rue Drummond, Montréal, H3G 1Z6, ☎(514) 849-8351, ⊷(514) 499-9471.

Netherlands
Consulate General of the Netherlands: 1002 Rue Sherbrooke Ouest, Suite 2201, Montréal, H3A 3L6, ☎(514) 849-4247, ⊷(514) 849-8260.

Norway
Consulate General of Norway: 1155 Boul. René-Lévesque Ouest, Suite 3900, Montréal H3B 3V2, ☎(514) 874-9087.

Spain
Consulate General of Spain: 1 Westmount Square, Suite 1456, Montréal, H3Z 2P9, ☎(514) 935-5235, ⊷(514) 935-4655.

Sweden
Consulate General of Sweden: c/o Ericsson Communications, 8400 Boulevard Décairie, Ville de Mont-Royal, H4P 2N2, ☎(514) 345-2727, ⊷(514) 345-7972.

Switzerland
Consulate General of Switzerland: 1572 Avenue Dr Penfield, Montréal, H3G 1C4, ☎(514) 932-7181, ⊷(514) 932-9028.

United States
American Consulate General: Place Félix-Martin, 1155 Rue Saint-Alexandre, Montréal, H2Z 1Z2, ☎(514) 398-9695, ⊷(514) 398-9748.

Mailing address: C.P. 65 Stations Desjardins, Montréal, H5B 1G1.

Foreign Consulates in Vancouver

Australia
Australian Consulate: 999 Canada Place, Suite 602, Vancouver, BC, V6C 3E1, ☎(604) 684-1177,

Belgium
Honourary Consulate of Belgium: Birks Place, Suite 570, 688 West Hastings, Vancouver, BC, V6B 1P4, ☎(604) 684-6838

Finland
Consulate of Finland: 1188 Georgia Street West, Apt. 1100, Vancouver, BC, V6E 4A2, ☎(604) 688-4483

Germany
Consulate General of Germany: World Trade Centre, 999 Canada Place, Suite 704, Vancouver, BC, V6C 3E1, ☎(604) 684-8377, ⁼(604) 684-8334.

Great Britain
British Consulate General: 111 Melville St., Suite 800, Vancouver, BC, V6E 3V6, ☎(604) 683-4421

Italy
Consulate General of Italy: 1200 Burrard Street, Suite 705, Vancouver, B.C., V6Z 2C7, ☎(604) 684-7288, ⁼(604) 685-4263

Netherlands
Consulate General of the Netherlands: 475 Howe Street, Suite 821, Vancouver, BC, V6C 2B3, ☎(604) 684-6448

Norway
Royal Norwegian Consulate General: 1200 Waterfront Centre, 200 Burrard Street, Vancouver, BC, V6C 3L6, ☎(604) 682-7977, ⁼(604) 682-8376

Spain
Honourary Consul: 3736 Parker St., Burnaby, B.C., VC5 3B1, (604) 299-7760, ⁼(604) 255-2532.

Sweden
Consulate of Sweden: 1188 Georgia Street West, Apt. 1100, Vancouver, BC, V6E 4A2, ☎(604) 683-5838, ⁼(604) 687-8237.

Switzerland
Consulate General of Switzerland: 999 Canada Place, Suite 790, Vancouver, BC, V6C 3E1, ☎(604) 684-2231

United States
U.S. Consulate General: 1095 West Pender, 21st Floor, Vancouver, BC, V6E 2M6, ☎(604) 685-4311

 TOURIST INFORMATION

Each province has its own Ministry of Tourism that can provide you with a wealth of information and free brochures.

Different travel publishers have put out maps and guides about more specific areas of Canada. Ulysses Publications publish guides such as this one which take a closer look at these regions: *Atlantic Canada, Québec, Ontario* and *Western Canada*.

The addresses of the various regional tourist information offices are located in the "Practical Information" section of each chapter.

Tourist Information Offices Abroad

Belgium
Délégation Générale du Québec: 46 Avenue des Arts, 7e étage, 1040 Bruxelles, ☎(2) 512.00.36, Métro Art-Loi.

Société - Interface International: Amerikastraat 27, 1060 Bruxelles, ⁼(2) 539-2433.

Germany
Canada Tourismusprogramm: Postfach 200 247, 63469 Maintal 2, Deutschland, ☎(49) 6181 45178, ⁼(49) 6181 497558, Email: 06181441398-0001@t-online.de, http://www.dfait-maeci.gc.ca/~bonn/Tourism/eto2main.htm.

Great Britain
Visit Canada Centre: 62-65 Trafalgar Square, London, WC2N 5DT, ☎0891 715000 (calls charged at 50p/minute), ⁼(44) 171 389 1149, Email: vcc@dial.pipex.com.

PRACTICAL INFORMATION

Italy
Canadian Tourism Commission: Via Vittor Pisani 19, 20124 Milan, Italy, ☎(39) 2 6758-3900

Netherlands
Canadian Tourism Commission: Sophialaan 7, 2514 JP The Hague, Netherlands, ☎(70) 3111682.

Norway
Geelmuyden. Kiese: Lilleakervn.2d, Postboks 362, N-1324 Lysaker, NORDICS, ☎(47) 22 13 03 04.

Switzerland
Welcome to Canada!: 22, Freihofstrasse, 8700 Küsnacht, ☎(1) 910 38 24.

For more information, contact the Canadian embassy or consulate of your country.

AIRPORTS

Canada has several international airports. For information on each, see the Practical information section at the beginning of each chapter.

 GETTING TO CANADA

By Car

Good road conditions and cheaper oil prices than in Europe make driving an ideal way to travel all over Québec. Excellent road maps published in Québec and regional maps can be found in bookstores and in tourist information centres

Things to Consider

Driver's License: As a general rule, foreign driver's licenses are valid for six months from the arrival date in Canada.

Winter Driving: Although roads are generally in good condition, the dangers brought on by drastic climatic conditions must be taken into consideration. Roads are often transformed into virtual skating rinks by black ice. Wind is also a factor, causing blowing snow, and reducing visibility to almost nil. All these factors, which Canada is used to, require prudent driving. If you plan on driving through remote areas, be sure to bring along a blanket and some supplies should your car break down.

Driving and the Highway Code: There is no priority to the right. Traffic lights at intersections indicate priority to the right. Signs marked "Arrêt" or "Stop" against a red background must always be respected. Come to a complete stop even if there is no apparent danger.

Traffic lights are often located on the opposite side of the intersection, so be careful to stop on the stop line, a white line on the pavement before the intersection. When a school bus (usually yellow in colour) has stopped and has its signals flashing, you must come to a complete stop, no matter what direction you are travelling in. Failing to stop at the flashing signals is considered a serious offense, and carries a heavy penalty. Wearing of seatbelts in the front and back seats is compulsory at all times.

In all provinces except for Québec, right turns are permitted on red lights as long as there are no cars in the right lane.

The speed limit on highways is 100 km/h. The speed limit on secondary highways is 90 km/h, and 50 km/h in urban areas.

Gas Stations: Because Canada produces its own crude oil, gasoline prices are less expensive than in Europe, around $0.60 a litre. Some gas stations (especially in the downtown areas) might ask for payment in advance as a security measure, especially after 11 p.m.

Car Rentals

Many travel agencies have agreements with the major car rental companies (Avis, Budget, Hertz, etc.) and offer good values; contracts often include added bonuses (reduced ticket prices for shows, etc.).

When renting a car, find out if:

The contract includes unlimited kilometres and if the insurance offered provides full coverage (accident, property damage, hospital costs for you and passengers, theft).

Table of distances (km/mi)
Via the shortest route

© ULYSSES

Example: The distance between Montréal and Toronto is 542 km or 325 mi.

1 mile = 1.6 kilometre
1 kilometre = 0.6 mile

	Calgary (AB)	Charlottetown (PE)	Edmonton (AB)	Fredericton (NB)	Halifax (NS)	Montréal (QC)	Ottawa (ON)	Québec (QC)	Regina (SK)	Saskatoon (SK)	St. John's (NF)	Toronto (ON)	Vancouver (BC)	Whitehorse (YK)	Winnipeg (MB)
Charlottetown (PE)	4847/2908														
Edmonton (AB)	278/167	5125/3075													
Fredericton (NB)	4461/2677	386/232	4739/2843												
Halifax (NS)	4931/2959	265/159	5209/3125	469/281											
Montréal (QC)	3643/2186	1207/724	3921/2353	820/492	1290/774										
Ottawa (ON)	3508/2105	1403/842	3786/2272	1017/610	1487/892	197/118									
Québec (QC)	3894/2336	984/590	4173/2504	598/359	1068/641	254/152	449/269								
Regina (SK)	758/455	4092/2455	1036/622	3706/2224	4176/2506	2888/1733	2753/1653	3139/1884							
Saskatoon (SK)	825/495	4380/2628	523/314	3994/2396	4464/2678	3176/1906	3041/1825	3427/2056	257/154						
St. John's (NF)	5742/3445	957/574	6020/3612	1281/769	1020/612	2101/1261	2296/1378	1879/1127	4987/2992	5275/3165					
Toronto (ON)	3427/2056	1747/1048	3706/2224	1361/817	1833/1099	542/325	402/241	795/477	2673/1604	2961/1777	2642/1585				
Vancouver (BC)	967/580	5814/4888	1245/747	5428/3257	5898/3539	4610/2710	4475/2685	4861/2917	1725/1035	1792/1075	6709/4025	4387/2632			
Whitehorse (YK)	2330/1398	7177/4306	2051/1231	6791/4075	7261/4357	5973/3584	5838/3503	6224/3734	3088/1853	2579/1547	8072/4843	5750/3455	1919/1151		
Winnipeg (MB)	1329/797	3518/2111	1607/964	3131/1879	3601/2161	2314/1388	2179/1307	2565/1539	574/344	862/517	4412/2647	2098/1259	2296/1378	3659/2195	
Yellowknife (NT)	1733/1040	6580/3948	1454/872	6194/3716	6664/3998	5376/3226	5241/3145	5627/3376	2491/1495	1979/1187	7475/4485	5161/3097	2700/1620	2685/1611	3062/1837

Caution:

To rent a car, you must be at least 21 years of age and have had a driver's license for **at least** one year. If you are between 21 and 25, certain companies (for example Avis, Thrifty, Budget) will ask for a $500 deposit, and in some cases they will also charge an extra sum for each day you rent the car. These conditions do not apply for those over 25 years of age.

A credit card is extremely useful for the deposit to avoid tying up large sums of money.

Most rental cars have an automatic transmission, however you can request a car with a manual shift. Child safety seats cost extra.

Renting an R.V.
(Motorhomes or Camper-Trailers)

This is a fairly expensive way to get around, but beyond the price it is an excellent way to discover the great outdoors. As with the car rental, however, a package deal organized through a travel agency is the most inexpensive. Your travel agent can provide you with more information.

Because of high demand and the short camping season, it is necessary to reserve early to have a good choice of trailers. When planning a summer holiday it is best to reserve by January or February at the latest.

Remember to examine the insurance coverage carefully as these vehicles are very expensive. Make sure the kitchen utensils and the bedding are included in the rental price.

Here is a helpful address should you decide to rent on the spot. There are many other companies listed in the Yellow Pages phone book under the heading *Recreation Vehicles*:

Cruise Canada *(☎514-628-7093 or 1-888-278-1736, ⁼514-628-7103)* has offices in Vancouver, Calgary, Toronto and Montréal.

Accidents and Emergencies

In most parts of Canada, in case of serious accident, fire or other emergency, you can dial **911**. Where this service is not available, dial **0**.

If you run into trouble on the highway, pull onto the shoulder of the road and turn the hazard lights on. If it is a rental car, contact the rental company as soon as possible. Always file an accident report. If a disagreement arises over who was at fault in an accident, ask for police help.

By Bus

Besides cars, busses are the easiest way to get around, are relatively cheap, and provide access to most of Canada. It takes only three-and-a-half days to cross the country. Except for public transportation in cities, which is government-run, there is no national transportation company; many private coach lines share the road. **Greyhound** *(☎1-800-661-8747)* covers all of Western Canada to Ottawa. **Voyageur** *(☎514-842-2281)* is the big company in Québec.

Smoking is prohibited on most bus lines and pets are not allowed. In general, children under five travel free of charge and people aged 60 and over are granted significant discounts.

Travel Times

Montréal - Ottawa:	2 h 10 min
Montréal - Québec City:	2 h 45 min
Montréal - Toronto:	6 h 10 min
Calgary - Vancouver:	14 hours
Toronto - Vancouver:	3 days

Passes

Travellers wishing to cover a lot of ground might want to consider a pass. Greyhound offers a 15-day Canada Pass for travel in Western Canada all the way to Ottawa for $294. Greyhound and Voyageur offer the TourPass for 14 days of travel in Québec and Ontario for $230. Certain restrictions apply and extensions are possible. You can save up to 30% in some cases by purchasing your ticket in advance. A 50 % reduction is offered to children under 12, children under five travel free-of-charge.

Bus Tours

Some companies also offer package deals on excursions of a day or more, which (depending

VIA Rail: Discover Canada By Train!

In this part of North America where the highway is king, the train is often overlooked as a different and enjoyable way of exploring Canada. What better way to contemplate the spectacular and unique Western Canadian scenery than through huge picture windows while comfortably seated in your wide reclining chair?

The Routes

Modern and rapid (reaching up to 150 km/h), **VIA Rail** trains connect eastern Canadian cities in no time.

Preferred by businesspeople, the Québec-Windsor corridor, one of the busiest routes, connects the downtown metropolis's of Québec, Montréal, Ottawa, Toronto, Windsor and other towns quickly and comfortably.

VIA Rail also provides a regular service to New Brunswick and Nova Scotia. Particularly interesting is the transcontinental *Chaleur*, leaving from Montreal, which follows the river, taking passengers to Gaspé via Carleton, New Carlisle and Percé, among other cities. The *Abitibi* train, for its part, acquaints passengers with the Lanaudière, Mauricie and Abitibi-Témiscamingue regions. There is also the *Saguenay*, which travels to Saguenay—Lac-Saint-Jean, the land of Marie Chapdelaine. And of course, the train also links Montreal and Quebec City, travelling though Montérégie and Bois-Francs.

An exciting way of seeing the country is aboard the *Canadian*, which departs from Toronto and travels all the way to Vancouver running through Ontario's forests, the central Prairies and the mountains of the West. The *Skeena* offers just as spectacular a route, departing from Jasper in the Rockies and traversing the mountains travelling along the magnificent Skeena River all the way to Prince Rupert. Finally, the *Malahat* makes daily trips on Vancouver Island, between Victoria and Courtenay, serving up magnificent views along the way.

Economy or First Class?

Economy class carriages are equipped with comfortable seats and wide aisles and, for a slight surcharge, passengers can have something to eat as well. If you enjoy being waited on hand and foot, opt for first class, where the price of your ticket includes access to a waiting room, priority boarding and meals served with wine and spirits at your seat, in warmly decorated carriages.

Some trains are equipped with a Skyline carriage in which a café and saloon car allow you to enjoy yourselves in the company of other passengers. These carriages have large panoramic windows whence you can admire the passing landscape.

Save with *VIA*!

VIA offers several types of savings:

Up to 40% off on travel outside peak periods and tourist season, on certain days of the week and on advance bookings (five days), depending on the destination;

PRACTICAL INFORMATION

Student rebates (24 years and under, 40% year-round on advance booking except during Christmas period);

A 10% discount for people aged 60 and over, on certain days during off-peak travel times up to 50%, depending on the destination;

Special rates for children (2 to 11 years, half-price; free for 2 years and under, accompanied by an adult)

Special Tickets

With the **CANRAILPASS**, you can travel throughout Canada on one ticket. The ticket allows 12 days of unlimited travel in a 30-day period for $569 in high season and $369 in low season (Jan 1 to May 31 and Oct 16 to Dec 31).

The **North America Rail Pass**, valid on all *VIA* and *Amtrak* trains, is available in economy class for a 30-day period for $625 during off-peak periods and $895 during peak periods.

For further information, call your travel agent or closest *VIA* office, or visit the website at: www.viarail.ca

In Switzerland: Western Tours, ☎(01) 268 2323, ⇋(01) 268 2373

In Canada: ☎1-800-561-8630 or contact your travel agent.

In Australia: Asia Pacific/Walshes World, ☎(02) 9318 1044, ⇋(02) 9318 2753.

In Italy: Gastaldi Tours, ☎(10) 24 511, ⇋(10) 28 0354.

In the Netherlands: Incento B.V., ☎(035) 69 55111, ⇋(035) 69 55155.

In New Zealand: Walshes World, ☎(09) 379-3708, ⇋(09) 309-0725.

In the United Kingdom: Leisurail, ☎01733-335-599, ⇋01733-505-451.

In the United States: ☎1-800-561-3949 or contact your travel agent.

on the length of the tour) include accommodation and guided tours. There is quite a variety of tours available, too many to list here. For further information on these tours, contact the tourist information centres.

By Train

Travellers with a lot of time may want to consider the train, one of the most pleasant and impressive ways to discover Canada. Via Rail Canada (see box) is the only company that offers train travel between the Canadian provinces. VIA rail provides service between the Atlantic provinces, Québec, Ontario, Manitoba, Saskatchewan, Alberta and British Columbia, except for Prince Edward Island, Newfoundland, the Northwest Territories and the Yukon.

By Bicycle

Bicycling is very popular in Canada, especially big cities like Montréal, Vancouver and Ottawa. Bicycle paths have been set up so that cyclists can get around easily and safely, but caution is always recommended, even on these paths. Bicycle touring is possible throughout Canada (see p 92).

Hitchiking

Hitchiking is prohibited on highways and is more common, especially during the summer, to do outside the large city centres.

"Organized" hitchhiking, or ridesharing, with Allo-Stop in Québec *(☎514-985-3032)* works very well in all seasons. This efficient company pairs drivers who want to share their car for a small payment with passengers needing a ride. A membership card is required and costs $6 for a passenger and $7 for a driver per year. The driver receives part (approximately 60 %) of the fees paid by the passengers. Destinations include virtually everywhere in the province of Québec, as well as the rest of Canada and the United States.

Children under five cannot travel with Allo-Stop because of a regulation requiring the use of child safety-seats. Not all drivers accept smokers, and not all passengers want to be exposed to smoke, so check on this ahead of time.

CURRENCY

The monetary unit is the dollar ($), which is divided into cents (¢). One dollar = 100 cents.

Bills come in 2-, 5-, 10-, 20-, 50-, 100-, 500- and 1000-dollar denominations, and coins come in 1- (pennies), 5- (nickels), 10- (dimes), 25-cent pieces(quarters), and in 1-dollar (loonies) and 2-dollar coins.

In Québec, Francophones sometimes speak of *"piastres"* and *"sous"* which are dollars and cents respectively.

MONEY AND BANKING

Most banks readily exchange American and European currency but almost all will charge **commission**. There are exchange offices that have longer hours, and some don't take commission. Just remember to **ask about fees** and **to compare rates**.

Traveller's Cheques

Remember that Canadian dollars are different from American dollars. If you do not plan on travelling to the United States on the same trip, it is best to get your travellers cheques in Canadian dollars. Traveller's cheques are accepted in most large stores and hotels, however it is easier and to your advantage to change your cheques at an exchange office.

Credit Cards

Most major credit cards are accepted at stores, restaurants and hotels. While the main advantage of credit cards is that they allow visitors to avoid carrying a large sums of money, using a credit card makes leaving a deposit for car rental much easier, also some cards, gold cards for example, automatically insure you when you rent a car. In addition, the exchange rate with a credit card is generally better. The most commonly accepted credit cards are Visa, Master Card, and American Express.

Credit cards offer a chance to avoid service charges when exchanging money. By overpaying your credit card (to avoid interest charges) you can then withdraw against it. You can thus avoid carrying large amounts of money or travellers' cheques. Withdrawals can be made directly from an automatic teller if you have a personal identification number for your card.

Banks

Banks can be found almost everywhere and most offer the standard services to tourists. Visitors who choose to stay for a long period of time should note that **non-residents** cannot open bank accounts. If this is the case, the best way to have ready money is to use traveller's cheques. Withdrawing money from foreign accounts is expensive. However, several automatic tellers machines accept foreign bank cards, so that you can withdraw directly from your account. Money orders are another means of having money sent from abroad. No commission is charged but it takes time. People who have residence status, permanent or not (such as landed-immigrants,

Exchange Rates				
$1 US	=	$1.43 CAN	$1 CAN	=	$0.69 US
1 £	=	$2.40 CAN	$1 CAN	=	£0.41
$1 Aust	=	$0.93 CAN	$1 CAN	=	$1.07 Aust
$1 NZ	=	$0.79 CAN	$1 CAN	=	$1.25 NZ
1 fl	=	$0.71 CAN	$1 CAN	=	1.40 fl
1 SF	=	$0.96 CAN	$1 CAN	=	1.04 SF
10 BF	=	$0.40 CAN	$1 CAN	=	25.76 BF
1 DM	=	$0.80 CAN	$1 CAN	=	1.24 DM
10 pesetas	=	$0.10 CAN	$1 CAN	=	105 pesetas
1000 lire	=	$0.80 CAN	$1 CAN	=	1233 lire

students), can open a bank account. A passport and proof of residence status are required.

TAXES AND TIPPING

Taxes

The ticket price on items usually **does not include tax**. In most provinces there are two taxes, the G.S.T or federal Goods and Services Tax, of 7%, which is payable in throughout Canada, and a provincial sales tax which varies from province to province.

Newfoundland and Labrador 12%
Prince Edward Island 10%
New Brunswick 11%
Nova Scotia 11%
Québec 6.5%
Ontario 8%
Manitoba 7%
Saskatchewan 9%
Alberta has no provincial sales tax
British Columbia 7%

The provincial and federal sales taxes are cumulative in Newfoundland and Labrador, Prince Edward Island, New Brunswick, Nova Scotia and Québec.

Tax Reimbursements for Non-Residents

Non-residents can be refunded for taxes paid on their purchases made while in Canada. To obtain a refund, it is important to keep your receipts. A separate form for each tax (federal and provincial) must be filled out to obtain a refund. Conditions under which refunds are awarded are different for the GST and the PST. For further information, call ☎1-800-668-4748 (for GST).

Tipping

Tipping applies to all table services, that is in restaurants or other places in which customers are served at their tables (fast food service is therefore not included in this category). Tipping is also compulsory in bars, nightclubs and taxis.

Depending on the quality of the service, patrons must give approximately 15% of the bill before tax. Unlike in Europe, the tip is not included in the bill, and clients must calculate the amount themselves and give it to the waitress or waiter; service and tip are one and the same in North America.

BUSINESS HOURS AND HOLIDAYS

Business Hours

Stores

The law respecting business hours allows stores to be open the following hours:

Monday to Wednesday from 8am to 9pm; though most stores open at 10am and close at 6pm
Thursday and Friday from 8am to 9pm; though most open at 10am
Saturday from 8am to 5pm; though most open at 10am.
Sunday from 8am to 5pm; though most open at noon.

Convenience stores, variety stores or *dépanneurs* are found throughout Canada and are open later, sometimes 24 hours a day.

Banks

Banks are generally open Monday to Friday from 10am to 4pm. Most are open on Thursdays and Fridays, until 6pm or even 8pm.

Post Offices

Large post offices are open from 8am to 5:45pm. There are several smaller post offices throughout Canada, located in malls, convenience stores and pharmacies; these post offices are open much later than the larger ones.

Holidays

The following is a list of public holidays. Administrative offices and banks are closed on these days, some stores may be closed.

January 1 and 2 New Year's
Easter Monday
3rd Monday in May Victoria Day
June 24 Saint-Jean Baptiste Day (Québec)
July 1 Canada Day
1st Monday in August Civic Holiday (except in Québec)
1st Monday in September Labour Day
2nd Monday in October Thanksgiving
November 11 Remembrance Day
December 25 and 26 Christmas & Boxing Days

TIME DIFFERENCE

Canada has six time zones: from Halifax to Vancouver there are five (Pacific, Mountain, Central, Eastern and Atlantic), and then Newfoundland, which is a half-hour ahead of Atlantic Standard Time. Eastern Standard Time is five hours behind Greenwich Mean Time and six hours behind continental Europe.

CLIMATE

The climate of Canada varies widely from on region to the next depending which province

you're in and which season it is. Winters are generally very cold with temperatures reaching as low as -20°C throughout most of the country. British Columbia (temperatures range between 0°C and 15°C in Vancouver) is the biggest exception where they receive rain instead of snow. The Northwest Territories, the Yukon and the northern regions endure extremely cold temperatures in winter – it is not unusual to see the thermometre drop to -30°C. Throughout the country, summer is a beautiful season, and temperatures can reach above 30°C. In certain coastal areas, particularly in Newfoundland and Nova Scotia, it is often rainy and foggy.

HEALTH

Vaccinations are not necessary for people coming from Europe, the United States, Australia and New Zealand. On the other hand, it is strongly suggested, particularly for medium or long-term stays, that visitors take out health and accident insurance. There are different types so it is best to shop around. Bring along all medication, especially prescription medicine. Unless otherwise stated, the water is drinkable throughout Canada.

During winter, lip balm and moisturizers are often used by people with sensitive skin, since the air inside buildings is often very dry.

Emergencies

Many municipalities in Canada have the **911** service, allowing you to dial only three digits to reach the police, firefighters or ambulance service, in case of emergency. You can also dial **0** to contact an operator who will supply you with the appropriate numbers.

SECURITY

There is far less violence in Canada, compared to the United States. A genuine non-violence policy is advocated throughout the country. If you run into problems, **911** is the emergency number in most places, otherwise dial **0** to reach an operator.

TABLE OF TEMPERATURES IN CANADA
(Minimum and maximum in degrees Celsius)

	January	March	May	July	September	November
Victoria (BC)	0/6	2/10	7/17	11/22	9/19	3/9
Edmonton (AB)	-22/-11	-12/-1	3/17	9/22	3/17	-11/0
Régina (SK)	-23/-13	-13/-2	4/18	12/26	5/19	-10/0
Winnipeg (MB)	-24/-14	-14/-3	5/18	13/26	6/18	-9/0
Toronto (ON)	-8/-1	-3/4	9/18	17/27	13/21	2/8
Québec (QC)	-17/-8	-9/0	5/17	13/25	7/18	-4/3
Halifax (NS)	-7/-1	-4/4	5/14	14/23	12/20	2/9
Charlottetown (PE)	-11/-3	-6/1	4/14	14/23	10/18	0/7
St. John's (NF)	-7/0	-5/2	2/11	11/21	8/17	0/7
Fredericton (NB)	-15/-4	-8/3	4/17	13/26	7/20	-3/6
Yellowknife (NT)	-33/-25	-25/-13	0/10	12/21	4/10	-18/-10
Whitehorse (YK)	-25/-16	-14/-2	1/13	8/20	3/12	-12/-5

INSURANCE

Cancellation Insurance

Your travel agent will usually offer you cancellation insurance when you buy your airline ticket or vacation package. This insurance allows you to be reimbursed for the ticket or package deal if your trip must be cancelled due to serious illness or death. Healthy people are unlikely to need this protection, which is therefore only of relative use.

Theft Insurance

Most residential insurance policies protect some of your goods from theft, even if the theft occurs in a foreign country. To make a claim, you must fill out a police report. It may not be necessary to take out further insurance, depending on the amount covered by your current home policy. As policies vary considerably, you are advised to check with your insurance company. European visitors should take out baggage insurance.

Life Insurance

Several airline companies offer a life insurance plan included in the price of the airplane ticket. However, many travellers already have this type of insurance and do not require additional coverage.

Health Insurance

This is the most useful kind of insurance for travellers, and should be purchased before your departure. Your insurance plan should be as complete as possible because health care costs add up quickly. When buying insurance, make sure it covers all types of medical costs, such as hospitalization, nursing services and doctor's fees. Make sure your limit is high enough, as these expenses can be costly. A repatriation clause is also vital in case the required care is not available on site. Furthermore, since you may have to pay immediately, check your policy to see what provisions it includes for such situations. To avoid any problems during your vacation, always keep proof of your insurance policy on your person.

SENIOR CITIZENS

Reduced transportation fares and entertainment tickets are often made available to seniors. Do not hesitate to ask.

CHILDREN

Children in Canada are treated like royalty. Facilities are available almost everywhere you go, whether it be transportation or leisure activities. Generally children under five travel for free, and those under 12 are eligible for fare reductions. The same rules apply for various leisure activities and shows. Find out before you purchase tickets. High chairs and children's menus are available in most restaurants, while a few of the larger stores provide a babysitting service while parents shop.

TELECOMMUNICATIONS

Local area codes are clearly indicated in the "Practical Information" section of every chapter. Dialling these codes is unnecessary if the call is local. For long distance calls, dial 1 for the United States and Canada, followed by the appropriate area code and the subscriber's number. Phone numbers preceded by 800 or 888 allow you to reach the subscriber without charge if calling from Canada, and often from the US as well. If you wish to contact an operator, dial 0.

When calling abroad you can use a local operator and pay local phone rates. First dial 011 then the international country code and then the phone number.

Country codes

United Kingdom:	44
Ireland:	353
Australia:	61
New Zealand:	64
Belgium:	32
Switzerland:	41
Italy:	39
Spain:	34
Netherlands:	31
Germany:	49

For example, to call Belgium, dial 011-32, followed by the area code (Antwerp 3, Brussels 2, Ghent 91, Liège 41) and the subscriber's number. To call Switzerland, dial 001-41, followed by the area code (Bern 31, Geneva 22, Lausanne 21, Zurich 1) and the subscriber's phone number.

Another way to call abroad is by using the direct access numbers below to contact an operator in your home country.

United States:
AT&T, ☏1-800-CALL ATT,
MCI, ☏1-800-888-8000

British Telecom Direct:
☏1-800-408-6420 or 1-800-363-4144

Australia Telstra Direct:
☏1-800-663-0683

New Zealand Telecom Direct:
☏1-800-663-0684

Considerably less expensive to use than in Europe, public phones are scattered throughout the city, easy to use and some even accept credit cards. Local calls cost $0,25 for unlimited time. For long distance calls, equip yourselves with quarters ($0,25 coins), or purchase a $10, $15 or $20 smart card ("La Puce"), on sale at newsstands. As an example, a call from Montreal to Toronto will cost $2,50 for the first three minutes and $0,38 for every additional minute. Calling a private residence will cost even less. Paying by credit card or with the prepaid "HELLO!" card is also possible, but be advised that calling by such means is considerably more expensive.

 EXPLORING

Every chapter in this guide leads you through a Canadian region, territory or province, including major tourist attractions, followed by a historical and cultural description. Attractions are classified according to a star system, allowing you to make the optimum choice if time is lacking.

★ Interesting
★★ Worth a visit
★★★ Not to be missed

The name of each attraction is followed by its address and phone number. Prices included

PRACTICAL INFORMATION

therein are admission fees for one adult. It is best to make inquiries, for several places offer discounts for children, students, senior citizens and families. Several are only open during tourist season, as indicated within these same brackets. Even in the off-season, however, some of these places welcome groups in particular upon request.

 ## ACCOMMODATIONS

A wide choice of types of accommodation to fit every budget is available in most regions of Canada. Most places are very comfortable and offer a number of extra services. Prices vary according to the type of accommodation and the quality/price ratio is generally good, but remember to add the 7% G.S.T (federal Goods and Services Tax) and the provincial sales tax, which varies from province to province. The Goods and Services Tax is refundable for non-residents in certain cases (see p 56).

A credit card will make reserving a room much easier (strongly recommended in summer!), since in many cases payment for the first night is required.

Most tourist information centres provide a free hotel-room reservation service.

Hotels

Hotels rooms abound, and range from modest to luxurious. Most hotel rooms come equipped with a private bathroom. The prices we have listed are rack rates in the high season. In the majority of establishments, however, a whole slew of discounts, up to 50% in some cases, is possible. Weekend rates are often lower when a hotel's clientele is mostly business people. There are also corporate rates, rates for auto-club members, and seniors discounts to take advantage of. Be sure to ask about package deals, promotions and discounts when reserving.

Bed and Breakfasts

Unlike hotels or inns, rooms in private homes are not always equipped with a private bathroom. Bed and breakfasts are well distributed throughout Canada, in the country as well as the city. Besides the obvious price advantage, is the unique family atmosphere. Credit cards are not always accepted in bed and breakfasts.

Youth Hostels

Youth hostel addresses are listed in the "Accommodations" section for the cities in which they are located.

Motels

There are many motels throughout the country, and though they tend to be cheaper, they often lack atmosphere. These are particularly useful when pressed for time.

University Residences

Due to certain restrictions, this can be a complicated alternative. Residences are only available during the summer (mid-May to mid-August); reservations must be made several months in advance, usually by paying the first night with a credit card.

This type of accommodation, however, is less costly than the "traditional" alternatives, and making the effort to reserve early can be worthwhile. Visitors with valid student cards can expect to pay approximately $20 plus tax, while non students can expect to pay around $30. Bedding is included in the price, and there is usually a cafeteria in the building (meals are not included in the price).

Staying in Native Communities

The opportunities for staying in native communities are limited but are becoming more popular. As the reserves are managed by native groups, in some cases it is necessary to obtain authorization from the Band Council to visit.

Camping

Next to being put up by friends, camping is the most inexpensive form of accommodation. Unfortunately, unless you have winter-camping gear, camping is limited to a short period of the year, from June to August. Services provided by campgrounds can vary considerably. Campsites can be either private or publicly owned. The prices listed in this guide apply to campsites without connections for tents, and vary depending on additional services.

 RESTAURANTS

Many restaurants offer set menus, complete meals for one price, which is usually less expensive than ordering individual items from the menu. The price usually includes a choice of appetizers and main dishes, plus coffee and sometimes dessert.

Prices in this guide are for a meal for one person, before taxes and tip (See "Taxes and Tipping", p 56).

$	$10 or less
$$	$10 to $20
$$$	$20 to $30
$$$$	$30 or more

These prices are generally based on the cost of evening set menus, but remember that lunchtime meals are often considerably less expensive.

 BARS AND NIGHTCLUBS

Most pub-style bars do not have a cover charge (although in winter there is usually a mandatory coat-check). Expect to pay a few dollars to get into discos on weekends. Most provinces stop the sale of alcohol at 2am, except for Québec where it ends at 3am. Some bars remain open past these hours but serve only soft drinks. Drinking establishments that only have a liquor license must close at midnight. In small towns, restaurants also frequently serve as bars. Those seeking entertainment come nightfall should therefore consult the "Restaurant" sections in every chapter as well as those in the "Entertainment" sections.

Wine, Beer and Alcohol

In Canada, provincial governments are responsible for regulating alcohol, sold in special liquor stores throughout the country.

For example, Québec has the *Société des Alcohols du Québec* (S.A.Q.) with many branches all over the province. Also in Québec, convenience and grocery stores have the authorization to sell beer and a few wines, but the choice is slim and the quality of wines mediocre. Other provinces have State-run beer and wine stores, the only places where alcohol can be purchased.

The legal drinking age in Canada is 19, except in Québec where it is 18. Note that certain northern communities are dry towns, where the sale of alcohol os strictly forbidden.

GAY AND LESBIAN LIFE

In 1977, Québec became the second place in the world, after Holland, to include in its charter the principle of not discriminating on the basis of sexual orientation. Other Canadian provinces later followed suit (most recently in Alberta).

Canadians are generally open and tolerant towards homosexuality. Over the years legislation, particularly at the federal level, has been reformed, to an extent, in favour of gays and lesbians, thus reflecting changing attitudes in society, especially in Québec, Ontario and British Columbia. However, the government sometimes seems to be living in the dark ages when Canada Customs does everything in its power to ban the importation of Marcel Proust's novels in English Canada! Little Sisters bookstore in Vancouver has been putting up a brave legal battle against these inspectors who believe they are *the* authority on censorship.

Generally speaking, rural areas tend to be more homophobic and Western Canada is not as tolerant of gays and lesbians. Yet, the Prairies have their share of queer celebrities, including country-singer, k.d. lang. Atlantic Canada seems to display a similar attitude to the west, however, Nova Scotia has attracted some attention to this issue with the film *The Hanging Garden*, by Halifax playwright Thom Fitzgerald. Famous gay rocker Ashley MacIsaac is also from Cape Breton. In Québec, society on the whole is very tolerant; famous artists an politicians have come out about themselves at an early age, as did the renowned playwright, Michel Tremblay. Ontario's gay community tends to stand out in the news the most, since Toronto is the most populated city in Canada

PRACTICAL INFORMATION

and probably because the city has a more politically active nature.

Montréal constitutes one of the most important gay communities in the world along with San Francisco, New York and Amsterdam. The **Village**, regrouping most of the services and businesses catering to gays and lesbians, has become a tourist attraction. Québec City also has a gay quarter on Rue Saint-Jean, outside the walls.

In English Canada, Toronto, Ottawa and Vancouver have the largest established gay communities. In Toronto, it is found around Church Street and Wellesley Street, in Vancouver it is mainly in the West end.

Important celebrations mark gay pride each year in Toronto towards the end of June and in Montreal the first weekend of August (Divers Cité).

For more information on gay and lesbian life:

In Montreal: L'Androgyne Bookstore, 3636 Boulevard Saint-Laurent.
In Toronto: Glad Day Bookshop, 598a Yonge Street.
In Vancouver: Little Sister Book and Art Emporium, 1221 Thurlow Street.

 ADVICE FOR SMOKERS

Smoking is prohibited in most shopping centres, on buses and on subways and in government offices.

Most public places (restaurants, cafés) have smoking and non-smoking sections. Cigarettes are sold in bars, grocery stores, newspaper and magazine shops.

 SHOPPING

In most cases prices are fixed and as indicated. Do not be surprised, however, if you hear someone asking a store clerk if something is on sale.

What to Buy

Alcohol: Many kinds of products are sold in Québec and Ontario.

Electronics: Canada is one of the biggest manufacturers of telecommunications products. The industry is centred in Montréal. It therefore might be a good idea to buy some gadgets such as answering machines, fax machines or cordless telephones and cellular phones. However, be aware that these devices may require a special adaptor for use in your home country. Importing these items may be illegal in certain European countries.

Compact Discs: Compact discs are much less expensive than in Europe, however, they may be more expensive than in the United States.

Furs and Leather: Clothes made from animal skins are of very good quality and their prices are relatively low. Approximately 80% of fur items in Canada are made in the "fur area" of Montréal.

Local Arts & Crafts: These consist of paintings, sculptures, woodwork, ceramics, coppered enamel, weaving, etc.

Native Arts & Crafts: There are beautiful native sculptures made from different types of stone that are generally quite expensive. Make sure the sculpture is authentic by asking for a certificate of authenticity issued by the Canadian government. Good quality imitations are widely available and are much less expensive.

 FESTIVALS AND CULTURAL EVENTS

Canada is rich in cultural activities. Given the impressive number of festivals, annual expositions, exhibitions, fairs, gatherings and otherwise, it is impossible to list them all. We have, however selected a few of the highlights, which are described in the "Entertainment" sections of each chapter.

PETS

The restrictions on animal companion vary from one province to another. Québec provincial and national parks don't accept dogs, even on leashes, whereas the opposite is true of Ontario. Pets are not allowed in restaurants. Some hotel chains in Canada allow domestic animals; we have indicated these establishments with this symbol: ⚡; in some cases there is a charge for having a pet in the room so it is best to ask when making your reservations.

WEIGHTS AND MEASURES

Although the metric system has been in use in Canada for several years, some people continue to use the Imperial system in casual conversation. Here a some equivalents:

Weights
1 pound (lb) = 454 grams (g)
1 kilogram (kg) = 2.2 pounds (lbs)

Linear Measure
1 inch = 2.54 centimetres (cm)
1 foot (ft) = 30 centimetres (cm)
1 mile = 1.6 kilometres (km)
1 kilometre (km) = 0.63 miles
1 metre (m) = 39.37 inches

Land Measure
1 acre = 0.4 hectare
1 hectare = 2.471 acres

Volume Measure
1 U.S. gallon (gal) = 3.79 litres
1 U.S. gallon (gal) = 0.83 imperial gallon

Temperature
To convert °F into °C: subtract 32, divide by 9, multiply by 5
To convert °C into °F: multiply by 9, divide by 5, add 32.

DRUGS

Recreational Drugs are against the law and not tolerated (even "soft" drugs).

ELECTRICITY

Voltage is 110 volts throughout Canada, the same as in the United States. Electricity plugs have two parallel, flat pins, and adaptors are available here.

LAUNDROMATS

Laundromats are found almost everywhere in urban areas. Bring your own detergent. Although change machines are sometimes provided, it is best to bring plenty of change with you.

PHARMACIES

In addition to the smaller drug stores, there are large pharmacy chains which sell everything from chocolate to laundry detergent, as well as the more traditional items such as cough drops and headache medications.

RESTROOMS

Public washrooms can be found in most shopping centres. If you cannot find one, it usually is not a problem to use one in a bar or restaurant.

MARKETS

There are many, both outdoor and indoor. Besides good bargains and fresh produce and goods, they are often great places to get a feel for a place.

PRACTICAL INFORMATION

OUTDOORS

anada boasts vast, untouched stretches of wilderness protected by national and provincial parks, which visitors can explore on foot, by bicycle, by car, on horseback, on skiis or by snowmobile. You'll discover coasts washed by the waters of the Pacific and Atlantic oceans, vast rain forest harbouring centuries-old trees, majestic mountains that form the spine of the American continent, as well as prairies, coniferous forests and more. The following pages contain a description of the most popular outdoor activities that can be enjoyed in these unspoiled areas.

PARKS

Throughout Canada there are national parks administered by the federal government, and provincial parks administered by the provincial governments. Most of the parks offer a variety of services and facilities: information centres, maps of the parks, nature interpretation programs, guides, lodging information (B&B, inns, camping) and restaurant information. Since these services often depend on the season and are not available in all parks, it is best to check with the park offices ahead of time. Provincial parks are generally smaller and offer less services.

A number of parks are crisscrossed by marked trails stretching several kilometres, perfect for hiking, cycling, cross-country skiing and snowmobiling. Primitive camping sites or shelters can be found along some of these paths. Some of the camping sites are very rudimentary, and a few don't even have water; it is therefore essential to be well equipped. Take note, however, that in the national parks in the Rocky Mountains, wilderness camping is strictly forbidden due to the presence of bears and other large animals. Since some of the trails lead deep into the forest, far from all human habitation, visitors are strongly advised to heed all signs. This will also help protect the fragile plant-life. Useful maps showing trails, camping sites and shelters are available for most parks.

It is important to be well aware of the potential dangers before heading off into the wild of the provincial and national parks. Do not forget that each individual is ultimately responsible for his or her own safety. Dangers to watch out for include avalanches and rock slides, risks of hypothermia or sunstroke, rapid changes in temperature (especially in mountainous regions), non-potable water, glacier crevasses concealed by a thin layer of snow, strong waves or tides on the coasts and wild animals like bears and rattlesnakes.

Never stop in an avalanche or rock slide area. Cross-country skiers and hikers must take particular care when passing through these areas. It is always best to check with park staff about the stability of the snow before heading out.

Hypothermia begins when the internal body temperature falls below 36°C, at which point the body loses heat faster than it can produce it. Shivering is the first sign that your body is not able to warm itself. It is easy to discount the cold when hiking in the summer. However, in the mountains, rain and wind can lower the temperature considerably. Imagine sitting above the tree line in a downpour, with the wind blowing at 50 km/h. Then imagine that you are tired and have no raincoat. In such conditions your body temperature drops rapidly and you run the risk of hypothermia. It is therefore important to carry a change of warm clothes and a good wind-breaker with you at all times. When hiking, it is preferable to wear several layers instead of a big jacket that will prove too warm once you start exercising intensely, but too light when you stop to rest. Avoid wet clothes at all costs.

Water can be found in most Canadian parks, but it is not always clean enough to drink. For this reason, be sure to bring along enough water for the duration of your hike, or boil any water you find for about 10 minutes.

Visitors who enter the national and provincial parks run the risk of encountering wild, unpredictable and dangerous animals. It is irresponsible and illegal to feed, trap or bother wild animals in a national park. Large mammals like bears, elk, moose, deer and buffalo may feel threatened and become dangerous if you try to approach them. It is even dangerous to approach animals in towns where wild animals roam about in an urban setting. Stay at least 30 metres from large mammals and at least 50 metres from bears and buffalo.

 SUMMER ACTIVITIES

As soon as the temperature inches above 0°C and the ice starts to melt, Canadians and visitors alike start to look forward to days in the country. While your choice of clothing will vary with the season, do not forget that evenings and nights are often quite chilly throughout the year depending on which the latitude. In certain regions, regardless of the temperature, a long-sleeved shirt is indispensable unless you want to serve yourself as dinner to the mosquitoes and black flies. If you plan on venturing into the woods in the month of June, bring insect repellent and use it!

 Hiking

Hiking is accessible to all and is practised all over the country. Many of the parks have hiking trails of varying length and difficulty. A few have longer trails that head deep into the wilderness for 20 to 40 kilometres. Respect the trail markings and always leave well prepared when you follow these trails. Maps which show the trails, campsites and shelters are available.

 Biking

Visitors can go bicycling all over Canada, along the usually quiet secondary roads or the trails crisscrossing the parks. The roads offer prudent cyclists one of the most enjoyable means possible of touring these picturesque regions. Keep in mind, however, that distances in these two vast provinces can be very long.

If you are travelling with your own bicycle, you are allowed to bring it on any bus; just be sure it is properly protected in an appropriate box. Another option is to rent one on site. For bike rental locations, check under the "Bicycles-Rentals" heading in the *Yellow Pages*. Many bike shops also offer rentals and can direct you to tourist information offices. Adequate insurance is a good idea when renting a bicycle. Some places include insurance against theft in the cost of the rental. Inquire before renting.

 Canoeing

Canada's vast territory is spotted with a multitude of lakes and rivers, making it a canoe enthusiast's dream. Many of the parks and reserves are departure points for canoe trips of one or more days. For the longer trips backwoods campsites are available for canoeists. Maps of the canoe trips and trails, as well as canoe-rental services are available at the information centre of a park.

Kayaking

Kayaking isn't a new sport but its popularity is on the rise. More and more people are discovering this wonderful way to travel on water in a safe and comfortable vessel at a pace well suited to appreciating the surrounding nature. In fact, being in a kayak gives you the impression of sitting right on the water and being a part of nature: an experience that is both disorienting and fascinating! There are three types of kayaks with varying curvatures: lake kayaks, river kayaks and sea kayaks. This last kind can hold one or two people depending on the model, and is the most popular since it is the easiest to manoeuvre. Many companies offer kayak rental and organize guided expeditions on Canada's waterways.

 Rafting

Rafting, which involves tackling rapids in an inflatable dingy, is perfect for thrill seekers. These rafts hold around ten people and offer the strength and flexibility required to take on the rapids. People particularly relish the sport in the spring when river waters are high and the current is more lively. It goes without saying that you should be in good physical condition to take part in this type of excursion, all the more so because between rapids, the boat is manoeuvred by the strength of the rowers. A well-organized trip, however, with an experienced guide doesn't present an inordinate risk. Generally, companies that offer rafting provide all the equipment necessary to ensure the comfort and safety of the participants. So, hop in and let the freshly thawed rivers make you jump and twirl among huge splashes!

  Beaches and Swimming

Whether on the atlantic or pacific shores, or on a lake or tumultuous river in the forest, Canada's waterways await you. Soft white sand, pebble or rocky beaches are numerous. Don't expect warm waters everywhere; the more north, the more cold the water, especially that of rivers. Canadians and visitors alike can soak up the sun on the coasts, lakes and rivers of the country.

 Hunting and Fishing

Hunting and fishing are both strictly regulated. Given the complexity of the regulations it is a good idea to check with Natural Resources Canada, or with Environment Canada. Free brochures containing the essentials with respect to the hunting and fishing regulations and restrictions are available.

As a general rule the following applies:

A permit is required to hunt or fish. Hunting of migratory birds is only permitted with a federal permit which can be purchased in any post office. A certificate to bear fire-arms or a permit by the province or country of origin is required when requesting this type of permit.

At the time of this guide's publication, a fishing permit is around $20 (up to $50 for non-residents). The price of a hunting permit depends on the type of game hunted and can cost up to $300 for non-residents. Permits are issued depending on the hunting zone, time of year, the species and the existing quotas. It is a good idea to obtain your permit well in advance since there are numerous restrictions.

Fishing and hunting seasons are established by the government and must be respected at all times. While hunting, always wear an orange fluorescent singlet. Hunting at night is not permitted. In the interests of conservation, the number of game is limited, and protected species cannot be hunted. All hunters must declare their kill at one of the registration centres (most of which are located on access roads to the hunting zones) within 48 hours of leaving the zone.

Hunting and fishing are permitted in wildlife reserves and parks according to certain rules. Reservations are required for access to waterways. For more information check directly with the park or reserve office where you plan to hunt or fish.

 WINTER ACTIVITIES

In winter, most of Canada is covered with a blanket of snow creating ideal conditions for a slew of outdoor activities. Most parks with summer hiking trails adapt to the climate, welcoming cross-country skiers. Dress warmly

OUTDOORS

or the cold will bite you. Despite the low temperature, winter offers many possibilities for outdoor activities for your enjoyment.

 ## Downhill Skiing

There are many downhill skiing centres in the country. Known the world over for its downhill skiing, the Rocky Mountains attract millions of fans of powder skiing, who are whisked to the highest summits by helicopter, and deposited there to enjoy the ski of their lives.

Some of these have lighting systems and offer night skiing. The hotels located near the ski hills often offer package-deals including accommodation, meals and lift tickets. Check when reserving your room.

Lift tickets are very expensive; in an effort to accommodate all types of skiers most centres offer half-day passes, whole-day and night-passes. Some centres have even started offering skiing by the hour.

 ## Snowboarding

Snowboarding arrived in Canada at the beginning of the 90s. Although it had a limited following at the beginning, is continues to grow in popularity, so much so that North American ski resorts often have more snowboarders than skiers. It's easy to understand why! With a snowboard, there's so much more sensation during a run. Despite what many people believe, it's not only for young people; there's no age restriction to enjoying the pleasures of a slalom. For interested newcomers, a few lessons are recommended before hitting the slopes, and many resorts offer them and also rent equipment.

 ## Cross-country Skiing

There are many parks and ski centres with well kept cross-country trails. In most ski centres you can rent equipment by the day. Many places offer longer trails, with shelters alongside them offering accommodation for skiers. For skiers on longer trails, some ski centres offer a service that delivers food to the shelter by snowmobile.

 ## Snowmobiling

Now this is a popular Canadian sport! It was a Quebecer named Joseph-Armand Bombardier who invented the snowmobile, thereby giving life to one of the most important industries of Québec, now involved in the building of airplanes and railway materials.

Trails cross diverse regions and lead adventurers into the heart of the wilderness. Along the trails are all the necessities for snowmobiling: repair services, heated sheds, fuel, and food services. It is possible to rent a snowmobile and the necessary equipment in certain snowmobiling centres.Don't forget, that a permit is required. It is also advisable to take out liability insurance.

Certain safety rules apply. A helmet is mandatory and driving on public roads is forbidden unless the trail follows it. Headlights and brake lights must be lit at all times. The speed-limit is 70 km/h. It is preferable to ride in groups. Lastly, always stick to cleared trails.

 ## Dogsledding

Used by the Inuit for transportation in the old days, today dogsledding has become a respected sporting activity. Competitive events abound in northern countries all over the world. In recent years, tourist centres have started offering dogsled trips running anywhere from a few hours to a few days in length. In the latter case the tour organizer provides the necessary equipment and shelter. In general you can expect to cover 30 kilometres to 60 kilometres per day and this sport is more demanding than it looks, so good physical fitness is essential for long trips.

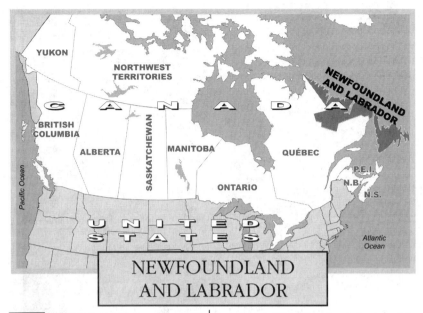

NEWFOUNDLAND AND LABRADOR

Still a little known corner of the world, the province of Newfoundland and Labrador is very different from Canada's other Atlantic provinces – not just geographically but historically and culturally as well. Made up on the island of Newfoundland and the territory of Labrador on the eastern edge of the Québec peninsula, the province's geographical isolation, at the northeasternmost edge of North America, has helped forge its unique character. "The Rock", as the island is aptly nicknamed, is rocky and ill-suited to agriculture, a hostile region whose landscape, often very rugged, is so splendid that you can't help but stand back and marvel. The west part of the island is shaped by the ancient Long Range Mountains, the tail end of the Appalachians. Gros Morne National Park, a UNESCO World Heritage Site, offers visitors a remarkable chance to explore these mountains, which in many places plunge straight into the limpid waters of deep fiords. Farther north, toward L'Anse aux Meadows, the site of a former Viking camp, the road runs along flat and strikingly desolate coastal landscapes. Elsewhere, lofty cliffs, pebble beaches and tiny fishing villages punctuate the shore, providing scenes of picturesque enchantment. The capital of the province, St. John's, lies in a magnificent natural setting on the shores of a long harbour rimmed with high, rocky hills. Newfoundland offers outdoor enthusiasts countless opportunities to explore a rich wilderness and to observe caribou and moose, colonies of puffins and gannets, and, from the coast, whales swimming about and icebergs slowly drifting by.

The numerous traces of indigenous communities that have been discovered along its shores indicate that this province has been inhabited almost continuously for over 8,000 years. The first Europeans whose presence here can actually be proved, however, were the Vikings, who, toward the year 1000, apparently used the island as a base for exploring the continent. It wasn't until the 15th century that Europeans rediscovered Newfoundland, when they learned of the teeming waters around the island through Basque fishermen. Officially, however, the credit for discovering Newfoundland goes to Giovanni Caboto (John Cabot), who came here in the service of England in 1497. Over the following centuries, the French and the English competed for control of Newfoundland and the rest of North America. The Seven Years' War (or French and Indian War) war ended with the last battle fought in St. John's and with the signing of the Treaty of Paris in 1763, under which France lost its North American empire. In 1949, Newfoundland became the tenth and final province to join Canadian Confederation.

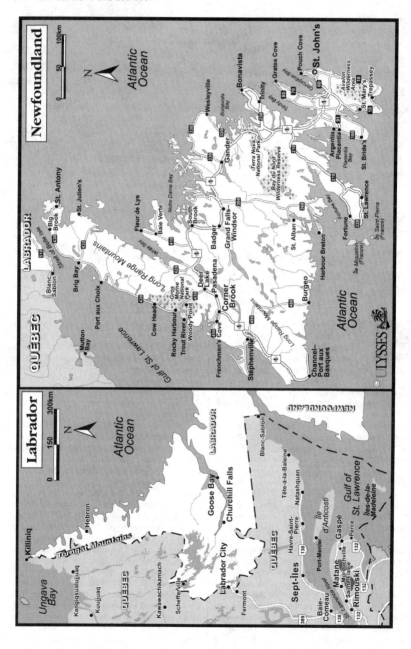

FINDING YOUR WAY AROUND

By Plane

The province's major airport is located in St. John's. There are direct flights between St. John's and a number of large Canadian cities, including Halifax, Montréal and Toronto. Air Canada also offers direct service to St. John's from London, England, while Royal Airlines offers a direct flight from Dublin, Ireland. The two main airlines that serve Newfoundland and Labrador are Air Canada, with its subsidiary Air Nova *(☎800-463-8620)* and Canadian Airlines, with its subsidiary Air Atlantic *(☎709-576-0274, 570-0800 or 722-0101)*. The airport is only six kilometres from downtown St. John's.

By Ferry

The island of Newfoundland is accessible by ferry from North Sydney, on Cape Breton Island, Nova Scotia. These ferries, operated by the Marine Atlantic company, offer service to Port aux Basques (in southwestern Newfoundland) and Argentia (on the Avalon Peninsula, in southeastern Newfoundland). The crossing between North Sydney and Port aux Basques usually takes about five hours. With a few exceptions, there is at least one crossing per day, each way, between North Sydney and Port aux Basques. The one-way fare is about $59 per car and $19 per adult. It takes about 14 hours to travel between North Sydney and Argentia. There is at least one crossing, each way, every Monday, Wednesday and Friday. The one-way fare is about $118 per car and $52 per adult. Reservations: ☎1-800-341-7981.

 PRACTICAL INFORMATION

Area code: 709

Tourist Information

Destination Newfoundland and Labrador: P.O. Box 215, St. John's, Newfoundland, A1C 5J2,

☎(709) 729-2830, 729-1965 or 1-800-563-6353.

 EXPLORING

St. John's ★★

St. John's, the provincial capital, occupies a spectacular site on the Avalon Peninsula, at the eastern tip of the island, and of Canada. The city is built like an amphitheatre around a well-protected harbour that opens onto the Atlantic Ocean by way of a narrow channel aptly known as the Narrows and flanked on either side by tall, rocky peaks. About 1.6 kilometres long and 800 metres wide, St. John's harbour is an excellent inland port, which is frequented by ships of all sizes flying the flags of various countries. Hidden behind the port installations lies a charming city whose winding streets are lined with pretty, brightly coloured wooden houses. European fishermen of various nationalities were already coming regularly to the site of modern-day St. John's as early as the 15th century. In 1583, Sir Humphrey Gilbert officially claimed the harbour and the rest of the island of Newfoundland for the Queen of England. Later, St. John's was often at the centre of rivalries between the French and the English and fell into the hands of the French on three different occasions. Signal Hill was subsequently fortified to protect the city.

Commissariat House ★ *(free admission; Jun to Sep; King's Bridge Road, ☎729-2460)*. This Georgian-style wooden building, completed in 1821, was first used as the residence of the commissariat of the local military base and then served as the vicarage of **St. Thomas Anglican Church** *(Military Road)*. This church, also known as the Old Garrison Church (1836), was the chapel of the British garrison of Fort William. Commissariat House and St. Thomas Church are among the few buildings in downtown St. John's to have survived the great fires of 1846 and 1892. Now a provincial historic site, Commissariat House was restored some time ago and furnished in the style of the 1830s.

Government House *(Military Road, ☎729-4494)*, another building that escaped the flames, was erected in 1831 as the official residence of the governor of Newfoundland. It has served as the lieutenant governor's house

NEWFOUNDLAND AND LABRADOR

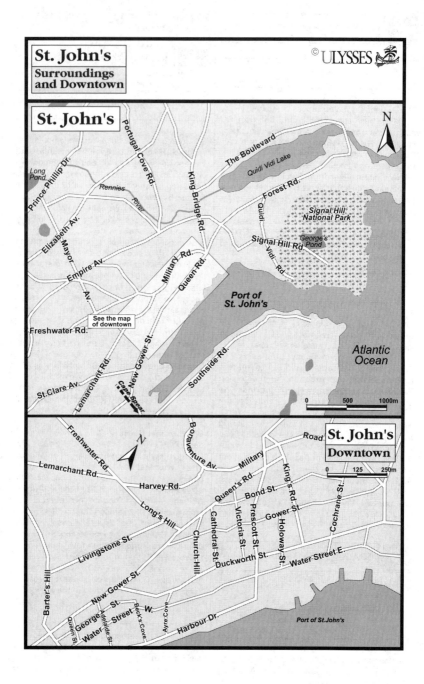

since the province joined the Canadian Confederation. The beautifully landscaped grounds are open to the public every day, but the house itself may only be visited by appointment. The frescoes adorning the ceiling were executed by Polish painter Alexander Pindikowski in 1880 and 1881. He would paint during the day then return for the night to the local prison, where he was serving a sentence for counterfeiting.

Built on a promontory overlooking the city, the **Roman Catholic Basilica of St. John the Baptist ★** *(Military Road)* was designed by Irish architect John Jones in 1855. Originally a cathedral, it was converted into a basilica in 1955. Its façade is graced with two 43-metre-high towers. The interior is richly decorated; the left transept contains a statue of Our Lady of Fatima, a gift from some Portuguese sailors who survived a shipwreck on the Grand Banks. The front of the basilica is a splendid vantage point from which to view the city.

The elegant **Anglican Cathedral of St. John the Baptist** *(at the corner of Church Hill and Gower Street)*, with its pure Gothic lines, was designed by English architect Sir George Gilbert Scott in 1847. It was completed in 1885 but was totally destroyed by a fire in 1892. The cathedral was rebuilt a few years later under the supervision of Sir George's son. Its magnificent stained-glass windows are particularly noteworthy. Established in 1699, the parish of St. John the Baptist is the oldest Anglican parish in Canada.

The **Newfoundland Museum ★** *(free admission; Duckworth Street, ☎729-0916)* houses permanent exhibitions that offer an excellent overview of the human history of Newfoundland and Labrador. The collections also examine the way of life of the six aboriginal nations who live or once lived in these regions: the Maritime Archaic who left traces of their existence in Port au Choix, among other places; the Dorset, who lived on the shores of the island until beginning of the first century AD; the Beothuk, the major Indian nation in Newfoundland when the Europeans arrived, who have since been completely wiped out; the Micmac, the largest group of natives in the Maritimes; the Inuit, often called Eskimos, who still inhabit the northernmost shores of Labrador; and the Montagnais, who live in Labrador, along the shores of the Gulf of St. Lawrence. The exhibitions also explore the lives of 19th-century settlers and fishermen.

Signal Hill National Historic Site ★★, visible from all over St. John's, is a rocky hill topped by a tower, which looks out over the mouth of the harbour. The hilltop commands magnificent **views ★★** of the Atlantic, the harbour and the city both day and night. Because of its strategic location, Signal Hill was long used as an observation and communications post. As early as 1704, flags were flown here to inform the military authorities and merchants of St. John's when ships were arriving. It was also on Signal Hill that the city's defences were erected, from the 18th century to the Second World War. Vestiges of 19th-century military installations can still be found here. In 1762, Signal Hill was the scene of the final North American battle of the Seven Years' War (also known as the French and Indian War). The French, who had been defeated in Québec City and Louisbourg several years earlier, managed to seize St. John's for a few months, after which they were ousted by English troops led by Lieutenant Colonel William Amherst. During summer, visitors can see the **Signal Hill Tattoo**, a re-enactment of 19th-century military exercises, complete with period costumes and gun and cannon salvos.

At the Signal Hill welcome centre, there is a small **museum** *($2.25; mid-Jun to early Sep, every day 9am to 5pm; ☎772-5567)* with an exhibition on fishing and the history of St. John's and Newfoundland. **Cabot Tower**, the main building on Signal Hill, was erected in 1897 in honour of the 400th anniversary of John Cabot's arrival in North America and Queen Victoria's diamond jubilee. The tower was a maritime signal station until 1960 and now houses an exhibition on the history of maritime signalling on this hill. The exhibition also takes a close look at the life of Guglielmo Marconi, who, on December 12, 1901, received the first transatlantic wireless message at Signal Hill. This message, an "S" in Morse code, was sent from Cornwall, England. From the top floor of Cabot Tower, visitors can enjoy a splendid view of the ocean. For a view of the harbour, head to the ruins of the **Queen's Battery**. From the foot of the cliff, you can see the rock to which the chain that sealed off the harbour in the 18th century was fastened. On the other side, you'll see the ruins of Fort Amherst, now topped by a lighthouse. Signal Hill's well laid out paths make it a pleasant place for a walk. Another trail runs along the harbour from Signal Hill to St. John's.

NEWFOUNDLAND AND LABRADOR

Standing proudly at the foot of Signal Hill, flanked by rock walls, is **Quidi Vidi ★**, one of the most picturesque villages in the province. It is made up of a few dozen brightly coloured houses, a small chapel and, of course, a fishing port, which has been in use since the 17th century. Nearby **Quidi Vidi Lake** is the scene of the annual **St. John's Regatta**, held on the first Wednesday in August. On a nearby promontory, visitors will find the remains of the **Quidi Vidi Battery** *(free admission; mid-Jun to early Sep, every day 9am to 5pm)*. Built in 1762 by the French, who occupied St. John's and its surrounding area for several months, this battery was later used by the British and was only abandoned in 1870.

The **Cape Spear National Historic Site ★★** *(11 km south of St. John's, on Highway 11)*. Cape Spear is the easternmost point on the North American continent. It was thus graced with a lighthouse (1863), which became the most important one in the province, after the lighthouse in St. John's harbour. Originally, the lighthouse was a square structure built around a tower, at the top of which were seven parabolic reflectors that reflected the light from seven lamps. The lighthouse was modernized over the years, then a new one was erected right near by in 1955. The **old lighthouse** *($2.25; all year, every day 9am to 5pm)*, furnished the way its keeper's house was in 1939, is open to the public. Close by, visitors can see the remnants of the extensive military installations built here during the Second World War. Cape Spear is also a pleasant place to stroll along the shore. In fine weather, the view of the ocean and the coast is spectacular.

The Avalon Peninsula

Witless Bay

The **Witless Bay Ecological Reserve ★** (see p 78) comprises three islands offshore from the villages of Witless Bay and Bauline. Each summer, these islands serve as a refuge for hundreds of thousands of seabirds, who come here to lay their eggs and raise their nestlings.

Ferryland

A pretty fishing village that feels as if it has been left behind by time, Ferryland was the site of one of the first English colonies in North America (1621). The settlers were sent here by George Calvert, who only stayed here for a few years then moved to present-day Maryland, thus becoming the first Lord Baltimore. Calvert's departure did not mean the end of the colony of Ferryland, which was taken in hand by English navigator David Kirke. At the **Colony of Avalon Archaeology Site** *(adults $2; mid-Jun to mid-Oct, every day 9am to 5pm; Highway 10; ☎432-3200)*, where excavations have been carried out over the past few years, visitors can see the foundations of the colony and tour the research and analysis facilities. To learn more about the history of Ferryland and its surrounding area, head to the **Historic Ferryland Museum** *(free admission; mid-Jun to mid-Sep, every day 9am to 5pm; Highway 10, ☎432-2711)*, whose exhibitions deal, most notably, with the colony's earliest days.

The 1,070-square-kilometre **Avalon Wilderness Reserve**, located in the southeastern part of the Avalon Peninsula, attracts fishing buffs and hikers. To visit the reserve, you must obtain a permit at La Manche Provincial Park (Highway 10, 11 kilometres from Cape Broyle). The Avalon Wilderness Reserve is the natural habitat of tens of thousands of caribou. In the southernmost part of it, families of **caribou** can frequently be seen crossing Highway 10.

Cape St. Mary's

The **Cape St. Mary's Ecological Reserve ★★** *(free admission; May to Oct, every day 9am to 5pm; along Highway 100, ☎729-2431)* (see p 79) protects the most spectacular and most easily accessible colony of seabirds in North America.

Placentia ★

This picturesque village on the shores of Placentia Bay became closely associated with the European presence on the island at a very early date. Basque fishermen were already stopping here by the early 16th century, as the pebble beach proved a particularly suitable spot for drying cod. Later, in 1662, the French established the first permanent settlement here. Known as Plaisance, it was the capital of the French colony of Terre-Neuve until the signing of the Treaty of Utrecht in 1713. Under the French Regime, Plaisance's role consisted of containing English expansion in Newfoundland, defending the French fleet based in Newfoundland, and protecting Canada from invasion in times of war. France kept only limited military forces in Plaisance, which didn't stop the little garrison from attacking St. John's, the English capital of Newfoundland, three times, in 1696, 1705 and 1709. The 1705 expedition was the only one on which the French failed to seize Fort William, which overlooked St. John's, though they did burn the city. **Castle Hill National Historic Park ★** *(free admission; mid-Jun to early Sep, every day 8:30am to 8pm; early Sep to mid-Jun, every day 8:30am to 4:30pm; on Highway 100, ☎227-2401)* protects the ruins of various 17th- and 18th-century French and English fortifications. To defend Plaisance, the French built the Vieux Fort in 1662, Fort Louis in 1691 and Fort Royal in 1693. The English, after seizing control of the region, erected little Fort Frederick in 1721, then, during the War of the Austrian Succession (1740-1748), the New Fort. Castle Hill commands an outstanding view of Placentia and its bay.

The Bonavista Peninsula

Trinity ★

A village with particularly well-preserved 19th-century architecture, Trinity sits on a promontory alongside an excellent natural harbour. The site was named by explorer Gaspar Corte Real, who explored its bay on Trinity Sunday in the year 1501. In 1558, the English made Trinity their first permanent settlement in Newfoundland. Thanks to its fisheries and its commercial ties with London, Trinity managed to attain a certain level of prosperity. In 1615, it became the seat of the first maritime court in the history of Canada, for a case involving a conflict between local and seasonal fishermen.

Trinity offers visitors all sorts of opportunities to step back into the past: the **Trinity Interpretation Centre** *(free admission; mid-Jun to early Sep, every day 9am to 5pm; Highway 239, ☎729-2460)* boasts an excellent collection of maps, illustrations and period photographs; the **Green Family Forge** *($2; mid-Jun to beginning of Sep, every day 9am to 5pm; Church Road, ☎464-3720)* presents an exhibition on the history of a forge dating back to the 1750s and **Hiscock House** *(free admission; mid-Jun to beginning of Sep, every day 9am to 5pm, Highway 239, ☎729-2460)*, open to the public, is a typical turn-of-the-century merchant's house. The most novel way to learn about Trinity's history, however, is the **Trinity Pageant ★**, a series of plays about local history, presented in different places around town. The shows are held daily during summer, starting at 2pm.

From May to August, several kinds of whales come to the waters off Newfoundland. They can often be spotted from the shore. For a closer look, we recommend going on a whale-watching excursion. Trinity is a good point of departure, and a number of tour agencies organize outings.

Cape Bonavista ★

Did John Cabot really open the way to the exploration of Canada? Newfoundlanders swear that he did, and maintain that it was at Cape Bonavista that Cabot and his crew stopped for the first time in the summer of 1497, after sailing across the Atlantic from Bristol, England. In reality, no one really knows where Cabot arrived in the New World. Cape Bonavista is fighting over the honour with several other sites along the Canadian coast. In any case, it was in Cape Bonavista that Newfoundlanders celebrated, with great pomp, the 500th anniversary of Cabot's landing in 1997.

The village of Bonavista is the largest community on the peninsula. Its pretty, brightly coloured houses are surrounded by a rolling landscape that opens onto a bustling port. Bonavista was frequented by fishermen of all different nationalities throughout the 16th century, before the English settled here around 1600.

At the beginning of the 19th century, the government of Newfoundland started building lighthouses along the shores of the island to make the waters safer for ships. In 1843, the first lighthouse on the north shore of the island was erected on Cape Bonavista. Today, you can visit the **old lighthouse** *(free admission; mid-Jun to early Sep, every day 9am to 5pm; Highway 230)*, which has been restored and furnished the way it was in the 1870s. It houses an exhibition on the history of lighthouses and the daily life of their keepers. The point offers a magnificent **view ★** of the sea and the rocky shoreline. Whales can often be spotted offshore in summer. If you keep your eyes peeled, you can see these giant mammals from many spots along Bonavista Bay.

NEWFOUNDLAND AND LABRADOR

Cape Bonavista

This little community is the gateway to **Terra Nova National Park** (see p 77).

The Viking Route

Gros Morne National Park ★★★, see p 77.

Port au Choix

Port au Choix, where fishing is still the major activity, was an important port for Basque fishermen for many years. Its name comes from "Portuchoa", which means "little port" in Basque. The Basques were not the first people to take advantage of Port au Choix's excellent location, however. The **Port au Choix National Historic Site ★** *($1; mid-Jun to mid-Sep, every day 9am to 5pm; ☎861-3522)* displays traces of peoples who inhabited this region long before any Europeans arrived. These vestiges were discovered during archaeological excavations. In the 1950s, in nearby Phillip's Gardens, archaeologists uncovered traces of a Dorset Eskimo community that occupied this site between the years 200 and 600. Dorset culture was sophisticated, as evidenced by the finely worked bone and stone carvings

discovered here. In 1967, other major digs in the region led to the uncovering of a Maritime Archaic burial ground containing human bones, tools and weapons and dating back 3,200 to 4,300 years. The Maritime Archaic survived essentially on fishing and hunting. They developed an artistic tradition and decorated their clothing with shells, seal's claws and pendants made of bone. The tools, weapons and ornaments found in the tombs indicate that these natives would prepare for a life after death not unlike their life on earth. At the Port au Choix National Historic Site, visitors can see some of the artifacts found in this area and watch a documentary on the lifestyle of these indigenous peoples. The short walk to the Phillip's Garden's archaeological site offers a chance to contemplate the region's rugged landscape.

L'Anse-aux-Meadows

The **L'Anse-aux-Meadows National Historic Site ★★** *($2.50; mid-Jun to early Sep, every day 9am to 5pm; Highway 436, ☎623-2608)* is the only place where traces of the presence of Norwegian sailors – or Vikings, as they are sometimes called in North America – have been discovered. L'Anse-aux-Meadows has been designated a World Heritage Site by UNESCO. A group of Norwegian sailors, led by Leif Eriksson, came here from Greenland and set up a camp around the year 1000. This camp, known as Leif's camp, consisted of eight buildings and was home to an estimated 80 to 100 people. The Norwegians used it as a base for their expeditions along the Atlantic coast. According to the sagas, on their expeditions from Leif's camp, Leif Eriksson and his family discovered the shores of Labrador, Newfoundland and regions farther south, on the Gulf of St. Lawrence. Eriksson named the southernmost lands Vinland, after the wild vines that grew back then. The L'Anse-aux-Meadows site was discovered by Helge Ingstad and Anne Stisne Ingstad in 1960. Visitors can see the foundations of the eight buildings uncovered by the Ingstads, and later by Parks Canada. Three buildings from Eriksson's era have been reconstructed right near by. Excellent guided tours are available. The welcome centre presents an interesting exhibition on the vestiges found on the site and also shows a film on the captivating story of the excavations conducted by Helge Ingstad and Anne Stisne Ingstad, and later by Parks Canada.

St. Anthony

Located on the shores of an excellent inland harbour, St. Anthony is the largest community in the northern part of the peninsula. Since 1922, it has been the headquarters of **Grenfell Mission**, which provides medical care for the isolated communities of northern Newfoundland and Labrador. The mission was founded by Dr. Wilfred Grenfell (1865-1940), who started developing the region's first real network of hospitals, infirmaries and orphanages in 1894. To finance his projects, Grenfell created a company called Grenfell Crafts, which sold winter clothing made by local craftspeople; the profits would go to the mission. Today, you can visit the **Grenfell House Museum** *($2; mid-Jun to mid-Sep, every day 9am to 5pm; Highway 430, ☎454-2281),* the Grenfell family's former home, which houses a collection of objects used by fishermen at the turn of the century. The museum's shop sells pretty clothing made on the premises, as well as local crafts. From the centre of St. Anthony, visitors can go to nearby **Fishing Point**, which offers a splendid **view ★** of the ocean. Whales and icebergs can often be spotted from here during the summer. There is also a good restaurant at Fishing Point.

OUTDOORS

Parks

Terra Nova National Park *(☎533-2801)* covers just over 400 square kilometres of wooded, gently rolling terrain. It is bounded by the Newman Sound and the Clode Sound, which are inlets of Bonavista Bay. The park is home to numerous animal species, including moose, black bears, martens, beavers and lynxes. The waters of the sounds, particularly during May and August, attract various species of whales, including humpbacks and finbacks. **Ocean Watch Tours** *(☎533-6024)* hosts cruises in the sounds for people interested in observing whales and other aquatic species. The main activities to be enjoyed in the park are camping, hiking, fishing, canoeing and, in winter, cross-country skiing; most organized outings start at Newman Sound. The Twin Rivers Golf Course is located at the park's south entrance. Two lookouts, both accessible by car, offer **panoramic views ★** of the park: the **Blue Hill Lookout** *(drive 7 km from the north entrance, then take a side road for 1.5 km)* and the **Ochre Hill Lookout** *(drive 23 km from the north entrance, then take a side road for 3 km).*

The internationally renowned **Gros Morne National Park ★★★** *(☎458-2417)* boasts 1,805 square kilometres of spectacular scenery: fiords, lakes, high plateaux, coastal dunes and boreal forests. The Long Range Mountains run the entire length of the park; Gros Morne is the highest, at 850 metres. In 1987, UNESCO designated Gros Morne National Park a World Heritage Site, primarily because of its geological make-up: in the southern part of the park, **Tablelands**, formed by the shifting of two tectonic plates, serves as an eloquent testimony to continental drift. The park's landscape was also shaped by the retreat of the glaciers at the end of the Glacial Epoch.

Gros Morne National Park protects numerous wild mammals, including bears, moose and caribou. It is not uncommon to see moose along the park's main roads, and various species of whales can be spotted from the shore during summer. In addition to wildlife observation, other activities to be enjoyed here are camping, hiking (over 100 kilometres of

NEWFOUNDLAND AND LABRADOR

Moose

trails), swimming, boat rides, fishing and, in winter, cross-country skiing. Lodgings are available at Trout River, Woody Point, Rocky Harbour and Cow Head.

Its splendid scenery and distinctive geological characteristics make the park's south sector well worth exploring. From the south entrance, Highway 431 runs through a rolling landscape, then along one of the arms of **Bonne Bay ★**, a deep fiord surrounded by the Long Range Mountains. The road leads to **Woody Point**, a pretty fishing village, then on to **Trout River ★★**. This 15-kilometre-long freshwater fiord lies in a glacial valley at the edge of the Gregory Plateau and **Tablelands ★★**, created by the shifting of the tectonic plates about 500 million years ago. Visitors can explore this part of the park by taking a **boat ride** *(mid-Jun to mid-Sep; three departures per day from Trout River; ☎951-2101)* on Trout River.

The landscape of the **north sector** is dominated by the Long Range Mountains. The park's welcome centre, on Highway 430, a few kilometres from **Rocky Harbour**, shows an excellent documentary on the flora, fauna and geological features of Gros Morne National Park. It also provides information on the various activities to be enjoyed in the park and hosts a number of nature talks. From Rocky Harbour, the road leads to the **Lobster Cove Head lighthouse**. The old lighthouse keeper's house now contains an exhibition on the history of the settlement of the coastline in this area. There is a trail leading from the lighthouse to a rocky beach. Much farther north in the park, a three-kilometre trail offers access to **Western Brook ★★**, a 16-kilometre-long, 165-metre-deep inland fiord created during the Glacial Epoch. The rock walls that plunge into its crystalline waters reach as high as 650 metres in places. A **cruise** is the most pleasant way to take in the fiord's spectacular beauty. The outing lasts about two and a half hours; for reservations, inquire at the Ocean View Motel *(☎458-2730)* in Rocky Harbour. Trimmed with beaches and sand dunes, **Shallow Bay ★**, at the north end of the park, is a good place to go swimming.

 Bird-Watching

At the **Witless Bay Ecological Reserve ★**, the main avian attraction is the Atlantic puffin, the provincial bird. Though bird colonies can be

Atlantic Puffin

seen from the shore, you can get a much closer look by taking a cruise. A number of tour agencies, including **Bird Island Charters** *($25 per person;* ☎*753-4850)* offer excursions from the villages along the coast.

The **Cape St. Mary's Ecological Reserve** ★★ *(free admission; May to Oct, every day 9am to 5pm; on Highway 100,* ☎*729-2431)*, on the southwest tip of the Avalon Peninsula and washed on three sides by the Atlantic Ocean, is home to some 60,000 seabirds. The most interesting place to observe them is along Bird Rock, a tall rock a few metres from the shore, where a number of species nest. Visitors will also find the largest gannet colony in Newfoundland, the southernmost colony of thick-billed murre in the world, and many other species of birds, including eagles. Furthermore, during July, humpback whales can be spotted offshore. The welcome centre provides fascinating information on the behaviour of seabirds.

  ACCOMMODATIONS

St. John's

The Roses B & B *($55 bkfst incl.; K; 9 Military Rd.,* ☎*726-3336,* ⌨*726-3483)*. Laid out in a

Victorian house that is typical of downtown St. John's, this bed and breakfast is a friendly and very charming spot. Its high ceilings, rich mouldings, and wood floors give it a warm atmosphere. Its always inviting rooms are decorated with a heterogenous mix of antiques of greater or lesser value and modern furniture. Some of the rooms are equipped with fireplaces. Days at this welcoming inn always begin on the right foot with a copious breakfast served on the top floor of the house, from which there is a panoramic view of the port.

Compton House *($60 bkfst incl.; pb,* ⊛*; 26 Waterford Bridge Rd., A1E 1C6,* ☎*739-5789)*. This majestic Victorian residence, converted into an inn, occupies a vast, prettily landscaped property near the Waterford River valley, about fifteen minutes by foot from the centre of the city. Guests quickly feel right at home in this lovely, simultaneously elegant and inviting house brimming with period charm. The front living room is particularly pleasant; as in the little library and the dining room, it is possible to enjoy the warmth of a crackling fireplace in it. Guest rooms are well furnished, very comfortable and all equipped with private washrooms. If a little extra luxury is in order, visitors can stay in suites, each of which is equipped with a balcony or a patio, a whirlpool and a fireplace.

Waterford Manor *($85;* ⊛*,* ℜ*; 185 Waterford Bridge Rd., A1E 1C7,* ☎*754-4139,* ⌨*754-4155)*. Built at the end of the last century for the family of a local merchant, this sumptuous Queen Anne house is now one of the province's beautiful inns. Recent renovation work has restored its former grandeur and adapted it to meet modern expectations of comfort. Guest rooms, each of which has its own special character, are furnished with antiques and decorated with meticulous attention to detail. They are all very pleasant, but the most beautiful of them, on the top floor, offers a fireplace and a whirlpool. Breakfast may be served in guests' rooms or in the dining room on the ground floor. The Waterford Manor, tucked away in a pretty residential neighbourhood on the outskirts of the Waterford River valley, is an approximately fifteen-minute walk from downtown St. John's.

Quality Hotel by Journey's end *($85;* ℜ*; 2 Hill O'Chips, A1C 6B1,* ☎*754-7788 or 1-800-228-5151,* ⌨*754-5209)* is always a sure bet. It is a welcoming, well-situated establishment near downtown that offers good value for your money. Although the rooms are

NEWFOUNDLAND AND LABRADOR

comfortable, well kept and functional, there is nothing especially original about them. Since it sits on a rise near the port, the Quality Hotel offers a lovely view of the bay.

Hotel Newfoundland *($105; ℜ; Cavendish Square, P.O. Box 5637, A1C 5W8, ☎726-4980, ⊷726-2025).* The most prestigious establishment in St. John's, a member of the Canadian Pacific hotel chain, is a modern, 301-room hotel in the heart of the city. Its interior decor is a brilliant success: it is both original and inviting. From the lobby visitors can go into the Court Garden, where terraced plant beds are embellished by interspersed waterfalls. The warmth and brightness of this spot are in singular contrast to the cool, rainy climate that so often shrouds the city. Guest rooms are spacious, charming and comfortable – they have been designed as much to please vacationers as to meet the needs of business travellers – and most of them offer breathtaking views of the port, the city and the bay.

The Avalon Peninsula

Ferryland

Lodging is available about an hour from St. John's at **Downs Inn** *($45 bkfst incl.; 4 rooms; Rte. 10, ☎432-2808),* a pleasant bed and breakfast laid out in an old Presbyterian convent. Erected in 1914, this building was home to about fifteen nuns until the 1980s, renovation work has managed to preserve the spirit of the house. Each of the spacious, clean, comfortable rooms is equipped with a fireplace, but none of them have private washrooms.

Placentia

Guests of the **Rosedale Manor** *($50 bkfst incl.; Riverside Dr., ☎227-3613),* one of the lovely inns on this part of the peninsula, feel right at home. Located in the heart of the village, just across from the bay, this pretty historic house offers carefully decorated rooms embellished with antique furniture and equipped with private bathrooms. The owner is both attentive and discreet. If you have an interest, she will be happy to fill you in on the local history.

The Bonavista Peninsula

Trinity

Campbell House *($70 bkfst incl.; 5 rooms; ☎464-3377 or 753-8945)* is a bed and breakfast set up in a lovely house that dates from the 1840s. The old-fashioned appeal of this stately residence, which stands in the middle of the town's historic area, has been well preserved thanks to meticulous renovation work. The rooms are charming and prettily decorated. From Campbell House there is a beautiful view of the town and the ocean.

The Village Inn *($39-$89; ℜ, tv; 12 rooms; ☎464-3269)* is, despite its relatively modest size, the largest hotel establishment in Trinity. It has occupied this building since the beginning of this century. Its room vary greatly in comfort and quality. There is a good family restaurant on the premises and whale-watching trips are organized here.

Terra Nova National Park

The **Terra Nova Park Lodge** *($79; 79 rooms; ℜ, ≈, ≡, tv; ☎543-2525)* stands on a large lot near the national park and close to an excellent 18-hole golf course. Naturally, it attracts a clientele of golfers, but it also appeals to travellers who simply want to enjoy its peaceful setting. This luxurious establishment offers all of the comforts and the excellent cuisine served in its restaurant adds to the pleasure of a stay here.

The Viking Route

Norris Point

As you come to Norris Point, in the southern part of the park, the **Sugar Hill Inn** *($76; 7 rooms; ⌂, ℜ; Rte. 431, P.O. Box 100, A0K 3V0, ☎/⊷458-2147),* one of the best places to stay on the western half of the island, comes into view on a beautifully landscaped hillside. All of its rooms are charming and equipped with private washrooms. There are a sauna and a whirlpool at guests' disposal and excellent fare is served in the inn's dining room.

The **Ocean View Motel** *($65; 44 rooms; ℜ, tv; Main St., Rocky Harbour, ☎458-2730)* offers rooms that are spacious, comfortable and clean, but of no particular charm. This establishment is well kept and houses a good family restaurant.

Cape Onion

A little over half an hour from L'Anse-aux-Meadows road and from St. Anthony is the **Tickle Inn** *($50; ℜ, R.R. 1, AOK 4J0, ☎/≈452-4321)*, an appealing little inn in an enchanting setting facing the ocean and surrounded by valley landscapes. This spot is unquestionably perfect for long walks and for spotting whales and icebergs on the open sea. The rooms are well kept and inviting. The Tickle Inn's dining room serves some of the best cuisine in the area.

 RESTAURANTS

St. John's

Stella's *($; 183 Duckworth St., ☎753-9625)* is absolutely perfect for a quick bite or for a tea break. This warm and welcoming spot offers a menu made up of fish and chicken dishes, vegetarian dishes, sandwiches, salads and soups. The seafood chowder is especially comforting on a rainy day.

The **Boston Grill** *($$; 223 Duckworth St., ☎579-0096)* has an English pub decor and specializes in steaks and seafood. While the presentation of dishes is sometimes lacking, the food is always perfectly prepared.

The **Taj Mahal** *($$; 203 Water St., ☎576-5500)*, lavishly decorated in Victorian style, prepares authentic Indian cuisine. Its elaborate menu highlights various tandoori specialties. The chicken *tikka*, the *tandoori* shrimp and the *malai tikka* fish are especially delicious. The *nan* bread is succulent, as is the steamed rice. Most of the main dishes cost about $10. A complete dinner for two can be enjoyed here for under $40.

One of the best restaurants in the province, the **Cellar** *($$-$$$; Bird's Cove, ☎579-8900)* earns its reputation with an innovative menu that seduces the senses. Whether in a pasta, seafood or meat dish, the originality of the flavours and the freshness of the produce are as impressive as the beautiful presentation. The pleasant atmosphere of the dining room and its low-key lighting are perfect for intimate evenings.

The magnificent **Stone House** *($$$; 8 Kenoa's Hill, ☎753-2380)*, built in the 1830s, is comprised of four dining rooms and offers an interesting menu that mingles nouvelle cuisine with the culinary traditions of Newfoundland. It lists an appetizer of cod tongues, of course, as well as a wide selection of seafood- and fish-based main courses. In addition there is an excellent choice of game, such as caribou, moose, wild goose and pheasant. The wine cellar is well stocked and may be visited upon request.

The Avalon Peninsula

Trepassey

The **Trepassey Restaurant** *($-$$; Rte. 10, ☎438-2934)*, behind the façade of the Trepassey Motel, is the perfect spot for lunch. The dishes on offer, mainly seafood and fish, are simple but well prepared and inexpensive. The layout of the restaurant is inviting and offers a pretty view of the bay.

The Bonavista Peninsula

Trinity

Eriksson *($$; ☎464-3698)* simmers up simple dishes composed mainly of seafood and fish in the warm atmosphere of a stately old home.

The Viking Route

Gros Morne National Park

The **Seaside Restaurant** *($$-$$$; Trout River, ☎451-3461)* owes its renown to the freshness and quality of its fish and seafood, which take up the greater part of its menu. The cuisine is delicate and well-prepared, while the service allows for plenty of time (sometimes a bit too much) to contemplate the fascinating motion of the ocean through the dining room's large picture window.

NEWFOUNDLAND AND LABRADOR

An unpretentious family restaurant, **Fisherman's Landing** *($$; Rocky Harbour, ☎458-2060)* proposes a menu of seafood and fish, with some meat and poultry items for good measure. The service is courteous, although somewhat businesslike, and the prices are reasonable. In the morning copious breakfasts are served.

St. Anthony

There could be no better location for a restaurant than that of the **Lightkeepers' Café** *($$-$$$; Fishing Point, ☎454-4900)*: at the very tip of Fishing Point, it offers a remarkable view of the ocean, an entrancing tableau occasionally enhanced by the slow drift of an iceberg or the to and fro of a whale. This beautiful panorama is happily complemented by excellent fare. The menu lists mainly fish and seafood dishes, including succulent snow crab, and the wine list is quite varied. Sunrise over the sea is a sight that can be enjoyed here starting at 7am.

Labrador

Separated from Newfoundland by the Strait of Belle Isle, Labrador is an immense territory of close to 300,000 square kilometres inhabited by only a few thousand people: Inuit and other aboriginal peoples, and French and English Canadians, who live mainly in the fishing villages along the coast and in the little towns of the central and western parts of the region. In fact, almost the entire area remains a vast wilderness, largely undeveloped and underrated. The southern part of Labrador presents landscapes of rolling hills dotted by many lakes and lined by rivers. Further north, the Torngat Mountains reach heights of up to 1,676 metres. The land is covered with subarctic forests of shrubs and stunted trees and, in the more northerly regions, tundra.

Along the Strait of Belle Isle

An approximately 80-kilometre-long road links the coastal villages along the Strait of Belle Isle from Blanc-Sablon, in Québec, to Red Bay. Blanc-Sablon can be reached by ferry from St. Barbe, on the northern end of Newfoundland, along the Viking route. The ferry schedule permits a round-trip to Labrador to be completed in one day. The coastal road travels through rugged maritime landscapes, crossing tiny communities that subsist on fishing. As were many other shoreline communities, L'Anse-au-Clair, the first village on the route, was founded in the 17th century by the French. It has a pretty fishing harbour and a tourist information office in a turn-of-the-century church. Further along, at L'Anse-Amour, archeologists have discovered the remains of a funerary monument erected 7,500 years ago by maritime Archaic Indians. Nearby is **Point Amour Lighthouse Provincial Historic Site** *(free; mid-Jun to mid-Sep)* – with its height of over 30 metres, this is the tallest lighthouse in eastern Canada. Just near L'Anse-au-Loup, the **Labrador Straits Museum** *(adults $1.50; early Jul to mid-Sep)* presents a collection of objects relating the history of the region. Route 510 stretches to Red Bay, where travellers can visit the **Red Bay National Historic Site** *(free; mid-Jun to mid-Sep)*. In the 16th century, this was the largest station used by Basque whalers: at its busiest point, twenty boats might be moored here. An interpretive centre is open to the public and an excellent film on the history of whaling in the region is presented. In addition, a boat travels to Saddle Island, site of the area's most significant archeological digs.

The Labrador Coast

To this day, most of the Labrador coast is inaccessible by road; boat and plane are the only means of transportation to many of its communities. A boat shuttles up the coast regularly, departing once a week from the port of St. Anthony, on the northern tip of Newfoundland, and stopping at about 40 tiny, isolated communities to ensure that they are adequately resupplied. This service runs all the way to Nain, in northern Labrador, and the trip makes for a great opportunity to admire undisturbed natural landscapes and, in summer, to watch drifting icebergs.

Central and Western Labrador

Central and western Labrador are relatively easy to reach. A ferry links Lewisporte, on the northern part of Newfoundland, and Happy Valley-Goose Bay, in central Labrador. From there, a road runs to Labrador City and on to Baie-Comeau, Québec. Another option is to take the train from Sept-Îles, Québec, to Labrador City. This part of Labrador is rich in untamed natural beauty. There are a few small towns here, including Happy Valley, which serves as a military base for the air forces of many countries; Churchill Falls, near a huge hydroelectric dam; and Labrador City, the site of one of the largest iron mines in the world.

NEWFOUNDLAND AND LABRADOR

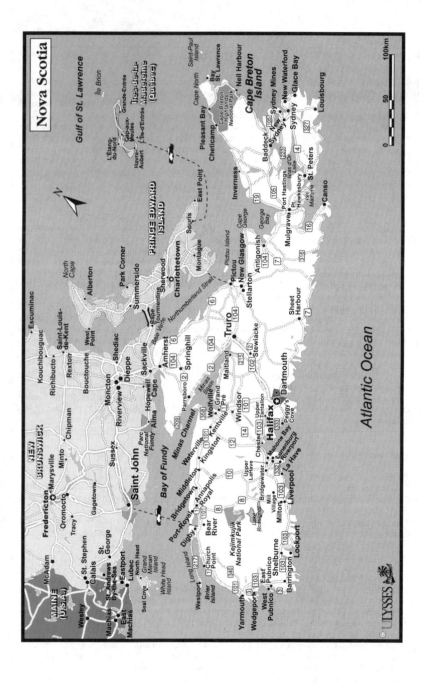

Nova Scotia

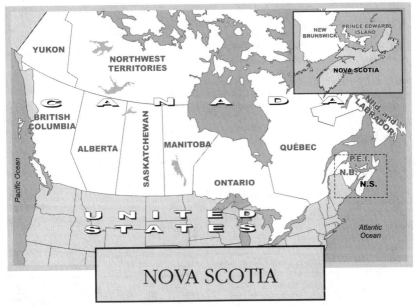

NOVA SCOTIA

he magnificent province of Nova Scotia looks like a long peninsula, connected to the continent by nothing more than the narrow strip of land known as the Chignecto Isthmus. In "Canada's Ocean Playground", the sea is never far away. In fact, no part of the territory of Nova Scotia is more than 49 kilometres from the water, be it the Atlantic Ocean, the Northumberland Strait or the Bay of Fundy. The proximity of the coast has shaped the character and lives of Nova Scotians as much as it has the splendid maritime landscape. The coastline, stretching hundreds of kilometres, is punctuated with harbours and bays, their shores dotted with fishing villages and towns. What is most striking about Nova Scotia is the way its architectural heritage blends so harmoniously with the natural setting. From the tiniest fishing village to Halifax, the capital, there are few places where the architecture of the houses and buildings, often dating back to the 19th century, does not fit in beautifully with the surrounding landscape.

There are countless reasons to visit Nova Scotia and many splendid sights to discover here. Everyone has heard of the legendary beauty of Cape Breton Island, whose mountainous landscape, with its magnificent cliffs overhanging the deep blue sea, is among the most spectacular in Eastern Canada. But Cape Breton is only one of many scenic regions in Nova Scotia. For example, tucked away along the Lighthouse Route, which runs from

Halifax to Yarmouth, is a multitude of picturesque villages steeped in history, such as Peggy's Cove, Mahone Bay and Lunenburg. Farther along, near the Bay of Fundy, visitors can explore the former Acadia, whose rich farmlands formed the heart of the Acadian territory from 1605 to 1755. Equally delightful is Halifax, the beautiful, vibrant capital of Nova Scotia and the largest city in the Atlantic Provinces.

FINDING YOUR WAY AROUND

By Car

Nova Scotia has a good road network. When following the tours outlined in this guide, visitors will usually have a choice between a picturesque route and an expressway. Keep in mind that the foggy conditions common along the coast call for prudent driving.

Visitors can reserve a car by contacting the provincial reservation service at ☎1-800-565-0000.

Halifax

Entering Halifax and reaching the downtown area is generally very easy by car, since the way is always clearly indicated. If in doubt, remember that Halifax lies on the southwest side of the harbour (Dartmouth is on the other side), and the downtown area faces right onto the port. Visitors will have little trouble finding their bearings downtown, since Citadel Hill and the port serve as landmarks. The most important downtown artery is Barrington Street.

Cape Breton Island

From Halifax, take Highway 7 to Antigonish, then take the TransCanada to Canso Strait, which separates Nova Scotia from Cape Breton Island.

Visitors can also reach Cape Breton Island by driving along the shoreline. From Halifax, take Highway 7, but instead of heading inland near Stillwater, continue along Route 211, and then the 316. When you reach Highway 16, take it to Highway 4.

Either of these routes will take you to Cape Breton Island. Once there, you can go either to Sydney, Louisbourg or near Baddeck, which marks the beginning of the Cabot Trail.

By Plane

Halifax International Airport *(☎902-873-2091)* is served by planes from Europe and the United States as well as elsewhere in Canada. Air Canada, Air Nova, Canadian Airlines, Air Atlantic, Icelandair offer flights from various capital cities to Halifax. There is a shuttle service from the airport to the big hotels downtown.

By Bus

A number of buses crisscross Nova Scotia. There are links between Montréal and Nova Scotia (departure aboard Voyageur with a transfer to SMT Bus Lines in New Brunswick and Acadian Lines in Nova Scotia).

Visitors can reach a variety of destinations within Nova Scotia, since there are buses running from Halifax to Yarmouth, Amherst and Sydney *(Acadian Lines, ☎454-9321)* and along the southern coast of the province, from Yarmouth to Halifax *(MacKenzie Bus Lines,*

☎543-2491) and from Halifax to Sherbrooke *(Zinck's Bus Co., ☎468-4342)*.

Cape Breton Island

From Halifax, visitors can take the bus as far as Sydney. It is worth noting, however, that no bus goes all the way around the island (aside from private tour buses). There is no way to get around easily, except in Sydney, so it is best either to rent a car or rely on your own resources (hitchhiking, cycling).

Acadian Lines (Halifax to Sydney): ☎454-9321. **Transit Cap Breton** (around Sydney): ☎539-8124.

By Train

There is a train that runs from Montréal across New Brunswick to Nova Scotia. This is a comfortable means of transportation, but relatively slow; the trip from Montréal to Halifax takes 20 hours. The train is equipped with a dining car and sleeping berths.

Via Rail Canada (Halifax): ☎1-800-561-3952.

By Ferry

Nova Scotia is linked to Prince Edward Island, Newfoundland and Maine by ferry.

The ferry linking Caribou (Nova Scotia) to Wood Islands (Prince Edward Island) provides daily service from May to December: **Northumberland Ferry**, Box 634, Charlottetown, P.E.I., C1A 7L3, ☎1-888-249-7245, from Nova Scotia and Prince Edward Island.

From Saint John (New Brunswick) to Digby (Nova Scotia): Three departures daily during summer with the **MV Princess of Acadia**, Box 250, North Sydney, N.S., B2A 3M3, ☎1-888-249-7245.

From Port-aux-Basques (Newfoundland) to North Sydney (Nova Scotia): One departure daily year-round, **Marine Atlantic**, Box 355 rue Purvers, North Sydney, B2A 3V2, ☎1-800-341-7981.

From Portland (Maine) to Yarmouth (Nova Scotia): Daily departures from May to October, **Prince of Fundy Cruise**, Box 4216, Station A, Portland, Maine, 04101, ☎1-800-341-7540 from Canada and the United States.

From Bar Harbor (Maine) to Yarmouth (Nova Scotia): One departure daily, mid-May to mid-September, **Marine Atlantic**, Box 250, North Sydney, Nova Scotia, B2A 3M3, ☎(888) 249-7245.

By Bicycle

Seasoned cyclists might consider a tour of the province, which promises some extremely pleasant excursions. Some regions, however, are quite difficult, with many steep hills. This is particularly true of Cape Breton Island. Not recommended for the casual cyclist.

 PRACTICAL INFORMATION

Area code: 902

Tourist Information Offices

The provincial government operates a reservation service for hotels, bed & breakfasts, campsites and car rentals. Information on festivals, ferry service and weather forecasts is also available. Dial ☎1-800-565-0000 in North America or ☎425-5781.

Halifax
By Mail: Tourism Halifax, Box 1749, Halifax, B3J 3A5, ☎421-8736, ⇒421-2842.
On site: Historic Properties, Lower Water Street, open all year.

Truro
By Mail: Central Nova Tourist Association, Box 1761, Truro, B2N 5Z5, ☎and ⇒893-8782.
On site: Highway 104, At the New Brunswick border, open all year.

By Mail: Yarmouth County Tourist Association, Box 477, Yarmouth, B5A 4B4, ☎742-5355, ⇒742-6644
On site: Annapolis Royal, Annapolis Tidal Project, Route 1, open from mid-May to mid-Oct.

Digby
On site: Shore Road, towards the ferry landing, open from mid-May to mid-Oct.

Yarmouth
On site: 228 Main Street, open from early May to late Oct.

Lunenburg
On site: Blockhouse Hill Road, Lunenburg, ☎634-8100, ⇒634-3194.

Sydney
By mail: Tourism Cape Breton, 20 Keltic Drive, Sydney River, ☎539-9876, ⇒539-8340.
On site: On the way onto the island, along the Canso Causeway, **Port Hastings**, open from mid-May to mid-Oct.
There are also booths in Louisbourg, Baddeck and Margaree Forks.

Antigonish
By Mail: Antigonish-Eastern Shore Tourist Association, Musquodoboit Harbour, B0J 2L0, ☎and ⇒889-2362.
On site: At the intersection of Highway 106 and Route 6, **Pictou**, open from mid-May to mid-Oct.

 EXPLORING

Halifax ★★★

A city with a rich architectural heritage, built at the foot of a fortified hill overlooking one of the longest natural harbours in the world, Halifax is a delightful place to visit. The city's location, which is outstanding from both a navigational and a strategic point of view, has been the deciding factor in its growth. In 1749 the British began developing the site, which had long been frequented by Micmac Amerindians. That year, 2,500 British soldiers and colonists led by Governor Edward Cornwallis settled here with the aim of securing Britain's claim to the territory of Nova Scotia. At the time, France and its North American colonies were the enemy. Over the following decades, Halifax served as a stronghold for British troops during the American Revolution and the War of 1812 against the United States. A military past is evident in the city's present-day urban landscape, its most striking legacy being, of course, the Citadel, whose silhouette looms over the downtown area. Not only a military city, Halifax has always been a commercial centre as well. Its access to the Atlantic, its

NOVA SCOTIA

Old Town Clock

excellent port and, starting in the late 19th century, its connection to the Canadian rail network have all favoured trade. Historic Properties, made up of warehouses built on the pier, is the oldest architectural grouping of its kind in the country, bearing witness to the city's long-established commercial tradition. Halifax is now the largest urban centre in the Maritime provinces, with a population of over 330,000 (including the inhabitants of its twin city, Dartmouth). It has a more varied, even cosmopolitan, appearance than the rest of the Maritimes, and boasts several superb museums and a whole slew of other attractions. Visitors are sure to enjoy strolling around Halifax and scouting out its restaurants, bustling streets and wide assortment of shops.

The Citadel and Its Surrounding Area

The **Halifax Citadel National Historic Site** ★★★ *($2; mid-May to mid-Jun, 9am to 5pm; mid-Jun to late Aug, 9am to 6pm; early Sep to mid-Oct, 9am to 5pm; Citadel Hill; ☎426-5080)* is the most striking legacy of the military history of Halifax, a city that has played an important strategic role in the defense of the East Coast ever since it was founded in 1749. The fourth British fort to occupy this site, this imposing star-shaped structure overlooking the city was built between 1828 and 1856. It was the heart of an impressive network of defenses intended to protect the port in the event of an attack, which incidentally never took place. Visitors can explore the Citadel alone or take part in an interesting guided tour, which traces the history of the various fortifications that have marked the city's landscape since 1749, and explains their strategic value. All of the rooms used to accommodate soldiers and store arms and munitions are open to the public, and visitors can move about through the corridors leading from one room or level to another. It is also possible to walk along the ramparts, which offer an incomparable view of the city and its port. In summer, students dressed and armed like soldiers of the 78th Highlanders and the Royal Artillery perform manœuvers within these walls. The site also includes a **military museum** *(☎427-5979)*, which houses an extensive collection of British and Nova Scotian arms and uniforms. A fascinating, 15-minute audio-visual presentation on the history of Halifax may be viewed as well.

Right in front of the Citadel, towards the port, stands one of the most famous symbols of Halifax, the **Old Town Clock** ★ *(Citadel Hill, opposite the main entrance of the Citadel)*, with its four dials. The clock was presented to the city in 1803 by Prince Edward, son of George III of Britain, who served as commander in chief of the Halifax garrison from 1794 to 1800. It serves as a reminder that the prince was a great believer in punctuality.

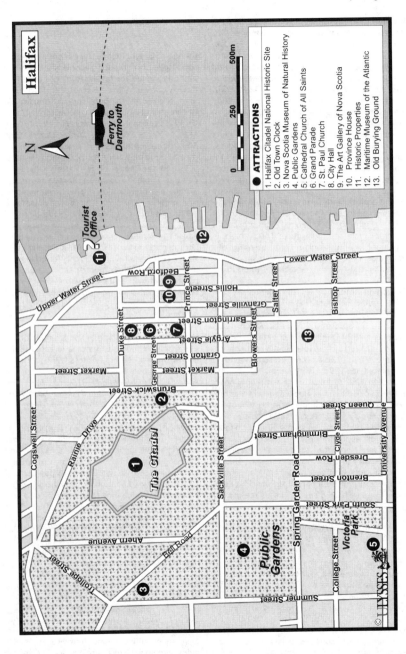

Halifax

N

Ferry to
Dartmouth

Tourist
Office

Upper Water Street

Lower Water Street

Bedford Row

Prince Street

Hollis Street

Granville Street

Salter Street

Bishop Street

Duke Street

George Street

Grafton Street

Barrington Street

Argyle Street

Market Street

Blowers Street

Brunswick Street

Market Street

Cogswell Street

Rainie Drive

The Citadel

Ahern Avenue

Bell Road

Sackville Street

Trollope Street

Queen Street

Birmingham Street

Dresden Row

Brenton Street

Clyde Street

University Avenue

South Park Street

Spring Garden Road

Public
Gardens

College Street

Summer Street

Victoria
Park

© ULYSSES

500m

250

0

● **ATTRACTIONS**

1. Halifax Citadel National Historic Site
2. Old Town Clock
3. Nova Scotia Museum of Natural History
4. Public Gardens
5. Cathedral Church of All Saints
6. Grand Parade
7. St. Paul Church
8. City Hall
9. The Art Gallery of Nova Scotia
10. Province House
11. Historic Properties
12. Maritime Museum of the Atlantic
13. Old Burying Ground

NOVA SCOTIA

Northwest of the Citadel, visitors will find the **Nova Scotia Museum of Natural History ★** *($3; Jun to mid-Oct, Mon, Tue, Thu and Fri 9:30am to 5:30pm, Wed 9:30am to 8pm, Sun 1pm to 5:30pm; mid-Oct to late May, Tue, Thu, Fri and Sat 9:30am to 5pm, Wed 9:30am to 8pm, Sun 1pm to 5pm; 1747 Summer St.; ☎424-7353)*, whose mission is to collect, preserve and study the objects and specimens most representative of Nova Scotia's geology, plant and animal life and archaeology. The museum features exhibits on subjects such as botany, fossils, insects, reptiles and marine life. One of the most noteworthy items on display is a whale skeleton. Visitors can also view a film on the birds living along the province's coast. The archaeology exhibit is particularly interesting, presenting the lifestyle and material possessions of the various peoples who have inhabited the province's territory over the centuries. The exhibit is organized in chronological order, starting with the Palaeolithic age, then moving on to the Micmacs, the Acadians and finally the British.

Stretching southwest of the Citadel are the lovely, verdant **Public Gardens ★★** *(main entrance on South Park St.)*, a Victorian garden covering an area of 7 hectares, which dates back to 1753. Originally a private garden, it was purchased by the Nova Scotia Horticultural Society in 1836. The present lay-out, completed in 1875, is the work of Richard Power. A fine example of British know-how, the Public Gardens are adorned with stately trees concealing fountains, statues, charming flowerbeds, a pavilion and little lakes where ducks and swans can be seen swimming about. This is an absolutely perfect place to take a stroll, far from the occasionally turbulent atmosphere of downtown Halifax. During summer, concerts are held here on Sunday afternoons, and the Friends of Public Gardens organization offers guided tours of the garden *(☎422-9407)*.

South of the Public Gardens, near Victoria Park, stands the **Cathedral Church of All Saints ★** *(free admission; 1720 Tower; ☎424-6002)*, whose remarkable stained-glass windows and exquisite woodwork will take visitors' breath away. The structure was completed in 1910, two centuries after the first Anglican service was held in Canada. It is located in a pretty part of the city, where the streets are flanked by stately trees. Some of Halifax's most prominent educational establishments can be found nearby.

Downtown Halifax and the Port

As early as a decade after Halifax was founded, **Grand Parade** *(between Harrington and Argyle Streets)* had become a trading and gathering place for residents of the city. It is now a garden in the heart of the downtown area, flanked by tall buildings on all sides. At the south end of Grand Parade, visitors will find **St. Paul Church ★** *(free admission; Jun to Sep, Mon to Sat 9 30am to 4:30pm; Oct to May, Mon to Fri 9am to 4:30pm; Grand Parade)*, the oldest Protestant church in Canada, built in 1750 on the model of St. Peter's Church in London, England. Despite the wearing effects of time and the addition of several extensions, the original structure has been preserved. Inside, visitors can examine a piece of metal from the *Mont Blanc*, one of the ships that caused a terrible explosion in Halifax in 1917. On the north side of Grand Parade stands **City Hall** *(free admission)*, an elegant Victorian style building dating back more than a century. In summer, Mayor Moira Ducharme invites both residents and visitors here to meet her and have tea *(Jul and Aug, Mon to Fri 3:30pm to 4:30pm)*.

In the Dominion Building, a fine example of the city's rich architectural heritage, erected at the end of the last century, visitors will find the **Art Gallery of Nova Scotia ★★★** *($2.50; Jun to early Sep, Tue, Wed and Fri 10am to 5pm, Thu 10am to 9pm, Sat and Sun 12pm to 5pm; early Sep to May, Tue to Fri 10am to 5pm, Sat and Sun 12pm to 5pm; 1741 Hollis, opposite Province House; ☎424-7542)*, four flours of modern exhibition space containing the most remarkable art collection in Nova Scotia. The permanent collection, consisting of nearly 3,000 pieces, is devoted to both popular and contemporary art. Although many works are by painters and sculptors from Nova Scotia and the Maritime Provinces in general, artists from other Canadian provinces, the United States and Europe are also represented. The Art Gallery presents the occasional touring exhibition as well. Lastly, there is a wonderful boutique selling local crafts.

Seat of the government of Nova Scotia, **Province House ★** *(free admission; Jul and Aug, Mon to Fri 9am to 5pm, Sat and Sun 10am to 4pm; Sep to Jun, Mon to Fri 9am to 4pm; Hollis St.; ☎424-4661)*, an elegant Georgian style edifice dating from 1819, is the oldest provincial legislature building in Canada. Visitors can take a guided tour through the Red

Chamber, the library and the legislative assembly chamber.

The buildings and old warehouses along the Halifax pier, the oldest of their kind in Canada, have been renovated and now form an attractive and harmonious architectural grouping known as **Historic Properties ★★** *(bordered by Duke and Lower Water Streets)*. Numerous shops, restaurants and cafés have set up business here, along with an excellent provincial tourist information office. This is a very popular, pleasant place, whose narrow streets lead to a promenade along the pier. The *Bluenose II* is often moored here during the summer. Built in Lunenburg in 1963, the *Bluenose II* is a replica of the most beloved ship in Canadian history, the *Bluenose*, which sailed the seas from 1921 to 1946 and is depicted on the Canadian ten-cent piece. When it is moored here, the *Bluenose II* offers two-hour cruises in the Halifax harbour. A tour of Halifax's impressive port aboard this or any other ship offering similar excursions is a marvellous way to get to know the city *(for more information, contact the tourist information office, Historic Properties; ☎424-4247)*.

Looking right out onto the harbour, the **Maritime Museum of the Atlantic ★★** *($3; Jun to Sep, Mon to Tue and Thu to Sat, 9:30am to 5:30pm, Wed 9:30am to 8pm, Sun 1pm to 5:30pm; Oct to May, same hours as summer, closed Sun; 1675 Lower Water St., near the port; ☎424-7490)* presents a wonderful exhibition offering a comprehensive overview of the city's naval history. On the ground floor, there is a reconstruction of *William Robertson and Son*, a store that furnished shipowners, shipbuilders and captains with materials for a century. On the same floor, visitors will find an assortment of historical artifacts related to Halifax's military arsenal and a varied collection of small craft, particularly lifeboats. The second floor features an absolutely extraordinary assortment of boat models, from sailboats to steamships. Visitors can also tour the *Acadia*, which is moored at the pier behind the museum. This ship first sailed out of Newcastle-on-Tyne, England back in 1913 and spent most of the following 57 years gathering information for charts of the Atlantic coast and the shores of Hudson Bay. The *HMCS Sackville* is a convoy ship that was used in World War II and has now been converted into a museum dedicated to the sailors who served in that war. At the interpretive centre, located in an adjacent building, visitors can view a 15-minute film on the Battle of the Atlantic.

Farther south, on Barrington Street, at the corner of Spring Garden Road, lies the **Old Burying Ground ★** *(free admission; Jun to Sep, 9am to 5pm; Barrington St. and Spring Garden Rd.)*, Halifax's first cemetery, which is now considered a national historic site. Some of the old tombstones are veritable works of art. The oldest, marking the grave of John Connor, was erected in 1754. A map containing information on the cemetery is available at St. Paul Church *(Grand Parade)*.

While visiting Halifax, make sure to stroll along **Spring Garden Road ★**, the busiest and most pleasant commercial street in the Maritimes. Lined with all sorts of interesting shops, restaurants and cafés, it looks like the local Latin Quarter. Parallel to Spring Garden Road, but farther north, **Blowers Street** is another attractive artery, flanked by somewhat less conventional shops and businesses.

On the Outskirts of Halifax

Point Pleasant Park ★ *(free admission; at the end of Young Ave.)* covers an area of 75 hectares on Halifax's south point. Here, visitors will find kilometres of hiking trails along the coast, offering lovely views through the forest. Due to its location at the entrance of the harbour, Point Pleasant was of great strategic importance to the city for many years. The first Martello tower in North America, now the **Prince of Wales Tower National Historic Site ★** *(free admission; Point Pleasant Park; ☎426-5080)*, was erected here in 1796-97. Drawing inspiration from a supposedly impregnable tower on Corsica's Martello Point, the British erected this type of structure in many places along their country's and colonies' shores. The Prince of Wales Tower was part of Halifax's extensive network of defenses. It now houses a museum, where visitors can learn about its history.

McNabs Island, measuring 4.8 kilometres by 1.2 kilometres and located right at the entrance of the harbour, was also part of the city's defenses. The British erected Fort McNab here between 1888 and 1892, equipping it with what were then the most powerful batteries in all of the city's fortifications. Visitors can examine the vestiges of the structure at the **Fort McNab Historic Site ★** *(☎426-5080)*, while enjoying a stroll around this peaceful, pretty island, which features a number of hiking trails. The ferry to McNabs Island leaves from Cable Wharf. For the schedule, contact the tourist information office *(Historic Properties, ☎424 -4247)*.

Dartmouth

From the pier in front of Historic Properties in Halifax, visitors can take a **ferry** *(about $1)* to Dartmouth, on the opposite shore, which offers a splendid view of both the port and McNabs Island. The town of Dartmouth boasts an attractive waterfront, beautiful residences, a variety of shops and restaurants and several tourist attractions, including the **Historic Quaker House ★** *(free admission; 57-59 Ochterlaney St., ☎464-2253)*. This is the only remaining example among some 22 similar houses built around 1785 by Quaker whalers who came to Dartmouth from New England. Guides in period dress tell visitors about the Quaker lifestyle.

Springhill

Springhill was founded in 1790 by Loyalist colonists who intended to support themselves by farming. The area did not actually develop, however, until 1871, when the Springhill Mining Company's coal mine opened. For nearly a century after, Springhill was one of the largest producers of coal in Nova Scotia. This difficult and dangerous task was not carried out without accidents or loss of life. In 1891, 125 men and boys perished in an accident in one of the galleries, and then two catastrophes, one in 1956, the other in 1958, claimed the lives of 39 and 75 men respectively. After that, several mines remained in operation, but large-scale coal mining came to an end in Springhill. To cap off this string of bad luck, the city was also the victim of two devastating fires (1957 and 1975).

To find out everything there is to know about popular singer Anne Murray, a Springhill native, head to the **Anne Murray Centre** *($5.50; late May to early Oct, 9am to 5pm; Main St.; ☎597-8614)*. Fans of the singer will be delighted by the exhaustive collection of objects that either belonged to her at one time or summon up key moments in her life and career. Audiovisual aids frequently complement the presentation. Few details have been neglected; the exhibit starts off with a family tree tracing Murray's family origins back two centuries.

The **Springhill Miners' Museum ★★** *($4.50; late May to early Oct, 9am to 5pm; on Route 2, take Black River Rd.; ☎597-3449)* offers an excellent opportunity to discover what life was like for Springhill's miners. A visit here starts out with a stop at the museum, which explains the evolution of coal mining techniques and tells the often dramatic history of Springhill's mining industry. Visitors are then invited to tour an old gallery.

Parrsboro

At the edge of Minas Basin, marking the farthest end of the Bay of Fundy, Parrsboro is a small community graced with several pretty buildings dating back to the last century. The region's often dramatic shoreline, which has been sculpted by the tides, is a treasure-trove for geologists. It is therefore no surprise that Parrsboro was chosen as the location for the **Fundy Geological Museum ★** *($3; early Jun to mid-Oct, every day 9:30am to 5:30pm, Sun 1pm to 5:30pm; Two Island Rd., near the centre of Parrsboro; ☎254-3814)*, a provincial museum devoted to the geological history of Nova Scotia and other regions. The exhibits, which include various types of fossils, rocks and stones, are lively and interesting, and have been created with the lay person in mind. There is also a fun video, designed to teach children about geography.

Windsor ★

The site now occupied by Windsor, at the confluence of the Avon and Sainte-Croix Rivers, was frequented by Micmac Amerindians for many years before being colonized. They referred to it as Pisiquid, meaning "meeting place." Acadians began settling here in 1685 and succeeded in cultivating the land by creating a network of dykes. Although this part of Acadia was ceded to Great Britain under the terms of the Treaty of Utrecht in 1713, the British presence was not felt in the area until Charles Lawrence erected Fort Edward here in 1750. By building the fort, Lawrence was attempting to strengthen Britain's authority over the territory and protect the British from the Acadians. In 1755, about 1000 of the region's Acadians were rounded up here before being deported. During the 19th century, Windsor was an important centre for shipbuilding and the exportation of wood and gypsum. Despite major fires in 1897 and 1924,

The Great Upheaval

In the 1670s, a small group of Acadians moved from the region of Port-Royal, the first Acadian settlement, founded in 1605, to the fertile land along Minas Basin. These industrious farmers managed to free up excellent grazing grounds alongside the basin by developing a complex system of dykes and aboideaus. The area became relatively prosperous, and its population grew steadily over the following decades.

Not even the signing of the Treaty of Utrecht in 1713, under which France ceded Acadia to Great Britain, could hinder the region's development. Relations between the Acadian colonists and British authorities remained somewhat ambiguous, however. When France and Great Britain were preparing for a final battle for control of North America, the Acadians declared themselves neutral, refusing to swear allegiance to the British crown. The British accepted this compromise at first. However, as the tension mounted between the two colonial powers, the British began to find the Acadians' neutrality more and more irritating.

Various events, such as the surprise attack on the British garrison at Grand-Pré by troops from Québec—with the help, it was suspected, of Acadian collaborators—increased British doubts about the Acadians' sincerity. In 1755, the governor of Nova Scotia, Charles Lawrence, decided to take an extraordinary step, ordering the expulsion of all Acadians. With 5,000 inhabitants, the region along Minas Basin was the most populated part of Acadia, and Grand-Pré the largest community. That year, British troops hastily rounded up the Acadians, confiscated their land and livestock and burned their houses and churches.

The Acadians were put on boats, often separated from their families, and deported. Of the approximately 14,000 colonists living in Acadia at the time, about half were sent away. Some of the ships went down at sea, while others deposited their passengers at ports in North America, Europe and elsewhere. After years of wandering, some of these Acadians, the ancestors of today's Cajuns, found refuge in Louisiana. Those who escaped deportation had to hide, fleeing through the woods to the northeast coast of present-day New Brunswick, all the way to Québec or elsewhere. One thing is for sure: the deportation order issued by Charles Lawrence succeeded in wiping Acadia from the map. In the following years, the land was offered to Planters from New England, who were joined by Loyalists at the end of the American Revolution, in 1783.

the town has managed to preserve some lovely residences. It is the starting point of the Evangeline Route.

The **Fort Edward National Historic Site** ★ *(free admission; early Jun to early Sep, 10am to 6pm; in the centre of Windsor;* ☎*542-3631)* consists only of a blockhouse, the oldest fortification of its kind in Canada. This structure is all that remains of Fort Edward, erected in 1750. An interpretive centre provides information on the history of the fort. The site also offers a gorgeous view of the Avon River.

Erected in 1835, **Haliburton House** ★ *(free admission; early Jun to mid-Oct, Mon to Sat 9:30am to 5:30pm, Sun 1pm to 5:30pm; Clifton Ave.;* ☎*798-2915)*, also known as **Clifton House**, was the residence of Thomas Chandler Haliburton (1796-1865), judge, politician, businessman, humorist and successful author. This plain-looking wooden house is adorned with magnificent Victorian furniture. It stands on a large, attractively landscaped piece of property, which covers 10 hectares. Haliburton made a name for himself in Canada and elsewhere by writing novels featuring the character Sam Slick, an American merchant who comes to Nova Scotia to sell clocks. Through this colourful character, Haliburton offered a harsh but humorous critique of his fellow Nova Scotians' lack of enterprise. A number of the expressions Haliburton created for his character such as "Truth is stranger than fiction" are commonly used today in both French and English.

Shand House *(free admission; early Jun to mid-Oct, Mon to Sat 9:30am to 5:30pm, Sun 1pm to 5:30pm; Avon St.;* ☎*798-8213)*, a fine example of Victorian architecture, was built between 1890 and 1891. The furniture inside

NOVA SCOTIA

belonged to the family of Clifford Shand, the house's original owner.

Grand-Pré ★

The **Grand-Pré National Historic Site ★★** *(free admission; open all year, church open mid-May to mid-Oct, 9am to 6pm; Route 1 or Route 101, Exit 10; ☎542-3631)* commemorates the tragic deportation of the Acadians. Here, visitors will find a replica of the Acadian church that occupied this site before the Deportation, Église Saint-Charles, which houses a museum. The walls are hung with six large and extremely moving paintings by Robert Picard, depicting life in colonial Acadia and the Deportation. The stained-glass windows, designed by Halifax artist T.E. Smith-Lamothe, show the Acadians being deported at Grand-Pré. Visitors will also find a bust of American author Henry Wadsworth Longfellow and a statue of Evangeline. In 1847, Longfellow wrote a long poem entitled "Evangeline: A Tale of Acadie," which told the story of two lovers separated by the Deportation. The site also includes a smithy and a placard explaining the principal behind the dykes and aboideaus developed by the Acadians before they were expelled from the region.

Wolfville ★

Wolfville is a charming little university town. Its lovely streets are lined with stately elms concealing sumptuous Victorian residences. The city has about 3,500 permanent residents, while the university, **Acadia University**, founded in 1838, welcomes about 4,000 students a year. With its Victorian atmosphere, excellent cafés and restaurants and magnificent inns, this beautiful town is a perfect place to stay during a tour of the region. Wolfville was founded in 1760, several years after the deportation of the Acadians, by Planters from New England, who were attracted by the excellent farmlands available here. The community was known as Upper Horton and then Mud Creek before being christened Wolfville in honour of local judge Eilsha DeWolf in 1830. Twice a day, from the shores of the small, natural harbour, visitors can observe the effects of the high tides in the Bay of Fundy. Aboideaus constructed by the Acadians in the 17th century can be seen nearby.

While touring the pretty university campus, take the time to stop in at the **Acadia University Art Gallery** *(free admission; early Jun to mid-Sep, 12pm to 5pm; mid-Sep to late May, Tue 11am to 8pm, Wed to Fri 11am to 5pm, Sat and Sun 1pm to 4pm; Beveridge Art Centre, at the corner of Main St. and Highland Ave.; ☎542-2200 ext. 1373)*, which often presents interesting exhibitions of contemporary art, as well as works from other periods.

The **Randall House Historical Museum** *(free admission; mid-June to mid-Sep, 10am to 5pm, Sun 2pm to 5pm; 161 Main St.; ☎542-9775)* displays objects, furniture, paintings and photographs from the region dating from 1760 to the present day.

The Route to Cape Split ★★

After passing through some of the region's magnificent rolling landscape and picturesque little villages, take a few moments to stop at the **Lookoff ★** *(Route 368)*, which offers an extraordinary view of Minas Basin and the Annapolis valley. Then go to the end of Route 358, where a trail (13 km return) leads to the rocky points of **Cape Split ★★**.

Port-Royal

In 1604, one year after the king of France granted him a monopoly on the fur trade in Acadia, Pierre du Gua, Sieur de Monts, accompanied by Samuel de Champlain and 80 men, launched the first European attempt to colonize North America north of Florida. In the spring of 1605, after a difficult winter on Île Sainte-Croix, De Monts and his men settled at the mouth of the waterway known today as the Annapolis River, where they founded Port-Royal. From 1605 to 1613, the settlement of Port-Royal occupied the area now known as the Port-Royal National Historic Site. After efforts to colonize this region were abandoned, the capital of Acadia was moved first to La Have (on the Atlantic coast) for several years, and then to the present site of Annapolis Royal.

The **Port-Royal National Historic Site ★★** *($2; mid-May to mid-Oct, 9am to 6pm; from Route 1, take the Road leading to Granville Ferry; ☎532-2898)* is an excellent reconstruction of the small wooden fortification known as "*Abitation*" as it appeared in 1605. It was here that fruitful, cordial relations were established between the French and the Micmacs. This site also witnessed the first performance of the Neptune Theatre and the founding of the first social club in North America, known as *L'Ordre du Bon Temps*. Today, visitors can see the various facilities that enabled the French to survive in North America. Staff in period costume take visitors back to those long-lost days. One of the guides is of Micmac origin and can explain the nature of the relationship between the French and the Micmacs, who were always allies. Acadian visitors can ask to see a map of the region, which shows where each Acadian family resided in the mid-17th century.

The **Annapolis Tidal Project** *(free admission; Route 1, ☎532-5454)* is an experimental project where visitors can discover how the powerful tides in the Bay of Fundy can be used to produce electricity. There is a tourist information office here as well.

Annapolis Royal ★★

It was here that Port-Royal, the capital of Acadia, was established in 1635. Because of its advantageous location, the settlement was able to control maritime traffic. In 1710, the British took over the site and renamed the town Annapolis Royal in honour of Queen Anne. Until Halifax was founded in 1749, Annapolis Royal was the capital of the British colony of Nova Scotia. Today, Annapolis Royal is a peaceful village with a rich architectural heritage, graced with residences dating back to the early 18th century. Wandering along its streets is a real pleasure. It is also possible to stay in some of the lovely houses here.

At the **Fort Anne National Historic Site ★★** *($2; mid-May to mid-Oct, 9am to 6pm, until 5pm the rest of the year; St.George St.; ☎532-2397)*, visitors will find an old fort, in the heart of which lie the former officers' quarters, now converted into a historical museum. The exhibition provides a detailed description of all the different stages in the history of the fort, which was French before being taken over by the British. Visitors can enjoy a pleasant stroll around the verdant grounds, which offer a lovely view of the surrounding area.

While in the area, make sure to take a walk in the **Annapolis Royal Historic Gardens ★★** *($3.50; late May to mid-Oct, 8am until dark; ☎532-7018)*, which have been carefully laid out according to British and Acadian horticultural traditions.

Digby ★

A charming town with a picturesque fishing port, Digby lies alongside Annapolis Basin and the Digby Strait, which opens onto the Bay of Fundy. It is known for its scallop fishing fleet, the world's largest. Its port is therefore a very lively place, where visitors will be tempted to linger, fascinated by the coming and going of the boats. From Digby, visitors can also head over to Saint John, New Brunswick aboard the ferryboat *MV Princess of Acadia*, which sets out from the port.

Long Island and Brier Island ★

Veritable havens of peace, Long Island and Brier Island attract thousands of visitors each year because the waters off their shores are frequented by sea mammals, especially whales, who come to the Bay of Fundy to feed during summertime. Whale-watching cruises set out from Westport (Brier Island) and Tiverton (Long Island) every day during summer.

Pointe-de-l'Église (Church Point) ★

Farther along the coast, the road passes through another little Acadian village, Pointe-de-l'Église (Church Point), which is home to the splendid **Église Sainte-Marie ★**. Built between 1903 and 1905, it is the largest and tallest wooden church in North America. The interior has a very harmonious appearance. Right next-door stands **Université Sainte-Anne**, Nova Scotia's only French-language university, which plays an important cultural role in the province's Acadian community. The university houses a museum containing objects related to the history of the local Acadians. A visit to Pointe-de-l'Église and its surroundings would not be complete without taking the time to eat a *pâté de râpure*, a local dish available at the university snack-bar, among other places.

Yarmouth

Yarmouth was founded in 1761 by colonists from Massachusetts. Life here has always revolved around the town's bustling seaport, which is the largest in western Nova Scotia. Now a major port of entry for visitors from the United States, Yarmouth has a large selection of hotels and restaurants, as well as an excellent **tourist information office** *(288 Main St.)*. Two ferries link Yarmouth to the state of

Maine: the *Bluenose* (☎1-800-341-7981), which shuttles back and forth between Yarmouth and Bar Harbor all year round, and the *MS Scotia Prince* (☎1-800-341-7540), which offers service between Yarmouth and Portland from the beginning of May to the late October.

A good way to learn about Maritime history and the town's heritage is to view the extraordinarily rich collection on display at the **Yarmouth Country Museum** ★ (*$2.50, ☎742-5539*), a small regional museum set up inside a former Presbyterian church. This vast jumble of objects includes miniature replicas of ships, furniture, old paintings, dishes, etc. The museum's most important piece, however, is an octagonal lamp formerly used in the Cape Fourchu lighthouse.

Equally remarkable is the **Firefighters Museum** ★ (*$2; Jun, Mon to Sat 9am to 5pm; Jul and Aug, Mon to Sat 9am to 9pm, Sun 10am to 5pm; Sep, 9am to 5pm; Oct to May, Mon to Fri 10am to 12pm and 2 PM to 4pm; 451 Main St.; ☎742-5525*), which displays two full floors of fire engines. The oldest vehicle, which the firefighters had to pull, dates back to the early 19th century.

Cape Fourchu ★ *(turn left after the hospital and continue for 15 kilometres)* is undeniably less spectacular than Peggy's Cove, but much more peaceful. Its lighthouse, erected in 1839, stands on a rocky promontory. Visitors who arrive at the right time will be able to see Yarmouth's impressive fishing fleet pass by just off shore.

Shelburne ★

Shelburne was founded in 1783, the final year of the American Revolution, when about thirty ships carrying thousands of Loyalists arrived in Nova Scotia. By the following year, the town already had over 10,000 inhabitants, making it one of the most densely populated communities in North America. Today, Shelburne is a peaceful village. **Dock Street** ★, which runs alongside the natural harbour, is flanked by lovely old buildings, which form a harmonious architectural ensemble.

This historic section features several points of interest, including the **Ross Thomson House** *(free admission; early Jun to mid-Oct, 9:30am to 5:30pm; Charlotte Line; ☎875-3141)*, whose general store dates back to the late 19th century. It is furnished in a manner typical of that type of business in those years. In the same neighbourhood, visitors can stop in at the **Dory Shop** *(free admission; mid-Jun to mid-Sep, 9:30am to 5:30pm; Dock St.; ☎875-3219)*, a workshop where fishing vessels were built in the last century. Also noteworthy is the **Shelburne County Museum** *(free admission; mid-May to late Oct; Dock St.; ☎875-3219)*, whose collection deals with the arrival of the Loyalists and the history of shipbuilding in this area, among other subjects.

The lovely beaches nestled along the coast between Shelburne and Liverpool are safe for swimming. Near Port Joli, visitors can also stop at **Kejimkujik Seaside Adjunct National Park** ★ (see p 102), and hike a few kilometres along one of the trails there.

Lunenburg ★★

Lunenburg is definitely one of the most picturesque fishing ports in the Maritimes. Founded in 1753, it was the second British settlement in Nova Scotia, Halifax being the first. Its original population consisted mainly of "foreign Protestants" from Germany, Montbeliard and Switzerland. German was commonly spoken in Lunenburg up until the end of the last century, and various culinary traditions have survived to the present day. The village occupies a magnificent site on the steep shores of a peninsula with a natural harbour on either side. A number of the colourful houses and buildings here date back to the late 18th and early 19th centuries. In fact, because of the architecture, parts of Lunenburg are somewhat reminiscent of the Old World. A very busy fishing port, Lunenburg also has a long tradition of shipbuilding. The celebrated *Bluenose*, a remarkable schooner never once defeated in 18 years of racing, was built here in 1921. Lunenburg is an extremely pleasant place to visit in the summertime. Its streets are lined with shops selling quality products. The art galleries are particularly interesting. The atmosphere here is also enlivened by all sorts of activities, including the **Nova Scotia Fisheries Exhibition and Fisherman Reunion**, a celebration of the world of fishing, which has been held each year at the end of August since 1916.

The **Fisheries Museum of the Atlantic** ★★ (*$7; mid-May to mid-Oct, 9:30am to 5:30pm; mid-Oct to mid-Nov, Mon to Fri 9:30am to 4:30pm; on the waterfront; ☎634-4794*), set up inside an old fish-processing plant, commemorates the heritage of the fishermen of the Atlantic provinces. Visitors will find an exhaustive, three-floor introduction to the world of fishing, including an aquarium, an exhibit on the 400-year history of fishing in the Grand Banks of Newfoundland, a workshop where an artisan can be observed building a small fishing boat, an exhibit on whaling and another on the history of the *Bluenose*, etc. Three ships are tied to the pier behind the building, including the *Theresa E. Connor*, a schooner built in Lunenburg in 1938 and used for fishing on the Banks for a quarter of a century. Expect to spend at least three hours for full tour of the museum.

Make sure to take the opportunity to visit the little fishing hamlet of **Blue Rock** ★, located a short distance from Lunenburg. Peaceful and picturesque, this handful of houses lies on a rocky cape overlooking the ocean.

Mahone Bay ★

Mahone Bay is easily recognizable by its three churches, each more than a century old, built side by side facing the bay. Like Lunenburg, it was first settled by "Protestant foreigners" in 1754, and like a number of other communities on the Atlantic coast, its port served as a refuge for privateers. Until 1812, these individuals pillaged enemy ships and villages, while paying British authorities to protect them. Later, until the end of the 19th century, Mahone Bay enjoyed a period of great prosperity due to fishing and shipbuilding. The lovely old houses lining the streets of the village bear witness to this golden era. Mahone Bay has a pretty sailing harbour and several good inns and bed & breakfasts. Visitors can also go to the **Settlers Museum** *(free admission; mid-May to early Sep, Tue to Sat 10am to 5pm, Sun 1pm to 5pm; 578 Main St.; ☎624-6263)*, which features a collection of antique furniture, dishes and other old objects from the area. The house itself dates back to 1850.

Chester ★

Chester was founded in the 1760s by families from New England. It has been a popular vacation spot since the beginning of the last century. Many well-heeled residents of Halifax have secondary homes here, and visitors will find a number of quality hotels and restaurants, an 18-hole golf course, three sailing harbours, several craft shops and a theatre, the **Chester Playhouse**. Perched atop a promontory overlooking Monroe Bay, Chester cuts a fine figure with its lovely residences and magnificent trees.

From Chester, Route 12 leads to the **Ross Farm Museum** ★ *($4.25; early Jun to mid-Oct, 9:30am to 5:30pm; New Ross; ☎689-2210)*, a 23-hectare farm inhabited by five successive generations of the Ross family from 1916 onwards. Guides in period dress liven up the museum, which has about 10 buildings typical of those found on large farms in the 19th century.

Peggy's Cove ★★

The picturesque appearance of the tiny coastal village of Peggy's Cove has charmed many a painter and photographer. The little port, protected from turbulent waters, is lined with warehouses standing on piles. Farther along, visitors can stroll across the blocks of granite that serve as a base for the famous lighthouse of Peggy's Cove, which houses a post office during summertime. It is best to be careful when walking here, especially when the water is rough. On the way out of Peggy's Cove, visitors can stop at the **William F. deGarthe Memorial Provincial Park** ★ to see a sculpture of 32 fishermen, along with their wives and children, carved into a rock face 30 metres long. William de Garthe, who spent five years creating this sculpture, was fascinated by the beauty of Peggy's Cove, where he lived from 1955 until his death in 1983, and by the lifestyle and courage of the local fishermen.

Cape Breton Island

In addition to its historic sites, Cape Breton boasts marvellous stretches of wilderness, to the delight of countless nature lovers each year. One of these is Cape Breton Highlands National Park, with its hiking trails and spectacular vantage points. The Cabot Trail is the best way to enjoy and appreciate the beauty of Cape Breton Island. This steep winding road makes a complete circle around the island, passing through dense forests and charming villages along the way. No visit to Nova Scotia would be complete without seeing Cape Breton Island.

NOVA SCOTIA

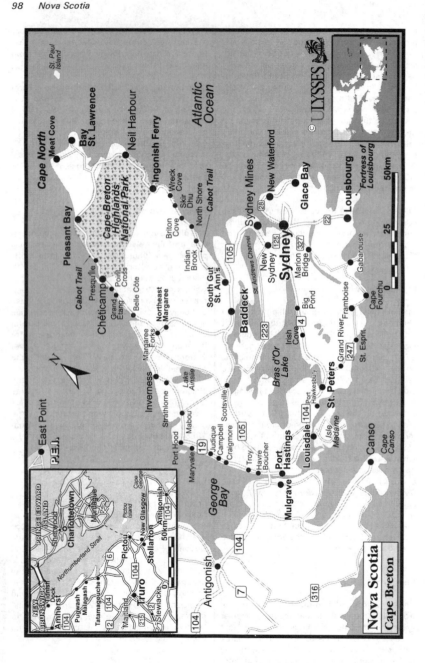

Port Hastings

The small town of Port Hastings is the gateway to Cape Breton Island. Although not a particularly pretty town, it is a major crossroads for travellers, with highways leading to both Baddeck and Sydney. Port Hastings does offer many practical facilities, including restaurants, service stations and most importantly, a tourist information office (see p 87).

Isle Madame

This tranquil peninsula covers an area of 42.5 square kilometres and has some nice picnic areas. Isle Madame was settled by the Acadians and a francophone presence still remains today.

St. Peters

St. Peters is situated on the narrow strip of land that separates the Atlantic Ocean from Bras d'Or Lake. Colonists settled here in 1630 and built a fort called Fort Saint-Pierre. About twenty years later, Nicolas Denys took over the fort and turned it into a trading and fishing post. To learn more about this French pioneer, visit the **Nicolas Denys Museum** *($2; Jun to Sep, open everyday 9am to 5pm).*

The trading post developed gradually, but business really began to take off when 140 years ago, a canal was dug between Bras d'Or Lake and the ocean to provide a passage for boats. Each year, many ships (maximum tonnage 4.88 t) can be seen passing through the canal from the park on either side. An outdoor display shows how the locks work.

Bras d'Or Lake ★

Bras d'Or Lake is an inland sea with 960 kilometres of shoreline. It thus occupies a good part of the island, dividing it into two areas, the Cape Breton Lowlands and Highlands. This vast expanse of salt water attracts many animal species, including the magnificent bald eagle which can be seen on occasion. For those who like to fish, trout and salmon abound in the lake and its many channels (St. Andrews Channel, St. Patrick Channel).

Native peoples have long been attracted to the shores of this lake with its abundance of fish. It was the Micmac Amerindians who established themselves permanently here. Their presence remains constant to this day on the four reserves that have been created—the Whycocomagh, Eskasoni, Wagmatcook and Chapel Island. Besides the reserves, there are several villages around the lake, including St. Peters. The **Bras d'Or Scenic Drive ★** *(follow the signs marked with a bald eagle)* goes all the way around the lake.

From St. Peters to Sydney

The road to Sydney passes through small towns along the shores of Bras d'Or Lake. It also goes through the Chapel Island Micmac Reserve.

This road winds along the coast and passes through several charming fishing villages, including l'Archevêque. Unfortunately, the road is in poor condition.

Bald Eagle

Sydney

With a population of 25,000, Sydney is the largest town in the area. J.F.W. DesBarres, a Loyalist from the United States, founded the town in 1785. A few years later, Scottish immigrants settled here. Sydney grew quickly at the beginning of the century, when coal-mining industries were established here. Coal-mining is still Sydney's primary industry. The town has all the services necessary to accommodate visitors and is a good place to stop for a rest before going on to Louisbourg. Otherwise, Sydney offers few attractions.

NOVA SCOTIA

Cossit House *(free admission; Jun to mid-Oct, 9:30am to 5:30pm; 75 Charlotte St., ☎539-7973)* is the oldest house in town. Restored and decorated with period furniture, it looks just as it did long ago. Guides dressed in period costume lead tours through the house and are available to answer any questions.

Nearby, also on Charlotte Street, is the **Jost House** *(free admission; Jul and Aug, Mon to Sat 10am to 4pm; Sep to Jun, Tue to Fri 10am to 4pm, Sun 1pm to 4pm; 54 Charlotte St., ☎539-0366)*, which was the home of a rich merchant.

To find out more about Sydney's history, visit **St. Patrick's Church** *(87 Esplanade)*. Built in 1828, this Catholic church is the oldest in Cape Breton. It features an exhibit on the town's past.

Louisbourg

Visitors are drawn to Louisbourg because of the nearby Fortress of Louisbourg, the area's main attraction. Many of the local businesses, including hotels, motels and restaurants, are geared towards tourists. It takes a full day to see the fortress, while the town itself offers few attractions.

The **Fortress of Louisbourg** ★★★ *($6.50, children $3.25, family $16; Jun and Sep 9:30am to 5pm, Jul and Aug 9am to 7pm; ☎733-2280)* was built at a strategic point at the water's edge, from where enemy ships could be seen and attacks could be countered. The fortress is ideally-located since it was built outside of the town itself and is removed from all the modern development. It has therefore been easier to recreate the atmosphere of the fledgling French colony back in 1744. Cars are not permitted close to the fortress, and a bus provides transportation to the site.

During the 18th century, France and England fought over territory in America. The French lost Acadia, which then became Nova Scotia. It was during this turbulent period in 1719, that French authorities decided to build a fortified city on Île Royale and began construction of the Fortress of Louisbourg. As the most complex system of fortifications in New France, this undertaking presented some major challenges.

Besides being a military stronghold, Louisbourg was also a fishing port and a commercial centre. Within a short time, its population had grown to 2,000 inhabitants. Everything was designed to enable colonists and soldiers to adjust to their new environment and barracks, houses and garrisons were all erected. Nevertheless conditions were rough, and colonists sometimes had difficulty adapting. Despite the hardships, the colony grew and local business flourished.

The French presence on Île Royale was a thorn in the side of the English colonies stationed further south. In 1744, when war was declared in Europe between France and England, the Louisbourg garrison took advantage of its position to attack the English villages in the area and thus take over an English outpost. The situation incensed the English in New England, and provoked William Shirley, governor of Massachusetts, to send his troops to attack the offending French bastion in 1745. Four thousand New England soldiers ventured an attack on the Fortress of Louisbourg, which was said to be impenetrable. Despite this reputation, the French troops were under-equipped and poorly organized. They had never even imagined such an attack possible, and could not defend themselves. After a six week-long siege, the Louisbourg authorities surrendered to the British troops.

A few years later, in 1748, Louisbourg was returned to France when the two nations signed a peace treaty. Life carried on in the fortress, and within a year, Louisbourg was as active as ever before. This renewed prosperity was short-lived, however, since in 1758 the fortress was conquered once and for all by British troops, thus ending the French presence in the area.

Hardly 10 years after this conquest, the fortress was left to ruin, and only much later was it rebuilt. Today, almost one quarter of the fortress has been restored, and during the summer, people dressed in period costume bring it to life again, recreating the Louisbourg of long ago. There are soldiers, a baker baking bread and a fisherman with his family. The scene is most convincing, and a stroll down the streets of this old French fortress is a fascinating experience.

Glace Bay

Glace Bay lies on the Atlantic coast. The area is rich in coal which forms the base of Glace Bay's industry. The name of this town is of French origin and refers to the pieces of ice *(glace)* that can be seen drifting along the coast. This small town, which has a population of about 20,000, features two interesting attractions.

Guglielmo Marconi (1874-1937) became famous for proving that it was possible to send messages using a wireless telegraph. At the age of 22, Marconi had already developed a wireless station from which a message could be sent over a short distance. In 1902, he sent the first trans-Atlantic message from his transmitting station at Table Head. At the **Marconi National Historic Site** ★ *(free admission; Jun to mid-Sep, 10am to 6pm)* visitors can learn about Marconi's discoveries and see his work table, as well as the radio station from which the first message was sent. The Glace Bay area's mining industry dates back many years. As long ago as 1790, French soldiers from Louisbourg were already coming to Port Morien for coal. The industry really took off at the beginning of the 20th century, when mines were dug here, most importantly at New Waterford. Today, Glace Bay produces more coal than any other town in Eastern Canada.

To learn more about this industry, visit the **Miner's Museum** ★★ *($2.75; Jun to early Sep, 10am to 6pm, Tue until 7pm; rest of the year Mon to Fri 9am to 4pm; 42 Birkley St., ☎849-4522)*, which has exhibits showing the various tools and techniques used in coal mining. There is also a recreation of a typical mining town from the beginning of the century. Finally, the most fascinating part of the museum is a guided tour of a coal mine.

Baddeck ★★

Baddeck is a charming village, perfect for taking a stroll or enjoying a bite to eat on a terrace. Whether you decide to stay for a few days to enjoy the comfortable hotels and calm atmosphere, or simply stop for a few hours before heading off on the Cabot Trail, Baddeck offers many attractions that make it worth the detour. One fascinating sight is the summer home of the inventor Alexander Graham Bell.

The **Alexander Graham Bell National Historic Site** ★★ *($3.50; Jul and Aug, 9am to 8pm; Sep, 9am to 6pm; rest of the year, 9am to 5pm; town's east exit, Chebucto St. ☎295-1512)*. Many of Bell's inventions are on display, as are the instruments he used in his research. Bell's life story is also told. Visitors will learn, for example, that after teaching sign language for many years, he created an artificial ear that recorded sounds. This experiment led to his invention of the telephone.

The Cabot Trail ★★★

The Cabot Trail follows steep precipitous cliffs that plunge out over the Atlantic Ocean, and passes through some picturesque little villages. Leaving Baddeck, the road follows the shore before climbing up to the plateau on the north end of the island. The many lookouts along this road offer magnificent panoramic views. It's worth taking the time to stop and appreciate the wild beauty of the landscape, where a restless sea with steep hills and a dense forest are home to a variety of animal species.

The first village after Baddeck is tiny **South Gut St. Ann's**, home to the **Gaelic College**, an institution devoted to the survival of Gaelic culture in North America. Courses are offered in Gaelic language, singing and bagpipe playing.

The road continues along the coast to **Ingonish Ferry**, where it starts climbing the vast plateau occupying the north end of the island at an elevation of 366 metres. The natural scenery grows increasingly spectacular. **Cape Breton Highlands National Park** ★★★ (see p 102) begins near here. The park spreads over 950 square kilometres and features many hiking trails through the forest.

This road leads first to a charming fishing village called **Bay St. Lawrence** ★. Built at the water's edge, the village has little wooden houses and a picturesque port, where cormorants can be seen gliding above the waves. The road climbs along the **cliffs** ★★ and winds its way to **Meat Cove**, a perfect place to stop for a picnic and enjoy the **superb view** ★ over the ocean waves.

The road continues west. From Cape North to Pleasant Bay, visitors can gaze at the canyon formed by the sides of the hills. The **view** ★★ is stunning.

The plateau ends near Petit Étang. The road heads back down and follows the Gulf of St. Lawrence to the Acadian region of Cape Breton. The landscape is surprising, as forests and steep cliffs give way to a barren plateau studded with Acadian villages. Among these is Chéticamp, a quiet village with simple little houses and a fishing port. It is a departure point for seal and whale-watching excursions. More villages with French names follow,

NOVA SCOTIA

including Grand Étang, Saint-Joseph du Moine, Cap-Lemoine and Belle Côte.

The west part of the Cabot Trail ends at Margaree Harbour. You can continue your journey by cutting across the plateau to return to Baddeck. The highlight along this route is the **Margaree Salmon Museum** *($0.50, mid-Jun to mid-Aug, 9am to 5pm; ☎248-2848)* in **Northeast Margaree**. The museum displays the various implements used for salmon fishing.

Ceildish Trail

The road along the west coast of the island leads to the Ceildish Trail. This region was settled by Scots, and vestiges of Gaelic culture still remain. Here, the warm waters wash up against a few of the island's beautiful beaches, especially near Mabou. There are a number of modest little villages along the Gulf of St. Lawrence. A few kilometres past Mabou is the **Glenora Distillery**, which recently began producing a single malt whisky.

Pictou ★

Pictou has a symbolic importance in Nova Scotia's history. This is where the *Hector*, a ship carrying the first Scottish settlers to Nova Scotia, dropped anchor. Many Scots later followed, seduced by the climate and geography reminiscent of home. They colonized other parts of the coast and Cape Breton Island. Pictou's lively downtown streets are lined by handsome buildings dating back to those early years of colonization. A ferry service runs between Caribou, just beside Pictou, to Wood Islands, on Prince Edward Island. Not far away, **Caribou Provincial Park** has a beautiful beach that is perfect for swimming.

Hector Heritage Quay ★★ *($3.50; Jun to mid-Oct 10am to 8pm; downtown, at the port, ☎485-8028)* is an interpretive centre devoted to the history of the *Hector*, the schooner that carried the first Scottish settlers to Pictou in 1773. The exhibition is very thorough. Behind the building, visitors can watch artisans reconstructing an exact replica of the *Hector*.

The **McCulloch House ★** *(free admission; early Jun to mid-Oct, Mon to Sat 9:30am to 5:30pm, Sun 1:30pm to 5:30pm; Old Haliburton Rd., ☎485-4563)* is a modest house that was built in 1806 for Reverend Thomas McCulloch, one of the most influential people in the Pictou area at the time. The house is furnished with original pieces.

Housed in the old railway station, the **Northumberland Fisheries Museum ★** *(free admission; late Jun to early Sep; Front St.)* contains a collection of items related to the history of fishing in this region, and features an authentic fishing hut.

 OUTDOORS

 Parks

Kejimkujik National Park ★★ *($5 per day; mid-Jun to mid-Oct; P.O. Box 236, Maitland Bridge, BOT 1B0; ☎682-2772)* covers 381 square kilometres in the heart of Nova Scotia. Crisscrossed by peaceful rivers teeming with fish, this territory was once inhabited by Micmac tribes, who established their hunting and fishing camp here. It is still considered a prime location for canoeing. The park also features camping sites, a pleasant beach (Merrymakedge) and various trails leading into the forest.

A part of the park, **Kejimkujik Seaside Adjunct National Park ★**, stretches 22 kilometres along the shoreline, near Port Mouton. The landscape here is more rugged than in the rest of the park. Although the area is bordered by steep cliffs sculpted by glaciers, there are a few coves nestled here and there, with sandy beaches tucked inside. Trails have been cleared to enable visitors to explore the park and observe the local plant and animal life; seals can sometimes be spotted along the shore.

Created in 1936, **Cape Breton Highlands National Park ★★★** protects 950 square kilometres of wilderness inhabited by moose and bald eagles. A wide range of activities are offered throughout this the oldest park in Eastern Canada, with just about everything an outdoor-enthusiast could desire: magnificent views, a forest inhabited by fascinating animal life, 27 hiking trails, beaches, campsites and even a golf course.

Beaches

Sandy beaches that are ideal for swimming can be found in various parts of Nova Scotia. Two regions have pleasant beaches: the north coast of the province, along the Northumberland Strait, where the shore is washed by delightfully warm waters, and the Atlantic coastline. A number of provincial parks have been established in order to protect these areas, and we have selected some of those with the loveliest beaches.

Whale-Watching

Every year, whales come to the Gulf of St. Lawrence and the waters south of the island, in the Atlantic Ocean. During this period, visitors can take part in one of the whale-watching expeditions organized by various local companies (approx. 3 h).

Lunenburg Whale Watching Tours: Box 475, Lunenburg, ☎525-7175.

Brier Island Whale & Seabird Cruises *(two departures daily)*: Westport, ☎839-2995.

Pirate's Cove *($33; two departures daily 9am and 1pm)*: Tiverton, ☎839-2242.

Cape Breton

Atlantic Whale Watch *($20, children $10; departures at 10am, 1:30pm and 4:30pm)*: Ingonish Beach, ☎285-2320.

Whale Watch *($25, children $12; departures at 10:15am, 1:30pm and 4:30pm)*: Bay St. Lawrence, ☎383-2981.

Aspy Bay Tour *(departures at 9:30am, 1pm and 4:30pm)*: Box 87, Dingwall, ☎383-2847.

Pleasant Bay *($24, children $10; Jul and Aug, departures at 9am, 1pm and 6pm)*: ☎224-1315.

Seaside Whale & Nature Watch *($25, children $10; three departures daily)*: Laurie's Motor Inn, Chéticamp, ☎224-3376 or 1-800-95-WHALE.

Whale Cruisers *($25, children $10; Jul and Aug, departures at 9am, 1pm and 6pm)* Grand Étang, ☎224-3376.

Deep-Sea Fishing

Various outfits organize deep-sea fishing expeditions. Participants are provided with all necessary equipment and instruction.

Whale Island *($25, children $12)*: Ingonish, ☎285-2338 or 1-800-565-3808, ⇒285-2338.

Deep-Sea Fishing Chéticamp *($25, children $12)*: P.O. Box 221, Chéticamp, B0E 1H0, ☎224-3606.

ACCOMMODATIONS

Halifax

Several hundred metres from the train station and about fifteen minutes by foot from the city's main attractions, the **Halifax Heritage House Hostel** *($15 for members, $18 for non-members; 15 rooms, 1253 Barrington St., B3J 1Y3, ☎422-3863)* is part of the International Youth Hostel Federation. A pretty, historic building, it can accommodate about 50 people and is equipped with a kitchenette.

Comfortable but somewhat lacking in charm, the **Citadel Inn Halifax** *($85; 270 rooms, tv, ℜ, ≈; 1960 Brunswick St., B3J 2G7, ☎422-1391 or 1-800-565-7162, ⇒429-6672)* is attractively located just a stone's throw away from the Citadel. Guests have access to an indoor pool and a gym, as well as a dining room and a bar. Breakfast is included in the price of the room. Furthermore, the parking is free, which is a real bonus in Halifax.

The **Waverley Inn** *($87; 32 rooms, tv, ℜ; 1266 Barrington St., B3J 1Y5, tel 423-9346, ⇒425-0167)* boasts a rich tradition of hospitality dating back more than a century. This sumptuous house, built in 1865-66, was the personal residence of wealthy Halifax merchant Edward W. Chipman until 1870, when a reversal of fortune plunged him into bankruptcy. A few years later, sisters Sarah and Jane Romans purchased the house for the sum of $14,200. In October 1876, the Waverley Inn threw open its doors and was considered the most prestigious hotel in the city for several decades to follow. It has welcomed many famous individuals, including English author Oscar Wilde, who stayed here in 1882. Despite the passing of time, the Waverley Inn has managed to preserve most of its original grandeur. Of course, it is no longer as luxurious, since its rooms, decorated in a rather heavy style, are now outmoded according to modern standards of comfort. However, this inn is sure to interest visitors seeking a truly authentic Victorian atmosphere. The price of the room includes breakfast and an evening snack. The Waverley Inn is located near the train station, about fifteen minutes' walk from the city's major attractions.

Halliburton House Inn *($110; 30 rooms, tv, ℜ; 5184 Morris St., B3J 1B3; ☎420-0658, ⋫423-2324)* lies tucked away on a quiet residential street near the train station, just a short distance from Halifax's main attractions. A pleasant, elegant place, it offers an interesting alternative to the large downtown hotels. In terms of comfort, Halliburton House Inn has all angles covered. The pleasant rooms are well-decorated and adorned with period furniture, giving them a lot of character. There are also several lovely common rooms, including a small living room to the left of the entrance, a library and an elegant dining room where guests can enjoy excellent cuisine (breakfast is included in the price of the room). The inn's three buildings look out on a peaceful, pretty garden full of flowers, where guests can sit at a table beneath a parasol. Halliburton House Inn, erected in 1809, was originally the home of Sir Brenton Halliburton, chief justice of the Supreme Court of Nova Scotia.

A member of the Canadian Pacific hotel chain, the **Chateau Halifax** *($125; 300 rooms, tv, ℜ, △, ⊛, ≈; 1990 Barrington St., B3J 1P2, ☎425-6700 or 1-800-441-1414, ⋫425-6214)* offers superior accommodation in spacious, sober and very comfortably furnished rooms. The friendly, pleasant hotel bar, Sam Slick's Lounge, is a perfect spot to enjoy a drink with friends or hold an informal meeting. The Chateau features an indoor pool and numerous sports facilities. It allows access to a shopping centre containing stores and restaurants, and lies just minutes away from the city's main sights and the World Trade and Convention Centre.

Halifax is home to a good number of luxury hotels. None of these, however, boasts a more spectacular or enchanting site than the

Sheraton Halifax *($139; 353 rooms, tv, ℜ, △, ≈; 1919 Upper Water St., B3J 3J5, ☎421-1700 or 1-800-325-3535, ⋫422-5805)*, located right on the pier, next to Historic Properties. Furthermore, particular care was taken to ensure that the building would blend harmoniously with its surroundings, which make up the oldest part of the city. The rooms are spacious, well-decorated and inviting. There hotel has two restaurants, conference rooms, an indoor pool and several other athletic facilities.

Wolfville

The superb **Tattingstone Inn** *($85; 10 rooms, tv, ≈, △, ℜ, pb; 434 Main St., B0P 1X0, ☎542-7696 or 1-800-565-7696, ⋫542-4427)* offers tastefully decorated rooms, some containing 18th-century furniture. The accent here is on comfort and elegance. Guests can stay in one of two buildings; the main residence has the most luxurious rooms.

At the elegant **Blomidon Inn** *($80; 26 rooms, ℜ, tv; 127 Main St., B0P 1X0, ☎542-2291 or 1-800-565-2291, ⋫542-7461)*, visitors can stay in a sumptuous manor built in 1877. At the time, costly materials were used to embellish the residence, which still features marble fireplaces and a superb staircase made of carved wood. This place has all the ingredients of a top-quality establishment: a splendid dining room where guests can enjoy refined cuisine; impeccable, friendly service and richly decorated sitting rooms. This majestic building stands in the centre of a large property bordered by stately elms. The Blomindon Inn is a veritable symbol of Nova Scotian hospitality. All of the rooms are adorned with antique furniture and include a private bath.

Annapolis Royal

Several bed & breakfasts and excellent inns offer visitors the pleasure of staying in the heart of Annapolis Royal, one of the oldest towns in North America. One of these is the **Garrison House Inn** *($55; open Apr to Dec; 7 rooms, ℜ, K, pb and sb; 350 George St., B0S 1A0, ☎532-5750, ⋫532-5501)*, is a magnificent hotel located in the heart of Annapolis Royal, just facing Fort Anne. Its antique-filled rooms are simply gorgeous. The room on the top floor with a view out the back is definitely the most stunning with its large windows and many skylights; advance reservations are a good idea for this room in particular. Very inviting common areas, including a delightful library and a restaurant on the ground floor, contribute to the pleasure of a stay here.

Digby

The impressive **Pines Resort Hotel** *($135; 87 rooms, ≈, K, tv; Shore Rd., B0V 1A0, ☎245-2511 or 1-800-667-4637, ↻245-6133)* stands on a hill overlooking the bay, in a lovely natural setting. Every part of this hotel was conceived to ensure an excellent stay, from the superb interior design and pretty, comfortable rooms to the excellent restaurant and inviting bar. Guests also have access to a wide range of athletic facilities, including tennis courts, a swimming pool and a gym; there is also a golf course nearby.

Yarmouth

The **Rood Colony Harbour Inn** *($85; 65 rooms, tv, ℜ; 6 Forest St., B5A 3K7, ☎742-9194 or 1-800-565-7633, ↻742-6291)* lies directly opposite the boarding point for the ferry to Maine. Since it is located on the side of a hill, there is a lovely view from the back. The rooms are spacious and well-designed. The bar is a pleasant place for a drink.

Shelburne

Located in the very heart of Shelburne's historic section, looking out on the harbour, the lovely **Cooper's Inn** *($65; 5 rooms, ℜ; 875 Dock St., B0T 1W0, ☎875-4656 or 1-800-688-2011)* is one of the best hotels in the province. It occupies a magnificently renovated old house that was originally built for a wealthy Loyalist merchant in 1785. The decor of each room and the choice of furniture for the house were carried out with such minute attention to detail that a simple visit to Cooper's Inn constitutes a pleasure in itself. All of the rooms are comfortable and equipped with private bathrooms. A splendid, very bright suite has been laid out on the top floor; it is well worth the $135 rate it demands. In addition, one of the rooms is easily accessible to disabled travellers. Each room is named for one of the house's former owners. To top it all off, the inn's dining room serves up cuisine that pleases the most distinguishing palates.

White Point

The **White Point Beach Resort** *($80; 47 rooms, tv, ℜ, ≈; Route 3. Exit 20A or 21 off of Hwy 103, B0T 1G0, ☎354-2711 or 1-800-565-5068, ↻354-7278)* offers luxurious modern accommodation in small cottages or in a large building facing directly onto a beach that stretches a kilometre and a half. The complex is attractive, and has been carefully and tastefully laid out in order to make the most of the surrounding beauties. In addition to swimming at the beach or in the pool, visitors can play golf or tennis or go fishing. The bar, which offers a magnificent view of the ocean, is especially pleasant.

Lunenburg

A visit to Lunenburg offers an opportunity to discover the old-fashioned charm of the town's numerous 19th-century residences, many of which have been converted into pleasant inns. One good, relatively inexpensive option is the **Compass Rose Inn** *($60; open mid-Feb to Dec; 4 rooms, ℜ; 15 King St., B0J 2C0, ☎1-800-565-8509)*, a lovely Victorian house built around 1825. The decor remains quite typical of that era, when tastes leaned towards heavily furnished rooms. Breakfast is included in the price of the room. In the evening, guests can enjoy a delicious meal in the dining room.

The **Bluenose Lodge** *($55; 9 rooms, ℜ, tv; at the corner of Falkland Ave. and Dufferin St., B0J 2C0, ☎634-8851 or 1-800-565-8851)* is a splendid Victorian house located a few minutes' walk from the centre of Lunenburg. Furnished with antiques, the rooms have a lot of character, and all include a private shower. Guests can enjoy an excellent meal in the dining room on the ground floor. This place is highly prized by individuals who relish an authentic Victorian atmosphere and fine food. Excellent service is a priority here.

The **Brigantine Inn** *($59; 7 rooms, ℜ, tv; 82 Montague St., B0J 2C0, ☎634-3300 or 1-800-360-1181)* is extremely well-located in front of the port. Most of the spotless, attractively decorated rooms feature large windows and a balcony with a splendid view. Breakfast is included in the price of the room.

Mahone Bay

The village of Mahone Bay is sure to please visitors with a taste for large 19th-century houses. Some of these residences are now high-quality bed & breakfasts. One of the best is the **Sou'Wester Inn** *($75; 4 rooms; 788 Main St., BOJ 2EO, ☎624-9296)*, a magnificent Victorian residence originally owned by a ship-builder. The entire house is furnished in the style of the era in which it was built. Guests are invited to relax on the terrace overlooking the bay.

Chester

A charming residence built at the end of the 19th century, the **Mecklenburg Inn** *($59; open late May to late Oct; 4 rooms; 78 Queen St., BOJ 1J0, ☎275-4638)* has adorable rooms, a terrace and a charming sitting room where guests will enjoy relaxing. Breakfast is included in the price of the room, and the dining room is open in the evening.

Sydney

Downtown Sydney consists mainly of a few streets alongside the river, and it is here that most of the town's hotels are located. One of these is the **Delta Sydney** *($79; 152 rooms, ≈, ℜ, tv, ◇, ☺, ◉; 300 Esplanade, B1P 6J4, ☎562-7500 or in Canada 1-800-268-1133 or in the United States 1-800-887-1133, ⇒562-3023)*, whose façade looks out on the Sydney River. The rooms are a bit lacking in charm, but thoroughly functional. As a bonus, the hotel features a lovely swimming pool with a slide, a sure hit with the children.

Right next-door stands the **Cambridge Suites Hotel** *($89; 150 rooms, tv, ≈, K, ℜ, ◇, ☺; 380 Esplanade, B1P 1B1, ☎562-6500 or 1-800-565-9466, ⇒564-6011)*, which is about as comfortable as the Delta, although more care has been taken with the decor. The rooms are actually small apartments equipped with a kitchenette.

For charming accommodation in a peaceful environment that is nevertheless close to the downtown area, head to the **Rockinghorse Inn** *($65; 8 rooms, tv; 259 Kings Rd., B1S 1A7, ☎539-2696 or 1-800-664-1010, ⇒539-2696)*. This renovated Victorian residence has eight charming rooms, each with its own private bath. Staying here makes it easy to forget that Sydney is an industrial town.

Baddeck

Also on the shores of Bras d'Or Lake, offering rooms with a lovely view, the **Auberge Gisèle** *($75; open early May to late Oct; 19 rooms, ℜ, ◉, ≈, ◇; Route 205 exit 8, BOE 1BO, ☎295-2849 or 1-800-304-0466, ⇒295-2033)* is a good place to keep in mind. Upon arriving, visitors will be enchanted by the pine-bordered lane leading up to this lovely residence, whose rooms are all attractively decorated. There are a few more rooms in a nearby annex.

At the cozy **Inverary Inn** *($80; 150 rooms, tv, ℜ; Hwy 105 exit 8, BOE 1BO, ☎295-3500 or 1-800-565-5660, ⇒295-3527)*, guests can stay either in the main building or in charming little wooden cottages. The decor and the vast grounds give this place a rustic feel well-suited to the Nova Scotian countryside.

Ingonish Beach

The **Keltic Lodge** *($259; open Jun to Oct and Jan to Mar; 98 rooms, ≈, K, ℜ, tv; Middle Head Peninsula, BOC 1LO, ☎285-2880 or 1-800-565-0444, ⇒285-2859)* boasts a spectacular location alongside a cliff overlooking the sea. Slightly removed from the access roads, in the heart of a veritable oasis of peace, the Keltic Lodge offers top-notch accommodation just a short distance from the Cabot Trail. The buildings are handsome and the rooms, some of which are in cottages, are both charming and comfortable. The dining room features a gourmet menu.

Dingwall

An excellent place to relax, admire the sea, walk along the beach or set off to explore the Cabot Trail, the **Markland Coastal Resort** *($90; K, ℜ, tv; 3 km from Dingwall, BOC 1GO, ☎383-2246 or 1-800-872-6084, ⇒383-2092)* offers comfortable accommodation in wooden cottages with a cozy, rustic-looking interior. Each cottage has several rooms equipped with a terrace. The large, grassy piece of land opposite the cottages leads to an untouched beach. The Markland is an ideal spot for couples or families who enjoy a peaceful, secluded setting and wide open spaces. The fine food served in the dining room hits the spot after a long day in the fresh air.

Chéticamp

There are several places to stay in the centre of the Acadian community of Chéticamp. One of these is **Laurie's Motor Inn** *($85; 61 rooms, K, ℜ, tv; Main St., BOE 1H0, ☎224-2400 or for reservations: 1-800-95-WHALE, ≈224-2069)*, a motel stretching alongside the Gulf of St. Lawrence. Although the decor is not very original, the rooms are clean and comfortable. If you're famished or just want to enjoy a satisfying meal, don't hesitate to stop in at the motel's dining room, which has a very decent menu. The seafood is especially good.

Pictou

Located in the heart of Pictou, the **Walker Inn** *($75; 10 rooms, ℜ, tv; 34 Coleraine St., BOK 1H0, ☎485-1433 or 1-800-370-5553 for reservations)* is a pretty brick building dating back to 1865. This place has a great deal of charm. The rooms have been renovated in order to furnish each with a private bath. Breakfast is included in the price of the room. The Walker Inn is kept by a very likeable French Canadian couple. By reservation only, evening meals may be enjoyed in the inn's beautiful dining room.

 RESTAURANTS

Halifax

What a pleasure it is to enjoy an excellent cup of coffee while poring over a book! That's the concept behind the **Trident Booksellers & Café** *($; 1570 Argyle St., ☎423-7100)*, an extremely friendly, airy place located a few steps away from Blowers Street. The menu is limited to an extensive choice of coffees, hot chocolates, teas and, during summertime, cold drinks. A small assortment of pastries tops off the offerings. Newspapers are always available for customers, and books (often second-hand), are sold at modest prices.

Much more than a simple French restaurant, **La Maison** *($$-$$$; 1541 Birmingham St., ☎492-4339)* offers a whirlwind tour of the flavours of French-speaking America and Europe. There are many appetizers to choose from, including steak tartar, warm goat-cheese salad, and an excellent bouillabaisse of mussels, scallops and shrimp. Mouth-watering lamb chops, seafood papillote, duck in Grand Marnier sauce and a variety of steaks are some of the main dishes prepared at La Maison. The food is served either in the relaxing atmosphere of the dining room, which has a classic decor, or, when the weather is fair, on the peaceful terrace.

The dining room of the elegant **Halliburton House Inn** *($$$; 5184 Morris St., ☎420-0658)* is a perfect place to enjoy a long, intimate dinner for two or linger over a meal among friends. Furnished in a tasteful, elegant manner, the place has a lot of style and emanates an atmosphere of opulence. Aside from a few exceptions, like the alligator appetizer, the menu is made up of classics, including an excellent *steak au poivre* flambéd with brandy, lamb *à la provençale*, Atlantic salmon and *coquilles Saint-Jacques*.

Set up inside one of the oldest buildings in town, an old school that has now been renovated, the **Five Fishermen** *($$$; 1740 Argyle St., ☎422-4421)* is a one of the great favourites with fish and seafood lovers. Lobster obviously gets top billing on the menu. Other dishes include Atlantic salmon and trout, as well as a variety of steaks. It is worth noting that the kitchen closes later than most others in town, around 11 PM on Sunday and at midnight during the rest of the week. The wine list, furthermore, is very extensive.

Wolfville

If you're craving a good cup of coffee, head over to the **Coffee Merchant** *($; at the corner of Main and Elm)*, which serves good cappuccino and espresso. This is a pleasant place, where it is tempting to linger, reading the newspaper of gazing out the window at the comings and goings of the people on the street. The menu is fairly limited, but nevertheless lists a few sandwiches and muffins.

The **Blomidon Inn** *($$-$$$; 127 Main St., ☎542-2291)* has two dining rooms—a small, very cozy one in the library and a larger one richly decorated with mahogany chairs. The latter is embellished by a picture window that looks out onto a beautiful landscape. The menu is equally exceptional, featuring such delicious

NOVA SCOTIA

dishes as poached salmon and scallops and salmon Florentine.

Digby

Digby's famous scallops are of course *the* local specialty, and most of the town's restaurants are in proximity of the port. The **Red Raven Pub** *($-$$; Water St., ☎245-5533)*, a family restaurant, dishes up simple, inexpensive fare.

Shelburne

Cooper's Restaurant *($$$; Cooper's Inn, Dock St., ☎875-4656)* offers the elegance and ambiance of a historic house built in 1785 and the flavours of refined regional cuisine. For starters there is a choice of dishes such as smoked salmon wrapped in a spinach crepe. About ten main dishes are offered, including succulent sauteed scallops and excellent pasta topped with lobster. A selection of about twenty wines, including some excellent vintages, as well as a great variety of aperitifs and *digestifs*, rounds out the menu.

Lunenburg

The **Bluenose Lodge** *($$; 10 Falkland Ave., at the corner of Dufferin Ave., ☎634-8851)*, which has been set up inside of a large Victorian house, has a lovely dining room on the ground floor. The menu consists mainly of fish and seafood, The Atlantic salmon and haddock with spinach sauce are especially delicious. The service is both friendly and professional and the staff will readily chat with guests about the world of fishing and the history of Lunenburg.

Lunenburg boasts a magnificent location overlooking a natural harbour. The **Boscawen Inn** *($$; 150 Cumberland St., ☎634-3325)*, a Victorian house standing on the side of a hill, is a good place to appreciate the natural beauty of the surroundings and the harmoniousness of the local architecture. The dining room menu consists mainly of excellent fish and seafood dishes.

Sydney

On Charlotte Street, there are a number of little snack-bars serving hamburgers and fries.

Don't be scared off by the Western look of **Joe's Warehouse** *($$; 424 Charlotte St., ☎539-6686)*, which happens to be a local institution. Although the decor is not exactly sophisticated and the music sounds like what you'd hear in a shopping mall, the atmosphere is still very inviting. In any case, people come to Joe's for the generous portions of delicious prime rib. Seafood is also included on the menu.

The Delta Hotel's restaurant, **Des Barres** *($$; 300 Esplanade, ☎562-7500)*, has a very decent menu featuring a fair number of fish dishes. With its large picture windows looking out onto the water, the place also boasts a lovely view. Breakfast served.

Louisbourg

At the fortress, a restaurant has been set up in one of the buildings facing the water. The food is no more than decent, but at least visitors can eat lunch without leaving the site.

Baddeck

In the centre of the village, visitors will spot a lovely terrace with a few tables on it. This belongs to the charming **Highlandheeler Café** *($; Chebucto St.)*, which serves delicious soups, healthy sandwiches, quiche and all sorts of desserts—everything it takes to put together an excellent picnic. Those who prefer to take advantage of the terrace can eat on the premises.

The Silver Dart Lodge is pleasantly located on the shores of Bras d'Or Lake. Its restaurant, **McCurdy's** *($$; Silver Dart Lodge, Shore Rd., ☎295-2340)*, which looks out onto this magnificent body of water, offers its guests an unbeatable atmosphere. In addition to the view, people come here to sample the tasty seafood dishes and savour the Scottish cuisine.

Dingwall

The restaurant of the **Markland Hotel** *($$; ☎383-2246)* has a pine-panelled dining room with a decor that is stylish without being extravagant. The menu is extremely interesting, however; simply reading it over will whet your appetite. The offerings include grilled salmon with Mousseline sauce and grilled filet of pork with plums in a red wine and onion sauce.

Chéticamp

At **Laurie's** *($-$$;* ☎224-2400), visitors might be surprised to discover that the menu lists both lobster and hamburgers. In fact, this restaurant has something for everyone, in terms of both taste and budget. Guests are offered such succulent dishes as the fisherman's platter, which includes lobster, crab and shrimp. The Acadian staff is as friendly as can be, amiably telling their guests to "enjoy *le repas.*"

Pictou

Established in a lovely stone house in Pictou's historic district, the **Stone House Café and Pizzeria** *($-$$; 11 Water St.)* is a very appealing family restaurant that serves simple, well-prepared fare and which is especially pleasing to fans of American-style pizza. In nice weather it is possible to sit on the restaurant's terrace facing the port.

  ENTERTAINMENT

Halifax

Bars and Nightclubs

To enjoy traditional Maritime music in an extremely relaxed atmosphere, head to the **Lower Deck Pub** *(Privateer's Warehouse, Historic Properties,* ☎425-1501), a pleasant, friendly place with live music in the evening.

Theatres

Halifax's most renowned theatre company, the **Neptune Theatre** *(5216 Sackville St.,* ☎429-7070) is devoted to presenting classic plays to the public.

Large-scale rock concerts are held at the **Halifax Metro Centre** *(1284 Duke St.,* ☎451-1221). For that matter, when artists of international renown come to the Maritimes, they usually choose to play in Halifax. To know what concerts are scheduled, dial the number indicated above.

Fans of classical music can attend concerts given by the **Symphony Nova Scotia** *(1646 Barrington St.,* ☎421-7311).

 SHOPPING

Halifax

Without a doubt, the most pleasant place to shop is **Historic Properties** *(bordered by Duke and Lower Water Streets)*, the historic neighbourhood alongside the Halifax wharves. Shops selling crafts and clothing take up a large portion of the space in this harmonious architectural grouping built in the 19th century.

The **Gallery Shop** *(Art Gallery of Nova Scotia, 1741 Hollis,* ☎424-2836) offers an excellent selection of local crafts, as well as works by painters, sculptors and other artists from Nova Scotia. Pieces by Micmac artists are also available.

The **Micmac Heritage Gallery** *(Barrington Place Shops, Granville Level,* ☎422-9509) is the most impressive gallery dedicated to Micmac arts and crafts in the Maritime Provinces. Articles on display include leather mittens and moccasins, woven baskets, jewelry and paintings.

The **Houston North Gallery** *(Sheraton Hotel, 1919 Upper Water St.)* presents a remarkable collection of Amerindian and Inuit sculptures and paintings.

The **Book Room** *(1664 Granville St.)* is a large store with a wide selection of books published in Canada and abroad. Right nearby, the **Government Bookstore** *(1700 Granville St.)* sells all of the books and publications put out by the government of Nova Scotia. Many of these deal with plant and animal life, geology, history—in short, all sorts of subjects that might interest travellers curious to know more about Nova Scotia.

NOVA SCOTIA

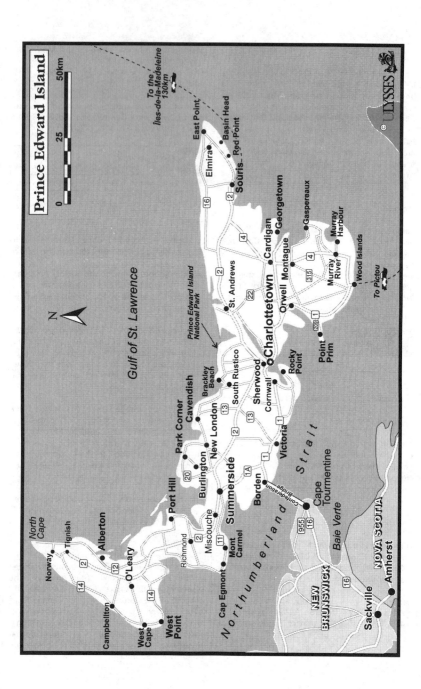

Prince Edward Island

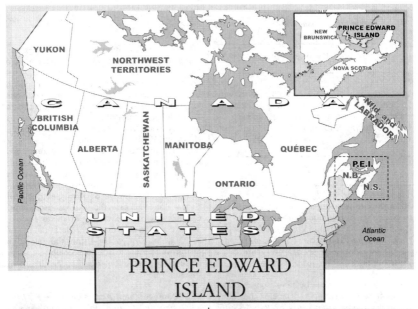

PRINCE EDWARD ISLAND

hink Prince Edward Island and many people envision a rare harmony of rural and maritime landscapes, the epitome of a gentle serene life. Set back from the peaceful roads and tucked away behind rolling valleys of farmland, lie picturesque little fishing villages, adorable white clapboard churches, or the pulsing glow of a lighthouse towering over the sea from isolated rocky outcrops. Most striking in these charming scenes is the brilliant palette of colours: the vibrant yellow and green of the fields falling over the cliffs of deep rust red into the lapis blue of the sea. Bathed to the north by the Gulf of St. Lawrence and to the south by the Strait of Northumberland, this island is above all known for its magnificent white sand dunes and beaches, often deserted and extending between sea and land as far as the eye can see. It goes without saying that these ribbons of sand are among the most beautiful on the east coast of the continent. They offer great spots for swimming, long walks and discoveries. The beaches may be what initially attracts most visitors, but they quickly discover the many other treasures Prince Edward Island (P.E.I.) has to offer. For starters, the small capital city of Charlottetown, whose architecture and unique atmosphere give it an antique charm; from there the possibilities are virtually endless, the friendliest fresh lobster feasts you can imagine, the storybook world *Anne of Green Gables*, or the richness of the magnificent plants and wildlife of Prince Edward Island National Park.

 FINDING YOUR WAY AROUND

By Car

Prince Edward Island is accessible from Cape Tormentine, New Brunswick, via the 13-kilometre-long **Confederation Bridge** *($35 per car, round-trip)* which spans Northumberland Strait. For islanders, the bridge's inauguration in 1997 marked a veritable revolution: crossing the strait now takes 10 minutes by car compared to a half hour by ferry.

By Plane

Visitors arriving on the island by plane, come in to **Sherwood** airport, about 4 km north of downtown Charlottetown *(☎566-7992)*. Air Canada *(☎894-8825 or 892-1007)*, and its partner Air Nova, as well as Canadian Airlines *(☎892-5358)*, and its partner Air Atlantic are the major airline companies serving this airport. Four car rental agencies have offices in the airport.

By Bus

Bus service to Prince Edward Island is very limited. However, there is bus service to Cavendish from the big hotel chains in Charlottetown: Departure at 9am, return at 6pm.

By Ferry

From May to November, You can reach P.E.I. by taking the **Northumberland Ferries** which link Caribou (Nova Scotia) to Wood Islands *(May to Nov, no reservation; car $30.50, passenger $9.50; ☎1-888-249-7245)*. The trip takes 75 minutes.

P.E.I. is also accessible by ferry from the Îles-de-la-Madeleine (Québec) aboard the **Lucy Maud Montgomery** *(car $64.25, adults $33.75; one ferry per day, reserve if possible; ☎418-986-3278)* which arrives in Souris, near the northeastern point of the island.

 PRACTICAL INFORMATION

Area Code: 902

Tourist Information Offices

The main tourist information office of the island is located in Borden-Carleton, right at the foot of the Confederate Bridge, ☎629-2428 or (800) 463-4734.

Charlettetown: at the corner of Water and Prince Streets.

 EXPLORING

Charlottetown ★★

Charming and quaint, Charlottetown has a unique atmosphere. Despite its size, Charlottetown is not just a small Maritime town like any other; it is also a provincial capital with all the prestige, elegance and institutions one would expect. Though everything here seems decidedly scaled down, the capital of Prince

Edward Island has its parliament buildings and sumptuous Lieutenant-Governor's residence, a large complex devoted to the stage and visual arts, pretty parks and rows of trees concealing beautiful Victorian residences, a prestigious hotel and several fine restaurants. Adding to its charm is its picturesque location on the shores of a bay at the confluence of the Hillsborough, North and West Rivers. A meeting place of the Micmac, the site was known to explorers and French colonists in the 18th century. It was not until 1768, however, that the British settlers actually founded the city, named Charlottetown in honour of the wife of King George III of Great Britain. Less than a century later, Charlottetown made its way into history books as the cradle of Canadian Confederation. It was in this little town, in 1864, that the delegates of the North American British colonies met to discuss the creation of the Dominion of Canada.

The **Confederation Arts Centre ★★** *(free admission; Jul to Aug, 9am to 9pm; Sep to Jun, Mon to Sat 9am to 5pm, Sun 2pm to 5pm; Grafton Street, corner Queen Street, ☎628-1864)* was constructed in 1964, one century after the decisive meeting of the Fathers of Confederation in Charlottetown. The complex was designed to increase public knowledge of Canadian culture today and its evolution over the last 130 years. The Arts Centre has many facets, including a museum with several impressive exhibits, an art gallery and a public library. There are also several beautiful auditoriums where visitors can take in a performance of *Anne of Green Gables.* Presented every summer for more than three decades, this musical is a fun way to spend an evening in Charlottetown and become immersed in the world of Prince Edward Island's most famous author, Lucy Maud Montgomery.

The **Province House National Historic Site ★★** *(free admission; Jul and Aug, 9am to 6pm; Sep to Jun, Mon to Fri 9am to 5pm; corner of Great George and Richmond Streets, ☎566-7626)* can honestly be considered the cradle of Canadian Confederation. It was here that the 23 delegates from United Canada (Ontario and Québec today), Nova Scotia, New Brunswick and Prince Edward Island assembled in 1864 to prepare the Confederation of 1867. Ironically, the host of this decisive conference, Prince Edward Island, did not join the Dominion of Canada until a few years later, in 1873. Visitors can see the rooms where the Canadian Confederation was worked out and watch a

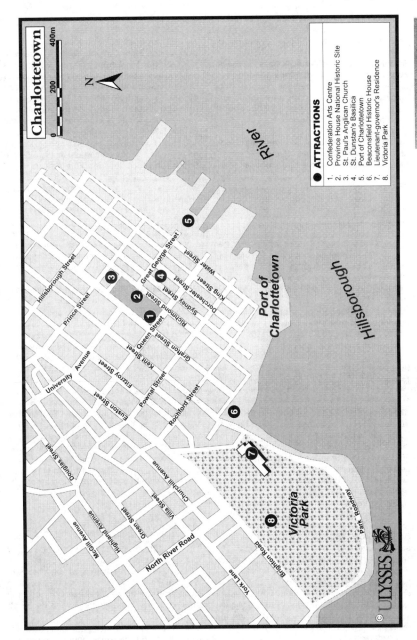

Charlottetown

0 200 400m

N

● **ATTRACTIONS**

1. Confederation Arts Centre
2. Province House National Historic Site
3. St. Paul's Anglican Church
4. St. Dunstan's Basilica
5. Port of Charlottetown
6. Beaconsfield Historic House
7. Lieutenant-governor's Residence
8. Victoria Park

River

Port of Charlottetown

Hillsborough

Hillsborough Street
Prince Street
Great George Street
Sydney Street
Dorchester Street
King Street
Water Street
Richmond Street
Queen Street
Grafton Street
Kent Street
Fitzroy Street
University Avenue
Euston Street
Pownal Street
Rochford Street
Douglas Street
Churchill Avenue
Villa Street
Green Street
Highland Avenue
McGill Avenue
North River Road
York Lane
Brighton Road
Park Roadway

Victoria Park

© ULYSSES

short film explaining the significance of the event. Province House is now the seat of the Legislative Assembly of Prince Edward Island.

St. Paul's Anglican Church ★ *(free admission; corner of Grafton and Prince Streets)* was erected in 1896 to replace several other Anglican churches built in the previous century. Its interior is splendid, especially the wooden vault and stained-glass windows.

St. Dunstan's Basilica ★ *(free admission; corner of Great George and Sydney Streets)*, a beautiful example of the Gothic style, is the most impressive religious building on Prince Edward Island. Its construction began in 1914, on the same site occupied by three Catholic churches successively during the previous century.

Pretty Great George Street, where you can browse through many shops and second-hand stores, ends up at the small **port of Charlottetown**, a pleasant area where visitors will find not only a park and marina, but also **Peake's Wharf ★** *(at the end of Great George Street)*, a collection of shops in charming renovated old buildings. Close by stands the classy **Prince Edward Hotel** (see p 120), as well as a few restaurants.

Beaconsfield Historic House ★ *($2.50; mid-Jun to early Sep, Tue to Sun 10am to 5pm; Sep to late Oct, Tue to Fri and Sun 1pm to 5pm; early Nov to mid-Jun, Tue to Fri 1pm to 5pm; 2 Kent Street, ☎368-6600)* was built in 1877 for wealthy shipbuilder James Peake and his wife Edith Haviland Beaconsfield. It is one of the most luxurious residences in the province, with 25 rooms and 9 fireplaces. After James Peake declared personal bankruptcy in 1882, his creditors, the Cunall family, moved in. The family had no descendants, so Beaconsfield House served as a training school from 1916 on, and was converted into a museum in 1973.

On the other side of Kent Street, shielded behind a stately row of trees, stands the splendid **Lieutenant-Governor's residence** *(corner of Kent Street and Pond Road)*. It has been the official residence of the British crown's representative on Prince Edward Island since 1835. Magnificent, beautifully designed **Victoria Park ★** which spreads out before the residence, is a lovely place for a stroll.

Rocky Point ★

Rocky Point is located at the end of a point of land, at the mouth of the West River and in front of the Hillsborough River, which was always a strategic point in the defense of Charlottetown and the back-country against an eventual attack from the sea. This site was of particular interest early on to the colonial empires who would fight battles to win control of the island. The French were the first to establish themselves here in the 1720s, by founding Port la Joye, captured in 1758 by the British who then founded Fort Amherst. The fine-tuning of the fort came that same year when the war between France and England began in earnest. The British garrison had the important role of protecting the island from French invasion and controlling maritime traffic in the Northumberland Strait throughout the whole war. However, as of 1763, with the end of the war, the fort's importance decreased significantly and was abandoned by the British in 1768. The **Port La Joye - Fort Amherst National Historic Site ★** *(free admission; late Jun to early Sep 10am to 6pm; Route 19; ☎675-2220)* houses a small interpretive centre presenting an exhibit on the various documents related to the French colony (Port La Joye) and the British presence at the site (Fort Amherst). There is also a short documentary film on the history of the Acadians of Prince Edward Island. Very little remains today of Fort Amherst. There is however a lovely view of the surrounding fields and of the city of Charlottetown from the site. The **Micmac Village** *($3.25; Jun, 10am to 5pm, Jul, 9:30am to 7pm, Aug, 9:30am to 6pm; Route 19, ☎675-3800)* is also worth a stop, when visiting Rocky Point. There is a small museum, a gift shop and a reconstruction of a Micmac village, the natives that inhabited the island before the arrival of European colonists.

Victoria ★

The beautiful residences lining the streets of this charming and peaceful coastal town are evidence of the opulence of another era. Founded in 1767, this seaport played a significant role in the local economy up until the end of the 19th century, when bit by bit the development of the railway on Prince Edward Island outmoded it. Fishing trawlers can still be seen, however bobbing about just beyond the once busy harbour. Today the interest in Victoria lies mostly in its old-fashioned character and in the friendliness of

Lucy Maud Montgomery

Lucy Maud Montgomery was born, in New London, P.E.I. November 30th, 1874. But early in her childhood she had to leave New London to live with her grandparents, Alexander and Lucy MacNeill, in Cavendish, who raised her after the death of her mother. Her first novel Anne of Green Gables, inspired by her own orphan life, was a huge success as soon as it appeared in 1908, it has since been translated into 16 languages. L.M. Montgomery, later published 23 novels up until her death in 1942. Her most famous work remained however the story of Anne, that enchanting little orphan with the red hair and freckled face.

its residents. Country life on the island is best represented here. There are two inns, a few restaurants, and a famous chocolatier...

When arriving from the east you'll first come to **Victoria Provincial Park**, extending to the water and including a small beach and a picnic area. The **Victoria Seaport Museum** *(free admission; Jul to early Sep, Tue to Sun 10am to 5pm; Route 116; ☎658-2602)* is located close by in a lighthouse. Besides the several photographs of Victoria on display, you can also climb to the top of the lighthouse for a view of the village, the coast and surroundings.

Just a few streets make up the centre of Victoria. Here and there are several shops, restaurants as well as The **Victorian Playhouse** which presents, good quality concerts and theatre all summer long, adding to the charm of town.

Park Corner

Anne of Green Gables Museum at Silver Bush ★ *($2.50; Jun, 9am to 6pm; Jul and Aug, 9am to 8pm; Sep and Oct, 9am to 6pm; ☎886-2807)* was actually a favourite house of Lucy Maud Montgomery, it belonged to her aunt and uncle, Annie and John Campbell. She adored it and was married here in July, 1911. Today it is a historic house, decorated with period furniture and many of the author's and her family's personal effects.

New London

The small community of New London has the distinguished honour of being the birthplace of the writer who has done the most for Prince Edward Island abroad. The main attraction is the house where she was born, the **Lucy Maud Montgomery Birthplace** *($2; late May and Jun, 9am to 5pm; Jul and Aug, 9am to 7pm; early Sep to Oct, 9am to 5pm; intersection of Routes 6 and 8, ☎886-2099 or 436-7329)*. Personal objects, including L.M. Montgomery's wedding dress, can be viewed in this simple house.

Cavendish ★

The Cavendish area is a sacred spot for tourists to P.E.I.. Located next to some of the most beautiful beaches on the island, and several big tourist attractions, Cavendish has many lodging possibilities, restaurants and shops. It is for many a gateway to the national park, and therefore has an excellent tourist information centre.

Green Gables House ★ *($2.50; mid-May to late Jun, 9am to 5pm; late Jun to late Aug, 9am to 8pm; late Aug to late Oct, 9am to 5pm; Route 6, west of Cavendish, ☎672-6350)* is the house that inspired Lucy Maud Montgomery, and it is also where she situates the action of her famous novel *Anne of Green Gables*. Built towards the middle of the last century, the house belonged to David and Margaret MacNeil, older cousins of the author's. L.M. Montgomery used to love strolling down "lover's lane", located in the woods on her cousins' property. She was so inspired by the surroundings that it became the backdrop for her novel. By 1936 the novel was so popular that the federal government made a classified site of the house, and thus today it can be visited.

Prince Edward Island National Park ★★★ (see p 119)

South Rustico ★

Two significant institutions in the history of the Acadian community on the north of the island, are actually located right next to each other: The **Banque des Fermiers** ★ or Farmer's Bank, a museum today *($1; late Jun to early Sep,*

Green Gables

Mon to Sat 9:30am to 5pm, Sun 11:30am to 4pm; Route 243, ☎963-2505), was founded in 1864 by Father George-Antoine Belcourt, with the aim of providing Acadians with the opportunity to take their place in the economic development. It was the first people's bank in the country, and for a certain time, the smallest chartered bank in Canada. The exhibit tells of Father Belcourt's work, the building is located on a historic site. Right next door, the modest **Saint Augustine Church** *(Church Street)* is the oldest Acadian church on the island.

Brackley Beach ★

This small hamlet on the shores of Rustico Bay is worth a visit to see the **Brackley Beach Lighthouse** *($1.50, early Jun to mid-Sep, 10am to 10pm; at intersection of Routes 15 and 16, ☎672-3478)* and its exhibit of photographs of lighthouses on the island. Another recommended stop, close by is The **Dunes Art Gallery** *(free admission; May, 10am to 6pm; Jun to Sep, 9am to 10pm; Oct, 10am to 6pm; Route 15, ☎672-2586)* where the works of the biggest artists of the island are on display. There is also a charming little restaurant. Since Prince Edward Island national park is nearby, Brackley Beach provides plenty of accommodations.

Orwell Corner

A visit to the **Orwell Corner Historic Village ★** *($3; mid-May to late Jun, Mon to Fri 10am to 3pm; late Jun to late Aug, Tue to Sun 9am to 5pm; early Sep to early Oct, 10am to 3pm; TransCanada Highway, 30 km east of Charlottetown; ☎651-2013)* is a must for anyone interested in discovering what life was like in rural Prince Edward Island back in the 19th century. This delightful village is made up of restored buildings, including a pretty little school that looks as if it came straight out of an L.M. Montgomery novel, a church, a shingle factory, several barns, a forge and a farmhouse that doubles as a general store and a post office. The atmosphere is enlivened by characters in period dress, who are available to answer visitors' questions. Orwell Corner may be smaller than other similar historic villages, such as Kings Landing in New Brunswick, but its size gives it a charming authenticity.

A few hundred metres from Orwell Corner, tucked away in an enchanting setting, lies the **Sir Andrew Macphail Homestead** *(free admission, donations appreciated; Jun and Sep, Tue to Sun 10am to 5pm; Jul and Aug, Wed to Sun 10am to 8pm; 30 km east of Charlottetown, Route 1, ☎651-2589).* A native of Prince Edward Island, Andrew Macphail (1864-1938) had an extraordinary career in the fields of research and medicine, and also as an author and journalist. His house, furnished as it was at the beginning of the century, is a lovely part of the local heritage. There is a small dining room, where light meals are served. Visitors can also explore the vast grounds by taking a pleasant walk along a 2 km trail.

Point Prim

Not far from the village of Eldon, Route 1 intersects with Route 209, a small road leading to the **Point Prim Lighthouse** *(free admission; Jul and Aug, 9am to 7pm; Route 209, ☎659-2312)*, designed and built by Isaac Smith, architect of Charlottetown's Province House, in 1845. The lighthouse is open to the public, and the surrounding area is perfect for a picnic. The **view ★** of the sea is worth the short detour.

Montague ★

Montague might not be very big, but it is nevertheless one of the largest communities in the eastern part of the province. It is home to several businesses, shops and restaurants, as well as the interesting **Garden of the Gulf Museum ★** *($2.50; mid-Jun to late Sep, Mon to Sat 10am to 5pm, Sun 1pm to 5pm; 2 Main Street South, ☎838-2467)*, set up inside the former post office. The exhibit deals with both local and military history. Montague is also the point of departure for excursions organized by **Cruise Manada Seal Watching Boat Tours** *($15; mid-May to late Aug; on Main Street, near the bridge, ☎838-2444)* (see p 119). Other excursions start at the Brudenell Marina.

Souris

The little town of Souris, with its 1,600 or so inhabitants, is the largest community in the eastern part of Prince Edward Island. Accordingly, it offers a range of services, several restaurants and hotels and a tourist information centre. Not far away lies **Souris Beach Provincial Park** , where visitors will find a picnic area and an unsupervised beach. The town's Main Street is graced with several pretty buildings, which bear witness to Souris' prominent role in this region. The most striking of these are the **Town Hall** and **St. Mary's Church**. The town port is the boarding point for the ferry (see p 112) to Québec's Îles-de-la-Madeleine.

Basin Head ★

Ideally located on one of the island's loveliest **sandy beaches ★★**, not far from some magnificent dunes, the **Basin Head Fisheries Museum ★★** *($3; mid-June and late Sep, Mon to Fri, 10am to 5pm; Jul and Aug, 10am to 7pm; Route 16, ☎357-2966)* offers visitors an opportunity to learn about all different facets of the wonderful world of fishing around Prince Edward Island. The museum exhibits an interesting collection of artifacts related to the lives and occupation of the fishermen of old. The building itself is flanked by sheds, in which vessels of various sizes and periods are displayed, as well as a workshop where local artisans make wooden boxes like those used in the past for packing salted fish. An old canning factory stands a little farther off. In all respects, this is one of the most interesting museums in the province. To make the most of a visit, however, don't miss a chance to stroll along the neighbouring beaches and dunes as well.

East Point

For a magnificent view of the ocean and the area's coastal landscape, head to the **East Point Lighthouse ★** *(free admission, guided tours $2.50; Jul to mid-Aug; Route 16; ☎357-2106)*, which stands on the easternmost tip of the island. During summer, visitors can climb to the top of this old lighthouse, which dates back to 1867.

Elmira

A tiny rural village near the easternmost tip of the island, Elmira is home to one of the Prince Edward Island Museum and Heritage Foundation's six museums, the **Elmira Railway Museum ★** *($1.50; mid Jun to early Sep, Tue to Sun 9am to 5pm; Route 16A, ☎357-2481)*. Located in a bucolic setting, it occupies the town's former train station, which has been closed since 1982. In addition to the main building, there is a warehouse and a railway car, which is stationed on one of the tracks. This museum's excellent exhibit is a reminder of the glorious sense of adventure that accompanied the construction of Prince Edward Island's railway.

The Acadian Presence

Although Acadians didn't settle in the Evangeline region until 1812, their presence on Prince Edward Island dates back to the 1720s, when the island was a French colony named Île-Saint-Jean. These first colonists, who came from the area then known as Acadia (present-day Nova Scotia), founded the settlements of Port-LaJoye, Pointe-Prime and Malpèque, among others. In the following decades, the Acadian population gradually increased, then began growing rapidly in 1755, due to the arrival of refugees fleeing deportation from Nova Scotia (the former Acadia). In 1758, however, Ile-Saint-Jean also fell into the hands of the British, who deported about 3,000 of the 5,000 Acadians living on the island. After the war, the remaining Acadians, along with those who returned to the island, lived mainly in the area around Malpèque Bay. It wasn't until 1812 that some families left this region to settle in the southwest, founding La Roche (Baie-Egmont) and Grand-Ruisseau (Mont-Carmel).

Summerside ★

With a population of about 10,000, Summerside is Prince Edward Island's second largest town. It is presently experiencing an economic boom, due to the nearby construction of the bridge that will soon link the island to the province of New Brunswick. It is a pleasant town, graced with lovely Victorian residences and a pretty waterfront. As the chief urban centre on the western part of the island, Summerside also has a number of shops, restaurants and places to stay.

Eptek ($2; Tue to Sun 10am to 5pm; on the waterfront, Water Street, ☎888-8373) is a national exhibition centre, which presents travelling exhibits of Canadian art. The same building houses Prince Edward Island's Sports Hall of Fame.

Through a collection of photographs and other articles, the International Fox Museum ★ (free admission, contributions accepted; May to Oct, 10am to 6pm; 286 Fitzroy Street, ☎436-2400) traces the history of fox-breeding on Prince Edward Island. After a timid start at the end of the last century, this activity represented 17% of the province's economy by the 1920s. In those years, a pair of silver foxes could fetch as much as $35,000. Efforts are now being made to revive this once prosperous industry.

Mount-Carmel

Mont-Carmel, known for many years as Grand-Ruisseau, was founded in 1812 by the Arseneault and Gallant families. The splendour of the Église Notre-Dame-du-Mont-Carmel ★ (Route 11), which lies in the heart of the parish, bears eloquent witness to the prominent role played by Catholicism in Acadian culture.

Located on the site of the very first settlement, Grand-Ruisseau (now known as Mont-Carmel), the Acadian Pioneer Village ★ ($3.50; Jun to mid-Sep, 9am to 7pm; Route 11; 1.5 km west of the church, ☎854-2227) recreates the rustic lifestyle of early 19th century Acadians. The village includes a church and presbytery, two family homes, a smithy, a school and a barn. Most of the furniture in the buildings was donated by citizens of neighbouring villages. A comfortable hotel stands at the entrance of the pioneer village, along with the restaurant Étoile de Mer, which offers visitors a unique opportunity to enjoy Acadian cuisine.

West Point ★

A stop at West Point offers an opportunity to explore one of the most peaceful, picturesque spots on the island, Cedar Dunes Provincial Park ★ (Route 14), which features endless deserted beaches and dunes. Another interesting spot nearby is the West Point Lighthouse ($2.50; late Jun to late Aug, 8am to 9:30pm; May to mid-Jun and Sep, 8am to 8pm; Route 14; ☎859-3606), which dates back to 1875 and is one of the largest in the province. In addition to housing a museum and a restaurant, it is the only lighthouse in Canada to be used as an inn.

North Cape ★

The scenery around North Cape, the northernmost tip of the island, is not only pretty, but often spectacular, with red sandstone cliffs plunging into the blue waters of the Gulf of St. Lawrence. North Cape itself occupies a lovely site along the coast. Here, visitors will find the Atlantic Wind Test Site

($2; Jul and Aug, 10am to 8pm; at the end of Route 12; ☎882-2746), where wind technology is tested and evaluated. A small exhibit explains the advantages of using this type of energy.

Port Hill

The **Green Park Shipbuilding Museum** ★ *(adults $2.50; June to early Sep, 9am to 5pm; Route 12; ☎831-2206)* reminds visitors that shipbuilding was the mainspring of Prince Edward Island's economy for the greater part of the 19th century. It presents an exhibit on the various techniques used in shipbuilding and the history of the trade. The site includes a reconstructed shipyard, complete with a ship in progress. Right nearby stands the Yeo house, the lovely former home of James Yeo, Jr., who owned a shipyard in the 19th century.

OUTDOORS

Parks

A visit to the island wouldn't be complete without a trip of at least one day to **Prince Edward Island National Park ★★★** *(three welcome centres: in Cavendish, near the intersection of Routes 6 and 13, ☎963-2391; opposite the Dalvay-by-the-Sea Hotel, ☎672-6350; Brackley welcome centre, at the intersection of Routes 6 and 15, ☎672-2259)*, which stretches 40 km along the northern coast of the island, from Blooming Point to New London Bay. The park was created in 1937 with the goal of preserving a unique natural environment, including sand dunes, with their fragile ecosystem, red sandstone cliffs, magnificent beaches and salt-water marshes. While exploring the park, visitors will be constantly delighted by stunning views of the sheer coastline, the sudden appearance of a red fox or one of the many activities that may be enjoyed here.

There are trails leading right into the heart of the park. On the Reeds and Rushes trail, visitors can observe the animal life in a pond from a floating footbridge. Other species of plant and animal life may be discovered on one of the four other marked trails, suitable for all ages, that crisscross the park. The beaches here are also terrific for families. Be careful around the neighbouring sand dunes, however, since the piping plover, a small, endangered species of bird, sometimes nests there. Footbridges have been laid out in order to protect this fragile environment; please respect the signs.

Cruises

Visitors wishing to head out to sea can take part in one of a variety of short cruises offered by local companies.

Mill River Boat Tour (adults $15): ☎856-3820
Cardigan River: Cardigan (sailing), ☎583-2020

Seal-Watching

Groups of seals regularly swim near the shores of the island. Visitors interested in observing these large sea mammals can take part in an excursion organized for that express purpose.

Cruise Manada (adults $13.50, children under 12 $7): ☎838-3444,
Departures: From the Montague Marina, everyday 2pm. (mid-May to Jun), everyday 1pm, 3:30pm and 7pm, (early Jul to Aug).
From the Brudenell Marina, everyday 2:30pm (Jul and Aug).

Garry's Seal Cruises: ☎962-2494 or 1-800-561-2494,
Departures: Murray River pier, everyday 1pm, 3:30pm and 6:30pm (Jun), everyday 8:30am, 10:30am, 1pm, 3:30pm and 6:30pm (Jul to mid-Sep).

Deep-Sea Fishing

Several companies offer deep-sea fishing excursions, giving visitors a chance to test their fishing skills while enjoying an exciting outing on the water. Excursions of this type set out from **Covehead Harbour:**

Richard's Deep-Sea Fishing ($15): ☎672-2376
Salty Seas Deep-Sea Fishing ($15): ☎672-3246

A company in Alberton arranges similar outings:

Andrew's Mist ($25): Alberton, ☎853-2307

Seals

 ACCOMMODATIONS

Charlottetown

The **Youth Hostel** *($12.50 members $15 non-members; 153 Mount Edward Road, ☎894-9696)* provides the least expensive lodging in the provincial capital region. It's a friendly spot set up in a barn-like building about 3 km west of downtown, near the university. During summer, rooms are also available at the **University of Prince Edward Island** *($29.50; ☎566-0442)*.

The **Heritage Harbour House Inn** *($65; early Jun to late Sep; 5 rooms; 9 Grafton Street, C1A 1K3, ☎892-6633 or 1-800-405-0066)* is an excellent bed and breakfast located on a residential street, just a stone's throw from the Arts Centre. The rooms are impeccably clean, as are the shared bathrooms. The house itself is warm and inviting, and guests have use of a day room where they can relax, read or watch television. Each morning, Bonnie, the owner and a charming hostess, serves a continental breakfast.

The **Charlottetown Rodd Classic** *($85; 109 rooms, tv, ℜ, ≈; corner of Kent and Pownal Streets, C1A 1L5, ☎894-7371 or 1-800-565-7633)* is an excellent downtown hotel with a rather stately appearance, built to meet the needs of both businesspeople and vacationers. The inviting rooms are modern and

tastefully furnished. The hotel also houses a good restaurant.

The **Dundee Arms** *($95; 18 rooms, tv, ℜ; 200 Pownal Street, ☎892-2496)* is an elegant inn set up inside a large Queen-Anne style residence built at the beginning of the century. The beautifully-decorated bedrooms and common rooms will take you back in time. The inn also features a highly-reputed dining room. Finally, there are comfortable, slightly less expensive motel rooms available in an adjoining building.

Part of the Canadian Pacific hotel chain, The **Prince Edward Hotel** *($135; 211 rooms, ℜ, ≈; 18 Queen Street, C1A 8B9, ☎566-2222 or 1-800-441-1414, ≈566-2282)* is without a doubt the ritziest and most comfortable hotel on the island. It is also perfectly situated, looking out over the port of Charlottetown. The interior is modern and well designed, with four restaurants and all the facilities one would expect to find in a hotel of this calibre. Business meetings and conferences are often held at the Prince Edward. Its conference rooms can accommodate up to 650 people.

Victoria

The **Orient Hotel** *($75 bkfst incl.; mid-May to mid-Oct; 6 rooms; ℜ, tv; Main Street, C0A 2G0, ☎658-2503)* fits in perfectly with Victoria's old-fashioned atmosphere. Built at the beginning of the century, it is a delightful place with decorations and furniture from days gone by. It is comfortable without being overly luxurious, and guests receive a warm welcome. The Orient also has a dining room and a pretty tea room, which looks out onto the street. Breakfast is included in the price of the room.

Cavendish

In the heart of Cavendish, the **Shining Water Country Inn** (*$75; may to mid-Oct; 10 rooms, Route 13, C0A 1N0, ☎963-2251*) combines comfort with charm. A lovely old house with spacious porches all around, this inn features comfortable rooms and friendly service. Guests can relax in a pleasant, airy living room. There are cottages behind the house, which are available for about $15 extra.

In the heart of what could be considered the village of Cavendish, the **Cavendish Motel** (*$72; early Jun to mid-Sep; 35 rooms, tv, ℜ; at the intersection of Routes 6 and 13, C0A 1M0, ☎963-2244 or 1-800-565-2243*) offers clean, pleasant, modern rooms.

Furnished with antiques and exquisitely decorated, the **Kindred Spirits Country Inn** (*$65; mid-May to mid-Oct; 14 rooms, tv, Route 6, C0A 1N0, ☎963-2434*) offers quality accommodation less than a kilometre from the Cavendish beach. Guests can relax in one of several common rooms, including a superb living room.

South Rustico

The **Barachois Inn** (*$95; May to late Oct; 7 rooms, Church Road, C1A 7M4, ☎963-2194*), a magnificent house built in the 1870s, has superb rooms furnished with antiques and adorned with works of art. It offers guests an excellent opportunity to savour the atmosphere of a sumptuous 19th century home.

Little Rock

Dalvay-by-the-Sea (*$135; early Jun to late Sep; including breakfast and dinner; 27 rooms, tv, ℜ; Route 2, C0A 1P0, ☎672-2048*) is probably the most highly renowned establishment in northern Prince Edward Island. A big, beautiful Victorian house built around 1885, it lies less than 200 m from a magnificent beach. The

interior is exquisite, the decor, tasteful and the food, excellent.

Little Pond

A haven of peace, the **Ark Inn** (*$70; mid-Jun to Sep; 8 rooms, ℜ, tv; R.R.4, C0A 2B0, ☎583-2400, ≈583-2176 or 1-800-665-2400*) stands on a large property with access to a private beach. The comfortable rooms feature futons, modern furniture and large windows. One thing that sets the Ark Inn apart is that most of its rooms are split-level, with the upper portion affording a lovely view. Some rooms are also equipped with a whirlpool. There is a pleasant restaurant on the ground floor.

Bay Fortune

One of the most sumptuous and charming inns on the island, the **Inn at Bay Fortune** (*$120; late May to mid-Oct; 11 rooms, ℜ, tv; Route 310, C0A 2B0, ☎687-3745, ≈687-3540*) offers high-quality food and accommodation. The building has a unique architectural design, it stands on a lovely, verdant site, offering a superb view of the bay after which it is named. The rooms are furnished in an elegant and original, fashion, each one different from the last. Some even have a fireplace. An excellent choice!

Summerside

The beautiful **Silver Fox Inn** (*$69; 6 rooms, ℜ; 61 Granville Street, C1N 2Z3, ☎436-4033*) lies a short distance from the port in an old residential neighbourhood, and is surrounded by a pretty little garden. All of the rooms are well-furnished, inviting and equipped with a private bath. Overall, the inn is elegantly decorated. The atmosphere is reminiscent of turn-of-the-century high-society.

The most comfortable hotel in Summerside, the **Loyalist Country Inn** (*$86; 50 rooms, tv, ℜ; 195 Harbour Drive, C1N 5B2, ☎436-3333, ≈436-4304*) boasts an excellent location in the heart of town, with a view of the nearby port. Although they are modern, the rooms still have character, and are tastefully furnished. This hotel is a real favourite with businesspeople. Its restaurant, furthermore, is highly recommended (see p 123).

West Point

The only inn in Canada set up inside a lighthouse (only one room is actually inside the lighthouse; the others are in the adjoining building), the **West Point Lighthouse** *($70; late may to late Sep; 10 rooms, tv, ℜ; O'Leary, R.R.2, COB 1V0,* ☎*859-3605 or 1-800-764-6854)* is a good spot to stop for a day or two, long enough to explore the magnificent dunes and beaches along the nearby shore. This is a friendly place, and the rooms are decent.

Woodstock

The **Rodd Mill River Resort** *($67; May to Oct; 90 rooms, tv, ℜ, O'Leary, R.R.2, COB 1V0,* ☎*859-3555 or 1-800-565-7663)* is ideal for sports buffs. Not only is there an excellent golf-course nearby, but the resort itself has an indoor pool, tennis courts, a gym and squash courts. The rooms, furthermore, are very comfortable.

Tyne Valley

The **Doctor's Inn Bed & Breakfast** *($55; 2 rooms, ℜ; Route 167, COB 2C0,* ☎*831-3057)* is a country home typical of the 1860s with a pleasant garden. Its two decent, but not very luxurious rooms are available year-round. The place is very calm, and excellent evening meals are available.

 RESTAURANTS

Charlottetown

Just outside the Prince Edward Hotel, on the same side as Peake's Wharf, the **Anchor and Oar House Grub & Grog** *($; mid-May to mid-Oct, behind the Prince Edward Hotel, Water Street,* ☎*566-2222)* has a simple menu ideal for lunch. Most dishes are less than $6. There is a selection of salads and sandwiches, and several fish and seafood dishes round out the offerings.

Centrally located, **Cedar's Eatery** *($; 81 University Street,* ☎*892-7377)* offers an inexpensive, change of pace. *Kebab, falafel, shawarma* and *shish taouk,* Lebanese cuisine's most famous exports, are the headliners. The atmosphere is young, friendly and unpretentious, and the portions are generous.

Peake's Quay *($-$$; May to Sep; 36 Water Street,* ☎*368-1330)* should win the trophy for the best-situated restaurant in Charlottetown. The pleasant terrace looks directly out over the city's marina. An economical menu of simple dishes, including excellent seafood crepes, is offered at breakfast time. In the evening, the menu is more elaborate but still affordable. For less than $20, you can have, among other things, a delicious plate of lobster. Peake's Quay is also a pub where people linger over a drink or two.

Perhaps surprisingly for a city of this size, Charlottetown does hide a few gems in terms of restaurants, namely the **Off Broadway Café** *($$; 125 Sydney Street,* ☎*566-4620).* Its relaxing, romantic and tasteful atmosphere and excellent, deliciously-concocted menu make it the hottest restaurant in town. A variety of dishes, many with a French touch, are served. And seafood connoisseurs will not be disappointed by the main dishes and appetizers featured. Rounding up the menu is a choice selection of desserts including many crepes.

Victoria

In the centre of the charming little village of Victoria, near the two inns and almost directly opposite the chocolate shop, visitors will find the **Landmark Café & Craft** *($; mid-Jul to mid-Sep; Main Street,* ☎*658-2286)* an extremely friendly, warm and simple place whose walls are adorned with pretty handicrafts. The menu consists of light home-made dishes—quiche, *tourtière,* pasta, salads, desserts, etc.

St. Ann

For more than 30 years now, **St. Ann's Church Lobster Supper** *($$; Jun to Oct; Route 224,* ☎*621-0635),* a non-profit organization, has been serving lobster everyday from 4pm to 9pm. The menu, like those of other similar local restaurants, consists of a salad, fish soup, mussels, lobster and dessert— all for about $20. This is the type of tradition that visitors to Prince Edward Island should definitely not miss out on.

New Glasgow

The **Prince Edward Island Preserve Co.** *($; Route 13 at the intersection of Routes 234 and 258, ☎964-2524)* is actually a shop selling delicious natural products. It also has a café, which serves good sandwiches and salads, as well as other dishes, including lobster quiche, a smoked fish platter and mussels *à la provençale*.

Looking out on the Clyde River, the **New Glasgow Lobster Suppers** *($$; Jun to mid-Oct; Route 258, ☎964-2870)* is one of the island's classic eateries. Since opening, it has served over a million customers! During summer, hundreds of people pass through its two dining rooms every evening between 4pm and 8:30pm. The charm of this place lies in its simplicity; in the dining rooms, there are rows of plain tables covered with red and white checked tablecloths. The menu, obviously, revolves around lobster. Each meal includes an all-you-can-eat appetizer, one lobster and a home-made dessert. Prices vary depending on the size of the lobster you choose, but $20 per person is about average.

North Rustico

A well-known local institution, **Fisherman Wharf Lobster Suppers** *($$; mid-May to mid-Oct; Route 6, ☎963-2669)* also serves traditional lobster meals, with unlimited fish and seafood soup, a vast choice of salads, bread, a lobster and a dessert for about $20. The place can seat approximately 500 people, which doesn't exactly make it intimate, but that's part of its charm.

Oyster Bed Bridge

Both elegant and inviting, the **Café St-Jean** *($$; early Jun to late Sep; Route 6, ☎963-3133)* is a small restaurant set up inside a rustic-looking house looking out on the Wheatley River. In the evening, the food is fairly elaborate, with not only seafood on the menu, but also a fair number of other well-prepared, original dishes. The less expensive lunch menu consists of light dishes. The name of the café refers to the time before the British conquest, when the island was known as Île-St-Jean and the Acadian presence was very strong in this region.

Brackley Beach

The **Dunes Café** *($$; Jun to Sep; Route 15, ☎672-2586)* is the only place of its kind on the island. Set up in a complex with original modern architecture, which also houses a remarkable art gallery, it serves local and international cuisine in an airy decor. The lunch menu is less elaborate and easier on the pocketbook. Live music is often featured in the evening.

Orwell Corner

Located on the historic site of the Sir Andrew Macphail Homestead, the **Tea Room Restaurant** *($; Route 1, ☎651-2789)* is a pleasant place to enjoy a good, light meal at lunchtime or take a break in the afternoon. Though the menu is simple, the food is tasty. Reservations are required for dinner. The elegance and atmosphere of the Macphail Homestead make this a very appealing little restaurant.

Summerside

The **Prince William Dining Room** *($$; 195 Harbour Drive, ☎436-3333)* offers well-prepared food and a fairly elaborate menu, including a wide choice of appetizers and main dishes. Seafood and fish make up a good part of the offerings, but various steak and chicken dishes are also available. On some evenings, a specific dish is featured, such as the excellent surf and turf, consisting of a small steak and a lobster tail. The service is courteous, and the atmosphere, elegant but relaxed.

West Point

A good place to stop for a break during a tour of western Prince Edward Island, the **West Point Lighthouse** is an inn whose **restaurant** *($-$$; late May to late Sep; Route 14, ☎859-3605)* is open from daybreak to 9:30pm. The lunch menu consists of a variety of light dishes, including the usual lobster rolls, chowders and other seafood. In the evening, the cuisine is a bit more sophisticated, with more elaborate appetizers and main courses, such as a fisherman's platter, made up of five different kinds of seafood or fish for less than $20. The menu also lists steak, chicken Kiev and pasta. The restaurant is laid out in a simple fashion in the building adjoining the lighthouse. Guests can also eat on the terrace outside.

ENTERTAINMENT

Charlottetown

Each summer, for more than three decades now, the Confederation Arts Centre has presented the musical *Anne of Green Gables* *(Confederation Arts Centre, ☎566-1267 or 1-800-566-1207)*, inspired by the work of Prince Edward Island's foreign ambassador Lucy Maud Montgomery. Both funny and touching, the story of little "Anne with an e" is now a classic of children's literature all over the world. It is amazing to see to what point Anne has affected young Japanese, who now make up an important percentage of tourists to the island. The musical is well done and makes for a fun night out.

Victoria

Almost every night in July and August, the **Victoria Playhouse** *(about $12; ☎658-2025 or 1-800-925-2025)* presents enjoyable plays and concerts in its little theatre. With its quality performances, the Victoria Playhouse is as charming as the city itself.

 ## SHOPPING

Charlottetown

In Charlottetown, visitors can go to **Peake's Wharf** to stroll along the pier and enjoy the seashore while getting in some shopping in one of the pretty boutiques. There is something for everyone here—crafts, souvenirs, t-shirts, etc.

Clothing

Both children and their parents will enjoy picking out one of the funny t-shirts and sweatshirts available at **Cow's** *(opposite the Confederation Arts Centre)*. Make sure to sample the store's excellent ice cream at the same time.

La Cache *(119 Kent Street, ☎368-3072)* sells comfortable cotton clothing, as well as kitchen goods and tablecloths.

Anyone who likes Liz Claiborne clothing won't want to miss the low prices at the **Liz Claiborne Factory Outlet** *(on the TransCanada, opposite the Rodd hotel)*.

Visitors looking for warm woolens should head over to the **Wool Sweater Factory Outlet** *(Prince Edward Hotel, ☎566-5850)*, which offers a lovely selection of high-quality, casual sweaters.

Crafts

All sorts of beautiful crafts, books and souvenirs are available at **The Two Sisters** *(150 Richmond Street, ☎894-3407)*.

Anne fans can poke around in one of the two **Anne of Green Gables Souvenirs** shops *(Confederation Court Mall and Peake's Wharf)*.

Victoria

The melt-in-your-mouth home-made chocolates at **Island Chocolate** *(Main Street)* are an absolute delight.

Cavendish

The **Cavendish Boardwalk** *(Route 6)* has all kinds of adorable little shops, some, like **Two Sisters**, specializing in t-shirts and souvenirs. Visitors will also find a branch of **Roots** (sportswear) and **Cow's**, with its cute clothing and terrific ice cream. At the front of the store, there is a selection of slightly flawed Cow's clothing at reduced prices.

NEW BRUNSWICK

New Brunswick, gateway to the Maritimes, is enchanting in its diversity. Geographically, it is remarkably varied, combining more than a thousand kilometres of shoreline and seascapes with picturesque farmlands and endless stretches of often mountainous wilderness. Forests cover a full 85% of the territory, which is traversed from north to south by the majestic St. John River, whose source lies in the Appalachian foothills. This river has always been essential to the province's development, and charming town and villages have sprung up along its richly fertile banks. Among these are Fredericton, New Brunswick's pretty capital, with its aura of a bygone era, and Saint John, the province's chief port city and industrial centre. After winding its way through a pastoral landscape, the St. John River empties into the Bay of Fundy, whose often spectacularly steep shores mark the southern border of New Brunswick. An amazing natural phenomenon occurs in this bay twice a day when the highest, most powerful tides in the world surge up onto the shores, reshaping the landscape in sometimes unusual ways, and actually reversing the current of the rivers! Without question, the Bay of Fundy's giant tides constitute one of the greatest natural attractions in the eastern part of the continent. The bay's shoreline, furthermore, is of incomparable beauty. Be that as it may, New Brunswick's other coast, on the Atlantic Ocean, has charms of its own. It is here, from the border of Nova Scotia to that of

Québec, that visitors will find the province's most beautiful sandy beaches, washed by uncommonly warm waters that are perfect for swimming. Most importantly, however, this is the Acadian coast. It is here, in towns and villages like Caraquet, Shippagan and Shediac, that visitors can learn about Acadia and its warm, hospitable inhabitants.

 FINDING YOUR WAY AROUND

By Car

The city of Fredericton grew up on either side of the St. John River, but the downtown area and most tourist attractions lie on the west bank. Visitors will have no difficulty finding their way around the small city centre, which may be explored on foot. The two main downtown arteries are Queen and King Streets, both of which run parallel to the river. Most attractions, as well as many restaurants and businesses, lie on one or the other of these streets.

To reach the Bay of Fundy, from St. Stephen to Saint John, and then on to Sussex, the major road is Highway 1. In Sussex, Highway 1 connects with Highway 2, which leads to Moncton and Aulac, at the border of Nova Scotia, where the tour ends. To reach Deer

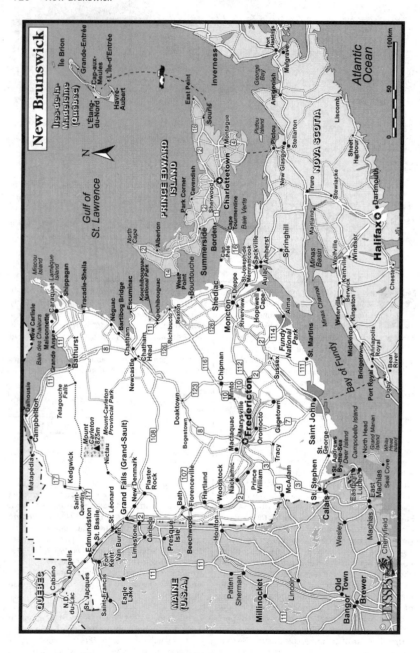

Island, take the exit for St. George from Highway 2, then follow the signs to the tiny village of Letete. A ferry crosses from there to Deer Island. It is possible to reach Campobello Island from the state of Maine by taking the road from Calais to Lubec. To go to Grand Manan Island, visitors must take the ferry from Blacks Harbour.

Prince Edward Island is accessible from Cape Tormentine, New Brunswick, via the 13-kilometre-long **Confederation Bridge** *($35 per car, round-trip)*, inaugurated in the summer of 1997, which spans Northumberland Strait. The crossing takes under 10 minutes by car.

By Plane

Fredericton: Located about 16 kilometres southeast of the city, on Lincoln Road *(☎444-6100)*, Fredericton's airport is served mainly by Air Canada *(☎458-8461 or 452-0166)* and its partner, Air Nova, and Canadian Airlines *(☎446-6034)* and its partner, Air Atlantic. Visitors can take a taxi to the downtown area.

Saint John: About ten kilometres east of the city. A shuttle carries passengers from the large downtown hotels to the airport several times a day. The airport is served mainly by Air Canada *(☎652-1517)* and its partner, Air Nova, and Canadian Airlines *(☎698-2630)* and its partner, Air Atlantic.

Moncton: Located on Champlain Street, in Dieppe. The downtown area may be reached by taxi. The airport is served mainly by Air Canada *(☎857-1044)* and its partner Air Nova, and Canadian Airlines *(☎857-0620)* and its partner, Air Atlantic.

Bus Stations

Fredericton: At the corner of Brunswick and Regent Streets, ☎458-6000.
Saint John: 300 Union Street, at the corner of Carmarthen Street, ☎648-3555.
Moncton: Well-located downtown, at 961 Main Street, ☎859-5060.

Train Stations

Saint John: Station Street, ☎(800) 561-3952.

Moncton: Downtown, on the west side, near Main Street, ☎382-7892.

By Ferry

A ferry makes the crossing from Saint John to Digby, Nova Scotia three times a day except for Sunday, setting out from a dock on the west bank of the St. John River; ☎636-4048.

 PRACTICAL INFORMATION

Area Code: 506

Tourist Information Offices

Regional Office

Tourist Information Centre: ☎1-800-561-0123.

Fredericton
On the TransCanada Highway, ☎460-2191. City Hall, Queen Street, ☎460-2129 or (888) 888-4768.

St. Stephen
King Street, ☎466-7390.

Saint John
Highway 1, ☎658-2940. Near the Reversing Falls, ☎658-2937. Downtown, in the market, ☎658-2855.

Moncton
Main Street, facing Boreview Park, ☎856-4399. City Hall, 774 Main Street, ☎853-3540.

 EXPLORING

Fredericton ★★

Fredericton is definitely one of the most precious jewels in the province's crown. Capital of New Brunswick, it has managed to preserve the remarkable historical legacy and

NEW BRUNSWICK

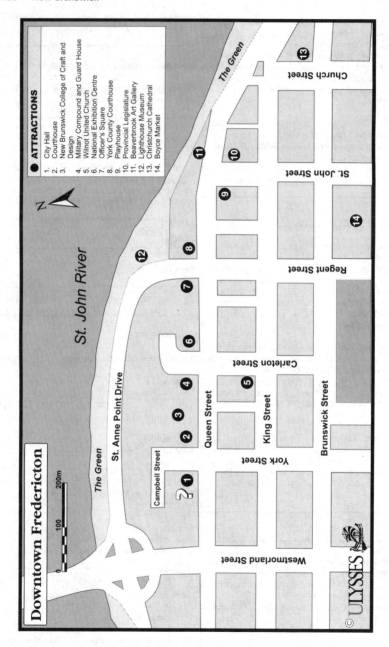

Downtown Fredericton

● **ATTRACTIONS**

1. City Hall
2. Courthouse
3. New Brunswick College of Craft and Design
4. Military Compound and Guard House
5. Wilmot United Church
6. National Exhibition Centre
7. Officer's Square
8. York County Courthouse
9. Playhouse
10. Provincial Legislature
11. Beaverbrook Art Gallery
12. Lighthouse Museum
13. Christchurch Cathedral
14. Boyce Market

St. John River

The Green

St. Anne Point Drive

Campbell Street

Westmorland Street

York Street

Queen Street

King Street

Carleton Street

Regent Street

St. John Street

Church Street

Brunswick Street

© ULYSSES

Cape Spear in Newfoundland, the eastern-most point in continental North America. (Sean O'Neil)

Lunenberg is one of the most picturesque fishing ports of Nova Scotia. (Tibor Bognar)

Old and new in Montréal: St. George's Anglican Church and the Tour I.B.M.
(Roger Michel)

NEW BRUNSWICK

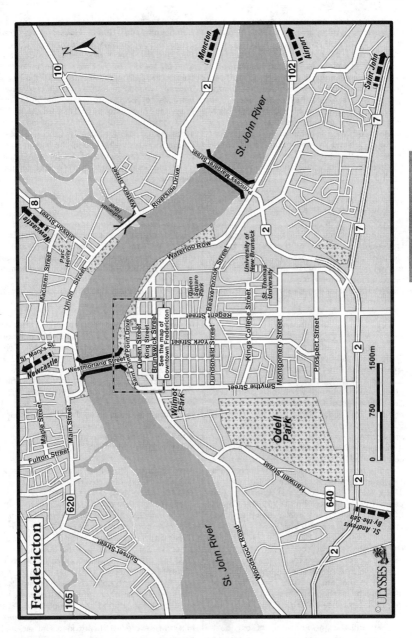

Fredericton

architectural harmony handed down to it from the previous century, giving it a subtle elegance and old-fashioned character. Adorned with magnificent churches and government buildings, as well as large green spaces, some of which lie alongside the St. John River, Fredericton is one of those cities that charms visitors at first sight. Its quiet streets, lined with stately elms, are graced with vast, magnificent Victorian residences. These pretty houses, with their invariably well-tended front gardens, abound in Fredericton, contributing greatly to the city's charm. The site now occupied by the city was originally an Acadian trading post named Sainte-Anne, which was founded in the late 17th century. Acadians lived here until 1783, when they were driven away by the arrival of the Loyalists. The city of Fredericton was founded the following year. It became the provincial capital and was named Fredericton in honour of the second son of George III, Great Britain's king at the time. Over the years, very few industries have set up shop here, opting instead for Saint John. Today, Fredericton's chief employers are the provincial government and the universities.

Downtown

The best place to start off a tour of downtown Fredericton is the excellent tourist office located inside City Hall (at the corner of Queen and York Streets, ☎452-9616), which also offers very good guided bus tours of the city. The oldest part of **City Hall ★** (free admission; mid-May to early Sep, everyday 8am to 7:30pm; early Sep to mid-May, by appointment) was built in 1876, at which time it included not only the municipal offices and council rooms, but also an opera house, a farmer's market and a number of prison cells. The fountain in front of City Hall dates from 1885, while the building's second wing was erected between 1975 to 1977. The Council Chamber, open to the public during summer, makes for an interesting visit.

On the other side of York Street, visitors will see the **Courthouse** (no tours; at the corner of Queen and York Streets), a large stone building erected in the late 1930's. The edifice was used as a high-school before being adopted for its present purpose in 1970. Right next to the Courthouse stands the **New Brunswick College of Craft and Design** (no tours), the only post-secondary school in Canada to offer a program devoted entirely to training artisans.

A little farther, visitors will see the **Military Compound and Guard House ★★** (free admission; Jun to early Sep, everyday 10am to 6pm; at the corner of Queen and Carleton Streets, ☎453-3747). These stone buildings, erected in 1827 as replacements for the city's original, wooden military buildings, served as barracks for British troops until 1869. One room has been restored to illustrate the building's initial use, and a soldier in period dress serves as a guide. A sundial was reconstructed on the barracks wall. Up until the beginning of this century, residents of Fredericton could check the time by referring to devices such as this one.

Head up Carleton Street to the corner of King Street, where **Wilnot United Church ★★** (at the corner of Carleton and King Streets) is located. Its rather austere façade conceals a superb, exceptionally colourful interior abounding in hand-carved woodwork. This church was built in 1852, although the Fredericton Methodist Society, which joined the United Church of Canada in 1925, was founded back in 1791.

A beautiful Second Empire style building erected in 1881 houses the **National Exhibition Centre ★** (free admission; Jun to early Sep, everyday 10am to 6pm; Sep to early Jun, Tue to Sun noon to 5pm; at the corner of Queen and Carleton Streets, ☎453-4737), which presents exhibits on history, crafts, the arts, sciences and technology. The second floor of the building is occupied by the **New Brunswick Sports Hall of Fame** (free admission; ☎453-3747), dedicated to New Brunswick's finest athletes.

Also on Queen Street, **Officer's Square ★★** ($1; May to Jun, Mon to Sat 10am to 6pm; Jul and Aug, Mon, Wed, Fri and Sat 10am to 6pm, Tue and Thu 10am to 9pm, Sun 12pm to 6pm; Sep to mid-Oct, Mon to Fri 9am to 5pm; mid-Oct to Apr, Mon, Wed and Fri 11am to 3pm; Queen St., near Regent St., ☎455-6041) is an attractive park. Facing it is the building once used as officers' quarters, erected in two stages, from 1839 to 1840 and in 1851. Its bow-shaped stone columns, railings and iron stairs are typical of architecture designed by royal engineers during the colonial era. The former quarters now house the **York-Sunbury Museum**, devoted to the province's military and domestic history.

Continue along Queen Street to the pretty **York County Courthouse ★** (no tours; Queen St., *after Regent St.)*, erected in 1855. In those years, there was a market on the ground floor. Today, the building houses the services of the Ministry of Justice, as well as a courtroom.

A little farther along Queen Street, on the opposite side of the street, stands the **Playhouse** *(Queen St., at the corner of St. John St.)*, built in 1964. Since 1969, it has served as home base for the only English-speaking theatre company in the province, The New Brunswick Theatre. Construction of the Playhouse was financed by Lord Beaverbrook, a British newspaper tycoon who lived in New Brunswick as a child.

Not far from the Playhouse, visitors will see the **Provincial Legislature** ★★ *(free admission; Jun to Aug, everyday 9am to 8pm; late Aug to early Jun, Mon to Fri 9am to 4pm; Queen St., at the corner of St. John St., ☎453-2527)*, seat of the provincial government since 1882. Inside, an impressive spiral staircase made of wood leads to the library, which contains over 35,000 volumes, some very rare. Of particular interest are the Assembly Chamber, where the members of Parliament gather, and the portraits of King George III and Queen Charlotte, by British painter Joshua Reynolds.

Across from the Legislative Building stands the **Beaverbrook Art Gallery** ★★★ *($3; Jul and Aug, Sun to Wed 10am to 5pm, Thu to Sat 10am to 7pm; Sep to Jun, Tue to Sat 10am to 5pm, Sun and Mon noon to 5pm; Queen St., ☎458-8545)*, another of Lord Beaverbrook's gifts to the city of Fredericton. The gallery houses, among other things, a superb collection of works by highly renowned British painters, as well as a number of other lovely canvases by Canadian artists such as Cornelius Krieghoff and James Wilson Morrice. Without question, however, the most impressive piece on display is Catalan artist Salvador Dali's *Santiago el Grande*.

After touring the fascinating Beaver-brook Art Gallery, summer visitors can enjoy a delightful stroll on Fredericton's splendid **Green** ★, which stretches 4 kilometres alongside the St. John, enabling both walkers and cyclists to explore the banks of the river. The Green contributes greatly to the quality of life in the city. Visitors can stop at the **Lighthouse Museum** *($2; Oct to May, Mon to Fri 9am to 4pm; Jun to Sep, Mon to Fri 9am to 4pm, Sat and Sun noon to 4pm; Jul and Aug, everyday 10am to 9pm; ☎459-2515)*, which presents a historical exhibit.

Take Queen Street to Church Street in order to visit the Gothic style **Christ Church Cathedral** ★★ *(at the corner of Queen St. and Church St.)*, whose construction, completed in 1853, was largely due to the efforts of Fredericton's first Anglican bishop, John Medley.

From the cathedral, take Brunswick Street to Regent Street. On the left-hand side stands **Boyce Market** *(at the corner of Brunswick and Regent Streets)*, a public market where farmers, artisans and artists sell their products every Saturday morning. Right next door, on the right side of Brunswick Street, lies Fredericton's **Old Loyalist Cemetery**. It was here that the most notable figures in Fredericton's early history were buried from 1787 to 1878.

Outside the Downtown Area

The **University of New Brunswick** *(at the end of University St.)*, founded in 1785 by newly arrived Loyalists, is made up of several different edifices. Its arts building is the oldest university building still in use in Canada.

On the same site, visitors will also find **St. Thomas University**, a Catholic institution originally located in Chatham, on the Miramichi River. The two universities are attended by a total of 8,000 students each year. This is a wonderful spot from which to view the city below.

Odell Park ★ *(Rookwood Ave., northwest of the city)* covers over 175 hectares and includes 16 kilometres of trails. This beautifully preserved, peaceful natural area has been enhanced by the addition of an enclosure for deer, duck ponds, picnic tables and a play area for children.

Saint-Jacques

This is the first village that many travellers (or at least those arriving from Québec) will encounter on their tour of New Brunswick. It is therefore no coincidence that Saint-Jacques is home to one of the province's largest tourist information centres, as well as a provincial park, **Les Jardins de la République**, which includes two interesting attractions.

The République de Madawaska

The origins of the mythical République de Madawaska date back to the region's early coloni-zation, a time when the British and the Americans were continuously redefining the border between Maine and New Brunswick after skirmishes and tortuous political negotiations. Tired of being mere pawns in all of this, the people of Madawaska, scorning the authorities, event-ually decided to "found" their own republic, which had the very vaguest of borders, but more or less encompassed the French-speaking population in this part of the country. Pushing the fantasy even further, they decided that the republic would have its own president, namely, the mayor of Edmundston. Behind this peculiar historical legacy lies a very strong cultural bond bet-ween French-speakers on both sides of the border, which can best be appreciated during Edmundston's Foire Brayonne, a festival held each year at the end of July.

The **New Brunswick Botanical Garden** ★★ *($3; Jun to Sep; Hwy 2, Exit 8,* ☎*735-2699)*, destined to become one of the region's greatest draws, is worth visiting for a number of reasons. Some 75,000 plants have been distributed over a well laid-out area of 7 hectares, which offers a lovely panoramic view of the region's gentle, wooded valleys. The garden's designers had the clever idea of installing an unobtrusive sound system, enabling visitors to explore the garden with the music of Bach, Chopin or Mozart in the background.

The **Antique Automobile Museum** ★ *($2.50; late May to mid-Sep; right beside the Garden,* ☎*735-4871)* grew up around the private collection of Edmundston resident Melvin Louden. It displays a lovely selection of antique cars, some of which are very rare nowadays, including the Bricklin—the only automobile made in New Brunswick—and the 1933 Rolls Royce Phantom.

Grand Falls (Grand-Sault) ★★

A charming little town on the banks of the St. John, at the point where the river plunges 23 metres, Grand Falls is a dynamic, engaging community whose mostly French-speaking population has Québecois and Acadian roots. This pretty spot was frequented by Malecite Indians for many years before becoming a British military post in 1791. The city was final-ly established in 1896. In addition to its attractive location, Grand Falls has a charming town centre. Its wide boulevard, flanked by low houses facing right onto the street, gives it a slightly midwestern character. It is worth noting that Grand Falls is the only town in Canada with an officially bilingual name—Grand Falls-Grand Sault. With its field-covered valleys,

the surrounding region, known for its potatoes, makes for a lovely outing.

The magnificent **waterfall** ★★ that inspired the town's name is the largest and most impressive to be found in the Maritimes. The waters of the St. John plunge 23 metres, then rush for about 2 kilometres through a gorge whose sides reach as high as 70 metres. At the far end of the gorge, the turbulent water has eroded the rock, creating cavities known here as "wells," since water stays in them after the river rises. Visitors can start off their tour by dropping by the **Malobiannah Centre** *(on Chemin Madawaska, alongside the falls)*, which is both an interpretive centre and a regional tourist information centre. From here, there is a splendid **view** ★ of the falls and the hydroelectric dam. A footpath heading out from the centre makes it possible to observe the falls and the gorge from all different angles. At the **Centre La Rochelle** *($1; Centennial Park)*, on the opposite bank, right in the centre of town, there is a staircase that leads down to the river bed, offering a lovely **view** ★★ of the gorge, the wells and the waterfall.

Hartland ★

Home town of Richard Hatfield, the province's eccentric former prime minister, Hartland is an adorable village typical of the St. John River Valley. It is known for its remarkable **covered bridge** ★★, the world's longest. Stretching 390 metres across the river, the structure was built in 1899, at a time when simply covering a bridge made its skeleton last up to seven times longer. Today there are more covered bridges in New Brunswick than anywhere else on Earth. Visitors who would like to stop for a picnic and admire the local scenery will find an attractive park on the west bank of the river.

NEW BRUNSWICK

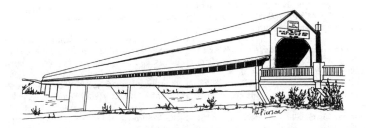

Covered Bridge at Hartland

Prince William

A wonderful open-air museum covering 120 hectares on the banks of the St. John, **Kings Landing** ★★★ *($6; Jun to mid-Oct, everyday 9am to 5pm; along the TransCanada Hwy in Prince-William, ☎363-4999)* is a reproduction of an early 19th century Loyalist village. It includes more than 20 historic buildings and about 30,000 objects that help illuminate the area's past, including furniture, clothing and tools. To enliven the atmosphere, there are people dressed in period clothing, who perform the daily tasks of 19th century villagers, as well as answering visitors' questions. There is no more pleasant, effective means of learning about Loyalist history than a visit to Kings Landing, the best museum devoted to that subject.

Gagetown ★

After winding its way through the fields of a prosperous farming region, the little road heading out from Oromocto leads to Gagetown, a tiny village on the banks of the majestic St. John. Everything here—the church, the general store, the handful of houses, the very location—is so pretty that it appears to have come straight out of a fairy tale. This peaceful spot has retained the old-fashioned character of a Loyalist village, as well as an atmosphere that couldn't possibly be more Anglo-Saxon. With all that charm, it is hardly surprising that each year Gagetown attracts artists seeking inspiration, as well as vacationers looking for a place to relax. Sailors stop here, too, tying their yachts or sailboats to the village wharf. Although Gagetown is a tiny

village, it nevertheless boasts several bed & breakfasts, a very good inn, an art gallery and several craft shops. There is also a free ferry service, enabling visitors to cross over to the other side of the river.

The **Tilley House** ★ *($2, mid-Jun to mid-Sep, everyday 10am to 5pm; Front St., ☎488-2066)* was built in 1786, making it one of the oldest residences in New Brunswick. It now houses the Queens County Museum, which displays all sorts of objects relating to local history and the life of the house's most illustrious owner, Samuel Leonard Tilley, one of the Fathers of Canadian Confederation (1867).

At the **Loomcrofter Studio** ★ *(south of the village, near the school, ☎488-2400)*, visitors will find the studios of various designers and weavers of tartan cloth. The building itself is one of the oldest in the St. John River Valley.

St. Stephen

The most important border town in the Maritimes, St. Stephen is a small, lively community, which was founded in 1784 by American colonists wishing to remain loyal to the British crown after the Revolutionary War. Today, ironically, St. Stephen and Calais, its twin town in the state of Maine, could easily be mistaken for a single town if it weren't for the St. Croix River, which forms a natural border. This lively community is celebrated on both sides of the border each year during the **International Festival**, which takes place at the end of August. In early August, another festival, this time dedicated to **chocolate**, is held only in St. Stephen, which has the distinction of being the birthplace of the chocolate bar, invented here in 1910 by the Ganong company. The ever successful **Ganong Chocolatier** *(73 Milltown Blvd., ☎465-5611)* shop is a must for anyone with a sweet tooth.

The **Charlotte County Museum** *(free admission; Jun to Aug, Mon to Sat 9:30am to 4:30pm; 443 Milltown Blvd., ☎466-3295)* is set up inside a Second Empire style residence built in 1864 by a prosperous local businessman. It now houses a collection of objects related to local history, especially the period when St. Stephen and the small neighbouring villages were known for shipbuilding.

The **Crocker Hill Garden & Studio** *(2.4 km east of St. Stephen, on Ledge Rd., ☎466-4251)* is a magnificent garden looking out on the St. Croix River.

St. Andrews By-the-Sea ★★

The most famous vacation spot in Southern New Brunswick, St. Andrews is a lovely village facing the bay. It has managed to benefit from its popularity by highlighting its astonishingly rich architectural heritage. Like many other communities in the area, St. Andrews was founded by Loyalists in 1783, and then enjoyed a period of great prosperity during the 19th century as a centre for shipbuilding and the exportation of billets. A number of the opulent houses flanking its streets, particularly **Water Street ★**, date back to that golden era. At the end of the century, St. Andrews began welcoming affluent visitors, who came here to drink in the invigorating sea air. St. Andrews' new vocation was clearly established in 1889 with the construction of a magnificent hotel, the **Algonquin ★★** on a hill overlooking the village. In addition to the picturesque charm of its many historic buildings and its location alongside the bay, with its giant tides, St. Andrews now boasts a wide selection of accommodations and fine restaurants, numerous shops and a famous golf-course. All of this makes St. Andrews By-the-Sea a perfect place to stay during a tour of the region and its islands.

Erected in 1820, **Sheriff Andrews' House ★** *(free admission; late Jun to early Sep 9:30am to 4:30pm; 63 King St., ☎453-2324)* is one of the town's best-preserved homes from that era. It was built by Elusha Shelton Andrews, sheriff of Charlotte County and son of a distinguished Loyalist, Reverend Samuel

Andrews. Since 1986, it has belonged to the provincial government, which has turned it into a museum. Guides in period costume explain the sheriff's life and times.

A sumptuous 19th century neoclassical residence, the **Ross Memorial Museum ★** *(free admission, late May to early Oct, Tue to Sat 10am to 4:30pm, Sun 1:30pm to 4:30pm; 188 Montague St., ☎529-1824)* contains an antique collection, which Henry Phipps Ross and Sarah Juliette Ross, an American couple who lived in St. Andrews from 1902 until they died, assembled over their lifetime. The Rosses had a passion for travelling and antiques, and acquired some magnificent pieces of Chinese porcelain and other now priceless imported objects, as well as some lovely furniture made in New Brunswick.

There are several remarkable churches in St. Andrews. The most flamboyant is **Greenock Church ★★** *(at the corner of Montague and Edward Streets)*, a Presbyterian church completed in 1824. Its most interesting feature is its pulpit, a good part of which is made of Honduran mahogany.

Until very recently, the **St. Andrews Blockhouse** *(on the west end of Water St.)*, a national historic site, was the last surviving blockhouse from the War of 1812. It was unfortunately damaged by fire, but necessary repairs have been completed. Pretty **Centennial Park** lies opposite.

The **Sunbury Shores Arts & Nature Centre** *(139 Water St., ☎529-3386)* houses a small art gallery, where visitors can admire the work of New Brunswick artists. The centre is better known, however, for its summer courses on art, crafts and nature, which are open to groups of children and adults.

At the **Huntsman Marine Science Centre and Aquarium ★★** *($4; May to Oct 10am to 4:30pm; Brandy Cove Rd.; ☎529-1202)*, visitors can learn about the bay's natural treasures. Several animal species may be observed here, including seals, who are fed every day at 11 AM and 4 PM There is also a touch-tank, where visitors can touch various live species of shellfish. This is an important research centre.

The **Ministers Island Historic Site ★** *($5 per car includes tour of house; Jun to mid-Oct; Mowat Drive Rd., take Bar Rd. only at low tide until the end)* was originally, back at the very beginning of the 19th century, the property of Reverend Samuel. It was purchased in 1890 by Sir WIlliam Van Horne, a Montréal resident famous for building the first railroad linking Montréal to Vancouver. On this large estate, Van Horne erected an immense summer home with about 50 rooms. Minister's Island is only accessible at low tide. To arrange a visit, contact the tourist information office *(☎529-3000 or 529-5081)*.

At the **Atlantic Salmon Centre** *($1; Chamcook, 8 km from St. Andrews on Route 127, ☎529-4581)*, visitors can learn about the life cycle of the Atlantic salmon, most importantly by viewing the fish in its natural environment through a window.

Deer Island

After cruising through a scattering of little islands covered with birds, the free ferry from Letete lands at Deer Island, with its wooded landscape, untouched beaches and tiny fishing villages. Three hours before high tide each day, visitors can view an interesting natural phenomenon from the southern point of the island—one of the largest whirlpools in the world, known locally as the **Old Sow ★**. In summertime, a private ferry makes the crossing between Deer Island and Campobello island about once an hour.

Campobello Island ★★

Campobello, the beloved island of former American president Franklin D. Roosevelt (1882-1945), is a good place for fans of history and the great outdoors to unwind. People come here to enjoy the lovely untouched beaches, go cycling on the quiet roads or walk along the well-maintained trails that follow the shoreline. On the eastern tip, the picturesque lighthouse at **East Quoddy Head ★** occupies a magnificent site on the bay, from which it is sometimes possible to spot whales and other sea mammals. In the early 19th century, Campobello's beauty began to attract the attention of wealthy families living in the northeastern cities of the United States, who built lovely summer homes here. The most famous of these families was that of Franklin D. Roosevelt, whose father, James, purchased 1.6 hectares on the island in 1883. Franklin himself, and then his own family, spent most of his summers here from 1883 to 1921, the year he contracted polio. He

returned on several occasions later to visit his friends on the island while serving as President of the United States. Although Campobello lies within Canadian lines, it is most easily accessible from the border town of Lubec, Maine. During the summer months, a private ferry also shuttles back and forth from Deer Island to Campobello about once an hour.

Roosevelt-Campobello International Park ★★ *(free admission; late May to early Oct, 10am to 6pm; Route 774, ☎752-2922)* is a joint project of the Canadian and American governments, launched in 1964 with the aim of increasing public awareness of Roosevelt's special attachment to Campobello Island and his magnificent property there. The visitors' centre shows a short film on Roosevelt's sojourns on the island. Afterward, visitors can tour the extraordinary **Roosevelt House**, most of whose furnishings belonged to the former American president, then stop at the **Prince House**, the site of the **James Roosevelt House** and the **Hubbard House**. The park also includes a beautiful natural area, south of the visitors' centre, where lovely hiking trails have been cleared along the shore.

Grand Manan Island ★

For many years, Grand Manan attracted mainly scientists, including the famous James Audubon in the early 19th century, due to the 275 or so species of birds that land here each year and the island's unique rock formations. More recently, however, Grand Manan has begun to benefit from the current craze for ecotourism, since the island obviously has a lot to offer nature lovers. It is a pleasant place to explore by bicycle, and even better on foot, thanks to the excellent network of trails running alongside the jagged shoreline with its often spectacular scenery. Without question, one of the most picturesque places on the island is the lighthouse known as **Swallowtail Light ★**, which stands at the tip of a peninsula at North Head. From here, whales can be seen regularly swimming off the shores of the island. Grand Manan also features a **museum** *(Grand Harbour, ☎662-3524)* and serves as the point of departure for numerous whale watching excursions and expeditions to **Machias Seal Island ★**, a remarkable bird sanctuary. To reach Grand Manan Island, visitors must take the ferry from Blacks Harbour *(☎662-3724)*, which makes five or six trips a day.

NEW BRUNSWICK

Saint John ★★

New Brunswick's largest city, Saint John occupies a hilly area on either side of the St. John River, at the point where it flows into the Bay of Fundy. A perfect example of the old, industrial port cities in the eastern part of North America, it has a unique, slightly mysterious charm. Lofty cranes and warehouses line the docks, which look strangely like wooden fences rising high out of the river at low tide. To add to its mysterious character, Saint John is often blanketed with a thick fog that can envelop the city at any moment, and then disappear just as quickly. The growth of the city's industries is due largely to its port, which is ice-free all year long. The site itself was scouted out for the first time on June 24, 1604 by explorer Samuel de Champlain, who christened the river St. John (Saint-Jean) in honour of the patron saint of that day. Later, in 1631, Charles de La Tour established a trading post here. The city's history didn't really start, however, until 1783, under the English regime. That year, from May 10 to May 18, about 2,000 Loyalists landed in Saint John, seeking a fresh start in life after the defeat of British forces by American revolutionaries. More arrived before winter, doubling the population of Saint John. The city then absorbed a large number of immigrants, most from the British Isles. In those years, Partridge Island, in the port, was Canada's chief point of entry and quarantine station for immigrants. Today, Saint John has a higher concentration of Irish-Canadians than any other city in the country. It is a pleasant place to visit, particularly in mid-July during **Loyalist Days**, which commemorate the arrival of the Loyalists in 1783. The excellent **By-the-Sea Festival**, in August, celebrates the performing arts, while the **Franco-Frolic**, held in June, honours Acadian culture and traditions.

Downtown Saint John ★★, with its narrow streets lined with historic buildings and houses, lies on a hill on the east side of the river. A tour of the area usually starts at **Market Square**, laid out a little more than a decade ago as part of an effort to revitalize the city centre. The square includes a shopping mall, a convention centre, several restaurants and a hotel, which combines modern construction with 19th century buildings. An excellent **tourist information office** is located at the entrance to Market Square. The **New Brunswick Museum ★** *($4; every day 10am to 5pm; Market Square, ☎643-2300)* recently moved and is now also located in Market Square. The oldest museum in Canada, it is devoted not only to the work of New Brunswick artists, but also to the history of the province's inhabitants—Amerindians, Acadians, Loyalists, and others. The permanent collection features certain imported objects as well, including pieces of Chinese porcelain.

On the south side of Market Square stands **Barbour's General Store** *(free admission; mid May to mid Oct; ☎658-2939)*, a small brick building displaying consumer goods typically available in this type of shop during the 19th century. Guided tours of the city are offered from here. Visitors can head up Union Street to the **Loyalist House National Historic Site ★** *($2; open all year; 120 Union St., ☎652-3590)*, a very simple house built in the first decade of the 19th century, which is decorated with elegant period furniture.

Union Street later intersects with Charlotte Street, where visitors can turn right to reach **King's Square ★**, a pretty urban park marking the centre of Saint John. The paths in the park are laid out in the pattern of the Union Jack; what better way for the inhabitants of Saint John to express their attachment to their mother country? Standing opposite the park on Charlotte Street is the **Old City Market ★** *(free admission; open all year, Mon to Thu 7:30am to 6pm, Fri 7:30am to 7pm, Sat 7:30am to 5pm; 47 Charlotte St., ☎658-2820)*, dating back to 1876, where shoppers can still purchase fresh produce from local farms. Some merchants sell dulse, a type of seaweed that people in Saint John make generous use of as an accompaniment to various dishes. On another side of the park, visitors will find the sumptuous **Imperial Theatre ★** *(24 King St., ☎634-8355)*, built in 1913 and restored in 1994, which is dedicated to the performing arts.

The **Aitken Bicentennial Exhibition Centre** *(free admission; Jun to Sep, everyday 10am to 5pm; Sep to Jun, Tue to Sun 11:30am to 4:30pm; 20 Hazen Ave., ☎633-4870)* presents exhibits specifically designed to teach children about various facets of science in a dynamic fashion.

The **Reversing Falls ★★** *(on Route 100, at the river)* is a unique natural phenomenon that occurs twice a day at high tide. The current of the river, which, at this point drops 4 metres at low tide, is reversed at high tide when the water level of the bay is several metres higher than that of the river. This counter-current is felt as far up-river as Fredericton.

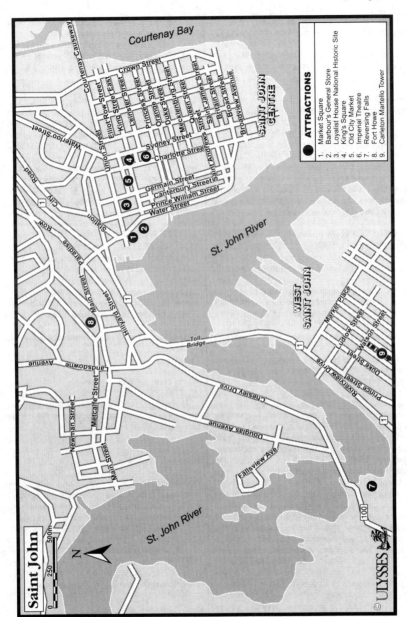

Saint John

N

0   250   500m

Courtenay Bay

SAINT JOHN
CENTRE

WEST
SAINT JOHN

St. John River

St. John River

Crown Street
Courtenay Causeway
Elliot Row Street
King Street East
Lanster Street
Princess Street
Orange Street
Duke Street
Mecklenburg Street
Queen Street
Saint James Street
Britain Street
Broad Street
Broadview Avenue
Sydney Street
Charlotte Street
Germain Street
Canterbury Street
Prince William Street
Water Street
Saint Andrews Street
Union Street
Waterloo Street
City Road
Station
Paradise Row
Hillyard Street
Main Street
Lansdowne Avenue
Metcalfe Street
Newman Street
Main Street
Chesley Drive
Douglas Avenue
Fallsview Ave.
Market Place
Ludlow Street
Watson Street
Duke Street
Prince Street
Riverview Drive
Toll
Bridge

⓵ ⓶ ⓷ ⓸ ⓹ ⓺ ⓻ ⓼ ⓽

● ATTRACTIONS

1. Market Square
2. Barbour's General Store
3. Loyalist House National Historic Site
4. King's Square
5. Old City Market
6. Imperial Theatre
7. Reversing Falls
8. Fort Howe
9. Carleton Martello Tower

NEW BRUNSWICK

© ULYSSES

100

For an excellent **view ★** of the city, head to the site of **Fort Howe** *(Main St., ☎658-2090)*. At the same location, there is a wooden blockhouse, which was built in Halifax and moved here in 1777 to protect the port of Saint John in the event of an American attack.

The **Carleton Martello Tower ★★** *(free admission; Jun to Oct 9am to 5pm; on the west bank, Charlotte St., ☎636-4011)* is a circular tower built during the War of 1812 to protect the port from American attacks. It was also used as a command post for the Canadian army during the Second World War. Guides in 19th century dress explain the history of both the tower and the city of Saint John. From the top, visitors can enjoy a magnificent panoramic view of the city, the port and the bay.

If Saint John were a person, **Rockwood Park** *(main entry on Mt. Pleasant Ave.)* would be its lungs. Covering 890 hectares, it is Canada's largest city park. All sorts of outdoor activities may be enjoyed here, including hiking, swimming, fishing, canoeing and pedal-boating. A number of other activities are organized just for children. In the north section of the park, is the **Cherry Brook Zoo** *($3.25; open all year 10am to nightfall; Sandy Point Rd., in the north part of Rockwood Park, ☎634-1440)*, the only zoo in the Maritimes featuring exotic animals. Some one hundred or so different species may be found here.

For many years, **Partridge Island ★** *($10; May to Nov; from the port of St. John, for information ☎635-0782)* was the main point of entry for immigrants coming to Canada from the British Isles and the European continent. Between 1785 and 1942, it was the transition point and quarantine station for some three million immigrants who then settled in Saint John or, more commonly, elsewhere in Canada or the United States. About 2,000 of these individuals, having survived the often difficult journey across the Atlantic, never had the chance to see anything beyond Partridge Island. They died and were then buried in one of the six cemeteries located here. The island is also the site of New Brunswick's oldest lighthouse, as well as a historical museum.

The perfectly marvellous **Irving Nature Park ★★** *(free admission; at the end of Sand Cove Rd., ☎632-7777)* has a great deal to offer nature lovers. Located just a few kilometres west of the industrial city of Saint John, this magnificent park covers a 225-hectare peninsula trimmed with untouched beaches. The

city seems a million miles away from here. Visitors can also enjoy a pleasant stroll along one of the park's trails, communing with nature and observing the plant and animal life in Southern New Brunswick. See also p 144.

St. Martins ★

St. Martins is one of New Brunswick's best kept treasures. An idyllic fishing village looking out on the Bay of Fundy, St. Martins is adorned with numerous houses built in the last century, when it was known as a major producer of large wooden ships. Today, the village is very picturesque, with the boats of local fishermen moored in its little port. It also has two covered bridges, one of which leads to the famous **echo caves ★**, cavities created in local cliffs by the action of the tides in the Bay of Fundy. Nature lovers will find long, untouched beaches in St. Martins, as well as the attractive **Lions Park**, which is a good place to take a walk or go swimming. As home to one of the province's best inns (see p 147), the village also has something to offer connoisseurs of fine cuisine. Finally, to enjoy a **spectacular view ★** of the local red cliffs, head to the **Quaco Head lighthouse**, located several kilometres west of St. Martins.

Fundy National Park ★★★

This national park covers a densely-wooded, mountainous area of 206 square kilometres along the Bay of Fundy (see p 144).

Hopewell Cape ★★

Hopewell Cape's rock formations, nicknamed the **flower pots ★★**, are one of the province's most famous attractions. All by themselves, they symbolize the massive force of the tides in the bay. At high tide, they look like small wooded islands right off the coast. As the waters recede at low tide, they expose lofty rock formations sculpted by the endless coming and going of the tides. When the tide is at its lowest, visitors can explore the sea bed.

Moncton ★

Due to its location in the heart of the Maritimes, as well as its qualified, bilingual workforce, Moncton is now New Brunswick's rising star. Up until the Acadians were expelled

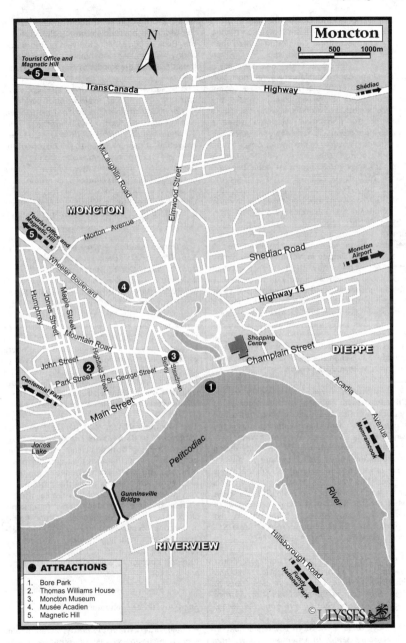

Moncton

NEW BRUNSWICK

● ATTRACTIONS

1. Bore Park
2. Thomas Williams House
3. Moncton Museum
4. Musée Acadien
5. Magnetic Hill

from the region, this site on the banks of the Petitcodiac River was a small Acadian trading post. Colonists from the United States then settled here and founded the city, which thrived in the mid-19th century as a shipbuilding centre and later as a transportation hub for the Intercolonial Railway. The economy is now based chiefly on commerce and the service sector. For Acadians, who constitute 35% of the population, Moncton offers a unique opportunity to face the challenges and savour the pleasures of city living. Despite their minority status, they have made Moncton a base for their most important economic and social institutions and the home of the province's only French-speaking university, the Université de Moncton. Ironically, the city and by extension the university were named after officer Robert Monkton, commander of the British forces during the capture of Fort Beauséjour in 1755, an event that heralded the fall of the French Empire in North America. In any case, Moncton is now the centre of Acadian rebirth and the vibrant energy in the air here is due in good part to the entrepreneurial spirit that characterizes today's Acadians. Moncton's immediate surroundings include such varied communities as **Dieppe**, most of whose inhabitants are Acadian, and the very anglophone **Riverview**. An excellent time to visit the city is in early July, when the atmosphere is enlivened by the **Moncton Jazz Festival**.

The Petitcodiac River, known locally as the Chocolate River because of the colour of its waters, empties and then fills back up again twice a day, in accordance with the tides in the Bay of Fundy. The rise in the river's water level is always preceded by an interesting phenomenon known as a **tidal bore ★**, a wave up to several dozen centimetres high that flows upriver. The best spot to watch this wave is **Bore Park** *(downtown on Main St.)*. To know what time of the day the tidal bore will occur during your stay, contact Moncton's tourist information office *(at the corner of Main St., facing Bore Park, ☎856-4399)*.

The Second Empire style **Thomas Williams House ★** *(free admission; May, Mon, Wed and Fri 10am to 5pm; Jun, Tue to Sat 10am to 5pm, Sun 1pm to 5pm; Jul and Aug, Mon to Sat 9am to 5pm, Sun 1pm to 5pm; Sep, Mon, Wed and Fri 10am to 5pm; 103 Park St., ☎857-0590)* is a 12-room residence built in 1883 for the family of Thomas Williams, who was an accountant for the Intercolonial Railway at the time. His heirs then lived here for nearly a century. Today, the house is a museum

where visitors can learn about the lifestyle of the Moncton bourgeoisie during the Victorian era. Back in 1883, Moncton was no more than a tiny village, and the house lay outside its boundaries, in the middle of the countryside.

The **Moncton Museum ★** *(free admission; Jul and Aug, Mon to Sat 10am to 5pm, Sun 1pm to 5pm; Sep to Jun, Tue to Fri 1pm to 5pm, Sat 10am to 5pm, Sun 1pm to 5pm; 20 Mountain Rd., ☎856-4383)* houses a lovely collection of objects linked to the history of the city and its surrounding area. During summertime, the museum often presents large-scale temporary exhibits. The sumptuous façade was salvaged from the city's former City Hall. Moncton's oldest building, dating back to 1821 and very well preserved, stands right next door.

The **Musée Acadien ★** *(free admission; Jun to Sep, Mon to Fri 10am to 5pm, Sat and Sun 1pm to 5pm; Oct to May, Tue to Fri 1pm to 4:30pm, Sat and Sun 1pm to 4pm; Université de Moncton, Clément Cormier Bldg., ☎858-4088)* displays over 30,000 objects, including a permanent collection of Acadian artifacts dating from 1604 up to the last century. The museum was founded in Memramcook in 1886 by Père Camille Lefebvre of the Collège Saint-Joseph, and was moved to its present location in 1965. In the same building as the museum, visitors will find the **Centre d'Art de l'Université de Moncton ★★**, where works by Acadian artists are exhibited.

The **Magnetic Hill ★** *($2 per car; west of Moncton, Exit 88 from the Trans-Canada Hwy)* is an intriguing optical illusion, which gives people the impression that their car is climbing a slope. The staff ask drivers to stop their engines at what seems to be the bottom of a very steep hill. Then, as if by miracle, the car seems to climb the slope. This remarkable illusion is a must for families. Other family attractions have sprung up around the Magnetic Hill, including a terrific water park, a zoo, a mini-train, a go-kart track and a miniature golf course, as well as shops, restaurants and a hotel.

Saint-Joseph-de-Memramcook

A small rural town in the pretty Memramcook valley, Saint-Joseph is of great symbolic importance to the Acadian people. This is the only region on the Bay of Fundy where Acadians still live on the farmlands they occupied before the Deportation. It thus serves as a bridge between pre- and post-Deportation Acadia. Collège Saint-Joseph, where the Acadian elite was educated for many years, was founded here in 1864. The college hosted the first Acadian national convention in 1881. At the **Acadian Odyssey National Historic Site** ★ *(free admission; Jun to early Sep, everyday 9am to 5pm; Monument Lefebvre, ☎758-9783)*, visitors can learn about Acadian history by viewing an exhibition on the key factors and pivotal moments leading to the survival of the Acadian people.

Sackville ★

A subtle aura of affluence and a unique awareness of the past emanate from Sackville, whose beautiful residences lie hidden behind the stately trees that flank its streets. The city is home to **Mount Allison University**, a small, highly reputable institution whose lovely buildings stand on beautiful, verdant plots of land in the centre of town. On campus, visitors will find the **Owens Art Gallery** ★ *(on campus, ☎364-2574)*, which displays a large collection of paintings by New Brunswick artists, including several works by master Alex Colville.

Waterfowl Park ★★ *(free admission; every day until nightfall; entrance on East Main St.)* is an interpretive centre focussing on the plant and animal life in salt-water marshes. Thanks to two kilometres of trails and wooden footbridges, visitors can enter a world of unexpected richness and diversity. In addition to being exceptionally informative, this park is a wonderful place to relax.

Aulac

After British forces captured Fort Beauséjour in 1755, that tragic event in Acadian history, the Deportation, was initiated in Aulac. Built in 1751, Fort Beauséjour occupied a strategic location on Chignecto Bay, on the border of the French and British colonial empires. The **Fort Beauséjour National Historic Site** ★ *(free admission; mid-May to mid-Oct; Hwy 2, Exit 550A, ☎536-0720)* includes an interpretive centre, which deals with Acadian history and the Deportation. Visitors can also stroll around several of the star-shaped structure's remaining fortifications. The view of the bay, New Brunswick and Nova Scotia is excellent from here.

Cap-Pelé ★

Cap-Pelé offers visitors a wonderful opportunity to discover the fascinating world of fishing. Founded at the end of the 18th century, this Acadian community still depends on the riches of the sea for its survival. The village is also home to about a dozen *boucanières* (smokehouses), barn-like buildings where fish is smoked before being exported. Beautiful **Plage de l'Aboiteau** ★ is not far from Cap-Pelé. This splendid beach, located in proximity to a fishing port, is ideal for swimming and much less crowded than Parlee Beach Provincial Park. It is hidden from the road by an embankment of boulder and rock that is the inspiration of the beach's name (*Aboiteau* refers to a type of seawall that extends and protects coastal farmland and is a word primarily used in Acadia.) There are also two other beautiful beaches in the Cap-Pelé area: Gagnon Beach and Sandy Beach. The region occupies a little plateau that is almost completely bare of vegetation and offers lovely views of the ocean. Farther along the same road, visitors will reach **Barachois**. In the centre of the village stands the oldest Acadian church in the Maritimes, the **historic church of Saint-Henri-de-Barachois** ★ *(free admission; Jul and Aug; Route 133, ☎532-2976)*.

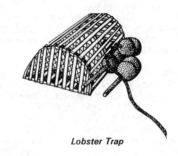

Lobster Trap

Shediac ★

The town of Shediac is the best-known vacation spot on the east coast of New Brunswick. Its popularity is due largely to the magnificent beach in **Parlee Beach Provincial Park** ★★ *(Route 15, see also p 144)*, whose surprisingly warm waters are perfect for swimming. Because of this popularity, a number of recreational facilities have sprung up in and around Shediac, including a lovely golf course and some amusement parks. The town's reputation, however, is also due in good measure to the abundance of lobster found off its shores, which can be savoured fresh any time. The town has even proclaimed itself the lobster capital of the world and holds an annual **lobster festival** in mid-July. Shediac was founded as a fishing port in the 19th century. A handful of lovely buildings have endured from that era, contrasting sharply with the chaotic atmosphere that characterizes the town during the busy summer season. Heading northward along the coast, visitors will pass through several tiny Acadian communities, which survive mainly on fishing.

Bouctouche ★★

A pleasant little town looking out on a large, calm bay, Bouctouche was founded at the end of the 18th century by Acadians driven from the Memramcook valley. It has the distinction of being the birthplace of two celebrated New Brunswickers, Antonine Maillet and K.C. Irving. Winner of the 1979 Prix Goncourt for her novel *Pélagie-la-Charrette*, Antonine Maillet has gained more international recognition than any other Acadian author. She first came into the public eye in the 1960's with *La Sagouine*, a remarkable play that evokes the lives and spirit of Acadians at the beginning of the century. K.C. Irving, who died recently, built a colossal empire with widely diversified operations, most importantly in the oil industry. He started out with nothing and died one of the wealthiest individuals in the world.

The brand new **Pays de la Sagouine ★★** *($6.50; mid-Jun to early Sep, everyday 10am to 6pm; at the southern entrance of the village on Route 134; ☎743-1400, ≈743-1414)* is an effort to recreate early 20th century Acadia, drawing inspiration from Antonine Maillet's highly successful play, *La Sagouine*. Its creators cleverly decided to enliven the atmosphere with characters from the famous play, who perform theatrical and musical pieces. The highlight is Île-aux-Puces, in the centre of the bay. It is here that the Pays de la Sagouine is the liveliest, and visitors can learn what they wish about the lifestyle of early 20th century Acadians by talking with the characters on site. The restaurant l'Ordre du Bon Temps, located at the entrance, serves tasty, traditional Acadian cuisine.

The **Kent County Museum ★** *($2; late Jun to early Sep; on the east side of the village, 150 Convent St., ☎743-5005)* is one of the most interesting regional museums in the prov-

ince. The building itself was used as a convent until 1969. Its various rooms contain period furniture and pieces of sacred art, evoking the history of the convent and the daily life of the nuns and their students. The museum's friendly guides give interesting tours.

Tracadie-Sheila

After passing through the villages of **Néguac** and **Val-Comeau**, each of which has beaches and a provincial park, Route 11 leads to Tracadie-Sheila, a little town with numerous restaurants and hotels, as well as an attractive wharf. As the institutional buildings attest, the town's history was marked for many years by the presence of the *Religieuses Hospitalières de Saint-Joseph* (Sisters of Mercy), who nursed the sick—especially lepers— here from 1868 to 1965. Every year in late June and early July, Tracadie-Sheila hosts the **Festival International de la Francophonie**, which highlights French-language music and arts.

The **Tracadie Historical Museum ★** *(free admission; Jun to mid-Aug; on the 3rd floor of the Académie Sainte-Famille, Rue du Couvent, ☎395-2212)* houses an exhibit on the various stages in the history of Tracadie and its surroundings. Visitors will find a selection of Micmac artifacts, religious objects and 19th century tools. Not far from the museum lies the **leper cemetery**, where about sixty identical crosses stand in rows.

Shippagan ★

Protected by the strait that separates it from Île Lamèque, the site now occupied by Shippagan was originally a trading post, which gave way to a sea port at the end of the 18th century. Now a bustling little community, Shippagan boasts several industries and, more importantly, a port that accommodates one of the largest fishing fleets on the Acadian penin-sula. Its charm lies not only in its seaside loca-tion, but also in the unique atmosphere created by its port. Anyone interested in learning more about the fishing industry—the mainspring of the Acadian economy for over two hundred years now—should stop in Shippagan, explore the town, stroll along the wharf and visit the marine centre. In addition, each year around the third week of July, the town holds a **Fisheries Festival**, made up of a number of fishing-related activities, including the blessing of the boats.

Most Acadians who succeeded in avoiding deportation fled from the fertile shores of the Bay of Fundy through the woods to the province's east coast. Since the soil there was much poorer, they turned to the sea for survival, taking up fishing, an economic activity that has long been an integral part of Acadian culture. To discover the fascinating world of modern fishing in Acadia and the Gulf of St. Lawrence, especially the rich animal life inhabiting the sea bed in this region, visitors can head to the **Marine Centre and Aquarium ★ ★** *($4; mid-May to Sep; near the Shippagan wharf, ☎336-3013)*. This complex is also used for scientific research.

Île Lamèque ★

A ramp connects Shippagan to Île Lamèque. With its flat landscape and handful of tiny hamlets made up of pretty white or coloured houses, this island is a haven of peace where time seems to stand still. A visit to the **Église Sainte-Cécile ★** in Petite-Rivière-de-l'île is a must. This charming, colourful wooden church provides an enchanting setting for the **International Baroque Music Festival**, a wonderful event held each year during the third week of July.

Île Miscou ★

Just a short ferry ride from Île Lamèque lies Île Miscou, another sparsely populated haven of peace, renowned for its lovely, often deserted beaches. At the far end of the island stands the **Île Miscou Lighthouse ★** *(at the end of Route 133)*, one of the oldest in New Brunswick and a marvellous spot from which to view the ocean. A few kilometres before the lighthouse, on the same road, visitors will find an **interpretive site ★** *(Route 133)* with a path and footbridges leading through a peat bog.

Caraquet ★ ★

Caraquet's charm lies mainly in the warmth and vitality of its inhabitants. The largest town on the peninsula, equipped with a number of hotels and restaurants, Caraquet is also considered the cultural hub of Acadia — and with good reason. It is probably this town and its residents' lifestyle that best illustrate modern Acadian culture, which draws on a variety of influences without, however, renouncing its rich past. August is by far the best time to visit Caraquet, since August 15 is the Acadian national holiday, the culmination of the **Festival Acadien**, a series of about ten different events. The Tintamarre and Frolic (August 15) alone make for a memorable experience. At other times, visitors can attend performances by the excellent theatre company of the **Théâtre Populaire d'Acadie** *(276 Blvd. Saint-Pierre Ouest, ☎727-0920)*, relax on one of the town's little beaches or set off on a cruise from the **Carrefour de la Mer** *(51 Blvd. Saint-Pierre Est)*.

The **Acadian Museum ★** *(free admission; mid Jun to mid Sep; 15 Blvd. Saint-Pierre Est, ☎727-1713)* houses a small collection of everyday objects from the past two centuries.

An important place of pilgrimage in a lovely natural setting, the **Sanctuaire Sainte-Anne-du-Bocage ★** *(free admission; everyday, all year round; Blvd. Saint-Pierre Ouest)* includes a small wooden chapel, the Stations of the Cross and a monument to Alexis Landry, ancestor of most of the Landrys in Acadia.

No history book on Acadia could ever be as an effective an educational tool as the **Village Historique Acadien ★ ★ ★** *($7.50; mid-Jun to early Sep; on Route 11, about 10 km west of Caraquet, ☎726-2600)*. Here, on a vast piece of land, visitors will find a reconstructed village, including about twenty houses and other buildings, most of which are authentic, dating from 1780 to the end of the 19th century. The atmosphere is enlivened by performers in period costume, who carry out everyday tasks using traditional methods and gladly inform visitors about the customs of the past. A film at the interpretive centre presents a brief history of the Acadian people.

Grande-Anse

At Grande-Anse, another tiny coastal village, visitors will find pretty **Ferguson Beach**, which lies at the foot of a cliff, and the unique **Pope Museum ★** *($2; Jun to Sep; 184 Rue Acadie, ☎732-3003)*. The museum's exhibit includes a model of Saint Peter's in Rome, clothing and pieces of sacred art, as well as a collection of papal iconography. A number of these objects are both rare and interesting. The museum serves as a reminder of the important role religion has played in Acadian history.

NEW BRUNSWICK

OUTDOORS

Parks

The perfectly marvellous **Irving Nature Park** ★★ *(free admission; at the end of Sand Cove Rd.,* ☎632-7777*)* has a great deal to offer nature lovers. Located just a few kilometres west of the industrial city of Saint John, this magnificent park covers a 225-hectare peninsula trimmed with untouched beaches. The city seems a million miles away from here. Visitors can also enjoy a pleasant stroll along one of the park's trails, communing with nature and observing the plant and animal life in Southern New Brunswick.

Fundy National Park ★★★ *(Route 114, near Alma,* ☎887-6000 or 887-2005*)* is the ultimate place to explore the shores of the bay, observe its plant and animal life and grasp the power of its tides. It covers a densely wooded, mountainous territory of 206 square kilometres, abounding in spectacular scenery, lakes and rivers and nearly twenty kilometres of shoreline. All sorts of athletic activities can be enjoyed here. The park is a hiker's paradise, with its 120 kilometres of trails running through the forest, near lakes and alongside the magnificent bay. Visitors can also enjoy fishing, camping on one of many equipped or natural sites, playing a game on the excellent golf course or swimming in the heated pool. Travellers pressed for time should make sure at the very least to visit **Pointe Wolfe** ★★, where nearby trails offer spectacular views of cliffs plunging straight into the waters of the bay. At each entrance to the park, employees offer information on the various activities available.

Blanketed by a forest of cedars and other conifers and studded with peat bogs, magnificent **Kouchibouguac National Park** ★★ *(Route 11 or 134,* ☎876-2443*)*, boasts over 26 kilometres of spectacular coastline made up of salt-water marshes, lagoons, dunes and golden, sandy beaches. It is the natural habitat of several hundred animals, including the extremely rare piping plover. The park is laced with hiking trails and bicycle paths, and may also be explored by canoe or rowboat. All equipment necessary for these sports is available on site, along with a campground. The park is a perfect place for salt-water swimming, especially at Lagoon Beach, which is washed by the warmest salt-water in the province, and the excellent Kelly's Beach and Collanders Beach.

Beaches

Murray Beach Provincial Park ★ *(Route 955)* has a lovely beach, a campground and various games.

Aboiteau Beach ★ *(Route 15)* stretches 2.5 kilometres and features lovely sand dunes. On top of being an excellent spot for swimming, the beach itself is extremely enchanting. Between Cap Pelé and Shediac, there are three more pretty beaches along the coast.

Parlee Beach Provincial Park ★★ *(near Exit 17 on Route 15)* is probably New Brunswick's most famous beach. It is patrolled by life guards and stretches several kilometres. Visitors can camp nearby.

Some of the most beautiful beaches in the province are to be found in **Kouchibouguac National Park** *(Route 134 and 11)*. Visitors can also rent a canoe or rowboat, go hiking or cycling and, in winter, enjoy cross-country skiing here. There are campings sites as well.

Whale-Watching

Because of its rich feeding grounds, the Bay of Fundy is one of the best places in the world to observe certain species of whales. Whale-watching excursions are organized throughout the summer, starting from the following places: St. Andrews By-the-Sea, Deer Island, Campobello Island and Grand Manan Island, in the southwestern part of the province.

Cline Marine: Departures from St. Andrews, Deer Island and Campobello Island: ☎529-4188 or 747-2287.

Atlantic Marine Wildlife Tours: Departures from St. Andrews, ☎459-7325.

Island Coast Boat Tours: Departures from Grand Manan Island, ☎662-8181.

Ocean Search: Departures from Grand Manan Island, ☎662-8488.

Seawatch: Departures from Grand Manan Island, ☎662-8552.

Starboard Tours: Departures from Grand Manan Island, ☎662-8545 or 663-7525.

ACCOMMODATIONS

Fredericton

During the summer, student residence rooms can be rented at the **University of New Brunswick** *(at the end of University Ave., ☎453-4891)*. Expect to pay around $40 for a double occupancy room, or $28 for a single room.

The charm of Fredericton is due to the many opulent Victorian residences lining its streets. The **Carriage House Inn** *($60; 10 rooms, tv; 230 University Ave., E3C 4H7, ☎ 452-9924 or 1-800-267-6068, ≈458-0799)* is one of these magnificent houses, which has been transformed into an inn with a unique atmosphere that transports guests to another era. There are several large rooms including a ballroom, a library and a solarium, as well as ten guest rooms furnished with antiques. The inn looks out onto a quiet, well-to-do street shaded by large elm trees and lies just a few minutes walk from downtown. It is best to reserve in advance, regardless of the season.

The elegant **Sheraton Inn** *($89; 223 rooms, tv, ℜ, ≈; 225 Woodstock Rd., E3B 2H8, ☎457-7000 or 1-800-325-3535, ≈457-4000)* is beautifully located on the shores of the St. John River, just outside of downtown Fredericton. It is by far the most luxurious hotel in the capital and one of the nicest in the province. The architects made the most of the location including a superb terrace looking out over the river, the ideal spot for cocktails, a dip in the pool or a relaxed meal while taking in the scenery. The rooms are very comfortable, pretty and functional, and several offer great views. Built recently, the Sheraton is of course equipped with an indoor pool and exercise facilities, a very good restaurant, a bar and conference rooms. It has clearly been designed to please both business people and travellers.

You won't find a hotel more centrally located than the **Lord Beaverbrook Hotel** *($89; 175 rooms, tv, ℜ, ≈; 659 Queen St., E3B 5A6, ☎455-3371 or 1-800-561-7666, ≈455-1441)* which has been a landmark in downtown

Fredericton for half a century. With its back to the St. John River, it faces the Legislative Assembly of New Brunswick. The hotel's prestigious history is evident in the richly decorated entrance hall and the aristocratic air about the Governor's Room, a small dining room tucked away. Despite renovations, the rooms are a bit disappointing.

Grand Falls (Grand-Sault)

Along the TransCanada Highway, 2.5 kilometres north of Grand Falls the **Motel Léo** *($66; 34 rooms, tv, ℜ; 2.5 km north of Grand Falls, EOJ 1M0, ☎473-2090 or 1-800-661-0077, ≈573-6614)* rents inexpensive well-appointed rooms. It is a fairly typical motel, where most guests only stop for one night to take a break on a long trip. The staff is very friendly.

Right next door to the Motel Léo is the **Motel Près du Lac** *($74; 100 rooms, tv, ℜ, ≈; 2.5 km north of Grand Falls, EOJ 1M0, ☎471-1300 or for reservations: 1-800-528-1234, ≈473-5501)*, offering quality lodging. The complex includes motel rooms as well as cottages on the shores of an artificial lake. Guests can choose a standard room or a wedding suite. Activities ranging from pedal-boating on the lake, to mini-golf, basketball, working out and swimming in the indoor pool make this a popular spot for families.

Hartland

It is hard to imagine a more peaceful spot than **Campbell's Bed & Breakfast** *($35; 3 rooms, tv, K; 1 km north of Hartland, EOJ 1NO, ☎375-4775, ≈375-4014)*, a farmhouse built along the St. John River near the town of Hartland. Sitting on the large porch, it is easy to appreciate the tranquility of Richard Hatfield country. The rooms are comfortable, although a bit over-decorated, and guests have use of a fully-equipped kitchen at all times. Mrs. Campbell doesn't actually live in the B&B, but rather in a little house about 200 metres away on the same property.

Gagetown

A rather austere house in appearance in the heart of town along the shore of the St. John River, the **Steamers Stop Inn** *($65; 7 rooms, tv, ℜ; Front St., EOG 1VO, ☎488-2903,*

NEW BRUNSWICK

☞488-1116) fits right in with the pastoral charm that characterizes Gagetown. There is definitely no better place to get a real feel for this little vacation spot, since everything is close by. Rooms are well appointed, and five of them provide a view of the river. The inn also has a decent restaurant.

St. Andrews By-the-Sea

Considered one of the oldest hotels in the country, in operation since 1881, the **Best-Western Shiretown Inn** *($68; 26 rooms, tv, ℜ, K; 218 Water St., EOG 2XO,* ☎*529-8877 or for reservations: 1-800-528-1234,* ☞*529-3044)* is centrally located near the St. Andrews pier. This picturesque historic building has cosy rooms, an excellent restaurant and a beautiful front balcony where guests can dine or enjoy drinks. Nicely-appointed apartments with kitchenettes can also be rented close by.

Set in the middle of a large property overlooking the surrounding countryside, the **Rossmount Inn** *($75; 17 rooms, tv, ≈, ℜ; a few kilometres from St. Andrews on Hwy 127 heading east, EOG 2XO,* ☎*529-3351,* ☞*529-1920)* is a magnificent inn with antique furniture in each room. The Rossmount Inn also offers an excellent dining room.

Dominating the quaint setting of St. Andrews By-The-Sea is the best and most reputed hotel in the Maritimes, the **Algonquin Resort** *($149, open May to Oct; 240 rooms, tv, ℜ, K, ≈; Hwy 127, EOG 2XO,* ☎*529-8823 or 1-800-441-1414,* ☞*529-4194)*. A majestic neo-Tudor grouping in the centre of a large property, this dream hotel has withstood the test of time by carefully preserving the aristocratic refinement and Anglo-Saxon character of an elite resort of the late 1800s. Built in 1889, the Algonquin was completely devastated by fire in 1914. Most of it was rebuilt the next year. Then, in 1991, a new convention centre was added, followed by a new wing with 54 rooms and suites in 1993. The Algonquin offers superb, modern and very comfortable rooms and suites, excellent food at the Passamaquoddy Veranda dining room, flawless service and a whole slew of activities. If the nightly rate is beyond your budget, do at least visit the hotel and treat yourself to Sunday brunch, lunch or supper, a drink in the Library Bar or stop at the gift shop.

Campobello Island

Well situated near the park, the **Lupin Lodge** *($50, open Jun to Oct; 10 rooms, tv, ℜ; EOG 3HO,* ☎*752-2555)* offers relatively comfortable accommodation. The neighbouring restaurant is busy during the summer season, all day long until evening falls.

Grand Manan Island

Lots of families spend at least a few days of their vacation on Grand Manan Island. A popular option for such vacationers is to rent a cottage like the ones offered at **Fisherman's Haven Cottages** *($80; 5 rooms, Grand Harbour, EOG 1XO,* ☎*662-8919 or 662-3389,* ☞*662-6246)* which have two or three bedrooms. Weekly rates are available.

Saint John

If you don't see Saint John as an idyllic spot to take a relaxing and revitalizing vacation it must be because you've never come across the **Inn on the Cove** *($65; 5 rooms, tv; 1371 Sand Cove Rd., E2M 4X7,* ☎*672-7799,* ☞*635-5455)*, probably one of the best inns in the province. Located in a quiet setting with a spectacular view of the Bay of Fundy, the inn is actually only 5 minutes by car from downtown. Nature-lovers will find beautiful wild beaches to explore close by and trails leading to Irving Nature Park. The house is furnished with taste and a particular attention to detail, and the comfortable rooms are decorated with antiques. All of the rooms are nice, but the two located on the second floor and facing over the back of the house are even better: they are larger, have their own bathrooms and offer a stunning view of the bay. The owners are friendly but discreet, and prepare excellent breakfasts.

In the heart of downtown on the busiest street, the **Delta Brunswick Hotel** *($87; 225 rooms, tv, ℜ, ≈; 39 King St., E2L 4W3,* ☎*648-1981 or 1-800-268-1133,* ☞*658-0914)* is the largest hotel in Saint John, with 255 deluxe rooms and suites. Attached to a shopping mall, the building itself lacks a bit of charm. The hotel is best known for the gamut of services for vacationers and business people.

The Saint John **Hilton** *($134; 197 rooms, tv, ℜ, ≈; 1 Market Square, E2L 4Z6,* ☎*693-8484 or 1-800-561-8282,* ☞*657-6610)*, offering high quality accommodation, lies in a beautiful setting at the edge of the pier close to the market. It is a great spot to enjoy the singular beauty of this sea port whose activity is dictated by the continuous ebb and flow of the tides. Its rooms are spacious and decorated with furniture that is simultaneously modern and inviting. Obviously, the rooms at the back of the building, which look out over the port of Saint John, are most desirable. The Hilton also has a good restaurant, Turn of the Tide (see p 149).

St. Martins

The divine **St. Martins Country Inn** *($70; 12 rooms, tv; Hwy 111, EOG 2ZO, ☎833-4534 or 1-800-565-5257, ≈833-4725)* is situated in the enchanting setting of a large property overlooking the town. Built in 1857 for the most important shipbuilder in St. Martins, it has maintained the serene and perhaps slightly snobby atmosphere befitting the residence of a highly-visible member of the Anglo-Saxon upper class of that era. Everything to satisfy the discerning tastes of the epicurean traveller is in place: beautifully decorated rooms filled with period furniture, a highly-reputed kitchen, three splendid dining rooms and impeccable service. Reserve in advance.

Fundy National Park

Visitors to Fundy National Park can choose between campsites and **Fundy Park Chalets** *($50; 29 rooms, tv, K, ℜ; EOA 1BO, ☎887-2808)*. These rather rustic-looking cottages are located near the park administration office and the golf course, not far from the coast. Each one is equipped with a room with two beds, a bathroom and a kitchenette. Provisions are available just a few kilometres away in Alma.

Moncton

Set in a quiet neighbourhood not far from the city's liveliest streets, the **Canadiana Inn** *($65, open Mar to Nov; 17 rooms, tv; 46 Archibald St., E1C 5H9, ☎382-1054)* occupies a large, lovely Victorian house built at the end of the last century. Its rooms, equipped with comfortable furnishings, are handsomely decorated and inviting. The establishment has a pleasant upstairs terrace, as well as two dining rooms in which generous breakfasts are served. The service here is very congenial.

For those travellers in need of some pampering and in search of elegance and comfort, there is the **Hotel Beauséjour** *($150; 314 rooms, tv, ℜ, ≈; 750 Main St., E1C 1E6, ☎854-4344 or 1-800-441-1414, ≈858-0957)*, Moncton's finest establishment and a member of the Canadian Pacific hotel chain. The quality of service that has made the reputation of this chain is here, as well as beautifully-decorated and spacious rooms, an excellent restaurant and piano bar and a lovely indoor swimming pool where it is easy to put the bustle of urban life behind, or perhaps below, you. Right in the heart of Moncton, the hotel could not be more suitably located for business people and travellers hoping to take advantage of the nearby restaurants and bars.

Sackville

The charm of Sackville is due in good part to the multitude of large, beautiful houses from the 1800s. One of these has been converted into the outstanding **Marshlands Inn** *($55; 21 rooms, tv, ℜ; 59 Bridge St., EOA 3CO, ☎536-0170, ≈536-0721)*, once a sumptuous residence offered as a wedding gift by William Crane, an important man of that era, to his daughter. The inn has more than 20 rooms, each one impeccably furnished; several have private bathrooms.

Shediac

Located on a beautifully-maintained piece of property in the heart of Shediac, **Chez Françoise** *($55, open Apr to Dec; 19 rooms, tv; 93 Main St., EOA 3GO, ☎532-4233)* is a wonderful inn. Built at the turn of the century, it was originally the residence of a wealthy family. The elegant interior, with its wood trim and sumptuous staircase, and the large front porch, ideal for coffee or an apéritif, make for a charming little spot.

Near the entrance to the provincial park, the **Four Seas Motel** *($60; 42 rooms, tv, ℜ, K; 762 Main St., EOA 3GO, ☎532-2585, ≈855-0809)* is a good choice for families. The service is efficient and friendly, the restaurant is very good and the rooms are clean and well furnished, mostly with modern pieces. During the summer season, it is best to reserve early in the morning if you want one of the less expensive rooms since they go fast.

A member of the Association des Auberges du Patrimoine du Nouveau-Brunswick, **Belcourt Inn** *($79; 7 rooms, tv; 112 Main St., EOA 3GO, ☎532-6098)* occupies a sumptuous patrician house that has belonged to such notables as former premier of New Brunswick Judge Allison Dysart. Erected in 1912, this three-story Victorian building has preserved all of its olden-day splendour and charm, both inside and out. The common rooms are spacious, furnished with antiques and richly ornamented with woodwork. The inn's seven individually decorated guestrooms are also decked out in period furniture. A very inviting porch provides an ideal setting for reading and relaxing. Belcourt Inn is situated in the heart of Shediac, just across from Chez Françoise.

Bouctouche

The **Old Presbytery of Bouctouche** *($57, open May to Oct; 22 rooms, ℜ; 157 Chemin du Couvent, EOA 1GO, ☎743-5568, ⟛743-5566)* actually occupies a presbytery constructed at the end of the 19th century. Today it is a superb family inn just outside the centre of Bouctouche, with a beautiful view of the bay. The atmosphere is first-rate, ideal for relaxation, and the building, which has been renovated several times is full of charm. An old chapel has been converted into a reception hall. The restaurant has an excellent reputation as well.

Caraquet

Also part of the Caraquet skyline for many years, the **Hôtel Paulin** *($45, open May to Oct; 9 rooms, tv, ℜ; 143 St. Pierre Blvd W., E1W 1B6, ☎727-9981, ⟛727-3165)* is actually a pleasant inn run by the Paulin family for the last three generations. The rooms vary in quality: some have recently been nicely renovated while others are quite out of date but still very clean; in all cases, however, the quality/price ratio is very good. There is a very pretty suite at the back of the building with a view of the ocean. Guests can relax in the sitting room and enjoy the restaurant's excellent food.

There is truly something for all tastes and all budgets at the **Maison Touristique Dugas** *($55; 18 rooms, tv; 683 St. Pierre Blvd W.,* E1W 1A1, ☎727-3195, ⟛722-3193*)*. The main building, a beautiful, massive house built in 1926, numbers over 10 impeccable, pretty rooms of varying sizes. In addition to these rooms, campsites and fully equipped rental cottages are available on the grounds. The Maison Touristique Dugas offers a very friendly welcome and excellent breakfasts in the morning. From the house, located a little bit west of Caraquet, a trail winds through the woods to the Dugas's private beach, just a ten-minute walk away.

The **Auberge de la Baie** *($59; 54 rooms, tv, ℜ; 139 St. Pierre Blvd W., E1W 1B7, ☎727-3485, ⟛727-3634)* provides comfortable and modern motel-style accommodation. Strangely enough, most of the rooms open onto an interior hallway instead of outdoors. There is a good restaurant with polite, friendly and attentive service. Finally the ample grounds offer access to a small deserted beach located behind the inn.

 RESTAURANTS

Fredericton

The **Café du Monde** *($; 608 Queen St.)* is a cosy café-style restaurant close to the main attractions of Fredericton. Light dishes, sandwiches and a small choice of breads and buns are served. This is the perfect spot for an afternoon break, an inexpensive meal or a good cup of coffee to start off the day.

The **Lobster Hut** *($$; 1216 Regent St., City Motel)* could almost be listed as a Fredericton attraction, due to its bizarre, almost psychedelic decor, made up of an eclectic collection of photos, posters and gadgets all having to do with maritime life. The restaurant is as friendly as can be, and as you may have guessed specializes in fish and seafood. The food is good and relatively inexpensive.

In summertime when the weather is mild, it would be hard to imagine a better spot for a drink, light snack or meal than **The Dip** *($$-$$$; Sheraton Inn)*, a terrace restaurant with a bistro menu. Besides the attentive and courteous service, The Dip offers an absolutely unbeatable view of the St. John River. If the weather proves prohibitive, you can always take shelter at **Bruno's Seafood Café** *($$$)*, the indoor restaurant at the Sheraton Inn (see p 145). The cuisine is just as good, the service, impeccable and the ambiance, cosy. The highlights of the menu are excellent scallops Florentine and pepper shrimp. There is also a children's menu. In addition, Bruno's usually offers a seafood buffet on Friday evenings for about $20 per person.

St. Andrews By-the-Sea

Imagine America in the fifties and you've got the decor of the **Chef Café** *($; 180 Water St., ☎529-8888)*, a popular but rinky-dink restaurant that clashes with the inherent chic that is St. Andrews. The menu includes simple dishes like fish and chips and lobster rolls, as well as several inexpensive breakfasts. For a more sophisticated menu, pick a spot at the back of the restaurant, in the cosier dining room known as the Captain's Table.

For many visitors, fresh lobster at a reasonable price is in itself enough of a reason to visit the Maritimes. When passing through St. Andrews, these seafood fanatics converge on **The Lighthouse Restaurant** *($$-$$$, Patrick St., ☎529-3082)*. This pretty spot looking out over Passamaquoddy Bay is on the last street at the eastern edge of St. Andrews.

The **Passamaquoddy Veranda** *($$$; Algonquin Hotel, ☎529-8823)* offers an outstanding dining experience, as much for the elegance of its decor as for the exceptional quality of its international and regional cuisine. A meal at the Veranda is not within everyone's budget, but fortunately there is a much less expensive lunch menu and a Sunday brunch, which starts at $18.50.

Saint John

Grannan's Seafood Restaurant and Oyster Bar *($$; Market Square, ☎634-1555)* has become an institution in Saint John. The restaurant, whose decor is a hodgepodge of eccentric maritime-related relics and photos, a real fishmonger's paradise, opens onto an outdoor terrace, perfect for those warm summer evenings. The menu of this restaurant, which is often very crowded in the evening, is predictably composed mainly of seafood and fish dishes.

Without question one of the trendiest spots in Saint John, the **Incredible Edibles Café** *($$; 42 Princess St.)* serves excellent continental cuisine and superb desserts. Feasters can sit out in the garden or in the delightful interior dining room. The menu includes excellent pasta with mussels as well as a succulent filet of salmon, among other dishes. To top off a delectable meal, or simply to satisfy a mid-afternoon craving, the raspberry cheesecake hits the spot. This café also has a reasonably priced lunch menu.

The **Turn of the Tide** *($$$; Hilton Hotel, see p 146)* offers a varied menu, typical of a hotel of this calibre, with a vast choice of meat, game, and of course the prerequisite fresh seafood and fish. The menu is a bit pricey, but the food is sure to please, and the view of the port makes it all the more worthwhile. The decor is classic, airy and tasteful. Turn of the Tide proves to be an ideal place for romantic evenings and special occasions.

Moncton

Practically facing the Café Robinson, the **Café Joe Moka** *($; at the corner of Robinson St. and Main St.)* offers a similar menu and a patio that is just as pleasant as the Robinson's.

In business for more than half a century, **Cy's Seafood** *($$; 170 Main St., ☎857-0032)* has adopted one of the Maritimes' treasures, the lobster, as its house specialty. The menu lists other types of seafood as well, all prepared simply and deliciously.

Shediac

When the owners of the **Café Péché Mignon** *($; 15 Queen St., ☎532-6555)* opened for business in the summer of 1994, they did so believing there was space for a little French café, in Shediac. They couldn't have been more right! Besides excellent desserts and coffees, the menu includes a good choice of simple dishes like excellent quiche and some Acadian specialties. The atmosphere is particularly friendly and reflects the bohemian spirit of the owner, who is a painter.

About 5 kilometres outside of Shediac, towards Cap-Pelé, a small road leads to the famous **Paturel** *($$-$$$; Cape Bimet Rd., ☎532-4774)*, a simple restaurant with a view of the ocean, which serves fresh seafood at prices that are reasonable, all things considered. Portions are generous, especially the Seafood Platter, which includes samples the abundant variety of seafood of the region. To add to the maritime atmosphere, the restaurant lies right next to Paturel Seafood Ltd., a seafood processing plant.

Undeniably one of the best restaurants in the region, **Chez Françoise** *($$$; 93 Main St., ☎532-4233)* offers refined French cuisine and an excellent selection of wine. And to add to your dining pleasure, the dining room is decorated with elegance and style. On lazy summer afternoons, the establishment's front porch is the perfect place for sipping a cool drink.

Bouctouche

L'Ordre du Bon Temps *($-$$; at the entrance to the Pays de la Sagouine, ☎743-1400)* the restaurant at the *Pays de la Sagouine* offers visitors the chance to sample traditional Acadian specialties like *fricot de poulet*, *poutine râpée* or *poutine à trou*, *pâté à la râpure* or *pâté aux palourdes*. The menu probably has the most extensive selection of Acadian dishes in all of Acadia, so take advantage of it.

Acadian hospitality is at its best at **Tire-Bouchon** *($$-$$$; Old Presbytery, ☎743-5568)* the excellent dining room in the Old Presbytery, where chef, Marcelle Albert introduces diners to the most refined regional specialties. The name, which means "corkscrew", is quite fitting considering the fine bottles stocked in the wine cellar.

Shippagan

Very elegant and endowed with a splendid view of the port, the **Jardin de la Mer** *($$-$$$; next to the Aquarium, ☎336-8454)* is, as one might expect, an excellent fish and seafood restaurant. Lunchtime, when the lobster rolls and other small meals are available at relatively reasonable prices, is a good time to stop in for a bite. Evenings, gourmets benefit from a wide choice. Those with a big appetite can attempt to discover all the wonders of the sea in one meal with the *Sea in Your Plate*.

Caraquet

Airy and modern, but at the same time friendly and inviting, the **Auberge de la Baie dining room** *($$; 139 St. Pierre Blvd, ☎727-3485)* offers a good variety of dishes, including seafood and steaks. The service is very

attentive. Some of this restaurant's specialties are baked scallops, Coquilles St. Jacques au gratin and Provençale frogs' legs.

Paquetville

If your tummy starts to grumble as you pass through the little town of Paquetville, silence it with a stop at **La Crêpe Bretonne** *($-$$; 1085 rue Du Parc, ☎764-4344)*, a small restaurant whose specialties are crepes and seafood. These two are sometimes combined in scallops and béchamel crepes, lobster and béchamel crepes, crab and béchamel crepes, etc. A good place for an inexpensive lunch or a good evening meal.

  ENTERTAINMENT

Fredericton

Always hopping, even on a Sunday night, **The Upper Deck Sport's Bar** *(2nd floor, Queen St.)* is one of the most popular spots with young Frederictonians. The place features pool tables and regular live music. This bar has a large back patio where people can eat and sip drinks in a relaxing atmosphere.

Saint John

The Irish influence is known to be very strong in Saint John. It is therefore no surprise to find **O'Leary's** *(46 Princess St.)*, an excellent Irish pub. The clientele is generally young, and musicians are often presented.

Moncton

The sumptuous **Capitol Theatre** *(811 Main St., ☎856-4377)* is the main performing arts centre in Moncton. Since its reopening in 1993, after renovations restored the panache of days gone by, the theatre has presented a variety of quality productions.

 SHOPPING

Fredericton

No visit to Fredericton would be complete without a stop at **Gallery 78** *(796 Queen St.)*, which exhibits and sells works by some of the most well-known New Brunswick artists. It is also a wonderful way to visit a sumptuous Victorian house overlooking the St. John River. With its high ceilings, large rooms, hardwood floors and stately staircase, you'll be wishing it was for sale too!

The **Arts Council of New Brunswick** *(103 Church St.)* (Conseil d'Artisanat du Nouveau-Brunswick) boutique exhibits and sells a superb collection of high quality products created by the province's artists and crafts-people. It is one of the best craft boutiques in New Brunswick.

Gagetown

The charming contemporary **Acadia Gallery of Canadian Art** *(☎488-1119)*, located in the centre of Gagetown, exhibits a particularly interesting selection of works by artists using a variety of media. Since the gallery also serves

as a workshop, it is often possible to meet some of the artists inspired by this enchanting site along the St. John River.

St. Stephen

The oldest candy maker in Canada (1873), **Ganong Chocolatier** *(73 Milltown Blvd., ☎465-5611)* is also the first producer of chocolate bars. Today, the shop sells about 75 different varieties of chocolate; just try to choose...

St. Andrews By-the-Sea

North of Sixty Art *(238 Water St., ☎529-4148)* is an Inuit art gallery that can be visited like a museum. Works exhibited include uniquely diverse and beautiful sculptures. Among the dozens of boutiques along Water Street, this one is probably the most interesting.

NEW BRUNSWICK

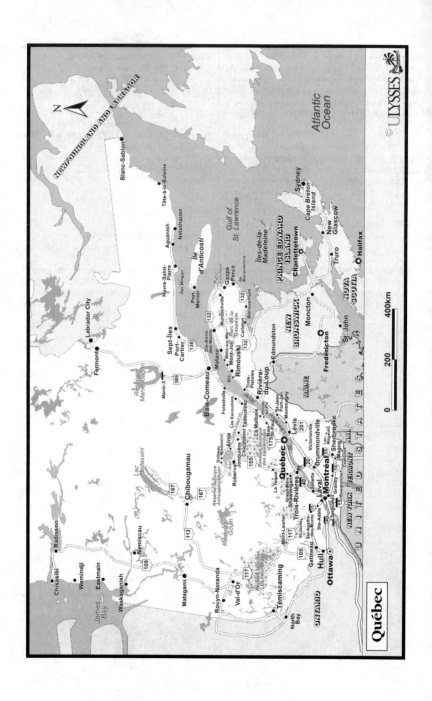

Québec

© ULYSSES

MONTRÉAL

 A city of paradoxes at the crossroads of America and Europe, seen as both Latin and northern, cosmopolitan and unmistakably the metropolis of Québec, **Montreal ★★★** holds nothing back. It succeeds in delighting American tourists with its so-called European charm, but also manages to surprise overseas travellers with its haphazard character and nonchalance. Montréal is an enchanting city to visit, an exhilarating place to discover; it is generous, friendly and not at all mundane. And, when it comes time to celebrate jazz, film, humour, singing or Saint-Jean-Baptiste Day, hundreds of thousands of people flood into the streets, turning events into warm public gatherings. This festive spirit lasts all year in the city's countless cafés, nightclubs and bars of all different kinds, which are constantly packed by a joyful, urban crowd. While Montrealers know how to party, they also enjoy celebrating the arts. With French and North American influences, as well as the vitality of new arrivals, Montréal is an international city and the primary centre of culture in Québec. The abundance of high quality work produced here, most notably in the fields of theatre, fashion, literature and music, attests to the dynamism and creativity of the local population. The city has also earned an enviable reputation among food-lovers; many believe that one can eat better in Montréal than anywhere else in North America.

 FINDING YOUR WAY AROUND

There are 28 municipalities on the island of Montréal, which measures 32 kilometres at its longest point by 16 kilometres at its widest. Montréal proper, with a population of about one million, is the main urban area in the Communauté Urbaine de Montréal (Montréal Urban Community), which encompasses all of the boroughs on the island. Greater Montréal also includes the Rive-Sud (South Shore), Laval and the Rive-Nord (North Shore), for a grand total of 3,200,000 inhabitants (1991). The downtown area runs along the St. Lawrence, south of Mont Royal (234 m), which is one of the 10 hills of the Montérégie region.

By Car

There are two possible routes from Québec City. The first is via Highway 20 W. to the Pont Champlain, then follow Autoroute Bonaventure (10) straight into the centre of town, the other route is via Highway 40 W. to Autoroute Décarie (15), and follow the signs for downtown, *centre-ville.*

Visitors arriving from Ottawa should take Highway 40 E. to Autoroute Décarie (15), then follow the signs for downtown, while those arriving from Toronto should take Highway 20

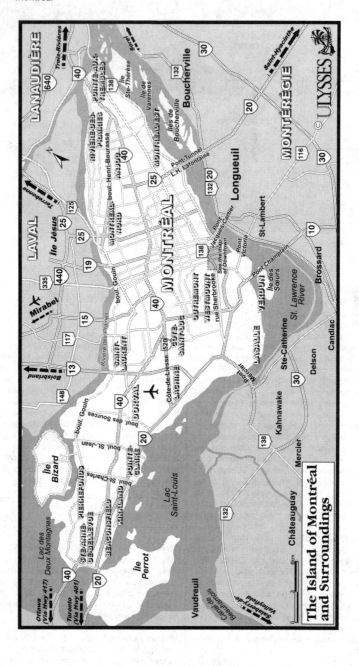

The Island of Montréal
and Surroundings

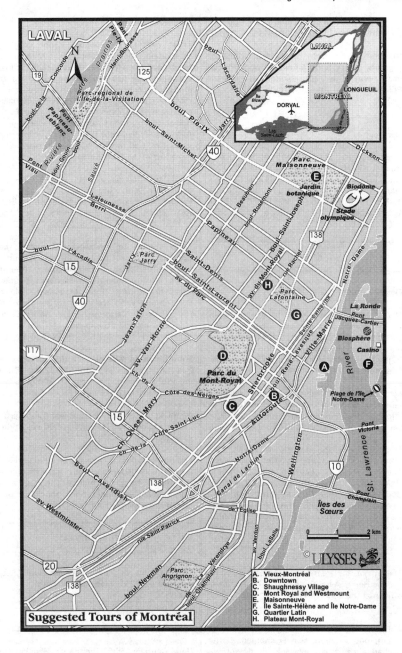

Suggested Tours of Montréal

A. Vieux-Montréal
B. Downtown
C. Shaughnessy Village
D. Mont Royal and Westmount
E. Maisonneuve
F. Île Sainte-Hélène and Île Notre-Dame
G. Quartier Latin
H. Plateau Mont-Royal

QUÉBEC

E. onto the island, then follow the signs for downtown via Autoroute Ville-Marie (720).

Visitors arriving from the United States on Highway 10 (Autoroute des Cantons de l'Est) or Highway 15 will enter Montréal by way the Pont Champlain and Autoroute Bonaventure (10).

Car Rentals

Avis: 1225 Rue Metcalfe, ☎(514) 866-7906
Budget: 1240 Rue Guy, ☎(514) 937-9121; Complexe Desjardins, ☎(514) 842-9931
Hertz: 1475 Rue Aylmer, ☎(514) 842-8537
Tilden: 1200 Rue Stanley, ☎(514) 878-2771
Via Route: 1255 Rue Mackay, ☎(514) 871-1166

Airports

Dorval Airport

Dorval airport is located approximately 20 kilometres from downtown Montréal, and is 20 minutes by car. To get downtown from here, take Highway 20 E. to the junction of Highway 720 (the Ville-Marie), follow signs for "Centre-ville, Vieux-Montréal".

For information regarding airport services (arrivals, departures, other information), an information counter is open from 6am to 10pm seven days a week; ☎(514) 633-3105.

From Dorval to downtown: with the Connaisseur Bus Company. Schedules vary. The bus stops at the Hôtel Reine-Elizabeth *(900 Boul. René-Lévesque Ouest, Métro Bonaventure)*, the Château Champlain, the Centre Sheraton and the Voyageur Bus Terminal *(505 Boul. de Maisonneuve Est, Métro Berri-UQAM)*. Free for children under five. Cost: $9 one way and $16.50 return, ☎(514) 934-1222.

The major car rental companies, including Tilden, Hertz, Avis, Budget and Thrifty, have offices at the airport.

A Thomas Cook counter is open from 6am to 11pm, but a commission is charged. Better exchange rates are available in downtown Montréal (see p 158).

Mirabel Airport

This airport is located approximately 50 kilometres north of Montréal, in Mirabel. To reach downtown Montréal from Mirabel, follow the Autoroute des Laurentides (Hwy 15) S. until it intersects with Autoroute Métropolitaine (Hwy 40) E., which you follow for a few kilometres, then continue once again on the 15 S. (which is now called Autoroute Décarie) until Autoroute Ville-Marie (Hwy 720). Follow the signs for "Centre-ville, Vieux-Montréal". The trip takes 40 to 60 minutes.

For information on airport services (arrivals, departures, and other information), visit the information counter, it is open daily from 8am to 11:30pm. There is also a 24-hour telephone service *(☎514-476-3010 or 1-800-465-1213)*.

From Mirabel to downtown Montréal: the Connaisseur Bus Company offers a shuttle service. The schedule changes often. The bus stops at the Hôtel Reine-Elizabeth (Queen Elizabeth Hotel), (Rue Mansfield, Métro Bonaventure) and at the Voyageur Bus Terminal *(505 Boul. de Maisonneuve Est, Métro Berri-UQAM)*. Cost: $7.25 one-way, $10.25 return (free for children under five, ☎514-934-1222).

From Dorval to Mirabel: with the Connaisseur Bus Company *(☎514-934-1222)*. Daily departures from 9:20am to 10:30pm. Cost: $12 one-way and $16 return.

All the large car rental companies: Avis, Hertz, Tilden, Budget, and Thrifty, have offices at the airport.

The Royal Bank of Canada is open during flight arrivals and departures, but they charge a commission to change money. This bank also has various automatic teller machines for currency exchange.

Bus Terminals

---

505 Boulevard de Maisonneuve Est, ☎(514) 842-2281, Métro Berri-UQAM.

Train Station

Gare Centrale: 935 Rue de la Gauchetière Ouest: ☎514-871-7765, 1-800-361-5390

QUÉBEC

(from Québec) or 1-800-561-8630 (from Canada), ☎871-7766, Métro Bonaventure.

Public Transportation

Montréal's Métro (subway) and bus network covers the entire metropolitan region. A $45 pass entitles the holder to unlimited use of these services on the island for one month. For shorter stays, visitors can purchase six tickets for the price of $7.75, or single tickets at $1.85 apiece. If a trip involves a transfer (from the bus to the Métro or vice versa), the passenger must ask the bus driver for a transfer ticket when boarding or take one from a transfer machine in the Métro station. Free subway maps and timetables for each line are available inside all stations.

For more information on the public transportation system, call: **STCUM**, ☎288-6287 (A-U-T-O-B-U-S).

Taxis

Co-op Taxi: ☎(514) 725-9885.
Diamond: ☎(514) 273-6331.
Taxi LaSalle: ☎(514) 277-25.52

 PRACTICAL INFORMATION

Area code: 514

Tourist Information

Centre Infotouriste (Peel Métro station): 1001 Rue du Square-Dorchester (at the corner of Metcalfe and Square-Dorchester), ☎(514) 873-2015, www.tourisme-montreal.org

The centre is open from 8am to 7pm, every day during summer, and from 9am to 6pm every day from November to April.

There is a small tourist booth in old Montréal, which provides information only on Montréal, at 174 Rue Notre-Dame Est (Champ-de-Mars Métro station)

Foreign Exchange

A number of downtown banks offer currency exchange services. In most cases, there is a service charge. Foreign exchange offices don't always charge a fee, so it is best to inquire beforehand. Most banks are able to exchange U.S. currency.

Bank of America Canada: 1230 Rue Peel, ☎392-9100
National Bank of Canada: 1001 Rue Sainte-Catherine Ouest, ☎281-9640.
Forexco: 1250 Rue Peel, ☎879-1300.
Thomas Cook: 625 Boulevard René-Lévesque Ouest, ☎397-4029.

Automatic teller machines capable of exchanging foreign currency have been installed in Complexe Desjardins (on Sainte-Catherine Ouest, between Jeanne-Mance and Saint-Urbain). They are open from 6am to 2am. These machines can provide Canadian funds in exchange for various foreign currencies, or American or French funds for Canadian currency. There are similar machines at Mirabel Airport.

Post Office

1250 Rue University: ☎283-4506.
1250 Rue Sainte-Catherine Est: ☎522-5191.

 EXPLORING

Vieux-Montréal ★★★

In the 18th century, Montréal, like Québec City, was surrounded by stone fortifications. Between 1801 and 1817, these ramparts were demolished due to the efforts of local merchants, who saw them as an obstacle to the city's development. The network of old streets, compressed after nearly a century, nevertheless remained in place. Today's Vieux-Montréal, or Old Montréal, thus corresponds quite closely to the area covered by the for-tified city. During the 19th century, this area became the hub of commercial and financial activity in Canada. Banks and insurance com-panies built sumptuous head offices here,

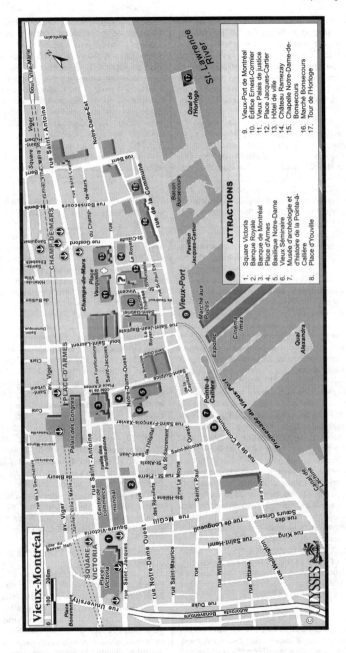

Vieux-Montréal

0 100 200m

St. Lawrence River

ATTRACTIONS

1. Square Victoria
2. Banque Royale
3. Banque de Montréal
4. Place d'Armes
5. Basilique Notre-Dame
6. Vieux Séminaire
7. Musée d'archéologie et d'histoire de la Pointe-à-Callière
8. Place d'Youville
9. Vieux-Port de Montréal
10. Édifice Ernest-Cormier
11. Vieux Palais de justice
12. Place Jacques-Cartier
13. Hôtel de ville
14. Château Ramezay
15. Chapelle Notre-Dame-de-Bonsecours
16. Marché Bonsecours
17. Tour de l'Horloge

QUÉBEC

leading to the demolition of almost all the buildings erected under the French Regime. The area was later abandoned for nearly 40 years in favour of the modern downtown area of today. Finally, the long process of putting new life into Old Montréal got underway during the preparations for Expo '67, and continues today with numerous conversion and restoration projects.

In the 19th century, **Square Victoria** was a Victorian garden surrounded by Second-Empire and Renaissance-Revival-style stores and office buildings. The narrow building at 751 Rue McGill is the only one to survive from that era. North of Rue Saint-Antoine, visitors will find a **statue of Queen Victoria**, executed in 1872 by English sculptor Marshall Wood, as well as an authentic Art-Nouveau-style **Parisian Métro railing**. The latter, designed by Hector Guimard in 1900 and given to the city of Montréal by the city of Paris for Expo '67, was installed at one of the entrances to the Square-Victoria Métro station.

Rue Saint-Jacques was the main artery of Canadian high finance for over a century. This role is reflected in its rich and varied architecture, which serves as a veritable encyclopedia of styles from 1830 to 1930. In those years, the banks, insurance companies and department stores, as well as the nation's railway and shipping companies, were largely controlled by Scottish Montrealers, who had come to the colonies to make their fortune.

Begun in 1928 according to plans by New York skyscraper specialists York and Sawyer, the former head office of the **Banque Royale ★★** *(360 Rue Saint-Jacques)*, or Royal Bank, was one of the last buildings erected during this era of prosperity. The base of the 22-floor tower is inspired by Florentine palazzos and corresponds to the scale of the neighbouring buildings. Inside the edifice, visitors can admire the high ceilings of this "temple of finance", built at a time when banks needed impressive buildings to win customers' confidence. The walls of the great hall are emblazoned with the heraldic insignia of eight of the 10 Canadian provinces, as well as those of Montréal (St. George's cross) and Halifax (a yellow bird), where the bank was founded in 1861.

The square, which is in fact shaped more like a trapezoid, is surrounded by several noteworthy buildings. The **Banque de Montréal ★★** *(119 Rue Saint-Jacques, Métro Place-d'Armes)*, or Bank of Montreal, founded in 1817 by a group of merchants, is the country's oldest banking institution. Its present head office takes up an entire block on the north side of Place d'Armes. A magnificent building by John Wells built in 1847 and modelled after the Roman Pantheon, it occupies the place of honour in the centre of the block and offers customer banking. Its Corinthian portico is a monument to the commercial power of the Scottish merchants who founded the institution. The capitals of the columns, severely damaged by pollution, were replaced in 1970 with aluminum replicas. The pediment includes a bas-relief depicting the bank's coat of arms carved out of Binney stone in Scotland by Her Majesty's sculptor, Sir John Steele.

Under the French Regime, **Place d'Armes ★★** was the heart of the city. Used for military manoeuvres and religious processions, the square was also the location of the Gadoys well, the city's main source of potable water. In 1847, the square was transformed into a lovely, fenced-in Victorian garden, which was destroyed at the beginning of the 20th century in order to make room for a tramway terminal. In the meantime, a **monument to Maisonneuve** was erected in 1895. Executed by sculptor Philippe Hébert, it shows the founder of Montréal, Paul de Chomedey, Sieur de Maisonneuve, surrounded by prominent figures from the city's early history, namely Jeanne Mance, founder of the Hôtel-Dieu (hospital), Lambert Closse, along with his dog Pilote, and Charles Lemoyne, head of a family of famous explorers. An Iroquois warrior completes the tableau.

In 1663, the seigneury of the island of Montréal was acquired by the Sulpicians from Paris, who remained its undisputed masters up until the British conquest of 1760. In addition to distributing land to colonists and laying out the city's first streets, the Sulpicians were responsible for the construction of a large number of buildings, including Montréal's first parish church (1673). Dedicated to Notre Dame (Our Lady), this church had a beautiful Baroque façade, which faced straight down the centre of the street of the same name, creating a pleasant perspective characteristic of classical French town-planning. At the beginning of the 19th century, however, this rustic little church cut a sorry figure when compared to the Anglican cathedral on Rue Notre-Dame and the new Catholic cathedral on Rue Saint-Denis, neither of which remains today. The Sulpicians therefore decided to make a decisive move to surpass their rivals once and for all. In 1823, to the great displeasure of local architects, they commissioned New York architect James O'Donnell, who came from an Irish Protestant background, to design the largest and most original church north of Mexico.

Basilique Notre-Dame ★★★ *(110 Rue Notre-Dame Ouest, ☎842-2925)*, built between 1824 and 1829, is a true North American masterpiece of Gothic-Revival architecture. It should be seen not as a replica of a European cathedral, but rather as a fundamentally neoclassical structure characteristic of the Industrial Revolution, complemented by a medieval-style decor, which foreshadowed the historicism of the Victorian era. These elements make the building remarkable. O'Donnell was so pleased with his work that he converted to Catholicism before dying so that he could be buried under the church. Between 1874 and 1880, the original interior, considered too austere, was replaced by the fabulous polychromatic decorations found today. Executed by Victor Bourgeau, then the leading architect of religious buildings in the Montréal region, along with about 50 artists, it is made entirely of wood, painted and gilded with gold leaf. Particularly noteworthy features include the baptistery, decorated with frescoes by Ozias Leduc, and the powerful electro-pneumatic Casavant organ with its 5,772 pipes, often used during the numerous concerts given at the basilica. Lastly, there are the stained-glass windows by Francis Chigot, a master glass artist from France, which depict various episodes in the history of Montréal. They were installed in honour of the church's 100th anniversary.

To the right of the chancel, a passage leads to the Chapelle du Sacré-Cœur (Sacred Heart Chapel), added to the back of the church in 1888. Nicknamed the Chapelle des Mariages (Wedding Chapel) because of the countless nuptials held there every year, it was seriously damaged by fire in 1978. The spiral staircases and the side galleries are all that remain of the exuberant, Spanish-style Gothic-Revival decor of the original. The architects Jodoin, Lamarre and Pratte decided to tie these vestiges in with a modern design, completed in 1981, and included a lovely sectioned vault with skylights, a large bronze reredos by Charles Daudelin and a Guilbault-Thérien mechanical organ.

The **Vieux Séminaire** ★ *(116 Rue Notre-Dame Ouest)*, or old seminary, was built in 1683 in the style of a Parisian *hôtel particulier*, with a courtyard in front and a garden in back. It is the oldest building in the city. For more than three centuries, it has been occupied by Sulpician priests, who, under the French Regime, used it as a manor from which they managed their vast seigneury. At the time of the building's construction, Montréal had barely 500 inhabitants, and was constantly being terrorized by Iroquois attacks. Under those circumstances, the seminary, albeit modest in appearance, represented a precious haven of European civilization in the middle of a wild, isolated land. The public clock at the top of the façade was installed in 1701, and may be the oldest one of its kind in the Americas.

The **Musée d'Archéologie et d'Histoire de la Pointe-à-Callière** ★★ *(8$; Sep to Jun, Tue to Fri 10am to 5pm, Sat and Sun 11am to 5pm; Jul to Sep, Tue to Fri 10am to 6pm, Sat and Sun 11am to 6pm; 350 Place Royale, Pointe-à-Callière, ☎872-9150)*. This archaeology and history museum lies on the exact site where Montréal was founded on May 18, 1642. The Rivière Saint-Pierre used to flow alongside the area now occupied by Place d'Youville, while the muddy banks of the St. Lawrence reached almost as far as the present-day Rue de la Commune. The first colonists built Fort Ville-Marie out of earth and wooden posts on the isolated point of land created by these two bodies of water. Threatened by Iroquois flotillas and flooding, the leaders of the colony soon decided to establish the town on Coteau Saint-Louis, the hill now bisected by Rue Notre-Dame. The site of the fort was then occupied by a cemetery and the château of Governor de Callière, hence the name.

The museum uses the most advanced techniques available to provide visitors with a survey of the city's history. Attractions include a multimedia presentation, a visit to the vestiges discovered on the site, excellent models showing the different stages of Place Royale's development, holographic conversations and thematic exhibitions. Designed by architect Dan Hanganu, the museum was erected for the celebrations of the city's 350th anniversary in 1992.

Stretching from Place Royale to Rue McGill, **Place d'Youville** owes its elongated shape to its location on top of the bed of the Rivière Saint-Pierre, which was canalized in 1832. In the middle of the square stands the **Centre d'Histoire de Montréal** *($4.50; May to Sep, every day 9am to 5pm; Sep to May, closed Mon 10am to 5pm, closed Dec 8 to Jan 5; 335 Place d'Youville, ☎872-3207)*, a small, unpretentious historical museum presenting

QUÉBEC

temporary exhibitions on various themes related to life in Montréal. The building itself is the former fire station number 3, one of only a few examples of Flemish-style architecture in Québec. The Marché Sainte-Anne once lay to the west of Rue Saint-Pierre and was, from 1840 to 1849, the seat of the Parliament of United Canada. In 1849, the Orangemen burned the building after a law intended to compensate both French and English victims of the rebellion of 1837-38 was adopted. The event marked the end of Montréal's political vocation.

The Port of Montréal is the largest inland port on the continent. It stretches 25 kilometres along the St. Lawrence, from Cité du Havre to the refineries in the east end. The **Vieux-Port de Montréal ★★**, or old port, corresponds to the historic portion of the port, located in front of the old city. Abandoned because of its obsolescence, it was revamped between 1983 and 1992, following the example of various other centrally-located North American ports. The old port encompasses a pleasant park, laid out on the embankments and coupled with a promenade, which runs alongside the piers or *quai*, offering a "window" on the river and the few shipping activities that have fortunately been maintained. The layout accents the view of the water, the downtown area and Rue de la Commune, whose wall of neoclassical, grey stone warehouses stands before the city, one of the only examples of so-called "waterfront planning" in North America.

From the port, visitors can set off on an excursion on the river and the Lachine canal aboard **Le Bateau Mouche** *($18, children $9; May to Oct, departures every day at 10am, noon, 2pm, 4pm, 7pm; Quai Jacques-Cartier; ☎849-9952)*, whose glass roof enables passengers to fully appreciate the beauty of the surroundings.

From the time it was inaugurated in 1926 until it closed in 1970, the **Édifice Ernest-Cormier ★** *(100 Rue Notre-Dame Est)* was used for criminal proceedings. The former courthouse was converted into a conservatory, and was named after its architect, the illustrious Ernest Cormier, who also designed the main pavilion of the Université de Montréal and the doors of the United Nations Headquarters in New York City. The Courthouse is graced with outstanding bronze sconces, cast in Paris at the workshops of Edgar Brandt. Their installation in 1925 ushered in the Art Deco style in Canada. The main hall, faced with travertine and topped

by three dome-shaped skylights, is worth a quick visit.

The **Vieux Palais de Justice ★** *(155 Rue Notre-Dame Est)*, the oldest courthouse in Montréal, was built between 1849 and 1856, according to a design by John Ostell and Henri-Maurice Perrault, on the site of the first courthouse, which was erected in 1800. It is another fine example of Canadian neoclassical architecture. After the courts were divided in 1926, the old Palais was used for civil cases, judged according to the Napoleonic Code. Since the opening of the new Palais to its left, the old Palais has been converted into an annex of City Hall, located to the right.

Place Jacques-Cartier ★ was laid out on the site once occupied by the Château de Vaudreuil, which burned down in 1803. The former Montréal residence of the governor of New France was without question the most elegant private home in the city. Designed by engineer Gaspard Chaussegros de Léry in 1723, it had a horseshoe-shaped staircase, leading up to a handsome cut-stone portal, two projecting pavilions (one on each side of the main part of the building), and a formal garden that extended as far as Rue Notre-Dame. After the fire, the property was purchased by local merchants, who decided to give the government a small strip of land, on the condition that a public market be established there, thus increasing the value of the adjacent property, which remained in private hands. This explains Place Jacques-Cartier's oblong shape.

The **Hôtel de Ville ★** *(275 Rue Notre-Dame Est)*, or City Hall, a fine example of the Second-Empire or Napoleon III style, is the work of Henri-Maurice Perrault, who also designed the neighbouring courthouse. In 1922, a fire destroyed the interior and roof of the building, later restored in 1926, after the model of the city hall in Tours, France. Exhibitions are occasionally presented in the main hall, which is accessible via the main entrance. Visitors may also be interested to know that it was from the balcony of City Hall that France's General de Gaulle cried out his famous "*Vive le Québec libre!*" ("Freedom for Québec!") in 1967, to the great delight of the crowd gathered in front of the building.

The humblest of all the "châteaux" built in Montréal, the **Château Ramezay ★★** *($5; summer, every day 10am to 6pm; rest of the year, Tue to Sun 10am to 4:30pm; schedule subject to change; 280 Rue Notre-Dame Est,*

QUÉBEC

Hôtel de Ville

☎861-3708), is the only one still standing. It was built in 1705 for the governor of Montréal, Claude de Ramezay, and his family.

In 1896, after serving as the first building of the Montréal branch of the Université Laval in Québec City, the château was converted into a museum, under the patronage of the Société d'Histoire et de Numismatique de Montréal (Montréal Numismatic and Antiquarian Society), founded by Jacques Viger. Visitors will still find a rich collection of furniture, clothing and everyday objects from the 18th and 19th centuries here, as well as a large number of native artefacts. The Salle de Nantes is decorated with beautiful Louis XV-style mahogany panelling, designed by Germain Boffrand and imported from the Nantes office of the Compagnie des Indes (circa 1750).

The present **Chapelle Notre-Dame-de-Bonsecours** ★ *(400 Rue Saint-Paul Est, ☎845-9991)* dates back to 1771, when the Sulpicians wanted to establish a branch of the main parish in the eastern part of the fortified city. In 1890, the chapel was modified to suit contemporary tastes, and the present stone façade was added, along with the "aerial"

chapel looking out on the port. Parishioners asked God's blessing on ships and their crews bound for Europe from this chapel. The interior, redone at the same time, contains a large number of votive offerings from sailors saved from shipwrecks. Some are in the form of model ships, hung from the ceiling of the nave. At the back of the chapel, the little **Musée Marguerite-Bourgeoys** *($2; May to Oct, Tue to Sun 9am to 4:30pm; Nov to Apr 10:30am to 4:30pm)* displays mementos of the saint. From there, visitors can reach a platform adjoining the "aerial" chapel, which offers an interesting view of the old port.

The **Marché Bonsecours** ★★ *(350 Rue Saint-Paul Est, ☎872-7730)* was erected between 1845 and 1850. The lovely grey stone neoclassical edifice with sash windows, was erected on **Rue Saint-Paul**, for many years Montréal's main commercial artery. The building is adorned with a portico supported by cast-iron columns moulded in England, and topped by a silvery dome, which for many years served as the symbol of the city at the entrance to the port. The public market, closed since the early sixties following the advent of the supermarket, was transformed into municipal offices then an exhibition hall before finally reopening partially in 1996. The building originally housed both the city hall and a concert hall upstairs.

The **Tour de l'Horloge** ★ *(at the end of the Quai de l'Horloge; May to Oct)* is visible to the east from the end of Quai Jacques-Cartier. Painted a pale yellow, the structure is actually a monument erected in 1922 in memory of merchant marine sailors who died during the First World War.

Downtown ★★★

The downtown skyscrapers give Montréal a typically North American look. Nevertheless, unlike most other cities on the continent, there is a certain Latin spirit here, which seeps in between the towering buildings, livening up this part of Montréal both day and night. Bars, cafés, department stores, shops and head offices, along with two universities and numerous colleges, all lie clustered within a limited area at the foot of Mont Royal.

At the beginning of the 20th century, Montréal's central business district gradually shifted from the old city to what was up until then a posh residential neighbourhood known as The Golden Square Mile, inhabited by upper-class Canadians. Wide arterial streets such as Boulevard René-Lévesque were then lined with palatial residences surrounded by shady gardens. The city centre underwent a radical transformation in a very short time (1960-1967), marked by the construction of Place Ville-Marie, the Métro, the underground city, Place des Arts, and various other infrastructures which still exert an influence on the area's development.

The **Musée des Beaux-Arts de Montréal** ★★★ *(free admission for permanent collection; $10, students $5 for temporary exhibits, half-price Wed 5:30pm to 9pm; Tue to Sun 11am to 6pm, Wed until 9pm; 1380 Rue Sherbrooke Ouest, ☎285-1600)*, Montréal's Museum of Fine Arts, the oldest and most important museum in Québec, was founded in 1860 by the Art Association of Montreal, a group of Anglo-Saxon art lovers. The Pavillon Beniah-Gibb, on the north side of Rue Sherbrooke *(1379 Rue Sherbrooke Ouest)*, opened its doors in 1912. Its façade, made of white Vermont marble, is the work of the Scottish merchants' favourite architects, the prolific Edward and William Sutherland Maxwell. The building

became too small for the museum's collection, and was enlarged towards the back on three different occasions. Finally, in 1991, architect Moshe Safdie designed the Pavillon Jean-Noël-Desmarais, just opposite on the south side of Rue Sherbrooke. This new wing includes the red brick façade of a former apartment building, and is linked to the original building by tunnels under Rue Sherbrooke. The museum's main entrance is now in the new wing, at the corner of Rue Crescent.

At Montréal's **Musée des Arts Décoratifs** *($4; Tue to Sun 11am to 6pm, Wed 11am to 9pm; 2200 Rue Crescent, ☎259-2575)*, visitors can see International-style (1935 to the present day) furniture and decorative objects from the Liliane and David Stewart collection, as well as travelling exhibitions on glass, textiles, etc.

The last of Montréal's grand old hotels, the **Ritz-Carlton Kempinski** ★ *(1228 Rue Sherbrooke Ouest)* was inaugurated in 1911 by César Ritz himself. For many years, it was the favourite gathering place of the Montréal bourgeoisie. Some people even stayed here year-round, living a life of luxury among the drawing rooms, garden and ballroom. The building was designed by Warren and Wetmore of New York City, the well-known architects of Grand Central Station on New York's Park Avenue. Many celebrities have stayed at this sophisticated luxury hotel over the years, including Richard Burton and Elizabeth Taylor, who were married here in 1964.

Montréal has the most extensive **underground city** in the world (see p 184). Greatly appreciated in bad weather, it provides access to over 2,000 shops and restaurants, as well as movie theatres, apartment and office buildings, hotels, parking lots, the train station, the bus station, Place des Arts and even the Université du Québec à Montréal (UQAM) via tunnels, atriums and indoor plazas. The **Cours Mont-Royal** ★★ *(1455 Rue Peel)* are duly linked to this sprawling network, which centres around the various Métro stations. A multi-purpose complex, the Cours consist of four levels of stores, offices and apartments laid out inside the former Mount Royal Hotel.

The **Édifice Sun Life** ★★ *(1155 Rue Metcalfe)*, erected between 1913 and 1933 for the powerful Sun Life insurance company, was for many years the largest building in the British Empire. It was in this "fortress" of the Anglo-Saxon establishment, with its colonnades reminiscent of ancient mythology, that the

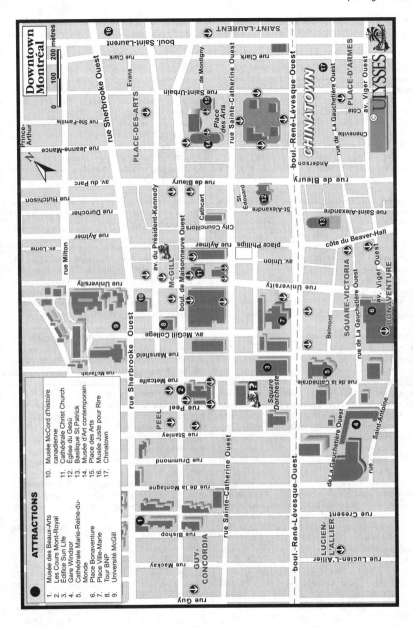

ATTRACTIONS

1. Musée des Beaux-Arts
2. Les Cours Mont-Royal
3. Édifice Sun Life
4. Gare Windsor
5. Cathédrale Marie-Reine-du-Monde
6. Place Bonaventure
7. Place Ville-Marie
8. Tour BNP
9. Université McGill
10. Musée McCord d'histoire canadienne
11. Cathédrale Christ Church
12. Église du Gesù
13. Basilique St-Patrick
14. Musée d'Art contemporain
15. Place des Arts
16. Musée Juste pour Rire
17. Chinatown

Downtown Montréal

0   100   200 mètres

© ULYSSES

British Crown Jewels were hidden during the Second World War. In 1977, the company's head office was moved to Toronto, in protest against provincial language laws excluding English. Fortunately, the chimes that ring at 5pm every day are still in place and remain an integral part of the neighbourhood's spirit.

A number of churches clustered around Square Dorchester before it was even laid out in 1872. Unfortunately, only two of the eight churches built in the area between 1865 and 1875 have survived. One of these is the beautiful Gothic-Revival-style **St. George's Anglican Church ★★** *(at the corner of Rue de la Gauchetière and Rue Peel)*. Its delicately sculpted sandstone exterior conceals an interior covered with lovely, dark woodwork. Particularly noteworthy are the remarkable ceiling, with its exposed framework, the woodwork in the chancel, and the tapestry from Westminster Abbey, used during the coronation of Elizabeth II.

In 1887, the head of Canadian Pacific, William Cornelius Van Horne, asked his New York friend Bruce Price (1845-1903) to draw up the plans for **Gare Windsor ★** *(at the corner of Rue de la Gauchetière and Rue Peel)*, a modern train station, which would serve as the terminus of the transcontinental railroad, completed the previous year. At the time, Price was one of the most prominent architects in the eastern United States, where he worked on residential projects for high-society clients, as well as skyscrapers like the American Surety Building in Manhattan. Later, he was put in charge of building the Château Frontenac in Québec City, thus establishing the Château style in Canada.

Cathédrale Marie-Reine-du-Monde ★★ *(Boulevard René-Lévesque Ouest at the corner of Mansfield)* is the seat of the archdiocese of Montréal and a reminder of the tremendous power wielded by the clergy up until the Quiet Revolution. It is exactly one third the size of St. Peter's in Rome. In 1852, a terrible fire destroyed the Catholic cathedral on Rue Saint-Denis. The ambitious Monseigneur Ignace Bourget (1799-1885), who was bishop of Montréal at the time, seized the opportunity to work out a grandiose scheme to outshine the Sulpicians' Basilique Notre-Dame and ensure the supremacy of the Catholic Church in Montréal. What could accomplish these goals better than a replica of Rome's St. Peter's, right in the middle of the Protestant neighbourhood? Despite reservations on the part of architect Victor Bourgeau, the plan was carried out. The bishop even made Bourgeau go

to Rome to measure the venerable building. Construction began in 1870 and was finally completed in 1894. Copper statues of the 13 patron saints of Montréal's parishes were installed in 1900.

An immense, grooved concrete block with no façade, **Place Bonaventure ★** *(1 Place Bonaventure)*, which was completed in 1966, is one of the most revolutionary works of modern architecture of its time. Designed by Montrealer Raymond Affleck, it is a multi-purpose complex built on top of the railway lines leading into the Gare Centrale. It contains a parking area, a two-level shopping centre linked to the Métro and the underground city, two large exhibition halls, wholesalers, offices, and an intimate 400-room hotel laid out around a charming hanging garden, worth a short visit.

A railway tunnel leading under Mont Royal to the downtown area was built in 1913. The tracks ran under Avenue McGill College, then multiplied at the bottom of a deep trench, which stretched between Rue Mansfield and Rue University. In 1938, the subterranean **Gare Centrale** was built, marking the true starting point of the underground city. Camouflaged since 1957 by the **Hôtel Reine-Elizabeth**, the Queen Elizabeth Hotel, it has an interesting, streamline-Deco waiting hall. **Place Ville-Marie ★★★** *(1 Place Ville-Marie, Métro Bonaventure)*, was erected above the northern part of the formerly open-air trench in 1959. The famous Chinese-American architect Ieoh Ming Pei (Louvre Pyramid, Paris; East Building of the National Gallery, Washington, D.C.) designed the multipurpose complex built over the railway tracks and containing vast shopping arcades now linked to most of the surrounding edifices. It also encompasses a number of office buildings, including the famous cruciform aluminum tower, whose unusual shape enables natural light to penetrate all the way into the centre of the structure, while at the same time symbolizing Montréal, a Catholic city dedicated to the Virgin Mary.

In the middle of the public area, a granite compass card indicates true north, while **Avenue McGill College**, which leads straight toward the mountain, indicates "north" as perceived by Montrealers in their everyday life. This artery, lined with multicoloured skyscrapers, was still a narrow residential street in 1950. It now offers a wide view of Mont Royal, crowned by a metallic cross erected in 1927 to commemorate the gesture of Paul Chomedey de Maisonneuve, founder of

Montréal, who climbed the mountain in January 1643 and placed a wooden cross at its summit to thank the Virgin Mary for having spared Fort Ville-Marie from a devastating flood.

The **Tour BNP** ★ *(1981 Avenue McGill College)*, certainly the best designed building on Avenue McGill College, was built for the Banque Nationale de Paris in 1981, by the architectural firm Webb, Zerafa, Menkès, Housden Partnership (Tour Elf-Aquitaine, Paris; Royal Bank, Toronto). Its bluish glass walls set off a sculpture entitled *La Foule Illuminée* (The Illuminated Crowd), by the Franco-British artist Raymond Mason.

McGill University ★★ *(805 Rue Sherbrooke Ouest, McGill Métro)* was founded in 1821, thanks to a donation by fur-trader James McGill. It is the oldest of Montréal's four universities. Throughout the 19th century, the institution was one of the finest jewels of the Golden Square Mile's Scottish bourgeoisie. The university's main campus lies nestled in greenery at the foot of Mont Royal. The entrance is located at the northernmost end of Avenue McGill College, at the Roddick Gates, which contain the university's clock and chimes. On the right are two Romanesque-Revival-style buildings, designed by Sir Andrew Taylor to house the physics (1893) and chemistry (1896) departments. The Faculty of Architecture now occupies the second building. A little farther along, visitors will see the Macdonald Engineering Building, a fine example of the English baroque-revival style, with a broken pediment adorning its rusticated portal (Percy Nobbs, 1908). At the end of the drive stands the oldest building on campus, the Arts Building (1839). For three decades, this austere neoclassical structure by architect John Ostell was McGill University's only building. It houses Moyse Hall, a lovely theatre dating back to 1926, with a design inspired by antiquity (Harold Lea Fetherstonaugh, architect).

The **Musée McCord d'Histoire Canadienne** ★★ *($8, free on Sat 10am to noon; Jun to mid-Oct, every day 10am to 6pm; mid-Oct to May, Tue to Fri 10am to 6pm, Sat and Sun 10am to 5pm; 690 Rue Sherbrooke Ouest, McGill Métro, ☎398-7100)*, the McCord Museum of Canadian History, occupies a building formerly used by the McGill University Students' Association. Designed by architect Percy Nobbs (1906), this handsome building of English baroque inspiration was enlarged toward the back in 1991. Along Rue Victoria, visitors can see an interesting sculpture by Pierre Granche

entitled *Totem Urbain/Histoire en Dentelle* (Urban totem/History in lace). For anyone interested in aboriginals and daily life in Canada in the 18th and 19th centuries, this is *the* museum to see in Montréal. It houses a large ethnographic collection, as well as collections of costumes, decorative arts, paintings, prints and photographs, including the famous Notman collection, composed of 700,000 glass plates and constituting a veritable portrait of Canada at the end of the 19th century.

The first Anglican cathedral in Montréal stood on Rue Notre-Dame, not far from Place d'Armes. After a fire in 1856, **Christ Church Cathedral** ★★ *(at the corner of Rue University)* was relocated nearer the community it served, in the heart of the nascent Golden Square Mile. Using the cathedral of his hometown, Salisbury, as his model, architect Frank Wills designed a flamboyant structure, with a single steeple rising above the transepts. The soberness of the interior contrasts with the rich ornamentation of the Catholic churches included in this walking tour. A few beautiful stained-glass windows from the workshops of William Morris provide the only bit of colour.

After a 40-year absence, the Jesuits returned to Montréal in 1842 at Monseigneur Ignace Bourget's invitation. Six years later, they founded Collège Sainte-Marie, where several generations of boys would receive an outstanding education. **Église du Gesù** ★★ *(1202 Rue de Bleury)* was originally designed as the college chapel. The grandiose project begun in 1864 according to plans drawn up by architect Patrick C. Keely of Brooklyn, New York was never completed, due to lack of funds. Consequently, the church's Renaissance-Revival-style towers remain unfinished. The *trompe-l'œil* decor inside was executed by artist Damien Müller. Of particular interest are the seven main altars and surrounding parquetry, all fine examples of cabinet work. The large paintings hanging from the walls were commissioned from the Gagliardi brothers of Rome. The Jesuit college, erected to the south of the church, was demolished in 1975, but the church was fortunately saved, and then restored in 1983.

Fleeing misery and potato blight, a large number of Irish immigrants came to Montréal between 1820 and 1860, and helped construct the Lachine canal and the Victoria bridge. **St. Patrick's Basilica** ★★ *(Rue Saint-Alexandre)*, was thus built to meet a pressing new demand for a church to serve the Irish Catholic community. When it was inaugurated in 1847, St. Patrick's dominated the city below. Today, it is well hidden by the skyscrapers of the business centre. Architect Pierre-Louis Morin and Père Félix Martin, the Jesuit superior, designed the plans for the edifice, built in the Gothic Revival style favoured by the Sulpicians, who financed the project. One of the many paradoxes surrounding St. Patrick's is that it is more representative of French than Anglo-Saxon Gothic architecture. The high, dark interior encourages prayer. Each of the pine columns that divide the nave into three sections is a whole tree trunk, carved in one piece.

Formerly located at Cité du Havre, the **Musée d'Art Contemporain ★★** *($6; Tue to Sun 11am to 6pm, half-price on Wed 6pm to 9pm; 185 Rue Sainte-Catherine Ouest, at the corner of Rue Jeanne-Mance, ☎847-6212)*, Montréal's modern art museum, was moved to this site in 1992. The long, low building, erected on top of the Place des Arts parking lot, contains eight rooms, where post-1940 works of art from both Québec and abroad are exhibited. The interior, which has a decidedly better design than the exterior, is laid out around a circular hall. On the lower level, an amusing metal sculpture by Pierre Granche entitled *Comme si le temps... de la rue* (As if time... from the street), shows Montréal's network of streets crowded with helmeted birds, in a sort of semicircular theatre.

During the rush of the Quiet Revolution, the government of Québec, inspired by cultural complexes like New York's Lincoln Center, built **Place des Arts ★** *(260 Boulevard de Maisonneuve Ouest, through to Rue Sainte-Catherine Ouest, Métro Place-des-Arts)*, a collection of five halls for the performing arts. Salle Wilfrid Pelletier, in the centre, was inaugurated in 1963 (2,982 seats). It accommodates both the Montreal Symphony Orchestra and the Opéra de Montréal. The cube-shaped Théâtre Maisonneuve, on the right, contains three theatres, Théâtre Maisonneuve (1,460 seats), Théâtre Jean-Duceppe (755 seats) and the intimate little Café de la Place (138 seats). The Cinquième Salle (350 seats) was built in 1992 in the course of the construction of the Musée d'Art Contemporain. Place des Arts is linked to the governmental section of the underground city, which stretches from the Palais des Congrès convention centre to Avenue du Président-Kennedy. Developed by the various levels of government, this portion of the underground

network distinguishes itself from the private section, centred around Place Ville-Marie, further west.

Set up inside the former buildings of the Ekers brewery, the **Musée Juste Pour Rire ★★** *(opens in Jun, call for schedule and exhibition information; 2111 Boulevard Saint-Laurent, Saint-Laurent Métro, ☎845-4000)*, or Just for Laughs Museum, opened in 1993. This museum, the only one of its kind in the world, explores the different facets of humour, using a variety of film clips and sets. Visitors are equipped with infrared headphones, which enable them to follow the presentation. The building itself was renovated and redesigned by architect Luc Laporte, and has some 3,000 square meters of exhibition space.

Montréal's **Chinatown ★** may be rather small, but it is nonetheless a pleasant place to walk around. A large number of the Chinese who came to Canada to help build the transcontinental railroad, completed in 1886, settled here at the end of the 19th century. Though they no longer live in the neighbourhood, they still come here on weekends to stroll about and stock up on traditional products. Rue de la Gauchetière has been converted into a pedestrian street lined with restaurants and framed by lovely Chinese-style gates.

Shaughnessy Village ★★

When the Sulpicians took possession of the island of Montréal in 1663, they kept a portion of the best land for themselves, then set up a farm and a native village there in 1676. Following a fire, the aboriginal village was relocated several times before being permanently established in Oka. A part of the farm, corresponding to the area now known as Westmount, was then granted to French settlers. The Sulpicians planted an orchard and a vineyard on the remaining portion. Starting around 1870, the land was separated into lots. Part of it was used for the construction of mansions, while large plots were awarded to Catholic communities allied with the Sulpicians. It was at this time that Shaughnessy House was built — hence the name of the neighbourhood. During the 1970s, the number of local inhabitants increased considerably, making Shaughnessy Village the most densely populated area in Québec.

The Sulpicians' farmhouse was surrounded by a wall linked to four stone corner towers, earning it the name Fort des Messieurs. The house was destroyed when the **Grand Séminaire** ★★ (1854-1860) *(2065 Rue Sherbrooke Ouest)* was built, but two towers, erected in the 17th century according to plans by François Vachon de Belmont, superior of the Montréal Sulpicians, can still be found in the institution's shady gardens. It was in one of these that Saint Marguerite Bourgeoys taught young native girls. Around 1880, the long neoclassical buildings of the Grand Séminaire, designed by architect John Ostell, were topped by a mansard roof by Henri-Maurice Perrault. Information panels, set up on Rue Sherbrooke, directly in line with Rue du Fort, provide precise details about the farm buildings.

Founded in 1979 by Phyllis Lambert, the **Centre Canadien d'Architecture** ★★★ *($5, students $3, free Thu 6pm to 8pm; Jun to Sep, Tue to Sun 11am to 6pm, Thu to 9pm; Oct to May, Wed to Fri 11am to 6pm, Thu to 8pm; Sat and Sun 11am to 5pm; address, ☎939-7026)*, or Canadian Centre for Architecture, is both a museum and a centre for the study of world architecture. Its collections of plans, drawings, models, books and photographs are the most important of their kind in the entire world. The Centre, erected between 1985 and 1989, has six exhibition rooms, a bookstore, a library, a 217-seat auditorium and a wing specially designed for researchers, as well as vaults and restoration laboratories. The main building, shaped like a "U," was designed by Peter Rose, with the help of Phyllis Lambert. It is covered with grey limestone from the Saint-Marc quarries near Québec City. This material, which used to be extracted from the Plateau Mont-Royal and Rosemont quarries in Montréal, adorns the façades of many of the city's houses.

The centre surrounds the **Maison Shaughnessy** ★, whose façade looks out on Boulevard René-Lévesque Ouest. This house is in fact a pair of residences, built in 1874 according to a design by architect William Tutin Thomas. It is representative of the mansions that once lined Boulevard René-Lévesque (formerly Boulevard Dorchester). In 1974, it was at the centre of an effort to salvage the neighbourhood, which had been torn down in a number of places.

The amusing **architecture garden**, by artist Melvin Charney, lies across from Shaughnessy House, between two highway on-ramps. It illustrates the different stages of the neighbourhood's development, using a portion of the Sulpicians' orchard on the left, stone lines to indicate borders of 19th-century properties and rose bushes reminiscent of the gardens of those houses.

The **Couvent des Sœurs Grises** ★★ *(1185 Rue Saint-Mathieu)* is the product of an architectural tradition developed over the centuries in Québec. The chapel alone reveals a foreign influence, namely the Romanesque Revival style favoured by the Sulpicians, as opposed to the Renaissance and baroque revival styles preferred by the church.

Mont Royal and Westmount ★★

Montréal's central neighbourhoods are distributed around Mont Royal, an important landmark in the cityscape. Known simply as "the mountain" by Montrealers, this squat mass, measuring 234 metres at its highest point, is composed of intrusive rock. It is in fact one of the seven hills studding the St. Lawrence plain in the Montérégie region. A "green lung" rising up at the far end of downtown streets, it exerts a positive influence on Montrealers, who, as a result, never lose touch with nature. The mountain actually has three summits; the first is occupied by Parc du Mont-Royal, the second by the Université de Montréal, and the third by Westmount, an independent city with lovely English-style homes. In addition to these areas, there are the Catholic, Protestant and Jewish cemeteries, which, considered as a whole, form the largest necropolis in North America.

From the **Belvédère Camilien-Houde** ★★ *(Voie Camilien-Houde)*, a lovely scenic viewpoint, visitors can look out over the entire eastern portion of Montréal. The Plateau Mont-Royal lies in the foreground, a uniform mass of duplexes and triplexes, pierced in a few places by the oxidized copper bell towers of parish churches, while the Rosemont and Maisonneuve quarters lie in the background, with the Olympic Stadium towering over them. In clear weather, the oil refineries in the east end can be seen in the distance. The St. Lawrence River, visible on the right, is actually 1.5 kilometres wide at its narrowest point. The Belvédère Camilien-Houde is Montréal's version of Inspiration Point and a favourite gathering place of sweethearts with cars.

QUÉBEC

Pressured by the residents of the Golden Square Mile (see p 164), who saw their favourite playground being deforested by various firewood companies, the City of Montréal created **Parc du Mont-Royal** ★★★ in 1870. Frederick Law Olmsted (1822-1903), the celebrated designer of New York's Central Park, was commissioned to design the park. He decided to preserve the site's natural character, limiting himself to a few lookout points linked by winding paths. Inaugurated in 1876, the park, which covers 101 hectares on the southern part of the mountain, is cherished by Montrealers as a place to enjoy the fresh air.

The **Chalet du Mont Royal** ★★★ *(Mon to Fri 9:30am to 8pm; Parc du Mont-Royal, ☎844-4928)*, located in the centre of the park, was designed by Aristide Beaugrand-Champagne in 1932, as a replacement for the original structure, which was threatening to collapse. During the 1930s and 1940s, big bands gave moonlit concerts on the steps of the building. The interior is decorated with remounted paintings depicting scenes from Canadian history. These were commissioned from some of Québec's great painters, such as Marc-Aurèle Fortin and Paul-Émile Borduas. Nevertheless, people go to the chalet mainly to stroll along the lookout and take in the exceptional view of downtown, best in the late afternoon and in the evening, when the skyscrapers light up the darkening sky.

Both the cemetery and the roads leading to it offer a number of views of the **Oratoire Saint-Joseph** ★★ *(free admission; every day 9am to 5pm, mass between 6:30 am and 9:30pm, nativity scene Nov 15 to Dec 15; 3800 Chemin Queen Mary, ☎733-8211 for information)*. The enormous building topped by a copper dome, the second largest dome in the world after that of St. Peter's in Rome, stands on a hillside, accentuating its mystical aura. From the gate at the entrance, there are over 300 steps to climb to reach the oratory. Small buses are also available for worshippers who do not want to climb the steps. It was built between 1924 and 1956, thanks to the efforts of the blessed Frère André, porter of Collège Notre-Dame (across the street), to whom many miracles are attributed. A veritable religious complex, the oratory is dedicated to both Saint Joseph and its humble creator. It includes the lower and upper basilicas, the crypt of Frère André and two museums, one dedicated to Frère André's life, the other to sacred art. Visitors will also find the porter's first chapel,

built in 1910, a cafeteria, a hostelry and a store selling devotional articles.

After many attempts, Québec City's Université Laval, aiming to preserve its monopoly on French-language university education in Québec, finally opened a branch of its institution in the Château Ramezay. A few years later, it moved to Rue Saint-Denis, giving birth to the Quartier Latin (see p 174). The **Université de Montréal** ★ *(2900 Boulevard Édouard-Montpetit)* finally became autonomous in 1920, enabling its directors to develop grandiose plans. Ernest Cormier (1885-1980) was approached about designing a campus on the north side of Mont Royal. The architect, a graduate of the École des Beaux-Arts in Paris, was one of the first to acquaint North Americans with the Art Deco style.

Westmount is like a piece of Great Britain in North America. Its **City Hall** ★ *(4333 Rue Sherbrooke Ouest)* was built in the Neo-Tudor style, inspired by the architecture of the age of Henry VIII and Elizabeth I, which was regarded during the 1920s as the national style of England, because it issued exclusively from the British Isles. The style is characterized, in part, by horizontal openings with multiple stone transoms, bay windows and flattened arches. The impeccable green of a lawn-bowling club lies at the back, frequented by members wearing their regulation whites.

Westmount Park ★ and the **Westmount Library** ★ *(4575 Rue Sherbrooke Ouest)*. The park was laid out on swampy land in 1895. Four years later, Québec's first public library was erected on the same site. Up until then, religious communities had been the only ones to develop this type of cultural facility, and the province was therefore somewhat behind in this area. The red-brick building is the product of the trends toward eclecticism, picturesqueness and polychromy that characterized the last two decades of the 19th century.

Maisonneuve ★★

In 1883, the city of Maisonneuve was founded in the east part of Montréal thanks to the initiative of farmers and French-Canadian merchants; port facilities expanded into the area and the city's development picked up. Then, in 1918, the formerly autonomous city was annexed to Montréal, becoming one of its major working-class neighbourhoods, with a 90% francophone population. In the course of its history, Maisonneuve has been profoundly influenced by men with grand ideas, who wanted to make this part of the country a place where people could thrive together. Upon taking office at the Maisonneuve town hall in 1910, brothers Marius and Oscar Dufresne instituted a rather ambitious policy of building prestigious Beaux-Arts-style public buildings intended to make "their" city a model of development for French Québec. Then, in 1931, Frère Marie-Victorin founded Montréal's Jardin Botanique (botanical garden) in Maisonneuve; today, it is the second largest in the world. The last major episode in the area's history was in 1971, when Mayor Jean Drapeau initiated construction on the immense sports complex used for the 1976 Olympic Games.

The **Jardin Botanique, Maison de l'Arbre** and **Insectarium** ★★★ *(8.75$ high season, 6.50$ low season; Sep to late Jun, every day 9am to 5pm, summer 9am to 7pm; 4101 Rue Sherbrooke Est, ☎872-1400).* The Jardin Botanique, covering an area of 73 hectares, was begun during the economic crisis of the 1930s on the site of Mont-de-La-Salle, home base of the brothers of the Écoles Chrétiennes. Behind the Art Deco building occupied by the Université de Montréal's institute of biology, visitors will find a stretch of 10 connected greenhouses, which shelter, notably, a precious collection of orchids and the largest grouping of bonsais and *penjings* outside of Asia. The latter includes the famous Wu collection, given to the garden by master Wu Yee-Sun of Hong Kong in 1984.

Thirty outdoor gardens, open from spring through autumn, and designed to inform and amaze visitors, stretch to the north and west of the greenhouses. Particularly noteworthy are the symmetrical display gardens around the restaurant, the Japanese garden and its *sukiya*-style tea pavilion, as well as the very beautiful Chinese Lac de Rêve, or Dream Lake, garden, whose pavilions were designed by artisans who came here from China specifically for the task. Since Montréal is twinned with Shanghai, it was deemed appropriate that it should have the largest such garden outside of Asia.

The northern part of the botanical garden is occupied by an arboretum. The **Maison de l'Arbre**, literally the tree house, was established in this area to familiarize people with the life of a tree. The interactive, permanent exhibit is actually set up in an old tree trunk. There are

displays on the yellow birch, Québec's emblematic tree since 1993. The building's structure, consisting of beams of different types of wood, reminds us how leafy forests really are. Note the play of light and shade from the frame onto the large white wall, meant to resemble trunks and branches. A terrace in the back is an ideal spot from which to contemplate the arboretum's pond; it also leads to a charming little bonsai garden. To reach the Maison de l'Arbre, climb on board the Balade, the shuttle which regularly tours the garden, or use the garden's northern entrance located on Boulevard Rosemont.

The complementary **Insectarium** *(☎872-8753)* is located to the east of the greenhouses. This innovative, living museum invites visitors to discover the fascinating world of insects.

The **Château Dufresne** ★★ *(2929 Rue Jeanne-d'Arc, métro Pie-IX)* is, in fact, two 22-room private mansions behind the same façade, built in 1916 for brothers Marius and Oscar Dufresne, shoe-manufacturers and authors of a grandiose plan to develop Maisonneuve. The plan was abandoned after the onset of the First World War, causing the municipality to go bankrupt. Their home, designed by Marius Dufresne and Parisian architect Jules Renard, was supposed to be the nucleus of a residential upper-class neighbourhood, which never materialized. It is one of the best examples of Beaux-Arts architecture in Montréal. From 1979 to March of 1997, the château was home to the Musée des Arts Décoratifs de Montréal *(☎259-2575)* now located downtown.

The **Stade Olympique** ★★★ *(guided tour $5.25, package with tour and funicular $10.25; guided tours in French at 11am and 2pm, and in English at 12:40pm and 3:40pm; closed mid-Jan to mid-Feb; 4141 Avenue Pierre-de-Coubertin, ☎252-8687)* is also known as the Olympic Stadium and the "Big O". Jean Drapeau was mayor of Montréal from 1954 to 1957, and from 1960 to 1986. He dreamed of great things for "his" city. Endowed with exceptional powers of persuasion and unfailing determination, he saw a number of important projects through to a successful conclusion, including the construction of Place des Arts and the Métro, Montréal's hosting of the World's Fair in 1967 and, of course, the 1976 Summer Olympics. For this last international event, however, it was necessary to equip the city with the appropriate facilities. In spite of the controversy this caused, the city sought out a Parisian visionary to design something

QUÉBEC

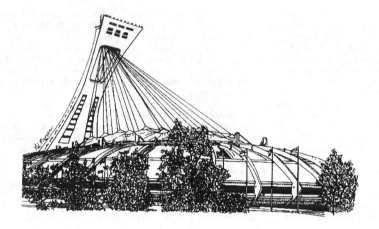

Stade Olympique

completely original. A billion dollars later, the major work of architect Roger Taillibert, who also designed the stadium of the Parc des Princes in Paris, stunned everyone with his curving, organic concrete shapes. The 56,000-seat oval stadium is covered with a kevlar roof supported by cables stretching from the 190-metre leaning tower. In the distance, visitors will see the two pyramid shaped towers of the **Olympic Village**, where the athletes were housed in 1976. Every year, the stadium hosts different events, such as the Salon de l'Auto (Car Show) and the Salon National de l'Habitation (National Home Show). From April to September, Montréal's National League baseball team, the Expos, plays its home games here.

The stadium's tower, which is the tallest leaning tower in the world, was rebaptised the **Tour de Montréal**. A funicular *($7.25; schedule changes frequently, please call for information ☎252-8687)* climbs the structure to an interior observation deck which commands a view of the eastern part of Montreal. Exhibits on the Olympics are presented on the upper levels. There is also a rest area with a bar.

The foot of the tower houses the swimming pools of the Olympic Complex, while the former cycling track, known as the Vélodrome, located nearby, has been converted into an artificial habitat for plants and animals called the **Biodôme** ★★★ *($9.50; every day 9am to 5pm; mid-Jun to early Sep, to 7pm; 4777 Avenue Pierre de Coubertin; ☎868-3000)*. This

new type of museum, associated with the Jardin Botanique, contains four very different ecosystems — the Tropical Rainforest, the Laurentian Forest, the St. Lawrence Marine Ecosystem and the Polar World — within a space of 10,000 square metres. These are complete microcosms, including vegetation, mammals and free-flying birds, and close to real climatic conditions. Be careful not to catch a cold!

Île Sainte-Hélène and Île Notre-Dame ★★

When Samuel de Champlain reached the island of Montréal in 1611, he found a small rocky archipelago located in front of it. He named the largest of these islands in the channel after his wife, Hélène Boulé. Île Sainte-Hélène later became part of the seigneury of Longueuil. Around 1720, the Baroness of Longueuil chose the island as the site for a country house surrounded by a garden. It is also worth noting that in 1760, the island was the last foothold of French troops in New France, commanded by Chevalier François de Lévis. Recognizing Île Saint-Hélène's strategic importance, the British army built a fort on the eastern part of the island at the beginning of the 19th century. The threat of armed conflict with the Americans having diminished, the Canadian government rented Île Sainte-Hélène to the City of Montréal in 1874, at which time the island was turned into a park and linked to Old

Montréal by ferry, and, from 1930 on, by the Jacques-Cartier bridge.

In the early 1960s, Montréal was chosen as the location of the 1967 World's Fair (Expo '67). The city wanted to set up the event on a large, attractive site near the downtown area; a site such as this, however, did not exist. It was thus necessary to build one: using earth excavated during the construction of the Métro tunnel, Île Notre-Dame was created, doubling the area of Île Sainte-Hélène. From April to November 1967, 45 million visitors passed through Cité du Havre, the gateway to the fairground, and crisscrossed both islands. Expo, as Montrealers still refer to it, was more than a jumble of assorted objects; it was Montréal's awakening, during which the city opened itself to the world, and visitors from all over discovered a new art of living, including miniskirts, colour television, hippies, flower power and protest rock.

Parc Hélène-de-Champlain ★★ lies on Île Sainte-Hélène, which originally covered an area of 50 hectares, but was enlarged to over 120 hectares for Expo '67. The original portion corresponds to the raised area studded with boulders made of breccia. Peculiar to the island, breccia is a very hard, ferrous stone that takes on an orange colour when exposed to air for a long time. In 1992, the western part of the island was transformed into a vast open-air amphitheatre, where large-scale shows are presented. On a lovely park bordering the river, across from Montréal, visitors will find *L'Homme* (Man), a large metal sculpture by Alexandre Calder, created for Expo '67.

After the War of 1812 between the United States and Great Britain, the **Fort de l'Île Sainte-Hélène** ★★ was built so that Montréal could be properly defended if ever a new conflict were to erupt. The construction, supervised by military engineer Elias Walker Durnford, was completed in 1825. Built of breccia stone, the fort is in the shape of a jagged "U", surrounding a drill ground, used today by the Compagnie Franche de la Marine and the 78th Regiment of the Fraser Highlanders as a parade ground. These two costumed mock regiments delight visitors by reviving Canada's French and Scottish military traditions. The drill ground also offers a lovely view of both the port and **Pont Jacques-Cartier**, inaugurated in 1930, which straddles the island, separating the park from La Ronde.

The arsenal is now occupied by the **Musée David-M.-Stewart** ★★ *($5; Sep to May, Wed to Mon 10am to 5pm; Jun to Aug, Wed to Mon 10am to 6pm; ☎861-6701)*, which exhibits a collection of objects from the 17th and 18th centuries, including interesting collections of maps, firearms, and scientific and navigational instruments put together by Montréal industrialist David Stewart and his wife Liliane. The latter heads both the museum and the Macdonald-Stewart Foundation, which also manages the Château Ramezay and the Château Dufresne (the former Musée des Arts Décoratifs).

La Ronde ★ *($17.30, children 3 to 12 years old $8.55, families $40; Jun to Sep, every day 11am to 11pm, Fri and Sat to midnight.; ☎872-6222)*, an amusement park set up for Expo '67 on the former Île Ronde, opens its doors to both the young and the not so young every summer. For Montrealers, an annual trip to La Ronde has almost become a pilgrimage. An international fireworks competition is held here on Saturdays or Sundays during the months of June and July.

Very few of the pavilions built for Expo '67 have survived the destructive effects of the weather and the changes in the islands' roles. One that has is the former American pavilion, a veritable monument to modern architecture. The first complete geodesic dome to be taken beyond the stage of a model, it was created by the celebrated engineer Richard Buckminster Fuller (1895-1983). The **Biosphere** ★★ *($6.50; Jun 24 to Sep 1, every day 10am to 6pm; off-season, Tue to Sun, 10am to 5pm; ☎283-5000, Métro Île-Sainte-Hélène)*, built of tubular aluminum and measuring 80 metres in diameter, unfortunately lost its translucent acrylic skin in a fire back in 1978. An environmental interpretive centre on the St. Lawrence River, the Great Lakes and the different Canadian ecosystems, is now located in the dome. The permanent exhibit aims to sensitize the public on issues of sustainable development and the conservation of water as a precious resource. There are four interactive galleries with giant screens and hands-on displays to explore and delight in. A terrace restaurant with a panoramic view of the islands completes the museum.

Île Notre-Dame emerged from the waters of the St. Lawrence in no less than 10 months, with the help of 15 million tons of rocks and soil transported here from the Métro construction site. Because it is an artificial island, its creators were able to give it a fanciful shape by playing with both soil and water. The island, therefore, is traversed by pleasant **canals and gardens** ★★, laid out for the 1980 Floralies Internationales, an international flower show. Boats are available for rent, enabling visitors to ply the canals and admire the flowers mirrored in their waters.

Montréal's **Casino** ★ *(free admission, parking and coat check; every day 24 hours; Métro Île-Sainte-Hélène, bus #167; ☎392-2746)* occupies the former French and Québec pavilions of Expo '67. The main building corresponds to the old **French Pavilion** ★, an aluminum structure designed by architect Jean Faugeron. It was renovated in 1993 at a cost of $92.4 million in order to accommodate the Casino. The upper galleries offer some lovely views of downtown Montréal and the St. Lawrence Seaway.

Immediately to the west of the former French pavilion, the building shaped like a truncated pyramid is the former **Québec pavilion** ★ *(every day 9am to 3am)*. It was incorporated into the Casino after being raised and recovered with gold-tinted glass in 1996.

Visitors will find all sorts of things to do at the Casino, and all this in a very festive atmosphere among some of the 15,000 people that visit the casino each day. With 2,700 slot machines and 107 gaming tables, this is one of the 10 largest casinos in the world. This is also a popular spot thanks to its bars and cabaret (see p 184), along with its four restaurants, including Nuances (see p 180), which is rated as one of the best in Canada. Entrance is reserved for 18 and over. Dress code.

Nearby, visitors will find the entrance to the **Plage de l'Île Notre-Dame**, a beach enabling Montrealers to lounge on real sand right in the middle of the St. Lawrence. A natural filtering system keeps the water in the small lake clean, with no need for chemical additives. The number of swimmers allowed on the beach is strictly regulated, however, so as not to disrupt the balance of the system.

Quartier Latin ★★

People come to this university neighbourhood, centred around Rue Saint-Denis, for its theatres, cinemas and countless outdoor cafés, which offer a glimpse of the heterogeneous crowd of students and revellers. The area's origins date back to 1823, when Montréal's first Catholic cathedral, Église Saint-Jacques, was inaugurated on Rue Saint-Denis. This prestigious edifice quickly attracted the cream of French-Canadian society, mainly old noble families who had remained in Canada after the conquest, to the area. In 1852, a fire ravaged the neighbourhood, destroying the cathedral and Monseigneur Bourget's palace in the process. Painfully reconstructed in the second half of the 19th century, the area remained residential until the Université de Montréal was established here in 1893, marking the beginning of a period of cultural turmoil that would eventually lead to the Quiet Revolution of the 1960s. The Université du Québec, founded in 1974, has since taken over from the Université de Montréal, now located on the north side of Mont Royal. The prosperity of the quarter has thus been ensured.

After the great fire of 1852, a reservoir was built at the top of the hill known as Côte-à-Barron. In 1879, it was dismantled and the site was converted into a park by the name of **Square Saint-Louis** ★★. Developers built beautiful Second-Empire-style residences around the square, making it the nucleus of the French-Canadian bourgeois neighbourhood. These groups of houses give the area a certain harmonious quality rarely found in Montréal's urban landscape. To the west, **Rue Prince-Arthur** extends west from the square. In the 1960s, this pedestrian mall (between Boulevard Saint-Laurent and Avenue Laval) was the centre of the counterculture and the hippie movement in Montréal. Today, it is lined with numerous restaurants and terraces. On summer evenings, street performers liven up the atmosphere.

The **Bibliothèque Nationale** ★ *(1700 Rue Saint-Denis)*, the national library, was originally built for the Sulpicians, who looked unfavourably on the construction of a public library on Rue Sherbrooke. Even though many works were still on the *Index*, and thus forbidden reading for the clergy, the new library was seen as unfair competition. Known in the past as Bibliothèque Saint-Sulpice, this branch of the Bibliothèque Nationale du Québec was designed in the Beaux-Arts style by architect Eugène Payette in 1914. This style, a synthesis of classicism and French Renaissance architecture, was taught at the Paris École des Beaux-Arts, hence its name in North America. The interior is graced with lovely stained-glass windows created by Henri Perdriau in 1915.

The screening room and rental service of the **Office National du Film du Canada (ONF) (National Film Board of Canada)** *(1564 Rue St-Denis)* are located at the corner of Boulevard de Maisonneuve. The ONF-NFB has the world's only *cinérobothèque ($5 for two hours, 3$ for one hour; Tue to Sun noon to 9pm; ☎496-6887)*, enabling about 100 people to watch different films at once. The complex also has a movie theatre *($5; every day, monthly schedule)* where various documentaries and NFB films are screened. Movie lovers can also visit the **Cinémathèque Québécoise** *(335 Boulevard de Maisonneuve Est)*, a little further west, which has a collection of 25,000 Canadian, Québec and foreign films, as well as hundreds of pieces of equipment dating back to the early history of film (see p 183). The Cinémathèque recently re-opened after extensive renovations. UQAM's new concert hall, **Salle Pierre-Mercure**, is across the street.

Unlike most North American universities, with buildings contained within a specific campus, the campus of the **Université du Québec à Montréal (UQAM)** ★ *(405 Rue Sainte-Catherine Est, at the corner of rue Saint-Denis)* is integrated into the city fabric like French and German universities built during the Renaissance. It is also linked to the underground city and the Métro. The university is located on the site once occupied by the buildings of the Université de Montréal and the Église Saint-Jacques, which was reconstructed after the fire of 1852. Only the wall of the right transept and the Gothic-Revival steeple were integrated into Pavillon Judith-Jasmin (1979), and have since become the symbol of the university. UQAM is part of the Université du Québec, founded in 1969 and established in different cities across the province. Every year, over 40,000 students attend this flourishing institution of higher learning.

Plateau Mont-Royal ★

If there is one neighbourhood typical of Montréal, it is definitely this one. Thrown into the spotlight by writer Michel Tremblay, one of its illustrious sons, the "Plateau," as its inhabitants refer to it, is a neighbourhood of penniless intellectuals, young professionals and old francophone working-class families. Its long streets are lined with duplexes and triplexes adorned with amusingly contorted exterior staircases leading up to the long, narrow apartments that are so typical of Montréal. Flower-decked balconies made of wood or wrought iron provide box-seats for the spectacle on the street below. The Plateau is bounded by the mountain to the west, the Canadian Pacific railway tracks to the north and east, and Rue Sherbrooke to the south. It is traversed by a few major streets lined with cafés and theatres, such as Rue Saint-Denis and Avenue Papineau, but is a tranquil area on the whole. A visit to Montréal would not be complete without a stroll through this area to truly grasp the spirit of Montréal. This tour starts at the exit of the Mont-Royal Métro station. Turn right on Avenue du Mont-Royal, the neighbourhood's main commercial artery.

At the end of Rue Fabre, visitors will find **Parc Lafontaine**, the Plateau's main green space, laid out in 1908 on the site of an old military shooting range. Monuments to Sir Louis-Hippolyte Lafontaine, Félix Leclerc and Dollard des Ormeaux have been erected here. The park covers an area of 40 hectares, and is embellished with two artificial lakes and shady paths for pedestrians and bicyclists. There are tennis courts and bowling greens for summer sports enthusiasts, and in the winter, the frozen lakes form a large rink, which is illuminated at night. The Théâtre de Verdure (Outdoor Theatre) is also located here. Every weekend, the park is crowded with people from the neighbourhood, who come here to make the most of beautiful sunny or snowy days.

Église Saint-Jean-Baptiste ★★ *(309 Rue Rachel Est)*, dedicated to the patron saint of French Canadians, is a gigantic symbol of the solid faith of Catholic working-class inhabitants of the Plateau Mont-Royal at the turn of the 20th century, who, despite their poverty and large families, managed to amass considerable amounts of money for the construction of sumptuous churches. The exterior was built in 1901, according to a design by architect Émile Vanier. The interior was redone after a fire, and is now a veritable baroque-revival masterpiece designed by Casimir Saint-Jean that is not to be missed. The pink-marble and gilded wood baldaquin in the chancel (1915) shelter the altar, made of white Italian marble, which faces the large Casavant organs — among the most powerful in the city — in the jube. Concerts are frequently given at this church. It can seat up to 3,000 people.

QUÉBEC

OUTDOORS

 Cycling

The area around the **Canal de Lachine** has been redesigned in an effort to highlight this communication route, so important during the 19th and early 20th centuries. A pleasant bike path was laid out alongside the canal. Very popular with Montrealers, especially on Sundays, the path leads out to **Parc René-Lévesque**, a narrow strip of land jutting out into Lac Saint-Louis, and offering splendid views of the lake and surroundings. There are benches and picnic tables in the park and plenty of seagulls to keep you company. The path leads around the park, returning beside the river and the Lachine rapids. Many birds frequent this side of the park, and if you are lucky you might see some great herons.

Île Notre-Dame and **Île Sainte-Hélène** are accessible from Old Montréal. The path runs through an industrial area, then through the Cité du Havre before reaching the islands (cyclists cross the river on the Pont de la Concorde). It is easy to ride from one island to the other. The islands are well maintained and are a great place to relax, stroll and admire Montréal's skyline.

 ACCOMMODATIONS

Gîte Montréal *($45-$55 per person, $65 for two people; 3458 Avenue Laval, H2X 3C8, ☎289-9749 or 1-800-267-5180, ≈287-7386)* is an association of nearly 100 bed & breakfasts (*gîtes*), mostly Victorian houses in the Latin Quarter. In order to make sure that all rooms offered are comfortable, the organization visits each one. Reservations required.

About 30 bed & breakfasts are also registered with the **Relais Montréal Hospitalité** *($35 single and double to $55 double; 3977 Avenue Laval, H2W 2H9, ☎287-9635 or 1-800-363-9635, ≈287-1007)*. All have been carefully inspected, and the rooms are clean and comfortable. The establishments are located throughout Montreal, though many are on Rue Laval.

Vieux-Montréal

The **Auberge Alternative** *($15-$45; 358 Rue Saint-Pierre, H2Y 2M1, ☎282-8069; http://odyssee.net/eber/intro.html)*, located in Old Montréal, opened in April 1996. Run by a young couple, it is a renovated building dating from 1875. The 34 beds in the rooms and dormitories are rudimentary but comfortable, and the bathrooms are very clean. Brightly coloured walls, lots of space and a large common room and kitchenette with stone walls and old wooden floors complete the facilities. A blanket costs $2 per night, and guests have laundry machines at their disposal. Twenty-four hour access.

Even though Old Montréal is visited by thousands of tourists, it has little to offer in the way of accommodation. There is, however, set in the heart of the old city, the **Passants du Sans-Soucy** *($95 to $120 bkfst incl.; 9 rooms; 171 Rue Saint-Paul Ouest, ☎842-2634, ≈842-2912, Métro Place d'Armes)*, an extremely pleasant inn whose charming rooms are furnished with antiques. Built in 1723, the building was renovated eight years ago. Reservations required.

Except for one of its wings, the **Hôtel Inter-Continental** *($139-$230 bkfst incl.; 357 rooms, ≈, ☉, ⌂, ℜ, ℙ; 360 Rue Saint-Antoine Ouest, H2Y 3X4, ☎987-9900 or 1-800-327-0200, ≈847-8550, www.interconti.com)*, located on the edge of Old Montréal, is a fairly new building (1991) that is linked to the Centre de Commerce Mondial (World Trade Centre) and several shops. The Palais des Congrès (convention centre) is right nearby. It has an original appearance, due to its turret with multiple windows, where the living rooms of the suites are located. The rooms are tastefully decorated with simple furniture. Each one is equipped with a spacious bathroom, among other nice touches. Guests are courteously and attentively welcomed. Business people will enjoy all the necessary services, such as computer hook-ups, fax machines and photocopiers.

Built in 1725, the **Maison Pierre-du-Calvet** *($165-$195 bkfst incl.; 6 rooms, pb, ℜ; 405 Rue Bonsecours, ☎282-1725, ≈282-0456, Métro Champ-de-Mars)* is one of Montréal's oldest homes, discreetly tucked away at the intersection of Bonsecours and Saint-Paul streets. It has recently been entirely renovated, as have many other older houses in the neighbourhood. The rooms and suites, each different from the next and each with its own fireplace, exude an irresistible charm, with lovely antique wood panelling accentuated by oriental rugs, stained glass and beautiful antiques; the ancestral yet refined setting gives visitors the illusion of travelling back in time.

Downtown

The **Auberge de Jeunesse** (*$18-$21 per person for members, $24-$40 per person for non-members; 1030 Rue Mackay, H3G 2H1, ☎843-3317 or 1-800-663-3317, ≈934-3251*), or youth hostel, located a stone's throw from the downtown area, is one of the least expensive places to sleep in Montréal. Two-hundred and fifty beds occupy rooms that can accommodate from four to ten people as well as fifteen private rooms. Breakfast is served in the café, which opened in 1996. Guests have access to a laundry room, a tv room, a pool table and a kitchen. Finally, a variety of reasonably priced activities and excursions are organized by the hostel; these can include anything from trips to a sugar-shack to guided tours of the city. This is a non-smoking hostel.

The downtown **YMCA** (*$40-$56; tv, ≈, ⊙, ◖; 1450 Rue Stanley, H3A 2W6, Peel Métro, ☎849-8393, ≈849-8017*), the oldest YMCA in North America, was built in 1851 and has 331 basic but comfortable rooms with one or two beds each. Men, women and children are welcome. Most of the rooms are equipped with a telephone and a television; some have a sink or a bathroom. The cafeteria on the ground floor serves morning and evening meals (*$3-$6*). Guests enjoy free access to the YMCA's swimming pool, fully equipped gym and locker room. The Young Men's Christian Association (YMCA) was founded in London in 1844 to help young English workers.

Manoir Ambrose (*$45-$75, bkfst incl.; 22 rooms, sb or pb, tv, ☎; 3422 Rue Stanley, H3A 1R8, ☎288-6922, ≈288-5757, http://interresa.ca/hotel/mambrose.htm*) is set in two big, beautiful Victorian houses made of hewn stone, side by side on a peaceful street. It has several little rooms, scattered all over the house. The outdated decor will amuse some guests, but the rooms are well-kept and the service is friendly. Laundry service for a fee (*$5*).

The **Hôtel du Complexe Desjardins** (*$99-$170, less expensive packages available on weekends with bkfst $129; 572 rooms, ≈, ◖, ⊙, ℜ; 4 Complexe Desjardins, H5B 1E5, ☎285-1450 or 1-800-361-8234, ≈514-285-1243*), formerly the Meridien, is part of Complexe Desjardins. Consequently, on the main floor, there is a series of shops, movie theatres and restaurants. Located a few steps from Place des Arts and the Musée d'Art Contemporain, the hotel has a prime downtown location right next to all the action of the Jazz Festival along Rue Ste-Catherine. The large, comfortable rooms correspond with what one would expect from a hotel in this category.

Standing over 30 stories high, the **Centre Sheraton** (*$119-$295; ≈, ⊙, ◖, ℜ; 1201 Boulevard René-Lévesque, H3B 2L7, ☎878-2000 or 1-800-325-3535, ≈878-3958*) has 824 rooms. A number of little extras (coffee maker, hair dryer, iron and ironing board, non-smoking floors) are evidence of the meticulous service provided here. Some rooms are equipped for businesspeople with fax machines, modem hook-ups, voice mailboxes, etc. The rooms are pretty without being luxurious. Take some time to admire the beautiful lobby, decorated with picture windows and tropical plants. Several renovations were completed in 1996.

Besides its 134 rooms spread over 19 floors, the **Hôtel de la Montagne** (*$129-$195; ℜ, ≈, ≡; 1430 Rue de la Montagne, H3G 1Z5, ☎288-5656 or 1-800-361-6262, ≈288-9658*) also offers a pool, an excellent restaurant and a bar, as well as friendly and courteous staff. The pool is found outside, on the roof, and is only open in the summer.

The **Marriott Château-Champlain** (*$110-$226; 611 rooms, ≈, ⊙, ◖, ℜ, ♿; 1 Place du Canada, H3B 4C9, ☎878-9000 or 1-800-228-9290, ≈878-6761*) is a very original-looking white building with semicircular windows, much resembling a cheese-grater. Unfortunately, this renowned hotel has small rooms, which are less attractive than one might expect from an establishment in this class. Guests nevertheless enjoy a slew of services, including a masseuse. Direct access to the underground city (see p 184).

The **Queen Elizabeth** (*$149-$275; 1022 rooms, ≈, ℜ, ◖; 900 Boulevard René-Lévesque Ouest, H3B 4A5, www.cphotels.ca/qehindex.htm, ☎861-3511 or 1-800-441-1414, ≈954-2256*) is one Montréal hotel that has set itself apart over the years. Its lobby, decorated with fine wood panelling, is magnificent. Visitors will find a number of shops on the main floor. Two of the hotel's floors, designated "Entrée Or", boast luxurious suites and are like a hotel within the hotel. Numerous renovations were completed in 1996. The hotel has the advantage of being located in the heart of downtown, and its underground corridors, furthermore, provide easy access to the train station and the underground city.

The **Ritz Carlton Kempinski Montréal** *($205 to $235;* ⊙, ℜ; *1228 Rue Sherbrooke Ouest, H3G 1H6,* ☎842-4212 *or 1-800-363-0366,* ≈842-4907, *http://ritz-carlton-montreal.com)* was inaugurated in 1912. Renovated over the years in order to continue offering its clientele exceptional comfort, it has managed to preserve its original elegance. The rooms are decorated with superb antique furniture. The marble bathrooms, moreover, add to the charm of this outstanding establishment.

Guests of the **Bonaventure Hilton** *($214-$302; 367 rooms,* ≈, ⊙, ℜ; *1 Place Bonaventure, H5A 1E4,* ☎878-2332 *or 1-800-267-2575,* ≈878-3881 *or 878-1442),* located on the boundary between downtown and Old Montréal, enjoy a number of little extras that make this hotel a perfect place to relax; these include, among other things, a massage service. The rooms are decorated in a simple manner, without a hint of extravagance, and the bathrooms are small. The hotel has a heated outdoor swimming pool, where guests can swim all year round, as well as a lovely garden and access to the underground city (see p 184).

At first sight, the **Loews Hôtel Vogue** *($240-$285; 126 rooms, 16 suites,* ≈, ⊛, ℜ; *1425 Rue de la Montagne, H3G 1Z3,* ☎285-5555 *or 1-800-465-6654,* ≈849-8903, *www.loewshotels.com/vogue.html),* a glass and concrete building with no ornamentation, looks bare. The lobby, embellished with warm-coloured woodwork, gives a more accurate idea of the luxury and elegance of this establishment. The large rooms, with their elegant furniture, are very comfortable. Each room has a whirlpool bath and two suites have a sauna.

Plateau Mont-Royal

The **Auberge de la Fontaine** *($109-$175 bkfst and parking included; 21 rooms, tv, pb;*

1301 Rue Rachel Est, H2J 2K1, ☎597-0166, ≈597-0496) lies opposite lovely Parc Lafontaine. Designed with a great deal of care, it has a lot of style. A feeling of calm and relaxation emanates from the rooms, all of which are nicely decorated. Guests are offered a complimentary snack during the day. All these attractive features have made this a popular place — so much so that it is best to make reservations.

Near the Airports

Mirabel Airport

Directly accessible from Mirabel Airport, the **Château de l'Aéroport-Mirabel** *($89-$115, suite for $175;* ⊙, ≈, ◻, ℜ; *12555 Rue Commerce, A4, J7N 1E3,* ☎476-1611 *or 1-800-361-0924,* ≈476-0873, *www.châteaumirabel.com)* was built to accommodate travellers with early morning flights. Unlike its downtown cousins, this hotel's high season is from November to May. A massage service is particularly appreciated by nervous flyers. The rooms are very functional and comfortable.

Dorval Airport

Entirely renovated in 1996, the rooms in the **Best Western Hôtel International** *($79-$99;* ⊙, ⊛, ◻, ≈, ℜ; *13000 Chemin Côte-de-Liesse,* ☎514-631-4811 *or 1-800-361-2254,* ≈631-7305) are pleasant and affordable. The hotel also offers an interesting service: after passing the night here, guests can park their car here for up to a month, free of charge.

The **Hilton International** *($158-$202, weekends $109-$129, bkfst incl.; 482 rooms,* ⊙, ⊛, ≈, ◻, ℜ; *12505 Côte-de-Liesse, H9P 1B7,* ☎631-2411 *or 1-800-268-9275,* ≈631-0192) has pleasant rooms. Its main advantage is its proximity to the airport.

 RESTAURANTS

Vieux-Montréal

The varied menu of the French restaurant **Bonaparte** *($$; 443 Rue Saint-François-Xavier,* ☎844-4368) always includes some delicious surprises. The tables on the mezzanine offer a lovely view of Old Montréal.

The unique **Café Electronique** *($$; 405 Rue St-Sulpice, corner Rue St-Paul, ☎849-1612)* allows everyone the chance to discover the joys of computing while at the same time sipping a coffee or having a bite to eat. Expect to shell out about $5 for half an hour on the Internet or $4 to use the CD-ROM. Classes are offered to demystify accessing the Internet and CD-ROM.

Gibby's restaurant *($$$; closed at noon; 298 Place d'Youville, ☎282-1837)* is located in a lovely, renovated old stable and its menu offers generous servings of beef or veal steaks served at antique wooden tables set around a glowing fire and surrounded by low brick and stone walls. In the summer months, patrons can eat comfortably outdoors in a large inner courtyard. All in all, an extraordinary decor, which is reflected in the rather high prices. Vegetarians beware.

Claude Postel *($$$-$$$$; closed Sat noon and Sun; 443 Rue Saint-Vincent, ☎875-5067)* enjoys an established reputation in the old part of town. An extensive menu boasts some true triumphs of French cuisine that are rather pricey; the *table d'hôte* is just as tasty, and much more reasonable. The decor is simple and refined. The chef and owner also runs a pastry shop next door, so save some room for dessert.

Following a disagreement, the Filles du Roi restaurant closed its doors to reopen under the name **Maison Pierre-du-Calvet** *($$$$; closed Sun and Mon; 405 Rue Bonsecours, ☎282-1725)*. This jewel among Montréal restaurants has given way to a magnificent inn (see p 176) boasting one of the best dining rooms in the city. The new establishment is to be particularly recommended for its delicious and imaginative French cuisine. Its menu, based on game, poultry, fish and beef, changes every two weeks. The elegant surroundings, antiques, ornamental plants and discrete service further add to the pleasure of an evening meal here.

Downtown

At the beginning of the century, a Lithuanian immigrant modified a recipe from his native country to suit the needs of workers, and thus introduced the smoked meat sandwich to Montréal, and in the process created **Ben's Delicatessen** *($; 900 Boulevard de Maisonneuve Ouest, ☎844-1000)*. Over the years, the restaurant has become a Montréal institution, attracting a motley crowd from 7am to 3:30am. The worn, Formica tables and photographs yellowed by time give the restaurant an austere appearance.

The **Brûlerie Saint-Denis** *($; 2100 Rue Stanley, in the Maison Alcan, ☎985-9159)* serves the same delicious coffee blends, simple meals and sinful desserts as the other two Brûleries. Though the coffee is not roasted on the premises, it does come fresh from the roasters on Saint-Denis.

Le Commensal *($; 1204 McGill College, ☎871-1480)* is a buffet-style restaurant. The food, all vegetarian, is sold by weight. Le Commensal is open every day until 11pm. The inviting modern decor and big windows looking out on the downtown streets make it a pleasant place to be. See also p 180.

Café du TNM *($$; 84 Rue Ste-Catherine Ouest, ☎866-8668)* is a wonderful addition to this somewhat rundown area. You can enjoy a simple drink, coffee or dessert in the deconstructivist decor on the ground floor or a good meal upstairs, where the atmosphere is like a Parisian *brasserie*. The menu goes with the decor: classic French bistro cuisine. Impeccable service, attractive presentation and flawless food, what more could you ask for?

The superb dining room at **Eaton, le 9^e** *($$; 677 Rue Sainte-Catherine, 9th floor, ☎284-8421)* is worth a brief visit, if only to experience the sensation of stepping back into another era. The restaurant is open for lunch and, on Thursdays and Fridays, for dinner. Unfortunately, the cuisine is nothing to rave about.

The **Jardin du Ritz** *($$; 1228 Rue Sherbrooke Ouest, ☎842-4212)* is the perfect escape from the summer heat and the incessant downtown bustle. Classic French cuisine is featured on the menu, with tea served on a patio surrounded by flowers and greenery, next to the pond with its splashing ducks. Only open during the summer months, the Jardin is an extension of the hotel's other restaurant, Le Café de Paris (see below).

Made up of several large dining rooms, the restaurant **La Mère Tucker** *($$; 1175 Place du*

QUÉBEC

Frère André, ☎*866-5525)* is ideal for families and large groups. The all-you-can-eat roast beef has developed a solid reputation with big eaters. The atmosphere is relaxed.

Located on the 42nd floor of Place Ville-Marie, the **Club Lounge 737** restaurant *($$$; closed Sat and Sun noon; 1 Place Ville-Marie,* ☎*397-0737)* boasts large windows allowing for an unobstructed view of Montreal and its surroundings. It's buffet consists of a variety of French-inspired creations. Be warned that the prices here are as high as the restaurant is.

Arguably one of Montreal's best restaurants, **Chez la Mère Michel** *($$$$; closed Sat noon, Sun, Mon noon; 1209 Rue Guy,* ☎*934-0473)* is the definition of fine French dining. Inside the lovely old house on Guy Street lie three exquisitely decorated, intimate dining rooms. At the front, banquettes and chairs covered in richly printed fabrics welcome patrons to their elegantly laid tables, while in the back a cosy fireplace and profusion of plants set the mood. Market-fresh ingredients are combined with excellence by Chef Micheline to create delightful French regional specialties as well as a changing five-course seasonal *table d'hôte.* The service is friendly and attentive. The impressive wine cellar boasts some of the finest bottles in the city.

Beautiful wood-panelling lend an atmosphere of refinement to the internationally renowned **Beaver Club** *($$$$; 900 Boulevard René-Lévesque Ouest, in the Queen Elizabeth Hotel,* ☎*861-3511),* which elevates the hotel dining room to a whole new level. A changing *table d'hôte* can feature anything from fresh lobster to fine cuts of beef or wild game. Everything is prepared with the utmost attention to detail, right down to the exquisite presentation. Knowledgeable wine steward. There is music and dancing on Saturday evenings.

Île Sainte-Hélène and Île Notre-Dame

Festin des Gouverneurs *($$$;* ☎*879-1141),* recreates feasts like those prepared in New France at the beginning of colonization. Characters in period costumes and traditional Québec dishes bring patrons back in time to these celebrations. The restaurant only serves groups and reservations are necessary.

On Île Sainte-Hélène, the restaurant **Hélène-de-Champlain** *($$$; closed noon;* ☎*395-2424)* lies in an enchanting setting, without question one of the loveliest in Montréal. The large dining room, with its fireplace and view of the city and the river, is extremely pleasant. Each corner has its own unique charm, overlooking the ever-changing surrounding landscape. Though the restaurant does not serve the fanciest of gastronomic cuisine, the food is good. The service is courteous and attentive.

Ensconced on the fifth floor of Montréal's Casino, **Nuances** *($$$$; every day 5:30pm to 11pm; Casino de Montréal, Île Notre-Dame,* ☎*392-2708 or 1-800-665-2274, ext 4322)* is one of the best dining establishments in the city, perhaps even the country. Refined and imaginative cuisine is served in a decor rich in mahogany, brass, leather and views of the city's lights. Of particular note on the menu are the creamy lobster *brandade* in flaky pastry, brochette of grilled quail, roast cutlet of duck, tenderloin of Québec lamb or striped polenta with grilled tuna. The delectable desserts are each presented exquisitely. The plush and classic ambiance of this award-winning restaurant is perfect for business meals and special occasions.

Quartier Latin

Le Commensal *($; 1720 Saint-Denis,* ☎*845-2627)* just moved into its new location, the former Grand Café. See description p 179.

Tiny **La Paryse** *($; 302 Rue Ontario Est,* ☎*842-2040)* is often crowded with students, for a very simple reason: it serves delicious hamburgers and home-made French fries in generous portions.

Plateau Mont-Royal

L'Anecdote *($; 801 Rue Rachel Est,* ☎*526-7967)* serves hamburgers and vegetarian club sandwiches made with quality ingredients. The place has a 1950s-style decor, with movie posters and old Coke ads on the walls.

With its decor made up of four tables and a counter, the **Binerie Mont-Royal** *($; 367 Avenue Mont-Royal Est,* ☎*285-9078)* is a very modest little neighbourhood restaurant. It is known for its specialty, baked beans (*fèves au lard* or "*binnes* ") and also as the backdrop of

Yves Beauchemin's novel, *Le Matou* (*The Alley Cat*).

At the charming **Le Daphnée** tea room *($; closed Mon; 3803 Rue Saint-Denis, ☎849-3042)*, visitors can enjoy dainty little treats of the sweet or savoury variety. During summer, the balcony offers a choice view of Rue Saint-Denis. The staff is sometimes a bit pretentious.

The meeting place of an entire contingent of thirty-something yuppies, the terrace and dining room at the **Café Cherrier** *($$; 3635 Rue Saint-Denis, ☎843-4308)* is always packed. The bustling French *brasserie* ambiance is enjoyable. The menu features respectable bistro-style cuisine. A brunch is served on weekends.

Chu Chai *($$; 4088 Rue St-Denis, ☎843-4194)* dares to be innovative and you have to congratulate them for it. So many restaurants are just like so many others! Here, the Thai vegetarian menu they've come up with is quite a pastiche: vegetarian shrimp, vegetarian fish and even vegetarian beef and pork. The resemblance to the real thing is so extraordinary that you will spend the evening wondering how they do it! The chef affirms that they really do consist of vegetable-based products like seitan, wheat, etc. The results are delicious and delight the mixed clientele that squeezes into the modest dining room or onto the terrace. They offer economical lunch specials.

The staging is very subtle at the **Continental** *($$; closed noon; 4169 Saint-Denis, ☎845-6842)*. Some evenings, the restaurant is positively charming, with its attentive, courteous staff, stylish clientele and updated 1950s-style decor. The varied menu includes a few surprises such as crispy oriental noodles. The cuisine is sublime and the presentation is always very original.

The yuppie gathering place during the mid-eighties, **L'Express** *($$-$$$; 3927 Rue Saint-Denis, ☎845-5333)* is still highly rated for its dining-car decor, lively Parisian bistro atmosphere, which few restaurants have managed to recreate, and consistently appealing menu. Over the years, this restaurant has developed a solid reputation.

Set up inside a superb residence, **Laloux** *($$-$$$; closed noon; 250 Avenue des Pins Est, ☎287-9127)* resembles a chic and elegant Parisian-style bistro. People come here to enjoy consistently high-quality nouvelle cuisine. A reasonably priced *menu théâtre,* which includes three light courses is offered.

If you're looking for a new culinary experience, **Toqué** *($$$; 3842 Rue Saint-Denis, ☎499-2084)* is without a doubt the address to remember when in Montréal. The chef, Normand Laprise, insists on having the freshest ingredients in his kitchen, where dishes are always prepared with great care, and beautifully presented. Not to mention the desserts, which are veritable modern sculptures. The service is exceptional, the wine list good, the new decor elegant, and the high prices do not seem to deter anyone. One of the most original dining establishments in Montréal.

  ENTERTAINMENT

Bars and Nightclubs

L'Air du Temps *(194 Rue Saint-Paul Ouest)* ranks among the most famous jazz bars in Montréal. Set in the heart of Old Montréal, it has a fantastic interior decorated with scores of antiques. As the place is often packed, it is necessary to arrive early to get a good seat. The cover charge varies according to the show. Call for information on upcoming acts.

Dark, smoky, jam-packed, hot, hectic and noisy, **Le Balattou** *(4372 Boulevard Saint-Laurent)* is without a doubt the most popular African nightclub in Montréal. On weekends, the cover charge is $7 (including one drink). Shows are presented only during the week, when the cost of admission varies.

A bar with a modest decor, **Les Beaux Esprits** *(2073 Rue Saint-Denis)* presents good jazz and blues shows.

A clientele composed mainly of junior executives crowds into the **Belmont sur le Boulevard** *(4483 Boulevard Saint-Laurent)*. On weekends, the place is literally overrun with customers. Cover charge: $3 Thursdays, $4 Fridays and Saturdays.

Obliged to move from its location in front of the Université de Montréal, **Café Campus** *(57 Prince Arthur)* has settled into a large place on Rue Prince Arthur. Over the years, it had

QUÉBEC

become a Montréal institution, and had to prove itself all over again. The decor is still quite plain. Good musicians frequently give shows here.

Di Salvio's *(3519 Boulevard Saint-Laurent)* art deco interior and fifties-style furniture create a unique and original setting. Patrons lucky enough to get picked from the line-up (it can be difficult to get in) dance to acid-jazz music.

Les Foufs *(87 Rue Sainte-Catherine Est)* is a fantastic, one-of-a-kind bar-nightclub pick-up joint. The best bar in Québec for dancing to alternative music, it attracts a motley crowd of young Montrealers, ranging from punks to medical students. The decor, consisting of graffiti and strange sculptures, is wacky, to say the least. Don't come here for a quiet night.

Thursday's *(1449 Rue Crescent)* bar is very popular, especially among the city's English-speaking population. It is a favourite meeting place for business people and professionals.

The **Whisky Café** *(5800 Boulevard Saint-Laurent)* has been so conscientiously decorated that even the men's bathrooms are on their way to becoming a tourist attraction. The warm colours used in a modern setting, the tall columns covered with woodwork and pre-1950s-style chairs all create a sense of comfort and elegance. The well-off, well-bred clientele consists of a gilded youth between the ages of 20 and 35.

Gay and Lesbian Bars

The **Cabaret l'Entre-Peau** *(1115 Rue Sainte-Catherine Est, ☎525-7566)* puts on transvestite shows. The place attracts a lively, mixed clientele.

The **O'Side** *(4075 A Rue Saint-Denis, ☎849-7126)* is for women only (men will be politely turned away at the door). The atmosphere is relaxed, making this a good place for a drink and some conversation. There are pool tables.

Sisters *(1450 Rue Sainte-Catherine Est, ☎523-0064)* is for lesbians. The latest mainstream hits get things moving and shaking on the dance floor.

With its four dance floors that each play a different type of music: alternative, commercial, techno, retro, etc., the two-storey

Sky Pub *(1474 Rue Sainte-Catherine Est, ☎529-6969)*, is the biggest gay club in Montreal. Obviously, in such an immense place, there is more than one atmosphere. The crowd is mostly young. The cover charge frequently changes.

La Track *(1584 Rue Sainte-Catherine Est)* is a lively men's gay bar.

Theatres

Club Soda *(5240 Avenue du Parc, ☎270-7848)*, presents great shows, particularly during the Just for Laughs Festival and the Jazz Festival. During the latter festival, the shows are free after 11pm.

Place des Arts *(260 Boulevard de Maisonneuve Ouest, ☎285-4200, box office ☎842-2112, Métro Place-des-Arts)*. The complex contains five theatres: Salle Wilfrid-Pelletier, Théâtre Maisonneuve, Théâtre Jean-Duceppe, Théâtre du Café de la Place and the Cinquième Salle, opened in 1992. The **Orchestre Symphonique de Montréal** *(for subscription information call ☎849-0269, otherwise call the Place des Arts box office)* and **Grands Ballets Canadiens** *(for subscription information call ☎842-9951, otherwise call the Place des Arts box office)* both perform in this venerable hall.

Centaur Theatre *(453 Rue Saint-François, ☎288-3161)* presents musicals.

Saidye Bronfman Centre *(5170 Côte Sainte-Catherine, ☎739-7944)* exhibits artwork by local and internationally renowned names and hosts theatrical performances such as Yiddish plays. Fine-arts courses are also given, and there is a drama camp for children in summer.

Théâtre Saint-Denis *(1594 Rue Saint-Denis, ☎849-4211 Métro Berri-UQAM)* presents concerts, plays and musicals.

Shows at the **Spectrum** *(318 Rue Sainte-Catherine Ouest, ☎861-5851, Métro Place-des-Arts)* usually begin around 11pm. Count on at least $10 to get in. As with Club Soda, shows after 11pm are usually free during the Festival de Jazz.

Théâtre du Nouveau Monde *(84, rue Ste-Catherine Ouest, ☎861-0563)*. See p 179.

Ticket Sales

There are three major ticket agencies in Montréal, which sell tickets for shows, concerts and other events over the telephone. Service charges, which vary according to the show, are added to the price of the ticket. Credit cards are accepted.

Admission
☎(514) 790-1245
☎1-800-361-4595

Telspec
☎(514) 790-2222

Billetterie Articulée (an Admission ticket outlet)
☎ 844-2172

Information on the Arts

Info-Arts (Bell): ☎790-ARTS. This service's operators provide information on current cultural and artistic events in the city.

Movie Theatres

The following show films in English:

Égyptien *(Cours Mont-Royal, 1455 Rue Peel, ☎849-3456, Métro Peel).*

Loews *(954 Rue Sainte-Catherine Ouest, ☎861-7437, Métro Peel).*

Palace *(698 Rue Sainte-Catherine Ouest, ☎866-6991, Métro McGill).*

The following show films in French:

Berri *(1280 Rue Berri, ☎849-3456, Métro Berri-UQAM).*

Complexe Desjardins *(Rue Sainte-Catherine Ouest, between Jeanne-Mance and Saint-Urbain, ☎849-3456, Métro Place-des-Arts).*

Le Parisien *(480 Rue Sainte-Catherine Ouest, ☎866-3856, Métro McGill).*

Quartier Latin *(350 Rue Émery, ☎849-4422).*

The following are repertory theatres:

La Cinémathèque Québécoise *(335 Boulevard de Maisonneuve Est, ☎842-9763, Métro Berri-UQAM)* is known for its outstanding projection

quality. French-language repertory and art films are shown here.

Le Cinéma Parallèle *(3682 Boulevard Saint-Laurent, ☎843-6001)* shows films in French and English.

Impérial *(1430 Rue de Bleury, ☎848-0300, Métro Place-des-Arts)* is the oldest movie theatre in Montréal.

Cinéma du Parc *(3575 Avenue du Parc, ☎287-7272, Métro Place-des-Arts, bus 80)* shows English-language films or films dubbed or subtitled in English.

Office National du Film (National Film Board) *(1564 Rue Saint-Denis, ☎496-6301).* A *cinérobothèque* allows several people to watch NFB films at once. A robot, the only one like it in the world, loads each machine. The complex is dedicated to Québec and Canadian cinema.

You can also see large-screen productions at:

Le Cinéma Imax *(Vieux-Port de Montréal, Rue de la Commune corner Boulevard Saint-Laurent, ☎496-4629).* Films are presented on a giant screen.

Festivals and Cultural Events

The **Tour de l'Île** *(1251 Rue Rachel Est, H2J 2J9, ☎514-847-8356)* takes place in early June. The event can accommodate a maximum of 45,000 cyclists, who ride together for some 65 kilometres around the island of Montréal.

June is marked by an international event that captivates a large number of fans from all over North America: the **Grand Prix Players du Canada** *(to reserve seats, call ☎514-392-0000)*; it takes place at the Circuit Gilles Villeneuve on l'Île Notre-Dame during the second week of June.

The **Concours International d'Art Pyrotechnique** (International Fireworks Competition) *(☎872-6222)* starts in mid-June and runs until mid-July. The world's top pyrotechnists present high-quality pyro-musical shows every Saturday in June and every Sunday in July.

During the **Festival International de Jazz de Montréal** *(☎871-1881)*, hundreds of shows set to the rhythm of jazz and its variations are presented on stages erected around Place des

QUÉBEC

Arts. From late June to the second week in July, this part of the city and a fair number of theatres are buzzing with activity. The event offers people an opportunity to take to the streets and be carried away by the festive atmosphere of the fantastic, free outdoor shows that attract Montrealers and visitors in large numbers.

Humour and creativity are highlighted during the **Festival Juste pour Rire - Just for Laughs Festival** (☎845-3155 or 790-HAHA), held the last two weeks of July.

The **FrancoFolies** (last two weeks of June, ☎871-1881) are organized to promote French-language music and song.

During the last week of August, the **Festival International des Films du Monde** (World Film Festival) (☎848-3883) is held in various Montréal movie theatres. During this competition, films from different countries are presented to Montréal audiences.

Spectator Sports

The **Centre Molson** (1250 Rue de la Gauchetière, ☎989-2841). In the fall, the hockey games of the famous Montreal Canadiens hockey team start in the new Centre Molson. There are 42 games during the regular season. The play-offs follow, at the end of which the winning team walks away with the legendary Stanley Cup.

Spring signals the beginning of baseball season at the **Stade Olympique** (4141 Avenue Pierre-de-Courbertin, ☎846-3976). The Expos play against the various teams of the National Baseball League at the Olympic Stadium.

Casino

With 2,700 slot machines and one hundred gaming tables (blackjack, roulette, baccarat, poker, etc.), the **Casino de Montréal** (free admission, every day 9am to 5am, Métro Île Sainte-Hélène and Bus 167, ☎392-2746) is without a doubt a major player in the city's nightlife. Following the addition of a new wing in 1996 in the former Québec pavilion, the casino is now one of the 10 biggest casinos in the world in terms of its gaming equipment. A cabaret show, also added in 1996, has seen

the likes of Liza Minelli, André-Philippe Gagnon and Jean-Pierre Ferland to name but a few, and has brought a new vitality to the place.

 SHOPPING

The Underground City

The 1962 construction of Place Ville-Marie, with its underground shopping mall, marked the origins of what is known today as the underground city. The development of this "city under the city" was accelerated by the construction of the Métro, which opened in 1966. Soon, most downtown businesses and office buildings, as well as a few hotels, were strategically linked to the underground pedestrian network and, by extension, to the Métro.

Today, the underground city, one of the largest in the world, has five distinct sections. The first lies at the very heart of the Métro system, around the Berri-UQAM station, and is connected to the buildings of the Université du Québec à Montréal (UQAM), the Galeries Dupuis and the bus station. The second stretches between the Place-des-Arts and Place-d'Armes stations, and is linked to Place des Arts, the Musée d'Art Contemporain, Complexe Desjardins, Complexe Guy Favreau and the Palais des Congrès, forming an exceptional cultural ensemble. The third, at the Square-Victoria station, serves the business centre. The fourth, which is the busiest and most important one, is identified with the McGill, Peel and Bonaventure stations. It encompasses the Bay and Eaton department stores; the Promenades de la Cathédrale, Place Montréal Trust and Cours Mont-Royal shopping centres, as well as Place Bonaventure, 1000 de la Gauchetière, the train station and Place Ville-Marie. The fifth and final area is located in the commercial section around the Atwater station; it is linked to Westmount Square, Collège Dawson and Place Alexis Nihon (see detailed map of underground city).

Shopping Centres and Department Stores

Several downtown shopping centres and department stores offer a good selection of clothing by well-known fashion designers, including Jean-Claude Chacok, Cacharel, Guy Laroche, Lily Simon, Adrienne Vittadini, Mondi, Ralph Lauren and many others.

Holt Renfrew
1300 Rue Sherbrooke Ouest, ☎842-5111

Ogilvy
1307 Rue Sainte-Catherine Ouest, ☎842-7711

Place Montréal Trust
1600 Avenue McGill College, ☎843-8000

Place Ville-Marie
5 Place Ville-Marie, ☎861-9393

Westmount Square
4 Westmount Square, ☎932-0211

The Bay
Square Phillips (on Rue Sainte-Catherine Ouest), ☎281-4422

Eaton
677 Rue Sainte-Catherine Ouest, ☎284-8411

Sports and Outdoor Gear

Those who are going on an expedition in the great outdoors should make their first stop at **La Cordée** *(2159 Rue Sainte-Catherine Est, ☎524-1106).*

For warm, fashionable clothing that is perfectly suited to the outdoors, see the creations at **Kanuk** *(485 Rue Rachel, ☎527-4494)*

Bookstores

General

Champigny (French)
4380 Rue Saint-Denis, ☎844-2587

Chapters (French and English)
1171 Rue Sainte-Catherine Ouest, ☎849-8825

Librairie Gallimard (French)
3700 Boulevard Saint-Laurent, ☎499-2012

Paragraphe Books and Café (English)
2220 McGill College, ☎845-5811

Librairie Renaud-Bray (French)

5252 Chemin de la Côte-des-Neiges, ☎342-1515
4301 Rue Saint-Denis, ☎499-3656
5117 Avenue du Parc, ☎276-7651

WH Smith (French and English)
Place Ville-Marie, ☎861-1736
Promenades de la Cathédrale, ☎289-8737

Specialized

Librairie Allemande (German books)
3434 Chemin de la Côte-des-Neiges, ☎933-1919

Librairie Las Americas (Spanish books)
10 Rue Saint-Norbert, ☎844-5994

Librairie l'Androgyne (gay and feminist literature)
3636 Boulevard Saint-Laurent, ☎842-4765

Librairie C.E.C. Michel Fortin (education, languages)
3714 Rue Saint-Denis, ☎849-5719

Librairie du Musée des Beaux-Arts (art)
1368 Rue Sherbrooke Ouest, ☎285-1600, ext 350

Librairie Olivieri (contemporary art)
185 Rue Sainte-Catherine Ouest, ☎847-6903

Librairie Olivieri (foreign literature, art)
5200 Rue Gatineau, ☎739-3639

Librairie Renaud-Bray (children)
5219 Chemin de la Côte-des-Neiges, ☎342-1515

Librairie Ulysse (travel)
4176 Rue Saint-Denis, ☎843-9447
560 Avenue du Président-Kennedy, ☎843-7222

Music

Archambault Musique
500 Rue Sainte-Catherine Est, ☎849-6201
175 Rue Sainte-Catherine Ouest, Place des Arts, ☎281-0367

HMV
1020 Rue Sainte-Catherine Ouest, ☎875-0765
Annexe at 1035 Rue Ste-Catherine Ouest, ☎987-1809 (sale-priced merchandise)

QUÉBEC

Sam the Record Man
399 Rue Sainte-Catherine Ouest, corner Rue
Saint-Alexandre, ☎281-9877

Québec Crafts

Craft shops, known as *boutiques d'artisanat* in
French, offer an impressive selection of pieces
illustrating the work and specific themes dear
to artisans from here and abroad.

Local crafts include Canadian, Native and Inuit,
as well as Québec works. Each year during the
month of December, the *Salon des Métiers
d'Art du Québec* (Québec Art and Crafts show)
is held at Place Bonaventure *(901 Rue de la
Gauchetière Ouest)*. The show lasts about 10
days and provides Québec artists the
opportunity to display and sell their work.

Throughout the year, it is also possible to
purchase several beautifully crafted items by
Quebec artists and on of the **Le Rouet**
boutiques *(136 Rue Saint-Paul Est,
☎875-2333; 4201 Rue Saint-Denis,
☎842-4306; 1500 Avenue McGill College in
Place Montréal-Trust, ☎843-5235 or
289-0803)*.

Le Chariot *(446, Place Jacques-Cartier,
☎875-6134)* offers a good selection of Inuit
and Native art and crafts.

Guilde Canadienne des Métiers d'Arts *(2025
Rue Peel, ☎849-6091)* is a small boutique sells
pieces of Canadian and Quebecois art, and two
small galleries exhibit Inuit and Native art and
crafts.

The **Galerie d'Objets d'Art du Marché
Bonsecours** *(350 Rue St-Paul E., ☎878-2787)*
is another great place to buy Quebec art.

Gifts and Gadgets

Boutique du Musée d'Art Contemporain
(185 Rue Sainte-Catherine Ouest, ☎847-6226)
and **Boutique du Musée des Beaux-Arts de
Montréal** *(1390 Rue Sherbrooke Ouest,
☎285-1600)* have a whole store of splendid
reproductions and trinkets of all kinds: t-shirts,
decorative objects and more. A great find for
beautiful souvenirs.

La Mouette Rieuse *(4418 Rue St-Denis,
☎843-4851)* will surpirse comic fans of Tintin,
Gaston Lagaffe, Bidochon and Asterix.

At **Valet de Cœur** *(4408 Rue Saint-Denis,
☎499-9970)*, you will find parlour games,
puzzles and chess and checker boards among
other things.

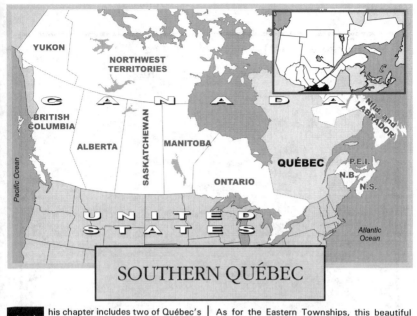

SOUTHERN QUÉBEC

This chapter includes two of Québec's tourist regions, namely Montérégie and the Eastern Townships. The six hills in Montérégie: Mont Saint-Bruno, Mont Saint-Hilaire, Mont Yamaska, Mont Rigaud, Mont Saint-Grégoire and Mont Rougemont, are the only large hills in this flat region. They do not rise much over 500 metres, are spread out and were long considered ancient volcanoes. Actually, they are metamorphic rocks that did not break through the upper layer of the earth's crust, and became visible as the neighbouring land eroded over a long period of time.

The Montérégie area is a beautiful plain, rich in history and agriculture, located between Ontario, New England and the foothills of the Appalachians in the Eastern Townships. Located just south of Montréal, with many natural communication routes such as the majestic Rivière Richelieu, Montérégie has always played an important military and strategic role. The many fortifications that can now be visited in the area were once outposts that served to protect the colony from the Iroquois, the British and the Americans respectively. It was also in Montérégie that the American nation experienced its first military defeat, in 1812. The *Patriotes* and the British confronted each other in Saint-Charles-sur-Richelieu and Saint-Denis, during the 1837 rebellion.

As for the Eastern Townships, this beautiful region in the Appalachian foothills, in the southernmost part of Québec. Its rich architectural heritage and mountainous countryside give it a distinctive character reminiscent in many ways of New England. Picturesque villages marked by what is often typically Anglo-Saxon architecture, lie nestled between mountains with rounded summits and lovely little valleys.

As may be gathered from many place names, such as Massawippi and Coaticook, this vast region was originally explored and inhabited by natives of the Abenaki tribe. Later, when New France came under English control and the United States declared its independence, many American colonists still loyal to the British monarchy (known as Loyalists) settled in the Eastern Townships. Throughout the 19th century, these settlers were followed by waves of immigrants from the British Isles, mainly Ireland, and French colonists from the overpopulated St. Lawrence lowlands. Though the local population is now over 90% French-speaking, the area still bears obvious traces of its Anglo-Saxon past, most notably in its architecture. Many towns and villages are graced with majestic Anglican churches surrounded by beautiful 19th-century Victorian or vernacular American-style homes. The Townships are still home to a handful of prestigious local institutions, like Bishop's University in Lennoxville.

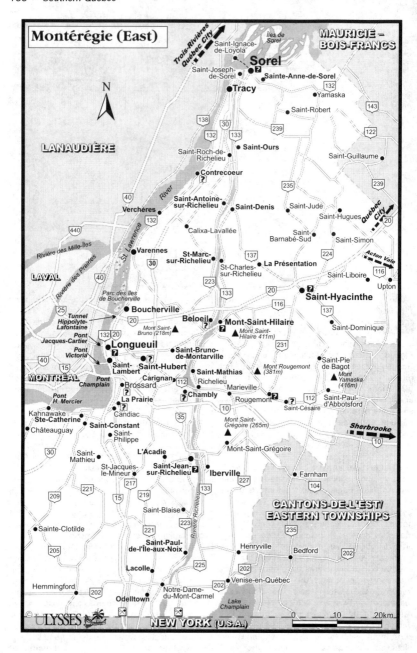

Montérégie (East)

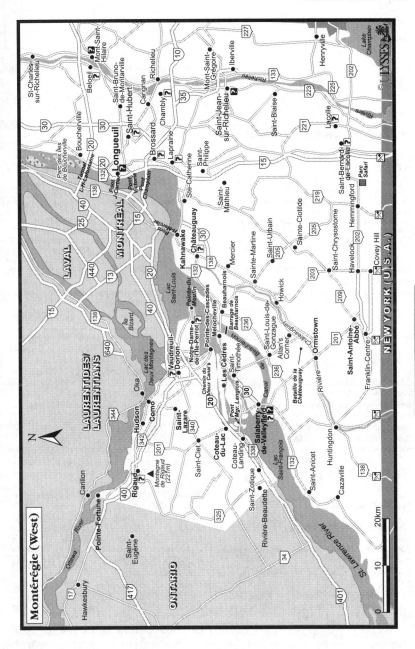

Montérégie (West)

FINDING YOUR WAY AROUND

Ferries

Montérégie

St-Paul-de-l'île-aux-Noix – **Île-aux-Noix** ☎291-5700, seasonal
St-Denis – **St-Antoine-sur-Richelieu:** ☎787-2759, seasonal.
St-Marc-sur-Richelieu – **St-Antoine-sur-Richelieu:** ☎584-2813, seasonal.
St-Roch-de-Richelieu – **St-Ours:** ☎785-2161, seasonal.
Sorel – **St-Ignace-de-Loyola:** ☎743-3258, open all year.
Ferry Longueuil - **Île Charron:** ☎442-9575, seasonal.
River shuttle Longueuil - **Montréal:** ☎281-8000, seasonal.
Hudson - **Oka:** ☎458-4732, seasonal.

Bus Stations

Montérégie

Saint-Jean-sur-Richelieu: 600 Boulevard Pierre-Caisse, ☎359-6024.
Saint-Hyacinthe: 1330 Rue Calixa-Lavallée, ☎778-6090.
Sorel: 191 Rue du Roi, ☎743-4411.
Longueuil: bus terminal: 1001 Rue de Sévigny, ☎670-3422.
STRSM (Métro terminal, Longueuil station): 100 Place-Charles-Lemoyne, ☎463-0131.

Eastern Townships

Bromont: 624 Rue Shefford (dépanneur Shefford), ☎534-2116.
Sutton: 28 Rue Principale (Esso station), ☎538-2452.
Magog-Orford: 67A Rue Sherbrooke (Terminus Café), ☎843-4617.
Sherbrooke: 20 Rue King Ouest, ☎569-3656.
Lac-Mégantic: 6630 Rue Salaberry (Dépanneur 6630 Fatima), ☎819-583-2717.

PRACTICAL INFORMATION

Unless otherwise indicated the **area code** for this region is **450**.

Tourist Information Offices

Montérégie

Association Touristique Régional de la Montérégie 989, Rue Pierre-Dupuy, Longueuil, J4K 1A1, ☎674-5555, ⁓463-2876.
Saint-Jean-sur-Richelieu: 315 Macdonald, suite 225, J3B 8J3, ☎358-4849.
Mont-Saint-Hilaire: 1080 Chemin des Patriotes Nord, ☎536-0395 or 1-888-748-3783, ⁓536-3147
Saint-Hyacinthe: Parc des Patriotes, 2090 Rue Cherrier, ☎774-7276 or 1-800-849-7276, ⁓774-9000.
Sorel: 92 Chemin des Patriotes, ☎746-9441 or 1-800-474-9441, ⁓780-5737
Longueuil: 989 Rue Pierre-Dupuy, ☎674-5555.
Office du Tourisme de la Rive-Sud (convention bureau) 205 Chemin Chambly, ☎674-2977.
Salaberry-de-Valleyfield: 980 Boulevard Mgr-Langlois, ☎377-7676.
Sûroit Tourism Office: 30 Avenue du Centenaire, office 126, ☎377-7676 or 1-800-378-7648, ⁓377-3727

Eastern Townships

Tourisme Cantons de l'Est 20 Rue Don-Bosco S., Sherbrooke, J1L 1W4, ☎(819) 820-2020 or 1-800-355-5755, ⁓566-4445, www.tourisme-estrie.qc.ca.
Bromont: 83 Boulevard Bromont, J0E 1L0, ☎534-2006.
Granby: 650 Rue Principale, J2G 8L4, ☎372-7273.
Rougemont: 11 Chemin Marieville, J0L 1M0, ☎469-3600
Magog-Orford: 55 Rue Cabana, J1X 2C4, ☎(819) 843-2744.
Sherbrooke: 48 Rue du Dépôt, J1H 5G1, ☎(819) 821-1919 or 1-800-561-8331.
Sutton: 11 Rue Principale, J0E 2K0, ☎538-8455 or 1-800-565-8455.
Lac-Mégantic: 3295 Rue Laval N., G6B 2S6, ☎(819) 583-5515.

EXPLORING

Montérégie

Chambly ★★

The town of Chambly is located on a privileged site alongside the Richelieu. The river widens here to form the Bassin de Chambly at the end of the rapids that once hindered navigation on the river and making the area a key element in New France's defence system.

In 1665, the Carignan-Salières regiment, under the command of Captain Jacques de Chambly, built the first pile fort to drive back the Iroquois who made frequent incursions into Montréal from the Mohawk River. In 1672, the captain was granted a seigneury in his name for services rendered to the colony.

The town that gradually formed around the fort flourished during the Canadian-American war of 1812-14, while a sizeable British garrison was stationed there. Then, in 1843, the Canal de Chambly opened, allowing boats to bypass the Richelieu Rapids and thereby facilitating commerce between Canada and the United States. Many transportation and import-export companies opened in the area at this time. Today, Chambly is both a suburb of Montréal and a getaway and leisure spot.

Fort Chambly National Historic Site ★★★ *(adults $3.50; Feb, Sat and Sun 10am to 5pm; early Mar to mid-May, Wed to Sun 10am to 5pm; mid-May to mid-Jun, every day 9am to 5pm; late Jun to early Sep, every day 9:30 to 6pm; Sep, Mon 1pm to 5pm, Tue to Sun 10am to 5pm; Oct, Wed to Sun 10am to 5pm; closed from late Oct to early Feb; 2 Rue Richelieu, ☎658-1585).* Also called Lieu Historique National du Fort Chambly, this is the largest remaining fortification of the French Regime. It was built between 1709 and 1711 according to plans drawn by engineer Josué Boisberthelot de Beaucours at the request of the marquis de Vaudreuil. The fort, defended by the *Compagnies Franches de la Marine,* had to protect New France against a possible British invasion. It replaced the two pile forts that had occupied this site since 1665.

Saint-Paul-de-l'Île-aux-Noix

This village is known for its fort, built on Île aux Noix (literally, island of nuts) in the middle of the Richelieu. Farmer Pierre Joudernet was the first occupant of the island, and he payed his seigneurial rent in the form of a bag of nuts, hence the island's name. Towards the end of the French Regime, the island became strategically important because of its proximity to Lake Champlain and the American colonies. The French began to fortify the island in 1759, but had such poor resources that the fort was taken by the British without difficulty. In 1775, the island became the headquarters for the American revolutionary forces, who attempted to invade Canada. Then, during the war of 1812-14, the reconstructed fort served as a base for the attack on Plattsburg (New York State) by the British.

Fort Lennox National Historic Site ★★ *($5; mid-May to late Jun, Mon to Fri 10am to 5pm, Sat and Sun 10am to 6pm; late Jun to early Sep, Mon noon to 6pm, Tue to Sun 10am to 6pm; 1 61e Avenue, J0J 1G0, Saint-Paul-de-l'Île-aux-Noix, ☎291-5700),* also called Lieu Historique National du Fort Lennox. Taking up two-thirds of Île aux Noix and significantly altering its face, Fort Lennox was built on the ruins of previous forts between 1819 and 1829 by the British, prompting the construction of Fort Montgomery by the Americans just south of the border. Behind the wall of earth and surrounded by large ditches are a powder keg, two warehouses, the guardhouse, the officers' residences, two barracks and 19 blockhouses. This charming cut-stone ensemble, built according to the plans of engineer Gother Mann, is a good example of the colonial neoclassical architectural style of the British Empire.

The two-story **Blockhaus de Lacolle ★**, a squared wooden building with loopholes *(free admission; late May to late Aug every day 9am to 5pm; early Sep to early Oct, Sat and Sun 9am to 5pm; 1 Rue Principale, ☎246-3227),* is found at the southernmost point of the Saint-Paul-de-l'Île-aux-Noix municipality. Its construction dates back to 1782, making it one of the oldest wooden structures in Montérégie. It is also one of the few buildings of this type to survive in Québec.

Manoir Rouville-Campbell

Mont-Saint-Hilaire ★

This small town, located at the foot of Mont Saint-Hilaire, was originally part of the seigneury of Rouville, granted to Jean-Baptiste Hertel in 1694. It remained in the hands of the Hertel family until 1844, when it was sold to Major Thomas Edmund Campbell, secretary to the British governor, who operated an experimental farm, which remained in operation until 1942.

Mont-Saint-Hilaire has two urban centres, one along the Richelieu, where the parish church is located, and the other on the southeast side of the mountain, an area that enjoys a mild microclimate and is home to orchards and maple groves.

Though recently scarred by the addition of parking lots and an ostentatious gate, the **Manoir Rouville-Campbell** ★ *(125 Chemin des Patriotes Sud)* remains one of the most magnificent seigneurial residences in Québec. It was built in 1854 according to the plans of British architect Frederick Lawford, who also contributed to the interior decor of the Église de Saint-Hilaire. During the eighties, the house and the stables were transformed into an inn (see p 202).

The **Église Saint-Hilaire** ★★ *(260 Chemin des Patriotes Nord)* was originally supposed to have two façade towers topped with spires. As a result of internal arguments, only the bases of the towers were erected in 1830, and a steeple, placed in the centre of the façade, was later installed. The interior decor, done in the Gothic-Revival style, was completed over a long period of time, between 1838 and 1928. The masterpiece of this interior is the work of painter Ozias Leduc (1864-1955), completed at the end of the 19th century.

Saint-Hyacinthe ★★

Saint-Hyacinthe's main attraction is the vitality of the city and its inhabitants. The city is divided into the upper part of town, which is more administrative, religious, and middle-class, and the lower part of town, more working-class and commercial. Rarely in rural Québec have the liveliness of a town centre and the monuments that dominate its landscape been so successfully preserved as here. It is best to explore downtown Saint-Hyacinthe on foot.

The town specializes in the construction of large pipe organs. The Casavant brothers set up their famous organ factory outside the city in 1879 *(900 Rue Girouard Est)*. Approximately 15 electro-pneumatic organs are made here every year and are installed throughout the world by the house experts. Guided tours are sometimes organized. Guilbault-Thérien organ-builders have been building mechanical traction organs since 1946 according to French and

German models of the 18th century *(2430 Rue Crevier)*. Saint-Hyacinthe also has a music bookstore dedicated solely to the organ and the harpsichord *(Ex Arte, 12790 Rue Yamaska)*.

The **Cathédrale Saint-Hyacinthe-le-Confesseur ★** *(1900 Rue Girouard Ouest)* is a squat building despite its 50-metre-high spires. It was built in 1880 and modified in 1906 according to designs by Montréal architects Perrault and Venne. They contributed the Romanesque Revival style and interesting rococo interior, reminiscent of some of the subway stations in Moscow.

La Présentation

The beautiful church in this modest village was built shortly after the La Présentation parish was created, following the division of part of Saint-Hyacinthe in 1804.

The **Église de La Présentation ★★** *(551 Chemin de L'Église)* is unique among other temples built in Montérégie during the same era because of its finely sculpted stone façade, completed in 1819. Note the inscriptions written in Old French above the entrances. The vast presbytery, hidden in the greenery, as well as the modest sexton house, complete this landscape typical of Québec rural parishes.

Saint-Denis ★

Throughout the 1830s, Saint-Denis was home to large political gatherings as well as the headquarters of the Fils de la Liberté (Sons of Freedom), a group of young French Canadians who wanted Lower Canada (Québec) to become an independent country. But even more important, Saint-Denis was the site of the only Patriotes victory over the British during the 1837-38 rebellion. On November 23, 1837, General Gore's troops were forced to withdraw to Sorel after a fierce battle against the Patriotes, who were poorly equipped but determined to defeat the enemy. The British troops took revenge a few weeks later, however, by surprising the inhabitants while they slept, pillaging and burning the houses, businesses and industries of Saint-Denis.

The town of Saint-Denis, founded in 1758, experienced an intense period of industrialization in the early 19th century. Canada's largest hat industry was located here, where the famous beaver pelt top hats worn by men throughout Europe and America, were made. Other local industries in Saint-Denis included pottery and earthenware. The repression that followed the rebellion put an end to this economic expansion, and from then on, the town became a small agricultural village.

A monument was unveiled in 1913 in **Parc des Patriotes** to honour the memory of the Saint-Denis Patriotes. It is located in the middle of the square that was once known as Place Royale before becoming Place du Marché, a market place, and then a public park in the early 20th century.

The **Maison Nationale des Patriotes ★** *($3.50; early May to early Jun and early Sep to late Nov, Tue to Sun 10am to 5pm; early Jun to late Aug, Tue to Sun 11am to 6pm; 610 Chemin des Patriotes, ☎787-3623)*. To the south of the park stands a former stone inn built for Jean-Baptiste Mâsse, in 1810. The building's irregular shape is characteristic of urban homes of the late 18th century (firebreak walls with corbels, veranda on the main floor, optimum usage of the land). It is one of the rare examples of this type found outside of Montréal and Québec City.

Sainte-Anne-de-Sorel ★

This village is oriented more towards hunting and fishing than other communities in Montérégie because of its proximity to the Sorel islands. Writer Germaine Guèvremont (1893-1968), who lived on one of these islands, introduced this archipelago located in the middle of the St. Lawrence to the literary world in her novel *Le Survenant*.

The best way to explore the **Îles de Sorel ★** is by taking one of the cruise boats that crosses the archipelago of approximately 20 islands *(two types of cruises are offered: Croisière des Îles de Sorel, 1665 Chemin du Chenal-du-Moine, and Excursions et Expéditions de Canots, ☎743-7227 or 743-7807)*. The hour and a half-long cruises begin at the Chenal du Moine. This large waterway was named in the 17th century following the discovery of the frozen body of a Recollet monk *(moine)* who had been travelling from Trois-Rivières to Sorel along the channel *(chenal)*.

The islands are an excellent place to observe aquatic birds, especially during the spring and

QUÉBEC

fall. A few houses on piles with individual piers dot the flat landscape, which offers views of the vast expanse of Lac Saint-Pierre downstream. There are two restaurants at the end of the Île d'Embarras (accessible by car) that serve *gibelotte*, a fish fricassee typical of this region.

Saint-Constant

This municipality has a large railway museum, the Musée Ferroviaire Canadien, as well as an ecomuseum, considered a forerunner in its field.

The **Musée Ferroviaire Canadien** ★★ *($5.75; early May to early Sep, every day 9am to 5pm; early Sep to mid-Oct, Sat and Sun 9am to 5pm; 120 Rue Saint-Pierre, ☎632-2410)* displays an impressive collection of railway memorabilia, locomotives, freight cars, and maintenance vehicles. The famous *Dorchester* locomotive, put into service in 1836 on the country's first railway between Saint-Jean-sur-Richelieu and La Prairie, is worth noting, as well as many luxurious passenger cars of the 19th century that belonged to Canadian Pacific. Also on display are foreign locomotives such as the powerful *Châteaubriand* from the SNCF (French Railway System), put into service in 1884.

La Prairie ★

The streets of Vieux-La Prairie ★★ have an urban character rarely found in Québec villages during the 19th century. Several houses were carefully restored after the Québec government declared the area an historical district in 1975. A stroll along Saint-Ignace, Sainte-Marie, Saint-Jacques and Saint-Georges streets reveals this distinctive flavour. Some of the wood houses are reminiscent of those once found in Montréal districts *(240 and 274 Rue Saint-Jacques)*. Other homes draw their inspiration from French Regime architecture (two sided roofs, firebreak walls, dormer windows), except for the fact that they are partially or totally built of brick instead of stone *(234 and 237 Rue Saint-Ignace, 166 Rue Saint-Georges)*. Lastly, the stone house covered with wood at number 238 Rue Saint-Ignace is the only surviving testimony of the French Regime in Vieux-La Prairie.

Longueuil ★

Located across from Montréal, this city is the most populous in Montérégie. It once belonged to the Longueuil seigneury, granted to Charles Le Moyne (1624-1685) in 1657. He headed a dynasty that played a key role in developing New France. Many of his 14 children are famous, such as Pierre Le Moyne d'Iberville (1661-1706), first governor of Louisiana, Jean-Baptiste Le Moyne de Bienville (1680-1768), founder of New Orleans, and Antoine Le Moyne de Châteauguay (1683-1747), governor of Guyana.

The eldest son, Charles Le Moyne de Longueuil, inherited the seigneury upon the death of his father. Between 1685 and 1690, he had a fortified castle built on the site of the current Église Saint-Antoine-de-Padoue. The castle had four corner towers, a church and many wings. In 1700, Longueuil was raised to the rank of barony by Louis XIV, the only such case in the history of New France. The baron of Longueuil saw to the development of his land, which continued to grow until it reached the banks of the Richelieu.

The 1810 church, was demolished in 1884 to make room for the present building, the **Église Saint-Antoine-de-Padoue** ★★ *(Rue Saint-Charles, at the corner of Chemin de Chambly)* the largest church in Montérégie. The exterior is inspired by flamboyant Gothic art, but remains close to Victorian eclecticism.

Kahnawake

In 1667, the Jesuits set up a mission for the converted Iroquois at La Prairie. After moving four times, the mission settled permanently in Sault-Saint-Louis in 1716. The Saint-François-Xavier mission has now become Kahnawake, a name that means "where the rapids are". Over the years, Iroquois Mohawks from the State of New York joined the mission's first inhabitants, so that English is now the first language on the reserve, even though most inhabitants stilll use the French names given to them by the Jesuits. In 1990, Mohawk Warriors demonstrated by blocking the Pont Mercier for months in a show of support for the demands made by the Mohawks of Kanesatake (Oka). Tension between Québec authorities and the natives still exists in the area surrounding the reserve, but visitors need not worry as they are generally warmly welcomed in Kahnawake.

The **Enceinte, Musée** and **Église Saint-François-Xavier** ★★ *(Main Street)* Saint-François-Xavier wall, museum and church. Villages and missions were required under the French Regime to surround themselves with fortifications. Very few of these walls have survived. The wall of the Kahnawake mission, still partially standing, is the kind of ruin rarely found north of Mexico. It was built in 1720, according to plans of the King's engineer, Gaspard Chaussegros de Léry, to protect the church and the Jesuit convent, built in 1717. The guardroom, powder magazine and officers' residences (1754) are also still standing. From the platform behind the Jesuit convent, visitors can enjoy spectacular views of the seaway, Lachine and Montréal.

The church was modified in 1845 according to the plans of Jesuit Félix Martin, and redecorated by Vincent Chartrand (1845-47), who also made some of the furniture. Guido Nincheri designed the polychromatic vaulted ceiling in the 20th century. Also found here is the tomb of Kateri Tekakwitha, a young native. The convent houses the museum of the Saint-François-Xavier mission, where visitors can see some of the objects that belonged to the Jesuits.

Châteauguay

The Châteauguay seigneury was granted to Charles Le Moyne in 1673. He immediately had Château de Guay built on Île Saint-Bernard, at the mouth of the Rivière Châteauguay. One hundred years later, a village stood out around the Église Saint-Joachim. The roads and Boulevards that run along the river and Lac Saint-Louis are still dotted with pretty farm homes built between 1780 and 1840, when the seigneury belonged to the Sœurs Grises (the Grey Nuns). The municipality has developed considerably since 1950, making it a large component of the Montréal suburbs.

When the first church in Châteauguay was built in 1735 it was the westernmost parish on the south shore of the St. Lawrence. Work on the present **Église Saint-Joachim** ★★ (*1 Boulevard Youville*) began in 1775 in order to more easily serve a growing number of parishioners. The **Hôtel de Ville** neighbours the church to the north. It is located in the former convent of the Congrégation de Notre-Dame (1886).

Salaberry-de-Valleyfield

This industrial city came into being in 1845 around a saw and paper mill purchased a few years later by the Montréal Cotton Company. This growing industry led to an era of prosperity in the late 19th century in Salaberry-de-Valleyfield, making it one of Québec's main cities at the time. The old commercial and institutional centre on Rue Victoria recalls this prosperous period, and gives the city more of an urban atmosphere than Châteauguay whose population is higher. The city is cut in half by the old Canal de Beauharnois, in operation from 1845 to 1900 (not to be confused with the current Canal de Beauharnois located to the south of the city.)

A diocese since 1892, Salaberry-de-Valleyfield was graced with the current **Cathédrale Sainte-Cécile** ★ (*31 Rue de la Fabrique*) in 1934, following a fire in the previous church. The cathedral is a colossal piece of work. Architect Henri Labelle designed it in the late Gothic Revival style, narrower and closer to the historical models, and combined the result with elements of Art Deco.

The **Battle of the Châteauguay National Historic Site** ★ (*$2.50; late Jun to late Aug, every day 10am to 6pm; Sep and Oct, Wed to Sun 9am to 5pmk; 2371 Chemin Rivière-Châteauguay Nord)*, also called the Lieu Historique National de la Bataille de la Châteauguay. During the American War of Independence (1775-76), the Americans attempted their first take-over of Canada, a British colony since 1760. They were forced back by the majority French population. In 1812-13, the Americans tried once again to take over Canada. This time, it was loyalty to the Crown of England and the decisive battle of Châteauguay that bungled the Americans' attempt. In October 1813, troops of American General Hampton, 2,000-men strong, gathered at the border. They entered Canadian territory during the night along the Rivière Châteauguay. But Charles Michel d'Irumberry de Salaberry, seigneur of Chambly, was waiting for them along with 300 militiamen and a few dozen natives. On October 26, the battle began. Salaberry's tactics got the better of the Americans, who retreated, putting an end to a series of conflicts and inaugurating a lasting friendship between the two countries.

Highway 15 leads to the town of Hemmingford near the American border. **Parc Safari** ★ is located here (*$19; $66 per car; early May to*

QUÉBEC

early Sep, every day 10am to 5pm; 850 Route 202, ☎247-2727). The park is an interesting zoological garden, where animals from Africa, Europe and America, wander freely, as visitors tour the grounds in their cars.

Eastern Townships

The Wine Route ★

European visitors might consider it quite presumptuous to call the road between Dunham and Stanbridge East *(Route 202 W.)* the "Wine Route", but the concentration of vineyards in this region is unique in the province, and Québec's attempts at wine-making have been so surprisingly successful that people have been swept away by their enthusiasm. There are no châteaux or distinguished old counts here, only growers who sometimes have to go as far as renting helicopters to save their vines from freezing. The rotor blades cause the air to circulate, preventing frost from forming on the ground during crucial periods in May. The region is, however, blessed with a microclimate and soil favourable for grape growing (slate). The various wines are sold only at the vineyards where they are produced.

You can visit the **L'Orpailleur** *(1086 Route 202, JOE 1MO, Dunham, ☎295-2763, ⌐295-3112)* winery, whose products include a dry white wine and Apéridor, an apéritif similar to Pineau des Charentes.

The **Domaine des Côtes d'Ardoises** *(879 Route 202, Dunham, JOE 1MO, ☎295-2020)* is one of the few Québec vineyards that produces red wine. Here, as at other wineries, the owner will give you a warm welcome.

Les Blancs Coteaux *(1046 Route 202, Dunham, JOE 1MO, ☎294-3503)* not only makes quality wine but also has a lovely craft shop.

Bromont

Developed in the 1960s, Bromont has become a favourite resort area among Montrealers. It is renowned for its downhill ski resort, its sports facilities, and also for having hosted the 1976 Olympic equestrian competitions.

Valcourt

Bombardier was not the only mechanic in Québec to develop a motor vehicle for use on snow-covered surfaces. Residents had to come up with something, since many roads in the province were not cleared of snow until the beginning of the 1950s. As automobiles were, for all practical purposes, somewhat unreliable, people had to depend on the same means of transportation as their ancestors, namely, the horse-drawn sleigh. Bombardier, however, was the only individual to succeed in making a profit from his invention, most notably because of a lucrative contract with the army during World War II. Though the company later diversified and underwent considerable expansion, it never left the village of Valcourt—to this day the site of its head office.

The **Musée J.-Armand-Bombardier** ★ *($5; mid-Jun to late Apr, Tue to Sun 10am to 5pm; 1001 Avenue Joseph-Armand-Bombardier; ☎532-5300)* is a museum that traces the development of the snowmobile, and explains how Bombardier's invention was marketed all over the world. Different prototypes are displayed, along with a few examples of various snowmobiles produced since 1960. Group tours of the factory are also available.

Granby

A few kilometres from the verdant Parc de la Yamaska, **Granby**, the "princess of the Eastern Townships", basks in the surrounding countryside's fresh air. In addition to its Victorian-style houses, this city boasts grand avenues and parks graced with fountains and sculptures. Transected by the Yamaska Nord river, it is also the point at which the Montérégiade and Estriade bicycle trails converge. The city's youth and dynamism are reflected through its multiple festivals, notably the celebratory Festival International de la Chanson, an international song festival that has exposed the French-speaking world to a number of excellent performers.

Visitors to the **Granby Zoo** ★★ *($15; mid-May to early Sep, every day 10am to 6pm; take Exit 68 or 74 from Hwy 10 and follow the signs; ☎372-9113)* can see some 250 animal species from various different countries, in particular North America and Africa. This is an old-style zoo, so most of the animals are in cages and there are few areas where they can roam freely. It is nevertheless interesting.

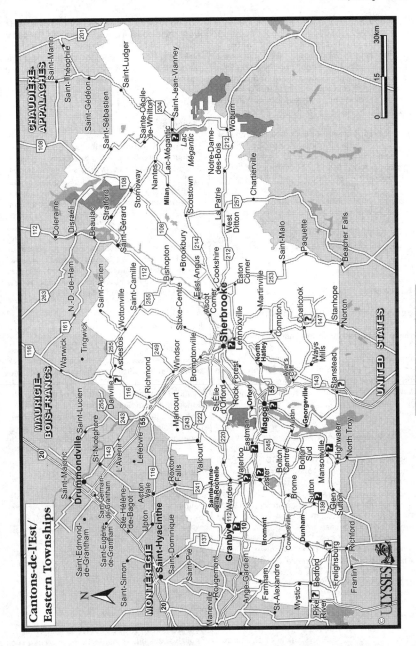

Cantons-de-l'Est/
Eastern Townships

Knowlton ★★

Lac Brome ★, a circular body of water, is popular among windsurfers, who can use a parking lot and a little beach on the side of the road near Knowlton. The duck from this lake is known for its flavour and is featured on the menus of local inns and restaurants when in season.

The **Musée Historique du Comté de Brome ★** (*$3; mid-May to mid- Sep, Mon to Sat 10am to 4:30pm, Sun 11am to 4:30pm; 130 Rue Lakeside; ☎243-6782)*, the historical museum of Brome County, occupying five Loyalist buildings, traces the lives and history of the region's inhabitants. In addition to the usual furniture and photographs, visitors can see a reconstructed general store, a 19th- century court of justice, and what's more unusual, a collection of military equipment, including a World War I airplane.

Sutton ★

Sutton, which is located at the base of the mountain of the same name, is one of the major winter resorts in the Eastern Townships. The area also has several well-designed golf courses Among the local houses of worship, the Gothic Revival Anglican **Grace Church**, built out of stone in 1850, is the most noteworthy. Unfortunately, though, its steeple no longer has its pointed arch.

Lac Memphrémagog ★★

Lac Memphrémagog, which is 40 kilometres long and only one to two kilometres wide, will remind some visitors of a Scottish loch. It even has its own equivalent of the Loch Ness monster, named "Memphre"; sightings go back to 1798! The southern portion of the lake, which cannot be seen from Magog, is located in the United States. The name Memphrémagog, like Massawippi and Missisquoi, is an Abenaki word. Sailing enthusiasts will be happy to learn that the lake is one of the best places in Québec to enjoy this sport.

Saint-Benoît-du-Lac ★★

This municipality consists solely of the estate of the **Abbaye de Saint-Benoît-du-Lac**, an abbey founded in 1913 by Benedictine monks who were driven away from the Abbaye de Saint-Wandrille-de-Fontenelle in Normandy. Aside from the monastery itself, there are the guest quarters, the abbey chapel and the farm buildings. However, only the chapel and a few corridors are open to the public. Visitors will not want to miss the Gregorian chants sung at vespers at 5pm every day.

Magog ★

Equipped with more facilities than any other town between Granby and Sherbrooke, Magog has a lot to offer sports lovers. It is extremely well situated on the northernmost shore of Lac Memphrémagog, but has unfortunately been subjected to unbridled development for several years now. The town's cultural scene is worth noting. Visitors can go to the theatre or the music complex, set in the natural mountain surroundings. The textile industry, once of great importance in the lives of local residents, has declined, giving way to tourism. Visitors will enjoy strolling down Rue Principale, which is lined with shops and restaurants.

North Hatley ★★

Attracted by North Hatley's enchanting countryside, wealthy American vacationers built luxurious villas here between 1890 and 1930. Most of these still line the northern part of Lac Massawippi, which, like Lac Memphrémagog, resembles a Scottish loch. Beautiful inns and gourmet restaurants add to the charm of the place, ensuring its reputation as a vacation spot of the utmost sophistication. In the centre of the village, visitors will notice the tiny Shingle-style **United Church**, which appears more Catholic than Protestant.

Manoir Hovey ★ (*Chemin Hovey*), a large villa built in 1900, was modelled on Mount Vernon, George Washington's home in Virginia. It used to be the summer residence of an American named Henry Atkinson, who entertained American artists and politicians here every summer. The house has since been converted into an inn.

Lennoxville ★

This little town, whose population is still mainly English-speaking, is home to two prestigious English-language educational institutions, Bishop's University and Bishop's College. Established alongside the road linking Trois-

Rivières to the American border, it was named after Charles Lennox, the fourth Duke of Richmond, who was governor of Upper and Lower Canada in 1818. Once off the main road (Route 143) explore the town's side streets to see the institutional buildings and lovely Second Empire and Queen Anne houses nestled in greenery.

Bishop's University ★ *(College Road)*, one of three English-language universities in Québec, offers 1,300 students from all over Canada a personalized education in an enchanting setting. It was founded in 1843, through the efforts of a minister named Lucius Doolittle. Upon arriving at the university, visitors will see **McGreer Hall**, built in 1876 according to a design by architect James Nelson and later modified by Taylor and Gordon of Montréal to give it a medieval look. **St. Mark's Anglican Chapel**, which stands to its left, was rebuilt in 1891 after a fire. Its long, narrow interior has lovely oak trim, as well as stained-glass windows by Spence and Sons of Montréal.

Sherbrooke ★★

Sherbrooke, the Eastern Townships' main urban area, is nicknamed the Queen of the Eastern Townships. It spreads over a series of hills on both sides of the Rivière Saint-François, accentuating its disorderly appearance. The city nevertheless has a number of interesting buildings, the majority of which are located on the west bank. Sherbrooke's origins date back to the beginning of the 19th century; like so many other villages in the region, it grew up around a mill and a small market. However, in 1823, it was designated as the site of a courthouse intended to serve the entire region, which set it apart from the neighbouring communities. The arrival of the railroad here in 1852, as well as the downtown concentration of institutions, such as the head office of the Eastern Township Bank, led to the construction of prestigious Victorian edifices thereby transforming Sherbrooke's appearance. Today, the city is home to an important French-language university, founded in 1952 in order to counterbalance Bishop's University in Lennoxville. Despite the city's name, chosen in honour of Sir John Coape Sherbrooke, governor of British North America at the time it was founded, the city's population has been almost entirely French-speaking (95 %) for a long time.

An important financial institution in the last century, now merged with the CIBC (Canadian Imperial Bank of Commerce), the former **Eastern Townships Bank ★★** *(241 Rue Dufferin)* was established by the region's upper class, who were unable to obtain financing for local projects from the banks in Montréal. Its Sherbrooke head office, erected in 1877, was designed by Montréal architect James Nelson, involved at the time in building Bishop's University. It is considered the finest Second Empire building in Québec outside of Montréal and Québec City. Following a donation from the Canadian Imperial Bank of Commerce (CIBC) and major renovations, the building now houses the **Musée des Beaux-Arts** *($2.50; mid-Jun to Aug, Tue to Sun 11am to 5pm; Sep to mid-Jun, 1pm to 5pm; 241 Rue Dufferin, ☎819-821-2115).* Gérard Gendron's work, which greets visitors in the main hall, parallels the building's former tenants and its present vocation. Besides the museum's large collection of naive art, there are several works by local contemporary artists. Volunteers are available to answer questions on the exhibitions, which usually change every two months.

Some of the loveliest houses in Sherbrooke are located on **Parc Mitchell ★★**, which is adorned with a fountain by sculptor George Hill (1921). **Maison Morey** *(not open to visitors; 428 Rue Dufferin)*, is an example of the bourgeois Victorian style favoured by merchants and industrialists from the British Isles and the United States. It was built in 1873 for Thomas Morey.

Notre-Dame-des-Bois

Located in the heart of the Appalachians at an altitude of over 550 metres, this little community acts as a sort of gateway to Mont Mégantic and its observatory, as well as Mont Saint-Joseph and its sanctuary.

The **Astrolab du Mont-Mégantic ★★** *($10; mid-Jun to Sep, every day 10am to 6pm, 8pm to 11pm with reservations; 189 Route du Parc, ☎819-888-2941 or 1-888-881-2941)* is an interpretation centre on astronomy. The interactive museum's various rooms and multimedia show reveals the beginnings of astronomy with the latest technology. A guided tour to the summit of Mont Mégantic, lasting approximately 1 hour and 15 minutes, walks visitors through the facilities. Famous for its observatory, Mont Mégantic was chosen for its strategic position between the Universities of Montreal and Laval, as well as its distance from urban light sources. The second highest summit

QUÉBEC

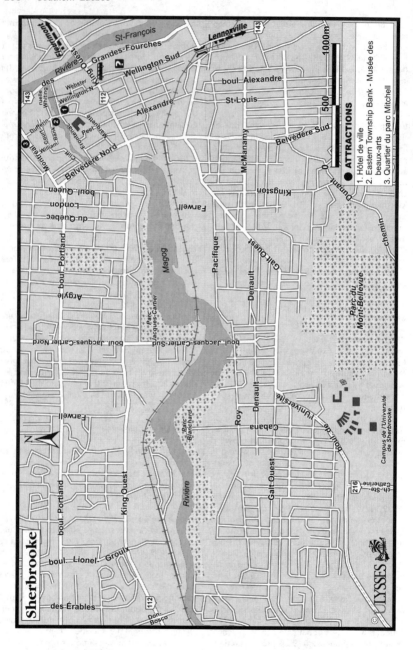

Sherbrooke

ATTRACTIONS

1. Hôtel de ville
2. Eastern Township Bank - Musée des beaux-arts
3. Quartier du parc Mitchell

in the Eastern Townships, it stands at 1105 metres. During the **Festival d'Astronomie Populaire du Mont Mégantic**, a local astronomy festival held the second week of July, astronomy buffs can observe the heavens through the most powerful telescope in eastern North America. Otherwise, the latter is only available to researchers. In summer, however, basic celestial mechanics workshops are given. These begin at 8pm and include giant-screen presentations and observation of the sky. Reservations required.

A vast expanse of crystal-clear water stretching 19 kilometres, **Lac Mégantic** ★★ is teeming with all sorts of fish, especially trout, and attracts a good many vacationers eager to go fishing or simply enjoy the local beaches. Five municipalities around the lake, Lac-Mégantic being the most well-known, welcome visitors lured by the lovely mountainous countryside.

OUTDOORS

Parks

Montérégie

Centre de Conservation de la Nature du Mont Saint-Hilaire ★★ *($4; every day 8am until sundown; 422 Rue des Moulins, Mont-Saint-Hilaire, J3G 4S6, ☎467-1755)*. Situated on the upper half of Mont Saint-Hilaire, this nature conservation centre is a former estate that brigadier Andrew Hamilton Gault passed on to Montréal's McGill University in 1958. Scientific research is conducted here and recreational activities (hiking, cross-country skiing) are permitted throughout the year on half of the estate, which covers 11 square kilometres. The Centre was also recognized as a Biosphere Reserve by UNESCO in 1978, because it is covered by a mature forest that has remained virtually untouched over the centuries. An information centre on the formation of the Montérégie hills and a garden of indigenous plants can be found at the park's entrance.

Eastern Townships

The **Parc du Mont-Orford** ★★ *(C.P. 146, Magog, J1X 3W7; ☎819-843-6233)* stretches over 58 square kilometres and includes—in addition to the mountain—the area around Lac

Stukely. During the summer, visitors can enjoy the beach, the magnificent golf course ($30 a round), back-country campsites, and some 50 kilometres of hiking trails (the most beautiful path leads to Mont Chauve). The park also attracts winter sports lovers with its cross-country ski trails and 33 downhill ski runs ($34 a day).

The **Parc de la Gorge de Coaticook** ★★ *($6; May to Nov, every day 9am to 8pm; 135 Rue Michaud; ☎819-849-2331)* protects the part of the impressive 50-metre gorge created by the Rivière Coaticook. Trails wind across the entire area, enabling visitors to see the gorge from all different angles. Cross the suspension bridge over the gorge, if you dare!

Known foremost for its famed observatory (see p 199), the **Parc de Conservation du Mont-Mégantic** *(189 Route du Parc, Notre-Dame-des-Bois, ☎819-888-2800)* covers an area of 58.8 square kilometres and is an example of the different types of mountainous vegetation characteristic of the Eastern Townships. Heavy infrastructure has not even been able to disturb the tranquillity of this park whose goal is an educational one. Hikers and skiers can take advantage of the Park's interpretive trails, cabins and campsites and, if lucky, observe up to 125 species of migrating birds. Snowshoeing in winter and mountain-biking in summer. Its summits, Mont Mégantic and Mont Saint-Joseph, are accessible by car.

Hiking

Eastern Townships

The **Sentier de l'Estrie** *(☎819-868-3889)* network of trails winds over 150 kilometres through the Chapman, Kingsbury, Brompton, Orford, Bolton, Glen, Echo and Sutton areas. You can obtain a topographical guide of the trail and the membership card necessary to walk it for $20. Keep in mind that most of the trail runs across private property. The various landowners have accorded an exclusive right of way to members.

QUÉBEC

Horseback Riding

Eastern Townships

The **Centre Équestre de Bromont** *(100 Rue Laprairie, ☎534-3255)* hosted the 1976 Olympic equestrian events, for which a variety of stables and rings, both exterior and interior, were built. Some of these facilities are now used for riding classes.

 Downhiill Skiing

Eastern Townships

The **Station de Ski Bromont** *($32; 150 Rue Champlain, ☎534-2200)* has 23 runs, 20 of which are lit until 11:30pm for night-skiing. The mountain has a vertical drop of over 400 metres.

Mont Sutton ★ *($39; 671 Chemin Mapple; ☎450-866-2545, ☎538-2339 during summer)* has 53 downhill ski runs and a vertical drop of 460 metres. It is known for its magnificent glade runs.

Mont Orford ★ *($32.75; Magog, ☎819-843-6549)* is among the prettiest ski centres in Québec. It boasts 40 trails.

Owl's Head ★ *($30; Chemin du Mont Owl's Head, Mansonville, ☎292-3342)* is one of the most beautiful ski resorts in the Eastern Townships region, with sweeping views of Lac Memphrémagog and the surrounding mountains. There are 27 runs for skiers of all different levels.

 ACCOMMODATIONS

Montérégie

Chambly

La Maison Ducharme *($90-$110 bkfst incl.; ≈; 124 Rue Martel, ☎447-1220, ☎447-1018)*. This pleasant B&B occupies an old 19th-century barracks, right near Fort Chambly. Tastefully decorated, the house is steeped in the antique luxury of an era, when people took the time to make every detail in the house immaculate. A lovely English garden and pool add to this large property next to the Rivière Richelieu rapids.

Saint-Jean-sur-Richelieu

The **Auberge des Trois Rives** *($55, ℜ; 297 Rue Richelieu, J3B 6Y3, ☎358-8077, ☎358-8077)* is a pleasant B&B set up in a rustic home. A restaurant and a terrace offer a pretty view of the water. There are 10 modestly-decorated but comfy rooms spread over two floors. Take note that prices may be higher during the hot-air balloon festival.

Mont-Saint-Hilaire

The **Manoir Rouville Campbell** *($105; ≡, ≈, ℜ; 125 Chemin des Patriotes, ☎446-6060, ☎446-4878)* has a certain mystical air about it; as you enter the manor it's as though time has stopped or even gone back a century. This place, now 200 years old, has seen many chapters of Québec history unfold. It was converted into a luxury hotel in 1987 and is now owned by Québec comedian Yvon Deschamps. The dining room, bar and gardens overlooking the Richelieu complement this lordly manor.

Saint-Hyacinthe

In a building next to the highway, the **Auberge des Seigneurs** *($70-$120, ≈, ⊙, △, ℜ; 1200 Daniel-Johnson, J2S 7K7, ☎774-3810 and 1-800-363-0110, ☎774-6955)* offers pretty rooms as well as other services, to ensure its visitors a pleasant stay. Tennis and squash courts are available, and the peaceful lobby is decorated with plants and a fountain.

Saint-Marc-sur-Richelieu

The **Hostellerie les Trois Tilleuls** *($90-$390; ≈, tv, ℜ; 290 Rue Richelieu J0L 2E0, ☎584-2231 or 1-800-263-2230, ☎584-3146)* is a member of the prestigious Relais et Châteaux association. Built next to the Richelieu, it enjoys a tranquil rural setting. The name of the establishment comes from the three grand linden trees, called *tilleul* in French, that shade the property. The rooms are decorated with rustic furniture and they each have a balcony overlooking the river. Outside, guests have access to gardens, a lookout and a heated pool.

Eastern Townships

Dunham

With its 0.5 hectares of land, the **Pom-Art B&B** *($55, sb, $75 pb, bkfst incl.; 677 Chemin Hudson, ☎295-3514)*, built in 1820, is a real gem. Denis and Lise offer guests a warm welcome, not to mention an exceptional breakfast where apples from the region figure prominently. An ideal abode in which to seek refuge after a tiring day on the slopes of Mont Sutton, located 15 kilometres away. Indeed, the most luxurious of the three rooms boasts a fireplace and a window looking out on the surrounding mountains.

Bromont

Those looking for comfort can head to the **Château Bromont** *($140; ≈, ○, ℜ; 90 Stanstead, JOE 1L0; ☎534-3433 or 1-800-304-3433, ⊷534-0514)*, where both the main rooms and the bedrooms are elegantly decorated with antique furniture. It is located alongside Mont Bromont, providing skiers with easy access to the slopes.

Around Lac Brome

Joli Vent *($80 bkfst incl.; ≈; 667 Chemin Bondville, Foster, JOE 1R0; ☎243-4272, ⊷243-0202)* is a lovely inn within a pleasant setting, despite being alongside the road. The modestly furnished rooms have a rustic charm.

Knowlton

Ideally located near ski resorts and golf courses, the **Auberge Lakeview** *($125 bkfst incl. Fri to Sun, $88 bkfst incl. Mon to Thu; ⊛, ≈, ℜ, ⊛; 50 Rue Victoria, ☎243-6183 or 1-800-661-6183, ⊷243-0602)* offers an altogether Victorian atmosphere. Indeed, the 1986 renovations have restored some of the noble antiquity to this historic monument, built in the latter half of the 19th century. Rates for rooms, both comfortable and spacious, include the continental breakfast.

Sutton

La Paimpolaise *($76 bkfst incl.; ℜ; 615 Maple, C.P. 548, JOE 2K0; ☎538-3213, ⊷538-3970)* inn near the ski slopes is set up in two separate buildings. The reception is in a small, wooden, Swiss chalet-style house, and the rooms are in a long concrete annex. These are somewhat austere. This is a very plain hotel with a clientele consisting mainly of skiers.

Magog

Surrounded by wild flowers and cats, **Aux Jardins Champêtres** *($65 sb, $90 pb, $126 ½ b; 1575 Chemin des Pères, ☎819-868-0665)* recalls summers spent at grandma's. Located a few minutes from Magog and l'Abbaye St-Benoit-du-Lac, this B & B boasts comfortable rooms as well as a swimming pool. The welcoming little farm also owes its reputation to its excellent and varied country cooking.

Mont-Orford

Situated near the Centre d'Arts d'Orford, the **Auberge La Grande Fugue** *($15/person; May to Oct; 3166 Chemin du Parc, ☎819-843-8595 or 1-800-567-6155)* consists of a series of small cottages surrounded by nature. A communal kitchen is available to guests. In the early afternoon, a shuttle service ($2 return trip) takes visitors from Magog to the Centre d'Arts. For information about timetables, contact the tourist office or call at ☎819-847-0151.

The **Village Mont-Orford** *($95; ≈, K; 5015 Chemin du Parc, J1X 3W8, ☎819-847-2662 or 1-800-567-7315, ⊷847-2487)* is comprised of several buildings, each containing a few lovely, equipped condos. Approximately 200 metres from there, a quadruple chair lift takes skiers up to Mont Orford's runs.

In the shadow of Mont Orford is the very opulent and modern **Manoir des Sables** *($119 to $134; ≡, ℜ, ○, ⊙, ≈, tv; 90 Avenue des Jardins, ☎819-847-4747 or 1-800-567-3514, ⊷847-3519)*. The hotel features a multitude of services and facilities such as indoor and outdoor swimming pools, an 18-hole golf course, tennis courts and a health spa. Several rooms boast fireplaces, and those on the top floor offer magnificent views of the lake and of the 60-hectare property. Rooms in the "Privilège" wing come with exemplary service and include continental breakfasts.

QUÉBEC

Ayer's Cliff

Set on a natural, six-hectare property facing Lac Massawippi, the **Auberge Ripplecove** (*$234 ½b; ≈, ◎, ≈, ℜ; 700 Rue Ripplecove,* ☎*819-838-4296 or 1-800-668-4296,* ⇔*819-838-5541*), is wonderfully peaceful. Its elegant Victorian-style dining room and tasteful rooms ensure comfort in unparalleled, intimate surroundings. Moreover, the more luxurious rooms boast their own fireplaces and whirlpool baths. A variety of outdoor activities is offered. The place becomes absolutely magical in winter.

North Hatley

The **Auberge Hatley** (*$200 ½b; ≈, ℜ; Route 108, J0B 2C0;* ☎*819-842-2451,* ⇔*842-2907*) occupies a superb residence built in 1903. The spacious living room looking out on the lake is decorated with beautiful antiques. A vast garden surrounds the inn and its pool. A magical place to escape to.

Built in 1900, the **Manoir Hovey** (*$250 ½b; ⊖, ≈, ℜ; Chemin Hovey, J0B 1C0;* ☎*819-842-2421,* ⇔*842-2248*) reflects the days when wealthy families spent their vacations in the beautiful country houses of the Townships (see p 198). Converted into an inn 40 years ago, it is still extremely comfortable. The 40 rooms are decorated with lovely antique furniture, and most offer a magnificent view of Lac Massawippi. The property retains much of the old, natural charm of the site.

Sherbrooke

Recently converted into a B&B, **Le Vieux Presbytère** (*$55 sb, $65 pb, bkfst incl.; 1162 Boulevard Portland,* ☎*819-346-1665*) has five tastefully decorated rooms. Several of the proprietors' finds will delight antique lovers, as will the beautiful lobby and reception on the ground floor. Moreover, safe storage is provided for bicycles.

The pinkish **Delta Hotel** (*$78; ≈, ⊖, △, ℜ; 2685 Rue King Ouest, J1L 1C1;* ☎*819-822-1989 or 1-800-268-1133*) is also on the way into town. Recently built, it offers its guests a wide range of facilities, including an indoor pool, a whirlpool and an exercise room.

RESTAURANTS

Montérégie

Chambly

Crêperie du Fort Chambly (*$$; 1717 Rue Bougogne,* ☎*447-7474*), on the edge of Bassin de Chambly, occupies a wooden house that recalls the sea. They serve crêpes, of course, but also cheese fondues. Waterfront terrace and friendly service.

Les Fous de Bassin (*$$-$$$; 1574 Rue Bourgogne,* ☎*447-6945*) serves mouthwatering, innovative French cuisine in a pleasant, unpretentious atmosphere.

Saint-Jean-sur-Richelieu

Le Manneken Pis (*$; every day 9am to 9pm; 320 Rue Champlain,* ☎*348-3254*). With a name like that, Belgian waffles are sure to be nearby – and what delicious waffles they are, and with such fine chocolate! The coffees, roasted on site, are also excellent. A pleasant terrace faces a little marina. They also serve bread with various spreads and salads.

Chez Noeser (*$$$; wine; 236 Rue Champlain,* ☎*346-0811*). A few years ago, Denis and Ginette Noeser left Montréal and their Rue Saint-Denis restaurant to settle in Saint-Jean-sur-Richelieu. Their latest restaurant offers particularly courteous service and delicious classic French cuisine. There is a terrace during the summer months.

Saint-Hyacinthe

In Saint-Hyacinthe there are two restaurants that everyone knows about, and they both have the same owner. Although it's not *haute cuisine*, **Chez Pépé** (*$$; 1705 Rue Girouard Ouest,* ☎*773-8004*) and **Grillade Rose** (*$$; 494 Rue Saint-Simon,* ☎*771-0069*) both offer simple tasty meals in a pleasant decor and both places have terraces. Each restaurant is based on a different theme; Pépé's is Italian and offers a selection of pastas, and Grillade Rose is Santa Fe-style with grill dishes and nachos.

Saint-Marc-sur-Richelieu

The restaurant in the **Hostellerie des Trois Tilleuls** *($$$$; 290 Rue Richelieu, ☎584-2231)*, serves up some gems of fine French gastronomy. The artfully prepared menu offers traditional and sophisticated meals, and the dining room has a nice view of the river. The beautiful terrace is open to guests during the summer.

Eastern Townships

Dunham

The restaurant at the **L'Orpailleur** *($$; early Jun to mid-Oct, closed Mon and Tue; 1086 Route 202; ☎295-3763)*, vineyard, open only in the summer, has a short, but high-quality menu. A pleasant terrace looking out on the vineyard enables guests to enjoy the lovely countryside while they eat. The service is extremely friendly.

Granby

The name **Ben la Bédaine** *($; 599 Rue Principale; ☎378-2921)*, which means "Potbelly Ben" is certainly evocative; this place is a veritable shrine to the French fry.

The owner of **Maison de Chez Nous** *($$$-$$$$; closed Mon and Tue; 847 Rue Mountain; ☎372-2991)* gave up his wine cellar so that his customers, who may now bring their own wine, could save a little money. Furthermore, the menu offers the best and most refined of Québec cuisine.

Cowansville

A must in the region, the **McHaffy** restaurant *($$$; 351 Rue Principale, ☎266-7700)*, whose menu changes every two months, offers fine, international cuisine made with local ingredients and accompanied by a Blancs Coteaux wine chosen by Alain Bélanger, one of Quebec's best sommeliers. At lunch, patrons enjoy lighter meals on a pleasant terrace. Not to be missed is the duck festival, from mid-October to mid-November, when chef Pierre Johnston creates excellent dishes for the occasion.

Bromont

The **Etrier Rest-O-Bar** *($$; closed Mon; 547 Shefford; ☎534-3562)* serves excellent cuisine to an established clientele. The restaurant is located a short distance outside the city in a pleasant, though unsophisticated setting.

Chez Simon *($$$; Wed to Sun 5:30pm to 9pm; 632 Rue Shefford, ☎534-4626)* is the perfect place for an intimate dinner. Located in a small country-style house, the restaurant's three dining rooms can only accommodate about ten people each. Chef Giovanni Costanzo, one of the initiators of the Lac Brome duck festival, prepares European dishes with regional products. Portions are generous and the menu is varied. Reservations required.

Sutton

Il **Duetto** *($$$; every day from 5pm; 227 Académie-Élie, ☎819-538-8239)* serves fine Italian cuisine in a quiet country setting in the hills around Sutton. The pasta is home-made and the main dishes are inspired by the regional cuisines of Italy. The five-course menu is a good sampling of the variety of Italian cooking.

Magog

La Grosse Pomme *($$; 276 Principale Ouest, ☎819-843-9365)* is a friendly restaurant serving good bistro-style food. In the evening, the ambiance is livened up by chatty patrons both young and old.

Though it is located on a very busy street, **La Paimpolaise** *($$$; closed Mon; Route 112; ☎819-843-1502)* still has character. A friendly restaurant in a charming little house, it serves a wide selection of crepes and other French dishes. This is without question one of the best places to eat in the city.

Orford

With its modern decor, the restaurant at the Manoir des Sables, **Les Jardins** *($$$$; 90 Avenue des Jardins, ☎819-847-4747 or 1-800-567-3514, ⌐847-3519)* is somewhat lacking in character. Fortunately, its large windows look out on Mont Orford. The menu features gourmet cuisine, including a "*table*

QUÉBEC

estrienne", allowing guests to sample regional flavours.

Ayer's Cliff

Recognized as a four-diamond establishment, the **Auberge Ripplecove**'s restaurant *($$$$; 700 Rue Ripplecove, ☎819-838-4296 or 1-800-668-4296, ↦838-5541)* offers fine gourmet cuisine of great distinction. Its Victorian atmosphere and elegant decor make it an excellent place for a romantic meal.

North Hatley

Located inside a large house on the shores of Lac Massawippi, the **Pilsen** *($$; 55 Rue Principal; ☎819-842-2971)* serves good, simple food, such as salads and hamburgers, in a warm, friendly atmosphere. Its attractive country decor gives it a very pleasant old-fashioned character.

The restaurant at the **Auberge Hatley** *($$$$; Route 108; ☎819-842-2451)*, which has received numerous awards, is without question one of the region's best places to eat. The skillfully prepared gourmet meals will please even the most delicate palate. Not to mention that the dining room is beautifully decorated and offers a magnificent view of Lac Massawippi.

Graced with antique furniture and a fireplace, the dining room of the **Manoir Hovey** *($$$$; 575 Chemin Hovey; ☎819-842-2421)* has a soft atmosphere which makes for a lovely evening. The cuisine, as refined as the Auberge Hatley's, has also earned a lot of praise.

Sherbrooke

A laid-back clientele frequents the **Presse Boutique Café** *($; 4 Rue Wellington Nord, ☎819-822-2133)*. In addition to visual-art exhibitions and shows by local and other musicians, patrons can enjoy a wide variety of imported beers, a simple menu (salads, *croque-monsieur*, sandwiches, etc.) and vegetarian dishes. Moreover, two Internet stations are available ($6/hour, $1/10 minutes).

Located right in the heart of the new downtown area, the opulent **Da Toni** restaurant *($$$-$$$$; 15 Belvédère Nord, Sherbrooke, ☎819-346-8441)* has a well-established

reputation. Indeed, for 25 years now, patrons have been enjoying its fine French and Italian cuisine, served with a wide selection of wines in a classical decor. The table d'hôte features five excellent, reasonably priced main courses. Though somewhat noisy, a terrace allows guests to enjoy a drink outside during the summer.

Notre-Dame-des-Bois

Located close to verdant Mont Mégantic, the intimate and very charming **Aux Berges de l'Aurore** restaurant *($$$-$$$$; May to Oct, Wed to Sun 6pm to 9pm; July and Aug everyday; 139 Route du Parc, ☎819-888-2715)* serves excellent Québec cuisine. Seasoned with wild herbs gathered in the surrounding countryside, its dishes are most original. From the very first bite, guests will appreciate why it received the *Mérite de la Fine Cuisine Estrienne* award!

  ENTERTAINMENT

Montérégie

Upton

Unique in North America, the concept of **La Dame de Coeur** *(Jun to late Aug; 611 Rang de la Carrière, ☎549-5828)* is sure to fascinate both young and old alike. Located in a magnificent historical site, the "Queen of Hearts" puts on terrific marionette shows complete with striking visual effects. The outdoor theatre has an immense roof and pivoting seats that are heated on chilly evenings.

Saint-Jean-sur-Richelieu

The **Festival de Montgolfières**, a hot-air-balloon festival *(☎346-6000)*, fills the sky over Saint-Jean-sur-Richelieu with approximately one hundred multicoloured hot-air balloons. Departures take place every day from 6am to 6pm, weather permitting. Exhibitions and shows make up some of the other activities that take place during the festival.

Valleyfield

In early July, Valleyfield hosts the **Régates de Valleyfield** *($15 before Jun 24, $19.50 afterward, ☎371-6144)*. The competition involves several categories of hydroplane races, with speeds reaching 240 km/h. The regattas always attract a large number of visitors.

Kahnawake

Various traditional aboriginal events (dances, songs, etc.) are organized as a part of the **Pow Wow** *(☎632-8667)*, held in Kahnawake every year during the second weekend of July. Most of the activities are held on Île Kateri Tekakwitha.

Eastern Townships

Magog

Located inside an old Protestant church built in 1887, the **Théâtre du Vieux-Clocher** *(64 Rue Merry Nord Magog-Orford; ☎819-847-0470)* staged many shows that later became very successful in both Québec and France. Those interested in attending a show should reserve their seats well in advance. The theatre is attractive, but small.

A few days of festivities are organized as part of the **Traversée Internationale** *($5; mid-July; ☎819-843-5000, ⊶843-5621)*, including performances by Québec theatrical artists, exhibits of all kinds and folk singers. The highlight of the celebrations is the arrival of swimmers from Newport, USA. The 42-kilometre swim is undertaken by athletes considered among the best in the world. In the summer of 1998, this event will be celebrating its 20th anniversary.

Sherbrooke

Located in the old downtown area, the **Au Vieux Quartier** pub *(252 Rue Dufferin)* has a relaxed ambiance. The place remains faithful to classic rock, as evidenced by photographs of various rock stars covering the walls. Moreover, every Sunday night, different local musicians perform here.

The Université de Sherbrooke's cultural centre houses the **Salle Maurice O'Bready**, *(2500 Boulevard Université, ☎819-820-1000)*, where concerts, be they classical or rock, are put on.

A former church converted into a concert hall, the **Vieux Clocher de Sherbrooke** *(1590 Galt Ouest, ☎819-822-2102)* now welcomes music lovers and entertainment-seekers. Taking on the same role as its predecessor in Magog, the new hall, accommodating approximately 500 spectators, offers "discovery-shows" featuring young Quebecers and well-established performers. Performance listings can be found in the Sherbrooke daily *La Tribune*.

Orford

The **Centre d'Arts Orford** *(3165 Chemin du Parc, ☎819-843-3981 or 1-800-567-6155)* provides advanced training courses to young musicians during summertime. An annual festival also takes place at the centre, which is made up of several buildings designed in the 1960s by Paul-Marie Côté. The exhibition room that completes the whole was originally the Man and Music *(l'Homme et la Musique)* pavilion at Expo 67, and was designed by Desgagné and Côté.

During the months of July and August, the **Festival Orford** *(3165 Chemin du Parc, ☎819-843-2405 or 1-888-310-3665, ⊶843-7274)* offers a series of concerts featuring ensembles and world-famous virtuosos. Several excellent free concerts are also presented by young musicians, here for the summer to hone their skills at the Centre d'Arts Orford. This high-calibre festival is an absolute must for all music lovers.

QUÉBEC

YUKON
NORTHWEST TERRITORIES
CANADA
BRITISH COLUMBIA
ALBERTA
SASKATCHEWAN
MANITOBA
ONTARIO
QUÉBEC
Nfld. and LABRADOR
P.E.I.
N.B.
N.S.
Pacific Ocean
UNITED STATES
Atlantic Ocean

WESTERN QUÉBEC

This chapter includes the part of the province extending north and west of Montréal that corresponds to the tourist regions of Lanaudière, the Laurentians and the Outaouais. The Lanaudière region extends north of Montréal, from the plains of the St. Lawrence to the Laurentian plateau. Except for the part of the region engulfed in the urban sprawl of Montréal, Lanaudière is a peaceful area of lakes, rivers, farmland, wild forests and huge open spaces. It is a great place to kick back and try your hand at the various sports and activities the area has to offer like skiing, canoeing, snowmobile rides, hiking, hunting and fishing. One of the first colonized areas in New France, your visit will most certainly also include a tour of the region's rich architectural heritage.

Continuing west you'll come to the most renowned resort area in Québec, the beautiful Laurentides region, also called the Laurentians, attracts a great many visitors all year round. For generations now, people have been "going up north" to relax and enjoy the beauty of the Laurentian landscape. The lakes, mountains and forests provide a particularly good setting for a variety of physical activities or outings. As the region boasts the highest concentration of ski resorts in North America, skiing gets top billing here when winter rolls around. The villages scattered at the foot of the mountains are often both charming and friendly.

The southern part of the region, known as the Basses-Laurentides, was settled early on by French colonists, who came here to cultivate the rich farmland. A number of local villages reveal this history through their architectural heritage. The settling of the Laurentian plateau, engineered by the now legendary Curé Labelle, began much later, toward the middle of the 19th century. The development of the Pays d'En Haut, or highlands, was part of an ambitious plan to colonize the outlying areas of Québec in an effort to counter the exodus of French-Canadians to industrial towns in the northeastern United States. Given the poor soil, farming here was hardly profitable, but Curé Labelle nevertheless succeeded in founding about twenty villages and attracting a good number of French Canadian colonists to the region.

Still further west is the Outaouais region. Discovered early on by explorers and trappers it was not settled by whites until the arrival of Loyalists from the United States in the early 19th century. Forestry was long the region's main economic activity. Of particular importance to the industry were red and white pine; trees used in ship building. The logs were sent down the Ottawa River and the St. Lawrence to Québec City, where they were loaded onto ships headed for Great Britain. Forestry still plays an important role here, but service industries and government offices are also a major source of jobs, a situation resulting from the proximity of Canada's capital region.

FINDING YOUR WAY AROUND

Lanaudière

By Car

Highway 25 is the extension of Boulevard Pie-IX and leads towards Terrebonne, the first stop on this tour. It continues east to Assomption on Route 344. Next take Route 343 N. to Joliette and Route 158 W. to Berthierville.

Bus Stations

Terrebonne: Galeries de Terrebonne.
Joliette: 250 Rue Richard (at the Point d'Arrêt restaurant), ☎759-1524.
Repentigny: 435 Boulevard Iberville (at the *hôtel de ville*) ☎654-2315.
Rawdon: 3168 1re Avenue (at the Patate à Gogo) ☎834-2000
Saint-Donat: 751 Rue Principale (Dépanneur Boni-Soir) ☎(819) 424-1361

Train Station

Joliette: 470 Rue Champlain, ☎759-3252

Laurentides (Laurentians)

By Car

From Montréal follow Highway 13 N. Take the exit for Route 344 W. towards Saint-Eustache. This road continues to Oka. A ferry from Oka leads to Hudson (see p 190) in the Montérégie region. Or take Highway 15 (the *Autoroute des Laurentides*) to Saint-Jérôme (Exit 43). Landmarks along the way include the imposing Collège de Sainte-Thérèse (1881) and its church, on the right, and the only General Motors automobile assembly plant in Québec, on the left. A little further, before Saint-Jérôme, is Mirabel Airport. Highway 15 and then Route 117 lead to Saint-Jovite. Mont-Tremblant is north of here on Route 327, Continue on the 117 to reach Labelle and Mont-Laurier.

Bus Station

Saint-Eustache: 550 Arthur Sauvé, ☎(514) 472-9911.
Saint-Sauveur: 166 Rue Principale (in front of the municipal garage).
Sainte-Adèle: 1208 Rue Valiquette (Pharmacie Brunet) ☎(514) 229-6609.
Mont-Tremblant: Chalet des Chutes, ☎(819) 425-2738.
Mont-Laurier: 555 Boulevard Paquette (Dépanneur Provi-Soir) ☎(819) 623-5538.

The Outaouais

By Car

From Montréal, there are two options for reaching the departure point of the tour; one through the valley of the Ottawa River, and a faster way through Ontario.

1. Take Highway 13 N., then Route 344 W., which corresponds to part of the Lac des Deux-Montagnes tour (see p 245). Finally take Route 148 W. toward Ottawa.

2. Take Highway 40 W., which becomes Route 17 W. over the Ontario border. In Hawkesbury, cross the Ottawa River to return to Québec. Turn left on Route 148 W., toward Montebello and Ottawa.

Bus Stations

Montebello: 570 Rue Notre-Dame, ☎423-6900.
Hull: 238 Boulevard Saint-Joseph, ☎771-2442.
Ottawa (Ontario): 265 Catherine Street, ☎613-238-5900.

By Train

The small Hull-Chelsea-Wakefield steam train is a great way to see part of the rural Gatineau valley. The 32-kilometre trip takes approximately five hours and stops for two hours in Wakefield. In general however, the best ways to explore the valley are by car and bicycle.

PRACTICAL INFORMATION

The Lanaudière region and the southern part of the Laurentians region use the **450** area code. The Outaouais and the northern part of the Laurentians region use the **819** area code. To avoid confusion, the area code has been given only for Laurentian's telephone numbers in this guide. This code is not required for local calls.

Tourist Information Offices

Lanaudière

Tourisme Lanaudière 2643 Rue Queen, C.P. 1210, Rawdon, J0K 1S0, ☎843-2535 or 1-800-363-2788, ⬝843-8100, http://tourisme-lanaudiere.qc.ca.
Berthierville: 760 Rue Gadoury, ☎836-1621
Joliette: 500 Rue Dollard, ☎759-5013 or 1-800-363-1775
Terrebonne: 1091 Boulevard Moody, ☎964-0681
Rawdon: 3588 Rue Metcalfe, ☎834-2282.
Saint-Donat: 536 Rue Principale, ☎(819) 424-2883

Laurentides (Laurentians)

Maison du Tourisme des Laurentides 14142 Rue de la Chapelle, R.R. 1, Sainte-Antoine, J7Z 5T4, ☎(450) 436-8532, ⬝(450) 436-5309.
Saint-Eustache: 600 Rue Dubois, J7P 5L2, ☎(450) 472-5825 (summer only).
Saint-Sauveur-des-Monts: 100 Rue Guindon, Local M, 3e Étage, J0R 1R6, ☎(450) 227-2564.
Sainte-Adèle: 333 Boulevard Sainte-Adèle, J0R 1L0, ☎(450) 229-5399.
Mont-Tremblant: C.P. 248, 140 Rue du Couvent, J0T 1Z0, ☎(819) 425-2434.
Labelle: 7404 Boulevard du Curé-Labelle, ☎(819) 686-2606
Mont-Laurier: 177 Boulevard Paquette, J0T 1H0, ☎(819) 623-4544.

The Outaouais

Association Touristique de l'Outaouais 103 Rue Laurier, Hull, J8X 3V8, ☎778-2222 or 1-800-265-7822, ⬝778-7758, www.achilles.net/~ato/

Montebello: 502-A Rue Notre-Dame, ☎423-5602.
Hull: 103 Rue Laurier, ☎778-2222.
Maniwaki: 156 Rue Principale Sud, ☎449-6291.

 EXPLORING

Lanaudière

Terrebonne ★★

Located along the banks of the rushing Rivière des Mille-Îles, this municipality gets its name from the fertile soil (*terre* meaning earth, and *bonne* meaning good) from which it grew. Today it is included in the ribbon of suburbia surrounding Montréal, yet the old town, divided into an *haute-ville* and *basse-ville* (upper and lower town), has preserved some of its residential and commercial buildings. Terrebonne is probably the best place in Québec to get an idea of what a prosperous 19th-century seigneury was really like.

Île des Moulins ★★ *(free admission; late Jun to early Sep, every day 1pm to 9pm; at the end of Rue des Braves, ☎471-0619)* is an impressive concentration of mills and other pre-industrial equipment from the Terrebonne seigneury. Most of the buildings, located in a park, have been renovated and now serve as community and administrative buildings. Upon entering, the first building on the left is the old flour mill (1846) then the saw mill (restored in 1986) which houses the municipal library. Next is the Centre d'Accueil et d'Interprétation de l'Île des Moulins (information centre) in what used to be the seigneurial office. This cut stone building was constructed in 1848 according to plans by Pierre-Louis Morin.

Joliette ★

At the beginning of the 19th century, the notary Barthélémy Joliette (1789-1850) opened up logging camps in the northern section of the Lavaltrie seigneury, at the time, still undeveloped land. In 1823 he founded "his" town around the sawmills and called it "L'Industrie", a name synonymous with progress and prosperity. The settlement grew so rapidly that in just a few years it had eclipsed its two rivals, Berthier and L'Assomption. In 1864 it was

QUÉBEC

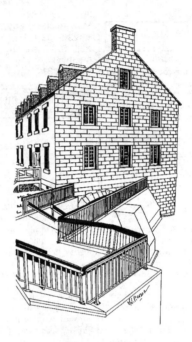

Île des Moulins

renamed Joliette in honour of its founder. Barthélémy Joliette completed many other ambitious projects, most notably the construction of the first railroad belonging to French Canadians, and a bank where money bearing the Joliette-Lanaudière name was printed.

Père Wilfrid Corbeil c.s.v. founded the exceptional **Musée d'Art de Joliette ★★** *($4; late Jun to early Sep, Tue to Sun 11am to 5pm; the rest of the year, Wed to Sun noon to 5pm; 145 Rue Wilfrid-Corbeil,* ☎*756-0311)* with works collected during the forties by the clerics of Saint-Viateur that show Québec's place in the world. This is the most important regional museum in Québec. Since 1976 it has been located in a rather menacing building on Rue Corbeil. On display are major pieces from Québec and Canadian artists like Marc-Aurèle de Foy Suzor-Côté, Jean-Paul Riopelle and Emily Carr, as well as works by European and American artists like Henry Moore and Karel Appel. One section of the museum is devoted to Québec religious art, while another section contains religious art of the Middle Ages and Renaissance periods, with some excellent examples from France, Italy and Germany.

The Festival International de Lanaudière was begun by Père Fernand Lindsay c.s.v. Each year during the months of July and August, a variety of music concerts and opera singers are presented as part of the festival. In 1989 the 2,000-seat open-air **Amphithéâtre de Lanaudière** *(1575 Base-de-Roc,* ☎*759-7636 or 1-800-561-4343)* was constructed in order to increase the capacity and accessibility of the event, which up to that time was limited to the churches of the area. Artist Georges Dyens completed the interior design of the aisles and the exquisite sculptures.

Berthierville ★

The modest Autray Seigneury was conceded to Jean Bourdon, an engineer of the King, in 1637. The land corresponds to the sector Berthier-en-bas, or Berthierville, along the shores of the St. Lawrence. The Berthier Seigneury, which was much more extensive, was conceded to Sieur de Berthier in 1672 before passing through several hands. It corresponds in part to Berthier-en-haut, or Berthier. In 1765 both these tracts of land were

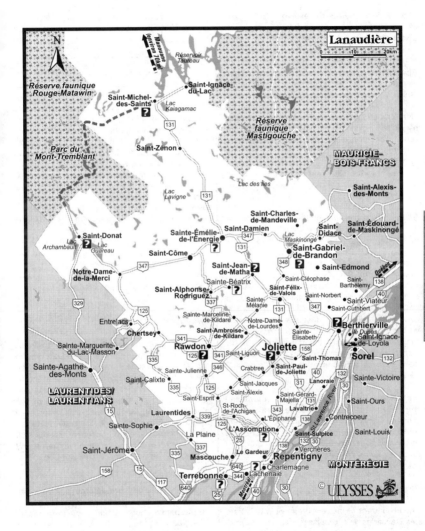

acquired by James Cuthbert, an aide de camp of General Wolf during the battle of the Plains of Abraham in Québec City, as well as a friend of the Duke of Kent. He developed the land mainly for use as a vacation spot.

The **Église Sainte-Geneviève** ★★ *(780 Montcalm)* is a Lanaudière treasure. Constructed in 1781 it is one of the oldest churches in the region. The interior's Louis-XVI styling was designed by Amable Gauthier and Alexis Millette between 1821 and 1830. Many elements in the decor combine to make this building truly exceptional. The decor has a richness rarely seen at that time, comprising elements such as the original high altar, crafted by Gilles Bolvin in 1759, the shell-shaped retable and the diamond-pattern ornamenting the vault. There are also several paintings, including one of Sainte-Geneviève (a French canvas from the 19th century hanging over the high altar), and six paintings by Louis Dulongré, painted in 1797.

Gilles Villeneuve, the championship race car driver who was killed tragically during the qualifying trials for the 1982 Grand-Prix of Belgium, was from Berthierville. The **Musée Gilles-Villeneuve** *($6; Mar to Oct, every day 10am to 4pm; 960 Avenue Gilles Villeneuve, ☎836-2714)* is dedicated to the illustrious career of the Ferrari Formula 1 driver, his prizes, his souvenirs and his cars. In the last few years, Gilles' son Jacques, has taken up where his father left off and become a top-ranked Formula 1 driver, at the heart of the British Williams-Renault team. The museum now devotes a new section to the career of Jacques Villeneuve.

Farther on, take Route 158 to Île Dupras and the village of **Saint-Ignace-de-Loyola**, from which a ferry leads to Sorel on the south shore of the St. Lawrence *(in summer departures every half hour between 5:30am and 3pm, the crossing takes 10 min; ☎836-4600)*.

Rawdon ★

The other spot of interest in the vicinity is **Parc des Cascades** ★ *($6 per car; mid-May to mid-Oct, every day; ☎834-4149)*, which can be reached on Route 341, the extension of Boulevard Pontbriand. Also on the bank of Rivière Ouareau, which runs in lovely cascades over the rocky riverbed here, this park includes a picnic area where sunbathers stretch out during the hot months of summer.

Saint-Donat ★

Minutes away from Mont-Tremblant, tucked between mountains reaching up to 900 metres and the shores of Lac Archambault, the small town of Saint-Donat extends east to the shores of Lac Ouareau. Saint-Donat is also a departure point for the **Parc du Mont-Tremblant** (see p 220).

Laurentides (Laurentians)

The Laurentians has been the favourite playground of Montrealers since the thirties. Located less than an hour and a half from the big city, it encompasses a multitude of lakes, wooded mountains and villages equipped to accommodate visitors. Montrealers "go up north" to their cottage in the summer to relax, go canoeing—in short, to enjoy the natural surroundings. In winter, visitors from Ontario, New York or Atlanta join the numbers of Montrealers in the charming local inns and luxury hotels. They come here not only to go downhill skiing, but also to snowshoe, cross-country ski or snowmobile across the white snow, and spend pleasant evenings by the fireside. The Laurentians boast the largest concentration of ski runs in North America.

Saint-Jérôme

This administrative and industrial town is nicknamed La Porte du Nord (The Gateway to the North), because it marks the passage from the St. Lawrence valley into the mountainous region that stretches north of Montréal and Québec City. The Laurentians are one of the oldest mountain ranges on earth. Compressed by successive glaciations, the mountains are low, rounded, and composed of sandy soil. Colonization of this region began in the second half of the 19th century, with Saint-Jérôme as the starting point.

The **Cathédrale de Saint-Jérôme** ★ *(every day 8:30am to 4:30pm; in front of Parc Labelle)*, a simple parish church when it was erected in 1899, is a large Roman-Byzantine style edifice reflecting Saint-Jérôme's prestigious status as the "headquarters" of the colonization of the Laurentians. A bronze statue of Curé Labelle, sculpted by Alfred Laliberté, stands in front of the cathedral.

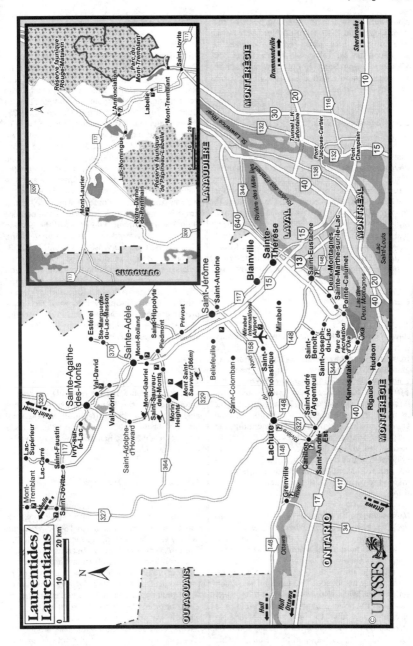

Laurentides/
Laurentians

QUÉBEC

© ULYSSES

Saint-Jérôme is also the starting point of the **Parc Linéaire le P'tit Train du Nord ★★**. This extraordinary bike path, which becomes a cross-country ski trail in winter, stretches 200 kilometres, from Saint-Jérôme to Mont-Laurier, along the same route once followed by the Laurentian railroad.

Saint-Sauveur-des-Monts ★

Located perhaps a little too close to Montréal, Saint-Sauveur-des-Monts has been over-developed in recent years, and condominiums, restaurants and art galleries have sprung up like mushrooms. Rue Principale is very busy and is the best place in the Laurentians to mingle with the crowds. This resort is a favourite among entertainers, who own luxurious secondary residences on the mountainside. The Église Saint-Sauveur is also very popular with future couples, who have to put their namesdown on a long waiting list in order to be married there.

Sainte-Adèle ★

The Laurentians were nicknamed the Pays-d'En-Haut (the Highlands) by 19th-century colonists heading for these northern lands, far from the St. Lawrence valley. Writer and journalist Claude-Henri Grignon, born in Sainte-Adèle in 1894, used the region as the setting for his books. His famous novel, *Un homme et son péché* (A Man and his Sin), depicts the wretchedness of life in the Laurentians back in those days. Grignon asked his good friend, architect Lucien Parent, to design the village church, which graces Rue Principale to this day. On August 27, 1997, the villages of Mont-Rolland and Sainte-Adèle merged to form the new municipality of Sainte-Adèle.

Musée-Village de Séraphin ★ *($9; mid-Jun to mid-Oct, every day from 10am to 6pm; Montée à Séraphin, ☎450-229-4777)*. Séraphin Poudrier is the main character of Claude-Henri Grignon's novel, *Un homme et son péché*. Miserly and unlikable, Séraphin has supreme control over his village. The film and television series (*Les Belles Histoires des Pays-d'en-Haut*) based on the novel proved so successful that a village was built to recreate the era of colonization in the Laurentians. In all, about 20 furnished buildings are open to the public. This is an interesting place to visit, even for those unfamiliar with Grignon's work.

Ville d'Estérel ★

In Belgium, the name Empain is synonymous with financial success. Baron Louis Empain, who inherited the family fortune in the early 20th century, was an important builder, just like his father, who was responsible for the construction of Heliopolis, a new section of Cairo (Egypt). During a trip to Canada in 1935, Baron Louis purchased Pointe Bleue, a strip of land that extends out into Lac Masson. In two years, from 1936 to 1938, he erected about 20 buildings on the site, all designed by Belgian architect Antoine Courtens, to whom we also owe the Palais de la Folle Chanson and the façade of the Église du Gésu in Brussels, as well as the Grande Poste in Kinshasa, Zaïre. Empain named this entire development **Domaine de l'Estérel**. The onset of the Second World War thwarted his plans, however, and afterwards, the land was divided up. In 1958, a portion of it was purchased by a Québec businessman named Fridolin Simard, who began construction of the present **Hôtel L'Estérel** alongside Route 370, and then divided the rest of the property into lots. On these pieces of land, visitors will find lovely modern houses made of stone and wood, designed by architect Roger D'Astou.

Val-David

Val David attracts visitors not only because it is located near the Laurentian ski resorts, but also because of its craft shops, where local artisans display their work. The village, made up of pretty houses, has managed to retain its own unique charm.

Sainte-Agathe-des-Monts ★

Set in the heart of the Laurentians, this is a business and tourist oriented town, which sprang up around a sawmill in 1849. When the railway was introduced into the region in 1892, Sainte-Agathe-des-Monts became the first resort area in the Laurentians. Located at the meeting point of two waves of colonization, the Anglo-Saxon settling of the county of Argenteuil and the French-Canadian settling of Saint-Jérôme, the town succeeded in attracting wealthy vacationers, who, lured by Lac des Sables, built several beautiful villas around the lake and in the vicinity of the Anglican church. The region was once deemed a first-class resort by important Jewish families of Montréal and New York. In 1909, the Jewish community founded Mount Sinai Sanitarium (the present building was erected in 1930) and in the following years, built synagogues in Sainte-Agathe-des-Monts and Val-Morin.

Mont-Tremblant Resort ★★★

Some of the largest sports and tourist complexes in the Laurentians were built by wealthy American families with a passion for downhill skiing. They chose this region for the beauty of the landscape, the province's French charm and above all for the northern climate which makes for a longer ski season than in the United States. The Station de Ski du Mont-Tremblant was founded by Philadelphia millionaire Joseph Ryan in 1938. The resort is now owned by Intrawest, which also owns Whistler Resort in British Columbia, and which has invested a considerable amount of money in Tremblant in order to put it on a par with the huge resorts of western Canada and the United States. At the height of the season, 74 trails, including several new ones, attract downhill skiers to Tremblant's slopes (914 m), in the summer the magnificent new golf course is just as popular. Not only does this place have the longest and most difficult vertical drops in the region, it also boasts a brand-new resort complex set in a cute little village of traditional Quebecois-style buildings at the base of the mountain. The Disney-ish appearance of these colourful units is not for everyone, but there is certainly lots to keep you busy... The ultimate goal, to create a one-of-a-kind vacation spot, was achieved.

Mont-Tremblant Village ★

On the other side of Lac Tremblant lies the charming Mont-Tremblant Village, not to be confused with the resort area that Intrawest started developing in 1993. Here, in a more authentic setting, visitors will find attractive shops and restaurants, as well as a number of other places to stay, including the famous Club Tremblant (see p 224).

The Outaouais

Montebello ★

The Outaouais region did not experience significant development under the French Regime. Located upstream from the Lachine Rapids, the area was not easily accessible by water, and was thus left to hunters and trappers until the early 19th century and the beginning of the forestry operations. The Petite-Nation seigneury, granted to Monseigneur de Laval in 1674, was the only attempt at colonization in this vast region. Not until 1801, when the seigneury passed into the hands of notary Joseph Papineau, was the town of Montebello established. Papineau's son, Louis-Joseph Papineau (1786-1871), head of the French-Canadian nationalist movement in Montréal, inherited the Petite-Nation seigneury in 1817. Returning from an eight-year exile in the United States and France following the rebellion of 1837-38, disillusioned and disappointed by the stand taken by the Catholic clergy during the rebellion, Papineau retired in Montebello, where he built an impressive manor.

The **Manoir Louis-Joseph-Papineau ★★** *($3.50; mid-May to mid-Jun and early Sep to mid-Oct, Wed to Sun 10am to 5pm; mid-Jun to early Sep, every day 10am to 6pm; mid-Oct to mid-Nov, Sat and Sun 10am to 5pm; 500 Rue Notre-Dame, ☎423-6965)* was erected between 1846 and 1849 in the monumental neoclassical villa style. The house was designed by Louis Aubertin, a visiting French architect. The towers added in the 1850s give the house a medieval appearance. One of the towers houses a precious library that Papineau placed here to protect it from fire. The house has approximately 20 staterooms, through which visitors can now stroll, and features rich Second Empire decor. It is located on lovely tree-shaded grounds, and is owned by the Canadian Pacific hotel chain, which also manages the nearby Château Montebello. A small wooden walkway leads to the **Chapelle Funéraire des Papineau** (1853), where 11 members of the family are buried. Note that this is an Anglican chapel. Papineau's son joined the Church of England when his father died and was refused a Catholic burial. A bust of the elder Papineau by Napoléon Bourassa made from the funeral mask of the deceased, is one of the interesting objects found in the chapel.

The **Château Montebello ★★** *(392 Rue Notre-Dame; ☎423-6341)* is a large resort hotel on the Papineau estate. It is the largest log building in the world. The hotel was erected in 1929 (Lawson and Little, architects) in a record 90 days. The impressive lobby has a central fireplace with six-hearths, each facing one of the building's six wings. See also p 224.

QUÉBEC

Manoir Papineau

Hull

The modest wood-frame houses that line the streets of Hull are nicknamed "matchboxes" because they once housed many employees of the Eddy match factory, and because they have had more than their fair share of fires. In fact, Hull has burned so many times throughout its history that few of the town's historical buildings remain. The former town hall and beautiful Catholic church burned down in 1971 and 1972, respectively. Ottawa has the reputation of being a quiet city, while Hull is considered more of a fun town, essentially because legal drinking age is a year younger and the bars stay open later in Québec. It is not uncommon to see crowds of Ontarians along the **Promenade du Portage** on Saturday nights.

The **Musée Canadien des Civilisations** ★★★ *($5, free admission on Sun 9am to noon; May to mid-Oct, every day 9am to 6pm; mid-Oct to late Apr, every day 9am to 5pm; Jul to Sep, Fri to 9pm; open Thu until 9pm all year; 100 Rue Laurier, ☎776-7000).* Many parks and museums were established along this section of the Québec-Ontario border as part of a large redevelopment program in the National Capital Region between 1983 and 1989. Hull became the site of the magnificent Musée Canadien des Civilisations, dedicated to the history of Canada's various cultural groups. If there is one museum that must be seen in Canada it is this one. Douglas Cardinal of Alberta drew up the plans for the museum's two striking curved

buildings, one housing the administrative offices and restoration laboratories, and the other the museum's collections. Their undulating design brings to mind rock formations of the Canadian shield, shaped by wind and glaciers. There is a beautiful view of Ottawa River and Parliament Hill from the grounds behind the museum.

The Grande Gallerie (Great Hall) houses the most extensive collection of native totem poles in the world. Another collection brilliantly recreates different periods in Canadian history, from the arrival of the vikings around 1000 AD to life in rural Ontario in the 19th century and French Acadia in the 17th century. Contemporary native art, as well as popular arts and traditional crafts are also on display. In the Musée des Enfants (Children's Museum), young visitors choose a theme before being led through an extraordinary adventure. Screening rooms have been equipped with OMNIMAX technology, a new system developed by the creators of the large-screen IMAX. Most of the movies shown here deal with Canadian geography.

The **Casino de Hull** ★★ *(11am to 3am; 1 Boulevard du Casino, ☎1-800-665-2274 or 772-2100)* has an impressive location between two lakes; Leamy Lake, in the park of the same name, and Lac de la Carrière, which is in the basin of an old limestone quarry. The theme of water is omnipresent all around the superb building, inaugurated in 1996. The magnificent

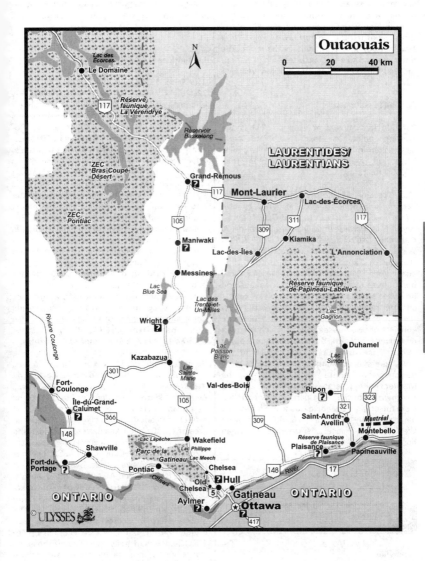

walkway leading to the main entrance is dotted with towering fountains, and the harbour has 20 slips for boaters. The gambling area, which is 2,741 square metres in size, includes 1,300 slot machines and 58 playing tables spread around a simulated tropical forest. Quebec painter Jean-Paul Riopelle's famous 40-metre-long painting, **Hommage à Rosa Luxembourg** ★★★, dominates the room. The artist created this immense triptych in honour of Joan Mitchell, his partner of many years.

Parc de la Gatineau

Parc de la Gatineau ★ (see p 221) is the starting point for this tour. The park, established in 1934, is an area of rolling hills, lakes and rivers, that measures more than 35,000 hectares.

The **Domaine Mackenzie-King** ★★ *($6 for parking; mid-May to mid-Jun, Wed to Sun 11am to 5pm; mid-Jun to mid-Oct, 11am to 5pm; Rue Barnes in Kingsmere, Parc de la Gatineau, ☎613-239-5000 and 827-2020).* William Lyon Mackenzie King was Prime Minister of Canada from 1921 to 1930, and again from 1935 to 1948. His love of art and horticulture rivalled his interest in politics and he was always happy to get away to his summer residence near Lac Kingsmere, which today is part of Parc de la Gatineau. The estate consists of two houses (one of which is now a charming tea room), a landscaped garden and follies, false ruins that were popular at the time. However unlike most follies, which were designed to imitate ruins, those on the Mackenzie-King estate are authentic building fragments. For the most part, they weretaken from the original Canadian House of Parliament, destroyed by fire in 1916, and from Westminister Palace, damaged by German bombs in 1941.

 OUTDOORS

 Parks

Lanaudière

The **Réserve Faunique Rouge-Matawin** *(26 km west of Saint-Michel-des-Saints; ☎819-424-3026 in Saint-Donat or 833-5530 in Saint-Michel-des-Saints)* is 1,394 square kilometres of greenery, through which flow about 450 lakes and waterways. It is home to an abundant and fertile wildlife. There is no lack of things to do, from hiking, hunting, fishing, canoe-camping tripping and wild-berry-picking, all the way to snowmobiling in the winter.

Laurentides (Laurentians)

The **Parc d'Oka and the Calvaire d'Oka** ★ *(2020 Chemin d'Oka, ☎450-479-8337)* encompasses about 45 kilometres of trails for hikers in the summer and cross-country skiers in the winter. Most of the trails lie south of Route 344, crisscrossing a relatively flat area. North of Route 344, there are two other trails, which lead to the top of the Colline d'Oka (168 m), where visitors can drink in a view of the entire region. The longer trail (7.5 km) ends at a panoramic viewing area, while the shorter one (5.5 km) guides visitors past the oldest stations of the cross in the Americas. This calvary was set up by the Sulpicians back in 1740, in an effort to stimulate the faith of natives recently converted to Catholicism. Humble and dignified at the same time, the calvary is made up of four trapezoidal oratories and three rectangular chapels built of whitewashed stone. These little buildings, now empty, once housed wooden bas-reliefs depicting the Passion of Christ. The park also has campsites *($18.75 per day, ☎450-479-8337)* and an information centre.

Parc du Mont-Tremblant ★★ *(Chemin du Lac Tremblant, ☎819-688-2281 or 1-800-461-8711)*, created in 1894, was originally known as Parc de la Montagne Tremblante (Trembling Mountain Park) in reference to an Algonquian legend. It covers an area of 1,250 square kilometres, encompassing the mountain, seven rivers and some 500 lakes. The ski resort opened in 1938, and has been welcoming skiers ever since. Today, it has modern facilities and 45 trails, with a vertical drop of up to 710 metres. A day of skiing costs $44. The park also includes nine cross-country ski trails, which stretch over 50 kilometres. The resort caters to sports enthusiasts all year round. Hiking buffs, can explore up to 100 kilometres of trails here. Two of these, La Roche and La Corniche, have been rated among the most beautiful in Québec. The park also has bicycle paths, mountain bike circuits, and offers water sports like canoeing and wind-surfing.

The Outaouais

Parc de la Gatineau ★ *(visitor centre is located in Chelsea, also accessile via Boulevard Taché in Hull;* ☎*827-2020)* is not far from downtown Hull. The 35,000 hectare park was founded during the Depression in 1934 in order to protect the forests from people looking for firewood. It is crossed by a 34 kilometre long road dotted with panoramic lookout points, including as **Belvédère Champlain**, which offer superb views of the lakes, rivers and hills of the region. Outdoor activities can be enjoyed here throughout the year. Hiking and mountain biking trails are open during the summer. There are many lakes in the park, including Lac Meech, which was also the name of a Canadian constitutional agreement drawn up nearby but never ratified. Watersports such as windsurfing, canoeing and swimming are also very popular and the park rents small boats and camp sites. **Lusk Cave**, formed some 12,500 years ago by water flowing from melting glaciers can be explored. During the winter, approximately 190 kilometres of cross-country skiing trails are maintained *(approx. $7 per day)*. **Camp Fortune** *(*☎*827-1717)* has 19 downhill skiing runs, 14 are open at night. It costs $24 during the day and $20 at night.

Rock-climbing

Laurentides (Laurentians)

The **Val-David** area is renowned for its rock faces. A number of mountains here are fully equipped to accommodate climbers' needs; **Mont King**, **Mont Condor** and **Mont Césaire** are among the most popular. For more information, equipment rentals or guide services, contact **Passe Montagne** *(1760 Montée 2e Rang, Val-David, JOT 2NO,* ☎*819-322-2948)*, a trailblazing rock-climbing outfit in the Val-David region. Their team of experts offer excellent advice.

Biking

Laurentides (Laurentians)

The former railway line of the **P'tit Train du Nord** *(300 Rue Longpré, Bureau 110, St-Jérôme, J7T 3B9,* ☎*450-436-4051,* ⌨*436-2277)*, which carried Montrealers up North for many years, has been transformed into a superb 200-kilometre bike path from Saint-Jérôme to Mont-Laurier. It leads through a number of little villages where accommodations and restaurants in all price ranges can be found.

Rafting

Laurentides (Laurentains)

Thanks to the thrilling Rivière Rouge, the Laurentians offer excellent conditions for whitewater rafting — among the best in Canada, according to some experts. Of course, there is no better time to enjoy this activity than during the spring thaw. Rafting during this period can prove quite a challenge, however, so previous experience is recommended. The best season for novices is summer, when the river is not too high and the weather is milder. For further information, contact **Nouveau Monde, Expéditions en Rivière** *($85 per person; 100 Chemin de la Rivière Rouge, Calumet, JOV 1B0,* ☎*819-242-7238 or 1-800-361-5033,* ⌨*242-0207)*, which offers group outings every day.

Downhill Skiing

Laurentides (Laurentians)

A small mountain with a vertical drop of only 210 metres, **Mont Saint-Sauveur** *($34; 350 Rue Saint Denis,* ☎*450-227-4671)* attracts a large clientele because of its proximity to Montréal. It offers 26 downhill ski trails, a few of which are lit for night-skiing.

The **Station de Ski Mont-Blanc** *($30; Route 117,* ☎*819-688-2444 or 1-800-567-6715)*, in Saint-Faustin, has 35 runs and the second highest vertical drop in the Laurentians (300 metres).

Gray Rocks *($25; Route 327,* ☎*819-425-2771 or 1-800-567-6767)* is another resort in the region. It has about 20 trails, with a vertical drop of 191 metres (much lower than at Mont-Tremblant). A major overhaul of the facilities is scheduled for the spring of 1998. New accommodations (apartments and chalets) will be added, along with a new golf course.

QUÉBEC

ACCOMMODATIONS

Lanaudière

Joliette

In a large red brick building by the river, the **Château Joliette** *($75; ℜ; 450 Rue St-Thomas, J6E 3R1, ☎752-2525 or 1-800-361-0572, ⇌752-2520)* is the largest hotel in town. Though the long corridors are cold and bare, the modern rooms are large and comfortable.

Saint-Alphonse-Rodriguez

Ten kilometres from the village of Saint-Alphonse-Rodriguez, after a long climb past peaceful Lac Long and into what seems like another world, is the marvellous **Auberge sur la Falaise** *($89-154; ≡, ≈, ℜ, Δ; 324 Av. Du Lac Long Sud, J0K 1W0, ☎883-2269 or 1-888-325-2437, ⇌883-0143)*. The inn, perched on a promontory, dominates this serene landscape, reserving exceptional views for its guests. The 25 rooms in this modern building are luxurious, some of them with whirlpool baths and fireplaces. The hotel does double duty as a spa and offers many sports activities. Finally, the cuisine served in the dining room is among the best in the area (see p 225).

Saint-Jean-de-Matha

Another exceptional establishment, **Auberge de la Montagne Coupée** *($110-$195; ≡, ≈, ℜ, Δ; 1000 Ch. de la Montagne-Coupée, J0K 2S0, ☎886-3891 or 1-800-363-8614, ⇌886-5401)* appears after what seems like an interminable climb. Reward is at hand though in this immense white building with huge bay windows. The hotel has 50 comfortable, modern rooms bathed in natural light, some of which have fireplaces. In the dining room and the lounge, large windows reveal a breathtaking panorama. There is an equestrian centre and a summer theatre at the bottom of the grounds, and the hotel has a remarkable restaurant (see p 225).

Saint-Donat

The Pimbina section of **Parc du Mont-Tremblant** *($18; 2951 Route 125 Nord, C.P. 1169, J0T 2C0, ☎424-7012, ⇌424-2413)*, near Saint-Donat and accessible via Route 125, includes 341 campsites.

The **Manoir des Laurentides** *($70; 290 Rue Principale, J0T 2C0 or 1-800-567-6717, ⇌424-2621)*, well located by the water's edge, offers good value for your money. The rooms in the three-story main building are comfortable but boring, though each has its own balcony. There are also two rows of motel rooms that stretch to the lakefront and about forty cottages equipped with kitchenettes. Since this spot is often quite lively, visitors who value peace and quiet should opt for motel rooms or cottages. A beach and a small marina at the water's edge are available to guests.

Laurentides (Laurentians)

Saint-Sauveur-des-Monts

A beautiful row of fir trees graces the garden of the **Hôtel Châteaumont** *($85;≡, tv, ☺; 50 Rue Principale, J0R 1R6, ☎450-227-1821, ⇌227-1483)*, forming an attractive entranceway. The rooms have modern furnishings, and all but two are equipped with a fireplace, a real plus after a day of skiing.

The long green and white building of the **Relais Saint-Denis** *($84; ≈, ≡, tv, ℜ; 61 Rue Saint-Denis, J0R 1R4, ☎450-227-4602, ⇌227-8504)* is modern-looking for a country inn. Fortunately, the attractively decorated rooms are more inviting. Behind the building is a pleasant garden with a swimming pool.

Sainte-Adèle

At **Le Chanteclerc** *($89 bkfst incl., $170 ½b; ≈, ≡, tv, Δ, ☺, ♿; 1474 Chemin du Chanteclerc, J0R 1L0; ☎450-229-3555, ⇌229-5593)*, whose name and emblem (a rooster) were inspired by Edmond Rostand's play, guests can enjoy a multitude of activities in an pristine lakeside setting at the foot of Mont Chanteclerc. The golf course is picturesque, with mountains on either side. The sizeable sports complex and the handsome stone building with its 300 or so rooms attracts quite a crowd.

A member of the prestigious Association des Relais et Châteaux, the hotel **L'Eau à la Bouche** *($125, $255 ½b; ≈, ≡, tv, ℜ, ᕗ; 3003 Boulevard Sainte-Adèle, JOR 1LO, ☎450-229-2991, ≈229-7573)* is known for its excellent gourmet restaurant and extremely comfortable rooms. Don't be fooled by the building's rustic appearance, the rooms are elegantly furnished. The hotel itself dates from the mid-1980s and is set back from the road. It offers a splendid view of the ski slopes of Mont Chanteclerc. The restaurant, for its part, is in a separate building. The complex is located on Route 117, a fair distance north of the village of Sainte-Adèle.

Ville d'Estérel

At the **Hôtel l'Estérel** *($238 ½b; ≈, ☉, ◯, ℜ, ᕗ; Boulevard Fridolin-Simard, JOT 1EO; ☎450-228-2571 or 1-888-378-3735, ≈228-4977)*, a large complex located on the shores of Lac Masson, guests can enjoy a variety of water sports and diverse athletic activities such as tennis, golf and cross-country skiing. The accent is placed mainly on these activities; the rooms, although comfortable, are decorated with outmoded colours.

Val-Morin

Making the most of its extensive grounds, the **Far Hills** *($200 ½b; ≈, ◯, ℜ, ᕗ; Far Hills; ☎819-866-2219 or from Montréal 990-4409, ≈322-1995)* has an extremely peaceful country setting. Its clientele includes cross-country skiers, who come to enjoy over 100 kilometres of trails. Not only are the rooms adorable, but the hotel also has a very good restaurant.

Val-David

The **Chalet Beaumont** *($23 per person sb, $26 per person pb; K; 1451 Beaumont, JOT 2N0, ☎819-322-1972; from the bus stop, take Rue de l'Eglise across the village to Rue Beaumont and turn left; it's about a 2-km walk)*, located in a peaceful mountain setting, is one of only two youth hostels in the Laurentians. A log building with two fireplaces, it's a very appealing, comfortable place.

The comfortable **Auberge du Vieux Foyer** *($194 ½b; ⊛, ℜ, ≈, ᕗ; 3167 R.R. 1, JOT 2N0, ☎819-322-2686 or 1-800-567-8327, ≈322-2687)* is ideal for travellers looking for a peaceful getaway. The service is impeccable, the rooms are comfortable and the food is highly rated. Guests can borrow bicycles.

La Sapinière *($250 ½b; ≈, ≡, tv, ℜ, ᕗ; 1244 Chemin de la Sapinière, JOT 2N0, ☎819-322-2020 or 1-800-567-6635, ≈322-6510)*, in a rustic log building, is far from luxurious. The rooms have nevertheless been entirely renovated. The hotel is therefore a comfortable place to stop during a tour of the region, especially thanks to its beautiful location.

Sainte-Agathe-des-Monts

The **Auberge La Saint-Venant** *($85-130 bkfst incl.; pb, tv; 234 Rue Saint-Venant, J8C 2Z7, ☎819-326-7937, 1-800-697-7937 or 819-326-4848)* is one of the best-kept secrets in Sainte-Agathe. A big, beautiful, yellow house perched atop a hill, it has nine large, tastefully decorated rooms whose big windows let lots of light flood in. The service is friendly yet discreet.

The **Auberge La Calèche** *($110-$240; pb, ≈, ℜ; 125 Rue du Tour du Lac, J8C 1B4, ☎819-326-3753 or 1-800-567-6700)* has built itself a solid reputation over the years. A large inn with some 70 comfortable rooms, it is located a short distance from the village, on Lac des Sables.

Lac-Supérieur

The **Base de Plein Air le P'tit Bonheur** *($314 fb for 2 nights; ℜ; 1400 Chemin du Lac Quenouille, Lac-Supérieur, JOT 1P0, ☎819-326-4281, ≈326-9516)* is nothing less than an institution in the Laurentians. Once a children's summer camp, it now caters to families looking to take an "outdoor vacation". Set on a vast piece of property on the shores of a lake, right in the heart of the forest, there are four buildings containing a total of nearly 450 beds, most in dormitories. About 20 of the beds are in separate rooms, each equipped with a private bathroom and able to accommodate up to four people. Of course, this is the perfect place to enjoy all sorts of outdoor activities: sailing, hiking, cross-country skiing, skating, etc.

QUÉBEC

Mont-Tremblant Resort

The prestigious, international Marriot chain has also joined the action at Tremblant, with its **Marriott Residence Inn** *($109-$229; pb, ≡, ≈, ℜ, ☉, tv, K; 170 Chemin Curé-Deslauriers, JOT 1Z0, ☎819-681-4000, ∞681-4099)*, a large building located right at the start of the village. The place rents out studios and one- or two-bedroom apartments, each equipped with a kitchenette. Some units even have a fireplace.

Overlooking the village, the Mont-Tremblant, the **Château Mont Tremblant** *($135-$199; pb, ≡, ≈, ℜ, ☉, ☉, tv; 3045 Chemin Principal, JOT 1Z0, ☎819-681-7000, ∞681-7099)* is one of only two additions to have been made to the prestigious Canadian Pacific hotel chain in a century, the other being located in Whistler, British Columbia. This imposing 316-room hotel manages to combine a genuine rustic warmth, well-suited to the surroundings, with all the comforts one expects from a top-flight establishment. It also houses a large convention centre and numerous conference rooms.

The **Station Touristique du Mont-Tremblant** *($99-$279; ☎819-681-3000 or 1-800-461-8711, ∞681-5999)* manages a whole assortment of lodgings directly. Visitors may rent a room or an apartment in the **Kandahar** complex *($99-$238; pb, ≡, ≈, ☉, tv, K)*, located near a pond in the "Vieux-Tremblant" area, or in the luxurious **Deslauriers, Saint-Bernard** and **Johanssen** *($99-$279; pb, tv, ≡, K)* complexes, which face onto Place Saint-Bernard. Families will be better off with a fully equipped condo in **La Chouette** *($92-$130)*. These units are small but flooded with natural light. What's more, they offer excellent value for the money, making them an option well worth considering in this area.

Mont-Tremblant Village

The **Auberge de Jeunesse Mont-Tremblant** *($15.50; sb, ℜ; 2213 Chemin Principal, P.O. Box 1001, JOT 1Z0, ☎819-425-6008, ∞425-3760)* youth hostel opened in the fall of 1997. Formerly the L'Escapade hotel, it has 84 dormitory beds. The common areas include a kitchen, a café/bar/restaurant and a living room with a fireplace.

There are nearly 600 campsites in the Diable sector of **Parc du Mont-Tremblant** *($21; ☎819-688-2281)*. Restrooms and showers.

On the first floor of the **Hôtel Mont Tremblant** *($60, $90 with ≡, bkfst incl.; 1900 Chemin Principale, JOT 1Z0, ☎819-425-3232, ∞425-9755)*, visitors will find a bar; and on the second, rooms that are modest but satisfactory given the price and the location—all in the heart of the village, near the ski resort.

The **Auberge Gray Rocks** *($240 ½b; ≈, ≡, ℜ, ☉, ☉, tv, ♿; Route 327, JOT 2H0, ☎819-425-2771 or 1-800-567-6767, ∞425-3474)* also offers a range of activities and facilities, aiming to satisfy vacationers' every desire. Particular care has been taken to provide guests with the widest range of activities possible.

At the **Club Mont-Tremblant** *($300; ≈, ≡, ☉, ☉, tv, ℜ, ♿, K; Avenue Cuttles, JOT 1Z0, ☎819-425-2731 or 1-800-567-8341, ∞425-5617)*, guests are offered the choice of renting a very functional, well-equipped condo or a conventional room. The vast peaceful site is perfect for outdoorsy types (Parc du Mont-Tremblant is right nearby), as well as those who prefer to relax far from the city in a beautiful natural setting.

The Outaouais

Montebello

Christened the **Château Montebello** *($145; ℜ, ≈, ☉, ☉, ♿; 392 Rue Notre-Dame; ☎423-6341 or 1-800-268-9411, ∞423-5283)*, this beautiful pine and cedar building stands next to Ottawa River. It is the largest log building in the world and is equipped with several facilities including an indoor and outdoor swimming pool, squash courts and an exercise room.

Hull

The **Auberge de la Gare** *($74 bkfst incl.; 205 Boulevard St-Joseph, J8Y 3X3, ☎778-8085 or 773-4273, ∞595-2021)* is a simple, conventional hotel that offers good value for your money. The service is both courteous and friendly, and the rooms are clean and well kept, albeit nondescript.

Parc de la Gatineau

Without a doubt one of the most beautiful places in the area to camp, **Parc de la Gatineau** *($18 Camping du Lac Philippe, Route 366, ☎456-3016; $15 Camping du Lac La Pêche, Route 366, ☎456-3494)*, with over 350 campsites, has everything for people who want to sleep in the great outdoors. There are also facilities for recreational vehicles.

 RESTAURANTS

Lanaudière

Terrebonne

Le Folichon *($$$-$$$$; closed Mon; 804 Rue Saint-François-Xavier, ☎492-1863)*, which means playful and lighthearted, lives up to its name in the historic quarter of Terrebonne. In the summer, the shaded terrace is the best place to relax. The five course table d'hôte menu has a solid reputation. Particularly tasty are the escargot and grilled duck. Impressive wine list.

L'Étang des Moulins *($$$-$$$$; closed Mon; 888 Rue St-Louis, ☎471-4018)* occupies a magnificent stone house. The inventive French menu oozes refinement from the lobster Thermidore to the frog's legs in puff pastry. Without doubt, one of the best restaurants in Lanaudière.

Joliette

Amongst the many fine restaurants, **Antre Jean** *($$$; closed Mon; 385 St-Viateur; ☎756-0412)* seems to be the undeclared favourite with the locals. French cuisine specialties, as they are prepared in France are served as part of a table d'hôte menu. The decor is warm and inviting and the atmosphere is unpretentious.

Saint-Alphonse-Rodriguez

At the extraordinary **Auberge sur la Falaise** *($$$-$$$$; 324 Av. Du Lac Long Sud, ☎883-2269)*, meals are served in a setting of perfect tranquillity. Nestled in the deep forest, overlooking the calm surface of a lake, this establishment is a perfect retreat from the hectic rhythm of modern life (even if it is just for a meal). With a great deal of skill, the chef adapts French cuisine with Québec flavours – *médaillon de caribou aux bleuets du Lac* (caribou with blueberries), loin of lamb, pike *mousseline*, maple custard, etc. The obvious choice for epicureans is the five-course gourmet menu – a memorable experience indeed!

Saint-Jean-de-Matha

Auberge de la Montagne Coupée *($$$$; 1000 Ch. de la Montagne-Coupée, ☎886-3891)*, another spot famous for its peaceful setting, offers an exciting menu of innovative Québecois cuisine. The dining room is surrounded by two-story bay windows that look out on an absolutely breathtaking scene. And this is just the beginning – the best part of the evening (the meal!) is yet to come. To imaginatively presented game dishes are added succulent treasures such as grain-fed poultry with leeks, Oka cheese in *dijonnaise* sauce and crispy lamb with goat cheese. The service is doting; the wine list is excellent. Very copious breakfasts are also served.

Saint-Donat

La Petite Michèle *($; 327 Rue St-Donat, ☎819-424-3131)* is just the place for travellers looking for a good family restaurant. The atmosphere is relaxed, the service, friendly and the menu, traditional Québécois.

The food is always delicious at the **Maison Blanche** *($$; 515 Rue Principale, ☎819-424-2222)*. The house specialty, a divine juicy, rare steak, is known far and wide.

The **Auberge Havre du Parc** *($$$; 2788 Route 125, Lac-Provost, ☎819-424-7686)* not only boasts an exceptionally peaceful setting, but also has an excellent selection of French specialties.

Laurentides (Laurentians)

Saint-Jérôme

Le Jardin d'Agnès *($$$; 401 Rue Laviolette, ☎450-431-2575)* is set up inside a pretty stone house overlooking the Rivière du Nord. Its four-

QUÉBEC

course table d'hôte is $59.95 for two and includes such promising dishes as breast of chicken with old-fashioned mustard and filet of lamb with basil cream. Waterfront terrace out back.

Saint-Sauveur-des-Monts

Le Chrysanthème *($$; 173 Rue Principale, ☎450-227-8888)* has a beautiful, spacious outdoor seating area, a wonderful place to dine on a fine summer evening. The restaurant serves authentic Chinese cuisine, making for a nice change of pace in this area.

The menu at Papa Luigi *($$$; 155 Rue Principale, ☎450-227-5311)* is made up of – you guessed it – Italian specialties, as well as seafood and grill. Set up inside a lovely, blue, wooden house, this restaurant draws big crowds, especially on weekends. Reservations strongly recommended.

Near by, on the other side of the street, you'll see the green house that is home to Le Mousqueton *($$$; closed Mon and Tue; 120 Rue Principale, ☎450-227-4330)*. Innovative, contemporary Québec cuisine is served here in a warm, unpretentious atmosphere. Game, fish and even ostrich appear on the menu.

Mont-Rolland

The enchanting natural setting of the Auberge La Biche au Bois *($$$$; closed Sun and Mon in winter, Mon in summer; 1806 Route 117, ☎450-229-8064)* on the banks of the Rivière Simon is sure to give you an appetite. The menu is made up of Québec and French specialties like duck with Québec blueberries, veal Roquefort and smoked salmon with eggplant. Romantic ambiance.

Sainte-Adèle

There are several small restaurants on the little road leading to the Chanteclerc. The most appealing is La Scala *($$; closed Mon and Tue; 1241 Chemin Chanteclerc, ☎450-229-7453)*. Guests can sit in the cozy, inviting dining room or, weather permitting, outside on the shady terrace, which offers a lovely view of Lac Rond. The menu is made up of Italian and French specialties. The lamb tenderloin is a tried and true favourite.

The Clef des Champs *($$$$; 875 Chemin Sainte-Marguerite; ☎450-229-2857)* serves French cuisine fit for even the most delicate palate. The warmly decorated dining room is just right for an intimate dinner for two. The wine cellar is excellent.

One of the finest restaurants not only in the Laurentians but in all of Québec can be found at the hotel L'Eau à la Bouche *($$$$; 3003 Boulevard Sainte-Adèle, ☎450-229-2991)*. Chef Anne Desjardins takes pride in outdoing herself day after day, serving her clientele outstanding French cuisine made with local ingredients. Her Abitibi trout, Atlantic salmon and Far North caribou all bear witness to her exceptional finesse. Two menus, one with three courses, the other with six, are offered each evening. Excellent wine list. An unforgettable gastronomic experience!

Sainte-Marguerite-du-Lac-Masson

Don't be put off by the uninspired exterior of the Bistro à Champlain *($$$$; closed Fri and Sat in winter; 75 Chemin Masson, ☎450-228-4988)*, in Sainte-Marguerite-du-Lac-Masson. The place is actually one of the best restaurants in the Laurentians. It serves excellent nouvelle cuisine made with fresh local ingredients. The interior is absolutely extraordinary – a veritable art gallery, where you can admire a number of paintings by Jean-Paul Riopelle, a close friend of the owner's, as well as works by other artists like Joan Mitchell and Louise Prescott. The restaurant also boasts one of the province's most highly reputed wine cellars, which may be toured by appointment. Everyone can sample some of the wines in this impressive stock, since even the finest are available by the glass.

Val-Morin

The Hôtel Far Hills *($$$$; Rue Far Hills, ☎819-322-2014 or from Montréal 990-4409)* still has one of the finest restaurants in the Laurentians. The gourmet cuisine is positively world-class. Make sure to try the salmon *aux herbes folles du jardin* (with homegrown wild grasses), a sheer delight.

Val-David

The restaurant in La Sapinière *($$$; 1244 Chemin La Sapinière, ☎819-322-2020)* (see p 223) has been striving for over 60 years now to concoct creative dishes inspired by the culinary repertoires of both Québec and France. Among the house specialties, the *lapereau* (young rabbit), *porcelet* (piglet) and the gingerbread are particularly noteworthy, and the *tarte au sucre à la crème* (sugar pie) is an absolute must. Very good wine list.

Sainte-Agathe-des-Monts

At the restaurant **Le Havre des Poètes** *($$; 55 Rue Vincent, ☎819-326-8731)*, singers perform French and Québec classics. The food is well-rated, but people come here mainly for the ambiance.

At the restaurant **Chez Girard** *($$$-$$$$; 18 Rue Principale Ouest; ☎819-326-0922)*, set back a little from the road and not far from Lac des Sables, guests can enjoy delicious French cuisine in an extremely pleasant setting. It has two floors, the first being the noisiest.

Sauvagine *($$$$; 1592 Route 329 Nord, ☎819-326-7673)* is a French restaurant cleverly set up inside what used to be the chapel of a convent. Extremely well thought out, it is decorated with large pieces of period furniture.

Mont-Tremblant Resort

Aux Truffes *($$$$; 3035 Chemin Principal, ☎819-425-4544)* is the best restaurant in the Mont-Tremblant resort. In an inviting modern decor, guests dine on succulent nouvelle cuisine. Truffles, foie gras and game are among the predominant ingredients.

La Légende *($$$$; closed May and from Oct 15 to Nov 15; Mont Tremblant, ☎819-681-3000 or 1-800-461-8711, ext. 5500)* is a gourmet restaurant located at the top of Mont Tremblant in the Grand-Manitou complex, which also has a cafeteria. Of course, the spectacular view of the area is the main attraction. Don't underestimate the restaurant's Québec cuisine, though; game, fish, veal, beef and pork are all prepared with a great deal of finesse here. Outdoor seating available.

Mont-Tremblant Village

The magnificent dining room of the **Club Tremblant** *($$$$; Avenue Cuttles, ☎819-425-2731)* (see p 224) offers a panoramic view of the lake and Mont Tremblant. The chef prepares traditional French gastronomic cuisine. On Thursday and Saturday nights, the restaurant serves a lavish buffet. The Sunday brunch is also very popular. Reservations strongly recommended.

The Outaouais

Hull

A pleasant café/restaurant/bar/gallery/movie theatre/terrace with a very laid-back atmosphere, **Aux Quatre Jeudis** *($; 44 Rue Laval, ☎771-9557)* is patronized by a young, slightly bohemian clientele. It shows movies, and its pretty terrace is very popular in the summertime.

Le Tartuffe *($$$; closed Sun; 133 Rue Notre Dame, ☎776-6424)* is a marvelous little gourmet French restaurant located just steps from the Musée Canadien des Civilisations. With its friendly, courteous service and delightful, intimate ambiance, this place is sure to win your heart.

The Casino has all the facilities for your gambling pleasures – two restaurants serve excellent meals away from all the betting: **Banco** *($$)* offers a reasonably priced, quality buffet and various menu items; the more chic and expensive **Baccara** *($$$$; closed for lunch; 1 Boulevard du Casino, ☎772-6210)* has won itself a place among the best restaurants of the region. The set menu always consists of superb dishes that you can enjoy along with spectacular views of the lake. The well-stocked wine cellar and impeccable service round out this memorable culinary experience.

The stylish **Café Henry Burger** *($$$$; 69 Laurier, ☎777-5646)* specializes in fine French cuisine. The menu changes according to the availability of the freshest ingredients, and always offers dishes to please the most discerning palate. The restaurant has long maintained an excellent reputation.

Chelsea

It would be unheard of to visit the Outaouais without going to the Parc de la Gatineau — if only for a meal. **L'Orée du Bois** *($$$; closed Sun and Mon in winter; 15 Kingsmere Road, Old Chelsea, ☎827-0332)* is set up inside a

QUÉBEC

rustic house in the country. The crocheted curtains, wood and brick inside add to the ambiance. This is the kind of family business that you find all over France. For 17 years now, gentle, cheerful Manon has been welcoming guests and overseeing the dining rooms, while Guy focuses his expertise on the food. Guy has developed a French cuisine featuring ingredients from the various regions of Québec. The menu thus lists dishes made with wood mushrooms, fresh goat cheese, Lac Brome duck, venison and fish smoked on the premises, using maple wood. The prices are very reasonable, and the portions generous. A pleasant evening is guaranteed for all!

Papineauville

La Table de Pierre Delahaye *($$$-$$$$; closed Mon and Tue; 247 Papineau; ☎427-5027)* is worth a stop. Forget Montebello! This restaurant is sure to linger in your memory. It's run by a couple — Madame greets the guests and Monsieur takes care of the food. The welcome is always warm and cordial, the Norman-style cuisine succulent. If the thought of sweetbreads makes your mouth water, look no farther. The rooms in this historic house (1880) are oozing with atmosphere. Parties of eight or more can even have one all to themselves.

  ENTERTAINMENT

Bars and Nightclubs

Saint-Sauveur-des-Monts

The bar **Les Vieilles Portes** *(Rue Principale)* is a nice place to get together with friends for a drink. It has a pleasant outdoor terrace which is open during the summer.

Bentley's *(235 Rue Principale)* is often full of young people, who come here to have a drink before going out dancing.

Mont-Rolland

Bourbon Street *(Route 117, Mont-Rolland)* hosts good live music and is frequented by a relatively young clientele.

Mont-Tremblant Resort

The **Petit Caribou** is a young, energetic bar that really fills up after a good day of skiing.

Hull

Everyone knows about the bars along the Promenade du Portage, including Ontarians, who come here to top off a night of partying. The crowd is relatively young.

For many years now, **Aux Quatre Jeudis** *(44 Laval)* has been *the* place for the café crowd. It has lots of atmosphere, and there's a big, attractive terrace to hang out on in the summer.

Le Bop *(5 Aubry)* is a pleasant little place in old Hull. You can kick off your evening with a reasonably priced, decent meal. The music ranges from techno and disco to soft rock and even a little hard rock.

Le Fou du Roi *(253 Boulevard St-Joseph)* is where the thirty-something crowd hangs out. There's a dance floor, and the windows open onto a little terrace in the summertime. This place is also a popular after-work gathering place.

The Casino de Hull has two beautiful bars: the **777** and the **Marina** *(1 Boulevard du Casino)* which serve no less than 70 Canadian microbrews.

Theatres

Laurentides (Laurentians)

Pavillon des Arts de Sainte-Adèle *(1364 Chemin Sainte-Marguerite, ☎450-229-2586)* is a 210-seat concert hall in a former chapel. Twenty-five classical concerts are presented here annually. Each is followed by a music lover's wine and cheese in the adjoining gallery.

Festivals and Cultural Events

Lanaudière

The most important event on the regional calendar is the **Festival International de Lanaudière** *(early Jul to early Aug; ☎759-4343* *or 1-800-561-4343).* During the most beautiful weeks of the summer, dozens of classical, contemporary and popular music concerts are presented in the churches of the area and outdoors at the superb Amphithéâtre de Lanaudière.

When autumn arrives, the forests of the Saint-Donat region turn into a multicoloured natural extravaganza. To celebrate this spectacular burst of colour, various family activities are organized during **Week-ends des Couleurs** *(Sep and Oct;* ☎*819-424-2833 or 1-888-783-6628).*

Laurentides (Laurentians)

The **Festival des Couleurs** *(*☎*450-436-8532)* takes place from mid-September to the beginning of October, when the landscape is ablaze with flamboyant colours. Countless family activities are organized in Saint-Sauveur, Sainte-Adèle, Sainte-Marguerite-du-Lac-Masson, Sainte-Adolphe-d'Howard, Sainte-Agathe and Mont-Tremblant to celebrate this time of the year.

Casino

The Outaouais

If you want to have fun and possibly win some money, the **Casino de Hull** *(11am to 3am; 1 Boulevard du Casino,* ☎*1-800-665-2274 or 772-2100)* has what you're looking for. This huge casino has slot machines, Keno, blackjack and roulette tables, as well as two restaurants (see p 227).

QUÉBEC

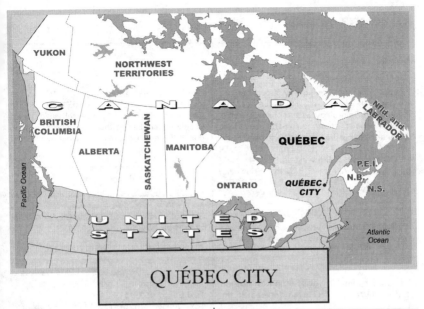

QUÉBEC CITY

Q uébec City ★★★ stands out as much for the stunning richness of its architectural heritage as for the beauty of its location. The Haute-Ville quarter covers a promontory more than 98 metres high, known as Cap Diamant, and juts out over the St. Lawrence River, which narrows here to a mere one kilometre. In fact, it is this narrowing of the river which gave the city its name: in Algonquian, *kebec* means "place where the river narrows". Affording an impregnable vantage point, the heights of Cap Diamant dominate the river and the surrounding countryside. From the inception of New France, this rocky peak played an important strategic role and was the site of major fortifications early on. Dubbed the "Gibraltar of North America", today Québec is the only walled city north of Mexico.

The cradle of New France, Québec is a city whose atmosphere and architecture are more reminiscent of Europe than of America. The stone houses that flank its narrow streets and the many spires of its churches and religious institutions evoke the French Regime. In addition, the old fortifications of the Haute-Ville, the Parliament and the grand administration buildings attest eloquently to the importance of Québec in the history of the country. Indeed, its historical and architectural richness are such that the city and its historic surroundings were recognized by UNESCO in 1985 as a World Heritage Site, the first in North America.

 FINDING YOUR WAY AROUND

By Car

Québec City can be reached from Montréal along either shore of the St. Lawrence River. Highway 40 E. runs along the north shore, becoming the 440 on the outskirts of Québec City and then Boulevard Charest once you get downtown. On the south shore, Highway 20 runs east until the Pont Pierre-Laporte. Across the bridge, Boulevard Laurier continues in the direction of Québec City, becoming Grande-Allée Est as you enter the downtown area.

Hertz
Airport: ☎871-1571
Québec City: 580 Grande-Allée, ☎647-4949
Vieux-Québec: 44 Côte du Palais ☎694-1224,
≈692-3713

Tilden
Airport: ☎871-1224
Québec City: 295 Rue Saint-Paul, ☎694-1727,
≈694-2174

By Plane

Though small, the Québec City airport handles international flights. It is located on the periphery of Sainte-Foy and Ancienne-Lorette. To get there from Vieux-Québec, take Boulevard Laurier heading west to Autoroute Henri-IV (Hwy 40 N.). From there take Boulevard Hamel going west and follow it until the Route de l'Aéroport: 510 Rue Principale, Sainte-Foy, G2E 5W1, ☎640-2600, ≈640-2656.

A company called La Québécoise (☎872-5525, ≈872-0294), travels between the airport and several hotels in downtown Québec City. A one-way trip costs $8 to Sainte-Foy and $9 to Québec for adults.

Various car rental agencies, such as Budget, Thrifty, Hertz and Tilden, are located at the airport.

The Thomas Cook foreign exchange office is open every day from 8am to 9pm.

By Bus

A network of bus routes covers the entire city. A $50 monthly pass allows for unlimited travel. A single trip costs $2 (exact change only) or $1.60 with the purchase of tickets (sold at newspaper stands). Transfers, if needed, should be requested from the driver upon boarding. Take note that most bus routes are in operation between 6am and 12:30am. Fridays and Saturdays, there is additional "late-night" bus service for #800, #801, #7, #11 and #25; all leave from Place d'Youville at 3am. For more information : ☎627-2511.

Bus Station

320 Rue Abraham-Martin (Gare du Palais), ☎525-3000.

Train Station

450 Rue de la Gare-du-Palais, ☎524-4161

By Ferry

The ferry (adults $1.75; cars $3; 10 Rue des Traversiers, ☎644-3704), from Lévis to Québec City takes 20 min. As the schedule varies widely depending on the season, it is best to check the times of crossings when planning a trip.

Ridesharing

Rides are organized to Québec City with Allo-Stop (☎522-3430)

Taxis

Taxi Coop: ☎525-5191
Taxi Québec: ☎525-8123

 PRACTICAL INFORMATION

Area code: 418

Tourist Information Office

The information centre of the **Office du Tourisme et des Congrès de la Communauté Urbaine de Québec**, which used to be on Rue d'Auteuil, is now located near the Manège Militaire and the Plains of Abraham. Unfortunately, it is only open during normal business hours: 835 Avenue Wilfrid-Laurier, G1R 2L3, ☎649-2608, ≈692-1481, www.quebec-region.cuq.qc.ca

The Infotouriste is right in the old city on 12 Rue Sainte-Anne, in front of the Château Frontenac.

Post Office

300 Rue Saint-Paul, ☎694-6176

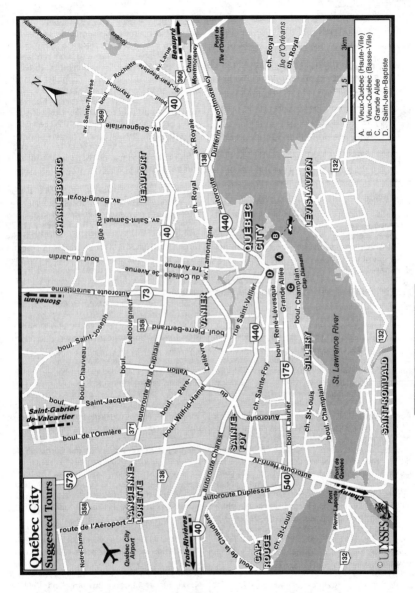

Québec City
Suggested Tours

A. Vieux-Québec (Haute-Ville)
B. Vieux-Québec (Basse-Ville)
C. Grande Allée
D. Saint-Jean-Baptiste

0   1.5   3km

QUÉBEC CITY

CHARLESBOURG

BEAUPORT

VANIER

SAINTE-FOY

SILLERY

LÉVIS-LAUZON

SAINT-ROMUALD

CAP-ROUGE

L'ANCIENNE-LORETTE

St. Lawrence River

QUÉBEC

© ULYSSES

Banks

Banque Royale: 700 Place d'Youville.
Caisse Populaire Desjardins du Vieux-Québec:
19 Rue des Jardins.

 EXPLORING

Vieux-Québec
(Haute-Ville) ★★★

Haute-Ville, or upper town, covers the plateau atop Cap Diamant. As the administrative and institutional centre, it is adorned with convents, chapels and public buildings whose construction dates back, in some cases, to the 17th century. The walls of Haute-Ville, dominated by the citadel, surround this section of Vieux-Québec and give it the characteristic look of a stronghold. These same walls long contained the development of the town, yielding a densely built-up bourgeois and aristocratic milieu. With time, the picturesque urban planning of the 19th century contributed to the present-day image of Québec City through the construction of such fantastical buildings as the Château Frontenac and the creation of such public spaces as Terrasse Dufferin, in the *belle époque* spirit.

Porte Saint-Louis *(at the beginning of the street of the same name)*. This gateway is the result of Québec City merchants' pressuring the government between 1870 and 1875 to tear down the wall surrounding the city. The Governor General of Canada at the time, Lord Dufferin, was opposed to the idea and instead put forward a plan drafted by the Irishman William H. Lynn to showcase the walls while improving traffic circulation. The design he submitted exhibits a Victorian romanticism in its use of grand gateways which bring to mind images of medieval castles and horsemen. The pepper-box tower of Porte Saint-Louis, built in 1878, makes for a striking first impression upon arriving in downtown Québec City.

Lieu Historique National des Fortifications-de-Québec ★. Québec City's first wall was built of earth and wooden posts. It was erected on the west side of the city in 1693, according to the plans of engineer Dubois Berthelot de Beaucours, to protect Québec City from the Iroquois. Work on much stronger stone fortifications began in 1745, according to the plans of engineer Chaussegros de Léry, when England and France entered a new era of conflict. However, the wall was unfinished when the city was seized by the British in 1759. The British saw to the completion of the project at the end of the 18th century. Work on the citadel began in 1693 to a minor extent. However, the structure as we know it today was essentially built between 1820 and 1832. Nevertheless, the citadel is largely designed along the principles advanced by Vauban in the 17th century, principles that suit the location admirably.

Walking along **Terrasse Dufferin ★★★**, overlooking the St. Lawrence, provides an interesting sensation compared to the pavement we are used to. It was built in 1879 at the request of the Governor General of the time, Lord Dufferin. The boardwalk's open-air pavilions and ornate streetlamps were designed by Charles Baillargé and were inspired by the style of French urban architecture common under Napoleon III. Terrasse Dufferin is one of Québec City's most popular sights and is the preferred meeting place for young people. The view of the river, the south shore and Île d'Orléans is magnificent. During the winter months, a huge ice slide is set up at the western end of the boardwalk.

Château Frontenac ★★★ *(1 Rue des Carrières)*. The first half of the 19th century saw the emergence of Québec City's tourism industry when the romantic European nature of the city began to attract growing numbers of American visitors. In 1890, the Canadian Pacific Railway company, under Cornelius Van Horne, decided to create a chain of distinguished hotels across Canada. The first of these hotels was the Château Frontenac, named in honour of one of the best-known governors of New France, Louis de Buade, Comte de Frontenac (1622-1698).

The Château Frontenac was built in stages. The first section was completed in 1893 and three sections were later added, the most important of these being the central tower (1923), the work of architects Edward and William Sutherland Maxwell. To fully appreciate the Château, one must go inside to explore the main hall, decorated in a style popular in 18th-century Parisian *hôtels particuliers*, and visit the Bar Maritime in the large main tower overlooking the river. The Château Frontenac has been the location of a number of important events in history. In 1944, the Québec

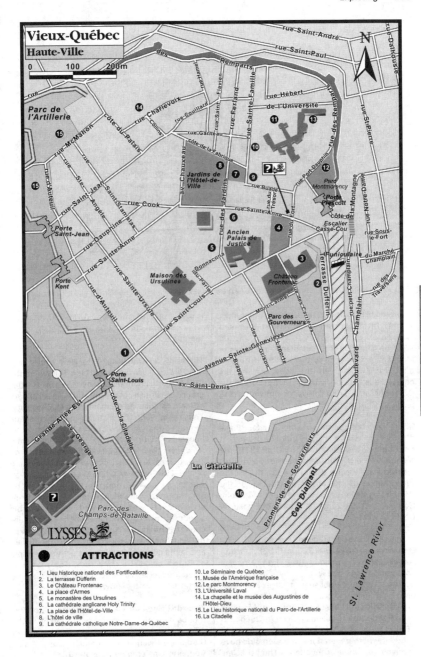

Vieux-Québec
Haute-Ville

0   100   200m

Parc de
l'Artillerie

Jardins de
l'Hôtel-de-
Ville

Ancien
Palais de
Justice

Maison des
Ursulines

Château
Frontenac

Parc des
Gouverneurs

Porte
Saint-Jean

Porte
Kent

Porte
Saint-Louis

Parc des
Champs-de-Bataille

La Citadelle

Parc
Montmorency

Porte
Prescott

Escalier
Casse-Cou

Côte de
Sous-
le-Fort

St. Lawrence River

Cap Diamant

© ULYSSES

QUÉBEC

ATTRACTIONS

1. Lieu historique national des Fortifications
2. La terrasse Dufferin
3. Le Château Frontenac
4. La place d'Armes
5. Le monastère des Ursulines
6. La cathédrale anglicane Holy Trinity
7. La place de l'Hôtel-de-Ville
8. L'hôtel de ville
9. La cathédrale catholique Notre-Dame-de-Québec

10. Le Séminaire de Québec
11. Musée de l'Amérique française
12. Le parc Montmorency
13. L'Université Laval
14. La chapelle et le musée des Augustines de
    l'Hôtel-Dieu
15. Le Lieu historique national du Parc-de-l'Artillerie
16. La Citadelle

Chateau Frontenac

Conference was held at the Château Frontenac. At this historic meeting, American President Franklin D. Roosevelt, British Prime Minister Winston Churchill and Canadian Prime Minister Mackenzie King met to discuss the future of post-war Europe. On the way out of the courtyard is a stone with the inscription of the Order of Malta, dated 1647, the only remaining piece of Château Saint-Louis.

Until the construction of the citadel, **Place d'Armes ★** was a military parade ground. It became a public square in 1832. In 1916, the Monument de la Foi (Monument of Faith) was erected in Place d'Armes to mark the tricentennial of the arrival in Québec of the Récollet religious order. Abbot Adolphe Garneau's statue rests on a base designed by David Ouellet.

Monastère des Ursulines ★★★ *(18 Rue Donnacona; ☎694-0413)*. In 1535, Sainte Angèle Merici founded the first Ursuline community in Brescia, Italy. After the community had established itself in France, it became a cloistered order dedicated to teaching (1620). With the help of a benefactor, Madame de la Peltrie, the Ursulines arrived in Québec in 1639 and, in 1641, founded a monastery and convent where generations of young girls have received a good education. The Ursuline convent is the longest running girls' school in North America. Only the museum and chapel,

a small part of the huge Ursuline complex, where several dozen nuns still live, are open to the public.

The **Anglican Cathedral of the Holy Trinity ★★** *(31 Rue des Jardins)* was built following the British acquisition of Québec, when a small group of British administrators and military officers established themselves in Québec City. These men wanted to distinguish their presence through the construction of prestigious buildings with typically British designs. However, their small numbers resulted in the slow progress of this vision until the beginning of the 19th century when work began on an Anglican cathedral designed by Majors Robe and Hall, two military engineers. The Palladian-style church was completed in 1804. This significant example of non-French architecture changed the look of the city. The church was the first Anglican cathedral built outside Britain and, in its elegant simplicity, is a good example of British colonial architecture. The roof was made steeper in 1815 so that it would not be weighted down by snow.

Place de l'Hôtel-de-Ville ★, a small square, was the location of the Notre-Dame market in the 18th century. A monument in honour of Cardinal Taschereau, created by André Vermare, was erected here in 1923.

The American Romanesque Revival influence seen in the **Hôtel de Ville** *(2 Rue des Jardins)* stands out in a city where French and British traditions have always predominated in the construction of public buildings. The building was completed in 1895 following disagreements among the mayor and the city councillors as to a building plan. Sadly, a Jesuit college dating from 1666 was demolished to make room for the city hall. Under the pleasant gardens outside the building, where popular events are held in the summer, is an underground parking lot, a much needed addition in this city of narrow streets.

Cathédrale Catholique Notre-Dame-de-Québec ★★★ *(at the other end of Place de l'Hôtel-de-Ville)*. The history of Québec City's cathedral underscores the problems faced by builders in New France and the determination of the Québécois in the face of the worst circumstances. The cathedral as it exists today is the result of numerous phases of construction and a number of tragedies which left the church in ruins on two occasions. The first church on this site was built in 1632 under the orders of Samuel de Champlain, who was buried nearby four years later. This wooden church was replaced in 1647 by Église Notre-Dame-de-la-Paix, a stone church in the shape of a roman cross that would later serve as the model for many rural parish churches. In 1674, New France was assigned its first bishop in residence. Monseigneur François-Xavier de Montmorency-Laval (1623-1708) decided that this small church, after renovations befitting its status as the heart of such an enormous ministry, would become the seat of the Catholic Church in Québec. A grandiose plan was commissioned from architect Claude Baillif, which, despite personal financial contributions from Louis XIV, was eventually scaled-down. Only the base of the west tower survives from this period. In 1742, the bishop had the church remodelled according to the plans of engineer Gaspard Chaussegros de Léry, who is responsible for its present layout, featuring an extended nave illuminated from above. The cathedral resembles many urban churches built in France during the same period.

During the siege of Québec, in 1759, the cathedral was bombarded and reduced to ruins. It was not rebuilt until the status of Catholics in Québec was settled by the British crown. The oldest Catholic parish north of Mexico was finally allowed to begin the reconstruction of its church in 1770, using the 1742 plans. The work was directed by Jean Baillargé (1726-1805), a member of the well-known family of architects and craftsmen. This marked the beginning of the Baillargé family's extended, fervent involvement with the reconstruction and renovation of the church. In 1789, the decoration of the church interior was entrusted to Jean Baillargé's son François (1759-1830), who had recently returned from three years of studying architecture in Paris at the Académie Royale. He designed the chancel's beautiful gilt baldaquin with winged caryatids four years later. The high altar, the first in Québec to be designed to look like the façade of a Basilica, was put into place in 1797. The addition of baroque pews and a plaster vault created an interesting contrast. Thus completed, the spectacular interior emphasized the use of gilding, wood and white plasterwork according to typically Québécois traditions.

In 1843, Thomas Baillargé (1791-1859), the son of François, created the present neoclassical façade and attempted to put up a steeple on the east side of the church. Work on the steeple was halted at the halfway point when it was discovered that the 17th-century foundations were not strong enough. Charles Baillargé (1826-1906), Thomas Baillargé's cousin, designed the wrought iron gate around the front square in 1858. Between 1920 and 1922, the church was carefully restored, but just a few weeks after the work was completed a fire seriously damaged the building. Raoul Chênevert and Maxime Roisin, who had already come to Québec from Paris to take on the reconstruction of the Basilica in Sainte-Anne-de-Beaupré, were put in charge of yet another restoration of the cathedral. In 1959, a mausoleum was put into place in the basement of the church. It holds the remains of Québec bishops and various governors (Frontenac, Vaudreuil, de Callière). In recent years, several masters' paintings hanging in the church have been stolen, leaving bare walls and an increased emphasis on ensuring the security of the remaining paintings, including the beautiful *Saint-Jérôme*, by Jacques-Louis David (1780), now at the Musée de l'Amérique Française.

Séminaire de Québec ★★★ *(end of Jun to end of Aug, contact the museum for the schedule of guided tours; 2 côte de la Fabrique, ☎692-2843)*. During the 17th century, this religious complex was an oasis of European civilization in a rugged and hostile territory. To get an idea of how it must have appeared to students of the day, go through the old gate (decorated with the seminary's coat of arms)

QUÉBEC

and into the courtyard before proceeding through the opposite entryway to the reception desk. The seminary was founded in 1663 by Monseigneur Francois de Laval, on orders from the Séminaire des Missions Étrangères de Paris (Seminary of Foreign Missions), with which it remained affiliated until 1763. As headquarters of the clergy throughout the colony, it was at the seminary that future priests studied, that parochial funds were administered, and that ministerial appointments were made. Louis XIV's Minister, Colbert, further required the seminary to establish a smaller school devoted to the conversion and education of native people. Following the British Conquest and the subsequent banishing of the Jesuits, the seminary became a college devoted to classical education. It also served as housing for the bishop of Québec after his palace was destroyed by the bombardment. In 1852, the seminary founded the Université Laval, the first French-language university in North America. Today most of Laval's campus is located in Sainte-Foy. The vast collection of buildings of the seminary is home to a priests' residence facing the river, a private school and the Faculty of Architecture of Université Laval, which returned to its former location in 1987.

Musée de l'Amérique Française ★ *($3; late Jun to early Sep, every day, 10am to 5pm; early Sep to late Jun, Tue to Sun, 10am to 5pm; 2 côte de la Fabrique,* ☎*692-2843)* is a museum devoted to the history of French America. It contains a wealth of over 450,000 artifacts including silverware, paintings, oriental art and numismatics, as well as scientific instruments, collected for educational purposes over the course of the last three centuries by the priests of the seminary. The museum occupies five floors of what used to be the residences of the Université Laval. The first Egyptian mummy brought to America is on view, as are several items that belonged to Monseigneur de Laval.

Parc Montmorency ★ was laid out in 1875 after the city walls were lowered along Rue des Remparts and the Governor General of Canada, Lord Dufferin, discovered the magnificent view from the promontory. George-Etienne Cartier, Prime Minister of the Dominion of Canada and one of the Fathers of Confederation is honoured with a statue here, as are Louis Hébert, Guillaume Couillard and Marie Rollet, some of the original farmers of New France. These last three disembarked in 1617 and were granted the fiefdom of Sault-au-Matelot, on the future site of the seminary, in 1623. These

attractive bronzes are the work of Montréal sculptor Alfred Laliberté.

The halls of the old **Université Laval** ★ can be seen through a gap in the wall of the ramparts. Built in 1856 in the gardens of the seminary, they were completed in 1875 with the addition of an impressive mansard roof surmounted by three silver lanterns. When the spotlights shine on them at night, it creates the atmosphere of a royal gala.

The Augustinian nurses founded their first convent in Québec in Sillery. Uneasy about the Iroquois, they relocated to Québec City in 1642 and began construction of the present complex, the **Chapelle et Musée de l'Hôtel-Dieu** ★★ *(32 Rue Charlevoix)*, which includes a convent, a hospital and a chapel. Rebuilt several times, today's buildings mostly date from the 20th century. The oldest remaining part is the 1756 convent, built on the vaulted foundations from 1695, hidden behind the 1800 chapel. This chapel was erected using material from various French buildings destroyed during the Seven Years' War. The stone was taken from the palace of the intendant, while its first ornaments came from the 17th-century Jesuit church. Today, only the iron balustrade of the bell tower bears witness to the original chapel. The present neoclassical façade was designed by Thomas Baillargé in 1839 after he completed the new interior in 1835. The nun's chancel can be seen to the right. Abbot Louis-Joseph Desjardins used the chapel as an auction house in 1817 and again in 1821, after he purchased the collection of a bankrupt Parisian banker who had amassed works confiscated from Paris churches during the French Revolution. *La Vision de Sainte-Thérese d'Avila* (Saint Theresa of Avila's Vision), a work by François-Guillaume Ménageot which originally hung in the Carmel de Saint-Denis near Paris, can be seen in one of the side altars.

Artillery Park National Historic Site ★★ *($3; hours vary according to the season; 2 Rue d'Auteuil,* ☎*648-4205)*, also called Lieu Historique National du Parc-de-l'Artillerie, takes up part of an enormous military emplacement running alongside the walls of the city. The reception and information centre is located in the old foundry, where munitions were manufactured until 1964. On display is a fascinating model of Québec City built between 1795 and 1810 by military engineer Jean-Baptiste Duberger for strategic planning. The model has only recently been returned to

Québec City, after having been sent to England in 1813. It is an unparalleled source of information on the layout of the city in the years following the British Conquest.

The walk continues with a visit to the Dauphine redoubt, a beautiful white roughcast building near Rue McMahon. In 1712, military engineer Dubois Berthelot de Beaucours drafted plans for the redoubt which was completed by Chaussegros de Léry in 1747. A redoubt is an independent fortified structure that serves as a retreat in case the troops are obliged to fall back. The redoubt was never really used for this purpose but rather as military barracks. Behind it can be seen several barracks and an old cartridge factory constructed by the British in the 19th century. The officer's barracks (1820) which has been converted into a children's centre for heritage interpretation makes a nice end to the visit.

Citadelle ★★★ *(at the far end of the Côte de la Citadelle; ☎694-2815).* Québec City's citadel represents three centuries of North American military history and is still in use. Since 1920, it has housed the Royal 22nd Regiment of the Canadian Army, a regiment distinguished for its bravery during the Second World War. Within the circumference of the enclosure are some 25 buildings including the officer's mess, the hospital, the prison, and the official residence of the Governor General of Canada, as well as the first observatory in Canada. The citadel's history began in 1693, when Engineer Dubois Berthelot de Beaucours had the Cap Diamant redoubt built at the highest point of Québec City's defensive system, some 100 metres above the level of the river. This solid construction is today included inside the King's bastion.

Throughout the 18th century, French and then British engineers developed projects for a citadel that remained unfulfilled. Chaussegros de Léry's powderhouse of 1750, which now houses the Museum of the Royal 22nd Regiment, and the temporary excavation works to the west (1783) are the only works of any scope accomplished during this period. The citadel that appears today was built between 1820 and 1832 according to the plans of Colonel Elias Walker Durnford. Dubbed the "Gibraltar of North America", and built according to principles expounded by Vauban in the 17th century, the citadel has never borne the brunt of a single cannonball, though it has acted as an important element of dissuasion.

Vieux-Québec (Basse-Ville) ★★★

Vieux-Québec's port and commercial area, Basse-Ville, or lower town, is a narrow U-shaped piece of land wedged between the waters of the St. Lawrence and the Cap Diamant escarpment. The cradle of New France, Basse-Ville's Place Royale is where, in 1608, Samuel de Champlain (1567-1635) founded the settlement he called Abitation that would become Québec City. In the summer of 1759, three quarters of Basse-Ville was badly damaged by British bombardment. It took twenty years to repair and rebuild the houses. In the 19th century, the construction of multiple embankments allowed the expansion of the town and the linking by road of the area around Place Royale with the area around the intendant's palace. The decline of the port at the beginning of the 20th century led to the gradual abandonment of Place Royale; restoration work began in 1959.

Funiculaire *(☎692-1132).* The funicular began operating in November of 1879. It was put into place by entrepreneur W. A. Griffith in order to bring the lower and upper towns closer together. It is an outdoor elevator that obviates the need to take the Escalier Casse-Cou, "break-neck stairway", or to go around Côte de la Montagne. Due to an unfortunate accident in the summer of 1996, the funicular is being completely overhauled and should be back in operation in April 1998. In the meantime, the business owners of Petit-Champlain have set up a shuttle service between their neighbourhood and Haute-Ville.

The **Escalier Casse-Cou** *(Côte de la Montagne)* (literally, "the break-neck strairway") has been here since 1682. Until the beginning of the 20th century, it had been made of planks that were in constant need of repair or replacement. At the foot of the stairway is **Rue du Petit-Champlain**, a narrow pedestrian street flanked by charming craft shops and pleasant cafés located in 17th and 18th century houses. Some of the houses at the foot of the cape were destroyed by rockslides prior to the reinforcement of the cliff in the 19th century.

Place Royale ★★★ is the most European quarter of any city in North America, resembling resembles a village in northwestern France. Place Royale is laden with symbolism, as it was on this very spot that New France was founded in 1608. After many unsuccessful

QUÉBEC

attempts, this became the official departure point of the French exploits in America. Under the French Regime, Place Royale was the only densely populated area in a vast and untamed colony. Today, it contains the most significant concentration of 17th and 18th century buildings in the Americas north of Mexico.

The square itself was laid out in 1673 by Governor Frontenac as a market. It took the place of the garden of Champlain's Abitation, a stronghold that went up in flames in 1682, along with the rest of Basse-Ville. In 1686, Intendant Jean Bochart de Champigny erected a bronze bust of Louis XIV in the middle of the square, hence the name of the square, Place Royale. In 1928, François Bokanowski, then the French Minister of Commerce and Communications, presented Quebecer Athanase David with a bronze replica of the marble bust of Louis XIV in the Gallerie de Diane at Versailles to replace the missing statue. The bronze, by Alexis Rudier, was not set up until 1931, for fear of offending England.

Small, unpretentious **Église Notre-Dame-des-Victoires** ★★ (*mid-May to mid-Oct, every day 9am to 4:30pm, closed Sat in case of weddings; Place Royale)* is the oldest church in Canada. Designed by Claude Baillif, it dates from 1688. It was built on the foundations of Champlain's Abitation, and incorporates some of its walls. Initially dedicated to the Baby Jesus, it was rechristened Notre-Dame-de-la-Victoire after Admiral Phipps' attack of 1690 failed. It was later renamed Notre-Dame-des-Victoires (the plural) in memory of the misfortune of British Admiral Walker, whose fleet ran aground on Île-aux-Oeufs during a storm in 1711. The bombardments of the conquest left nothing standing but the walls of the church, spoiling the Levasseurs' lovely interior. The church was restored in 1766, but was not fully rebuilt until the current steeple was added in 1861.

The **Musée de la Civilisation** ★★ *($6; Tue free admission, except in summer; end of Jun to early Sep, every day 10am to 7pm; early Sep to end of Jun, every day 10am to 5pm; 85 Rue Dalhousie, ☎643-2158)* is housed in a building, completed in 1988, that interprets the traditional architecture of Québec City with its stylized roof, dormer windows and a belltower which evokes those of the surroundings. The architect Moshe Safdie, who also designed the revolutionary Habitat '67 in Montreal, Ottawa's National Gallery and Vancouver's Public Library, has created a sculptural building with a

monumental exterior staircase at its centre. The lobby provides a charming view of Maison Estèbe and its wharf while preserving a contemporary look that is underlined by Astri Reuch's sculpture, *La Débâcle*.

The ten rooms of this "sociological" museum present a collection of everyday objects relating to the Québec culture of the present and the past. The random grouping of this extensive collection tends to overwhelm, so it is a good idea to select a few rooms that seem particularly interesting. Some of the more remarkable items are the aboriginal artefacts, the large French Regime fishing craft unearthed during excavations for the Museum itself, some highly ornate 19th-century horse-drawn hearses, and some Chinese objets d'art and pieces of furniture, including an imperial bed, from the collection of the Jesuits.

Vieux-Port ★ *(160 Rue Dalhousie)*. The old port is often criticized for being overly American in a city of such European sensibilities. It was refurbished by the Canadian government on the occasion of the maritime celebration "Québec 1534-1984". There are various metallic structures designed to enliven the promenade, at the end of which is the handsome **Édifice de la Douane** (1856), the old customs building, designed by William Thomas of Toronto. All of the port area between Place Royale and the entrance of **Bassin Louise** is known as **Pointe-à-Carcy**.

Marché du Vieux-Port ★ *(corner of Rue Saint-Thomas and Rue Saint-André)*. Most of Québec City's public markets were shut down in the sixties, because they had become obsolete in an age of air-conditioned supermarkets and frozen food. However, people continued to want fruit and vegetables fresh from the farm as well as the contact with the farmers. Moreover, the market was one of the only non-aseptic places people could congregate. Thus, the markets gradually began to reappear at the beginning of the eighties. Marché du Vieux-Port was built in 1987 by the architectural partners Belzile, Brassard, Galienne and Lavoie. It is the successor to two other Basse-Ville markets, Finlay and Champlain, that no longer exist. In the summer, the market is a pleasant place to stroll and take in the view of the Marina Bassin Louise at the edge of the market.

For over 50 years, the citizens of Québec City clamoured for a train station worthy of their city. Canadian Pacific finally fulfilled their wish in 1915. Designed by New York architect Harry

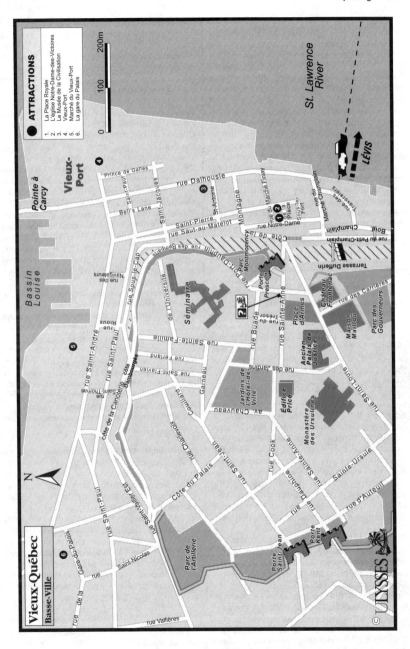

Vieux-Québec
Basse-Ville

ATTRACTIONS

1. La Place Royale
2. L'église Notre-Dame-des-Victoires
3. Le Musée de la Civilisation
4. Vieux-Port
5. Marché du Vieux-Port
6. La gare du Palais

0   100   200m

St. Lawrence River

QUÉBEC

Edward Prindle in the same style as the Château Frontenac, the **Gare du Palais** ★ *(Rue de la Gare)* gives visitors a taste of the romance and charm that await in Québec City. The 18-metre-high arrival hall that extends behind the giant window of the façade is bathed by sunlight passing through the leaded glass skylight of the roof. The faïence tiles and multicoloured bricks of the walls lend a striking aspect to the whole. The station was closed for almost ten years (from 1976 to 1985) at the time when railway companies were imitating airlines and moving their stations to the suburbs. Fortunately, it was reopened, with great pomp, and now houses the bus and train stations. The building on the right is Raoul Chênevert's 1938 post office. It illustrates the persistence of the Château style of architecture that is so emblematic of the city.

Grande Allée ★★

The Grande Allée appears on 17th-century maps, but it was not built up until the first half of the 19th century, when the city grew beyond its walls. It was originally a country road linking the town to the Chemin du Roi and thereby to Montréal. At that time, it was bordered by the large agricultural properties of the nobility and clergy of the French Regime. After the British Conquest, many of the domains were turned into country estates of English merchants who set their manors well back from the road. Then the neoclassical town spilled over into the area before the Victorian city had a chance to stamp the landscape with its distinctive style. Today's Grande Allée is the most pleasant route into the downtown area and the focus of extramural Haute-Ville. Despite the fact that it links the capital's various ministries, it is a cheery street as many of the bourgeois houses which front onto it have been converted into restaurants and bars.

The **Hôtel du Parlement ★★★** *(free admission; guided tours every day end of Jun to early Sep, 9am and 4:30pm; early Sep to Jun, Mon to Fri, 9am to 4:30pm; at the corner of Dufferin and Grande Allée, ☎643-7239)* is known to Quebecers as the Assemblée Nationale, the National Assembly. The seat of the government of Québec, this imposing building was erected between 1877 and 1886. It has a lavish French Renaissance Revival exterior intended to reflect the unique cultural status of Québec in the North American context. Eugène-Étienne Taché (1836-1912) looked to the Louvre for his

inspiration in both the plan of the quadrangular building and its decor. Originally destined to incorporate the two houses of parliament characteristic of the British system of government, as well as all of the ministries, it is today part of a group of buildings on either side of the Grande Allée.

The numerous statues of the parliament's main façade constitute a sort of pantheon of Québec. The 22 bronzes of important figures in the history of the nation were cast by such well-known artists as Louis-Philippe Hébert and Alfred Laliberté. A raised inscription on the wall near the central passage identifies the statues. In front of the main entrance a bronze by Hébert entitled *La Halte dans la Forêt* (The Pause in the Forest) depicts an aboriginal family. The work, which is meant to honour the original inhabitants of Québec, was displayed at Paris's World's Fair in 1889. *Le Pêcheur à la Nigog* (Fisherman at the Nigog), by the same artist, hangs in the niche by the fountain.

Place George-V and the **Manège Militaire ★** *(opposite Parc Le Pigeonnier)*. This expanse of lawn is used as the training area and parade ground of the military's equestrians. There are cannons and a statue in memory of the two soldiers who perished attempting to douse the flames of the 1889 fire in the suburb of Saint-Sauveur. Otherwise, the grounds serve mainly to highlight the amusing Château-style façade of the Manège Militaire, the Military Riding Academy, built in 1888 and designed by Eugène-Étienne Taché, the architect of the Hôtel du Parlement.

Behind the austere façade of the mother house of the Soeurs du Bon-Pasteur, a community devoted to the education of abandoned and delinquent girls, is the charming, baroque-revival-style **Chapelle Historique Bon-Pasteur ★★** *(free admission; Jul and Aug, Tue to Sat, 1:30pm to 4:30pm; 1080 Rue de la Chevrotière)*. Designed by Charles Baillargé in 1866, this tall, narrow chapel houses an authentic baroque tabernacle dating from 1730. Pierre-Noël Levasseur's masterpiece of New France carving is surrounded by devotional miniatures hung on pilasters by the nuns.

The **Grand Théâtre** *(269 Boulevard René-Lévesque Est, ☎643-8131)* is located at the far end of the park. Inaugurated in 1971, the theatre of Polish architect Victor Prus was to be a meeting place for the cream of Québec City society. There was quite a scandal,

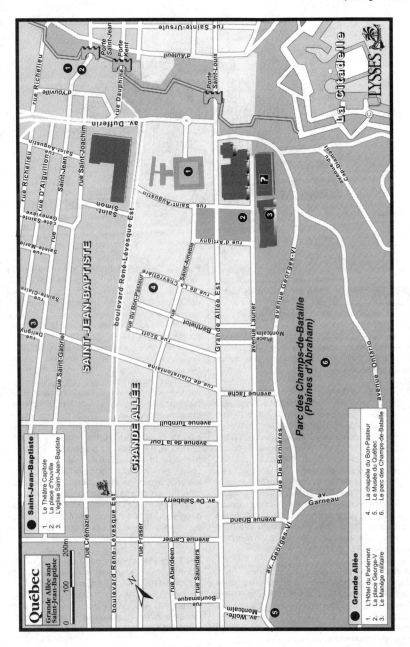

Québec

Grande Allée and Saint-Jean-Baptiste

0   100   200m

N

● **Saint-Jean-Baptiste**

1.   Le Théâtre Capitole
2.   La place d'Youville
3.   L'église Saint-Jean-Baptiste

● **Grande Allée**

1.   L'Hôtel du Parlement
2.   La place George-V
3.   Le Manège militaire
4.   La chapelle du Bon-Pasteur
5.   Le Musée du Québec
6.   Le parc des Champs-de-Bataille

QUÉBEC

Porte Saint-Jean
Porte Kent
Porte Saint-Louis

rue Sainte-Ursule
d'Auteuil

rue Richelieu
d'Youville
rue Dauphine

av. Dufferin

rue Richelieu
rue D'Aiguillon
Saint-Augustin
Saint-Jean
rue Saint-Joachim
Côte Sainte-Geneviève
rue Sainte-Marie
Saint-Simon
rue Saint-Augustin

rue Sainte-Claire
Sainte-Claire
rue Delligny

SAINT-JEAN-BAPTISTE

rue Saint-Gabriel
boulevard René-Lévesque Est
rue du Bon-Pasteur
rue de la Chevrotière
Saint-Amable
rue d'Artigny

rue Berthelot
rue Scott
Grande Allée Est
avenue Laurier
avenue Georges-VI

GRANDE ALLÉE

rue de Claire-Fontaine
avenue Taché
Place Montcalm

avenue Turnbull
avenue de la Tour
av. De Salaberry

Parc des Champs-de-Bataille
(Plaines d'Abraham)

rue De Bernières
av. Garneau
avenue Briand
av. Georges-VI

rue Crémazie
rue Fraser
avenue Cartier
rue Aberdeen
rue Saunders
rue Bourlamaque
av. Wolfe-Montcalm

avenue Ontario

La Citadelle

ULYSSES

Musée du Québec

therefore, when Jordi Bonet's mural was unveiled and the assembled crowd could read the lines from a poem by Claude Péloquin: *Vous êtes pas tannés de mourir, bande de caves*, which roughly translates, "You bunch of straights ain't sick of dying". The theatre has two halls (Louis-Fréchette and Octave-Crémazie) and stages the concerts of the symphony orchestra as well as theatre, dance and variety shows.

The **Musée de Québec** ★★★ *($5.75; late May to early Sep, every day 10am to 5:45pm, Wed to 9:45pm; early Sep to late May, Tue to Sun 11am to 5:45pm, Wed to 8:45pm; 1 Avenue Wolfe-Montcalm, ☎643-2150)* was renovated and enlarged in 1992. The older, west-facing building is on the right. Parallel to Avenue Wolfe-Montcalm, the entrance is dominated by a glass tower similar to that of the Musée de la Civilisation. The 1933 Classical Revival edifice is subterraneously linked with the old prison on the left. The latter has been cleverly restored to house exhibits and has been rebaptized Édifice Ballairgé in honour of its architect. Some of the cells have been preserved.

A visit to this important museum allows one to become acquainted with the painting, sculpture and silverwork of Québec from the time of New France to today. The collections of religious art gathered from rural parishes of Québec are particularly interesting. Also on display are official documents, including the original surrender of Québec (1759). The museum frequently hosts temporary exhibits from the United States and Europe.

Parc des Champs-de-Bataille ★★ takes visitors back to July 1759: the British fleet, commanded by General Wolfe arrives in front of Québec City. The attack is launched almost immediately. In total, almost 40,000 cannonballs crash down on the besieged city. As the season grows short, the British must come to a decision before they are surprised by French reinforcements or trapped in the December freeze-up. On the 13th of September, under cover of night, British troops scale the Cap Diamant escarpment west of the fortifications. The ravines which here and there cut into the otherwise uniform mass of the escarpment allow them to climb and to remain concealed. By morning, the troops have taken position in the fields of **Abraham Martin**, hence the name of the battlefield and the park. The French are astonished, as they had anticipated a direct attack on the citadel. Their troops, with the aid of a few hundred Indian warriors, throw themselves against the British. The generals of both sides are slain, and the battle draws to a close in bloody chaos. New France is lost!

The **Tours Martello** ★, two towers designed by the eponymous engineer, are characteristic of British defenses at the beginning of the 19th century. Tower number 1 (1808) is visible on the edge of Avenue Ontario; number 2 (1815) blends into the surrounding buildings on the corner of Avenue Laurier and Avenue Taché.

Saint-Jean-Baptiste ★

A student hangout complete with bars, theatres and boutiques, the Saint-Jean-Baptiste quarter is perched on a hillside between the upper and lower towns. The abundance of pitched and mansard roofs is reminiscent of parts of the old city, but the orthogonal layout of the streets is quintessentially North American. Despite a terrible fire in 1845, this old Québec City suburb retains several examples of wooden constructions, forbidden inside the walls of the city.

At the beginning of the 20th century, Québec City was in dire need of a new auditorium, its Académie de Musique having burnt to the ground in March of 1900. With the help of private enterprise, the mayor undertook to find a new location. The Canadian Government, owner of the fortifications, offered to furnish a strip of land along the walls of the city. While narrow, the lot grew wider as it grew deeper, making possible the construction of a fitting hall, the **Capitole** ★ *(972 Rue Saint-Jean)*. W. S. Painter, the ingenious Detroit architect already at work on the expansion of the Château Frontenac, devised a plan for a curved façade, giving the building a monumental air despite the restriction of the lot. Inaugurated in 1903 as the Auditorium de Québec, the building is one of the most astonishing beaux-arts realizations in the country.

Place d'Youville is the public space at the entrance of the old section of town. Formerly an important market square, it is today a bustling crossroads and cultural forum. A recent redevelopment has given the square a large promenade area with trees and benches. The counterscarp wall, part of the fortifications removed in the 20th century, has been highlighted by the use of black granite blocks.

The Montcalm Market was levelled in 1932 in order to build the multifunctional space called the **Palais Montcalm** *(995 Place d'Youville)*. Also known as the Monument National, this is the venue of choice for political rallies and demonstrations of all kinds. The auditorium has a sparse architecture which draws on both neoclassical and Art-Deco schools.

The **Église Saint-Jean-Baptiste** ★ *(Rue Saint-Jean on the corner of Rue de Ligny)* stands out as Joseph Ferdinand Peachy's masterpiece. A disciple of French eclecticism, Peachy was an unconditional admirer of the Église de la Trinité in Paris. The resemblance here is striking, as much in the portico as in the interior. Completed in 1885, the building caused the bankruptcy of its architect, who was, unfortunately, held responsible for cracks that appeared in the façade during construction.

 OUTDOORS

 Tobogganing

During winter, a hill is created on **Terrasse Dufferin**. You can glide down it comfortably seated on a toboggan. First purchase your tickets at the little stand in the middle of the terrace *($1 per ride; mid-Dec to mid-Mar, every day 11am to 11pm; 692-2955)*, then grab a toboggan and climb to the top of the slide. Once you get there, make sure to take a look around: the view is magnificent!

 ACCOMMODATIONS

Hospitalité Canada Tours is a free telephone service operated by the Maison du Tourisme de Québec *(12 Rue Ste-Anne, ☎694-1602 or 1-800-665-1528)*. Depending on what kind of accommodations you're looking for, the staff will suggest various places belonging to the network and even make reservations for you.

Vieux-Québec (Haute-Ville)

The **Centre Internationale de Séjour** youth hostel *($17 Canadians, $20 non-Canadians; 19 Rue Sainte-Ursule, G1R 4E1, ☎1-800-461-8585, ☎694-0755)* has 250 beds for young people during the summer months. The rooms can accommodate from three to eight people, the dormitories from 10 to 12; there are also private double rooms.

Behind its lovely white facade in Vieux-Québec, **Auberge de la Paix** *($18 bkfst incl., plus $2 for bedding if you don't have your own; sb, K; 31 Rue Couillard, G1R 3T4, ☎694-0735)* has a youth-hostel atmosphere. It has a total of 59 beds in rooms able to accommodate from two to eight people, as well as a kitchenette and a

QUÉBEC

living room. The pretty back yard is all abloom in the summer. Children welcome!

A number of old houses on Rue Sainte-Ursule have been made into hotels. Among these, **Maison Acadienne** *($77; ⊛, ≡, K; 43 Rue Sainte-Ursule, G1R 4E4, ☎694-0280)* is easily spotted by its large, white facade. The rooms are rather lacklustre, although some of them have been renovated.

Au Jardin du Gouverneur *($90 bkfst incl.; ≡; 16 Rue Mont-Carmel, G1R 4A3, ☎692-1704, ⌁692-1713)* is a charming little hotel in small blue and white house opposite Parc des Gouverneurs. Rooms are a good size but the decor is nothing special. No smoking.

Built in 1870, the **Clarendon** *($140 bkfst incl., $190 ½b; ≡, ℜ, &; 57 Rue Sainte-Anne, G1R 3X4, ☎1-800-463-5250, ☎692-4652, ⌁692-4652)* is one of the oldest hotels in the city. The hotel has an unpretentious exterior while the elegant interior is decorated in Art Deco style. The entrance hall is very attractive. Over the years, the rooms in this hotel have been renovated many times and are spacious and comfortable. This a very good place to stay in Vieux-Québec.

The **Château Frontenac** *($189 bkfst incl., $249 ½b; ℜ, ≡, &, ⊛, ≈, ⊘; 1 Rue des Carrières, G1R 4P5, ☎1-800-268-9420, ☎692-3861, ⌁692-1751)* is by far the most prestigious hotel in Québec City (see p 234). Its elegant entrance hall is decorated with wood panelling and warm colours. The reception, unfortunately, is often somewhat cooler. The rooms are decorated with classic refinement and are very comfortable. A new wing has recently been completed and, besides guest rooms, houses an indoor pool.

Vieux-Québec (Basse-Ville)

The pleasant **Hôtel Particulier Belley** *($45-$65; K; 249 Rue Saint-Paul, G1K 3W5, ☎692-1694, ⌁692-1696)* stands opposite the market at the Vieux-Port. A hotel since 1877, this handsome building will leave you with fond memories for years to come. It has eight simply decorated, cozy rooms, some with exposed brick walls, others with wooden beams and skylights. The ground floor is home to a bar called Taverne Belley, whose breakfasts and lunches, served in two lovely rooms, are very popular with locals. A number of extremely comfortable and attractively decorated lodgings, some with terraces, are also available in another house across the street. These may be rented by the night, by the week or by the month.

The **Priori** *($125 bkfst incl.; ⊛, ℜ; 15 Rue du Saul-au-Matelot, G1K 3Y7, ☎522-8108, ⌁692-0883)* is located on a quiet street in Basse-Ville. The building is very old but has been renovated in a very modern style. The decor successfully contrasts the old stone walls of the building with up-to-date furnishings. The appearance is striking and even the elevator is distinctive. The Priori comes highly recommended.

Auberge Sainte-Antoine *($189 bkfst incl.; ⊛, ≡; 10 Rue Saint-Antoine, G1K 4C9, ☎692-2211, ⌁ 692-1177)* is located near the Musée de la Civilisation. This lovely hotel is divided into two buildings. Guests enter through a tastefully renovated old stone building. The entrance hall is distinguished by exposed wooden beams, stone walls and a beautiful fireplace. The hotel serves breakfast. Each room is decorated according to a different theme and has its own unique charm.

Grande Allée

Also just outside Vieux-Québec is the **Hôtel Loews Le Concorde** *($165; &, ≡, ≈, ⊘, △, ℜ; 1225 Place Montcalm, G1R 4W6, ☎647-2222, ⌁647-4710)*. It is part of the Loews hotel chain and has spacious, comfortable rooms with spectacular views of Québec City and the surrounding area. There is a revolving restaurant on top of the hotel.

Saint-Jean-Baptiste

Adjoining the newly renovated theatre is the **Hôtel du Théâtre Capitole** *($135; ℜ, ≡, ⊛; 972 Rue Saint-Jean, G1R, ☎694-9930 ⌁647-2146)*. The hotel is located in the part of the building surrounding the theatre. While not luxurious, the room's are amusing, the decor resembling a stage set. At the entrance is the restaurant Il Teatro (see p 248).

RESTAURANTS

Vieux-Québec (Haute-Ville)

At **Chez Temporel** *($; 25 Rue Couillard)* all the food is prepared on the premises. Whether you opt for a butter croissant, a *croque-monsieur*, a salad or the special of the day, you can be sure that it will be fresh and tasty. To top it all off, the place serves some of the best espresso in town! The waiters and waitresses sometimes have more work than they can handle, but a touch of understanding on your part will be rewarded a hundred times over. Tucked away in a bend in little Rue Couillard, the two-story Temporel has been welcoming people of all ages and all stripes for over 20 years now. Open early in the morning until late at night.

The **Frères de la Côte** *($$; 1190 Rue Saint-Jean, ☎692-5445)* serves delectable bistro fare, including pasta, grill, and thin-crust pizzas baked in a wood-burning oven and topped with delicious fresh ingredients. All-you-can-eat mussels and fries on certain evenings. The atmosphere is lively and laid-back, and the place is often packed, which is only fitting here on bustling Rue Saint-Jean. Guests can take in the action outside through the restaurant's big windows.

Chez Livernois *($$-$$$; 1200 Rue Saint-Jean, ☎694-0618)* is a bistro located inside Maison Serge-Bruyère. It is named for photographer Jules Livernois, who set up his studio in this imposing 19th-century house in 1889. The excellent cuisine consists mainly of pasta and grill dishes, and the atmosphere is a bit more relaxed than at La Grande Table (see below).

The **Élysée-Mandarin** *($$$; 65 Rue d'Auteuil, ☎692-0909)*, which also boasts prime locations in Montréal and Paris, serves excellent Szechuan, Cantonese and Mandarin cuisine in a decor featuring a small indoor garden and Chinese sculptures and vases. The food is always succulent and the service, extremely courteous. If you are in a group, try the tasting menu: it would be a shame not to sample as many of the dishes as possible!

Located in one of the oldest houses in Québec City, the restaurant **Aux Anciens Canadiens** *($$$-$$$$, 34 Rue Saint-Louis, ☎692-1627)* serves up-scale versions of traditional Québec

specialities. Dishes include ham with maple syrup, pork and beans and blueberry pie.

Le Saint-Amour *($$$-$$$$; 48 Rue Sainte-Ursule, ☎694-0667)* has been one of the best restaurants in Québec for several years now. Chef and co-owner Jean-Luc Boulay creates succulent, innovative cuisine that is a feast for both the eyes and the palate. The desserts concocted in the *chocolaterie*, on the second floor, are positively divine. A truly gastronomic experience! To top it all off, the place is beautiful, comfortable and has a warm atmosphere. The solarium, open year-round and decorated with all sorts of flowers and other plants, brightens up the decor. On fine summer days, its roof is removed, transforming it into a sun-drenched patio. Valet parking.

Le Champlain *($$$$; 1 Rue des Carrières, ☎692-3861)* is the Château Frontenac's restaurant. Needless to say, its decor is extremely luxurious, in keeping with the opulence of the rest of the hotel. The outstanding French cuisine also does justice to the Château's reputation. Chef Jean Soular, whose recipes have been published, endeavours to add an original touch to these classic dishes. Impeccable service provided by waiters in uniform.

La Grande Table *($$$$; 1200 Rue Saint-Jean, ☎694-0618)*, in Maison Serge-Bruyère, has a solid reputation that extends far beyond the walls of the old city. Located on the top floor of a historic house between Couillard and Garneau Streets, it serves gourmet French cuisine that delights both the eye and the palate. The attractive decor includes paintings by Québec artists. Valet parking.

Vieux-Québec (Basse-Ville)

The **Cochon Dingue** *($-$$; 46 Boulevard Champlain, ☎692-2013)* is a charming café-bistro located between Boulevard Champlain and Rue du Petit-Champlain. Mirrors and a checkerboard floor make for a fun, attractive decor. The menu features bistro fare, such as *steak-frites* and *moules-frites* combos (steak and fries or mussels and fries). The desserts will send you into raptures. The Cochon Dingue has two other locations, one on the Grande Allée Tour *(46 Boulevard René-Lévesque Ouest, ☎523-2013)* and another in Sillery, outside Québec City *(1326 Avenue Maguire, ☎684-2013)*.

QUÉBEC

Café du Monde *($$-$$$; 57 Rue Dalhousie,*
☎692-4455) is a large Parisian-style brasserie
serving dishes one would expect from such a
place, including steak tartar and *magret de*
canard (duck filet). There is a singles bar at the
entrance. The waiters, dressed in long aprons,
are attentive.

The chef and co-owner of **Laurie Raphäel** *($$$-*
$$$$; 17 Rue Dalhousie, ☎692-4455), Daniel
Vézina, was named the best chef in Québec in
1997. The same year, a book of his tempting
recipes was published. When creating his
mouthwatering dishes, Vézina draws inspiration
from culinary traditions from all over the world,
preparing sweetbreads, scallops, ostrich, etc.,
in innovative ways. It goes without saying,
therefore, that the food at Laurie Raphaël is
delicious! In May 1996 the restaurant moved
into newer, more spacious quarters with a
semi-circular exterior glass wall. The chic decor
includes creamy white curtains, sand- and
earth-tones and a few decorative, wrought-iron
objects.

Grande Allée

Le Louis-Hébert *($$$; 668 Grande Allée Est,*
☎525-7812), a chic restaurant with a plush
decor, serves French cuisine and delectable
seafood. There is a solarium be decked with
greenery at the back. Courteous, attentive
service.

Located at the top of one of the city's largest
hotels, the revolving **L'Astral** restaurant *($$$-*
$$$$; Hotel Loews Le Concorde, 1225 Place
Montcalm, ☎647-2222) serves excellent French
food and provides a stunning view of the river,
the Plains of Abraham, the Laurentian
mountains and the city. It takes about one hour
for the restaurant to revolve completely. This is
a particularly good place to go for Sunday
brunch.

Saint-Jean-Baptiste

Il Teatro *($$$; 972 Rue Saint-Jean,*
☎694-9996), inside the magnificent Théâtre
Capitole, serves excellent Italian cuisine in a
lovely dining room with a long bar at its far end
and big, sparkling windows all around. The
courteous service is on a par with the delicious
food. During summer, guests can dine in a

small outdoor seating area sheltered from the
hustle and bustle of Place d'Youville.

 ENTERTAINMENT

Bars and Nightclubs

Vieux-Québec (Haute-Ville)

Le Chanteuteuil *(1001 Rue Saint-Jean)*, at the
foot of the hill on Rue d'Auteuil, is a pleasant
bistro. People spend hours here chatting away,
seated around bottles of wine or beers.

The oldest hotel in the city houses the **Emprise**
(Hôtel Clarendon, 57 Rue Sainte-Anne;
see p 354). This elegant bar is recommended
to jazz fans. There is no cover charge.

The **Saint-Alexandre** *(1087 Rue Saint-Jean)* is
a typical English pub serves 175 types of beer,
19 of which are on tap. The decor is appealing
and the ambiance pleasant.

Vieux-Québec (Basse-Ville)

L'Innox *(37 Rue Saint-André)* is a big place at
the Vieux-Port that brews good beer and serves
other drinks. Its lager, *blanche* (white) and
rousse (red) beers are all as delicious as can be.
There is also a small *économusée* on the
premises.

Grande Allée

Chez Dagobert *(600 Grande Allée Est)* is an
immense and popular disco located in an old
stone house. There is always a crowd and
there is no cover-charge.

Chez Maurice *(575 Grande Allée Est)*, which
occupies an old house on Grande Allée, is a
big, chic, trendy discotheque. The place to go
to see and be seen and dance to the latest hits.
Chez Maurice hosts theme nights as well,
including a very popular disco night. Inside,
you'll also find a cigar room called **Chez**
Charlotte, which truly merits the label *bar*
digestif (cocktail lounge)!

Gay and Lesbian Clubs

The gay disco **Ballon Rouge** *(811 Rue Saint-Jean)* has an exclusively male clientele. Its several rooms each have their own particular ambience.

Drague *(804 Rue St-Augustin)* is a large, loud, smoky tavern for men only.

Theatres

The Québec City edition of the French-language magazine *Voir* is distributed free of charge every Thursday and provides information on the principal events of the city.

Music

The **Orchestre Symphonique de Québec,** Canada's oldest symphony orchestra, performs regularly at the Grand Théâtre de Québec *(269 Boulevard René-Lévesque Ouest, ☎643-8131),* where you can also catch the **Opéra de Québec.**

Theatres

Grand Théâtre de Québec: 269 Boulevard René Lévesque Est, ☎643-8131. This theatre has two halls.

Le Palais Montcalm: 995 Place d'Youville, ☎691-2399, ticket service ☎670-9011.

Théâtre de la Bordée: 1143 Rue Saint-Jean, ☎694-9721, ticket service ☎694-9631.

Théâtre Capitole: 972 Rue Saint-Jean, ☎694-4444.

Le Périscope, 2 Rue Crémazie Est, ☎529-2183.

Théâtre de la Bordée, 1143 Rue Saint-Jean, ☎694-9631.

Théâtre du Trident, at the Grand Théâtre de Québec, 269 Boulevard René-Lévesque Ouest, ☎643-8131.

Movie Theatres

Cinéma de Paris: Place d'Youville, ☎694-0891

Les Galeries: 5401 Boulevard des Galeries, ☎628-2455

Place Charest: 500 Rue Dupont, ☎529-9745

Festivals and Cultural Events

Carnaval de Québec *(☎626-3716),* Québec City's winter carnival, takes place annually during the first two weeks of February. It is an opportunity for visitors and residents of Québec City to celebrate the beauty of winter. It is also a good way to add a little life to a cold winter that often seem interminable. Various activities are organized. This can be a bitterly cold period of the year, so dressing very warmly is essential.

The **Festival d'Été de Québec** *(mid-Jul; ☎692-4540)* is generally held for 10 days in early July, when music, dancing and other kinds of entertainment from all over the world liven up Québec City. The festival has everything it takes to be the city's most important cultural event. The outdoor shows are particularly popular.

 SHOPPING

Bookstores

La Maison Anglaise:
Place de la Cité, Sainte-Foy,
☎654-9523.
The best selection of English books around Québec City.

Librairie Ulysse:
4 Boulevard René-Lévesque Est,
☎529-5349; travel bookshop

CDs and Cassettes

Sillons Le Disquaire: 1149 Avenue Cartier, ☎524-8352.

Archambault: 1095 Rue Saint-Jean, Vieux-Québec, ☎694-2088

Craft Shops and Artisans' Studios

Atelier La Pomme: 47 Rue Sous-le-Fort, ☎692-2875. Leather goods.

Boutique Sachem: 17 Rue des Jardins, ☎692-3056. Native crafts.

Galerie-Boutique Métiers d'Art: 29 Rue Notre-Dame, Place Royale, ☎694-0267. Québec-made crafts.

Galerie d'Art Indien Cinq Nations: 25½ Rue du Petit-Champlain, ☎692-3329. Native crafts.

Les Trois Colombes: 46 Rue Saint-Louis, ☎694-1114. Handcrafted items and quality clothing.

L'Oiseau du Paradis: 80 Rue du Petit-Champlain, ☎692-2679. Paper and paper objects.

Pot-en-Ciel: 27 Rue du Petit-Champlain, ☎692-1743. Ceramics.

Verrerie d'Art Réjean Burns: 156 Rue St-Paul, ☎694-0013. Stained glass, lamps.

Verrerie La Mailloche: Escalier Casse-cou, ☎694-0445. Glass objects.

Jewellery and Decorative Arts

Lazuli: 774 Rue Saint-Jean, ☎525-6528.

Origines: 54 Côte de la Fabrique, Vieux-Québec, ☎694-9257.

Pierres Vives: 23½ Rue du Petit-Champlain, ☎692-5566.

Louis Perrier Joaillier: 48 Rue du Petit-Champlain, ☎692-4633.

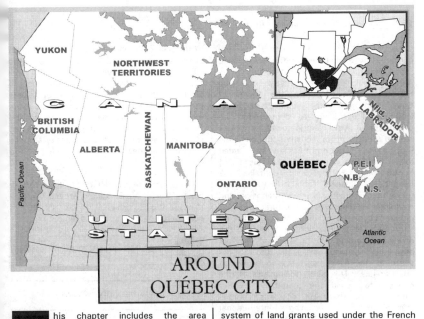

AROUND QUÉBEC CITY

This chapter includes the area immediately outside Québec City, as well as the Charlevoix, Mauricie-Bois-Francs and Chaudière-Appalaches regions. Under the French Regime, Québec City was the main urban centre of New France and was the seat of the colonial administration. To supply produce to the city and its institutions, farms were introduced to the area in the middle of the 17th century. The farming region on the periphery of the city was the first populated rural zone in the St. Lawrence Valley. Traces of the first seigneuries granted to settlers in New France are still visible in this historically rich rural area. The farmhouses are the oldest of New France and the descendants of their first residents are now scattered across the American continent.

For years, artists have been captivated by the beauty of the Charlevoix region. From the town of Saint-Joachim to the mouth of the Rivière Saguenay, dramatic mountainous countryside contrasts sharply with the expansive open water of the St. Lawrence. A scattering of charming villages and towns dots the coastline, dwarfed by mountains that fall away into the salt water of the river and steep-sided valleys. Away from the river, Charlevoix is a wild, rugged region where Boreal forest sometimes gives way to taiga. The old houses and churches found throughout the region are vestiges of Charlevoix's history as a French colony. In addition, the division of farmland in the area continues to reflect the seigneurial

system of land grants used under the French Regime.

The rich architectural heritage and exceptional geography are complemented by a dazzling variety of flora and fauna. The Charlevoix region was named a "World Biosphere Reserve' in 1988 by UNESCO, and is home to many fascinating animal and plant species. A number of whale species feed at the mouth of the Rivière Saguenay during the summer. In the spring and fall, hundreds of thousands of snow geese make migratory stops, creating a remarkable sight near Cap-Tourmente, farther west. Deep in the hinterland the territory has all the properties of taiga, a remarkable occurrence at this latitude. This area is home to a variety of animal species such as the caribou and the large Arctic wolf. Charlevoix's plant life is rich in species not found in other parts of eastern Canada.

The Mauricie–Bois-Francs region is an amalgam of diverse regions on either side of the St. Lawrence. Located about halfway between Montréal and Québec City, this large region runs from north to south and includes terrain of the three types that make up the province: the Canadian Shield, the St. Lawrence plains, and part of the Appalachian mountain range. The city of Trois-Rivières is generally considered the heart of this region. Trois-Rivières was the second city founded in New France (1634). First a fur-trading post, it became an industrial centre with the founding of the Saint-Maurice ironworks in 1730. Since the end of the 19th century, the exploitation of the surrounding forests has made Trois-Rivières the hub of the provincial pulp and paper industry. Further up the Rivière Saint-Maurice, the towns of Shawinigan and Grand-Mère, also major industrial sites, serve as centres for the production of hydro-electric power, as well as a centre for the major industries that consume that power. To the north lies a vast untamed expanse of lakes, rivers and forest. This land of hunting and fishing also contains the magnificent Mauricie National Park, reserved for outdoor activities such as canoeing and camping. To the south lie the rural zones on either side of the St. Lawrence. Opened up very early to colonization, the land is still divided according to the lines of the old seigneurial system. Finally, in the extreme south of the region lies the area known as "Bois-Francs". The gently rolling hills of this countryside herald the mountains of the Appalachians. There are interesting annual festivals in the area including an international music festival in Victoriaville and an international folklore festival in Drummondville.

The Chaudière-Appalaches region is made up of several small areas with very distinct geographical features. Located opposite Québec City, on the south shore of the St. Lawrence, it stretches across a vast fertile plain before slowly climbing into the foothills of the Appalachian Mountains, all the way to the American border. The Rivière Chaudière, which originates in Lac Mégantic, runs through the centre of this region, then flows into the St. Lawrence across from Québec City.

A pretty pastoral landscape unfolds along the river between Leclercville and Saint-Roch-des-Aulnaies, an area occupied very early on by the French. There are attractive villages, including Saint-Jean-Port-Joli, an important provincial crafts centre. Out in the gulf adventure awaits in the Archipel de l'Île-aux-Grues.

Further south, the picturesque Beauce region extends along the banks of the Rivière Chaudière. The river rises dramatically in the spring, flooding some of the villages along its banks almost every year, providing muddied local inhabitants with the nickname "*jarrets noirs*", which translates somewhat inelegantly as "black hamstrings". The discovery of gold nuggets in the river bed attracted prospectors to the area in the middle of the last century. Farms have prospered in the rolling green hills

of the Beauce for hundreds of years. Church steeples announce the presence of little villages, scattered evenly across the local countryside. The Beauce region is also home to Québec's largest concentration of maple groves, making it the true realm of the *cabane à sucre*, sugar shack. The spring thaw gets the flowing and signals the sugaring-off season. Local inhabitants, called Beaucerons, are also known for their sense of tradition and hospitality.

The asbestos region, located a little further west of the Rivière Chaudière, around Thetford Mines, has a fairly varied landscape, punctuated with impressive open-cut-mines.

 FINDING YOUR WAY AROUND

Québec City Region

By Car

From Québec City, take the Autoroute Dufferin-Montmorency (Hwy 440) towards Beauport (Exit 24).

To go to Île d'Orléans from Québec, take Autoroute Dufferin-Montmorency (Hwy 440) to the Pont de l'Île. Cross the river and turn right on Route 368, also called Chemin Royal, which circles the island.

By Bus

Sainte-Anne-de-Beaupré *(9687 boul. Ste-Anne, Irving,* ☎*827-5169)* is accessible by bus *(320 Rue Abrahahm-Martin,* ☎*525-3000)*.

Sainte-Foy: 925 De Rochebelle, ☎650-0087.

Public Transportation

Bus number 53 leaves from Place Jacques-Cartier *($1.85, Rue du Roi, at the corner of Rue de la Couronne)* and drops visitors near the Chute Montmorency.

To reach Wendake from Québec City, take bus #801, the métrobus, whose stops are clearly indicated (for example, at Place d'Youville). From the Charlesbourg terminus, take bus #72 to Wendake. The historic village of Onhoüa

Chetek8e is north of the reserve and accessible by taxi.

By Ferry

Sainte-Foy: 3255 Chemin de la Gare (corner Chemin St-Louis), ☎658-8792.

Charlevoix

By Car

To get to Charlevoix from Québec City, take Route 138, which is the main road in the region.

Bus Stations

Baie-Saint-Paul: 2 Route de l'Équerre (Centre Commercial Le Village), ☎418-435-6569.
Saint-Hilarion: 354 Route 138, ☎418-457-3855.
Clermont: 83 Boulevard Notre-Dame, ☎418-439-3404.
La Malbaie—Pointe-au-Pic: 46 Ste-Catherine, ☎418-665-2264

By Ferry

The ferry to **Île aux Coudres** *(free; ☎418-438-2743)* leaves from Saint-Joseph-de-la-Rive. There is usually a half-hour wait before boarding during the summer months. The crossing takes approximately fifteen minutes; cars can be transported. The 26-kilometre island tour takes about half a day. The roads that runs along the river are ideal for bike rides (bikes can be rented on the island).

Saint-Siméon: The ferry *($10, cars $25; ☎418-638-5530)* from Rivière-du-Loup travels to Saint-Siméon in one hour and five minutes.

Baie-Sainte-Catherine: The ferry *(adults and cars free, ☎418-235-4395)* travels between Tadoussac and Baie-Sainte-Catherine in approximately 10 minutes.

Mauricie–Bois-Francs

By Car

From Montréal, take Highway 40 (Félix-Leclerc), followed by Highway 55 S. for a short while, and then turn onto Route 138 E. to Trois-Rivières.

Bus Stations

Trois-Rivières: 1075 Rue Champflour, ☎374-2944
Grand-Mère: 800 6ᵉ Avenue, ☎533-5565.
La Tuque: 530 Rue St-Louis, ☎523-2121, Dépanneur Provi-Soir.
Shawinigan: 1563 Boulevard Saint-Sacrement, ☎539-5144
Victoriaville: 64 Boulevard Carignan, ☎752-5400.
Drummondville: 330 Rue Hériot, ☎477-2111.

By Ferry

La Tuque: 550 Rue Saint-Louis, ☎523-3257.
Shawinigan: 1560 Rue de la Station, ☎537-9007.
Drummondville: 263 Rue Lindsay, ☎472-5383.

Chaudière-Appalaches

By Car

From Montréal, take Highway 20 East. From Québec City, cross the river to take Route 132 in either direction.

Bus Stations

Lévis: 5401 Boulevard Rive-Sud, ☎837-5805
Montmagny: 5 Boulevard Taché Ouest, ☎248-3292
Saint-Jean-Port-Joli: 27 Avenue de Gaspé Ouest, ☎598-6808
Saint-Georges: 11655 Promenade Chaudière, ☎228-4040.
Thetford Mines: 127 Rue Saint-Alphonse, ☎335-5120.

QUÉBEC

Train Stations

Lévis: 5995 Rue St-Laurent, ☎833-8056
Montmagny: 4 Rue de la Station, ☎248-7875

By Ferry

The ferry between Québec City and Lévis *($1.75; car $3,* ☎*644-3704)* takes only 15 minutes. The schedule is subject to change, but there are frequent crossings.

The ferry to Île aux Grues, the **Grue des Îles** *(free;* ☎*248-3549)*, leaves from the Montmagny dock and takes about 20 minutes. The schedule varies with the tide.

The following companies also ferry people to Île aux Grues or to Grosse Île. The boats of **Taxi des Îles** *($15 round-trip to Île aux Grues; 124 Rue Saint-Louis, Montmagny, G5V 1M8,* ☎*248-2818)* are recognizable by their yellow and black colour scheme and frequently travel to the islands from the Montmagny dock. **Croisières Lachance** *($16 round-trip to Île aux Grues; 110 de la Marina, Berthier-sur-Mer, G0R 1E0,* ☎ *259-2140 or 1-888-476-7734)*, has two boats, one of them a pleasure steamer, and offers ferry service and cruises between Montmagny or Berthier-sur-Mer and the islands.

PRACTICAL INFORMATION

The Québec City, Charlevoix and Chaudière-Appalaches regions use the **418** area code; Mauricie-Bois-Francs uses **819**.

Tourist Information Offices

Québec City Region

Centre d'Information de l'Office du Tourisme et des Congrès de la Communauté Urbaine de Québec 3300 Avenue des Hôtels, Québec, G1W 5A8, ☎651-2882, ⊷651-7135, www.quebec-region.cuq.qc.ca
Sainte-Anne-de-Beaupré: 9310 Boulevard Ste-Anne, ☎827-5281.
Île d'Orléans: 490 Côte du Pont, Saint-Pierre, ☎ 828-9411
Deschambault: 12 Rue des Pins, ☎285-4616.
Charlesbourg: 7960 Boulevard Henri-Bourassa, ☎624-7720.

Charlevoix

Association Touristique de Charlevoix: 630 Boulevard de Cornporté, C.P. 275, La Malbaie, G5A 1T8, ☎665-4454 or 1-800-667-2276, ⊷665-3811.
Baie-Saint-Paul: 444 Boulevard Mgr-de-Laval (Belvédère Baie-Saint-Paul), ☎435-4160.

Mauricie-Bois-Francs

Tourism-Mauricie-Bois-Francs 1180 Rue Royale, 3rd floor, Trois-Rivières Ouest, G9A 4J1, ☎375-1222 or 1-800-567-7603, ⊷375-0301.
Trois-Rivières: 168 Rue Bonaventure, ☎375-9628; 1457 Rue Notre-Dame, G9A 4X4, ☎375-1122.
Cap-de-la-Madeleine: 170 Rue des Chenaux, ☎375-5346.
Victoriaville: 122 Rue Aqueduc, P.C. 641, ☎758-6371.
Drummondville: 1350 Rue Michaud, ☎477-5529.
Nicolet: 30 Rue Notre-Dame, ☎293-4537.

Chaudière-Appalaches

Association Touristique Chaudière-Appalaches 800 Autoroute Jean-Lesage, St-Nicolas, G7A 1C9, ☎831-4411, ⊷831-8442, www.chaudapp.qc.ca
Lévis: 7 Mgr Gosselin, ☎838-4126.
Montmagny: 45 Avenue du Quai, C.P. 71 G5V 3S3, ☎248-9196 or 1-800-463-5643, ⊷248-1436.
Saint-Jean-Port-Joli: 7 Place de l'Église, G0R 3G0, ☎598-3747, ⊷598-3085.
Saint-Georges: 11700 Boulevard Lacroix, G5Y 1L3, ☎227-4642, ⊷228-2255.
Thetford Mines: 682 Rue Monfette Nord, G6G 7G9, ☎335-7141, ⊷338-4984.

EXPLORING

Québec City Region

The long, narrow strip of land, nestled between the St. Lawrence and the undeveloped wilderness of the Laurentian massif, and called Côte-de-Beaupré, is the ancestral home of many families whose roots go back to the beginning of the colony. It illustrates how the spread of the population was limited to the

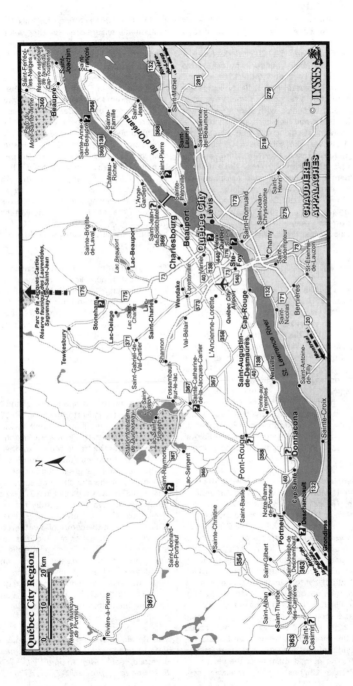

QUÉBEC

riverside in many regions of Québec, and recalls the fragility of development in the era of New France. From Beauport to Saint-Joachim, the colony's first road, the Chemin du Roy, or king's road, built under orders from Monseigneur de Laval during the 17th century, follows the Beaupré shore. A typical style characterized by a raised main floor covered in stucco, long balconies with intricately carved wood balusters and lace-curtained windows is repeated in houses along this road. Since about 1960, however, the suburbs of Québec City have gradually taken over the shore, marring the simple beauty of the area. Nevertheless, the Chemin du Roy is still an extremely pleasant route; whether rounding a cape, making one last jaunt in the Laurentians, or exploring the plains of the St. Lawrence, this route offers magnificent views of the mountains, fields, the river and Île d'Orléans.

Beauport ★

The large white house known as **Manoir Montmorency** *(2490 Avenue Royale,* ☎*663-3330)* was built in 1780 for British governor, Sir John Haldimand. At the end of the 18th century, the house became famous as the residence of the Duke of Kent, son of George III and father of Queen Victoria. The manor, which once housed a hotel, was severely damages by fire in May 1993. It has been restored according to the original plans and now hosts an information centre, a few shops and a restaurant, which offers exceptional view of the Montmorency Falls, the St. Lawrence and Île d'Orléans. The small Sainte-Marie chapel on the property and the gardens are open to the public.

The Manoir Montmorency is nestled in the **Parc de la Chute Montmorency ★★** *(free admission, parking $6, cablecar $4 one-way $6 return; accessible all year; for opening hours and parking* ☎*663-2877,* ☎*663-1666, www.chutemontmorency.qc.ca).* The Rivière Montmorency, which has its source in the Laurentians, flows along peacefully until it reaches a sudden 83-metre drop, at which point it tumbles into a void, creating one of the most impressive natural phenomena in Québec. One and a half times the height of Niagara Falls, the Montmorency Falls flow at a rate which can reach 125,000 litres-per-second during the spring thaw. Samuel de Champlain, the founder of Québec City, was impressed by the falls and named them after the viceroy of New France, Charles, Duc de Montmorency.

During the 19th century, the falls became a fashionable leisure area for the well-to-do of the region who would arrive in horse-drawn carriages or sleighs.

To take in this magnificent spectacle, a park has been set up, and a tour of the falls is possible. From the manor follow the pretty cliff walk, location of the Baronne lookout. You'll soon reach two bridges, the Pont Au-dessus de la Chute and the Pont Au-dessus de la Faille, which cross the falls and the fault respectively, with spectacular results. Once in the park you'll find picnic tables and a playground. The bottom of the falls are reached by the 487-step panoramic staircase or the trail. The cable-car provides a relaxing and picturesque means of regaining the top. In winter, the water freezes into a cone of ice, called a sugar-loaf, making a good ice-wall that anyone feeling adventurous can climb.

The lower part of the park is also accessible by car, though a complicated detour is required: continue along Avenue Royale, turn right on Côte de l'Église, then right again on Highway 40. The parking lot is on the right. To get back to Avenue Royale, take Boulevard Sainte-Anne west, Côte Saint-Grégoire and finally Boulevard des Chutes to the right.

Sainte-Anne-de-Beaupré ★

This long, narrow village is one of the largest pilgrimage sites in North America. In 1658, the first Catholic church on the site was dedicated to Saint Anne after sailors from Brittany, who had prayed to the Virgin Mary's mother, were saved from drowning during a storm on the St. Lawrence. Soon, a great number of pilgrims began to visit the church. The second church, built in 1676, was replaced in 1872 by a huge temple, which was destroyed by fire in 1922. Finally work began on the present basilica which stands at the centre of a virtual complex of chapels, monasteries and facilities as varied as they are unusual. They include the **Bureau des Bénédictions**, blessings office, and the Cyclorama. Each year, Sainte-Anne-de-Beaupré welcomes more than a million pilgrims, who stay in the hotels and visit the countless souvenir boutiques, of perhaps dubious taste, along Avenue Royale.

The **Basilique Sainte-Anne-de-Beaupré ★★★** *(information counter is loctated near the entrance, early May to mid-Sep, every day 8:30am to 5pm; 10018 Avenue Royale,*

☎827-3781), towering over the small, metal-roofed wooden houses that line the winding road, is surprising not only for its impressive size, but also for the feverish activity it inspires all summer long. The church's granite exterior, which takes on a different colour depending on the ambient light, was designed in the French Romanesque Revival style by Parisian architect Maxime Roisin, who was assisted by Quebecer Louis Napoléon Audet. Its spires rise 91 metres into the sky above the coast, while the nave is 129 metres long, and the transepts over 60 metres wide. The wooden statue gilded with copper sitting atop the church's façade was taken from the 1872 church. When the fire destroyed the former basilica, the statue stayed in place while everything collapsed around it.

The basilica's interior is divided into five naves, supported by heavy columns with highly sculpted capitals. The vault of the main nave is adorned with sparkling mosaics designed by French artists Jean Gaudin and Auguste Labouret, recounting the life of Saint Anne. Labouret also created the magnificent stained glass, found all along the perimeter of the basilica. The left transept contains an extraordinary statue of Saint Anne cradling Mary in her right arm. Her tiara reminds the visitor that she is the patron saint of Quebecers. In a beautiful reliquary in the background, visitors can admire the Great Relic, part of Saint Anne's forearm sent over from the San Paolo Fuori le Mura in Rome. Finally, follow the ambulatory around the choir to see the ten radiant chapels built in the 1930s, whose polychromatic architecture is Art-Deco inspired.

The **Cyclorama de Jérusalem** ★★ *($6; early May to Oct; every day 8:30am to 8pm, 8 Rue Régina, near the parking lot ☎827-3101)*. This round building with oriental features houses a 360° panorama of Jerusalem on the day of the crucifixion. This immense *trompe l'œuil* painting, measuring 14 metres by 100 metres, was created in Chicago in about 1880 by French artist Paul Philippoteaux and his assistants. A specialist in panoramas, Philippoteaux produced a work of remarkable realism. It was first exhibited in Montréal before being moved to Sainte-Anne-de-Beaupré at the very end of the 19th century. Very few panoramas and cycloramas, so popular at the turn of the century, have survived to the present day.

The **Musée de Sainte Anne** ★ *($6; Apr to Oct, every day 10am to 5pm; Oct to Apr, Sat and*

Sun 10am to 5pm; 9803 Boulevard Ste-Anne, ☎827-6873, ☞827-6870) is dedicated to sacred art honouring the mother of the Virgin Mary. These interestingly diverse pieces were acquired over many years from the basilica but have only recently been put on display for the public. Sculptures, paintings, mosaics, stained-glass windows and goldworks are dedicated to the cult of Saint Anne, as well as written works expressing prayers or thanks for favours obtained. The history of pilgrimages to Sainte-Anne-de-Beaupré is also explained. The exhibition is attractively presented and spread over two floors.

Cap Tourmente ★★

The pastoral and fertile land of Cap Tourmente is the eastern-most section of the St. Lawrence plain, before the mountains of the Laurentian Massif reach the shores of the St. Lawrence. The colonization of this area at the beginning of the 17th century represented one of the first attempts to populate New France. Samuel de Champlain, the founder of Québec City, established a farm here in 1626, the ruins of which were recently unearthed. The land of Cap Tourmente was acquired by Monseigneur François de Laval in 1662, and was cultivated by the Société des Sieurs de Caen. Soon the land passed into the hands of the Séminaire de Québec which eventually built a retreat for priests, a school, a summer camp and, most importantly, a huge farm which met the institution's nutritional needs and brought in a substantial income. Following the British Conquest, the seminary moved the seat of its Beaupré seigneury to Cap Tourmente, leaving behind the ruins of the Château Richer. The **Château Bellevue** ★ was built between 1777 and 1781. This superb building is endowed with a neoclassical cut stone portal. The property's Saint-Louis-de-Gonsague Chapel (1780) is well hidden in the trees.

Located in the middle of the St. Lawrence River, downstream from Québec City, **Île d'Orléans**, this 32-kilometre-by-5-kilometre island, is famous for its old-world charm. Of all regions of Québec, the island is the most evocative of life in New France. When Jacques Cartier arrived in 1535, the island was covered in wild vines, which inspired its first name: Île Bacchus. However, it was soon renamed in homage to the Duc d'Orléans. With the exception of Sainte-Pétronille, the parishes on the island were established in the 17th century. The colonization of the entire island followed

QUÉBEC

soon after. In 1970, the government of Québec protected Île d'Orléans as a historic district. The move was made in part to slow down the development that threatened to turn the island into yet another suburb of Québec City, and also as part of a widespread movement among Quebecers to protect the roots of their French ancestry by preserving old churches and houses. Since 1936, the island has been linked to the mainland by a suspension bridge, the Pont de l'Île.

Sainte-Pétronille ★★

Paradoxically, Saint-Pétronille was the site of the first French settlement on Île d'Orléans and is also its most recent parish. In 1648, François de Chavigny de Berchereau and his wife Éléonore de Grandmaison established a farm and a Huron mission here. However, constant Iroquois attacks forced the colonists to move further east, to a spot facing Sainte-Anne-de-Beaupré. It was not until the middle of the 19th century that Sainte-Pétronille was consolidated as a village, as its beautiful location began attracting numerous summer visitors. Anglophone merchants from Québec City built beautiful second homes here, many of which are still standing along the road.

Saint-Laurent

Until 1950, Saint-Laurent's main industry was the manufacturing of *chaloupes*, boats and sailboats which were known as the in United States and Europe. Though production of these boats has ceased, some traces of the industry, such as abandoned boatyards, can still be seen off the road, near the banks of the river. The village was founded in 1679, and still has some older buildings, such as the beautiful **Maison Gendreau** built in 1720 *(2387 Chemin Royal, west of the village)* and the **Moulin Gosselin**, which now houses a restaurant *(758 Chemin Royal, east of the village)*.

Saint-Jean ★★

In the mid-19th century, Saint-Jean was the preferred homebase of nautical pilots who made a living guiding ships through the difficult currents and rocks of the St. Lawrence. Some of their neoclassical or Second Empire houses remain along Chemin Royal and provide evidence of the privileged place held by these

seamen who were indispensable to the success of commercial navigation.

The most impressive manor from the French Regime still standing is in Saint-Jean. The **Manoir Mauvide-Genest** ★★ *($ 4; late May to late Sep, every day 10am to 5.30pm, early Sep to mid-Oct by appointment only; 1451 Chemin Royal, ☎829-2630)* was built in 1734 for Jean Mauvide, the Royal Doctor, and his wife, Marie-Anne Genest. This beautiful stone building has a rendering coat of white roughcast, in the traditional Norman architectural style. The property officially became a seigneurial manor in the middle of the 18th century, when Mauvide, who had become rich doing business in the Caribbean, bought the southern half of the Île d'Orléans seigneury.

In 1926, Camille Pouliot, descendant of the Genest family, bought the manor house. He then restored it, adding a summer kitchen and a chapel. He later transformed the house into a museum, displaying furniture and objects from traditional daily life. Pouliot was one of the first people to be actively interested in Québec's heritage. The manor still has a museum on the second floor devoted to antique furniture and everyday objects, while the main floor is taken up by a restaurant.

Saint-François ★

This, the smallest village on Île d'Orléans, retains many buildings from its past. Some, however, are far from the Chemin Royal and are therefore difficult to see from Route 368. The surrounding countryside is charming, and offers several pleasant panoramic views of the river, Charlevoix and the coast. The famous wild vine that gave the island its first name, Île Bacchus, can also be found in Saint-François.

As you leave the village, on the roadside is an **observation tower** ★★, which offers excellent views to the north and east. Visible are the Îles Madame et au Ruau, which mark the meeting point of the fresh water of the St. Lawrence and the salt water of the gulf. Mont Sainte-Anne's ski slopes, Charlevoix on the north shore and the Côte-du-Sud seigneuries on the south shore can also be seen in the distance.

Sainte-Famille ★

The oldest parish on Île d'Orléans was founded by Monseigneur de Laval in 1666 in order to establish a settlement across the river from Sainte-Anne-de-Beaupré for colonists who had previously settled around Sainte-Pétronille. Sainte-Famille has retained many buildings from the French Regime. Among them is the town's famous church, one of the greatest accomplishments of religious architecture in New France, and the oldest two-towered church in Québec.

The beautiful **Église Sainte-Famille ★★** *(3915 Chemin Royal)* was built between 1743 and 1747, to replace the original church built in 1669. Inspired by the Église des Jésuites in Québec City, which has since been destroyed, Father Dufrost de la Jemmerais ordered the construction of two towers with imperial roofs, which explains the single steeple sitting atop the gable. Other unusual elements such as five alcoves and a sun dial by the entrance (which has since been destroyed) make the building even more original. In the 19th century, new statues were installed in the alcoves, and the imperial roofs gave way to two new steeples, bringing the total number of steeples to three.

Though modified several times, the interior decor retains many interesting elements. Sainte-Famille was a wealthy parish in the 18th century, thus allowing the decoration of the church to begin as soon as the frame of the building was finished. In 1748, Gabriel Gosselin installed the first pulpit, and in 1749 Pierre-Noël Levasseur completed construction of the present tabernacle of the high altar. Louis-Basile David, inspired by the Quévillon school, designed the beautiful coffered vault in 1812. Many paintings adorn the church, among them are *La Sainte Famille* (The Holy Family) painted by Frère Luc during his stay in Canada in 1670, the *Dévotion au Sacré Coeur de Jésus* (Devotion to the Sacred Heart of Jesus, 1766) and *Le Christ en Croix* (Christ on the Cross) by François Baillargé (circa 1802). The church grounds offer a beautiful view of the coast.

Saint-Pierre

The most developed parish on Île d'Orléans had already lost some of its charm before the island was declared a historic site. Saint-Pierre is particularly important to the people of Québec, as the home for many years of the renowned poet and singer Félix Leclerc (1914-1988). The singer and songwriter, who penned *P'tit Bonheur*, was the first musician to introduce Quebecois music to Europe. He is buried in the local cemetery.

The **Chemin du Roy** is the first maintained road between Montréal and Québec City and built in 1734. This road, running along the St. Lawrence (some parts parallel to Route 138), and lined with beautiful 18th century French-style houses, churches and windmills, is one of the most picturesque drives in Canada.

Sillery ★★

This well-to-do suburb of Québec City retains many traces of its varied history, influenced by the town's dramatic topography. There are actually two sections to Sillery, one at the base and the other at the top of a steep cliff which runs from Cap Diamant to Cap-Rouge. In 1637, the Jesuits built a mission in Sillery on the shores of the river, with the idea of converting the Algonquins and Montagnais who came to fish in the coves upriver from Québec City. They named the fortified community for the mission's benefactor, Noël Brûlart de Sillery, an aristocrat who had recently been converted by Vincent de Paul.

By the following century, Sillery was already sought after for its beauty. The Jesuits converted their mission to a country house, and the bishop of Samos built Sillery's first villa (1732). Following the British Conquest, Sillery became the preferred town of administrators, military officers and British merchants, all of whom built themselves luxurious villas on the cliff, in architectural styles then fashionable in England. The splendour of these homes and their vast English gardens were in stark contrast to the simple houses lived in by workers and clustered at the base of the cliff. The occupants of these houses worked in the shipyards, where a fortune was being made building ships out of wood coming down from the Outaouais region to supply the British navy during Napoleon's blockade, which began in 1806. The shipyards, set up in Sillery's sheltered coves, had all disappeared before Boulevard Champlain, now running along the river's edge, was built in 1960.

The **Bois-de-Coulonge ★** to the east borders Chemin Saint-Louis. This English park once surrounded the residence of the lieutenant-governor of Québec, the King or Queen's representative in Québec until the title was abolished in 1968. The stately home was destroyed in a fire in 1966, though some of its outbuildings survived, notably the guard's house and the stables. The Saint-Denys stream flows through the eastern end of the grounds at the bottom of a ravine. British troops gained access to the Plains of Abraham, where a historic battle decided the future of New France, by climbing through this ravine. Now Bois de Coulonge, one of the Jardins du Québec, has magnificent gardens and a well-arranged arboretum to walk through.

The **Maison des Jésuites de Sillery** ★★ (*$2; mid-Mar to late Dec, Tue to Sun 11am to 5pm, Thu to 7pm; 2320 Chemin du Foulon, ☎654-0259, ⊷654-0991)* built of stone and covered with white plaster, occupies the former site of a Jesuit mission, a few ruins of which are still visible. In the 17th century, the mission included a fortified stone wall, a chapel, a priest's residence and native housing. As European illnesses, such as smallpox and measles, devastated the indigenous population, the mission was transformed into a hospice in 1702. At the same time work began on the present house, a building with imposing chimney stacks. In 1763, the house was rented to John Brookes and his wife, writer Frances Moore Brookes, who immortalized it as the setting for her novel, *The History of Emily Montague*, published in London in 1769. It was also during this time that the structure was lowered and the windows were made smaller in size, in the New England saltbox tradition. The house now has two stories in front and one in back and is covered with a catslide roof.

By 1824, the main building was being used as a brewery and the chapel had been torn down. The house was later converted to offices for various shipyards. In 1929, the Maison des Jésuites became one of the first three buildings designated as historic by the government of Québec. Since 1948, it has housed a museum detailing the 350-year history of the property.

The **Aquarium du Québec** (*$8; every day 9am to 5pm; 1675 Avenue des Hôtels, in Sainte-Foy, ☎659-5266)*, home to some 250 species of fish, marine mammals and reptiles, is full of fascinating sights. Of particular interest among the indigenous animals are the four species of seal. The area around the aquarium has walking trails and picnic areas.

Neuville ★

A vein of limestone, traversing the region from Neuville to Grondines, has been tapped since the French Regime for the construction of prestigious buildings across the province since the French Regime. This explains the large number of rubble-stone houses dotting the villages in the area. Today most of the jobs related to the extraction and cutting of this grey stone are concentrated in the town of Saint-Marc-des-Carrières, west of Deschambault.

The village of Neuville was formerly part of the Pointe-aux-Trembles seigneury, granted to the royal engineer Jean Bourdon, in 1653. The houses of Neuville are built into the hills at varying elevations so that most of them have a view of the St. Lawrence. This terraced layout lends this section of the Chemin du Roy a certain charm.

Rue des Érables ★★ has one of the largest concentrations of old stone houses outside Québec's large urban centres. The abundance of the necessary raw material and the hom-owners' desire to make use of the talents of local builders and stonemasons explains this. Number 500 on Rue des Érables was built for Édouard Larue, who acquired the Neuville seigneury in 1828. The huge house is representative of traditional rural Québec architecture, with its raised stone foundation and gallery covered with flared eaves, running the whole length of the façade.

In 1696 the villagers undertook the construction of the simple **Église Saint-François-de-Sales** ★★ (*guided tours; Rue des Érables)*. It was added to and altered during the following centuries, to the point where the original elements of the building have all but disappeared. A new chancel was built in 1761, the nave was expanded in 1854, and finally, a new façade was added in 1915. The present church is the result of these transformations. The interior of the church houses an impressive piece of baroque art from the period of the French Regime: a wood baldaquin (richly ornamented canopy over the altar) ordered in 1695 for the chapel of the episcopal palace in Québec City.

Cap-Santé ★

The construction of the **Église Sainte-Famille** ★★ (*guides tours; Rue du Quai)* went on between 1754 and 1764 under the auspices of curate Joseph Filion, but was seriously disrupted by the British Conquest. In 1759, materials intended for the finishing touches on the building were requisitioned for the construction of Fort Jacques-Cartier. Nevertheless, the completed church, with its two

Vieux Presbytère

steeples and its high nave lit by two rows of windows, is an ambitious piece of work for its time, and was possibly the largest village church built under the French Regime. The three beautiful wooden statues placed in the alcoves of the façade in 1775 have miraculously survived Québec's harsh climate. The imitation cutstone done in wood covering the stone walls was added in the 19th century. Before stepping inside the church, be sure to visit the wooded cemetery and presbytery built according to plans by Thomas Baillargé in 1850.

Today the **Vieux Chemin** ★, the old road, is nothing more than a simple road passing in front of the church, but it was once part of the Chemin du Roy that linked Montréal and Québec City. Numerous well-preserved 18th-century houses facing the river can still be seen along the road, making it one of the most picturesque drives in Canada.

Deschambault ★★

The charming tranquillity of this agricultural village on the banks of the St. Lawrence was a bit disturbed recently by the development of an aluminum smelter. Deschambault was founded thanks to the efforts of Seigneur Fleury de la Gorgendière who had previously had a church built in nearby Cap Lauzon in 1720. Because the village has grown slowly, it retains its small-town charm.

The **Maison Deschambault** *(128 Route 138)* is visible at the end of a long tree-lined lane. The stone building equipped with fire-break walls was practically built in the late 18th century. It was practically in ruins in 1936 when the Québec government, who owned the building at the time, undertook its restoration, a rarity in an era when many elements of Québec's heritage had already been lost. The building now houses a charming inn (see p 387), and a fine French restaurant (see p 285).

The **Vieux Presbytère** *($1.50; mid-Jun to late Sep every day 10am to 5pm; 117 Rue Saint-Joseph, ☎286-6891)* occupies a prime location behind the church offering a beautiful panoramic view of the river and the south shore. The small presbytery building, set apart in the centre of a large lawn, was built in 1815 to replace the first presbytery dating from 1735. The foundations of the original building are visible near the entrance. In 1955, an antique dealer saved the presbytery from destruction, then, in 1970, a residents' association began using the building as an exhibition centre, demonstrating a dynamic community commitment to preserving its heritage.

QUÉBEC

Charlesbourg ★

The Notre-Dame-des-Anges seigneury was granted to the Jesuits in 1626, making it one of the first permanent settlements inhabited by Europeans in Canada. Despite this early settlement and original seigneurial design, few buildings built before the 19th century remain in Charlesbourg. The fragility of early buildings and the push to modernize are possible explanations for this void. Since 1950, Charlesbourg has become one of the main suburbs of Québec City, and has lost much of its original character.

The **Église Saint-Charles-Borromée ★★** *(135 80ᵉ Rue Ouest)* revolutionized the art of building in rural Québec. Architect Thomas Baillargé, influenced by the Palladian movement, showed particular innovation in the way he arranged the windows and doors of the façade, to which he added a large pediment. Construction of the church began in 1828 and was uninterrupted. The original design has remained intact since. The magnificent interior decor by Baillargé was done in 1833.

A visit to the zoo is always guaranteed to fill both adults and children with wonder. The **Jardin Zoologique du Québec ★** *($5.50; year-round, every day 9am to 5pm; 9300 Rue de la Faune, Charlesbourg, ☎622-0312, ≈644-9004, www.spsnq.qc.ca)* is on an attractive site overrun by greenery and flowers. In winter the area can be covered on cross-country skis. The buildings that house the animals are made of stone, reminiscent of Quebec's old constructions and include the **Maison des Insectes** *(☎626-0445)*, the insect house, aviaries with over 150 species of birds and a pavilion for big cats and primates. You can also attend seal performances and see many other mammals. All of this can be explored along three trails: the Hibou (owl), Ours (bear) and Orignal (moose). Many educational activities are organized throughout the year.

Wendake ★

Forced off their land by the Iroquois in the 17th century, 300 Huron families moved to various places around Québec before settling in 1700 in Jeune-Lorette, today known as Wendake. Visitors will be charmed by the winding roads of the village in this native reserve located on the banks of the Rivière Saint-Charles. The museum and gift shop provide a lot of information on the culture of this peaceable and sedentary people.

The **Église Notre-Dame-de-Lorette ★** *(140 Boulevard Bastien)*, the Huron church, completed in 1730, is reminiscent of the first churches of New France. This humble building with a white plaster façade conceals unexpected treasures in its chancel and in the sacristy. Some of the objects on display were given to the Huron community by the Jesuits, and come from the first chapel in Ancienne-Lorette (late 17th century). Among the works to be seen are several statues by Noël Levasseur, created between 1730 and 1740, an altar-facing depicting a native village, by the Huron sculptor François Vincent (1790) and a beautiful *Vierge à l'Enfant* (Madonna and Child) sculpture, by a Parisian goldsmith (1717). In addition, the church has a reliquary made in 1676, chasubles from the 18th century and various liturgical objects by Paul Manis (circa 1715). However, the most interesting element remains the small, Louis XIII-style gilded tabernacle on the high altar, sculpted by Levasseur in 1722.

The Huron village of **Onhoüa Chetek8e** *($5; late May to early Oct, every day 9am to 5pm; 575 Rue Stanislas-Koska, ☎842-4308)* is a replica of a Huron village from the time of early colonization. The traditional design includes wooden longhouses and fences. Visitors are given an introduction to the lifestyle and social organization of the ancient Huron nation. Various native dishes are also served and worth a taste.

Charlevoix

The Charlevoix countryside could have been created for giants – the villages tucked into bays or perched atop summits look like dollhouses left behind by a child. Rustic farmhouses and luxurious summer houses are scattered about, and some have been converted into inns. Although Charlevoix was one of the first regions in North America where tourism flourished, further inland it is still a wilderness area of valleys and quiet lakes.

Baie-Saint-Paul ★★

Charlevoix's undulating geography has proved a challenge to agricultural development. Under the French Regime, only a few attempts at

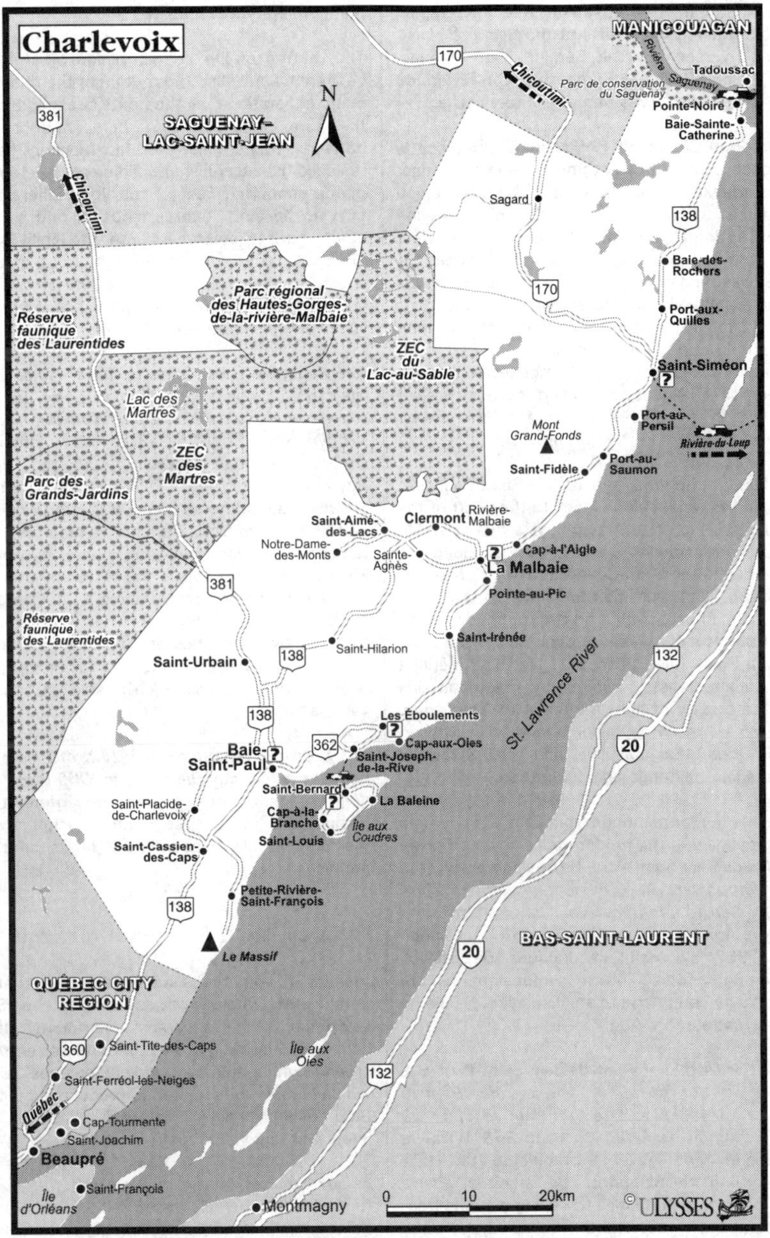
Charlevoix
MANICOUAGAN
SAGUENAY–LAC-SAINT-JEAN
Chicoutimi
Tadoussac
Rivière Saguenay
Parc de conservation du Saguenay
Pointe-Noire
Baie-Sainte-Catherine
Sagard
Baie-des-Rochers
Port-aux-Quilles
Saint-Siméon
Port-au-Persil
Rivière-du-Loup
Mont Grand-Fonds
Port-au-Saumon
Saint-Fidèle
Parc régional des Hautes-Gorges-de-la-rivière-Malbaie
Réserve faunique des Laurentides
ZEC du Lac-au-Sable
Lac des Martres
ZEC des Martres
Parc des Grands-Jardins
Saint-Aimé-des-Lacs
Clermont
Rivière-Malbaie
Notre-Dame-des-Monts
Sainte-Agnès
Cap-à-l'Aigle
La Malbaie
Pointe-au-Pic
Saint-Irénée
Saint-Hilarion
Saint-Urbain
St. Lawrence River
Les Éboulements
Cap-aux-Oies
Saint-Joseph-de-la-Rive
Baie-Saint-Paul
Saint-Bernard
La Baleine
Cap-à-la-Branche
Île aux Coudres
Saint-Louis
Saint-Placide-de-Charlevoix
Saint-Cassien-des-Caps
Petite-Rivière-Saint-François
Le Massif
BAS-SAINT-LAURENT
QUÉBEC CITY REGION
Saint-Tite-des-Caps
Saint-Ferréol-les-Neiges
Québec
Cap-Tourmente
Saint-Joachim
Beaupré
Île aux Oies
Île d'Orléans
Saint-François
Montmagny
381
170
138
362
132
20
360
0 10 20km
© ULYSSES

QUÉBEC

colonisation were made in this vast region which, along with parts of the Beaupré coast, was overseen by the Séminaire de Québec. Baie-Saint-Paul, at the mouth of the Rivière du Gouffre valley, was home to a few settlers.

Although Charlevoix has some of the planet's oldest rock formations, several major earthquakes have rocked the pastoral region since it was first colonized. The following description by Baptiste Plamondon, then vicar of Baie-Saint-Paul, appeared in the October 22, 1870 edition of the *Journal de Québec:* "It was about half an hour before noon... a tremendous explosion stunned the population. Rather than simply tremble, the earth seemed to boil, such that it caused vertigo... The houses could have been on a volcano, the way they were tossed about. Water gushed fifteen feet into the air through cracks in the ground...'

A bend in the road reveals Baie-Saint-Paul in all its charm, and a slope leads to the heart of the village, which has maintained a quaint small-town atmosphere. Set out on foot along the pleasant Rue Saint-Jean-Baptiste, Rue Saint-Joseph, and Rue Sainte-Anne, where small wooden houses with mansard roofs now house boutiques and cafés. For over 100 years, Baie-Saint-Paul has attracted North American landscape artists, inspired by the mountains and a quality of light particular to Charlevoix. There are many art galleries and art centres in the area that display and sell beautiful Canadian paintings and sculptures.

A selection of paintings from Charlevoix artists is displayed in the modern building, the **Centre d'Art de Baie-Saint-Paul** ★ *(free admission; late of Jun to late Aug, every day 9am to 7pm; early Sep to late Jun, every day 9am to 5pm; 4 Rue Ambroise-Fafard, ☎435-3681)*, designed in 1967 by architect Jacques DeBlois. A painting and sculpture symposium, where works by young artists are displayed, is held by the Centre every August.

The **Centre d'Exposition de Baie-Saint-Paul** ★★ *($3; late Jun to late Aug, every day 9am to 7pm, early Sep to late Jun 9am to 5pm; 23 Rue Ambroise-Fafard, ☎435-3681)* is a museum and gallery, completed in 1992 according to blueprints by architect Pierre Thibault, which houses travelling exhibits from around the world. The Centre also houses the René Richard gallery, where several paintings by this Swiss-born artist are on display (see below).

Saint-Joseph-de-la-Rive ★

The rhythm of life in this village on the St. Lawrence parallelled the rhythm of the river for many generations, as the boats beached along the shore testify eloquently. In recent decades, however, tourism and the craft business have replaced fishing and ship-building as the staples of the economy. East of the dock where the ferry to Île aux Coudres lands, a fine sandy beach tempts swimmers into the chilly salt water. A little wood building in front of the church is a reminder of the fragility of human endeavours within the immense marine landscape of Charlevoix.

The **Papeterie Saint-Gilles** ★ *(free admission; May to Dec, every day 8am to 5pm; Jan to May, every day 1am to 5pm; 304 Rue Félix-Antoine-Savard, ☎635-2430)*. This traditional papermaking workshop was founded in 1966 by priest and poet Félix-Antoine Savard (1896-1982, author of *Menaud Maître-Draveur)* with the help of Mark Donohue, a member of a famous Canadian pulp and paper dynasty. Museum guides explain the different stages involved in making paper using 17th century techniques. Saint-Gilles paper has a distinctive thick grain and flower or leaf patterns integrated into each piece, producing a high quality writing paper which is sold on site in various packages.

The **Exposition Maritime** ★★ *($2; mid-May to mid-Oct, every day 9am to 5pm; 305 Place de l'Eglise)*, located in a shipyard, recaptures the golden era of the schooner. Visitors are welcome to climb aboard the boats on the premises.

Île aux Coudres ★★

Visitors are sometimes surprised to learn that a number of whale species live in the St. Lawrence. For several generations the economic livelihood of Île aux Coudres centred around whale hunting, mainly belugas, and whale blubber was melted lo produce lamp oil. Ship building, mainly small craft, was also an important regional industry.

Île-aux-Coudres is the municipality that was formed when the villages of Saint-Bernard and Saint-Louis merged *(arrival and departure point on Ile-aux-Coudres)*. The ferry docks at the Quai de Saint-Bernard, where the following tour of the island begins. The dock is the best place to contemplate the Charlevoix mountains. One

Goélette

of the last shipyards still in operation in the region can also be seen from here.

The **Musée Les Voitures d'Eau** ★ *($4; mid-May to mid-Jun and mid-Sep to mid-Oct, Sat and Sun 9:30am to 5pm; mid-Jun to mid-Sep, every day 9:30am to 6pm; Chemin des Coudriers, Saint-Louis, ☎438-2208)* presents exhibits dealing with the history, construction and navigation of the small craft once built in the region. The museum was founded in 1973 by Captain Éloi Perron, who recovered the wreck of the schooner *Mont-Saint-Louis,* now on display.

The **Moulins Desgagné** ★★, or **Moulins de l'Isle-aux-Coudres** *($2.50; mid-May to mid-Jun and early Sep to mid-Oct, every day 10am to 5pm; mid-Jun to early Sep, every day 9am to 6:30pm; 247 Chemin du Moulin, Saint-Louis, ☎438-2184).* It is extremely rare to find a water mill and a windmill operating together. Indeed, the Saint-Louis mills are a unique pair in Québec. The mills, erected in 1825 and 1836 respectively, complement one another by alternately generating power according to prevailing climatic conditions. Along with a forge and milling house, the mills were restored by the Québec government, which has also established on-site information centres. The machinery necessary for operation is still in perfect condition, and is now back at work

grinding wheat and buckwheat into flour. Bread is made in an antique wood oven.

Les Éboulements ★

In 1663, a violent earthquake in the region caused a gigantic landslide; it is said that half a small mountain sank in the river. The village of les Éboulements is named after the event (*éboulements* means landslide in English).

Saint-Irénée ★

Saint-Irénée, or Saint-Irénée-les-Bains, as it was known during the Belle Époque, is the gateway to the part of Charlevoix, usually considered the oldest vacation spot in North America. In the late 18th century, British sportsmen were the first Europeans to enjoy the pleasures of the simple life the wild region had to offer. They were followed by wealthy Americans escaping the heat of summer in the United States. Wealthy English- and French-Canadian families also had summer houses with lovely gardens built for them in Charlevoix. Saint-Irénée is renowned for its picture-perfect landscapes and classical music festival.

QUÉBEC

La Malbaie—Pointe-au-Pic ★

On his way to Québec City in 1608, Samuel de Champlain anchored in a Charlevoix bay for the night. To his surprise, he awoke the next morning to find his fleet resting on land and not in water. Champlain learned that day what many navigators would come to learn as well: et low tide in this region the water recedes a great distance and will trap any boat not moored in deep enough water. In exasperation, he exclaimed *"Ah! La malle baye!"* (Old French which translates roughly to "Oh what a bad bay!"), inadvertently providing the name for many sites in the region. The towns of Pointe-au-Pic, La Malbaie, and Cap-à-l'Aigle now form a continuous web of streets and houses lining the bay.

The Malbaie seigneurs passed through three sets of hands before being seriously developed. Jean Bourdon received the land for services rendered to the French crown, in 1653. Too busy with his job as prosecutor for the King, he did nothing with it. The seigneury was then granted to Philippe Gaultier de Comporté, in 1672. Following his death, it was sold by his family to merchants Hazeur and Soumande, who harvested wood on the property for the construction of ships in France. The seigneury became crown property in 1724. Exceptionally, it was then granted, under English occupation, to Captain John Nairne and Officer Malcolm Fraser in 1762, who began colonizing it.

Seigneurs Nairne and Fraser initiated a longstanding tradition of hospitality in Charlevoix. They hosted, in their respective manors, friends and even strangers from Scotland and England. Following the example of these seigneurs, French Canadians began welcoming visitors from Montréal and Québec during the summer months. Eventually, larger inns had to be built to accommodate the increasing number of urban vacationers now arriving on steamships that moored et the dock in Pointe-au-Pic. Among the wealthy visitors was American President Howard Taft and his family, who were very fond of Charlevoix.

In the early 20th century, a wave of wealthy Americans and English Canadians built summer houses along **Chemin des Falaises**, a street well worth exploring. The houses reflect popular architectural styles of the period, including the charming Shingle Style characteristic of seaside resorts on the American east coast, which is distinguished by a cedar shingle exterior. Another popular trend at the time was to build houses that resembled 17th-century French manor houses, complete with turrets and shuttered casement windows. Beginning in 1920, the architecture of summer residences started to incorporate traditional local building styles. La Malbaie architect Jean Charles Warren (1869-1929), became known for designing a style of rustic furniture, inspired by local traditions and the English Arts and Crafts movement. Owning one of his creations became a must among summer residents. The most important and impressive building from the turn-of-the-century construction boom is the Manoir Richelieu, et the west end of Chemin des Falaises.

La Malbaie is now the regional administrative centre and, since its amalgamation with the neighbouring municipality of Pointe-au-Pic in 1995, has confirmed its position of strength within the region's tourist industry. It is henceforth officially known as "La Malbaie—Pointe-au-Pic".

The original wood building of the **Manoir Richelieu ★★** *(181 Avenue Richelieu),* the only grand hotel in Charlevoix to survive, was built in 1899. Destroyed in a fire, however, it was replaced by the current cement building in 1929. The hotel plans were drawn by architect John Smith Archibald in the Château Style. Many famous people have stayed at the hotel, from Charlie Chaplin to the King of Siam, to the Vanderbilt of New York City. The casino is a reconstruction of the Château Ramezay in Montréal. Visitors not staying at the Manoir can nevertheless discreetly walk through its hallways, elegant salons and gardens overlooking the St. Lawrence.

The region's number-one attraction is the **Casino de Charlevoix** *(183 Avenue Richelieu,* ☎665-5300 *or 1-800-665-2274),* an attractively designed European-style casino located next to the Manoir Richelieu. Proper dress required.

Cap-à-l'Aigle

From Boulevard de Comporté in La Malbaie, visitors can catch a glimpse of a stately stone house sitting high on the Cap-à-l'Aigle escarpment. The building is the old manor house of the Malcolm Fraser seigneurs, a property also known as Mount Murray. It is matched to the east of Rivière Malbaie by the John Nairne seigneury, established west of the waterway and simply named Murray Bay in honour of James Murray, British Governor at the time. Cap-à-l'Aigle, whose tourism industry dates back to the 18th century, forms the heart of the Mount Murray seigneury.

Jardins aux Quatre Vents ★★ *(by appointment only, on the left hand side of Route 138)*, on the grounds of the Cabot family estate, is one of the most beautiful private gardens in Québec. The garden is meticulously tended and is expanded annually. Unfortunately it is open to the public for only a few days every year. Strictly speaking, the gardens comprise 22 separate gardens, each one having its own theme. For example, there is the Potager en Terrasses (terraced vegetable garden), the Jardin du Ravin (ravine garden), Les Cascades (waterfalls), and the Lac des Libellules (dragonfly lake). The Quatre Vents (or four winds) garden began in 1928 with the planting of the Jardin Blanc (white garden), where all the flowers are, naturally, white as snow.

Mauricie–Bois-Francs

The Valley of the Rivière Saint-Maurice is located halfway between Montréal and Québec City, on the north shore of the St. Lawrence River. The cradle of Canada's first major industry, Mauricie has always been an industrial region. Its towns feature fine examples of architecture of the industrial revolution. Nevertheless, the vast countryside surrounding the towns remains primarily an area of mountain wilderness covered in dense forest, perfect for hunting, fishing, camping and hiking.

The Bois-Francs region, on the other side of the St. Lawrence river, takes its name from the hardwood, *(bois-francs)*, forests that made the reputation of cabinet-making businesses in the surrounding villages. The population of the area is a mix of French, British, Acadian and Loyalist colonists. Up until the mid-19th century, there was not much going on here. However, the arrival of the Grand Trunk Railway began a process of industrialization that has yet to taper off. In the course of the last twenty years, some of Canada's largest and most modern factories have been built here. Paradoxically, there remains nothing of the railway but the strip of land it occupied. Plans are underway to turn the rail bed into a cycling path that will link the Eastern Townships to Québec City.

Trois-Rivières ★★

The aspect of the town, once similar to Vieux-Québec, was completely changed by a fire in June 1908. Now, it more resembles a town of the American Midwest. However, Trois-Rivières remains a city redolent of Old-World charm with its many cafés, restaurants and bars on Rue des Forges, and the terrace overlooking the St. Lawrence. Halfway between Montréal and Québec City, this urban centre is home to 100 000 people.

Located at the confluence of the St. Lawrence and Saint-Maurice rivers, where the latter divides into three branches, giving the town its name, Trois-Rivières was founded in 1634 by Sieur de Laviolette. From the outset, the town was surrounded by a stone wall which now marks the city's historic area. In the 17th century, there were three regional governments in the St. Lawrence valley apart from the Governor of New France: Québec City's, Montréal's, and Trois-Rivières's. More modest than its two sister cities, the latter boasted a population of a mere 600 and a total of 110 houses. The real boom took place in the middle of the 19th century with the creation of the pulp and paper industry. For a time, Trois-Rivières was the world's leading paper producer.

The **Cathédrale de l'Assomption ★** *(every day 7am to 11:30am and 2pm to 5:30pm, Sun open at 8:30am; 362 Rue Bonaventure ☎374-2409)* was built in 1858 according to the plans of architect Victor Bourgeau, well known for the many churches he designed in the Montréal area. The cathedral's massive Gothic-Revival style is vaguely reminiscent of London's Westminster Abbey, also designed in the mid-19th century. Guido Nincheri's stained-glass windows, executed between 1923 and 1934, are certainly the most interesting element in what is otherwise an austere interior.

The **Musée des Arts et Traditions Populaires du Québec** *($6; guided tours; Jul and Aug, every day 10am to 7pm; Sep to Jun, Tue to Sun 10am to 5pm; 200 Rue Laviolette, ☎372-0406 or 1-800-461-0406)*, south of Rue Hart, was inaugurated in 1996. The town's old prison, a handsome neoclassical building erected in 1822 according to plans by François Baillargé, is incorporated into the post-modern structure. The museum presents exhibitions on the customs and daily life of Quebecers over the centuries. In addition to traditional quilts, it displays old toys, whale bones and a 17th-

QUÉBEC

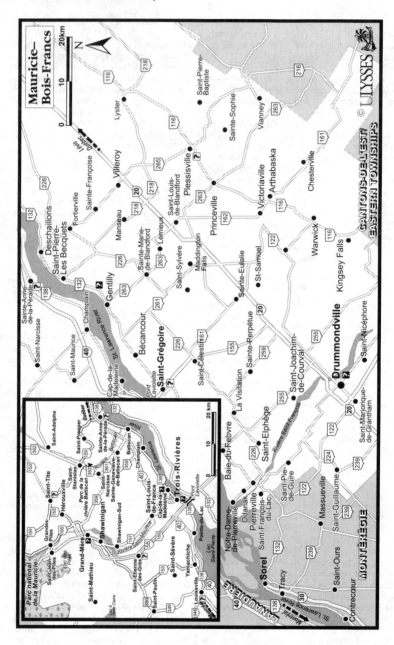

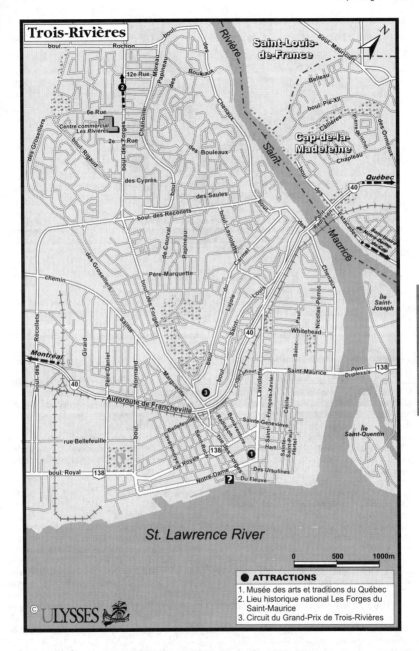

Trois-Rivières

Saint-Louis-de-France

Cap-de-la-Madeleine

Québec

Montréal

St. Lawrence River

Île Saint-Joseph

Île Saint-Quentin

0   500   1000m

QUÉBEC

● **ATTRACTIONS**
1. Musée des arts et traditions du Québec
2. Lieu historique national Les Forges du Saint-Maurice
3. Circuit du Grand-Prix de Trois-Rivières

© ULYSSES

Sanctuaire Notre-Dame-du-Cap

century aboriginal dugout canoe, as well as a number of small buildings from the collection of Robert-Lionel Séguin, one of the pioneers of Québec ethnology.

The **Forges du Saint-Maurice National Historic Site ★★** *($4, May to mid-Oct, every day 9am to 5pm; 10000 Boulevard des Forges, ☎378-5116)* is also called Lieu Historique National Les Forges du Saint-Maurice. These ironworks began in 1730, when Louis XV granted permission to François Poulin de Francheville to work the rich veins of iron-ore that lay under his land. The presence of dense wood lots from which to make charcoal, of limestone, and of a swift-running waterway favoured the production of iron. The workers of this first Canadian ironworks came for the most part from Burgundy and Franche-Comté in France. They were kept busy making cannons for the King and wood-burning stoves for his subjects in New France.

After the British Conquest (1760), the plant passed into the hands of the colonial government of the British, who ceded it in turn to private enterprise. The works were in use until 1883. At that time, the plant included the smelter and forges, as well as the Grande Maison, the foreman's house, at the centre of a worker's village. Following the 1908 fire, the residents of Trois-Rivières recuperated the material necessary to rebuild their town from the forge, leaving only the foundations of most

buildings. In 1973, Parks Canada acquired the site and rebuilt the foreman house to serve as an information centre. They set up a second, very interesting centre on the site of the smelting forge.

A visit begins at the foreman's house, a huge white building said to have been inspired by the architecture of Burgundy. Various aspects of life at the ironworks are presented, as are the products of the works. On the second floor is a model depicting the layout of the works in 1845. The model is used as the basis of a sound and light show, after which the site can be perused by walking along various footpaths.

Cap-de-la-Madeleine

As the heartland of Catholicism in North America, Québec is home to a number of major pilgrimage destinations visited by millions every year from all over the world. The **Sanctuaire Notre-Dame-du-Cap ★★** *(626 Rue Notre-Dame, ☎374-2441)*, a shrine under the auspices of the Oblate Missionaries of the Virgin Mary, is consecrated to the worship of the Virgin. The history of this sanctuary began in 1879 when it was decided a new parish church in Cap-de-la-Madeleine was needed. It was the month of March, and the stones for the new church had to be transported from the south side of the river. Strangely, the river had not yet frozen. Following the prayers and rosaries addressed to the statue of the Virgin presented to the parish in 1854, an ice-bridge formed "as if by miracle", allowing the necessary stones to be transported in one week. The parish priest, Father Désilet, decided to preserve the old church and to turn it into a sanctuary devoted to the Virgin. Built between 1714 and 1717, the sanctuary is one of the oldest churches in Canada. Visitors meditate before the statue of the Virgin. It is recounted that in 1888, the statue opened its eyes in front of several witnesses.

The miraculous ice-bridge is today symbolized by the **Pont des Chapelets** (1924), visible in the garden of the sanctuary. A stations of the cross, a calvary, a holy sepulchre and a small lake complete this riverside garden. Surrounded by an expanse of asphalt and looking like something from the set of a Cecil B. DeMille epic is the enormous **Basilique Notre-Dame-du-Rosaire**. Work on the basilica was begun in 1955, according to the plans of the architect Adrien Dufresne, a disciple of Dom Bellot. The Dutch master glazier Jan Tillemans created three sets of windows depicting the history of the sanctuary, that of Canada, and the mysteries of the rosary.

Grand-Mère ★

The town was named after a rock bearing a strong resemblance to the profile of an old woman. Found on an island in the middle of the Saint-Maurice, the rock was transported piece by piece to a park in downtown Grand-Mère when the hydro-electric dam was constructed in 1913. The town and its neighbour Shawinigan are good examples of "company towns" where life revolves around one or two factories. The omnipresence of the factories extends to the residential patterns, the towns being divided into two distinct sections, one for management (mostly anglophone in the beginning) and one for workers (almost exclusively francophone). The town features many well thought-out industrial buildings designed by talented architects brought in from outside the area.

Grand-Mère came into being at the end of the 19th century as a result of the forestry industry. Pulp and paper factories processed trees cut down in the logging camps of Haute-Mauricie. The town was developed in 1897 by the Laurentide Pulp and Paper Company, the property of John Foreman, Sir William Van Horne and Russell Alger, hero of the American War of Secession. After the 1929 stock market crash, the town's economy diversified and moved away from the pulp and paper industry which had helped it grow.

The television miniseries *Les Filles de Caleb* (*Émilie* in English), based on Arlette Cousture's novel, was immensely successful across Canada. **Le Village d'Émilie ★** (*$8.95; mid-May to late Sep, every day 10am to 6pm; Route 55 Exit 226, ☎538-1716 or 1-800-667-4136)* is a showcase for the sets used in the shooting of the series *Shehaweh*, *Les Filles de Caleb* (*Émilie*) and *Blanche*. It features, among other things, the Ovila log house, the Bourdais schoolhouse, the Shehaweh native village, the Caleb farms and Desjardins hall. There is a park for children and carriage rides are also available.

Shawinigan

In 1899, Shawinigan became the first city in Québec to be laid out according to the principles of urban planning, thanks to the powerful Shawinigan Water and Power Company, which supplied electricity to all of Montréal. The name of this hilly town means "portage at the peak" in Algonquian. The town itself was hard hit by the recession of 1989-93, which left indelible marks on its urban landscape: abandoned factories, burnt-out buildings, empty lots and so on. Nevertheless, Shawinigan boasts many architecturally interesting buildings from the first third of the 20th century. Some of its residential streets resemble those of interwar English suburbs.

Inaugurated in the spring of 1997, the **Cité de l'Énergie** (*$10; late Jun to mid-Sep, every day 10am to 7pm; mid-Sep to late Jun, Tue to Sun 10am to 5pm; 1000 Avenue Melville, ☎536-4992, 536-2982 or 1-800-383-2483)* promises to acquaint many a visitor, child and adult alike, with the history of industrial development in Québec, in general, and in Mauricie, in particular. The hub of this development is the town of Shawinigan, singled out by aluminum factories and electric companies at the beginning of the century thanks to the strong currents in the Rivière Saint-Maurice and the 50-metre-high falls nearby. A huge theme park, the Cité de l'Énergie features several attractions: two hydroelectric power stations, one of which, the Centrale Shawinigan 2, is still in operation; a science pavilion and a 115-metre-high observation tower, which needless to say

QUÉBEC

offers a sweeping view of the area, including the frothy Chutes Shawinigan Waterfronts.

The Cité de l'Énergie provides transportation (by trolley bus and by boat) to make it easier to visit these attractions. A multimedia show is also presented. During your tour of the Cité, you will learn how various regional industries, such as hydroelectricity, pulp and paper, aluminum, etc., have evolved over the past hundred years. The development of innovations that led to scientific advances in these fields is explained step by step. Interactive exhibitions are presented in the Centre des Sciences, which also has a restaurant and a shop.

Victoriaville

The economic heartland of the Bois-Francs, Victoriaville owes its development to the forestry and steel industries. Named after Queen Victoria, who reigned at the time of the town's establishment (1861), Victoriaville now incorporates the surrounding municipalities of Arthabaska et Sainte-Victoire-d'Arthabaska.

Arthabaska ★, the southern portion of Victoriaville, means "place of bulrushes and reeds" in the native language. It has produced or welcomed more than its share of prominent figures in the worlds of art and politics. Its residential sectors have always boasted a refined architecture, notably in the European and American styles. The town is especially known for its Victorian houses, particularly those along Avenue Laurier Ouest. In 1859, Arthabaska became the judicial district of the township. Construction of the courthouse, the prison and the registry office, that would make the fortune of the town, followed. Arthabaska was superseded by Victoriaville at the turn of the century, and though these buildings have now been demolished it still retains a good part of its Belle Époque charm.

The **Maison Suzor-Côté** (*846 Boulevard Bois-Francs Sud*) is the birthplace of landscape painter Marc-Aurèle de Foy Suzor-Côté (1869-1937). His father had built the humble home 10 years earlier. One of Canada's foremost artists, Suzor-Côté began his career decorating churches, including Arthabaska's, before leaving to study at Paris' École des Beaux-Arts in 1891. After taking first prize at both the Julian and Colarossi academies, he worked in Paris before moving to Montréal in 1907. From then on, he returned annually to the family house, gradually turning it into a studio. His impressionist winter scenes and July sunsets are well known. The house is still a private residence (*not open to the public*).

The **Musée Laurier ★** (*$3.50; Jul to Aug, Mon to Fri 9am to 6pm, Sat and Sun 1pm to 5pm; Sep to May, Mon to Fri 9am to noon and 1pm to 5pm, Sat and Sun 1pm to 5pm; 16 Rue Laurier Ouest, ☎357-8655*) occupies the house of the first French-Canadian Prime Minister (1896 to 1911). Sir Wilfrid Laurier (1841-1919) was born in Saint-Lin in the Basses-Laurentides but moved to Arthabaska as soon as he finished his legal studies. His house was turned into a museum in 1929 by two admirers. The ground floor rooms retain their Victorian furniture, while the second floor is partly devoted to exhibits. Paintings and sculptures by Québéc artists encouraged by the Lauriers are on view throughout the house. Of particular interest are the portrait of Lady Laurier by Suzor-Côté and the bust of Sir Wilfrid Laurier by Alfred Laliberté.

Drummondville

Drummondville was founded in the wake of the War of 1812 by Frederick George Heriot, who gave it the name of the British Governor of the time, Sir Gordon Drummond. The colony was at first a military outpost on the Rivière Saint-François, but the building of mills and factories soon made it a major industrial centre.

The **Village Québécois d'Antan ★★** (*$10; early Jun to early Sep, every day 10am to 5pm; Sep, Sat and Sun; 1425 Rue Montplaisir, ☎478-1441*) traces 100 years of history. Some 70 colonial-era buildings have been reproduced to evoke the atmosphere of village life from 1810 to 1910. People in period costume make *ceintures fléchées* (v-design sashes), candles and bread. Many historical television shows are shot on location here.

The **Parc des Voltigeurs ★** has recently been undergoing a facelift. The only heritage building between Montréal and Québec, which happens to be visible from Highway 20, lies in the southern part of the park. The **Manoir Trent**, built in 1848 for retired British Navy officer George Norris Trent, is not really a manor, but a large farmhouse. It was acquired by the Compagnons de l'École Hotelière, a hostel school, which turned it into the **Centre Québécois des Vins et Fromages**. A reference centre and training school, this unusual information centre is the site of wine and cheese tastings.

Chaudière-Appalaches

This tour is dotted with charming villages at regular intervals along the majestic St. Lawrence. It encompasses both the Rive-Sud of Québec City and the Côte-du-Sud (the southern shore and coast), gradually taking on a maritime flavour as the river widens. In many places, visitors will enjoy stunning views of this vast stretch of water as its colour varies with the time of day and temperature, as well as Île d'Orléans and the mountains of Charlevoix. The tour also features a few of the loveliest examples of traditional architecture in Québec, including churches, seigneurial manors, mills, or old houses, whose windows open onto vast open spaces. It is perhaps this region that best represents rural Québec. It also includes the Beauce region which follows the Chaudière River south until the Appalachian Mountain.

Lotbinière ★

Granted to René-Louis Chartier de Lotbinière in 1672, the seigneury of Lotbinière is one of the few estates to have always remained in the hands of the same family. Because he had a seat on the Conseil Souverain, the sovereign council, the first seigneur did not actually live on the premises; but he did see to it that the land and the village of Lotbinière were developed. At the heart of Lotbinière, which quickly became one of the most important villages in the region, visitors will find a number of old houses made of stone and wood. This area is now protected by the provincial government.

Along with its presbytery and former convent, the monumental **Église Saint-Louis ★★** *(7510 Rue Marie-Victorin)*, set parallel to the St. Lawrence, provides a lovely setting in which to enjoy a view of the river. The present building is the fourth Catholic church to be built in the seigneury of Lotbinière. Designed by François Baillargé, it was begun in 1818. The spires, as well as the crown of the façade, are the result of modifications made in 1888. Its polychromatic exterior—white walls, blue steeples and red roof—creates a surprising (and very French) tricolour effect.

The decor of the church is a masterpiece of traditional religious art in Québec. Without question, the key piece is the neoclassical reredos shaped like a triumphal arch, sculpted by Thomas Baillargé in 1824. In the middle of it hang three paintings dating back to 1730, which are attributed to Frère François Brékenmacher, a Récollet monk from the Montréal monastery. The organ in the jube, originally intended for the Anglican cathedral in Québec City, was built in London by the Elliott Company in 1802. Too high for the Anglican church, it was put into storage before being acquired by Père Faucher, the parish priest, in 1846. A century later, it was restored and equipped for electric power by the Casavant Company of Saint-Hyacinthe.

Sainte-Croix

The Chartier de Lotbinière lineage dates back to the 11th century. In the service of French kings for many generations, the family preserved its contacts with the motherland once established in Canada, despite the British Conquest and the distance between the two lands. In 1828, Julie-Christine Chartier de Lotbinière married Pierre-Gustave Joly, a rich Huguenot merchant from Montréal. In 1840, Joly purchased a part of the Sainte-Croix land from the Québec City Ursulines in order to build a seigneurial manor there, which would be known as the Manoir de la Pointe Platon, or the Domaine Joly de Lotbinière.

Domaine Joly de Lotbinière ★★ *($4.50; late Jun to Sep, every day 10am to 6pm; mid-May to late Jun and Sep to mid-Oct on weekends; Route de la Pointe-Platon, ☎926-2462)* is part of the Jardins de Québec association. The main attraction here is the superb setting on the banks of the St. Lawrence. It is especially worthwhile to take the footpaths to the beach in order to gaze out at the river, the slate cliffs and the opposite shore, where the Église de Cap Santé is visible. Numerous rare century-old trees, floral arrangements and bird gardens adorn the grounds of the estate. There is also a boutique and café with a patio. The manor, which was built in 1840 to overlook the river, is designed as a villa with wraparound verandas. Though the interior is disappointing, it does include a small exhibition on the family of the Marquis de Lotbinière. Visitors will learn, for example, that the son of Pierre-Gustave Joly, Henri-Gustave, was born in Épernay (France), and later became Premier of Québec

Domaine Joly de Lotbinière

(1878-79), federal Revenue Minister and finally Lieutenant-Governor of British Columbia. The Domaine Joly de Lotbinière came under the care of the provincial government in 1967, when the last seigneur, Edmond Joly de Lotbinière, had to vacate the premises.

Lévis ★★

Founded by Henry Caldwell in 1826, Lévis developed rapidly during the second half of the 19th century, due to the introduction of the railroad (1854) and the establishment of several local shipyards, supplied with wood by sawmills owned by the Price and Hamilton families. Because there was no railway line on the north shore of the St. Lawrence at the time, some of Québec City's shipping activities were transfered to Lévis. Originally known as Ville d'Aubigny, Lévis was given its present name in 1861, in memory of Chevalier François de Lévis, who defeated the British in the Battle of Sainte-Foy in 1760. The upper part of the city, consisting mostly of administrative buildings, offers some interesting views of Vieux-Québec, located on the opposite side of the river, while the very narrow lower part welcomes the trains and the ferry linking Lévis to the provincial capital. Lévis merged with its neighbour, **Lauzon**, in 1990.

Built during the stock market crash of 1929, the **Terrasse de Lévis** ★★ *(Rue William-Tremblay)* offers spectacular views not only of downtown Lévis, but also of Québec City. Visitors will note, for example, Vieux-Québec's Place Royale, located alongside the river, and the Château Frontenac and Haute-Ville above. A few modern skyscrapers stand out in the background, the tallest being the Édifice Marie-Guyart, located on Québec City's Parliament Hill.

Maison Alphonse-Desjardins *(free admission; Mon to Fri 10am to noon and 1pm to 4:30pm, Sat and Sun noon to 5pm; 6 Rue du Mont-Marie, ☎835-2090)*. Alphonse Desjardins (1854-1920) was a stubborn man. Eager for the advancement of the French-Canadian people, he struggled for many years to promote the concept of the *caisse populaire* (credit union), a cooperative financial institution controlled by its members, and by all the small investors who hold accounts there. In the family kitchen of his house on Rue Mont-Marie, Desjardins and his wife Dorimène conceived the idea and set up the first *caisse populaire*. The Caisses Desjardins aroused suspicion at first, but eventually became an important economic lever. Today there are more than 1,200 across Québec, with more than 5 million members.

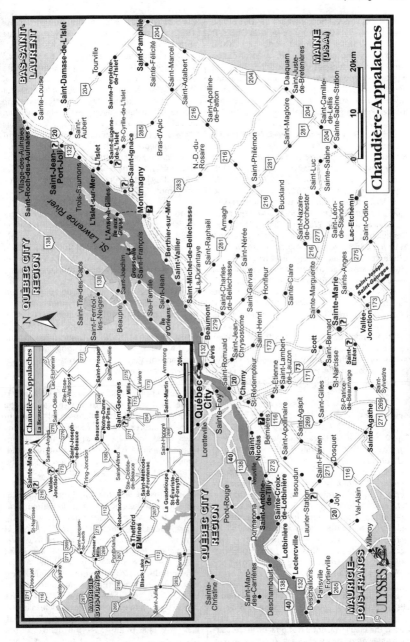

Chaudière-Appalaches

© ULYSSES

QUÉBEC

The Gothic Revival house where the Desjardins lived for nearly 40 years was built in 1882. It was beautifully restored on its 100th anniversary and converted into an information centre which focuses on Desjardins's career and achievements. Visitors can watch a video and see several restored rooms. The offices of the Société Historique Alphonse-Desjardins are located on the second floor.

The **Fort No.1 at Pointe de Lévy National Historic Site** ★ *($2.75; mid-May to mid-June, Sun to Fri 9am to 4pm; mid-Jun to late Aug, every day 10am to 5pm; early Sep to late Oct, Sun noon to 4pm; 41 Chemin du Gouvernement, ☎835-5182)* is also called the Lieu Historique National du Fort-Numéro-Un. Fearing a surprise attack from the Americans at the end of the Civil War, the British (and later Canadian) government built three separate forts in Lévis, which were incorporated into Québec City's defence system. Only Fort No.1 remains intact. Made of earth and stone, it illustrates the evolution of fortified structures in the 19th century, when military techniques were advancing rapidly. Visitors will be particularly interested by the rifled bore, an imposing piece of ordnance, as well as the vaulted pillboxes and the caponiers, masonry structures intended to ditch the moat. The site also includes an exhibition on the history of the fort. Finally, from the top of the wall, visitors can enjoy a lovely view of Québec City and Île d'Orléans.

Montmagny

The **Centre Éducatif des Migrations** ★ *($6; late Apr to mid-Nov, every day 9:30am to 5:30pm; 53 Rue du Bassin-Nord, ☎248-4565)* is located near the former seigneurial mill, which has been converted into a residence. This information centre on bird migrations deals with the *sauvagine*, or snow goose; it also has a theatre presenting a sound and light show about the colonization of the region and the arrival of immigrants at Grosse-Île. Though the link between these two subjects seems somewhat tenuous, the exhibits and the show are extremely instructive.

Grosse Île and the Irish Memorial National Historic Site ★★ *(guided tours only; May to Oct; ☎248-8888 or 1-800-463-6769)* is also called the Lieu Historique National de la Grosse-Île-et-le-Mémorial-des-Irlandais. An excursion to Grosse Île is to step back into the sad history of North American immigration. Fleeing epidemics and famine, Irish emigrants to Canada were particularly numerous from the 1830s to the 1850s. In order to limit the spread of cholera and typhus in the New World, authorities required transatlantic passengers to submit to a quarantine before allowing them to disembark at the port of Québec. Grosse Île was the logical location for this isolation camp, far enough from the mainland to effectively sequester its residents, but close enough to be convenient. On this "Quarantine Island" each prospective immigrant was inspected with a fine-tooth comb. Travellers in good health stayed in "hotels", the luxury of which depended on the class of the berths they had occupied on the ships. The sick were immediately hospitalized.

In total, four million European immigrants passed through the port of Québec between 1832 and 1937. It is impossible to ascertain how many of these resided for a period on Grosse Île, but close to 7,000 people perished there. In 1847, the year of the Great Potato Famine, a principle cause of Irish emigration, the typhus epidemic was particularly virulent and especially hard on Irish immigrants. In memory of this sad year, people of Irish descent have made pilgrimages to Grosse Île every year since 1909. A Celtic cross stands on the island, in memory of those who came here and of those unfortunates who did not survive the experience.

The guided tour of Grosse Île, part of which is made on a small motorized train, reveals the natural beauty of the island and its human-made structures. The barracks still stand, as does the imposing disinfection building, recently opened to the public for the first time. Together, these buildings recount a page of the history of this part of the continent.

Île aux Grues ★★ is the only island of the Isle-aux-Grues archipelago that is inhabited year round. It is an excellent spot for watching snow geese in the spring, for hunting in autumn, and for walking in summer. In winter the island is locked in by ice and residents can only access the mainland by airplane. A few rural inns dot this 10-kilometre-long agricultural island. A bicycle trip through its golden wheat fields along the river is one of the most pleasant ways to explore the area. The island is also accessible by car thanks to the Grue des Îles ferry (see p 254). At the centre of the island is the village of **Saint-Antoine-de-l'Isle-aux-Grues**, with its little church and its lovely houses. There is a craft shop, a cheese store that sells a delicious locally produced cheese, and a small museum that reveals past and present traditions of island life. To the east is the **Manoir Seigneurial McPherson-LeMoine**, which was rebuilt for Louis Liénard Villemonde Beaujeu after the island was sacked by the British army in 1759. This attractive house, fronted by a long gallery, was the summer home of historian James McPherson-LeMoine at the end of the 19th century. Today it is the haven of painter Jean-Paul Riopelle.

There is a small tourist information stand at the end of the dock that is staffed during the high season. If you plan to spend a few days on the island bring enough cash since there is only one small bank on the island and it does not have an automatic teller machine.

L'Islet-sur-Mer ★

As its name, which translates as Islet by the Sea, suggests this village's activities centre around the sea. Since the 18th century, local residents have been handing down the occupations of sailor and captain on the St. Lawrence from father to son. Some have even become highly skilled captains and explorers on distant seas. In 1677, Governor Frontenac granted the seigneury of L'Islet to two families, the Bélangers and the Couillards, who quickly developed their lands. They turned both L'Islet-sur-Mer, on the banks of the St. Lawrence, and L'Islet, further inland, into prosperous communities which still play an important role in the region.

The wind coming in off the sea is a gauge of the immensity of the nearby river. A good place to breathe this sea air is from the front step of the **Église Notre-Dame-de-Bonsecours** ★★ *(15 Rue des Pionniers Est, Route 132)*. The present church, begun in 1768, is a large stone building with no transepts. The interior decor, executed between 1782 and 1787, reflects the teachings of the Académie Royale d'Architecture in Paris, where the designer François Baillargé had recently been a student. Consequently, unlike earlier churches, the reredos mirrors the shape of the semicircular chancel, itself completely covered with gilded Louis-XV and Louis-XVI-style wood panelling. The coffered ceiling was added in the 19th century, as were the spires on the steeples, which were redone in 1882. The tabernacle was designed by Noël Levasseur and came from the original church in 1728. Above it hangs *L'Annonciation* (The Annunciation), painted by Abbé Aide-Créquy in 1776. The

glass doors on the left open onto the former congregationist chapel, added to the church in 1853, where occasional summer exhibitions with religious themes are put on.

With objects related to fishing, ship models, an interpretive centre and two real ships, the **Musée Maritime Bernier** ★★ *($7.50; mid-May to mid-Oct, every day 9am to 5pm; the rest of the year, Tue to Fri 9am to noon and 1:30pm to 5pm; 55 Rue des Pionniers Est, ☎247-5001)* recounts the maritime history of the St. Lawrence from the 17th century to the present day. The institution, founded by the Association des Marins du Saint-Laurent, occupies the former Couvent de l'Islet-sur-Mer (1877) and bears the name of one of the village's most illustrious citizens, Captain J. E. Bernier (1852-1934). Bernier was one of the first individuals to explore the Arctic, thus securing Canadian sovereignty in the far north.

Saint-Jean-Port-Joli ★

Saint-Jean-Port-Joli has become synonymous with handicrafts, specifically wood carving. The origins of this run back to the Bourgault family, who made their living carving wood in the early 20th century. On the way into the town, Route 132 is lined with an impressive number of shops, where visitors can purchase a wooden-pipe-smoking grandfather or knitting woman. Museums exhibit the finest pieces. Though the handicraft business is flourishing now more than ever, the village is also known for its church, and for Philippe Aubert de Gaspé's novel *Les Anciens Canadiens* (Canadians of Old), written at the seigneurial manor.

The charming **Église Saint-Jean-Baptiste** ★★ *(2 Avenue de Gaspé Ouest)*, built between 1779 and 1781, is recognizable by its bright red roof topped by two steeples, placed in a way altogether uncommon in Québec architecture: one in the front, the other in the back at the beginning of the apse. The church has a remarkable interior made of carved, gilded wood. Pierre Noël Levasseur's rocaille tabernacle, crowned with a wood shell supported by columns, comes from the original chapel and dates back to 1740. The building of side galleries on the nave in order to increase the number of pews is somewhat rare in Québec. Those in Saint-Jean-Port-Joli, dating back to 1845, are the only ones to have survived the waves of renovation and restoration of the past 40 years.

QUÉBEC

Saint-Roch-des-Aulnaies ★★

This pretty village on the banks of the St. Lawrence is actually made up of two neighbourhoods. The one around the church is called Saint-Roch-des-Aulnaies, while the other, not far from the manor, is known as the Village des Aulnaies. The name Aulnaies refers to the abundance of alder trees (*aulnes*) all along the Rivière Ferrée, which powers the seigneurial mill. Nicolas Juchereau, the son of Jean Juchereau, Sieur de Maur from Perche, was granted the seigneury in 1656. Most of the old residences in Saint-Roch-des-Aulnaies are exceptionally large, a sign that local inhabitants enjoyed a certain degree of prosperity in the 19th century.

The manor and its mill are located on the right, after the bridge that spans the Rivière Ferrée.

Seigneurie des Aulnaies ★★ *($5; mid-Jun to early Sep, every day 9am to 6pm; early Sep to mid-Oct; every day, 10am to 4pm; 525 Chemin de la Seigneurie, ☎354-2800).* The Dionne estate has been transformed into a fascinating information centre, focusing on the seigneurial era. Visitors are greeted in the former miller's house, converted into a shop and café whose menu includes pancakes and muffins made with flour ground in the neighbouring mill, a large stone structure rebuilt in 1842 on the site of an older mill. Guided tours of the mill in operation enable visitors to understand its complex gearing system, set in motion by the Rivière Ferrée. Its main wheel is the largest in Québec.

A long staircase leads to the manor, which stands on a promontory. Like the manor in Lotbinière, this looks more like a charming villa than an austere seigneurial residence. Interactive display units, set up in different rooms in the basement, provide a detailed explanation of the principles behind the seigneurial system and its impact on the rural landscape of Québec. The more sober main floor contains reception rooms furnished according to 19th century tastes.

Saint-Georges

Divided into Saint-Georges-Ouest and Saint-Georges-Est, on either side of the Rivière Chaudière, this industrial capital of the Beauce region is reminiscent of a New England manufacturing town. A German-born merchant by the name of Georges Pfotzer is considered the true father of Saint-Georges for having taken advantage of the opening of the Lévis-Jackman route in 1830 in order to launch the forest industry here. In the early 20th century, the Dionne Spinning Mill and various shoe manufacturers established themselves in the region, creating a significant increase in population. Today, Saint-Georges is a sprawling city. Though the outskirts are somewhat grim, there are a few treasures nestled in the centre of town.

The **Église Saint-Georges ★★** *(1ʳᵉ Avenue, in Saint-Georges-Ouest)* stands on a promontory overlooking the Rivière Chaudière. Begun in 1900, it is unquestionably Québec City architect David Ouellet's masterpiece (built in collaboration with Pierre Lévesque). The art of the Belle Époque is beautifully represented here by the central steeple towering 75 metres and the magnificent three-level interior, which has been lavishly sculpted and gilded. In front of the church stands an imposing statue entitled *Saint Georges Terrassant le Dragon* (St. George Bringing Down the Dragon). This is a fibreglass copy of the fragile original. Louis Jobin's original metal-covered wooden (1909), is now exhibited at the Musée du Québec in Québec City.

Thetford Mines

Asbestos is a strange ore with a whitish, fibrous appearance that is valued for its insulating properties and heat resistance. It was discovered in the region in 1876, promoting the development of a portion of Québec that had previously been considered extremely remote. Large American and Canadian companies developed the mines in Asbestos, Black Lake and Thetford Mines (before the mines were nationalized in the early 1980s), building industrial empires which made Québec one of the highest-ranking producers of asbestos in the world.

Mine Tours ★★ *($10; late Jun to early Sep, every day at 1:30pm; Jul 1:30pm and 3:30pm; 682 Rue Mofette N., ☎335-7141 and 335-6511)* provide a unique opportunity to see an asbestos mine in operation. In addition to visiting extraction sites and going down into an open-cut mine, participants can attend an information session on asbestos-based products.

PARKS

Québec City Region

The **Station Mont Sainte-Anne ★** *(Route 360, C.P. 400, Beaupré, GOA 1E0, ☎827-4561, ☎827-3121, www.mont.sainte.anne.com)* cover 77 square kilometres and includes 800-metre-high Mont Sainte-Anne, one of the most beautiful downhill skiing sites in Québec (see p 280). Various other outdoor activities are possible the park has 200 kilometres of mountain bike trails, which become 200 kilometres of cross-country trails in winter. Access to these is $5 per day. Sports equipment is rented on site. There are a few hotels close to the ski hill and to the park.

The **Cap-Tourmente National Wildlife Area ★★** *(Saint-Joachim, Apr-Oct ☎827-4591, Nov-Apr ☎827-3776)* is located on pastoral, fertile land. Each spring and autumn its sand-bars are visited by countless snow geese, who stop to gather strength for their long migration. The reserve also has birdwatching facilities and naturalists on hand to answer your questions about the 250 species of birds and 45 species of mammals you might encounter on the hiking and walking trails that traverse the park.

Throughout the year, hordes of visitors come to **Parc de la Jacques-Cartier ★★** *(Route 175 Nord, ☎848-3169)*, located in the Réserve Faunique des Laurentides, 40 kilometres north of Quebec. The area is called Vallée de la Jacques-Cartier, after the river of the same name that runs through it, winding between steep hills. Benefitting from the microclimate caused by the river being hemmed in on bothsides, the site is suitable for a number of outdoor activities. The vegetation and wildlife are abundant and diverse. The winding and well-laid-out paths sometimes lead to interesting surprises, like a moose and its offspring foraging for food in a marsh. Before heading out to discover all the riches the site has to offer, you can get information at the nature centre's reception area. Campsites, chalets and equipment are all available to rent.

At the park, specialists organize **Safaris d'Observation de l'Orignal**, moose observation safaris, from mid-September to mid-October as well as **Écoute des Appels Nocturnes des Loups**, nocturnal wolf call-listening sessions *(☎/☎-848-5099)* at night (7:30pm to midnight) from the beginning of July until mid-October, in order to familiarize people with these animals. Reservations are required for these educational excursions, which usually last three hours; it costs $15 for adults; each of these activities lasts at least three hours and requires that you walk through the forest. Reservations necessary.

Charlevoix

Located at the eastern edge of the Réserve Faunique des Laurentides, the **Parc des Grands-Jardins ★★** *(166 Boulevard de Comporté, Baie-St-Paul, ☎846-2057 and 457-3945)* is rich with flora and fauna characteristic of taiga and tundra, a very unusual occurance at such a southern latitude. Hikes led by naturalises are organized throughout the summer. Caribou have been spotted from some of the trails. The park's Mont du Lac des Cygnes (Swan Lake Mountain) trail is among the most beautiful in Québec. Visitors can also go on canoe-camping trips.

Parc Régional des Hautes-Gorges-de-la-Rivière-Malbaie ★★ *(from Baie-Saint-Paul, take Route 138 to Saint-Aimé-des-Lacs, ☎439-4402)*, which covers over 233 square kilometres of land, was created in order to protect the area from commercial exploitation. Over 800 million years ago, a crack in the earth's crust formed the magnificent gorges after which the park is named; later the terrain was shaped by glaciers. The park features an incredible diversity of vegetation, ranging from maple stands to alpine tundra. The rock faces, some of which are 800 metres high, tower over the river and are used for rock-climbing. The best known climb, 'Pomme d'Or', is a 350-metre high expert-level trail. Other park activities include snowmobiling, hiking (the Acropole trail is particularly scenic), and canoe-camping. The park's rental centre has mountain bikes and canoes. **River boat cruises** are also offered for $20 *(duration: 1 hr 30 min, ☎665-7527)*. A trip down the river is the best way to truly appreciate the park.

Mauricie–Bois-Francs

The **Mauricie National Park ★** *($3.50 per person for one day; Grand-Mère, ☎538-3232)* is also known as Parc national de La Mauricie.

QUÉBEC

It was created in 1970 to preserve a part of the Laurentians. It is a perfect setting for outdoor activities such as canoeing, hiking, mountain biking, snowshoeing and cross-country skiing. Hidden among the woods are several lakes and rivers, as well as natural wonders of all kinds. Visitors can stay in dormitories year-round for $21 per person. Reservations can be made at ☎537-4555.

 OUTDOORS

 Rafting

Québec City Region

In spring and early summer the Rivière Jacques-Cartier has been giving adventurers a good run for their money. Two longstanding companies offer well-supervised rafting expeditions with all the necessary equipment. At **Nouveau Monde Québec** *(three hours $45, per day with lunch $69; 1440 Chemin du Hibou, C.P. 455, Stoneham, ☎848-4144 or 1-800-267-4144)*, they promise lots of excitement. With **Excursions Jacques-Cartier** *(½ day $45, isothermal suit $16; 978 Av. Jacques-Cartier, Tewkesbury, ☎848-7238, ⇝848-5687)*, you can also experience some very exciting runs.

 Downhill Skiing

Québec City Region

Station Mont-Sainte-Anne *($37.38 per day; Mon 9am to 4pm, Tue to Fri 9am to 10pm, Sat 8:30am to 10pm, Sun 8:30pm to 4pm; Route 360, C.P. 400, Beaupré, GOA 1E0, ☎827-4561, ⇝827-3121, www.mont.sainte.anne.com)* is one of the biggest ski resorts in Québec. Among the 51 runs, some reach 625 metres in height and 14 are lit for night skiing. It's also a delight for snowboarders. Instead of buying a regular ticket, you can buy a pass worth a certain number of points, valid for two years, and each time you take the lift, points are deducted. Equipment rentals are also available *(skiing $21 per day, snowboarding $33 per day)*.

The **Station Touristique Stoneham** *($36; Stoneham, ☎848-2411)* welcomes visitors year-round. In the winter there are 25 runs, 16

of which are lighted. For cross-country skiers there are 30 kilometres of maintained trails, which in the summer are at the disposal of hikers, mountain-bikers and horseback riders.

Charlevoix

The **Massif** ★★★ *($32.25; 1350 Rue Principale; C.P. 47, Petite-Rivière-Saint-François, GOA 2L0, ☎632-5876)* is a ski hill boasting a vertical drop of approximately 700 metres, one of the highest in Québec, making it a popular destination among downhill skiers. Until recently, skiers were brought to the top of the hill by bus. Two mechanical lifts, including a quadruple lift, were installed in order to service more skiers. The mountain can now accommodate up to 2,500 people per day and has 14 intermediate- and advanced-level runs. It is a good idea to reserve lift tickets in advance. The view from atop is mind-blowing.

Parc Régional du Mont Grand-Fonds ★ *($25; 1000 Chemin des Loisirs, La Malbaie, ☎665-0095)* has thirteen 355-metre runs. The longest run is 2,500 metres.

 Ice-fishing

Mauricie–Bois-Francs

From December to February, thousands of devotees of **ice-fishing**, converge on the Rivière Sainte-Anne to fish for tomcod. The river is covered with fishing huts in the winter. These can be rented, along with the necessary equipment, from the Comité de Gestion de la Rivière Sainte- Anne, the river's management committee *(Ste-Anne-de-la-Pérade, ☎418-325-2475)*. The price is $15 per person per day (four per cabin, maximum), $18 on the weekend.

 ACCOMMODATIONS

Québec City Region

Château-Richer

For over 50 years, **Auberge Baker** *($59 sb, $85 pb; bkfst incl., ℜ, K; 8790 Avenue Royale, GOA 1N0, ☎666-5509, ⇝824-4412)* has existed in this hundred-year-old Côte-de-Beaupré house. Its stone walls, low ceilings, wood floors and wide-frame windows enchant visitors. The five bedrooms are on the dimly-lit upper floor but there's also a kitchenette, a bathroom and an adjoining terrace on the same floor. The rooms are meticulously decorated in authentic fashion and furnished with antiques. They serve delicious food.

Beaupré (Mont Sainte-Anne)

Many chalets have recently been built around the base of the Mont Sainte-Anne, in newly developed areas. Among these is the **Hôtel Val des Neiges** *($95, $160 ½b; ≈, ☉, ⌂, ℜ, ᕮ; 201 Val des Neiges, GOA 1EO, ☎827-5711 or 1-800-463-5250, ⊷827-5997)*. The decor is rustic and the rooms are comfortable. The complex also includes small, well-equipped condos. They also offer cruise packages.

La Camarine *($98, $240 ½b; ≈, ℜ; 10947 Sainte-Anne, GOA 1EO, ☎827-5703, ⊷827-5430)* faces the St. Lawrence River. This charming high-quality inn has thirty rooms. The decor successfully combines the rustic feel of the house with the more modern wooden furniture. This is a delightful spot.

Île d'Orléans

On Île d'Orléans, there are about 50 bed and breakfasts! A list can be obtained from the tourist office. There are also a few guesthouses with solid reputations and a campground. There are plenty of options therefore for getting the most out of your stay on this enchanting island.

Le Vieux-Presbytère guesthouse *($60 bkfst incl., $118 ½b; pb, sb, ℜ; 1247 Avenue Monseigneur-d'Esgly, St-Pierre, GOA 4EO, ☎828-9723 or 1-888-282-9723, ⊷828-2189)* is in fact located in an old presbytery just behind the village church. The structure is predominantly made out of wood and stone. Low ceilings with wide beams, wide-frame windows and antiques such as woven bedcovers and braided rugs take you back to the era of New France. The dining room and the lounge are inviting. It's a tranquil spot with rustic charm.

Le Canard Huppée *($125 bkfst incl., $175 ½b; ℜ; 2198 Chemin Royal, St-Laurent, GOA 3ZO, ☎828-2292 or 1-800-838-2292, ⊷828-0966)*

has enjoyed a very good reputation over the last few years. Their eight clean, comfortable, country-style rooms are scattered with wooden ducks. The restaurant is also just as renowned and appealing. The service is conscientious, and the surrounding, beautiful.

Deschambault

The **Maison Deschambault** *($95 bkfst incl., $165 ½b; ℜ; 128 Chemin du Roy, GOA 1SO, ☎286-3386, ⊷286-4064)* offers five luxurious rooms, decorated with flowered patterns and pastel colours. There's also a small bar, a dining room that serves fine cuisine (see p 285), a conference room, and a massage service all in an enchanting old manor house (see p 261). Relaxing in this peaceful setting is no trouble at all.

Charlevoix

Baie-Saint-Paul

The least expensive place to stay in town is the **Auberge de Jeunesse Le Balcon Vert** *($15; Route 362, GOA 1SO, ☎435-5587)*. This youth hostel offers small chalets that sleep four people, as well as camp sites. It is only open during the summer.

The **Parc des Grands-Jardins** *($14-$20; 166 Boulevard de Comporté, Baie-St-Paul, ☎1-800-665-6527)* rents out small cottages and shelters This park is a popular place for fishing, so if you want to stay here during summer, you'll have to reserve early.

The **Le Genévrier** campground *($20; Route 138, at the Baie-Saint-Paul exit, GOA 1BO, ☎435-6520)* is a vast recreational-tourist complex in perfect harmony with its natural environment. Campers of all stripes are sure to find what they are looking for here. The campground boasts 450 sites, mostly on forested land, for all types of lodging and shelter, from the biggest motorhomes to tents for those who prefer camping in the wild. Several fully equipped, modern and comfortable cottages are situated by the river or lake. In summer, two more rustic but fully equipped log cabins with bedding and showers are also for rent. Every day, an extensive programme of sports and leisure activities is offered. Hiking and mountain-biking trails along the river.

QUÉBEC

The strange circular building housing the **Auberge la Pignoronde** *($124; $184 ½b; ≈, ℜ; 750 Boulevard Mgr de Laval, GOA 180, ☎435-5505 or 1-800-463-5250)* may be less than appealing from the outside, but the interior decor is quite charming, and the lobby features a welcoming fireplace. There is also an excellent view of the bay.

The **Auberge La Maison Otis** *($180 ½b; ≈, △, ℜ; 23 Rue St-Jean-Baptiste, GOA 1B0, ☎435-2255)* has a suave ambiance, is tastefully decorated and serves divine food. The old section has small, snug rooms with bunk-beds, whereas in the new section, the rooms are large and cosy. This former bank is an example of classic Québec architecture and is located in the heart of the city.

Île aux Coudres

A long building, with several skylights, the **Cap-aux-Pierres** hotel *($190 ½b; ≈, ℜ; 246 Route Principale, La Baleine, GOA 2AO, ☎438-2711 or 1-800-463-5250)* offers pleasant rustic rooms.

Saint-Irénée

The charming **Auberge des Sablons** *($168 ½b; sb or pb, ℜ; 223 Chemin Les Bains, GOT 1VO, ☎452-3240)* is a pretty white house with blue shutters, located in a peaceful spot nextto Domaine Forget. The rooms are pleasant, but not all have private bathrooms.

La Malbaie – Pointe-au-Pic

A veritable institution in Quebec, the **Manoir Richelieu** *($69-$159; ≈, K, ℜ; 181 Avenue Richelieu, GOT 1MO, ☎665-4431 or 1-888-270-0111, ≈665-3093)* remains one of the choicest and most highly-rated resorts in Québec. This architectural gem in the Norman style boasts 350 rooms and numerous suites in the rear section. Several boutiques are on the ground floor as is an underground link to the Casino. A good many of the rooms have been renovated since the opening of the Casino.

The **Auberge Les Trois Canards et Motels** *($75.; ℜ, ≈, △; 49 Côte Belleveue, GOT 1MO, ☎665-3761 or 1-800-461-3761, ≈675-4727)* has a magnificent view of the entire region. The inn offers nine rooms, each warmly decorated with a fireplace, thick carpets, and a

whirlpool. The motel rooms are not as nice but still offer a great view of the water.

Cap-à-l'Aigle

The **Auberge des Peupliers** *($172 ½b; △, ℜ; 381 Saint-Raphaël, GOT 180, ☎665-4423, ≈665-3179)* sits on a hillside overlooking the St. Lawrence. The rooms are decorated with wooden furniture that creates a warm, charming atmosphere. The inn also has pleasant, quiet living rooms.

The luxurious **La Pinsonnière** hotel *($130, $230 ½b; △, ≈, ☉, ℜ; 124 Saint-Raphaël, GOT 180, ☎665-4431)* boasts a wonderful location on a headland overhanging the river. The rooms are tastefully decorated, each different from the next. This is a very pleasant place. Their restaurant is very popular.

Mauricie–Bois-Francs

Trois-Rivières

The **Auberge de Jeunesse la Flotille** *($18 for dormitories, $36 for private rooms; 497 Rue Radisson, G9A 2C7, ☎378-8010)*, the youth hostel, is right downtown. There are some 40 beds in the summer season, this number dwindles to 30 in the winter.

The high tower of the **Hôtel Delta** *(84 $, ≈, ☉, △, ℜ; 1620 Notre-Dame, G9A 6E5, ☎376-1991, ≈372-5975)* is easy to spot next to the downtown area. The rooms are spacious. The hotel also has sports facilities.

Grand-Mère

The **Auberge Le Florès** *($45 in the old wing, $60 in the new wing; tv, ≈, ≡, ℜ; 4291 50e Avenue, G9T 6S5, ☎538-9340, ≈538-1884)* is a superb period house. Though not spectacular, the rooms are quite comfortable.

Shawinigan

A well-kept place on the way into town, the **Auberge l'Escapade** *($58; ℜ; 3383 Rue Garnier, G9N 6R4, ☎539-6911 or 539-7669)* has several different personalities. The choice of accommodations here ranges from basic, inexpensive rooms *($48)* to luxurious rooms decorated with period furniture *($145)*. In between the two, there are pretty, comfortable rooms that offer good value for the money *($63-$80)*. What's more, the restaurant serves tasty food.

Pointe-du-Lac

The **Auberge du Lac Saint-Pierre** *($180;* ℜ, ≈, ≡, ⊛, △, ⊖; *1911 Route 138, P.O. Box 10, GOX 1Z0,* ☎*377-5961, 371-5579 or 1-888-377-5971)* is located in Pointe-de-Lac, a small village at the north end of Lac Saint-Pierre, which is actually just a widening in the St. Lawrence. The flora and fauna that make their home in and around the "lake" are characteristic of marshy areas. Perched atop a promontory that slopes down to the shore, this large inn boasts an outstanding location. It has comfortable modern rooms, some of which have a mezzanine for the beds, leaving more space in the main room. The dining room serves excellent food (see p 286). There are bicycles on hand if you feel like exploring the area.

Saint-Paulin

Located alongside a river, **Le Baluchon** *($97;* ⊖, △, ≈, ℜ, ⊛); *350 Chemin des Trembles, J0K 2J0,* ☎*268-2555, 268-5234 or 1-800-789-5968)* is the place in the area for active types. The vast grounds highlight the beautiful natural surroundings. There are plenty of ways to occupy your time here: hiking or skiing along the river or through the woods, kayaking, canoeing, etc. Guests sleep in one of two buildings, each containing nearly 40 pleasant and comfortable modern rooms. style. You can also relax at the well-equipped fitness centre or tempt your palate in the dining room (see p 287).

Bécancour

The **Auberge Godefroy** *($150;* ⊛, ℜ, ≈, ≡, △, ⊖, K; *17575 Boulevard Bécancour, GOX 2T0,* ☎*233-2200, 233-2288 or 1-800-361-1620)* is an imposing building with lots of windows. During winter, a crackling fire awaits guests in the stately lobby. The 70 rooms are spacious and offer all the comforts one would expect from an establishment in this category. The hotel also has a fitness centre and offers a variety of packages. Go ahead and indulge yourself in the dining room as well (see p 287)!

Drummondville

The **Motel Blanchette** *($55; 225 Boulevard St-Joseph Ouest, J2E 1A9,* ☎*477-1222 or 1-800-567-3823)* has a good location and pretty, reasonably priced rooms.

The **Hôtellerie Le Dauphin** *($74;* ≈, ℜ; *600 Boulevard St-Joseph, J2C 2C1,* ☎*478-4141,* ⇔*478-7549)* is located on a very busy street, near a number of shopping centres. It has large, well-kept rooms decorated with modern furnishings.

Victoriaville

The modern **Le Suzor** hotel *($76; 1000 Boulevard Jutras, G6S 1E4,* ☎*357-1000,* ⇔*357-5000)* is in a quiet part of town. The pleasant, spacious rooms are equipped with new furniture.

Chaudière-Appalaches

Saint-Antoine-de-Tilly

La Maison Normand *($60 bkfst incl.; 3894 Chemin de Tilly, GOS 2C0,* ☎*886-2218)* is a lovely residence dating back to 1894, that has been tastefully renovated. It has a magnificent living room with a piano, and a pretty terrace in the back. The hosts are extremely friendly, and the breakfasts are both copious and delicious.

Manoir de Tilly *($175 ½b;* ⊖, ⊛, ℜ: *3854 Chemin de Tilly, C.P. 28, GOS 2C0,* ☎*886-2407 or 1-888-862-6647,* ⇔*886-2585)* is a historic home that dates from 1788. The rooms that are available to guests are not, however, in the older part of the building, but in a modern wing that nonetheless offers all of the comfort and peace one could desire. Each room has a fireplace and a beautiful view. The service is attentive and the dining room offers fine cuisine (see p 287). The inn also has a gym and conference rooms.

Beaumont

Perched high on a hill and surrounded by trees, the **Manoir de Beaumont** *($100 bkfst incl.; ≈; 485 Route du Fleuve, GOR 1CO, ☎833-5635, ≈833-7891)* offers bed-and-breakfast accommodations in perfect calm and comfort. Its five rooms are attractively decorated in period style, matching the house itself. A large, sunny living room and a swimming pool are at guests' disposal.

Montmagny

The **Manoir des Érables** *($99, $196 ½b; ⊛, ≈, ⊛, ℜ; 220 Boulevard Taché E., G5V 1G5, ☎248-0100 or 1-800-563-0200, ≈248-9507)* is an old, English-style seigneurial abode. The opulence of its period decor and the warm, courteous welcome it lends make guests feel like royalty. The rooms are beautiful and comfortable, and many of them have fireplaces. On the ground floor there is pleasant cigar lounge decorated with hunting trophies where guests can choose from a great variety of scotches and cigars. There is also a dining room and a bistro (see p 287), both of which serve excellent cuisine. Motel rooms under the maples, set off from the hotel, and a few rooms in a lodge that is just as inviting as the manor itself are also available.

Saint-Eugène de l'Islet

Auberge des Glacis *($165 ½b; ℜ; 46 Route Tortue, GOR 1X0, ☎247-7486, ≈247-7182)* has a special charm about it, set as it is in an old seigneurial mill at the end of a tree-lined lane. Each of the comfortable rooms has a name and its own unique decor. Delicious French cuisine is featured in the dining room (see p 287). The stone walls and wood-framed windows of the mill have been preserved as part of the finery of the establishment, which whose property includes a lake, bird-watching trails, a small terrace, and, of course, the river. This is an especially peaceful spot, perfect for relaxation.

Saint-Jean-Port-Joli

In an old, red and white house with four corner towers and a wraparound with a view of the river, the inn at **Maison de L'Ermitage** *($65 bkfst incl.; sb; 56 Rue de l'Hermitage, GOR 1GO, ☎598-7553)* offers five cozy rooms

and a tasty breakfast. The house is full of sunny spots furnished for reading and relaxing, and its yard slopes down to the river. The annual Sculpture festival held just next door (see p 288).

Saint-Georges

Auberge-Motel Benedict-Arnold *($59; ≈, ≡, ℜ; 18255 Bd. Lacroix, G5Y 5B8, ☎228-5558 or 1-800-463-5057, ≈227-2941)* has been a well-known stopover near the United States border for many generations. The inn has over 50 rooms, each of them decorated with privacy in mind. Motel rooms are also available. Two dining rooms offer quality fare. The staff is very obliging.

RESTAURANTS

Québec City Region

Beauport

The **Manoir Montmorency** *($$$-$$$$; 2490 Avenue Royale, ☎663-3330)* (see p 256) benefits from a superb location above the Montmorency Falls. From the dining room surrounded by bay windows, there's an absolutely magnificent view of the falls, the river and Île d'Orléans. Fine French cuisine, prepared with the best products in the region, is served in pleasant surroundings. A wonderful experience for the view and the food! The entrance fee to the Parc de la Chute Montmorency (where the restaurant is located) and the parking fees are waived upon presentation of your receipt or by mentioning your reservation.

Beaupré (Mont Sainte-Anne)

The **La Camarine** Inn *($$$$; 10947 Sainte-Anne, ☎827-5703)* also houses an excellent restaurant which serves Quebecois nouvelle cuisine. The dining room is peaceful, with a simple decor. The innovative dishes are a feast for the senses. In the basement of the inn is another small restaurant, the **Bistro**, which offers the same menu and prices as upstairs; but it is only open in the winter. Equipped with a fireplace, it is a cozy spot for après-ski. It is open in the evening for drinks.

Île d'Orléans

The dining room at **La Goéliche** *($$$; 22 Chemin du Quai, Ste-Pétronille, ☎828-2248)* is a little small. It's still pleasant though, and you can still get one of the most beautiful views of Quebec City. They serve fine French cuisine: stuffed quail, nuggets of lamb and saddle of hare.

Located in a 17th-century house **L'Âtre** *($$$$; 4403 Chemin Royal, ☎829-2474)* provides a unique atmosphere. The employees, all dressed in period clothing, and the charming old-fashioned decor will make you think you have been transported back in time. The rather pricey menu consists of good traditional Quebecois cuisine.

Sainte-Foy

At **La Fenouillère** *($$$-$$$$; 3100 Chemin St-Louis, ☎653-3886)* the menu of refined and creative French cuisine promises a succulent dining experience. This restaurant is also proud to possess one of the best wine cellars in Quebec. The decor is simple and comfortable.

The **Michelangelo** *($$$-$$$$; 3111 Chemin Saint-Louis, ☎651-6262)* serves fine Italian cuisine that both smells and tastes wonderful. The classically decorated dining-room, although busy, remains warm and intimate. The courteous and attentive service adds to the pleasure of the food.

Deschambault

The restaurant in the **Maison Deschambault** Inn *($$$-$$$$; 128 Route 138, ☎286-3386, ≈286-4711)* is well-known for its excellent menu, which consists mainly of fine French cuisine as well as various specialties of the region. The setting is particularly enchanting (see p 261).

Wendake

At the Huron village (see p 262), there's a pleasant restaurant whose name means "the meal is ready to serve". Nek8arre *($$; Mon to Fri 9am to 5pm; 575 Rue Stanislas-Kosca, ☎842-4308, ≈842-3473)* introduces you to traditional Huron cooking. Wonderful dishes such as clay trout, caribou or venison *brochettes* with mushrooms accompanied by wild rice and corn, are some of the items on the menu. The wood tables have little texts explaining the eating habits of native cultures embedded in them. Numerous objects scattered here and there will arouse your curiosity, and luckily, the waitresses act as part-time "ethnologists" and can answer your questions. All this in a pleasant atmosphere. The entry fee to the village will be waived if you're only going to restaurant.

Charlevoix

Baie-Saint-Paul

The country decor of the **Le Mouton Noir** restaurant *($; 43 Rue Sainte-Anne, ☎435-3075)* was recently renovated, causing it to lose a bit of its charm. While the restaurant has a good reputation, the food can be a little unimaginative. Nevertheless, it is a pleasant place with a view of the river.

Graced with an exceptional decor, the dining room of the **Auberge La Pignoronde** *($$$-$$$$; 750 Boulevard Mgr-de-Laval, ☎435-5505 or 1-800-463-5250)* looks out on the Vallée du Gouffre and Île aux Coudres. The restaurant serves absolutely delicious fare, where meat, fish and seafood share the stage with panache. Service is particularly attentive.

The finest and most sophisticated of cuisines is featured at **La Maison Otis** *($$$-$$$$; 23 Rue Saint-Jean-Baptiste, ☎435-2255)*, which has developed an avant-garde gourmet menu where regional flavours adopt new accents and compositions. In the inviting decor of the oldest part of the inn, where a bank once stood, guests are treated to a delightful culinary experience and a relaxing evening. The service is impeccable, and several ingredients on the menu are home-made. Fine selection of wines.

Saint-Joseph-de-la-Rive

The warm and intimate dining rooms of the **La Maison sous les Pins** inn *($$$; 352 Rue F.-A.-Savard, ☎635-2583)* can accommodate about twenty guests that come here to discover the refined aromas emanating from a medley of regional and French dishes, with an emphasis on local products. Friendly reception and romantic ambiance. Non-smoking.

QUÉBEC

Île aux Coudres

La Mer Veille *($; Pointe de lislet, west side of the island,* ☎*438-2149)* is a very popular restaurant that serves light meals and an appealing table d'hôte.

Saint-Irénée

Charm, romanticism and good taste are in perfect harmony with culinary quality at the **Auberge des Sablons** *($$$-$$$$; 223 Chemin Les Bains,* ☎*452-3594)*, ensuring a delightful dining experience. Guests here can savour excellent French cuisine while admiring the ocean from the terrace or dining room.

La Malbaie – Pointe-au-Pic

With a most pleasant atmosphere, the **Le Passe Temps** creperie *($$-$$$; 34 Boulevard Bellevue, Route 362,* ☎*665-7660)* constitutes an excellent choice for both lunch and dinner. The menu features a great variety of buckwheat or whole-wheat flour crêpes as main courses and desserts. The fresh pasta is exquisite, particularly the spaghetti with fresh tomatoes and Migneron cheese. The terrace is also welcome treat.

A spacious house with a nice garden, the **Auberge des Falaises** *($$$-$$$$; 18 Chemin des Falaises,* ☎*665-3731)* specialises in refined cuisine. The restaurant is among the most popular in the region, and won the *Prix Québécois de la Gastronomie.*

The chefs at the **Auberge des Trois Canards** *($$$$; 49 Côte Bellevue,* ☎*665-3761 or 1-800-461-3761)* have always been daring and inventive in integrating local ingredients or game with their refined cuisine. Invariably succeeding with panache, they have endowed the restaurant with an enviable nationwide reputation. The service, for its part, is outstanding, and the staff is genuinely cordial and knowledgeable about the dishes served. Good wine list.

For the last few years, the Manoir Richelieu's dining room, **Le Saint-Laurent** *($$$$; 181 Avenue Richelieu,* ☎*665-3703 or 1-888-294-0111)*, has raised its standards of quality considerably, to the point of making a name for itself as one of the four or five best gourmet restaurants in the area. In addition to its unobstructed view of the river, the glass-

walled dining hall boasts a superb menu, generally composed of five-course meals with three choices of meat dishes and three of fish. The Sunday morning brunch is quite an experience in Charlevoix, even for those not staying at the hotel.

Cap-à-l'Aigle

The **Auberge des Peupliers** *($$$-$$$$; 381 Rue Saint-Raphaël,* ☎*665-4423 or 1-888-282-3743)* has many wonderful surprises in store for its guests, fruits of its chef's fertile imagination and audacity. Patrons have only to abandon themselves to these intoxicating French and regional flavours, sure to delight any palate.

The food at **La Pinsonnière** *($$$$; 124 Rue Saint-Raphaël,* ☎*665-4431 or 1-800-387-4431)* has long been considered the height of gastronomic refinement in Charlevoix and, despite increasingly fierce competition, is still worthy of the title in many respects. La Pinsonnière offers a very upscale, classic gourmet menu, worthy of a veritable gustatory experience that requires dedicating an entire evening to. The wine cellar remains the best-stocked in the region and one of the finest in Québec.

Mauricie–Bois-Francs

Trois-Rivières

The Auberge Castel des Près *(5800 Boulevard Royal,* ☎*375-4921)* has two different restaurants: **L'Étiquette** *($-$$)* serves bistro-style cuisine and **Chez Claude (Castel des Prés)** *($$-$$$)* offers traditional French cuisine making it an excellent choice in this area. The chef has won a number of culinary awards. The menu includes pasta, meat and fish dishes with rich, flavourful sauces. During the warm weather, guests can enjoy a sheltered outdoor terrace cooled by summer breezes.

Pointe-du-Lac

If you go to the **Auberge du Lac Saint-Pierre** *($$$-$$$$; 1911 Route 138,* ☎*377-5971 or 1-888-377-5971)* (see p 283) for dinner, star your evening with a short walk on the shore to work up an appetite, or perhaps have an apéritif on the terrace, with its view of the river. The modern decor of the dining room is a bit cold, but there's nothing bland about the presentation of the dishes, much less their flavour. The menu, made up of French and Québec cuisine, includes trout, salmon, lamb and pheasant, all artfully prepared.

Saint-Paulin

Located on a magnificent estate, **Le Baluchon** *($$$-$$$$; 350 Chemin des Trembles, ☎268-2555 or 1-800-789-5968)* (see p 283) offers choice French and Québec cuisine, as well as a "health-conscious" menu that will leave you feeling anything but deprived. The dining room has a soothing decor and a view of the river.

Bécancour

The spacious dining room of the **Auberge Godefroy** *($$$-$$$$; 17575 Boulevard Bécancour, ☎233-2200 or 1-800-361-1620)* (see p 283) looks out onto the river. The delicious French cuisine varies from classic dishes to original creations made with regional produce. Succulent desserts!

Victoriaville

The restaurant **Plus Bar** *($; 192 Boulevard Des Bois-Francs Sud, ☎758-9927)* serves a splendid *poutine* (French fries, gravy and curd cheese) deemed one of these best in these parts. You can savour this magnificent "culinary" creation taking in the latest sporting events on a giant screen. Watch out: the "plus" size might be a little more "plus" than you're expecting!

Drummondville

The restaurant of the **Le Dauphin** hotel *($$; 600 Boulevard Saint-Joseph, ☎478-4141)* has a good seafood buffet. The helpings are large and there is also an "all you can eat" option. The decor is a little bleak but the atmosphere nice and relaxed.

Chaudière-Appalaches

Saint-Antoine-de-Tilly

The restaurant of **Manoir de Tilly** *($$$$; 3854 Chemin de Tilly, ☎886-2407)* proposes refined French cuisine with a base of local products such as lamb and duck or, for more imaginative dishes, ostrich and deer. The renovated dining room preserves not even a hint of the historic building, but it is pleasant nonetheless. In it, diners savour carefully prepared and finely presented dishes complemented by the view through the large windows on the north wall.

Lévis

Lévis is home to a link in the popular **Piazzeta** *($-$$; 5410 Boulevard de la Rive-Sud, ☎835-5545)* restaurant chain; this one unfortunately located in a rather commercial setting along Route 132 with none of the charm of Vieux-Lévis. Nonetheless, the ambiance is pleasant. Delicious, creatively garnished thin-crust pizza and tasty side dishes such as prosciutto and melon are served.

Montmagny

Bistro Saint-Gabriel *($$; 220 Boulevard Taché Est, ☎248-0100)* occupies the basement of the Manoir des Érables (see p 284). The old walls, made of very large stones, and the low ceiling confer on the spot a very unique atmosphere. During the summer, meals are served in the open air, on a terrace where fish and meat are grilled before your eyes.

The dining room of **Manoir des Érables** *($$$$; 220 Boulevard Taché E., ☎248-0100)* (see p 284) features fish and game. Goose, sturgeon, burbot, lamb and pheasant are lovingly prepared in traditional French style. Served in the inn's magnificent dining room, these local foods enchant guests, who, in fall and winter, dine in the warm glow of a fireplace. One of the finest restaurants in the region.

Saint-Eugène-de-l'Islet

Auberge des Glacis *($$$; 46 Route Tortue, ☎247-7486)* serves fine French cuisine that is likely to become one of the best memories of

QUÉBEC

any trip! The dining room, in a historic mill (see p 284), is bright and pleasantly laid out. Diners savour meat and fish dishes as easy on the eyes as they are on the taste buds. The restaurant also serves a light lunch, which may be enjoyed on a riverside terrace.

L'Islet-sur-Mer

The restaurant **La Paysanne** *($$$; 497 Rue des Pionniers E.,* ☎*247-7276)* is set right on the riverbank and so offers a spectacular view of the St. Lawrence and the north shore. The fine French cuisine plays on regional flavours and is attractively presented.

St-Jean-Port-Joli

The **Coureuse des Grèves** *($$; 300 Route de l'Église,* ☎*598-9111)* is a friendly restaurant-café in a very attractive old house named for a seafarers' legend. Tasty light meals such as spinach squares served with celeriac salad are served. In summer, diners take advantage of a large sheltered patio. This is a popular spot, and the service is business-like but courteous. The upstairs bar is also quite a draw in the evening.

Saint-Georges

The new restaurant-bar **Il Mondo** *($$; 11615 1ʳᵉ Avenue,* ☎*228-4133)* presents a lovely decor in the latest style with ceramic, wood and wrought-iron elements. Internationally inspired cuisine, including nachos and pannini, is featured, as is delicious coffee from a popular Montreal roaster. If you order a bowl of coffee be forewarned – it will be garnished with marshmallows!

La Table du Père Nature *($$-$$$; 10735 1ʳᵉ Avenue,* ☎*227-0888)* is definitely one of the best restaurants in town. Guests enjoy innovative French cuisine prepared with skill and sophistication. Just reading the menu is enough to make your mouth water. The restaurant occasionally serves game.

ENTERTAINMENT

Festivals and Cultural Events

Charlevoix

The **Symposium de la nouvelle peinture au Canada** *(*☎*435-3681)* is held annually in Baie-Saint-Paul. Throughout the month of August, visitors can thus admire large-scale works based on a suggested theme and created here by approximately 15 artists from Québec, Canada and abroad.

Mauricie–Bois-Francs

In mid-July, Drummondville hosts a 10-day **Festival Mondial du Folklore à Drummondville** *(*☎*472-1184 or 1-800-265-5412)*. The goal of this festival of world folklore is to encourage exchanges between the different traditions and cultures of the world.

The **Festival de Musique Actuelle de Victoriaville** *(*☎*758-9451)* takes place each year in May. This festival starts off where the others end, in that it is an exploration of new musical forms. Of course, this event won't appeal to everyone, but it is always interesting to go to check out the new directions in which music is heading. This festival is an adventure, for musicians and spectators alike, and all sorts of surprises await.

Chaudière-Applaches

In the fall, snow geese leave the northern breeding grounds where they have spent the summer and head south toward more clement climates. On the way, they stop on the banks of the St. Lawrence River, especially in spots that provide abundant food for them, like the sand bars of Montmagny. These avian visitors are the perfect excuse to celebrate the **Festival de l'Oie Blanche** *(*☎*284-3954)*, which features all sorts of activities related to watching and learning about these beautiful migrating birds.

Every year, at the end of June, Saint-Jean-Port-Joli welcomes sculptors from all over the world to the lively **Fête Internationale de la Sculpture** *(*☎*598-7288)*. Renowned artists create works

Architectural treasures of the National Capital Region: Canadian Parliament in Ottawa and the Musée des Civilisations in Hull. (T.B.)

Toronto, the Canadian megacity, with its skyscrapers and famous CN Tower.
(T.B.)

before your eyes, some of which are then exhibited throughout the summer.

Casino

Charlevoix

The **Casino de Charlevoix** *(183 Avenue Richelieu, ☎665-5300 or 1-800-665-2274)*, in Pointe-au-Pic, next to the Manoir Richelieu, is a European-style casino. Formal dress required.

 SHOPPING

Québec City Region

Île d'Orléans has a handful of craft shops, antique dealers and cabinet-making studios. One of these, the **Corporation des Artisans de l'île** *(☎828-2519)*, is located in the Saint-Pierre church. There are about half a dozen art galleries on the island too, many in the village of Saint-Jean.

The shop of the **Forge à Pique-Assaut** *(2200 Chemin Royal, St-Laurent, ☎828-9300)* sells various forged-metal objects, from candlesticks and knick-knacks to furniture. They also sell other crafts.

The **Chocolaterie de l'Île d'Orléans** *(196 Chemin Royal, Ste-Pétronille, ☎828-2252)* offers a whole range of little delectable treats. Their home-made ice-cream is also delicious.

Charlevoix

Baie-Saint-Paul

Baie-Saint-Paul is particularly noteworthy for its **art galleries**. There is a little of everything here, as each shop has its own specialty. Oils, pastels, watercolours, etchings... paintings by big names and the latest artists, originals and reproductions, sculpture and poetry... whatever your heart desires! Take an enjoyable stroll along Rue St-Jean-Baptiste and the neighbouring streets where you'll find countless beautiful galleries staffed by friendly and chatty art dealers.

Saint-Joseph-de-la-Rive

The wonderful paper made at the **Papeterie Saint-Gilles** *(304 Rue Félix-Antoine-Savard, ☎635-2430)* is sold on the premises. The quality of the cotton paper is remarkable. Some of the paper is decorated with maple or fern leaves. You can also purchase a collection of narratives, stories and Québec songs printed on this fine paper.

Chaudière-Appalaches

Saint-Jean-Port-Joli

Saint-Jean-Port-Joli is renowned for its crafts and many of its shops offer the products of local artisans – if this sort of shopping interestsyou, this town has much to offer. There are also a few second-hand stores here, to the delight of treasure hunters, many of them along Route 132.

At **Boutique Jacques-Bourgault** *(326 Av. de Gaspé Ouest)*, between Musée des Anciens Canadiens and Maison Médard-Bourgaut, the son of the latter sells contemporary and religious art.

Artisanat Chamard *(mid-Mar to late Dec, 8am to 5pm; 601 Avenue de Gaspé Est, ☎598-3425)*, whose fine reputation dates back nearly half a century, sells woven goods and ceramics, as well as native and Inuit works of art.

QUÉBEC

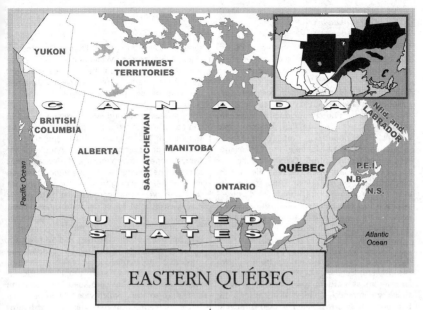

EASTERN QUÉBEC

This chapter covers a vast region, which includes the tourist regions of Bas-Saint-Laurent, Gaspésie, Îles-de-la-Madeleine, Saguenay-Lac-Saint-Jean, Manicouagan and Duplessis. The picturesque Bas-Saint-Laurent region extends east along the St. Lawrence River from the little town of La Pocatière to the village of Sainte-Luce, and south to the borders of the United States and New Brunswick. Besides the particularly fertile agricultural land next to the river, much of the Bas-Saint-Laurent is composed of farming and forestry development areas stretched over gently rolling hills glittering with lakes and streams.

The shores of the vast Gaspé peninsula are washed by the waters of Baie des Chaleurs, the St. Lawrence River and the Gulf of St. Lawrence. Many Quebecers cherish unforgettable memories of their travels in this mythical land in the easternmost part of Québec. People dream of touring Gaspésie and discovering its magnificent coastal landscape, where the Monts Chic-Chocs plunge abruptly into the cold waters of the St. Lawrence. They dream of going all the way to the famous Rocher Percé, heading out to sea toward Île Bonaventure, visiting the extraordinary Forillon National Park, and then slowly returning along Baie des Chaleurs and through the valley of Rivière Matapédia in the hinterland. This beautiful part of Québec, with its strikingly picturesque scenery, is inhabited by friendly, fascinating people, who still rely mainly on the sea for their living. The majority of Gaspesians live in small villages along the coast, leaving the centre of the peninsula covered with dense Boreal forest. The highest peak in southern Québec lies here, in the part of the Appalachians known as the Chic-Chocs.

The word *Gaspé* means "land's end" in the language of the Micmacs, who have been living in this region for thousands of years. Despite its isolation, the peninsula has attracted fishermen from many different places over the centuries, particularly Acadians driven from their lands by the English in 1755. Its population is now primarily francophone.

Gaspésie's main attractions are its rugged, mountainous landscape and the Gulf of St. Lawrence which is so huge that it might as well be the ocean. The coastline is studded with a string of fishing villages, leaving the interior devoid of towns and roads, much as it was when Jacques Cartier arrived in 1534.

The Îles-de-la-Madeleine (sometimes referred to in English as the Magdalen Islands) emerge from the middle of the Gulf of St. Lawrence more than 200 kilometres from the Gaspé Peninsula. They constitute a 65-kilometre-long archipelago of about a dozen islands, many connected to one another by long sand dunes. Swept by winds from the open sea, these small islands offer superb colourful scenery. The golden dunes and the long wild beaches blend with the red sandstone cliffs and the blue sea.

Villages with brightly painted houses, lighthouses and harbours add the finishing touches to the islands' beautiful scenery.

The 15,000 *Madelinots* (as residents are called) have always earned their livelihood from the sea, and continue to do so today by fishing for crab, bottom-feeding fish, mackerel and lobster. The population, mostly of French origin, live on seven islands of the archipelago: Île de la Grande Entrée, Grosse Île, Île aux Loups, Île du Havre aux Maisons, Île du Cap aux Meules, Île du Havre Aubert and Île d'Entrée. Among them, only Île d'Entrée, where a few families with Scottish roots live, is not attached by land to the rest of the archipelago.

Lac Saint-Jean is a veritable inland sea with a diameter of over 35 kilometres; from it flows the Rivière Saguenay, the location of the southernmost fjord in the world. In a way, these two impressive bodies of water form the backbone of this magnificent region. Moving swiftly toward the St. Lawrence River, the Rivière Saguenay flows through a rugged landscape studded with cliffs and mountains. Aboard a cruise ship or from the banks of the river, visitors can enjoy a series of gorgeous panoramic views of this untouched natural setting. The Saguenay is navigable, as far as Chicoutimi, and governed by the eternal rhythm of the tides. Its rich marine animal life includes various species of whale, in the summer. In the heart of the region, visitors will find the bustling city of Chicoutimi, the main urban centre in this part of Québec. The region's first settlers came here in the 19th century, attracted by the beautiful fertile plains and excellent farmland around the lake. The hard life of these pioneers, who were farmers in the summer and lumberjacks in the winter, was immortalized in Louis Hémon's novel *Maria Chapdelaine*. Sweet and delicious blueberries abound in the area and have made the region of Lac Saint-Jean famous. The fruit is so closely identified with the region that Quebecers all over the province have adopted the term *bleuets*, blueberries, as an affectionate nickname for the local inhabitants. Residents of both the Saguenay and Lac Saint-Jean regions are renowned for their friendliness and spirit.

The Manicouagan region borders the St. Lawrence for some 300 kilometres, extends north into the Laurentian plateau to include the Monts Groulx and the Réservoir Manicouagan, and is joined to the Duplessis region, forming

what is called the "Côte Nord". Covered by thick Boreal forest, Manicouagan also has an extensive river system that powers the eight generating stations of the Manic-Outardes hydroelectric complex.

Duplessis is a vast and remote region bound to the south for almost a thousand kilometres by the Gulf of St. Lawrence and to the north by the Labrador border. Its small population of francophones, anglophones and Montagnais is concentrated along the St. Lawrence coast and in a few inland mining towns. The region is far from any large urban centres, and its economy has always been based on natural resources. Aboriginals have lived in the region for thousands of years. In the 16th century Basque and Breton fishermen and whalers set up seasonal posts in the region. Today, the important economic activities are fishing, forestry and iron and titanium mining. Additional jobs are provided by a large aluminum smelter, which was built in Sept-Îles to take advantage of the availability of hydro-electricity.

 FINDING YOUR WAY AROUND

Bas-Saint-Laurent

By Car

Get off Highway 20 and take Route 132 E. Highways 232, 185 and 289 run through the Bas-St-Laurent, allowing you to reach the heart of this region and see its spectacular forests and valleys.

Bus Stations

Rivière-du-Loup: 83 Boulevard Cartier, ☎862-4884.
Rimouski: 90 Rue Leonidas, ☎723-4923.

Train Stations

La Pocatière: 95 Rue Principale, ☎856-2424.
Rimouski: 57 de l'Évêché Est, ☎722-4737.
Rivière-du-Loup: 615 Rue Lafontaine, ☎867-1525.
Trois-Pistoles: 231 Rue de la Gare, ☎851-2881.

By Ferry

Isle-Verte: The *La Richardière (adults $5, cars $20, ☎989-2843)* ferries passengers from Isle-Verte to Notre-Dame-des-Sept-Douleurs in 30 minutes. If you don't have a car, you can take a taxi-boat *($6.50; ☎898-2199).* The schedule varies according to season, so call ahead.

Trois-Pistoles: A ferry runs between Trois-Pistoles and Les Escoumins *($25 per car, $10 per person; ☎233-2202).* The crossing takes 90 minutes and if you're lucky you might see some whales. Reserve in advance for summer.

Gaspésie

Bus Stations

Matane: 750 Avenue du Phare O., ☎562-1177 (Irving station).
Saint-Anne-des-Monts: 90 Boulevard Sainte-Anne, ☎763-3321.
Gaspé: 2 Rue Adams, ☎368-1888.
Percé: 50 Route 132 O., ☎782-2140 (Petro-Canada station)
Bonaventure: 118 Rue Grand Pré, ☎534-2053 (Motel Grand-Pré).
Carleton: 561 Rue Perron, ☎364-7000.
Amqui: 9 Boulevard Saint-Benoit, ☎629-4898.

Train Stations

Gaspé: 3 Boulevard Marina, ☎368-4313
Percé: 44 L'Anse au Beaufils, ☎782-2747
Bonaventure: 217 Rue de la Gare, ☎534-3517
Carleton: 116 Rue de la Gare, ☎364-7734
Matapédia: 10 Rue MacDonnell, ☎865-2327

By Ferry

Baie-Comeau - Matane *(adults $10, cars $26; ☎562-2500)* the crossing takes 2 hours and 30 minutes. The schedule varies from year to year so be sure to check when planning your trip. Reservations are a good idea during summer.

Godbout - Matane *(adults $10, cars $26; ☎562-2500)* the crossing takes 2 hours and 30 minutes. Reservations are a good idea during summer.

Miguasha - Dalhousie *(cars $13; mid-Jun to mid-Sep, on the hour as of 8am in Dalhousie and 6:30am in Miguasha; ☎794-2596)* the crossing take 15 minutes and saves you about 70 kilometres of driving.

Îles-de-la Madeleine

By Car

Of the seven inhabited islands of the Îles-de-la-Madeleine, six are linked together by Route 199.

The seventh island, Île d'Éntrée, is only accessible by boat, and is a trip in itself. The *S. P. Bonaventure (☎986-5705)* boat leaves the Cap-aux-Meules pier from Monday to Saturday, and the trip takes approximately one hour.

Car rentals are available for visitors who want to drive around the islands.

Cap-aux-Meules Honda: 199 Rue La Vernière, ☎418-986-4085. They also rent motorcycles.
Tilden: Airport, ☎418-969-2590

By Plane

Air Alliance *(☎418-969-2888 or 800-361-8620)* and **Inter-Canadian** *(☎800-665-1177)* both offer daily flights to the Îles-de-la-Madeleine. Most flights make stopovers in Cluébec, Mont-Joli or Gaspé, so count on a four-hour trip. Considerable price reductions can be found by booking well in advance.

By Ferry

The *M.V. Lucy Maud Montgomery* ferry *($33.75, car $65, motorcycle $22.50, bicycle $7.75; ☎418-986-6600 or 888-986-3278, ☎986-5101)* leaves from Souris (Prince Edward Island) and reaches Cap-aux-Meules in about five hours. Try to reserve in advance if possible; if not, arrive at the pier a few hours before departure, or to be extra sure, go to Souris the day before your departure and reserve seats. Ask for the ferry crossing schedule, as it changes from one season to the next.

The cargo and passenger vessel *CTMA Voyageur ($480 one-way in high season, includes meals; ☎418-986-6600)* leaves the port of Montréal every Sunday and sails down the St. Lawrence to the Îles-de-la-Madeleine;

the boat can take about 15 people, and the trip takes 48 hours.

By Bicycle

Bikes are, without a doubt, the best way to visit the islands. Here is bike rental outfit:

Le Pédalier: 365 Chemin Principal, Cap-aux-Meules, ☎418-986-2965.

Saguenay–Lac-Saint-Jean

By Car

From Québec City, take Route 138 E. to Saint-Siméon. Turn left on to Route 170, which passes through the village of Sagard on its way to the Parc du Saguenay. This road continues onto Chicoutimi.

Bus Stations

Chicoutimi: 55 Rue Racine E., ☎543-1403.
Jonquière: 2249 Rue Saint-Hubert, ☎547-2167.
Roberval: 336 Boulevard Marcot (Valentine restaurant), ☎275-1555.
Alma: 439 Rue du Sacré-Cœur (Coq-Rôti restaurant), ☎662-5441.

Train Stations

Hébertville: 15 Rue Saint-Louis, ☎343-3383.
Jonquière: 2439 Rue Saint-Dominique, ☎542-9676.
Chambord: 78 Rue de la Gare, ☎342-6873.

Manicouagan

By Car

From Beauport (near Québec), take Route 138 that runs along the north shore of the Saint Lawrence River to Natashquan, in Duplessis. At Baie-Sainte-Catherine, a ferry crosses the Rivière Saguenay to Tadoussac. To follow the Manicouagan tour, continue on Route 138: You can't go wrong – there's only one highway!

Bus Stations

Tadoussac: 443 Rue Bateau-Passeur, ☎235-4653.
Bergeronnes: 138 Route 138 (Station Irving): ☎232-6330.
Baie-Comeau: 212 Boulevard LaSalle, ☎296-6921.

By Ferry

Except for the Baie-Ste-Catherine–Tadoussac ferry, it is better to reserve a spot a few days in advance in the summer.

Tadoussac: The ferry ride from Baie Sainte-Catherine to Tadoussac (free, ☎235-4395) takes only 10 min. The schedule varies greatly from one season to the next, so make sure to double-check the times before planning a trip.

Baie-Comeau: The ferry ride from Baie-Comeau to Matane (adults $10, cars $27, motorcycles $10, ☎296-2593) takes 2 hours 30 min.

Godbout: The ferry ride from Godbout to Matane, in Gaspésie (adults $10, cars, $27, motorcycles $10; ☎568-7575) takes 2 hours 30 min.

Les Escoumins: There is a ferry from Trois-Pistoles to Les Escoumins ($10, car $25; ☎233-2202) that lasts one hour and 30 minutes.

Duplessis

By Car

Route 138 provides access to much of this region. In 1996, Route 138 was expanded to reach Natashquan. However, during the summer, only hydroplanes and weekly supply boats from Havre-Saint-Pierre link the inhabitants of the scattered villages farther east to the rest of Québec. In the winter, snow and ice provide a natural route for snowmobiles between villages.

By plane

Inter-Canadien (☎1-800-665-1177) serves Port-Menier on Ile d'Anticosti. There are usually three flights per week from Montréal, through Québec City.

In summer and during the Christmas season, **Air Satellite** *(☎589-8923 or 1-800-463-8512)* offers daily flights from Rimouski, Sept-Îles, Baie-Comeau, Havre-Saint-Pierre and Longue-Pointe-de-Mingan.

Confortair *(☎968-4660)* offers charter flights to Ile d'Anticosti.

In summer, **Air Schefferville** *(☎1-800-361-8620)* offers direct flights from Montreal to Schefferville.

Bus Stations

Sept-Îles: 126 Rue Monseigneur Blanche, ☎962-2126.
Havre-Saint-Pierre: 1130 Rue de l'Escale, ☎538-1666.
Natashquan: 183 Chemin d'En Haut (Auberge La Cache), ☎726-3347.

By Train

QNS&L: ☎962-9411. The train links Sept-Îles to Schefferville and runs once a week. The trip lasts from 10 to 12 hours and crosses the Canadian Shield to the outlying tundra.

By Boat

The **Nordik Express** cargo boat *(adults $40, cars according to their weight between $200 and $400; ☎723-8787 or 1-800-463-0680 from outside area code 418)* leaves from Sept-Îles and travels to Port-Menier, Havre-Saint-Pierre, Natashquan, Kegaska, La Romaine, Harrington Harbour, Tête-à-la-Baleine, La Tabatière, Saint-Augustin, Vieux-Fort and Blanc-Sablon. There is only one departure a week, so check the schedule before planning a trip.

 PRACTICAL INFORMATION

Area code: 418.

Tourist Information Offices

Bas-Saint-Laurent

Association Touristique du Bas-St-Laurent 189 Rue Hôtel-de-Ville, Rivière-du-Loup, G5R 5C4, ☎867-3015 or 1-800-563-5268, ≈867-3245, www.tourismebas-st-laurent.com.
Saint-Fabien: 33, Route 132 Ouest, G0L 2Z0, ☎869-3333.
Rimouski: 50 Rue St-Germain Ouest, G5L 4B5, ☎723-2322 or 1-800-746-6875.

Gaspésie

Association Touristique de la Gaspésie 357 Route de la Mer, Sainte-Flavie, G0J 2L0, ☎775-2223 or 1-800-463-0323, ≈775-2234, www.tourisme.gaspesie.qc.ca.
Sainte-Flavie: 357 Route de la Mer, G0J 2L0, ☎775-2223, ≈775-2234.
Matane: 968 Avenue du Phare O., G4W 3P5, ☎562-1065.
Gaspé: 27 Boulevard York E., ☎368-6335.
Percé: 142 Route 132 O., G0C 2L0, ☎782-5448.
Carleton: 629 Boulevard Perron, G0C 1J0, ☎364-3544.
Pointe-à-la-Croix: 1830 Rue Principale G0C 1L0, ☎788-5670.

Îles-de-la-Madeleine

Association Touristique des Îles de la Madeleine: 128 Chemin du Débarcadère, Cap-aux-Meules, ☎986-2245, ≈986-2327, www.ilesdelamadeleine.com; mailing address: C.P. 1028, Cap-aux-Meules, G0B 1B0.

Saguenay–Lac Saint-Jean

Association Touristique du Saguenay - Lac-Saint-Jean 198 Rue Racine E., Bureau 210, Chicoutimi, G7H 1R9, ☎543-9778 or 1-800-463-9651, ≈543-1805.
La Baie: 1171 7e Avenue, G7B 1S8, ☎697-5050, ≈697-5180.
Chicoutimi: see above.

QUÉBEC

Jonquière: 2665 Boulevard du Royaume, G7S 5B8, ☎548-4004, ♒548-7348.
Alma: 715 Rue Harvey O., G8B 7H2, ☎669-5030, ♒669-5043.
Saint-Félicien: 1209 Boulevard du Sacré-Cœur, C.P. 7, G8K 2R3, ☎679-9888.

Manicouagan

Association Touritique Régionale de Manicouagan: C.P. 2366, Baie-Comeau, G5C 2T1, ☎589-5319 or 1-888-463-5319, ♒589-9546.
Tadoussac: 197 Rue des Pionniers, GOT 2AO; ☎235-4744.
Baie-Comeau: 847 Rue de Puyjalon, G5C 1N3; ☎589-5319 or 888-463-5319.

Duplessis

Association Touristique Régionale de Duplessis: 312 Avenue Brochu, Sept-Îles, G4R 2W6, ☎962-0808, ♒962-6518, www.bbsi.net/atrd
Sept-Îles: 1401, Boulevard Laure Ouest, G4R 4K1, ☎962-1238, ♒968-0022.
Havre-Saint-Pierre: 1081 Rue de la Digue, GOG 1PO, ☎538-2717, ♒538-3439.
Natashquan: 33 Allée des Galets, ☎726-3756 (seasonal office).

 EXPLORING

Bas-Saint-Laurent

Kamouraska ★★

On January 31, 1839, the young Seigneur of Kamouraska, Achille Taché, was murdered by a former friend, Doctor Holmes. The Seigneur's wife had plotted with Holmes, her lover, to do away with her husband and flee to distant lands. The incident inspired Anne Hébert's novel *Kamouraska,* which was made into a film by prominent Québécois director Claude Jutra. The novel, and later the film, brought a level of fame to the village. Kamouraska, an Algonquin word meaning "bulrushes by the water" earned a place in the colourful history of rural Québec. For many years, the village was the easternmost trading post on the Côte-du-Sud. Kamouraska stands on several ranges of rocky hillocks that provide a striking contrast to the adjacent coastal plain. The unusual rocky terrain, a remnant of ancient mountains long worn down by glaciers, is typical of the area.

Rivière-du-Loup ★

Rivière-du-Loup is set on several ranges of rolling hills. It has become one of the most important towns in the Bas-Saint-Laurent region. Its strategic location made it a marine communication centre for the Atlantic, the St. Lawrence, Lac Témiscouata and the St. John River in New Brunswick. Later, it was an important railway centre, when the town was the eastern terminus of the Canadian train network. Rivière-du-Loup is the turn-off point for the road to New Brunswick and is linked by ferry to Saint-Siméon on the north shore of the river.

Manoir Fraser ★ *($3.50; late Jun to mid-Oct, every day 10am to 5pm; 32 Rue Fraser, ☎867-3906).* The Rivière du Loup seigneury was granted to a wealthy Québec merchant named Charles Aubert de la Chesnaye in 1673. It later passed through several owners, all of whom showed little interest in the remote region. The house, originally built in 1830 for Timothy Donahue, became the Fraser family residence in 1835. In 1888, it was modified to suit contemporary tastes by Québec architect Georges-Émile Tanguay. The house was renovated in June 1997 with the help of local residents, and it is now open to the public with guided tours as well as a multi-media presentation of an official dinner of the time.

Église Saint-Patrice ★ *(121 Rue Lafontaine)* was rebuilt in 1883 on the site of an earlier church erected in 1855. It houses several treasures, including a representation of the stations of the cross designed by Charles Huot, stained-glass windows created by the Castle company (1901) and statues by Louis Jobin. Rue de la Cour, in front of the church, leads to the **Palais de Justice** *(33 Rue de la Cour),* the courthouse constructed in 1882 by architect Pierre Gauvreau. A number of judges and lawyers built beautiful houses along the shady streets nearby.

The **Musée du Bas-Saint-Laurent ★** *($3.50; all year, every day, 1pm to 5pm, Wed to 9pm; 300 Rue Saint-Pierre, ☎862-7547)* displays objects characteristic of the region, and holds contemporary art exhibits (these are often more interesting). The building itself, made of concrete, is a work of modern Brutalist architecture.

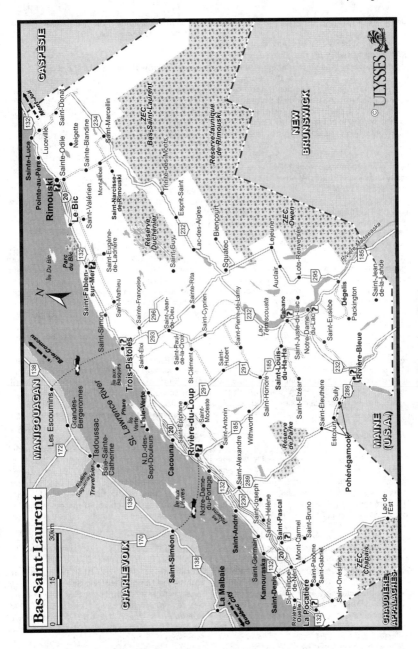

Bas-Saint-Laurent

GASPÉSIE

NEW BRUNSWICK

MAINE (U.S.A.)

CHARLEVOIX

CHAUDIÈRE-APPALACHES

MANICOUAGAN

St. Lawrence River

© ULYSSES

QUÉBEC

Isle-Verte ★

The village of Isle-Verte was once an important centre of activity in the Bas-Saint-Laurent region; several buildings remain from this period. For its part, life in the surrounding countryside follows a traditional pattern that keeps time with the continuing rhythm of the tides. Just off shore lies Île Verte, the island, named by the explorer Jacques Cartier, who, upon spotting the lush island, exclaimed, *"Quelle île verte!"*, literally "What a green island!". The only island in the Bas-Saint-Laurent inhabited year-round, Île Verte is more easily accessible than the other islands in the area (see below).

Though 12 kilometres long, only 40 people live on Île Verte. Its isolation and constant winds have discouraged many colonists over the years.

Visitors to the island have the opportunity to watch sturgeon and herring being salted in little smokehouses, test excellent local lamb, watch beluga and blue whales and photograph the waterfowl, black ducks and herons. The **Lighthouse ★★** *(free admission; Jun to Oct, every day 10am to 5pm; Route du Phare, ☎898-2757)*, or *phare*, located on the eastern tip of the island, is the oldest on the St. Lawrence (built in 1806). Five generations of the Lindsay family tended the lighthouse from 1827 to 1964. From the top of the tower, the view can seem almost endless.

Trois-Pistoles

According to legend, a French sailor passing through the region in the 17th century dropped his silver tumbler, worth three pistols, in the nearby river, giving the river its unusual name. The name was adopted by the small industrial town that sprung up next to the river.

When the colossal **Église Notre-Dame-des-Neiges ★★** *(mid-May to mid-Sep, every day 9am to 6pm; mid-Oct to mid-May, 1pm to 5pm; 30 Rue Notre-Dame Est, ☎851-4949)* was built in 1887, the citizens of Trois-Pistoles believed their church would soon be named the cathedral of the diocese. This explains the size and splendour of the building, topped by three silver steeples. The honour eventually fell to the Rimouski church, the masterpiece of architect David Ouellet, to the great dismay of the congregation of Notre-Dame-des-Neiges. An Ottawa canon by the name of Georges

Bouillon, designed the elaborate Roman Byzantine interior decor.

Saint-Fabien-sur-Mer and Le Bic ★★

The landscape in this area becomes rugged, giving visitors a test of the Gaspé region farther east. In Saint-Fabien-sur-Mer, a line of cottages is wedged between the beach and a 200-metre high cliff. An octagonally-shaped barn built around 1888, is located inland in the village of Saint-Fabien. This type of farm building, originated in the United States and, while interesting, proved relatively impractical and enjoyed limited popularity in Québec.

Rimouski ★

At the end of the 17th century, a French merchant named René Lepage, originally from Auxerre, France, undertook the monumental task of clearing the Rimouski *seigneury*. The land thus became the eastern-most area on the Gulf of St. Lawrence to be colonized under the French Regime. In 1919, the Abitibi-Price company opened a factory, turning the town into an important wood processing centre. Today, Rimouski is considered the administrative capital of eastern Québec, and prides itself on being on the cutting edge of the arts. Rimouski means "Land of the moose" in Micmac.

The **Canyon des Portes de l'Enfer** *($5; mid-May to mid-Oct, every day 10am to 5pm; Saint-Narcisse-de-Rimouski, 5.6 km along a dirt road, ☎750-1586)* is a fascinating natural spectacle, especially in winter. Literally, the "gates of hell", this canyon starts at the 18-metre Grand Saut falls, and stretches nearly five kilometres on either side of the Rivière Rimouski, with cliffs reaching as high as 90 metres in places. Guided boat tours are conducted in the canyon.

Pointe-au-Père

Musée de la Mer and the **Pointe-au-Père Lighthouse National Historic Site ★★** *($5.50; mid-Jun to end of Aug, every day 9am to 6pm; Sep to mid-Oct, every day 10am to 5pm; 1034 Rue du Phare Ouest, ☎724-6214)*, also known as the Lieu Nationale Historique du Phare-Pointe-au-Père. It was off the shores of Pointe-au-Père that the *Empress of Ireland* went down in 1914, claiming the lives of 1,012 people. The Musée de la Mer houses a fascinating collection of objects recovered from the wreck and provides a detailed account of the tragedy. The nearby lighthouse, which is open to the public, marks the exact spot where the river officially becomes the Gulf of St. Lawrence.

Gaspésie

Grand-Métis ★

Grand-Métis is blessed with a micro-climate which attracted wealthy summer visitors to the area in the past, and also made it possible for horticulturist Elsie Reford to plant a landscape garden here. The garden is now the town's main attraction. It contains a number of species of trees and flowers that cannot be found anywhere else at this latitude in North America. The word "Métis" is derived from the Malecite name for the area, "Mitis" meaning "little poplar".

The **Jardins de Métis ★★** *($6; early Jun to late Aug, every day 8:30am to 6:30pm; Sep and Oct, every day 8:30am to 5pm; 200 Route 132, ☎775-2221, ≈775-6201).* In 1927, Elsie Stephen Meighen Reford inherited an estate from her uncle, Lord Mount Stephen, who had made his fortune by investing in the Canadian Pacific transcontinental railroad. The following year, she began laying out a landscape garden which she maintained and expanded until her death in 1954. Seven years later, the government of Québec purchased the estate and opened it to the public. The garden is divided into eight distinct ornamental sections-the Floral Massif, the Rock Garden, the Rhododendron Garden, the Royal Walkway, the Primrose Garden, the Crab Apple Garden, *the Muret* (low wall) overlooking Baie de Mitis, and the Underbrush which contains a collection of indigenous plants. The mosquitoes are pretty voracious here, so don't forget your insect repellent.

The **Musée de la Villa Reford ★★** *(Jun to mid-Sep, every day 9:30am to 6:30pm; in the Jardins de Métis, ☎775-3165)*, a 37-room villa set in the midst of the Jardins de Métis, offers a glimpse of what life was like for turn-of-the-century Métissiens. Visitors can tour a number of rooms, the servants' quarters, the chapel, the general store, the school and the doctor's office. There is also a restaurant and gift shop.

Matane

The main attraction in Matane, whose name means "Beaver Pond" in Micmac, is the salmon and the famous local shrimp, cause for an annual festival. The town is the region's administrative centre and economic mainspring, due to its diversified industry based on fishing, lumber, cement-making, oil refining and shipping. During the Second World War, German submarines came all the way to the town pier.

Gaspé ★

It was here that Jacques Cartier claimed Canada for King Francis I of France in early July 1534. But it was not until the beginning of the 18th century that the first fishing post was established in Gaspé, and the town itself didn't develop until the end of that century. Throughout the 19th century, the lives of an entire population of poorly-educated, destitute French-Canadian and Acadian fishermen were regulated by the large fishing companies run by the merchants from the island of Jersey. During the Second World War, Gaspé prepared to become the Royal Navy's main base in the event of a German invasion of Great Britain, which explains why there are a few military installations around the bay. Today, Gaspé is the most important town on the peninsula, in addition to being the region's administrative centre. The city follows the waterfront in a narrow ribbon of development.

In 1977, upon the initiative of the local historical society, the **Musée de la Gaspésie ★★** *($3.50; late Jun to early Sep, every day 8:30am to 8:30pm; early Sep to mid-Oct, Mon to Fri 9am to 5pm, Sat and Sun noon to 5pm; mid-Oct to late Jun, Tue to Fri 9am to 5pm; 80 Boulevard Gaspé, ☎368-5710)* was erected on Pointe Jacques Cartier, overlooking Baie de Gaspé. A museum of history and popular tradition, it houses a permanent exhibit entitled *Un Peuple de la Mer* (A People of the Sea), tracing life in Gaspésie from the first native inhabitants, members of the Micmac tribe, all the way up to the present day. Temporary exhibits are also featured in the museum.

Cathédrale du Christ-Roi ★ *(20 Rue de la Cathédrale)*, the only wooden cathedral in North America, has a contemporary design characteristic of Californian "shed" architecture, that is foreign to the east coast of the

QUÉBEC

continent. Designed by Montréal architect Gérard Notebaert, it was erected in 1968 on the foundations of an earlier basilica, which was begun in 1932 to commemorate the 400th anniversary of Jacques Cartier's arrival in Canada, but was never completed due to a lack of funds. The interior is bathed in soft light from a lovely stained glass window by Claude Théberge, who made it with antique glass. Visitors will also find a fresco showing Jacques Cartier taking possession of Canada, which was received as a gift from France in 1934.

Percé ★★

A famous tourist destination, Percé lies in a beautiful setting, which has unfortunately been somewhat marred by the booming hotel industry. The majestic scenery features several naturel phenomena, the most important being the famous Rocher Percé, which is to Québec what the Sugar Loaf is to Brazil. Since the beginning of the 20th century, artists have been flocking to Percé every summer, charmed by the beautiful landscape and the local inhabitants.

Upon arriving in Percé, visitors are greeted by the arresting sight of the famous **Rocher Percé ★★★**, a wall of rock measuring 400 metres in length and 88 metres in height at its tallest point. Its name, which translates as pierced rock, comes from the two entirely natural arched openings at its base. Only one of these openings remains today, since the eastern part of the rock collapsed in the mid-19th century. At low tide, starting from Plage du Mont Joli, it is possible to walk around the rock and admire the majestic surroundings and the thousands of fossils trapped in the limestone *(inquire about the time of day and duration of the tides beforehand).*

At the Percé docks, there are a number of boats that take people out to **Parc de Île Bonaventure ★★**. During the high season, there are frequent departures from 8am to 5pm. Often, the crossing includes a short ride around the island and Rocher Percé, so that passengers can get a good look at the park's natural attractions. Most of these outfits let you spend as long as you want on the island and come back on any of their boats, which travel back and forth regularly between the island and the mainland.

The **Centre d'interprétation de Percé** *(free admission; early Jun to mid-Oct, every day 9am to 5pm)* shows a short film on the history of Île Bonaventure and the gannets that nest there. Visitors will also find an exhibition area, saltwater aquariums and two short footpaths. Finally, there is a shop run by the local birdwatching, which sells books and souvenirs.

Gannet

Paspébiac

This little industrial town used to be the headquarters of the Robin company, which specialized in processing and exporting cod. The business was founded in 1766 by Charles Robin, a merchant from the island of Jersey, and then expanded to several spots along the coast of Gaspésie and even along the Côte-Nord. In 1791, Robin added a shipyard to his facilities in Paspébiac, in order to build vessels to transport fish to Europe. Around 1840, the company began to face fierce competition from an enterprise owned by John LeBoutillier, one of Robin's former employees. Then the failure of the Bank of Jersey in 1886 had a severe impact on fishing enterprises in Gaspésie, which never regained their former power.

The **Site Historique du Banc-de-Paspébiac ★★** *($5; Jun to early Sep, every day 9am to 6pm; Route du Banc, ☎752-6229).* A *banc* is a strip of sand and gravel used for drying fish. Paspébiac's *banc,* along with the town's deep, well-protected natural port, lent itself to the development of a fishing industry. In 1964, there were still some 70 buildings from the Robin and LeBoutillier companies on the *banc.*

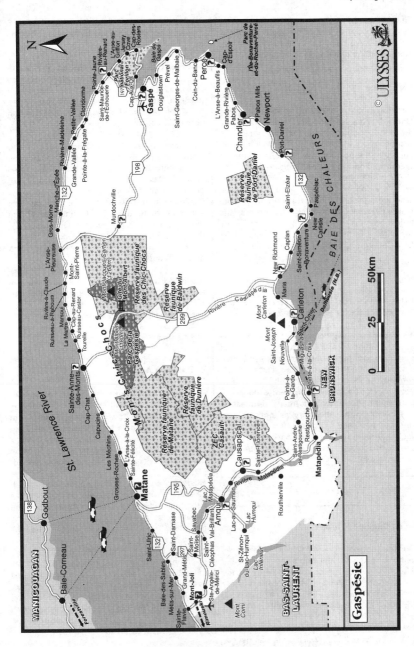

Gaspésie

QUÉBEC

That year, however, most of them were destroyed by a fire. The eight surviving buildings have been carefully restored in this historic site and are open to the public.

Carleton ★

Carleton is a stronghold of Acadian culture in Québec, and a seaside resort with a lovely sandy beach washed by calm waters, which are warmer than elsewhere in Gaspésie and account for the name of the bay (chaleur means warmth). The Mountains rising up behind the town give it a distinctive character. Carleton was founded in 1756 by Acadian refugees, who were joined by deportees returning from exile. Originally known as Tracadièche, the little town was renamed in the 19th century by the elite of British extraction, in honour of Sir Guy Carleton, Canada's third governor.

Miguasha

Palaeontology buffs will surely be interested in Parc de Miguasha ★★ (free admission; early Jun to late Sep, every day 9am to 6pm; 231 Miguasha O., Nouvelle, ☎794-2475), the second largest fossil site in the world. The park's palaeontology museum displays fossils discovered in the surrounding cliffs, which formed the bottom of a lagoon 370 million years ago. The information centre houses a permanent collection of many interesting specimens. In the laboratory visitors can learn the methods used to remove fossils from the rock and identify them. The park also has an amphitheatre, used for audiovisual presentations.

Îles-de-la-Madeleine

Île du Cap aux Meules

Our tour begins on Île du Cap aux Meules ★, since it is the archipelago's most populated island as well as the docking point for all the ferries (Cap-aux-Meules). Home to the region's major infrastructures, (hospital, high school, CÉGEP), this island is the centre of local economic activity. This activity does not take away from the island's charm, however, with the brightly painted houses that some say allow sailors to see their homes from the sea.

A climb to the top of the Butte du Vent ★★ reveals a superb panorama of the island and the gulf.

The beautiful Chemin de Gros-Cap ★★, south of Cap-aux-Meules, runs alongside the Baie de Plaisance and offers breathtaking scenery. If possible, stop at the Pêcherie Gros-Cap, where the employees can be seen at work in this fish processing plant.

For a long time, Étang-du-Nord was home to almost half the Îles-de-la-Madeleine population and it constituted the largest fishing village. With the foundation of Cap-aux-Meules (1959) and Fatima (1954), however, it lost a significant part of its population, and now only has a bit more than 3,000 inhabitants. The municipality, with its beautiful port, welcomes many visitors every year who come to take advantage of the region's tranquillity and natural beauty.

North of Étang-du-Nord, visitors can take in a splendid view by walking along the magnificent Falaises de la Belle Anse ★★. There is an impressive sight of the violent waves crashing relentlessly along the coast, from the top of this rocky escarpment.

Île du Havre Aubert

The beautiful Île du Havre Aubert ★★★, dotted with beaches, hills and forests, has managed to keep its picturesque charm. From early on it was home to various colonies. Even today, buildings testify to these early colonial years. Prior to this, it was populated by Micmac communities, and relics have been discovered.

Havre-Aubert, the first stop on the island, stretches along the sea, and benefits from a large bay, ideal for fishing. Apart from the magnificent scenery, the most interesting attraction is without a doubt the La Grave ★★★ area, which has developed along a pebbly beach and gets its charm from the traditional cedar-shingled houses. It is the heart of a lively area, and home to several cultural events. Boutiques and cafés line the streets, which are always enjoyable, even in bad weather. The few buildings along the sea were originally stores and warehouses that received the fish caught by locals.

Sandy Hook Dune ★★★ (see p 314)

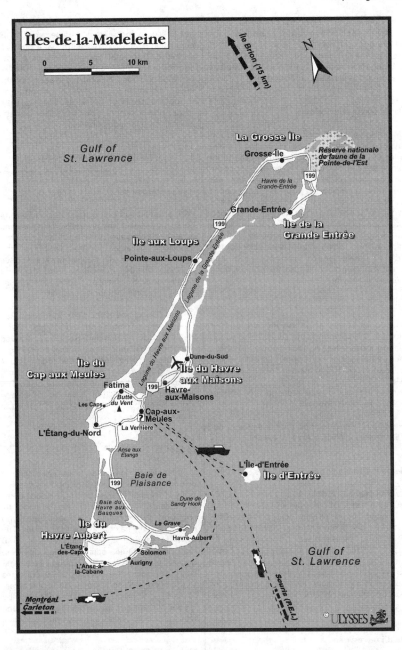

Îles-de-la-Madeleine

0   5   10 km

Île Brion (15 km)

N

Gulf of
St. Lawrence

La Grosse Île

Grosse-Île

Réserve nationale
de faune de la
Pointe-de-l'Est

Havre de la
Grande-Entrée

199

Grande-Entrée

199

Île de la
Grande Entrée

Île aux Loups

Pointe-aux-Loups

Dune-du-Sud

Île du
Cap aux Meules

Île du Havre
aux Maisons

Fatima

Butte
du Vent

199

Havre-
aux-Maisons

Les Caps

Cap-aux-
Meules

L'Étang-du-Nord

La Vernière

Anse aux
Étangs

L'Île-d'Entrée

Île d'Entrée

Baie de
Plaisance

199

Baie du
Havre aux
Basques

Dune de
Sandy Hook

Île du
Havre Aubert

La Grave

Havre-Aubert

L'Étang-
des-Caps

Solomon

L'Anse-à-
la-Cabane

Aurigny

Gulf of
St. Lawrence

Souris (P.É.I.)

Montréal
Carleton

© ULYSSES

QUÉBEC

The road that runs along the sea between the Pointe à Marichite and the Étang-des-Caps offers a magnificent view ★★ of the Gulf of St. Lawrence. From the small village of **L'Étang-des-Caps**, the small Île Corps Mort is visible in the distance on clear days.

Île du Havre aux Maisons

Île du Havre aux Maisons ★★ is characterized by its bare landscape and its small attractive villages with pretty little houses scattered along the winding roads. The steep cliffs at the southern end of the island overlook the gulf and offer a fascinating view of this immense stretch of water. The Dune du Nord and the Dune du Sud are two long strips of sand found at both extremities of the island, and are home to beautiful beaches. In the centre of the town also named **Havre-aux-Maisons** stands the Vieux Couvent (old convent) and the presbytery; the town is also the island's main centre of activity.

Grosse Île

The rcoky coasts of **Grosse Île** have caused numerous shipwrecks, the survivors of which have settled here. A good number of these accidental colonists were Scottish, and approximately 500 of them still live here today. Most earn their living from fishing and agriculture; some also work in the Seleine saltworks, which opened in 1983.

Highway 199 continues until the **Pointe-de-l'Est National Wildlife Area ★** (see below).

Île de la Grande Entrée

Île de la Grande Entrée ★, colonized in 1870, was the last of the Îles-de-la-Madeleine to be inhabited. Upon arriving, cross Pointe Old-Harry, to check out a striking view of the gulf. This tip of the island was named in honor of Harry Clark, who was the area's only inhabitant for many years. The island's main town, **Grande-Entrée,** has an active port that serves as a departure point for many brightly painted fishing boats, usually for lobster fishing.

Île d'Entrée ★★

Île d'Entrée stands out from the rest of the islands not only because of its geographic location (it is the only inhabited island that is not linked to the others), but because of its population (some 200 residents, all of Scottish descent). This small community lives almost entirely from the sea, and has managed to settle on this land despite the waves and the wind. The island has its own infrastructure to meets the needs of its residents (electricity, roads, and telephone). An incredible serenity prevails on this undulating islet.

Saguenay–Lac-Saint-Jean

Rivière-Éternité ★

With a poetic name that translates as Eternity River, how could anyone resist being carried away by the stunning beauty of the Saguenay, especially because Rivière-Éternité is the gateway to **Parc du Saguenay ★★★** (see p 314) and the marvelous **Parc Marin du Saguenay ★★★** (see p 314), where whales can be observed in their natural habitat.

On the first of the three cliffs that form Cap Trinité, is a statue of the Virgin Mary, christened **Notre-Dame-du-Saguenay**. Carved out of pine by Louis Jobin, it was placed here in 1881 in thanks for a favour granted to a travelling salesman, who was saved from certain death when he fell near the cape. The statue is tall enough (8.5 m) to be clearly visible from the deck of ships coming up the river.

La Baie ★

La Baie is an industrial town occupying a beautiful site at the far end of the Baie des Ha! Ha! Old French for *impasse* (means dead-end), the colourful term "Ha!Ha!" was supposedly employed by the region's first explorers, who headed into the bay thinking it was a river. The town of La Baie is the result of the 1976 merging of three adjacent municipalities, Bagotville, Port-Alfred and Grande-Baie. The latter was founded in 1838 by the Société des Vingt-et-Un, making it the oldest of the three. At La Baie, the Saguenay is still influenced by the salt-water tides, giving the town a maritime feel. La Baie also has a large **sea port,** which is open to the public.

Musée du Fjord ★ *($3.50; late Jun to early Sep, Mon to Fri 9am to 6pm, Sat and Sun 10am to 6pm; early Sep to late Jun, Mon to Fri*

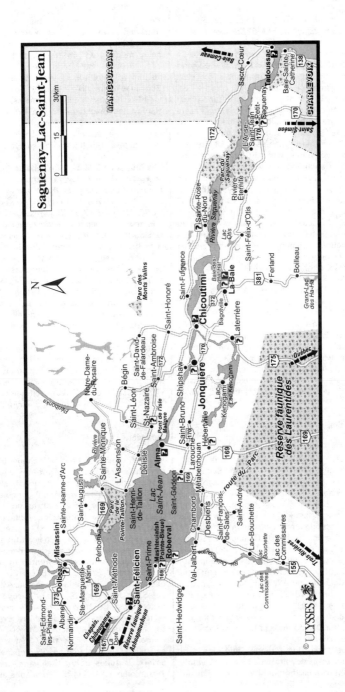

Saguenay–Lac-Saint-Jean

QUÉBEC

8:30am to noon and 1:30pm to 5pm; Sat and Sun 10am to 5pm; 3346 Boulevard de la Grande-Baie S., ☎697-5077, ☎697-5079). The Société des Vingt-et-Un was founded in La Malbaie (Charlevoix) in 1837 with the secret aim of finding new farmlands to ease overcrowding on the banks of the St. Lawrence. Under the pretext of cutting wood for the Hudson's Bay Company, the Société cleared the land around a number of coves along the Saguenay, and settled men, women and children there. On June 11, 1838, Thomas Simard's schooner, with the first settlers on board, set anchor in the Baie des Ha! Ha! The colonists disembarked and, under the supervision of Alexis Tremblay, built the region's very first wood cabin (4m x 6m), thus marking the birth of the present town of La Baie. The Musée du Fjord houses an interesting permanent exhibition, describing the settling of the Saguenay region from an ethnographic angle. Temporary art and science exhibits are also presented here each year.

At the **Palais Municipal** ★ *($27; late Jun to early Aug, Thu to Sat and some Sun at 8:30pm; 591 5e Rue, ☎544-0404 and 1-800-667-4582)*, visitors can see *La Fabuleuse Histoire d'un Royaume*, an elaborate historical pageant similar to those presented in some provincial French towns. Bringing this colourful extravaganza to life involves over 200 actors and 1,400 costumes, along with animals, carriages, lighting effects and sets.

Chicoutimi ★

In the language of the Montagnais, "Chicoutimi" means "there where it is deep", a reference to the waters of the Saguenay, which are navigable as far as this city, the most important urban area in the entire Saguenay-Lac-Saint-Jean region. For over 1,000 years, nomadic native tribes used this spot for meetings, festivities and the trading of goods. Starting in 1676, Chicoutimi became one of the most important fur-trading posts in New France. The post remained active up until the mid-19th century, when two industrialists, Peter McLeod and William Price, opened a sawmill nearby (1842). This finally enabled the development of a real town on the site, graced with the presence of three powerful rivers, the Moulin, the Chicoutimi and the Saguenay.

Religious and institutional buildings are predominant in downtown Chicoutimi, who's main commercial thoroughfare is Rue Racine.

Very little remained of the 19th century Victorian town after most of Chicoutimi was destroyed by a raging fire in 1912, the rest has been "modernized" or stripped of its character over the past 30 years. Along the streets, visitors will notice shop signs bearing typical Saguenay names, like Tremblay and Claveau, as well as English-sounding names, such as Harvey and Blackburn; this is indicative of a phenomenon found only in this part of the country, the assimilation of English-speaking families into French-speaking society.

The **Musée de Site de la Pulperie de Chicoutimi** ★★ *($8.50; mid-May to mid-Oct, every day 9am to 6pm; Jul until 8pm; mid-Oct to late nove, Mon to Fri noon to 4pm; 300 Rue Dubuc, ☎698-3100, ⬏698-3158).* This vast industrial complex, built alongside the turbulent Rivière Chicoutimi, included four pulp mills equipped with turbines and digesters, two hydroelectric stations, a smelter, a repair shop and a railway platform. The decline of pulp prices in 1921 and the crash of 1929 led to the closing of the pulp mill. It remained abandoned until 1980. In the meantime, most of the buildings were ravaged by fire, which, if nothing else, showed the strength of their thick stone walls.

Since 1996, the whole complex has become a gigantic museum covering an area of over one hectare. In addition to stopping in at the Maison-Musée du Peintre Arthur-Villeneuve, visitors can go on a 12-stop self-guided tour of the site and take in a thematic exhibition.

Jonquière

In 1847, the Société des Défricheurs (meaning land-clearers) du Saguenay received authorization to set up business alongside Rivière aux Sables. The name Jonquière was chosen in memory of one of the governors of New France, the Marquis de Jonquière. The town's early history is marked by the story of Marguerite Belley of La Malbaie, who escorted three of her sons to Jonquière on horseback to prevent them from being tempted to emigrate to the United States. In 1870, the territory between Jonquière and Saint-Félicien, in the Lac-Saint-Jean region, was destroyed by a major forest fire. It took over 40 years for the region to recover. Today, Jonquière is regarded as an essentially modern town, whose economic mainspring is the Alcan aluminum smelter. This multinational company owns several factories in the Saguenay–Lac-Saint-Jean region, replacing the Price sons and their wood empire as the largest local employer. The towns of Arvida and Kénogami merged with Jonquière in 1975, forming a city large enough to rival nearby Chicoutimi. Jonquière is known for its industrial tours.

The **Centrale Hydroélectrique de Shipshaw** ★★ *(free tour; Jun to Aug, Mon to Fri 1:30pm and 3pm; 1471 Route du Pont, ☎699-1547)*, which began operating in 1931, is a striking example of Art-Deco architecture. It supplies electricity to the local aluminum smelters.

Val-Jalbert

The **Village Historique de Val-Jalbert** ★★ *(\$8.50; mid-May to mid-Jun and early Sep to late Oct, every day 9am to 5pm; mid-Jun to early Sep 9am to 7pm; Route 169, ☎275-3132, ≈275-5875)* is a rich slice of North America's industrial heritage. Part of the village still looks like a ghost town, while the rest has been carefully restored to provide visitors with accommodations and an extremely informative interpretation centre. Various viewing areas, linked by a gondola *(adults \$3.25)*, have been built to enable visitors to fully appreciate the surroundings. There is a campground beside the village, and accommodations are available in some of the restored houses.

Saint-Félicien

At the **Jardin Zoologique de Saint-Félicien** ★★ *(\$17; late May to late Sep, every day 9am to 5pm; Jul until 7pm; Jan and Feb, Sun 9am to 5pm; Mar, Sat and Sun 9am to 5pm; last tour departs at 3:30pm; 2230 Boulevard du Jardin, ☎679-0543 or 1-800-667-5687, ≈679-3647)*, visitors can observe various species of Québec's indigenous wildlife in their natural habitat. What makes this zoo unusual is that the animals are not in cages, but roam about freely, while visitors tour the zoo in small, screened buses. A lumber camp, a fur-trading post, a Montagnais encampment, and a settler's farm have all been reconstructed, and along with the authentic buildings onsite, add a historical feel to this untraditional zoo.

Péribonka ★

Louis Hémon was born in Brest (France) in 1880. After attending the Lycée Louis-LeGrand in Paris, he obtained his law degree from the Sorbonne. In 1903, he settled in London, where he started his career as a writer. His adventurous spirit eventually led him to Canada. He lived in Québec City, then in Montréal, where he met some investors who wanted to build a railroad in the northern part of the Lac-Saint-Jean region. He headed off to scout out a location, but became fascinated instead by the local inhabitants' daily life. In June 1912, he met Samuel Bédard, who invited him to his home in Péribonka. Hémon helped out on the farm, secretly recording his impressions of the trip in a notebook, these impressions later formed the basis of his masterpiece, the novel *Maria Chapdelaine*. Hémon did not, however, have time to enjoy his novel's tremendous success; on July 8, 1913, he was hit by a train while walking on the railroad tracks near Chapleau, Ontario, and died a few minutes later in the arms of his travelling companions.

Musée Louis-Hémon ★★ *(\$4.50; Jun to Sep, every day 9am to 5:30pm; Sep to Jun, Mon to Sat 9am to 4pm, Sun 1pm and 5pm; 700 Route 169, ☎374-2177, ≈374-2516)* is located in the house where Louis Hémon spent the summer of 1912 with Samuel Bédard and his wife Eva (née Bouchard). It is still visible alongside Route 169 and is one of a few rare examples of colonial homes in the Lac-Saint-Jean region to have survived the improvements in the local standard of living. The extremely modest house that inspired Hémon was built in 1903. As it was converted into a museum in 1938, its furnishings have remained intact, and are still laid out in their original positions in the humble rooms. A large postmodern building was erected nearby in order to house Hémon's personal belongings, as well as various souvenirs of the villagers who inspired his work, and memorabilia relating to the success of *Maria Chapdelaine*.

Alma

This industrial town lies along the edge of the Lac-Saint-Jean region. It is home to a large aluminum smelter and a paper mill, all surrounded by working- and middle-class neighbourhoods. Parc Falaise serves as a reminder that Alma has been the twin town of the town of Falaise in Normandy since 1969.

Tour guides at the **Aluminerie Alcan** ★ *(Mon to Fri before noon, with reservation; 1025 Rue des Pins Ouest, ☎668-9472)* lead visitors through the factory and explain the different steps

QUÉBEC

involved in the making of aluminum. Visitors sometimes have the opportunity to watch the aluminum being casted. The tour lasts about an hour, and participants should wear long pants, a long-sleeved shirt or sweater and flat shoes that cover the entire foot.

Tours of the facilities of the **Papeterie Alma** ★ *(with reservation; 1100 Rue Melançon, ☎668-9400, ext. 9348)* are also offered. The tour includes a visit to the pulp department and the machine room and an explanation of the manufacturing process.

Manicouagan

Tadoussac ★★

In 1600, eight years before Québec City was founded, Tadoussac was established as a trading post; it was chosen for its strategic location at the mouth of the Saguenay river. Tadoussac was the first permanent white settlement north of Mexico. In 1615, the Récollet religions order established a mission that operated until the mid-19th century. The town's tourism trade received a boost in 1864 when the original Tadoussac Hotel was built to better accommodate the growing number of visitors coming to the area to enjoy the sea air and breathtaking landscape. Although the town is old (by North American standards), it has a look of impermanence, as if a strong wind could sweep the entire town away.

Dominating the town, the **Hôtel Tadoussac** ★ *(165 Rue du Bord-de-l'Eau, ☎418-235-4421)* is to this community what the Château Frontenac is to Québec City: its symbol and landmark. The current hotel was built between 1942 and 1949 by the Canada Steamship Lines, following the destruction of the first hotel. Reminiscent of the resort hotels built in New England during the second half of the 19th century, Hôtel Tadoussac is long and low and its weathered wood siding exterior contrasts sharply with the bright red roof. The polished wood panelling and antique furniture that characterize the interior decor reflect traditional rural French-Canadian tastes.

The **Centre d'Interprétation des Mammifères Marins** ★ *($4.75; mid-May to late Oct, every day noon to 5pm, late Jun to late Sep, every day 9am to 8pm; 108 Rue de la Cale-Sèche, ☎235-4701)* is an information centre that was created to provide an understanding of the whales that migrate to the region every summer. The centre features skeletons of various sea mammals, video presentations, and an aquarium with specimens of fish species that live in the St. Lawrence; naturalists are on hand to answer questions.

The **Centre d'interprétation et d'observation de Cap-de-Bon-Désir** ★ *($4; mid-Jun to mid-Sep, every day 8am to 8pm; 166 Route 138, ☎232-6751)* is an information and observation centre located around the Cap Bon-Désir lighthouse (still in operation). It has an interesting exhibit on whales as well as a whale observation point.

Baie-Comeau

In 1936, when Colonel Robert McCormick, publisher and senior editor of *The Chicago Tribune,* no longer wanted to be dependant upon foreign paper-making companies, he chose to build his own paper factory in Baie-Comeau, sparking the transformation of a quiet village into a bustling mill. Over the years, other large companies were attracted to Baie-Comeau by the abundance and low cost of local hydro-electric power. The young town is named after Napoléon Comeau (1845-1923), famed trapper, geologist and naturalist of the Côte-Nord.

The **Centrales Manic 2 et Manic 5 (Barrage Daniel Johnson)** ★★★ *(free admission; mid-Jun to Labour Day, every day: Manic 2, 9am, 11am, 1pm and 3pm; Manic 5, 9am, 11am, 1:30pm and 3:30pm; 135 Boulevard Comeau, ☎294-3923),* the generating stations and dam, are located on the Rivière Manicouagan. A 30-minute drive through the beautiful Canadian Shield landscape leads to the first dam of the complex Manic 2, the largest hollow-joint gravity dam in the world. A guided tour of the dam brings visitors inside the imposing structure. A three-hour drive farther north leads to the more impressive Manic 5 and the Daniel-Johnson dam. Built in 1968, the dam is named after a Québec Premier who died on the morning the dam was declared officially completed. With a 214-metre central arch and measuring 1,314 metre in length, it is the largest multiple-arch structure in the world. The dam regulates the water supply to the generating stations of the Manic-Outardes complex. Visitors can walk to the foot of the dam as well as to the top, where there is a magnificent view of the Vallée de la Manicouagan and the reservoir, which measures 2000 square kilometres.

Barrage Daniel-Johnson

Duplessis

Sept-Îles

This town extending along the vast Baie de Sept-Îles (45 km²) is the administrative centre of the Côte Nord. A fur-trading post under the French Régime, Sept-Îles experienced an industrial boom in the early 20th century sparked by the development of the forestry industry. By about 1950, Sept-Îles had become an important relay point in the transport of iron and coal, resources extracted from the Schefferville and Fermont mines and sent to Sept-Îles by railroad. The town's deep-water port is ice-free during the winter and ranks second in Canada after Montréal in terms of tonnage handled annually. Sept-Îles is named after the archipelago of seven islands in the entrance to the bay. The town is a good starting point for exploring the northern regions of Labrador and Nouveau-Québec.

The **Vieux-Poste** ★ *($3.25; late Jun to late Aug, every day 9am to 5pm; Boulevard des Montagnais, ☎968-2070)* is a reconstruction of the important Sept-Îles fur-trading post established during the French Régime. Based on archeological excavations and documents from the period, the compound appears as it would have in the mid-18th century, complete with chapel, stores, houses and protective wooden fence. Montagnais culture is explored through exhibits and according to season, various outdoor activities.

The **Musée Régional de la Côte-Nord** ★ *($3.25; late Jun to Labour Day, every day 9am to 5pm; rest of the year, Mon to Fri 9am to noon, 1pm to 5pm, Sat and Sun 1pm to 5pm; 500 Boulevard Laure, ☎968-2070)*, displays some 40,000 objects of anthropological and artistic importance found during the many archeological digs carried out along the Côte-Nord, as well as stuffed wildlife, aboriginal objects and contemporary artistic works (paintings, sculptures and photographs) from various regions of Québec.

Mingan

Montagnais and whites live together in this village located on the mainland opposite the Îles de Mingan. The name Mingan, of Celtic origin *(Maen Cam)*, means "curved stone", and refers to rock formations on the islands. The formations made an impression on early visitors from Brittany, reminding them of ancient stones and dolmens. Mingan is also a major salmon-fishing location.

Havre-Saint-Pierre ★

This small picturesque town was founded in 1857 by fishermen from the Îles-de-la Madeleine. In 1948, following the discovery of large titanium deposits 43 kilometres inland, the town's economy was transformed overnight by the QIT-Feret-Titarle company. It became an active industrial centre and port. Since the opening of the Mingan Archipelago National Park Reserve in 1983, Havre-Saint-Pierre has also developed a significant tourism

QUÉBEC

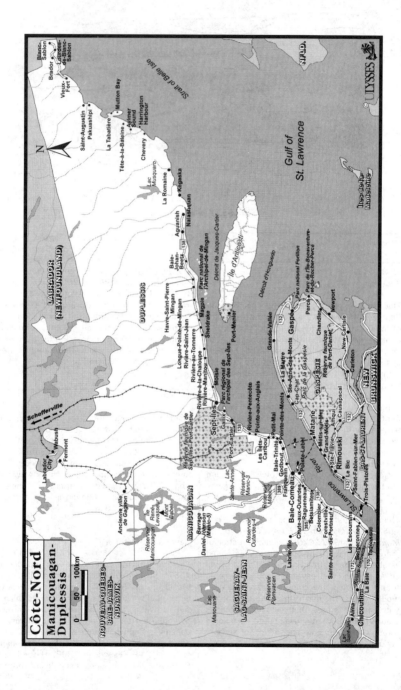

industry. The town is an excellent starting point for visitors who want to explore the Îles de Mingan and the large Île d'Anticosti.

The **Centre Culturel et d'interprétation de Havre-St-Pierre ★** *(free admission; mid-Jun to early Sep, every day 10am to 10pm; 957 Rue de la Berge, ☎538-2512)* is an information centre in the Clark family's former general store, which has been skilfully restored. Local history is recounted with an exhibit and slide show.

Centre d'Accueil et d'interprétation, Réserve du Parc National de l'Archipel-de-Mingan *(mid-Jun to early Sep, every day 1pm to 5pm and 6pm to 9pm; 975 Rue de l'Escale , ☎538-3285)* is the information centre for the Mingan Archipelago park. Here visitors will find a photo exhibit as well as all the information they will need concerning the flora, fauna and geology of the Mingan islands.

Île d'Anticosti ★★

The presence of natives on Île d'Anticosti goes back many years. The Montagnais made sporadic visits to the island, but the harsh climate discouraged permanent settlement. In 1542, Basque fishermen named the island "Anti Costa", which roughly translates as "anti-coast", or "after travelling all this way across the Atlantic, we still haven't reached the mainland!" In 1679, Louis Jolliet was given the island by the King of France for leading important expeditions into the middle of the North American continent. Jolliet's efforts to settle Anticosti were limited by the island's isolation, poor soil and high winds. To make matters much worse, British troops returning from a failed bid to take Québec City in 1690 were shipwrecked on the island and slaughtered most of the settlers living there. Anticosti is feared by sailors, thanks to the more than 400 ships that have run aground here since the 17th century.

In 1895, Île d'Anticosti became the exclusive property of Henri Menier, a French chocolate tycoon. The "Cocoa Baron" introduced white-tailed deer and foxes to the island to create a personal hunting preserve. In addition, he established the villages of Baie-Sainte-Claire (later abandoned) and Port-Menier, now the only settlement on the island. Menier governed the island like an absolute monarch reigning over his subjects. He established forestry operations on the island and commissioned a

cod-fishing fleet. In 1926, his heirs sold Anticosti to a consortium of Canadian forestry companies named Wayagamack, which continued operations until 1974, when the island was sold to the Québec government and became a wildlife reserve. Not until 1983 were residents given the right to purchase land and houses on the island. Anticosti, still unexplored in parts, holds many surprises, such as the **Grotte à la Patate** (cave), discovered in 1982.

Port-Menier, where the ferry from Havre-Saint-Pierre docks, is the only inhabited village on the island, with a populations of 340. Most village houses were built during the Menier era, giving the village a certain architectural sameness. Foundations of the **Château Menier** (1899), an elaborate wooden villa, built in the American shingle-style tradition can be seen from Route de Baie-Sainte-Claire. Because the villagers could not adequately maintain the spectacular estate, they set fire to it in 1954, reducing an irreplaceable historical building to ashes. In **Baie-Sainte-Claire,** visitors can see the remains of a lime kiln built in 1897, the only vestige of the short-lived village that once stood on this site.

Baie-Johan-Beetz

Originally known as "Piastrebaie", due to its location at the mouth of the Rivière Piashti, this village was renamed after the learned Belgian naturalist Johan Beetz in 1918. Piastrebaie was founded around 1860 by Joseph Tanguay, who, along with his wife, Marguerite Murdock, earned a living here fishing salmon. Over the following years, a number of immigrants from the Îles-de-la-Madeleine arrived. These included the Bourque, Loyseau, Desjardins and Devost families, whose descendants still live mainly on hunting and fishing.

Maison Johan-Beetz ★ *(early May to mid-Oct every day, reservations required; ☎539-0137).* Johan Beetz was born in 1874 at the Oudenhouven castle in Brabant, Belgium. Grief-stricken over the death of his fiancée, he wanted to take off for the Congo, but a friend convinced him to emigrate to Canada instead. A hunting and fishing fanatic, he visited the Côte-Nord, and soon set up residence. In 1898, he married a Canadian and built this charming Second-Empire-style house, which can be visited by appointment. Beetz painted lovely still-lifes on the doors inside. In 1903, he became something of a pioneer in the fur industry when he started breeding animals for their pelts, which he sold to the Maison Revillon in Paris. Johan Beetz contributed greatly his neighbours' quality of life. Thanks to his university studies, during which he had learned the rudiments of medicine, he became the man of science in whom the villagers placed their trust. Equipped with books and makeshift instruments, he treated as best he could, the ills of the inhabitants of the Côte-Nord. He even managed to save the village from Spanish influenza with a skilfully monitored quarantine. If you ask the elderly people here to tell you about Monsieur Beetz, you'll hear nothing but praise.

Natashquan ★

This small fishing village, with its wooden houses buffeted by the wind, is where the famous poet and songwriter Gilles Vigneault was born in 1928. Many of his songs describe the people and scenery of the Côte-Nord. He periodically returns to Natashquan for inspiration, where he still owns a house. In the Montagnais language, Natashquan means "place where bears are hunted". The neighbouring village of Pointe-Parent is inhabited by Montagnais.

Blanc-Sablon

This isolated region was visited as early as the 16th century by Basque and Portuguese fishermen. They established camps where they melted seal blubber and salted cod before shipping it to Europe. It has been suggested that Vikings, who are known to have established a settlement on the nearby island of Newfoundland, might have set up a village near Blanc-Sablon around the year 1000. However, archeological digs have only just begun. Brador, a fishing camp used by Frenchmen from Courtemanche, has recently been reconstructed.

Blanc-Sablon is only 1.5 kilometres from Labrador, a large, mostly arctic territory. Much of Labrador was once part of the province of Québec; it is now the mainland half of the province of Newfoundland. It is accessible by road from Blanc-Sablon. The former British colony of Newfoundland did not become a part of Canada until 1949. A ferry links Blanc-Sablon and the island of Newfoundland.

 # OUTDOORS

 ## Parks

Bas-Saint-Laurent

Parc du Bic ★★ *(free admission; closed to cars in winter; for a schedule of summer activities, contact reception, ☎869-3502)* is an area of 33 square kilometres featuring a jumble of coves, jutting shoreline, promontories, hills, escarpments and marshes, as well as deep bays rich in a tremendously wide variety of plant and animal life. The park is a good place for hiking, cross-country skiing and mountain biking, and also has an information centre.

Gaspésie

Parc de la Gaspésie ★★★ *(free admission; year-round, every day 8am to 8pm; 124 1re Avenue O., ☎763-3301)* covers an area of 800 square kilometres, and encompasses the famous Monts Chic-Chocs. It was established in 1937, in an effort to heighten public awareness regarding nature conservation in Gaspésie. The park is composed of conservation zones, devoted to the protection of the region's natural riches, and an ambient zone, made up of a network of roads, trails and lodgings. The park's trails run through three levels of terrain, leading all the way to the summits of the four highest mountains in the area, Mont Jacques-Cartier, Mont Richardson, Mont Albert and Mont Xalibu. This is the only place in Québec where white-tailed deer (in the rich vegetation of the first level), moose (in the Boreal forest) and caribou (in the tundra, at the top of the mountains) co-exist. Hikers are required to register before setting out.

The motto of **Forillon National Park ★★★** *($2.50 per person, $6 family; early Jun to mid-Oct, every day 9am to 4pm; 122 Boulevard Gaspé; ☎368-5505)* is "harmony between man, land and sea". Many an outdoor enthusiast daydreams about this series of forests, mountains and cliff-lined shores all crisscrossed by hiking trails. Home to a fairly wide range of animals, this national park abounds in foxes, bears, moose, porcupines and other mammals. Over 200 species of birds live here, including herring gulls, cormorants, finches, larks and

White-tailed deer

QUÉBEC

gannets. Depending on the season, visitors might catch a glimpse of whales or seals from the paths along the coast. A variety of rare plants also lie hidden away in Forillon National Park, contributing to a greater understanding of the soil in which they grow. Visitors will find not only natural surroundings here in the park, but also traces of human activity. This vast area (245 square kilometres) once included four little villages. The 200 families inhabiting them were relocated – not without a fight – when the park was established in 1970. The buildings of the greatest ethnological interest were kept and restored, namely the ten or so **Maisons de Grande-Grave**, the **Phare de Cap-Gaspé** (the lighthouse), the **former Protestant Church of Petit-Gaspé** and the **Fort Péninsule**, part of the fortifications erected during the Second World War to protect Canada from attacks by German submarines.

At **Parc de l'Île Bonaventure** ★★ *(transportation fee, but free admission to the island itself; early Jun to late Aug, every day 8:30am to 5pm; early Sep to mid-Oct, every day 9am to 4pm; 4 Rue du Quai, ☎782-2240, ⇌782-2241)*, visitors will find large bird colonies, as well as numerous footpaths lined with rustic houses. The trails range from 2.8 to 4.9 kilometres in length, and cover a total of 15 kilometres. Due to the aridity of the surroundings, there are no stinging insects on the island. There is also no water along the trails,

so be sure to bring a canteen. All trails end at an impressive bird sanctuary, where some 200,000 birds, including about 55,000 gannets, form a wildlife exhibition.

Îles-de-la-Madeleine

The eastern tip of Grosse Île, made up of dunes and beaches, is home to the rich bird life typical of these islands. It is one of the best sites for spotting various species, such as the rare piping plover (which only nests on the islands) the northern pintail, the betted kingfisher, the atlantic puffin and the horned lark, but take care not to damage the nesting sites (generally clearly marked). This entire zone is protected by the **Pointe-de-l'Est National Wildlife Area** ★, also known as the Réserve Nationale de Faune de la Pointe-de-l'Est.

One of the most beautiful beaches of the islands, the **Plage de la Grande Échouerie** ★★, stretches for about 10 kilometres in the Pointe-de-l'Est wildlife area.

The **Plage de l'Hôpital**, located along the Dune du Nord on Île du Cap aux Meules, is a good place to go for a dip and watch the seals. You'll also find the wreckage of a ship here. It should be noted that the currents become dangerous toward Pointe-aux-Loups. The Anse the l'Hôpital, Cap de l'Hôpital, Plage de l'Hôpital and Étang-de-l'Hôpital are all named after a boat that came into the cove (*anse*) carrying passengers suffering from a contagious illness (typhus). The boat was put into quarantine, and only doctors and nurses were allowed on board.

Like a long strip of sand stretching into the gulf on Île du Havre Aubert, **Sandy Hook Dune** ★★★ is several kilometres long and its beach is among the nicest on the islands. This spot is a favourite with nudists, who come to swim in complete tranquillity.

The **Plage de l'Ouest** ★ stretches from the northwest part of Île du Havre Aubert to the southwest part of Île du Cap aux Meules. Perfect for swimming and shell collecting, it is renowned for its magnificent sunsets.

The **plage de la Dune du Sud** ★ on Île du Havre aux Maisons offers several kilometres of beach, great for swimming.

Saguenay–Lac-Saint-Jean

The **Parc du Saguenay** ★★★ *(accessible from Route 170, ☎272-2267)* extends across a portion of the shores of the Rivière Saguenay. It stretches from the banks of the estuary (located in the Manicouagan tourist region) to Sainte-Rose-du-Nord. In this area, steep cliffs plunge into the river, creating a magnificent landscape. The park has about one-hundred kilometres of hiking trails, providing visitors with an excellent opportunity to explore this fascinating region up close. A few of the more noteworthy trails include a short, relatively easy one along the banks of the Saguenay (1.7 kilometres); the Sentier de la Statue, which stretches 3.5 kilometres and includes a difficult uphill climb, and the superb, 25-kilometre Sentier des Caps, which takes three days (registration required). During winter, the trails are used for cross-country skiing. Accommodation in the form of campsites and shelters is available.

Manicouagan

The **Parc Marin du Saguenay** ★★★ *(182 Rue de l'Eglise, Tadoussac, ☎235-4703 or 1-800-463-6769)* features the Fjord du Saguenay, the southern-most fjord in the world, and was created to protect the area's exceptional aquatic wildlife. The fjord was carved out by glaciers; it is 276 metres deep near Cap Éternité, and just 10 metres deep at the mouth. The distinctive geography in the fjord, created by glacial deposits, includes a basin where fauna and flora, indigenous to the Arctic, can be found. The top 20 metres of water in the Saguenay is fresh and its temperature varies between 15°C and 18°C, whereas the deeper water is saline and maintains a temperature of approximately 1.5°C. This environment, a remainder of the ancient Goldthwait sea, supports wildlife such as the arctic shark and the beluga, creatures otherwise seen farther north. A number of whale species frequent the region to feed on the marine organisms that proliferate here due to the constant oxygenation in the water. One of these, the blue, reaches lengths of 30 metres and is the largest mammal in the world. Seals and occasionally dolphins can be seen in the park as well. From early on, European fishermen took advantage of the abundance of marine life, with the result that some species were overhunted. Today, visitors can venture out on the river to observe the whales at close range. However, strict rules have been set to protect the animals from being mistreated, and boats must maintain a certain distance.

Duplessis

The **Parc Régional de l'Archipel des Sept-Îles** ★★ is made up of several islands: Petite Boule, Grande Boule, Dequen, Manowin, Corossol, Grande Basque and Petite Basque. There is also an abundance of cod in the area, making fishing a popular activity. Trails and camp sites have been set up on Île Grande Basque. For cruises around the archipelago, see p 316.

A series of islands and islets stretching over a 95-kilometre long area, the **Mingan Archipelago National Park Reserve** ★★ *(Havre-St-Pierre, ☎538-3331)* is also called the Réserve de Parc National de l'Archipel-de-Mingan. It boasts incredible natural riches. The islands are characterized by distinctive rock formations, made up of very soft stratified limestone that has been sculpted by the waves. The formations are composed of marine sediment that was swept into the area some 250 million years ago from equatorial regions before being washed up on land and covered by a mantle of ice, several kilometres thick. As the ice melted some 7000 years ago, the islands re-emerged with their impressive stone monoliths. In addition to this fascinating element, the marine environment encouraged the development of varied and unusual plant life. Approximately 200 species of birds nest here, including the Atlantic puffin, the gannet, and the Arctic tern. The river is also home to several whale species, including the blue whale. There are two visitor information centres, one in Longue-Pointe-de-Mingan (*124 Rue du Bord-de-la-mer, GOG 1VO, ☎949-2126*) and the other in Havre-Saint-Pierre (*975 Rue de l'Escale, GOG 1PO, ☎538-3285*). Both are open only the summer. There are camp sites on the island. Some of the islands have hiking trails.

In addition to natural attractions, the park also contains the vestiges of a very old native settlement, dating back over 4,000 years. Montagnais from the village of Mingan were the first to visit this spot regularly, to hunt for whales and gather berries.

Measuring 222 kilometres in length and 56 kilometres in width, the **Réserve Faunique de l'île d'Anticosti** ★★ is big enough to accommodate a number of activities including hunting, walking, swimming and fishing. The island has belonged to the Québec government since 1974, but was not open to hikers until 1986. The reserve is very popular among hunters, and is known for its white-tailed deer. Contributing to the magnificent scenery are breathtaking panoramas, long beaches, waterfalls, caves, cliffs, and rivers.

The **Chute and Canyon de la Vauréal** ★★ are two of the major natural sites on Île Anticosti. The waterfall (*chute*) flows into the canyon from a height of 70 metres, offering a truly breathtaking spectacle. You can take a short (*1 hour*) hike along the river, inside the canyon, to the base of the falls. This will give you a chance to see some magnificent grey limestone cliffs streaked with red and green shale. If you continue 10 kilometres on the main road, you'll come to the turn-off for **Baie de la Tour** ★★, which lies another 14 kilometres away. There, you'll find a long beach with majestic limestone cliffs rising up behind it.

 Cruises and Whale-watching

Bas-Saint-Laurent

The **Excursions du Littoral** (*$30; Jun to Oct, every day 9am and 1pm; 518 Route du Fleuve, Notre-Dame-du-Portage, ☎862-1366*) offer visitors a chance to observe grey seals and migratory birds near the Îles Pélerins during a three-hour cruise.

The **Duvetnor** (*$10-$40; mid-May to mid-Sep, every day; 200 Rue Hayward, Rivière-du-Loup, ☎867-1660*) company offers a variety of cruises. You can visit the Îles du Bas-Saint-Laurent and see black guillemots, eider ducks and razorbills. The cruises start at the Rivière-du-Loup marina and last anywhere from an hour and a half to eight hours, depending on your destination. You can even stay overnight in a lighthouse on one of the islands (see p 317).

The **Croisières Navimex** (*$35; Jul to Oct, departures at 9am, 1pm and 5pm, Exit 507 off the 20, 200 Rue Hayward, Rivière-du-Loup, ☎867-3361*) take passengers on whale-watching cruises aboard the *Cavalier des Mers*. You'll get to see belugas, lesser rorquals and maybe even a blue whale. Make sure to bring some warm clothing. The cruises last about three and a half hours.

The **Excursions dans les Îles du Bic** (*$25; Jun to Sep; Parc du Bic marina, ☎736-5739*) enable visitors to explore the islets, cliffs and reefs of the Bic. During this two-hour cruise, you'll see lots of birds, as well as grey and common seals.

Écomertours Nord-Sud (*606 des Ardennes, Rimouski, G5L 3M3, ☎724-6227, 724-2527 or 1-888-724-8687*) offer a variety of packages that showcase the river and the islands dotting it as far as the Gulf of St. Lawrence and the Basse-Côte-Nord. The boat used for these cruises, which range in length from two to eight days, is called the *Écho des Mers* (Echo of the Seas). It can carry up to 49 passengers and about 15 crew members and has comfortable cabins.

Gaspésie

Croisières Découverte (*$16; mid-Jun to mid-Sep; at the Cap-des-Rosiers harbour, Forillon National Park, ☎892-5629*) takes passengers out on the *Félix-Leclerc* to see a seal colony and the birds that nest in the cliffs. A guide is present on all cruises, which last nearly two hours. If you're lucky, you might get to see some whales. Make sure to dress warmly, as the wind is often very cold. The departure schedule varies greatly depending on the date, so call beforehand.

QUÉBEC

Observation Littoral Percé *($30; mid-May to mid-Oct; near the Hôtel Normandie; Route 132, Percé,* ☎782-5359*)* hosts whale-watching excursions. With a little luck, you might also meet up with a school of white dolphins. Don't expect to see whale tails like those in photographs; usually, only the whale's back is visible, and often the animal is far away. The companies that organize these excursions must adhere to strict laws and have to pay large fines if they don't keep their distance. The outings start early in the morning and last two to three hours. Make sure to bundle up and wear a good windbreaker.

Iles-de-la-Madeleine

A boat ride on the *Le Ponton III* of the **Excursions de la Lagune** *($20; daily departures in the summer at 11am, 2pm, and 6pm; Île du Havre aux Maisons,* ☎969-4550 or 969-2088*)*, is an exciting two-hour trip on the waves, during which visitors can observe the sea floot and occasionally some shellfish through the boat's glass bottom.

La Gaspésienne 26 ($40; Mon-Sat during the tourist season; La Grave marina, Ile du Havre Aubert, ☎937-2213*)*, a schooner, is one of a handful of the 50 *Gaspésiennes* to have been restored. A veritable floating work of art, this schooner will carry you off to contemplate the sea in absolute silence. There are two cruises per day, each four hours long.

Saguenay–Lac-Saint-Jean

The cruise-company **La Marjolaine** *($30; Boulevard Saguenay, C.P. 203, Port de Chicoutimi, G7H 587,* ☎543-7630 or 1-800-363-7248, ☞693-1701*)* organizes cruises on the Saguenay, providing one of the most enjoyable ways to take in the spectacular view of the fjord. The ship sets out from Chicoutimi, en route to Sainte-Rose-du-Nord. Passengers return by bus, except during June and September, when the return trip is by boat. Each cruise lasts an entire day. It is also possible to take the trip in the opposite direction, from Sainte-Rose-du-Nord to Chicoutimi.

Manicouagan

Many agencies near the dock organize boat trips onto the river:

Croisières AML *($30; Tadoussac,* ☎237-4274*)*, offers whale-watching trips in large, comfortable boats that accommodate up to 300 people. The expedition lasts approximately four hours.

For the more adventurous, **Compagnie de la Baie de Tadoussac** *($30; up to four departures every day, Tadoussac,* ☎235-4548*)* organizes trips in inflatable boats. The boats are smaller than those used by Croisière Navimex, bringing passengers closer to the whales. As a precaution, dry suits, provided by the company, must be worn. The boats may seem a bit crude, but they are quite safe. The air out on the water is significantly colder, so dress warmly. The expedition takes approximately three hours.

The **Croisières Neptune** *(adults $30, children $15; Jun to mid-Oct; 9am, 11:30am, 2pm and 4:30pm; 498 Rue de la Mer, C.P. 194, Bergeronnes, GOT 1G0,* ☎232-6716 or 232-6692 during the low season*)* whisks thrill-seekers into the heart of the fjord aboard eight-metre long, well-equipped rubber dingies to watch the magnificent sea mammals frolicking about.

Les Croisières Baie-Comeau *(adults $25, children $15; 9am, 1:30pm, 6pm; 194 Rue Laval, Baie-Comeau,* ☎294-2300 or 296-2708*)* based at the Baie-Comeau marina, near the ferry to Matane, will take you out to explore some magnificent spots along the coast near town. The 7.5-metre outboard stops at the breathtaking Baie de Pancrasse, where passengers can go swimming and tuck into a feast. Seafood dinner in the evening and on weekends (reserve a day ahead).

Duplessis

The **Virée des Iles** *($20; 140 Boulevard Laure Ouest, Sept-Iles,* ☎968-1818 or 962-1238*)*, a three-hour cruise through the Archipel des Sept-Iles, offers a glimpse of the rich marine life of the St. Lawrence, home to many kinds of aquatic mammals, particularly whales. The boat goes to Île Corossol, a large bird sanctuary.

Visitors wishing to tour the Archipel-de-Mingan have a choice of cruises. A little boat by the name of *Le Moyac* *(*☎949-2069*)* stops at several islands; a full cruise costs $30, a half-cruise, $25. **La Tournée des Iles** *($25;*

☎*538-3397)*, another guided cruise, starts at Havre-Saint-Pierre.

For whale-lovers, the most wonderful experience the Côte-Nord has to offer is to set out with the biologists of the **Station de Recherche des Iles de Mingan** for a close encounter with some **humpback whales**. Seated aboard seven-metre, **dinghies** passengers take part in a day of research, which involves identifying the animals by the markings under their tails. Biopsies are occasionally carried out as well, and useful data is compiled. These outings are not recommended for anyone prone to seasickness, however, as they start at the research station at 7am and last a minimum of six hours (sometimes much longer) in turbulent waters.

 Hiking

The numerous short and medium-length trails that lace the Tadoussac area are fantastic, since they lead through radically different ecosystems.

Tadoussac is also the starting point of one of the most remarkable long trails in Québec: the strikingly beautiful **Sentier du Fjord**. This 12-kilometre, intermediate trail starts near the welcome centre in Parc du Saguenay *(☎235-4238)*, next to the **fish-breeding pond**. For almost its entire length, it offers a view of the mouth of the Saguenay, the cliffs, the capes, the river and the village. There is a rudimentary campground about nine kilometres from the start. When you reach the end of the trail, you can continue hiking to Passe-Pierre, where you'll find another campground, superbly laid out in an idyllic spot.

 ACCOMMODATIONS

Bas-Saint-Laurent

Kamouraska

The **Motel Cap Blanc** *($50; K, tv; 300 Avenue Morel, GOL 1MO, ☎492-2919)* has simple, comfortable rooms with lovely views of the river. Pets are allowed.

Saint-André

A large house dating from the late 19th century, **La Solaillerie** *($60 bkfst incl.; sb, ℜ; 112 Rue Principale, GOL 2HO, ☎493-2914)* has a magnificent white façade and a big wraparound porch on the second story. Inside, the sumptuous decor evokes the era in which the house. The five guest rooms are cozy, comfortable and tastefully decorated in pure "old inn" tradition: one even has a canopy bed! Each has a sink and a claw-footed bathtub and offers a lovely view of the river. There are plans to construct an outbuilding with six well-equipped rooms. As far as the cuisine is concerned, gourmets can expect some delightful surprises (see p 322).

Rivière-du-Loup

The **Auberge de Jeunesse Internationale** in Rivière-du-Loup *($24; 46 Rue Hôtel-de-Ville, G5R IL5, ☎862-7566 or 1-800-461-8585)* is a youth hostel that offers the most affordable accommodation in town. The rooms are simple but clean.

The **Auberge de la Pointe** *($70; ≈, ◊, ⊖, ℜ, tv; 10 Boulevard Cartier, G5R 3Y7, ☎862-3514 or 1-800-463-1222, ≈862-1882)* is particularly well located. In addition to comfortable rooms, guests can indulge in a hydrotherapy, algotherapy or massage therapy sessions, and enjoy spectacular sunsets from the balcony. There is also a summer theatre.

Îles du Pot à L'Eau-de-Vie

The **Phare de l'Île du Pot à L'Eau-de-Vie** *($135 per person, ½b incl. Cruise; 200 Rue Hayward, Rivière-du-Loup, G5R 3Y9, ☎862-9454, ≈867-3639)*, a lighthouse on an island in the middle of the St. Lawrence, exposes its white façade and red roof to the four winds. Owned by Duvetnor, a non-profit organization dedicated to protecting birds, the Pot à L'Eau-de-Vie archipelago is swarming with water birds. Duvetnor offers package rates that include accommodations, meals and a cruise on the river with a naturalist guide. The lighthouse, over a century old, has been carefully restored. It has three cozy guestrooms The food is delicious. If you're looking for a peaceful atmosphere, this is the place to stay.

QUÉBEC

Trois-Pistoles

Motel Trois-Pistoles *($50;   ℜ,   tv; 64 Route 132 Ouest, GOL 4KO, ☎851-2563)* has 32 comfortable rooms, some affording a lovely view of the river; the sunsets from this spot are absolutely magnificent.

Le Bic

The nine-room **Auberge du Mange Grenouille** *($50-$80 bkfst incl.; ℜ; 148 Rue Sainte-Cécile, GOL 1SO, ☎736-5656)* has a good reputation in Québec and beyond. Guests are warmly welcomed, served succulent food, and stay in 15 cozy rooms decorated with antiques. The inn also hosts murder-mystery parties.

Rimouski

The **Hôtel Rimouski** *($85;   ≈,   ≡,   ℜ,   tv; 225 Boulevard René-Lepage Est, G5L IP2, ☎725-5000 or 1-800-463-0755, ↝725-5725)* has a somewhat unique design; its big staircase and long pool in the lobby will appeal to many visitors. Children under 18 can stay in their parents' room for free.

Pointe-au-Père

Auberge La Marée Douce *($50 bkfst incl., $85 for rooms in the new modern wing, $125 ½b; ℜ; 1329 Boulevard Sainte-Anne, G5R 8X7, ☎722-0822, ↝736-5167)* is a riverside inn located in Pointe-au-Père, near the Musée de la Mer. Built in 1860, it has comfortable rooms, each with its own decor.

Gaspésie

Matane

Visitors will find the perfect place to relax at the confluence of the St. Lawrence and Matane rivers, namely, **L'Auberge de La Seigneurie** *($70 bkfst incl.; 621 Rue Saint-Jérôme, G4W 3M9, ☎562-0021, ↝562-4455)*, an inn with comfortable rooms, located on the former site of the Fraser seigneury.

The **Hôtel des Gouverneurs** *($150; ℜ, ≈, △, ☉; 250 Avenue du Phare E., G4W 3N4; ☎566-2651 or 1-888-910-1111, ↝562-7365)* makes a charming first impression. Upon arrival, visitors will notice the care that has been taken to make the place both attractive and comfortable. The wooden spiral staircase and leather armchairs are just a hint of what lies further on. On their way through the restaurant and bar, guests will enjoy an exquisite view of the St. Lawrence. The rooms on the 3rd floor are among the newest in the hotel, which also has a tennis court and a golf course.

Parc de la Gaspésie

There are a number of different **campgrounds** *($16; mid-Jun to late Sep)* in Parc de la Gaspésie, as well as 19 **cabins** *($59-$169)* able to accommodate four, six or eight people *(☎763-2288 or 1-888-270-4483, ↝763-7803)*.

For panorama views, head to the **Gîte du Mont-Albert** *($85;   ≈,   △;   ☎763-2288 or 888-270-4483, ↝ 763-7803)*, located in Parc de la Gaspésie. The building is U-shaped, so each comfortable room offers a sweeping view of Mont Albert and Mont McGerrigle.

Forillon National Park

There are four campgrounds in the park, with a total of 368 sites. To reserve one, dial ☎368-6050 *(May to late Jul, Mon to Fri 9:30am to noon and 1pm to 3:30pm, or from April on write to Forillon National Park, P.O. Box 1220, Gaspé, GOC 1R0)*. Only half the sites may be reserved; for the rest, the park follows a first come, first served policy. The **Camping Des-Rosiers** *($15; Jun 11 to 10 Oct; Secteur Nord)*, a partially wooded area by the sea, has 155 tent and RV sites *(42 with electricity: $18)*. The **Camping Bon-Ami** *($15; Jun 11 to Sep 5; Secteur Sud)* has 135 tent and RV sites on a wooded stretch of land covered with fine gravel.

Gaspé

The **residence hall of the CÉGEP de la Gaspésie et des Îles** *($36 a night or $180 a week; K; 94 Rue Jacques-Cartier, C.P. 2004, GOC 1RO; ☎368-2749)* rents out its rooms between June 15 and August 15. Guests are provided with a kitchenette, bedding, towels and dishes.

The **Auberge des Commandants** *($80; ℜ; 178 Rue de la Reine, GOC 1RO, ☎368-3355, ↝368-1702)* is downtown, next to a shopping centre. The rooms are pleasant and comfortable.

Percé

The **Camping du Gargantua** *($16; 222 Route des Failles,* ☎782-2852) is definitely the most beautiful campground in the Percé area. It offers a view not only of Rocher Percé and the sea, but also of the verdant surrounding mountains.

The **Auberge du Gargantua** *($45; ℜ; Jun to mid-Oct; 222 Route des Failles, GOL 2LO,* ☎782-2852, ↩782-5229) has been looking out over Percé from atop its promontory for 30 years now and is well-known to anyone familiar with the Gaspé peninsula. Its restaurant (see p 324) is one of the best in the region, and its location and view are unforgettable. The small, motel-style rooms are simply decorated but comfortable.

The hotel-motel **La Normandie** *($58-$125; ℜ, ≈; 221 Route 132 O., GOC 2LO,* ☎782-2112 *or 1-888-463-0820,* ↩782-2337) has a well established reputation in Percé. During the high season, this luxury establishment is full most of the time. Both the restaurant and the rooms offer a view of the famous Rocher Percé.

Paspébiac

The **Auberge du Parc** *($150; ◯, ℜ, ≈; 68 Boulevard Notre-Dame, GOC 2KO;* ☎752-3555 *or 1-800-463-0890,* ↩752-6406) occupies a 19th-century manor erected by the Robin company. It stands in the midst of a wooded area, providing a perfect place to relax. Whirlpools, body wraps, therapeutic massages, acupressure and a saltwater pool enhance the stay.

New Carlisle

There's a pretty room waiting for you at the **Maison du Juge Thompson** *($60 bkfst incl.; Jul and Aug; 105 Rue Principale,* ☎752-6308 *or 752-5744),* a lovely old villa dating from 1844, complete with walking paths and a beautiful period garden. You can relax and admire the sea on the veranda. The tasty English-style breakfasts are an added bonus.

Carleton

The **Centre de Thalassothérapie Aqua-Mer** *($1095 for seven days, including treatments, meals and return transportation from Charlo airport in New Brunswick; ≈;* ☎364-7055 *or 1-800-463-0867,* ↩364-7351) located in an enchanting setting, offers a number of seven-day packages.

Pointe-à-la-Garde

The **Auberge de Jeunesse** and **Château Bahia** *($24 per person; ℜ; 152 Boulevard Perron, GOC 2MO,* ☎788-2048) are set back from the road, halfway between Carleton and Matapédia. This youth hoste is a great place to relax. During the high season, the clientele consists mainly of Europeans. Guests are offered high-quality regional dishes such as fresh salmon and maple-flavoured ham, all at modest prices, and may sleep either in the hostel or in the château behind it.

Îles-de-la-Madeleine

Île du Cap aux Meules

The very warm welcome at the **Auberge Chez Sam** *($35; sb; 1767 Chemin de L'Etang-du-Nord, L'Étang-du-Nord, GOS 1EO,* ☎986-5780) will quickly make guests feel et home. There are five attractive and well-kept rooms here.

Auberge Maison du Cap-Vert *($49 bkfst incl.; year round; 202 Chemin L'Aucoin, P.O. Box 521, Fatima, GOB 1KO,* ☎986-5331) is a family inn with five absolutely charming rooms with comfy beds and a unique decor. This place has managed to carve out an enviable place for itself on the island inn scene in just a short period of time. With its delicious, all-you-can-eat breakfasts, this place is definitely a good deal.

Visitors might first be surprised to find that the **Château Madelinot** *($109; ℜ, ≈, ℝ, ⊗, ◯; 323 Highway 199, C.P.44, GOB 180,* ☎986-3695, *or 1-800-661-4537,* ↩986-6437) is really a large house. But the comfortable rooms and superb view of the sea make it easy to forget this first impression. The château offers many services including a saltwater spa and a large swimming pool, and is without a doubt the most well-known accommodation on the islands.

QUÉBEC

Île du Havre Aubert

Located close to La Grave, **La Marée Haute** *($60; sb, ℜ; 25 Chemin des Fumoirs, GOB 1J0, ☎937-2492)*, is a lovely little inn where guests receive an extremely warm welcome. The rooms are cosy and attractively decorated. One of the owners also cooks; you won't regret trying one of these lovingly and meticulously prepared dishes. The view from the inn is absolutely ravishing!

The **Havre Sur Mer** inn *($95; ℜ; 1197 Chemin du Bassin, L'Anse à la Cabane, GOS 1AO, ☎937-5675, ⇔937-2540)*, near the cliff's edge, enjoys a magnificent location. The rooms have a communal terrace from which everybody can enjoy the beautiful view. The inn is decorated with antique furniture, and attracts many visitors. If you are interested in staying here, it is best to make reservations in advance.

Île du Havre aux Maisons

Set up in a charming hundred-year-old house, the **La P'tite Baie** inn *($70 bkfst incl.; 187 Highway 199, Havre-aux-Maisons, GOS 1EO, ☎969-4073, ⇔969-4900)* is made of wood and enjoys a warm and comfortable atmosphere. The impeccable rooms offer a superb view of the surrounding area.

Île de la Grande Entrée

The **Club Vacances "Les Îles"** *($236 per person, ½b for 3 days including all activities; Grande-Entrée, ☎985-2833 or 1-888-537-4537, ⇔985-2226)*, in addition to offering comfortable rooms, organizes several activities and excursions so that visitors can discover the area's natural riches. Guests can also take advantage of the cafeteria for their meals, where they are served generous portions of food.

Saguenay–Lac-Saint-Jean

La Baie

La Maison de la Rivière *($50; ℜ, ⊛; 9122 Chemin de la Batture, G7B 3P6, ☎544-2912 or 1-800-363-2078, ⇔544-2912)* lies in an enchanting setting, surrounded by beautiful greenery. Its peaceful atmosphere makes it a daydreamers' paradise. Guests are

warmly received. Unique, specialized packages focusing on regional and native gastronomy, wild plants, the outdoors, cultural activities, romanticism and alternative medicine. Guide service. Comfortable, tastefully decorated rooms designated by names taken from nature rather than by numbers. Ten of them have private balconies with stunning views of the fjord. Modern architecture with an environmentalist slant.

The charming **Auberge des 21** *($100; ⊛, ≈, ℜ, tv; 335 Rue Mars, G78 4N1, ☎544-9316, ⇔544-3360)* offers a magnificent recently renovated rooms at reasonable view of the Baie des Ha! Ha!. In addition to comfortable rooms and a health club, to help travellers relax as much as possible.

Chicoutimi

Located in the heart of town, the **Hôtel des Gouverneurs** *($65; ≈, ℜ, ≡, tv; 1303 Boulevard Talbot, G7H 4CI, ☎549-6244 or 1-800-463-2820, ⇔549-55227)* is a meeting place frequented by businesspeople looking for rooms with all the modern conveniences.

Jonquière

Though outside the centre of town, the **Hôtel Holiday Inn Saguenay** *($80; ≈, ≡, ℜ, ⊘, tv; 2675 Boulevard du Royaume, G7S 5B8, ☎548-3124, ⇔548-1638)* nevertheless very well located on the road between Jonquière and Chicoutimi, and has nice rooms.

Val-Jalbert

This ghost town has an outstanding **campground** *($20, ☎275-3132)*. A vast stretch of land, dotted with beautiful natural sites that will delight fans of rustic camping.

Lodgings and hotel rooms are available in the historical village *($55, ☎275-3132)*.

Saint-Félicien

As may be gathered from its name, the **Camping du Zoo** *($25; ≈; ☎679-1719)* is located beside the zoo; so you might be awakened by animal noises at night. It occupies a large piece of land, and is equipped with all the necessary facilities.

Péribonka

Alone on an island, the **Auberge de l'Île-du-Repos** (*$17 per person in dormitory, $83 ½b; ℜ; Route 169, ☎347-5649)* offers beautiful surroundings, an environment that stimulates conversation and a fascinating cultural programme.

Alma

The **Complexe Touristique de la Dam en Terre** (*$96 for 4 people; 1385 Chemin de la Marina, G8B 5Wl, ☎668-3016)* rents out well-designed cottages with a beautiful view of Lac Saint-Jean. Campers can opt for the more economical campsites.

Manicouagan

Tadoussac

No place offers a more stunning panoramic view than **Camping Tadoussac** (*$17; 428 Rue du Bateau-Passeur, GOT 1AO, ☎235-4501)*, which looks out over the bay and the village.

The **Maison Majorique** is Tadoussac's youth hostel (*$16; 158 Rue du Bateau-Passeur, GOT 2AO, ☎235-4372, ⋈235-4608)* is located less than one kilometre from the bus station. It has dormitories, private rooms, even campsites in summer, and they offer a whole variety of outdoor activities as well as reasonably priced cafeteria meals.

Located by the river, the **Hôtel Tadoussac** (*$129, $260 ½b and cruise; ℜ; 165 Rue du Bord-del'Eau, GOT 2AO, ☎235-4421)* resembles a late 19th-century manor house and is distinguished by its bright red roof. The hotel, made famous as the backdrop for the movie *Hotel New Hampshire,* is not as comfortable as one might expect.

Baie-Comeau

Anyone who visits Baie-Comeau regularly knows about **La Caravelle** (*$55; ≈, ℜ; 202 Boulevard LaSalle, G4Z 2L6, ☎296-4986, 296-4622 or 1-800-463-4968)*, a hotel-motel that looks out over the town from atop a hill. It has 70 renovated rooms, a number of which are available at low rates. Some rooms are equipped with a water bed and some with a fireplace.

What, you might ask, is that splendid house in its own little Garden of Eden right in the middle of town? **Le Petit Château** (*$78 bkfst incl.; ℜ; 2370 Boulevard Laflèche, G5C 1E4, ☎295-3100 or 295-3225)*, a *gîte*, has a simple, country atmosphere but is nonetheless inviting.

Godbout

Any way you look at it, **Aux Berges** (*$45 bkfst incl.; sb, ℜ; 180 Rue Pascal-Comeau, GOH 1GO,, ☎568-7748 May to Sep, ☎568-7816 Sep to May)* is one of the best *gîtes* on the Côte-Nord. The rooms are simple and the place is far from luxurious, but the graciousness of the hosts, the tourist services available to guests and the sophisticated regional cuisine make all the difference. This is a place to kick back and relax in the heart of a fascinating village. Aux Berges also rents out log cabins, located near the main building.

Duplessis

Sept-Îles

Many city-dwellers dream of camping on an unspoiled island in the peaceful wilderness. The **Camping Sauvage de l'Ile Grande-Basque** (*$20; Jul and Aug; accessible by ferry; Corporation Touristique de Sept-Iles, 1401 Boulevard Laure Ouest, G4R 4K1, ☎962-1238 or 968-1818 in summer, ☎968-0022)* can make such dreams a reality in the magnificent setting of the Baie de Sept-Iles. This island is the closest to the shore, making it a good stopping place for kayakers and canoeists. Firepits; firewood available. No drinking water.

Havre-Saint-Pierre

The friendly **Auberge de la Minganie** youth hostel (*$15; K; May to Oct; Route 138, GOG 1PO, ☎538-2944)* is located on the outskirts, beside the Mingan Archipelago National Park Reserve. Visitors arriving by bus can ask the bus driver to let them off here. There are many cultural and outdoor activities here.

You can't miss the **Hôtel-Motel du Havre** (*$62; ℜ, K; 970 Boulevard de l'Escale, GOG 1PO,*

☎538-2800 or 538-3438), located at the intersection of the main road and Rue de l'Escale, which runs through town to the docks. This place is definitely *the* big hotel in town. Though some rooms have benefited from recent attempts at renovation, others remain drab and a bit depressing. Friendly service.

Île d'Anticosti

The **Auberge Au Vieux Menier** *($17.50 per person in the dormitory, $45 bkfst incl. in the gîte; sb, ℜ; P.O. Box 112, Port-Menier, G0G 2Y0, 535-0111)* falls somewhere between a B&B and a youth hostel. Located on the site of the former Saint-Georges farm. Exhibitions. Low rates.

The **Auberge Port-Menier** *($66; ℜ, ctv; P.O. Box 160, Port-Menier, G0G 2Y0, ☎535-0122 or 535-0204)*, a venerable institution on the island, offers clean rooms and excellent food in a modest setting. The lobby is decorated with magnificent wooden reliefs from the Château Meunier. The inn serves as the starting point for a number of guided tours. Bicycle rentals.

Baie-Johan-Beetz

You can stay at the historic **Maison Johan-Beetz** *($50 bkfst incl.; 15 Johan-Beetz, ☎539-0137)*. This truly exceptional hotel is a veritable monument decorated with Beetz's own artwork. The rooms are comfortable but basic.

Natashquan

The **Auberge La Cache** *($85; 183 Chemin d'En Haut, G0G 2E0, ☎726-3347, ⌑726-3508)* has about ten pleasant rooms.

As many villages don't have any hotels, a home-stay network has been set up. Local families will welcome you into their houses, enabling you to share in the day-to-day life of the residents of the Côte-Nord:

Aylmer Sound	☎242-2115
Bonne Espérance	☎379-2911
Baie-Johan-Beetz	☎539-0125
Chevery	☎787-2389
Harrington-Harbour	☎795-3376 or
	☎795-3354
Kagaska	☎726-3291
La Tabatière	☎773-2263 or
	☎773-2596
Rivière-St-Paul	☎379-2911
Saint-Augustin	☎947-2501 or
	☎947-2404
Tête-à-la-Baleine	☎242-2115,
	☎242-2045 or
	☎242-2002
Vieux-Fort	☎379-2260

 RESTAURANTS

Bas-Saint-Laurent

Saint-André

The dining room at **La Solaillerie** *($$$; 112 Rue Principale, ☎493-2914)* has been carefully decorated to highlight the historic character of the old house in which it is located. In this inviting setting, guests savour excellent cuisine lovingly prepared and served by the owners of the inn. Drawing his inspiration from the French culinary repertoire, the chef uses fresh regional foodstuffs like quail, lamb and fresh and smoked salmon to create new dishes according to his fancy.

Rivière-du-Loup

The **Saint-Patrice** *($$$, 169 Rue Fraser, ☎862-9895)* is one of the best restaurants in town. Fish, seafood, rabbit and lamb are specialities. Another restaurant at the same address, **Le Novello** *($$)*, serves pasta and thin-crust pizza in a bistro setting.

The restaurants in the Hôtel Lévesque, **La Terrasse** and **La Distinction** *($$, 171 Rue Fraser, ☎862-2790 or 862-6927)*, serve a variety of delicious Italian dishes, as well as smoked salmon prepared according to a traditional method in the hotel's smokehouse.

Trois-Pistoles

The café/restaurant **L'Ensolleillé** *($; 138 Rue Notre-Dame Ouest, ☎851-2889)* is a vegetarian restaurant with a very simple à la carte menu. The three-course lunch and dinner menus are a good deal.

Michalie *($$, 55 Rue Notre-Dame Est,* ☎851-4011) is a charming little restaurant serving some of the best regional cuisine to be found, as well as gourmet Italian food.

Saint-Fabien

In the warm, traditional atmosphere of the **Auberge Saint-Simon** *($$$-$$$$; 18 Rue Principale,* ☎738-2971), guests will enjoy another excellent Bas-Saint-Laurent dining experience. Rabbit, lamb, halibut and seafood are paired with fresh vegetables grown in the restaurant garden.

Le Bic

The **Auberge du Mange Grenouille** *($$$-$$$$; 148 Sainte-Cécile,* ☎736-5656) is one of the best restaurants in the Bas-Saint-Laurent. It was once a general store and is decorated with old furniture carefully chosen to complement the architecture. Guests are offered a choice of six daily tables d'hôte that include fowl, lamb and fish dishes. Everything served here is delicious, and the service is always attentive.

Rimouski

The **Café-Bistro Le Saint-Louis** *($$; 97 Rue St-Louis,* ☎723-7979) looks just like its Parisian cousins, and is filled with all the same aromas. It offers a large selection of imported beer and microbrews. The menu, which changes daily, is delicious, and the dishes are served in a pleasant atmosphere.

Serge Pouly *($$; 284 Rue Saint-Germain Est,* ☎723-3038) serves game, seafood, steak and French specialties. The relaxed atmosphere and attentive service make this the perfect place for an intimate dinner for two.

Gaspésie

Grand-Métis

The restaurant **Les Ateliers Plein Soleil** *($-$$; Jardins de Métis)* takes pride in making sure everything is perfect: the waiters and waitresses, dressed in period clothing, are attentive; the decor is picturesque and the Métis and Québécois cuisine is served in generous portions.

Métis-sur-Mer

The restaurant **Au Coin de la Baie** *($$$; 1140 Route 132,* ☎936-3855) opens its doors between May and September. Here, visitors can treat themselves to smoked salmon royale and "cedar" sorbet. The wine list is excellent.

Matane

The restaurant **Le Vieux Rafiot** *($$-$$$; 1415 Avenue du Phare, alongside Route 132,* ☎562-8080) attracts lots of visitors to its incredible dining room, which is divided into three sections by partitions with portholes and decorated with paintings by local artists. In addition to the novel decor, guests can enjoy a variety of delicious dishes.

At **La Maison Sous le Vent** *($$$$; 1014 du Phare O.,* ☎562-7611), opened in 1992, you will dine on exquisite refined cuisine; beef, lamb and fish are prepared with wine, herbs and citrus fruits.

Parc de la Gaspésie

The **Gîte du Mont-Albert** *($$$$;* ☎762-2288) offers innovative seafood dishes that are definitely worth a try. During the Game Festival, in September, you can sample more unusual meats like guinea hen, bison and partridge.

Gaspé

The bistro/bar **Brise-Brise** *($-$$; 2 Côte Cartier, Place Jacques-Cartier,* ☎368-1456) is probably the nicest café in Gaspé. The menu includes sausages, seafood, salads and sandwiches. The place also features an assortment of beer and coffee, an enjoyable happy hour, live shows all summer long, and dancing late into the evening.

The café-restaurant **La Belle Hélène** *($$$-$$$$; 135A Rue de la Reine,* ☎368-1455) serves what is undoubtedly the best food in the entire Gaspé area. The menu includes not only fish and seafood, but also Breton crepes and originally-prepared game. For dessert, try the maple syrup and hazelnut pie. The service is pleasant, and the music, exquisite. The tables are decorated with bouquets of regional flowers.

QUÉBEC

Fort Prével

At **Fort Prével** *($$$-$$$$; 2053 Boulevard Douglas, ☎368-2281 or 1-888-377-3835)* guests are not only plunged into an historic atmosphere, but also get to savour delicious French and Québec cuisine. These skillfully prepared and elegantly presented dishes are served to guests in a huge dining room. The menu includes fish and seafood, of course, as well as all sorts of specialties that could turn any gourmet green with envy.

Percé

Though there are lots of restaurants in Percé, few fall into the gourmet category. One that does, however, is the **Auberge à Percé** *($$$; 1 Promenade du Bord de Mer, ☎782-5055 or 1-888-782-5055)*, which serves divinely prepared scallops, lobster, fish and red meat. The restaurant's charming address seems tailor-made for the beautiful setting.

Regarded by many as one of the best restaurants in Percé, **La Normandie** *($$$$; 221 Route 132 O.; ☎782-2112)* serves delicious food in an altogether charming spot. Diners rave about the *feuilleté de homard au champagne* lobster in puff pastry with champagne) and the *pétoncles à l'ail* (scallops with garlic). The restaurant also features an extensive wine list.

The decor of the **Auberge Gargantua** *($$$$; 222 Rue des Failles; ☎782-2852)* is reminiscent of the French countryside where the owners were born. The dining room offers a splendid view of the surrounding mountains, so be sure to arrive early enough enjoy it. The dishes are all gargantuan and delicious, and usually include an appetizer of periwinkle, a plate of crudités, and soup. Guests choose their main dish from a long list, ranging from salmon to snow crab, to a selection of game.

Bonaventure

The **Café Acadien** *($$-$$$; early Jun to mid-Sep; 168 Rue Beaubassin, ☎534-4276)* serves good food in a charming setting. Open throughout the summer season, this place is very popular with locals and tourists alike, which might explain why the prices are a little high.

Carleton

La Seigneurie *($$-$$$; 482 Boulevard Perron; ☎364-3355)*, the restaurant in the Hôtel-Motel Baie Bleue, serves a wide variety of delicious dishes based on game, fish and seafood. The view from the dining room is superb.

Îles-de-la-Madeleine

Île du Cap aux Meules

The **P'tit Café** *($$; ☎986-2130)*, in the Château Madelinot (see p 319), serves Sunday brunch from 10am to 1:30pm. Those with a taste for novelty can order seafood, red meat or chicken cooked on a hot stone. The menu includes a large selection of appetizers, soups and charbroiled offerings. In addition to a view of the sea, the decor is enhanced by temporary exhibitions by artists from the islands and elsewhere in Québec.

Since 1978, the **La Table des Roy** *($$$$; mid-May to mid-Sep from 6pm, closed Mon; La Vernière, ☎986-3004)*, restaurant has offered refined cuisine to delight every visitor's tastebuds. The seafood, prepared in a multitude of ways, such as grilled scallops and lobster with *coralline sauce*, naturally highlights this tempting menu. The dining room is charming and adds a particular style to this excellent restaurant that also offers dishes adorned with edible flowers and plants of the islands. It is advised to reserve in advance.

Île du Havre Aubert

Decorated like an old general store, the **Café de la Grave** *($$; early May to end of Oct 8:30am to 3pm; Havre-Aubert, ☎937-5765)* has one of the most pleasant atmospheres, and on days when the weather is bad, you can spend hours here chatting. In addition to muffins, croissants and a wide variety of coffees, the menu offers healthy and sometimes unusual dishes, such as *pâté de loup marin*, which are always good. This café is delightfully welcoming and will leave you with lasting memories.

The chef and co-owner of **La Marée Haute** *($$$; 25 Chemin des Fumoirs, ☎937-2492)*, knows how bring out the best in fish and seafood. In this pretty inn, you can sample sea perch, shark or mackerel while drinking in the magnificent view. You can taste the ocean in these dishes, whose expertly enhanced flavour will send you into raptures. The menu also includes a few equally well-prepared meat dishes and some succulent desserts.

Île du Havre aux Maisons

La P'tite Baie *($$$; year round; 187 Route 199, ☎969-4073)* serves well-prepared grill, seafood and fish, as well as a number of beef, pork and chicken dishes. *Loup-marin* is served up here in season. In addition to the à la carte menu, there is a table-d'hôte with a choice of two main dishes. The service is courteous and a great deal of care has gone into the decor.

Saguenay–Lac-Saint-Jean

La Baie

With its succulent game dishes, the restaurant **Le Doyen** *($$-$$$; Auberge des 21, 335 Rue Mars, ☎544-9316)* boasts one of the region's best menus. The dining room commands a remarkable, sweeping view of the Baie des Ha! Ha! The Sunday brunch is excellent. Run by renowned chef Marcel Bouchard, who has won numerous regional, national and international awards, Le Doyen is making a tangible contribution to the evolution and refinement of regional cuisine.

The head chef at **La Maison de la Rivière** *($$-$$$; 22630 Chemin de la Batture, ☎544-2912)* has developed a menu centred around aboriginal traditions, regional dishes and international cuisine. This superb inn lies in an extremely pleasant setting, featuring a lovely view of the fjord.

Chicoutimi

The scent of freshly ground coffee permeates the air at **La Cuisine** *($$; 387 Rue Racine Est, ☎698-2822)*. We especially recommend the steak tartare, mussels, rabbit, sweetbreads and "steak-frites".

Le Privilège *($$ wine; 1623 Boulevard St-Jean-Baptiste, ☎698-6262)* ranks among the finest restaurants in the region. A feast for the senses in this picturesque hundred-year-old house. Intuitive cuisine with market fresh ingredients for a lucky few at a time. Friendly and relaxed ambiance and service. Reservations required.

The newly opened **Chez Pachon** *($$$; 230 Rue Lafontaine, ☎693-0227)*, whose chef has already made a name for himself throughout the region, serves gourmet food seasoned with the culinary traditions of France and influenced by regional flavours. House specialties include *cassoulet de Carcassonne, confit de magret de canard,* filet and loin of lamb, sweetbreads, fish and seafood.

Jonquière

L'Amandier *($$; 5219 Chemin Saint-André, ☎542-5395)* has an astonishing dining room decorated with carved plaster and an overabundance of woodwork. The restaurant serves regional cuisine made with fresh ingredients. Somewhat removed from town, it is not easy to find. Reservations required. Good food is joined here by a unique ambiance well-suited to dining among friends: the inviting decor and the hosts' hospitality create a festive mood.

One of the finest restaurants in Jonquière, **Le Bergerac** *($$$; 3919 Rue Saint-Jean, ☎542-6263)* has developed an excellent repertoire of dishes. Lunchtime menu du jour and evening table d'hôte.

Saint-Félicien

The fine regional cuisine served at the **Hôtel du Jardin** *($$-$$$; 1400 Boulevard du Jardin, G8K 2N8, ☎679-8422)* is never disappointing.

Alma

People don't come to the **Bar Restaurant Chez Mario Tremblay** *($$-$$$; 534 Collard Ouest, ☎668-6431)* to enjoy the meal of their life; they are attracted by the owner's reputation as a hockey player and coach, which earned him the nickname '*le bleuet bionique*' (the Bionic Blueberry). This brasserie-style restaurant is a popular gathering place for hockey devotees.

Manicouagan

Tadoussac

Try the **Crêperie La Bolée** *($; 164 Morin, ☎235-4750)* for simple but tasty meals like stuffed crepes. It is also a good place to come later on in the evening for a drink. There is a bakery below the restaurant.

The **Café du Fjord** *($$; 154 Rue du Bateau-Passeur,* ☎*235-4626)* is located in an uninteresting-looking house, but it is very popular. They offer a seafood buffet for lunch, and nights are livened up with shows or with disco music.

Bergeronnes

An inn with a unique charm about it, the **Auberge La Rosepierre** *($$-$$$; 66 Rue Principale,* ☎*232-6543)* has a tastefully decorated dining room with a table d'hôte featuring regional flavours and cooking methods. Naturally, fish and seafood dishes occupy a large part of the menu and are always prepared with flair.

Baie-Comeau

La Cache d'Amélie *($$$-$$$$; 37 Avenue Marquette, G4Z 1K4,* ☎*296-3722 or 1-800-544-3722)* is the place for gastronomic cuisine in Baie-Comeau. In the picturesque former presbytery of the loveliest parish in town, guests enjoy a delightfully intimate atmosphere that enhances their dining experience.

The hotel restaurant at **Le Manoir** *($$$-$$$$; 8 Rue Cabot, G4Z 1L8,* ☎*296-3391 or 1-800-463-8567)* has a well-established reputation. In an extremely inviting and luxurious decor, guests dine on expertly prepared cuisine worthy of the most elaborate praise. A meeting place for businesspeople and industrialists, it will also appeal to tourists, who will enjoy the unique view of the bay and the holiday atmosphere that pervades the outdoor seating area. Outstanding wine list.

Pointe-des-Monts

The **Restaurant du Fort de Pointe-des-Monts** *($$; Route du Vieux Fort,* ☎*939-2332)*, located in a quiet little bay, has a menu consisting mainly of fresh seafood dishes. The cuisine is excellent and the service, impeccable.

Duplessis

Sept-Îles

The charming **Café du Port** *($-$$; 495 Avenue Brochu,* ☎*962-9311)* prepares simple and delicious dishes. It is one of the area's most popular restaurants.

The newly opened **Le Bon Bistro** *($$-$$$; closed Mon; 588 Avenue Brochu,* ☎*968-3777)* is in an old house that is rich in style and character. Seafood dishes and regional cuisine.

Havre-Saint-Pierre

Chez Julie *($$; 1023 Rue Dulcinée,* ☎*538-3070)* has an excellent reputation for seafood. The coffee shop decor, including vinyl seat covers, does not seem to discourage the customers who flock to the restaurant for seafood and smoked salmon pizzas.

Île d'Anticosti

The **Auberge Au Vieux Menier** *($-$$; Port-Menier,* ☎*535-0111)* and its café/bar serve Anticosti specialties, seafood, home-made baked goods and grilled fare. Outdoor seating available.

The dining room of the **Pointe-Carleton** *($-$$; SÉPAQ)* is the best and most pleasant place to eat on the island. Whether you're sitting in the bright dining room or outside on the terrace, the view is spectacular and the cuisine, succulent. A different specialty is featured every evening. If you happen to be around on a "Bacchante" night (fisherman's platter), don't miss it.

Natashquan

A good meal can be had et the **Auberge La Cache** *($$-$$$; 183 Chemin d'En Haut,* ☎*726-3347)*; meat and seafood dishes are featured.

ENTERTAINMENT

Festivals and Cultural Events

Iles-de-la Madeleine

The **Concours des Châteaux de Sable** (Sand Castle Contest) takes place annually during the month of August on the Havre-Aubert beach. Participants work for hours to build the nicest sand castle. Visitors wanting to put their talent to the test can register by calling Artisans du Sable at ☎937-2917.

Saguenay–Lac-Saint-Jean

The **Carnaval-Souvenir de Chicoutimi** *(mid-Feb;* ☎*543-4438)* celebrates the customs of winter in days gone by with period costumes and traditional activities.

Since 1955, the last week in July has been devoted to the **Traversée Internationale du Lac Saint-Jean** *(*☎*275-2851)*. Swimmers cover the 40 kilometres between Péribonka and Roberval in eight hours, and some even make the return trip in 18 hours.

SHOPPING

Gaspésie

Grand-Métis

Les Ateliers Plein Soleil *(every day 9am to 6:30pm; Jardins de Métis,* ☎*775-3165)*, a

group of artisans from Grand-Métis, runs the Maison Reford. They make all sorts of hand-woven tablecloths, doilies and napkins, which may be purchased in their shop, along with herbs, locally produced honey and home-made tomato ketchup.

Percé

Thanks to its central location, you can't miss the Place du Quai, a cluster of over 30 shops and restaurants, as well as a laundromat and an S.A.Q. (liquor store).

Causapscal

Le Kiosque d'Artisanat de la Matapédia *(early Jun to mid-Oct, every day 9am to 9pm; 51 Rue Saint-Jacques Sud,* ☎*756-3062)* has a wide choice of fabrics and knitwear, toys, jewellery, home-made preserves made with wild fruit and all sorts of other souvenirs to take back home. Local artisans have joined forces to offer customers items that truly reflect the traditions of the region.

Îles-de-la-Madeleine

Les Artisans du Sable *(La Grave, Havre-Aubert,* ☎*937-2917)* offer several sand items, made using a special technique unique to Madelinot artisans. These items, which vary from decorations to lampshades, are wonderful souvenirs of the islands. You can also learn more about sand here.

QUÉBEC

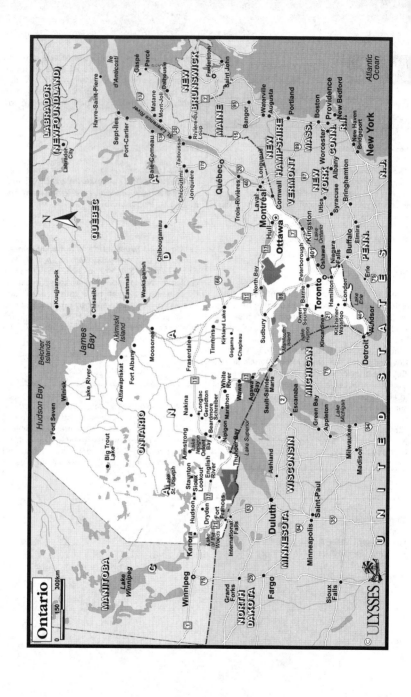

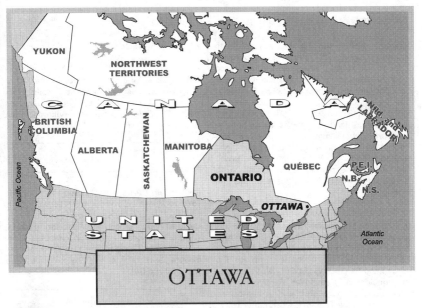

OTTAWA

Who would have thought, less than 200 years ago, that at the confluence of the Ottawa and Rideau rivers, in the heart of a dense forest, a city would develop that would become the capital of Canada?

The history of Ottawa goes back to the days after the War of 1812, in which British forces in Canada were pitted against American troops. During these difficult years, the English authorities recognized the importance of protecting the navigable waters of the St. Lawrence between the newly built towns along the river, in particular between Montréal and Kingston. Defending this waterway was not a simple matter since, over a sizable distance, one shore lay on the Canadian side and the other on the American side. A canal between the Ottawa River and Kingston that would bypass the St. Lawrence between the present-day cities of Ottawa and Kingston was proposed as a solution. This strategic military decision was the impetus for the founding of Ottawa.

An early agricultural settlement led by Philmeon Wright had begun on the site of what is today Hull, on the Québec side of the border, around the year 1800. Construction of the canal began in 1826, under the supervision of Lieutenant-Colonel By. A tiny hamlet developed with the workers brought to build the canal and the managers brought to oversee the construction as its residents. It was called Bytown after the lieutenant-colonel.

It took seven years to complete the canal; in 1832, a little village was built at the confluence of the Ottawa River and the Rideau Canal. The town flourished, mostly because of the dense forest surrounding it; wood-cutting gave work to many people.

Two very distinct areas developed on each side of the canal: the upper town, on the west side, where the more affluent inhabitants had sumptuous dwellings built, and the lower town, on the east side, which became home to the town's poorer residents, mostly French and Irish, both groups being predominantly Catholic. There was rivalry and tension between these two groups and Bytown's first years were tumultuous ones. The 19th century profoundly transformed this small city of just a few thousand souls.

After the War of 1812, the threat of an American attack ended, and contrary to the original plans for the canal, it never served in wartime. The waterway was instead used by pleasure-boaters out enjoying fine summer days.

Kingston was the capital of United Canada between 1841 and 1844, but its proximity to the United States worried the authorities who feared eventual attacks on this important, yet vulnerable colonial administrative centre. They sought another site for the capital, with Toronto, Québec City, Montréal and Bytown. Though it was gritty and violent, Bytown had a lot to recommend it: it was located at the boundary between Upper and Lower Canada, it had an equally English-speaking and French-speaking population and the British government owned ideal land for the construction of governmental buildings. In 1857, Bytown was chosen as the capital of United Canada and was thus know as Ottawa. Ottawa remained capital with the signing of the British North America Act in 1867, and has kept the title ever since.

Forestry allowed the town and the surrounding region to prosper in the 19th century, but this industry went into decline during the 20th century. At the same time, however, its status as national capital enabled it to attract the burgeoning federal civil service, which became the principal local employer. A city plan was adopted at the turn of the 20th century to beautify the area. Though it wasn't until 1937, when French architect and town planner Jacques Greber was appointed to develop a new layout for the city centre, that Ottawa was transformed and took on the grand appearance it has today. Today, the elegant buildings of Parliament Hill and the broad avenues lined with splendid Victorian dwellings bear witness to the success of this plan that brought Ottawa among the ranks of Canada's most beautiful cities.

 FINDING YOUR WAY AROUND

By Car

An excellent system of highways and expressways makes Ottawa easy to reach from many points in Ontario and Quebec.

From Toronto, follow Highway 7, which crosses Peterborough and goes directly to Ottawa. It is also possible to drive along the St. Lawrence, taking Highway 401 to Prescott and, from there, Highway 16 to Ottawa.

From Montréal, take Highway 40 and then the 417, taking the Nicholas St. exit to reach the downtown area.

Along the Rideau Canal

From Ottawa, take Colonel Drive along the Rideau Canal for a fair distance. At the end of the road, turn left on Brookfield Road, then right on Riverside Drive, which becomes Route 19. Follow this to Kemptville and then Route 43 to Merrickville.

By Plane

MacDonald-Cartier International Airport *(50 Airport Drive, ☎613-998-5213, ⇒954-2136)* is fairly small, but nonetheless is the destination of domestic and international flights. It is located about 20 minutes from downtown and easy to reach by car (there are several car-rental agencies), by taxi or by bus (OC Transpo 96).

By Train

VIA Train Station: 200 Tremblay St., ☎(613) 244-1660.

The train station is about 10 minutes from downtown by car (Hwy 417). You can take OC Transpo Bus 95 from the station to downtown for $1.85.

A taxi costs about $10.

By Bus

Ottawa is also accessible by bus, with fast, punctual service from Montréal or Toronto. Between Montréal and Ottawa, there are frequent departures every hour from 6am to late evening.

Bus terminal: 265 Catherine St., ☎238-6668.

To get downtown from the bus station, take OC Transpo Bus 4 or Kent and Bank Streets by car.

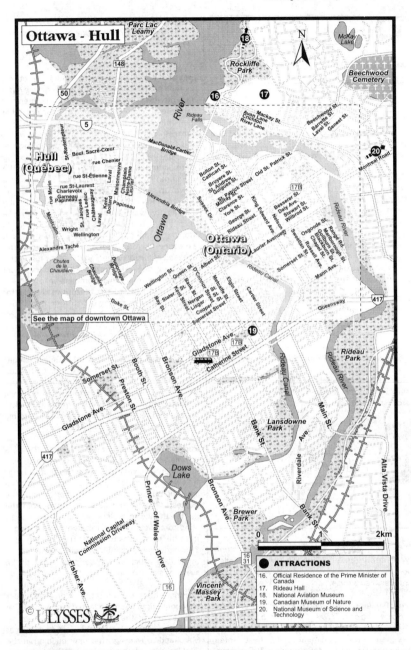

Ottawa - Hull

Parc Lac
Leamy

McKay
Lake

Rockliffe
Park

Beechwood
Cemetery

148

50

5

River

Rideau
Falls

MacDonald-Cartier
Bridge

Avon Lane
Crichton
River Lane

Mackay St.

Beechwood St.
Barrette St.
Laval St.
Genest St.

Hull
(Québec)

St-Redempteur

Boul. Sacré-Cœur

rue Chenier

rue St-Étienne

rue St-Laurent

rue Morin

Charlevoix
Garneau
Papineau

St. rue Leduc

Maisonneuve
Notre-Dame
Champlain
Laurier

Kent
Dollard

Laval

Papineau

Chateauguay

Alexandria Bridge

Sussex Dr.

Bolton St.
Cathcart St.
Bruyere St.
St-Andre St.
Guigues St.
St. Patrick Street
Murray St.
Clarence St.
York St.
George St.
Rideau Street

Old St. Patrick St.

17B

Besserer St.
Daly Ave.
Stewart St.
Wilbrod St.

Rideau River

Montreal Road

20

Jacques

Laval

Ottawa

Ottawa
(Ontario)

Laurier Avenue

King Edward Ave.
Nelson
Cumberland

Osgoode St.
Sweatland St.
Russell Ave.
Marlborough St.
Blackburn Ave.
Goulburn Ave.

Range Rd.
Chapel St.

Montcalm

Wright

Wellington

Alexandre Taché

Chutes
de la
Chaudière

Chaudière
Bridge

Duke St.

Portage
Bridge

Ottawa

Wellington St.

Queen St.
Albert St.

Bay St.

Booth St.

Bronson Ave.

Preston St.

Somerset St.

Duke St.

Metcalfe St.

Kent Street

O'Connor Street

Bank Street
Nergan St.
Lisgar
Cooper St.
Somerset Street

Slater

Elgin Street

Carter Street

Rideau Canal

Somerset St.

Mann Ave.

Queensway

417

Rideau
Park

19

Gladstone Ave.

17B

Gladstone Ave.

17B

Catherine Street

Rideau Canal

Rideau River

417

Gladstone Ave.

Bank St.

Lansdowne
Park

Main St.

Riverdale Ave.

Alta Vista Drive

Dows
Lake

Bronson Ave.

Brewer
Park

Bank St.

0   1   2km

16
31

National Capital
Commission Driveway

Prince of Wales Drive

16

© ULYSSES

Fisher Ave.

Vincent
Massey
Park

● ATTRACTIONS

16. Official Residence of the Prime Minister of
     Canada
17. Rideau Hall
18. National Aviation Museum
19. Canadian Museum of Nature
20. National Museum of Science and
     Technology

See the map of downtown Ottawa

ONTARIO

PRACTICAL INFORMATION

Area code: 613

Tourist Information Offices

There is a new tourist office just a few steps from Parliament Hill. Brochures, information and a hotel reservation service are all available.

Capital Information Office: 90 Wellington St., ☎239-5000, ☎(800) 465-1867 (within Canada), open May to early Sep, every day 8:30am to 9pm; rest of the year, every day 9am to 5pm.

The internet is another source of information. Check out the following sites:
www.ottawakiosk.com
www.tourottawa.org

Guided Tours

Several companies provide city tours offering a good glimpse of the most attractive areas.

Capital Double-Decker and Trolley Tours *($20;* ☎*729-6888 or 1-800-823-6147),* departures from Infocentre.

Gray Line: *($16;* ☎*725-1441 or 1-800-440-0317).*

 EXPLORING

Around Parliament Hill ★★

This tour starts at Parliament Hill along Wellington Street. "The Hill," as it is called locally, truly dominates the city and is almost impossible to miss.

The **Parliament Buildings ★★★** *(information about activities* ☎*239-5000 or 1-800-465-1867)* truly dominate Ottawa. Perched atop Parliament Hill, these three buildings are distributed around a 200-square-metre garden. The central building, or Centre Block, houses the Senate and the House of Commons, the seat of the federal government. The two other edifices, known as the East and West Blocks, contain various administrative offices.

Erecting some of these splendid structures seemed necessary to the city's authorities, who had nowhere to accommodate members of Parliament, when Ottawa became the capital of the United Province of Canada in 1857. A contest was held and won by Thomas Fuller and Chilion Jones, whose plans proposing the erection of a High Victorian Gothic building were adopted. The time allotted for the development of these plans was very limited, however, and work got under way before all the problems posed by a construction of such complexity were solved. Moreover, barely a year later, the impressive 250,000-pounds sterling budget allowed had already been exceeded. The authorities were consequently accused of mismanaging government funds and work had to be interrupted. Three years would pass before the Royal Commission of Inquiry authorized to get to the bottom of the matter recommended resuming construction. In 1866, the first session was held here, even though construction had yet to be completed. Work only really concluded as of 1876.

Though the development of the Parliament Buildings was a difficult task, the end result was enough to make Ottawa residents proud: three magnificent High Victorian Gothic-style buildings now marked the horizon in their city, which had essentially consisted of humble wooden houses up to that point.

Barely 40 years later, on February 3, 1916, a terrible fire broke out in the Centre Block. The offices on the west side were the first to burn, followed by those on the east side. The splendid building was entirely destroyed by the flames, save for the library, spared from the flames thanks to a clerk with the presence of mind to close the thick iron doors separating it from the rest of the building. This magnificent, 16-sided, High Victorian Gothic-style structure, topped by a lantern copper roof, can still be seen today.

Reconstruction of the Centre Block got under way some time later and lasted nine years. The architecture of the East and West Blocks led architects John A. Pearson and J. Omer Marchand to redesign the new building in the Gothic style, while retaining its original aspect. Its façade is adorned with the 90-metre-high Peace Tower, which boasts, among other

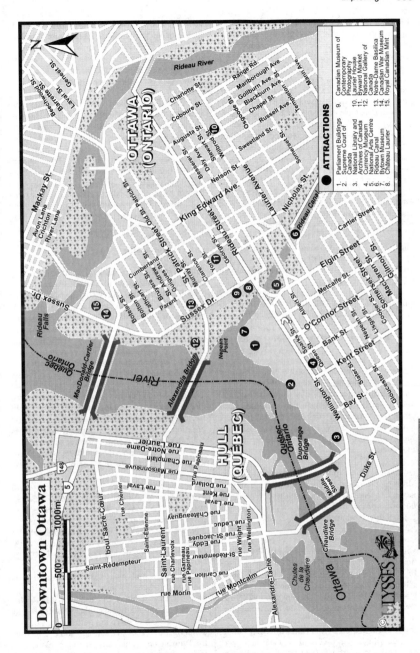

Downtown Ottawa

0   500   1000m

● **ATTRACTIONS**

1. Parliament Buildings
2. Supreme Court of Canada
3. National Library and Archives of Canada
4. Currency Museum
5. National Arts Centre
6. Rideau Canal
7. Bytown Museum
8. Château Laurier
9. Canadian Museum of Contemporary Photography
10. Laurier House
11. Byward Market
12. National Gallery of Canada
13. Notre-Dame Basilica
14. Canadian War Museum
15. Royal Canadian Mint

ONTARIO

things, a 53-bell carillon. No effort was spared in beautifying this magnificent building's interior, notably adorned with grand sculptures and wainscoting.

The central building has been flanked by the East and West Blocks from the very beginning. The latter two are the work of Thomas Stent and Augustus Laver. The East Block is a lovely structure with asymmetrical elevations; of hewed, cream- to ochre-coloured stones and graced with towers, chimneys, pinnacles, ogive windows, gargoyles and various sculptures. It was originally built to accommodate the Canadian Civil Service; it henceforth contains the offices of senators and members of Parliament. A guided tour is offered, giving visitors the opportunity to see the offices once occupied by John A. Macdonald and George-Étienne Cartier, as well as every prime minister having succeeded them, from Laurier to Trudeau. The building also houses the original Governor General's office as well as the Privy Council Chamber.

Guided tours are available of the centre and east blocks *(free admission; late May to early Sep, Mon to Fri 9am to 7:30pm, Sat and Sun 9am to 4:30pm; Sep to May, every day 9am to 3:30pm).*

Parliament is also the scene of numerous events, notably the **changing of the guard**, which takes place every day from late June to late August at 10am, when you can see soldiers parading in their ceremonial garb. A **sound and light show** *(free admission; May to Sep 9:30pm and 10:30pm)* presents the history of Canada.

On the vast lawn graced with beautiful flowers stretching in front of the parliament buildings, is the centennial flame, inaugurated in 1967 to commemorate the 100th anniversary of Canadian confederation.

Continuing along Wellington Street, you will see the massive, simple, austere building housing the **Supreme Court of Canada** *(corner of Wellington and Kent Sts.).* This Art Deco structure was designed by architect Ernest Cormier, with construction beginning in 1939. Only one alteration was made to the original plan, which called for a flat roof. Changes to the roof requested by the Department of Public Works, which then favoured the Château style, and perhaps at the behest of Prime Minister Mackenzie King, were thus made, giving it its current appearance.

At the end of Wellington Street are the buildings of the **National Library and Archives of Canada** *(395 Wellington St.),* containing an impressive collection of documents dealing with Canada, as well as Canadian publications. Temporary exhibitions are presented here.

From the city's earliest days, two districts have vied for the title of shopping precinct: the area surrounding Byward Market, downtown, and **Sparks Street**, uptown. To this end, huge efforts were made by the area's residents and merchants to beautify Sparks. This elegant main thoroughfare, graced with five-to six-story buildings, was consequently one of the very first to be paved, criss-crossed by the tramway and to be lit by street lights. It was thus dubbed Ottawa's Broadway. Its long commercial tradition has never waned, and it is now a lovely pedestrian street (between Kent and Elgin Streets).

The first stop on Sparks is the **Currency Museum** ★ *($2; Mon to Sat 10:30am to 5pm; 245 Sparks St., ☎782-8914),* , inside the Bank of Canada; visitors can reach the museum through the back door. The exhibit, displayed throughout eight rooms, recounts the history of money. The first room deals with the first objects to be used as currency. Among these are Native-American *wampum* belts adorned with sea-shell beads. Visitors can then follow the evolution of the coin, from those of the Chinese, who were the first to use them, to the Florentines' (florins), the first to make them from precious metals. Rooms 3 to 6 relate the creation of Canadian currency. Numismatists will also have the opportunity to admire a beautiful collection of old coins and paper money in the 8th and final room.

The **National Arts Centre** *(between Confederation Square and the Rideau Canal, ☎996-5051)* presents excellent concerts and plays all year long (see p 342). It also has the advantage of being built at the edge of the Rideau Canal, with its splendid site used aptly for outdoor cafés during the summer.

The **Rideau Canal** snakes through the city, to the great delight of people who come for a breath of fresh air in the urban mêlé. In the summer, its banks boast parkland dotted with picnic tables, and there are paths alongside the canal for the use of pedestrians and cyclists. In the winter, once the canal is frozen over, it is transformed into a vast skating rink that crosses the city. Facing the National Arts Centre is a pavilion open year-round where, in the summer, you can rent pedalboats and canoes and, in the winter, tie on your skates or simply warm up.

Visitors will reach the shores of **Dows Lake** by following Queen Elizabeth Drive. There is another small pavilion here, where you can rent pedal boats and canoes in summer, or warm up and lace up your skates or rent some in winter.

On a fine summer day, there is nothing quite like a stroll along the locks, where pleasure boats abound. This walk is all the more pleasant because it leads across the canal (little bridges are set up atop the gates of the locks) to Major's Hill Park, a vast garden stretching from the National Gallery of Canada to Nepean Point, with its fine **view** ★ of Parliament Hill.

Right next to the locks, you will notice a stone house; from 1827, it is oldest building in the city. Inside the **Bytown Museum** *($2.25; Apr and May, Oct and Nov, Mon to Fri 10am to 4pm; May to Oct, Mon to Sat 10am to 4pm, Sun 2pm to 5pm; next to the locks, ☎234-4570)*, which retraces the history of the city from its rough beginnings following the war of 1812 up until it became Ottawa, the Canadian capital. An interesting exhibit highlights the progress of the building of the Rideau Canal.

Lower Town ★★★

Early on, two distinct neighbourhoods developed on either side of the Rideau Canal. Lower Town, on the east side of the canal, around the present-day By Ward Market, was inhabited mostly by poor Irish, drawn by construction work on the canal, and by French Canadians, who came some years later to work in the prosperous lumber industry. This part of the city presented a tougher, less affluent face than the grand avenues of the upper town. Life was not always rosy, and skirmishes between Irish and French, often competing for the same jobs, were a frequent occurrence. Today these rivalries are ancient history, and this district of Ottawa is one of the most pleasing in the city.

The bridge crossing the canal becomes Rideau Street on this side, lined by rows of shops.

You will first see the imposing **Château Laurier**, which has overlooked the Rideau Canal since 1912 and remains among the city's most prestigious hotels (see p 340). This hotel presents the chateau-style architecture typical of the Canadian Pacific hotel chain, of which it is part.

Next to this is the **Canadian Museum of Contemporary Photography** *(free admission; May to Sep, Mon and Tue, Fri and Sun 11am to 5pm, Wed 4pm to 8pm, Thu 11am to 8pm; Sep to Apr, Wed and Fri-Sun 11am to 5pm, Thu 11am to 8pm; 1 Rideau Canal, ☎993-4497)*, with a collection containing more than 158,000 images created from the photographic resources of the National Film Board of Canada.

Laurier House ★ *($2.50; Apr to Sep, Tue to Sat 9am to 5pm, Sun 2pm to 5pm; Oct to Mar, Tue to Sat 10am to 5pm, Sun 2pm to 5pm; 335 Laurier Avenue East, ☎992-8142)*, a delightful residence built in 1878, belonged to Sir Wilfrid Laurier. He was elected Prime Minister of Canada in 1896, and that year his party, the Liberal Party of Canada, offered him this house. Laurier was the first French-speaker to become Canadian Prime Minister, a post he held until 1911; he lived in this house until his death in 1919. Later, Lady Laurier gave it to William Lyon Mackenzie King, who succeeded her husband as Liberal leader. When King died in 1950, the house was bequeathed to the government as part of Canada's heritage. Visiting it today, you can explore several rooms decorated according to King's tastes and a few others decorated with the Laurier family's furniture.

One of Ottawa's liveliest places, the **By Ward Market** ★★ *(around York and George Sts.)* is a pleasant open-air market where various merchants assemble to sell fruits, vegetables, flowers and all sorts of other treasures and knick-knacks. All around, and on the neighbouring streets, there are many shops, restaurants, bars and cafés, some of them with pretty outdoor terraces. On fine summer days, the area is at its most lively, with crowds of people out for a stroll or a little shopping.

The **National Gallery of Canada** ★★★ *(free admission to the permanent collection; Jun to early Oct, every day 10am to 6pm, Wed-Fri 10am to 8pm; Oct to late May, Wed to Sun 10am to 5pm, Thu 10am to 8pm; 380 Sussex Drive, ☎990-1985 or 1-800-318-ARTS)*, with its collection of 45,000 works of art, 1,200 of which are on display, offers a fabulous trip through the art history of Canada and elsewhere.

ONTARIO

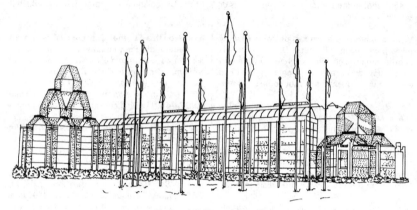

National Gallery of Canada

Rising above the Ottawa River, this modern glass, granite and concrete building, a masterpiece by architect Moshe Safdie, is easily identified by its harmonious tower, covered with glass triangles, recalling the shape of the parliamentary library visible in the distance.

Once inside, the museum seems to draws you in. You'll first walk up the Colonnnade, stopping for a minute to contemplate the Boreal Garden outside, inspired by the work of the Group of Seven. Once in the Grand Hall, the spectacular view of the Parliament Buildings and the Ottawa River unfolds before you.

The first rooms of the museum, on the ground floor, are devoted to the works of Canadian and American artists. Fifteen of these rooms trace the evolution of Canadian artistic movements. Some of the finest canvasses from the 19th century are exhibited there, notably *Sister Saint Alphonse* by Antoine Plamondon, recognized as one of the earliest Canadian masterpieces. You can also see works by Cornelius Krieghoff, an artist of Dutch descent who portrayed the lives of ordinary people in the early days of colonization with great brio.

The following rooms present important works by artists who made their mark in the early 20th century. Among them, are canvasses by the Ontario painter Tom Thomson (*The Jack Pine*) and by members of the Group of Seven (including *The Red Maple* by A.Y. Jackson), who created unique works in the modern interpretation of natural scenes from the Canadian Shield. Space is also given to artists who gained acclaim by creating painting techniques and exploiting themes that were particular to them, including British Columbian artist Emily Carr (*Indian Hut, Queen Charlotte Islands*). You can also contemplate canvasses by great 20th-century Québec painters, notably Alfred Pellan (*On the Beach*), Jean-Paul Riopelle (*Pavane*), Jean-Paul Lemieux (*The Visit*), and Paul-Émile Borduas (*Leeward of the Island*).

The ground floor also includes the Inuit art galleries, which are worthy of special attention. With about 160 sculptures and 200 prints, they provide an occasion to admire several masterpieces of Inuit art. Among them, *The Enchanted Owl* by Kenojuak and the beautiful sculpture *Man and Woman Seated with a Child*.

The museum also houses an impressive collection of American and European works. The collection of works of the great masters is presented in chronological order, and in the course of your visit you can contemplate creations by famous painters such as the Pierre-Paul Rubens work *The Entombment*. The rooms containing 19th-century canvasses present several surprises, including *Mercury and Argus* by Turner, *Woman an Unmbrella* by Edgar Degas, *Waterloo Bridge: The Sun in the Fog* by Claude Monet, *Forest* by Paul Cézanne, and *Hope I* by Gustav Klimt. The achievements of 20th-century artists are also highlighted; the museum exhibits canvasses including *Nude on Yellow Sofa* by Matisse, *The Small Table* by Picasso, *The Glass of Absinth* by Georges

Braque, *Number 29* by Jackson Pollock, and *In the Line of Fire* by Barnett Newman. The collection of American art includes several lithographies by Roy Lichtenstein and Andy Warhol.

The string of rooms on the ground floor surrounds a very special gallery housing an unusual work: the beautiful interior of the **chapel of Notre Dame du Sacré Coeur convent**, made of gracious vaults ending in wood panelling. It was rebuilt in the museum and then restored to save it from otherwise certain destruction.

In 1841, **Notre Dame Basilica ★** *(Sussex Drive at the corner of Saint Patrick Street)*, topped by two elegant steeples, was built to serve Catholics in Lower Town, French-speakers as well as the English-speaking Irish. In the choir stall, you will notice the presence of Saint John the Baptist and of Saint Patrick. This is the oldest church in the city. Its magnificent choir stall of finely worked wood and statues of the prophets and evangelists by Louis-Philippe Hébert are still in perfect condition.

The **Canadian War Museum ★** *($3.50; May to Sep, every day 9:30am to 5pm; Sep to May closed Mon; 330 Sussex Dr., ☎776-8600)* traces the history of the armed forces in Canada from their early battles at the beginning of the colonial period to the great world events that have marked the 20th century. You can also observe various weapons manufactured and used by the Canadian army over the years, notably heavy artillery pieces.

The **Royal Canadian Mint** *($2; May to Aug, Mon to Fri 9am to 4pm, Sat-Sun 10am to 5pm; 320 Sussex Dr., ☎993-5700)*. This building houses equipment used to make coins. In the past couple of decades, only collector's items such as the gold or silver maple leaf coins have been made here. Visitors can observe the production process.

Outside the downtown area ★

Some of the main attractions of the city are situated near the Rideau Canal where it reaches the Ottawa River, and are easily accessible on foot. There are also other attractions farther out which are easier to explore if you have a car or bicycle.

Beyond the Royal Canadian Mint, Sussex Drive continues alongside the Ottawa River. It goes past Green Island, where the Rideau River flows into the Ottawa River, forming two waterfalls that descend like a curtain. Rideau is the French word for curtain, hence the river's name.

Next you will reach one of the city's most opulent neighbourhoods, with its many fine mansions. Among them, at 24 Sussex Drive, an immense stone residence surrounded by a beautiful garden. This is the **official residence of the Prime Minister of Canada**. Built in 1867 for businessman Joseph Currier, it became the home of Canadian Prime Ministers in 1949. Visitors are not admitted.

Not far off is the magnificent **Rideau Hall ★** *(free admission; garden schedule varies; 1 Sussex Dr., ☎998-7113)* is the official residence of the governor-general, the representative of Queen Elizabeth II in Canada. In practice, the powers of the governor-general are more symbolic than real. Thomas Mackay had this sumptuous dwelling built in 1838, and it was named the Chateau Mackay. In 1865 the government rented it for the use of Lord Monck, the governor-general of the time, and then bought it in 1868. Since then, several modifications have been made to the original building, which has long served as an official residence. Visitors are allowed to roam about the vast, pleasant garden, which covers 35.6 hectares (88 acres) and surrounds the house. During the summer, it is also possible to go on a guided tour of the house, five of whose rooms are open to the public.

Facing Rideau Hall is a lovely green space, **Rockliffe Park**, with lookouts offering fine views of Hull and the Gatineau River.

Going inside the **National Aviation Museum ★★★** *($5; Apr to Oct, every day 9am to 5pm, Thu until 8pm; Oct to Apr every day 10am to 5pm; Rockliffe Airport, ☎993-2010)*, you will immediately be struck by the very special atmosphere emanating from this gigantic triangular building, which houses a stunning and marvellously laid out collection of aircraft. You can admire more than a hundred of these flying machines, ranging from the earliest models to fighters and bombers from the two world wars to airplanes that played a role in civil aviation. Besides the aircraft, the museum features the interesting "Walkway of Time", a trip through the history of aviation, full of reconstructions and clear

ONTARIO

explanations on technical and historical matters.

The **Canadian Museum of Nature** ★ *($4; May to Sep, every day 9:30am to 5pm, Thu until 8pm; Sep to May, every day 10am to 5pm, Thu until 8pm; at the corner of McLeod and Metcalfe Sts., ☎566-4700)* is set in a spacious, three-floor building, with each floor presenting a particular natural facet. The museum covers all aspects of nature, from geology and the formation of the planet, to reconstitutions of prehistoric animals that lived in Canada, to mammals and birds that originate in Canada and still inhabit its forests, without forgetting the wonderful world of insects as well as plant life in general.

The **National Museum of Science and Technology** ★★ *($6; May to Sep, every day 9am to 6pm, Fri until 9pm; Sep to Apr, 9am to 5pm; 1867 Saint Laurent Blvd., ☎991-3044)* covers these fascinating topics, making it accessible to all. The attraction of this museum lies not in any particular collection but in its interactive presentation of a great variety of subjects as varied as computers, printing, transport, astronomy and communications. Thanks to numerous games, explanatory panels and scale models of all sorts, visitors will become familiar with the subjects at hand.

Along the Rideau Canal ★

Winding its way through Eastern Ontario's undulating countryside, the Rideau Canal lead to the development of various important industrial centres when it was built in the 1830s. Now just peaceful villages, these centres are as charming as can be. This 100-kilometre-plus ride leads along attractive back-country roads; after Merrickville it leads to Peterborough.

Merrickville ★★

A surprising number of splendid stone buildings line the streets of this small village. Dating back to the 19th century, they bear witness to the former wealth of this hamlet. In 1793, William Mirick undertook the construction of mills next to the waterfalls located at this point on the Rideau River, and this led to the village's prosperity. During the 19th century, development gained pace with the building of the Rideau Canal. The advent of the railway,

however, curtailed Merrickville's prosperity, when the town was bypassed by railroad builders. One positive repurcussion of this decline, however, is that the village was spared from modernization, and its distinct character seems frozen in time.

Walking alongside the Rideau Canal, the first building you come to is the **Merrickville Public Library** ★ *(Main St.)*, built around the 1890s by William Pearson. This elegant brick building has a gable and a verandah. It was Pearson's daughter Mary who bequeathed this superb dwelling to the town to house its library.

In front, the **Sam Jakes Inn**, now converted to a stylish and comfortable inn, is the former residence of Samuel Jakes, who had it built in 1861.

The **Blockhouse** *($1; mid-May to mid-Oct, every day; ☎692-2581)* is the biggest military building erected along the Rideau Canal to protect war boats that used this waterway. It could accommodate up to 50 soldiers, and today houses a small museum.

At the edge of the Rideau River is the Merrickville **industrial zone** ★, with ruins of the mills that once assured the village's prosperity. Among these buildings, the oldest of them built in 1793 by William Mirick, you will see a sawmill, a weaving mill, a flour mill and an oat-processing mill. Not far from this area, on Mill Street, is William Mirick's last residence.

Saint Lawrence Street is lined with a cluster of shops, each more charming than the last, where you can linger for hours in front of the tempting show windows. For those who wish to explore the other treasures in this delightful village, a small brochure entitled *Merrickville Walking Tour* is also available.

 OUTDOORS

 Hiking

It is possible to set out on the 400 km of hiking trails forming the **Rideau Trail** alongside the Rideau Canal, through the undulating lands and forests of eastern Ontario at the edge of the Canadian Shield, extending from Kingston to Ottawa. In some places there are parallel trails.

Maps are available from the **Rideau Trail Association**: P.O. Box 14, Kingston, K7L 4V6.

 Biking

In Ottawa, there is nothing quite like following the Rideau Canal by bicycle, using the cycling paths running alongside this waterway. The ride is easy and if you like, you can stop for a few moments at one of the benches set out along the trail to enjoy the refreshing shade of a tree while contemplating the lively atmosphere that reigns along the canal. Bike rentals are available at **RentABike**: Chateau Laurier, 1 Rideau St., Ottawa, ☎241-4140.

 Cruises

As soon as the fine weather arrives, cruises are operated along the waterways surrounding Ottawa. You can take part, seeing the city from a different angle and drifting quietly on the waves. Several companies offer such excursions, notably **Ottawa Riverboat**: 30 Murray St., Ottawa, Ontario, K1N 5M4, ☎562-4888.

 Skating

Imagine lacing on a pair of skates and gliding uninterrupted over 8 km of ice. Every winter, as soon as the Rideau Canal has frozen over, in late December or early January, the canal is transformed into a vast skating rink, one of the longest in the world. The ice surface is cleared and maintained for the pleasure of skaters of all ages. A heated cabin is at the disposal of visitors just a few steps from the National Arts Centre to allow skaters to lace up in warmth.

 ACCOMMODATIONS

Right next to the Rideau Centre, in the heart of the action, is Ottawa's **Youth Hostel** *($18.75 for a bed, $42 for a room; 75 Nicholas St., Ottawa K1N 7B9;* ☎*235-2595)*, with fully equipped common kitchen and showers. It is interesting to note that it occupies the site of a former prison.

Right in the city, on the Lebreton flats, travellers will find a small, friendly **campground** *($, free for children under 12; June to early Sept; tents only;* ☎*724-6096 or 1-800-465-1867)* easily reached by a bicycle path as well as by car or bus. It is run by the National Capital Commission and has 200 campsites. Toilets, showers and picnic tables. Reservations are not accepted.

Around Parliament Hill

It is possible to find lodgings not far from the Parliament Buildings along a stretch of Albert Street where businesses and the downtown bustle give way to a quiet residential neighbourhood. There you will find two charming inns. The **Doral Inn** *($60; 468 Albert Street, Ottawa K1R 5B5,* ☎*230-8055)*, whose decor is a tad uninspired, is set in a pretty Victorian house. The rooms, each with a private bathroom, are well kept. Next door, the **Albert House** *($50 bkfst; 478 Albert Street, Ottawa K1R 5B5,* ☎*236-4479)* is also located in an appealing residence. There are only 17 rooms, giving it a pleasant family atmosphere. Each of the rooms is perfectly maintained and decorated with care.

The classic **Lord Elgin Hotel** *($90;* ℜ, ዼ, ✕; *100 Elgin St., K1P 5K8,* ☎*235-3333 or 1-800-267-4298,* ≈*235-3223)* has dominated the Rideau Canal for the last 50 years. This sumptuous hotel, among the most elegant in the city, has more than 300 rooms. Recently renovated for the utmost in comfort, the hotel has nevertheless kept its old-fashioned charm.

As you enter the **Delta** *($99;* ≈, ℜ, ◌, ◑; *361 Queen St., K1R 7S9,* ☎*238-6000,* ≈*238-2290)* you will straightaway notice the efforts made to create a more intimate atmosphere than at the standard downtown chain hotel. The glass ceiling allows plenty of light to penetrate the vast lobby. It also boasts large plants, mahogany chairs and a cosy fireplace. The rooms are of a good size and are furnished with comfortable mahogany pieces. Finally, children will be thrilled with the pool's long waterslide.

Some prefer older establishments filled with antiques and an elegant decor, still others opt for modern styling and the utmost in service. Those who fit into the latter category will appreciate the very modern **Sheraton** *($119;* ≈, ℜ, ◌, ◑, ዼ;*150 Albert St., K1P 5G2,*

ONTARIO

☎238-1500, 1-800-489-8333, ⇝235-2723), with its conference halls, large rooms with offices, telephones with voice-mail, hair dryers and fitness centre with pool, sauna and whirlpool bath.

Set in an imposing old house, the **Carmichael Inn & Spa** *($125 bkfst incl.; ℜ; 46 Cartier St., Ottawa K2P 1J3,* ☎236-4667, ⇝563-7529) is part of Ottawa's heritage. This non-smoking establishment has 11 rooms, decorated with antiques and fitted with queen-size beds.

Lower Town

Around the By Ward Market

Dating back to the early 20th century but entirely renovated, **L'Auberge du Marché** *($60 bkfst incl.; 87 Guigues St., Ottawa, K1N 5H8,* ☎241-6610 or 1-800-465-0079) is a little house that reflects the charm of its proprietor. There are three rooms upstairs and a shared bathroom, as well as a suite on the ground floor with a private bathroom, a full kitchen, and a small lounge with sofa-bed and cable television. Breakfast varies each day, but is always plentiful and refined. Guests have a private entrance allowing them to come and go as they please.

Located in a quiet neighbourhood and affording a superb view of Strathcona Park, the **Olde Bytown Bed and Breakfast** *($75 brkfst incl.; pb, sb; 459 Laurier Ave. E., K1N 6R4,* ☎565-7939, ⇝565-7981) is a choice place for those who appreciate the cachet of turn-of-the-century Victorian houses. The B & B's every room is meticulously kept and graced with beautiful antiques, flowered wallpaper and old artifacts. There are seven wonderfully cosy rooms in which guests could easily spend hours daydreaming.

The **Westin Hotel** *($135; ≈, ℜ, △, ⊛, ⊙, ⎈, ✗; 11 Colonel By Dr.,* ☎560-7000, ⇝569-2013) has what may be the most enviable location in Ottawa, facing the Rideau Canal, opposite the National Arts Centre and right in the heart of Ottawa's bustle. It is part of the complex that includes the Rideau Centre shopping mall and the Ottawa Convention Centre. Rooms are very spacious and extremely comfortable, offering magnificent views of the canal. The hotel has a very good restaurant, **Daly's** (excellent atmosphere, interesting and refined cuisine),

and even a happening night club. Very good weekend packages are usually available.

Part of the Canadian Pacific hotel chain, the **Château Laurier** *($150; ≈; △; ⎈; 1 Rideau St., Ottawa K1N 8S7,* ☎241-1414 or 1-800-441-1414, ⇝562-7030) does not need any introduction. Service reflects the long tradition of the grand hotels of this chain. Rooms are elegant, and the attentive service is impeccable. Nothing more needs to be said about the quality of the hotel, which also has several fine restaurants (see p 342).

Along the Rideau Canal

Merrickville

The **Sam Jakes Inn** *($129 bkrfs; ℜ, ⊛; 118 Main St. E., K0G 1N0,* ☎269-3711 or 1-800-567-4667, ⇝269-3713) occupies a splendid and very elegant early 19th-century residence. Rooms are comfortable and decorated with fine old furniture. Excellent meals are available in big dining rooms on the ground floor. The courteous hospitality and quiet atmosphere make this inn a choice spot for a restful stay.

 RESTAURANTS

Ottawa offers a variety of cuisines from around the world. The atmosphere is are relatively quiet, however, except on Friday and Saturday evenings!

Around Parliament Hill

If you are looking for a good but simple Mexican meal, the friendly **Pancho Villa** *($-$$; 361 Elgin St.,* ☎234-8872) can provide it. Just next door is **Lois and Frimas**, whose excellent home-made ice creams keep people coming back again and again.

For excellent Indian dishes, make a reservation at the **New Delhi** *($$; 417 Bank St.,* ☎237-4041). The friendly owner offers dishes prepared with fresh quality ingredients, and the food is never too spicy. The chicken tikka, a Tandoori specialty, is absolutely delicious. There is a buffet for under $10, every day except Saturday. It is also possible to order take-out items by telephone or at the counter.

Elgin Street is home to an institution known to just about everyone in town, the **Ritz** *($$;* *237 Elgin St., ☎235-7027)*. Waiting is almost obligatory at this Italian restaurant, which does not accept reservations. Its pasta dishes are deservedly renowned. Fortunately, this restaurant now has younger siblings. The **Ritz Uptown** *(226 Nepean, ☎238-8752)* is set in an old house, and reservations are accepted. In the summer, many people prefer the **Ritz on the Canal** *(375 Queen Elizabeth Dr., at the corner of 5th Ave., ☎238-8998)*, with a slightly different menu from the other two, including gourmet pizza from a wood-burning oven. Its exceptional setting, at a spot where the canal widens and resembles a bay, explains the great popularity of its huge terrace. These restaurants are for non-smokers only.

The first of them, **Le Métro** *($$$;* *315 Somerset St. W., ☎230-8123)* is doubtless one of the best eating spots in town. The *escargots* with roquefort in pastry are a true joy, as are the steak tartare or simple beef fillet with *béarnaise* sauce. The opulent, harmonious decor, quiet atmosphere and big, comfortable leather chairs assure you a relaxing and delicious evening.

The Café of the National Arts Centre *($$$;* *Elgin St., ☎594-5127)* offers an unbeatable view of the teeming activity on the Rideau Canal, with boats in the summer and skaters in the winter. During the summer months, meals are served on a comfortable, well-designed terrace. Beyond a doubt, this is one of the most pleasant outdoor terraces in town. Refined Canadian cooking is offered; the chef makes inventive use of quality products from various regions of Canada. Grilled Atlantic salmon is a specialty. Not to be missed are the wonderful desserts. Prices are on the high side, however, unless a fixed-price menu is offered, which is unfortunately rare.

Lower Town

To satisfy your sweet tooth, try **Beaver Tails**. Fear not: these delicious and sweet snacks are really something of a cross between doughnuts and biscuits.

Memories *($; 7 Clarence St., ☎232-1882)* is almost always packed. Why? Because almost everyone in Ottawa comes to try the many desserts that have made its reputation. The selection of cakes and pies of all sorts is so impressive that it can be hard to choose. But the greatest temptation may fall on the delicious, oversized portions of apple pie. Light meals (interesting soups, sandwiches, salads) are also available. The coffee is good.

Having a good meal in a shopping centre may seem illusory... And yet, **MarcheLino Mövenpick** *($; Rideau St., at Sussex Dr.)*, in the Rideau Centre, attracts crowds of happy diners. The restaurant's recipe for success is simple: a large dining-room, attractively decorated with plants and wooden tables, and delicious, quickly-prepared dishes from fresh, quality ingredients. In this lively place, everyone is free to stroll about, choosing their dishes from one of the various stations where sushi, salads, pasta, quiches and all sorts of other dishes sure to please the most demanding palates are prepared before your eyes.

Some spots draw attention more for their decor than for their food. This is the case of **Zak's Diner** *($; 89 Clarence St., ☎238-7182)*, whose bright lights and Coca-Cola signs are meant to make it look like a 1950s American diner. The menu seems not to have evolved since that time, with the usual hamburgers, milk shakes and fries, all served in large portions. This is a pleasant spot for breakfast.

If you don't feel like trying anything new, have been craving some family-style cooking and just want a good menu with ordinary dishes, consider **Mother Tucker's** *($$; 61 York St., ☎238-6525)*. Among the choices is the all-you-can-eat roast beef.

Another institution in Ottawa is **The Fish Market** restaurant *($$-$$$; 54 York St., ☎241-3474)*, set up on the approaches to the Byward Market and known throughout the capital since 1979. The dining-room is decorated with nets, buoys and other objects related to fishing, as is only right and proper in an establishment specializing in fish, shellfish and seafood, always impeccably fresh. Two other rooms on the first floor meet other needs. **Coasters**, whose large picture windows look out on the bustling market, is just as pleasant. Dishes here are less sophisticated (fish n' chips) and more moderately priced, but quite good. The third room, **Vineyards**, is the place to go if all you want is a drink (good selection of wine by the glass) and a bite to eat. Shows are sometimes featured here.

ONTARIO

Spending a little time at the Château Laurier sounds appealing? If you enjoy this sort of treat but do not wish to spend a fortune on a meal, head to **Wilfrid's** restaurant *($$-$$$; 1 Rideau St., ☎241-1414)* for lunch. A cosy dining-room, comfortable armchairs, an unobstructed view of the Rideau Canal and an affordable, delicious lunch menu (à-la-carte dishes are around $10) await you here. Having breakfast here can also be very pleasant, but will cost you at least $10.

Domus Café *($$$; 85 Murray St., ☎241-6007)* is undoubtedly one of the best restaurants in Ottawa. The food is refined and innovative, made with the freshest of ingredients; its success is derived from original combinations of international flavours. Recipes are drawn from the many cookbooks sold at the adjacent store. The menu changes every day, but some of the most popular items keep reappearing. The choice is never exhaustive, but the selection is interesting enough to make it difficult to decide. The desserts, limited to a choice of four or five, are of a calibre unequalled in Ottawa. The wine list includes excellent California wines, some of them available by the glass. And finally, try the Sunday brunch. It is divine and well worth the wait (reservations are not accepted for brunch).

  ENTERTAINMENT

Bars and Nightclubs

Near downtown Ottawa, there are several bars and pubs along Elgin Street, which is quite lively in the evening.

Maxwell's *(340 Elgin St., ☎232-5771)*, upstairs from a restaurant, is popular with trendy youth. In the summer, there are tables on a large balcony facing the street scene.

Across the street is a very popular pub, **Lieutenant's Pump** *(361 Elgin St., ☎238-2949)*. There are a few tables outside in the summer, and food is available.

Friday's Piano Bar *(150 Elgin St., ☎237-5353)* is more of a meeting spot for business people. It has an older clientele, some of whom end their evening here after dining at the restaurant of the same name.

The area around the By Ward Market is home to several bars, many of them clustered along George and York streets.

Stoney's *(62 York Street, ☎241-8858)* probably holds the record of longevity for disco-bars. It seems young people have been coming here forever to have a drink and let loose on a small dance floor. In the summer, it is open in back. The music generally tends towards rock and roll.

Vineyard's Wine Bar Bistro *(54 York St., ☎241-4270)* is a friendly, congenial little bar where you can enjoy wine, beer and cheese. Musicians often perform here, with jazz at the top of the list.

Gay bars

Briefs *(151 George St., ☎241-9667)* is a very popular establishment with the local gay community. Set on three floors, there are theme evenings. The dance floor is vast and very crowded on weekends.

Festivals and Cultural Events

The **National Arts Centre** *(between Confederation Square and the Rideau Canal, ☎996-5051)* is Ottawa's cultural headquarters, with an opera house and two theatres where top-notch performances are offered year-round.

For information on activities going on in the region, contact the **National Capital Commission** *(☎239-5555 or 1-800-465-1867)*.

Winterlude no longer needs an introduction: its reputation is well established in Canada. It consists of 10 days of winter festivities of all sorts in early February and is centred on what is billed as the world's longest skating rink.

The **tulip festival** is held in May, around the Victoria Day holiday. Tulips are offered each year by the Netherlands as a gesture of thanks to Canada for having sheltered Queen Wilhelmina during the Second World War. The city blooms with profusions of magnificent tulips everywhere, while programs of all sorts, including shows and various activities, are put on in different parts of the city, notably Confederation Park and Dows Lake.

The **Ottawa Jazz Festival** takes place in July, near the National Arts Centre.

 SHOPPING

Around Parliament Hill

Canada Books *(Sparks St.)* has a fine selection of Canadian books, whether it be literature, arts, photography or other topics.

The boutique at the **National Gallery** *(380 Sussex Dr.)* sells prints of all the masterpieces exhibited at the museum, as well as art books, crafts and native sculptures.

Lower Town

For window shopping and some interesting finds, nothing beats a stroll around the By Ward Market. Winter or summer, the central pavillion, where vegetable dealers gather in the summer, houses a multitude of handicraft stalls on two floors. You can buy all sorts of items: jewellery, leather goods, scarves, paintings, and so on. The vegetable market lies at the heart of the action in the summer. It is a pleasant spot to shop or merely to linger.

The **Rideau Centre** *(50 Rideau St.)*, with its 200 boutiques including the Eaton department store, has everything. Among the stores worth mentioning: HMV (music), the Disney store, Oh Yes Ottawa (souvenirs), Mrs. Tiggy Winkles (toys) and Roots (clothing and leather goods). The shopping centre also has two pharmacies, banks, plus lots of fast-food restaurants and the MarcheLino Mövenpick (see p 341).

ONTARIO

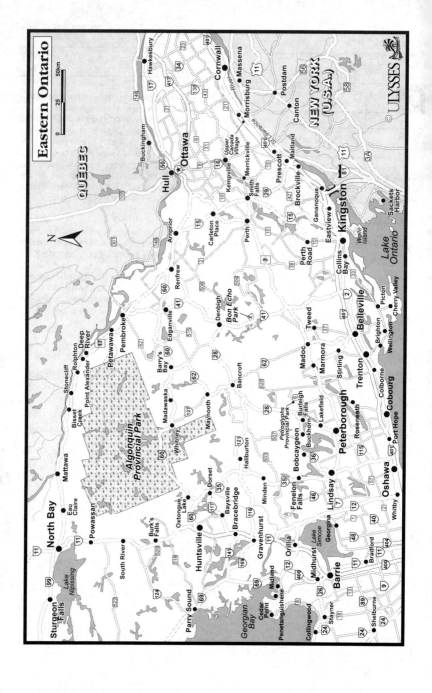

Eastern Ontario

SOUTHEASTERN ONTARIO

outheastern Ontario, a rich plain between the St. Lawrence River and the Canadian Shield, has always been favourable to human habitation. Natives were drawn here by the fertile land and abundant supply of fresh water; French colonists, by the region's strategic location along the lucrative fur route. Later, Loyalists arriving from the newly independent United States chose to establish their new villages in these vast spaces. This hospitable region has been welcoming new inhabitants ever since, and some villages have developed into lovely cities, like Kingston, while others, having preserved their old-fashioned character, have become popular vacation spots.

Vast, rolling fields greet visitors who explore this magnificent region. Splendid old houses that seem to have been there since the earliest days of colonization pop up around every other bend in the road. The region's first hamlets, now cities like Brockville, remain virtually unchanged and are still graced with lovely Victorian buildings. In some places, where the human presence is less obvious, the landscape consists largely of a forest of hardwoods and conifers strewn with lakes and rivers.

 FINDING YOUR WAY AROUND

By Car

From the Quebec border, Highway 401 runs all the way to Oshawa, in the Toronto area. If you have more time, however, we recommend Route 2, which runs alongside the St. Lawrence and then Lake Ontario, leading through lovely pastoral scenery and offering some magnificent views. It runs through or near all the stops on this tour (Cornwall, Morrisburg, Prescott, Brockville, Gananoque, Kingston, Cobourg and Oshawa).

Visitors starting out from Ottawa can take the 417 and then the 138 to Cornwall.

By Train

The train through the Montreal-Windsor corridor runs alongside part of the area covered by this tour, so visitors can easily reach Cornwall, Kingston and Oshawa stations by train.

Cornwall: Station St.
Kingston: 800 Counter St.
Oshawa: On Thornton St. S.

By Bus

There is bus service to every little town along this tour.

Cornwall: 120 Tolgate Rd. W., ☎(613) 932-9511.
Kingston: 175 Counter St., ☎(613) 547-4916.
Oshawa: 47 Brown St. W., ☎(905) 723-2241.

 PRACTICAL INFORMATION

Area Code: 613, except for Oshawa 905.

Tourist Information Offices

Eastern Ontario Travel Association: R.R.1, Lansdowne, ON, K0E 1L0, ☎659-4300, ☎(800) 567-EAST, ≈659-4306.

Lakelands: HTA- Simcoe County Building, Midhurst, ON, L0L 1X0, ☎(705) 726-9300.

Quinte's Isle Tourist Association: P.O. Box 50, Picton, ON, K0K 2T0, ☎476-2421, ≈476-7461.

 EXPLORING

Following the St. Lawrence ★★★

The shores of the St. Lawrence River were among the very first parts of Ontario to be colonized on the Great Lakes route. As early as the 17th century, a number of French forts were built here, most notably Fort Frontenac (1673), on the site now occupied by Kingston. Long before any forts were erected, however, Iroquoian tribes (Hurons and Iroquois) fought over the borders of this vast territory, delimited by the southern part of the St. Lawrence River and the shores of the Great Lakes. This tour will guide you alongside the majestic St. Lawrence, which meets Lake Ontario at Kingston. In addition to picturesque towns like Kingston, this tour features a visit to Upper Canada Village, a reconstructed pioneer village that will transport you 100 years back in time,

and to outstanding natural sites like the Thousand Islands.

Cornwall

In 1784, in the wake of the American Revolution, a number of Scots left the United States and settled on the shores of the St. Lawrence River, where they founded Cornwall. This rather grim-looking industrial city is now the largest Ontarian town on the St. Lawrence. Located on the Quebec border, it is populated by both English- and French-speakers. The pulp and paper industry, hydroelectric dams and the cotton industry form the backbone of the local economy but have never brought the town any real prosperity. Some particularly gloomy sectors and an uninteresting industrial zone ring the nondescript downtown area made up of uninspiring buildings. A bridge links Cornwall to New York State, and for many, Cornwall is just a place to pass through on their way somewhere else.

If you do decide to spend some time in Cornwall, however, there are a few interesting tourist attractions, including the **Inverarden Regency Cottage Museum** *(free admission; Apr to Nov, Tue to Sat 11am to 5pm, Sun 2pm to 5pm; Montreal Rd., east of Boundary, ☎938-9585)*. This magnificent house, erected in 1816 for fur merchant John McDonald, is one of the finest examples of Regency architecture in Ontario. It has no fewer than 14 rooms, all decorated with lovely period furniture. The museum's splendid garden, which looks out onto the St. Lawrence, is an exquisite place to stroll about on a fine summer day.

The little **United Counties Museum in the Wood House** *(free admission; Apr to Nov, Tue to Sat 11am to 5pm, Sun 1pm to 5pm; 2nd St. W., ☎932-2381)*, better known locally as the Wood House Museum, displays a number of paintings by Canadian artists, as well as various everyday objects from the early days of colonization, including toys and tools.

Morrisburg

Morrisburg would be just another little town if it weren't for its proximity to Upper Canada Village, a remarkable tourist attraction consisting of houses from eight little villages that were flooded when the water level of the river was raised during the construction of the

St. Lawrence Seaway. The houses were moved to Crysler Farm Battlefield Park, where they now make up a fascinating historical reproduction of a 19th century community. The park also has a small monument commemorating the Canadian victory over American troops in the War of 1812.

With 35 buildings, **Upper Canada Village ★★★** *($9.50; May to Oct, every day 9:30am to 5pm; Crysler Farm Battlefield Park, 11 km east of Morrisburg, on Rte. 2, ☎613-543-3704)* is an outstanding reconstruction of the type of village found in this part of Canada back in the 1860's. The place has a remarkably authentic feel about it, and you will be continually surprised by the extraordinary attention to the detail that went into building it. A sawmill, a general store, a farm, a doctor's house – nothing is missing in this village that you can explore on foot or by horse-drawn cart. To top off this almost idyllic tableau, the "villagers" are costumed guides able to answer all your questions. Their carefully designed outfits reflect both their trade and social class. You can spend several hours exploring Upper Canada Village and watching the various inhabitants go about their business (running the sawmill, working on the farm, using the flour mill, etc.).

The Parks of the St. Lawrence, see p 352.

Prescott

For many years, Prescott occupied a key location on the St. Lawrence Seaway because the rapids at this point on the river prevented boats from going any farther, forcing them to unload their merchandise here. A fort was thus built to defend the area. Today, this charming little town still has an active port, since it has the only deep-water harbour between Montreal and Kingston. Most people come here to see the fort, however.

In 1838-1839, **Fort Wellington ★** *($2.25; May to Sep, every day 10am to 5pm; head east on Rte. 2, ☎925-2896)* was erected on the site of an earlier military structure built during the Canadian-American War of 1812. The fort, with its massive stone walls and blockhouse, was designed to protect the seaway. It remained in use until the 1920's, and has since been restored and opened to the public, complete with guides to liven up the atmosphere.

Brockville ★

Brockville boasts a number of splendid buildings, which bear witness to the golden era of the Loyalists. From the late 18th century, when it was founded, up until the beginning of the 20th, Brockville, like many other towns along the St. Lawrence, enjoyed a long period of opulence, which is reflected in its magnificent residences.

Gananoque

Upon entering Gananoque, you will be greeted by a long commercial artery lined with scores of fast-food restaurants and motels. The place is not especially inviting, but it does serve as a departure point for cruises in the Thousand Islands region, and several lovely houses from the last century line its waterfront.

The Thousand Islands ★★

Islands, islands and still more islands... the Thousand Islands, which actually number 1,865, boast some remarkably beautiful scenery. The Cataraquis Indians, who inhabited this region before the colonists arrived, called it "The Garden of the Great Spirit" While exploring the area, you will discover all sorts of islands, ranging from tiny islets (two trees and 2.5 square metres of land are the minimum requirements for an island to be categorized as such) to big islands adorned with opulent houses.

A cruise on the St. Lawrence is an extremely pleasant way to enjoy a close look at this veritable maze of islands, some of which are particularly interesting. In addition to taking in the fascinating scenery, you can actually visit some of the islands, such as Gordon Island, the smallest national park in Canada, and Heart Island, home of Boldt Castle; don't forget, however, that the latter is in American territory, so European passengers must show their passport before disembarking there.

The **Thousand Islands** region is the perfect place for a pleasant trip on the St. Lawrence. Cruises from **Gananoque** offer a chance to take in some lovely scenery.

From Gananoque: **Gananoque Boat Line**, ☎382-2144 or 382-2146; 3-hour cruise, $15.

ONTARIO

From Kingston: **Island Queen**, ☎549-5544; 3-hour cruise, $15.95.

Kingston ★★

In 1673, the Comte de Frontenac sent René-Robert Cavelier de La Salle up the St. Lawrence River to scout out the perfect location for a trading post. La Salle chose to erect a fort, which he named Fort Frontenac, at the point where the river met Lake Ontario. The site was a strategic one, since it was located along the route taken by both explorers and *coureurs des bois* (trappers). From that point on, the French began to develop lucrative commercial ties with the natives. They remained in the region for nearly a century, until 1758, when the fort was captured by the English under Colonel Bradstreet, putting an end to French colonization in the area.

After the English conquest, the area was abandoned until 1783, when Loyalists arriving from the United States founded Kingston here. As a stopping point on the Great Lakes Route, the town enjoyed renewed prosperity, and Fort Henry was built to protect the area during the War of 1812. Kingston gradually became bigger and bigger, and was even the capital of Upper and Lower Canada for a few years (1841-1844). Due to its proximity to the U.S. border and the fear of an American invasion, however, it lost the title to Montreal, which only held it itself until 1849, when Ottawa was finally named capital.

A number of magnificent Victorian buildings bear witness to the city's glorious past, as do several large military schools, most importantly the Royal Military College and the National Defense College. Furthermore, Kingston lies on the shores of Lake Ontario and has an extremely attractive downtown area, which is bustling with life when the weather is fine. We have outlined a walking tour to help you explore this town, one of Eastern Ontario's jewels.

Fort Henry ★★ *($9.50; May to Oct, every day 10am to 5pm; Rte. 2,* ☎542-7388*)* was built between 1832 and 1837 on a promontory overlooking Lake Ontario, in order to protect Upper Canada in the event of an American invasion. This large military post was never attacked, however, and was abandoned after the 1870's, when an invasion no longer seemed likely. Later, in the 1930's, the building underwent renovations.

Upon entering, you will be greeted by guides in period costume, who will tell you about life at the fort in the 19th century. You will also have a chance to attend shooting drills performed by the Fort Henry Guard, whose uniforms are similar to those worn by English soldiers in 1867. This is definitely the most memorable part of the visit. After watching these demonstrations, you can tour the barracks, whose rooms still contain 19th century furnishings and tools, offering a good idea of what daily life was like here back then. Finally, you can spend some time admiring the museum's fine collection of 19th century English military equipment.

The Royal Military College is visible on nearby Point Frederick. Not far from there, a Martello tower dating from 1846 houses the **Royal Military College of Canada Museum** *(free admission;* ☎541-6000, ext. 6664*)*, where you can learn about the history of the college and the first military conflicts to take place in this region.

Kingston's era of prosperity during the 1840s and 1850s corresponds to the apogee of neoclassicism in Canada. It is therefore not surprising to find a significant collection of buildings in this style, the majority of which are of grey limestone extracted from local quarries. This is the case with the Kingston's **City Hall ★** *(216 Ontario St.)*. This vast building was constructed between 1842 and 1844 when the town was the seat of government for United Canada. Following the decision to move the colonial capital to Montreal, the town councillors graciously, though unsuccessfully, offered the government this city hall in the hopes that it might change its mind. City Hall overlooks the water and is reminiscent of the grand public buildings of Dublin, Ireland. The Council Room and Ontario Hall on the second floor have what are considered the most beautiful interior neoclassical decors in Canada.

Just opposite City Hall, on the banks of the Cataraqui River, lies **Confederation Park**. This vast stretch of greenery is perfect for a stroll. Right beside the park, you'll find the tourist office, where you can catch the **Confederation Tour Train** *($7.50; mid-May to Sep, 10am to 7pm)*, a small train that runs through the old parts of Kingston.

Cruises to the Thousand Islands set out from the marina by the park (see p 347).

Kingston City Hall

Keep walking on **Ontario Street**, Kingston's major downtown artery, which is lined with all sorts of little shops and restaurants with pretty terraces. You'll come first to the **Prince George Hotel** whose original section was built in 1809. Two additions were added later and the building as it stands now was completed in 1867. It was further renovated and transformed into a hotel in 1978.

St. George's Cathedral is the seat of the anglican bishopric of Kingston. This lovely neoclassical building was completed in 1825 and designed by Thomas Rogers. The portico, tower and clock were added in 1846, while the cupola dates from 1891. On the same block, the former **post office** and **customs house** are reminiscent of the 17th century England of Inigo Jones. These two edifices were built in 1856 according to designs by Montreal architects Hopkins, Lawford and Nelson.

At the beginning of the 19th century, the Catholic bishopric of Kingston covered all of Upper Canada (Ontario). In 1843, **St. Mary's Roman Catholic Cathedral ★** *(corner of Johnson and Clergy Sts.)* was built so that the bishopric would have a worthy house of worship. The 60-metre-high neo-Gothic tower was added in 1887.

You will eventually come to two little museums located almost side by side. The first, the **Marine Museum of the Great Lakes** *(at the corner of Ontario and Union, ☎542-2261)*, deals with the history of navigation on the Great Lakes, from 1678 on. Moored in front of the museum is the *Alexander Henry*, an icebreaker that has been converted into an inn (see p 353).

The second museum, the **Pump House Station Museum** *(23 Ontario St., ☎546-4696)* is a fully restored pumping station containing different models of steam pumps, as well as other machinery dating from 1849. These huge pumps were one of the most important sources of energy in the 19th century.

Martello towers, invented by the engineer of the same name, were a common part of the British defense system in the early 19th

ONTARIO

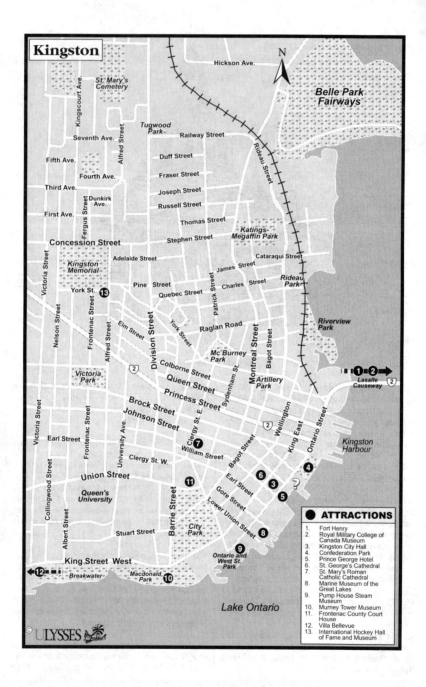

Kingston

Hickson Ave.

N

Belle Park Fairways

St. Mary's Cemetery

Kingscourt Ave.

Tugwood Park

Railway Street

Seventh Ave.

Alfred Street

Duff Street

Fifth Ave.

Fraser Street

Fourth Ave.

Joseph Street

Third Ave.

Dunkirk Ave.

Russell Street

Fergus Street

First Ave.

Thomas Street

Rideau Street

Katings-Megaffin Park

Concession Street

Stephen Street

Victoria Street

Adelaide Street

Cataraqui Street

Kingston Memorial

James Street

Rideau Park

Pine   Street

Charles   Street

York St.

Quebec Street

⑬

Nelson Street

Frontenac Street

Patrick Street

Riverview Park

Elm Street

Raglan Road

York Street

Alfred Street

Division Street

Montreal Street

Bagot Street

Victoria Park

2

Colborne Street

Mc Burney Park

Queen Street

Artillery Park

Lasalle Causeway

❶ ❷

2

Princess Street

Sydenham St.

Frontenac Street

Victoria Street

Brock Street

Johnson Street

University Ave.

Clergy St.

2

Wellington

King East

Ontario Street

Kingston Harbour

Earl Street

❼

William Street

Clergy St. W.

Bagot Street

❹

?

Collingwood Street

Union Street

❶❶

Earl Street

❻

❸

Albert Street

Queen's University

Stuart Street

Barrie Street

Gore Street

❺

Frontenac Street

City Park

Lower Union Street

❽

❾

Ontario and West St. Park

King Street West

❶❷ ▪▪▪

Breakwater

Macdonald Park

❶⓪

Lake Ontario

© ULYSSES

● ATTRACTIONS

1. Fort Henry
2. Royal Military College of Canada Museum
3. Kingston City Hall
4. Confederation Park
5. Prince George Hotel
6. St. George's Cathedral
7. St. Mary's Roman Catholic Cathedral
8. Marine Museum of the Great Lakes
9. Pump House Steam Museum
10. Murney Tower Museum
11. Frontenac County Court House
12. Villa Bellevue
13. International Hockey Hall of Fame and Museum

century. The Murney Tower, located in **Macdonald Park**, was erected in 1846 to defend the port. This squat stone tower now houses the **Murney Tower Museum** *($2; May to Sep every day 10am to 5pm; at the corner of King and Barrie, ☎544-9925)*, which displays an assortment of 19th-century military articles.

Built entirely of local sandstone, the **Frontenac County Court House** ★ designed by Edward Horsey, is a fine example of the neoclassical architecture of the mid-19th century. It was originally supposed to be the Parliament building, but was never used for that purpose. The huge fountain in front of it was erected in 1903.

The Court House looks out onto a pleasant park, which is flanked by a few magnificent Victorian houses.

When it was built back in the 1840s, **Bellevue House** ★ *($2.50; Jun to Sep, every day 9am to 7pm; Apr to May and Sep to Oct, every day 10am to 5pm; 35 Centre St., ☎545-8666)* was the subject of much discussion. Its Tuscan-style architecture, being somewhat novel at the time, earned it a variety of nicknames, including "the pagoda". In 1848 and 1849, it was the family residence of John A. Macdonald, Canada's first prime minister (1867-1873). Upon entering the house, you will discover a splendid interior adorned with furniture dating back to the time when Macdonald lived here. You can visit the elegant dining room and the bedroom where Macdonald's ailing wife lay confined to her bed, and enjoy a stroll in the pretty garden surrounding the house.

Hockey fans won't want to miss the **International Hockey Hall of Fame** *($2; at the corner of York and Alfred, ☎544-2355)*, which displays photographs and equipment, thus showing how the sport has evolved over the years. It is located a short distance from downtown Kingston.

Quinte's Isle ★

Quinte's Isle (pop. 45,000) abounds in lovely pastoral scenes, which you'll discover as you round a bend in the road or explore the shores of the island. With its peaceful hamlets, vast, fertile fields and long sandy beaches, Quinte's Isle is sure to appeal to city-dwellers in search of beautiful natural landscapes. Although large numbers of visitors come here to savour the

bucolic atmosphere in summer, the island has not become touristy. It is crisscrossed by a few roads, which are perfect for bicycling.

Cobourg

Cobourg lies in the heart of the countryside on the shores of Lake Ontario. At first glance, it looks like a simple little town. On your way through, however, you will discover some impressive buildings, which bear witness to a prosperous past, when Cobourg's port was one of the busiest in the region, and flour mills, sawmills and car factories fuelled the local economy. One of the most noteworthy of these elegant edifices is the majestic, Palladian-style **town hall** ★ *(Victoria Hall, 55 King St. W.)*, designed by architect Kivas Tully in 1860. This large building houses the provincial courts, a concert hall and an art gallery whose exhibits include handicrafts and paintings by Canadian artists. A few steps away stands St. Peter's Church, a lovely example of Early Gothic Revival architecture, begun in 1851.

For a relaxing stroll or picnic next to the peaceful waters of Lake Ontario, head to the lovely sandy beach at **Victoria Park**. You can also enjoy a pleasant stroll on the pretty streets around the park, which are shaded by elms and willows.

Oshawa ★

Oshawa, the last town on this tour, lies about fifty kilometres from Toronto, whose presence is already tangible. This town has flourished as a result of its automobile industry, which was launched at the beginning of the century, when Robert McLaughlin began manufacturing cars here, and which has since become the most highly developed in Ontario. When General Motors purchased his plant, he became director of the company's Canadian division. Since then, GM has been the town's largest employer.

Like many industrial towns in North America, Oshawa is a drab-looking place. It does, however, have a few interesting attractions, mostly related to McLaughlin and the automobile industry.

The **Robert McLaughlin Gallery** ★ *(free admission; Tue to Fri 10am to 5pm, Tue until 9pm, Sat and Sun noon to 4pm; Civic Centre, Centre St., ☎576-3000)* displays some lovely

ONTARIO

paintings by contemporary Canadian artists, including abstract pieces by members of the Painters Eleven, who made a name for themselves in the 1950s. These artists' technique was to paint quickly, drawing only on the inspiration of the moment, in order to infuse their work with a feeling of intensity.

You can step into the world of automobiles at the **Canadian Automotive Museum** ★ *($5; Mon to Fri 9am to 5pm, Sat and Sun 10am to 6pm, closed Mon Oct to Mar; 99 Simcoe St. S., ☎576-1222)*, a totally nondescript building containing over sixty antique cars.

If you only have time to see one attraction in Oshawa, head straight to **Parkwood Estate** ★★ *($5; Jun to Sep, Tue to Sun 10:30am to 4:30pm; 270 Simcoe St. N., ☎579-1311)*, the sumptuous former residence of R.S. McLaughlin. The house stands in the midst of a magnificent garden featuring a harmonious combination of stately trees, hedges and verdant stretches of lawn, crowned by a lovely fountain. The outstanding garden is an indication of the opulence of the house itself, whose 55 beautifully decorated rooms make for a captivating visit.

 OUTDOORS

The Parks of the St. Lawrence *(R.R.1, Morrisburg, K0C 1X0, ☎543-3704)* are a group of tourist attractions, including historic sites such as Upper Canada Village (see p 347), Fort Henry (see p 348) and the Upper Canada Migratory Bird Sanctuary (see p 352) and the beautiful **St. Lawrence Islands National Park** ★★, whose 23 islands and countless islets lie strewn across a distance of 80 kilometres, from Gananoque to Lancaster. These islands are actually the crests of mountains that were submerged when the glaciers receded and the St. Lawrence River was formed. Their vegetation is very distinctive, featuring species usually found either much farther north or south. As you go from one island to the next, you might be surprised by the diversity of the plant-life, which makes for a patchwork of remarkable settings.

Most of the islands have been adapted with tourists in mind. Some, like those along the Long Sault Parkway, are accessible by car, others only by boat. Picnic areas, beaches (Crysler Beach) and campgrounds (Ivy Lea and

Mallorytown) are scattered here and there, enabling visitors to enjoy a variety of outdoor activities while exploring the fascinating natural surroundings. For further information, stop by at the park headquarters in Mallorytown.

Route 2 and the Thousand Islands Parkway run alongside the river, offering some magnificent views of the St. Lawrence and the islands. Some of the islands have hiking trails, which are very pleasant to walk along. If you are pressed for time and don't want to go onto the islands, you can explore the banks of the St. Lawrence by taking the Mainland Nature Trail, which starts at the park headquarters in Mallorytown. Finally, if you prefer cycling to canoeing, go for a ride on the beautiful bike path that runs alongside the Thousand Islands Promenade.

Presqu'île Provincial Park ★ *(R.R. 4, Brighton, K0K 1H0, ☎475-2204)* was created in order to protect a thin strip of land that extends into Lake Ontario and is flanked by vast swamps, which attract a variety of bird species. There are wooden piers, from which ornithologists of all ages can view some of the local species at close range. Wooden benches and panels providing information on the wildlife make an outing here both pleasant and instructive. Visitors eager to enjoy the refreshing waters of Lake Ontario won't be disappointed either, since the park has long sandy beaches. Campsites are available for those wishing to stay the night.

 Beaches

Sandbanks Provincial Park ★ *(R.R. 1, Picton, Quinte's Isle, K0K 2T0, ☎393-3319)* is known mainly for its magnificent sandy beaches, which stretch along the shores of Lake Ontario and are literally overrun with sun-worshippers and water sports enthusiasts on hot summer days. It also boasts some remarkable sand dunes, some over 25 metres high.

 Bird-watching

In spring and fall, various species of migratory birds stop along the St. Lawrence River, especially along the stretch protected by the **Upper Canada Migratory Bird Sanctuary** *(14 km east of Morrisburg, ☎543-3704)*, where you

can observe them. A variety of other species can also be spotted here all summer long.

 ACCOMMODATIONS

Cornwall

Vincent Massey Street and Brookdale Avenue, both of which are lined with hotels and small motels are located near the entrance to town. The local inns have sacrificed old-fashion charm for modern comfort, but it is easy to find decent accommodation. The **Ramada Inn** *($80; ≡, ≈, ⌂, ⊚, ✕; 805 Brookdale, K6J 4P3, ☎933-8000, ⇨933-3392)* and Best Western *($90; ≡, ≈, ℜ, ⌂, ⊚, ✕; 1515 Massey, K6H 5R6, ☎932-0451 or 1-800-528-1234, ⇨938-5479)* are noteworthy for their wide range of amenities.

Morrisburg

At the **Upper Canada Migratory Bird Sanctuary Nature Awareness Campsite** *(☎543-3704 or 537-2024, ⇨543-2847)*, which is park of the Parks of the St. Lawrence, fifty campsites have been laid out in a lovely natural setting.

You can also camp at one of the other campgrounds in the Parks of the St. Lawrence, which are beautifully situated on the banks of the river.

Reservations:
Glengarry, ☎(613) 347-2595.
Mille Roches, Woodlands and McLaren, ☎(613) 534-8202.
Riverside/Cedar, ☎(613) 543-3287.
Ivy Lea ☎(613) 659-3057.

Gananoque

When entering Gananoque by the highway, you'll find yourself on the main street lined with mundane fast-food restaurants. Continue on however, towards the river and you'll discover a delightful inn. The **Victoria Rose Inn** *($80 brkfs incl.; 279 King St. W., K7G 2G7, ☎382-3368)*, located in a magnificent Victorian residence, has nine spacious and inviting rooms.

Kingston

The **Kingston International Hostel** *($15,75; 75 Nicholas St., K1N 7B9, ☎546-7203)*, located close to the downtown area, welcomes visitors in both summer and winter. Fewer beds are available during winter.

The ***Alexander Henry*** *($65; 55 Ontario St., K7L 2Y2, ☎542-2261)*, which you are sure to have noticed on your way past the Maritime Museum, is a restored icebreaker that has been converted into a very unusual inn. Don't expect a luxurious room; people stay here for the experience, not the comfort.

Downtown, the **Queen's Inn** *($85; 125 Brock, K7L 1S1, ☎546-0429)*, a 19th-century stone house with a restaurant on the ground floor, offers pleasant accommodations. Although well-kept, the rooms are decorated with imitation-wood furniture, and therefore don't have the old-fashioned charm visitors might hope to find.

Continuing down Princess Street, you'll also notice the **Best Western Fireside Inn** *($130; ≡, ≈, ℜ, ⊚; 1217 Princess St., K7M 3E1, ☎549-2211 or 1-800-567-8800, ⇨549-4523)*. Its main building, made of logs, has a rustic appearance that is somewhat unusual for this type of establishment. In keeping with the rural theme, the interior is decorated with flowered wallpaper and pine furniture. To top it all off, there is a switch-operated fireplace in every room! The result is an altogether inviting ambiance. Not surprisingly, the place is often full during the cold winter months.

Kingston boasts some magnificent 19th century houses, which have been carefully restored over the years. A number of these have been converted into inns, which manage to combine charm and comfort. You will have little trouble tracking down a few of these masterpieces of Victorian architecture in the area around downtown Kingston. The beautifully maintained **Hochelaga Inn** *($130; 24 Sydenham St. S., K7L 3G9, ☎549-5534)* is a fine example. Built in the 1880's, this superb red-brick house has an ornately decorated green and white façade with a pretty turret and a large balcony. It offers a peaceful atmosphere and 23 tastefully decorated rooms furnished with lovely antiques.

ONTARIO

Picton (Quinte's Isle)

The **Merrill Inn** *($$$$; 343 Main St. E., K0K 2Y0, ☎476-7451 or 1-800-567-5969)* occupies one of Picton's lovely Victorian houses. Built in 1878 for Edwards Merrill and his family, this red-brick building is reminiscent of Hansel and Gretel. The pretty rooms of this appealing little inn are all decorated with antiques.

Oshawa

Being an industrial town, Oshawa is hardly a vacation spot. Visitors can nevertheless find comfortable accommodation at the **Travelodge** *($75; ≡, ≈, ⊚, ✖; 940 Champlain Ave., L17 7A6, ☎905-436-9500 or 1-800-578-7878, ≈436-9544)*.

 RESTAURANTS

Cornwall

If you are staying in town for a while, you can opt for something a little more interesting than fast food. The **Gemini Café** *($; 241 Pitt St., ☎936-9440)* has a daily menu listing a variety of tasty dishes.

Kingston

The **Café Max** *($$; Brock St., at the corner of King, ☎547-2233)* offers an inexpensive nightly *table d'hote*, with a choice of soup or Caesar salad, a main course such as Tandoori chicken served with pasta, and coffee. The food is honest and always served in generous portions, making the place extremely popular with the local residents, who willingly line up for a table on Saturday nights.

Le Caveau *($$; 354 King St. E., ☎547-1617)* is an unpretentious place with a very relaxed mood, probably because of the small number of tables and intimate decor, featuring woodwork and an exposed brick wall. This cozy atmosphere certainly adds to the enjoyment of your meal, especially since the menu lists mouthwatering specialties like sole stuffed with shrimp. Lighter dishes are served at lunchtime. There is a **wine bar** on the first floor, with a tempting selection of about forty wines, each sold by the glass (the hard part is choosing one).

To enter **Chez Piggy** *($$; 68 Princess St., ☎549-7673)*, you must first pass through a small inner courtyard, where you will see the terrace and the lovely, 19th-century stone buildings that house the restaurant. These superb buildings have been tastefully renovated, and Chez Piggy has long been a favourite of Kingston residents, who readily line up for a delicious meal, both at lunchtime, when the restaurant serves simple fare like quiche and salads, and at dinnertime, when the menu is more sophisticated, listing a variety of dishes, notably chicken and lamb.

Ontario Street runs alongside the lake, and a number of restaurants have set up terraces here to take advantage of the lovely view. **Stoney's** *($$; 189 Ontario St., ☎546-9424)* has probably one the prettiest terraces of all; at lunchtime, it is a highly coveted spot from which to observe the nonstop activity on the street while enjoying a slice of quiche or a salad.

If you aren't worried about breaking your budget and want to spend a memorable evening out, go to the **River Mill** *($$$; 2 Cataraqui St., ☎549-5759)*. Upon entering the elegant dining room, you will be greeted by the enchanting view over the lake through the big picture windows. The menu, whose delicious offerings change with the seasons, is sure to whet your appetite.

Bloomfield (Quinte's isle)

The charming town of Bloomfield is a wonderful place to satisfy your hunger. **Mrs. Dickenson's** *($; 55 Main St., ☎393-3356)*, a cafe open only during the day, has a simple menu featuring sandwiches and succulent desserts. This is a perfect place to relax.

Year after year, **Angeline's** *($$$; 433 Main St., ☎393-3301)* manages to live up to its long-standing reputation as the best restaurant on the island. People come here to savour a handful of specialties, such as lamb with garlic. The restaurant, furthermore, is a charming place to spend a delightful evening.

Oshawa

There's nothing like a good, healthy meal, which is what you'll find at **Culture** *($; Simcoe St., at the corner of Athol St., ☎728-5356)*, where hearty sandwiches and salads dominate the menu.

For a good, nourishing meal, try **Fazio** *($$; 33 Simcoe St.,* ☎*571-3042)*, where you can savour simple Italian dishes in a large, somewhat impersonal dining room.

 ENTERTAINMENT

Kingston

The **Grand Theatre** *(218 Princess St.,* ☎*530-2050)* is the hub of cultural activity in Kingston, presenting plays and classical-music concerts.

The Dukes *(331 King E.,* ☎*542-2811)*, an unpretentious Irish pub, is very popular with university students. It has a good selection of imported beer on tap, and hosts live music on some evenings.

Toucan-Kirkpatricks *(76 Princess St.,* ☎*544-1966)*, located right nearby, has a similar clientele and also hosts live music.

 SHOPPING

Kingston

Downtown Kingston centres around Ontario Street, with Brock and Princess as secondary arteries. If you hunt around a little, you're sure to find a few little treasures here.

If you like unusual decorative objects, stop in at **Buston & Grace** *(66 Princess St.)*, where you'll find wrought-iron candlesticks, Dali-esque clocks and oddly-shaped frames.

Brock Street boasts some of Kingston's prettiest storefronts, many seemingly right out of another era. **Cooke's**, a typical turn-of-the-century general store, is perfectly charming. It sells specialty foods like Rogers chocolates from Victoria (British Columbia) and delicious preserves.

On the other side of the street, relive some happy childhood memories at **Doll Attic** *(Brock St.)*, which sells some of the most beautiful dolls imaginable.

ONTARIO

CENTRAL ONTARIO

T he lands on both sides of the St. Lawrence were among the first to be colonized by Loyalists fleeing the newly independent United States. They settled on a small strip of land; forests to the north were unsuitable to agriculture and farming, and thus only little hamlets developed. Today, the human presence is scarce, and forests of broad-leafed and coniferous trees crisscrossed by lakes and rivers set the backdrop for this region.

 FINDING YOUR WAY AROUND

By Car

The Kawartha Lakes and the Haliburton Highlands

This tour circles Kawartha Lakes and crosses Haliburton Highlands to Peterborough.

The Muskoka Lakes

Take the 400 from Toronto to Barrie, then pick up the 11.

By Bus

The Kawartha Lakes and the Haliburton Highlands

Peterborough: Simcoe St., ☎(705) 743-1590.

The Muskoka Lakes

Barrie: 15 Maple Ave., ☎(705) 728-5571.
Orillia: 150 Front St., ☎(705) 326-4101.
Gravenhurst: On 2nd St., ☎(705) 687-2301.
Huntsville: At the corner of Main and Centre.

Georgian Bay

Owen Sound: 1020 3rd Ave. E., ☎(519) 376-5375.
Collingwood: 70 Hurontario, ☎(705) 445-4231.

By Train

Barrie: 15 Maple Ave., ☎(705) 728-5571.
Orillia: 150 Front St., ☎(705) 326-4101.
Gravenhurst: On 2nd St., ☎(705) 687-2301.
Huntsville: At the corner of Main and Centre.

PRACTICAL INFORMATION

Area Code: 705, except for Owen Sound 519

Tourist Information Offices

The Kawartha Lakes and the Haliburton Highlands

Peterborough Kawartha Tourism: 175 George St. N., Peterborough, ON, K9J 3G6, ☎(705) 742-2201, ☎(800) 461-6424.

The Muskoka Lakes

Simcoe County Building: Midhurst, ON, L0L 1X0, ☎(705) 726-8502, ≈(705) 726-3991.

EXPLORING

The Kawartha Lakes and the Haliburton Highlands

The verdant plains of the St. Lawrence gradually give way to a dense forest, and then to hills and rocky escarpments, offering a glimpse of the landscape that characterizes the Canadian Shield to the north. Some 600 lakes and rivers lie strewn across this territory, which attracts fans of outdoor activities like canoeing in the summer and skiing in the winter. The region is also scattered with a handful of peaceful hamlets like **Minden** and **Haliburton**, each of which is equipped with restaurants and hotels.

To the north lies the region's pride and joy, **Algonquin Provincial Park** ★★★ (see p 363, 365), with its numerous canoe routes and trails for both hiking and cross-country skiing.

Bobcaygeon ★

After passing through a dense, seemingly uninhabited forest, you'll come to Bobcaygeon, a picturesque hamlet well worth a visit. In addition to its charming main street, it boasts the first lock to be built on the canal (1883).

Peterborough

In 1825, Governor Peter Robinson led 2,000 Irish immigrants to the site of present-day Peterborough, on the shores of Little Lake and the Otonabee River, and founded the town that still bears his first name. Peterborough itself is a rather gloomy-looking place, which serves as a stopping point for motorists travelling between Ottawa and Toronto. Visitors using the Trent-Severn Waterway, however, will see the town in a more attractive light, since it has three locks, including an amazing **hydraulic lift lock** ★, an elevator dating back to 1904, which still lifts boats some 20 metres above water so that they can continue on to Georgian Bay. Peterborough is also the home of Trent University.

In the centre of town, the modern shopping centre, **Peterborough Square Complex** ★ was built in 1973 and integrated in to old Market Hall. This former market, dominated by its clock tower, was built in 1889 and designed by architect John Belcher.

If you have a little time to spare, you can visit **Hutchison House Museum** *($2; May to Dec, Tue to Sun 1pm to 5pm; Jan to Mar, Sat and Sun 1pm to 5pm; Aylmer St., ☎743-9710)*, the former home and office of Peterborough's first resident doctor. Now restored, it contains some mementos of the city's early days.

Centennial Museum *(free admission; Mon to Fri 9am to 5pm, Sat and Sun 10am to 5pm; Armour Hill, ☎748-3666)* traces the history of the city, from the beginning of colonization to the 20th century, with particular emphasis on the difficult life of its early immigrants.

The Muskoka Lakes ★★

For nearly a century now, the lovely Muskoka Lakes region has been attracting vacationers, who come here for the charming villages and unobtrusive but well-developed tourist infrastructure. This tour will take you from Toronto to Barrie and Orillia, and then farther north, into the Muskoka Lakes region as such, from Gravenhurst to Huntsville.

Barrie

Outside the greater Toronto area, the highway continues north along Lake Simcoe. It skirts round Kempenfelt Bay, which stretches westward like a long arm of the sea, at the end of which lies Barrie, the most populous town in the region. Although the outskirts of Barrie can seem somewhat stark at first sight, you will be pleasantly surprised by the downtown area, which is attractively located alongside the bay.

Those fond of water sports can head to **Centennial Park**, whose lovely sandy beach is often packed on hot summer days.

The **Simcoe County Museum** *($3.25; Mon to Sat 9am to 4:30 pm, Sun 1pm to 4:30pm; R.R.2, Mingesing,* ☎*728-3721)*, located some 8 km north of town, offers a survey of local history, starting with the region's first inhabitants and continuing up to the 20th century. The reconstruction of an 1840's commercial street is by far the most interesting of the major displays.

Orillia ★

The site of present-day Orillia, located at the meeting point of Lakes Simcoe and Couchiching, was inhabited by Ojibwa Indians for many years. Around 1838, the natives were driven out of the region by European colonists, at which point an urban area began to develop. Surrounded by woods and water, it was naturally geared toward the forest industry and agriculture. Then, toward the end of the 19th century, another lucrative industry began to flourish here: tourism. Ever since, visitors have been flocking to Orillia, lured by its attractive location on the shores of Lake Couchiching. The town also became known through the writings of Stephen Leacock (1869-1944), who lived here.

In 1908, Stephen Leacock purchased a plot of land on Lake Couchiching and had a magnificent house built. At the **Stephen Leacock Museum ★** *($4; Jun to Sep, every day 10am to 5pm, Sep to Dec and Apr, to Jun 10am to 5pm; 50 Museum Dr.,* ☎*326-9357)*, now open to the public, visitors can see where the author wrote some of his works, and even examine a few of the actual manuscripts. The rooms are decorated with period furniture.

Leacock taught history and economics at McGill University (Montreal), but is known primarily for his literary output, characterized by wit and irony. *Sunshine Sketches of a Little Town* will be of particular interest to visitors, since the stories take place in a fictional town called Mariposa which was later revealed to be the town of Orillia.

Near the marina, stretched along Lake Couchiching, is a beautiful **park ★** with a promenade, a few benches and a small beach. The *Island Princess*, which docks at the marina, takes visitors on cruises on the lake.

Gravenhurst ★

Gravenhurst was once a modest lumberjack village. Like the neighbouring towns, however, it has been reaping the benefits of the public's infatuation with this region since the late 19th century. Visitors began coming here for the lovely natural setting and built the beautiful Victorian homes that still grace the streets. As the gateway to the Muskoka Lakes region, Gravenhurst welcomes throngs of summer visitors attracted by its peaceful atmosphere and air of days gone by. Gravenhurst lies on the shores of Lake Muskoka, short cruises of the lake aboard the *R.M.S. Segwun* are offered (see p 365).

Gravenhurst was the birthplace of the eminent Canadian doctor Norman Bethune. To learn more about his accomplishments, stop by **Bethune Memorial House** *($2.25; mid-May to Oct, mon to Fri 10am to noon and 1pm to 5pm; 235 John St. N.,* ☎*687-4261)*, where he grew up. Here, you'll find articles relating to different aspects of his life, as well as some of the technical innovations for which he was responsible, including the mobile blood-transfusion unit.

Bracebridge

Located on the banks of the Muskoka River, Bracebridge is a very pretty town graced with elegant houses and attractive shops and centred around a magnificent park shaded by stately trees. At the edge of town, the Muskoka River empties into Lake Muskoka. Visitors are well served here, as the charming streets are lined with comfortable hotels and B&Bs.

Huntsville ★

Huntsville is a picturesque town located at the meeting point of Vernon and Fairy Lakes. In order to make the most of the setting, the downtown area has been laid out on the shores of both lakes, which are linked by a small bridge. On one side, you can browse through charming shops, while on the other, you can enjoy lunch on one of several attractive waterfront terraces. The town has a few decent places to stay, but most visitors opt for the superb hotel complexes in the surrounding countryside.

The **Muskoka Pioneer Village** *($6; Jul to oct, every day 11am to 4pm; Brunel Rd., ☎789-7576)* is a reconstruction of an early 19th century village. It is made up of about a dozen little buildings, including a smithy, an inn and a general store, where the local settlers' daily life is re-enacted.

Georgian Bay ★★

Bruce Peninsula extends into Lake Huron, forming one side of magnificent Georgian Bay, whose shores are dotted with vacation spots. This tour will take you through a few of the region's prettiest villages and into the heart of what was once Huronia.

Bruce Peninsula ★★

The Bruce Peninsula, the continuation of the Niagara Escarpment, extends into Lake Huron, rising up here and there to form islands, most importantly Manitoulin Island. This ridge is as high as 100 metres in some places, making for some remarkably beautiful scenery that you can enjoy during an outing in one of the parks that protect this unique area (see p 364).

The Niagara Escarpment

The Niagara Escarpement is actually a huge geological basin created about 400 million years ago, when shallow seas covered this area. Over the years, the sea bed became carpeted with coral and bone fragments, which formed a solid layer of dolomite, a calcareous mineral. When the water receded, the dolomite did not erode as rapidly as the rocks below it. Eventually there was nothing left to support it and it collapsed, forming a vast bowl, whose rim runs from New York State all the way to Georgian Bay.

Tobermory

Tobermory lies at the tip of the peninsula. Although the village itself is rather ordinary, it attracts large numbers of visitors because of its location. Not only is it the point of departure for outings to Fathom Five National Marine Park (see p 364) and the ferry ride to Manitoulin Island aboard the *Chi-Cheemaun*, but it also marks the end of the Bruce Trail (see p 410).

Owen Sound

This little town, formerly known as Sydenham, was renamed after Admiral Owen, who made the first hydrographic studies of Georgian Bay, thus making it safer for boats to sail on the Great Lakes. Although Owen Sound has the advantage of being located alongside this magnificent body of water, with its lovely scenery, a number of factories have been built along part of the shoreline here, giving some sections of town a gloomy look.

For a stroll through a pleasant stretch of greenery, go to **Harrisson Park ★**, which has picnic tables, a restaurant and a number of ponds with ducks and wild geese paddling about in them.

Owen Sound is also known as the birthplace and childhood home of the great Canadian landscape painter Tom Thomson (1877-1917). The **Tom Thomson Museum ★** *(donations welcome; Tue to Sat 10am to 5pm, Wed until 9pm, Sun noon to 5pm; 840 1st Ave. W., ☎376-1932)* is devoted to this artist, whose magnificent paintings reveal a highly personal interpretation of the Canadian wilderness, particularly the Canadian Shield. The museum displays a fine collection of his paintings, as well as a number of works by other Canadian painters, including members of the Group of Seven.

Collingwood ★

Collingwood, also located on the shores of Georgian Bay, was an important shipbuilding centre at the beginning of this century. When that industry started to decline, the town managed to capitalize on its location near the Blue Mountains and the lovely beaches on the bay, and develop a prosperous tourist industry. This little town now has everything a vacationer could ask for — pretty shops, a comfortable inn and delicious restaurants.

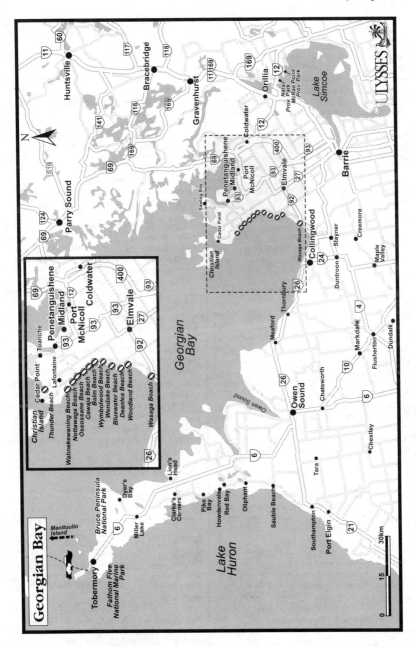

Georgian Bay

ULYSSES

ONTARIO

Wasaga Beach ★★

Magnificent Wasaga Beach, a strip of sand stretching about 14 kilometres along Georgian Bay, is a virtual paradise for vacationers looking for places to enjoy water sports. Although there are some lovely summer homes along the beach, part of it has unfortunately been overdeveloped, so a jumble of cheap-looking souvenir shops and unattractive motels detracts somewhat from the beauty of the landscape. This area is nonetheless a good place to have fun, and is popular with a younger crowd.

The **Nancy Island Historic Site** *(Moseley St., ☎429-2728)* tells the story of the *HMS Nancy*, a sailing ship that went down in the bay in 1814 during the War of 1812. In addition to seeing the wreckage of the ship, visitors will learn about 19th-century fur-traders and their way of life.

Midland ★

Now a peaceful little town, Midland once lay at the heart of Huronia, just a few kilometres from the site where the fearsome Iroquois martyrized and killed a large number of Hurons, as well as Jesuit priests who had come here to convert them to Christianity. Thanks to several fascinating historical reconstructions, visitors can relive the colony's early days.

Although it is not as big as Sainte-Marie Among the Hurons, the **Huronia Museum and Huron Village** *(King St. S., Little Lake Park)* nevertheless offers an introduction to Huron society, complete with a reconstructed Amerindian village.

You can board the ***Miss Midland*** *($13; town dock, ☎526-0161)* for a cruise in the bay, during which you can take in the magnificent sight of the 30,000 Islands.

Standing by the side of the highway is the **Martyr's Shrine** *(Hwy 12, near Sainte-Marie)*, a Catholic sanctuary dedicated to the first Canadian martyrs, including Jean de Brébeuf, Gabriel Lalemant and Antoine Daniel. The fascinating historic site of Sainte Marie Among the Hurons lies on the opposite side of the road.

Sainte-Marie Among the Hurons ★★ *($7.25; May to Oct every day 10am to 5pm; Hwy 12, 5 km east of Midland, ☎526-7838)*. When

colonists first arrived here, the Georgian Bay region was inhabited by Hurons, who were among the first native nations in Ontario to come into contact with Europeans (Étienne Brûlé came here around 1610). The natives and the French were on such good terms with each other that Jesuit missionaries came to the region in 1620 to try to convert the Hurons to Christianity, and founded a mission here in 1639. Their efforts had profound repercussions on Huron society, which split into two groups — those who had been converted and those who hadn't. The resulting disputes upset the social structure. In addition, many natives fell victim to illnesses brought over by the Europeans (influenza, smallpox, etc.), further destabilizing their society.

The Hurons were thus in a weakened state when it came time to fight the ferocious Iroquois, who were determined to take control of the fur trade. In 1648, the Iroquois attacked the mission, captured, tortured and killed Jesuit missionaries Jean de Brébeuf, Antoine Daniel and Gabriel Lalemant, and massacred the Hurons. In 1649, the last Hurons and Jesuits abandoned the mission and fled to Quebec City.

Sainte-Marie Among the Hurons is an exact replica of the mission as it appeared in the 1630s. The site includes the village, its longhouses and the various tools used by the Hurons. Guides in period dress (Jesuit priests, colonists, natives) offer an idea of what daily life was like here. After touring the mission, you can further increase your knowledge of Huron society by visiting the museum located on the premises.

Wye Marsh Wildlife Centre (see p 364).

 OUTDOORS

 Parks

The Kawartha Lakes and the Haliburton Highlands

The Ojibwa who once lived in this region left behind scores of petroglyphs carved in white marble. They used these symbols to tell the young the story of life. **Petroglyphs Provincial Park ★** *(Woodview, KOL 3EO, ☎705-877-2552)* was founded in order to protect these

Loon

testimonies to the Ojibwa past, which are five to ten centuries old. Visitors can admire a few of the 900 petroglyphs found in the park, which are now sheltered by a large building.

In 1893, **Algonquin Provincial Park ★★★** *(P.O. Box 219, Whitney, K0J 2M0, ☎705-633-5572)* was created, thus protecting 7,700 square kilometres of Ontario's territory from the forest industry. This vast stretch of wilderness boasts some fantastic scenery, which has charmed many a visitor. Back in 1912, it was a source of inspiration for Canadian painter Tom Thomson, whose presence will linger here forever, since he not only created his most beautiful works in the park, but also died here mysteriously in 1917. Shortly after, following in Thomson's footsteps, the Canadian landscape painters known as the Group of Seven came here in search of subject matter.

For over a century, Algonquin Park has been captivating outdoor enthusiasts, who are drawn here by the shimmering lakes with their small population of loons, the rivers that wind around the bases of rocky cliffs, the forest of maples, birches and conifers, the clearings covered with blueberry bushes, and the varied animal life that includes beavers, racoons, deer, moose, black bears and more. As you set out by foot or by canoe into the heart of this untamed wilderness, you will be embarking on one of the most enchanting journeys imaginable.

Only one road (Route 60, which is 60 kilometres long), starting in Pembroke and leading as far as Huntsville, runs through the southern part of the park. The information office is located along the way. You can only go deeper into the wilderness by foot, on skis or by canoe. The park obviously attracts a lot of visitors, and a limited number of people are allowed access to certain sites. It is therefore advisable to make reservations.

Equipment Rental:

Portage Algonquin
R.R. 6 K8A 6W7, ☎(613) 735-1795.

Portage Store
Route 60, ☎(705) 633 5622.

Algonquin Outfitter
Route 60, ☎(705) 635-2243.

If you do not know how to canoe but are willing to learn the basics:

Algonquin Paddling School
Ostongue Lake, Dwight, ☎(705) 635-1167.

Camping is permitted in the park, and eight areas have been laid out for that purpose.

ONTARIO

Georgian Bay

Bruce Peninsula National Park ★★ *(P.O. Box 189, Tobermory, NOH 2RO, ☎519-596-2233)* covers a large portion of the 80-kilometre peninsula that stretches into Lake Huron, forming part of the shoreline of Georgian Bay. Within this vast park, there are tracts of private property as well as stretches of untouched wilderness where you can find a mixed forest and unusual flowers, including about forty different kinds of orchids. The animal life is no less fascinating; the park is home to deer, beavers, the dangerous massasauga (a venomous snake), and as many as 170 species of birds. You can venture into the heart of the park on one of a number of hiking trails, including the Bruce Trail and the Cyprus Lake trails. Visitors also have access to beaches (on Cyprus Lake and Dorcas Bay) and campsites.

A series of islands, 19 in all, trail off the tip of the Bruce Peninsula; these are actually the last peaks of the Niagara Escarpment. These limestone masses have been eroded over the years, and now form odd-looking rocky pillars, the best known and most strangely shaped of all being Flowerpot Island. **Fathom Five National Marine Park ★★** *(P.O. Box 189, Tobermory, NOH 2RO, ☎519-596-2233)* encompasses this entire area.

All these rocky islets are completely wild, except for Flowerpot Island, where campsites and paths have been cleared. Hidden around them lie the wrecks of a number of ships that went down in the sometimes treacherous waters of Lake Huron in the late 19th and early 20th centuries. You can take part in a scuba diving excursion or go for a ride on a glass-bottomed boat to view these sunken ships.

The scenery of the 30,000 islands that dot Georgian Bay is typical of the Canadian Shield, featuring twisted pines and bare rocks of the same type that inspired Tom Thomson and the Group of Seven. In fact, many people have been enchanted by the landscapes here, including wealthy vacationers who began purchasing the islands one by one until 1929, when the **Georgian Bay Islands National Park ★** *(P.O. Box 28, Honey Harbour, POE 1EO, ☎705-756-2415)* was created in order to keep 59 of these in the public domain. These unspoiled areas are only accessible by boat; if you don't have one, you can take a water taxi from Honey Harbour or one of the private boats that set out from the marinas of coastal towns like Penetanguishene and Midland. The only campsites and hiking trails you'll find are on Beausoleil Island. No matter where you go, however, always make sure to bring along sufficient food and water.

 Hiking

Georgian Bay

One hiking trail follows the railroad from Collingwood to Meaford-Heberg; in the winter, it becomes a cross-country ski trail. The 32-kilometre **Georgian Trail** runs along the Niagara Escarpment.

 Bird-watching

The dual purpose of the **Wye Marsh Wildlife Center ★** *($6; late May to Sep every day 10am to 6pm, until 4pm during the rest of the year; Hwy 12, near Sainte Marie Among the Hurons, ☎526-8709)* is to protect the marshes in this area and increase public awareness of the importance, and fragility, of this fascinating world. There are trails through the woods and the swamps so that visitors can observe all sorts of birds like chickadees; some of which get along particularly well with human beings, and will not hesitate to eat seeds out of your hand.

Chickadee

Cruises

The Kawartha Lakes and the Haliburton Highlands

The **Trent-Severn Waterway** stretches 386 kilometres, and offers a unique and enjoyable way of exploring the Ontario landscape. For further information or to plan a trip, write to the Trent-Severn Waterway, P.O. Box 567, Peterborough, K9J 6Z6, ☎(705) 742-9267

If you don't have a boat but would like to spend a few hours on the Waterway, you can take a cruise from Lindsay or Fenelon Falls.

Skylark VIII Boat Tours: Wellington St., Lindsay, ☎(705) 324-8335, $15.

Fenelon Falls Cruise: Tickets available on Oak Street, ☎(705) 887-9313, $14.

The Muskoka Lakes

In Gravenhurst, you can set out to discover some of the beautiful scenery of the Muskoka Lakes on a real 19th-century steamboat (reservations recommended), the *R.M.S. Segwun ($17.25; Town Pier, ☎687-6667).*

Georgian Bay

A cruise around the Georgian Bay Islands (from Midland, Penetanguishene or Parry Sound) is a wonderful opportunity to get a taste of magnificent scenery.

PCML Cruises: town dock, ☎(705) 526-0161.

Georgian Queen **Cruises:** town dock, ☎(705) 549-7795.

Island Queen: town dock, ☎(705) 746-5365.

 Nocturnal Excursions

The Kawartha Lakes and the Haliburton Highlands

Imagine yourself seated in the heart of a peaceful forest shrouded in darkness; suddenly, a howl rings out into the night. If this image appeals to you, you can contact Algonquin Daytrippers, which organizes excursions in **Algonquin Provincial Park** for visitors interested in learning more about wolves and listening to them howl at night (you won't see any, of course). You will also learn about other nocturnal species, such as owls.

Algonquin Daytrippers: Baysville, ☎(905) 898-5949.

 Downhiill Skiing

For downhill skiing, the place to go is the **Blue Mountain Resort** *(R.R.3, Collingwood, L9Y 3Z2, ☎705-445-0231)*, which has the highest vertical drop in the region (219 metres). Some of the trails are open for night skiing as well.

A number of shops in the area sell, rent and repair equipment, so you'll have no trouble finding everything you need.

 ACCOMMODATIONS

The Kawartha Lakes and the Haliburton Highlands

Bobcaygeon

The building now known as the **Bobcaygeon Inn** *($75; ≡, ℜ; 31 Main St., KOM 1AO, ☎738-5433)* has been accommodating visitors since the 1920s. Although it has been renovated, its attractively decorated rooms still have an old-fashioned charm about them. The place also boasts an outstanding location, right at the edge of the water.

Set right in the country, **Eganridge** *($150; ℜ, ⊛, ঊ; R.R. 3, KOM 1NO, ☎738-5111)* is the ideal place for nature-lovers who are looking for rustic yet comfortable lodgings. Guests have two options here, they can either stay in one of the rooms in Dunsfort House, a large, renovated wood building from the 19th century, or in one of the small chalets.

Peterborough

Peterborough's **Holiday Inn** *($100; ≡, ≈, ℜ, ⊛, ◠, ঊ, ✈; 50 George St., N., K9J 3G5,*

ONTARIO

☎743-1144 or 800-465-4329, ⊶740-6559) is easy to find located right at the edge of town. This big hotel is fully equipped to accommodate families, and also has two swimming pools.

Algonquin Provincial Park

Imagine spending the night in the heart of Algonquin Park's forest, far from the crush of the city at the **Arowhon Pines** (*$348 fb; POA 1B0, ☎633-5661, ⊶633-5795)* hotel. You will slip into sweet slumber in a rustic decor that is just as inviting as big-city luxury hotels. Destined to become one of those special memories you will cherish long after returning to the bustle of the regular day-to-day.

The Muskoka Lakes

This region has been welcoming visitors for many years, and thus has all sorts of charming inns and luxurious hotel complexes. It is nonetheless possible to find inexpensive accommodation here, although the choice is somewhat limited.

Orillia

The **Lakeside Inn** (*$70; 86 Creighton St., L3V 1B2, ☎325-2514)* is more like a motel than a charming inn, but its location on the banks of Lake Couchiching makes it a pleasant place to stay.

Gravenhurst

The **Muskoka Sands Inn** (*$139; ≡, ≈, ℜ, ⊛, ◯, ♿; Muskoka Beach Rd., P1P 1R1 ☎687-2233 or 1-800-461-0236, ⊶687-7474)* lies in a very peaceful setting outside of Gravenhurst, on the shores of Lake Muskoka. The cabins and buildings containing the rooms are scattered across its extensive grounds. Guests will also find lots to do here, since the complex has a beach, swimming pools and tennis courts.

Bracebridge

On your way into town, you'll pass the **Muskoka Riverside Inn** (*$79; ≡, ℜ, ◯, ♿; 300 Ecclestone Dr., ☎645-8775 or 1-800-461-4474, ⊶645-8455)*, a large, uninspiring place that nonetheless meets modern standards of comfort and even has a few bowling lanes.

The more elegant **Inn at the Falls** (*$98; ≈, ℜ; 17 Dominion St., P1L 1R6, ☎645-2245, ⊶645-5093)* offers antique-furnished rooms. It is made up of several old houses, each more charming than the last, and all facing onto a quiet little street that leads to the Muskoka River, near the falls.

Huntsville

The most attractive places to stay, however, are located in a small valley a few kilometres outside of town. Take Route 60 to the 3, which will take you to a vast stretch of greenery punctuated by large hotel complexes.

The elegant **Grandview** (*$125; ≡, ≈, ℜ, ◯, ⊛; 939 Hwy 60, P1H 1Z4, ☎789-4417 or 1-800-461-4454, ⊶789-6882)* was once a private residence. It has since been converted into a magnificent hotel complex where everything has been designed to ensure guests' satisfaction. The charmingly decorated rooms and varied choice of activities, ranging from golf to walks in the woods, make a stay here both fun and relaxing.

The **Deerhurst** (*$200; ≡, ≈, ℜ, ◯, ⊛; 1235 Deerhurst Dr., P1H 2E8, ☎789-6411 or 1-800-441-1414, ⊶789-2431)* hotel complex lies on the shores of Peninsula Lake, in an outstanding natural setting where you can savour clean air and a tranquil atmosphere. The complex is made up of three-story buildings with extremely comfortable rooms, some of which are equipped with kitchenettes and fireplaces. To ensure that guests are entertained as well as comfortably lodged, all sorts of activities are planned.

Georgian Bay

Owen Sound

The **Inn on the Bay** (*$99; ℜ, ♿; 1800 2nd Ave. E., N4K 2S7, ☎519-371-9200)* stands at the far end of a dreary-looking industrial area, overlooking the waters of Owen Sound. The building has been cleverly designed so that every room has a lovely view of the bay. This place boasts the most attractive setting in town, and is therefore often full on weekends.

Collingwood

There are several places to stay at the foot of the Blue Mountains, the least expensive being the **Blue Mountain Auberge** *($; R.R.3, L9Y 3Z2, ☎445-1497, ⋈444-1497)*, whose no-frills dormitories are decent for the price.

The **Blue Mountain Inn** *($135; ≈, ℜ, △, ⊛, ⊖, ♿; R.R.3, L9Y 3Z2, ☎445-0231, ⋈444-5619)* complex boasts a prime location for skiing, right at the foot of the slopes. The comfortable rooms are located inside a long building, which is a bit too modern-looking for the setting. Guests can also opt for an apartment with kitchenette. Ski packages available.

In the centre of town, the magnificent **Beild House Inn** *($359 fb for 2 nights; 64 Third St., L9Y 1K5, ☎444-1522, ⋈444-2394)*, with its pretty brick façade is easy to spot. Surrounded by a splendid garden shaded by majestic trees, it has 16 rooms, all extremely appealing and elegant.

Wasaga Beach

All sorts of nondescript, charmless motels lie close to the beach. For more peace and quiet, we recommend staying in one of the neighbouring towns instead.

On Mosley Street, the **Lakeview Motel** *($75; 44 Mosley St., L0L 2P0, ☎429-5155)* is one possibility, but don't expect a very warm welcome from the owner. The place does have the advantage of being located alongside the beach, however.

 RESTAURANTS

The Kawartha Lakes and the Haliburton Highlands

Peterborough

The youthful, unpretentious atmosphere at **Hot Belly Mama's** *($; at the corner of Simcoe and Water)* lends itself well to enjoying a good meal at lunchtime. The menu features quiche and skewered shrimp.

Algonquin Provincial Park

The **Arowhon Pines** *($$$$; ☎633-5661)* restaurant boasts an exceptional setting next to one of Algonquin Park's many lakes. The only thing that might interrupt your meal as you contemplate the enchanting surroundings, is the echo of the forest. Besides the cosy fireplace in the centre of the dining room, you will savour an excellent cuisine prepared with the freshest of ingredients.

The Muskoka Lakes

Barrie

Weber's *($; 11 Victoria St., ☎734-9800)* is a veritable burger institution in town that is sure to satisfy ravenous and mild hunger attacks.

Tara *($$; 128 Dunlop St. E., ☎737-1821)*, locate downtown, serves up delicious Indian food. All the effort is concentrated on the excellent cuisine, such that the uninspired decor is soon forgotten.

Orillia

Weber's *($)* is a local road-side institution at the edge of town, where you can enjoy a good charbroiled burger.

For breakfast or a quick snack, try **Café au Lait** *($; Mississaga St.)*, which serves tasty baked goods and cappuccinos.

If you're more in the mood for a healthy meal, head downtown to the aptly named **Evergreen** *($; Mississaga St.)*, which serves delicious, nutritious sandwiches, salads and the like.

Frankie's *($$; 83 Mississaga St. W., ☎327-5404)*, a lovely restaurant with a relaxed atmosphere serves delicious, innovative Italian cuisine with fresh ingredients.

Bracebridge

In fine weather, the terrace at the **Muskokan** *($; at the corner of Kimberley and Manitoba)* is definitely one of the most pleasant places in the area for lunch. Seated in the delightful shade offered by stately trees and parasols, you can start off your day with a good, simple meal.

ONTARIO

The well-located restaurant of the **Inn at the Falls** *($$$$; 17 Dominion St.,* ☎*645-2245)* boasts a beautiful view of the Muskoka River. Comfortably seated in the elegant dining room, you can enjoy this magnificent setting while savouring such irresistible dishes as beef tournedos in a chanterelle sauce and grilled swordfish. Although each dish is more delicious than the last, try to save some room for dessert — you'll be glad you did.

Huntsville

The banks of the Muskoka River, with its wooden terrace and string of restaurants, whose main attraction is their idyllic location, is the perfect spot for a noontime meal. **Blackburn's Landing** *($)* serves simple fare like hamburgers, pasta and salads, as does the **Pasta & Grill** *($)*, next door.

Georgian Bay

Owen Sound

The **Inn on the Bay** *($-$$; 1800 2nd Ave. E.,* ☎*371-9200)* is perfect for breakfast and a glorious sunrise over the water.

Norma Jean *($-$$; 243 8th St. E.,* ☎*376-2232)* is a pleasant little restaurant whose walls are adorned with posters and statuettes of Marilyn Monroe. The perfect place to go for a bite with friends, it has quite a strong following, no doubt drawn by the tasty burgers, salads and beef dishes.

Collingwood

Christopher's *($$-$$$; 167 Pine,* ☎*445-7117)* is sure to catch your eye, as it occupies a magnificent house built in 1902 as a wedding present. It has lost none of its character over the years, and is perfectly suited to an intimate meal at lunchtime *($-$$)*, when quiche and pasta dishes are served, or in the evening, when the menu is more elaborate.

 SHOPPING

The Muskoka Lakes

Orillia

On your way through the Rama reserve, you'll pass by the **Rama Moccasin & Craft Shop**, which is typical of the stores found on native reserves. Don't be put off by the building's wacky appearance (the parking lot is adorned with wooden bears and tepees); the place sells lovely native crafts, including Ojibwa moccasins, *mukluks*, Inuit and Iroquois sculptures, prints and all sorts of jewellery.

Georgian Bay

Collingwood

At **Clerkson's** *(94 Pine St.)*, set up inside a big, beautiful house, you can treat yourself to some handicrafts, decorative objects or perhaps even a piece of antique-style furniture.

TORONTO

The first European to discover Lake Ontario and to set foot on the ground that would become the largest city in Canada was Étienne Brûlé, a French explorer sent by Samuel de Champlain. Brûlé's expedition took place in 1615, at the beginning of the French colonization of North America. Like many of his predecessors, Brûlé was in search of a navigable route across the continent to the riches of the Orient.

As of 1720, the French set up a fur-trading post. About 30 years later, the British, in an attempt to counter competition from their commercial rivals, constructed a fort. The French ultimately burned their Fort Rouillé in 1759 as they beat a hasty retreat from advancing British troops.

In order to realize the potential of this excellent site, the British purchased it from the Mississauga natives in 1787 for 1,700 pounds sterling. John Graves Simcoe, the first governor of Upper Canada, needed a capital for the new province; the location had to be well protected and far enough from the American border to avoid potential invasion. In 1793, he chose this site. A small fort called York was built, and the area's new status as capital attracted a few colonists. The 700 people that had settled here by 1812 succeeded in pushing back the Americans, who had declared war on Britain the year before, but not before the town had been seized for a few days and then destroyed.

In 1834, the city was incorporated and renamed Toronto. Its population was 9,000 at the time. During the 19th century, Toronto underwent rapid expansion, particularly from 1850-1860 with the construction of the railway between Montréal and New York.

At the beginning of the 20th century, Toronto gained a reputation that it just couldn't seem to shake. It became known as "Toronto the Good", rather fitting especially after the 1906 legislation on the "Day of Lord" which forbade the city's residents from any work or diversions on Sundays.

Toronto's growth over the last 20 years has redefined the city, both literally and figuratively. Figuratively, in the sense that nowhere else in Canada are there as many different ethnic communities, a characteristic that distinguishes the city from the rest of Ontario and also from the Toronto of old. Toronto is not only the financial centre of Canada but also the heart of culture in English-speaking Canada. The city was redefined literally on January 1, 1998, when the new Megacity of Toronto officially came into existence. Despite wide anti-amalgamation protests and a No-win in a referendum, the six municipalities (Scarborough, North York, York, East York, Etobicoke and Toronto), which each had their own council along with a metropolitan government, are now joined and form one huge city; a city that is bigger than any American city except New York, Los Angeles and

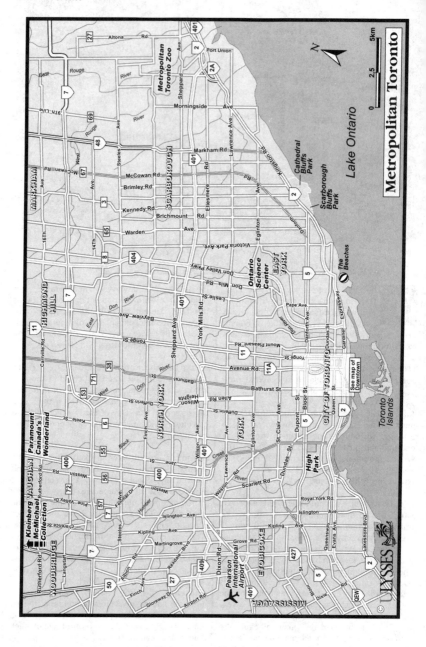

Metropolitan Toronto

Toronto's Subway

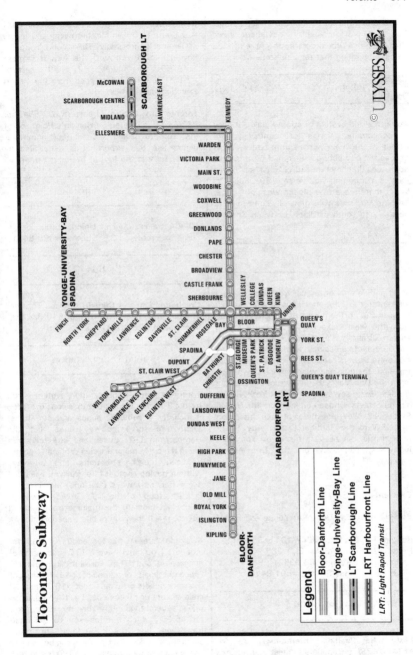

© ULYSSES

Legend

	Bloor-Danforth Line
	Yonge-University-Bay Line
	LT Scarborough Line
	LRT Harbourfront Line

LRT: Light Rapid Transit

ONTARIO

Chicago and that has about 2.3 million people. The "Vote No to megacity" movement feared that the move would destroy the fibre of their cities, something that remains to be seen...

 FINDING YOUR WAY AROUND

Toronto's grid-system of streets makes it easy to get around. Yonge (pronounced *young*) Street is the main north-south artery and it divides the city between east and west. Street addresses that have the suffix "East" or "E." lie east of Yonge and vice versa; 299 Queen St. W. is therefore a few blocks west of Yonge. Toronto's downtown is generally considered to be the area south of Bloor, between Spadina and Jarvis.

By Car

Most people arriving by car from east or west will enter the city on Highway 401, which crosses the northern part of the city. Coming from the west, take Hwy 427 south to the Queen Elizabeth Way (QEW), continue east to the Gardiner Expressway, and exit at York, Bay or Yonge Streets for downtown. Coming from the east, the quickest way to reach downtown is on the Don Valley Parkway; continue to the Gardiner Expressway, then exit at York, Bay or Yonge Streets. Those coming from the United States will follow the shores of Lake Ontario on the QEW to the Gardiner Expressway. Rush-hour traffic can be very heavy on Toronto's highways, especially on the Don Valley Parkway.

Car Rentals

Avis: Hudson Bay Centre at Yonge and Bloor, ☎964-2051.
Budget: 141 Bay St., ☎364-7104 or 363-1111.
Hertz: 128 Richmond St. E., ☎363-9022.
Thrifty: 134 Jarvis, ☎868-0350.
Tilden: 40 Dundas St. W., ☎591-8414.

By Plane

Lester B. Pearson International Airport (☎247-7678) is Canada's biggest and busiest airport. Fifty airlines fly into one of three terminals here. The airport is 27 kilometres from downtown Toronto. By car, take Highway 427 South to Queen Elizabeth Way and follow it Gardiner Expressway. Take York, Yonge or Bay exit for downtown. The **Airport Express** *($12.50 one way, $21.50 return,* ☎1-800-387-6787*)* bus goes from the airport to various city hotels.

Toronto City Centre Airport *(*☎203-6945 or 868-6942*)* is located on Hanlan's Point, on of the Toronto Islands. Short-haul commuter flights use this airport. It is accessible by special ferry at the foot of Bathurst Street.

By Train

All VIA trains arrive at Union Station at the corner of Front and Bay Streets, ☎366-8411.

By Bus

Greyhound Lines of Canada services Toronto. The bus station is downtown at 610 Bay St., Information ☎367-8747.

Public Transportation

Toronto's public transportation system is run by the **Toronto Transit Commission**, the **TTC**; it includes a subway, buses and streetcars. There are three subway lines and the Harbourfront LRT. Buses and streetcars run along the city's major arteries. You can transfer between buses, streetcars and subways without paying another fare, but you will need a transfer, so always take one, just in case. Pick up a copy of the *Ride Guide*, as well. It points out most of the major attractions and how to reach them by public transportation.

A single **fare** is $2 for adults, $1.35 for students (you must have a TTC student card) and seniors and $0.50 for children under 12. Five adult tickets or tokens cost $8, 10 student or senior tickets or tokens cost $10.70 and 10 child tickets or tokens cost $4. If you plan on taking several trips in one day, buy a Day Pass for $6.50, which entitles you to unlimited travel on that day. Sundays are really economical, since one Day Pass can be used by two adults, or by a family (two adults and four children, or one adult and five children). A monthly pass costs $83 for adults and $73 for students and seniors.

For route and schedule information call ☎393-4636; for fare and general information call ☎393-TONE(8663).

On Foot

Toronto's underground city, called the **PATH**, is one of the largest in the country. It weaves its way under the streets from Union Station on Front Street all the way to the Atrium on Bay at Dundas Street. The perfect escape for those cold winter days, it provides access to shops and restaurants.

 PRACTICAL INFORMATION

Area Code: 416.

Tourist Information Offices

Tourism Toronto: Queen's Quay Terminal, 207 Queen's Quay, Suite 590, M5J 1A7, ☎203-2500 or 1-800-363-1990.

Ontario Travel: lower level of the Eaton Centre at Queen and Yonge Streets, ☎1-800-668-2746; open year-round, Monday to Friday 10am to 9pm, Saturday 10am to 5pm and Sunday noon to 5pm; this office is more accessible than the Tourism Toronto office.

Foreign Exchange

Foreign Exchange Centre: 289 Yonge St. (Eaton Centre), ☎599-8984.

Thomas Cook Foreign Exchange: 9 Bloor St. W., ☎923-6549.

Post Office

General Information ☎979-8822.

Main Post Offices: 36 Adelaide St. E. or 1117 Queen St. W.

 EXPLORING

The Waterfront ★★★

Being near a major body of water often determines the location of a city, and Toronto is no exception. For many years, however, the city of Toronto neglected its waterfront. The Gardiner Expressway, the old railway lines and the numerous warehouses that disfigured the shore of Lake Ontario offered few attractions in the eyes of residents. Fortunately, efforts were made to revive this area, and it is now home to luxury hotels, many shops, and numerous cafés bustling with constant activity.

Harbourfront Centre ★ *(free admission, Queen's Quay W.; ☎973-4000 or 973-3000 for information on special events)* is a good example of the changes on Toronto's waterfront. It is easily reached by the Union Station trolley running west toward Spadina Avenue. Since the federal government purchased 40 hectares (100 acres) of land along the shores of Lake Ontario, dilapidated old factories and warehouses have been renovated, turning this into one of Toronto's most exciting areas. Apart from the pretty little cafés and the numerous shops, a variety of shows and cultural events are also the pride of Torontonians.

Formerly located in an old military complex dating back to 1814 and formerly known as the Marine Museum, the new **Waterfront Interpretive Centre** is set to open in July 1998 in Harbourfront Centre. Like its predecessor, the new facility will focus on the city's historical and modern role as a centre of marine activity in the Great Lakes region and will feature the last steamship on Lake Ontario, the *Ned Hanlan*. The ship should be rigged up for harbour tours in time for the grand opening.

A few steps away, at the foot of York Street, is **Queen's Quay Terminal ★★★** *(207 Queen's Quay W.)*, where boats leave for trips around the bay and the Toronto Islands. This former warehouse has been completely renovated and modified to house a dance theatre, as well as about 100 restaurants and shops.

At the foot of Bay Street, a ferry transports passengers back and forth to the **Toronto Islands Park ★★★**. The dock is just behind the

ONTARIO

Harbour Castle Westin Hotel. The Toronto Islands are the ideal spot to relax, take a little sun, go for a bike ride, go in-line skating, take a stroll, or go for a swim.

The **SkyDome** ★★ *(guided tour: $9; every day 9am to 4pm; tour schedules may vary depending on events; 1 Blue Jay Way, Suite 3000, ☎341-3663)*, the pride of Toronto, is the first sports stadium in the world with a fully retractable roof. In poor weather, four panels mounted on rails come together in 20 minutes, despite their 11,000 tonnes, to form the SkyDome's roof. Since opening in 1989, this remarkable building has been home to the American Baseball League's Toronto Blue Jays team and to the Canadian Football League's Toronto Argonauts. Daily 30-minute guided tours are offered on SkyDome's technical aspects *(☎341-2770)*.

The **CN Tower** ★★★ *(observation deck $12: every day, summer 10am to midnight, autumn 9am to 11pm, winter 10am to 10pm; Q-Zar, Simulator Theatre, Virtual World: every day, summer 10am to 10pm, autumn Sun-Thu 10am to 8pm, Fri-Sat 10am to 10pm; winter Sun-Thu 11am to 8pm, Fri-Sat 11am to 10pm; Front Street W., ☎360-8500)*. No doubt the most easily recognizable building in Toronto, the CN Tower dominates the city from a height of 553.33 metres (1,815 feet), making it the highest observation tower in the world. Originally built by the Canadian National Railway company to help transmit radio and TV signals past the numerous downtown buildings, it has become one of the city's main attractions. To avoid long lines, go early in the morning or late in the day, especially in the summer and on weekends. On an overcast day, it is best to postpone your visit.

The foot of the tower offers a panoply of activities. You can also climb to the observation deck in an elevator that lifts you off the ground floor at a speed of six metres per second, equivalent to the takeoff of a jet aircraft. Located 335.25 metres up and set on four levels, the observation deck is the nerve centre of the tower. The view from the top is splendid, of course. On a clear day, you can see over a distance of 160 kilometres and even make out Niagara Falls. Because of the great height, you may feel the tower sway in the wind. This is perfectly normal and enhances the resistance of the entire structure.

CN Tower

1. Harbourfront Centre
2. Queen's Quay Terminal
3. Skydome
4. CN Tower
5. Fort York
6. Ontario Place
7. Princess of Wales Theatre
8. Royal Alexandra
9. Roy Thompson Hall
10. Sun Life Tower
11. First Canadian Place
12. Toronto-Dominion Centre
13. Bank of Nova Scotia
14. National Club Building
15. Bank of Commerce Building
16. Toronto Dominion Bank
17. Number 15
18. Original Toronto Stock Exchange
19. Royal Bank Plaza
20. Union Station
21. Royal York Hotel
22. BCE Place
23. Hockey Hall of Fame
24. Gooderham Building
25. St. Lawrence Hall
26. St. James Cathedral
27. King Edward Hotel
28. The Bay
29. Elgin and Wintergarden Theatres
30. Pantages Theatre
31. Eaton Centre
32. Old City Hall
33. New City Hall
34. City TV and MuchMusic
35. Art Gallery of Ontario
36. Provincial Parliament
37. Bata Shoe Museum
38. Royal Ontario Museum
39. Gardiner Museum of Ceramic Art
40. Yorkville Public Library
41. Firehall No. 10
42. Village of Yorkville Park

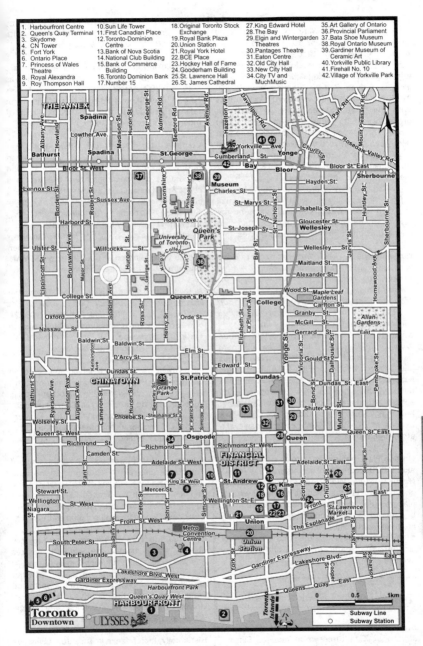

ONTARIO

It was on the shores of Lake Ontario, at **Fort York** *($4.75; Oct 1 to May 15, Tue-Fri 9:30am to 4pm, May 16 to Sept 30, Tue-Sun 9:30am to 5pm; ☎366-6127)* that Toronto was born. Built in 1783 by Governor John Graves Simcoe in response to a looming American threat, Fort York was destroyed by American invaders in 1813 and rebuilt soon afterward. As relations with the United States improved rapidly, it gradually lost its purpose. In the 1930s, the city of Toronto renovated it extensively to turn it into a tourist attraction. Nowadays, Fort York is the site of the largest Canadian collection of buildings dating from the War of 1812. A visit includes a tour of the barracks, which are furnished as they were when they housed officers and soldiers, as well as a small museum with a short informative video on the history of the fort. In the summer, guides in period dress perform military manoeuvres.

Ontario Place ★ *(free admission except during special events; day passes offer unlimited access to various attractions except for bungee-jumping and sailboarding; May to Sep, Mon to Sat 10:30am to midnight, Sun 10:30am to 11pm; 955 Lakeshore Boulevard West, ☎314-9900; from late May to early September, a bus service links Union Station with Ontario Place).* Designed by Eberhard Zeidler, Ontario Place consists of three islands joined by bridges. Five structures are suspended several metres above the water and bustle with activities. An enormous white sphere stands out clearly from the other buildings; inside is the **Cinesphere**, an **IMAX cinema** *(☎965-7722)* with an impressive six-story-high movie screen.

Ontario Place has a marina with a capacity for about 300 boats, centred around the *HMCS Haida*, a World War II destroyer. If you have children, head to the **Children's Village**, with its playgrounds, pool, waterslides, waterguns, bumper-boats, Nintendo centre, LEGO creative centre, cinema and other attractions. The not-so-young will appreciate the **Forum**, an outdoor amphitheatre with musical shows every evening.

The Theatre and Financial Districts ★★

Start at the corner of King and John, the stretch of King Street from here to Simcoe Street is also known as Mirvish Walkway, after the father and son duo of discount-store magnates who refurbished the area by saving

the Royal Alex from the wrecking ball and by filling in the empty warehouses with restaurants for hungry theatre-goers.

The spanking new **Princess of Wales Theatre** *(300 King St. W., ☎872-1212)* theatre was built in 1993 expressly for the musical *Miss Saigon*. Though no tours are offered, it is worth taking a peak inside at the minimalist decor of moon and stars in the lobby.

Continue to **The Royal Alexandra** ★★ *(260 King St. W., ☎872-3333)*. Plastered on the walls of Ed Mirvish's various food emporiums between these two theatres is a collection of newspaper articles attesting to the entrepreneur's various exploits. The Royal Alexandra was named after the king's consort, and is now popularly known as the Royal Alex. Its rich Edwardian styling and beaux-arts decor of plush red velvet, gold brocade and green marble were restored in the 1960s by Toronto discount-sales magnate Ed Mirvish.

Across the street rises **Roy Thompson Hall** ★★★ *(45-min guided tours Mon to Sat 12:30pm; $3; 60 Simcoe St., ☎593-4822)*, one of the most distinctive buildings in Toronto's cityscape. The space-age 40,000-square-foot mirrored-glass exterior was designed by Canada's Arthur Erickson and gets mixed reviews, having been compared to an upside-down mushroom and a ballerina tutu. The interior, however, is another story, boasting striking luminosity, a glamorous lobby and exceptional acoustics that the resident Toronto Symphony and Mendelssohn Choir show off beautifully.

A large courtyard stretches out to the west of Roy Thompson Hall, it is bordered to the west by **Metro Hall** (facing the Princess of Wales), and to the south by Simcoe Place (the large square building to the left) and the **CBC Broadcast Centre** (the tall building to the right).

Continue into Toronto's heart, to its **financial district**, where money, the thing that makes many local residents run themselves ragged, is the leading preoccupation. The district stretches from Adelaide Street to the north and Front Street to the south and between University Avenue to the west and Yonge Street to the east.

Historically, high finance in Toronto has always been centred around this area. It all started at the intersection of Yonge and Wellington in the mid-1800s, when the only form of advertising available to financial organizations was architecture. Image was everything in those days, and a sense of solidity and permanence was achieved through majestic entrance halls, cornices, porticoes and the like. By the early 1900s the hub had shifted north to King and Yonge, and the sleek Art Deco was in vogue. As the district expanded to the west, skyscrapers were built right up against the road on Bay Street, creating a northern version of the Wall Street canyon. In the last three decades, the steel and glass towers have become the centrepieces of vast windswept courtyards. In recent years, these concrete parks have come in direct competition with the ever-expanding underground walkway system known as the PATH, and the debate continues as to the merits of these impersonal tunnels, which shuttle office workers hither and thither.

As you walk east along King Street, the first tower of steel and mirror is the **Sun Life Tower** ★ *(150-200 King St. W.)*, standing opposite St. Andrew's Church at the corner of Simcoe and King Streets. At the northeast corner of York and King stands the august-marble tower known as **First Canadian Place** ★★. Though its stark exterior and squat base are not very appealing, the interior commercial space is bright and airy. The **Toronto Stock Exchange** ★★ *(free admission; Mon to Fri 9:30am to 4pm, guided tours at 2pm; 130 King St., ☎947-4670)* is the focal point of Canadian high finance, The Visitors' Centre is located on the ground floor of the Exchange Tower, in the reception area. This is one of the more interesting stops in the district as visitors can watch the action on the trading floor from an observation gallery.

Halfway between York and Bay, the **Standard Life** and **Royal Trust** buildings stand on the south side of King Street next to the impressive **Toronto-Dominion Centre** ★★★ *(55 King St. W.)*, on the southwest corner of King and Bay. The work of famous modernist Ludwig Mies van der Rohe, it was the first International-Style skyscraper built in Toronto in the mid-1960s.

At the northeast corner of King and Bay is the Art-Deco **Bank of Nova Scotia** ★ *(44 King St. W.)*. A few gems lie up Bay Street, notably the **National Club Building** *(303 Bay St.)*, the **Bank of Montreal** *(302 Bay St.)* and the **Canada Permanent Building** *(320 Bay St.)* with its splendid Art Deco lobby.

Back on King Street, the **Bank of Commerce Building** ★★★ *(25 King St. W.)* is seen by many as the best bank building and office tower in Toronto's financial district. Enter the immense banking hall to view the roseate stone, gilt mouldings and blue-coffered barrel vault. To the east, on the corner of King and Bay, is the **"Old" Bank of Commerce Building**, which for many years was the tallest building in the British Commonwealth. In between and facing Bay Street is **Commerce Court** *(243 Bay St.)*, which encompasses the two aforementioned buildings and a slick glass and steel skyscraper built in the early 1970s.

The **Toronto Dominion Bank** ★★★ *(55 King St. W.)* lies on the southwest corner of King and Yonge. Its interior is a veritable feast for the eyes. A central staircase leads down to the vault, touted as the largest in Canada when it was built, while another, even more formal staircase to the right leads up to the main banking hall.

At number 15 Wellington Street is the oldest building on this tour. Originally the Commercial Bank of Midland District (1845), then the Merchant's Bank, it is now simply known as **Number 15** ★★, or depending who you talk to, Marché Mövenpick (see p 389). Make your way to Bay. About halfway up the block towards King Street, on the east side, is the **Original Toronto Stock Exchange** ★★★ *(234 Bay St.)* the city's most typically Art Deco building. The 74-foot stone frieze above the door mixes irony and humour as only a Canadian stock exchange building could. Located in the magnificently restored interior, the **Design Exchange** *($5; Wed and Thu 10am to 9pm, Fri 10am to 6pm, Sun 10am to 5pm; ☎216-2150)* features exhibits of international and national designers.

The lavish and imposing **Royal Bank Plaza** ★★★ *(200 Bay St.)* is below Wellington. The gold-enriched mirrored exterior is like a breath of fresh air amidst the sober white-collar demeanour of Toronto's financial district, especially at twilight; the gold also acts as an insulator.

ONTARIO

Front Street and St. Lawrence ★

It was in the rectangular area formed by George, Berkley, Adelaide and Front streets that Commander John Graves Simcoe of the British army founded the town of York in 1793.

Today it is better known as Toronto. This part of the city, close to Lake Ontario, was for many years the business centre of the growing city. At the end of the 19th century, economic activity slowly moved toward what is today known as the financial district, leaving behind a partially deserted area. Like Harbourfront, the St. Lawrence neighbourhood has undergone major renovations over the last couple of decades, financed by the federal, provincial and municipal governments. Today a cheerful mixture of 19th- and 20th-century architecture characterizes an area where the city's various socio-economic groups converge.

Union Station ★★ *(65-75 Front St. W.)* ranks first among Canadian railway stations for its size and magnificence. It was built in the spirit of great American railway terminals, with columns and coffered ceilings inspired by the basilicas of ancient Rome. Work on the station began in 1915 but was completed only in 1927. This was one of the masterpieces of Montréal architects Ross and Macdonald. Its façade on Front Street stretches over 250 metres, concealing the port and Lake Ontario in the background.

The **Royal York Hotel ★★** *(100 Front St. W.)* is a worthy introduction to downtown Toronto for anyone arriving by train at Union Station. Its message to new arrivals is clear: the Queen City is indeed a major metropolis that will play second fiddle to nobody. This hotel, the biggest in the Canadian Pacific chain, has more than 1,500 rooms on 25 floors. Like the station, it was designed by Montréal architects Ross and Macdonald. Here the château style of the railway hotels is combined with Lombard and Venetian elements (see also p 388).

Enter **BCE Place ★★★** by the courtyard located east of the Canada Trust Tower. BCE Place stretches from Bay Street to Young Street and is made up of twin towers linked by a magnificent five-story glass atrium supported by enormous white metal ribs. This bright and airy space is a delightful place to rest for a few moments or grab a bite. There are fast-food counters on the lower level, or for something unique, head instead to the **Marché Mövenpick** (see p 389), a happy blend of restaurant and market.

BCE Place also encloses the entrance to the famous **Hockey Hall of Fame ★** *($8.50; summer, Mon to Sat 9:30am to 6pm, Sun 10am to 6pm; rest of the year, Mon to Fri 10am to 5pm, Sat 9:30am to 6pm, Sun 10:30am to 5:30pm; 30 Yonge St., ☎360-7765)*, a veritable paradise for hockey fans. Do not miss the Bell Great Hall, at the centre of which is the original Stanley Cup, North America's oldest professional sports trophy, donated by Lord Stanley of Preston in 1893. Other highlights inside include a reconstitution of the Montréal Canadiens' dressing room as well as some of hockey's most exciting moments on video.

At the corner of Yonge and Front Streets is the old **Bank of Montreal Building ★★**. The Hockey Hall of Fame is actually located in this building, though the only entrance is through BCE Place. Built in 1886 by architects Darling and Curry, the Bank of Montreal building is one of the oldest 19th-century structures still standing in Toronto. Designed during a prosperous and optimistic period, its architecture which conveys a sense of power and invulnerability was typical of the era, with imposing masonry, splendid porticoes and gigantic windows.

A little further east along Front Street beyond Berczy Park is the amusing *trompe l'oeil* fresco painted on the back of the **Gooderham Building ★** *(49 Wellington St.)*. This mural, created by Derek Besant in 1980, has become a well-known sight in Toronto. Contrary to popular belief, it does not portray the windows of the Gooderham Building but rather the façade of the Perkins Building, located across the street at 41-43 Front Street East. The Gooderham is often called the Flatiron Building because of its triangular structure that recalls the shape of its famous younger New York namesake.

Look back now from where you came and contemplate the interesting vista of the Flatiron Building framed by the office towers of the financial district and the CN Tower. Across Front Street, the gleaming façades that now harbour shops and cafes are merely those of simple warehouses.

At the corner of Jarvis Street is the **St. Lawrence Market ★★** *(91 Front St. E.)*. Built in 1844, it housed the city hall until 1904, the year Henry Bowyer Lane converted it into a public market. Expanded in 1978, St. Lawrence Market is famed today for the freshness of the fruits and vegetables, fish, meats, sausages and cheeses sold inside. Actually, this giant red-brick building completely envelops the former city hall, which is still perceptible in the façade. The best time to go is on Saturday, when the fish is freshest and local farmers

Gooderham Building

ONTARIO

arrive at 5am to sell their products across the street at the **Farmer's Market**.

St. Lawrence Hall ★ *(151 King St. E.)* was Toronto's community centre in the latter half of the 19th century. This Victorian structure was built to present concerts and balls. Among the celebrities who performed here were Jenny Lind, Andelina Patti, Tom Thumb and P.T. Barnum. For several years, St. Lawrence Hall was also home the National Ballet of Canada.

Lovely **St. James Park**, a 19th-century garden with a fountain and annual flower beds, lies a few steps to the west. While seated on one of its many benches, you can contemplate **St. James Cathedral** ★★ at the corner of Church and King Streets, Toronto's first Anglican cathedral. Built in 1819, it was destroyed in

the 1849 fire that levelled part of the city. The St. James Cathedral you see today was built on the ruins of its predecessor. It has the highest steeple in all of Canada and the second highest in North America, after St. Patrick's Cathedral in New York. The interior is far more elaborate than the sober, yellow-brick Gothic exterior suggests.

The splendid **King Edward Hotel** ★★ *(37 King St. E.)* (see p 388), between Church Street and Leader Lane, was designed in 1903 by E.J. Lennox, architect of the Old City Hall (see p 380), Massey Hall (see p 392) and Casa Loma (see p 385). With its Edwardian style, its wonderful mock marble columns on the ground floor and its magnificent dining rooms, the King Edward was one of Toronto's most luxurious hotels for nearly 60 years, until, with the decline of the surrounding area, it fell into disrepair. Splendid Café Victoria (see p 390) ultimately saved the hotel from the wrecker's ball.

Queen West, Kensington and Chinatown ★★★

This tour starts at the corner of Yonge and Queen Streets where Queen West begins. **The Bay** department store occupies the southwest corner and the whole south side of Queen all the way to Bay. The stunning Art Deco entrance at Richmond and Yonge was added in 1928.

Head north on Yonge Street. On the left is the exterior of the six-story shopping mecca, the Eaton Centre (see below); on the right you'll soon come upon two more of Toronto's majestic theatres, the Elgin and Wintergarden and the Pantages.

The **Elgin and Wintergarden Theatres** ★★ *(one-hour tours, $4; Thu 5pm, Sat 11am; 189 Yonge St., ☎363-5253 or 872-5555)* together form the last operating double-decker theatre complex in the world. Opened in 1914 as vaudeville theatres, the Elgin downstairs was opulence galore, while the Wintergarden upstairs was one of the first "atmospheric theatres", with trellised walls and columns disguised as tree trunks supporting a ceiling of real leaves. After a stint as a movie house, these landmarks were restored by the Ontario Heritage Centre and again serve as live theatres.

Once the biggest vaudeville house in the British Empire, the **Pantages Theatre** *(one-hour tours Mon, Tue and Fri 11:30am, Sat 10:30am; $4; 263 Yonge St., ☎362-3218)* went through many reincarnations as a picture palace and then a six-theatre movie house, and finally in 1988-89, was restored to its original splendour. It is perhaps best-known, however, as the home of Andrew Lloyd Webber's *Phantom of the Opera*.

Even if you have no desire to go shopping, at least take a peek inside the **Eaton Centre** ★★, which runs along Yonge Street between Queen and Dundas. And if you do need something, by all means linger in this glass-roofed arcade, which a few sparrows have even decided is more pleasant than outside. Here, so-called streets have been stacked five-stories high and lined with pristine benches and trees. Look up

and you will see Michael Snow's exquisite flock of fibreglass Canada geese, called *Step Flight*, suspended over the Galleria. Framed by two 30-story skyscrapers and two subway stations (Dundas and Queen Stations) and occupying six million square feet, the Eaton Centre contains more than 320 stores and restaurants, 2 indoor parking lofts and a 17-theatre cinema complex.

Once you've had your fill of the shops, exit the Eaton Centre via Trinity Square, at the northwest corner of the mall.

This lovely space was almost never created. The **Church of the Holy Trinity** ★★ (1847), the **Rectory** (1861) and the **Scadding House** (1857) are some of Toronto's oldest landmarks, and the original plans for the Eaton Centre called for their demolition. Fortunately, enough people objected and the huge mall was built around the building trio.

Head down James Street towards the back of **Old City Hall** ★★ *(60 Queen St. W.)* designed by E. J. Lennox in 1889. As you make your way around the building towards the front on Queen Street, look up at the eaves, below which the architect carved the letters "E J LENNOX ARCHITECT" to ensure that his name would be remembered. Lennox won a contest to design the building, but the city councillors denied his request to engrave his name on a cornerstone; in retaliation, he had disfigured versions of their faces carved above the front steps so that they would have to face their gargoyle-like selves every day! By the time all these insulting personal touches were revealed, it was too late to do anything about them.

In 1965, the municipal administration of Toronto moved out of its Victorian city hall and into **New City Hall** ★★ *(100 Queen St. W.)*, a modernist masterpiece that quickly gained a certain notoriety and became as symbolic of Toronto as the CN Tower. Once again, a contest was held to choose the city's most avant-garde architect and this time the winner was Finn Viljo Revell, a master of Scandinavian post-war rationalist thinking. Its two curved towers of unequal length are like two hands protecting the saucer-shaped structure that houses the Council Room.

Nathan Phillips Square ★, a vast public space in front of New City Hall, is named after the mayor of Toronto who blessed the city with many new facilities at the beginning of the 1960s. A large pool of water straddled by three arches is transformed into a skating rink in the winter. Nearby stands "*The Archer*", by Henry Moore, and the Peace Garden.

Make your way along Queen Street West, lined with trendy shops, cafés and bars for most of its length, it is also the home of **CityTV and Muchmusic** *(299 Queen St. W.)*, "the nation's music station". The former Wesley Building was built for a publishing company in 1913-15; note the grotesque readers and scribes that adorn its façade. In the Speakers' Corner video booth you can applaud or criticize any cause you like, and maybe even end up on national television.

Take the time to stroll along **Queen West** ★★ and admire the hip and avant-garde boutiques. There are even a few interesting architectural highlights, as most of these shops occupy late-19th-century buildings.

Now you can head north on Spadina. The five blocks between Queen and Dundas might not look like much, but they contain some of the best bargains in town, from designer clothes to designer food, and from evening wear to kitchenware. At the intersection of Spadina and Dundas, you will find yourself in the heart of Toronto's **Chinatown** ★★★. The community radiates from this point north to College Street, south to Queen and east to Bay, and is the largest Chinatown in North America. The neighbourhood actually began around Elizabeth Street where New City Hall now stands. It gradually moved west to Spadina, though remnants of it remain all along Dundas. The best time to explore the fascinating tea shops, herbalists and Chinese grocers is on Sunday, when sounds of Cantonese pop music, mounds of fresh vegetables, racks of roasted duck and smells of ginseng transport you to another world. Sunday is also the day when most Chinese families head out for brunch, though they call it dim sum, and there are no scrambled eggs or baked beans to wade through!

Before straying too far along Dundas, however, check out **Kensington Market** ★★, located along Kensington Street. This bazaar epitomizes Toronto's multi-ethnicity. It began as a primarily Eastern European market, but is now a wonderful mingling of Jewish, Portuguese, Asian and Caribbean culture. The lower half of Kensington is mostly vintage clothing shops, while the upper portion boasts international grocers peddling fresh and tasty

morsels from all over the world. Perfect for picnic fixings!

Whether you decide on a picnic or dim sum, make sure to save time for an edifying afternoon at the Art Gallery of Ontario and The Grange.

The Art Museum of Toronto was founded in 1900, but was without a permanent home until 1913, when The Grange (see below) was bequeathed to the museum. A new building was added in 1918, and the first exhibition of Canada's renowned Group of Seven was held in 1920 at what was by then known as the Art Gallery of Toronto. A significant chapter in Canada's and Toronto's cultural histories was thus written. In 1966, the museum received provincial support and was officially rebaptized the **Art Gallery of Ontario** ★★★ *(admission is on a pay-what-you-can basis, $5 per person is suggested; special exhibitions are priced individually; May to Oct, Tue and Thu to Sun 10am to 5:30pm, Wed 10am to 10pm, holiday Mon 10am to 5:30pm; Oct to May, Wed 10am to 10pm, Thu to Sun 10am to 5:30pm, holiday Mon 10am to 5:30pm; 317 Dundas St. W., ☎977-0414)*. Successive renovations and additions over the years have all tried to reinvent the AGO, by introducing new elements in place off old ones. Exhibits feature contemporary art and Inuit sculptures, and the beautiful Tanenbaum Sculpture Atrium, exposes a façade of The Grange. The Henry Moore Sculpture Centre is one of the museum's greatest treasures. The Canadian historical and contemporary collections contain major pieces by such notables as Cornelius Krieghoff, Michael Snow, Emily Carr, Jean-Paul Riopelle, Tom Thomson and the Group of Seven — Frederick Varley, Lawren Harris, Franklin Carmichael, A. Y. Jackson, Arthur Lismer, J. E. H. MacDonald and Frank H. Johnson. The museum also boasts masterpieces by Rembrandt, Van Dyck, Reynolds, Renoir, Picasso, Rodin, Degas and Matisse, to name a few.

Adjacent to the Art Gallery of Ontario stands its original home, **The Grange** ★ *(admission included with AGO ticket; May to Oct, Tue and Thu to Sun noon to 4pm, Wed noon to 9pm; Oct to May, Wed noon to 9pm, Thu to Sat noon to 4pm; Grange Park, south of the AGO, ☎977-0414)*. The Georgian-style residence was built in 1817-18 by D'Arcy Boulton Jr., a member of Toronto's ruling elite, the much-reviled Family Compact. The city of Toronto was barely thirty years old at the time, yet by

ONTARIO

1837, the year of Mackenzie's rebellion, The Grange had become the virtual seat of political power and thus symbolized the oppressive colonial regime in Upper Canada. The house was willed to the Art Museum of Toronto in 1910. It was restored to its 1830s grandeur and the whole house was opened to the public in 1973. This aristocrat's house, with its grand circular staircase and fascinating servants' quarters, was one of Toronto's first brickwork buildings.

End your day with a hearty meal on Baldwin Street in Chinatown's residential area. The block to the east of McCaul harbours some fantastic little restaurants.

Around Queen's Park ★★

Each of the ten provinces has its own legislative assembly. Ontario's is located in the **Provincial Parliament** ★★ *(1 Queen's Park)*, at the centre of Queen's Park in the middle of University Avenue. The red sandstone building (1886-1892) was designed in the Richardsonian neo-Romanesque style by architect Richard A. Waite of Buffalo, who is also responsible for several Canadian buildings, including the old headquarters of the Grand Trunk Railway on McGill Street in Montreal.

The forty or so buildings of the **University of Toronto** ★★ *(between Spadina Rd. to the west, Queen's Park Cresc. to the east, College St. to the south and Bloor to the north)* are dot a vast and very green English-style campus. Granted a charter in 1827, the institution didn't really get going until the construction of its first building in 1845 (no longer standing). Today, the University of Toronto is considered one of the most important in North America.

The oldest building on campus is **University College** *(15 Kings College Circle)*, built in 1859 by architects Cumberland and Storm. The result is a picturesque neo-Romanesque ensemble with remarkably detailed stone carving.

A winding road called **Philosopher's Walk** ★ heads north from Hoskins. The Taddle Creek once flowed here where the philosopher now walks to the wafting sounds of music students practising their scales at the **Royal Conservatory of Music** *(273 Bloor St.)*. A contemplative stroll next to the newly planted oak trees leads to the Alexandra Gates (which originally stood at Bloor and Queen's Park).

Bloor and Yorkville ★★★

This tour covers the area around Bloor and Yorkville, two names that are now synonymous with expensive, up-scale and trendy. The tour has a little something for everyone, including some of Toronto's finest museums and best shopping.

The area north and west of Bloor and Bedford was once the Village of Yorkville, which was incorporated in 1853 and existed as a separate town until 1883, when it was annexed to the city of Toronto. The first signs of the area's trend-setting status began to appear in the postwar era, as the 19th-century residences were transformed into coffeehouses and shops, and Yorkville became the focus of Canada's folk music scene in the 1960s. The gentrification of the area took off in the seventies and eighties, and on Bloor Street multi-purpose complexes and high rises have sought to make optimal use of now outrageously expensive rental properties.

Start at the corner of St. George and Bloor Streets, just a few steps from the St. George subway station. This corner lies at the southwestern extremity of The Annex (see p 385), an area containing many wonderfully preserved 19th-century homes.

The new home of the **Bata Shoe Museum** ★★★ *($6; Tue to Sat 10am to 5pm, Thu until 8pm, Sun noon to 5pm; 327 Bloor St. W, ☎979-7799)* is a whimsical start to a serious museum-touring excursion and a great place to get a few ideas before you hit the major shopping! The first museum of its kind in North America, it holds 10,000 shoes and provides an extraordinary perspective on the world's cultures. The new building was designed by architect Raymond Moriyama to look like a shoe box, and the oxidized copper along the edge of the roof is meant to suggest a lid resting on top. Some of the more memorable pieces of footwear on display include space boots of Apollo astronauts, geisha platform sandals and a pair of patent-leather beauties that once belonged to Elvis Presley.

The **Royal Ontario Museum** ★★★ *($10; Mon to Sat 10am to 6pm, Tue 10am to 8pm, Sun*

11am to 6pm; 100 Queen's Park, ☎586-5549 or 586-5551; Museum subway; parking is expensive) is actually two museums in one since admission to the ROM, as it is called, also includes admission to the George R. Gardiner Museum of Ceramic Art (see below). Canada's largest public museum, as well as a research facility, the ROM preserves some six million treasures of art, archaeology and natural science. After extensive renovation, restoration and the opening of new galleries, the ROM can now display these treasures using techniques that benefit their inestimable worth; upon entering the impressive free-Romanesque-style building, visitors' eyes are drawn up to the Venetian glass ceiling that depicts a mosaic of cultures. The ceiling is the only part of the museum that was not built using materials from Ontario. Continuing into the museum, the eyes are drawn up once again by the towering totem poles flanking the lobby, one of which is 24 metres tall, and whose top is just 15 centimetres shy of ceiling! With exhibits on Romans and Nubians, Chinese art and antiquities including a Ming tomb, and evrything from bats to dinosaurs, your first stop should be at the Mankind Discovering Gallery, where the layout and workings of the ROM are explained.

On the east side of Queen's Park Avenue, the **George R. Gardiner Museum of Ceramic Art** ★★★ (admission included with ROM ticket; year-round Tue to Sat 10am to 5pm, Sun 11am to 5pm; in summer, Tue until 7:30pm; 111 Queen's Park, ☎593-9300) boasts a striking collection of porcelain and pottery. Four galleries span history from the pre-Colombian Mayans and Olmecs to European treasures of the last 500 years.

The luxurious **Park Plaza Hotel** (4 Avenue Rd.), built in 1926, stands at the northwest corner of Avenue and Bloor. The rough stone walls, sweeping slate roof and belfry of the **Church of the Redeemer** (162 Bloor Ste. W.) occupy the northeast corner of Bloor and Avenue.

The stretch of Bloor Street from Queen's Park/Avenue Road to Yonge is a collection of modern office buildings, shopping malls and ultra-chic boutiques and galleries including such notables as Holt Renfrew, Chanel, Hermès, Tiffany's and Hugo Boss. According to some, Bloor Street is Toronto's Fifth Avenue, so make your way along it as quickly or as leisurely as you wish.

Heading west along Yorkville, you'll come to the grand **Yorkville Public Library** (22 Yorkville Ave.) built in 1907 and remodelled in 1978. The bold porticoed entrance still dominates the façade just as it did when this library served the village of Yorkville.

Right next door is the old **Firehall No. 10** ★ (34 Yorkville Ave.), built in 1876 and then reconstructed (except for the tower, used to dry fire hoses) in 1889-90. This red- and yellow-brick hose house is still in use. The coat of arms on the tower was salvaged from the town hall; the symbols on it represent the vocations of the town's first councillors: a beer barrel for the brewer, a plane for the carpenter, a brick mould for the builder, an anvil for the blacksmith and a bull's head for the butcher.

An exceptional collection of galleries, shops and cafés line Yorkville, Hazelton and Cumberland. More architectural gems, too numerous to list, remain on Hazelton Avenue. These have all been faithfully restored, some to the extent that they look like new buildings; nevertheless, the results are aesthetically pleasing and worth a look.

One block south is Cumberland Street, lined with fancy boutiques and galleries on one side, and the **Village of Yorkville Park** ★★ on the other. This urban park, which lies over a subway station, is an uncommon mix of urban ecology, local history and regional identity. It is divided into 13 zones, each representing a different part of the province's geography. The huge boulder toward the centre is native Canadian Shield granite.

Toronto: City of Neighbourhoods

Many people view Toronto as a bastion of Anglo-Saxon culture, as Canada's financial hub or as the home to the Blue Jays and the CN Tower, but few realize that it is also a city of tremendously diverse neighbourhoods. While some areas are defined by their architectural extravagance or lack thereof, a perhaps more interesting handful are defined by the people that live there. Toronto's ethnicity is a marvel; with some 70 nationalities and more than one hundred languages, the city is emblematic of the Canadian mosaic, and restaurant-goers are all the happier for it!

Chinatown

Toronto's best-known ethnic neighbourhood is Chinatown (see p 381). There are actually six Chinatowns in greater Toronto, but the most exciting and vibrant is probably the one bound by University, Spadina, Queen and College. During the day, fresh vegetables line the sidewalks around the intersection of Spadina and Dundas, the area's core, while at night, the bright yellow and red lights are reminiscent of Hong Kong. Picturesque, adjacent **Kensington Market** is often associated with Chinatown. The vintage clothing stores and specialty food shops from Europe, the Caribbean, the Middle East and Asia are veritable must-sees.

Little Italy

Italians make up the city's largest ethnic group, and their spiritual home is Little Italy, located on College Street near Bathurst, where trattorias and boutiques add a bit of the Mediterranean to this Canadian metropolis. The neighbourhood extends to **Corso Italia**, on St. Clair Avenue, west of Bathurst. This vibrant mix of traditional shops and designer Italian boutiques is a marvellous spot for a real cappuccino or Italian *gelato*.

Greektown

Greektown is also known as The Danforth, after the street that runs through it. Greektown is perhaps a misnomer anyway since the community is now home to Italians, Greeks, East Indians, Latin Americans and Chinese. The Greeks still dominate, however, when it comes to restaurants, and Greektown, with its late night fruit markets, specialty food shops, taverns and summer cafés, is a real culinary experience.

Little Poland

Between the Lakeshore and Dundas Street West, Roncesvalles Avenue is known as Little Poland, a pleasant area of grand trees and stately Victorians. This is where you can catch an Eastern European film or savour traditional home-made cabbage rolls and pirogies at one of the many cafés.

Portugal Village

The traditional *azulejos* (ceramic tiles) and a glass of port will make you think you are in Portugal when you visit the area around Dundas Street West, Ossington Avenue, Augusta Avenue and College Street, known as Portugal Village. Bakeries here sell some of the best bread in town, while cheese stores, fish markets and lace and crochet shops occupy every other corner.

Little India

Little India is a collection of spice shops, clothing stores, restaurants and movie houses along Gerrard Street, east of Greenwood Avenue. These establishments are frequented by Toronto's East Indian community, which is now spread throughout the city.

Caribbean Village

The area around Bathurst Street north of Bloor Street is the commercial district known as the Caribbean Community. Great food shops sell delicious treats, including savoury patties (pastry turnovers with spicy meat fillings) and *roti* (flat bread with meat, fish or vegetable filling) of the islands.

Gay Village

Toronto has the largest population of gays and lesbians in Canada, and is a surprisingly welcoming place considering the city's occasionally stodgy reputation. The Gay Village is centred around the corner of Church and Wellesley Streets. Another popular hangout is Hanlan's Point on the Toronto Islands.

Rosedale

Both of Toronto's most distinguished and affluent neighbourhoods lies just north of the downtown area. The first one, Rosedale, is bound by Yonge Street to the west, the Don Valley parkway to the east, Bloor Street to the south and St. Clair Avenue to the north. Rosedale began as the estate of Sheriff William Jarvis, and was so named by his wife Mary after the wild roses that once abounded here. The wild roses and the original house overlooking the ravine are now gone, replaced by a collection of curved streets lined with

Grain elevators, railroad tracks and fields as far as the eye can see: classic images of the Canadian prairie. (Walter Bibikow)

Herbert La
framed by
snowy pea
the Rocky
Mountains
one of the
spectacula
sights alon
the Icefield
Parkway. (T

Vancouver,
between sea
and sky, where
Asia meets
America. (P.L.)

exquisite residences representing quite a variety of architectural styles. Rosedale was once considered too far from town, but today its natural ravine setting is one of its major assets. Some of the prettiest residences lie on South Drive, Meredith Crescent, Crescent Road, Chestnut Park Road, Elm Avenue and Maple Avenue.

Forest Hill

North of St. Clair Avenue, the second posh area, known as Forest Hill, begins. It extends north to Eglinton, east to Avenue Road and west to Bathurst Street. The former village of Forest Hill was incorporated into the city of Toronto in 1968. Perhaps in keeping with its name, one of the village's first bylaws back in the twenties was that a tree be planted on every lot. This haven of greenery is home to some of the city's finest dwellings; many of the loveliest grace Old Forest Hill Road. The community is also home to one of the country's most prestigious private schools, Upper Canada College, which has produced such luminaries as authors Stephen Leacock and Robertson Davies.

Cabbagetown

Cabbagetown was once described as the "biggest Anglo-Saxon Slum" and was for many years an area to be avoided. The area has been transformed in recent years, however, and is now the epitome of gentrification in Toronto. Its name originated with Irish immigrants who arrived here in the mid-19th century and grew cabbages right on their front lawns. Cabbagetown's residential area lies around Parliament Street (its commercial artery), and extends east to the Don Valley, and between Gerrard and Bloor Streets. It contains grand trees and quaint small-scale Victorian homes, many of which have historic markers. Winchester, Carlton, Spruce and Metcalfe Streets are all lined with these true gems.

The Annex

Extending north and west of the intersection of Bloor Street and Avenue Road to Dupont and Bathurst Streets is an area that was annexed by the city of Toronto in 1887, and is now appropriately called The Annex. As this was a planned suburb, a certain architectural homogeneity prevails; even the unique gables, turrets and cornices are all lined up at an equal distance from the street. Take a stroll along Huron Street, Lowther Avenue and Madison Avenue to get a true feel for the Annex's architectural character, which residents have long fought to preserve. Save a few ugly apartment high-rises along St. George Street, their efforts have been quite successful.

Torontonians can be known sometimes for their reserve, modesty and discretion. Of course there are exceptions to every rule, and one of these is certainly **Casa Loma ★★** *($9; every day 9:30am to 4pm; 1 Austin Terrace, ☎923-1171)* an immense Scottish castle with 98 rooms built in 1914 for the eccentric colonel Sir Henry Mill Pellatt (1859-1939) who made his fortune by investing in electricity and transportation companies. Pellatt owned, among other things, the tramways of São Paolo, Brazil! His palatial residence, designed by the architect of Toronto's Old City Hall, E.J. Lennox, includes a vast ball room for 500 guests with a pipe organ, a library with 100,000 volumes and an underground cellar. The self-guided tour leads through various secret passages and lost rooms. Great views of downtown Toronto can be seen from the towers.

To the east of Casa Loma, atop the Davenport hill and accessible by the Baldwin Steps is **Spadina ★** *($5; Jun to Dec, Mon to Fri 9:30am to 5pm, Sat and Sun noon to 5pm; Jan to May, Tue to Fri 9:30am to 5pm, Sat and Sun noon to 5pm; 285 Spadina Rd., ☎392-6910)* another house-turned museum of Toronto's high society. This one is smaller but just as splendid for those who want to get a taste of the Belle Époque in Canada. The grounds include a solarium overflowing with luxuriant greenery and a charming Victorian garden, in bloom from May to September. The residence has been renovated several times and features several glassed-in overhangs, which offered its owners panoramic views of the surroundings that the natives called *Espanidong*, and the English *Spadina* (the correct pronunciation is *Spadeena*).

The Beaches

Last but not least, there are The Beaches (Toronto really does have everything!). This is perhaps Toronto's most charming neighbourhood, for obvious reasons — sun, sand, a beach-side boardwalk, classic clapboard and shingle cottages and the open

ONTARIO

water all lie just a streetcar ride away from the hectic pace of downtown. Bound by Kingston Road, the old Greenwood Raceway grounds, Victoria Park Avenue and Lake Ontario, The Beaches are more than just a neighbourhood, they are a way of life. Weary travellers will revel in the chance to sunbathe on the hot sand, take a quick dip in the refreshing water and, as the sun sets, do some window-shopping and lounge about on a pretty patio.

Other Sights

Ontario Science Centre ★★★ *($8; every day 10am to 5pm, 770 Don Mills Rd., ☎429-4100, www.osc.on.ca).* Since its opening, September 27, 1969, the Science Centre has welcomed over 30 million visitors, young and old alike. Designed by architect Raymond Moriyama, it houses 650 different expositions. The best part about the centre is its many hands-on exhibits and experiments. One of the biggest crowd-pleasers is the electricity ball that makes your hair stand on end. The brand new OMNIMAX theatre, which is an improved version of the IMAX, seats 320 people under an enormous 24-metre-wide dome with a powerful hi-fidelity sound system.

For an enjoyable change of scenery within 30 minutes of downtown Toronto head to the **Toronto Metropolitan Zoo ★★** *($12; Meadowvale Rd. West Hill, Scarborough, follow Hwy 401 to Exit 389, then take Meadowvale Dr. ☎392-5900, www.torontozoo.com)* where you can see some 4,000 animals from the four corners of the globe and take advantage of this lovely 300-hectare park. The African pavillion is particularly interesting. Canadian wildlife is also well represented, and several species that are adapted to the local climate roam free in large enclosures.

The first one of its kind in the country, **Paramount Canada's Wonderland (6)** *(Pay One Price Passport: guests aged 7-59 $37.95; May, Sep and Oct, Sat and Sun 10am to 8pm; Jun to Labour Day, every day 10am to 10pm; 9580 Jane St., Vaughan, ☎905-832-7000, Rutherford exit from Hwy 400 and follow the signs, or Yorkdale or York Mills subway then take special GO express bus)* is the answer if you have a day to kill and children to please. Gut-wrenching rides include the Vortex, the only suspended roller coaster in Canada, and the renowned Days of Thunder, which puts you behind the driver's seat for a simulated stock-car race. The park also features a waterpark called Splash Works with 16 rides and slides, and live shows at the new Kingswood Theatre *(☎905-832-8131).* The restaurant facilities may not be to everyone's liking so pack a lunch.

The **McMichael Collection ★★★** *($7; mid-Oct to May, Tue to Sun 10am to 4pm, May to mid-Oct, everyday 10am to 5pm; take Hwy 400, then Major Mackenzie Dr. to Islington Ave., ☎893-1121)* houses one of the most magnificent collections of Canadian and native art in Canada and draws many visitors to the peaceful hamlet of Kleinberg on the outskirts of Greater Toronto. A magnificent stone and log house built in the 1950s for the McMichaels is home to the collection. Art-lovers from the start, their initial collection of paintings by grand Canadian masters are at the heart of the museum's present collection. Large and bright galleries present an impressive retrospective of the works of Tom Thomson as well as of the Group of Seven, those artists who strove to reproduce and interpret, Ontario's wilderness through their own perspective. Inuit and native art is also well represented, notably the work of Ojibwa painter Norval Morrisseau, who created his own "pictographic" style.

 ## OUTDOORS

High Park *(for information ☎392-1111),* located in the western part of the city and bound by Bloor Street to the north, The Queensway to the south, Parkside Drive to the east and Ellis Avenue to the west, is Toronto's Central Park. It is accessible by both subway (Keele or High Park stations) and streetcar (College or Queen). The city's largest park, High Park features tennis courts, playgrounds, bike paths and nature trails; skating and fishing on Grenadier Pond; rare flora; wildlife indigenous to the area plus animal paddocks where buffaloes, llamas and sheep are kept; a beach on Lake Ontario; a swimming pool and finally historic Colborne Lodge and the Howard Tomb and Monument. "Shakespeare Under the Stars" is one of the park's most popular summer attractions (for park information ☎392-1111).

Scarborough Heights Park and **Cathedral Bluffs Park** command breathtaking views of Lake Ontario from atop the scenic bluffs, while **Bluffer's Park** offers scenic and spacious beaches and picnic areas.

Toronto Islands Park *(open year-round; Metro Parks general information ☎392-8186; ferry return fares $4; schedule: May to Sep, first departure 8am then every 30 min or 15 min during peak hours, last ferry to the city from Hanlan's Point is at 9:30pm, from Centre Island 11:45pm, from Ward's Island 11:30pm; call for departure times for rest of the year ☎392-8193; to reserve picnic sites for large groups ☎392-8188)* lies on a group of 17 islands collectively known as the Toronto Islands, a short, 8-minute ferry ride from Toronto Harbour. Three ferries, each departing from the Mainland Ferry Terminal at the foot of Bay Street, service the three biggest islands, Hanlan's Point, Centre Island and Ward's Island; bridges connect the other islands that are occupied by private homes, yacht clubs and an airport. Bicycles are permitted on all of the ferries, except, on occasion, the Centre Island ferry, which gets very crowded on weekends. Bikes can be rented at Hanlan's Point and at the pier, while canoes, rowboats and pedal-boats can be rented on Long Pond east of Manitou Bridge.

 Biking

The Martin Goodman Trail, a 22-km jogging and cycling path, follows the shore of Lake Ontario from the mouth of the Humber River west of the city centre, past Ontario Place and Queen's Quay to the Balmy Beach Club in The Beaches. Call ☎367-2000 for a map of the trail.

Toronto Island Bicycle Rental: Centre Island ☎203-0009, $5 an hour, tandem $10.

In-line Skate rentals: Rent 'n' Roll *(Queen's Quay Terminal, ☎203-8438)* rents skates and all necessary equipment (pads) for $10/hour. You will need at least 3 hours to tour the islands. They also offer lessons.

 Ice-Skating

There are several enchanting places to go ice-skating in the city. These include the rink in front of New City Hall, Grenadier Pond in High Park and York Quay at Harbourfront. For information on city rinks call ☎392-1111.

 Golf

There are five municipal golf courses (two executive and three regulation), which operate on a first-come first-served basis. For general information on public courses call ☎367-8186.

For something more challenging, take a little jaunt out to Oakville, to the Glen Abbey Golf Club *(green fees and cart $145, discount rates in off-season and on weekends after 2pm $85; ☎905-844-1800)*. This spectacular course was the first to be designed by Jack Nicklaus. The rates are high, but it's a real thrill to play where the pros tee off. This is the home of the Canadian Open Championship.

 ACCOMMODATIONS

The Waterfront

The SkyDome Hotel *($179-$239; ≡, ℜ, ≈, ☉, pb, △, tv, ⅃, ✕; 1 Blue Jays Way, M5V 1J4, ☎341-7100 or 1-800-441-1414, ≈341-5090 or 341-5091)* has 346 rooms with panoramic views and 70 of these overlook the inside of the stadium. The latter cost more, but what a view! You have a choice of restaurants and a bar that also offers a view of the playing field. The rooms, decorated in modern style, are adequate but nothing special. Valet and room service are available day and night.

If you like the sea, you will feel at home at the Radisson Plaza Hotel Admiral *($205; ≡, ◉, ≈, pb, ⅃; 249 Queen's Quay W., M5J 2N5, ☎364-5444 or 1-800-333-3333, ≈364-2975)*. The decor of this charming hotel displays a seafaring motif, with the rooms giving guests the impression they are aboard a cruise ship. The view of the bay from the fifth-floor pool is quite magnificent. Regular shuttle service is offered between the hotel and the downtown area.

The Westin Harbour Castle *($290; ≡, ≈, ℜ, ☉, pb, △, tv, ⅃, ✕; 1 Harbour Sq., M5J 1A6, ☎869-1600 or 1-800-228-3000, ≈869-0573)* used to be part of the Hilton hotel chain. In 1987, Westin and Hilton decided to swap their respective Toronto hotels. Located on the shore of Lake Ontario, in a calm and peaceful spot, the Westin Harbour Castle is just a few steps

ONTARIO

from Harbourfront Centre and the ferry to the Toronto Islands. To help guests reach the downtown area, the hotel offers a free shuttle service; it also lies along a streetcar line.

The Theatre and Financial Districts

For a pleasant hotel located in the heart of downtown, just a few steps from the Royal York Hotel and a few minutes' walk from the waterfront, head to the **Strathcona Hotel** (*$85; ≡; 60 York St., M5J 1S8, ☎363-3321, ⊶363-4679*).

Front Street and St. Lawrence

The French **Novotel** (*$185; ≡, ⊛, ℜ, ⊘, pb, △, tv; 45 The Esplanade, M5E 1W2, ☎367-8900 or 1-800-668-6835, ⊶360-8285*) enjoys an ideal Toronto location, just minutes from the Harbourfront, the St. Lawrence and Hummingbird centres, and Union Station. Comfort is assured at this hotel, except perhaps for the rooms facing The Esplanade, whose peace and quiet may be disturbed by sounds from the outdoor bars.

Built in 1903, the **Royal Meridien King Edward Hotel** (*$220; ≡, ℜ, ⊘, pb, tv, ₺, ✻; 37 King St. E., M5C 1E9, ☎863-9700 or 1-800-225-5843, ⊶367-5515*) is the oldest hotel in Toronto and still one of the most attractive. Rooms at this very elegant spot each have their own character but do not, unfortunately, offer much in terms of views. The magnificent lobby and the two ballrooms make up for this, however. Airport buses stop here regularly.

With its renovated guest rooms, its 34 banquet rooms (each decorated differently), and its 10 restaurants, it is easy to understand why the **Royal York Hotel** (*$159-$299; ≡, ≈, ⊘, pb, △, tv; 100 Front St. W., M5J 1E3, ☎863-6333, 1-800-828-7447 or 800-441-1414*) is one of Toronto's most popular hotels. The impressive, sumptuously decorated lobby is an indication of the elegance of the rooms.

Queen West, Kensington and Chinatown

The **Bond Place Hotel** (*$95; ≡, ℜ, tv; 65 Dundas St. E., M5B 2G8, ☎362-6061, ⊶360-6406*) is undoubtedly the best-located hotel for enjoying the city beat and for mixing with the varied throng at the corner of Dundas and Yonge streets.

The **Beaconsfield** (*$69 sb, $99 pb bkfst incl.; tv; 38 Beaconsfield Ave., M6J 3H9, ☎535-3338*), a superb Victorian house dating from 1882 in a quiet little neighbourhood near Queen Street, is a good place to turn if you are looking for something different from big hotels. Rooms are charming and imaginatively decorated. Perhaps best of all, though, are the delightful musical breakfasts.

If you prefer to have everything under the same roof, the brand-new **Toronto Marriott Eaton Centre** (*$179; ≡, ≈, ℜ, ⊛, △, ⊘, pb, tv, ₺; 525 Bay St., M5G 2L2, ☎597-9200, ⊶598-9211*) will fit the bill. Linked to the famous Eaton Centre, a shoppers' mecca and one of the city's attractions (see p 380), the Marriott offers huge, well-equipped rooms (they even have irons and ironing boards). If you wish to relax, there are two ground-floor lounges, one with pool tables and televisions.

Around Queen's Park

Hostelling International (*$26.50; K, tv, ℜ; 223 Church St., M5B 1Y7, ☎971-4440 or 1-800-668-4487, ⊶368-6499*), open day and night, offers 175 beds in semi-private rooms or dormitories at very affordable prices. Guests will find a television lounge, a laundromat, a kitchen and a restaurant with a pool table and dart board, as well as an outdoor terrace.

Bloor and Yorkville

Just a few steps from the Royal Ontario Museum (see p 382) and from Yorkville Street, the **Inter-Continental Toronto** (*$235; ≡, ≈, ℜ, ⊘, pb, △, tv, ₺; 220 Bloor St. W., M5S 1T8, ☎960-5200, ⊶920-8269*) is sure to seduce you with its vast, tastefully decorated rooms and its exemplary service.

If you are looking for top-of-the-line luxury accommodation, the **Four Seasons Hotel Toronto** (*$280; ≡, ⊛, ≈, ℜ, ⊘, pb, tv, ₺; 21 Avenue Rd., M5R 2G1, ☎964-0411 or 1-800-268-6282, ⊶964-2301*) is one of the most highly rated hotels in North America. This complex is faithful to its reputation, with impeccable service and beautifully decorated rooms. It also has a sumptuous ballroom with

Persian carpets and crystal chandeliers. The hotel restaurant, Truffle, with Uffizi sculptures at the entrance portraying two wild boars, will satisfy your desires with some of the best food in Toronto.

Neighbourhoods

Annex

Global Guest House *($59 sb, $69 pb; no-smoking, ≡; 9 Spadina Rd., M5R 2S9, ☎923-4004, ⬅923-1208, kth@echo-on.net)* is a popular, inexpensive and ecologically sound alternative, ideally located just north of Bloor Street. The nine rooms are all spotless and simply decorated.

Lowther House *($75 sb, $100 pb, bkfst incl.; tv, ≡; 72 Lowther Ave., M5R 1C8, ☎323-1589 or 1-800-265-4158, ⬅962-7005)* is a charming, beautifully restored Victorian mansion in the heart of the Annex and just minutes from many of the city's best sights. A double jacuzzi tub, sun room, fireplace, claw-footed tub and delicious Belgian waffles are just some of the treasures that await visitors at this home away from home. Private and shared bathrooms.

High Park

An alternative to the big, expensive hotels, the **Marigold Hostel** *($22 bkfst incl.; 2011 Dundas St. W., M6R 1W7, ☎536-8824 after 7pm, ⬅533-4402)* is a charming little hotel that is often filled with young travellers and students who prefer to save a bit of cash and will forego a private bathroom.

Near the airport

If you want to be close to the airport, the **Best Western Carlton Place Hotel** *($155; ≡, ⊛, ≈, ℜ, △, tv, pb, ⬥; 33 Carlson Court, Etobicoke M9W 6H5, ☎675-1234 or 1-800-528-1234, ⬅675-3436)* offers decent, comfortable rooms at reasonable prices.

The **Sheraton Gateway Hotel at Terminal Three** *($99-$155; ≡, ⊛, ℜ, ⊘, pb, tv ⬥; AMF, P.O. Box 3000, Mississauga L5P 1C4, ☎905-672-7000 or 1-800-565-0010, ⬅905-672-7100)*, linked directly to Terminal 3 at Toronto's Pearson International Airport, is the best located hotel for in-transit passengers. It has 474 attractively decorated, fully soundproof rooms, with panoramic views of the airport and the city.

 RESTAURANTS

The Waterfront

Wayne Gretzky's *($$; 99 Blue Jays Way, ☎979-PUCK)* is a sports bar par excellence, complete with the great-one's sweaters, trophies and skates. Burgers, all taste-tested by Wayne himself, and a good selection of pastas round out the regular pub fare on the menu.

Imagine having a meal with Toronto at your feet. This is what awaits you atop the CN Tower, at the **360 Revolving** restaurant *($$$$; CN Tower, 301 Front St. W., ☎362-5411)*, which offers good food as well as one of the finest views in town.

The Theatre and Financial Districts

At the **Marché Mövenpick** *($$-$$$; inside BCE Place, ☎366-8986)*, you can choose from a tasty array of dishes each more tempting than the last and each prepared right before your eyes. After finally deciding on your meal, you may face the problem of finding a table, for this spot is very popular (see below).

At **Acqua** *($$$; BCE Place, 10 Front St. W., ☎368-7171)*, as the name suggests, the decor has water as its theme. While observing the fine and rather unusual decor of this fashionable restaurant, you will enjoy succulent dishes drawn from Mediterranean and California culinary traditions.

Mövenpick Restaurant *($$$; 165 York St., ☎366-0558)* serves the same delicious Swiss specialties as the Marché (see above) but with table service and without the hectic cafeteria ambiance.

Fenice *($$$-$$$$; 319 King St. W., ☎585-2377)* invites you to enjoy delicious Italian dishes prepared with fresh ingredients, and to delight in a warm atmosphere cradled by the sounds of classical music.

ONTARIO

Front Street and St. Lawrence

C'est What *($$; 67 Front St. E., ☎867-9499)* A wonderful medley of cuisines is served into the wee hours at this before- and after-theatre stop. The exciting menu features exotic salads and original sandwiches. The ambiance is almost pub-like, with cosy chairs, board games and mood music that runs the gamut from folk to jazz.

You are sure to be satisfied at **Le Papillon** restaurant *($$-$$$; 16 Church St., ☎363-0838)*, for the menu offers a tempting variety of dishes combining the delicacies of French and Québécois cuisines. The *crêpes* are especially good.

Café Victoria *($$$-$$$$; King Edward Hotel, 37 King St. E., ☎863-9700)* is enchanting with its classically decorated dining room and symetrically placed, intimate tables. The meal, a veritable feast ending with a delicious dessert, is sure to be memorable.

The **Senator** *($$$$; closed Monday; 249 Victoria, ☎364-7517)* has survived the recent explosion of the Toronto restaurant scene and still serves one of the best steaks in town. Classy, refined setting.

Queen West, Kensington and Chinatown

Future Bakery *($; 739 Queen St. W., ☎504-8700)* is a lofty café where the air is infused with the wonderful aromas of bread baking and coffee brewing. You can stop in for picnic fixings, stay for a piece of one the sumptuous cakes or pies or settle in for a hearty meal of varenyky, cabbage rolls and borscht. You can even settle in with a good book and a coffee for hours on end!

Swatow *($; 309 Spadina, ☎977-0601)* is a no-fuss eatery with an extensive menu that is guaranteed to satisfy your palate. There is nothing fancy about this place, but you can't beat it for its genuine Cantonese cooking served up fast and good, just like in China.

On Sunday morning, the **Chinatown International** *($-$$; 421 Dundas St. W., ☎593-0291)* bustles with activity as Chinese families come for the traditional dim sum. This

is a special occasion to enjoy a unique and succulent experience.

La Hacienda *($-$$; 640 Queen St. W., ☎703-3377)*, a charming restaurant with a retro decor recalling the 1960s, offers a menu consisting mostly of Mexican dishes, many of which will satisfy vegetarian gourmets.

Queen Street West is one of Toronto's liveliest streets after dark, and the **Bamboo** restaurant *($$; 312 Queen St. W., ☎593-5771)* is one of the most colourful spots around. To reach the dining rooms, you have to squeeze through a narrow passageway linking the "temple" to the street. You can then choose between a two-level outdoor terrace or one of two indoor dining rooms. This one-of-a-kind restaurant, with food spanning Caribbean, Malay, Thai and Indonesian flavours, also offers reggae and salsa shows.

Margaritas Fiesta Room *($$; 14 Baldwin St., ☎977-5525)* provides quite an escape with its infectious Latin music and its tasty dishes including Toronto's best *nachos* and delicious *guacamole*. This piece of Mexico will transport you far from the rush of urban Toronto.

Cavernous and austere decor, exquisite presentation, attitude, mood lighting and an interesting interpretation of southwestern cuisine: that pretty much sums up the dining experience at **Left Bank** *($$-$$$; 567 Queen St. W., ☎504-1626)*.

Peter Pan *($$$; 373 Queen St. W., ☎593-0917)* offers a beautiful 1930s decor, as well as delicious and imaginative dishes. Pastas, pizzas and fish take on an original look here. Service is courteous.

The **Bodega** *($$$; 312 Baldwin St., ☎977-1287)* serves resolutely gastronomic French dishes made with the freshest of ingredients. The wall coverings, the lace and the music that wafts across the dining room help create an authentic French atmosphere.

Around Queen's Park

The relaxed setting at **Kalendar's Koffee House** *($; 546 College, ☎923-4138)* is ideal for an intimate tête-à-tête over coffee and cake, or a light lunch. The menu lists an array of interesting sandwiches and simple dishes.

The friendly **College Street Bar** *($$; 574 College St.,* ☎*533-2417)* boasts a tasty Mediterranean menu and lively atmosphere. This hot spot is frequented by a young crowd, most of whom just stop in to have drinks and soak up the atmosphere.

There is nothing quite like a tender-grilled sirloin steak from **Barberian's** *($$$$; 7 Elm St.,* ☎*597-0225).* Steak dominates the menu here, which may seem a little scanty to anyone hoping for other choices. It is preferable to reserve in advance.

Bloor and Yorkville

In the Yorkville district, among the chic stores, you might be surprised to discover a traditional diner. **Flo's Diner** *($; 10 Bellair St.,* ☎*961-4333),* like most establishments of this type, is a good spot for hamburgers. In the summer, there is a rooftop terrace.

It is really worth taking the trouble to find **Jacques L'Omelette**, also called **Jacques Bistro du Parc** *($$-$$$; 126-A Cumberland Ave.,* ☎*961-1893).* This charming little spot is located upstairs in a fine Yorkville house. The very friendly French owner offers simple but high-quality food. The fresh Atlantic salmon and the spinach salad are among the pleasant surprises on the menu.

The **Bistro 990** *($$$$; 990 Bay St.,* ☎*921-9990)* is quite simply one of the best eating spots in Toronto. Delicious items of *nouvelle cuisine* are offered in a Mediterranean setting, with outstanding preparations of lamb, salmon and duck.

Neighbourhoods

The Annex

At the **Kensington Kitchen** *($$$; 124 Harbord St.,* ☎*961-3404),* you can enjoy Mediterranean dishes while seated comfortably in a pretty New Age dining room. This is a good spot to remember for fine summer days, when you can enjoy the same specialties on the rooftop terrace.

Le Paradis *($$-$$$; 166 Bedford Rd.,* ☎*921-0995)* serves authentic French-bistro cuisine at authentic bistro prices. The decor is

simple and the service reserved, but a devoted following and the delicious cooking make it a must.

The Beaches

Whitlock's *($$; 1961 Queen St. E.* ☎*691-8784)* is a longstanding tradition in the Beach. Located in a lovely old building, the atmosphere is simple, casual and unpretentious. The menu is varied and down-to-earth. It typifies the real "Beach", as compared to the glitz and trendiness of what some like to call the "Beaches".

 ENTERTAINMENT

Bars and Nightclubs

The Big Bop *(651 Queen St. W.,* ☎*504-6699)* is packed every week-end night with a young crowd (the capacity is 800 people!), who let loose to oldies on the first floor and rock 'n' roll, dance and house upstairs. The decor is eclectic to say the least. This is a major meat market for young adults.

A rich and lavish decor sets the tone at **Bemelman's** *(83 Bloor St. W.,* ☎*960-0306).* A trendy crowd of young professionals appreciates the extensive list of martinis (shaken or stirred) and the outdoor terrace, for hot summer nights.

Whiskey Saigon *(250 Richmond St. W.,* ☎*593-4646)* is one of Toronto's consummate dance halls. Retro, rap, reggae and rock all have there place here.

Toronto's most popular student hangout is the **Brunswick House** *(481 Bloor St. W.,* ☎*964-2242).* Large-screen televisions, shuffleboard, billiard tables, lots of beer and a character named Rockin' Irene are the mainstays here in this historical building, the oldest party spot in town.. Jazz and blues create a more mellow atmosphere at **Albert's Hall** upstairs.

Toronto's highest piano lounge, **The Acquarius Lounge** *(55 Bloor St. W., 51st floor,* ☎*967-5225)* sits atop the ManuLife Centre. The drinks and cocktails are pricey, but then

ONTARIO

again the view is spectacular. Proper dress required.

Gay Bars

Woody's *(467 Church St., ☎972-0887)* is a popular meeting place for gay men. Set in the heart of the gay village, the atmosphere is casual and friendly.

Boots *(592 Sherbourne, ☎921-0665)* is a popular and intense dance bar frequented by a gay and straight clientele. Theme nights include fetish nights and other intriguing possiblities.

Theatres

The Toronto Symphony Orchestra and Toronto Mendelssohn Choir both perform in the exceptional acoustic space of **Roy Thompson Hall** *(60 Simcoe St., ☎593-4828)*.

For **theatre**, **ballet** and **opera** look into the offerings at the following theatres: **Royal Alexandra** *(360 King St. W., ☎872-3333)*, **Princess of Wales Theatre** *(300 King St. W., ☎872-1212)*, **Pantages Theatre** *(263 Yonge St., ☎872-3333)*, **Théâtre Français de Toronto** *(231 Queen's Quay W., ☎534-6604)*, **Young People's Theatre** *(165 Front St. E., ☎864-9732)*, **Massey Hall** *(178 Victoria St., ☎593-4828)*, **O'Keefe Centre** *(1 Front St. E., ☎872-2262)*, and the **Canadian Opera Company** *(239 Front St., ☎363-8231 or 393-7469)*

For popular music concerts: **SkyDome** *(1 Blue Jay Way, ☎963-3513)* and **Maple Leaf Gardens** *(60 Carlton St., ☎977-1641)*.

Tickets for these and other shows are available through:

Ticketmaster: ☎870-8000

T.O. Tix: at the corner of Yonge and Dundas streets, ☎596-8211. Reduced-price tickets for same-day musical and theatrical events.

Spectator Sports

The National Hockey League's Toronto Maple Leafs play at Maple Leaf Gardens from November to April. The play-offs follow the regular season and last right into June.

The Toronto Blue Jays of the American Baseball League, the Toronto Argonauts of Canadian Football League (CFL) and the Toronto Raptors of the National Basketball Association (NBA) all play their matches at the SkyDome.

The Molson Indy car races *(☎260-9800)* take place in mid-July.

Festivals and Cultural Events

Benson & Hedges International Fireworks Festival: Mid-June through July, ☎442-3667

Du Maurier Downtown Jazz: end of June, ☎363-8717 or 363-5200

The **Caribana** Caribbean festival *(☎925-5435)* from late July to beginning of August, features the largest parade in Canada – it lasts 12 hours!

Canadian National Exhibition: End of August beginning of September, ☎393-6000

Toronto's **International Film Festival** *(☎967-7371, for tickets: Film Festival Box Office, ☎968-FILM)* at the beginning of September is becoming a truly star-studded event.

 # SHOPPING

Downtown Toronto is a shoppers-paradise, from big designers to discount bonanzas, there is certainly a store that has what you are looking for.

Shopping Areas and Malls

Kensington Market on Kensington St., north of Dundas St. W., vintage clothing and international foods.

Queen's Quay Terminal (207 Queen's Quay) gift shops in Harbourfront.

Eaton Centre *(Yonge, between Queen and Dundas St.)* Huge shopping complex.

Bloor Street and Yorkville Avenue are both lined with exclusive shops and boutiques including **Holt Renfrew** *(50 Bloor St. W.,* ☎*922-2333)* and **Hazelton Lanes** *(Hazelton, near Yorkville).*

Garish yet delightful in all its neon splendour, **Honest Ed's** *(581 Bloor St. W., at the corner of Bathurst St.,* ☎*537-1547)* discount store opened for business more than 40 years ago, and is a Toronto institution. It is the flagship enterprise of philanthropist Ed Mirvish, the man behind the historic Royal Alexandra and The Princess of Wales Theatres.

Fur

Birger Christensen at Holt Renfrew
Holt Renfrew Centre, 50 Bloor St. W., ☎960-2863
Dufferin Street and Hwy. 401, Yorkdale Shopping Centre, ☎789-5377

General Bookstores

World's Biggest Bookstore
20 Edward St., ☎977-7009

Litchman's News & Books
at the corner of Yonge St. and Richmond St.. ☎368-7390

Specialized Bookstores

Open Air Books and Maps (travel)
25 Toronto St., ☎363-0719

Maison de Presse Internationale (newspapers)
124-126 Yorkville Ave., ☎928-0418

Ulysses Travel Bookshop (travel)
101 Yorkville Ave., ☎323-3609

Antiques

Harbourfront Antique Market
390 Queen Quay W., ☎260-2626

Antiques — Michel Taschereau
176 Cumberland St., ☎923-3020

Native Art

The Arctic Bear
125 Yorkville, Queen's Quay Terminal, ☎967-7885.

The Guild Shop
118 Cumberland St., ☎921-1721.

ONTARIO

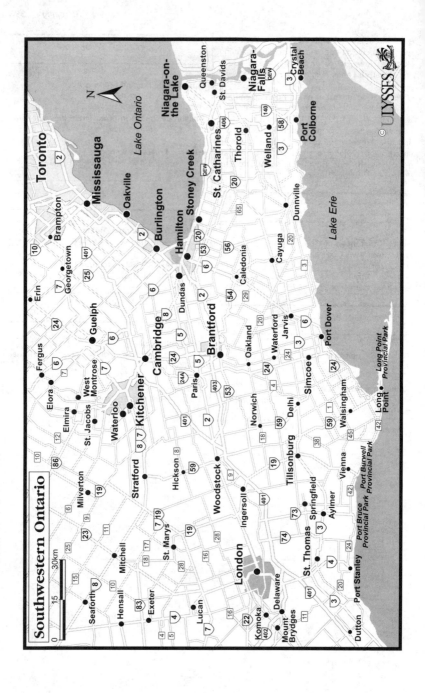

Southwestern Ontario

SOUTHWESTERN ONTARIO

Southwestern Ontario was once inhabited only by Huron, Erie, Petun and Neutral Indians, and was highly coveted by the Iroquois, whose territory lay south of Lake Erie. Once Europeans began arriving here, the situation erupted into a bloody war, which was at its worst between 1645 and 1655, when the Iroquois, armed with guns, attacked the other Amerindian nations. By the end of the conflict, all but a handful of the tens of thousands of Hurons, Eries, Petuns and Neutrals living in the region had been wiped out, and the victorious Iroquois took over the territory. They did not stay for long, however; in the following years, other native tribes, most importantly the Mississaugas, succeeded in recapturing the land and in driving the Iroquois back to their original territory. Although their numbers had been diminished by armed conflicts and illnesses (influenza, smallpox, etc.) brought over by the Europeans, the natives remained in control of southwestern Ontario until the end of the 18th century, when the English began colonizing the region. Although relatively few natives live in the area today, numerous tourist sites have been established in an effort to familiarize visitors with the culture of those who once inhabited this part of the province.

Most of the first colonists were farmers, who worked the fertile soil, gradually turning the region into the Ontario's granary. Due to the unique microclimate here on the shores of Lake Erie, they were able to plant vineyards and orchards as well. Little by little, the population grew, and lovely towns like London, Kitchener-Waterloo, Windsor and Hamilton developed. Finally, southwestern Ontario is also home to one of the natural wonders of the world, Niagara Falls.

 FINDING YOUR WAY AROUND

By Car

Mennonite Country

From Toronto: Take Highway 401 to Kitchener-Waterloo.

Hamilton and Surroundings

From Toronto: Take the Queen Elizabeth Way (QEW).

The Wine Route

From Toronto: Take the Queen Elizabeth Way (QEW), which leads to Hamilton and St. Catharines.

London and Surroundings

From Toronto: Head west on Highway 2, which leads to London via Brantford.

The Far Southwest

From Toronto: Take the 401 West, towards Chatham, then pick up the 40, which leads to the 3, the starting point of the tour.

Train Stations

Mennonite Country

Kitchener-Waterloo: 126 Weber St.
Stratford: 101 Shakespeare St.

Hamilton and Surroundings

Hamilton: 380 James St. N., ☎(800) 361-1235.

London and Surroundings

Brantford: 5 Wadworth St.
London: 197 York, at the corner of the street.

The Far Southwest

Windsor: 298 Walker Rd., ☎(519) 256-5511.
Sarnia: 125 Green St.

Bus Stations

Mennonite Country

Kitchener-Waterloo: 15 Charles St., ☎(519) 741-2600.
Stratford: 101 Shakespeare, ☎(519) 271-7870.

Hamilton and Surroundings

Hamilton: 36 Hunter St., ☎(800) 387-7045.

The Wine Route

St. Catharines: 7 Carlisle St.

In summer, there is daily bus service between Niagara-on-the-Lake and both St. Catharines and Niagara Falls. If you don't have a car, the only way to get to Niagara-on-the-Lake during the rest of the year is by taxi.

Niagara Falls: 4555 Erie Ave., ☎(905) 357-2133.

London and Surroundings

Brantford: 64 Darling St., ☎(519) 756-5011.
London: 101 York, ☎(519) 434-3245.

The Far Southwest

Windsor: 44 University St. E., ☎(519) 254-7575.
Sarnia: 461 Campbell St., ☎(519) 344-2211.

 PRACTICAL INFORMATION

Area Codes: 519 for the regions covered in Tour A: Mennonite Country, Tour D: London and Surroundings and Tour E: The Far Southwest and most of Tour F: The Shores of Lake Huron.

The area code is **905** for the regions covered in Tour B: Hamilton and Surroundings and Tour C: the Wine Route.

Tourist Information Offices

Niagara and Mid-Western Travel Association: 160 Greenwich Street, Brantford, ON, N3S 2X6, ☎(519) 756-3230, ☎(800) 267-3399, ≈(519) 756-3231,

Southwestern Ontario Travel Association: 4023 Meadowbrook Drive, Suite 112, London, ON, N6L 1E7, ☎(519) 652-1391, ☎(800) 661-6804, ≈(519) 652-0533.

EXPLORING

Mennonite Country

This tour will lead you on the trail of the Mennonites, the first communities to colonize southwestern Ontario. These farmers, who came here from the United States to work the region's fertile land, were followed by other settlers, mostly of English, Scottish and German descent, who founded lovely towns. Despite all the years that have gone by, people here have managed to preserve some of their ancestors' traditions.

Kitchener-Waterloo ★★

In the wake of the American Revolution, those individuals who had declined to fight alongside the American troops were persecuted. The Mennonites, who had refused to take up arms for religious reasons, thus decided to emigrate to Ontario, where they could purchase fertile land at low prices. This first wave of immigrants arrived at the very end of the 18th century. Other colonists, mainly of German origin, also settled in the region, founding towns like Kitchener. Even today, a good part of the population of Kitchener-Waterloo is of German descent. In fact, every year the city hosts the largest *Oktoberfest* outside Germany.

Originally, Kitchener and Waterloo were simply neighbouring towns, but as they both grew, they merged into one large urban area, so authorities decided to join them officially. Kitchener-Waterloo thus has two downtown areas, one on King Street, near Erb Street East (Waterloo) and the other along King Street West, around Queen Street (Kitchener); although there are places where the two towns still seem like separate entities rather than a united whole. Kitchener-Waterloo is a pleasant city with several noteworthy tourist attractions.

Right near the Seagram Museum, is the **Canadian Clay and Glass Gallery** ★ *(Erb Street)*, which houses several collections of ceramic and glass objects, including one donated by the Indusmin silica company. Also on display are a number of works by Canadian artists like Denise Bélanger-Taylor, Irene Frolic, Joe Fafard and Sadashi Inuzuka. The museum has occupied the present building, designed by

Vancouver architects John and Patricia Patkau, since 1993.

City Hall stands at the corner of King and Queen, along with a shopping arcade known as Market Square, where the local **Farmer's Market** is held every Saturday morning (see p 418).

A visit to the **Joseph Schneider Haus** *($1.75; May to Sep, Mon to Sat 10am to 5pm, Sun 1pm to 5pm; closed Mon during the rest of the year; 466 Queen St. S., ☎742-7752)*, the former home of a German Mennonite, will give you an idea how simply 19th-century Mennonites lived. Guides on the premises explain the rustic, austere lifestyle of members of this community.

Next, you will come to the **Kitchener-Waterloo Art Gallery** *(donations welcome; Tue to Sat 10am to 5pm, Sun 1pm to 5pm; 101 Queen St. N., Kitchener ☎579-5860)*, whose collection, distributed amongst seven rooms, is quite modest on the whole. Most of the works exhibited are paintings by contemporary artists. The gallery regularly hosts temporary exhibitions as well.

The **Woodside National Historic Site** ★ *($2; May to Dec, every day 10am to 5pm; 528 Wellington St. N., ☎742-5273)*. William Lyon Mackenzie King, Prime Minister of Canada from 1921 to 1930 and from 1935 to 1948, spent part of his childhood here, between the ages of five and eleven. After touring the house, which has been restored and refurnished to look just as it did when Mackenzie lived here, you can take a stroll around the magnificent wooded grounds.

St. Jacobs ★

The charm of St. Jacobs, or Jacobstettel, as it used to be called, is in its main street, which is lined with crafts shops whose windows alone are fascinating enough to capture your attention for hours. This Mennonite village, which has managed to preserve its old-time appearance, is overrun year-round by visitors lured here by the pretty shops and the peaceful atmosphere pervading the streets.

Those interested in learning more about the Mennonites can go to the **Meeting Place** *($2; May to Oct, Mon to Fri 11am to 5pm, Sat 10am to 5pm, Sun 1:30pm to 5pm; Nov to Apr, Sat 11am to 4:30pm, Sun 2pm to*

ONTARIO

4:30pm; 33 King St., ☎*664-3518),* which presents a half-hour film on the subject.

Twice a week, local farmers gather at the **St. Jacobs Farmer's Market** to sell farm produce and handicrafts. Not only is this a picturesque scene, but it's also the perfect opportunity to purchase some delicious local foodstuffs.

Elora ★

Elora was founded in 1832 on the banks of the Grand River, on a site suitable for a mill. This magnificent stone structure has since been converted into a charming inn, which serves as a focal point for the local tourist industry. It is surrounded by shops in little stone houses, where you can purchase all sorts of knick-knacks.

Guelph ★

Scottish novelist John Galt, known for his works on Lord Byron, made several trips to Upper Canada for the Canada Company. He even lived here from 1826 to 1829, at which time he founded the town of Guelph (1827) on the shores of the Speed River. To create a pleasant environment, he incorporated large parks and wide arteries into the town's design, something highly unusual in those days. Today, this dynamic city is known for its university, the **University of Guelph**, whose magnificent buildings are located south of the Speed River.

The **MacDonald Stewart Arts Centre ★** *(358 Gordon St.,* ☎*836-1482),* located on the university campus, has a lovely collection of Canadian and Inuit art, which is displayed in spacious, well laid-out rooms and complemented by clear written commentaries.

On the winding streets of downtown Guelph, you'll find several interesting commercial and public edifices, including **Guelph City Hall ★** *(59 Carden St.),* which looks out onto a small public square. This elegant neo-Renaissance style building, designed by architect William Thomas, was erected in 1857.

An imposing church, **Our Lady of the Immaculate Conception ★★**, towers over City Hall. In the 19th century, most parishioners of Ontario's Catholic churches were Irish who had fled the potato famine and French Canadians who had come here from Quebec in search of a brighter future. This church is the masterpiece of Irish architect Joseph Connolly, and owes its existence to an enterprising French-Canadian priest by the name of Father Hamel. Since the families of the local communities were larger than average, the place had to be big. Its construction lasted from 1876 to 1926. Connolly opted for the Neo-Gothic style of the cathedral of Cologne in Germany. The only part of the church that truly reflects a Germanic influence, however, is the upper apse at the back of the building, which is surrounded by numerous apsidioles.

Stratford ★★

A man named Tom Patterson, a shopkeeper with a passion for Shakespeare, is the one who came up with the idea of starting a Shakespeare festival (see p 417) here in 1951. Then a modest hamlet, Stratford has since become an enchanting little town, where crowds of visitors flock each year to see the plays and enjoy the charming setting. Its downtown area is very attractive, and splendid **Queen's Park ★★** lies stretched along the banks of the Avon, where ducks, swans and barnacle geese paddle about. The park is also home to the **Festival Theatre**, where some of the plays are presented.

St. Marys ★

St. Marys, nicknamed Stonetown, is home to a number of magnificent old buildings, which bear witness to its prosperous past. A few of these, including the **town hall**, built in 1891 of stone from the local quarries, are located along Church Street, in the centre of town. A little farther along, the **Opera House** is sure to catch your eye. Erected in 1879 by James Elliott, it originally had shops on the ground floor, with a theatre above, and was later converted into a mill. Since being renovated, it now houses shops and private apartments.

Hamilton and Surroundings

There are two large cities to the west of Lake Ontario, Toronto and Hamilton. The stretch of road leading through Toronto's suburbs and Hamilton's industrial outskirts is not very appealing, but you can't avoid it if you want to go to Niagara Falls. There are, however, a few noteworthy attractions along the way, including the Royal Botanical Gardens in Hamilton.

Burlington

The westernmost shore of Lake Ontario is occupied by Burlington to the north, and Hamilton to the south. Set side by side, these two cities linked by Beach Boulevard, could almost be considered a single urban area. Burlington, the less populous of the two, is a peaceful residential town with little to offer in terms of tourist attractions, except perhaps for the little **Joseph Brant Museum** *($2.75; Tue to Sat 10am to 4pm, Sun 1pm to 4pm; 1240 North Shore E. Blvd., ☎634-3556)*, the last home of the Mohawk captain for which it is named.

Hamilton ★

Up until the arrival of the first colonists, who did not begin settling this area until the end of the 18th century, the site now occupied by Hamilton was the focal point of an Amerindian conflict. The Iroquois had virtually wiped out the Neutrals who had first inhabited the area. In turn, however, the Iroquois were driven out by white colonists. In 1815, George Hamilton drew up the plans for the city. Hamilton flourished in the 20th century, thanks to the steel, automobile and home-appliance industries, among others. These industries left their mark on the city, whose surrounding landscape is vast, stark and dreary.

Hamilton is nonetheless pleasantly located on Lake Ontario, whose shores are lined with lovely parks, including **Bayfront Park** and **Dundurn Park** where you can enjoy a stroll or a bike ride, relax on a bench or at a picnic table, and watch the lively activity at the marina. Along with the residential neighbourhood on the hillside with its superb Victorian homes, this is definitely the prettiest part of town. Downtown Hamilton and its surroundings, along King Street, are not particularly attractive places to explore on foot, except for **Hess Village ★**, a cluster of elegant houses, shops and restaurants.

There are, however, a few interesting places to visit in the centre of town, including the **Art Gallery of Hamilton ★** *(donations welcome; 9:30am to 6pm, greenhouses every day 9am to 5pm; 123 King St. E., ☎527-6610)*. Open since 1914, it houses paintings, prints and other works of art. Its collection of contemporary art is particularly rich, and makes for some fascinating viewing. Unfortunately, however, the written commentary accompanying the pieces can be a bit vague.

The classically inspired, Georgian-style **Whitehern** *(41 Jackson St. E., ☎546-2018)* was erected in the late 1840s. In 1852, one Dr. McQueston purchased it, and the splendid house remained in his family's possession until 1968. Now open to the public, it has been restored to its original state, complete with period furnishings, and thus reflects the tastes of a prosperous 19th-century family.

Founded in Toronto in the mid-19th century, **McMaster University** moved to Hamilton in 1928. The following year, construction was begun on **University Hall ★**, a lovely building similar to those found on the campuses of Oxford and Cambridge in England. Its façade is adorned with numerous gargoyles and masks symbolizing the various disciplines taught at the university.

Hamilton's most interesting attractions are hidden away outside the downtown area.

Dundurn Castle ★★ *($6, Jun to Sep, Tue to Sun 10am to 5pm; noon to 4pm during the rest of the year; York Blvd. ☎546-2872)*, generally viewed as the jewel of Hamilton, truly deserves to be called a castle, with its impressive dimensions and its architecture, a skillful blend of English Palladianism and the Italian Renaissance style characteristic of Tuscan villas. It was built in 1835 for Sir Allan MacNab, Prime Minister of the United Provinces of Canada from 1854 to 1856. Restored, furnished and decorated as it was back in 1855, this castle, with its 35 opulent rooms, reveals a great deal about upper-class life in the 19th century. The former servants' quarters in the basement are perhaps the most fascinating rooms of all, since they offer an idea of how difficult life was for those without which the castle wouldn't have functioned.

Another, smaller building on the castle grounds houses the **Hamilton Military Museum** *($2; Jun to Sep every day 11am to 5pm, closed Sun during the rest of the year; ☎546-4974)*. Here, you will find a collection of the various uniforms worn by Canadian soldiers over the years.

You can enjoy a unique outing just a step away from downtown Hamilton, at the **Royal**

ONTARIO

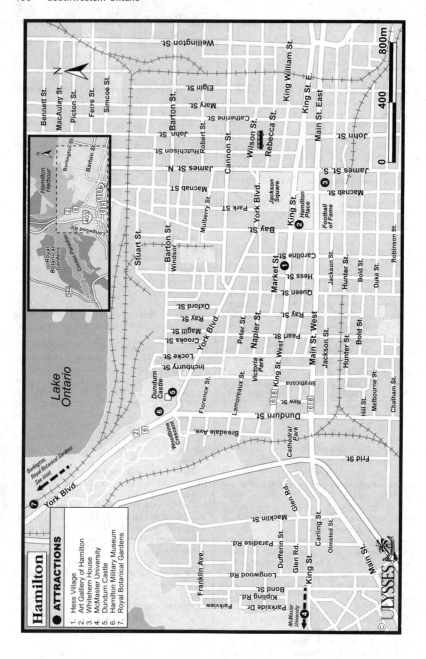

Hamilton

● **ATTRACTIONS**

1. Hess Village
2. Art Gallery of Hamilton
3. Whitehern House
4. McMaster University
5. Dundurn Castle
6. Hamilton Military Museum
7. Royal Botanical Gardens

Botanical Gardens ★★ *($7; Plains Rd., at the intersection of Hwy 6 and Hwy 403; ☎527-1158)*, where you can stroll about amidst luxuriant flowers and explore wonderfully preserved natural habitats. A large section of the park, which covers some 1,000 hectares in all, is known as "Cootes Paradise", a stretch of marshes and wooded ravines crisscrossed by footpaths. In addition to this untouched area, you will find a variety of gardens, including a rose garden, the largest lilac garden in the world and a rock garden, where thousands of flowers bloom in the spring. The Royal Botanical Gardens are enchanting year round; in the winter, when the outdoor gardens are bare, you can visit the greenhouses, where various flower shows are presented.

The Wine Route

This tour covers the region to the west of the Niagara River, along the U.S. border. Control over this area was once crucial as far as shipping on Lakes Ontario and Superior was concerned, and the two forts that were built to protect it still stand on either side of the river. Nowadays, however, the region is best known for its wineries and orchards, and for being home to the extraordinary Niagara Falls, which have continued to amaze people of all ages and inspire lovers and daredevils for decades.

St. Catharines

St. Catharines flourished with the construction of the Welland Canal. There have been four of these canals in all, the first of which was dug in 1829 and the last, still in use, in 1932. The Welland Canal, which links Lakes Ontario and Lake Erie, was designed to surmount a natural obstacle, the 99.5-metre Niagara Escarpment, which would otherwise be impassable. Forty-two kilometres long and equipped with eight locks, the canal enables ships to travel from St. Catharines to Port Colborne. There are viewing areas all along it, the most interesting being the **Lock 3 Viewing Complex** ★ *(free admission; the canal is closed to ships from Dec to Mar; take the Glendale Avenue exit from the QEW and follow the signs, ☎684-2361)* in St. Catharines, where visitors can watch ships go through the lock from a large observation deck. At the neighbouring **St. Catharines Museum** *($3; summer, every day 9am to 9pm; rest of the year, Mon to Fri 9am to 5pm, Sat and Sun 11am to 5pm; ☎984-8880)*, you can learn

about the history of the canal and see a short documentary that explains how the lock works.

Niagara-on-the-Lake ★★

The history of Niagara-on-the-Lake dates back to the late 18th century, when the town, then known as Newark, was the capital of Upper Canada from 1791 to 1796. Nothing remains of that time, however, for the town was burned during the War of 1812, which pitted the British colonies against the United States. After the American invasion, the town was rebuilt, and graced with elegant English-style homes, which have been beautifully preserved and still give this community at the mouth of the Niagara River a great deal of charm. Some of these houses have been converted into elegant inns, which welcome visitors to the celebrated Shaw Festival (see p 418), or those who are simply lured here by the town's English atmosphere.

After the American Revolution, the British abandoned Fort Niagara, which stands on the east side of the Niagara River. To protect their remaining colonies, however, they decided to build another fort. Between 1797 and 1799, Fort George was erected on the west side of the river. Within a few years, the two countries were fighting again. In 1812, war broke out, and the Niagara-on-the-Lake region, which shared a border with the United States, was in the eye of the storm. Fort George was captured, then destroyed in 1813, only to be reconstructed in 1815.

At the **Fort George National Historic Park** ★ *($3.50; Jul to Sep, every day 10am to 5pm; mid-May through Jun and Sep and Oct, every day 9:30am to 4:30pm; Nov to Mar, Mon to Fri 9am to 4pm; Apr to mid-May, every day 9:30am to 4:30pm; Niagara Parkway S., ☎468-4257)*, you can tour the officer's quarters, the guard rooms, the barracks and other parts of the restored fort.

There are a number of vineyards in the Niagara-on-the-Lake region, set amidst large, striped fields all along the side of the highway. Some of these offers tours.

Queenston

A pretty hamlet on the banks of the Niagara River, Queenston consists of a few little houses

ONTARIO

and verdant gardens. It is best known as the former home of Laura Secord.

The **Laura Secord Homestead** *($1; late May to early Sep every day 10am to 5:30pm; Queenston Heights St.,* ☎*684-1227).* Laura Secord, née Ingersoll, was born in Massachusetts in 1775, married James Secord in 1795 and moved to Queenston several years later. She became famous during the War of 1812, when, upon learning that the Americans were about to attack, she ran 25 km to warn the British army, which was thus able to drive back the enemy troops. Today, her name is associated first and foremost with a brand of chocolate, which you can sample at the chocolate shop adjoining the museum.

Farther south, you'll reach the foot of Queenston Heights. If you're feeling energetic, you can climb the steps to the statue of Isaac Brock, a British general who died in this area during the War of 1812, while leading his men to victory. You will also enjoy a splendid **view ★** of the region.

A few kilometres before Niagara Falls, lie the **Niagara Parks Botanical Gardens** *(Niagara Parkway,* ☎*356-8554),* a horticulture school whose beautifully kept gardens are open to the public.

Niagara Falls

The striking spectacle of Niagara Falls has been attracting crowds of visitors for many years, a trend supposedly started when Napoleon's brother came here with his young wife. Right beside the falls, the town of the same name is entirely devoted to tourism, and its downtown area is a series of nondescript motels, uninteresting museums and fast-food restaurants, accented by scores of colourful signs. These places have sprung up in a chaotic manner, and no one seems to have given a second thought to aesthetics. There's no denying that the Niagara Falls are a natural treasure, but the town is best avoided.

The **Niagara Falls ★★★** were created some 10,000 years ago, when the glaciers receded, clearing the Niagara Escarpment and diverting the waters of Lake Erie into Lake Ontario. This natural formation is remarkably beautiful, with two falls, one on either side of the border. The American Falls are 64 metres-high and 305 metres-wide, with a flow of 14 million litres per minute, while Canada's Horseshoe Falls, named for their shape, are 54 metres-high and 675 metres-wide, with a flow of 155 million litres of water per minute. The rocky shelf of the falls is made of soft stone, and it was receding at a rate of 1 metre per year until some of the water was diverted to nearby hydroelectric power stations. The rate of erosion is now about .3 metres per year.

It would be hard not to be impressed by the sight of all that raging water crashing down into the gulf with a thundering roar. This seemingly untameable natural force has been a source of inspiration to many a visitor. In the early 20th century, a few daring souls tried to demonstrate their bravery by going over the falls in a barrel or walking over them on a tightrope, resulting in several deaths. In 1912, these types of stunts were outlawed.

In 1885, **Victoria Park ★** was created, in order to protect the natural setting around the falls from unbridled commercial development. This beautiful green space alongside the river is scored with hiking and cross-country ski trails.

There are **observation decks ★★★** in front of the falls, which can also be viewed from countless other angles:

The *Maid of the Mist* **★** *($9.55; May to Oct, departures every 30 min; 5920 River Rd.,* ☎*358-5781)* takes passengers to the foot of the falls, which make the boat seem very small indeed. Protected by a raincoat, which will prevent you from getting drenched during the outing, you can view the American side of the falls and then the Canadian side, right in the middle of the horseshoe.

If you climb to the top of the **Skylon Tower** *($7.50; every day from 9am on; 5200 Robinson St.,* ☎*356-2651),* you can view the falls **★★** at your feet, a truly unique and memorable sight. You can enjoy a similar view from the **Minolta Tower** *($5.95; every day from 9am on; 6732 Oakes Prom.,* ☎*356-1501).*

The **Spanish Aero Car** *($4.75; Mar to Nov 9am to 9pm; Niagara Parkway,* ☎*356-2241)* offers a bird's-eye view of the falls from a height of 76.2 metres.

For a closer look at the falls, head to the **Table Rock Panoramic Tunnels**, which lead behind the Canadian side.

How about soaring through the air over the falls? You can do just that, thanks to **Niagara**

Helicopter *($80; every day from 9am on, weather permitting; 3731 Victoria Ave., ☎357-5672).*

An elevator transports visitors all the way down to the rapids *(Great Gorge Adventure $4.50; May to Oct from 9am on; 4330 River Rd., ☎356-1221).*

Niagara has countless museums, some of little interest. A number of them are located in the downtown area known as Clifton Hill.

If you have a little time to spare, visit the **Niagara Falls Museum** *($6,75; May to Sep every day 9am to 11pm, Oct to Apr 10am to 5pm; 5651 River Rd., ☎356-2151)*, whose collection ranges from Egyptian mummies to souvenirs of daredevils who have tried to conquer the falls.

The **IMAX Theatre** *($7.50; May to Oct every day; 6170 Buchanan Ave., ☎374-4629)* shows a giant-screen film on the falls.

If you'd like to forget about the falls for a little while and watch some performing sea-lions, dolphins and whales instead, head to **Marineland** *(prices vary, $20.95 during summer; Apr to Oct 10am to 5pm, Jul and Aug 9am to 6pm; 7657 Portage Rd., ☎356-9565)*. The little zoo and carousels are sure to be a hit with the kids.

London and Surroundings ★

A major centre of Iroquois culture in Ontario, the London area boasts fascinating tourist attractions that enable visitors to learn about Native history, customs and traditions. Over 150 years ago, the Iroquois began sharing this territory with English colonists, who were lured here by the fertile land. Once a modest hamlet, London now has a rich architectural heritage that makes it one of the loveliest towns in the region.

Brantford

This rather gloomy-looking town was named after Joseph Brant, whose native name was Thayendanegea. Its downtown area appears to have been abandoned by the local shopkeepers. Anyway, people come here to learn more about Iroquois culture, not for the buildings.

In the 17th century, the Iroquois confederation known as the Five Nations managed to wipe out the native tribes living in southwestern Ontario and take over their land. In the late 1800s, however, the Mississaugas drove the Iroquois back to their original territory south of the Great Lakes.

During the American Revolution, the Six Nations (the Tuscaroras had since joined the other five), based in the northeastern United States, declared themselves neutral, with the exception of a few warriors, like Joseph Brant, who fought alongside the British. Nevertheless, in the wake of the English defeat, all of the Iroquois had to leave the United States. As a gesture of thanks for the Iroquois' assistance during the war, Great Britain granted them 202,350 hectares of land along the Grand River. Two thousand natives thus returned to the region, and 450 of them settled on the site now occupied by Brantford. In 1841, British colonists purchased back part of the land and took up residence here.

At the edge of town, you will see a small white church known as the **Royal Chapel of the Mohawks ★**, which is the oldest Protestant church in Ontario. It was erected by King George III to thank the Iroquois for their assistance during the American Revolution.

The **Woodland Cultural Centre ★** *($3; Mon to Fri 8:30am to 4pm, Sat and Sun 10am to 5pm; 184 Mohawk St., ☎759-2650, ext. 241)* traces the history of the Six Nations. Articles on display include tools, clothing, *wanpum* (traditional belts) and handicrafts. A short visit here is a pleasant way to learn about Iroquois customs and traditions.

Alexander Graham Bell was born in Edinburgh, Scotland in 1847 and moved to Brantford with his parents in 1870. The **Bell Homestead** *($2; Tue to Sun 10am to 6pm; 94 Tutela Heights, ☎756-6220)*, where he lived from 1870 to 1881, is open to the public. It is decorated the same way it was in those years, and houses a number of Bell's inventions.

To learn more about the colonization of this region, head to the **Brant County Museum** *($2; Tue to Fri 9am to 5pm, Sat 1pm to 4pm, May to Aug Sun as well 1pm to 4pm; 57 Charlotte St., ☎752-2483)*, which displays various tools and other articles that belonged to the early settlers. The museum is particularly informative in regards to Iroquois captain Joseph Brant (1742-1807).

ONTARIO

London ★★

The industrious Colonel John Graves Simcoe, the first Lieutenant-Governor of Upper Canada, played an important role in the development of the young British colony. It was he who decided to divide the present-day London region into townships. His plan also included the founding of London itself (1793), which was supposed to become the capital of Upper Canada, but never did. He also lured farmers here from the United States by selling them fertile land at low prices. These so-called "Eleventh Hour Loyalists", who arrived after 1791, included a number of Quakers and Mennonites (especially in the Kitchener-Waterloo area).

Unlike most towns that go through a period of slow, steady growth before any prestigious public buildings are erected, London sprang immediately to life with the construction of an impressive government edifice known as the **Middlesex County Building** *(399 Ridout St. N.)* on a previously undeveloped piece of land that had been scouted out in the late 18th century as a potential site for a large town. This picturesque building was begun in 1828, and the town grew up around it over the following years. London is home to a number of other magnificent 19th-century buildings, the most beautiful of which are included in the following walking tour.

The tour starts at **Victoria Park**, a large and beautiful stretch of greenery in the heart of town. After the Rebellion of 1837, the British troops who had been sent to London set up their quarters here. When they left in 1868, the town took over the land and turned it into a magnificent park.

At the corner of Richmond and Fullarton, you will see the **Grand Theatre** *(471 Richmond St.)*, erected in 1901 on the site of the Masonic Temple and the Grand Opera House, which burned down in 1900. Since 1982, the building has undergone major renovations, and visitors can now take in a play here.

On the banks of the Thames River, is the elegant white **Eldon House** ★ *($3; Tue to Sun noon to 5pm; 481 Ridout St. N., ☎672-4580)*, the oldest private residence in London, built for the Harris family in 1834. Now open to the public, it is still decorated with 19th-century furnishings. On Ridout Street, you will find a number of other lovely homes dating back to the town's first few years.

If you keep heading south on Ridout, you'll come to the **London Regional Art and Historical Museums** *(free admission; Tue to Sun noon to 5pm; 421 Ridout St. N., ☎672-4580)*, a large, rather unusual-looking building designed by architect Moriyama. It is shaped like a cross, with big picture windows that let in a lot of natural light. The art collection consists primarily of works by Canadian painters, while the second-floor rooms are devoted to an exhibit on the history of London.

London, England has the Thames and the Tower; London, Canada, the Thames and the **Middlesex County Courthouse** ★ *(399 Ridout St. N.)*. This former courthouse has a prison whose Neo-Gothic architecture is reminiscent of a medieval castle with crenelated towers.

The Middlesex County Courthouse is a solid brick building covered with stucco made to look like freestone. Like Montreal's Notre-Dame, built around the same time, it is an excellent example of the first attempts at architectural historicism in Canada. In the case of the courthouse, medieval accents have been added to a fundamentally neoclassical building.

The central tower, added in 1878, was modelled after the tower of the Canadian Parliament in Ottawa.

Nineteenth-century Canadian and American courthouses were usually inspired by ancient Greek and Roman architecture. The more medieval style of the Middlesex County Courthouse can be explained by the association between the building and the name of the town in which it is located, as well as by the building's dominant presence in a community once governed by citizens from rural Scotland, where traditional clan leaders lived in medieval castles enshrouded in the Highland mists.

At the corner of Wellington stands the **Old City Hall**, a neoclassical building erected in 1918 and enlarged by T.C. McBride in 1927.

Located in the midst of a pleasant stretch of greenery, the **First St. Andrew's United Church** ★ *(350 Queens Ave.)* was originally built for one of London's many Presbyterian communities. A brick building erected between 1868 and 1871, it has all the traditional Neo-Gothic elements typical of Protestant churches, including ogival openings and a steeple topped by a spire. Inside, the nave has an austere, exposed wooden skeleton. Nearby, you'll find

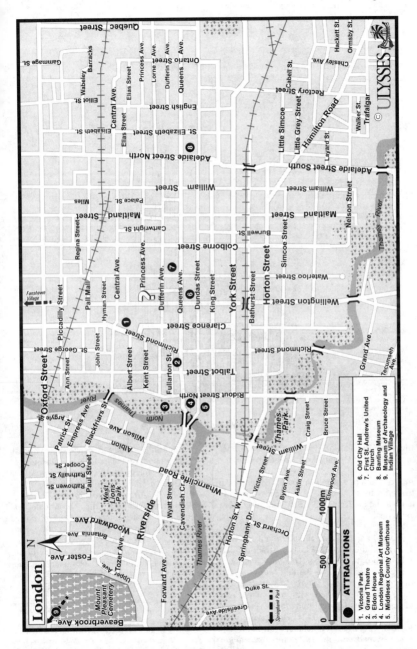

London

N

ULYSSES

ONTARIO

ATTRACTIONS

1. Victoria Park
2. Grand Theatre
3. Eldon House
4. London Regional Art Museum
5. Middlesex County Courthouse
6. Old City Hall
7. First St. Andrew's United Church
8. Banting Museum
9. Museum of Archaeology and Indian Village

0   500   1000m

Fanshawe Village

Springbank Park

First St. Andrew's United Church

the Neo-Renaissance manse, the former residence of the minister or Reverend Doctor.

As you continue along Waterloo Street, take the time to admire the magnificent Victorian homes dating from the 19th and early 20th centuries.

If you have a little time to spare, you can take Dundas all the way to Adelaide Street instead of turning onto Waterloo. This will give you a chance to see the little **Banting Museum** (*$3; Tue to Sat noon to 4:30pm; 442 Adelaide N., ☎673-1752*), devoted to the life and achievements of celebrated doctor Frederick Grant Banting (1891-1941), who, along with Scottish doctor John Macleod, won the Nobel Prize in medicine in 1923 for discovering insulin.

After passing through a peaceful residential neighbourhood, you'll reach the **Museum of Indian Archaeology** ★ (*$3.50; museum: every day 10am to 5pm, village: May to Aug 10am to 5pm; 1600 Attawandaron Rd., ☎473-1360*), which focuses on the archaeological excavations that revealed traces of native tribes dating back to well over 10,000 years. Through a survey of this research, the museum teaches visitors about the history, way of life and traditions of the First Nations. Outside, you'll find a reconstructed Iroquois village, complete with a longhouse.

The Far Southwest

This tour covers the strip of land flanked by Lakes Erie and St. Clair, alongside the United States, whose proximity has had a profound

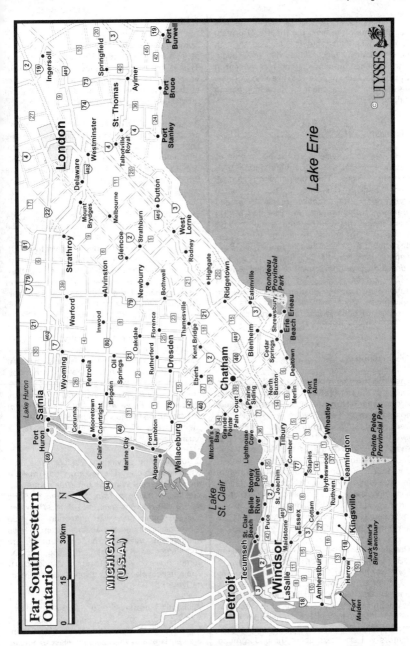

Far Southwestern Ontario

ONTARIO

© ULYSSES

influence on the history of the region. Not only has the area often been the theatre of British-American conflicts, but it was also through here that many black slaves fled to Canada. The American influence is still very evident in this region, and some towns, like Windsor, live very much in the shadow of their imposing neighbour.

Kingsville

Each year, Kingsville is visited by crowds of barnacle geese, who stop here during their migratory flight. This phenomenon can be traced back to one Jack Miner, who began trying to attract these graceful winged creatures to his property in 1904. His efforts were successful, and this area, one of the first in Canada to be set aside for birds, was designated a national bird sanctuary in 1917. Today, **Jack Miner's Bird Sanctuary ★** *(free admission; year-round; north of Kingsville, west of Division Rd., ☎733-4034)* is still open to the public, and you can go there to observe the wild geese. Open year-round, it attracts large numbers of birds in late March and from the end of October through November.

Amherstburg ★

The little town of Amherstburg, located at the mouth of the Detroit River, played an important role in local history when British troops were posted here at **Fort Walden ★** *($2; May to Dec, 10am to 5pm; Jan to Apr, Mon to Fri 1pm to 5pm, Sat and Sun 10am to 5pm; 100 Laird Ave., ☎736-5416)* during the War of 1812, with orders to protect the English colonies in this area. Unfortunately, they were no match for the enemy forces, which succeeded in capturing the fort and destroying part of it. After being returned to Canada in 1815, it was reconstructed, and still stands guard over the river—symbolically, at least.

The **North American Black Historical Museum** *($3; mid-Apr to late Oct, Wed to Fri 10am to 5pm, Sat and Sun 1pm to 5pm; 277 King St., ☎736-5433)* was built in memory of the black slaves who fled to Canada from the United States. It tells the sad epic tale of the men and women who were taken by force from Africa and brought to America to work on plantations. Visitors will also learn about the underground railway taken by slaves to reach Canada.

Windsor ★

Some people say that Windsor's greatest attraction is the Detroit skyline on the horizon. This is not simply a snide remark; Detroit, which stands on the opposite shore of the river of the same name, really does have something magical about it when viewed from here.

At the end of the 17th century, the French decided to set up a small trading post on the banks of the Detroit River. Due to their friendly relations with local natives the fort prospered. When France lost its American colonies to the British in 1763, however, the settlement was abandoned.

Later, in 1834, the English began settling the east bank of the river, founding a village named Sandwich, which later became Windsor. The town enjoyed its first period of prosperity with the construction of the Welland Canal, which enabled boats to sail into Lake Erie, and then with the arrival of the railway. It wasn't until the beginning of the 20th century, however, that the town really flourished; its population grew from 21,000 inhabitants in 1908 to 105,000 in 1928. This boom was largely due to the local automobile industry. Today, this industrial city has a rather depressing downtown area. There are a few pleasant spots, however, especially along the river, where a number of parks have been laid out. These include the magnificent **Coventry Gardens ★** *(Riverside Dr., at the corner of Pillette Rd.)*, adorned with beautiful flowers and the **Fountain of Peace**. Windsor also has a **casino** (see p 418).

If you are only staying in Windsor for a little while and can only visit one attraction, make it the **Art Gallery of Windsor ★★** *(free admission; Tue to Fri 10am to 7pm, Sat 10am to 5pm; 445 3100 Howard Ave., ☎969-4494)*, which has an amazingly rich collection of true masterpieces by great Canadian artists. These magnificent paintings and sculptures are complemented by clear, detailed written commentary on various facets of Canadian art. The museum also boasts a superb collection of native art.

Willistead Museum *($3.25; 1899 Niagara St., ☎253-2365)*, a splendid Tudor-style house built for Edward Walker, son of distiller Hiram Walker, is one of the city's loveliest examples of early 20th-century architecture. Its opulent rooms are elegantly decorated with furnishings from the 1900s.

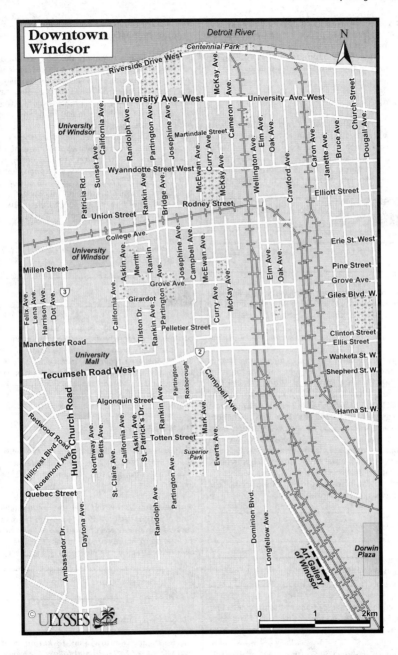

Downtown Windsor

Detroit River

Centennial Park

Riverside Drive West

University Ave. West

University of Windsor

University Ave. West

Martindale Street

Wyanndotte Street West

Rodney Street

Union Street

College Ave.

University of Windsor

Millen Street

Grove Ave.

Girardot

Manchester Road

University Mall

Tecumseh Road West

Algonquin Street

Totten Street

Superior Park

Quebec Street

Erie St. West

Pine Street

Grove Ave.

Giles Blvd. W.

Clinton Street

Ellis Street

Wahketa St. W.

Shepherd St. W.

Hanna St. W.

Pelletier Street

Dorwin Plaza

Art Gallery of Windsor

© ULYSSES

0   1   2km

ONTARIO

If you'd like to spend a day outdoors without leaving Windsor, go to the **Ojibwe Park and Nature Centre** *(free admission; ☎966-5852)*, where you'll find nature trails crisscrossing the forest and the vast, tall-grass prairie.

Sarnia

Sarnia is a rather dreary town, whose outskirts have a futuristic look, due to the area's thriving petrochemical industry. Fortunately, the parks along Lake Huron and the St. Clair River make it easy to forget about the factories, which are no doubt useful but disfigure the landscape.

     PARKS AND BEACHES

The Far Southwest

At the southwestern tip of Ontario, a finger of land known as Point Pelee stretches into Lake Erie; this is the southernmost part of the Canadian territory. Surrounded by marshes, this point is home to a variety of wildlife, including all sorts of birds, especially in the spring and the fall, when a number of migratory species stop here. The area has been set aside as **Point Pelee National Park** ★★ *(from Leamington, take Hwy 33; R.R.1, N8H 3V4, ☎519-322-2365, ≈322-1277)*, which has some pleasant hiking trails. As an added attraction, there are long wooden docks that lead deep into marshes, making it possible to observe some of the nearly 350 species of birds found here in their natural environment. In September, monarch season, the park is filled with these orange and black butterflies. There are several beaches on Point Pelee as well.

    OUTDOORS

    Hiking

In addition to hiking trails in the provincial and national parks, various other trails wind their way through southwestern Ontario, covering distances of several kilometres. **Hike Ontario** *(1185 Eglinton Ave. E., North York, M3C 3C6, ☎416-426-7362)*, the association that maintains these trails, can provide you with heaps of information.

The **Bruce Trail** is definitely the best known of all these trails, since it is the oldest and longest. It runs along the Niagara Escarpment, starting at Niagara Falls and ending at Tobermory, some 736 kilometres away. This trip obviously can't be made in a day and requires considerable preparation, but some wonderful surprises await hikers along the way. From Niagara, the trail follows the shoreline of Lake Ontario to Hamilton, heads north to Collingwood, then crisscrosses through fields to Owen Sound. From there, it leads out onto the Bruce Peninsula, running alongside the cliffs and affording some spectacular views. For more information, contact:

Bruce Trail Association
P.O. Box 857, Hamilton, ON, L8N 3N9, ☎(905) 529-6821.

    Biking

The quiet, charming country roads on the southwest peninsula are perfect for cycling. You can enjoy a ride through the fields in the St. Jacobs area, tour the local vineyards or follow the shoreline of Lake Huron. In most towns, you'll have no trouble finding a bike shop for any necessary repairs.

The Wine Route

Niagara Bicycle Touring *(tours start at the Pillar & Post Hotel ☎468-1300)* arranges three-hour bike trips through the Niagara-on-the-Lake region.

A road reserved for cyclists and pedestrians runs along the Niagara River (and the Niagara Parkway) from Niagara-on-the-Lake to Fort Erie, a distance of about 40 kilometres. Cyclists of all levels can enjoy this pleasant, peaceful ride.

    Bird-watching

Mennonite Country

The **Kortright Waterfowl Park** *(8 km north of Hwy 401; take Exit 195 and follow the signs, ☎824-6729)* is both a wilderness preserve and a research centre. This lovely, well laid-out area is a birder's paradise, with nearly one hundred species to spot.

The Far Southwest

Large numbers of migratory birds stop alongside Lake Erie to gather their strength before setting out across this huge body of water and, as a result, outstanding bird-watching areas dot the shoreline.

Jack Miner's Bird Sanctuary *(north of Kingsville, west of Division Rd., ☎519-733-4034)* was created in 1904 in order to protect certain species of birds, particularly ducks and barnacle geese, which come here in large numbers.

Point Pelee National Park is another outstanding place to observe all sorts of birds—as many as 350 different species during the migration seasons. It is laid out so that visitors can see as many birds as possible, with trails leading into the forest and wooden docks crisscrossing the marshes.

 ACCOMMODATIONS

Mennonite Country

Kitchener-Waterloo

There are several full-comfort hotels in town, but if you're looking for a charming inn, the neighbouring villages have more to offer.

The **Sheraton** *($85; ≈, ⊚, △, ₺, ✕; 105 King St. E., N2G 3W9, ☎744-4141, ⇒578-6889)*, located alongside Market Square, is unquestionably one of the most elegant places to stay in town. A modern hotel complex, it has spacious rooms and all the amenities. Large picture windows in the lobby look out onto a magnificent indoor swimming pool.

The nearby **Walper Terrace Hotel** *($89 bkfst incl.; ℜ, ₺; 1 King St. W., N2G 1A1, ☎745-4321)*, by contrast, is a handsome building dating back to 1893, whose charms are perhaps a bit outdated. Although not as luxurious as the more modern hotels, it is nevertheless comfortable.

St. Jacobs

The **Countryside Manor** *($65 bkfst incl.; 39 Henri St., N0B 2N0, ☎664-2622)* is one of those places you'll want to come back to. The owners are friendly, and you'll feel right at home in the pleasant rooms of their charming little house. The breakfasts, both copious and delicious, are equally memorable.

Benjamin's Inn *($95; ℜ; 17 King St., St. Jacobs, N0B 2N0, ☎664-3731)* is a pretty building that has stood in the centre of town for over a century; it has been renovated in order to accommodate visitors. The rooms are furnished with antiques, and have a cozy charm that adds to the pleasure of being on vacation.

Stately trees adorn the garden of the **Jacobstettel Guest House** *($115; ℜ; 126 Isabella, N0B 2N0, ☎664-2208)*, a splendid Victorian house with about a dozen charming rooms, all decorated with antiques.

Elora

The stone mill by the falls around which the town of Elora grew is now the splendid **Elora Mill Country Inn** *($135 bkfst incl.; 77 Mill St. W., N0B 1S0, ☎846-5356, ⇒846-9180)*. The place still plays a central role in the community, for its excellent reputation has long been attracting visitors, who come here for the tastefully decorated rooms and succulent cuisine.

Guelph

Although somewhat drab-looking, the **Best Western Carden Place** *($86 bkfst incl.; 106 Carden St., N1H 3A3, ☎836-1331, ⇒836-9627)*, has comfortable rooms and is well-located in the heart of downtown Guelph.

Stratford

During the finest months of the year, when the Shakespeare festival is in full swing, the local hotels are often full. Fortunately, there are plenty of B&Bs in town, each more attractive than the last. You can reserve a room in many of these places through the Stratford Festival Accommodation Bureau: P.O. Box 520, Stratford, N5A 6V2, ☎273-1600 or (800) 567-1600, ⇒273-6173.

ONTARIO

You might try your luck at one of the following B&Bs, which are all pleasant and centrally located:

On peaceful Church Street, the magnificent yellow brick **Stone Maiden Inn** *($135; 123 Church St.,* ☎*271-7129)* and the more modest but nonetheless charming **Maples of Stratford** *($75 sb; 220 Church,* ☎*273-0810)* are two possibilities. Another good choice is **Angel's Inn** *($85; 208 Church St.,* ☎*271-9651)*, a superb Victorian house.

Despite its name, there's nothing very Victorian about the **Victorian Inn** *($110; ≈, ℜ, ⊙, ᕃ; 10 Romeo St., N5A 5M7,* ☎*271-2030)*, a big, nondescript building made of white brick. It does, however, boast a superb view of the Avon River, as well as luxurious rooms and sports facilities.

Bentley's Inn *($140; ℜ; 99 Ontario St., N5A 3H1,* ☎*271-1121,* ≈*272-1853)*, located in the heart of downtown Stratford, is a lovely brick building dating back to the beginning of the century. The rooms are well-kept and have an old-fashioned charm about them. This may not be the height of luxury, but it's still quite pleasant.

St. Marys

The **Westover Inn** *($95; ≈, ℜ; 300 Thomas St., N4X 1B1,* ☎*284-2977,* ≈*284-4043)*, a true haven of peace, lies in a positively breathtaking setting in the heart of the countryside, surrounded by stately trees. If the location isn't enough to win your heart over completely, you're sure to be enchanted by the bright rooms, with their big windows and antique furnishings.

Hamilton and Surroundings

Hamilton

Hamilton has surprisingly few hotels and motels for a city of its size. The options are essentially limited to big chain hotels, which lack character, but are nonetheless quite comfortable. If you're on a tight budget and don't mind staying in a generic motel, you might be better off in Burlington.

The **Admiral Inn** *($64; ℜ; 149 Dundurn St. N.,* ☎*905-529-2311)* has comfortable, modern rooms that are fairly typical of this kind of hotel, located on the way into a city. Its façade, on the other hand, is more unique, with lots of picture windows, as a result the lobby and restaurant are wonderfully bright and sunny.

Those who would rather stay downtown can choose from one of three Hamilton mainstays. The old **Royal Connaught** *($89; ≈, ℜ, ⌂, ⊛, ᕃ, ➤; 112 King St. E., L8N 1A8,* ☎*905-546-8111,* ≈*546-8144)* looks as if it has seen better days, but the rooms are nonetheless pleasant. If its old-fashioned look puts you off, head to the nearby **Ramada Hotel** *($89 brkfs incl.;≈, ⌂, ⊛, ᕃ, ➤; 150 King st. E.,* ☎*905-528-3451 or 1-800-228-2828,* ≈*522-2281)*, whose more modern-looking architecture and lobby might be more your style. In terms of comfort, the rooms are at par with those at the Royal Connaught.

The Wine Route

Niagara-on-the-Lake

If you have money to spare, you can really spoil yourself in Niagara-on-the-Lake, which has scores of top-notch inns. Visitors on a tight budget will have a harder time finding a place to stay, however.

One of the local B&Bs is a popular solution, especially at an affordable $60 or so per night for two people. For a complete list, write to:

B&B Association
P.O. Box 1515, Niagara-on-the-Lake, Ontario, L0S 1J0, ☎(416) 468-4263.

The **Moffat Inn** *($80; ℜ; 60 Picton St., L0S 1J0,* ☎*905-468-4116)*, located near the centre of town, is a charming little white building adorned with green shutters. It has about twenty well-kept rooms, some with an attractive fireplace.

A real local institution, the **Prince of Wales** *($140; ≈, ℜ, ⌂, ⊛, ᕃ; 6 Picton St., L0S 1J0,* ☎*905-468-3246 or 1-800-263-2452,* ≈*468-5521)* stands at the end of Queen Street, a commercial artery. This superb building, erected in 1864, has managed to retain its charm over the years. In spite of its age, it remains extremely elegant, from its richly decorated sitting and dining rooms to its impeccable guest rooms.

The vast, enchanting lobby of the **Pillar and Post Inn** *($160; ≈, ⊘, ℜ, ⊛, ◌, ⏚; 48 John St., L0S 1J0, ☎905-468-2123, ⇾468-3551)* boasts plants, antiques and big skylights. The hushed atmosphere will make you feel like staying here for hours. This is just a foretaste of what you'll find in the rooms: beautiful wooden furniture, armchairs with floral patterns and even, in some cases, a fireplace. The place also has a gym, which can make a stay here that much more relaxing.

With its wide façade adorned with four white columns, the **Queens Landing Inn** *($160; ≈, ℜ, ⊛, ◌, ⏚; 155 Byron St., L0S 1J0, ☎905-468-2195 or 1-800-361-6645, ⇾468-2227)* is somewhat ostentatious, but nonetheless elegant, standing there proudly alongside the Niagara River. It has 137 large, tastefully decorated rooms, each with a whirlpool bath and a fireplace. A first-class hotel by any standard.

Niagara Falls

Niagara Falls, southwestern Ontario's tourist mecca, has at least a hundred hotels, most members of big North American chains, as well as a host of B&Bs. The local hotels are packed over summer vacation but empty during the low season, which is therefore a good time for bargain rates.

The most inexpensive place in town is without question the **Youth Hostel** *($18 per person; 4699 Zimmerman Ave., L2E 3M7, ☎905-357-0770)*, an excellent option for visitors who are watching their pennies.

If you drive along the river before coming into town, you will pass a series of hotels offering modern standards of comfort and a lovely view of the rapids. The **Comfort Inn** *($120; ≈, ℜ, ✻; 4009 River Rd. L2E 3E5, ☎905-356-0131, ⇾356-3306)*, the **Days Inn** *($130; ≈, ℜ, ⊛, ◌; 4029 River Rd., L2E 3E5, ☎905-356-6666 or 800-263-2543, ⇾356-1800)* and the **Best Western Fireside** *($130; ≈, ℜ, ◌; 4067 River Rd., L2E 3E4, ☎905-374-2027, ⇾774-7746)*, all in a row, have similar rooms, although those in the Fallsview are equipped with gas-burning fireplaces.

Other hotels are near all the action without being right in the middle of it, thus offering the advantage of being located on a somewhat quieter street than Clifton Hill. The **Travelodge** *($140; ≈, ℜ, ◌; 5234 Ferry St., L2G 1R5,* ☎905-374-7771 or 1-800-578-7878) and the **Comfort Inn** *($140; ≈, ℜ, ◌; 5257 Ferry Lane, L2G 1R6, ☎905-356-2842)* both have clean, even pleasant rooms.

The **Old Stone Inn** *($150; ≈, ℜ, ⊛; 5425 Robinson St., L2G 7L6, ☎905-357-1234, ⇾357-9299)* is one of the few hotels in Niagara Falls with a little character. The lobby and the restaurant are located inside an old mill dating from 1904; the rooms, quite comfortable, in a more recent annex.

At the very end of Oakes Street stands the beautiful **Sheraton Fallsview Hotel** *($150; 6755 Oakes St., L2G 3W7, ☎905-374-1077, ⇾374-6224)*, which definitely has the best location of all. Each of the rooms offers unimpeded views of the falls.

The finest hotels stand at the top of the hill overlooking the falls, enabling guests to enjoy a beautiful view. They also offer the added advantage of a peaceful location, set away from the downtown area. The **Days Inn Overlooking The Falls** *($160; 6361 Buchanan Ave., L2G 3V9, ☎905-357-7377)* has 239 comfortable rooms, the more expensive of which have views of the falls.

London and Surroundings

London

For lodgings right near downtown London, yet with the peace and quiet of a residential neighbourhood, head to the **Rose House B&B** *($50; 526 Dufferin, N6B 2A2, ☎433-9978)*, which has pretty, well-kept rooms. If the place is full, you can try one of the other twenty or so B&Bs in town. A complete listing is available at the tourist office *(300 Dufferin Ave., ☎432-2211)*.

If you prefer a hotel but don't want to spend a fortune, try Wellington Street, outside the downtown area, which is lined with modern hotels with somewhat impersonal but nonetheless decent rooms. These include a **Days Inn** *($60; ≈; 1100 Wellington, N6E 1M2, ☎681-1240)* and the **Best Western Lamplighter** *($79; 591 Wellington, N6C 4R3, ☎681-7151, ⇾681-3271)*.

The **Idlewyld Inn** *($110; 36 Grand Ave., N6C 1K8, ☎433-2891)*, a splendid 19th century house, has nothing in common with modern

ONTARIO

hotels. It has been renovated over the years, but has managed to retain its old-time charm. There are 27 rooms, each with its own unique decor.

There is one other top-notch hotel in town, the **Delta London Armouries** *($99; ≈, ℜ, ⊛, △, ✕; 325 Dundas, N6B 1T9, ☎679-6111 or 1-800-668-9999, ⇒679-3957)*, a converted armory topped by a tall glass tower. Although somewhat surprising at first sight, the combination is nonetheless harmonious. The rooms, furthermore, are impeccable.

The Far Southwest

Windsor

Windsor has neither a B&B association nor a youth hostel, so it can be hard to find an inexpensive place to stay in town. There are, however, a few average hotels with fairly reasonable rates, especially during the low season. Most of these are located on Huron Church Drive, a busy street with little to recommend it.

Closer to the downtown area, a stone's throw from the bridge to the United States, the **Holiday Inn** *($95; ⊛, △, &; 1855 Huron Church Dr., N9C 2L6, ☎966-1200, ⇒966-2521)* has pretty rooms with all the comforts and offers a wide range of amenities, including a pleasant restaurant and an indoor swimming pool. Good rates are available during the low season if you reserve three days in advance.

A handsome brick and glass building, the **Hilton** *($120; ℜ, ≈; 277 Riverside Dr. W., N9A 5K4, ☎973-5555 or 1-800-463-6655, ⇒973-1600)* boasts an excellent location by the riverside, steps away from the casino and downtown Windsor.

If you'd like to have your own kitchenette, try the **Quality Suites** *($130; ✕, K; 250 Dougall Ave., N9A 7C6, ☎977-9707, ⇒977-6404)*, whose modern rooms are not very cozy but extremely well kept. Not far from the downtown area.

RESTAURANTS

Mennonite Country

Kitchener-Waterloo

To make it easier for you to locate the following restaurants, we have specified whether each one is located in Kitchener or Waterloo.

Fed up with fried eggs and bacon for breakfast? Head over to **Especially Coffee** *($; 10 King St. E., Kitchener, ☎742-5272)*, which has a good selection of baked goods and coffee.

The façade of the **Harmony Lunch** *($; 90 King N., Waterloo, ☎886-4721)* looks as if it hasn't been touched since the place opened almost 50 years ago. Although this little restaurant looks rather uninviting at first, its "ham"burgers (literally made of ham) have won it a loyal clientele.

For a quick bite to eat, try **Reggies** *($; 1 King St. W., Kitchener)*, where you can get a sandwich made to order. Wide choice of toppings.

The dining room of the **Olde English Parlour** *($$; 77 King St. N., Waterloo, ☎886-1130)* is extremely cozy, with its comfortable armchairs, wallpaper and woodwork — just the kind of atmosphere that complements a good meal. The menu lists simple dishes like pasta, roast beef and hamburgers.

If you're in the mood for the kind of tender, juicy steak that is a hallmark of American cuisine, head to **Golf's Steak House** *($$$; 598 Lancaster W., Kitchener, ☎579-4050)*. The dining rooms are attractively decorated, and a meal includes a steak (try the New York Sirloin), unlimited salad from the salad bar and the soup of the day.

St. Jacobs

The **Stone Crock** *($$; 41 King St., ☎664-2286)*, a Mennonite restaurant, has a modest dining room and a pleasant family atmosphere. The setup is simple: an all-you-can-eat, full-course meal including soup, salad bar, a choice of three main dishes (roast turkey, fried chicken or spareribs) and dessert for $13.95 per person.

There's something captivating about the atmosphere at **Benjamin's Inn** *($$-$$$; 17 King, ☎664-3731)*, and once you've taken a seat in the dining room, you'll feel like staying there for hours. Perhaps it's the rustic charm of the place, or the lovely fireplace. Or maybe it's the meal itself, made up of a succession of delicious dishes. Whatever the reason, you're sure to have a wonderful time here.

Elmira

Elmira has a **Stone Crock** *($$; 59 Church St., ☎669-1521)* restaurant with the same setup as the one in St. Jacobs (see above).

Elora

The unpretentious **Desert Rose Café** *($; Metcalfe St.)* is the perfect place for a lunchtime snack, like a piece of quiche or a salad, or simply to treat yourself to a delicious dessert in the afternoon. The carrot cake and the butter tarts are especially worthy.

Alongside the river, is a real little gem called **La Cachette** *($$$; 13 Mill St. East, ☎846-8346)*, a French restaurant in a pretty house with two charming little dining rooms — one on the main floor, for smokers, and the other on the second floor, for non-smokers. The menu is even more appealing than the decor, listing succulent dishes like duck cutlet with apples and calvados and grilled lamb with *herbes de Provence*. During summer, you can enjoy your meal outside, by the side of the river, comfortably seated on the terrace.

Residents of Elora are truly spoiled when it comes to good restaurants. In addition to La Cachette, there's the **River Mill Inn** *($$$-$$$$; 77 Mill St. W., ☎846-5356)*, where you can enjoy a delicious meal in a dining room with a lovely view on the falls. The mouth-watering menu lists a variety of dishes, such as chateaubriand and lamb with a cheese filling.

Guelph

There are all sorts of charming places to enjoy a delicious meal in Guelph, which prides itself on having over a hundred restaurants. The following are a few of the finest and most pleasant ones on town.

The aptly named **Bookshelf Café** *($; 41 Quebec St., ☎821-3333)*, located at the back of a bookstore, is a cosy little spot with big picture windows, a relaxed, youthful atmosphere and an appetizing menu.

The **Woolwich Arms Pub** *($-$$; 176 Woolwich St., ☎836-2875)* is known for its delicious "specialty burgers" and attractive terrace, which is a pleasant place to eat on a fine summer day.

The **Georgian Creed's** *($$-$$$; 16 Douglas St., ☎837-2692)*, hidden away on a quiet street a few steps from downtown Guelph, has a beautiful decor and serves delicious dishes that are sure to satisfy your palate.

Stratford

With its wooden benches, wrought-iron tables and artists' drawings on the walls, **Down the Street** *($-$$; Ontario St.)* is more like a friendly cafe where people come to chat than a restaurant. It does have an appetizing menu, however, listing simple, tasty dishes like chicken linguine and Santa Fe Spicy Grilled Cheese.

Fellini's *($$; 107 Ontario St., ☎271-3333)* is a terrific, unpretentious restaurant decorated with checkerboard tablecloths. The menu lists a variety of pasta dishes, offering a good opportunity to sample some succulent Italian specialties.

The **Church** *(at the corner of Waterloo and Brunswick, ☎273-3424)*, a century-year-old converted church, has a unique ambiance that is truly irresistible. Add to that its delicious cuisine, and you've got the perfect recipe for a wonderful evening.

Hamilton and Surroundings

Hamilton

You'll have no trouble finding a place to eat downtown on King Street, which is lined with fast-food restaurants. One option is **Toby** *($; King St., on Jackson Sq.)*, known for its big, tasty burgers.

ONTARIO

For something a little more sophisticated, you can try the classier **Sundried Tomatoes** *($$; at the corner of St. John and Main St. E., ☎905-522-3155)*. The dining room, spacious enough so that guests have plenty of elbow room, is extremely pleasant. This place will appeal particularly to those with a penchant for oysters, which have top billing on the menu.

Hess Village consists of a few quiet streets, some superb Victorian houses and a number of delightful restaurants and terraces. If you only want a little snack, try **Moments Cafe** *($; George St.)*, which serves delicious coffee and desserts that will knock your socks off.

The **Amigo** *($$; George St., ☎522-3838)* definitely has one of the most inviting terraces in Hess Village. During winter, the veranda, with its big windows, is the perfect place for Sunday brunch. There are some cozier rooms inside as well. The menu is not exactly original, but features good chicken, beef and pasta dishes every day.

The Wine Route

St. Catharines

Beantrees *($; 204 St. Paul St., ☎682-3357)* must have the most eclectic clientele in St. Catharines. This little bistro, which is a perfect place for lunch, manages to attract students looking for a place to chat and while away the time; businesspeople, who stop in for a quick bite and shoppers lured inside by the impressive selection of tea.

Niagara-on-the-Lake

The pretty terrace of the **Buttery** *($; Queen St.)*, located in the heart of all the downtown action, is sure to catch your eye. You can enjoy a good meal here while watching the activity on the street.

The dining rooms of **The Oban** *(160 Front St., ☎468-2165)* occupy a good part of the ground floor of a magnificent house. Some of the tables are set on a long veranda with big picture windows, and it is in this section of the restaurant *($$$-$$$$)* that you can sample some of the succulent dishes that have conquered both the hearts and the palates of so many people. Another room inside *($$)*, is more of a pub, with pictures covering the walls, antique furniture, all sorts of knick-knacks, a piano and a fireplace. Seated in a captain's chair or on a love seat, plate on your knees or on a coffee table, you'll feel a bit like you're in your own living room. The menu lists simple dishes, such as chicken cacciatore and fried shrimp.

The elegant **Prince of Wales** *(6 Picton St., ☎468-3245)* has two dining rooms. The first *($$$$)*, and more ritzy of the two, has a refined menu and is harmoniously decorated with antiques. The second *($$)* has a more relaxed atmosphere, a pub-style decor and a simple menu that's perfect for lunch, with selections like chicken fingers and salads.

Niagara Falls

Clifton Hill is lined with fast-food restaurants, which are devoid of charm, but will suit your needs if you're simply looking for a quick bite.

For ribs or roast chicken, visit **Tony's Place** *($; 5467 Victoria Ave.)*.

For a refined meal, try the restaurant at the **Old Stone Inn** *($$-$$$; 5425 Robinson St., ☎357-1234)*, where you'll find a lovely dining room in a building dating back to the turn of the century. The menu lists an excellent selection of specialties from a number of different countries.

Finally, if your top priority is a view of the falls, your best bet is the restaurant in the **Skylon Tower** *($$$-$$$$; 5200 Robinson St., 356-2651)*. The menu features fish and meat dishes. Of course, you pay for the view, but what a view it is!

London and Surroundings

London

Mario's *($; 428 Clarence, ☎433-4044)* offers an appealing combination of spareribs and jazz.

The modest-looking **Jewel of India** *($$; 390 Richmond, ☎434-9268)* deserves its name, for it truly is a little jewel as far as Indian cuisine is concerned, complete with curries, Tandouris and *nan* bread. Not to mention that you can enjoy a real little feast here without spending a fortune.

The **Marienbad** *($$$; 122 Carling St., ☎679-9940)* has managed to keep up a good reputation over the years, attracting guests with its filling but tasty *goulaschs* and *schnitzels*.

The Far Southwest

Kingsville

The charming little **Vintage Goose** *($$$; 24 Main St.)* is without a doubt the most pleasant restaurant in town, with its appetizing menu and lovely dining room adorned with all sorts of bric-a-brac and statuettes and containing a handful of wooden tables with pretty flowered tablecloths.

Windsor

The **Old Fish Market** *($$; 156 Chatham W., ☎253-3474)* is decorated in an original manner with fishing nets, buoys, anchors and other such paraphernalia. This nautical atmosphere will help put you in the mood for one of the poached, grilled or fried fish dishes on the menu, which are all served in generous portions.

The façade of the **Plunkette Bistro** *($$-$$$; 28 Chatham St. E., ☎252-3111)*, with its orange-coloured columns, looks somewhat out of place in this part of town. Nevertheless, the menu features simple but tasty pasta and beef dishes.

  ENTERTAINMENT

Bars and Nightclubs

Kitchener-Waterloo

At the end of the day, people flock to the **Olde English Pub** *(77 King N., Waterloo, ☎886-1130)* for a good meal, then top off the evening with a drink. If you don't want to eat here, have a seat in the bar section. The place features live music on certain nights.

Stratford

Down the Street *(Ontario St.)* is both a pleasant little restaurant and pub with a good selection of draft beer. Its unpretentious atmosphere makes for a great place to chat.

Hamilton

The **Gown and Gavel** *(Hess St.)*, which occupies one of the lovely Victorian houses in Hess Village, is something of a local institution and has a steady student clientele.

Niagara-on-the-Lake

The **Oban** *(160 Front St., ☎468-2165)* is *the* place in town for a drink with friends, or even alone, ensconced in a comfortable armchair by the fireplace.

London

There are all sorts of places in town where a good time is guaranteed, whether you're in the mood to dance to popular tunes or sip a drink to the sounds of jazz.

For drinks and some R&B, **Chicago** *(Fullarton St.)* is the place to go, while jazz fans can head to **Underside of 5** *(York St. at the corner of Talbot St.)*. For rock and roll, go to **Brunswick**.

Festivals and Cultural Events

Kitchener-Waterloo

The **Oktoberfest**, the largest festival of its kind outside of Germany, serves as a reminder that a good part of the local population is of German descent. It is a major event in this region, during which all sorts of activities are organized, stalls selling sausages, sauerkraut and beer are set up and a festive atmosphere prevails.

Stratford

During the **Stratford Festival**, which takes place every year from May to November, various Shakespeare plays and other classics are presented. The festival is so popular that the town has no fewer than three theatres, the

ONTARIO

Festival Theatre *(55 Queen St.)*, the **Avon Theatre** *(99 Downie)* and the **Tom Patterson Theatre** *(Lakeside Dr.)*.

To reserve seats or obtain information on the festival calendar, call or write to:

Stratford Festival Box Office, P.O. Box 520, Stratford, ON, N5A 6V2, ☎(519) 273-1600, ☎(800) 567-1600, ⬝(519) 273-6173.

Niagara-on-the-Lake

The internationally renowned **Shaw Festival** *($22-$65, reservations ☎905-468-2153 or 1-800-511-7429, ⬝905-468-3804, www.shawfest.com/shaw.html)* has been held every year since 1962. From April to October, visitors can take in various plays by George Bernard Shaw at one of the three theatres in town, the **Festival Theatre**, the **Court House Theatre** and the **Royal George Theatre**.

London

Aeolian Hall hosts year-round concerts by the **London Symphony Orchestra**. For reservations, call ☎679-8778.

The town also has some wonderful playhouses, including the **Grand Theatre** *(471 Richmond St., ☎672-8800)*, where plays are presented year round.

Casinos

Niagara Falls

Visitors to Niagara Falls who feel lucky and who are looking for a bit of a distraction can now find it at the Niagara Falls Casino *(5705 Falls Ave., ☎905-374-5964 or 1-888-946-3255, ⬝374-5998)*. Spacious and housed in a beautiful modern building, it includes black-jack tables and baccara as well as many slot-machines, and is sure to please all kinds of players.

Windsor

Windsor's **Casino** *(445 Riverside Dr. W., ☎258-7878)*, a building devoid of charm and elegance, is the town's pride and joy. It is located on the shores of the Detroit River,

opposite the United States, and Americans make up the bulk of its clientele. Business is so good that another, even bigger casino is scheduled to open in 1997.

If you're in the mood to gamble, but the casino strikes you as a somewhat run-of-the-mill, head over to the **Northern Belle Casino** *(350 Riverside Dr. E., , ☎258-2141)*, located on a boat on the Detroit River, right near the downtown area.

 SHOPPING

Mennonite Country

Kitchener-Waterloo

Market Square, located at the corner of King and Queen Streets, looks like your average shopping mall, but the place really comes alive every Saturday morning when the local **Farmer's Market** is held here. On the ground floor, you'll find all sorts of handicrafts, quilts, knitted goods and clothing; in the basement, a variety of foodstuffs, including honey, preserves, sausages, bread, cheese, etc.

St. Jacobs

St. Jacobs is full of **craft shops**, each one more enticing than the last. Rather than tell you where to go, we'll leave you the pleasure of poking around this maze of little stores on your own.

The local **Farmer's Market** *(Hwy 17, at the west edge of town)*, where handicrafts, foodstuffs and livestock are sold, is a show like no other.

Guelph

There are some charming little shops on Quebec Street, including the **Bookshelf Café**, a restaurant and bookstore, and the **Maison de Madeleine**, where you can purchase unique and pretty decorative items for your home.

Stratford

You'll find some wonderful native art (sculptures and prints) at **Indigena** *(151 Downie St.)*.

Finally, if you're looking for a souvenir of the festival, make sure to stop by the **Theatre Store** *(96 Downie St.)*.

The Wine Route

Niagara-on-the-Lake

Downtown Niagara-on-the-Lake is home to all sorts of shops, each more enticing than the last, and a visit here wouldn't be complete without a little browsing.

J.W. Outfitters *(Queen St.)* looks like a simple souvenir shop, but inside you'll find terrific t-shirts and lovely posters of native art.

Greaves *(Queen St.)* specializes in jellies, jams and marmalades, all delicious.

For an unforgettable taste treat, stop by **Maple Leaf Fudge** *(Queen St.)*.

London and Surroundings

Brantford

The little shop in the **Woodland Cultural Centre** *(184 Mohawk St.)* has a good selection of native crafts, books and posters.

London

As far as native art is concerned, **Innuit** *(201 Queen Ave.,* ☎*672-7770)* is definitely one of the loveliest galleries in this part of the province. Inside, you'll find sculptures and lithographs by artists from all over Canada. A feast for the imagination, even if you can't afford to buy anything.

Novacks Travel Bookstore *(211 King St.,* ☎*519-434-2282)* has a vast array of travel guides and outdoor equipment.

The Far Southwest

Windsor

Downtown Windsor is located along Ouellette Avenue, which is lined with all sorts of shops. The Art Gallery of Windsor shop, **AGW**, has a lovely and unique selection of merchandise. There are two branches, one at 500 Ouellette Avenue and the other at the museum *(300 Howard Ave.)*.

ONTARIO

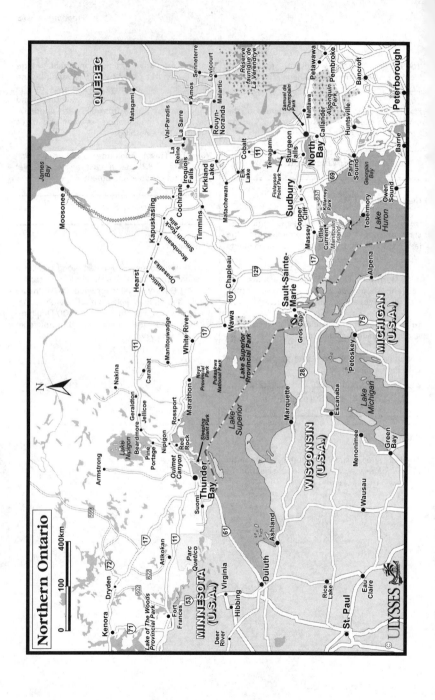

Northern Ontario

NORTHERN ONTARIO

 orth of the 46th parallel lies a vast, untamed stretch of territory dominated by forests, lakes and rivers. It was by exploring these rivers that Europeans first penetrated deep into this wilderness and discovered two virtual inland seas, Lakes Huron and Superior. They also encountered indigenous peoples who survived on hunting and fishing, and soon developed an interest in a luxury product in great demand in the Old World: fur. In the 17th century, the Europeans decided to set up trading posts so that they could do business with the northern natives tribes who were past masters in the art of hunting. It wasn't until the 19th century, however, that these first settlements, which were scattered all over the territory, began to grow into small towns. Even then, Northern Ontario remained sparsely populated, and though a wave of French-speaking immigrants, many of whom were poor, did begin to settle in the region in the early 20th century after rich mineral deposits were discovered here, the villages remained small and few in number.

Northern Ontario is bounded to the south by the Mattawa River and Lakes Huron and Superior. Its irregular landscape features a forest of leafy trees and conifers punctuated by rocky escarpments (typical of the Canadian Shield) to the south, and a boreal forest farther north. A tiny portion of the territory, all the way to the north, is tundra, distinguished by its sparse vegetation.

FINDING YOUR WAY AROUND

The territory covered in this chapter is vast, and its roads might cover dozens of kilometres before reaching a village. Driving is the best means of transportation here, although many towns and villages are served by buses. The train also goes to North Bay, Sudbury and a number of other towns farther north.

By Car

The 17 is the only highway that stretches all the way across northern Ontario. It starts in Ottawa and runs through North Bay, Sudbury, Sault Ste. Marie, Wawa and Thunder Bay, all the way to Kenora, on the Manitoba border.

If you are coming from Toronto, take the 440 to Barrie and then the 11 to North Bay.

By Train

One railway line links Toronto and North Bay, while another runs from Toronto to White River via Sudbury, passing alongside Georgian Bay.

North Bay: 100 Station Rd., ☎(705) 495-4200.
Sudbury: 233 Elgin St., ☎(800) 361-1235.

By Bus

You can easily get from one town to another by bus, but it might seem like a long ride, since there are frequent stops along the way.

Bus stations:

Pembroke: 213 Lake St., ☎(613) 732-2866.
North Bay: 100 Station Rd., ☎(705) 495-4200.
Sudbury: 854 Notre Dame Ave., ☎(705) 524-9900.
Sault Ste. Marie: 73 Brock St., ☎(705) 949-4711.
Thunder Bay: 815 Fort William Rd., ☎(807) 345-2194.
Kenora: 610 Lakeview Dr., ☎(807) 468-7172.

Manitoulin Island

There is bus service as far as Little Current. To visit the rest of the island, you'll have to find your own means of transportation (rental car, hitchhiking, bicycle).

Little Current: On Highway 540, ☎(705) 368-2540.

By Ferry

If you are coming from the southern part of the province, you can reach Manitoulin Island aboard the ferry *Chi-Cheemaun (car $23, adults $10.50;* ☎*1-800-461-2621)*, which links Tobermory (at the northern tip of the Bruce Peninsula) to South Baymouth from spring to fall. The crossing takes 1 hour 45 minutes. Reservations are accepted, but to keep them you must arrive one hour before boarding.

Summer schedule:

Tobermory - South Baymouth
7am; 11:20am; 3:40pm; 8pm

South Baymouth - Tobermory
9:10am; 1:30pm; 5:50pm; 10pm

Spring and fall schedule:

Tobermory - South Baymouth
8:50am; 1:30pm; 6:10pm (Fri only)

South Baymouth - Tobermory
11:10am; 3:50pm; 8:15pm (Fri only)

Visitors arriving from Northern Ontario on Highway 17 can reach the island via Highway 6, which links Espanola to Little Current.

 PRACTICAL INFORMATION

Area code 705, except for Pembroke 613 and the Thunder Bay area 807.

Tourist Information Offices

Almaquin Nipissing Travel Association: at the corner of Seymour Street and Highway 11, P.O. Box 351, North Bay, ON, P1B 8H5, ☎(705) 474-6634, ☎(800) 387-0516.

Rainbow Country Travel Association: 2726 Whippoorwill Ave., Sudbury, ON, P36 1E9, ☎(705) 522-0104, ☎(800) 465-6655, ⌐(705) 522-3132.

Algoma Kinniwabi Travel Association: 553 Queen Street East, Suite 1, Sault Ste. Marie, ON, P6A 2A4, ☎(705) 254-4293, ☎(800) 263-2540,

North of Superior Tourism: 1184 Rolland Street Thunder Bay, ON, P7B 5M4, ☎(807) 626-9420 ☎(800) 265-3951.

Ontario's Sunset Country: 102 Main Street, 2nd floor, P.O. Box P9N 3X6, ☎(807) 468-5853, ☎(800) 665-7567.

Manitoulin Island

Rainbow Country Travel Association: 2726 Whippoorwill Ave., Sudbury, ON, P3G 1E9, ☎(705) 522-0104, ☎(800) 465-6655.

 EXPLORING

On the Trail of the First Explorers ★★

In 1615, French explorers Samuel de Champlain and Étienne Brûlé along with a crew of Hurons sailed up the Ottawa River, crossed Lake Nipissing and continued to Huronia, at the edge of Georgian Bay (Lake Huron). The French remained on friendly terms with the Hurons for the next two decades, during which time they travelled quite frequently to this region, thus familiarizing themselves with the entire area, all the way to Lake Superior. Colonization was, nevertheless, a slow process, and no real settlements — neither French nor English — were established here for several decades.

This route through the middle of Northern Ontario nonetheless played a major role in the province's early history, for it enabled the *coureurs des bois* (trappers) to develop lucrative trading relations with the natives. This tour follows the trail of these first explorers, through the towns of North Bay, Sudbury, Sault Ste. Marie and Thunder Bay.

Pembroke

Pembroke, a rather nondescript town located on the banks of the Ottawa River, is the first stop on your journey north. Its main attraction is the river flowing alongside it, especially the rapids, which are popular with rafting buffs (see p 429).

North Bay

Upon arriving in North Bay, you will be greeted by long, uninspiring boulevards lined with motels and large shopping centres. These streets, however, are not representative of this northern city, which boasts some lovely homes and a picturesque downtown area (Main Street between Cassell's and Fisher), which is unfortunately fighting a losing battle against local malls. The beauty of this town lies in its simplicity, its spruce little houses with their well-kept gardens, and above all in its location on magnificent Lake Nipissing. A pleasant promenade ★ studded with benches runs along the shoreline. During summer, a peaceful crowd gathers here at the end of the day to savour the last rays of the sun as it slowly disappears into the shimmering waters of the lake. Visitors who so desire can take a cruise from the town dock to French River. Local inhabitants also enjoy access to another lovely body of water, Trout Lake, which lies east of town. Not that long ago, this lake was coveted as cottage country by local well-to-do families.

Beside the tourist office, you'll see the former home of the Dionne family, a modest log house that was moved here from Callander. It now houses the **Dionne Quintuplet Museum** *($2.75; May to Oct, 9am to 5pm; Seymour St., ☎472-8480)*, which displays photographs of Cecile, Emily, Yvonne, Annette and Marie, as well as a number of their personal belongings.

Sudbury ★

Although a few trading posts were set up in this region in the early days of colonization, it wasn't until the arrival of the railroad in 1883 that Sudbury truly began to thrive. When the railroad was being built, the largest nickel deposits in the world were discovered here, along with sizeable deposits of uranium and copper, thus ushering in a period of major development for the town. The metals came from the Sudbury basin, which was probably created by the impact of a meteorite. To this day, mining plays an important role in the local economy.

The source of Sudbury's prosperity is apparent all over town. Verdant, leafy forests give way to barren, almost lunar landscapes. Over the past few years, all sorts of measures have been taken to restore some of the local greenery, but the traces left by the mining industry seem to be indelible. The town is therefore somewhat lacking in charm. Fortunately, some interesting projects have been launched to compensate for the drab scenery, and attractions such as Science North are well worth a visit.

Science North ★★ *($9.50; Jun to early Sep, 9am to 6pm; May and Oct, 9am to 5pm; Nov to Apr, 10am to 4pm; 100 Ramsey Lake, ☎522-3701)* is an unusual-looking building shaped like a giant snowflake. Its architecture is appropriate, since its goal is to familiarize the public with the mysteries of science and nature. Inside, visitors will find a whole range of small-scale, thematic exhibitions, short films and interactive and educational games intended to make often complex scientific information easy to understand. Themes such as the biosphere, the atmosphere and the geosphere are explored in a manner that will satisfy the curiosity of both the young and the not so young. The top-floor laboratories are open to all, offering a unique opportunity to experiment with a variety of natural and scientific phenomena. The centre also has an **IMAX** theatre, which presents strikingly realistic films.

ONTARIO

To top it all off, Science North boasts a lovely setting on Lake Ramsey, and a pleasant park has been laid out along the shore. Wooden footbridges run through a swampy area, offering visitors a chance to take a stroll through tall grasses inhabited by scores of birds and other little animals. Finally, you can set out on a lake cruise aboard the *Cortina ($8)*.

Big Nickel Mine ★ *(same schedule as Science North, but closed Oct to May; take Lorne St. to Big Nickel Rd., ☎522-3701)*, designed solely for the tourist industry, contains no ore and has never been worked. Although this might seem like somewhat of a let-down, a tour of the "mine" is nonetheless interesting, as visitors are lead 20 metres underground to explore the type of installations generally found in real mines. A minibus provides free transportation to and from the Science North.

Next to the mine, you'll see a giant nickel, a reminder that these 5¢ coins were once made with local nickel.

Please note: Passes are available for Science North, the IMAX theatre and Big Nickel Mine, which have teamed up in order to make it more affordable to visit all three attractions. The price is $24.95 for an adult.

The **Path of Discovery** *(from Science North, ☎1-800-461-4898)*, a guided tour of the town and its surrounding area, enables visitors to learn about the geological history of the Sudbury basin. It also leads to the Inco Mine, one of the largest producers of nickel in the world.

A few small museums display various everyday objects from the early 20th century. These places will appeal to visitors interested in local culture, but don't expect to find any treasures. It is always wise to call before stopping by.

The **Copper Cliff Museum** *(free admission; Jun to Aug, 11am to 4pm; at the corner of Balsam and Power; ☎674-3141, ext. 457)* displays a wide array of typical tools found in a miner's shack at the beginning of the century.

Manitoulin Island ★

Manitoulin Island has been inhabited by native tribes for centuries — nearly 10,000 years, according to archaeological excavations. Their presence here has not been continuous, however; in the 1700s, for reasons that are still unclear, the local natives decided to leave the island and settle farther south. Over a century later, in the 1820s, they were driven back to the island when more and more colonists began settling in southern Ontario. For years, only a handful of natives lived on this huge territory, one of the largest freshwater islands in the world, with an area 1600 square kilometres. Little by little, however, Manitoulin Island began to attract English colonists, and in the 19th century, the natives had to negotiate with British authorities about sharing their land.

The native presence is quite evident on the island, with Odawa, Potawotami and Ojibwa tribes scattered across the territory. Many villages and lakes also bear native names, such as Sheguiandah, Manitowaning and Mindemoya, which can be traced back to legends that still haunt these areas. The name Manitoulin itself refers to one such legend, according to which the island is the land of the great spirit *Gitchi Manitou*.

A peaceful island with charming little villages, picturesque hamlets and over a hundred lakes, this place will delight visitors looking for rural areas and tranquil natural surroundings, but has little to offer big-city goers. With its long, white sand beaches, hiking trails and waters abounding in fish, it is a veritable playground for outdoorsy types.

Sault Ste. Marie ★★

The Ojibwa used to call this site Batawing in reference to its location on the banks of St. Mary's River, which forms a series of tumultuous waterfalls between Lake Huron and Lake Superior. The falls *(saults)* also prompted Jacques Marquette, a Jesuit priest, to name the mission he founded here Sainte-Marie du Sault. Its strategic location at the juncture of two of the Great Lakes made it an important supply stop for fur-traders, but up until 1840, it was essentially used to store merchandise. With the opening of the Bruce Mine in the 1850s, the town truly began to flourish.

Today, life in Sault Ste. Marie centres around the iron, steel and wood industries, as well as shipping, since large numbers of vessels pass through the local locks every day. You can watch these immense ships going through the locks from an attractive promenade along St. Mary's River. This park also attracts a lot of birds, especially barnacle geese. For a closer look at the lock mechanisms, take a tour with **Locks Tour Canada** *($15.50; Norgoma Dock, ☎253-9850).*

Canada Goose

Sault Ste. Marie, or the Soo, as it is popularly known, is a delightful place. A lovely, peaceful city with long, tree-shaded streets lined with opulent, old-fashioned houses, it has a unique charm and is no doubt one of the most attractive towns in Northern Ontario. Aside from its lovely downtown area and residential neighbourhoods, which you can explore at your leisure, it has a few interesting tourist attractions, and is the starting point for a magnificent excursion to the Agawa Canyon.

The historical retrospective of the **Sault Ste. Marie Museum** *($2; Mon to Sat 9am to 4:30pm, Sun 1pm to 4:30pm; 690 Queen St. E., ☎759-7278)* offers visitors a chance to step back 10,000 years in time. It begins with the first natives to inhabit the region and continues to the 20th century. Among other things, visitors will find a reconstructed wigwam and a collection of everyday objects from early colonial times. These articles are not particularly valuable, but the place is nonetheless quite interesting.

The pretty, stone **Ermatinger House** ★ *(free admission; Jun to Sep, every day 10am to 5pm; mid-Apr to May, Mon to Fri 10am to 5pm; Oct and Nov, 1pm to 5pm; 831 Queen St. E., ☎759-5443)* was erected in 1824 by a wealthy fur-trader named Charles Oakes Ermatinger as a gift for his Ojibwa wife. Built before the town developed, it is the oldest house in northwestern Ontario. Upon entering the house, which is decorated with antiques, you will be greeted by guides in period dress,

creating the impression that you are reliving a bygone era.

The **Algoma Art Gallery** *(donation appreciated; Mon to Sat 10am to 5pm, Sun 1:30pm to 4:30pm; 10 East St., ☎949-9067)* has two rooms containing works by artists from Canada and elsewhere. The collection is small, but some of the paintings are beautiful. The gallery also presents temporary exhibits.

Roberta Bondar Park was laid out on the shores of St. Mary's River as a tribute to Canada's first female astronaut, a native of Sault Ste. Marie. Its gigantic tent (1,347 square metres) is used for all sorts of events in both summer and winter, including the Winter Carnival.

Bellevue Park stretches alongside St. Mary's River east of town. It is very popular with local residents, who come here to stroll about and look at the bison, deer and other animals in the little zoo. The park also attracts large numbers of barnacle geese, who honk up a storm, detracting somewhat from the peacefulness of the setting.

For a memorable outing in the heart of the Northern Ontario wilderness, climb aboard the Algoma train for a visit to the **Agawa Canyon** ★★★ *($53; May to Sep, every day 8am to Sep, Jan to Mar, Sat and Sun 8am; the station is located in the Station Mall, ☎946-7300).* Comfortably seated in a charming little period train, you will wind through the forest, passing along hillsides and riverbanks and taking in some strikingly beautiful scenery that transforms with the seasons, changing from an intense green in summer to orange and red hues in fall and finally, a dazzling white in winter. The train departs early in the morning and travels through the woods for over three hours before reaching its destination in the heart of the forest. Passengers then have two hours to stroll about, visit the falls or climb the hills. Afterward, you will head back to town with your head full of images of majestic landscapes. Reservations are recommended, particularly in the fall.

Nipigon

A trading post was set up here at the mouth of the Nipigon River in 1678, making this the first site on the north shore of Lake Superior to be colonized by the French. Nipigon has the advantage of being located near a fascinating natural attraction, **Red Rock** ★, a series of

ONTARIO

200 metre-high red cliffs whose colour indicates the presence of hematite.

Ouimet Canyon ★

This breathtaking canyon, which is 107 metres-deep and about 150 metres-wide, can be viewed from two thrilling wooden lookouts. Stunted arctic flora is all that can survive in the perpetually cold temperature at the bottom of the canyon and along its steep sides.

Thunder Bay ★★

Natives settled in the Thunder Bay region over 10,000 years ago. When the first Europeans arrived in the area, Ojibwa tribes were still living here. These natives never left this territory, and still make up an important portion of the population.

Judging this to be a strategic site, the French founded (Fort) Caministiquoyan here in 1679 to make it easier for merchants to trade in this region. The development of Northern Ontario was a slow process, however, and it wasn't until 1803, with the establishment of the Fort William Company, that people of European descent began settling permanently in this region. The fort soon became the hub of the fur trade, and travellers came here all the way from Montreal to purchase furs from trappers. This naturally had a positive impact on the region's growth, since more and more colonists began taking up residence here. During the 19th century, Fort William and Port Arthur developed side by side. They finally joined in 1970 to form Thunder Bay. Because of the way it was founded, the town still has two downtown areas; the southern centre is located around Victoria and Brodie Streets, and the northern centre, between Algoma, Water and Keskus Streets.

Located about a hundred kilometres from Manitoba, Thunder Bay is the last sizeable town in western Ontario. It is a unique place, boasting all the advantages of a modern, dynamic and multicultural city, yet located just a short distance from stretches of untouched wilderness, which you can explore on foot, by canoe or on skis. Thunder Bay lies on the shores of magnificent Lake Superior, to which it owes some of its prosperity. Its port, the last stop for ships on the St. Lawrence Seaway, is one of the busiest in Canada. If you go to the port, you will not only find some gigantic ships,

but also 15 grain elevators used for storage, dotting the surrounding area for several kilometres. The biggest one of all is the Saskatchewan Wheat Pool Terminal. You can see a small part of the port by strolling along the promenade near the marina, behind the tourist office.

The promenade around the marina is very pretty, but for a closer look at the impressive ships or to view the port from another angle, take a seat aboard the *MV Welcome* ★ *($12.50; 10am departure from the marina; ☎344-2512)*, which takes passengers on a tour of the marina, then follows the Kaministkwia River through town to Fort William. This pleasant excursion takes two hours (one-way), with passengers returning to the marina by bus.

Old Fort William ★★ *(Broadway Ave. S., ☎577-2327)* is a fascinating reconstruction of original Fort William as it appeared in the early 19th century. The world's largest reconstruction of a fur-trading post, it is an enchanting place to visit. The fort is made up of about forty buildings, where guides in period dress (trappers, merchants and Ojibwa Indians) recreate everyday life in the 1800s, transporting visitors two centuries back in time.

The **Thunder Bay Museum** *(free admission; 219 May St., ☎623-0801)* displays a wide variety of objects related to local history, including articles used by early settlers, military and medical instruments and a collection of native artifacts. It offers an excellent opportunity to learn more about the daily life of the first native tribes and colonists to inhabit this region.

At the east edge of town, a **statue of Terry Fox** serves as a tribute to the courage of that young Canadian hero. Suffering from cancer, to which he had already lost a leg, Fox set off on a "Marathon of Hope" across Canada to raise money for research against the disease. He started in Newfoundland and made it across part of Canada, but had to stop here.

Centennial Park lies stretched along Boulevard Lake at the northeast edge of town; pretty trails follow the water and run through the woods. This is a pleasant place for the whole family, with picnic areas and a replica of a 1910 logging camp. Canoes and pedalboats can be rented at the lovely beach nearby.

Whole families go to **Chippewa Park** *(south of Hwy 61B)*, located alongside Lake Superior, for picnics or to ride the carousels in the amusement park. Camping.

The 183 metre-high **Mount McKay Lookout ★**, stands next to Thunder Bay, in the heart of the Fort William Ojibwa reserve. From the top, you can enjoy a magnificent view of the town and its surrounding area. Native crafts are sold here as well.

Ontario is rich in **amethysts**, the official stone of the province. The deposits in the Thunder Bay region were formed several million years ago by the intrusion of a boiling, silica-rich liquid into the granite here. As it cooled, the liquid formed crystals of this semi-precious stone, which is a type of quartz. You can tour the **Thunder Bay Amethyst Mine Panorama** *($1; mid-May to Oct 10am to 7pm; 58 km east of Thunder Bay, East Loon Rd.; 807-622-6908)* and the **Pearl Lake Amethyst Mines** *(free admission; 30 km east of Thunder Bay; May to Oct 9am to 6pm, ☎807-983-2047)*, and even rent tools so that you can chip off a few pieces for yourself.

Kenora

Kenora is located at the western edge of Ontario, a few kilometres from the Manitoba border. In the 19th century, both provinces tried to lay claim to this part of the territory. Ontario won out, and was officially granted the land in 1892. Kenora wasn't actually founded until 1905, with the union of three small municipalities, Keewatin, Norman and Rat Portage. Its name was formed by combining the first two letters of these three names (Ke-No-Ra).

The Kenora region is rich in natural resources, especially wood. The pulp and paper industry are thus mainstays of the local economy. The local lakes and forests have also led to the development of another prosperous industry, tourism, since this is a true paradise for fishing and hunting, not to mention lovely excursions in the great outdoors, on the shores of Lake of the Woods.

 OUTDOORS

Northern Ontario, a forest kingdom ruled by majestic evergreens, is a wonderful place to enjoy the outdoors — not only for intrepid explorers ready to set out for days into the heart of this imposing vegetation, but also for more timid nature-lovers looking for some easy trails to follow. Whether you're interested in hiking or cross-country trails or whether you would rather ride down tumultuous rivers in a canoe like the region's first explorers, the parks in this region have something for everyone with a taste for fresh air and vast expanses of wilderness.

Samuel de Champlain Park ★ *(Hwy 17, between Mattawa and North Bay, ☎705-744-2276)* lies along the banks of the Mattawa River, which early colonists used as a fur-trading route to travel deeper into Ontario, toward the Great Lakes. In memory of these explorers, the **Voyageur Museum** houses a small collection of objects related to their way of life, including an interesting replica of the kind of birch-bark canoe they used.

Most sports activities revolve around the Mattawa River, which is the nerve centre of the park. Visitors interested in hiking through the forest will find trails leading to the river and running alongside it for a fair distance, while those who know a bit about canoeing can paddle to their heart's content, either for a short trip or for a real adventure of several days. Backcountry campsites have been cleared throughout the park, which also has three campgrounds.

Canoes can be rented in North Bay at **Bob's Bait**: Trout Lake Rd., ☎705-472-7479.

To get to the little town of Killarney, take Highway 63, which runs alongside lovely **Killarney Park ★★** *(☎705-287-2800)*. This vast stretch of untouched wilderness extends into Georgian Bay and is strewn with scores of crystal-clear rivers and lakes, making it a canoeist's paradise. Exploring the park offers a chance to discover the magical landscapes that characterize the Canadian Shield, where lakes and rivers and birch and pine forests meet the cliffs of the La Cloche Mountains. The park has something for everyone, whether you want to canoe down a river with stretches of turbulent water or whether you prefer to hike or ski along a trail through the woods. The sites at the campground are equipped with electricity, and a number of other spots have been cleared for wilderness camping. You can rent all the necessary equipment for a canoe trip in the little village of Killarney.

Highway 17 runs through **Lake Superior Provincial Park ★★** *(after Sault Ste. Marie on Hwy 17, ☎705-856-2284)*, which covers some 80 kilometres of Lake Superior shoreline. A vast expanse of greenery, it boasts several lovely beaches, as well as hiking trails that lead deep into the heart of the forest that blankets part of its territory. The park also contains petroglyphs carved by Ojibwa Indians over 9,000 years ago; the best place to see them is on Agawa Rock. Those wishing to spend a few days in the park can set up camp at the Agawa Bay or Interior campground *(reservations: P.O. Box 1160, P0S 1K0, ☎705-856-2284)*.

Aside from a few trails, no road leads through **Pukaskwa National Park ★** *(take the 17 to Rte. 627, a few kilometres before Marathon; ☎807-229-0801)*, which is still more or less untouched. The magnificent **Coastal Hiking Trail ★★** stretches nearly 60 kilometres and offers some breathtakingly beautiful panoramic views. The park covers 1,878 square kilometres and is scored with rivers that are perfect for canoeing and kayaking. The park also protects a vast stretch of boreal forest. The cold temperatures generated by the lake affect the vegetation here; spruce is predominant in some areas, while only alpine species are able to survive in others. For some interesting information on the local vegetation, stop by the **Hattie Cove Interpretive Centre**, which is the starting point for a number of canoe routes. Camping.

Right near Thunder Bay, on Lake Superior, **Sleeping Giant Park ★** *(take Hwy 17 then turn onto Rte. 587)* protects a rocky peninsula, which was supposedly created by none other than Nanibijou, the "Great Spirit" of the Ojibwa Indians. Legend has it that Nanibijou showed the Ojibwa the location of a rich silver mine in order to reward them for their loyalty. He insisted, however, that the existence of the mine remain a secret from the white man; otherwise he would turn into stone and let them all perish. Unfortunately, the secret leaked out. All the men in the tribe were swallowed up by the waters of Lake Superior, and Nanibijou fell asleep and metamorphosed into a rocky headland, hence the name of the peninsula. Whether you believe the legend or not, there really is a silver mine here. Located about 40 kilometres from Thunder Bay, the park is an excellent place to enjoy the region's striking natural beauty. Its trails lead through enchanting landscapes and offer some splendid **views ★★** of the lake. The park also has some extremely pleasant beaches, which are occasionally overrun by local townspeople on hot summer days. Finally, visitors are welcome to camp here as well *(reservations. ☎807-933-4332)*. In winter, when the area is blanketed with snow, about 40 kilometres of cross-country trails crisscross this magnificent territory.

Quetico Park ★ *(take Hwy 11 from Shabaqua Corners, ☎807-597-2735)* covers a huge expanse of land along the Minnesota border. Its countless lakes and rivers have made it a big favourite with Ontarian canoeists. It is crisscrossed by nearly 1,500 kilometres of canoe routes, where you can encounter a variety of animal species. There are also a number of hiking trails for those who prefer walking.

Canoes can be rented at **Quetico North Tourist Services**: P.O. Box 100, Atikokan, P0T 1C0, ☎807-929-3561.

Lake of the Woods Provincial Park ★ *(take the 71 from Bergland, south of Kenora, then pick up the 600, ☎807-488-5531)* encompasses the magnificent lake after which it was named. This vast stretch of water has 105,000 kilometres of shoreline and attracts some remarkable avian species. With a little luck, you might spot a group of white pelicans or a majestic bald eagle. If the mood strikes you, you can take a walk on one of the many hiking trails along the shore or set out on the water to see a few of the 15,000 islands that stud the lake.

White Pelican

Rafting

In the **Pembroke** area, thrill-seekers can brave the turbulent waters of the Ottawa and Petawawa Rivers aboard a rubber raft. The ride is especially exciting during the spring thaw, when the waters are at their highest. Rafting excursions are organized by a number of different outfits, including:

Esprit Rafting Adventures: P.O. Box 463, K8A 6X7, ☎819-683-3241, ≈819-683-3641,

Owl Rafting: P.O. Box 29, Foresters Falls, K0J 1V0, ☎613-646-2263, ☎800-461-RAFT, ≈646-2307.

River Run: P.O. Box 179, Beachburg, K0J 1C0, ☎613-646-2501 or ☎800-267-8504.

Wilderness Tour: P.O. Box 89, Beachburg, K0J 1C0, ☎613-646-2291 or ☎800-267-9166.

 Hunting and Fishing

Salmon, trout, perch and muskie are just a few of the fish you can catch in the lakes and rivers of Northern Ontario. Some places are especially renowned, including Lake Nipissing and Trout Lake, in **North Bay**, the numerous lakes in **Missinaibi Park** *(north of Chapleau)*, which protects the river of the same name; **Lake of the Woods** *(south of Kenora, in Bergland)* and **Kettle Lake** *(32 km northwest of Timmins, Hwy 101,* ☎705-363-3511)*. **Manitoulin Island** is also very popular for fishing, since some good catches, including salmon, can be made off its shores.

A few parks in Northern Ontario also have something to offer hunting fans. Black bear, deer and moose are a few of the animals hunters can hope to bag, depending on the region. Some parts of northern Ontario, including the **Hearst** and **Kenora** areas, are reputed to be good for hunting.

Of course, permits are required for both hunting and fishing. To apply for one, or to obtain information regarding regulations, you can write to:

Ontario Ministry of Natural Resources: Information Centre, MacDonald Building, Office M1-73, 900 Bay Street, Toronto, M7A 2C1, ☎416-314-1177 (fishing), ☎416-314-2225 (hunting).

 Snowmobiling

A network of about 33,000 kilometres of snowmobile trails winds its way across the immense territory of Northern Ontario. These trails, which are interconnected, enable snowmobilers to travel from town to town, reach small villages and ride through the snow-covered forest, all the while enjoying the majestic scenery around them. To plan a snowmobile trip or to obtain further information, call ☎800-263-7533.

 ACCOMMODATIONS

Pembroke

Pembroke is a good place to stop along the Ottawa River, since there are several comfortable, reasonably priced hotels in town. These places don't have the charm of historic inns, but are perfectly acceptable for an overnight stay.

On your way into town, you are sure to notice the **Forest Lea Inn** *($80; ≡, ℜ; 1433 Pembroke St. E., K8A 7A5,* ☎613-732-9981)*, which, like many North American hotels, is surrounded by a parking lot. The place is nonetheless attractive, and its 28 well laid-out rooms meet modern standards of comfort.

North Bay

You'll have no trouble finding a place to stay in North Bay, which is the largest town in the region and has all sorts of hotels and motels.

The **Days Inn** *($80; ≡, ⌂; 255 McIntyre St. W., P1B 2Y9,* ☎474-4470)* is one of the few hotels in downtown North Bay. The building looks somewhat austere, but the rooms are perfectly adequate.

The hotels and motels lining Lakeshore Drive are perfect for visitors who have a car and are planning to spend a few days in town. One good choice is the **Venture Inn** *($79 bkfst incl.;*

ONTARIO

≡, ✕, ₺; *718 Lakeshore Dr., P1A 2G4,* ☎*472-7171 or 800-387-3933,* ⇒*472-8276),* since its well-kept rooms have a certain charm about them and it's located just steps away from the beaches on Lake Nipissing.

The nearby **Sunset Motel Park and Cottages** *($80;* ⊛, △, ℜ, ✕; *641 Lakeshore Dr., P1A 2E9,* ☎*472-8370 or 800-463-8370,* ⇒*476-5647)* has charmingly decorated rooms and little cottages with fireplaces, making for a cozy atmosphere. It is also located just a stone's throw away from Lake Nipissing and Sunset Beach.

Sudbury

There is no youth hostel or charming B&B in Sudbury, but several international hotel chains are represented here, so comfortable accommodation is readily available. One option is the Sheraton.

The various hotels near the Science North complex each seem to be trying to outdo the other by offering as many amenities as possible and attractive modern rooms. The **Travelodge** *($80;* ≡, ≈, ⊛, ⅖, ✕; *1401 Paris St., P3E 3B6,* ☎*522-1100 or 1-800-578-7878,* ⇒*522-1668)* offers package deals including accommodation and tickets to Science North. Guests also enjoy the use of an indoor swimming pool.

Another option is to stay in one of the hotels along Regent Street. You won't find any charming inns here, but some of the places have decent rooms. One of these is the **Venture Inn** *($79;* ≡, ℜ; *1956 Regent St., P3E 3Z9,* ☎*522-7600 or 1-800-387-3933,* ⇒*522-7648),* which is located near the highway, making it a convenient place to stop for the night.

Right nearby stands the **Sheraton** *($109;* ≡, ≈, △, ⊛, ℜ, ⅖; *1696 Regent St., P3E 3Z8,* ☎*522-3000 or 1-800-325-3535,* ⇒*522-8067),* a renowned establishment with lovely rooms and all sorts of amenities, including a pool and a sauna.

Manitoulin Island

There aren't any big hotel complexes on Manitoulin Island, nor are any major North American chains represented here. You will find a number of B&Bs and campgrounds, however.

Ruth's Bed and Breakfast *($50 bkfst incl.; 73 Campbell St. W., Little Current, POP 1K0,* ☎*368-3891)* is a good place to keep in mind, since it has pretty rooms and a central location in charming Little Current.

The **Rockgarden Terrace Resort** *($80; R.R.1, Spring Bay, POP 2B0,* ☎*377-4652)* offers comfortable rooms in a long building at the top of a cliff overlooking lovely Lake Mindemoya. Pretty, rustic cabins are available for those who want a little more space and privacy.

Sault Ste. Marie

There are a few inexpensive places to stay in town; one of the cheapest is the **Algonquin Hotel** *($23; 864 Queen St. E., P6A 2B4,* ☎*253-2311),* which is that much more of a bargain, since the rooms, albeit modest, are well-kept, and the place is conveniently located near the bus terminal.

A bit out of the way, but nonetheless attractively located on the banks of St. Mary's River, the local **Holiday Inn** *($114;* ≡, ≈, ℜ, △, ⊛, ⅖, ✕; *208 St. Mary's River Dr., P6A 5V4,* ☎*949-0611 or 1-800-HOLIDAY,* ⇒*945-6973),* like all the others across North America, offers functional rooms designed to meet travellers' needs. Guests also enjoy the use of a workout room.

Thunder Bay

The last major town in northern Ontario, Thunder Bay is a lovely place with a wide range of accommodations.

Located in a delightfully peaceful setting, the **Longhouse Village** *($16; R.R.13, 1594 Lakeshore Dr., P7B 5E4,* ☎*807-983-2042)* is actually a youth hostel with dormitories — the perfect place for visitors looking for a friendly atmosphere. If you have a tent, you can opt for one of the campsites instead.

On Arthur Street, you will find a good selection of modern hotels and motels, whose fully equipped rooms are perfect for anyone planning to spend a few days in town. We especially recommend the **Victoria Inn** *($80; 555 Arthur St. W.,* ☎*807-577-8481,* ⇒*475-8961),* whose relatively new rooms are well kept, and the **Best Western Crossroad Motor Inn** *($78;*

655 Arthur St. W., ☎807-577-4241), which has simple, but decent rooms.

The **White Fox Inn** *($130 brkst incl.; 1345 Mountain Rd., ☎807-577-FOXX or 1-800-603-FOXX)* is one of those B&Bs that you will remember for a long time. A relaxing atmosphere pervades the rooms, each of which is tastefully decorated with a different theme.

 RESTAURANTS

North Bay

El Greco *($$; 344 Algonquin, ☎474-3373)* has a simple decor and a clientele of all different ages. The menu, made up mainly of spaghetti and lasagna, is hardly original, but the food is consistently good. Part of what makes this place so popular is its friendly, relaxed atmosphere.

If you're looking for something a little dressier, **Churchill's** *($$$; 631 Lakeshore Dr., ☎476-7777)* is just the place. It serves what just may be the best prime rib in town.

The **Kabuki House** *($$$; 349 Main St. W., ☎495-0999)* is a charmingly decorated little place that serves succulent Japanese specialties like *sukiyaki* in a romantic atmosphere. A delicious change from the usual burgers and fries.

Sudbury

A modest-looking little house in downtown Sudbury, **Vesta Pasta** *($$; 49 Elgin, ☎674-4010)* is one of those charming places that are such a pleasure to discover. Not only does it have an adorable dining room, but it also serves delectable Italian cuisine. You can't go wrong on the menu; the veal and pasta dishes are all masterfully prepared.

Manitoulin Island

The **Old English Pantry** *($; Little Current, ☎368-3341)* is a relaxed, inviting place to linger over a cup of tea and scones.

The **School House** *($$; 46 McNiven St., Providence Bay, ☎377-4055)*, as its name suggests, is a charming old country school house. The dining room, which only has about twenty tables, is delightful and the food, delicious, making for a thoroughly enjoyable dining experience. The menu, which changes with the seasons, includes a number of fish dishes.

Sault Ste. Marie

A tiny house ingeniously decorated in the style of the 1960s, **Mr. B's** *($; 76 East St., ☎942-9999)* offers a unique atmosphere in which to enjoy a burger or a pizza.

For fine dining in a cozy restaurant with an inviting decor, try the **Thymely Manner** *($$$; 531 Albert St., ☎759-3252)*, which serves succulent French cuisine.

Thunder Bay

You can enjoy a good meal in a relaxed atmosphere at the **Port Arthur Brasserie and Brew Pub** *($; 901 Red River Rd., ☎767-4415)*.

The **Hoito Restaurant** *($$; 288 Bay St., ☎344-2922)* is well-known in Thunder Bay for its delicious, innovative cuisine. What makes the menu unique is an ingenious blend of Finnish and Canadian culinary traditions. The crêpes on the breakfast menu are truly delectable.

The atmosphere at some restaurants is so romantic that you can't help but have a lovely evening. This is true of **Armando Fine Italian Cuisine** *($$$)*, the perfect place to savour excellent Italian cuisine to the soothing sounds of violin music.

The restaurant at the **White Fox Inn** *($$$; take Hwy 61 to 1345 Mountain Rd., ☎577-FOXX)*, located just outside town, is worth the detour. Guests enjoy excellent food and a refined atmosphere, and the wine list will statisfy even the most demanding connoisseurs.

ONTARIO

ENTERTAINMENT

Festivals and Cultural Events

Bars and Nightclubs

North Bay

The **Lion's Heart Pub** *(147 Worthington E., ☎474-1772)* is a friendly little English pub, where you can wash down some munchies with an imported beer.

Sudbury

Pat and Mario's *(1463 LaSalle, ☎560-2500)* restaurant is known for its Italian cuisine, but its bar also attracts quite a crowd in the evening, and is a good place for a fun night out.

Sault Ste. Marie

The **Brickyard** *(714 Queen St. E.)* is one of the Soo's hot spots. Set up inside a pretty red brick house, it offers the perfect atmosphere for chatting with friends over a beer.

Thunder Bay

The **Port Arthur Brasserie and Brew Pub** *(901 Red River Rd., ☎767-4415)* is a pleasant place with an interesting selection of imported beer. Things pick up considerably during the summer when everyone heads outside on to the pretty terrace.

Merlin's Bistro and Boutiques *(127 May St., ☎622-3445)* is an engaging spot for a quiet evening out and a drink or two.

North Bay

The **Arts Centre** *(at the corner of Main and Wyld)* often hosts entertaining shows.

The **Winter Carnival**, held every year at the beginning of February, is an opportunity to enjoy a variety of sports activities.

Sudbury

The **Sudbury Theatre Centre** *(☎674-8381)* presents plays all year round.

Manitoulin Island

Every year, for the first few days of August, native families gather at the Wikwemigong reserve for a **Powwow**, during which numerous ceremonies and dances are performed.

Sault Ste. Marie

The **Bon Soo Winter Carnival**, held every year in late January and early February, livens up the cold winter days with all sorts of sports activities.

 ## SHOPPING

North Bay

North Western *(440 Wyld)* sells lovely native handicrafts.

Manitoulin Island

The **Ten Mile Point Trading Post** *(1651 SW 84th Ave., Sheguiandah)* has a large selection of beautiful native handicrafts.

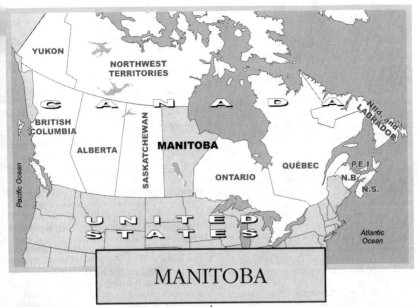

MANITOBA

Mention the word Manitoba and two images swiftly come to mind: professional hockey's Winnipeg Jets, who don't even reside here anymore, and polar bears — which certainly do. The popular impression of this place seems to be that it is mostly a place for passing through. But in fact, visitors have been coming to Manitoba — and staying — for more than a century, swelling its capital city of Winnipeg into the Canada's fourth-largest city and creating a surprising mix of immigrant culture more diverse than anything else between Vancouver and Toronto.

It did not always appear this would be so. In the beginning, the province consisted of a few aboriginal groups. It was they who gave the province its name: Manitou was chief among the spirits of the native religion, and the rapids of Lake Manitoba were believed to be his voice.

Once the English and French arrived, however, the story of Manitoba swiftly became the story of a running feud between two rival fur-trading companies: the English-owned Hudson's Bay Company on the one hand and the French-Indian North West Company — which sprung up later and, for a time, successfully out-competed the British — on the other.

The French-Canadian explorer Pierre de la Vérendrye made quite a mark in this regard. Vérendrye was the first European to penetrate the grasslands of Manitoba; his fur-trading posts established populations in what would eventually become the communities of Dauphin, La Pas, Selkirk and Portage la Prairie. This French influence is still pervasive today; in fact, the eastern Winnipeg suburb of St. Boniface is the largest French settlement in Canada outside of Québec.

The Métis made up a considerable part of this French-speaking population. The descendants of French trappers and natives, the French-speaking and Catholic Métis lived on the Red River and Assiniboine settlements, which were annexed to Canada in 1869. Fearing for their language, education and religious rights they were lead by Louis Riel in their pursuit of responsible government for the territory. What little they were granted was slowly chipped away at, leading settlers, both white and Métis, to set up their own provisional government. The outrage over the trial and execution of Ontarian Thomas Scott for defying the authority of said government forced Riel into exile in the United States. He did return to Canada, to Saskatchewan this time, to continue his fight. Riel, the man who might have been the first Premier of Manitoba, was executed for treason in 1885 and has been seen as a martyr by many ever since.

There are also considerable Ukrainian and Mennonite influences in Manitoba, and — surprisingly, the province is home to a sizeable immigrant population of Icelanders. The beginning of this influx can be precisely timed:

in 1875 a string of volcanic eruptions drove Icelanders to North America in search of another home. Many of them settled in eastern Manitoba, on the shores of Lakes Winnipeg and Manitoba, where they traded in their skills at saltwater fishing for the taking of whitefish. Manitobans have gone to great pains to preserve all these immigrants' stories, keeping their history alive in numerous museums and historic parks.

It's certainly true that the southern portion of the province is level, flattened by great glaciers during the most recent Ice Age. Where thousands of square miles of uninterrupted tallgrass prairie once rolled under the press of the wind, today colourful fields of hard wheat, flax, canola and sunflowers thrive. In wet places, thousands of pocket marshes, complete with full complements of resident and migrating waterfowl, replace the fields.

But whatever Manitoba may lack in topography, it makes up for with fertile farmland and enormous lakes that are home to countless birds. And, in fact, only about 40 percent of the province is flat. Most of the rest is comprised of hills and waterways carved out of the Canadian Shield, a massive pavement of hard ancient rock rimming Hudson Bay that surfaces most obviously here and in northern Ontario. This land is shot through with deep pine forests, cliffs, and lakes; it's not unusual to see elk, caribou or bears in the right places.

In the sparsely populated far north, taiga become predominant and the wildlife grows more spectacular still, as the luminous sub-Arctic summers, with their unique light, are filled with white whales and polar bears.

 FINDING YOUR WAY AROUND

By Plane

Winnipeg's airport is situated surprisingly close to the downtown area, only about five kilometres away.

Three major airlines handle traffic from both coasts: **Air Canada** *(2000 Wellington Ave., ☎943-9361)*, **Air Manitoba** *(☎ 783-2333)* and **Canadian Airlines** *(570 Ferry Rd., ☎632-1250)* are all located inside the airport complex.

By Bus

Greyhound Canada *(☎1-800-661-8747)* capably serves the major towns and cities. In Winnipeg, its terminal is located at the corner of Portage Avenue and Colony Street.

By Train

VIARail's *(☎1-800-561-8630 from western Canada)* cross-country Canadian service passes through the province, usually stopping in Winnipeg around 5pm (westbound) or 1:50pm (eastbound); if the train's on time, it can be an excellent way to arrive in Winnipeg before the dinner hour. Winnipeg's grand **Union Station** *(☎944-8780)*, located right in the centre of downtown at the busy crossing of Broadway and Main Street, is the largest station in Manitoba and the usual stopping point.

Smaller stations are located in Brandon, Portage la Prairie and other towns roughly parallel to the TransCanada Highway.

Public Transportation

Winnipeg Transit *(☎986-5054)*, located in an underground facility at the corner of Portage and Main, runs a good bus system around the city; rides cost $1.35, less if purchased in bulk-ticket blocks.

The city also maintains a transit information line *(☎986-5700)*.

Getting to Northern Manitoba

Special arrangements are required to reach far northern Manitoba. VIARail runs regular train service from Winnipeg to Churchill three times each week, taking a full day and two nights each way to get there. **Canadian Airlines** and its partner **Calm Air** *(☎632-1250)* operate regularly scheduled flights from Winnipeg each weekday year-round; in autumn, during polar bear season, there are additional flights on weekends. Once in Churchill, a variety of charter air and bus services can be hired for excursions out onto the tundra.

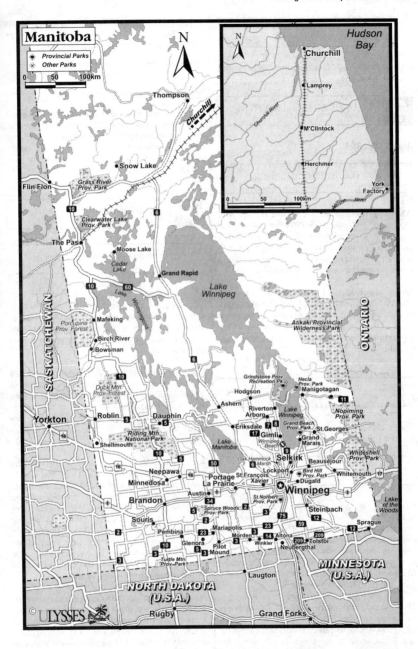

Manitoba

Provincial Parks
Other Parks

0   50   100km

Thompson

Churchill

Hudson Bay

N

Churchill

Lamprey

M'Clintock

Herchmer

Churchill River

York Factory

0   50   100km

Nelson River

Snow Lake

Grass River Prov. Park

Flin Flon

Clearwater Lake Prov. Park

The Pas

Moose Lake

Cedar Lake

Grand Rapid

Lake Winnipeg

Porcupine Prov. Forest

Mafeking

Birch River

Bowsman

Lake Winnipegosis

SASKATCHEWAN

ONTARIO

Atikaki Provincial Wilderness Park

Duck Mtn. Prov. Forest

Yorkton

Roblin

Dauphin

Riding Mtn. National Park

Shellmouth

Lake Manitoba

Grindstone Prov. Recreation Pk.

Hecla Prov. Park

Manigotagan

Hodgson

Ashern

Riverton

Arborg

Lake Winnipeg

Eriksdale

Gimli

Winnipeg Beach

Grand Beach Prov. Park

St.Georges

Grand Marais

Nopiming Prov. Park

Neepawa

Minnedosa

Brandon

Souris

Oak Hammock Marsh

Portage La Prairie

St.François Xavier

Austin

Lockport

Selkirk

Beausejour

Bird Hill Prov. Park

Dugald

Whitemouth

Whiteshell Prov. Park

Winnipeg

St.Norbert Prov. Park

Spruce Woods Prov. Park

Steinbach

Lake of the Woods

Pembina

Mariapolis

Glenora

Pilot Mound

Morden

Winkler

Altona

Neubergthal

Tolstoi

Sprague

Tuttle Mtn. Prov.Park

Laugton

MINNESOTA (U.S.A.)

NORTH DAKOTA (U.S.A.)

Rugby

Grand Forks

© ULYSSES

Taxis

Unicity (☎947-6611) is ubiquitous and speedy around Winnipeg.

 PRACTICAL INFORMATION

Area Code: 204.

Tourist Information

Winnipeg Tourism (320-25 Forks Market Rd., Winnipeg, ☎1-800-665-0204 or 943-1970) runs a year-round information centre in the Johnson Terminal, beside The Forks Market. It is open weekdays all year, and seven days a week during the summer months.

The **Manitoba Travel Ideas Centre** (☎945-1715), also beside The Forks Market, is open year round and longer hours. In other parts of the province, tourism office hours vary a great deal, but the larger ones are open year round.

Post Office

The main **post office** (266 Graham St.) is located right downtown.

Safety

Manitoba is generally very safe overall, although parts of downtown Winnipeg do experience car break-ins. The city's police department maintains 17 stations in six districts around the city; dial **911** for emergencies. There is also a **Royal Canadian Mounted Police** detachment (1901 Portage Ave., ☎983-5420) in the city.

The **Canadian Automobile Association** maintains offices in the province's most populous areas, offering roadside assistance and information to members. In Winnipeg, its offices are located at 870 Empress Street (☎987-6161), 501 St. Anns Road (☎987-6202) and 1353 McPhillips Street (☎987-6226). In Brandon, the CAA office is located at 20-1300 18th Street (☎727-1394); in Altona, it's at 61 Second Avenue NE (☎324-8474).

Climate

Summers are warm and dry. Winter, however, can bring dangerously low temperatures and blinding snowstorms; temperatures rarely rise above freezing during this time. As such, visitors should take careful precautions. For updated weather forecast information in Winnipeg, call 983-2050.

 EXPLORING

Downtown Winnipeg ★★

Manitoba boasts the largest city on the prairies, Winnipeg, a bona fide metropolis of more than 600,000 rising improbably from the plains at the convergence of three rivers, and the likely starting point for most visitors' journeys around the province.

The city was settled by a Scotsman named Thomas Douglas, 5th Earl of Selkirk, as a 187,000-square-kilometre settlement called the Red River Colony (a monument at the end of Alexander Avenue marks the spot). Douglas was an emissary of the Hudson's Bay Company.

All roads in Winnipeg seem to lead to **The Forks ★**, and they always have: this fertile confluence of the Red and Assiniboine rivers was the original camping ground of the indigenous peoples, and later the base camp for the North West Company, the area's original fur-trapping concern. The company's headquarters still stand across a busy street from the original site. Today, however, The Forks is synonymous with the covered market of the same name.

Inside, dozens of stalls house purveyors of everything from fresh fish, candy and East-Indian food to frozen yogurt and handmade jewellery. There's even a psychic. Future plans call for the addition of an amusement park and restaurants on the property in place of some green space, but for now it's a quiet introduction to the city's impressive diversity.

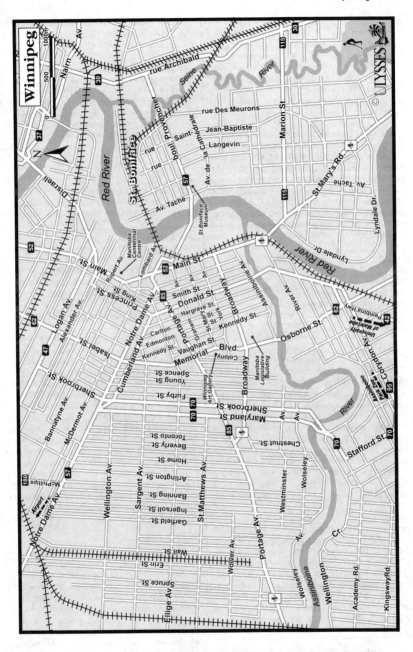

In the adjacent Johnson Terminal, a former rail station, the city's tourism office dispenses plenty of useful information. The **Manitoba Travel Idea Centre** ★ is short on information but long on inspiration, especially for kids, who love the intriguing (if strangely juxtaposed) dioramas. The Terminal also contains more stores, coffee shops and several small sports museums.

In the same complex but a different building is the **Manitoba Children's Museum** ★★★ (*$4; 45 Forks Market Rd., ☎956-1888*), the only children's museum in western Canada. The building was once a railway facility, containing an engine house and train repair shops as well as a blacksmith's shop. Today, there's a whimsical hand at work, creating such displays as a fully functioning television studio and a diesel engine from the 1950s.

Adjacent to the Forks complex and facing downtown sits **Union Station** ★, designed by the same team of architects that designed Grand Central Station in New York City. The station features a huge dome plastered inside in pink and white and arching semilunar windows. Walls are faced with the famous Tyndall limestone, mined nearby in Manitoba.

It's only a few blocks west up Assiniboine Street or along the river to Manitoba's **Legislative Building** ★★★ (*450 Broadway, ☎945-5813*). This is where the province's parliamentary business is taken care of, and it's an impressive property, full of interesting touches such as railways made of stone embedded with fossils, two bronze bisons, a statue of Cartier and so on. Up top, the dome is capped with the four-metre tall Golden Boy, a French sculpture of a boy's figure toting a sheaf of wheat underneath one arm and extending a torch toward the sky with the other.

Just down Assiniboine Avenue, **Dalnavert** ★ (*$3; Mar to May, noon to 5pm; Jun to Aug, 10am to 6pm; Sep to Dec, noon to 5pm; 61 Carlton St., ☎943-2835*) is an old brick Queen-Anne-Revival-style home built for Sir Hugh John Macdonald, former Premier of Manitoba. Its interest lies mainly in its period furnishings, and in the fact that it was among the very first homes in the city to be built with such amenities as indoor plumbing.

The **Exchange District** ★★★, close to downtown, is Winnipeg's former warehouse district — only today the smart industrial buildings have been given fresh coats of paint and new occupants such as print shops, bookstores, theatre companies and the like.

Some of the most striking buildings can be found by walking in the area of Albert Street and Notre Dame Avenue. The **Paris Building** (*269 Portage Ave.*) features many architectural flourishes such as scrolls, urns, Cupid figurines and other ornamental terracotta work. The nearby **Birks Building**, across Portage (*at Smith St. and Portage Ave.*) displays an Egyptian mosaic.

Around the corner, away from the busy traffic of Portage, the **Alexander Block** (*78-86 Albert St.*) was the first Edwardian-style construction in the neighbourhood and the only residence built here in that style; it was once a businessman's home. Finally, a few paces up Albert, the spectacular **Notre Dame Chambers** (*213 Notre Dame Ave.*), also known as the Electric Railway Chambers Building, is a terracotta, arch-topped building lit brightly at night with some 6,000 white lights.

The city's finest museums aren't far at all from the Exchange District. Located within a complex of science attractions in the same downtown building, the **Manitoba Museum of Man and Nature** ★★★ (*$4, mid-may to early Sep 10am to 6pm; rest of the year, Tue to Fri 10am to 4pm, Sat, Sun, Mon and holidays 10am to 5pm; 190 Rupert Ave., ☎956-2830*), is Winnipeg's showcase museum, a tour-de-force emphasizing natural history. Separate galleries teach the visitor about the province's geology, grasslands ecology, Arctic ecology — a polar bear diorama is the star here — and native history. Other special exhibit rooms describe the voyage of the English ship the *Nonsuch* (which established the Hudson's Bay Company's presence in western Canada in 1670) and the construction of a railroad to the far northern Manitoba port town of Churchill.

The tour ends with a very popular and well-designed two-story recreation of late-1800s downtown Winnipeg, including a cobbler, chapel, movie theatre and much more. Museum officials are excited about a new display that will open shortly, an impressive showing of Hudson's Bay Company items, but even before it arrives this museum is still a must-see. Other attractions on the lower floor of the same building include a **Planetarium** (*$3.50; same hours as museum; ☎943-3142*) and a **Science Centre** (*same hours as museum; $3.50*).

Nearby, the **Ukrainian Cultural and Educational Centre** ★★ *(free; Tue to Sat 10am to 4pm, Sun 2pm to 5pm; 184 Alexander Ave. E., ☎942-0218)*, also known as **Oseredok**, houses a number of Ukrainian-related services and exhibits under one roof, including a library, art gallery, gift shop and outreach program offices. The museum, located on the fifth floor, shows typical Ukrainian-decorated Easter eggs and other folk arts such as carving and embroidery.

The **Winnipeg Art Gallery** ★★★ *($3, Tue, Thu, Sat, Sun 11am to 5pm; Wed 11am to 9pm; summer Tue, Thu, Sat, Sun 10am to 5pm; Wed 10am to 9pm; 300 Memorial Boulevard, ☎786-6641)* is best known for its vast collection of Inuit art and sculptures. Founded in 1912, the museum boasts everything from 16th-century Flemish tapestry to modern art; it is particularly strong on Canadian artists, decorative porcelains and silver, and collections acquired from the Federal Department of Indian and Northern Affairs and the Hudson's Bay Company. Native works are exhibited in changing programs on the mezzanine level.

In the city's north end, on outer Broadway, the **Ukrainian Orthodox Church** ★★ is one of the city's most distinctive landmarks, decked in handsome burgundy and gold paint and possessing the trademark Ukrainian dome.

St. Boniface

Just across the Red River in St. Boniface, the unmistakable walls of the **St. Boniface Basilica** ★★★ are a must-see. The walls are all that remain of the church, which burned in 1968, but they are still mighty impressive. This was actually the fourth cathedral to stand on this spot. No wonder it remains a kind of shrine for Canada's largest French-speaking population outside of Quebec. The giant circular opening in the stone once contained a giant roseate stained-glass window.

Louis Riel's grave is marked by a simple red stone on the front lawn that belies the famous man who lies beneath it. Other stones on the lawn mark the graves of French settlers and Métis such as Chief One Arrow. There's also a glorious view of the river and the city skyline from this vantage point.

Next door, the **St. Boniface Museum** ★★ *($2; mid-May 17 to early Oct, 9am to 5pm, weekends 10am to 5pm; mid-Jun, to early Sept, Sun to Thu 10am to 8pm; early Oct to mid-May, weekdays only 9am to 5pm; 484 Tache Ave., St. Boniface; ☎237-4500)* was built in 1846 as a convent and tells a number of fascinating stories about the city's French roots; it is the oldest building in Winnipeg and its largest log structure. Of particular note is the tale of the four Grey Nuns (Les Soeurs Grises) who founded the convent — they travelled some 2,400 kilometres by canoe from Montreal, taking nearly two full months to accomplish the arduous journey.

Other highlights in the museum include holy water vessels and church objects, and a papier mâché Virgin Mary, decked in a blue shawl — western Canada's oldest statue. It was crafted by the artistic Sister Lagrave, one of the original Grey Nuns.

East of St. Boniface, on the edge of the city, sits the ultra-modern **Royal Canadian Mint** ★★ *($2; May to Aug, Mon to Fri, 9am to 5pm; 520 Lagimodiére Boulevard, ☎257-3359)*, the place where all of Canada's circulation coinage is minted. Tours and observation areas give insight into the process.

Greater Winnipeg

South of the Assiniboine River but easily reached via pedestrian walkways and Maryland Street, **Osborne Village** is acknowledged as the city's hippest address. It's more like a college campus than a throwback to the sixties, however; restaurants are everywhere. There are few buildings of architectural interest save the **Gas Station Theatre** ★ *(445 River Ave.)*, which presents plays and hosts visiting events such as a clown convention.

Assiniboine Park ★★ *(☎986-6921)* is a popular walking and cycling destination. Its extensive tree-lined paths wind along the river of the same name, and a steam train known as the **Prairie Dog Central** *(☎832-5259)* leaves for a 60-kilometre tour of the Winnipeg area twice each Sunday during summertime.

The park's most popular feature is the **Assiniboine Park Zoo** ★★★ *($3; Apr to mid-Oct 15, every day 10am to 8pm, Oct 15 to Mar, every day 10am to 6pm; ☎986-6921)*. More than 1,200 animals live here, including Russian lynx, a polar bear, kangaroo, snowy and great horned owls — even imported residents like the vicuña (a kind of South

MANITOBA

American camel) and Siberian tigers. As well, a statue of "Winnie-the-Bear" on the zoo grounds honours the famous Pooh's origins as a bear cub purchased by a Winnipeg soldier in Ontario and carried onward to England, where author A.A. Milne saw the cub and brought its story to a worldwide audience of children.

Close by, the park's **English Gardens ★★★** are a wonderful surprise when in bloom: colourful carpets of daisy, marigold, begonia, and more, artfully arranged beneath dark, shaggy columns of spruce trees.

The garden blends almost seamlessly into the **Leo Mol Sculpture Garden ★★** *(free admission; 10am to 8pm; ☎986-6531)*, an adjacent area containing the works of a single sculptor. Mol, a Ukrainian who immigrated to the city in 1949, has created whimsical polar bears, deer and nude bathing figures, among other forms. A glass-walled gallery displays hundreds more pieces of his work; a reflecting pool catches the grace of several posed figures; and Mol's studio, moved to a new home just behind the gallery, can be viewed by the curious.

Living Prairie Park, in a suburb west of downtown, is said to contain the last significant pocket of tallgrass prairie in Canada. If so, these 30 acres are a stark testament to the loss of the once vast prairie, for this is a rather small and unimpressive plot surrounded by an airfield, a school and housing developments. There's no sense at all of being out on the wide open plains. However, the adjacent **Living Prairie Museum ★** *($3; mid-Apr to late Jun, weekdays by appointment only, Sun 10am to 5pm; Jul and Aug, every day 10am to 5pm; Sep and Oct, by appointment only; 2795 Ness Ave., ☎832-0167)* does an adequate job of explaining and recapturing what once existed here. An annual festival, in August, draws further attention to the ecosystem.

Southwest of downtown, the **Fort Whyte Nature Centre ★★** *($3.50; Mon to Fri 9am to 5pm, Sat and Sun 10am to 5pm; 1961 McCreary Rd., ☎989-8355)* is a pocket of wilderness that's a bit more vital: its animal life includes foxes and muskrats; a number of birds are also present. An intrepretive centre on the premises featuring an aquarium, demonstration beehive and other exhibits designed to encourage the participation of children.

Finally, the **University of Manitoba ★**, just off the main southern entryway to the city, is Western Canada's oldest university and worth a brief look.

Eastern Manitoba

Dugald

Just east of Winnipeg, in little Dugald, is the **Dugald Costume Museum ★** *(Jun to Sep, 10am to 5pm, spring and fall, Wed to Sun 10am to 5pm; Highway 15, ☎853-2166)*, the first of its kind in Canada. A 15,000-piece collection dating to 1765, the costumes, housed in an 1886 pioneer home, are displayed in tableaus. Special exhibits illustrate aspects of costume; one recent exhibit, for instance, explained the long history of the silk trade. The museum somehow has also acquired some of Queen Elizabeth I's linen napkins dating from the late-16th century.

Oak Hammock

Birds are the most satisfied visitors to **Oak Hammock Marsh and Conservation Centre ★★** *($3.75; Mon to Fri 8:30am to 8:30pm, Sat and Sun 10am to 7:30pm; 1 Snow Goose Bay, ☎467-3300)*, a protected wetland (it was once farmland) a few miles north of downtown Winnipeg. Among the annual arrivals are Canada geese, ducks and more than 250 other species; mammals like the park, too, and all are visible while walking the centre's boardwalks (constructed so as not to disturb the marsh) and dikes.

A good **interpretive centre ★★** on site helps explain the value of the wetland and allows visitors to see it via remote-controlled cameras installed in the marsh. The Canadian headquarters of Ducks Unlimited are also located here.

Red River Heritage Road

From Route 9 heading north, the **Red River Heritage Road ★★** makes a nice meander off the beaten track. This territory once formed the heart of Thomas Douglas' "lower settlement" of Hudson's Bay Company charges; the dirt heritage road is beautifully laid out along the river banks and is well-marked with historic sites. It passes a number of old limestone buildings, including the William Scott farmhouse and the **Captain Kennedy Museum** and **Tea House** ★ *(free admission; Mon to Sat 10:30am to 5pm, Sun 10:30am to 6pm; ☎334-2498)*, an 1866 project of trader Captain William Kennedy with three restored period rooms, English gardens and a superb view of the river.

Near the end of the road lies **St. Andrews Rectory** ★★ *(☎334-6405 or 785-6050)*, a striking little building that is now a national historic park. Signs on the grounds tell the story, and interpreters are available during summertime to discuss the rectory's function.

Just across the road, the **St. Andrews-on-the-Red Anglican Church** ★★★ is the oldest stone church in western Canada still being used for public worship. It is handsome, with typically English pointed windows — the stained glass was supposedly shipped in molasses from England to protect it from breaking — and massive stone walls. Inside, benches are still lined with the original buffalo hide.

Selkirk

On Route 9A, Selkirk, a small river town marked by a giant green fish, is home to several important attractions. **Lower Fort Garry** ★ *($5; mid-May to early Sep, 10am to 6pm; Highway 9, ☎785-6050)*, just south of town, is a recreated pioneer village. It recalls the former importance of this post, built to replace the original Fort Garry in Winnipeg after it was carried away by flood waters. Exhibits include a recreated bake house, doctor's office, powder magazine, aboriginal encampment and blacksmith's shop; costumed characters interact with visitors while baking, trading and otherwise re-enacting their roles. A stone house on the property, constructed for the Hudson's Bay Company's Governor, displays housewares and an old piano.

Several area bridges over the Red River provide good views of the surrounding landscape. Downtown, hugging the river, lies **Selkirk Park** (see Outdoors). The world's largest Red River Ox Cart (6.5 metres high and 13.7 metres long) stands here, and the **Marine Museum of Manitoba** ★★ *($3.50; May to Sep, Mon to Fri 9am to 5pm, Sat and Sun 10am to 5pm; Highway 9, Selkirk, ☎482-7761)* occupies six ships – including Manitoba's oldest steamship – at the park entrance. An actual Lake Winnipeg lighthouse is also located here.

Just across the Red River, with a lovely view of it, sits **St. Peter's Dynevor Church** ★ in East Selkirk. The stone church, built in 1854, is a reminder of the first agricultural colony in Western Canada; it employed a combination of missionaries and native Canadians. Chief Peguis is buried in the churchyard, as are other settlers of the colony.

North of Selkirk

Netley Marsh, said to be one of the most important waterfowl nesting areas in North America, lies approximately 16 kilometres north of Selkirk on Route 320 inside **Netley Marsh Provincial Recreational Park** ★. At least 18 species of ducks and geese arrive each fall to fatten up for winter journeys.

North of Selkirk again, this time on Route 9, the **Little Britain Church** ★ is one of just five surviving Red River Settlement stone churches that remain standing in the province. It was constructed between 1872 and 1874.

Lockport

East of town, in Lockport at the foot of the large bridge, a park is home to the **Kenosewun Centre** *(free admission; Jun to Aug, noon to 8pm; ☎757-2864)*. The name means "there are many fishes" in the Cree language; the centre displays native horticultural artifacts and material on the history of the town, and offers tourist information. Pathways lead to the St. Andrews lock and dam.

Driving northeast from Selkirk, the traveller reaches a series of beautiful white sandy beaches; some of the province's finest, including Winnipeg Beach (see Outdoors) and Camp Morton.

Gimli

Gimli is still the heart of Manitoba's Icelandic population, and a Viking statue downtown welcomes visitors. The town was once the capital of a sovereign republic known as New Iceland. This heritage is perserved today with a popular annual festival and the small **Gimli Historical Museum** ★ *(Jul to Aug, every day 10am to 6pm; ☎642-4001)* on the harbour. The museum gives a good overview of local Icelandic and Ukrainian heritage, plus a

MANITOBA

Mennonite Carriage

discourse on the natural history of Lake Winnipeg and its fisheries.

Around Lake Winnipeg

Farther east around Lake Winnipeg, Route 59 passes through resort towns located on some of the province's best beaches: **Grand Beach, Grand Marais** and **Victoria Beach** are the places to go for summertime sand. Turning southeast again on Route 11, angling toward the Ontario border, the province's seemingly endless flatlands finally drop away all at once, replaced by rocks, rushing rivers and trees; as the road proceeds east, the towns become more and more woodsy, the fishing and canoeing and hiking more satisfying.

Pinawa is known for a paper mill and a festival celebrating paper, hydroelectric power and fish; **Lac du Bonnet** is home to an underground nuclear research facility; and a string of increasingly remote provincial parks compete for the attention of the traveller seeking off-the-beaten-track Manitoba.

Southern Manitoba

Directly south of Winnipeg, between the city and the United States border, lies the Pembina Valley — the province's Mennonite country. The drive is absolutely flat, but the monotony of the fields is interrupted by the leafy oasis of towns such as **Altona**. The town is famous for fields of sunflowers and an annual festival feting them (see Entertainment).

Steinbach

Steinbach, a bit southeast of Winnipeg, is the largest town in the region and features the popular **Mennonite Heritage Village** ★★ *($3.50; Mon to Sat 10am to 5pm; Highway 12, ☎326-9661).* A 16-hectare (40-acre) complex here focuses on the lives of Dutch and Germanic Mennonites who emigrated to the province beginning in 1874. Attractions include a restaurant offering authentic Mennonite food (plums and meat are featured); a general store selling such goods as stone-ground flour and old-fashioned candy; sod and log houses; an interpretative building; exhibition galleries, and a windmill with 20-metre-high sails.

Mariopolis

In Mariopolis, an unusually beautiful church reminds visitors of the strong French and Belgian culture in the province. **Our Lady of the Assumption Roman Catholic Church** ★★★ combines careful brickwork with a striking steeple whose alternating bands of black and white draw the eye upward to a simple cross.

Morden

Morden, another Mennonite stronghold, is known for its agricultural research facility and streets of graceful fieldstone mansions; various local tour operators will point out the homes for a small fee. The **Morden and District Museum ★** *($2; Jun to Aug, every day 1pm to 5pm; Sep to May, every day 1pm to 5pm; ☎822-3406)* displays a good collection of prehistoric marine fossils, reminders of the vast inland sea that once covered North America. Also in town, the **Agriculture Canada Research Station** *(Mon to Fri 8am to 4:30pm; ☎822-4471)* shows impressive ornamental gardens.

Winkler

A bit farther east on Route 14, Winkler is home to the unusual **Pembina Thresherman's Museum ★** *($3; 1pm to 5pm; ☎325-7497)*, filled with tools and machines from another era.

Neubergthal

Just southeast of Altona, Neubergthal is one of the province's best-preserved Mennonite towns, with its distinctive layout (just one street) and equally distinctive architecture, featuring thatched roofing and barns connected to houses.

Tolstoi

Just east of little Tolstoi on Route 209, a 320-acre **patch of tallgrass prairie ★★** *(☎945-7775)*, is maintained by the Manitoba Naturalists Society; this is the largest remaining such tract being protected in Canada.

Central Manitoba

Two main routes pass across central Manitoba. The TransCanada Highway (Hwy 1) is the faster of the two; though less visually rewarding, it does pass through the major population centres of Brandon and Portage La Prairie. The Yellowhead Highway (Hwy 16) is a marginally more scenic journey.

St. François-Xavier

Taking the TransCanada west from Winnipeg, it's not far to St. François-Xavier, a solidly French-Canadian village featuring two of Manitoba's most interesting restaurants (see p 453) as well as a mysterious Cree legend of a white horse. This is the oldest Métis settlement in the province, established in 1820 by Cuthbert Grant. Grant, legendary for his acumen at hunting buffalo, is buried inside the town's Roman Catholic church.

From here, **Route 26** makes a good short scenic detour along the tree-lined Assiniboine River, once home to a string of trapping posts.

Portage La Prairie

A little farther west lies small Portage La Prairie (pop. 20,000), founded in 1738 by French-Canadian explorer Pierre Gaultier de la Vérendrye as a resting stop on the riverine canoe journey to Lake Manitoba. The town's most interesting natural attraction is the crescent-shaped lake, a cutoff bend of the Assiniboine River, really, that nearly encircles the entire downtown.

Island Park ★ sits inside that crescent, providing beautiful tree-shaded picnic spots by the water and a host of attractions: a golf course, playground, deer and waterfowl sanctuary (watch for the Canada geese), fairgrounds and you-pick strawberry farm are among them. Canoeing is excellent here. Good relief from the heat and glare of driving.

The limestone **city hall ★★**, a former post office right on the main street, was designed by the same architect who planned Canada's first Parliament Buildings. It's surprisingly ornate, and has been declared a federal historic site.

Fort la Reine Museum and Pioneer Village ★ *($2; May to mid-Sep, Mon to Fri 9am to 6pm, Sat to Sun, 10am to 6pm; ☎857-3259)*, just east of town, recreates life in the 1800s. It is located on the site of the fort built by la Vérendrye in 1738 to serve as his base. Other attractions here include old rail cars and vehicles.

Austin

The highway west then passes through more fields and towns, reminders of the rich fertility of the local farmland. A few miles south of the one-street town of Austin, the **Manitoba Agricultural Museum** ★★ *($4; mid-May to Oct, every day 9am to 5pm;* ☎*637-2354,* ☎*637-2395)* reveals what life must have been like on the prairie in colonial times. The collection is housed in a number of buildings on a rambling fieldside property, and most of it dates at least back to the early 1900s.

The museum is particularly strong on farm equipment and old vehicles; John Deere tractors and implements and ancient snowmobiles are typical of the collection, which is the largest of operating vintage farm machinery in Canada. An old prairie schoolhouse, train station, general store and amateur radio museum have also been moved here to add atmosphere.

Every summer, as an added bonus, a festival brings the place alive with farm contests and a race between a turtle and an old-fashioned tractor. (Sometimes the turtle wins!) All in all, an excellent and educational way to pass an idle afternoon out in the heartland.

Glenboro

A detour 40 kilometres south of the TransCanada takes the traveller to **Glenboro**, gateway to Spruce Woods Provincial Park (see Outdoors) but also **Grund Church** ★, the oldest Icelandic Lutheran church in Canada. One of Manitoba's two remaining cable ferries still runs crosses the Assiniboine River.

Brandon

Brandon (pop. 40,000) is Manitoba's second-largest city, a city so tied to the fortunes of the surrounding wheatfields that wheat is still grown experimentally right downtown. Things are busy year round with hum of wheat trading, university life and the continuous festivals celebrating jazz, folk, pickles, anything.

The **Daly House Museum** ★★ *($2; Wed to Sun, 10am to 5pm, closed noon to 1pm; 122-18th St.,* ☎*727-1722)* is the best place to get an immediate feel for Brandon's history. Once home to Brandon's mayor, the home today includes a grocery store, recreated City Council chamber and research centre. Nearby, **Brandon University's** ★★ architecture is an unexpected treat: the oldest campus buildings date from 1901, and the student union building is particularly interesting.

Brandon's **experimental research farm** *(*☎*726-7650)*, on Grand Valley Road just west of Highway 10 (18th Street) was one of five original such farms in Canada established by law in 1886. Drive-through and guided tours are available Tuesdays and Thursdays at 1:30pm and 3:30pm; a variety of wheats are grown here.

Finally, there's a good aircraft museum housed in Hangar #1 of the city airport on the northern outskirts of Brandon. The **Commonwealth Air Training Plan Museum** ★ *($3; Mon to Sun, summer 10am to 4pm, winter 1pm to 4pm; Box 3, RR 5, Brandon,* ☎*727-2444)* features vintage planes from second-World-War Royal Canadian Air Force training schools that were held here; some of the more interesting articles include a restored vintage flight simulator, memorials, official telegrams announcing casualties and losses and biographies of flyers.

Souris

Southwest of Brandon, Souris is known for its **swinging suspension bridge** ★, Canada's longest at 177 metres; the bridge was constructed at the turn of the century and restored after a 1976 flood swept it away. The adjacent **Hillcrest Museum** *($1; Jul to early Sep, every day 10am to 6pm;* ☎*483-2008)* preserves items of local historical interest.

Neepawa

Another choice for touring central Manitoba is the Yellowhead Highway (Hwy 16). Coming west from Winnipeg, Neepawa touts itself as "Manitoba's Loveliest Town". No idle boast, but it is pretty and many lilies can be seen blooming here during the growing season. The oldest operating courthouse in Manitoba is here, as is the **Margaret Laurence Home** *($1; May 1 to mid-Oct, Mon to Fri 10am to 6pm; 312 First Ave.,* ☎*476-3612)*, a shrine to the beloved author who was born here. Laurence's typewriter and furniture are the highlights.

Minnedosa

Minnedosa, a tiny town to the west, surprises with its Czechoslavakian population. A series of prairie potholes, glacier-scraped depressions in the earth that later filled with rainwater, south of town on Route 262 provide optimum conditions for waterfowl such as drake, mallards and teal. Continuing north of Minnedosa on Route 262, the road enters a valley good for spotting white-tailed deer; a wildlife viewing tower provides even better opportunities to do so.

Dauphin

Just north of the Yellowhead, Dauphin (pop. 8,500) is transformed into the famous **Selo Ukrainia** ("Ukrainian Village") during the famous **National Ukrainian Festival** (see Entertainment) each summer. The event draws thousands in late July to the town.

Also in Dauphin, the fun **Fort Dauphin Museum ★** *($2; May to Sep, every day 9:30am to 5:30 pm; Jackson St., ☎638-6630)* recreates one of the French-run North West Company trading posts from the area, showcasing fur trapping and other pioneer activities. The displays and buildings include a trapper's cabin, blacksmith's shop, one-room rural schoolhouse, Anglican church and the trading post. There's even a birchbark canoe made entirely from natural materials, and a collection of fossils such as a bison horn, mammoth tusk and ancient canine skull.

Northern Manitoba

The Pas

The so-called Woods and Water Route shows another side of Manitoba. The Pas (pop. 6,000), with a large native Canadian population, is home to a large annual gathering of trappers and an exceedingly clear lake. Most visitors head for the **Sam Waller Museum ★★** *($2; 306 Fischer Ave., ☎623-3802)*. Built in 1916 and occupying the town's former courthouse, it offers a good orientation to local native peoples, fur traders and the like. Walking tours are offered.

A wall of **Christ Church ★★** *(Edwards Ave., ☎623-2119)* is inscribed with the Ten Commandments in the Cree language. The church was built in 1840 by Henry Budd, the first aboriginal in Canada ordained to the Anglican ministry, and still retains some furnishings fashioned by ships' carpenters and brought here during an 1847 expedition.

Flin Flon

Flin Flon (pop. 7,600), Canada's most whimsically named municipality, greets visitors with a jumble of streets climbing the rocky hills. Part in Manitoba, and a smaller part spilling over into Saskatchewan, Flin Flon is the most important mining centre in this part of the country, and has grown to become the province's sixth-largest city.

It was named by a group of gold prospectors in 1915 who found a copy of the mass-market science fiction paperback during a northern Manitoba portage. Later, on a lakeshore near here, they staked a mining claim and named it for the book's main character Josiah Flintabbatey Flonatin: "Flinty" to locals. Thus, the green 7.5-metre tall **Josiah Flintabbatey Flonatin statue** unmistakably marks the city's entrance; it was designed for the city by the renowned American cartoonist Al Capp.

A walk around town reveals old boomtown-era hotels, bright red headframes indicating mine shafts, and historic redwood cabins. Of all these historic sites, though, the **Flin Flon Station Museum ★★** *($1; mid-May to early Sept, every day 9am to 9pm; ☎687-2946)* might be the best: a small collection of local mining artifacts, including a diving suit and helmet for underwater prospecting; a Linn tractor; a train sweeper; and an ore car. The collection also includes a stuffed 63-pound lake trout that was caught near here.

Churchill

Special arrangements are required to reach far northern Manitoba (see Finding Your Way Around). Remote and cold, Churchill (pop. 1,100) nevertheless still beguiles the traveller with its remoteness and startling wildlife. The place is important historically, as well: this place helped the English first establish a foothold in Manitoba. They chose the site because of a superb natural harbour, so it's fitting that today the town-site's dominant feature is a huge **grain elevator** beside the docks. Recently purchased by an American firm, the terminal is experiencing an increase in business.

But that isn't why visitors come here. They come to see caribou, seals, birds and especially white **beluga whales** in summer. In autumn, thousands come to view **polar bears** beginning their annual migrations. And there is always the

MANITOBA

Polar Bear

possibility of an astonishing display of the aurora borealis, the northern lights.

The **Visitor Reception Centre**, in Bayport Plaza, orients visitors with an overview of the fur posts and forts. **Fort Prince of Wales ★★** (☎675-8863), an enormous, diamond-shaped stone battlement located at the mouth of the Churchill River, is historically interesting: after four decades of steady construction by the English it was surrendered to French-Canadian forces without a fight. The fort can only be reached by boat or helicopter; in summer, park staff lead interpreted tours of the site.

Sloop's Cove National Historic Site ★★ (☎675-8863), four kilometres upstream from the fort, is a natural harbour that provided safe haven for huge wooden sailing ships going at least as far back as 1689. When the Hudson's Bay Company set up shop here, its sloops were moored to these rocks with iron rings; some of the rocks also still bear inscriptions from the men posted there — men like explorer Samuel Hearne, who presided over the company's heyday. Like Fort Prince of Wales, the site can only be reached by boat or helicopter.

Across the river, **Cape Merry National Historic Site ★** preserves a gunpowder magazine, the only remnant of a battery built here back in 1746. It is reached via the Centennial Parkway.

The **Eskimo Museum ★★★** *(free admission; summer, Mon 1pm to 5pm, Tue to Sat 9am to 5pm; winter, Mon 1pm to 4:30pm, Tue to Fri 10:30am to 4:30 pm, Sat 1am to 4:30pm; ☎675-2030)* maintains one of the world's pre-eminent collections of Inuit artifacts. Founded in 1944 by the local Roman Catholic Diocese, it contains artifacts dating from as far back as 1700 BC. A set of ornately carved walrus tusks are among its most impressive pieces.

The **Northern Studies Centre** *(☎675-2307)*, 25 kilometres east of Churchill proper, is located in a former rocket-test range. Today students come here to study the northern lights, Arctic ecology, botany, meteorology, geology and more.

York Factory National Historic Site ★★★ *(☎675-8863)*, 240 kilometres southeast of Churchill, is what remains of the Hudson Bay Company fur-trade post that established the English in western Canada for the first time. A wooden depot built in 1832 still stands here, and there are ruins of a stone gunpowder magazine and a cemetery with markers dating back to the 1700s. Access can only be gained by charter plane or canoe, however; some guided tours are also offered in summer through Parks Canada.

Finally, there are those marvellous **polar bears ★★★**, easily Churchill's premier attraction. Autumn is the time to observe them and the only way is as part of a guided tour. There are at least a dozen operators in Churchill; the options include the following:

North Star Tours and Travel Agency *(Box 520, Churchill,* ☎*1-800-665-0690 or 675-2629;* ↬*675-2852)*. Mark Ingebrigtson leads natural history — and sometimes aboriginal culture — package tours along the shores of Hudson Bay.

Northern Expeditions Tours *(Box 662, Churchill,* ☎*1-800-544-5049 or 675-2121;* ↬*675-2877)*. Len and Beverly Smith lead polar bear safaris in both English and French; vehicles are specially outfitted to accommodate photographers.

Seal River Heritage Lodge *(Box 1034, Churchill,* ☎*1-800-665-0476 or 675-8875;* ↬*675-2386)*. Mike Reimer run eco-tours out of a remote wilderness lodge in the north country; sights include caribou, polar bears, beluga whales and seals.

 OUTDOORS

Greater Winnipeg

Birds Hill Provincial Park, just north of Winnipeg, is a gentle rise deposited by retreating glaciers. It makes for easy and popular cross-country skiing. In summer, visitors bike and hike the park's trails (one of which is wheelchair-accessible) to view prairie wildflowers — including several species of rare orchid — or head for a small beach. The park is also the site of the city's big and classy annual folk-music bash (see Entertainment).

Grand Beach Provincial Park is the most popular beach in Manitoba, hands down. Situated on Lake Winnipeg's eastern shore, it consists of pretty white sand and grassy eight-metre-high dunes that seem directly lifted from Cape Cod. As a bonus, the beach is wheelchair-accessible. Three self-guiding trails wind through the park — Spirit Rock Trail, Wild Wings Trail and the Ancient Beach Trail — enlightening beachgoers before they slap on the sunblock, and this is a good spot for windsurfing, as well. There are full tourist facilities here, including a restaurant, campground and outdoor amphitheatre for concerts. A golf course lies just outside the park.

St. Norbert Provincial Park *(free, mid-May to Sep, Thurs to Mon, 10:30am to 5:30 pm; 40 Turnbull Dr.,* ☎*269-5377,)* is a 17-acre, south-Winnipeg complex of buildings at the juncture of the Red and La Salle rivers, a former Métis and then French-Canadian settlement. The restored, gambrel-roofed Bohémier farmhouse and two more homes are on display; there's also a self-guiding trail here.

Eastern Manitoba

Winnipeg Beach Provincial Recreational Park ★★ *(*☎*389-2752)* has long been a favourite summer getaway for Winnipeg residents. Besides the well-known beach and a boardwalk, the park's grounds also include a marina, campground and bay that's a favourite with windsurfers.

Whiteshell Provincial Park ★★★ is one Manitoba's largest and best. Occupying some 2,500 square kilometres, it is rich in lakes, rapids, waterfalls, fish and birds. There's a little of something for everyone: **Alf Hole Goose Sanctuary ★** *(*☎*369-5470)* is among the best places in the province to see Canada geese, especially during migration; the rocks at **Bannock Point ★**, laid out by natives to resemble the forms of snakes, fish, turtles and birds, are of archaeological interest; the cliffs of **Lily Pond ★** are 3.75 billion years old. This is also the location of the province's deepest lake, which is popular with scuba divers. **Hiking** is also good in Whiteshell. Hikes include the Forester's Footsteps Trail, an easy walk through jackpine forest and then up a granite ridge, the Pine Point Trail, which is nice for cross-country skiing in winter, and the White Pine trail. A **Visitor Centre** and the **Whiteshell Natural History Museum** *(free, May to Sept,* ☎*348-2846)* help orient travellers and explain the park's ecology, geology and wildlife.

Nopiming Provincial Park shows a whole different Manitoba, a place of huge granite outcrops and hundreds of lakes. The surprising presence of woodland caribou here is an added bonus, as are the fly-in and drive-in fishing lodges scattered through the park. Nopiming is a local native word meaning "entrance to the wilderness".

Atikaki Provincial Wilderness Park ★★★, in the east of the province along the Ontario border, consists of a million-acre hodgepodge of cliffs, rock formation, pristine lakes and cascading rivers. It is extremely difficult to get to, however, requiring a canoe, floatplane or several-day hike to reach its interior; as a result, it contains the most unspoiled wilderness in the province's major parklands.

MANITOBA

Among the highlights are a series of rock murals painted by natives and a 20-metre waterfall well suited for whitewater canoeing. As Atikaki means "country of the caribou", moose and caribou sightings are quite possible.

Hecla Provincial Park ★★ *(☎279-2056)* is a beautiful and interesting park, combining lake ecology with dramatic island geology and the colours and creatures of the forest. Interpretive programs take place year-round, and there is a tower for viewing and photographing wildlife. The park's **Hecla Village** ★ adds a short trail with points of historical interest relating to Icelandic culture and architecture and a **heritage home museum** ★★ *(Thurs to Mon, 11am to 5pm)* — a restored 1920s home. Adjacent **Grindstone Provincial Park** ★★ is still being developed, and therein lies its beauty: it is not nearly so busy as Hecla.

East of Lake Winnipeg, the **Narcisse Wildlife Management Area** on Route 17 becomes wildly popular late each April when thousands of resident red-sided garter snakes emerge from their limestone dens to participate in a visceral mating ritual.

Selkirk Park, a riverside park in downtown Selkirk, has lots of recreational opportunities. There are campgrounds, boat-launching pads and an outdoor swimming pool. Snowshoeing and ice fishing are possible in winter; in spring and summer, the park home to a bird sanctuary with an observation deck for viewing Canada geese and other birds.

In Gimli there's a good rental agency for water and land sports. **H2O Beach and Adventure Sports** *(☎642-9781)*, located right on the sandy beach of Lake **Winnipeg**, rents bicycles, in-line skates, sailboats, kayaks, beach volleyballs, windsurfing equipment and just about everything else one could want or need.

It's purely manufactured fun, but **Skinner's Wet 'n' Wild Waterslide Park** *(☎757-2623)* in Lockport keeps packing them in anyway. The attractions contains four big waterslides, two smaller slides, a giant hot tub, mini-golf, batting cages and lots more. It's impossible to miss the complex, situated at the west end of the Lockport bridge.

Central Manitoba

Grand Valley Provincial Recreation Park ★ is best known for the **Stott Site** ★★, a designated provincial heritage site. Bones and artifacts from at least 1,200 years ago have been discovered here. A bison enclosure and camp have been reconstructed.

North of Portage la Prairie, on the shore of Lake Manitoba lies 18,000-hectare **Delta Marsh**, one of the largest waterfowl staging marshes in North America, stretching eight kilometres along the lake and a great place to bring binoculars. At Delta Beach, a waterfowl and wetlands research station studies ecological questions in a natural environment.

Riding Mountain National Park ★★★ *(☎1-800-707-8480 or 848-7275)* rises from the featureless plains and provides wonderful relief from the monotony. Its aspen-covered slopes provide habitats for wild animals such as elk, moose, deer, wolves and lynx. The largest black bear ever seen in North America was killed here by a poacher in 1992, and bison are contained within a large **bison enclosure** ★★ near Lake Audy. Route 10, running north-south, passes directly through the heart of the park and past the shores of its most beautiful lakes. The 12-metre-high wooden Agassiz lookout tower here gives a superb view of the surrounding territory. The remains of an old sawmill also fall within park boundaries, as do a series of geological formations called beach ridges — former edges of a giant lake.

Route 19 begins in the centre of the park and travels a switchback path up (or down) the park's steepest ridge. The naturalist Grey Owl, an Englishman who shed his old life for that of a native, lived here for 6 months, giving talks with his two beavers (he spent most of his time in Prince Albert National Park, however, see p 469); his remote **cabin** ★ is located 17 kilometres up a hiking trail off Route 19. More than 400 kilometres of trails have been cleared at Riding Mountain National Park, including the North Escarpment Loop, best for views, Whitewater Lake, giving a history of the prisoner-of-war camp that was once here, and the Strathclair Trail, formerly a fur trappers' route through the wooded hills. The park is also dotted with a number of pristine lakes superb for swimming. The sand beach at Clear Lake is the focus of human activity.

Duck Mountain Provincial Park ★★★ rises in long lumps near the Manitoba-Saskatchewan border; forests, meadows and lakes appear where the land has wrinkled upward in the Manitoba Escarpment formation. This is the home of **Baldy Mountain ★★**, at 831 metres the highest mountain in the province (there is also a tower up top to get a still longer view on things), as well as six hiking trails and a lake so clear the bottom can be seen from its surface 10 metres above.

Approximately 23 kilometres south of Roblin, the **Frank Skinner Arboretum Trail** commemorates the work of Dr. Frank Leith Skinner, a famous Canadian horticulturist. This farm served as Skinner's laboratory for breeding new strains of plants; visitors can walk atop a former dike, visit Skinner's greenhouse, and walk the Wild Willow Trail.

Turtle Mountain National Park ★★, partly composed of compacted coal and partly of glacial deposits, rises more than 250 metres above the surrounding prairie land. Vérendrye called it the "blue jewel of the plains", and its gentle hills lend themselves to mountain biking, horseback riding and hiking. There is also, of course, a considerable population of the beautiful painted turtles that give the mountain its name. Camping is available at three lakes here.

Northern Manitoba

At **Clearwater Lake Provincial Park ★**, the lake water is so clear that the bottom is visible 11 metres below the surface, making it one of the clearest lakes in the world. It is well known for its lake trout and northern pike. Also interesting are a series of enormous limestone slabs on the south shore: known as "the caves", they splintered off from the nearby cliffs and can be reached by a trail.

The **Cape Churchill Wildlife Management Area ★★** and the **Cape Tatnam Wildlife Management Area ★★** take in Hudson Bay's coastline from Churchill to the Ontario border — a tremendous stretch of wild country, nearly 6-million acres of land in all, harbouring polar bears, woodland caribou and many more birds and animals. They are accessible only by plane.

Grass River Provincial Park ★★ was explored by the aboriginal peoples for thousands of years, then explored anew by the English.

Countless islands and some 150 lakes interrupt the river, and a spring gushes out of a cliff.

Bird Cove ★, 16 kilometres east of Churchill, might be the area's best spot for observing the hundreds of bird species that pass through here, including possibly the rare Ross Gull. The wreck of the Ithaca, which sunk in a 1961 storm with a load of nickel ore en route to Montreal, sits at the western tip of the cove.

For addresses of polar-bear-observation outfitters see p 446.

 ## ACCOMMODATIONS

Bed and Breakfast of Manitoba *(Mon to Fri 8am to 3pm; 434 Roberta Ave., Winnipeg, ☎661-0300)* coordinates reservations for approximately 40 member B&Bs throughout the province.

The Manitoba Country Vacations Association *(☎667-3526; ⬦667-3526)* in Winnipeg provides a similar service but a different experience, booking rooms at around 40 farms or other rural vacation destinations.

Downtown Winnipeg

Guest House International Hostel *($26; sb, ≡; 168 Maryland St., Winnipeg; R3G 1L3, ☎772-1272, ⬦ 772-1272)*. Quirky old house in a good neighbourhood very close to downtown Winnipeg. Walls feature art by native children, and there are all kinds of room options. Game room in the somewhat crowded basement adds appeal, and the price is right.

Ivey House International Hostel *($30; sb, tv, K; 210 Maryland St., Winnipeg, R3G 1L6, ☎772-3022, ⬦784-1133)*. This extremely friendly and well-run Hostelling International-member facility is situated close to downtown (and very close to the other hostel). Classy operation, featuring a big kitchen, great staff and rooms that sometimes include handy desks.

Casa Antigua *($50; sb; 209 Chestnut St., Winnipeg; ☎775-9705)*. This quiet and reasonably priced bed-and-breakfast, in a residential neighbourhood near the two hostels, was built in 1906 and is furnished with nice antiques. Both English and Spanish are spoken

MANITOBA

here, and three bedrooms — all with shared bath — are offered.

Ramada Marlborough Hotel *($70; pb, tv, ≡, ℜ; 331 Smith St., Winnipeg, R3B 2G9, ☎1-800-667-7666 or 942-6411, ≈942-2017).* Also downtown, and home to an oft-lauded dining room in Gothic style, this elegant hotel has managed to maintain its circa-1910 lustre in the form of original architecture. Rooms are tasteful and spacious.

Hotel Fort Garry *($75; pb, tv, ≡, △, ≈, ⊛; 222 Broadway, Winnipeg, R3C 0R3; ☎1-800-665-8088 or 942-8521, ≈956-2351).* One of the most recognizable hotels on the city's skyline, this big-shouldered, neo-Gothic building was built by the Canadian National Railway in 1913. Now, however, it is much more famous as the home to a popular casino on the seventh floor. Rooms, foyer and fittings are all elegantly reworked.

The Delta Winnipeg *($75; pb, tv, ≡, ℜ, ≈, △, ⊛; 288 Portage Ave., Winnipeg, R3C 0B8, ☎1-800-268-1133 or 9456-0410, ≈947-1129).* Smack in the downtown business district, this posh hotel features an haute-cuisine restaurant, child care services and a valet laundry. For $15 more, Family Fun Rooms include in-room movies, bubble bath, tub toys, popcorn and cookies.

Place Louis-Riel All-Suite Hotel *($80; pb, tv, ≡, K, ℜ; 190 Smith St., Winnipeg, R3C 1JB, ☎947-6961, ≈947-3029).* Every unit in this downtown high-rise is a suite, meaning several rooms and usually a kitchenette. Sixteen of the suites have not one, but two bedrooms. Ideal for long-term visits.

Crowne Plaza Winnipeg Downtown *($120; pb, tv, ≡, K, ℝ, ℜ, ≈, ⊛, △; 350 St. Mary Ave., Winnipeg, R3C 3J2, ☎942-0551 or 1-800-2CROWNE, ≈943-8702).* Central and luxurious; some rooms have jacuzzis. Other facilities include an indoor pool, on-site restaurant, and aerobic instruction.

The Lombard *($170; pb, tv, ≡, ℜ, ≈, △, ⊛, ℝ, K; 2 Lombard Place, Winnipeg, R3B 0Y3, ☎957-1350 or 1-800-228-3000, ≈949-1486).* Under new ownership — it was formerly in the Westin chain — this landmark is among the top posh digs in the city. It's where the Rolling Stones stay when they're in town, though they sometimes get bumped by the convention business. Located at the busy and famous corner of Portage and Main streets.

St. Boniface

Gîte de la Cathédrale Bed and Breakfast *($45; sb; 582 rue Langevin, St. Boniface, ☎233-7792)* is located right across from Provencher Park in old St. Boniface. Five bedrooms are available; all are air-conditioned. Hostess Jacqueline Bernier's traditional French-Canadian breakfast might include pancakes with maple syrup, an omelette, or quiche with home-made baked beans. Service is in French.

Greater Winnipeg

Quality Inn *($65; pb, tv, ≡, ℜ, ⊛; 635 Pembina Highway, Winnipeg, R3M 2L4, ☎1-800-228-5151 or 453-8247, ≈287-2365).* Located on a strip highway south of the city, this is probably the most fun of Winnipeg's middle-range hotels: standard double rooms include sofas and closets, and two hopping bars include such diversions as golf simulations, video poker and plenty of pool tables. There are also six wacky (and a bit tacky) theme rooms that include hot tubs, though these cost considerably more.

Eastern Manitoba

Selkirk

Daerwood Motor Inn *($55; pb, tv, ≡; 162 Main St., R1A 1R3, ☎482-7722, ≈ 482-8655).* Reasonably priced accommodations located in central Selkirk, not far from several important local attractions. Rooms with kitchen units cost only $5 extra, and videocassette players are also available for an extra charge.

Riverton

Gull Harbour Resort *($90; pb, tv, ≡, ℜ, ≈, ⊛, △, ⊘; Box 1000, Riverton, R0C 1B0, ☎279-2030, ≈378-2784).* A beautiful resort on the tip of an island. This convention centre is especially well known for the golf courses nearby, as well as the natural scenery of Hecla and Grindstone parks. It's also located close to the Hecla Island Heritage Home Museum.

Gimli

Country Resort by Carlson *($100; tv, K,≋, ℜ, ≈, △; 10 Centre St., ☎1-800-456-4000 or 642-8565, ⇝642-4400).* Right on the harbour in Gimli. Guests can choose a countrified suite or room overlooking the small town or the large lake from which the town derives most of its business. Breaking with the tradition of impersonal rooms in most big hotel chains, rooms here feature quilts, a fresh scent, hardwood floors and in-room mini bars; there is a cosy fireplace in the lobby.

Southern Manitoba

Winkler

Winkler Inn *($70; tv, ≋, ℜ, ≈, ◉; 851 Main St., R6W 4B1, ☎1-800-829-4920 or 325-4381, ⇝325-9656).* The fertile Pembina valley draws visitors to Winkler, and the Winkler Inn accommodates them with a wide variety of amenities including queen-sized beds and poolside vistas. Also on site are a bar, restaurant, pool, and 10-person hot tub.

Central Manitoba

Lake Audy

Riding Mountain Guest Ranch *($50; Box 11, R0J 0Z0, ☎848-2265).* One of the better guest ranch experiences in the province. Host Jim Irwin takes groups or individuals into his three-and-a-half story ranch house, leading bison viewing tours and serving meals in a dining room. Special touches here include a billiards table, a hot tub overlooking the fields, air conditioning in summer and a wood-heated sauna in winter. The ranch is quite close to Riding Mountain National Park, and the property also includes groomed trails for cross-country skiing and tobogganing. Irwin specializes in hosting group events.

Roblin

Harvest Moon Inn *($60; pb, tv, K, ≋; 25 Commercial Dr., R0L 1P0, ☎937-3701; ⇝937-3701).* A new all-suite hotel with lots of room to stretch out. Each suite includes microwaves, refrigerators, televisions and videocassette recorders; a small selection of

free movies is available at the front desk. As a bonus, the family that runs the business are full of fishing advice and interesting stories about their travels. Emu jerky from the owners' farm is on sale in the lobby, too.

Brandon

Comfort Inn by Journey's End *($70; pb, tv, ≋; 925 Middleton Ave., R7C 1A8, ☎727-6232 or 1-800-288-5150, ⇝727-2246).* Super rooms and professional management right on the TransCanada Highway north of downtown Brandon. Rooms here feature work tables and sofas, a bonus for business travellers; only drawback is the place's popularity, often filling it months in advance.

Northern Manitoba

Churchill

Northern Lights Lodge *($68; pb, tv, ℜ; Box 70, R0B 0E0, ☎675-2403, ⇝675-2011).* This northern outpost caters to those in search of the polar bears who can usually be seen frolicking on the shores of Hudson Bay. The inn is only open from June until November, and there is a restaurant on premises. Small pets are allowed.

Polar Inn *($77; pb, tv; 15 Franklin St., R0B 0E0, ☎675-8878, ⇝675-2647).* The presence of polar bears has inspired a whole slew of motels and inns in Churchill, including this one. Rooms have been recently updated and include all modern amenities like telephone, television. Mountain bike rentals are a real bonus for outdoors types, and shoppers will find the on-site gift shop pleasant.

 RESTAURANTS

Downtown Winnipeg

Alycia's *($; 559 Cathedral Ave., Winnipeg; ☎582-8789).* This is likely the most popular of Winnipeg's half-dozen or so Ukrainian eateries. "It sticks with you," say customers of the food here; and, indeed, the place is well-known around town for thick soups, hearty perogies, cabbage rolls and other warming fare. Red

MANITOBA

creamy sodas and decorations such as Ukrainian Easter eggs and pictures of the Pope add to the festive mood, and the owners also run a deli of takeout meats and side dishes next door.

Blue Note Café *($; 875 Portage Ave., ☎774-2189).* A local hangout where the big-screen television serves up Canadian football while folks chow on burgers, chili and other bar food. Groovy jazz plays on the P.A. system each night until about 9pm, when some local musical act takes the stage. There's history here, too — the original location, downtown on Main Street, was the place where music star Neil Young and Canadian heroes Crash Test Dummies both got their starts.

Le Café Jardin *($; 340 Provencher Ave., Winnipeg; ☎233-9515).* This café attached to the Franco-Manitoban Cultural Centre serves French-Canadian cuisine, as well as light meals and pastries baked on-site. The outdoor terrace is popular in summertime.

d'8 Schtove *($$; 1842 Pembina Highway and 1277 Henderson Highway, Winnipeg; ☎275-2294 and ☎334-1200).* Three locations, one in the solidly Mennonite town of Morden and two more in north and south Winnipeg. This is the real deal, serving up unadulterated Russian Mennonite fare: two kinds of borscht (one tomato based, one potato and dill-based), plus more esoteric specialities like *kjielkje* and *rebspaa*. Desserts include a selection of strudels and cakes. And that unusual name? It means "the eating room."

Elephant and Castle *($$; 350 St. Mary Ave., Winnipeg; ☎942-5555).* Located in the lobby of the well-appointed Holiday Inn Crown Centre, this handsome English-style pub serves up the expected fare — turkey pot pie, bangers and mash, fish and chips, soups and sandwiches — but it's handled pretty well here, and brought to table with cheerful service. Dessert selection is especially good, including mousse, sherry trifle, deep-dish apple crisp, home-made pies and more. There's a full bar selection, as well.

Victor's *($$$; 331 Smith St., Winnipeg; ☎947-2751).* An elegant French restaurant with high vaulted ceilings located inside the Ramada Marlborough, this place is known for its creative kitchen. Meals include variations of such classics as chicken in mustard sauce, provençal bouillabaisse, and a mélange of lobster, shrimp, Manitoban whitefish and scallops known as Seafood Victor. Attracts a conservatively dressed crowd.

Hy's Steak Loft *($$$; 216 Kennedy St., Winnipeg, ☎942-1000).* The brick-warehouse appearance of this downtown institution is quite deceiving; it's one of those places where smoky backroom deals are forged over Alberta prime rib. Politicians and other bigshots head for the wood-panelled steak room to watch the beef char-grilled to order on an open grill right before their eyes. Those with real pull ask for one of the Loft's private dining rooms and discuss changes in insurance laws or whatever else needs to be free of the public's prying ears. There's also a smoking room and lounge on premises, good for relaxing before and after the big meal.

The Velvet Glove *($$$$; 2 Lombard Ave., Winnipeg, ☎985-6255).* Located inside the prestigious Lombard Hotel, this restaurant caters to Winnipeg's high rollers. Entrées might include choices of the chef's latest creations in beef, seafood or lamb; whatever's cooking, though, all meals begin with a simple soup and salad.

Eastern Manitoba

Gimli

Seagull's Restaurant *($$; 10 Centre St., ☎642-4145).* Filet mignon, lamb chops, locally caught whitefish and the like are featured of the menu of this hotel restaurant in downtown Gimli, near the harbour.

Central Manitoba

Brandon

Humpty's *($; Highway 1, ☎729-1902).* This restaurant, located in a gas station on a Brandon service road running parallel to the TransCanada, serves up solid stick-to-your-ribs food such as burgers, eggs and lots of filling sandwiches. Locals swear by it.

Casteleyn Cappuccino Bar *($; 908 Rosser Ave., ☎727-2820)* This place is an oasis on the prairie, well worth a detour to Brandon. The Belgian Casteleyn family has been making hand-dipped chocolates here for seven years; last year they opened a bright new space and added gelato, Italian sodas and a cappuccino bar. More a coffeehouse than a restaurant, but there's a tasty selection of meat and vegetable focaccia sandwiches each day. Other dessert options include Grand Marnier truffles, amaretto cheesecake and peach chocolate gateau. A wonderful lunch or snack experience.

St.François-Xavier

The Nun's Kitchen *($$; 1033 Highway 26, ☎864-2306)*. Located in — what else — a former convent, this restaurant is good high-end fare in a little French village outside of Winnipeg. Entrées run to buffalo, quiche, chicken, ribs and the like; prices are surprisingly reasonable.

Medicine Rock Café *($$$; 990 Highway 26, ☎864-2451)*. This place has of the more interesting menus in the province, including such entrées as emu, ostrich, boar, rabbit and the like. It's extremely popular, however, so reservations are usually recommended.

Shellmouth

The Church Caffe *($$; Box 15, ☎564-2626)*. Housed in a former United Church, this place serves up Austrian dinners in a scintillating lakeside location. Takes a bit of finding, but the reward is a selection of beef, pork and turkey entrées that come with soup and salad. The restaurant won the Flavour of Rural Manitoba Award in 1995.

  ENTERTAINMENT

Downtown Winnipeg

King's Head Pub *(120 King St., ☎957-7710)* might be Winnipeg's best bar. Located in the Exchange District, it features lots of imported beers and a wide selection of scotch, plus darts and pool for entertainment purposes. Food is also available.

The **Royal Winnipeg Ballet** *(380 Graham Ave., ☎1-800-667-4792 or 956-2792)* is Canada's best-known dance company, housed in their own performance building right downtown. The ballet company won a gold medal at the International Ballet Competition and sometimes hosts tours of its facility, in addition to regular performances.

There are also several casinos in Winnipeg. **Crystal Casino** *(222 Broadway, ☎957-2600)*, on the 7th floor of the famous Hotel Fort Garry, is a semi-formal, European-style casino. The games here include baccarat, roulette and blackjack — and more than 200 slot machines. **The Club Regent** *(1425 Regent Ave. W., ☎957-2700)*, east of the Red River rather than downtown, is far more laid-back; the palm trees and waterfalls set a Caribbean theme for this gaming establishment. The emphasis here is on electronic gaming: bingo, poker and Keno. There are slot machines here, as well.

Folkorama *(☎1-800-665-0234 or 982-6210)*, Winnipeg's huge annual summer bash, lasts two weeks each August and covers a lot of ground: representatives of the city's many cultures — French, Ukrainian, Hungarian, Chinese, Japanese, East Indian, to name a few — cook the food, sing the songs and dance the dances of their homelands.

St. Boniface

The **Festival du Voyageur** *(768 Ave. Taché, St. Boniface; ☎237-7692; email: voyageur@festivalvoyageur.mb.ca)* is a giant annual street party in St. Boniface each February celebrating winter and the voyageurs who settled the province. Action at the big outdoor pavilion includes sled-dog races, snow sculptures and children's activities.

Greater Winnipeg

Toad in the Hole *(112 Osborne St.)*, in funky Osborne Village, is a good pub with plenty of pints of various imported brews. Darts and pool are available here, as well.

The **Winnipeg Folk Festival** *(☎231-0096)* is one of North America's finest; the 200 or so performers invariably include national folk stars and musicians from places as far-flung as Australia. It's held each July in **Birds Hill Provincial Park** (see p 447), north of the city.

MANITOBA

Eastern Manitoba

Islendingadagurinn (the Icelandic Festival of Manitoba) occupies three days in late August, celebrating the local heritage from that far-off land right here in downtown Gimli. The festival includes a parade, music, poetry, Icelandic food and more.

Southern Manitoba

The **Manitoba Sunflower Festival** celebrates the tall yellow flower for three days each July with Mennonite foods, parades, dancing in the street and the like.

The **Morris Stampede and Exhibition** turns an otherwise slowpoke town into rodeo central for five days in early July. It's Canada's second-largest rodeo (after Calgary's), and features chuckwagon and chariot races, an agricultural fair, and (of course) bullriding and other rodeo contests.

Central Manitoba

The hugely popular **National Ukrainian Festival** *(119 Main St. S., Dauphin;* ☎*638-5645;* ‖*638-5851)* takes place three days each mid-summer in Dauphin, beginning on a Friday morning. Heritage village festivities include a bread-baking competition, embroidery contests, an Easter egg decorating competition, folk arts, lots of dancing and a beer garden.

The whole town of Brandon puckers up for the **International Pickle Festival**, held downtown each September. Besides the obvious pickle-tastings, attractions include expanded musical stages, classic car shows, kickboxing contests, and a full slate of children's events such as the "Oodles of Onions Contest". Truly quirky; but a real slice of small-town prairie life nevertheless.

While in Brandon, whatever's going on at the **Keystone Centre** is also probably interesting, since it's one of the largest convention centres in Canada — 10 acres under one roof, including five arenas.

In Portage la Prairie, it's the annual **Strawberry Festival** that draws visitors from all over the province. Held in mid-July, it features lots of street dances, entertainment and a flea market in addition to strawberry treats.

Northern Manitoba

The **Northern Manitoba Trappers' Festival** in The Pas occupies five days each February. Festivities here include a famous sled-dog race.

 ## SHOPPING

Downtown Winnipeg

Shopping options are well concentrated in the downtown area: within a few blocks it's possible to easily visit the big three department stores — Eaton Centre, Hudson's Bay Company and the North West Company. A series of covered elevated walkways downtown are well-used (and appreciated) in wintertime, connecting stores with office buildings, the library and other destinations.

Eaton Place, downtown at 234 Donald Street, has more than 100 shops connected by those walkways. **Portage Place** is another downtown mall spanning three blocks; it contains 160 shops or so, an IMAX theatre and an in-house theatre company. **Polo Park**, at 1485 Portage Avenue on the way to the airport, contains more than 180 shops and leans toward upscale department stores and the like. Among other stores downtown, The **Bayat Gallery** *(163 Stafford St.,* ☎*1-888-88INUIT or 475-5873)* is particularly interesting; it is the city's best gallery of Inuit art.

SASKATCHEWAN

aken at face value, Saskatchewan would appear to be one continuous wheat field, a place with little topography or cultural diversity. And the traveller passing through southern Saskatchewan in late summer can hardly be forgiven: this is Canada's breadbasket, after all, producing a full 60 percent of the nation's wheat in acres of golden fields that literally stretch to the horizon.

It is for this reason that the place is usually portrayed as nothing more than a cold monotonous patch of grassland between the lakes of Manitoba and the mountains of Alberta. And it's true the entire province is subject to such bitterly cold winters that "plug-ins" — electric connections that keep a car battery warm overnight — are standard at a good hotel.

However, a little probing reveals something beyond the stereotype. Venture a bit north, to Saskatchewan's two major cities, and surprising architectural touches are revealed. In other areas, a preponderance of Eastern European churches pop up — delicately painted church domes like elegant Easter eggs rising from the prairie, testament to the province's solid Ukrainian influence. (This influence is so strong that Ukrainian has been an optional language in the province's high schools since 1952.)

Farther north, the prairies abruptly give way to foothills and then genuine mountains, woods and lakes — making it a bit less surprising to learn that there is more forest, half a province worth, than farmland here. All of the major rivers in the province flow eastward into Manitoba, eventually emptying into Hudson Bay.

Saskatchewan's first peoples were organized in tribes such as the Assiniboine and the Blackfoot. Later, the Cree became the most active, pushing aggressively westward to satisfy traders' voracious appetite for furs. Later, it was to southern Saskatchewan that Sitting Bull came after routing General Custer of the United States Army at Little Big Horn. Eventually most native land in the province was sold or ceded to the government by treaty, but there are still more native reserves here than anywhere else in Canada.

Louis Riel and the Métis, descendants of French voyageurs and natives, made a significant mark on prairie history here in the hills and valleys of Saskatchewan. In 1884, after fighting for the rights of Métis and being exiled to the United States, Riel was called up by the settlers of present-day Saskatchewan, which at the time was part of the vast Northwest Territories. Riel's small band, fighting for provincial status for Saskatchewan and better treatment of natives and Métis, defeated Dominion troops in several early skirmishes. But Riel never wanted a military conflict, he hoped for negotiation. The Canadians, led by MacDonald waited for the inevitable and also had the advantage of numbers — especially since a new coast-to-coast railroad was continually bringing reinforcements. The Métis were finally defeated at Batoche in the last armed conflict on Canadian soil, and Riel was hanged as a traitor; he is still a hero in some quarters of the province for his unswerving determination to retain his people's sovereignty. Saskatchewan joined Confederation in 1905.

Since Riel's time, few other individuals have made such a personal mark on the province, save John Diefenbaker. Diefenbaker, who grew up in a tiny homestead near the Saskatchewan River, rose from the post of a country lawyer to become Prime Minister of Canada in the early 1960s. His law office, boyhood home, adult home and university office all are proud attractions. A lake also bears his name. Popular folk singer Joni Mitchell (born Joan Anderson) is probably the most famous modern daughter of the province: her formative years were spent in Saskatoon, and she is still known to drop by and sing an occasional set in a local club there.

Generally speaking, however, time still moves slowly in the province. Farmers are diversifying and growing such crops as flax now, and the mining of potash and the damming of rivers provide steady jobs, yet wheat and oil continue to power the economy. The province's two major cities both contain fewer than 200,000 residents and strive to fill the short summer with festivities. Regina is the elegant capital, so English it appears never to have left the Crown and choc-full of museums. Saskatoon, meanwhile, hosts a large university and offers a profusion of restaurants, sports, nightlife and culture.

 FINDING YOUR WAY AROUND

By Plane

The province's two largest airports are located in Regina and Saskatoon; several major carriers serve the province, shuttling air traffic to and from Calgary, Toronto, Vancouver and other Canadian cities.

Air Canada's offices in Regina (☎525-4711) are located at 2015 12th Avenue; in Saskatoon (☎652-4181), they are at the city airport.

Canadian Regional Airlines also maintains offices in Regina (☎569-2307) at 2002 Victoria Avenue and in Saskatoon (☎665-7688) at 123-2nd Avenue South.

To get to Saskatoon's airport, head directly north of the city approximately 7 kilometres. A chain of motels marks the approach. It is about a $12 taxi ride from downtown.

Regina's airport lies just southwest of the city, about 5 kilometres away; a cab costs $10 or a bit more.

By Bus

Greyhound Canada serves the province's major destinations. In Regina, the bus depot (☎787-3340) is located at 2041 Hamilton Street. In Saskatoon, the depot (☎933-8019) is at Pacific Avenue and 23rd Street East.

The **Saskatchewan Transportation Company** also serves lesser-visited parts of the province. In Regina, STC buses (☎787-3340) depart from the same depot at 2041 Hamilton Street; in Saskatoon, call ☎933-8000 to reach the company.

By Train

VIARail's (☎1-800-561-8630 from western Canada) cross-country Canadian service passes through the province during the night, making a stop here difficult although not impossible; coming from the east, for example, the thrice-weekly train stops in Saskatoon at 2:20am. Eastbound trains pass through at 3:25am.

The Saskatoon station (☎384-5665), located in the extreme southwest of the city at Cassino Avenue and Chappell Drive, is the largest station and usual point of embarking or disembarking in Saskatchewan; the cross-country train no longer runs through Regina. Smaller stations exist at Watrous and Biggar, stopping only on passenger request.

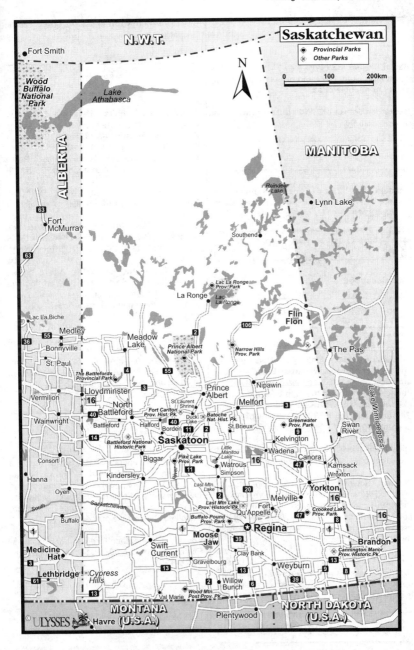

SASKATCHEWAN

Saskatchewan

⦿ Provincial Parks
⊗ Other Parks

0   100   200km

N.W.T.

Fort Smith

Wood
Buffalo
National
Park

Lake
Athabasca

MANITOBA

ALBERTA

63

Fort
McMurray

63

Reindeer
Lake

Lynn Lake

Southend

Lac La Biche

Medley

55

36

Bonnyville

St. Paul

Meadow
Lake

Lac La Ronge
Prov. Park

La Ronge

Lac
La Ronge

106

Flin
Flon

The Pas

Lake Winnipegosis

2

Prince Albert
National Park

Narrow Hills
Prov. Park

The Battlefords
Provincial Park

4

55

Lloydminster

3

Vermilion

16

North
Battleford

St Laurent
Shrine

Prince
Albert

Nipawin

Melfort

3

Fort Carlton
Prov. Hist. Pk.

Greenwater
Prov. Park

Swan
River

Wainwright

40

Battleford

Hafton

Ducks

40

Batoche
Nat. Hist. Pk.

St.Brieux

Borden

11

2

Kelvington

8

14

Battleford National
Historic Park

Saskatoon

Little
Manitou
Lake

Wadena

Canora

Kamsack

Consort

Biggar

Pike Lake
Prov. Park

16

47

Wroxton

Hanna

Kindersley

11

Watrous

Simpson

Yorkton

Oyen

South

Saskatchewan

Last Mtn
Lake

20

Melville

16

Buffalo

1

Last Mtn Lake
Prov. Historic Pk.

Fort
Qu'Appelle

47

Crooked Lake
Prov. Park

8

16

Buffalo Pound
Prov. Park

Regina

Brandon

Medicine
Hat

3

Lethbridge

61

Cypress
Hills

13

Moose
Jaw

Swift
Current

39

Clay Bank

Cannington Manor
Prov. Historic.Pk.

13

8

Gravelbourg

13

Weyburn

9

13

2

Willow
Bunch

6

39

Wood Mtn
Post Prov. Pk.

Val Marie

MONTANA

© ULYSSES   Havre (U.S.A.)

Plentywood

NORTH DAKOTA
(U.S.A.)

Public Transportation

Regina Transit *(333 Winnipeg St.,* ☎*777-7433)* covers the capital city and offers discounts for books of multiple rides.

Saskatoon Transit *(*☎*975-3100)* operates buses around that city.

Taxis

Capital Cab *(*☎*522-6621)* operates throughout Regina. In Saskatoon, try **Radio Cabs** *(*☎*242-1221)*.

 PRACTICAL INFORMATION

Area Code: 306.

Tourist Information Offices

Tourism Saskatchewan *(*☎*1-800-667-7191)* can be reached year-round. Provincial tourism information centres, scattered around the province on major highways, are only open during the summers; the lone exception is the centre in downtown Regina *(1919 Saskatchewan Dr.,* ☎*787-2300)*, which remains open all year.

Local tourism office hours vary a great deal, but the larger ones are open year-round.

Tourism Regina *(TransCanada Highway 1,* ☎*789-5099)* is way out on the eastern fringe of the city, impossible to reach except by driving but well-stocked and friendly. It is open all day weekdays, and all day weekends from May through August.

Tourism Saskatoon *(310 Idylwyld Dr. N. #102,* ☎*242-1206)* is located downtown and remains open weekdays all year. In summer months, it is also open all day Saturdays.

Post Offices

The main **post offices** are located at 2200 Saskatchewan Drive in Regina and at the corner of 4th Avenue North and 23rd Street East in Saskatoon.

Safety

The province is quite safe, even in its few urban areas. In the case of mishaps, the Regina Police Station *(*☎*569-3333)* and Saskatoon Police Station *(130 4th Ave. N.,* ☎*975-8300)* are the places to call. There is also a **Royal Canadian Mounted Police** depot *(*☎*975-5173)* in Saskatoon.

The **Canadian Automobile Association** maintains offices in the province's most populous areas, offering roadside assistance and information to members. In Regina, offices are located at 200 Albert Street North *(*☎*791-4321)*, 208 University Park Drive *(*☎*791-4323)* and at 3806 Albert Street *(*☎*791-4322)*; in Saskatoon, they are located at 3929 8th Street East #204 *(*☎*668-3770)* and 321 4th Avenue North *(*☎*668-3737)*.

Other offices are located in Moose Jaw *(80 Caribou St. W.,* ☎*693-5195)*; North Battleford *(2002-100th St.,* ☎*445-9451)*; Prince Albert *(68-13th St. W.,* ☎*764-6818)*; Swift Current *(15 Dufferin St. W.,* ☎*773-3193)*; Weyburn *(110 Souris Ave.,* ☎*842-6651)*; and Yorkton *(159 Broadway Street East,* ☎*783-6536)*.

Climate

Summers are generally warm and dry, with a great deal of sunshine. Winter, however, can bring dangerously low temperatures and blinding snowstorms; temperatures rarely rise above freezing during this time. As such, travellers should take precautions.

For updated weather forecast information in Regina, call ☎359-5749; in Saskatoon, call ☎975-4266.

⭐ EXPLORING

Regina ★

The **Wascana Centre ★★★** isn't obvious from downtown, but in fact it is a huge green space — reputedly the largest urban park in North America, even larger than New York City's Central Park — and the logical spot to begin exploring the city. This nearly 1,000-acre complex includes a lake, a university, bridges, lawns, gardens, a convention centre and even a bird sanctuary. Walking trails and bike paths wind throughout, and there is also ample parking and well-kept public washrooms.

A particularly interesting local institution here is the **Speaker's Corner ★★**, a podium on the lakeshore where opinions may be proffered to the public. This is a serious podium: the gas lamps and birches come from England.

Saskatchewan's cruciform **Legislative Building ★★★** *(free admission; May to Sep, every day 8am to 9pm; Oct to Apr, every day 8am to 5pm; Legislative Dr., ☎787-5358)*, facing Wascana Lake and landscaped gardens and lawns, may be Canada's most impressive provincial capital building. Its huge dome rises above the city; at the entrance, the fountain is one of a pair from London's Trafalgar Square (the other now resides in Ottawa).

Inside, ministers transact the business of the province — and in session, it's possible to sit in on the legislative machinations. A native heritage gallery and architectural flourishes such as a rotunda also occupy the building; guided tours leave every half hour from the front reception desk.

Wascana Waterfowl Park ★ is home to swans, pelicans and geese, some migrating and some who live here year-round. The small size of the pond here allows visitors to get very close to many of the birds.

The **John Diefenbaker Homestead ★★** *(May to Sep, every day 10am to 7pm; ☎522-3661)* commemorates Diefenbaker, who was born in northern Saskatchewan and served as Prime Minister of Canada. The homestead — which Diefenbaker actually helped his father build when he was just 10 years old — includes original family furnishings. A second, smaller building on the property belonged to Diefenbaker's uncle.

The **MacKenzie Art Gallery ★** *(free admission; every day 11am to 6pm; 3475 Albert St., ☎522-4242)*, located in the Wascana Centre at the corner of Albert Street and 23rd Avenue, showcases travelling exhibitions plus a permanent collection. The gallery, funded by the bequest of a local attorney, includes a painted bronze statue of John Diefenbaker standing on a chair.

Moving across the Prince Albert Bridge toward downtown, the **Royal Saskatchewan Museum ★** *(free admission; May to Sep, every day 9am to 8:30pm; Oct to Apr, every day 9am to 4:30pm; College Ave. and Albert St., ☎787-2815)* occupies a nice corner of parkland. This is Regina's natural history museum; the exhibits are heavy on sandbox-style dioramas of dinosaurs accompanied by stentorian voice overs, and there's more Saskatchewan geology here than a visitor could ever want or need to know. Still, this is the best place in town to see aboriginal Canadian artifacts and hear recorded aboriginal voices. An impressive selection of black-and-white photographs of native leaders, along with videotape of some dances and ceremonies, makes a fitting closing to the walk.

Toward downtown a few blocks north of the museum, you will come across lovely **Victoria Park ★★★** — an outstanding urban park, the best on the prairies, right in the centre of Regina with a fantastic view of downtown's modern skyscrapers. A series of pathways radiate like spokes of a wheel outward from the war memorial at the centre; spruce trees add a lovely contrast to the grass and gardens.

Nearby, Regina's **city hall ★★** *(free admission; Mon to Fri, 8am to 4:30pm; 2476 Victoria Ave., ☎777-7003)* is also worth a look while downtown. The lights on the roof are designed to resemble a queen's crown at night; tours, which must be booked in advance, offer a glimpse at the council chambers, foyer and forum. A souvenir shop is also maintained on the premises.

Scarth Street is downtown's pedestrian mall, ending at a large forgettable shopping centre called the Cornwall Centre. Just a few doors before the centre, the **Regina Plains Museum ★★** *($2; Apr to Sep, every day 10am to 4pm; Oct to Mar, every day Mon to Fri*

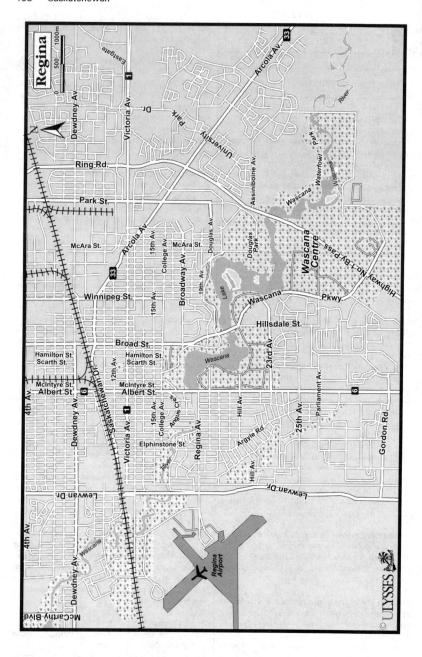

10am to 4pm; 1801 Scarth St., ☎780-9435) is a bit hard to find but worth the trip. Located four floors up inside the same downtown building that houses the Globe Theatre, this stop makes a good introduction to life on the plains.

The museum contains the obligatory plains chapel, schoolhouse, bedroom and post office recreations. More interesting are a small display describing native migrations through the province; an elegant glass sculpture of a wheatfield; a display concerning Louis Riel's trial; period surveyor's tools that were used to carve up the prairie (on paper, at least); and an old police mug book containing criminals' photographs. The cons' offenses, described in cursive handwriting as "cheating at cards", "resident of a bawdy house", and the like, make for entertaining reading.

The only two major sites requiring a drive are just a few minutes west of downtown and nearly adjacent to each other. The **Royal Canadian Mounted Police Centennial Museum ★★★** *(free admission; Jun to Sep 15, every day 8am to 6:45pm; Sep 15 to May, every day 10am to 4:45pm; Dewdney Ave. W., ☎780-5838)* is a popular, well-laid-out attraction located on the grounds of the R.C.M.P.'s training academy. Exhibits at this walk-through museum include many rifles, red-serge uniforms and other police artifacts dating from the formation of the R.C.M.P. force in 1873 to keep order and quell bootleggers in the Canadian Northwest. The story of the force's creation, march west across the prairies — their inaugural 3,200-kilometre walk from Montreal — and eventual relocation to the Regina post are all traced in detail here.

The museum is obviously strong on military items from all the historical periods, but as a bonus it also contains some truly interesting material relating to the darker side of the pioneers' resettling of the west: native land treaties, a buffalo skin incised with victories, Sitting Bull's rifle case, a buffalo skull paired with an ironic quote about the native buffalo hunt, the personal effects of Louis Riel, and so forth.

Government House ★ *(free admission; Tue to Sun, 1pm to 4pm; 4607 Dewdney Ave. W., ☎787-5717)*, close at hand to the R.C.M.P. training grounds, has been home to some of the province's highest officials since the late 19th century. It is still home to Saskatchewan's lieutenant governor, but tours are offered. On

some summer weekend afternoons, the staff also serves tea.

Southern Saskatchewan

The TransCanada Highway runs east to west through southern Saskatchewan, crossing wheatfields and the occasional town. Coming from the east, the road is uninspiring save the occasional small-town museum.

Fort Qu'Appelle River Valley ★★★

The Fort Qu'Appelle River Valley makes a surprising detour, however: the river has cut a little valley in the otherwise flat countryside. **Route 47**, barely known by tourists, parallels the river as it dips through the brown and green hills. It passes **Round Lake ★★** and then **Crooked Lake Provincial Park ★★**, beautiful lakes for swimming, fishing and sightseeing. A string of tiny tree-shaded resort towns provides campgrounds and the odd country store.

At a bend in the valley, where the river feeds into a series of lakes, the small town of **Fort Qu'Appelle** charms visitors with its setting — tucked among hills — as well as a smattering of historic sites. The tourist information centre is situated inside a former train station; a former Hudson's Bay Company log cabin for which the town is named is now a small **museum ★**. The fort was the site of a historic treaty ceding vast tracts of native lands in Saskatchewan to the Canadian government.

Moose Jaw

Moose Jaw (pop. 30,000), a former bootlegging capital during U.S. prohibition years, sprouts up in the flatlands west of Regina and offers little of interest besides the offbeat name, a series of downtown murals and a sprinkling of historic sites.

The **Western Development Museum's Transportation Museum ★** *($4.50; Apr to Dec, 10am to 7pm; 50 Diefenbaker Dr., ☎693-5989)*, north of downtown in a somewhat forlorn location, serves up the history of Canadian transportation — everything from canoe, Red River cart and pack horse to vintage rail cars, automobiles and airplanes. A narrow gauge railway runs behind the museum on weekends and holidays from late May to

Labour Day. Also popular is the **Snowbirds Gallery**, devoted to Canada's national aerobatic team. In the flight simulator, in the museum's cinema, the airplanes' artful manoeuvres come to life on a big movie screen.

Crescent Park ★, just east of downtown, surrounds the Moose Jaw River and makes a pleasant short walk beneath trees and over a bridge. The **Tunnels of Little Chicago** ★ *($3; ☎693-5261)* — a series of catacombs running beneath a downtown block of the town — are theoretically fascinating, since they were home to unsavoury characters like Al Capone, who used them as refuge from the long arm of the law. The Tunnels have been over-promoted, however, and an adjacent museum doesn't add much of interest. The half-hour tour is certainly worth a ticket; the big challenge is to imagine that Moose Jaw once bustled and bristled with so much activity.

Claybank

Southeast of Moose Jaw, on Route 339, is little Claybank and its historic **Claybank Brick Plant** ★ *($3; Jul to Aug, Sat to Sun 10am to 4pm; ☎799-4431)*. The plant operated from 1914 until 1989, one of Canada's two pre-eminent such plants during that time; its bricks faced such buildings as Quebec City's Chateau Frontenac. The complex of high chimneys and dome-like kilns can be toured by arrangement, and there is also a tearoom on the premises.

Gravelbourg

Southwest of Moose Jaw, a 115-kilometre detour off the TransCanada down routes 2 and then 43, Gravelbourg is the acknowledged centre of French culture in Saskatchewan. A French-Canadian culture centre and a dance troupe both make their homes here. Most prominent among downtown's buildings is the **Cathédrale Notre-Dame de l'Assomption** ★★ *(free admission; Jul to Aug, every day 9am to 5pm; ☎648-3322)*. Built in 1918, the church is a historic property and features wonderful interior murals painted by Charles Maillard, its founding pastor, over a 10-year period.

Nearby, on 5th Avenue East, the **Musée de Gravelbourg** ★ preserves mementos from the original French-speaking settlers of the region, including the missionary Father L.P. Gravel for whom the town is named.

Other Sights

Nearby, **Wood Mountain Post Provincial Historic Park** ★★ *(voluntary admission fee; Jun to Jul, Thu to Mon, 10am to 5pm; Aug to Sep, 10am to 4pm; ☎787-2700)*, a former Mountie post, is interesting particularly for its association with the Sioux chief Sitting Bull and his people. Sitting Bull came here in the spring of 1877 after defeating the United States Army at the battle of Little Big Horn; as many as 5,000 Sioux were already hiding in the surrounding hills.

The chief quickly forged a friendship with police Major James Walsh, but political pressure from both the Canadian and United States governments replaced Walsh with another officer who began a siege against the Sioux. The two buildings here, staffed with interpreters, explain the story in more detail.

Sitting Bull's former camp is located near the village of Willow Bunch in **Jean-Louis Legare Park** ★. Legare, a Métis trader, supplied food to the Sioux during their exile and also provisioned them for their long march back to the United States in 1881.

Approximately 40 kilometres north of Regina on Route 20 is **Last Mountain House Provincial Park** ★, a small but interesting recreation of a short-lived Hudson's Bay Company fur post. Built of wood and local white clay, the post was established near a buffalo herd in the adjacent river valley in 1869. But the buffalo moved west the following year, never to return.

Today the windswept park's displays include a fur press, trading store, icehouse for preserving meat, bunkhouse quarters for trappers and the more spacious quarters of the officers. During summer, park interpreters are on hand to recreate the experience.

Saskatoon ★

Saskatoon is Saskatchewan's hip address. Home to a large university, the place where the province's young people head for stimulation; as such, it possesses an astounding number of bars, restaurants and shopping malls, and lots of nightlife (for the prairies, that is). The city is beautifully situated, as well, occupying both banks of the much-loved South Saskatchewan River.

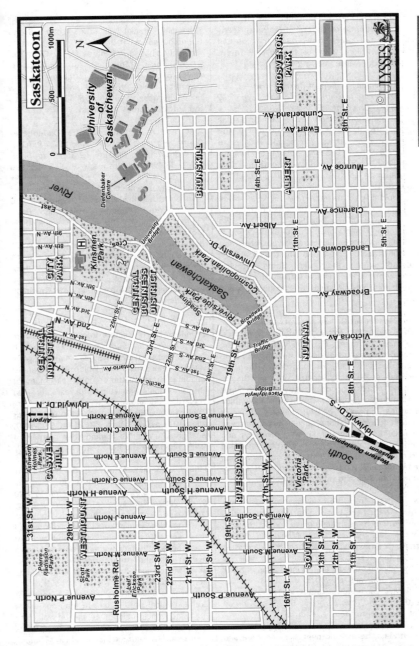

Saskatoon

University of Saskatchewan

0   500   1000m

N

River
East

Diefenbaker Centre

University Bridge

CITY PARK
9th Av. N
8th Av. N
Kinsmen Park
Cres.
5th Av. N
4th Av. N
3rd Av. N
2nd Av. N
1st Av. N

CENTRAL INDUSTRIAL

CENTRAL BUSINESS DISTRICT

25th St. E
23rd St. E
22nd St. E
20th St. E
19th St. E

Ontario Av.
Pacific Av.

Spadina Cres.

Riverside Park

Saskatchewan

Cosmopolitan Park

University Dr.

Broadway Bridge

Traffic Bridge

Place Idylwyld Bridge

1st Av. S
2nd Av. S
3rd Av. S
4th Av. S

Albert Av.
11th St. E
Landsdowne Av.

Broadway Av.

Victoria Av.

NUTANA

8th St. E

BRUNSKILL

14th St. E

ALBERT
Munroe Av.
Clarence Av.

Cumberland Av.
Ewart Av.

GROSVENOR PARK

8th St. E
5th St. E

Idylwyld Dr. N
Airport

Avenue B North
Avenue C North
Avenue E North
Avenue G North
Avenue H North
Avenue J North
Avenue M North

Ashworth Holmes Park
CASWELL HILL

Pierre Radisson Park
Scott Park
Leif Erickson Park

WESTMOUNT

31st St. W
29th St. W

Rusholme Rd.

23rd St. W
22nd St. W
21st St. W
20th St. W
19th St. W

Avenue P North

Avenue B South
Avenue C South
Avenue E South
Avenue G South
Avenue H South
Avenue J South
Avenue M South

RIVERSDALE

17th St. W
16th St. W

Avenue P South

South

Idylwyld Dr. S

Western Development Museum

Victoria Park

SOUTH
13th St. W
12th St. W
11th St. W

ULYSSES ©

Historical sites are harder to find. The city is, in fact, rather short on cultural attractions. Nearly all of the good ones are concentrated downtown along the river. It's possible to see everything of note in a single busy day.

The **Ukrainian Museum of Canada** ★★ *($2; Tue to Sat 10am to 5pm, Sun 1pm to 5pm; 910 Spadina Crescent E., ☎244-3800)* is a surprisingly good history lesson beneath a small roof. Through a series of walk-in rooms, the museum uses words and simple articles to describe the Ukrainian people's Eastern European origins and persecution, their migration to North America, their settlement of the prairies, and their subsequent endurance as a people. Highlights among the displays include a good section on the deep religious significance of the beautiful art of pysanka (Easter egg painting); a careful explanation of the distinctively domed Ukrainian churches; and a delineation of where and why the Ukrainians settled where they did. Some intricate ornamental breads and examples of rozpys — the decorative painting of furnishings, walls and doors — are also nice touches.

The **Mendel Art Gallery and Arts Centre** ★★★ *(free admission; every day 9am to 9pm; 950 Spadina Crescent E., ☎975-7610)* is the province's best art museum. Its exhibits rotate quite regularly, and whether drawn from the permanent collection or just on loan, they're always interesting; concurrently showing might be American James Walsh's astonishingly thick acrylics, in one gallery; several different multimedia installations, occupying another; and a collection of modern prints, paintings and other media works by native artists sprinkled throughout. The museum also contains such amenities as a children's room, coffeeshop, good gift shop and urban greenhouse.

A footpath from the back of the centre leads down to the river, hooking up with an extensive network of trails running north and south along both river banks. The **Meewasin Valley trails** ★★ extend more than 50 kilometres along the river, a joy for cyclists and walkers. The valley's other amenities include an outdoor skating rink and an urban grassland reserve. The **Meewasin Valley Authority headquarters** ★ *(402 Second Ave. S., ☎655-6888)* provide an introduction to the river and the city.

Southeast, across the river, lies the large and pretty **University of Saskatchewan** ★★ campus. Several attractions of historic interest are here, though some are only open during the summer when school is out of session. Especially quaint is the **Little Stone Schoolhouse** ★ *(☎966-8384)*, Saskatoon's first schoolhouse — it dates from 1887. The **St. Thomas More College** chapel ★ *(☎966-8900)* is worth a look for its mural by Canadian artist William Kurelek, and the university **observatory** *(☎966-6396)* opens to the public Saturday evenings.

Also not to be missed, the **Diefenbaker Centre** ★ *(free admission; Mon to Fri 9:30am to 4:30pm, Sat to Sun 12:30pm to 5pm; ☎966-8384)* preserves many of Diefenbaker's personal papers and effects, and his gravestone is located nearby on the university campus. Other displays include replicas of the former Prime Minister's office and Privy Council chamber. The centre — splendidly located with a view of the river and the downtown — is also famous for housing what is probably the most renowned piece of furniture in the province: a simple maple desk that once belonged to John A. Macdonald, the man considered the father of Canadian Confederation.

On the outskirts of town sits the **Western Development Museum's Boomtown 1910** ★ *($4.50; 9am to 5pm; ☎931-1910)*, which reconstructs a typical western mining town's main street in movie-set fashion. More than 30 buildings make up the complex; like many of the province's museums, its exhibits lean toward agricultural equipment and farm implements. Also outside the city, about four kilometres away, is **Valley Road** *(☎386-9544)*, an agricultural drive leading to a number of fruit, vegetable and herb farms in the area.

Finally, a 10-minutes drive to the north leads to the wonderful **Wanuskewin Heritage Park** ★★★ *($6; May to Sep, every day 9am to 9pm; Oct to Apr, Wed to Sun 9am to 5pm; ☎931-6767)*, perhaps the best native museum in the prairies. The area around Saskatoon had been settled continuously for thousands of years before the first white settlers arrived; a river valley just north of the city was long used as a "buffalo jump" where local native bands hunted and established winter camps. Now the property is open to the public as a series of archaeological sites — ancient tipi rings and a medicine wheel, for instance, can be walked to — plus an indoor museum and interpretive centre dealing with the history of First Nations people here.

Buffalo

"A people without history is like wind in the buffalo grass", says a panel in the museum, and the museum does indeed throw much light onto the native peoples of the Plains. The differences among Cree, Dene, Lakota, Dakota and Assiniboine are carefully explained in one display, and their recorded voices can be heard by pressing a button. Other rooms in the centre host art exhibits and slide shows; talks and conferences; and a native-foods café. Ongoing archaeological research is also conducted on the grounds.

The Yellowhead Highway

Yorkton

Yorkton would be rather uninteresting but for the **Western Development Museum's "Story of People" museum** ★★ *($4.50; May 3 to Sep 10, every day 9am to 6pm; Highway 16, ☎783-8361)*, which traces the various immigrant populations that have made the province as colourful as it is.

Yorkton is also notable as the site of western Canada's first brick Ukrainian church. **St. Mary's Ukrainian Catholic Church** ★★ *(155 Catherine St., ☎783-4594)*, built in 1914,

is topped with a distinctive 21-metre-high cathedral dome. The dome was painted in 1939-41 by Steven Meush and is considered one of the most beautiful such domes on the continent. Inside, there's beautiful icon work by Ihor Suhacev. If the church is not open, visitors can ask at the adjacent rectory for a look inside. The church also plays host to an annual "Vid Pust" (Pilgrimage Day) celebration each June.

Veregin

Approximately 50 kilometres north off the Yellowhead, Veregin houses the **National Doukhobour Heritage Village** ★★ *($2; mid-May to mid-Sep, every day 10am to 6pm; mid-Sep to mid-May, Mon to Fri, 10am to 4pm; ☎542-4441)*, an 11-building complex which throws light on one of the province's most intriguing immigrant groups. The Doukhobour came to Saskatchewan in 1899 and established a short-lived community here, eschewing meat, alcohol and tobacco in favour of an agrarian existence. They soon moved farther west, but this museum preserves the original prayer home and machinery shop. Also on display are a brick oven, bath house, agricultural equipment and blacksmith's shop.

Canora

Just 25 kilometres west of Veregin, Canora welcomes the traveller with a 7.6-metre statue in Slavic dress. A tourist booth, next to the statue, operates from June until September to orient visitors to local attractions. This little village is also home to a fine restored **Ukrainian Orthodox Heritage Church ★** *(Jun 1 to Sep 15, every day 8am to 6pm; 710 Main St., ☎563-5662)* Built in 1928, the church displays Kiev architecture and stained glass; visitors can obtain a key next door at 720 Main Street during times when the church isn't open.

Wroxton

Wroxton is some distance off of the Yellowhead — 35 kilometres north — but interesting for its two Ukrainian churches on opposite ends of the village. Both domes are visible just north of the main highway, and can be reached by driving one of the town's several dirt roads.

Around Wadena

In the Wadena area, **Big Quill Lake** and various other marshes on both sides of the Yellowhead offer good opportunities to view birds. The advocacy group Ducks Unlimited helps preserve many of these lands and interpret them for the general public. **Little Quill Lake Heritage Marsh ★**, best reached from Highway 35, was designated an international shorebird reserve in 1994 and is open year-round. This marsh hosts more than 150,000 migrating and resident shorebirds each year; visitors can hike, learn from interpretive signs and climb an observation tower.

St. Brieux

St. Brieux features a little **museum ★** *(May 1 to Aug 31, 10am to 4pm; 300 Barbier Dr., ☎275-2123)* in a former Roman Catholic rectory. It contains artifacts of early settlers from Quebec, France and Hungary; tours here are conducted in both English and French.

Meunster

Continuing west, also near the Yellowhead, the small town of Muenster is notable for a beautiful twin-towered cathedral and adjoining monastery. **St. Peter's Cathedral ★★** *(free; Mar to Dec, 9am to 9pm; winter, closed Jan and Feb; ☎682-1777)*, built in 1910, features paintings by Berthold Imhoff, a German-born count who later moved to St. Walburg, Saskatchewan, and became an artist. Approximately 80 life-sized figures grace the cathedral, with saints and religious scenes making up the interior. **St. Peter's Abbey ★★** *(March 1 to Dec 31, 8am to dusk; ☎682-1777)* gives a sense of what the monastic life is like: a self-guided tour reveals the abbey's farm, gardens, print shop and so on. It's also possible to sleep a night in the monastery for a small donation.

Little Manitou Lake ★

For centuries, travellers have been making a trip to Little Manitou Lake to "take the waters". This lake is so high in natural mineral salts that a person swimming can't sink — it is saltier here than in the Dead Sea, or in any ocean on Earth — and the salts are reputed to have restorative powers. That's why an strange little tourist town has sprung up around the lake, itself oddly placed among barren hills.

Borden

Borden, the boyhood home of John Diefenbaker — his house has been moved to downtown Regina — is interesting as a stop because one can take tours of a local **United Grain Growers (UGG) grain elevator ★** *(every day 8am to 5pm; ☎997-2010)* year-round. Guests are requested to phone ahead, however, to arrange these tours.

The Battlefords

Battleford (pop. 4,000), former capital of the North West Territories, was once important but is today overshadowed by its twin city of North Battleford across the Saskatchewan River. As usual, railway politics decided the fate of the twin towns. **Fort Battleford National Historic Site** *($3; May 18 to Oct 14, every day 9am to 5pm; Jul to Aug, every day 9am to 6pm; ☎937-2621)* recalls the original impetus for the townsite — a Mountie post — complete with four restored period buildings. The barracks house contains additional displays of historical interest, explained by guides in period police costume.

North Battleford (pop. 14,000) is often visited for the **Western Development Museum's Heritage Farm and Village** ★ *($4.50; May to mid-Sep, every day 8:30am to 7pm; ☎445-8033)*, a mostly agricultural museum featuring plenty of period farm machinery. The town is also famous as home to artist Allan Sapp. The **Allan Sapp Gallery** ★ *(May to Aug, every day 1pm to 5pm; Sep to May, Wed to Sunday 1pm to 5pm; ☎445-1760)* showcases the work of the prairies' best-known and loved native artist. Sapp's paintings, recollections of native life from a half-century ago, hang in the important museums of Canada and are displayed and sold here; the gallery, located on the ground floor of a restored Carnegie library, also contains hundreds of works by Sapp's mentor Allan Gonor.

West Central Saskatchewan

Poundmaker Trail

Route 40, the so-called Poundmaker Trail, is the former stronghold of the Poundmaker Cree Nation. **Cut Knife** sports what is said to be Canada's largest tomohawk, a suspended sculpture of wood and fiberglass whose fir handle is more than 16 metres long and supports a six-ton blade. The surrounding park contains the obligatory small museum. The legendary **Chief Poundmaker's grave** is also in town, on the Cree Reserve, testament to a man who favoured peace over war and surrendered his force of natives to the Mounties rather than continue to shed blood.

Hafford

Just northeast of Saskatoon, near the village of Hafford, the **Redberry Project Highway 40** ★ *(☎549-2400)* maintains one of the province's best waterfowl projects in a federal migratory bird sanctuary on Redberry Lake. Their motto is "we have friends in wet places", and the specialty here is pelicans. More than 1000 American white pelicans nest on the lake's New Tern Island; it's one of just 14 colonies of the birds in Saskatchewan.

Prince Albert

Prince Albert (pop. 34,000), oldest city in the province, is a gateway in more senses that one. It's the largest town near Prince Albert

Provincial Park, the site of a huge mill that converts the northern forests into pulp and paper, and the breeding ground for three Canadian Prime Ministers. Though the town began as a fur post for Northwestern explorer Peter Pond in 1776, the town as it exists today was established nearly a full century later by the Reverend James Nisbet as a mission for local Cree.

The **Diefenbaker House Museum** *(free admission; mid-May to Sep, Mon to Sat 10am to 6pm, Sun 10am to 9pm; 246-19th St. W., ☎953-4863)* is probably the most famous stop in town. It contains many of the former Canadian Prime Minister's personal effects and furnishings, and describes his relationship to the city.

The **Prince Albert Historical Museum** *($1; mid-May to Sep, Mon to Sat 10am to 6pm, Sun 10am to 9pm; ☎764-2992)* brings local history into focus, beginning with native and fur-trader culture from the mid-1800s. There's a second-floor tearoom with a balcony overlooking the North Saskatchewan River, as well.

Several more museums in Prince Albert are also worth a look. The **Evolution of Education Museum** *(free admission; mid-May to Sep, every day 10am to 8pm; ☎953-4386)*, located in a former one-room schoolhouse, and the **Rotary Museum of Police and Corrections** *(free admission; mid-May to Sep; ☎953-4386)*, which is inside a former North West Mounted Police guardhouse and includes a fascinating display of weapons fashioned by prisoners trying to break out of provincial jails.

Around Duck Lake

Southwest of Prince Albert, **Duck Lake** witnessed one of what was probably the most famous event in Saskatchewan history: the battle between Louis Riel and his band of Métis and the North West Police. The **Duck Lake Regional Interpretive Centre** ★★ *(mid-May to Sep, every day 10am to 5:30pm; ☎467-2057)* describes the events as they unfolded, displaying artifacts from the Métis Resistance campaign, you can also climb a viewing tower of the battlefield grounds. A series of painted outdoor murals welcome the visitor.

About 25 kilometres west of Duck Lake, **Fort Carlton Provincial Historic Park** ★★ *($2.50; May 18 to Sep 2; every day 10am to 6pm;*

☎953-2322) dates from 1810, another in the string of Hudson's Bay Company posts in Saskatchewan. An important land treaty was also signed here. Today the site consists of a reconstructed stockade and buildings; interpretive staff lead tours and explain how the fort was a Mountie post until the Battle of Duck Lake. Just outside the fort, a Plains Cree encampment — three tipis furnished in typical late-19th-century fashion — give a sense of what and how the natives traded with the English. The objects in these tipis include robes, skins, pipes, weapons and other ceremonial objects.

St. Laurent

St. Laurent Shrine ★ *(May 1 to Aug 31;* ☎467-2212), makes an enjoyable side trip in the area. Built in 1874 as an Order of the Oblate mission right on the South Saskatchewan River, and quite similar to the Our Lady of Lourdes shrine in France, it hosts Sunday services at 4pm during July and August. Annual pilgrimages also take place during those months; these date from 1893, when one Brother Guillet's leg miraculously healed after he prayed to the shrine.

Batoche National Historic Park ★★★ *($3; May 18 to Oct 14, 9am to 5pm; Jul to Aug, 10am to 6pm;* ☎423-6227) is the place where Riel's story came to its end in March of 1885. The site, a peaceful agricultural valley where the Métis had settled after ceding their lands, became capital of the Métis resistance when Riel challenged the English. Today, a walking path, museum and interpretive staff provide guidance to the remains of the village of Batoche, including the restored St. Antoine de Padoue church and rectory. There are also trenches and rifle pits used by the Mountie forces during their four-day siege of Batoche.

OUTDOORS

Southern Saskatchewan

Buffalo Pound Provincial Park ★ *(*☎694-3659), 23 kilometres northeast of Moose Jaw, presents a variety of recreational choices, including — most popularly — a chance to view grazing bison. A number of hiking trails wind through the dips and rises of the Qu'Appelle Valley: the trail tells the story of the Charles Nicolle Homestead, a stone dwelling constructed in 1930; another proceeds through a marsh; yet another traverses the junction of two rivers, an area rich with such wildlife as painted turtles, deer and great blue herons. The river is a popular beach and boating destination, as well.

Cannington Manor Provincial Historic Park ★ *(free admission; May to Sep, 10am to 6pm;* ☎577-2131) recounts a short-lived experiment by the Englishman Captain Edward Pierce. Pierce tried to form a utopian colony here, based on agriculture; and for awhile it worked, a combination of days working the fields and diversions such as fox hunts, cricket, horse races and afternoon tea. The experiment did not survive, but the manor features period antiques and farm tools used on the site. Six other buildings — some original, some reconstructed — complete the park.

Last Mountain Lake National Wildlife Area ★★ *(free admission; May 1 to Oct 31;* ☎836-2022), occupying the northern end of the lake with the same name, is believed to be the oldest bird sanctuary on the North American continent. More than 250 species of bird touch down here during their annual migrations south, including the spectacular whooping crane. These migrations are most spectacular during spring (mid-May) and fall (September); visitors either choose to follow a scripted auto tour or use their feet to climb the observation tower and walk the two hiking trails. The preserve is best reached by turning east off Highway 2 at the town of Simpson, then following signs to the lakeshore. There is talk that the site's administrators may soon begin charging a fee to visit the preserve.

Grasslands National Park ★★ *(*☎298-2257, year-round). This park was the first representative portion of original mixed-grass prairie set aside in North America. Among the variety of habitats represented here are grasslands, buttes, badlands and the Frenchman River Valley; spectacular views can be had from some of the butte tops, while the wildlife includes the rare swift fox, pronghorn antelopes and golden eagles. Most interesting, though, is the unique **prairie dog town** ★★, where colonies of black-tailed prairie dogs still live in their natural environment. Guided hikes are given from the park office in Val Marie on summer Sundays, and wilderness camping is permitted in the park — but permission must be obtained from private landowners to access certain parts of it.

Pike Lake Park ★ *(☎933-6966)*, a small recreation park about 30 kilometres southwest of Saskatoon, is a popular day trip for residents of Saskatchewan's largest city. The terrain here includes lawns shaded by aspen, ash and birch trees, a good beach and lots of wildlife. Watersports facilities include a pool, waterslide and canoes for hire; hiking trails, tennis courts, golf and mini-golf are also available here.

The Yellowhead Highway

Cumberland House Provincial Historic Park ★★★ *(☎888-2077)*, on an island in the North Saskatchewan River near the Manitoba border, was quite important historically: it was the first Hudson's Bay Company fur post in western Canada. Later, it served as a port for steamboat traffic along the river. An 1890s-era powderhouse and part of a sternwheeler paddleboat are all that remain, but it's still a fascinating stop.

Duck Mountain Provincial Park ★★ *(☎542-3482)* sits 25 kilometres east of Kamsack, right on the Manitoba border. Open year-round, the park completely surrounds popular Madge Lake. The mountain itself rises 240 metres above the surrounding terrain, covered with aspens. Full recreational facilities are here, including a campground, golf course, mini-golf course, fishing gear and beach. A lodge within park grounds provides accommodations.

The Battlefords Provincial Park ★ *(☎386-2212)* is considered one of the recreational jewels of the province. Its location on the northeast shore of Jackfish Lake provides easy access to fishing and sailing. Equipment is available for these watersports; there are also a golf course and mini-golf course on premises, as well as a store and year-round resort-style accommodations.

Greenwater Lake Provincial Park ★ *(☎278-2972)* is on Highway 38, north of Kelvington in the province's eastern Porcupine Forest. There's a marina with boat rentals and fishing gear in the summer, as well as tennis, golf, and horseback riding facilities; in winter, the park becomes a destination of cross-country skiers. Nice log cabins are available for rent, too.

West-Central Saskatchewan

Prince Albert National Park ★★★ *(☎663-5322)*, one million acres large, is one of Saskatchewan's finest parks. Entering from the south entrance on Route 263, you will pass through grassland and fields, then aspen parklands and finally forests.

Waskesiu Lake is the park area's largest and most popular body of water, including most of the services, beaches and activities. Farther off the beaten track, the park is noted for several good canoe routes and hiking trails that provide access to bird and plant life: bird enthusiasts, for instance, come to glimpse Canada's second-largest colony of American white pelicans, who nest on Lavallee Lake, while wolves, elk and buffalo also reside here. Hikers often choose to explore Boundary Bog Trail, which penetrates the park's muskeg territory — including carnivorous pitcher plants and dwarf stands of larch more than a century old — or the Treebeard Trail, winding among tall, aromatic groves of balsam fir and white spruce.

The park is most famous, however, for wise old Archibald Bellaney, an Englishman who came here in 1931, took the name of Grey Owl, and lived on a remote lake. **Grey Owl's Cabin** ★, a one-room log cabin on Ajawaan Lake, can only be reached by boat, canoe or — during summer — by foot via a 20-kilometre trail. It's the place Grey Owl lived for seven years; tours are available from park staff.

Waskesiu Riding Stables ★ *(☎663-5286 or 672-3547, May 17 to Sept 2, 9am to 9pm)*, just outside Waskesiu on Highway 264, offers guided trail rides through the wooded foothills for everyone from greenhorns to experts. Rides leave every hour on the hour, last five hours and include a packed lunch; rates range from $12 per hour for beginners to $13 per hour for more experienced riders.

Lac La Ronge Provincial Park ★★★ *(☎1-800-772-4064 or 425-4234)* lies just north of Prince Albert Park on Route 2, providing similar scenery — and more of it, as this is the province's largest provincial park — than its more well-known neighbourhood. More than 100 lakes are here, including enormous Lac La Ronge, dotted with what are said to be more than 1,000 islands. Cliffs, rock paintings and sand beaches can also be found in the park.

Additionally, Lac La Ronge Park contains one of the province's showcase historic sites, the **Holy Trinity Anglican Church Historic Site ★★★** — Saskatchewan's oldest standing building, an enormous structure in an oddly remote location. Built in the late 1850s from local wood, then completed with stained-glass windows shipped from England, the church was part of the historic Stanley Mission.

Narrow Hills Provincial Park ★★ *(☎426-2611)* lies just to the east of Prince Albert Park, although there is no direct connecting route; it can only be reached by a series of roads. It is famous for its eskers — the long, narrow glacially deposited hills that give the park its name — and more than 25 bodies of water, harbouring a number of species of game fish. One esker is topped by a fire tower, and its headquarters building includes a small museum.

Scenic **Anglin Lake ★★**, southwest of Prince Albert Park, has at least on particularly distinguishing feature: it harbours the continent's largest nesting loon population.

 ACCOMMODATIONS

Regina

Turgeon International Hostel *($34; K, tv, sb, ≡; 2310 McIntyre, Regina, S4P 2S2, ☎1-800-467-8357 or 791-8165, ≈721-2667).* A great value for the guest who enjoys interacting with other travellers, this friendly hostel provides accommodations in the way of bun rooms, a family room with space for five and a room for groups. The house once belonged to William Turgeon, an Acadian from New Brunswick who came to Regina and ran a successful law practice for many years; it was later purchased by Hostelling International and moved on a flatbed trailer. Its location is superb — the Royal Saskatchewan Museum is visible at the end of the street, for instance — and the family room is a super bargain. There's also a huge self-catering kitchen, delightful travel library, airy television room and great manager. The neighbourhood is within walking distance of all the city's major attractions and restaurants, as well. The office is closed during the day, however, and the facility closes completely during January.

Crescent House *($45 bkfst incl.; sb; 180 Angus Crescent, Regina, ☎352-5995, ≈352-5995; email: cheryl.mogg@dlcwest.com)* is a bed-and-breakfast located on a crescent-shaped street just minutes by foot from most of Regina's major attractions. Other touches include a fireplace, three friendly terrier dogs, and a backyard shaded by 50-foot ash and elm trees.

Imperial 400 *($56; pb, tv, ≡, ℜ, ⊛, ≈; 4255 Albert St., Regina, S4S 3R6, ☎584-8800, ≈584-0204).* Family-friendly Saskatchewan motel chain featuring basic rooms, on-site restaurant and waterslide/pool. Rates are modified for families and senior citizens.

Sands Hotel and Resort *($67; pb, tv, ≡, ℜ, ≈, ◊, ☺; 1818 Victoria Ave., Regina, S4P 0R1, ☎1-800-667-6500 or 569-1666, ≈525-3550).* Not exactly a luxury hotel, but this unusual place tries to make visitors feel like they're in one. Among the perks: jacuzzi suites and free guest access to the in-house driving range.

Country Inns & Suites *($78 bkfst incl.; pb, tv, ≡, K; 3321 Eastgate Bay, Regina, S42 1A4, ☎1-800-456-4000 or 789-9117, ≈789-3010).* This hotel chain strives to offer a more home-like atmosphere than most chains; rooms are done up with brass-style beds and duvets resembling quilts. Most rooms have honour bars; all guests receive free newspapers and can make free local calls. Suites come with a sitting room, sofa bed and microwave as well, and continental breakfast is included.

Travelodge *($81; pb, tv, ≡, ℜ, ≈, ☺; 4177 Albert St. South, Regina, S4N 7A9, ☎1-800-578-7878 or 565-0455, ≈586-9311).* A 200-room contemporary facility which caters to both business and leisure travellers. Rooms are large and comfortable with free in-room coffee. The huge indoor waterslide/pool with a play area for children is popular. Local calls are free, and there are no long distance surcharges. Meals are served in the authentic Irish pub, The Blarney Stone, where you can listen to Celtic music and relish a pint of Guinness.

Regina Inn Hotel and Convention Centre *($82; pb, tv, ≡, ℜ, ⊛, ☺; 1975 Broad St., Regina, S4P 1Y2, ☎525-6767 or 1-800-667-8162, ≈525-3630).* Another centrally located luxury hotel, this one's amenities include a dinner theatre, jacuzzi suites, a health club and winter plug-ins. Guests can choose from four on-site restaurants and lounges catering to fine or casual diners.

Ramada Plaza Hotel *($84; pb, tv, ≡, ℜ, ≈; 1919 Saskatchewan Dr., Regina, S4P 4H2, ☎1-800-272-6232 or 525-5255, ⇝781-7188).* Shopping and gambling attract guests to this luxury hotel as the property is near the Cornwall Centre Shopping Mall and Casino Regina. Whirlpools, satellite television, an indoor pool with adjacent waterslide complex cater those seeking entertainment on premises. On-site restaurant and bar, too.

Best Western Seven Oaks Inn *($90; pb, tv, ≡, ℜ, ≈, △; 777 Albert St., Regina, S4R 2P6, ☎1-800-667-8063 or 757-0121, ⇝565-2577).* Large, modern hotel located on the main city thoroughfare with many amenities including a licensed restaurant, sauna, indoor pool/whirlpool. Small pets are allowed, and there are winter plug-ins.

Hotel Saskatchewan-Radisson Plaza *($100; tv, pb, ≡, ℜ, △, ⊘, ⊛; 2125 Victoria Ave., Regina, S4P 0S3, ☎1-800-333-3333 or 522-7691, ⇝522-8988).* This hotel's fabulous location along one side of pretty Victoria Park, facing the city skyline, is only the beginning of the luxury that makes it Regina's crown jewel of accommodations. Built in 1927 by the Canadian Pacific Railroad, the hotel features such decorative notes as a chandelier from the Imperial Palace in St. Petersburg. More touches were added during a $28-million renovation in the early 1990s. There's also the original barbershop, a health club, massage therapists and an elegant dining room. How classy is it? Queen Elizabeth and Richard Chamberlain stay here whenever they're in town — not at the same time, of course — in the $995-per-night Royal Suite, where a special device heats towels as occupants bubble in the tub and the windows are fitted with bulletproof glass. It's 3,000 square feet of luxury and history.

Southern Saskatchewan

Swift Current

Heritage Inn Bed and Breakfast *($45; sb; Box 1301, ☎773-6305, ⇝773-0135).* Archaeologists and equine enthusiasts like this small bed-and-breakfast for its horses and Swift Current Petroglyph complex — both located on the property. There are two rooms containing queen-size beds, plus one family-style room with a set of bunks and a single bed.

Fort Qu'Appelle

Country Squire Inn *($50; pb, tv, ≡, ℜ; Highway 10, S0G 1S0, ☎332-5603, ⇝332-6708).* Probably the best affordable motel in the Fort Qu'Appelle Valley. Big clean rooms, cheerful help and a good restaurant (see below) all add up to an enjoyable experience. Short hiking trails beginning in back of the place snake to the top of surrounding hills. There are a lounge, a bar and 'offsales' — on-premises sale of beer — here, as well.

Bluenose Vacation Farm *($60; sb, ≡, ≈; Box 173, Qu'Appelle, S0g 4A0, ☎699-7192, ⇝699-7192; email: aalluhni@the.link.ca).* This bed-and-breakfast, located on a grain farm, aims to please with three-day vacation packages – including all meals and snacks – as well as single night stays. On the grounds are an Agricultural Interpretive Centre and mini-golf course, as well as a heated pool.

Moose Jaw

Temple Gardens Mineral Spa Hotel and Resort *($85; pb, tv, ≡, ℜ, ≈, △, ⊘; 24 Fairford St. E., Moose Jaw, ☎1-800-718-7727 or 694-5055, ⇝694-8310).* This resort, tucked improbably down a sidestreet off Moose Jaw's slow-moving main drag, offers true luxuries to the dusty prairie traveller. The big open lobby gives a hint of what's to come. Regular hotel rooms here are roomy enough, with big sofas, but the 25 full suites are the real hit: king-sized beds, cotton robes, tables, enormous walk-in bathrooms and a two-person mineral water jacuzzi create a romantic experience in each. Additionally, all resort guests receive free access to the resort's fourth-floor, 20,000 square-foot pool of mineral water. There's also a small health club featuring Nautilus machines and treadmills, a poolside café and an attached restaurant.

Saskatoon

Patricia Hotel Hostel *($30; sb, tv; 345 2nd Ave. N., Saskatoon, S7K 2B8, ☎242-8861, ⇝242-8861).* For hostel prices, visitors get very basic accommodations in a hotel that has frankly seen better days. The advantage here is the low, low price and the location close to downtown. However, there are no kitchen facilities or special touches, save a local bar beneath the dorm rooms. Rooms are very basic; some are equipped with bunkbeds, and hostel washrooms are shared with other guests.

Ramblin' Rose Bed and Breakfast *($45; sb, pb, tv, ℜ, ☜; Box 46, RR 3, Saskatoon, S7K 3J6, ☎668-4582).* Located south of Saskatoon, near popular Pike Lake Provincial Park, this cedar home offers two private suites with private baths and two with shared baths. Extras are plentiful — a jacuzzi, TV/VCR, video and book library among them. Pets are welcome here, and guests are also welcome to hike any of several nature trails on the property.

Brighton House Bed and Breakfast *($45 bkfst incl.; sb, tv, ☜; 1308 Fifth Ave. N., Saskatoon, S7K 2S2, ☎664-3278, ☞664-6822)* A house in Saskatoon's North Park neighbourhood, this bed and breakfast offers lots of amenities: an outdoor hot tub under a gazebo and free use of bicycles, for example. It's very close to Spadina Crescent's riverfront museums and other attractions, and the price is surprisingly low.

Imperial 400 *($50; pb, tv, K, ≡, ℜ, ≈, ☜; 610 Idylwyld Dr. N., Saskatoon, S7L 0Z2, ☎1-800-781-2268 or 244-2901, ☞244-6063).* This 176-room motel features an indoor waterslide complex, whirlpool, and in-house movies, making it a good deal for families. Even more attractive are kitchenettes in some rooms. There is also a restaurant on premises.

Country Inn and Suites by Carlton *($80 bkfst incl.; pb, tv, K, ≡; 617 Cynthia St., Saskatoon, S7L 3G8, ☎934-3900, ☞652-3100).* North of downtown Saskatoon, very near the airport, this is the best place in town to rent a full suite complete with a work desk, living room and kitchenette. Good staffing, too, and extra touches that are great for families such as a laundry room, free continental breakfast, videocassette recorders in each room and free morning newspapers. The staff is particularly courteous and helpful.

Sheraton Cavalier *($80; pb, tv, ≡, ℜ, ≈, △, ☜; 621 Spadina Crescent E., Saskatoon, S7K 3G9, ☎1-800-325-3535 or 652-6770, ☞244-1739).* This glamorous hotel boasts two indoor waterslides, the "Top of the Inn" ballroom, guest voicemail, and video checkout and breakfast order. All rooms are outfitted with mini bars, coffee makers and blow dryers. Recent additions include a cigar lounge.

Delta Bessborough *($84; pb, tv, ≡, ℜ, ≈, △, ☜, ☺; 601 Spadina Crescent E., Saskatoon,* S7K 3G8, ☎244-5521, ☞665-7262). This is the best-looking hotel in Saskatoon, according to many travellers. It was built by the Canadian National Railway in 1931 and features striking turrets and gables in faux-French style. Inside, rooms are standard with luxurious touches. In-house services include a newsstand, chocolatier and cosmetician, while special business-traveller rooms feature fax machines, printers and cordless telephones.

Radisson Hotel Saskatoon *($100; pb, tv, ≡, ℜ, ≈, △, ☜; 405-20th St. E., Saskatoon, S7K 6X6, ☎1-800-333-3333 or 665-3322, ☞665-5533).* This very new high-rise luxury hotel caters to everyone: there are three executive floors and six meeting rooms, not to mention waterslides, a sauna, whirlpool and gym. It's also located right on the South Saskatchewan River, which means good access to outdoor recreation. It includes 14 deluxe suites complete with a bar and an extra telephone connection and modem hook-up for your computer.

The Yellowhead Highway

Manitou Beach

Manitou Springs Resort *($85; pb, tv, ≡, ☜, ☺; MacLachlan Ave., Manitou Beach, S0K 4T0, ☎1-800-667-7672, ☞ 946-2233).* An old and well-known resort in western Canada, this facility is famous for its three pools of heated mineral water drawn from Little Manitou Lake. Other services at the resort include massage therapy, reflexology, and a fitness centre.

West Central Saskatchewan

North Battleford

Battlefords Inn *($48; pb, tv, ≡, ℜ, ≈, △; 11212 Railway Ave. E., S9A 2R7, ☎1-800-691-6076 or 445-1515, ☞445-1541).* Known for spacious rooms, this inn provides king- and queen-size beds, free local phone calls and free in-room coffee. Meals can be taken in the on-site restaurant, and alcohol can be purchased in the licensed beverage room. $$.

Prince Albert

South Hill Inn *($54; pb, tv, ≡, ℜ, ☜; 3245 2nd Ave. W., S6V 5G1, ☎1-800-363-4466 or*

922-1333; ⌐*763-6408).* Highlights of this conveniently located inn include big comfortable rooms, televisions with the option of in-house movies and free coffee. There is also a licensed restaurant on the premises.

 RESTAURANTS

Regina

Magellan's Global Coffee House *($; 1800 College Ave., Regina,* ☎*789-0009; email magellan@magellanscafe.com)* A place to sip some latte, cappuccino, or chai while browsing the Internet or sending e-mail. Patrons may get the keyboards a little sticky while eating the super-rich desserts, however.

Neo Japonica *($; 2167 Hamilton St., Regina,* ☎*359-7669).* A place for classic Japanese cooking in the form of sushi, pot dishes, teriyaki, and the ubiquitous sake.

Brown Sugar *($$; 1941 Scarth St., Regina,* ☎*359-7355).* A Caribbean eatery in the middle of the prairie? Absolutely. This blue-trimmed place, decorated in Caribbean prints, delivers authentic rotis (meat-filled pastry pockets), jerk chicken and dishes like fish cutter (fish on a bun) and ackee and salt fish that are otherwise impossible to find in western Canada. There's a great selection of imported Caribbean soft drinks and home-made libations such as ginger beer, mauby, sorrel and banana cow to consider, as well. The meal isn't over until the knockout tropical ice cream has been tasted.

Bushwakker *($$; 2206 Dewdney Ave., Regina,* ☎*359-7276)* A fun brewpub on the edge of an industrial area. Locals don't think twice about motoring over here to try the latest batch of Harvest Ale or some other concoction, buffered by a fancy hamburger or other typical bar fare. Well laid-out and super-friendly, plus the bar offers offsales (small and very large bottles of the brewery's beer) in addition to the usual taps.

Cathedral Village Free House *($$; 2062 Albert St., Regina).* Filling contemporary fare from all over the map — a concept that doesn't always work, but satisfies some of the time. Lunch might consist of straightforward buffalo burgers, salads, stir-fried vegetables, wood-fired oven pizza and the like; dinner leans toward pasta and other Italian dishes. The place gets extra points for eight beers on tap. The crowd here is young and hip despite the stodgy name, possibly explaining the erratic service; at least the location is central.

Heliotrope *($$$; 2204 McIntyre St., Regina,* ☎*569-3373).* The only vegetarian restaurant in Saskatchewan, and quite possibly one of the best in all Canada. The chairs and tables in this brick house are cozy in winter a fireplace keeps things warm too plus there's a great outdoor patio with a view of downtown Regina. Entrees are expertly handled, everything from lunches of falafel, vegetables and burgers to dinners of Moroccan stew, Thai curries and gado gado. Dessert is a real stunner too in-season fruit cheesecake and homemade gelato that consists only of fresh fruit and water. Stunning.

Orleans *($$$; 1822 Broad St., Regina;* ☎*525-3636).* A dash of Cajun cuisine on a busy downtown street, you'll find all the dishes that make the real New Orleans a mouth-watering destination; jambalaya, gumbo, étoufée, they're all represented here.

Southern Saskatchewan

Fort Qu'Appelle

The Country Squire *($12; Highway 10,* ☎*332-5603,* ⌐*332-6708).* Attached to the inn of the same name, this restaurant serves tasty, hearty portions in a convivial atmosphere; local folks often drop by for a bite of grilled salmon, burgers (choose from elk, bison, hamburger or ostrich!), salad or fish and chips.

Caronport

The Pilgrim *($12; TransCanada Highway 1,* ☎*756-3335, 7am to 11pm).* Yet another restaurant in a gas station, this one is located in the small town of Caronton, just west of Moose Jaw. This place serves family fare, accompanied by in-house breads and a salad bar. Its reputation for hearty prairie cooking and a 60-item salad and soup bar is solid. All bread is baked on the premises.

Saskatoon

Chocolatier Bernard Callebaut *($5; 125 Second Ave. N., Saskatoon, ☎652-0909 or 1-800-661-8367, ☛652-6606).* Right in the centre of downtown Saskatoon, a small Canadian chain based in Calgary serves up artful cream chocolates and bars of baking chocolate made of all-natural ingredients. A special treat here are the hand-dipped chocolate ice cream bars — delicious beyond words, and only a few dollars apiece.

Michel's Montreal Smoked Meats *($7; 101 - 129 2nd Ave. N., Saskatoon, ☎384-6664).* Fortuitously placed right next to Saskatoon's Belgian chocolate shop, this enterprising French-Canadian tries to match Montréal quality from 3,000 kilometres away — and nearly succeeds. The peppery smoked meat, stuffed between two slices of rye bread and embellished with generous squirts of mustard, doesn't have quite the bite of its Québec counterpart, but it's still very good. Other great touches include home-made sour pickles, a very basic (and therefore good and crunchy) coleslaw, and black-cherry cola and spruce beer imported from Quebec.

Wanuskewin Café *($8; R.R. #4, Saskatoon, ☎1-800-665-4600 or 931-6767).* Located inside the native heritage park of the same name just north of Saskatoon, this little café offers a good quick sampling of native-style cookery. Entrées aren't large here but they are tasty; the fare ranges from a warming, hearty cup of bison stew with a side of bannock (bread) to bison over wild rice. Dessert offerings include pastries featuring the tart local saskatoon berry, while the line of First Nation soft drinks — bottled by a native-owned company — are among the drink offerings.

Broadway Café *($; 814 Broadway Ave., Saskatoon, ☎652-8244).* This restaurant is located right in the heart of Saskatoon's hippest district, yes, but that's a bit misleading: this is merely a diner that serves up burgers, eggs and the like to swarms of locals. The snappy service is cheerful but a bit off-putting out here in laid-back Saskatchewan, and daring entrées should definitely be avoided. Diners will also want to note that the owner does not accept credit cards. Nevertheless, an authentic local experience.

Black Duck Freehouse *($; 154 Second Ave. S., Saskatoon, ☎244-8850).* More a bar than a restaurant, this downtown Saskatoon joint still manages a daily "snack menu" of lunch and dinner specials such as turkey sandwiches, fish and chips, salads and burgers. Nothing is spectacular, but there are nearly a dozen beers on tap at all times — and an extensive liquor selection — to wash it all down. The free popcorn is perfectly popped, too, for whatever that's worth.

Genesis *($$; 901D 22nd St. W., Saskatoon, ☎244-5516).* Widely acclaimed as Saskatoon's best healthy food, the menu leans toward Chinese food and macrobiotic cooking. Dim sum is available at lunchtime.

Saskatoon Station Place *($$; 221 S. Idylwyld Dr., Saskatoon, ☎244-7777).* Decorated with a train motif, this restaurant is set inside a mock train station and two dining cars. Very popular with locals, its menu includes burger, steaks, pastas — all the family favourites. The inside is decorated with still more train-related touches.

The Keg *($$; 301 Ontario Ave. N., Saskatoon, ☎653-3633).* This family restaurant offers solid steakhouse fare, including prime rib, plus lighter meals such as pasta and seafood.

West Central Saskatchewan

North Battleford

DaVinci's Ristorante Italiano *($$; 1001 Highway 16, ☎446-4700).* Even Leonardo himself might be surprised that the menu here is not exclusively Italian as suggests the name; traditional Louisiana cooking receives more than a few entrées, along with some continental European dishes.

Prince Albert

Amy's on Second *($$; 2990 Second Ave., ☎763-1515).* Fresh ingredients and a healthy approach to cooking make this restaurant a popular switch from the many local fast-food joints. Salads here are made to order, and come with home-made soups. Also featured are steaks, chicken and pasta dishes.

ENTERTAINMENT

Regina

The **Buffalo Days** festival occupies one week each summer, usually beginning in late July and stretching into early August. Festivities kick off with a Sunday picnic in lovely Wascana Park; from there, it's on to a raft of shows and, eventually, fireworks.

The **Saskatchewan Science Centre ★** *(at Winnipeg St. and Wascana Dr, Wascana Centre, ☎1-800-667-6300 or 352-5811)* is best known for its 50-foot high IMAX cinema with sound on all sides. Another section of the museum, the Powerhouse of Discovery, presents exhibits and live talks.

Southern Saskatchewan

The **Big Valley Jamboree** is a country music festival held just outside Regina each July in the tiny town of Craven. It lasts four days, swells the population of the town many times over, and often features national recording stars.

Saskatoon

Most of the pubs and clubs in Saskatoon are concentrated along Second Avenue South.

The **SaskTel Saskatchewan Jazz Festival** *(☎652-1421)* brings world-class jazz, gospel and world music to Saskatoon's riverbanks for 11 days each June. Musicians range from international stars to local provincial players. Some performances are held in the Delta Bessborough Gardens, adjacent to the landmark hotel.

The **Great Northern River Roar** is either an abomination or one great time, depending on your opinion of powerboats tearing up and down the river. Either way, there's no avoiding these races when they arrive in Saskatoon each July. Some 60,000 spectators are said to watch as the powerboats charge around courses at speeds of up to 225 kilometres per hour.

 SHOPPING

Regina

Shopping is concentrated downtown, with the **Scarth Street Mall** the usual starting point. All the major department stores (Eaton's, The Bay) are nearby.

Saskatoon

Shopping in Saskatoon is easy, with several downtown malls and streets focusing the activity. Perhaps the most popular area is the **Bayside Mall**, next to and including The Bay department store. The **Midtown Plaza**, on First Avenue South between 22nd Street East and 20th Street East, is another good option. **Second Avenue South** is the place to go for all the pubs, clubs and street life.

SASKATCHEWAN

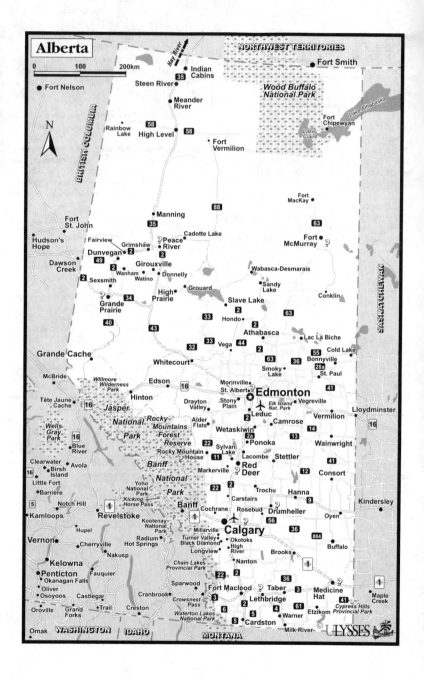

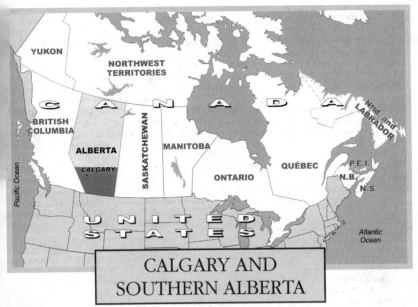

Map of Canada showing: YUKON, NORTHWEST TERRITORIES, BRITISH COLUMBIA, ALBERTA (CALGARY), SASKATCHEWAN, MANITOBA, ONTARIO, QUÉBEC, Nfld. and LABRADOR, P.E.I., N.B., N.S., CANADA, UNITED STATES, Pacific Ocean, Atlantic Ocean

CALGARY AND SOUTHERN ALBERTA

Calgary ★★★ is a thriving metropolis of concrete and steel, and a western city through and through; it is set against the Rocky Mountains to the west and prairie ranchlands to the east. This young, prosperous city flourished during the oil booms of the forties, fifties and seventies, but its nickname, Cowtown, tells a different story. For before the oil, there were cowboys and gentlemen, and Calgary originally grew thanks to a handful of wealthy ranching families.

When departing Calgary it is difficult to resist the pull of the Rocky Mountains and head south. However, southern Alberta boasts some of the best sights and scenery of the whole province, from Waterton Lakes National Park and the mining towns of Crowsnest Pass to the historic native gathering place at Head-Smashed-In, and the edge of the endless prairies.

 FINDING YOUR WAY AROUND

By Car

Calgary

The majority of Calgary's streets are numbered, and the city is divided into four quadrants, NE, NW, SE and SW. This may seem extremely unimaginative on the part of city-planners, but it makes it easy for just about anyone to find their way around. Avenues run east-west and streets run north-south. **Centre Street** divides the city between east and west, while the Bow River is the dividing line between north and south. The TransCanada Highway runs through the city, where it is known as 16th Ave. N. Many of the major arteries through the city have much more imaginative names, and not only are they not numbered but they are called trails, an appellation that reflects their original use. These are **Macleod Trail**, which runs south from downtown (ultimately leading to Fort Macleod, hence its name); **Deerfoot Trail** which runs north-south through the city and is part of Highway 2; and **Crowchild Trail** which heads northwest and joins **Bow Trail** before becoming Highway 1A.

Calgary's "Motel Village" is located along 16th Ave. NW between 18th St. NW and 22nd St. NW.

By Plane

Calgary

Calgary International Airport is located northeast of downtown Calgary. It is Canada's fourth-largest airport and houses a whole slew of facilities and services. It features restaurants, an information centre, hotel courtesy phones, major car-rental counters, currency exchange and a bus-tour operator.

Air Canada, Canadian Airlines, American Airlines, Delta Airlines, Northwest Airlines, United Airlines and KLM all have regular flights to the airport. Regional companies (Air B.C. and Canadian Regional) also serve Calgary International.

There is a shuttle from Calgary airport to the major downtown hotels; the **Airporter** (☎531-3909) charges $8.50 one-way and 15$ return, while a taxi will run about $25.

By Bus

Greyhound buses cover most of the province. Tickets can be bought on the spot; no reservations are taken but you will get a discount if you buy your tickets seven days in advance. Service is regular and relatively inexpensive, for example Calgary to Edmonton one-way is $35.31.

Brewster Transportation and Tours offers coach service from Calgary to Banff. Departures are from Calgary International Airport, for information call ☎221-8242.

Calgary

Calgary Greyhound Bus Depot: 877 Greyhound Way SW, off 16th St., ☎265-9111 or 1-800-661-8747. Services: restaurant, lockers, tourist information.

Southern Alberta

Lethbridge Greyhound Bus Depot 411 5th St. S, ☎327-1551; services: restaurant, lockers.

Medicine Hat Greyhound Bus Depot 557 2nd St. SE, ☎527-4418

By Train

Via does not service Calgary. The train passes through Edmonton, there is a bus connection between the two cities.

The only rail service from Calgary is offered by **Great Canadian Railtour Company – Rocky Mountain Railtours**. Trains leave three times a week from May to October for Vancouver, with a stop in Banff to pick up passengers (you cannot get off in Banff). The trip takes two days and includes two breakfasts and two lunches as well as a night in a hotel in Kamloops. The train only runs during the day, so you don't miss any of the spectacular scenery. It costs $700 per person, or $645 per person, double occupancy. Trains depart from the CP station in Calgary, located under the Palliser Hotel *(133 9th Ave. SW)*. For information and reservations call ☎1-800-665-7200 or (604) 606-7245 or send a fax to ☎(604) 606-7250.

Public Transit

Calgary

Public transit in Calgary consists of an extensive bus network and a light-rail transit system known as the **C-Train**. There are three C-Train routes: the Anderson C-Train follows Macleod Trail south to Anderson Road., the Whitehorn C-Train heads northeast out of the city and the Brentwood C-Train runs along 7th Avenue and then heads northwest. The C-Train is free in the downtown core. You can transfer from a bus to a C-Train, tickets are $1.60 for a single trip or $5.50 for a day pass. For bus information call **Calgary Transit** at ☎262-1000; they will gladly give you directions.

By Foot

Calgary

A system of interconnected, enclosed walkways links many of Calgary's downtown sights, shops and hotels. Known as the +15, it is located 15 feet above the ground. The malls along 7th Avenue SW are all connected as are the Calgary Tower, Glenbow Museum and Palliser Hotel.

PRACTICAL INFORMATION

Area Code: 403.

Information on everything from road conditions to movie listings to provincial parks is available from the **Talking Yellow Pages**. In Calgary call ☎521-5222. A series of recorded messages are accessible by dialling specific codes. The codes are listed in the front of the yellow pages phone book; there is usually a phone book in every phone booth.

Tourist Information Offices

Calgary

Calgary Tower Centre Tourist Information Centre St. and 9th Avenue SW, Mid-May to early Sep, every day 8:30am to 5pm; winter, Mon to Fri 8:30am to 5pm, Sat and Sun 9:30am to 5pm, ☎263-8510 or 1-800-661-1678.

Southern Alberta

Travel Alberta South ☎1-800-661-1222.

Lethbridge Tourist Information Centre 2805 Scenic Dr., ☎320-1222.

Medicine Hat Tourist Information 8 Gehring Rd. SE, ☎527-6422.

Drumheller Tourist Information at the corner of Riverside Dr. and 2nd St. W, ☎823-1331.

Big Country Tourist Association 170 Centre St., #28, Drumheller, ☎823-5885, ⊶823-7942.

EXPLORING

Calgary ★★

Calgary is also the only Child Friendly city in North America, which means that children rate all the sights, restaurants, etc. The city gives much to its residents, and the residents give back. In 1988, they were both rewarded when Calgary hosted the Winter Olympic Games.

After suffering through the drop in oil prices, the city flourished once again. The Olympics contributed something very special to the heritage of this friendly city; a heritage that is felt by Calgarians and visitors alike in the genuinely warm attitude that prevails.

Downtown

We recommend starting your tour of Calgary at the 190-metre, 762-step, 55-story **Calgary Tower ★★** *(adults $5.50; every day, summer 7:30am to 11pm; winter 8am to 10pm; 9th Ave, corner of Centre St SW, ☎266-7171)*. The city's most famous landmark not only offers a breathtaking view of the city, including the ski-jump towers at Canada Olympic Park, the Saddledome and the Canadian Rockies through high-power telescopes, but also houses the city's tourist information centre, a revolving restaurant and a bar. Photographers should take note that the specially tinted windows on the observation deck make for great photos.

Across the street at the corner of First Street SE is the stunning **Glenbow Museum ★★★** *(adults $5; every day 9am to 5pm during summer, closed Mon rest of year; 130 9th Ave. SE, ☎268-4100)*. Three floors of permanent and travelling exhibits chronicle the exciting history of Western Canada. The displays include contemporary and native art, and an overview of the various stages of the settling of the West, from the native peoples to the first pioneers, the fur trade, the North West Mounted Police, ranching, oil and agriculture. Photographs, costumes and everyday items bring to life the hardships and extraordinary obstacles faced by settlers. There is also an extensive exhibit on the indigenous peoples of the whole country. Check out the genuine teepee and the sparkling minerals, both part of the province's diverse history. A great permanent exhibit documents the stories of warriors throughout the ages. The museum also hosts travelling exhibitions. Free gallery tours are offered once or twice weekly. Great museum shop and café.

Built for the medal presentation ceremonies of the '88 Winter Olympics, the **Olympic Plaza ★★★** *(205 8th Ave. SE)* is a fine example of Calgary's potential realized. This lovely square features a large wading pool (used as a skating rink in winter) surrounded by pillars and columns in an arrangement reminiscent of a Greek temple. The park is now the site of concerts and special events, and is

ALBERTA

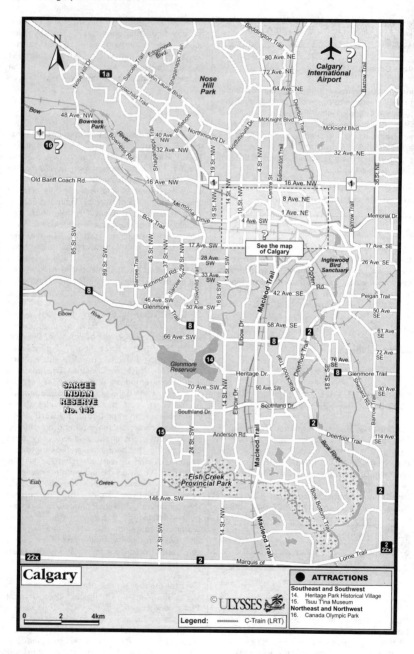

Calgary

ATTRACTIONS

Southeast and Southwest
14. Heritage Park Historical Village
15. Tsuu T'ina Museum
Northeast and Northwest
16. Canada Olympic Park

Legend: ======= C-Train (LRT)

0   2   4km

© ULYSSES

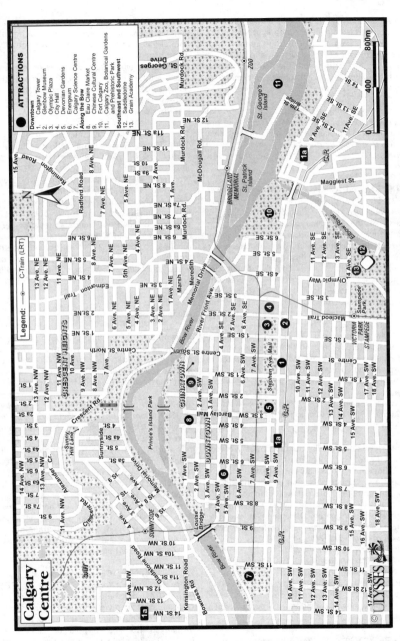

Calgary Centre

Legend:
⊶ C-Train (LRT)

© ULYSSES

ALBERTA

frequented by street performers throughout the year; it is also a popular lunch spot with office workers. Each pillar in the Legacy Wall commemorates a medal winner, and the paving bricks are inscribed with the names of people who supported the Olympics by purchasing bricks for $19.88 each!

Across from the Olympic Plaza is **City Hall** *(2nd St. SE, corner of Macleod Tr.)*, one of few surviving examples of the monumental civic halls that went up during the Prairies' boom. It was built in 1911 and still houses a few offices.

The **Stephen Avenue Mall** *(8th Ave between 1st St. SE and 6th St. SW)* is an excellent example not only of Calgary's potential, but also of the contrasts that characterize this cowtown metropolis — the mall is part vibrant pedestrian meeting place, part wasteland and unsavoury hangout. It has fountains, benches, cobblestone, restaurants and shops, but also more than its share of boarded-up storefronts and cheap souvenir and t-shirt shops. The beautiful sandstone buildings that line the Avenue are certainly a testament to better and different times, as are the businesses they house, including an old-fashioned shoe hospital and several western outfitters. One of these buildings is the **Alberta Hotel**, a busy place in pre-prohibition days. Other buildings house trendy cafés and art galleries, as the street once again becomes a meeting place for lawyers, doctors and the who's who of Calgary, just as it was at the beginning of the century.

Interconnected malls line the street west of First Street SW, including the Scotia Centre, TD Square, Bankers Hall, Eaton Centre and Holt Renfrew. Though this type of commercialism might not appeal to everyone, hidden within TD Square is a unique attraction — Alberta's largest indoor garden, **Devonian Gardens** ★★ *(free admission, donations accepted; every day 9am to 9pm; 317 7th Ave. SW, between 2nd and 3rd Sts. SW, Level 4, TD Square, ☎268-5207 or 268-3888)*. For a tranquil break from shopping, head upstairs, where 2.5 acres of greenery and blossoms await. Stroll along garden paths high above the concrete and steel and enjoy the art exhibitions and performances that are often presented here.

At the **Energeum** ★ *(free admission; summer, Sun to Fri 10:30am to 4:30 pm; rest of year, Mon to Fri 10:30am to 4:30pm; Energy Resources Building, 640 5th Ave. SW,* ☎297-4293) you can learn all about Alberta's number one resource, energy. Whether it is oil, natural gas, oil sands, coal or hydroelectricity, everything from pipelines to rigs to oil-sand plants is explained through hands-on exhibits and computer games. Across the street is the Renaissance Revival **McDougall Centre**, a government building that was declared a historic site in 1982.

The peculiar looking concrete building on 11th Street SW is **The Calgary Science Centre** ★★★ *(adults $9; every day 10am to 8pm; 701 11 St. SW,* ☎221-3700), a wonderful museum that children will love. Hands-on displays and multi-media machines cover a whole slew of interesting topics. The museum boasts a planetarium, an observatory, a science hall and two theatres that showcase mystery plays and special-effects shows. The recently completed, 220-seat, domed theatre features an exceptional sound system, all the better to explore the wonders of the scientific world.

Along the Bow

Kensington is a hip area that is hard to pin down. To get a true sense of the alternative attitude that pervades the coffee shops, bookstores and boutiques, explore Kensington Road between 10th and 14th Streets NW.

The recently built **Eau Claire Market** ★★ *(Mon to Wed 10am to 6pm, Thu and Fri 10am to 9pm, Sat 10am to 6pm, Sun 10am to 5pm; next to the Bow River and Prince's Island Park,* ☎264-6450) is part of a general initiative in Calgary to keep people downtown after hours. The large warehouse-like building houses specialty food shops that sell fresh fruit, vegetables, fish, meats, bagels and baked goods; neat gift shops with local and imported arts and crafts; clothing stores; a great bookstore; fast-food and fine restaurants; a movie theatre and a 300-seat **IMAX** *(*☎974-4600) giant-screen theatre.

Calgary's **Chinese Cultural Centre** ★★ *($2; every day 9:30am to 9pm; 197 1st St. SW,* ☎262-5071) is the largest of its kind in Canada. Craftsmen were brought in from China to design the building, whose central dome is patterned after the Temple of Heaven in Beijing. The highlight of the intricate tile-work is a glistening golden dragon. The centre houses a gift shop, a museum, a gallery and a restaurant.

Calgary's small **Chinatown** lies around Centre Street. Although it only has about 2,000 residents, the street names written in Chinese characters and the sidewalk stands selling durian, ginseng, lychees and tangerines all help to create a wonderful feeling of stepping into another world. The markets and restaurants here are run by descendants of Chinese immigrants who came to the west to work on the railroads in the 1880s.

Fort Calgary ★★★ *($3; May to mid-Oct, every day 9am to 5pm; 750 9th Ave. SE, ☎290-1875)* was built as part of the March West, which brought the North West Mounted Police to the Canadian west to stop the whisky trade. "F" Troop arrived at the confluence of the Bow and Elbow rivers in 1875, and chose to set up camp here either because it was the only spot with clean water or because it was halfway between Fort Macleod and Fort Saskatchewan. Nothing remains of the original Fort Calgary — the structures and outline of the foundations on the site today are part of an ongoing excavation project undertaken mostly by volunteers. In fact, the fort will never be completely rebuilt, as that would interfere with the archaeological work underway. An excellent interpretive centre includes great hands-on displays (the signs actually say "please touch"), woodworking demonstrations and the chance to try on a famous, scarlet Mountie uniform. Friendly guides in period costume provide tours.

The **Calgary Zoo, Botanical Gardens and Prehistoric Park** ★★ *(adults $9.50 summer, $8 winter; May to Sep, every day 9am to 6pm; Sep to May, every day 9am to 4pm; St. George's Island, 1300 Zoo Rd. NE, ☎232-9300 or 232-9372)* is the second largest zoo in Canada. It opened in 1920 and is known for its realistic re-creations of natural habitats, now home to over 300 species of animals and 10,000 plants and trees. Exhibits are organized by continent and include tropical birds, Siberian tigers, snow leopards and polar bears, as well as animals indigenous to this area. The Prehistoric Park recreates the world of dinosaurs with 27 full-size replicas set amidst plants and rock formations from prehistoric Alberta.

Southeast and Southwest

This tour explores Calgary immediately south of downtown, which for the purposes of this guide, we will delineate by the CPR tracks between 9th and 10th Avenues.

The aptly named **Saddledome** has the world's largest cable-suspended roof and is a giant testimony to the city's cowboy roots. Apparently, there was some controversy over its name, though it is hard to imagine what else it could have been called! It is home to the city's National Hockey League team, the Calgary Flames, and is also used for concerts, conventions and sporting events. The figure skating and ice-hockey events of the 1988 Olympics were held here. Tours are available *(☎777-1375)*. Also on the park grounds is the **Grain Academy** ★ *(free admission; year-round Mon to Fri 10am to 4pm; Apr to Sep, Sat noon to 4pm; on the +15 level of the Round-Up Centre, ☎263-4594)*, which traces the history of grain farming and features a working railway and grain elevator. Finally, thoroughbred and harness racing take place on the grounds year-round and there is also a casino.

Heritage Park Historical Village ★★ *($10, $16 with rides; May to Sep every day, Sep to Oct weekends and holidays only; 1900 Heritage Dr. SW, ☎259-1900)* is a 26-hectare park on the Glenbow Reservoir. Step back in time as you stroll through a real 1910 town of historic houses decorated with period furniture, wooden sidewalks, a working blacksmith, a teepee, an old schoolhouse, a post office, a divine candy store and the Gilbert and Jay Bakery, known for its sourdough bread. Staff in period dress play piano in the houses and take on the role of suffragettes speaking out for women's equality in the Wainwright Hotel. Other areas in the park recreate an 1880's settlement, a fur trading post, a ranch, a farm and the coming of the railroad. Not only is this a magical place for children, with rides in a steam engine and a paddlewheeler on the reservoir, but it is also a relaxing place to escape the city and enjoy a picnic.

The **Tsuu T'Ina Museum** ★ *(donation; Mon to Fri 8am to 4pm; 3700 Anderson Rd. SW, ☎238-2677)* commemorates the history of the Tsuu T'Ina, who are Sarcee Indians. Tsuu T'Ina means "great number of people" in their language and it is what they call themselves. Nearly wiped out several times in the 1800s by diseases brought by Europeans, the Tsuu T'Ina were shuffled around reserves for many years but persevered and were eventually awarded their reserve on the outskirts of Calgary in 1881. They held on to the land, spurning all pressures to sell it. Some of the pieces on

ALBERTA

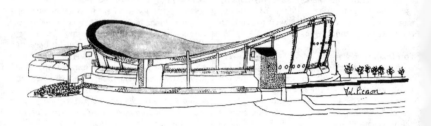

Saddledome

display were donated by Calgary families who used to trade with the Tsuu T'Ina, whose reserve lies immediately to the west of the museum. Other items, including a teepee and two headdresses from the thirties, were retrieved from the Provincial Museum in Edmonton.

Northeast and Northwest

North of the Bow River, the biggest draws in the Northwest are Canada Olympic Park, Nose Hill Park and Bowness Park, while in the Northeast there isn't much besides the airport.

Canada Olympic Park ★★★ *(museum $3.75, tours $6.50-$10; on 16th Ave. NW, ☎247-5452)*, or C.O.P., built for the 1988 Winter Olympic Games, lies on the western outskirts of Calgary. This was the site of the ski-jumping, bobsledding, luge, freestyle skiing and disabled events during the games, and it is now a world-class facility for training and competitions. Artificial snow keeps the downhill ski slopes busy in the winter, and the park also offers tours year-round and the chance to try the luge in the summertime *($13 for one ride, $22 for two)* or the bobsleigh in the winter, or view summer ski-jumping.

Visitors to C.O.P. have the choice of seven different guided tour packages ranging from a self-guided walking booklet to the Grand

Olympic Tour for $10, which includes a guided bus tour, chair lift ride, the Olympic Hall of Fame and the tower. It is worth taking the bus up to the observation deck of the 90-metre ski jump tower visible from all over the city. You'll learn about the refrigeration system, which can make 1,250 tonnes of snow and ice in 24 hours, the infamous Jamaican bobsleigh team, the 90- and 70-metre towers and the plastic-surface landing material used in the summer. If you do decide to take the bus, sit on the left for a better view of the towers and tracks. The **Naturbahn Teahouse** *(☎247-5465)* is located in the former starthouse for the luge. Delicious treats and a scrumptious Sunday brunch are served, but be sure to make reservations. The **Olympic Hall of Fame and Museum** *($3.75; mid-May to Sep, every day 8am to 9pm, call ahead for winter hours; ☎247-5452)* is North America's largest museum devoted to the Olympics. The whole history of the games is presented with exhibits, videos, costumes, memorabilia and a bobsleigh and ski-jump simulator. You'll find a tourist information office and a gift shop near the entrance.

Southern Alberta

The vast expanses and sometimes desert-like conditions you'll traverse while making your way from west to east in Southern Alberta are in stark contrast to the looming, snow-capped

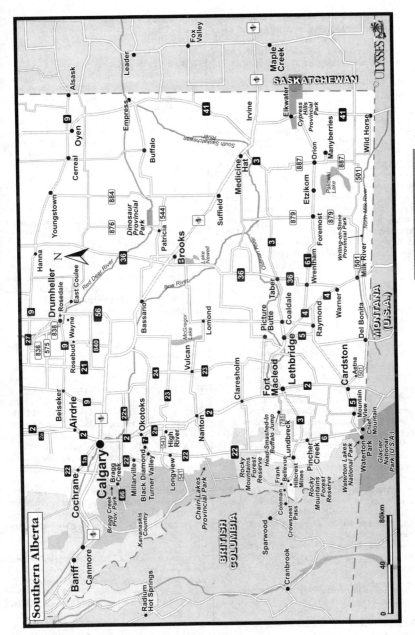

Southern Alberta

ALBERTA

Rocky Mountains to the west. Neat rows of wheat and other grains, perfectly round bales of hay, and the occasional grain elevator are about the extent of the relief across the slow-rolling terrain of this part of the province.

Okotoks

Okotoks is the largest city between Calgary and Lethbridge. It is also home to several antique and craft shops. The **Ginger Tea Room and Gift Shop** *(43 Riverside Dr., ☎938-2907)* is a Victorian mansion, where afternoon tea is served on weekdays and two floors of collectibles and crafts can be admired or purchased. A walking tour map is available at the tourist office *(53 N. Railway St., ☎938-3204)* and includes several historic buildings which date from when the town was a rest stop along the Macleod Trail between Fort Calgary and Fort Macleod.

Longview

The **Bar U Ranch National Historic Site** ★★ *($6; mid May to mid-Oct, every day 10am to 6pm; winter, call for group reservations; ☎395-2212 or 1-800-568-4996)* opened in the summer of 1995 and commemorates the contribution of ranching to the development of Canada. It is one of four ranches that once covered almost all of Alberta and, until recently, it was still a working ranch. Now, people are able to wander freely around the ranch and observe ranching operations on a scaled-down, demonstration level. "Bar U" refers to the symbol branded on cattle from this ranch. A beautiful new visitors centre features an interpretive display on breeds of cattle, the roundup, branding and what exactly a quirt is. A 15-minute video on the Mighty Bar U conveys the romance of the cowboy way of life and also explains how the native grasslands and Chinook winds unique to Alberta have been a perpetual cornerstone of ranching. The centre also houses a gift shop and a restaurant where you can savour an authentic buffalo burger.

Chain Lakes Provincial Park ★ is the only real attraction along this stretch of highway. It sits between the Rocky Mountains and the Porcupine Hills in a transition zone of spring-fed lakes. There is a campground. Farther south, the splendid pale yellow grasslands, dotted occasionally by deep blue lakes, roll off into the distant Rocky Mountains conveying an other-worldly look on the mountains looming across the horizon.

Waterton Lakes National Park

Waterton Townsite is home to restaurants, bars, shops, grocery stores, laundry facilities, a post office and hotels. There is also a marina, from which lake cruises depart. Things slow down considerably in the winter, though the cross-country skiing is outstanding. For more information see the Parks section, p 489.

Cardston

Cardston is a prosperous-looking town nestled in the rolling foothills where the grasslands begin to give way to fields of wheat and the yellow glow of canola. The town was established by Mormon pioneers fleeing religious persecution in Utah. Their move here marked one of the last great covered wagon migrations of the 19th century. Cardston might not seem like much of a tourist town, but it is home to one of the most impressive monuments and one of the most unique museums in Alberta. The monument is the **Mormon Temple** *(free admission; May to early Sep, every day 9am to 9pm; 348 3rd St. W., ☎653-1696)*, which seems a tad out of place rising up from the prairie. This truly majestic edifice took ten years to construct and was the first temple built by the church outside the United States. The marble comes from Italy and the granite was quarried in Nelson B.C. When it came time to do renovations recently, a problem arose because there was no granite left in Nelson; several blocks were fortuitously found in a farmer's field nearby, having been left there in storage after the temple was built. Only Mormons in good standing may enter the temple itself, but the photographs and video presented at the visitors centre should satisfy your curiosity.

The unique museum is the **Remington-Alberta Carriage Centre** ★★★ *($6.50; mid-May to early Sep, every day 9am to 8pm; Sep to May, every day 9am to 5pm; 623 Main St., ☎653-5139)*, opened in 1993. "A museum on carriages?", you may ask. The subject matter may seem narrow, but this museum is definitely worth a visit. Forty-nine of the approximately 260 carriages were donated by Mr. Don Remington of Cardston on the condition that the Alberta government build an interpretive centre in which to display them. The wonderfully restored carriages and enthusiastic, dedicated staff at this magnificent facility make this exhibit first-rate. Take a guided tour through the 1,675-square-metre display gallery, where town mock-ups and animated street scenes provide the backdrop for the collection, one of the best in the world among elite carriage facilities. The interesting film *Wheels of Change* tells the story of this once huge industry, which was all but dead by 1922.

Fort Macleod ★

The town of Fort Macleod centres around the fort of the same name, first set up by the North West Mounted Police in an effort to stop the whisky trade. Troops were sent to raid Fort Whoop-Up (see p 488) in 1874, but got lost along the way, and by the time they got to Whoop-Up the traders had fled. They continued west to this spot by the Oldman River and established a permanent outpost. The original settlement was on an island two miles east of the present town, but persistent flooding forced its relocation in 1882. The fort, as it stands now, was reconstructed in 1956-1957 as a museum. The **Fort Museum ★** *(adults $4; May and Jun, every day 9am to 5pm; Jul to Sep 9am to 8:30pm; Sep to mid-Oct, every day 9am to 5pm; mid-Oct to Dec 23rd and Mar to May, weekdays 10am to 4pm; 219 25th St. at 3rd Ave.,* ☎553-4703)* houses exhibits of pioneer life at the time of settlement, dioramas of the fort, tombstones from the cemetery and an interesting section of artifacts and photographs of the Plains Blood and Peigan tribes. A Mounted Patrol performs a musical ride four times a day in July and August.

Fort Macleod's downtown area is very representative of a significant period in history. Most of the buildings were erected between 1897 and 1914, except the Kanouse cabin, which lies inside the fort walls and dates from much earlier. Walking tour pamphlets are available at the tourist office. The tour includes such notable edifices as the **Empress Theatre**, which retains its original pressed-metal ceiling panels, stage and dressing rooms (complete with graffiti from 1913). Movies are still shown here, despite a ghost who haunts the place and occasionally gets upset with the way things are run. The **Silver Grill**, an old saloon across the street, has its original bar and bullet-pierced mirror.

The arrival of the horse in the mid-1700s signalled the end of a traditional way of hunting buffalo among Plains Indians. For 5,700 years before this, the Plains Indians had depended on **Head-Smashed-In Buffalo Jump ★★★** *($6.50; May to Sep, every day 9am to 8pm; Sep to May, every day 9am to 5pm; 15 km northwest of Fort Macleod on Hwy 785,* ☎553-2731)*. From it they got meat, fresh and dried for pemmican; hides for teepees, clothing and moccasins; and bones and horns for tools and decorations. Head-Smashed-In was an ideal spot for a jump, with a vast grazing area to the west. The Indians would construct drive lines with stone cairns, which led to the cliff. Some 500 people participated in the yearly hunt; men dressed in buffalo-calf robes and wolf skins lured the herd towards the precipice. Upon reaching the cliff, the leading buffalo were forced over the edge by the momentum of the stampeding herd behind them. The herd was not actually chased over the cliff, but rather fear amongst the herd led to a stampede. The area remains much as it was thousands of years ago, though the distance from the cliff to the ground drastically changed as the bones of butchered bison piled up, 10-metres deep in some places.

Today, the jump is the best preserved buffalo jump in North America and a UNESCO World Heritage Site. Many assume that the name comes from the crushed skulls of the buffalo, but it actually refers to a Peigan legend of a young brave who went under the jump to watch the buffalo topple in front of him. The kill was exceptionally good this particular day, and the brave was crushed by the animals. When his people were butchering the buffalos after the kill, they discovered the brave with his head smashed in — hence the name.

The interpretive centre, built into the cliff, comprises five levels and is visited from the top down. Start off by following the trail along the top of the cliff for a spectacular view of the plain and the Calderwood Jump to the left. Marmots can be seen sunning themselves on the rocks below and generally contemplating the scene. Continuing through the centre you'll learn about Napi, the mythical creator of people according to the Blackfoot. The centre leads through Napi's world, the people and their routines, the buffalo, the hunt, the contact of cultures and European settlement. An excellent film entitled *In Search of the Buffalo* is presented every 30 minutes. The tour ends with an archaeological exhibit of the excavation work at the site. Back outside the centre you

ALBERTA

can follow a trail to the butchering site. The annual Buffalo Days celebrations take place here in July. The centre has a great gift shop and a small cafeteria that serves buffalo burgers.

Lethbridge ★★

Lethbridge, known affectionately by locals as "downtown L.A.", is Alberta's third largest city, and a pleasant urban oasis on the prairies. Steeped in history, the city boasts an extensive park system, pretty tree-lined streets, interesting sights and a diverse cultural community. You're as likely to meet ranchers as business people, Hutterites or Mormons on the streets of L.A.

Indian Battle Park ★★, in the Oldman River valley in the heart of town, is where Lethbridge's history comes alive; it is the site of Fort Whoop-Up, the setting of a terrible Indian battle. On October 25, 1870, Cree Indians, displaced by European settlers into Blackfoot territory, attacked a band of Blood Blackfoot camped on the banks of the Oldman River. In the ensuing battle, the Blood were aided by a group of Peigan Blackfoot nearby; by the end some 300 Cree and 50 Blackfoot were dead.

A year earlier, American whisky traders had moved into Southern Alberta from Fort Benton, Montana. It was illegal to sell alcohol to natives in the United States, so the traders headed north into Canada, where there was no law against this. They set up Fort Hamilton nearby, at the confluence of the St. Mary's and Oldman rivers, and it became bootlegger headquarters in southern Alberta and Saskatchewan. This activity involved the trading of a particularly lethal brew which was passed off as whisky to the natives; besides whisky, this moonshine might also contain fortified grain alcohol, red pepper, chewing tobacco, Jamaican ginger and black molasses.

Fire destroyed the original fort, but **Fort Whoop-Up ★★**, was built in its place and whisky and guns continued to be traded for buffalo hides and robes. Fort Whoop-Up was the first and most notorious of 44 whisky trading posts. The American encroachment on Canadian territory, the illicit trading which had a demoralizing effect on the natives, and news of the Cypress Hills massacre prompted the formation of the North West Mounted Police by the Canadian government. Lead by scout Jerry Potts, the Mounties, under the command of Colonel Macleod, arrived at Fort Whoop-Up in October of 1874. Word of their arrival preceded them, however, and the place was empty by the time they arrived. A cairn marks the site of this fort. The present fort is a reconstruction and houses an interesting **interpretive centre** *(summer $2.50, winter $1; May to Sep, Mon to Sat 10am to 6pm, Sun noon to 6pm; Indian Battle Park, ☎329-0444)*, where visitors can experience the exciting days of the whisky trade. You can also taste fresh bannock, a round, flat Scottish cake made from barley and oatmeal and cooked on a griddle. Guides in period costume offer tours.

Paths weave their way through five traditional Japanese gardens at the **Nikka Yuko Japanese Garden ★★** *($3; mid-May to late Jun, every day 9am to 5pm; Jul and Aug every day 9am to 8pm; Sep, every day 9am to 5pm; 7th Ave. S. and Mayor Magrath Dr., ☎328-3511)*. These aren't bright, flowery gardens, but simple arrangements of green shrubs, sand and rocks in the style of a true Japanese garden — perfect for quiet contemplation. Created by renowned Japanese garden designer Dr. Tadashi Kudo of the Osaka Prefecture University in Japan, Nikka Yuko was built in 1967 as a centennial project and a symbol of Japanese and Canadian friendship (*Nikka Yuko* actually means friendship).

Across the prairie to Medicine Hat

The prairies seem to roll on forever along this stretch of highway surrounded by golden fields that are barren but for the occasional hamlet, grain elevator or abandoned farmhouse. Towns were set up every 10 miles or 16 kilometres because that was how far a farmer could haul his grain. As you drive along this road, you will come upon what was once the town of Nemiskam, about 16 kilometres out of Foremost. Another 16 kilometres further is Etzikom. With fewer than 100 inhabitants these days, Etzikom's days may be numbered. For a glimpse of the past, and a chance to stretch your legs, stop in at the **Etzikom Museum ★** *(donation; May to Sep, Mon to Sat 10am to 5pm, Sun noon to 6pm; Etzikom, ☎666-3737, 666-3792 or 666-3915)*. Local museums like this can be found throughout Alberta, but this is one of the best of its kind and makes for a pleasant stop off the highway. The museum is located in the Etzikom School, and houses a wonderful recreation of the Main Street of a typical town, complete with barber shop, general store and hotel. Outside is the **Windpower Interpretive Centre**, a collection of windmills including one from Martha's Vineyard, Massachusetts, U.S.A.

Medicine Hat ★

Rudyard Kipling once called Medicine Hat "a city with all hell for a basement", in reference to the fact that Medicine Hat lies above some of western Canada's largest natural gas fields. The town prospered because of this natural resource, which now supplies a thriving petro-chemical industry. Clay deposits nearby also left their mark, contributing to the city's once thriving pottery industry. Medicine Hat, like many towns in Alberta, boasts several parks. As for its name, legend has it that a great battle between the Cree and the Blackfoot took place here. During the battle, the Cree medicine man deserted his people and while fleeing across the river, he lost his headdress in mid-stream. Believing this to be a bad omen, the Cree abandoned the fight and were massacred by the Blackfoot. The battle site was called Saamis, which means medicine man's hat. When the Mounties arrived years later, the name was translated and shortened to Medicine Hat.

The **Saamis Tepee** is the world's tallest tepee. It was constructed for the 1988 Calgary Winter Olympics, and then purchased by a Medicine Hat businessman following the Games. The tepee symbolizes the First Nations way of life, based on spirituality, the circle of life, family and the sacred home.

You'll probably have seen the pamphlets for the **Great Wall of China**; this is not a replica of the real thing, but quite literally a wall of china produced by the potteries of Medicine Hat from 1912 to 1988. Though many of the pieces on display are priceless collector's items, the best part of the **Clay Interpretive Centre ★★** (☎529-1070) is the tour of the old Medalta plant and kilns. Medalta once supplied the fine china for all Canadian Pacific hotels. Today, workers' clothes and personal effects remain in the plant, which closed down unexpectedly in 1989. Medalta Potteries, Medicine Hat Potteries, Alberta Potteries and Hycroft China established Medicine Hat's reputation as an important pottery centre. Tour guides lead visitors through the plant and explain the intricate and labour-intensive work that went into each piece. The tour ends with a fascinating visit inside one of the six beehive kilns outside.

Historic Walking Tour pamphlets are available at the information office for those interested in exploring the turn-of-the-century architecture of Medicine Hat's downtown core.

 OUTDOORS

 Parks

Waterton Lakes National Park ★★★ *(for one day: groups $8, adults $4; camping from $10 to $21; for information call ☎859-5133 or write Waterton Lakes National Park, c/o Superintendent, Waterton Park, Alberta, TOK 2M0. Note that reservations are not accepted for campgrounds.)* is located right on the US-Canadian border and forms one half of the world's first International Peace Park (the other half is Glacier National Park, Montana). Waterton boasts some of the best scenery in the province and is well worth the detour required to visit it. Characterized by a chain of deep glacial lakes and upside-down mountains with irregularly shaped summits, this area where the peaks meet the prairies offers wonderful hiking, cross-country skiing, camping and wildlife-viewing opportunities. The unique geology of the area is formed by 1.5 billion year old sedimentary rock from the Rockies that was dumped on the 60-million year-old shale of the prairie during the last ice age. Hardly any transition zone exists between these two parks that are home to abundant and varied wildlife, where species from a prairie habitat mix with those of sub-alpine and alpine regions (some 800 varieties of plants and 250 species of birds). One thing to remember, and you will be reminded of it as you enter the park, is that wild animals here are just that — wild. While they may appear tame, they are unpredictable and potentially dangerous, and visitors are responsible for their own safety.

There is one park entrance accessible from Highway 6 or 5. On your way in from Highway 6, you will come upon a **buffalo paddock** shortly before the park gate. A small herd lives here and can be viewed by visitors from their cars along a loop road through the paddock. The sight of bison against the backdrop of the looming mountains of the park is truly spectacular. Fees must be paid at the gate, and

ALBERTA

information is available at the information centre a short distance inside the park beyond the gate. Park staff provide information on camping, wildlife-viewing and the various outdoor activities that can be enjoyed here, including hiking, cross-country skiing, golf, horseback riding, boating and swimming.

The park's trademark **Prince of Wales Hotel** (see p 492) was built in 1926-1927 by Louis Hill, head of the Great Northern Railway, to accommodate American tourists that the railway transported by bus from Montana to Jasper (today, the majority of visitors to the park are still American).

As you approach **Writing-on-Stone Provincial Park ★★** *(free admission; park office ☎647-2364)*, located only about 10 kilometres from the American border, you'll notice the carved out valley of Milk River and, in the distance, the Sweetgrass Hills rising up in the state of Montana. The Milk River lies in a wide green valley with strange rock formations and steep sandstone cliffs. The hoodoos, formed by iron-rich layers of sandstone that protect the softer underlying layers, appear like strange mushroom-shaped formations. These formations, along with the cliffs, were believed to house the powerful spirits of all things in the world, attracting natives to this sacred place as far back as 3,000 years ago. Writing-on-Stone Provincial Park protects more rock art — petroglyphs (rock carvings) and pictographs (rock paintings) — than any other place on the North American plains. Dating of the rock art is difficult and based solely on styles of drawing and tell-tale objects; for example, horses and guns imply that the drawings continued into the 18th and 19th centuries.

The majority of the rock-art sites are located in the larger part of the provincial park, which is an archaeological preserve. Access is provided only through scheduled interpretive tours, and for this reason, it is extremely important to call the park's **naturalist office** *(☎647-2364)* ahead of time to find out when the tours are heading out. They are given daily from mid-May to early September, and free tickets, limited in number, are required. These may be obtained from the naturalist office one hour before the tour begins. Wildlife checklists and fact sheets are also available at the naturalist office.

The park boasts an excellent campground (inquire at park office regarding fees). Visitors also have the opportunity to practise a whole slew of outdoor activities including hiking and

canoeing — this is a convenient place to start or end a canoe trip along the Milk River.

 Canoeing and Rafting

With hot summer temperatures and the possibility of spotting antelope, mule deer, white-tailed deer, coyotes, badger, beaver and cottontail rabbits, as well as several bird species, the Milk River is a great spot to explore by canoe. Set in arid southern Alberta, this river is the only one in Alberta that drains into the Gulf of Mexico. Canoes can be rented in Lethbridge.

Milk River Raft Tours *(Box 396, Milk River, Alberta, T0K 1M0, ☎647-3586)* organizes rafting trips along the river in the vicinity of Writing-on-Stone Provincial Park. Trips last from two to six hours, cost between $15 and $30 and can include lunch and hikes through the coulees.

 ACCOMMODATIONS

Calgary

There are often two rates for Calgary hotels and motels, a Stampede rate and a rest-of-the-year rate, and the difference between the two can be substantial in some cases.

The **Bed and Breakfast Association of Calgary** *(☎531-0065, ≈531-0069)* can arrange accommodation in nearly 40 bed and breakfasts throughout the city.

Downtown

The **Calgary International Hostel** *(members $15, non-members $19; 520 7th Ave. SE, Calgary, T2G 0J6, ☎269-8239, ≈283-6503)* can accommodate up to 114 people in dormitory-style rooms. Two family rooms are also available in winter. Guests have access to laundry and kitchen facilities, as well as to a game room and a snack bar. The hostel is advantageously located two blocks east of City Hall and Olympic Plaza. Reservations are recommended.

One of the most charming choices is **Inglewood Bed & Breakfast** *($70; 1006 8th Ave. SE, ☎/≈262-6570)*. Not far from downtown, this lovely Victorian house is also close to the Bow River pathway system. Breakfast is prepared by Chef Valinda.

The weekly, corporate and group rates of the all-suite **Prince Royal Inn** *($120, $135 with K; ℜ, △, ☉, tv, K; 618 5th Ave. SW, Calgary, T2P 0M7, ☎263-0520 or 1-800-661-1592, ≈298-4888)* make this perhaps the least expensive hotel accommodation right downtown. The fully equipped kitchens also help keep costs down.

Across the street is business-class **Calgary Mariott Hotel** *($159; ℜ, ≈, ≈, ◉, △, ☉, tv, ✖, ⅙; 110 9th Ave. SE, Calgary, T2G 5A6, ☎266-7331 or 1-800-228-9290, ≈262-8442)*, biggest of the downtown hotels. Its spacious rooms are decorated with warm colours and comfortable furnishings.

The **Palliser** *($280; ℜ, ≈, ◉, △, ☉, tv, ✖, ⅙; 133 9th Ave. SW, Calgary, T2P 2M3, ☎262-1234 or 1-800-441-1414, ≈260-1260)* offers distinguished, classic accommodations in true Canadian Pacific style. The hotel was built in 1914, and the lofty lobby, restored in 1997, retains its original marble staircase, solid-brass doors and superb chandelier. The rooms are a bit small but have high ceilings and are magnificently decorated in classic styles.

Southeast and Southwest

Another inexpensive accommodation option, only available in summer, is to stay at the residences of the **University of Calgary** *(single $28, double $38; 3330 24th Ave. NW, ☎220-3203)*.

Northeast and Northwest

Travellers just passing through or who have early or late flight connections to make should consider the convenience and reasonable prices of the **Pointe Inn** *($70; ℜ, ≈, tv, ✖; 1808 19th St. NE, Calgary, T2E 4Y3, ☎291-4681 or 1-800-661-8164, ≈291-4576)*. The rooms are clean but very ordinary. Laundry facilities.

Calgary's **Motel Village** is quite something: car rental offices, countless chain motels and hotels, fast-food and family-style restaurants and the Banff Trail C-Train stop. The majority

of the hotels and motels look the same, but the more expensive ones are usually newer and offer more facilities. Most places charge considerably higher rates during Stampede Week.

The **Red Carpet Motor Hotel** *($59-$79; ≈, ℜ, tv, ✖; 4635 16th Ave. NW, Calgary, T3B 0M7, ☎286-5111, ≈247-9239)* is one of the best values in Motel Village. Some suites have small refrigerators.

The Scottish decor of the **Highlander Hotel** *($85; ℜ, ≈, ≈, tv, ✖; 1818 16th Ave., Calgary, T2M 0L8, ☎289-1961 or 1-800-661-9564, ≈289-3901)* is a nice change from the typically drab motel experience. Close to services and a shopping mall. Airport shuttle service available.

The **Econo Lodge** *($89; ℜ, ≈, ≈, K, tv, ✖; 2231 Banff Tr. NW, Calgary, T2M 4L2, ☎289-1921, ≈282-2149)* is a good place for families. Children will enjoy the outdoor pool and playground, while the laundry facilities and large units with kitchenettes are very practical. The **Louisiana** family restaurant serves inexpensive *($)* Cajun and Creole food.

Southern Alberta

Waterton Townsite

Things slow down considerably during the winter months, when many hotels and motels close and others offer winter rates and packages.

The **Northland Lodge** *($50; sb or pb, ℜ; on Evergreen Ave., Waterton Lakes National Park, T0K 2M0, ☎859-2353)*, open from mid-May to mid-October, is a converted house with nine cosy rooms. Some rooms have balconies and barbecues.

The **Kilmorey Lodge** *($81; ⅙, ℜ, K; 117 Evergreen Ave., Box 100, Waterton Lakes National Park, T0K 2M0, ☎859-2334, ≈859-2342)* is open year-round. It is ideally located overlooking Emerald Bay, and many rooms have great views. Antiques and duvets contribute to the old-fashioned, homey feel. Two wheelchair-accessible suites have recently been added. The Kilmorey also boasts one of Waterton's finest restaurants, the Lamp Post Dining Room (see p 494).

ALBERTA

The venerable **Prince of Wales Hotel** *($175-$190 economy room, $347 suite; pb, ℜ; Waterton Lakes National Park, TOK 2M0, ☎859-2231 or (602) 207-6000, ⸗ 859-2630)*, open from mid-May until the end of September, is definitely the grandest place to stay in Waterton, with bell-hops in kilts and high tea in Valerie's Tea Room, not to mention the unbeatable view. The lobby and rooms are all adorned with original wood panelling. The rooms are actually quite small and unspectacular, however, with tiny bathrooms and a rustic feel. Those on the third floor and higher have balconies. Try to request a room facing the lake, which is, after all, the reason people stay here. Things will certainly change here if the rumours about expanding the Prince of Wales are true (see p 490).

Lethbridge

Built in 1937, the Art Deco **Heritage House B&B** *($50 bkfst incl.; sb; 1115 8th Ave. S, Lethbridge, T1J 1P7, ☎328-3824, ⸗328-9011)* is located on one of Lethbridge's pretty tree-lined residential streets, only a few minutes' walk from downtown. The guest rooms are uniquely decorated in accordance with the design of the house and include many of the house's original features. This house is an Alberta Provincial Historic Resource.

Days Inn *($60 bkfst. incl.; ≡, ⊛, K, ⊝, tv, ✘, ♿; 100 3rd Ave. S, Lethbridge, T1J 4L2, ☎327-6000, or 1-800-661-8085, ⸗320-2070)* is the best motel choice downtown. The typical motel-style rooms are non-descript, but modern and clean. A free continental breakfast is served. Coin laundry available.

The best hotel accommodation in Lethbridge is found at the **Lethbridge Lodge Hotel** *($87; ≡, ≈, ℜ, ⊛, tv, bar, ✘; 320 Scenic Dr., Lethbridge, T1J 4B4, ☎328-1123 or 1-800-661-1232, ⸗328-0002)*, overlooking the river valley. The comfortable rooms decorated in warm and pleasant colours seem almost luxurious when you consider the reasonable price. The rooms surround an interior tropical courtyard where small footbridges lead from the pool to the lounge and Anton's Restaurant (see p 494).

Medicine Hat

Besides the one central hotel, there is actually another, very pleasant place to stay that is close to downtown, along pretty First Street SE. The **Sunny Holme B&B** *($60; pb; 271 1st St. SE, Medicine Hat T1A 0A3, ☎526-5846)* is in a grand western Georgian house with a Victorian interior, and the three rooms are decorated in arts-and-crafts style. A large leafy lot surrounds the house. Sourdough pancakes are just one of the breakfast possibilities. Be sure to call ahead.

For about the same price, you can stay along the motel strip at the **Best Western Inn** *($79; ℜ, ⊝, ≡, ≈, ⌂, ⊛, K, tv, ✘; 722 Redcliff Dr., Medicine Hat, T1A 5E3, ☎527-3700 or 1-800-528-1234, ⸗526-8689)*, where the surroundings may not be as pleasant, but the facilities and rooms are more modern. Guests have access to an indoor pool and laundry facilities.

 RESTAURANTS

Calgary

Downtown

If you don't think you'll last until dinner, grab a bagel to go from **Schwartzie's Bagel Noshery** *($; 8th Ave. SW, ☎296-1353)*. Imagine the most typical and the most original bagels you can and they probably have one. You can also eat in; the interior is inviting and comfortable.

Drinkwaters Grill *($$; 237 8th Ave. SE, ☎264-9494)* is the new kid on the block when it comes to steakhouses in Calgary, and its self-billing as "contemporary" is appropriate. The huge sky-blue-coloured columns, modern tableaux, classic dark wooden chairs and upholstered banquettes are appealing. On the menu, there is everything from thin-crust pizza to spinach and strawberry salad, Chilean sea bass and, of course, a range of very acceptable sirloins, strips and other fine cuts, each with original accompaniments. They have theatre specials and a Happy Hour from 3:30pm to 7pm, Monday to Friday.

The **Silver Dragon** *($$; 106 3rd Ave. SE, ☎264-5326)* is one of the best of the many Chinese restaurants in Chinatown. The staff is particularly friendly and the dumplings particularly tasty.

Caesar's Steakhouse *($$$$; 512 4th Ave. SW; ☎264-1222 and 10816 Macleod Tr. S, ☎278-3930)* is one of Calgary's most popular spots to dig in to a big juicy steak, though they also serve good seafood. The elegant decor features Roman columns and soft lighting.

Hy's *($$$$; 316 4th Ave. SW,* ☎*263-2222),* around since 1955, is the other favourite for steaks. The main dishes are just slightly less expensive than Caesar's and the atmosphere is a bit more relaxed thanks to wood panelling. Reservations are recommended.

The Palliser Hotel's **Rimrock Room** *($$$$; 133 9th Ave. SW,* ☎*262-1234)* serves a fantastic Sunday brunch and, of course, healthy portions of prime Alberta beef. The Palliser's classic surroundings and fine food coalesce into one of Calgary's most elegant dining experiences.

Along the Bow

Good Earth Café *($; at Eau Claire Market, 200 Barclay Parade SW,* ☎*237-8684)* is a wonderful coffee shop with tasty, wholesome goodies all made from scratch. Besides being a choice spot for lunch, this is also a good source for picnic fixings.

The historic **Deane House Restaurant** *($$; year-round, Wed to Sun 11am to 2pm; 806 9th Ave. SE, just across the bridge from Fort Calgary,* ☎*269-7747)* is a pleasant tearoom located in the house of former commanding RCMP officer Richard Burton Deane. Soups and salads figure prominently on the menu.

Stromboli Inn *($$; 1147 Kensington Cresc. NW,* ☎*283-1166)* offers unpretentious service and ambiance and classic Italian cuisine. Locals recommend it for its pizza, though the menu also includes handmade gnocchi, plump ravioli and a delicious veal gorgonzola.

Buchanan's *($$$; 738 3rd Ave. SW,* ☎*261-4646)* gets the nod not only for its innovative steaks and chops in blue cheese sauce, but also for its excellent wine list (fine choices by the glass) and impressive selection of single malt scotches. This is a power-lunch favourite of Calgary's business crowd.

Southeast and Southwest

Everything is made from scratch at the informal **Nellie's Kitchen** *($; 17th Ave. SW between 7th and 6th Sts. SW),* a neat little rendezvous for lunch and people-watching.

The tiny **Kremlin** *($$; 2004 4th St. SW,* ☎*228-6068)* serves Russian "love food" that you will fall in love with. Hearty borscht with herb bread is a real deal, or maybe you'll go for the perogies with their filling of the day or the oh-so-tender tenderloin with rosemary, red wine and honey. For dessert, who could say no to perogies filled with Saskatoon berries and topped with orange brandy cream sauce? The decor is eclectic, cosy and perfect for "love food".

Entre Nous *($$-$$$; 2206 4th St. SW,* ☎*228-5525)* which means "between us", boasts a friendly and intimate bistro atmosphere, perfect for savouring some good French food. Special attention to detail, from the hand-selected ingredients to the *table d'hôte* menu, make for a memorable dining experience. Reservations recommended.

Cannery Row *($$$; 317 10th Ave. SW,* ☎*269-8889)* serves this landlocked city's best seafood. An oyster bar and casual atmosphere is intended to make you feel like you're by the sea, and it works. Fresh halibut, salmon and swordfish are prepared in a variety of ways. **McQueen's Upstairs** *($$$; upstairs,* ☎*269-4722)* has a similar seafood-oriented menu but is slightly more upscale.

The **Inn on Lake Bonavista** *($$$$; 747 Lake Bonavista Dr. SE,* ☎*271-6711)* is one of Calgary's finest dining rooms with fine menu selections like filet mignon and Châteaubriand, complemented by fine views over the lake.

Northeast and Northwest

The **Blue House Cafe** *($$; 3843 19th St. NW,* ☎*284-9111)* doesn't look like much, but the chef's Argentinian creations, especially the fish and seafood dishes, more than make up for it. Another plus is the flamenco and three-finger guitar performances on some evenings. The mood is fairly casual, but a bit dressier in the evenings.

Mamma's Ristorante *($$$; 320 16th St., NW,* ☎*276-9744)* has been serving Italian cuisine to Calgarians for more than 20 years. The ambiance and menu offerings are both equally refined, the latter including home-made pasta, veal and seafood dishes.

ALBERTA

Southern Alberta

Waterton

Pearl's Patio Café and Deli *($; 305 Windflower Ave.,* ☎*859-2284)* is a friendly place for a hearty breakfast. The home-made soups and breads are delicious. Take-out lunches are available. The place stays busy throughout the day, both inside and outside on the terrace.

The **Waterton Park Café** *($; Waterton Ave.,* ☎*859-2077)* is popular with the park's seasonal workers. Good sandwiches and lunch fare.

The **Lamp Post Dining Room** *($$$; in Kilmorey Lodge,* ☎*859-2334)* offers what some argue is the best dining room in Waterton. The traditional charm, coupled with award-winning food and relatively reasonable prices definitely make it one of the best.

The atmosphere at the **Garden Court Dining Room** *($$$$;* ☎*859-2231)* in the Prince of Wales Hotel, however, is unbeatable. This formal dining room serves a complete menu and a daily *plat du jour* that often includes delicious seafood or pasta. Reservations are not accepted. Also in the Prince of Wales, an enjoyable and equally elegant ambience can be found at the **Windsor Lounge** and **Valerie's Tea Room**, where afternoon tea and continental breakfast are both served along with stunning views of the park.

Lethbridge

The **Penny Coffee House** *($; 331 5th St. S,* ☎*320-5282)*, located next to B. Maccabee's bookseller is the perfect place to enjoy a good book; don't worry if you haven't got one, there is plenty of interesting reading material on the walls. This café serves delicious hearty soups and chilis, filling sandwiches, wonderful cheese and tomato scones, sodas and, of course, a great cup of Jo.

For a change from Alberta beef try the **O'Sho Japanese Restaurant** *($$; 1219 3rd Ave. S,* ☎*327-8382)* where classic Japanese fare is enjoyed in traditional style from low tables set in partitioned rooms.

The Lethbridge Lodge is home to **Anton's** *($$$$; Lethbridge Lodge,* ☎*328-1123)*, the city's finest restaurant. The pasta dishes are particularly well received, as is the setting, in the hotel's tropical indoor courtyard. Reservations are recommended. The **Garden Café** *($$)* is a less expensive alternative in the Lethbridge Lodge with the same lovely surroundings. It is open from 6:30am to 11:30pm and serves a hearty breakfast, as well as truly divine desserts.

Medicine Hat

The **City Bakery** *($; 5th Ave. SW, between 3rd and 4th St. SW,* ☎*527-2800)* bakes up wonderful fresh breads and New York bagels.

For lunch, try **Caroline's Pub & Eatery** *($-$$; 101 4th Ave. SE,* ☎*529-5300)*, a big, airy place that lacks a bit of ambience but serves good, inexpensive food.

Rustler's *($$; 901 8th St. SW,* ☎*526-8004)* is another spot that transports you back to the lawless wild west — the restaurant boasts a blood-stained card table preserved under glass for all to gawk at! The menu features steaks, chicken, ribs, pasta and several Mexican dishes. Breakfasts are particularly busy and copious.

  ENTERTAINMENT

Calgary

Avenue is a monthly publication that lists what's on throughout Calgary, including live acts around town and theatre offerings. It is available free of charge throughout the city. **The Calgary Mirror** and **ffwd** are free news and entertainment weeklies.

Bars and Nightclubs

Things have changed since the heyday of Electric Avenue (11th Avenue SW); the downtown core is picking up, as are 12th Avenue and 17th Avenue. **Senor Frog's** and **Crazy Horse** are popular with young professionals, with dance tunes at the former and classic rock and roll at the latter. **The Republic** *(219 17th Ave. SW)* and **The Warehouse** *(733 10th Ave. SW)* offer a more "alternative" alternative.

ALBERTA

The cocktail craze has hit Calgary, and the best places to lounge and sip martinis are the **Auburn Saloon** *(200 8th Ave. SW, ☎290-1012)*, the **Embassy** *(516C 9th Ave., ☎213-3970)*, **Quincy's** *(609 7th Ave. SW, ☎264-1000)*, which also has cigars, and finally **Diva** *(1154 Kensington Cresc., ☎270-3739)*, in Kensington.

Boystown *(213 10th Ave. SW)* attracts a gay crowd, while **The 318** and **Victoria's Restaurant** *(17th Ave. at 2nd St. SW)*, both located in the same building, cater to mixed crowds. **Rook's** is a relaxed bar with great 25¢ chicken wings and a mostly lesbian clientele.

Kaos Jazz Bar *(718 17th Ave. SW, ☎228-9997)* is a popular jazz club with live shows Thursday to Saturday; it is also a fun café with an interesting menu.

If you're itchin' to two-step then you're in luck. Calgary has two great country bars. At **The Ranchman's** *(9615 Macleod Tr. SW, ☎253-1100)*, the horseshoe-shaped dance floor is the scene of two-step lessons on Tuesdays and line-dancing lessons on Wednesday; the rest of the week it is packed. The **Rockin' Horse Saloon** *(7400 Macleod Tr. SE, ☎255-4646)* is where the real cowboys and cowgirls hang out. For some two-stepping downtown, head to **Cowboy's** *(826 5th St. SW, ☎265-0699)*.

Theatres

Alberta Theatre Projects *(☎294-7475)* is an excellent troupe that performs great contemporary plays.

Those in need of some culture may want to inquire about performances of the **Calgary Opera** *(☎262-7286)*, the **Calgary Philharmonic Orchestra** *(☎571-0270)* and the **Alberta Ballet** *(☎245-2274)*.

Uptown Screen *(612 8th Ave., ☎265-0120)* shows foreign films in an old, revamped theatre downtown. First-run movies can be seen at movie theatres throughout the city. Pick up a newspaper for schedules and locations, or call the Talking Yellow Pages ☎521-5222 (see p 479).

Festivals and Cultural Events

The **Calgary Exhibition and Stampede** is deservedly called the "Greatest Show on Earth". It began in 1912, at a time when many people expected that the wheat industry would eventually supercede the cattle industry, and was intended to be a one-time showcase for traditional cowboy skills. Of course, the cattle industry thrived, and the show has been a huge success ever since. Every July, around 100,000 people descend on Stampede Park for the extravaganza. It begins with a parade, which starts at 6th Avenue SE and Second Street SE at 9am, but get there early (by 7am) if you want to see anything. The main attraction is, of course, the rodeo where cowboys and cowgirls show off their skills. The trials take place every afternoon at 1:30pm and the big final is held on the last weekend. Reserved seats for this event sell out quickly, and you are better off ordering tickets in advance if you have your heart set on seeing the big event. There are also chuck-wagon races; heats for the Rangeland Derby are held every evening at 8pm, and the final is on the last weekend. Downtown's Olympic Plaza is transformed into Rope Square, where free breakfast is served every morning from the backs of chuck wagons. Festivities continue throughout the day in the Plaza. Back at Stampede Park, an Indian Village and agricultural fair are among the exhibits. Evening performances often feature some of the biggest stars in country music. A gate admission fee of eight dollars is charged and allows access to all live entertainment, except shows at the Saddledome, for which tickets must be purchased in advance. For information on the good rodeo seats write to Calgary Exhibition and Stampede, Box 1060, Station M, Calgary, Alberta, T2P 2L8, or call ☎261-0101 or 1-800-661-1260.

The **Calgary International Jazz Festival** *(☎233-2628)* takes place the last week of June. The **International Native Arts Festival** *(☎233-0022)* and **Afrikadey** *(☎283-7119)* both take place the third week of August, and both highlight entertainment and art from a variety of cultures from all over the world. The **Calgary Winter Festival** *(☎543-5480)* takes place in late January or February.

Spectator Sports

The Canadian Football League's **Calgary Stampeders** play their home games in McMahon Stadium *(1817 Crowchild Tr. NW, ☎289-0205 or 1-800-667-FANS)* from July to November. The National Hockey League's **Calgary Flames** play at the Olympic

Saddledome *(17th Ave. and 2nd St. SE, ☎777-4646 or 777-2177)* from October to April.

Southern Alberta

Fort Macleod

Every year in mid-July the **Annual Pow-wow** is held at Head-Smashed-In Buffalo Jump. A large teepee is set up on the grounds where visitors can see traditional native dancing and sample some native food. For information call ☎553-2731.

 SHOPPING

Calgary

The **Eaton Centre, TD Square, Scotia Centre** and **The Bay** department stores line 8th Avenue SW, as does a collection of swanky upscale shops including **Holt Renfrew** and the boutiques in **Penny Lane Hall.**

Not only are **Kensington Avenue** and the surrounding streets a pleasant place to stroll, but the area is also full of interesting specialty shops that are worth a look. One of these is **Heartland Country Store** *(940 2nd Ave. NW)* which sells beautiful pottery. There is a collection of shops, cafés and galleries along 17th Avenue SW, with a distinctly upbeat atmosphere. Along 9th Avenue SE, east of the Elbow River, in Inglewood, gentrified houses now contain antique shops and cafés.

The **Alberta Boot Co.** *(614 10th Ave. SW)* is the place to outfit yourself for the Stampede, with boots in all sizes and styles, just to make sure you fit in!

Mountain Equipment Co-op *(830 10th Ave. SW, ☎269-2420)* is a co-operative that is essentially open only to its members, but it only costs five dollars to join, and it is well worth it. High-quality camping and outdoor equipment, clothing and accessories are sold at very reasonable prices.

Arnold Churgin Shoes *(221 8th Ave. SW, ☎262-3366 and at the Chinook Centre, Macleod Tr. at Glenmore Tr., ☎258-1818)* sells high-quality women's shoes at reasonable prices and offers excellent service, a must for those with a weakness for footwear!

Callebaut Chocolates *(1313 1st St. SE, ☎265-5777)* makes delicious Belgian chocolates right here in Calgary. They are available throughout the city, but at the head office in the Southeast you can see them being made.

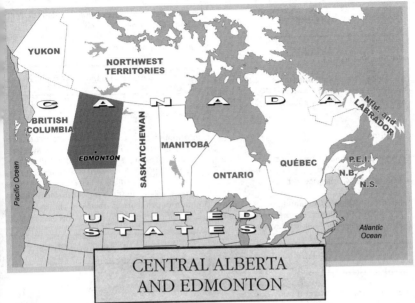

CENTRAL ALBERTA AND EDMONTON

C entral Alberta encompasses a vast swath of the province that includes the Red Deer River Valley, the foothills, the Rocky Mountains Forest Reserve and the heartland. A region that holds an inestimable amount of natural resources, forestry, farming and oil drive the economy of this area, as does tourism helped along tremendously by the occasional discovery of a dinosaur bone or two. Edmonton, the capital of the province, is easily accessible from anywhere in Central Alberta and has an unusually sophisticated atmosphere, with fine restaurants and a thriving arts community. Edmonton has become the technological, service and supply centre of Alberta.

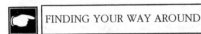 FINDING YOUR WAY AROUND

By Car

Edmonton's streets are numbered; the avenues run east-west and the streets run north-south. The major arteries include **Calgary Trail**, which runs north into the city (northbound it is also known as 103rd Street and southbound as 104th Street); **Whitemud Drive** runs east-west: it lies south of the city centre providing access to West Edmonton Mall, Fort Edmonton Park and the Valley Zoo; **Jasper Avenue** runs east-west through downtown where 101st Avenue would otherwise lie; Highway 16, the Yellowhead Highway, crosses the city north of downtown providing access to points in the tour of northern Alberta.

By Plane

Edmonton International Airport is located south of the city centre and offers many services and facilities including restaurants, an information centre, hotel courtesy phones, major car rental counters, currency exchange and a bus tour operator.

Air Canada, Canadian Airlines, American Airlines, Delta Airlines, Northwest Airlines, United Airlines and Lufthansa all have regular flights to the airport. Regional companies (Air B.C. and Canadian Regional) fly in and out of the municipal airport, located north of the city.

The **Sky Shuttle** (☎465-8515) travels to downtown hotels and to Edmonton's municipal airport. The trip is $11 one-way and $18 return. A taxi from the airport to downtown costs about $30.

By Bus

Central Alberta

Drumheller Greyhound Bus Depot: 1222 Hwy 9 South (Suncity Mall), ☎823-7566; services: restaurant, tourist information.

Edmonton

Edmonton Greyhound Bus Depot: 10324 103rd St., ☎413-8747, 420-2440 or 1-800-661-8747. Services: restaurant, lockers.

Edmonton South Greyhound Bus Depot: 5723 104th St., 2 blocks north of Whitemud Freeway on Calgary Trail, ☎433-1919

By Train

Via Rail's transcontinental railway passenger service makes a stop in Edmonton three times a week and either continues west to Jasper and Vancouver or east to Saskatoon and beyond. Via does not service Calgary. The train station in Edmonton is located under the CN Tower at 10004 104th Ave.

Public Transit

Edmonton's public transportation system also combines buses and a light-rail transit system. The LRT runs east-west along Jasper Avenue, south to the university and then north to 139th Street. There are only ten stops, and in the city centre the train runs underground. The LRT is free between Churchill and Grandin stops on weekdays from 9am to 3pm and Saturdays from 9am to 6pm. Fares are $1.60 for adults and a day pass is $4.75. Route and schedule information is available by calling ☎496-1611.

By Foot

Edmonton

Edmonton's downtown core has its own system of walkways known as the **pedway** system. It lies below and above ground and at street level and seems complicated at first, though is very well laid out and easy to figure out once you have picked up a map at the tourist information centre.

 # PRACTICAL INFORMATION

Area Code: 403.

Information on everything from road conditions to movie listings to provincial parks is available from the **Talking Yellow Pages**. In Edmonton, call ☎493-9000. A series of recorded messages is accessible by dialling specific codes. The codes are listed in the front of the yellow pages phone book; there is usually a phone book in every phone booth.

Tourist Information Offices

Central Alberta

Drumheller Tourist Information: at the corner of Riverside Dr. and 2nd St. W, ☎823-1331

Big Country Tourist Association 170 Centre St., #28, Drumheller, ☎823-5885, ☞823-7942

Red Deer Tourist Information Heritage Ranch on Cronquist Dr., ☎346-0180 or 1-800-215-8946

Rocky Mountain House tourist information in a trailer north of town on Hwy 11, summer only, ☎845-2414

Chamber of Commerce in Town Hall open year-round, ☎845-5450

Edmonton

Edmonton Tourism Civic Centre, 1 Sir Winston Churchill Square; also in Gateway Park, south of downtown on Calgary Trail (Hwy 2), ☎496-8423 or 1-800-463-4667.

EXPLORING

Central Alberta ★

Where the Red Deer River Valley now lies was once the coastal region of a vast inland sea; the climate probably resembled that of the Florida Everglades and was an ideal habitat for dinosaurs. After the extinction of the dinosaurs, ice covered the land. As the ice melted 10,000 years ago, it carved out deep trenches in the prairie; this and subsequent erosion have uncovered dinosaur bones and shaped the fabulously interesting landscape of hoodoos and coulees you'll see on this Dinosaur odyssey.

Brooks

The town of Brooks is a great jumping-off point for Dinosaur Provincial Park, declared a United Nations World Heritage Site in 1979. The landscape of this park consists of badlands, called *mauvaises terres* by French voyageurs because there was neither food nor beavers to be trapped there. These eerie badlands contain fossil beds of international importance, where over 300 complete skeletons have been found. Glacial melt water carved out the badlands from the soft bedrock, revealing hills laden with dinosaur bones. The erosion by wind and rain continues today, providing a glimpse of how this landscape of hoodoos, mesas and gorges was formed.

There are a loop road and two self-guided trails, but the best way to see the park is to follow a guided-tour into the restricted nature preserve, though this requires a bit of planning. Unless you plan to arrive early, it is extremely important to call ahead for the times of the tours, to make sure you are there in time to reserve yourself a spot (see Parks, p 507). Visitors can tour the **Field Station of the Tyrell Museum ★** (see p 507 for fee and schedule information) for an introduction to the excavation of dinosaur bones, and then head off on their own adventure.

Drumheller ★★★

The main attractions in Drumheller are located along the Dinosaur Trail and East Coulee Drive;

they include the Royal Tyrell Museum of Palaeontology, the Bleriot Ferry, the Rosedale Suspension Bridge, the Hoodoos, East Coulee, the Atlas Coal Mine and Last Chance Saloon. Erosion in the Red Deer River Valley has uncovered dinosaur bones and shaped the intricate landscape of hoodoos and coulees found in Drumheller. Besides the bones, early settlers discovered coal. Agriculture and the oil and gas industries now drive the local economy.

The **Dinosaur Trail ★★★** runs along both sides of the Red Deer River. The first stop on Highway 838 (the North Dinosaur Trail), the **Homestead Antique Museum** *(mid-May to mid-Oct, every day 10am to 5pm, ☎823-2600)*, which has a collection of 4,000 items from the days of the early settlers, is not the highlight of the tour. That honour falls on the **Royal Tyrell Museum of Palaeontology ★★★** *($6.50; mid-May to Sep, every day 9am to 9pm; Oct to mid-May, Tue to Sun 10am to 5pm; 6 km west of Drumheller on Hwy 838, ☎823-7707 or 1-888-440-4240)*. This mammoth museum contains over 80,000 specimens, including 50 full-size dinosaur skeletons. There are hands-on exhibits and computers, fibre-optics and audio-visual presentations. The Royal Tyrell is also a major research centre, and visitors can watch scientists cleaning bones and preparing specimens for display. There is certainly a lot to thrill younger travellers here; however, the wealth of information to absorb can be a bit overwhelming. You can participate in the **Day Dig** *(adults $85, children 10 to 15 $55, includes lunch, snacks, transportation and admission to the museum, reservations required; mid-May to late Jun, Sat and Sun, late Jun to end of Aug every day)*, which offers an opportunity to visit a dinosaur quarry and excavate fossils yourself, or the **Dig Watch** *($12; daily departures from the museum at 10am, noon, 2pm)*, a 90-minute guided tour to an actual working excavation site, where you'll see a dig in progress. Call ahead for tour times.

The next stop is the world's largest **Little Church**, which can accommodate "10,000 people, but only 6 at a time". The seven-by-eleven-foot house of worship, opened in 1958, seems to have been more popular with vandals than the devout and was rebuilt in 1990.

Once back in Drumheller, get on **East Coulee Drive ★★★**, also called the Hoodoo Trail, which heads southeast along Red Deer River. The town of **Rosedale** originally stood on the other side of the river next to the Star Mine.

ALBERTA

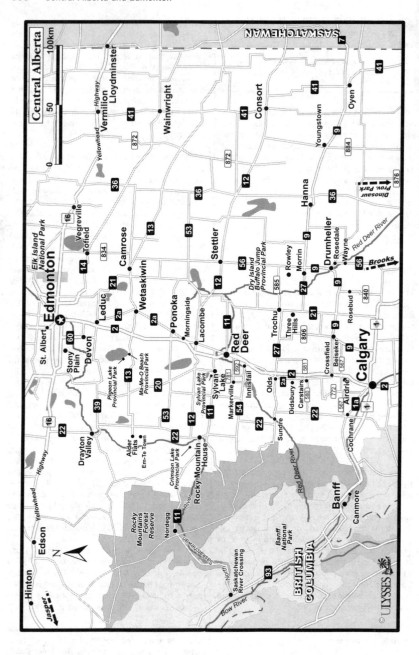

The suspension bridge across the Red Deer looks flimsy, but is said to be safe for those who want to venture across. Take a detour to cross the 11 bridges to **Wayne**. The bridges are perhaps the best part, as the main attraction in town, the Rosedeer Hotel, with its Last Chance Saloon, leaves a bit to be desired. Rooms are available for rent, but settle for a beer and some nostalgia instead. About halfway between Rosedale and East Coulee you'll see some of the most spectacular **hoodoos ★★★** in southern Alberta. These strange mushroom-shaped formations result when the softer underlying sandstone erodes. **East Coulee**, a town that almost disappeared, was once home to 3,000 people but only 200 residents remain. The **East Coulee School Museum** *(free admission; summer, every day 9am to 5pm; winter, closed Sat and Sun;* ☎*822-3970)* occupies a 1930s school house. Inside are a small tea room and gallery. Although the Atlas Coal Mine ceased operations in 1955, the **Atlas Coal Mine Museum** *($3; May to Oct, every day 9am to 6pm;* ☎*822-2220)* across the river from town keeps the place alive. The last standing tipple (a device for emptying coal from mine cars) in Canada stands amidst the mine buildings, which you can explore on your own or as part of a guided tour. The colourful owner of the Wildhorse Saloon, in front of the mine, was instrumental in saving the School Museum and the Atlas Coal Mine. Don't drink anything that's not bottled in this place.

Rocky Mountain House

Despite its evocative name, Rocky Mountain House is not a picturesque log cabin in the woods but rather a gateway town into the majestic Rocky Mountains. The town, known locally as Rocky, is home to just under 6,000 people and represents a transition zone between aspen parkland and the mountains. The exceptional setting is certainly one of the town's major attractions, which otherwise offers the gamut of services — hotels, gas stations and restaurants. Just outside Rocky lies the town's namesake, Rocky Mountain House National Historic Site, along with a wealth of outdoor possibilities, including river trips in voyageur canoes and fishing, hiking and cross-country skiing at Crimson Lake Provincial Park.

The **Rocky Mountain House National Historic Park ★★** *($2.25; May to Sep, every day 10am to 6pm, call for winter hours; 4.8 km southwest of Rocky on Hwy 11A,* ☎*845-2412)* is Alberta's only National Historic Park and encompasses four known historic sites. Rocky Mountain House is worth seeing because it exemplifies, perhaps better than any other trading post, the inextricable link between the fur trade and the discovery and exploration of Canada. Two rival forts were set up here in 1799, Rocky Mountain House by the Northwest Company and Acton House by the Hudson's Bay Company. Both companies were lured by the possibility of establishing lucrative trade with the Kootenai west of the Rockies. It was after the merging of the Hudson's Bay Company and the Northwest Company in 1821, that the area was called Rocky Mountain House. Trade with the Kootenai never did materialize; in fact, except for a brief period of trade with Blackfoot tribes in the 1820s, the fort never prospered, and actually closed down and was then rebuilt on several occasions. It closed for good in 1875, after the North West Mounted Police made the area to the south safe for trading. The Hudson's Bay Company thus set up a post in the vicinity of Calgary. An interesting fact: the Hudson's Bay Company, today the cross-Canada department store The Bay, makes more money on its real estate holdings than on its retail operations.

The visitors centre presents a most informative exhibit on the fur-trading days at Rocky Mountain House, including a look at the clothing of the Plains Indians and how it changed with the arrival of fur traders as well as artifacts and testimonies of early explorers. Visitors can also choose to view one of several excellent National Film Board documentaries. Two interpretive trails lead through the site to listening posts (in English and French) along the swift-flowing North Saskatchewan River. Stops include a buffalo paddock and demonstration sites where tea is brewed and a York Boat, once used by Hudson's Bay Company traders, is displayed (the Northwest Company traders preferred the birchbark canoe, even though it was much slower). All that remains of the last fort are two chimneys.

Alder Flats

Alder Flats itself is of little interest to visitors. A few kilometres south, however, is another town that is full of attractions, a place ironically called **Em-Te Town**. Here you'll find a saloon, jailhouse, harness shop, schoolhouse, church and emporium, located in a pretty setting at the end of a gravel road. Built from scratch in 1978, this is a neat place to experience life the way it was in the old west, with trail rides and home-cooked meals at the Lost Woman Hotel. Some may find the whole experience a bit contrived. In addition to the attractions, there are campsites and cabins for rent, as well as a restaurant.

The drive west from Rocky Mountain House runs along the edge of the Rocky Mountain Forest Reserve. Stunning views of the Rocky Mountains line the horizon. Highway 11, the **David Thompson Highway ★★★** continues west from Rocky Mountain House up into the Aspen Parkland and on into Banff National Park (see p 517). The town of **Nordegg** lies at the halfway point of the highway. In addition to an interesting museum, the Nordegg Museum, the town offers access to great fishing, the Forestry Trunk Road and camping and is also home to the Shunda Creek Hostel (see p 509). The only services available west of Nordegg before the Highway 93 are at the David Thompson Resort (see p 509).

Red Deer ★

Red Deer is another Alberta city whose extensive park system is one of its greatest attractions. The **Waskasoo Park System** weaves its way throughout the city and through the Red Deer River valley with walking and cycling trails. The information centre is located at **Heritage Ranch (1)** *(25 Riverview Park, at the end of Cronquist Dr., ☎346-0180)* on the western edge of town; take the 32nd Street Exit from Highway 2, left on 60th Street and left on Cronquist Drive. Heritage Ranch also features, among other things, an equestrian centre, picnic shelters and access to trails in the park system.

Fort Normandeau (2) ★ *(free; late May to end of Jun, every day 10am to 6pm; Jul to early Sep, every day noon to 8pm; ☎ 347-7550)* is located west of Highway 2, along 32nd Street. The present-day fort is a replica of the original.

Wetaskiwin ★

The city of Wetaskiwin is home to one of the finest museums in the province. Like the Remington-Alberta Carriage Centre in Cardston, the Reynolds-Alberta Museum proves again that there is more to Alberta than Calgary, Edmonton and the Rockies. Though there isn't much to see in Wetaskiwin besides the Reynolds-Alberta and the Aviation Hall of Fame, this pleasant city has an interesting main street, and respectable restaurants and hotels.

The **Reynolds-Alberta Museum ★★★** *($6.50; late Jun to early Sep, 9am to 7pm; Sep to Jun, Tue to Sun 9am to 5pm; west of Wetaskiwin on Hwy 13, ☎361-1351 or 1-800-661-4726)* celebrates the "spirit of the machine" and is a wonderful place to explore. Interactive programs for children bring everything alive. A top-notch collection of restored automobiles, trucks, bicycles, tractors and related machinery is on display. Among the vintage cars is one of the original 470 Model J Duesenberg Phaeton Royales. This one-of-a-kind automobile cost $20,000 when it was purchased in 1929. Visitors to the museum will also learn how a grain elevator works, and can observe the activity in the restoration workshop through a large picture window. Tours of the warehouse, where over 800 pieces are waiting to be restored, are offered twice daily *($1, call ahead for times, sign up at front desk)*; pre-booked, one-hour guided tours are also available.

Edmonton ★★

Edmonton seems to suffer from an image problem, and undeservedly so. People have trouble getting past the boomtown atmosphere and the huge mall! Admittedly it is a boomtown: a city that grew out of the wealth of natural resources that surround it. But this city of new money has more than struck oil with an attractive downtown core, a park system and cultural facilities including theatres and many festivals (see p 512). With all this going for it, though, the city's biggest attraction still seems to be its gargantuan shopping mall. You be the judge!

Downtown and North of the North Saskatchewan River

Begin your tour of Edmonton with a visit to the **Tourist Information Centre** *(Mon to Fri 8am to 5pm)* located in the **Civic Centre** *(1 Sir Winston Churchill Square)*; the hours may not be very practical, but the staff is very friendly and helpful. While there, pick up a *Ride Guide* to figure out the public transportation system. The impressive **City Hall** is the centrepiece of the Edmonton Civic Centre, a complex that occupies six city blocks and includes the Centennial Library, the Edmonton Art Gallery, Sir Winston Churchill Square, the Law Courts

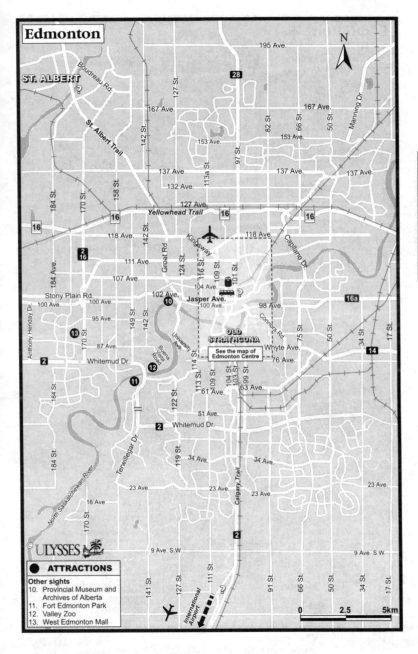

Edmonton

ALBERTA

Attractions

Other sights
10. Provincial Museum and Archives of Alberta
11. Fort Edmonton Park
12. Valley Zoo
13. West Edmonton Mall

© ULYSSES

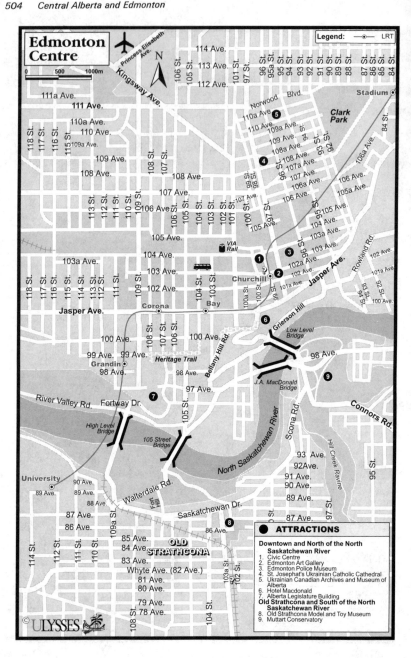

Edmonton Centre

Legend: ────●──── LRT

0   500   1000m

ATTRACTIONS

Downtown and North of the North Saskatchewan River
1. Civic Centre
2. Edmonton Art Gallery
3. Edmonton Police Museum
4. St. Josephat's Ukrainian Catholic Cathedral
5. Ukrainian Canadian Archives and Museum of Alberta
6. Hotel Macdonald
7. Alberta Legislature Building

Old Strathcona and South of the North Saskatchewan River
8. Old Strathcona Model and Toy Museum
9. Muttart Conservatory

© ULYSSES

Building, the Convention Centre and Citadel Theatre. City Hall, with its impressive 8-story glass pyramid, opened in 1992 on the site of the old city hall.

While City Hall may be the centrepiece of the Civic Centre, its biggest star these days is certainly the brand new **Francis Winspear Centre for Music ★★** *(4 Sir Winston Churchill Sq.)*, which will hopefully bring some life back to Edmonton's fading urban core. Built with a six-million-dollar gift from Edmonton businessman Francis Winspear, the 1,900-seat hall is faced with Manitoba tyndall limestone to match City Hall and brick to match the neighbouring Stan Milner Library. The Edmonton Symphony Orchestra now makes its home here.

On the eastern side of Sir Winston Churchill Square lies the **Edmonton Art Gallery ★★** *($3; Thu pm; Mon to Wed 10:30am to 5pm, Thu and Fri 10:30am to 8pm, Sat and Sun 11am to 5pm; ☎422-6223)*. Admission is free when the museum can find sponsorship. Fine art by local, Canadian and international artists is unfortunately a bit lost in this drab building, but a new curator and plans for exciting new shows promise to breathe new life into the gallery. Still, worth checking out.

The **Edmonton Police Museum ★** *(free admission; Mon to Sat 9am to 3pm; 9620 103A Ave., ☎421-2274)* is a bit of a change from your typical museum excursion as it traces law enforcement in Alberta's history. Located on the second floor of the Police Service Headquarters it houses displays of uniforms, handcuffs, jail cells and the force's former furry mascot!

The stretch of 97th Street from 105th to 108th Avenue is Edmonton's original Chinatown with plenty of shops and restaurants. Along 107th Avenue, from 95th Street to 116th Street is an area known as the Avenue of Nations with shops and restaurants representing a variety of cultures from Asia, Europe and the Americas. Rickshaws provide transportation during the summer months.

At the corner of 97th Street and 108th Avenue is **St. Josephat's Ukrainian Catholic Cathedral ★**. Among Edmonton's several Ukrainian churches, this is the most elaborate and is worth a stop for its lovely decor and artwork. One block to the east, 96th Street is recognized in *Ripley's Believe It or Not* as the

street with the most churches (16) in such a short distance. It is known as Church Street.

Head east to 96th Street then north to 110th Avenue to the **Ukrainian Canadian Archives and Museum of Alberta ★** *(donation; Tue to Fri 10am to 5pm, Sat noon to 5pm; 9543 110th Ave., ☎424-7580)* which houses one of the largest displays of Ukrainian archives in Canada. The lives of Ukrainian pioneers around the turn of the century are chronicled through artifacts and photographs. About ten blocks to the west, the smaller **Ukrainian Museum of Canada ★** *(free admission; Jun to Aug, Mon to Fri 9am to 4pm, winter by apt; 10611 110th Ave., ☎483-5932 or 434-6877)* displays a collection of Ukrainian costumes, Easter eggs, and household items.

In true Canadian Pacific tradition, the chateau-style **Hotel Macdonald ★★** is Edmonton's ritziest place to stay (see p 510) and was the place to see and be seen in Edmonton for many years. Completed in 1915 by the Grand Trunk Railway, it was designed by Montréal architects Ross and MacFarlane. The wrecker's ball came close to falling in 1983 when the hotel closed, but a $28-million-dollar restoration brought the Macdonald back in all its splendour. If you aren't staying here, at least pop in to use the facilities, or better yet, enjoy a drink overlooking the river from the hotel's suave bar, The Library.

The next stop on the tour is the Alberta Legislature Building. It is a fair walk to get there from the Hotel Macdonald, but nevertheless a pleasant one, along the tree-lined **Heritage Trail ★★★**. This historic fur-traders' route from Old Town to the site of Old Fort Edmonton is a 30-minute walk that follows the river bank for most of its length. A red brick sidewalk, antique light standards and street signs will keep you on the right track. The river views along Macdonald Drive are remarkable, especially at sunset.

The 16-story vaulted dome of the Edwardian **Alberta Legislature Building ★** *(mid-May to early Sep, weekdays 8:30am to 5pm, weekends 9am to 5 pm; Sep to May, weekdays 9am to 4:30pm, weekends noon to 5pm; Nov to Feb, closed Sat; 107th St. at 97th Ave., ☎427-7362)* is a landmark in Edmonton's skyline. Sandstone from Calgary, marble from Québec, Pennsylvania and Italy, and mahogany from Belize were used to build this, the seat of the Alberta government, in 1912. At the time, the Legislature stood next

ALBERTA

to the original Fort Edmonton. Today it is surrounded by gardens and fountains; be sure to visit the government greenhouses on the south grounds. Tours begin at the Interpretive Centre where Alberta and Canada's parliamentary tradition is explained.

Old Strathcona and South of the North Saskatchewan River

Old Strathcona ★★★, once a city independent of Edmonton, was founded when the Calgary and Edmonton Railway Company's rail line ended here in 1891. Brick buildings from that era still remain in this historic district, which is the best-preserved in Edmonton. While the area north of the North Saskatchewan River is clean, crisp and new with the unfinished feel of a boom town, south of the river, in Old Strathcona, a sense of character is much more apparent. Here an artistic, cosmopolitan and historic atmosphere prevails. Walking tour brochures are available from the **Old Strathcona Foundation** *(Mon to Fri 8:30am to 4:30pm; 10324 Whyte Ave., suite 401, ☎433-5866).*

On your way to the commercial centre of Old Strathcona, Whyte Avenue (82nd Avenue), stop in at the **Old Strathcona Model and Toy Museum ★★** *(donation; summer, Wed to Fri noon to 8pm, Sat 10am to 6pm, Sun 1pm to 5pm; winter, Wed to Fri noon to 5pm, Sat 10am to 6pm, Sun 1pm to 5pm; 8603 104 St., ☎433-4512),* housed in the Mackenzie Residence, one of the best-preserved buildings in Old Strathcona. This fascinating spot exhibits only models and toys made of paper or cardboard. These childhood treasures from the past will delight both young and old.

The four glass-pyramid greenhouses of the **Muttart Conservatory ★★★** *(\$4.25; Sun to Wed 11am to 9pm, Thu to Sat 11am to 6pm; Jun to Aug, every day 11am to 9pm; 9626 96A St., off 98 Ave., ☎496-8755)* are another of the landmarks of Edmonton's skyline. Flourishing beneath three of these pyramids are floral displays of arid, temperate and tropical climates, respectively. Every month, a new, vivid floral display is put together under the fourth pyramid. The conservatory is accessible from bus #51 south on 100th Street.

About six kilometres west as the crow flies, north of the river, is the **Provincial Museum and Archives of Alberta ★★** *(\$5.50; late May to early Sep, Sun to Wed 9am to 9pm, Thu to Sat 9am to 5pm; rest of year, Tue to Sun 9am to*

5pm; 12845 102 Ave, ☎453-9100). The natural and human history of Alberta is traced from the Cretaceous period, through the Ice Age to the pictographs of the province's earliest indigenous peoples. The merging of their cultures and those of the early explorers and pioneers is explained in the native display. The habitat gallery reproduces Alberta's four natural regions, while the Bug Room is abuzz with exotic live insects. Travelling exhibits complement the permanent collection. The displays are a bit dated, but nonetheless provide an interesting overview of the world of contrasts that is Alberta. Take bus #1 along Jasper Avenue, or bus #116 along 102 Avenue.

Government House ★ *(Sun 1pm to 5pm; free guided tours every half-hour ☎427-7362 or 427-2281),* the former residence of Alberta's lieutenant-governor, is located beside the Provincial Museum. The three-story sandstone mansion features the original library, oak-panelling along with newly renovated conference rooms. Take bus #1 along Jasper Avenue, or bus #116 along 102 Avenue.

Also north of the river is the **Edmonton Space and Science Centre ★** *(\$7; mid-Jun to Sep every day 10am to 6pm; Sep to mid-Jun, Tue to Sun 10am 6pm; 11211 142nd St., ☎451-3344).* All sorts of out-of-this-world stuff is sure to keep the young and old busy. You can embark on a simulated space mission at the Challenger Centre or create music on a giant piano. The Margaret Ziedler Star Theatre presents multi-media shows. The city's IMAX theatre is also on site.

In the North Saskatchewan River Valley, off Whitemud and Fox Drives, lies **Fort Edmonton Park ★★★** *(\$6.75; May and Jun, Mon to Fri 10am to 4pm, Sat and Sun 10am to 6pm; Jul to Sep, every day 10am to 6pm; over Christmas for sleigh rides; ☎496-8787),* Canada's largest historic park and home to an authentic reconstruction of Fort Edmonton as it stood in 1846. Four historic villages re-create different time periods here: the fur-trading era at the fort itself; the settlement era on 1885 Street; the municipal era on 1905 Street and the metropolitan era on 1920 Street. Period buildings, period dress, period automobiles and period shops, including a bazaar, a general store, a saloon and a bakery, bring you back in time. Reed's Bazaar and Tea Room serves a proper English tea with scones from 12:30pm to 5pm. Theme programs for children are put on Saturday afternoons. Admission is free after

4:30pm, but don't arrive any later or you'll miss the last train back to the fort, and take note that you'll be tight for time if you choose this frugal option, so it depends how much you want to see.

Across the river is the **Valley Zoo** ★ *($4.95, lower rate in winter; May to Jun, every day 9:30am to 6pm; Jul and Aug, until 8pm; Sep to mid-Oct, weekdays 9:30am to 4pm, weekends 9:30am to 6pm; winter, every day 9:30am to 4pm; at the end of Buena Vista Rd., corner 134th St., ☎496-6911)*, a great place for kids. It apparently began with a story-book theme but has since grown to include an African veldt and winter quarters which permit it to stay open in the winter. The residents include Siberian tigers and white-handed gibbons along with more indigenous species. Kids enjoy run-of-the-mill pony rides and more exotic camel rides.

Last, but certainly not least, is Edmonton's pride and joy the **West Edmonton Mall** ★★★ *(87th Ave. between 170th St. and 178th St.)*. You may scoff to hear that some visitors come to Edmonton and never leave the West Edmonton Mall, and then you may swear that you won't give in to the hype and visit it, but these reasons alone are enough to go, if only to say you've been. There are real submarines at the Deep-Sea Adventure; dolphin shows; underwater caverns and barrier reefs; the largest indoor amusement park; a National Hockey League-size rink where you can watch the Edmonton Oilers practise; an 18-hole golf course; a waterpark complete with wave pool, waterslides, rapids, bungee jumping and whirlpools; a casino, bingo room and North America's largest billiard hall; fine dining on Bourbon Street; a life-size, hand-carved, hand-painted replica of Columbus' flagship, the Santa Maria; replicas of England's crown jewels; a solid ivory pagoda; bronze sculptures; fabulous fountains including one fashioned after a fountain at the Palace of Versailles and finally, the Fantasyland Hotel (see p 510): lodging that truly lives up to its name... and, oh yeah, we almost forgot, there are also some 800 shops and services – this is a mall after all. It seems possible to come and never leave! Even though it is a shopping mall, the West Edmonton Mall simply has to be seen and therefore merits its three stars!

PARKS

Central Alberta

Kinbrook Island Provincial Park ★

The shores of Lake Newell, the largest man-made body of water in the province, are home to over 250 species of birds and fowl. Colonies of double-crested cormorants and American white pelicans occupy several of the protected islands on the lake. The best wildlife viewing is from the eastern shore. There are also walking trails through nearby Kinbrook Marsh. For information ☎362-2962.

Dinosaur Provincial Park ★★★

Dinosaur Provincial Park offers amateur palaeontologists the opportunity to walk through the land of these monstrous reptiles. Declared a UNESCO Heritage Site in 1979, this nature preserve harbours a wealth of information on these majestic former inhabitants of the planet. Today, the park is also home to more than 35 species of animals.

The small museum at the **Field Station of the Tyrell Museum** *($2; mid-May to early Sep, every day 9am to 9pm; Sep to May, Mon to Fri, 8:15am to 4:30pm; ☎378-4342 or 378-4344 for bus tour reservations)*, loop road and two self-guided trails (the Cottonwood Flats Trail and the Badlands Trail) will give you a quick introduction to the park. Two exposed skeletons left where they were discovered can be viewed. The best way to see the park, however, is on one of the guided tours into the restricted nature preserve that makes up most of the park. The 90-minute Badlands Bus Tour leads into the heart of the preserve for unforgettable scenery, skeletons and wildlife; the Centrosaurus Bone Bed Hike and Fossil Safari Hike offer close-up looks at excavation sites. Tickets for all of these tours go on sale the day of the event at 8:30am at the field station, and space is limited; arrive early in July and August. To avoid missing out, visitors are strongly advised to call ahead to find out when the tours leave.

ALBERTA

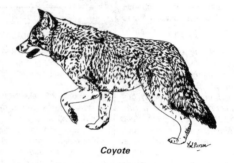

Coyote

The park also features campgrounds and a Dinosaur Service Centre with laundry facilities, showers, picnic tables and food. The cabin of John Ware, an important black cowboy, lies near the campground.

Elk Island National Park ★★

The magnificent Elk Island National Park *($4, groups $8; open year-round; park administration and warden Mon to Fri 8am to 4:30pm, ☎992-2984 or 992-2950; camping ☎992-2984)* preserves part of the Beaver Hills area as it was before the arrival of settlers, when Sarcee and Plains Cree hunted and trapped in these lands. The arrival of settlers endangered beaver, elk and bison populations, prompting local residents and conservationists to petition the government to set aside an elk reserve in 1906. The plains bison that live in the park actually ended up there by accident, having escaped from a herd placed there temporarily while a fence at Buffalo National Park in Wainwright, Alberta was being completed. The plains bison herd that inhabits the park began with those 50 escaped bison. Elk Island is also home to a small herd of rare wood bison, North America's largest mammal. In 1940, pure wood buffalo were thought to be extinct, but by sheer luck a herd of about 200 wood buffalo were discovered in a remote part of the park in 1957. Part of that herd was sent to a fenced sanctuary in the Northwest Territories. Today the smaller plains bison are found north of Highway 16, while the wood bison live south of the highway. While touring the park, remember that you are in bison country and that these animals are wild. Though they may look docile, they are dangerous, unpredictable and may charge

without warning, so stay in your vehicle and keep a safe distance (50 to 75 metres).

Elk Island became a national park in 1930 and is now a 195-square-kilometre sanctuary for 44 kinds of mammals, including moose, elk, deer, lynx, beaver and coyote. The park offers some of the best wildlife viewing in the province. It is crossed by major migratory fly ways – look for trumpeter swans in the fall.

The park office at the South Gate, just north of Highway 16, provides information on the two campgrounds, on wildlife viewing and on the twelve trails that run through the park, making for great hiking and cross-country skiing. Fishing and boating can be enjoyed on Astotin Lake, and the park even boasts a nine-hole golf course.

 ACCOMMODATIONS

Central Alberta

Brooks

There are campsites at **Kinbrook Island Provincial Park** *(☎362-2962)* as well as at **Dinosaur Provincial Park** *(☎378-3700)*. The latter has more facilities, including a snack bar, showers and a laundry.

Six and a half kilometres north of town on Highway 873 is the **Douglas Country Inn** *($77 bkfst incl.; ℜ, ≡, pb; Box 463, T1R 1B5, ☎362-2873, ≈362-2100)*. A casual country atmosphere is achieved in each of the seven beautifully adorned rooms and throughout the 'est of the inn. The only television is in the small TV room, which hardly ever gets used. Enjoy your complimentary sherry by the fire in the sitting room. The special occasion room *($99)* boasts a divine Japanese soaker tub with a view.

Drumheller

A converted downtown hotel now houses the **Alexandra International Hostel** *(members $13.65, non-members $17.85; 30 Railway Ave. N, T0J 0Y0, ☎823-6337, ⇒823-5327)*. It opened in 1991 after renovations and is independently operated in cooperation with Hostelling International. Most dorm rooms have eight beds, though there are some with fewer, and several even have private bathrooms. There are kitchen and laundry facilities on the premises, as well as all sorts of information brochures and a mountain-bike rental service.

By far the prettiest place to stay in town is the **Heartwood Manor** *($79; pb, ⊛, ≡, tv, ✗, ⚱; 320 Railway Ave. E, T0J 0Y4, ☎823-6495 or 1-888-823-6495, ⇒823-4935)*, a bed and breakfast in a restored heritage building, where a striking use of colour creates a cosy and luxurious atmosphere. Nine of the ten rooms have jet-tubs, and five even boast fireplaces. A spacious cottage is also available and a two-bedroom suite was added in the spring of 1997. Yummy home-made fruit syrups are served with the pancake breakfast. French and English spoken.

Rocky Mountain House

The **Voyageur Motel** *($50; ≡, K, ℜ, tv; on Hwy 11 S., Box 1376, T0M 1T0, ☎845-3381 or 1-888-845-3569, ⇒845-6166)* is a practical choice with spacious, clean rooms, each equipped with a refrigerator. Kitchenettes are also available for a surcharge.

The log exterior of the **Walking Eagle Motor Inn** *($66, cabins $35; ≡, ℜ, tv, bar; on Hwy 11, Box 1317, T0M 1T0, ☎845-2804, ⇒845-3685)* encloses 63 clean and large rooms decorated in keeping with the hotel's name.

Nordegg

Set against the stunning backdrop of the Rocky Mountains in David Thompson Country, and surrounded by countless opportunities for outdoor activities, is the **Shunda Creek Hostel** *(members $14, non-members $19; west of Nordegg, 3 km north of Hwy 11, on Shunda Creek Recreation Area Rd., ☎/⇒721-2140)*. The two-story lodge encloses kitchen and laundry facilities, a common area with a fireplace and 10 rooms that can accommodate a total of 48 people; it also adjoins an outdoor hot tub. Hiking, mountain biking, fishing, canoeing, cross-country skiing and ice-climbing are possible nearby.

David Thompson Resort *($65; pb, ≡, ≈; ☎721-2103)* is more of a motel and RV park than a resort, but regardless it is the only accommodations between Nordegg and Highway 93, the Icefields Parkway (see p 522), and you can't beat the scenery. The resort rents bicycles and even organizes helicopter tours of the area.

Red Deer

Many conventions are held in Red Deer, and as a result weekend rates in the many hotels are often less expensive.

The **Rainbow Motor Inn** *($53; ≡, ℜ, K, tv; 2803 Gaetz Ave., T4R 1H1, ☎343-2112 or 1-800-223-1993, ⇒340-8540)* is one of many hotels and motels along Gaetz Avenue. It houses pleasant, simple rooms. Kitchenette units are available for a surcharge.

Wetaskiwin

Close to the Reynolds-Alberta Museum, on 56th Street, the **Rose Country Inn** *($55; ≡, ℜ, ℝ, K, bar, tv; 4820 56th St., T9A 2G5, ☎352-3600, ⇒352-2127)* is one of the best deals in town. Each of the newly renovated rooms has a refrigerator and microwave oven.

Edmonton

Downtown

The **Edmonton International Hostel** *(members $13, non-members $18; ≡; 10422 91st St., T5H 1S6, ☎429-0140, ⇒421-0131)* is located close to the bus terminal, in a questionable area, so take care. The usual hostel facilities, including laundry machines, common kitchen and common room with fireplace are rounded out by a small food store and bike rentals.

ALBERTA

The **Edmonton House Suite Hotel** *($110; ℜ, K, ≈, △, tv, ⊘, ✕; 10205 100th Ave., T5J 4B5, ☎420-4000 or 1-800-661-6562, ⇝420-4008)* is actually an apartment-hotel with suites that boast kitchens and balconies. This is one of the better apartment-hotel options in town. Reservations are recommended.

Edmonton's grand chateau-style **Hotel MacDonald** *($179; ≡, ℜ, ≈, ⊛, △, ⊘, tv, bar, ✕, ⚫; 10065 100th St., T5J 0N6, ☎424-5181 or 1-800-441-1414, ⇝424-8017)* is simply stunning. Classic styling from the guest rooms to the dining rooms make this an exquisite place to stay. A variety of weekend packages are available including golf packages and romantic getaways. Call for details.

West of Downtown

For those who want to be close to the shopping, but aren't necessarily big-spenders, the **Edmonton West Travelodge** *($69; ≈, ≡, ⊛, tv, ✕; 18320 Stony Plain Rd., T5S 1A7, ☎483-6031 or 1-800-578-7878, ⇝484-2358)* is one of two relatively inexpensive hotels located close to the West Edmonton Mall. The rooms were recently redone and there is a big indoor pool.

The **West Harvest Inn** *($69; ≡, ℜ, ⊛, tv; 17803 Stony Plain Rd., T5S 1B4, ☎484-8000 or 1-800-661-6993, ⇝486-6060)* is the other inexpensive choice within striking distance of the mall. This hotel is relatively quiet and receives quite a few business travellers.

The **Best Western Westwood Inn** *($85; ≡, △, ⊘, ≈, ℜ, tv; 18035 Stony Plain Rd., T5S 1B2, ☎483-7770, 1-800-557-4767 or 1-800-528-1234, ⇝486-1769)* is also close to the mall. The rooms are more expensive here but they are also much larger and noticeably more comfortable and more pleasantly decorated.

Travellers on a shopping vacation will certainly want to be as close to the West Edmonton Mall as possible, making the **Fantasyland Hotel & Resort** *($155; ⊘, ✕, ≡, ℜ, ⊛, △, tv, bar; 17700 87th Ave., T5T 4V4, ☎444-3000 or 1-800-661-6454, ⇝444-3294)* the obvious choice. Of course, you might also choose to stay here just for the sheer delight of spending the night under African or Arabian skies or in the back of a pick-up truck!

Old Strathcona and South of the North Saskatchewan River

For a very reasonable rate, guests can stay at the **Southbend Motel** *($44; K, tv, ✕; 5130 Calgary Tr. Northbound, T6H 2H4, ☎434-1418, ⇝435-1525)*, where rooms are admittedly a bit dated, and for no extra charge use all the facilities at the Best Western Cedar Park Inn next door (see below). These include a pool, a sauna and an exercise room.

The **Best Western Cedar Park Inn** *($76; ≡, ℜ, ≈, △, ⊘, tv, ✕; 5116 Calgary Tr. Northbound, ☎434-7411, 1-800-661-9461 or 1-800-528-1234, ⇝437-4836)* is a large hotel with 190 equally spacious rooms. Some of these are called theme rooms *($150)*, which essentially means there are a hot-tubs for two, king-size beds, living rooms and a fancier decor. Weekend and family rates are available, and there is a courtesy limo service to the airport or the West Edmonton Mall.

 RESTAURANTS

Central Alberta

Brooks

Peggy Sue's Diner *($; 603 2nd St. W., ☎362-7737)* is neat little family-run eatery. Smoked meat, burgers, great fries and delicious mud pie can be eaten in or taken out.

Drumheller

Yavis Family Restaurant *($-$$; in the Valley Plaza, corner of 2nd St. W. and 3rd Ave., ☎823-8317)* has been around for years. The interior is fairly non-descript, and so is the menu. The selections are nonetheless pretty good, especially the great big breakfasts.

The **Sizzling House** *($$; 160 Centre St. ☎823-8098)* is also recommended by locals. They serve up tasty Thai cooking. A good place for lunch. The service is quick and friendly.

Cochrane

Cochrane's friendly **Home Quarter Restaurant & Pie Shoppe** *($$; 216 1st St. W, ☎932-2111)* is the home of the ever-popular Rancher's Special breakfast with eggs, bacon and sausage. Home-made pies are available all day long to eat in or take out. The lunch and dinner menu boasts filet mignon and chicken parmesan.

Red Deer

City Roast Coffee *($; 4940 50th St., ☎347-0893)* serves hearty soups, sandwich lunches and good coffee. The walls are decorated with posters announcing local art shows and events.

The **Good Food Company** *($-$$; at the corner of 50th St. and Gaetz Ave., ☎343-8185)* is located in the old Greene Block, a historic building in downtown Red Deer. Healthy meals including borscht and a peasant's platter are all served with home-made bread.

Wetaskiwin

The **MacEachern Tea House & Restaurant** *($-$$; Mon to Sat until 4:30pm, Jul and Aug also open Sun 10am to 4pm; 4719 50th Ave., ☎352-8308)* serves specialty coffees and over 20 teas. The menu boasts hearty home-made soups and chowders, as well as sandwiches and salads.

Edmonton

Downtown

Cheesecake Café Bakery Restaurant *($; 17011 100th Ave., ☎486-0440 or 10390 51st Ave., ☎437-5011)* serves a huge variety of cheesecakes — need we say more?

Vi's *($$; 9712 111th St., ☎482-6402)* is located in a converted house overlooking the North Saskatchewan River Valley. Innovative and delicious dishes are served in its several small dining rooms and, in the summer, on the terrace, from which you can enjoy great views and spectacular sunsets. Service can be slow if they are really busy, but the chocolate pecan pie on the dessert menu is worth the wait!

The **West Edmonton Mall**'s Bourbon Street harbours a collection of moderately priced restaurants. **Café Orleans** *($$; ☎444-2202)* serves Cajun and Creole specialties; **Sherlock Holmes** *($$; ☎444-1752)* serves typical English

pub grub; **Albert's Family Restaurant** *($; ☎444-1179)* serves Montréal smoked meat; the **Modern Art Café** *($-$$; ☎444-2233)* is a new-world bistro with pizzas, pasta and steaks where everything (the art, and furniture) is for sale.

Edmonton's first European bistro, **Bistro Praha** *($$$; 10168 100A St., ☎424-4218)* is very popular and charges accordingly. Favourites like cabbage soup, Wiener schnitzel, filet mignon, tortes and strudels are served in a refined but comfortable setting.

La Bohème *($$$; 6427 112th Ave., ☎474-5693)* is set in the splendidly restored Gibbard Building. A delicious variety of classic yet original French appetizers and entrées are enjoyed in a romantic setting complete with a cosy fire. Bed and breakfast accommodation is also offered upstairs.

Claude's on the River *($$$$; 9797 Jasper Ave., ☎429-2900)* is one of Edmonton's finest. An exceptional river valley view, menu offerings like Australian rack of lamb in a provençale crust and other distinguished French dishes, as well as an extensive wine list explain why.

Like its Calgary counterpart, **Hy's Steakloft** *($$$$; 10013 101A Ave., ☎424-4444)* serves up juicy Alberta steaks done to perfection. Chicken and pasta dishes round out the menu. A beautiful skylight is the centrepiece of the restaurant's classy decor.

Old Strathcona and South of the North Saskatchewan River

Barb and Ernie's *($; 9906 72nd Ave., ☎433-3242)* is an exceptionally popular diner-style restaurant with good food, good prices and a friendly, unpretentious ambience. Breakfast is a particularly busy time, expect to wait a bit for a table in the morning, though you can always come later since breakfast is served until 4pm.

Block 1912 *($; 10361 Whyte Ave., ☎433-6575)* is a European café that won an award for its effort to beautify the Strathcona area. The interior is like someone's living room with an eclectic mix of tables, chairs and sofas. Lasagna is one of the simple menu's best offerings. Soothing music and a relaxed mood are conducive to a chat with friends or the enjoyment of a good book.

Among the many cafés in Old Strathcona, the **Café La Gare** *($; 10308A 81st Ave., ☎439-2969)* seems to be the place to be. Outdoor chairs and tables are reminiscent of a Parisian café. The only food available are bagels and scones. An intriguing intellectual atmosphere prevails.

Turtle Creek *($$; 8404 109th St., ☎433-4202)* is an Edmonton favourite for several reasons, not the least of which are its California wines and its relaxed ambiance. The dishes follow the latest trends in Californian and fusion cuisine very well, though a little predictably. The weekend brunch is a good deal. Free indoor parking.

The Unheardof Restaurant *($$$$; 9602 82nd Ave., ☎432-0480)*: the name fits and it doesn't. This restaurant is no longer unheard of, yet it is an exception to Edmonton's dining norm. Recently expanded, it offers both à la carte and table d'hôte menus. The menu changes every two weeks, but usually features fresh game in the fall and chicken or beef the rest of the year. Inventive vegetarian dishes are also available. The food is exquisite and refined. Reservations are required.

   ENTERTAINMENT

Edmonton

See Magazine is a free news and entertainment weekly that outlines what's on throughout the city.

Bars and Nightclubs

Barry T's on 104th Street is a sports pub that attracts a young crowd with a mix of country and popular music. **Club Malibu** at 10310 85th Avenue attracts crowds of young professionals. The **Thunderdome** is another hot spot with top name rock and roll acts. There is always something happening at the **Sidetrack Cafe** *(10333 112th St., ☎421-1326)* resto-bar with its mix of comedy, rock and jazz acts.

The **Sherlock Holmes** *(10012 101A Ave., ☎426-7784)* has an impressive choice of British and Irish ales on tap. The relaxed atmosphere seems to attract a mixed crowd. The **Yardbird Suite** *(10203 86th Ave., ☎432-0428)* is the home base of the local Jazz Society, with live performances every night of the week. A small admission fee is charged. **Blues on Whyte** *(10329 82nd Ave., ☎439-5058)* showcases live acts.

The Roost *(10345 104th St., ☎426-3150)* is one of the few gay bars in Edmonton.

Well known as Edmonton's premiere country bar, the **Cook County Saloon** *(8010 103rd St., ☎432-2665)* offers lessons for amateur line-dancers and a mechanical bull for those closet cowboys looking for a wild eight seconds.

Theatres

The **Citadel Theatre** is a huge facility with five theatres inside. A variety of shows are put on from children's theatre to experimental and major productions. For information contact the box office at ☎426-4811 or 425-1820.

The **Northern Light Theatre** *(☎471-1586)* stages innovative and interesting works.

For some more classical culture, check out the offerings of the **Edmonton Opera** *(☎429-1000)*, the **Edmonton Symphony Orchestra** *(in the Frances Winspear Centre for Music, box office ☎428-1414)* and the **Alberta Ballet** *(☎428-6839)*.

Festivals and Cultural Events

Edmonton is touted as a city of festivals, and **Edmonton's Klondike Days** is possibly the city's biggest event. During the Yukon gold-rush, gold diggers were attracted to the "All-Canadian Route" which departed from here. The route proved almost impassable and none of the prospectors made it to the Yukon before the rush was over. This albeit tenuous link to the gold rush is, however, reason enough for Edmontonians to celebrate for 10 days in July. Starting the third Thursday in July, festivities, parades, bathtub road races, sourdough raft races and a casino bring the city to life. Every morning, free pancake breakfasts are served throughout the city. For information call ☎426-4055.

Other festival highlights include the **Jazz City International Festival** *(☎432-7166)*, which takes place during the last week in June. In late June and early July, **The Works: A Visual Arts Celebration** *(☎426-2122)* sees art exhibits take

The totem pole: the ultimate expression of West Coast natives.
(Pierre Longnus)

The Wats
Lake Sign
Forest has
more than
30,000 sig
(P.L.)

Dawson Creek, British Columbia, mile/kilometre 0 of the Alaska Highway. (P.L.)

to the streets. The **Edmonton Heritage Festival** *(☎433-3378)* features international singing and dancing during the first week in August. The **Edmonton Folk Music Festival** *(☎429-1899)* takes place the second week in August and tickets are recommended. The **Fringe Theatre Festival** *(☎448-9000)* is one of North America's largest alternative-theatre events; it takes place throughout Old Strathcona starting the second Friday in August for ten days. The **Dreamspeakers Festival** *(☎451-5033)* at the end of May celebrates native arts and culture.

 SHOPPING

Edmonton

Besides the obvious, the **West Edmonton Mall** (see Exploring, p 507) and its 800 shops and services located at 87th Avenue and 170th Street, there are regular malls scattered north, south and west of the city centre.

Downtown, the **Eaton Centre** and **The Bay** boast the usual department store offerings.

Old Strathcona makes for a much more pleasant shopping experience, with some funky specialty shops, bookstores and women's clothing stores along Whyte Avenue (82nd Avenue), including **Avenue Clothing Co.** and **Etzio**, and along 104th Street. **Strathcona Square** *(8150 105th St.)* is located in an old converted post office and boasts a bright assortment of cafés and boutiques all set in a cheery market atmosphere. The **Treasure Barrel** *(8216 104th St.)* is like a permanent craft fair showcasing arts and crafts of all kinds and for all tastes.

High Street at 124th Street *(124th St. and 125th St. between 102nd Ave. and 109th Ave.)* is an outdoor shopping arcade with galleries, cafés and shops located in a pretty residential area.

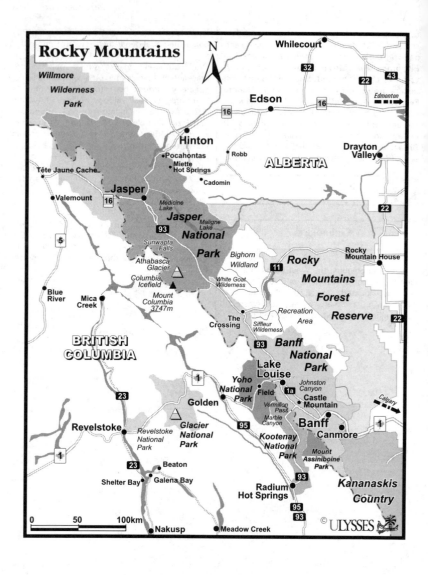

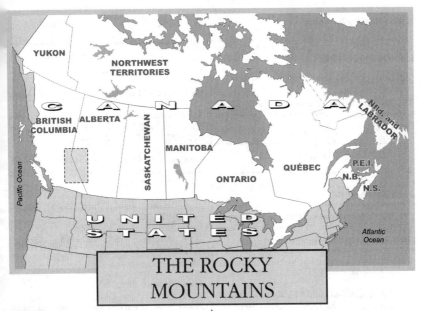

THE ROCKY MOUNTAINS

I n Canada, the term "Rockies" designates a chain of high Pacific mountains reaching elevations of 3,000 to 4,000 metres. These mountains consist of crystalline and metamorphous rock that has been thrust upwards by collision between the Pacific tectonic plate and the North American continental plate, and then later carved out and eroded by glaciers. The mountain chain runs east-west along the border between Alberta and British Columbia and covers Yukon territory. This vast region, which stretches more than 22,000 square kilometres, is known the world over for its natural beauty and welcomes some six million visitors each year. Exceptional mountain scenery, wild rivers sure to thrill white-water rafting enthusiasts, still lakes whose waters vary from emerald green to turquoise blue, parks abounding in all sorts of wildlife, world-renowned ski centres and quality resort hotels all come together to make for an unforgettable vacation.

 FINDING YOUR WAY AROUND

By Car

For information on road conditions in Banff, call **Environment Canada** (☎403-762-2088) or the Banff warden's office (☎403-762-1450); in Jasper, call the weather service (☎403-852-3185) or the **Alberta Motor Association** (Jun to Aug, ☎403-852-4444; year-round, ☎1-800-222-4357), where you can also call for roadside assistance. For Yoho National Park, call the tourist office (summer, ☎250-343-5324; winter, ☎250-343-6432) and for Kootenay National Park, the park office (☎250-347-9615).

This kind of information is also available at the entrance gates of the national parks and in all local offices of Parks Canada.

By Plane

Most people fly into the airports in Calgary, Edmonton or Vancouver and then drive to the national and provincial parks.

By Bus

Banff National Park

The **Bus Station** (☎403-762-6767), located on the way into Banff on Mount Norquay Road, at the corner of Gopher Road, is used by Greyhound (☎1-800-661-8747) and Brewster Transportation and Tours (☎403-762-6735). This latter company takes care of local transportation and organizes trips to the icefields and Jasper.

Jasper National Park

The **Greyhound Bus Station** *(☎403-852-3926)* is located right in the middle of Jasper, on Connaught Drive.

By Train

Banff National Park

The **Rocky Mountaineer** Train Station is right next to the bus station on Railway Drive. Taxis are available for the trip downtown.

Jasper National Park

The **VIA Rail** *(☎1-800-561-8630)* train station is located next to the Greyhound bus terminal. **Heritage Cabs** *(☎403-852-5558)* serves the area.

 PRACTICAL INFORMATION

Area Code: 403 for Alberta, and 250 for British Columbia.

Very reasonable fees are charged to gain access to the national parks of the Canadian Rockies, and these must be paid at the entrance gate of each park *($5 for one day, $35 per year)*.

Up until recently, the fees only applied to cars entering the parks, but from now on, every person must pay an individual fee. This allows Parks Canada to earn extra revenue from travellers arriving by foot, bike, train or bus, which contributes to maintaining park facilities.

Parks Canada also charges travellers wishing to practise certain activities (excursions of more than one day, rock-climbing, interpretive activities...) and for the use of certain facilities, like hot springs.

A complete list of annual fees is available at park entrance, at the parks' information centres (see addresses and telephone numbers below) or by calling 1-800-651-7959.

Tourist Information Offices

Banff National Park and The Icefields Parkway

Banff Visitor Centre: 224 Banff Avenue, Box 900, Banff, AB, T0L 0C0, ☎(403) 762-8421 or 762-0270, ⇌(403) 762-8163.

Banff National Park: 224 Banff Ave., Box 900, Banff, AB, T0L 0C0, ☎(403) 762-1550, ⇌(403) 762-3229.

Lake Louise Visitor Information Centre: ☎(403) 522-3833.

Lake Louise Parks Canada Office: ☎(403) 522-3833.

Jasper National Park

Jasper Tourism and Chamber of Commerce Box 98, 632 Connaught Drive, Jasper, AB, T0E 1E0, ☎(403) 852-3858, ⇌(403) 852-4932.

Parks Canada: 500 Connaught Drive, Box 10, Jasper, AB, T0E 1E0, ☎(403) 852-6220, ⇌(403) 852-5601.

Ski Jasper: ☎1-800-473-8135

Kootenay and Yoho National Parks

Kootenay National Park: Box 220, Radium Hot Springs, BC, V0A 1M0, ☎(250) 347-9615.

Golden and District Chamber of Commerce and Travel Information Centre: located in the centre of town, ☎250-344-7125.

Field Tourist Information Centre *(every day, 9am to 6pm; at the entrance of the city, ☎250-343-6324)*.

Kananaskis Country

Alberta Visitor Information Centre *(☎800-661-8888)* is located just off Highway 1A, at the west exit of Canmore, on Dead Mans Flats.

Kananaskis Country Head Office: Suite 100, 3115 12th St. NE, Calgary, AB, T2E 7J2, ☎(403) 297-3362.

Bow Valley Provincial Park Office: Located near the town of Seeby, ☎(403) 673-3663.

Peter Lougheed Provincial Park Visitor Information Centre: Located 3.6 kilometres from Kananaskis Trail (Hwy 40), ☎(403) 591-6344.

Barrier Lake Information Centre: ☎(403) 673-3985.

Elbow Valley Information Centre: ☎(403) 949-4261.

EXPLORING AND PARKS

Banff National Park ★★★

Banff ★★★

The history of the **Canadian Pacific** railway is inextricably linked to that of the national parks of the Rocky Mountains. In November of 1883, three workmen abandoned the railway construction site in the Bow Valley and headed towards Banff in search of gold. When they reached Sulphur Mountain, however, brothers William and Tom McCardell and Frank McCabe discovered sulphur hot springs instead. They took a concession in order to turn a profit with the springs, but were unable to counter the various land rights disputes that followed. The series of events drew the attention of the federal government, which sent out an agent to control the concession. The renown of these hot springs had already spread from railway workers to the vice-president of Canadian Pacific, who came here in 1885 and declared that the springs were certainly worth a million dollars. Realizing the enormous economic potential of Sulphur Mountain hot springs, then known as **Cave and Basin**, the federal government quickly purchased the rights to the concession from the three workers and consolidated its property rights on the site by creating a nature reserve the same year. Two years later, in 1887, the reserve became the first national park in Canada and was named Rockies Park, and then Banff National Park. In those days there was no need to protect the still abundant wildlife, and the mindset of government was not yet preoccupied with the preservation of natural areas. On the contrary, the government's main concern was to find an economically exploitable site with which to

replenish the state coffers, depleted by the construction of the railroad. To complement the springs, which were already in vogue with wealthy tourists in search of spa treatments, tourist facilities and luxury hotels were built. Thus was born the town of Banff, today a world-class tourist mecca.

At first glance, Banff looks like a small town made up essentially of hotels, motels, souvenir shops and restaurants all lined up along Banff Avenue. The town has much more to offer, however.

A bit farther along Banff Avenue, stop in at the **Natural History Museum ★** *($3; every day; Sep and May 10am to 8pm; Jul and Aug 10am to 10pm; Oct to Apr 10am to 6pm; 112 Banff Ave., ☎403-762-1558)*. This museum retraces the history of the Rockies and displays various rocks, fossils and dinosaur tracks, as well as several plant species that you're likely to encounter while hiking.

The **Whyte Museum of the Canadian Rockies ★★★** *($3; mid-May to Mid-Oct, every day 10am to 6pm; winter, Tue to Sun 1pm to 5pm, Thu 1pm to 9pm; 111 Bear St., ☎403-762-2291)* relates the history of the Canadian Rockies. You'll discover archaeological findings from ancient Kootenay and Stoney Indian settlements, including clothing, tools and jewellery. Museum-goers will also learn about local heros and famous explorers like Bill Peyto, and about the railway and the town of Banff. Personal objects and clothing that once belonged to notable local figures are exhibited. The museum also houses a painting gallery and extensive archives, in case you want to know more about the region. Right next to the Whyte Museum is the **Banff Public Library** *(Mon, Wed, Fri and Sat 11am to 6pm, Tue and Thu 11am to 9pm, Sun 1pm to 5pm; at the corner of Bear and Buffalo Sts., ☎403-762-2661)*.

Cave and Basin ★★★ *($2.25; Jun to Aug, every day 9am to 6pm; Sep to May 9:30am to 5pm; at the end of Cave Ave., ☎403-762-1556)* is now a national historic site. These springs were the origin of the vast network of Canadian national parks (see above). However, despite extremely costly renovations to the basins in 1984, the pool has been closed for security reasons since 1992. The sulphur content of the water actually deteriorates the cement, and the pool's paving is badly damaged in some places. You can still visit the cave into which three Canadian Pacific

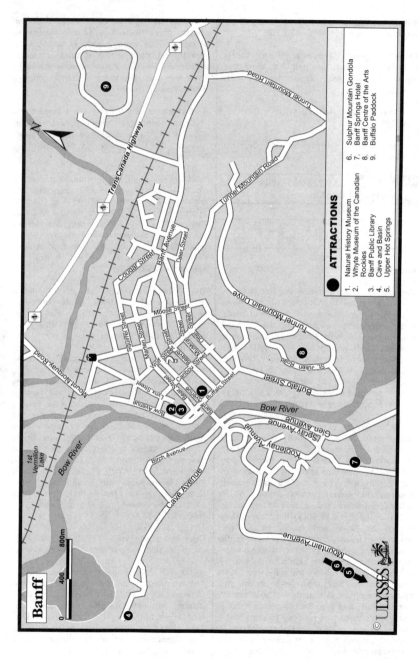

Banff

ATTRACTIONS

1. Natural History Museum
2. Whyte Museum of the Canadian Rockies
3. Banff Public Library
4. Cave and Basin
5. Upper Hot Springs
6. Sulphur Mountain Gondola
7. Banff Springs Hotel
8. Banff Centre of the Arts
9. Buffalo Paddock

© ULYSSES

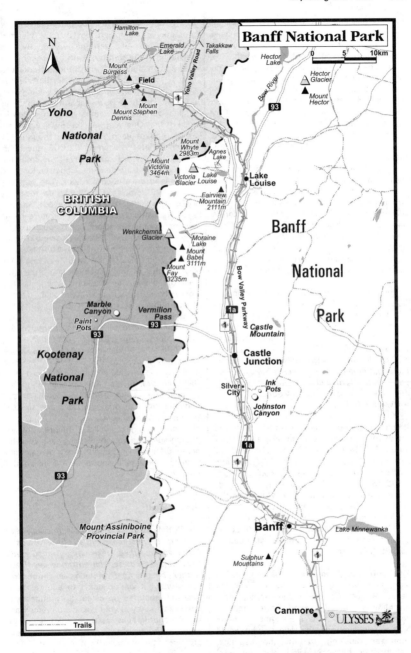

Banff National Park

N

Hamilton Lake

Emerald Lake

Takakkaw Falls

Hector Lake

Hector Glacier

Mount Hector

Bow River

Mount Burgess

Field

0   5   10km

Yoho

Mount Stephen
Mount Dennis

National

Park

Mount Whyte 2983m

Agnes Lake

Mount Victoria 3464m

Victoria Glacier

Lake Louise

Lake Louise

BRITISH COLUMBIA

Fairview Mountain 2111m

Banff

Wenkchemna Glacier

Moraine Lake

Mount Babel 3111m

Mount Fay 3235m

National

Park

Bow Valley Parkway

Marble Canyon

Vermilion Pass

Paint Pots

Castle Mountain

Kootenay

Castle Junction

National

Silver City

Ink Pots

Park

Johnston Canyon

THE ROCKY MOUNTAINS

Mount Assiniboine Provincial Park

Banff

Lake Minnewanka

Sulphur Mountains

Canmore

© ULYSSES

Trails

workers descended in search of the springs, and smell the odour of sulphurous gas, caused by bacteria that oxydize the sulphates in the water before it spurts out of the earth. The original basin is still there, but swimming is no longer permitted. If you watch the water, you'll see the sulphur gas bubbling to the surface, while at the bottom of the basin, you can see depressions appearing in the sand caused by this same gas (this is most obvious in the centre of the basin). In the theatre, there is a short film on Banff National Park and the history of the hot springs and their purchase by the government for only $900. You'll learn that the McCardell brothers and Frank McCabe were not actually the first to discover the springs – Assiniboine Indians were already familiar with their therapeutic powers. European explorers had also already spoken of them. However, the three Canadian Pacific workers, knowing a good thing when they saw it, were the first to try to gain exclusive rights over the springs and the government simply followed suit.

If you want to experience the sensation of Sulphur Mountain's waters (how rapturous it is to soak in them after a long day of hiking!), head up Mountain Avenue, at the foot of the mountain, to the hot spring facilities of **Upper Hot Spring** ★★★ *($7 for access to the pool; $20 for the whirlpool thermal baths and basins; bathing suit and towel rentals available; every day 9am to 11pm, call ahead to verify schedule and fees; up from Mountain Ave., ☎403-762-1515).*

If you haven't got the energy to hike up to the top of the mountain, you can take the **Sulphur Mountain Gondola** *($10; at the end of Mountain Ave., at the far end edge of the Upper Hot Springs parking lot, ☎403-762-2523).* The panoramic view of Banff, Mount Rundle, the Bow Valley and the Aylmer and Cascade Mountains is superb. The gondola starts out at an altitude of 1,583 metres and ascends 2,281 metres. Be sure to bring along warm clothes, as it can be cold at the summit.

The **Banff Springs Hotel** ★★★ is also worth a look. After visiting the springs at Cave and Basin, William Cornelius Van Horne, vice-president of the Canadian Pacific railway company, decided to have a sumptuous hotel built to accommodate the tourists who would soon be flocking to the hot springs. Construction began in 1887, and the hotel opened its doors in June 1888. Although the cost of the project had already reached

$250,000, the railway company launched a promotional campaign to attract wealthy visitors from all over the world. By the beginning of the century, Banff had become so well known that the Banff Springs Hotel was one of the busiest hotels in North America. More space was needed, so a new wing was built in 1903. It was separated from the original building by a small wooden bridge in case of fire. One year later, a tower was built at the end of each wing. Even though this immense hotel welcomed 22,000 guests in 1911, the facilities again proved too small for the ever-increasing demand. Construction was thus begun on a central tower. The building was finally completed as it stands today in 1928. The Tudor style interior layout, as well as the tapestries, paintings and furniture in the common rooms, are all original. If you decide to stay at the Banff Springs Hotel (see p 530) you may run into the ghost of Sam McAuley, the bellboy who helps guests who have lost their keys, or that of the unlucky young bride who died the day of her wedding when she fell down the stairs and who supposedly haunts the corridors of the hotel.

The **Banff Centre of the Arts** *(between St. Julien Rd. and Tunnel Mountain Dr., ☎403-762-6333)* was created in 1933. More commonly known as the Banff Centre since 1978, this renowned cultural centre hosts the **Banff Festival of the Arts** in the month of August. The festival attracts numerous artists and presents dance, opera, jazz and theatre performances. The centre also offers courses in classical and jazz ballet, theatre, music, photography and pottery. Finally, each year the centre organizes an international mountain film festival. There is a sports centre inside the complex as well.

Around Banff

The **Buffalo Paddock** ★★ *(free admission; May to Oct; to get there, head towards Lake Minnewanka, then take the TransCanada towards Lake Louise; the entrance lies 1 km farther, on the right)* provides an interesting opportunity, if you're lucky, to admire these majestic creatures up close. It is important, however, to stay in your car, even if you want to take photographs, as these animals can be very unpredictable and the slightest provocation may cause them to charge.

Twenty-two kilometres long and two kilometres wide, **Lake Minnewanka** ★★ is now the

Mountain Goat

biggest lake in Banff National Park, but this expanse of water is not completely natural. Its name means "lake of the water spirit". These days it is one of the few lakes in the park where motor boats are permitted. Originally, the area was occupied by Stoney Indian encampments. Because of the difficulties involved with diving in alpine waters and the scattering of vestiges that can be seen here, this lake is popular with scuba divers. Guided walks are given Tuesdays, Thursdays and Saturdays at 2pm. Besides taking a guided boat-tour with **Cruise and Tour Devil's Gap** *($22; Lake Minnewanka Boat Tours, Box 2189, Dept B, Banff, ☎403-762-3473, ≈762-2800)*, you can fish on the lake by first obtaining the appropriate permit from Parks Canada, and skating is possible in the winter. A 16-kilometre hiking trail leads to the far end of the lake. At the **Aylmer Lookout Viewpoint**, some mountain goats who frequent the area can be spotted.

Bow Valley Parkway ★★

To get from Banff to Lake Louise, take the Bow Valley Parkway (Hwy 1A), which is a much more picturesque route than the TransCanada. Meltwater no longer feeds the Bow, which can flow through the debris left behind by glaciers. Weaving its way along the mountains, the Bow Valley Parkway affords some exquisite views of the Bow River. It is important to heed the drive slowly warning as animals often approach the

road at sunrise and sunset. A stop at beautiful **Johnston Canyon**, located on the right-hand side about 20 kilometres beyond Banff, is a must. A small dirt trail has been cleared through the canyon, where you can behold the devastating effect even a small torrent of water can have on all kinds of rock.

The abandoned town of **Silver City** lies farther up the Bow Valley Parkway, on the left. Silver, copper and lead were discovered in the area in 1883. Prospectors arrived two years later, but the mineral deposits were quickly exhausted and ultimately the town was abandoned. In its glory days, this little city had some 175 buildings and several hotels, but just vestiges of these remain.

Lake Louise ★★★

Jewel of the Canadian Rockies, Lake Louise is known the world over thanks to its small, still, emerald-green lake. Few natural sites in Canada can boast as much success: this little place welcomes and average of about six million visitors a year!

Today, you can reach the lake by car, but finding a place to park here can be a real challenge. Stroll quietly around the lake or climb the mountain along the network of little trails radiating out from the lake's shore for a magnificent view of the Victoria Glacier, the lake and the glacial valley. Reaching **Lake Agnes** requires extra effort, but the **view ★★★** of **Victoria** (3,464 m), **Whyte** (2,983 m), **Fairview** (2,111 m), **Babel** (3,111 m) and **Fay** (3,235 m) **Mountains** is well worth the exertion.

If you aren't up to such a climb, you can always take the **Lake Louise Gondola**, which is open from 9am to 9pm and transports you to an altitude of 2,089 metres in just 10 minutes.

Though the present-day **Chateau Lake Louise ★★** has nothing to do with the original construction, it remains an attraction in itself. This vast Canadian Pacific Hotel can accommodate 700 visitors. Besides restaurants, the hotel houses a small shopping arcade with boutiques selling all kinds of souvenirs.

THE ROCKY MOUNTAINS

Moraine Lake ★★★

When heading to Lake Louise, you will come to a turnoff for Moraine Lake on the left. This narrow, winding road weaves its way along the mountain for about 10 kilometres before reaching Moraine Lake, which was immortalized on the old Canadian $20 bill. Though much smaller than Lake Louise, Moraine Lake is no less spectacular. Inaccessible in the winter, the lake often remains frozen until the month of June.

Canmore ★

This quiet little town of about 6,000 experienced its finest hour during the 1988 Winter Olympics. The cross-country, nordic combined and biathlon events were held here, along with the handicapped cross-country skiing demonstration event. Since the games, the facilities at the **Canmore Nordic Centre** *(every day; from the centre of town head up Main St., turn right on 8th Ave. and right to cross the Bow River. Turn left and head up Rundle Dr., then turn left again on Sister Dr. Take Spray Lake Rd. to the right and continue straight. The parking lot of the centre is located farther up on the right, ☎403-678-2400)* have been used for other international events like the World Cup of Skiing in 1995. In summer the cross-country trails become walking and mountain-biking trails. Dogs are permitted between April 11th and October 30th if they are on a leash. Bears are common in the region in the summer, so be extra careful.

Marvellously well situated at the entrance to Banff National Park and at the gateway to Kananaskis Country, Canmore welcomes many visitors each year, but it is often easier to find accommodations here than in Banff. Nevertheless, it is a good idea to reserve your room well in advance.

The **Canmore Recreation Centre** *(every day 6am to 10pm; 1900 8th Ave., ☎403-678-5597, ≈678-6661)* organizes all sorts of summer activities for children. The facilities include a municipal pool, a sports centre and an exercise centre.

The Icefields Parkway ★★★

The route through the icefields follows Highway 93 from Lake Louise for 230 kilometres to the continental divide, which is covered by glaciers, before ending up in Jasper. This wide, well-paved road is one of the busiest in the Rockies during the summer, with a speed limit of 90 kilometres per hour. It runs through some incredibly majestic scenery.

The **Hector Lake ★★** lookout on the left, 17 kilometres from Lake Louise, offers a great view of both the lake and Mount Hector. The lake is fed by meltwater from the Balfour Glacier and the Waputik Icefields.

One kilometre before **Mosquito Creek**, you can clearly see the Crowfoot Glacier from the road. Photographs reproduced on information panels by the road show just how much the glacier has melted in recent years. A bit farther along, you can stop to take in the magnificent view of Bow Lake, and then visit little **Num-Ti-Jah Lodge** ("Num-Ti-Jah" is an aboriginal name that means "pine marten"), built in 1922 by a mountain guide named Jimmy Simpson.

Bow Summit ★★ (2,609 metres) lies at the highest point of the Icefields Parkway and on the continental divide for the waters of the Bow and Mistayac rivers. At this point the vegetation changes drastically, giving way almost completely to sub-alpine plant-life. By the side of the road, there is a rest area that overlooks **Peyto Lake** (pronounced Pee-Toh). You can take a hike through an area of alpine vegetation, and if the weather is right, admire a lovely little lake.

At the intersection of Highways 93 and 11, called **The Crossing**, are a few souvenir shops, a hotel and some restaurants. Make sure your gas tank is full since there are no other gas stations before Jasper. This region was once inhabited by Kootenay Indians.

The **Castleguard Cave** is located 117 kilometres from Jasper. A network of underwater caves, the longest in Canada, extends over 20 kilometres under the Columbia Icefield. Because of frequent flooding and the inherent dangers of spelunking, you must obtain authorization from Parks Canada to enter the caves.

The **Parker Ridge ★★** trail, just 3 kilometres farther, makes for a wonderful outing. About 2.5 kilometres long, it leads up to the ridge, where, if you're lucky, you may spot some mountain goats. It also offers a great view of the Saskatchewan Glacier. Both the vegetation and the temperature change as you pass from

Grizzly Bear

Black Bear

the subalpine to the alpine zone. Warm clothing and a pair of gloves are a good idea.

At the **Sunwapta Pass** you can admire the grandiose scenery which marks the dividing line between Banff and Jasper National Parks. At 2,035 metres, this is the highest pass along the Icefields Parkway, after Bow Summit.

The **Athabasca Glacier** ★★★ and the **Columbia Icefield** are the focal points of the icefields tour. At the Athabasca Glacier, information panels show the impressive retreat of the glacier over the years. Those who wish to explore the ice on foot should beware of crevasses, which can be up to 40 metres deep. There are 30,000 of these on the Athabasca Glacier, some hidden under thin layes of snow or ice. Those without sufficient experience climbing on glaciers or lacking the proper equipment are better off with a ticket aboard the **Snow Coach** *($22.50; May to mid-Oct, every day; tickets sold at the Brewster counter, near the tourist information centre, ☎403-852-7031).* These specially equipped buses take people out onto the glacier.

The **Stutfield Glacier** ★★ lookout provides a view of one of the six huge glaciers fed by the Columbia Icefield, which continues one kilometre into the valley.

Seventeen kilometres farther, heading towards Jasper, you'll come across an area called

Mineral Lick, where mountain goats often come to lick the mineral-rich soil.

The trail leading to the 25-metre-high **Athabasca Falls** ★★, located seven kilometres farther along, takes about an hour to hike. The concrete structure built there is an unfortunate addition to the natural surroundings, but heavy traffic in the area would have otherwise destroyed the fragile vegetation. Furthermore, some careless types have suffered accidents because they got too close to the edge of the canyon. Travellers are therefore reminded not to go beyond the barriers; doing so could be fatal.

Jasper National Park

Jasper and Surroundings ★★

The town of Jasper takes its name from an old fur-trading post, founded in 1811 by William Henry of the Northwest Company. Jasper is a small town of just 4,000 residents which owes its tourist development to its geographic location and the train station built here in 1911. When the Icefields Parkway was opened in 1940, the number of visitors who wanted to discover the region's majestic scenery just kept growing. Although this area is a major tourist draw, Jasper remains a decidedly more tranquil and less commercial spot than Banff. This

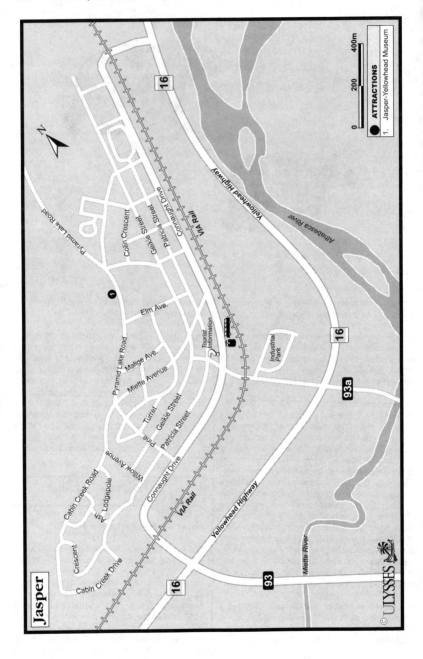

Jasper

ATTRACTIONS

1. Jasper-Yellowhead Museum

doesn't prevent hotel prices from being just as exorbitant as elsewhere in the Rockies, however.

The **Jasper-Yellowhead Museum and Archives** ★ *(free admission; mid-May to early Sep, every day 10am to 9pm; early Sep to mid-Oct, every day 10am to 5pm; winter, Thu to Sun 10am to 5pm; 400 Pyramid Lake Rd., facing the Aquatic Centre, ☎403-852-3013)* tells the story of the region's earliest First Nations inhabitants, as well as mountain guides and other legendary characters from this area.

Mount Edith Cavell ★★★ is 3,363 metres high. To get there, take the southern exit for Jasper and follow the signs for the Marmot ski hill. Turn right, then left, and you'll come to a narrow road, that leads to one of the most lofty summits in the area. The road snakes through the forest for about 20 kilometres before coming to a parking lot. Several hiking trails have been cleared to allow visitors to enjoy a better view of this majestic mountain, as well as its suspended glacier, the **Angel Glacier**.

In just a few minutes, the **Jasper Tramway** ★★ *($10; mid-Apr to late Oct; take the southern exit for Jasper and follow the signs for Mount Whistler, ☎403-852-3093)* whisks you up some 2,277 metres and deposits you on the northern face of **Mount Whistler**. You'll find a restaurant and souvenir shop at the arrival point, while a small trail covers the last few metres up to the summit (2,470 metres). The view is outstanding.

The road to Maligne Lake follows the valley of the river of the same name for 46 kilometres. Because of the tight curves of this winding road and the many animals which cross it, the speed limit is 60 kilometres per hour. Before reaching the lake, the road passes by one of the most beautiful resorts in Canada, the **Jasper Park Lodge**, run by Canadian Pacific. You can have a picnic, go boating or take a swim in one of the two pretty little lakes, **Agnes** and **Edith**, right next to this facility.

Maligne Canyon ★★★ lies at the beginning of Maligne Road. Hiking trails have been cleared so that visitors may admire this spectacular narrow gorge abounding with cascades, fossils and potholes sculpted by the turbulent waters. Several bridges span the canyon. The first offers a view of the falls; the second, of the effect of ice on rock; and the third, of the deepest point (51 metres) of the gorge.

Maligne Lake ★★ is one of the prettiest lakes in the Rockies. Water activities like boating, fishing and canoeing are possible here, and a short trail runs along part of the shore. The chalet on the shore houses a souvenir shop, a restaurant-café and the offices of a tour company that organizes trips to little **Spirit Island**, the ideal vantage point for admiring the surrounding mountain tops.

The road that heads north to Edmonton crosses the entire Athabasca Valley. A large herd of moose grazes in this part of the valley, and the animals can often be spotted between the intersection of Maligne Road and the old town of Pocahontas, near Miette Hot Springs.

By continuing on the road to Hinton, you'll soon reach the hottest springs in all of the parks in the Rockies, **Miette Hot Springs**. The sulphurous water gushes forth at 57°C and has to be cooled down to 39°C for the baths. A paved path follows Sulphur Stream past the water purification station to the old pool, built out of logs in 1938; the trail finally ends at one of three hot springs beside the stream. Several hiking trails have been cleared in the area for those who wish to explore the back country and admire the splendid scenery. The ruins of the town of **Pocahontas**, abandoned in 1921, lie at the turn-off for the road to Miette Hot Springs.

Kootenay and Yoho National Parks

Kootenay National Park ★★

Although less popular with the public than Banff and Jasper, Kootenay National Park nevertheless boasts beautiful, majestic landscapes and is just as interesting to visit as its more touristy neighbours. It contains two large valleys, the humid Vermillion River Valley and the drier Kootenay River Valley; the contrast is striking.

To reach Kootenay National Park from Banff, take the TransCanada to Castle Mountain Junction. Highway 93, on the left, runs the entire length of the park.

Vermillion Pass, at the entrance of Kootenay Park, marks the continental divide; from this point on, rivers in Banff Park flow to the east, while those in Kootenay Park flow west and empty into the Pacific.

THE ROCKY MOUNTAINS

A few kilometres farther lies **Marble Canyon ★★**, along with a tourist office where visitors can see a short film on the history of the park. Marble Canyon is very narrow, but you'll find a lovely waterfall at the end of the trail there. Several bridges span the gorge, and the erosion caused by torrential waters makes for some amazing scenery. Five hundred metres to the right, past the canyon, you'll find a trail leading to the famous **Paint Pots ★★**. These ochre deposits form by subterranian springs which cause iron oxide to rise to the surface.

One of the best places in the park for elk- and moose-watching is the **Animal Lick**, a mineral-rich salt marsh. The best time to go is early in the morning or at dusk. Viewing areas have been laid out along the road so that you can admire the scenery. The view is particularly lovely from the **Kootenay Valley Viewpoint ★★**, located at the park exit.

Radium Hot Springs

This little town, located at the entrance to the park, is surprisingly nondescript. You can, however, take a dip in the **Radium Hot Pools ★★** *($5; at the entrance of Kootenay Park,* ☎*250-347-9485)*, whose warm waters are apparently renowned for their therapeutic virtues. Whether or not you believe these claims, which have yet to be backed by any medical evidence, a soak in these 45°C non-sulphurous waters is definitely very relaxing.

Yoho National Park ★★

As in all the other parks in the Rockies, you must pay an entrance fee *($5 for one day, $35 a year)* if you wish to stay here. This fee does not apply if you are simply passing through the park.

A little farther along, you'll find another trail leading to the **Hoodoos**, natural rock formations created by erosion. The trail, which starts at the Hoodoo Creek campground, is very steep but only 3.2 kilometres long and offers an excellent view of the Hoodoos.

Hiking to **Emerald Lake ★★** has become a tradition here in Yoho National Park. A short trail (5.2 km) takes you around the lake. You can then visit the **Hamilton Falls**. Picnic areas have been laid out near the lake. Thanks to a small canoe-rental outfit, you can also enjoy

some time on the water. There is a small souvenir shop beside the boat-launching ramp.

The park's tourist office is located in Field, 33 kilometres east of the park entrance. During summer, visitors can learn more about the Yoho Valley by taking part in any number of interpretive activities. There are 400 kilometres of hiking trails leading through the valley deep into the heart of the region. Maps of these trails, as well as of those reserved for mountain bikes, are available at the **tourist office** *(Jul and Aug, every day 9am to 7pm; on the way into town,* ☎*250-343-5324, call 343-6432 for winter hours)* in **Field**. You can also purchase a topographical map of the park for $13. If you plan on staying more than a day here, you must register at the Parks Canada office, located in the same place. You can climb some of the mountains, but a special permit is required to scale Mount Stephen because fossils have been discovered in the area you must pass through to reach the top.

Kananaskis Country ★★

When Captain John Palliser led a British scientific expedition here from 1857 to 1860, the numerous lakes and rivers he found led him to christen the region Kananaskis, which means "gathering of the waters". Located 90 kilometres from Calgary, this region covers more than 4,000 square kilometres, including the **Bow Valley**, **Bragg Creek** and **Peter Lougheed** provincial parks. Because of its proximity to Calgary and thanks to the beautiful scenery and the huge variety of outdoor activities that can be enjoyed here, the area soon became one of the most popular destinations in the province, first with Albertans and then with visitors from all over the world.

No matter what season it is, Kananaskis Country has a great deal to offer. During summer, it is a veritable paradise for outdoor enthusiasts, who can play both golf and tennis here, or go horseback riding, mountain biking, kayaking, river rafting, fishing or hiking. With its 250 kilometres of paved roads and 460 kilometres of marked trails, this region is easier to explore than any other in Alberta. In winter, the trails are used for cross-country skiing and snowmobiling. Visitors can also go downhill skiing at Fortress Mountain or at Nakiska, speed down the toboggan runs, go skating on one of the region's many lakes or try dogsledding. Maps pertaining to these activities are available at the **Barrier Lake Information Centre** *(summer, every day 8:30am to 6pm, except Fri 8:30am to 7pm; autumn, Mon to Thu 9am to 4pm, Fri to Sun 9am to 6pm; winter every day 9am to 4pm; on Hwy 40 near Barrier Lake,* ☎*403-673-3985).*

The **Nakiska Ski Resort** *(near Kananaskis Village,* ☎*403-591-7777)* was designed specifically for the Olympic Games, at the same time as the Kananaskis Village hotel complex. It boasts top-notch, modern facilities and excellent runs.

Kananaskis Village consists mainly of a central square surrounded by three luxurious hotels. It was designed to be the leading resort in this region. Its construction was funded by the Alberta Heritage Savings Trust and a number of private investors. The village was officially opened on December 20, 1987.

The tourist office in **Peter Lougheed Provincial Park** *(near the two Kananaskis Lakes)* features an interactive presentation that provides all sorts of information on local flora, fauna, geographic, geologic and climatic phenomena.

 OUTDOORS

 Mountain Biking

Mountain bikes are permitted on certain trails. Always keep in mind that there might be people or bears around each bend. We also recommend limiting your speed on downhill stretches.

Banff National Park

You won't have any trouble renting a bicycle in Banff, since you can do so at a number of hotels. Just the same, here are a few places you can try: **Bactrax** *(from $5/hr or $16/day; every day 8am to 8pm; Ptarmigan Inn, 339 Banff Ave.,* ☎*403-762-8177)*; **Cycling the Rockies** *($50;* ☎*403-678-6770)* organizes mountain-bike trips in the Banff area (each package includes a bicycle, a helmet, transportation to the point of departure, refreshments and the guide services).

Jasper National Park

Freewheel Cycle rents out quality mountain bikes. Repairs are also done here *(618 Patricia St., Jasper,* ☎*403-852-3898).*

At **On-Line Sport & Tackle** you'll find bikes, helmets and bike-path maps *($18 per day; 600 Patricia St., Jasper,* ☎*403-852-3630).*

 Rafting

Banff National Park

The **Glacier Raft Company** organizes trips down Kicking Horse River. There is a special rate *($99, tax included)* for the **Kicking Horse Challenge**, which is a slightly wilder ride than the others *($85 per day, $49 for half a day; Banff, Alberta,* ☎*403-762-4347 and Golden, BC,* ☎*250-344-6521).*

Wet'n'Wild Adventure offers trips from Golden, Lake Louise and Banff. A half-day on Kicking Horse River will cost about $52. Those wishing to spend several days on the water can take advantage of some interesting package deals ranging in price from $130 to $160 per person. A minimum number of passengers is required, however *($50 and up; Golden, BC,* ☎*250-344-6546,* ≈*344-7650).*

Rocky Mountain Rafting, located in the Best Western, arranges trips down the Kicking Horse River *($49 and up; P.O. Box 1767, Golden, BC, V0A 1H0,* ☎*250-344-6979 or 1-800-808-RAFT).*

Jasper National Park

Maligne River Adventures, in addition to other excursions, offers an interesting three-day trip down the Kakwa River for $450 *(May and Jun).* Some experience is required, since these are class IV rapids, and are thus rather difficult to navigate *($50 and up; 626 Connaught Dr., P.O. Box 280, Jasper, T0E 1E0,* ☎*403-852-3370,* ≈*852-3405).*

Downhill Skiing

Banff National Park

Banff Mount Norquay was one of the first ski resorts in North America. It takes just 10 minutes to drive here from downtown Banff. For ski conditions, call ☎403-762-4421. The resort has both a ski school and a rental shop *($35 full day pass; on Norquay Rd., Box 219, Banff, AB, TOL OCO, ☎403-762-4421)*.

Sunshine Village is a beautiful ski resort located at an altitude of 2,700 metres on the continental divide between the provinces of Alberta and British Columbia. This resort has the advantage of being located above the tree line and thus gets lots of sun. Dial ☎403-277-SNOW for ski conditions. Ski rentals available *($46 full day; 8 km west of Banff, P.O. Box 1510, Banff, AB, TOL OCO, ☎403-760-5200 or 1-800-661-1676)*.

Lake Louise has the largest ski resort in Canada, covering four mountainsides and offering skiers over 50 different runs. Both downhill and cross-country equipment are available for rent here. For ski conditions, call ☎403-256-8473 *($46 per day; P.O. Box 5, Lake Louise, AB, TOL 1EO, ☎403-522-3555)*.

Jasper National Park

Marmot Basin is located about 20 minutes by car from downtown Jasper. Ski rentals available *($39 full day; take Highway 93 toward Banff, then turn right on 93A to get to the resort; P.O. Box 1300, Jasper, AB, TOE 1EO, ☎403-852-3816, or ☎488-5909 for ski conditions)*.

Kootenay and Yoho National Parks

The **Kimberley Ski Resort** is the only real attraction in Kimberley, an attractive little Bavarian village. It has some decent trails that are perfect for family skiing *($35 full day; P.O. Box 40, Kimberley, BC, V1A 2Y5, ☎250-427-4881 or 1-800-667-0871)*.

Whitetooth is relatively small, but getting bigger every year. It has a few good, well-maintained runs *($28 per day; P.O. Box 1925, Golden, BC, VOA 1HO, ☎250-344-6114)*.

Kananaskis Country

Nakiska *($36 full day; P.O. Box 1988, Kananaskis Village, AB, TOL 2HO, ☎403-591-7777, or ☎229-3288 for ski conditions)* hosted the men's and women's downhill, slalom and combination events during the 1988 Winter Olympics. Built specifically for that purpose, along with Kananaskis Village, this resort boasts an excellent, modern infrastructure and top-notch trails. Downhill and cross-country equipment are both available for rent here.

Fortress Mountain, located on the continental divide, at the edge of **Peter Lougheed Provincial Park**, is less popular than Nakiska but nevertheless has some very interesting runs *($32 full day; take Highway 40 past Kananaskis Village and turn right at Fortress Junction; Ste. 505, 1550 8th St. SW, Calgary, AB, T2R 1K1, ☎403-256-8473 or 591-7108; ☎244-4909 for ski conditions)*.

 Cross-country Skiing

There are countless cross-country trails in the parks of the Rockies, whose tourist information offices distribute maps of the major trails around the towns of Banff and Jasper and the village of Lake Louise. The **Canmore Nordic Centre**, which hosted the cross-country events of the 1988 Winter Olympics, deserves special mention for its magnificent network of trails *(1988 Olympic Way, ste. 100, Canmore, AB, T1W 2T6, ☎403-678-2400, ☎678-5696)*.

 Mountain Climbing

Banff National Park

Professional guides from the **Canadian School of Mountaineering (CSM)** can give you lessons in mountain and glacier climbing, as well as in telemark skiing *(629 10th St., P.O. Box 723, Canmore, AB, TOL OMO, ☎403-678-4134)*.

Jasper National Park

Peter Amann of the **Mountain Guiding and Schools** offers mountaineering lessons for novices and experienced climbers alike *(from $135 for 2 days; P.O. Box 1495, Jasper, AB, TOE 1EO, ☎/☎403-852-3237)*.

ACCOMMODATIONS

Banff National Park

Banff

A list of private homes that receive paying guests is provided at the tourist information office located at 224 Banff Avenue. You may obtain this list by writing to the following address: **Banff-Lake Louise Tourist Office**, P.O. Box 900, Banff, AB, TOL 0CO, ☎(403) 762-8421 or 762-0270, ☏(403) 762-8163.

It is impossible to reserve a campsite in advance in the park, which operates on a first-come, first-served basis, unless you are leading a fairly large group, in which case you should contact the Parks Canada offices in Banff.

Campsites generally cost between $13 and $16, according to the location and the facilities at the site. We advise you to arrive early to choose your spot. In high season, the Banff campgrounds are literally overrun with hordes of tourists. It is forbidden to pitch your tent outside the area set aside for this purpose. Camping at unauthorized sites is strictly prohibited, for reasons of safety and also to preserve the natural environment of the park.

Tunnel Mountain 1 and 2 *(toilets, showers, ☎; on Tunnel Mountain Rd. near the Banff Youth Hostel)* has about 840 spaces for trailers and for tents.

The two **Two Jack Lake Campgrounds** *($13; toilets, ☎; take the road going to Lake Minnewanka, then head toward Two Jack Lake, ☎403-762-1759)* are located on either side of the road that runs alongside Two Jack Lake. There are showers at the campground near the water. The other campground, deeper in the forest, offers a more basic level of comfort. It is easier to find spaces at these two campgrounds than at those in Banff.

Banff International Youth Hostel *($22 per person; on Tunnel Mountain Rd., Box 1358, Banff, AB, TOL 0CO, ☎403-762-4122, in Calgary ☎237-8282)* remains the cheapest solution, but it is often full. It is essential to reserve well in advance or else to arrive early. This friendly youth hostel is only about 20-minutes' walk from the centre of town. It offers a warm welcome, and the desk staff will be pleased to help you organize river rafting and other outdoor activities.

Tannanhof Pension *($80-$150 bkfst incl.; ☒; 121 Cave Ave., Box 1914, Banff, AB, TOL 0CO, ☎403-762-4636, ☏760-2484)* has eight rooms and two suites located in a lovely, big house. Some rooms have cable television and private baths, while others share bathrooms. Each of the two suites has a bathroom with tub and shower, a fireplace and a sofa-bed for two extra people. Breakfast is German-style with a choice of four dishes.

High Country Inn *($125; ⌂, ℙ, tv, pb, ≈, ⊛, heated underground; 419 Banff Ave., Box 700, Banff, AB, TOL 0CO, ☎403-762-2236 or 1-800-661-1244, ☏762-5084)*. Located on Banff's main drag, this inn has big, comfortable, spacious rooms with balconies. Furnishings are very ordinary, however, and detract from the beauty of the setting.

Inns of Banff, **Swiss Village** and **Rundle Manor** *($125-$195; pb, tv; 600 Banff Ave., Box 1077, Banff, AB, TOL 0CO, ☎403-762-4581 or 1-800-661-1272, ☏762-2434)*. These three hotels are really one big hotel, with a common reservation service. Depending on your budget, you have the choice of three distinct buildings. Inns of Banff, the most luxurious, has 180 very spacious rooms, each opening onto a small terrace. The Swiss Village has a little more character and fits the setting much better. The rooms, however, are a bit expensive at $150 and are less comfortable. Finally, Rundle Manor is the most rustic of the three but lacks charm. The Rundle's units have small kitchens, living rooms and one or two separate bedrooms. This is a safe bet for family travellers. Guests at the Rundle Manor and Swiss Village have access to the facilities of the Inns of Banff.

The **Bow View Motor Lodge** *($130; ⌖, ⊛, pb, tv, ≈, ℛ; 228 Bow Ave., P.O. Box 339, Banff, AB, TOL 0CO, ☎403-762-2261 or 1-800-661-1565, ☏762-8093)* has the enormous advantage of being located next to the Bow River and far from noisy Banff Avenue. Only a five minute walk from the centre of town, this charming hotel provides comfortable rooms; those facing the river have balconies. The restaurant, pretty and peaceful, welcomes guests for breakfast.

Rundle Stone Lodge *($165; ♿, P, pb, tv, ≈, ⊛; 537 Banff Ave., Box 489, Banff, AB, TOL OCO, ☎403-762-2201 or 1-800-661-8630, ⇒762-4501)* occupies a handsome building along Banff's main street. In the part of the building located along Banff Avenue, the rooms are attractive and spacious, each with a balcony. Some also have whirlpool baths. The hotel offers its guests a covered, heated parking area in the winter. Rooms for handicapped travellers are available on the ground floor.

Traveller's Inn *($170; ♿, P, pb, tv, ⌂, ⊛; 401 Banff Ave., Box 1017, Banff, AB, TOL OCO, ☎403-762-4401 or 1-800-661-0227, ⇒762-5905)*. Most rooms at the hotel have small balconies that offer fine mountain views. Rooms are simply decorated, big and cosy. The hotel has a small restaurant that serves breakfast, as well as heated underground parking, an advantage in the winter. During the ski season, guests have the use of lockers for skis and boots, as well as a small store for the rental and repair of winter sports equipment.

Banff Rocky Mountain Resort *($200, $375 for the presidential suite; pb, tv, ⊛, ≈, ⊙, squash courts, massage room, tennis courts; at the entrance to the town along Banff Ave., Box 100, Banff, AB, TOL OCO, ☎403-762-5531 or 1-800-661-9563, ⇒403-762-5166)* is an ideal spot if you are travelling as a family in Banff National Park. The delightful little chalets are warm and very well equipped. On the ground floor is a bathroom with shower, a very functional kitchen facing a living room and a dining room with fireplace, while upstairs are two bedrooms and another bathroom. These apartments also have small private terraces. Near the main building are picnic and barbecue areas as well as lounge chairs where you can lie in the sun.

Banff Springs Hotel *($207-$266; ⊛, ⊙, ≈, ⌂, ♿, 🐕, pb, tv, ℜ, ≈, bar; Spray Ave., Box 960, Banff, AB, TOL OCO, ☎403-762-2211 or 1-800-441-1414, ⇒762-4447)* is the biggest hotel in Banff. Overlooking the town, this five-star hotel, part of the Canadian Pacific chain, offers 770 luxurious rooms in an atmosphere reminiscent of an old Scottish castle. The hotel was designed by architect Price, to whom is also credited Windsor Station in Montréal and the Château Frontenac in Quebec City. Besides typical turn-of-the-century chateau style, old-fashioned furnishings and superb views from every window, the hotel offers its guests bowling, tennis courts, a pool, a sauna, a large whirlpool bath, and a massage room.

From afar, the **Rimrock Resort Hotel** *($225; ⊛, ≡, ℜ, ≈, ⌂, pb, tv; 100 Mountain Ave., Box 1110, TOL OCO, ☎403-762-3365 or 1-800-661-1587, ⇒403-762-4132)* stands out majestically from the mountainside much like the Banff Springs does. The rooms are equally well appointed though more modern. The various categories of rooms are based on the views they offer, the best view is of the Bow and Spray Valleys ($335). The hotel is right across the street from the Upper Hot Springs.

Between Banff and Lake Louise

Johnston Canyon Resort *($65-$125; vcr, 🐕, pb; from Banff, take the TransCanada Hwy to the Bow Valley exit, then take Hwy 1A, the Bow Valley Parkway, Box 875, Banff, AB, TOL OCO, ☎403-762-2971, ⇒762-0868)* constitutes a group of small log cabins right in the middle of the forest. The absolute calm is suitable for retreats. Some cabins offer a basic level of comfort, while others are fully equipped and have kitchens, sitting rooms and fireplaces. The biggest cabin can accommodate four people comfortably. A small grocery store with a basic range of products, is part of this tourist complex.

Near Silver City

Castle Mountain Youth Hostel *($11 for members, $16 for non-members; 27 km from Banff on Hwy 1A, at the Castle Junction crossroads, across from Castle Mountain Village; for reservations, call the Banff reservations office ☎403-762-4122, ⇒762-3441)* occupies a small building with two dormitories and a common room set around a big fireplace. The atmosphere is very pleasant, and the manager, who is from Québec, will be happy to advise you on hikes in the area.

Lake Louise

The Canadian Alpine Centre *($20-$24 for youth hostel members, $26-$30 for non-members; ♿, ⌂, sb; on Village Rd., Box 115, Lake Louise, AB, TOL 1EO, ☎403-522-2200, ⇒522-2253)* is a youth hostel offering rooms with two, four or six beds. Although fairly expensive, it is much more comfortable than other youth hostels. Guests have access to a laundry room, a common kitchen, a library, and little **Bill Peyto's Café**. The hostel is equipped to receive handicapped travellers. A piece of advice: reserve well in advance.

Lake Louise Inn *($128-$264; ✗, pb, tv, ≈, ℜ; 210 Village Rd., P.O. Box 209, Lake Louise, AB, TOL 1EO, ☎403-522-3791 or 1-800-661-9237, ⇒522-2018)* is located in the village of Lake Louise. The hotel offers very comfortable, warmly decorated rooms.

Deer Lodge *($135-$195; pb, ℜ, ⊛,; near the lake, on the right before reaching the Chateau Lake Louise, P.O. Box 100, Lake Louise, AB, TOL 1EO, ☎403-522-3747, ⇒522-3883)* is a very handsome and comfortable hotel. Rooms are spacious and tastefully decorated. The atmosphere is very pleasant.

Chateau Lake Louise *($215-$325; ♿, pb, tv, ≈, ℜ, △; Lake Louise, AB, TOL 1EO, ☎403-522-3511, ⇒522-3834)* is one of the best-known hotels in the region. Built originally in 1890, the hotel burned to the ground in 1892 and was rebuilt the following year. Another fire devastated parts of it in 1924. Since then, it has been expanded and embellished almost continuously. Today, this vast hotel, which belongs to the Canadian Pacific chain, has 511 rooms with space for more than 1,300 guests, and a staff of nearly 725 to look after your every need. Perched by the turquoise waters of Lake Louise, facing the Victoria Glacier, the hotel boasts a divine setting.

The magnificent **Post Hotel** *($240; tv, ≈, pb, ℜ; Box 69, Lake Louise, AB, TOL 1EO, ☎403-522-3989 or 1-800-661-1586, ⇒522-3966)* is part of the Relais et Châteaux chain. Everything at this elegant establishment, from the rooms to the grounds, is tastefully and carefully laid out. The restaurant is exquisite and the staff, friendly. If you can afford the extra cost and are looking to treat yourself, then this is the best place in Lake Louise.

Moraine Lake Lodge *($245-$375; ♿, pb, ℜ; Box 70, Lake Louise, AB, TOL 1EO, ☎403-522-3733, ⇒522-3719, Jun to Sep or 250-985-7456 Oct to May, ⇒250-985-7479)* is located at the edge of Lake Moraine. Rooms do not have phones or televisions. The setting is magnificent but packed with tourists at all times, detracting from its tranquillity.

Canmore

Restwell Trailer Park *($18; across Hwy 1A and the railway line, near Policeman Creek, ☎403-678-5111)* has 247 spaces for trailers and tents. Electricity, toilets, showers and water are available.

Ambleside Lodge *($70-$100; non-smokers only; 123A Rundle Dr., Canmore, AB, T1W 2L6, ☎403-678-3976, ⇒678-3916)* welcomes you to a large and handsome residence in the style of a Savoyard chalet just a few minutes from the centre of town. The big and friendly common room is graced with a beautiful fireplace. Some rooms have private baths.

Rocky Mountain Ski Lodge *($90-$220; pb, K, tv; 1711 Mountain Ave., Box 8070, Canmore, AB, T1W 2T8, ☎403-678-5445 or 1-800-665-6111, ⇒678-6484)* faces a pleasant little garden. Rooms are clean and spacious. Units with living-rooms, fireplaces, and fully equipped kitchens start at $120.

Georgetown Inn *($109 bkfst incl.; ♿, pb, tv, ℜ; 1101 Bow Valley Trail, Canmore, AB, T1W 1N4, ☎403-678-3439, ⇒678-6909)* has resolutely gone for an old-fashioned British ambiance. Rooms are comfortable, and some are equipped with whirlpool baths. Breakfast, which you can take in the Three Sisters dining room, is included in the price of your room. The fireplace, the old books and the reproductions hung on the walls give this place a warm atmosphere.

Lady MacDonald Country Inn *($110-$165; ♿, pb, tv; Bow Valley Trail, Box 2128, Canmore, AB, TOL OMO, ☎403-678-3665 or 1-800-567-3919, ⇒678-9714)* is a magnificent little inn established in a very pretty house. Eleven elegantly decorated rooms are placed at guests' disposal. Some rooms have been specially equipped to receive handicapped travellers; others are spread over two floors to welcome families of four. The superb "Three Sisters Room" offers a magnificent view of the Rundle Range and Three Sisters mountains, as well as a fireplace and a whirlpool bath.

The Icefields Parkway

Between Lake Louise and the Icefields Parkway

Rampart Creek Campground *($10; $3 extra to make a wood fire; a few kilometres from the* *intersection of Hwys 11 and 93)*. The entrance to the campground is unguarded. You must register yourself, and leave the payment for your stay in an envelope.

Wilcox Creek Campground and **Columbia Icefield Campground** *($10; $3 extra to make a wood fire; a few kilometres from the Columbia Icefield)*. These two campgrounds are equipped with the basics. You have to register yourself.

Waterfowl Lake Campground *($13; $3 extra to make a wood fire; above Lake Mistaya, just after the Mount Chephren lookout)*. As everywhere in the parks, it is first come, first served. Reservations are only possible for groups through the Parks Canada offices in Banff.

Athabasca Falls Youth Hostel *($10 per person for members, $15 for non-members; 32 km south of Jasper, ☎403-852-3215)*. In keeping with the rustic decor, this hostel has no running water, but it does have electricity and a kitchen. It is situated next to Athabasca Falls. Cyclists and hikers will appreciate this hostel's great location.

Hilda Creek Youth Hostel *($10 per person for members, $14 for non-members; closed Oct to Dec; a little before the entrance to Jasper National Park, ☎403-762-4122 or the Calgary reservations centre, ☎403-237-8282)*. This is a genuine mountain refuge, with no running water or electricity. This spot is heartily recommended for hikers, because of its proximity to the finest hiking areas around the Athabasca Glacier. Information is available here, and the staff will be happy to indicate the must-sees. The welcome is friendly, and the scenery will take your breath away.

Rampart Creek Youth Hostel *($10 per person for members, $14 for non-members; closed Oct to Dec; near the campground of the same name on Hwy 93, ☎403-762-4122 or the Banff reservations centre, ☎403-237-8282)* comes off as a little rustic, but it is very well situated for hikers and cyclists visiting the glaciers.

Mosquito Creek Youth Hostel *($11 per person for members, $15 per person for non-members; ⌂; on Hwy 93, a few kilometres after Lake Hector; to reserve, call the Banff Youth Hostel, ☎403-237-8282 or 762-4122)* offers a very basic level of comfort, with no running water or electricity. There is however a wood-fired sauna. Lodging is in mixed dormitories.

The Crossing *($88; ⌂, ℜ, pb, tv, ®, cafeteria, pub; at the crossroads of Hwys 93 and 11, 80 km from Lake Louise, Box 333, Lake Louise, AB, T0L 1E0, ☎403-761-7000, ⇛761-7006)* is a good place to stop along the Icefields Parkway.

Num-Ti-Jah Lodge *($95-$170; pb, on the shore of Bow Lake, about 35 km from Lake Louise, ☎403-522-2167, ⇛522-2425)* was built by Jimmy Simpson, a famous mountain guide and trapper from the region. Jimmy Simpson's two daughters also have a place in the history of the Rockies. Peg and Mary became world-class figure skaters in their time and toured in Canada and the United States extensively. The name Num-Ti-Jah comes from a Stoney Indian word for pine marten. The spot is popular with tourists, for Bow Lake is one of the most beautiful in the region.

Jasper National Park

Jasper

Athabasca Hotel *($89 sb or $129 pb; ℜ, bar, tv; Box 1420, Jasper, AB, T0E 1E0, ☎403-852-3386 or 1-800-563-9859, ⇛852-4955)* is located right in the centre of Jasper, facing the Via Rail station and the Brewster and Greyhound bus terminal. Decorated in old English style, the rooms are not very big, yet they are appealing. The least expensive are near a central bathroom, but the others have their own facilities. Neither flashy nor luxurious, this hotel is quite adequate, and the rooms are pleasant. This is the cheapest place to stay in Jasper, so you'll have to reserve in advance. The hotel does not have an elevator.

Marmot Lodge *($150; ♿, ⛟, tv, ≈, ℜ, K, ®; on Connaught Dr., at the Jasper exit, toward Edmonton; Box 1200, Jasper, AB, T0E 1E0, ☎403-852-4471 or 1-800-661-6521, ⇛852-3280)* offers very attractive rooms at what are considered reasonable prices in Jasper. The rooms are decorated in bright colours and old photographs hang on the walls, for a change from the normal decor. A terrace with tables has been set up in front of the pool, and this is a good spot for sunbathing. The decor, the friendly staff and the scenery all contribute to making this hotel a very pleasant place. It provides the best quality-to-price ratio in town.

Jasper Inn *($175; tv, ℜ, ≈, K, ◉, ℝ; 98 Geikie St., Box 879, Jasper, AB, TOE 1E0, ☎403-852-4461 or 1-800-661-1933, ≈852-5916)* offers spacious, attractive, comfortable rooms, some of them equipped with kitchenettes.

Jasper Park Lodge *($413; ⅄, ⋈, ≈, ℜ, ℝ, tv, ☺, ◉, △; P.O. Box 40, Jasper, AB, TOE 1E0, ☎403-852-3301 or 1-800-441-1414, ≈852-5107)* constitutes beyond a doubt the most beautiful hotel complex in the entire Jasper area. Now part of the Canadian Pacific chain, the Jasper Park Lodge has attractive, spacious, comfortable rooms. It was built in 1921 by the Grand Trunk Railway Company to compete with Canadian Pacific's Banff Springs Hotel. The staff are very professional, attentive and friendly. A whole range of activities are organized for guests. These include horseback riding and river rafting. You will also find one of the finest golf courses in Canada, several tennis courts, a big pool, a sports centre, and canoes, sailboards and bicycles for rent in the summer, plus ski equipment in the winter. Several hiking trails criss-cross the site, among them a very pleasant 3.8-kilometre trail alongside Lake Beauvert. Whether you're staying in a room in the main building or in a small chalet, you are assured of comfort and tranquillity. Each year Jasper Park Lodge organizes theme events, and hotel guests are invited to participate. Some weekends are dedicated to the mountains and relaxation, with yoga and aerobics classes as well as water gymnastics and visits to the sauna; while another weekend may be set aside for wine tasting Beaujolais Nouveau; other activities are organized for New Year's. Ask for the activities leaflet for more information.

Outside Jasper

Whistler Campground *($13-$19; open May 5 to Oct 10; 2.5 km south of Jasper; take Hwy 93, then turn on the road leading to the Whistler Mountain ski lift, taking the first left for the campground)*, with its 781 sites, has facilities for both trailers and tents. Water, showers and electricity are available. You can also find firewood on the site. The maximum stay at the campsite is 15 days. To reserve, call the Parks Canada office in Jasper (see p 516).

Wapiti Campground *($14-$15.50; open Jun 9 to Sep 11; 4 km from Jasper)*, with its 366 sites welcomes trailers and tents. Water, electricity and toilets are available.

Jasper's three youth hostels are located outside the town.

Mount Edith Cavell Youth Hostel *($9 per person for members, $14 per person for non-members; 26 km south of Jasper; take highway 93A and then go 13 km up the curvy road leading to Mount Edith Cavell, ☎403-852-3215)* constitutes a genuine high mountain refuge, without water or electricity. It is built on one of the most beautiful mountains in the area of Mount Edith Cavell. Take warm clothing and a good sleeping bag, for you are in a high mountain area, and the temperatures are unpredictable. If you enjoy tranquillity and beautiful walks, this is paradise.

Maligne Canyon Youth Hostel *($10 per person for members, $15 per person for non-members; closed Wed in winter; 11 km east of Jasper, on Maligne Lake road, ☎403-852-3215)* also comes across as the ideal spot for anyone who likes hiking and other outdoor activities. The Skyline hiking trail begins right near the hostel, leading experienced hikers through Alpine scenery. The hike takes two or three days, but the superb view over the Jasper valley is a good reward for your efforts. Also located near the hostel, the Maligne River canyon offers some fine rapid and waterfall photo opportunities. Do not hesitate to talk with the manager of the hostel: he is an expert on local fauna and conducts research for Jasper National Park.

Jasper International Youth Hostel *($15 per person for members, $20 per person for non-members; 7 km west of Jasper taking the Skytram road, ☎403-852-3215)* is quite a comfortable establishment. It is a few minutes' walk from the summer gondola that goes to the top of Whistler Mountain, where there is a superb view over the Athabasca Valley. Reserve well in advance.

Pine Bungalow Cabins *($75-$100; ⅄, K; on Highway 16, near the Jasper golf course, Box 7, Jasper, AB, TOE 1E0, ☎403-852-3491, ≈852-3432)* fit the motel category. The cabins are fully equipped, and some even have fireplaces, but furnishings are very modest and in rather poor taste. All the same, it is one of Jasper's cheapest places to stay.

Jasper House *($109; tv, pb, K, ℜ; a few kilometres south of Jasper on Icefields Parkway, at the foot of Mount Whistler, Box 817, Jasper, AB, TOE 1E0, ☎403-852-4535, ≈852-5335)* consists of a group of little chalet-style log houses built along the Athabasca River. Comfortable and quiet, the rooms are big and well equipped.

Pyramid Lake Resort *($120; summer only; &, tv, pb, ℜ; on the shore of Pyramid Lake, 5 km from Jasper; take Pyramid Lake Rd. to Jasper and follow the signs to Lake Patricia and Pyramid Lake, Box 388, Jasper, AB, TOE 1EO, ☎403-852-4900 or 852-3536, ≈852-7007)* offers simple but comfortable rooms facing Pyramid Lake, where you can enjoy your favourite nautical activities. Rentals of motorboats, canoes, and water-skis are available at the hotel.

Miette Hot Springs

Miette Hot Spring Bungalows *($67-$120; K, pb, ℜ; next to the Miette Hot Springs, Jasper East, Box 907, Jasper, AB, TOE 1EO, ☎403-866-3750 or 866-3760, in the off-season ☎852-4039, ≈866-2214)* offers accommodations in bungalows and a motel. The motel rooms are rather ordinary, but those in the bungalows offer good quality.

Outside Hinton

The **Overlander Mountain Lodge** *($140; pb, ℜ; 2 km to the left after leaving Jasper National Park toward Hinton; Box 6118, Hinton, AB, T7V 1X5, ☎403-866-2330, ≈866-2332)* has several charming cabins. This establishment is rendered more pleasant by the fact that it is set in a much calmer area than on the outskirts of Jasper, and the surrounding scenery is truly exquisite. This place stands out from the majority of motel-style establishments in this town. Reservations should be made far in advance, as Hinton is a common lodging alternative to lodging in Jasper.

Kootenay and Yoho National Parks

From Castle Junction to Radium Hot Springs

Kootenay Park Lodge *($74-$92 per cabin; mid-May to late Sep; ✗, pb, ℜ, ℝ; on Hwy 93 heading south, 42 km from Castle Junction, Box 1390, Banff, AB, TOL 0C0, ☎403-762-9196; in the off-season, phone Calgary ☎and ≈403-283-7482)* rents 10 small log cabins on the steep-sloped mountain cliffs of Kootenay National Park. On site, you will

find a small store offering sandwiches and everyday items. The restaurant is open only from 8am to 10am, 12 to 2pm and 6pm to 8:30pm.

Radium Hot Springs

Surprisingly, accommodations in Radium Hot Springs consist essentially of very ordinary motel rooms. All along the town's main strip you will find motel fronts that rival each other in ugliness. The region is popular with visitors, however, so here are a few suggestions.

Misty River Lodge *($55-$75; ✗, ≈, pb, tv, K; 5036 Hwy 93, Box 363, Radium Hot Springs, BC, VOA 1MO, ☎250-347-9912, ≈347-9397)* is the only exception to the "ugly-motel" rule in Radium Hot Springs. The rooms offer a decent level of comfort. The bathrooms are spacious and very clean. Without a doubt, the best motel in town.

The Chalet *($95; &, ⊙, △, pb, tv, ⊛; Box 456, Radium Hot Springs, BC, VOA 1MO, ☎250-347-9305, ≈347-9306)* offers several rooms with balconies, modestly furnished but comfortable. Perched above the little town of Radium Hot Springs, this big Savoy chalet-style house offers an interesting view of the valley below.

Fairmont Hot Springs Resort *($139; &, pb, ≈, ℜ, tv, ℝ, ⊛, △, ℜ; on Highway 93-95, near the Fairmont ski hills, Box 10, Fairmont Hot Springs, BC, VOB 1LO, ☎250-345-6311 or 1-800-663-4979, ≈345-6616)* is a magnificent hotel complex, wonderfully laid out, offering special spa, ski and golf packages. Hotel guests can also take advantage of tennis courts and a superb golf course. Guests have unlimited access to the hot springs. This establishment also has a vast adjacent campground *($15-$35)*.

Yoho National Park

Emerald Lake Lodge *($260-$410; Box 10, Field, VOA 1GO, ☎250-343-6321 or 1-800-663-6336, ≈343-6724)*, in Yoho National Park, was built by Canadian Pacific in the 1890s and today is an exquisite mountain hideaway. The central lodge built of hand-hewn timber is the hub of activity, while guests stay in one of 24 cabins. Each room features a fieldstone fireplace, willow-branch chairs, a down duvet, a private balcony and terrific lake views. Just 40 kilometres from Lake Louise.

Golden and Surroundings

McLaren Lodge *($60-$65 bkfst incl.; above Hwy 95 leaving Golden toward Yoho National Park, Box 2586, Golden, BC, VOA 1H0, ☎250-344-6133, ≈344-7650)* is an interesting spot in Golden for nature-lovers. The owners of this little hotel organize river rafting excursions. Rooms are rather small and have a pleasant old-fashioned air. This spot has the best quality-to-price ratio in Golden.

Prestige Inn *($130; ✗, ఉ, pb, K, ⊛, tv, ≈, ℜ, ☺; 1049 TransCanada Hwy, Box 9, Golden, BC, VOA 1H0, ☎250-344-7990, ≈344-7902)* is Golden's best hotel. Rooms are quite spacious, and bathrooms are well equipped.

Kananaskis Country

Mount Kidd RV Park *($16-$26; ✗, ఉ, toilets, showers, laundromat, △; on Hwy 40, a few kilometres south of Kananaskis Village, ☎403-591-7700)* has a unique set-up. Located at the edge of the river in a forested area, it is definitely the most pleasant campground in the region. Guests also have the use of tennis courts or can head off to any of the many hiking trails in the area. Be sure to reserve ahead (groups especially) at this popular spot.

Kananaskis Village

Ribbon Creek Youth Hostel *($12 per person for members, $16 per person for non-members; along the road leading to the central square of Kananaskis village, TOL 2H0, ☎403-762-4122)* is a pleasant little hostel that is almost always crowded. Do not wait to the last minute to reserve, or you will be disappointed. The common room, in front of the fireplace, is a pleasant spot to recover from the day's activities.

Kananaskis Inn Best Western *($155; ఉ, pb, tv, K, △, ⊛, ≈, ℜ; on the central square of Kananaskis Village, TOL 2H0, ☎403-591-7500 or 1-800-528-1234, ≈591-7633)* has 95 comfortable, pleasantly furnished rooms. The atmosphere at this hotel is quite pleasant, and the staff are friendly. However, the lobby is often besieged by visitors searching for souvenir shops or tea rooms.

 **RESTAURANTS**

Banff National Park

Banff

The restaurant of the Caribou Lodge, **The Keg** *($)*, serves American breakfasts and buffet-style food.

Joe BTFSPLK's (pronounced bi-tif'-spliks) *($; 221 Banff Ave., facing the tourist information centre, ☎403-762-5529)* is a small restaurant with a 1950s decor and good hamburgers. Joe BTFSPLK was a strange comic-book character who walked around with a cloud above his head causing disasters wherever he went. It seems the only way today to avoid annoyances (such as spending too much money) may be to come to this little restaurant, very popular with locals for the burgers, fries, salads, chicken fingers and milkshakes. The restaurant also serves breakfasts for under $6.

Grizzly House *($$; every day 11:30am to midnight; 207 Banff Ave., ☎403-762-4055)* specializes in big, tender, juicy steaks. The western decor is a bit corny, but your attention will quickly be diverted by your delicious meal.

Sukiyaki House *($$; every day; upstairs at 211 Banff Ave., ☎403-762-2002)* offers excellent Japanese cuisine at affordable prices. The sushi is perfect, and the staff is very courteous. The impersonal decor, however, leaves a bit to be desired.

Ticino *($$; 5:30pm to 10:30pm; 415 Banff Ave., ☎403-762-3848)* serves pretty good Italian cuisine as well as fondues. The decor is very ordinary, and the music tends to be too loud.

Le Beaujolais *($$$; every day; 212 Buffalo St., ☎403-762-2712)* prepares excellent French cuisine. The dining room is very elegant and the staff is highly attentive. British Columbia salmon baked with Pernod, is a true delicacy. The best food in Banff.

Caboose *($$$; every day 5pm to 10pm; corner of Elk St. and Lynx St., ☎403-762-3622 or 762-2102)* is one of Banff's better eateries. The fish dishes, trout or salmon, are excellent, or you may prefer the lobster with steak,

American style, or perhaps the crab. This is a favourite with regular visitors.

Lake Louise

The **Moraine Lake Lodge** *($$; every day; at the edge of Morraine Lake,* ☎403-522-3733) has a restaurant where you can enjoy good meals while contemplating the superb view over the long stretch of the lake and the Ten Peaks.

The **Edelweiss Dining Room** *($$$; every day; Chateau Lake Louise,* ☎403-522-3511) offers delicious Canadian continental cuisine in very elegant surroundings with a view over the lake. Reservations are recommended.

Post Hotel *($$$; at the edge of the Pipestone River, near the youth hostel,* ☎403-522-3989) houses an excellent restaurant recognized by the Relais et Châteaux association. Reservations are necessary, for this is one of the best dining rooms in Lake Louise. The setting of the hotel is enchanting.

Canmore

Nutter's *($; every day; 900 Railway Ave.,* ☎403-678-3335) is the best spot to find the fixings for sandwiches and other snacks for your back-country hikes. You will find a large selection of energizing natural foods to take out, or you can eat here at the small tables near the windows.

Chez François *($$; adjacent to the Best Western Green Gables Inn, Highway 1A,* ☎403-678-6111) is probably the best place to eat in Canmore. The chef, who comes from Québec, offers excellent French cuisine and a warm atmosphere in his restaurant.

Sinclairs *($$; every day; 637 8th St.,* ☎403-678-5370) offers good food in a warm ambiance enhanced by a fireplace. Reservations are recommended in high season, for the restaurant is often full. The restaurant also offers an excellent selection of teas, a rarity around here.

The Icefields Parkway

This tour crosses a sparsely populated area, and restaurants are few and far between. There

are, nonetheless, a few little cafés that serve light meals.

The Crossing *($; every day; at the junction of Hwys 93 and 11, 80 km from Lake Louise,* ☎403-761-7000) houses a fairly large cafeteria with light meals where just about every traveller seems to stop. As a result, it is very crowded, with long line-ups.

The café at the **Num-Ti-Jah Lodge** *($; every day; at the edge of Bow Lake, about 35 km from Lake Louise,* ☎403-522-2167) serves sandwiches, muffins and cakes. You can warm up in this little café with tea or other hot beverages. This spot is popular with tourists and is often crowded.

Jasper National Park

Jasper

Coco's Café *($; every day; 608 Patricia St.,* ☎403-852-4550) is a little spot that serves bagels, sandwiches and cheesecake.

Soft Rock Café *($; every day; in the Connaught Square Mall, 622 Connaught Dr.,* ☎403-852-5850) offers excellent breakfasts and sandwiches. Cake and ice-cream are the specialties for lazy afternoons.

Jasper Inn Restaurant *($$; every day; Jasper Inn, 98 Geikie St.,* ☎403-852-3232) serves up excellent fish and seafood. This is a very popular spot.

Tokyo Tom's Restaurant *($$; every day; 410 Connaught Dr.,* ☎403-852-3780) serves tasty Japanese food. The *sukiyaki* is excellent, but the gloomy decor is not.

Beauvallon Dining Room *($$$; every day; Charlton's Chateau Jasper, 96 Geikie St.,* ☎403-852-5644) prepares excellent French cuisine and is one of Jasper's finest dining establishments.

Beauvert Dining Room *($$$; every day; in Jasper Park Lodge, at the northern approach to Jasper,* ☎403-852-3301) is a rather fancy restaurant. The French cuisine offered is excellent. One of the best restaurants in Jasper.

Outside Jasper

The restaurant of the **Pyramid Lake Resort** *($; summer only, every day; at the edge of Pyramid Lake, 5 km from Jasper; take Pyramid Lake Rd. to Jasper and follow the signs to Lake Patricia and Pyramid Lake, ☎403-852-4900)* serves simple meals. The cuisine is good and unpretentious.

Hinton and Surroundings

Greentree Cafe *($; every day 5:30am to 11pm; in the Greentree Motor Lodge, ☎403-865-3321)* prepares delicious and copious breakfasts at unbeatable prices.

Ranchers *($; every day; in the Hill Shopping Centre, ☎403-865-4116)* prepares all sorts of pizzas. This spot is generally quite busy.

Fireside Dining Room *($$; every day; in the Greentree Motor Lodge, ☎403-865-3321)* is the best and most attractive restaurant in Hinton.

The **Overlander Mountain Lodge**'s *($$$; every day; in the Overlander Mountain Lodge, 2 km past the toll booths leaving Jasper National Park heading toward Hinton, go left toward the hotel, ☎403-866-2330)* attractive restaurant serves excellent food. The menu changes daily, but if you have the chance, give in to temptation and savour the rainbow trout stuffed with crab and shrimp and covered with *béarnaise* sauce.

Kootenay and Yoho National Parks

From Castle Junction and Radium Hot Springs

Kootenay Park Lodge Restaurant *($; every day 8am to 10am and 6pm to 8:30pm; mid-May to late Sep, noon to 2pm as well; on Hwy 93 heading south, 42 km from Castle Junction, ☎403-762-9196)* offers light meals in simple surroundings. Isolated amidst grandiose scenery, you may want to finish your meal with a stroll through the surrounding countryside.

Radium Hot Springs and Surroundings

The restaurant at the **Fairmont Hot Springs Resort** *($$; every day; on Hwy 93-95, near the Fairmont ski hill, ☎250-345-6311)* will satisfy the most demanding customers. Its healthy food is excellent, and the decor is pleasant.

Golden

The restaurant at the **Prestige Inn** *($$; every day; 1049 TransCanada Hwy, ☎250-344-7661)* encompasses the best of traditional cuisine in Golden.

Kananaskis Country

Chief Chiniki *($; every day; on Hwy 21, at Morley, ☎403-881-3748)* offers typical North American dishes at reasonable prices. The staff is very friendly and attentive.

Mount Engadine Lodge *($$; Spray Lakes Rd., ☎403-678-2880)* offers an interesting *table d'hôte*. The European-style cuisine is delicious.

L'Escapade *($$$; in the Hotel Kananaskis, ☎403-591-7711)* is the hotel's French restaurant. Prettily decorated with red carpeting, comfortable armchairs and bay windows, this spot exudes warmth, making your meal more appetizing.

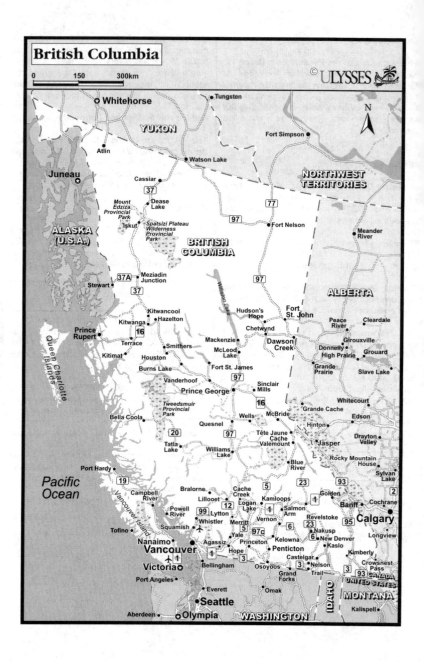

British Columbia

0   150   300km

©ULYSSES

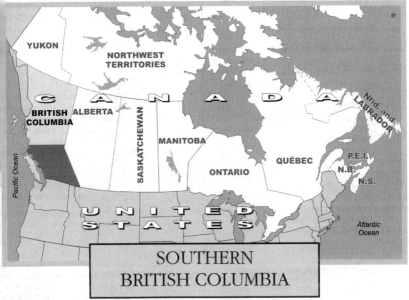

SOUTHERN
BRITISH COLUMBIA

T his region, which borders Washington state, is characterized by a blend of the urban and the undeveloped. The Vancouver area, for example, resembles a big American city, though it is set against a backdrop of green mountains and blue sea; here, you will find both wilderness and civilization. The Okanagan Valley is home to countless orchards and some of the best wineries in the country. As one majestic landscape succeeds another, your eyes will be dazzled by the sea, the everlasting snows and the spring colours, which appear very early in this region.

Communing with nature is a memorable experience of any trip in southern British Columbia. The waters that wash the deserted beaches beckon you to relax and let your mind wander. Stately trees stand guard over tranquil areas untouched by the forestry industry. Dotted with national and provincial parks that lie stretched across the loveliest parts of the province, this region has an extremely varied landscape, with everything from perpetual snows to desert valleys to rivers teeming with fish.

 FINDING YOUR WAY AROUND

By Car

Every highway in southern British Columbia is more spectacular than the last. One of these is the TransCanada (Highway 1), which runs east-west across mountains, rivers, canyons and desert valleys.

Highway 1, the TransCanada, provides an easy route eastward from Vancouver, although the traffic is always fairly heavy. The road leads to Calgary, running along the Fraser River, the Thompson River and Lake Shuswap at different points along the way. Another option is to take Highway 7 (the continuation of Broadway Avenue) out of downtown Vancouver, along the north bank of the Fraser River. If you're pressed for time, you can take the newly opened Coquihalla Highway, which runs between Hope and Kamloops. This is a toll highway, the only one in the province; what's more, it is not as attractive as the others.

By Ferry

The Sunshine Coast

To reach the Sunshine Coast, you must take a ferry from the coast or from Vancouver Island.

BC Ferry: 1112 Fort St., Victoria, V8V 4V2, ☎(250) 386-3431, ☎(888) 223-3779 from B.C., Saltery Bay, ☎(604) 487-9333, Powell River, ☎(604) 485-2943.

 PRACTICAL INFORMATION

Area Code: 604 in the Lower Mainland (Vancouver and suburbs), **250** in the rest of the province (north of Whistler, east of Hope, the islands).

Tourist Information Offices

Tourism Association of Southwestern B.C. 204-1755 West Broadway, Vancouver, BC, V6J 4S5, ☎604-739-9011 or 1-800-667-3306.

High Country Tourism Association 1-1490 Pearson Place, Kamloops, BC, V1S 1J9, ☎250-372-7770 or 1-800-567-2275.

Okanagan-Similkameen Tourism Association 1332 Water Street, Kelowna, BC, V1Y 9P4, ☎250-860-5999.

Kootenay Country Tourist Association 610 Railway Street, Nelson, BC, V1L 1H4, ☎250-352-6033.

 EXPLORING

The Sunshine Coast ★★

Most people get to the Sunshine Coast by boat. There are no roads linking Vancouver to these resort towns; the daily comings and goings are dictated by the ferry schedule. As a result, the mentality here is completely different. The towns that have grown up along this coast benefit from the sea and what it yields. The Sunshine Coast runs along the Strait of Georgia, and is surrounded by Desolation Sound to the north, the Coast Mountains to the east and Howe Sound farther south.

Langdale

It takes 40 minutes to reach **Langdale**, a small port city at the southern tip of the Sunshine Coast. Ferries shuttle back and forth several times a day, but you have to arrive at the Horseshoe Bay terminal at least an hour early for some weekend departures. **Horseshoe Bay** lies 20 kilometres northwest of Vancouver. You can save up to 15% on the price of your ticket if you return by way of Vancouver Island instead of opting for a round-trip. Ask for the Sunshine Coast Circlepac.

Gibsons ★

Visitors to Gibsons are sure to recognize the site of *The Beachcombers*, a Canadian Broadcasting Corporation (CBC) television series that was shot here for close to 20 years and broadcast in over 40 countries. On the way from Langdale to Gibsons, stop off at **Molly's Reach** to take a look at the photographs of the actors from the popular television show and to explore the little shops and restaurants along **Molly's Lane ★**. More recently Gibsons became Castle Rock for the film *Needful Things*, based on a Steven King novel.

A visit to the **Sunshine Coast Maritime Museum ★** *(at the end of Molly's Lane, ☎886-4114)* is a must. You will be greeted by a charming woman who will inspire you with her passion for the local marine life.

The Sunshine Coast has been developed in a thin strip alongside the forest. The area abounds in plant and animal life — orchids and wild roses, deer and black bears. River otters and beavers can be found near the coast, while sea-lions and seals swim about farther offshore.

Powell River ★

Powell River, an important waterfront town, boasts magnificent sunsets over Vancouver Island and the islands in the Strait of Georgia. The spotlight is on outdoor activities in this region, since the temperate climate is conducive to year-round fun and games.

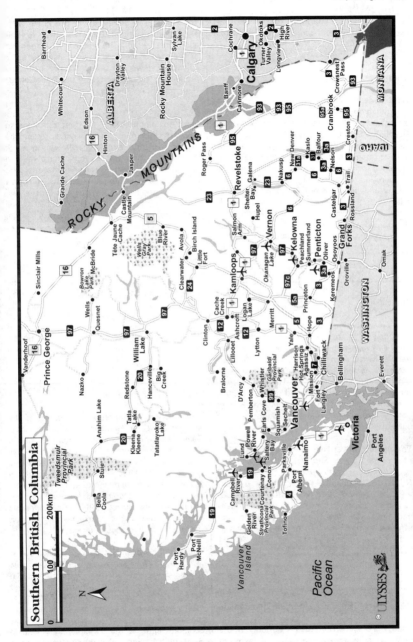

Southern British Columbia

BRITISH COLUMBIA

ULYSSES

Forestry plays an important role in the local economy, but visitors come here for the lakes, the woods, the wildlife and the views.

Lund ★

Lund, located at the beginning (or the end, depending on what direction you're heading in) of Highway 101, is the gateway to marvellous **Desolation Sound ★★**, a marine-life sanctuary easily accessible by canoe or kayak. The town port is magnificent, with its old hotel, its adjoining shops and its wooden promenade that skirts round the bay. Imagine a typical fishing village and your harbour will undoubtedly be filled with the fishing boats moored here. In terms of activities, there is much to do, from fishing and whale-watching trips to snorkelling and kayaking, sports everyone can enjoy.

Fraser River Loop ★★

Squamish

The **Soo Coalition for Sustainable Forests ★** *(4-hour walk in the woods $30; dryland sort tour, $14 for two people; mill tour $14 for two people with own car, $24 without car; reservations required; ☎604-892-9766)* is an organization that works toward preserving both the forest and the jobs related to the industry. It arranges tours of the forest and the lumber yard in order to educate the public on this subject.

The historic **Royal Hudson Steam Train** *($45 round-trip; Jun to Sep, Wed to Sun; 10am departure from North Vancouver; 1311 W. 1st St.; it is also possible to come back by boat $78; ☎604-688-7246 or 1-800-663-8238)* runs back and forth between North Vancouver and Squamish, following the coastline and offering unimpeded views of the island and of the snow-capped peaks of the Coast Mountains.

Yale

Three major historical events contributed to the development of Yale: the growth of the fur trade, the gold rush and the construction of the railway. The town also marks the beginning of the Fraser Canyon, so buckle your seatbelts and keep your eyes wide open.

The **Alexandria Bridge** spans the Fraser at a striking point along the river that is only accessible by foot. The bridge is no longer part of the road system, but you can enjoy some splendid views of the Fraser from its promenade. A sign alongside the TransCanada Highway shows the way.

Hell's Gate ★ *($9; ☎604-867-9277)* owes its name to Simon Fraser, the first European to navigate this river. For a while, even the salmon had trouble making their way through this gorge, which had become narrower and narrower as a result of major landslides. The current was so strong that the fish couldn't swim upstream to spawn. To solve the problem, a pass was cleared. A cablecar will take you down to the water's edge, 152 metres below.

Hope ★

Hope, located at the confluence of the Coquihalla, Fraser and Nicolum Rivers, marks the gateway to the Fraser Canyon. The Hudson's Bay Company established a fur-trading post named Fort Hope on this site in 1848; 10 years later, prospectors lured by the discovery of gold would stock up on supplies here.

Harrison Hot Springs ★

The **Harrison Hot Springs** are located at the southern end of Harrison Lake. The Coast Salish Indians used to come to here to soak in the warm mineral water, which supposedly has curative powers. Gold prospectors discovered the springs in 1858, when a storm on Lake Harrison forced them to return to shore and they happened to step into the warm water. The lake is surrounded by successive mountains peaks that contrast with the sky, making for a spectacular setting.

The indoor **Harrison Hot Springs Public Pool ★** *($7; May to Nov, every day 8am to 9pm; Dec to Apr, Sun to Thu 8am to 9pm, Fri and Sat 8am to 10pm; at the intersection of Hot Springs Rd. and Lilloet Ave., ☎604-796-2244)* offers access to the springs. In addition to running the public pool, the Harrison Hotel has acquired rights to the springs. Every year in September and October, sand-castle enthusiasts flock to the beaches on Harrison Lake, with impressive results. The road, which runs alongside the lake, leads to Sasquatch Provincial Park.

Mission

Xa:ytem Long House Interpretive Centre *(3 km east of Mission; donations accepted, ☎820-9725).* This First Nations archaeological site was discovered in 1990. Xa:ytem (pronounced HAY-tum) is a native word designating a boulder on a plateau on the Fraser River. According to geologists, the rock was deposited there by shifting glaciers. The Sto:lo Indians, who have inhabited this region for more than 4,000 years, explain the boulder's presence by saying that it is what became of three chiefs who had committed a sin. Hundreds of relics have been found in this area, including tools and weapons made of stone. These articles are displayed in the centre, whose guides are Sto:lo Indians.

Fort Langley

Fort Langley National Historic Site ★ *($4; every day 10am to 5pm; Exit 66 North of the TransCanada, towards Fort Langley, at the intersection of Mavis and Royal Streets; ☎888-4424).* Fort Langley was erected in 1827, four kilometres downriver from its present location, on the south bank of the Fraser. It was moved in 1839, only to be ravaged by fire the following year. The Hudson's Bay Company used the fort to store furs that were to be shipped out to Europe.

The Thompson River as far as Revelstoke ★

Ashcroft

Ashcroft lies a few kilometres east of Highway 1. In 1860, gold prospectors heading north set out from here. You can go back to the TransCanada 1 East and make your way to Kamloops, passing through Cache Creek on the way in order to skirt Kamloops Lake and see the ginseng fields (see below). We recommend taking Highway 97C to Logan Lake and the Copper Valley mine. As you make your way through a magnificent desert valley, you'll see the Sundance Guest Ranch (see p 550 for details on staying there), which looks out over the Thompson River. Ever since the 1950s, this ranch has been sending visitors off on horseback rides across thousands of hectares

of fields. Like most ranches in the region, it was once the home of stockbreeders.

Copper Valley ★★ *(May to Sep, Mon to Fri 9:30am and 12:30pm, Sat and Sun 9:30am, 12:30pm and 3:30pm; tours last 2 hrs 30 min; ☎250-523-2443).* Copper Valley is one of the largest open-cut copper mines in the world. The industrial machinery and equipment used to transport ore are completely outsized. Though you can't tour the mine, you'll notice its lunar landscape from the highway.

Kamloops

Kamloops (pop. 68,500), the capital of inland British Columbia, is a major stopover point. The local economy is driven chiefly by the forestry and tourism industries, with mining and stockbreeding playing subsidiary roles.

West of Kamloops, ginseng crops lie hidden in fields beneath big pieces of black cloth. Large farms produce this root, which is highly coveted by Asians for the health benefits it is supposed to procure. The variety grown here, known as American ginseng, was discovered in eastern Canada several hundred years ago by natives, who made potions with it. At the **Sunmore Company** *(925 McGill Place, ☎250-374-3017),* you can drop in and learn about ginseng farming in North America and how local methods differ from those employed in Asia.

Another activity that underlines the importance of the rivers in British Columbia is a cruise aboard the *Wanda-Sue*, which sails along the Thompson River through bare mountains. Natives, trappers, gold prospectors, lumberjacks and railway workers all travelled by boat before the railway lines and roads were laid here. The **Wanda-Sue ★** sets out from the Old Kamloops Yacht Club *($11.50; Apr to Sep; the trip lasts two hours; 1140 River St., near 10th Ave., ☎250-374-7447).*

Revelstoke ★★

The history of Revelstoke is closely linked to the construction of the transcontinental railway. Large numbers of Italians came here to apply their expertise in building tunnels. To this day, the town's 9,000 residents rely mainly on the railroad for their income. Tourism and the production of electricity also play important roles in the economy of this magnificent town.

BRITISH COLUMBIA

Revelstoke is a century-old town that has managed to retain its charm. Numerous Queen Anne, Victorian, Art Deco and neoclassical buildings here bear witness to days gone by. Pick up a copy of the **Heritage Walking & Driving Tour ★** at the Revelstoke Museum (see below) or at the Travel InfoCentre *(204 Campbell Ave., ☎250-837-5345)*.

The **Revelstoke Railway Museum ★** *($5; Jul and Aug, every day 9am to 8pm; Dec to Mar by apt.; call ahead for spring and autumn hours; 719 Track St., ☎250-837-6060)* focuses on the construction of the railway across the Rockies and the history of Revelstoke. The exhibit features old objects, photos from the local archives and most importantly, a 1940s locomotive and a company director's personal railway car, built in 1929.

At the **Revelstoke Dam ★** *(free admission; May to Jun, 9am to 5pm; Jun to Sep, 8am to 8pm; Sep and Oct, 9am to 5pm; closed Nov to May, although group visits are permitted during the low season; take Hwy 23 North, ☎250-837-6211)*, you can learn about the production of hydroelectricity and visit a number of rooms, as well as the dam itself, an impressive concrete structure.

Revelstoke is a crossroads between the Rockies and the Kootenays, to the south. If you plan on continuing east to Alberta, stay on the TransCanada to Golden, Field and Lake Louise (see p 515). We recommend driving down into the Kootenays, which are much less known than the Rockies, but equally fascinating. Before heading south, however, continue until you reach **Rogers Pass ★★**, named after the engineer who discovered it in 1881. This valley was originally supposed to serve as a passage between the east and the west, but after a number of catastrophes, during which avalanches claimed the lives of hundreds of people, the Canadian Pacific railway company decided to build a tunnel instead. At the **Rogers Pass Centre ★** *(☎250-814-5233)*, located an hour from Revelstoke in Glacier National Park, visitors can learn about the history of the railway. A trail that runs along the former tracks will take you past the ruins of a railway station destroyed by an avalanche.

Okanagan-Similkameen ★★★

All sorts of natural treasures await discovery in this part of British Columbia. With its stretches of water and blanket of fruit trees, the Okanagan Valley, which runs north-south, i one of the most beautiful areas in the province Okanagan wines have won a number of prizes the orchards feed a good portion of the country, and the lakes and mountains are a dream come true for sporty types. The climate is conducive to a wide variety of activities: the winters, mild in town and snowy in the mountains, can be enjoyed by all. In the spring, the fruit trees are in full bloom, and in summer and fall, a day of fruit-picking is often followed by a dip in one of the many lakes.

Princeton

American researchers come to the **Princeton Museum and Archives ★** *(Jul and Aug, every day 9am to 6pm; Sep to Jun, Mon to Fri 1pm to 5pm; Margaret Stoneberg, curator, ☎295-7588, home ☎295-3362)* to study its impressive fossil collection. You'll get caught up in curator Margaret Stoneberg's enthusiasm as she tells you about the pieces and how they bear witness to the region's history. Due to underfunding, the fossils pile up without being properly displayed, but it is nevertheless amazing to see how much the museum holds.

The **Maverick Cattle Drives Ltd.** *($125, reservations required; lunch, morning and afternoon outings, cattle driving; ☎250-295-6243 or 295-3753)* welcomes visitors who want to experience life on a ranch. You'll find yourself on the back of a horse, riding in the warm summer breeze across fields of wheat, taking in the view of the nearby glaciers. This wonderful experience also involves carrying out a number of tasks on the ranch. At the end of the day, all the cowboys get together at the saloon.

Osoyoos

Osoyoos lies at the bottom of a valley, flanked on one side by Osoyoos Lake and on the other by verdant slopes decked with vineyards and orchards. It is located a few kilometres from the U.S. border, in an arid climate more reminiscent of an American desert, or even southern Italy, than a Canadian town. The main attraction here is the exceptionally warm lake, where you can enjoy a variety of water sports during summer.

The wine route runs through the vast Okanagan region. North of Osoyoos and south of Oliver, you'll come across the **Domaine Combret** ★ *(32057-131st Rd. 13, Oliver, ☎250-498-8878, ⊷498-8879)*. In 1995, the *Office International de la Vigne et du Vin*, based in Burgundy, France, awarded this French-owned vineyard the highest international distinction for its Chardonnay. Its Reisling also won a prize in 1995. You must call beforehand for a tour of the premises, as the wine growers spend a good part of the day outside among the vines during the grape-picking season. Originally from the south of France, the Combrets come from a long line of vinters. Robert Combret first visited the Okanagan Valley in the 1950s. He returned in the early 1990s. His son Olivier runs the family business now. Stop by and enjoy a sample of his wine.

Keremeos

In Keremeos, history is recounted at the **Grist Mill** ★ *(May to Oct; R.R.1, Upper Bench Rd., ☎250-499-2888)*, founded in 1877 to produce flour for local native people, cowboys and miners. The water mill, equipment and original buildings have been restored and are now part of British Columbia's heritage.

Penticton ★

Penticton lies between Okanagan Lake, to the north, and Skaha Lake, to the south. The town has nearly 30,000 inhabitants and boasts a dry, temperate climate. Tourism is the mainspring of Penticton's economy. The area's First Nations named the site *Pen-tak-tin*, meaning "the place where you stay forever". A beach lined with trees and a pedestrian walkway run along the north end of town. The dry landscape, outlined by curves of the sandy shoreline, contrasts with the vineyards and orchards. People come to Penticton for outdoor activities, fine dining and local *joie de vivre*.

A visit to an orchard is a must, especially in the heat of summer, during the fruit-picking season. Not only is the fruit plentiful, but more importantly, it's delicious. From July to late September, the region is covered with fruit trees bursting with scents and colours. The **Dickinson Family Farm** *(turn left onto Jones Flat road from Hwy 97 North, then right onto Bentley Rd. 19208, ☎250-494-0300)* invites visitors to stroll through its rows of fruit trees. You can purchase fruit (apples, pears, etc.) and fruit-based products on the premises. For a real treat, try the peach butter and the freshly pressed apple juice. Head out of Penticton on Lakeshore Drive and take the 97 North toward Summerland.

An outing in the mountains along the former route of the **Kettle Valley Railway** ★★ offers another perspective of the Okanagan Valley. Laid at the turn of the century, these tracks connected Nelson, in the east, to Hope, in the west, and to the coast thus providing a link between the hinterland, where tons of ore used to be extracted. Mother Nature was a major obstacle throughout the railway's short existence; fallen debris, avalanches and snowstorms made the tracks impossible to use, and the line was abandoned. The 20 million dollar cost of building the railway was never recovered.

You can follow the tracks on foot or by bicycle. The railway runs through Penticton on either shore of Okanagan Lake, and the terrain is relatively flat, making for a pleasant outing. The directions, however, are not very clear. Start on Main Street, in downtown Penticton, and follow the signs for Naramata Road, then turn right onto MacMillan. At this point, the signs seem to disappear. Take the main road; as soon as its name becomes Chute Lake, keep right and then turn right again on Smethurst Road and keep going until you reach the end. You can either leave your car in town or drive the first six kilometres (at your own risk); pedestrians and cyclists have priority. You'll enjoy a direct view of Okanagan Lake along the way. After 4.8 kilometres, you'll pass through a small tunnel. Make noise as you walk to drive off any rattlesnakes, black bears or cougars. On the west shore, in Summerland, a part of the track is now used by a steam engine. Head toward Summerland on Highway 97 North, turn left on Solly Road and follow the signs for the **West Summerland Station of the Kettle Valley Steam Railway** *(May to Oct; ☎250-494-8422, ⊷494-8452)*. Maps for both areas are available at the Penticton tourist office on Lakeshore Drive.

Kelowna ★

Kelowna is the heart and mind of the Okanagan Valley. It was here that a French Oblate by the name of Father Charles Pandosy set up the first Catholic mission in the hinterland of British Columbia in 1859. He introduced apple and grape growing into the Okanagan Valley and

BRITISH COLUMBIA

was thus largely responsible for its becoming a major fruit-producing region.

The **Father Pandosy Mission** *(May to early Oct, every day; on Benvoulin Rd., at the corner of Casorso Rd.,* ☎*250-860-8369)*, which has been listed as a provincial historic site since 1983, includes a church and a number of farm buildings.

Located on the shores of Okanagan Lake, Kelowna boasts several waterfront parks. One of these is **Knox Mountain Park**, where you'll find a magnificent viewing area. You might even catch a glimpse of Ogopogo, the monster that supposedly inhabits the lake. To get to the park, take Ellis Street north out of downtown.

It takes about 20 minutes to reach the first metal bridge, which stretches across the **Myra Canyon** ★★. If you enjoy walking, you'll love this excursion. The local Chamber of Commerce *(544 Harvey Ave.,* ☎*861-1515)* or the Okanagan-Similkameen Tourism Association *(1332 Water St.,* ☎*860-5999)* can help you plan outings that take several days. Cyclists can pedal about to their heart's content; the more adventurous can spend a day riding to Penticton.

Almost all the wine produced in British Columbia comes from the Okanagan region. Over the past few years, local wines have won a number of international prizes. There are three vineyards along Lakeshore Road, south of Kelowna, including the **Cedar Creek Winery** *(5445 Lakeshore Rd.,* ☎*250-764-8866,* ☎*250-764-2603)*, which, like its competitors in the region, produces much more white wine than red. It is located on a pretty hill surrounded by vines and looking out onto Okanagan Lake. A free tour of the premises will give you a chance to sample some of the wines; the chardonnay is particularly noteworthy. You can also purchase a few bottles while you're there.

Vernon

Get back on the 97 North and continue on to Vernon, which is set amidst three lakes. The town started out modestly in the 1860s, when Cornelius O'Keefe established a ranch here. The northern part of Vernon is an important stockbreeding area. Stop by the **Historic O'Keefe Ranch** *(every day May to Oct; 12 km north of Vernon on Hwy 97,* ☎*250-542-7868)*, where you'll find the original ranch house,

wooden church and ranching equipment. Forestry and agriculture play greater economic roles here than in Kelowna and Penticton, where tourism is more important.

Kootenay Country ★★

Located off the beaten tourist track, this region is a gold mine for visitors with a taste for mountains, lakes, history and chance encounters. Once again, the landscape is one of the major attractions; this is British Columbia, after all! Because this region is underappreciated, it remains virtually unspoiled, making it that much more interesting to explore.

Located in the southeast part of the province, the Kootenays are a series of mountains (the Rockies, the Purcells, the Selkirks and the Monashees) stretching from north to south. The great Columbia River runs through this region, creating the vast body of water known as Arrow Lake on its way. Natural resources such as forests and mines have played a major role in the region's development. A number of towns bear witness to the different stages in the Kootenays' history.

New Denver

New Denver was the gateway to silver country at the turn of the century, when there was an abundant supply of the metal in this region. The history of that era is presented at the **Silvery Slocan Museum** *(Jul to Sep, every day 10am to 4pm; at the corner of 6th St. and Marine Dr.,* ☎*250-358-2201)*. When Canada declared war on Japan during the Second World War, Japanese residents of British Columbia were placed in internment camps in a number of towns in this region, including New Denver and Sandon. To learn more about their experiences, stop in at the **Nikkei Internment Memorial Centre** *(adults $4; May to Oct, every day 9:30am to 5pm; by appt. during winter; 306 Josephine St.,* ☎*250-358-7288)*.

Sandon ★★

At the turn of the century, 5,000 people lived and worked in Sandon. By 1930, the price of silver had dropped and the mine had been exhausted, prompting an exodus from the town. During World War II, Sandon became an internment centre for Japanese who had been living on the coast. Shortly after the war, it became a ghost town once again, and a number of buildings were destroyed by fire and floods. Today, visitors can observe what remains of a number of old buildings, as well as the first hydroelectric power plant constructed in the Canadian West, which still produces electricity.

Kaslo

Kaslo was built on the hills on the western shore of Kootenay Lake during the heyday of silver mining. A walk along the waterfront and a visit to the town hall will give you a glimpse of how beautiful the setting is. At the beginning of the century, people used to come here by paddle-boat. For nearly 60 years, up until 1957, the *SS Moyie* shuttled passengers back and forth across Kootenay Lake for Canadian Pacific. The boat has since been transformed into a museum.

At **Ainsworth Hot Springs** ★ *($6; swimsuit and towel rentals available;* ☎*229-4212)*, which is located in an enchanting setting along the shore to the south, bathers can alternate between very cold and very warm water. The swimming pool overlooks Kootenay Lake and the valley, which is brilliant at sunset. The U-shaped cave studded with stalactites, the humidity and the almost total absence of light will transport you to another planet. The temperature rises as you near the springs at the back of the cave, reaching as high as 40°C.

Nelson ★★

Make sure to park your car as soon as possible and explore this magnificent town on foot. Located at the southern end of the West Arm of Kootenay Lake, Nelson lies on the west flank of the Selkirk Mountains. In 1887, during the silver boom, miners set up camp here, working together to build hotels, homes and public facilities. Numerous buildings now bear witness to the town's prosperous past. Nelson has managed to continue its economic growth today, thanks to light industry, tourism and the civil service.

The Travel InfoCentre distributes two small pamphlets that will guide you through over 350 historic buildings. The town's elegant architecture makes walking about here a real pleasure. Classical, Queen Anne and Victorian buildings proudly line the streets. The stained-glass windows of the **Nelson Congregational Church** ★ *(at the corner of Stanley and Silica Sts.)*, the Chateau-style **town hall** ★ *(502 Vernon St.)*, the group of buildings on **Baker Street** and above all, the Italian-style **fire station** ★ *(919 Ward St.)* are eloquent reminders of the opulence of the silver mining era.

Its lovely architecture is not the only thing that sets Nelson apart from other inland towns in British Columbia. You will also find a number of art galleries here, many of which are integrated into restaurants, so you can contemplate works of art while looking over the menu. This setup is known as the **Artwalk**, which enables artists to exhibit their work in participating businesses each year. For further information, contact the **West Kootenay Regional Arts Council** *(☎250-352-2402)*.

Castlegar

Castlegar, which lies at the confluence of the Columbia and Kootenay Rivers, has no downtown area. While crossing the bridge in the direction of the airport, you'll see a suspended bridge built by the Doukhobors; turn left for a closer look.

Back on the highway, go uphill, then turn right to reach the **Doukhobor Museum** ★ *($3; May to Sep, every day 9am to 5pm,* ☎*250-365-6622)*. Fleeing persecution in Russia, the Doukhobors emigrated to Canada in 1898. They wanted to live according to their own rules rather than those of the state; for example, they were against participation in any war. They established communities on the prairies and farmed the land, adhering to their traditional way of life and gradually developing towns and setting up industries. One group, led by Piotr Verigin, left the prairies for British Columbia and took up residence in the Castlegar area. After the economic crisis of 1929 and the death of Verigin, the community diminished, but their descendants have taken up the task of telling visitors about their ancestors.

Rossland ★

Rossland is a picturesque little turn-of-the-century town that thrived during the gold rush and has managed to retain its charm. Located inside the crater of a former volcano, at an

BRITISH COLUMBIA

altitude of 1,023 metres above sea level, it attracts skiers and people who simply enjoy being in the mountains. Nancy Greene Provincial Park, named after the 1968 Olympic champion, a native of Rossland, boasts several majestic peaks. Red Mountain, renowned for its high-quality powder, is a world-class resort. Skier Kerrin Lee-Gartner, who won the gold medal in the 1992 Olympic Games, is also from Rossland.

All of the gold was mined from this region long before these Olympic skiers arrived. In 1890, a prospector discovered a large vein of gold here. The news spread, and hundreds of adventurers came to try their luck, resulting in a gold rush. Numerous hotels, offices and theatres were built, and Rossland flourished. Then came the crash of 1929, which hit the town hard; that same year, a major fire destroyed part of the downtown area. Rossland was on the decline; the famous **Le Roi** mine closed down, and the future did not look bright. Visitors can learn about the history of the gold rush at the **Le Roi mine** ★ and at the **Rossland Historical Museum** *($8 for mine tour and museum, $4 for museum; mid-May to mid-Sep, every day 9am to 5pm; at the intersection of the 3B and the 22; take Columbia Ave. east of the downtown area, ☎250-362-7722)*, which features an audiovisual presentation and a collection of objects from that era. The **Ski Hall of Fame**, located in the same building, highlights the careers of Nancy Greene and Kerrin Lee-Gartner.

 OUTDOORS

 Parks

The Sunshine Coast

Desolation Sound Marine Park ★★ *(north of Lund, accessible by boat; campsites, hiking, kayaking, swimming, fishing, scuba diving, potable water, toilets; B.C. Parks at Tenedos Bay, Sechelt Area Supervisor, ☎604-885-9019)* is popular with ocean lovers, who come here to observe the animal life inhabiting these warm waters. More and more people are coming here to go sea kayaking, something even novices can enjoy.

Fraser River Loop

Vast **Garibaldi Provincial Park** ★★ *(information Garibaldi/Sunshine District, Brackendale; 10 km north of Squamish, ☎604-898-3678)*, which covers 195,000 hectares, is extremely popular with hikers during summertime. Highway 99 runs along the west side of the park, offering access to the various trails.

The Thompson River as Far as Revelstoke

You can explore the woods on scores of paths in **Mount Revelstoke** ★★ and **Glacier** ★★ **National Parks** *(for maps, information and regulations, contact Parks Canada in Revelstoke, ☎250-837-7500)*. The level of difficulty varies; some trails run past centuries-old trees or lead to the tops of mountains, affording splendid panoramic views.

Okanagan-Similkameen

Manning Provincial Park ★★ *(tourist information: summer, every day 8:30am to 4:30pm; winter, Mon to Fri 8:30am to 4:30pm; ☎250-840-8836)* is located on the boundary of the southwestern part of the province and the huge Okanagan-Similkameen region. It lies 225 kilometres from Vancouver, making it a popular getaway for city-dwellers in search of vast green spaces.

Bighorn Sheep

Cathedral Provincial Park ★★ *(No dogs, no mountain bikes; for detailed maps and information, contact the BC Parks District Manager; Box 399, Summerland, B.C. V0H 1Z0, ☎250-494-6500)* is located 30 kilometres southwest of Keremeos, in the southern part of the province, right alongside the U.S. border. There are two distinct kinds of vegetation here — the temperate forest and the plant growth characteristic of the arid Okanagan region. At low altitudes, Douglas firs dominate the landscape, giving way to spruce and heather higher up. Deer, mountain goats and wild sheep sometimes venture out near the turquoise-coloured lakes.

Kootenay Country

Kokanee Glacier Provincial Park ★★ *(contact the BC Parks Kootenay District Area Office for maps; Nelson, ☎250-825-3500)* has about ten hiking trails of average difficulty, which require a total of about four hours of walking. The park, which looks out over two lakes (Kootenay and Slocan), is accessible from a number of different places.

 ## ACCOMMODATIONS

The Sunshine Coast

Gibsons

The **Maritimer Bed & Breakfast** *($80 bkfst incl.; pb, tv, children 12 and over, no smoking; 521 S. Fletcher Rd., ☎604-886-0664)*, run by Gerry and Noreen Tretick, overlooks the town and the marina. The charming scenery, friendly hosts and cozy atmosphere are sure to please. A private suite in the attic includes a sundeck. On the ground floor, there is a large room decorated with antique furniture and works of art by Noreen; a beautiful quilt graces one of the walls. Breakfast, served on the terrace that looks right out onto the bay, includes shrimp omelettes; this is the seashore, after all.

Powell River

Beacon Bed & Breakfast *($85-$125 bkfst incl.; pb, ᕕ, no smoking, ⊛, children 12 and over; 3750 Marine Ave., ☎604-485-5563, ⇝485-9450)*. Your hosts, Shirley and Roger Randall, will make you feel right at home. What's more, they will take great pleasure in telling you all about their part of the country. The Beacon faces west and looks out onto the sea, so you can enjoy the sunset while taking a bath, no less! The simply laid-out rooms each have fully equipped bathrooms. Breakfast includes a special treat: blueberry pancakes.

The **Beach Gardens Resort & Marina** *($99; pb, tv, tennis, interior ≈, △, pub, ℝ, ℙ, ℜ, marina, ✕; 7074 Westminster Ave., ☎604-485-6267 or 1-800-663-7070, ⇝485-2343)* All the rooms are on the water's edge and offer spectacular views of the coast. At the restaurant you can savour some of their excellent West Coast cuisine. An indoor pool and a fitness centre top off the list of facilities. Afterwards, you can go for a drink in the Canoe Room pub. The resort also has a liquor store.

The **Coast Town Centre Hotel** *($119; ℜ, ✕, pb, ℙ, ⊛, tv; 4660 Joyce Ave.; ☎604-485-3000 or 1-800-663-1144, ⇝485-3031)* is near Town Centre Mall, a large shopping centre in the heart of Powell River. The rooms are impeccable and spacious, and the hotel is equipped with a fitness centre. They also organize salmon-fishing excursions.

Lund

A relaxing atmosphere prevails at the century-old **Lund Hotel** *($77; pb, tv, ℜ, marina, at the end of Hwy 101, ☎483-3187)*, which opens onto the bay. The peaceful location and view of the boats coming and going more than compensate for the motel-style rooms.

Fraser River Loop

Harrison Hot Springs

At **Sasquatch Provincial Park** *($9.50 for four people; 177 wooded lots, beach, sb, playground, boat-launching ramp; cash only; Cultus Lake, ☎604-824-2300 or 796-3107)*, you choose your own campsite, and a park employee passes by to collect payment. Hidden in the mountains near Harrison Lake, this park has three campgrounds, which welcome nature lovers every year. According to a Coast Salish legend, the Sasquatch is half-man, half-beast and lives in the woods. To this day, some natives claim to have seen the creature around Harrison Lake.

Harrison Heritage House and Kottage *($50-$115 bkfst incl.; 2 rooms, pb, no smoking, one very large suite, pb and a small cottage, pb, K also available; 312 Lillooet Ave., ☎604-796-9552)*. Jo-Anne and Dennis Sandve will give you a warm welcome at their pretty house, located one street away from the beach and the public pool. Jo-Anne makes her own preserves. Certain rooms have whirlpools and fireplaces.

The **Harrison Hot Springs Hotel** *($119-$175; 306 rooms, ✸, ㄴ, pb, ≈, ℜ, Ѻ, dancing; 100 Esplanade; ☎604-796-2244 or 1-800-663-2266, ⋆796-3682)* offers the benefits of the lake and the mountain. It also has the advantage of being the only hotel with access to the mineral springs and as such it's a fun place where visitors get a sense of well-being. Outdoor hot-water pools, golf, food, dancing, children's playground and more.

The Thompson River as Far as Revelstoke

Ashcroft

Run by former clients, the **Sundance Guest Ranch** *($126 per person, low season Mar to Apr and Oct except on holidays; $148 per person, high season; fb, horseback riding twice a day (cowboy boots required, rentals available), ≈, tennis, tv; Highland Valley Rd., P.O. Box 489, V0K 1A0, ☎250-453-2422)* will take you back to a bygone era when cowboys roamed freely on horseback across as yet unexplored regions. The cost covers a stay of at least one day. Guests have access to a living room where they can bring their drinks; there is a separate living room just for children.

Kamloops

Sun Peaks Resort *($80-$169; ℜ; 45 min NE of Kamloops, 3150 Creekside Way, Ste. 50, Sun Peaks, B.C., V0E 1Z1, ☎1-800-807-3257, ⋆250-578-7843 at the top of the mountain)* is open all year and provides all the comforts. In the winter you can ski with Olympic champion Nancy Greene, but there are also a number of other activities, like swimming in the outdoor heated pool, snowmobile excursions, or the Christmas torch run. Families are welcome and young children can stay at the hotel and ski for free. There are plenty of summer activities, including golf and mountain biking. The complex also has a variety of dining establishments.

Located right near the TransCanada Highway on the way into town, the **Best Western Kamloops Towne Lodge** *($133; 122 rooms, ≈,*

®, Ѻ, ◉, ℜ, ㄴ; 1250 Rogers Way, ☎250-828-6660 or in western North America 1-800-665-6674, ⋆828-6698)* is a very comfortable, classic-style hotel that offers some splendid views of Kamloops and the Thompson River. You can also enjoy the scenery from one of the nearby motels, that vary only in price.

Revelstoke

The **Piano Keep Bed & Breakfast** *($75-$95 bkfst incl.; 3 rooms, no smoking, pb, ≈; 815 MacKenzie Ave., ☎/⋆250-837-2120)* is an imposing Edwardian house set in the midst of a garden. Host Vern Enyedy welcomes his guests in a charming setting featuring pianos from different eras. Both a collector and a music lover, Vern will demonstrate his musical skill.

The **Best Western Wayside Inn** *($109; 88 rooms, ≡, ✸, ㄴ, tv, ≈, ®, Ѻ, ℜ; 1901 Laforme Blvd., ☎250-837-6161, in B.C. and Alberta 1-800-663-5307, or 1-800-528-1234, ⋆837-5460)*, on the north side of the TransCanada, is not only close to everything, but offers the added attraction of a pastoral setting with views of Revelstoke and the Columbia River.

Okanagan-Similkameen

Manning Provincial Park *(four campgrounds and some wilderness camping sites; sb; tourist information: mid-Jun to late Sep, every day 8:30am to 4:30pm; Sep to mid-Jun, Mon to Fri 8:30am to 4pm; ☎250-840-8836)* is on the border between the western part of the province and the Okanagan-Similkameen region. Located 225 kilometres from Vancouver, this park attracts thousands of Vancouverites who come here to practise many sports, especially hiking and mountain-biking, as well as cross-country skiing in winter. In summer, you can drive up to the Cascade lookout observation point.

Cathedral Provincial Park

Cathedral Lakes Lodge *($96-$170; everything included; 10 rooms and 6 small cottages, sb, canoe and rowboat, fireplace, bar, transportation to and from the base of the mountain, no smoking; Jun to mid-Oct, rates* vary depending on the season, Jul and Aug high season; reservations required; for reservations ☎1-888-255-4453, administration ☎250-226-7560, ⌐226-7528, S4C8 Slocan Park, B.C., VOG 2EO). The road to the top of the mountain is only open to the lodge's all-terrain vehicle, so you have to leave your car on Ashnola River Road, in the lodge's base camp. If you go by foot, it will take you more than six hours to reach the lodge. Do not forget to reserve your seat in the vehicle. Turn left 4.8 kilometres west of Keremeos, cross the covered bridge and drive along Ashnola River Road for 20.8 kilometres. If you plan on taking the bus, call the lodge ahead of time to make arrangements for someone to pick you up. All this might seem complicated, but once you reach the top, you're sure to be enchanted by mountain goats, marmots and flowers, not to mention glaciers stretching as far as the eye can see.

Penticton

Olde Osprey Inn, Bed & Breakfast *($65-$70 bkfst incl.; 3 rooms, sb, ☒, no smoking; Sheep Creek Rd., ☎/⌐250-497-7134).* This magnificent log house was built by George Mullen, who astutely chose a site on a mountainside with an unimpeded view of Yellow Lake and the surrounding area. Joy Whitley, for her part, makes sure your stay is as comfortable as possible. She is a painter, and some of her work is on display here. Joy's daughter, furthermore, is a musician. This amiable family knows how to entertain their guests. The occasional osprey flies by, at which point everything comes to a halt as all eyes turn skyward.

Osoyoos

At the **Lake Osoyoos Guest House** *($95 bkfst incl.; 3 rooms, pb, garden and waterfront, K, pedalboat, cash only; 5809 Oleander Dr., ☎250-495-3297 or 1-800-671-8711, ⌐495-5310),* Sofia Grasso cooks up breakfast in her huge kitchen while guests sip freshly squeezed juice at the edge of Osoyoos Lake. Guests have use of a pedalboat to enjoy the lake and the changing colours of the valley as the day wears on.

Summerland

The **Illahie Beach** *($16-$20; 170 campsites, free showers, laundry facilities, pay phone, convenience store, beach; north of Penticton on Highway 97, Summerland, ☎494-0800)* campground welcomes vacationers from April to October. The beaches and views of the Okanagan Valley make for a heavenly setting.

Kootenay Country

Ainsworth Hot Springs

The **Ainsworth Hot Springs Resort** *($99; 43 rooms, ⅙, no smoking, ≈, tv, ℜ, ◯ in the caves, naturally warm water and ice-cold ≈; Hwy 31, ☎250-229-4212 or 1-800-668-1171, ⌐229-5600)* is part of the facilities surrounding the caves. Guests have free access to the caves, and can obtain passes for friends.

Nelson

The **Heritage Inn** *($64 bkfst incl.; 41 rooms, tv, ℜ, pub, ⅙; 422 Vernon St., ☎250-352-5331, ⌐352-5214)* was established in 1898, when the Hume brothers decided to build a grand hotel. Over the years, the building has been modified with each new owner. In 1980, major renovations breathed new life into the old place. The library is worth visiting; with its woodwork and fireplace, it has all the elements necessary to create a pleasant atmosphere. The walls of the rooms and corridors are covered with photographs capturing the highlights of Nelson's history.

Inn the Garden Bed & Breakfast *($70-$150 bkfst incl.; 6 rooms, sb or pb, adults only, no smoking, ℗, also a 3-bedroom cottage; 408 Victoria St., ☎250-352-3226, ⌐352-3284).* This charming Victorian house, renovated by owners Lynda Stevens and Jerry Van Veen, lies steps away from the main street. The couple's warm welcome will make your stay in Nelson that much more pleasant. Ask them to tell you about the town's architectural heritage: it is one of their passions.

Rossland

An inviting house owned by Tauna and Greg Butler, the **Ram's Head Inn** *($65-$85 bkfst incl.; 12 rooms, pb, ®, ◠, no smoking; at the foot of the slopes on Red Mountain Rd., Box 636, Rossland, V0G 1Y0, ☎250-362-9577, ⋯362-5681)* feels like a home away from home. The fireplace, woodwork, simple decor and pleasant smells wafting out of the kitchen create a pleasant, informal atmosphere.

 RESTAURANTS

The Sunshine Coast

Powell River

The dining room of the **Beach Gardens Resort Hotel** *($$-$$$; 7074 Westminster Ave., ☎604-485-6267 or 1-800-663-7070)* looks out onto the Malaspina Strait The menu lists divine seafood dishes flavoured with Okanagan wines.

The Thompson River as Far as Revelstoke

Kamloops

Internet Café *($; 462 Victoria, ☎828-7889)*, whose motto is "the world is at your fingertips invites you to check your e-mail, play the lottery or surf the Net while enjoying a salad or hamburger. The atmosphere is friendly and, if needed, the staff will help you on the computer.

Located in Riverside Park, the **Grass Roots Tea House** *($$; May to Sep, lunch 11:30am to 2:30pm, tea 2pm to 4pm, dinner 6:30pm (one service, reserve by 2pm); reservations required during winter; 262 Lorne St., ☎250-374-9890)* is a charming place surrounded by trees, where you can enjoy a cup of ginseng tea. Reservations are required for dinner, and the menu varies depending on what day of the week it is.

Déjà Vu *($$$; Tue to Sat 5pm to 10pm; 172 Battle St., ☎374-3227)* serves West Coast and French cuisine featuring an imaginative blend of fruit and seafood.

Revelstoke

At the **Frontier Restaurant** *($; every day 5am to midnight; right near the tourist office, at the intersection of the TransCanada Hwy and the 23, ☎250-837-5119)*, you chow down a big breakfast in a typically western setting.

The **Black Forest** *($$-$$$; 5 min west of Revelstoke, on the TransCanada, ☎250-837-3495)* is a Bavarian-style restaurant, which serves Canadian and European cuisine. Top billing on the menu goes to cheese and fish. The setting and view of Mount Albert are enchanting.

Okanagan-Similkameen

Penticton

The **Hog's Breath Coffee Co.** *($; every day; 202 Main St., ☎250-493-7800)* is the perfect place to start off your day with a good cup of coffee, and even more importantly, some peach muffins (in season): you'll love them! If you're looking for somewhere to go outdoors, the owner, Mike Barrett, will gladly offer some suggestions.

Seafood fans will find their favourite foods at **Salty's Beach House** *($-$$; 1000 Lakeshore Dr., ☎250-493-5001)*. Make sure to come here at lunchtime so you can enjoy the view of Okanagan Lake from the terrace. The pirate ship decor gives the place a festive atmosphere.

Theo's Restaurant *($$-$$$; 687 Main St., ☎250-492-4019)*. Fine Greek cuisine and a relaxed atmosphere make for a pleasant meal at this extremely popular spot.

Granny Bogners Restaurant *($$$; 302 Eckhardt Ave. W., ☎250-493-2711)*. This magnificent Tudor house was built in 1912 for a local doctor. In 1976, Hans and Angela Strobel converted it into a restaurant, where they serve fine French cuisine made with local produce.

Kelowna

Joey Tomato's Kitchen *($-$$; every day; 300-2475 Hwy 97 North, at the intersection of Hwy 33, ☎250-860-8999)* is located near a large boulevard in a neighbourhood of shopping malls. The people who run this place have successfully created a pleasant atmosphere. The terrace, with its plants, parasols and little Italian car will grab your attention. The dining room is also extremely attractive — a large space livened up by cans of food and bottles of oil, making you feel as if you're, well, in Joey's kitchen. And the pasta! Make sure to try the fettucine with salmon and tomatoes: it's a real treat.

Kootenay Country

Nelson

The successful **El Zocalo Mexican Cafe** *($$; 802 Baker St., ☎250-352-7223)* occupies a Mexican-style building and features live Mexican music. Guests enjoy delicious, traditional Mexican cuisine in a fiesta-like atmosphere.

The **All Seasons Cafe** *($$-$$$; every day, lunch 11:30am to 2:30pm, dinner 5pm to 10pm, Sun brunch 10am to 3pm, closed for lunch in winter; 620 Herridge Lane, behind Baker St., ☎250-352-0101)* is not to be missed. It lies hidden beneath the trees, so its terrace is bathed in shade. The soups mightsurprise you a bit — apple and broccoli (in season) is one example. The menu is determined by the season and what's available in the area, with lots of space accorded to the fine wines of British Columbia. The friendly, efficient service, elegant decor and quality cuisine make for an altogether satisfying meal. The walls are adorned with works of art.

Rossland

Elmer's Corner Café *($, corner of Elmer and Washington Sts.)* is a small restaurant that serves thin-crust pizza. Vegetarian and meat menus top the list of suggestions that this establishment has to offer including an outdoor terrasse in summer. The breads, baguettes and Montreal-style bagels come straight from the oven here.

BRITISH COLUMBIA

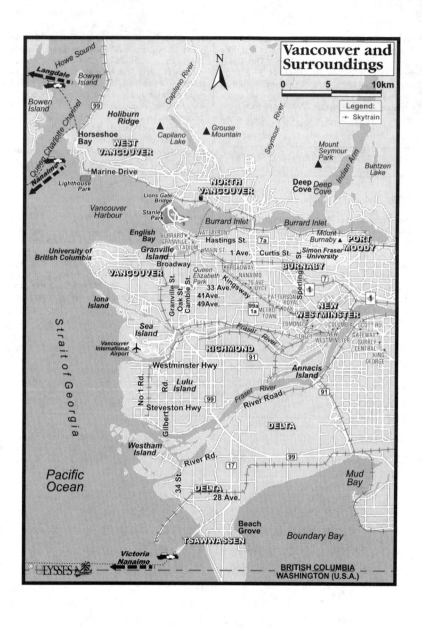

Vancouver and Surroundings

0 5 10km

Legend:
Skytrain

Howe Sound

Langdale

Bowyer Island

Bowen Island

99

Holiburn Ridge

Queen Charlotte Channel

Nanaimo

Horseshoe Bay

WEST VANCOUVER

Marine Drive

Lighthouse Park

Vancouver Harbour

Capilano River

Capilano Lake

Grouse Mountain

N

Seymour River

Mount Seymour Park

Deep Cove   Deep Cove

Indian Arm

Buntzen Lake

NORTH VANCOUVER

Lions Gate Bridge

Stanley Park

Burrard Inlet

WATERFRONT

BURRARD

GRANVILLE

Hastings St.

MAIN ST.

1 Ave.

Curtis St.

7a

Burrard Inlet

Mount Burnaby ▲

PORT MOODY

Simon Fraser University

English Bay

University of British Columbia

STADIUM

Granville Island

Broadway

VANCOUVER

Granville St.

Oak St.

Cambie St.

Queen Elizabeth Park

BROADWAY

NANAIMO

Kingsway

33 Ave.

41Ave.

49Ave.

20 AVE.

JOYCE

99a

1a

METRO-TOWN

OAK

PATTERSON

ROYAL

EDMONDS

COLUMBIA STREET

BURNABY

Sperling St.

1

7

1

NEW WESTMINSTER

NEW WESTMINSTER

SCOTT RD.

GATEWAY

SURREY CENTRAL

KING GEORGE

Iona Island

Sea Island

Vancouver International Airport

Fraser River

RICHMOND

91

Westminster Hwy

DELTA

No.1 Rd.

Gilbert Rd.

Lulu Island

99

Steveston Hwy

Fraser River

River Road

Annacis Island

91

Westham Island

River Rd.

17

34 St.

DELTA

28 Ave.

99

Mud Bay

Pacific Ocean

S t r a i t   o f   G e o r g i a

Beach Grove

TSAWWASSEN

Boundary Bay

Victoria Nanaimo

ⓒ ULYSSES

BRITISH COLUMBIA
WASHINGTON (U.S.A.)

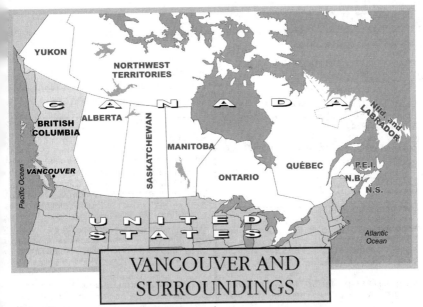

VANCOUVER AND SURROUNDINGS

ancouver ★★★ is truly a new city, one framed by the mighty elements of sea and mountains. As part of one of the most isolated reaches on the planet for many years, the city has, over the last 100 years, developed close ties with the nations of the largest ocean on Earth, and is fast becoming the multicultural metropolis of the Pacific Rim. Although its history is tied to the development of British Columbia's natural resources, most residents were lured here by the magnificent setting and the climate, which is remarkably mild in a country known for its bitter winters and stifling summers. Vancouver, where Asia meets America, is a city well worth discovering.

 FINDING YOUR WAY AROUND

By Car

Vancouver

Vancouver is accessible by the **TransCanada Highway 1**, which runs east-west. This national highway links all of the major Canadian cities. It has no tolls and passes through some spectacular scenery. Coming from Alberta, you will pass through the Rocky Mountains, desert regions and a breathtaking canyon. From

Calgary, Alberta to Vancouver, British-Columbia, it is around 975 kilometres.

Whistler

By **Highway 99 North**. From Vancouver: 120 km, 2 hours 15 min; from Kamloops: 400 km, 5 hours 30 min; from Seattle, WA: 338 km, 5 hours.

By Plane

Vancouver International Airport Vancouver International Airport (☎604-276-6101) is served by flights from across Canada, the United States, Europe and Asia. It takes about 30 minutes to get downtown by car or bus.

Take note: even if you have already paid various taxes included in the purchase price of your ticket, Vancouver International Airport charges every passenger an **Airport Improvement Fee** (AIF). The fee is $5 for flights within B.C. and to the Yukon, $10 for flights elsewhere in North America, and $15 for overseas flights; credit cards are accepted, and most in-transit passengers are exempted.

By Bus

Vancouver

Greyhound Lines of Canada: Pacific Central Station, 1150 Station St., ☎482-8747 or 1-800-661-8747.

Maverick Coach Lines *(☎604-662-8051)* offers services to Nanaimo.

By Train

Vancouver

Pacific Central Station *(Via Rail Canada, 1150 Station St., ☎1-800-561-8630)*.

BC Rail *(1311 W. 1st St., North Vancouver, ☎984-5246)* trains travel the northern west coast.

VIARail's Edmonton-Vancouver corridor is a spectacular journey through the Rocky Mountains and its rivers and valleys. Those in a hurry should abstain, since the trip takes about 24 hours and better suits tourist than business travellers. It costs less than $200 one way; call VIA for prices during the different seasons.

During the summer, the **Great Canadian Railtour Company Ltd.** offers **Rocky Mountain Railtours** *($700 per person, $645 per person double occupancy; ☎606-7200 or 1-800-665-7245, ☎606-7520)* between Calgary and Vancouver.

Whistler

With **BC Rail** *(Vancouver, ☎604-984-5246 or 1-800-663-8238)* from North Vancouver.

By Ferry

British Columbia Ferry Corporation (BC Ferries) *(☎1-888-BCFERRY, 250-386-3431 or 669-1211)*. Two ferry ports serve the greater Vancouver area for travellers coming from other regions in the province.

The Gulf Islands

BC Ferry *(☎888-223-3779)*. Reservations necessary in the summertime.

Public Transport

Vancouver

BC Transit bus route maps are available from the Vancouver Travel InfoCentre *(200 Burrard St., ☎683-2000)* or from the BC Transit offices in Surrey *(13401 108th Ave., 5th floor, Surrey, B.C., ☎1-800-903-4731 or 540-3450)*.

Tickets and passes are available for **BC Transit**, from the coin-operated machines at some stops, in some convenience stores or by calling ☎261-5100 or 521-0400.

BC Transit also includes a rail transit system and a marine bus. The **Skytrain** runs east from the downtown area to Burnaby, New Westminster and Surrey. These automatic trains run from 5am to 1am all week, except Sundays when they start at 9am. The **Seabus** shuttles frequently between Burrard Inlet and North Vancouver.

 PRACTICAL INFORMATION

Area Code: 604 except for the Gulf Islands 250.

Tourist Information Offices

Vancouver

The Tourism **Vancouver Tourist Info Centre** *(May to Sep, every day 8am to 6pm; Sep to May, Mon to Fri 8:20am to 5pm, Sat 9am to 5pm; Plaza Level, Waterfront Centre, 200 Burrard St., V6C 3L6, ☎683-2000)* provides brochures and information on sights and accommodations for the city as well as for the province.

Whistler

Whistler Travel InfoCentre: 2097 Lake Placid Road, ☎604-932-5528.

The Gulf Islands

Salt Spring Island Travel InfoCentre: year-round; 121 Lower Ganges Road, P.O. Box 111, Ganges, V8K 2T1, ☎537-5252.

Galiano Island Travel InfoCentre: seasonal; Sturdies Bay, P.O. Box 73, Galiano, V0N 1P0, ☎539-2233.

Emergencies

Vancouver

Police: ☎911

Vancouver Hospital: 855 West 12th Avenue, ☎875-4111
Saint Paul Hospital: 1081 Burrard Street, ☎682-2344

The Gulf Islands

Doctors: Mayne Island, ☎539-2312; Galiano Island, ☎539-9900.

 EXPLORING

Vancouver ★★★

Gastown ★

Just a few steps from downtown, Gastown is best discovered on foot. The area dates back to 1867, when John Deighton, known as Gassy Jack, opened a saloon for the employees of a neighbouring sawmill. Gastown was destroyed by fire in 1886. However, this catastrophe did not deter the city's pioneers, who rebuilt from the ashes and started anew the development of their city, which was incorporated several months later.

Architectural Institute of British Columbia ★ *(131 Water St., ste. 103; schedule and programme, ☎683-8588)*, offers guided tours of Vancouver during the summertime.

The intersection of Water and Carrall Streets is one of the liveliest parts of Gastown. Long **Byrnes Block** *(2 Water St.)*, on the southwest corner, was one of the first buildings to be

erected after the terrible fire of 1886. It was built on the site of Gassy Jack's saloon; a statue of the celebrated barkeep graces tiny **Maple Tree Square.** The thick cornice on the brick building is typical of commercial buildings of the Victorian era. Rising in front is the former **Hotel Europe** *(4 Powell St.)*, a triangular building erected in 1908 by a Canadian hotel-keeper of Italian descent.

Lonsdale Block (5) *(8-28 W. Cordova St.)*, built in 1889, is one of the most remarkable buildings on this street, which is undergoing a beautiful renaissance with the recent opening of several shops and cafés.

Chinatown and East Vancouver ★★

It is well worth stopping in at the **Dr. Sun Yat-Sen Garden ★** *(every day 10am to 7:30pm; 578 Carrall St., ☎689-7133)*, behind the traditional portal of the **Chinese Cultural Centre** at 50 East Pender Street. Built in 1986 by Chinese artists from Suzhou, this garden is the only example outside Asia of landscape architecture from the Ming Dynasty (1368-1644). The 1.2-hectare green space is surrounded by high walls which create a virtual oasis of peace in the middle of bustling Chinatown. It is worth noting that Dr. Sun Yat-Sen (1866-1925), considered the father of modern China, visited Vancouver in 1911 in order to raise money for his newly founded Kuomintang ("People's Party").

The next part of town you'll pass through is known as **Little Italy**, but is also home to Vancouverites of Portuguese, Spanish, Jamaican and South American descent. In the early 20th century, the Commercial Drive area became the city's first suburb, and middle-class residents built small, single-family homes with wooden siding here. The first Chinese and Slavic immigrants moved into the neighbourhood during World War I, and another wave of immigrants, chiefly Italian, arrived at the end of World War II.

Downtown ★★

The **Sinclair Centre ★** *(701 W. Hastings St.)* is a group of government offices. It occupies a former post office, and its annexes are connected to one another by covered passageways lined with shops. The main building, dating from 1909, is considered to be

Sinclair Centre

one of the finest examples of the neo-baroque style in Canada.

The **Marine Building** ★★ *(355 Burrard St.)*, which faces straight down West Hastings Street, is a fine example of the Art Deco style, characterized by vertical lines, staggered recesses, geometric ornamentation and the absence of a cornice at the top of the structure. Erected in 1929, the building lives up to its name, in part because it is lavishly decorated with nautical motifs, and also because its occupants are ship-owners and shipping companies. Its façade features terra cotta panels depicting the history of shipping and the discovery of the Pacific coast. The interior decor is even more inventive, however. The lights in the lobby are shaped like the prows of ships, and there is a stained glass window showing the sun setting over the ocean. The elevators will take you up to the mezzanine, which offers an interesting general view of the building.

Take Burrard Street toward the water to reach **Canada Place** ★★ *(999 Canada Place)*, which occupies one of the piers along the harbour and looks like a giant sailboat ready to set out across the waves. This multi-purpose complex, which served as the Canadian pavilion at Expo '86, is home to the city's Convention Centre, the harbour station where ocean liners dock, the luxurious Pan Pacific Hotel and an Imax theatre. Take a walk on the "deck" and drink in the magnificent panoramic view of Burrard Inlet, the port and the snow-capped mountains.

The imposing **Hotel Vancouver** ★ *(900 W. Georgia St.)*, a veritable monument to the Canadian railway companies that built it between 1928 and 1939, stands at the corner of West Georgia Street. For many years, its high copper roof served as the principal symbol of Vancouver abroad. Like all major Canadian cities, Vancouver had to have a château-style hotel. Make sure to take a look at the gargoyles near the top and the bas-reliefs at the entrance,

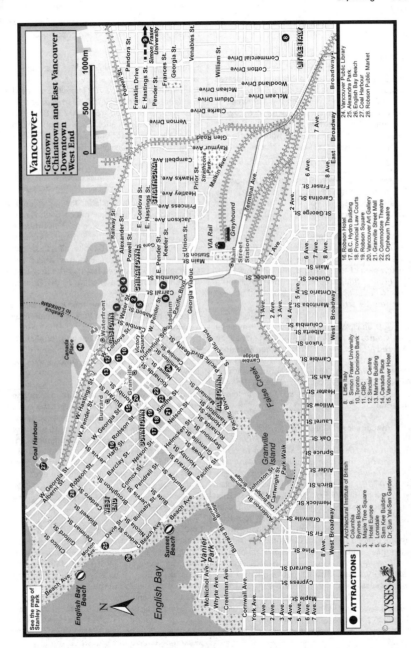

Vancouver
- Gastown
- Chinatown and East Vancouver
- Downtown
- West End

0 500 1000m

See the map of Stanley Park

BRITISH COLUMBIA

● **ATTRACTIONS**

1. Architectural Institute of British Columbia
2. Byrnes Block
3. Maple Tree Square
4. Hotel Europe
5. Lonsdale
6. Sam Kee Building
7. Dr. Sun Yat-Sen Garden

8. Little Italy
9. Simon Fraser University
10. Toronto Dominion Bank
11. CIBC
12. Sinclair Centre
13. Marine Building
14. Canada Place
15. Vancouver Hotel

16. Robson Hotel
17. B.C. Hydro Building
18. Provincial Law Courts
19. Robson Square
20. Vancouver Art Gallery
21. Granville Street Mall
22. Commodore Theatre
23. Orpheum Theatre

24. Vancouver Public Library
25. Alexandra Park
26. English Bay Beach
27. Coal Harbour
28. Robson Public Market

© ULYSSES

which depict an ocean liner and a moving locomotive.

Turn left on Thurlow Street and left again on **Robson Street** ★, which is lined with fashionable boutiques, elaborately decorated restaurants and West Coast-style cafés. People sit at tables outside, enjoying the fine weather and watching the motley crowds stroll by. In the mid-20th century, a small German community settled around Robson Street, dubbing it Robsonstrasse, a nickname it bears to this day.

The former **B.C. Hydro Building** ★ *(970 Burrard St.)*, at the corner of Nelson and Burrard, was once the head office of the province's hydroelectric company. In 1993, it was converted into a 242-unit co-op and renamed The Electra. Designed in 1955 by local architects Thompson, Berwick and Pratt, it is considered to be one of the most sophisticated skyscrapers of that era in all of North America. The ground floor is adorned with a mural and a mosaic in shades of grey, blue and green, executed by artist B.C. Binning.

Turn left on Howe Street to view the **Provincial Law Courts** ★ *(800 Smithe St.)*, designed by talented Vancouver architect Arthur Erickson. The vast interior space, accented with glass and steal, is worth a visit. The courthouse and **Robson Square** *(on the 800 block of Robson St.)*, by the same architect, form a lovely ensemble.

The **Vancouver Art Gallery** ★ *($7.50; May 3 to Oct 9, Mon to Wed 10am to 6pm, Thu 10am to 9pm, Fri 10am to 6pm, Sat 10am to 5pm, Sun and holidays noon to 5pm, closed Mon and Tue during winter; 750 Hornby St., ☎662-4700)*, located north of Robson Square, occupies the former Provincial Law Courts. This big, neoclassical-style building was erected in 1908 according to a design by British architect Francis Mawson Rattenbury, whose other credits include the British Columbia Legislative Assembly and the Empress Hotel, both located in Victoria, on Vancouver Island. Later, Rattenbury returned to his native country and was assassinated by his wife's lover. The museum's collection includes a number of paintings by Emily Carr (1871-1945), a major Canadian painter whose primary subjects were the native peoples and landscapes of the West Coast.

Turn right on West Georgia Street, then right again on the **Granville Street Mall** ★, the street of cinemas, theatres, nightclubs and retail stores. Its busy sidewalks are hopping 24 hours a day.

Stroll along the Granville Street Mall heading south towards Theatre Row. You'll pass the **Commodore Theatre** *(870 Granville St.)* and the **Orpheum Theatre** ★ *(884 Granville St., free tour upon reservation ☎665-3072)*. Behind the latter's narrow façade, barely eight metres wide, a long corridor opens onto a 2,800-seat Spanish-style Renaissance Revival theatre.

West End ★

Excluding Vancouver Island, farther west, the West End is the final destination of that quest for a better life that thousands of city-dwellers from Eastern Canada have been embarking upon for generations. Despite all its concrete skyscrapers, the West End has a laid-back atmosphere, influenced both by the immensity of the Pacific and the wisdom of the Orient.

Head west on Davie Street, then left on Bidwell Street to reach **Alexandra Park** ★, which forms a point south of Burnaby Street. This luxuriant park also offers a splendid view of **English Bay Beach** ★★ *(along the shore between Chilco and Bidwell Sts.)*, whose fine sands are crowded during the summer.

Head east on Robson Street, to the **Robson Public Market** ★ *(1610 Robson, at the corner of Cardero)*, a bustling indoor market with a long glass roof. You'll find everything here from live crabs and fresh pasta to local handicrafts. You can also eat here, as dishes from all over the world are served on the top floor. A pleasure for both the palate and the eyes!

Stanley Park ★★★

Lord Stanley, the same person for whom ice hockey's Stanley Cup was named, founded Stanley Park on a romantic impulse back in the 19th century, when he was Canada's Governor General (1888-1893). Stanley Park lies on an elevated peninsula stretching into the Georgia Strait, and encompasses 405 hectares of flowering gardens, dense woodlands and lookouts offering views of the sea and the mountains. Obviously Vancouver's many skyscrapers have not prevented the city from maintaining close ties with the nearby wilderness. Some species are held in captivity,

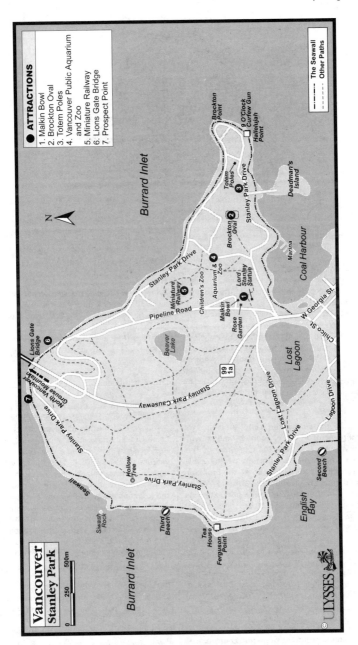

BRITISH COLUMBIA

Science World

but many others roam free — sometimes even venturing into the West End.

A ten-kilometre waterfront promenade known as the **Seawall** runs around the park, enabling pedestrians to soak in every bit of the stunning scenery here. The **Stanley Park Scenic Drive** is the equivalent of the Seawall for motorists. The best way to explore Stanley Park, however, is by bicycle. You can rent one from Stanely Park Rentals at the corner of West Georgia and Denman (☎688-5141) (see p 566). Another way to discover some of the park's hidden treasures is to walk along one of the many footpaths crisscrossing the territory. There are numerous rest areas along the way.

You'll be greeted by the sight of scores of gleaming yachts in the Vancouver marina, with the downtown skyline in the background. This is the most developed portion of the park, where you'll find the **Malkin Bowl**, the **Brockton Oval** and most importantly, the **Totem Poles** ★, reminders of the sizeable native population on the peninsula barely 150 years ago. The **9 O'Clock Gun** goes off every day at 9pm on Brockton Point (it is best not to be too close when it does). This shot used to alert fishermen that it was time to turn in.

On the left is the entrance to the renowned **Vancouver Public Aquarium and Zoo** ★★★ (*$12; Jul and Aug, every day 9:30am to 7pm; Sep to Jun, every day 10am to 5:30pm; ☎682-1118*), which has the undeniable advantage of being located near the ocean. It displays representatives of marine animal life of the West Coast and the Pacific as a whole, including magnificent killer whales, belugas, dolphins, seals and exotic fish. The zoo at the

back is home to sea lions and polar bears, among other creatures. The nearby **Miniature Railway** is a real hit with kids.

Head back to the Seawall under **Lions Gate Bridge** ★★, an elegant suspension bridge built in 1938. It spans the First Narrows, linking the affluent suburb of West Vancouver to the centre of town. **Prospect Point** ★★★, to the west, offers a general view of the bridge, whose steel pillars stand 135 metres high.

Other attractions

Head over to **Science World** ★ (*$10.50 or $13.50 with movie; 1455 Quebec St., ☎443-7440*), the big silver ball at the end of False Creek. Architect Bruno Freschi designed this 14-story building as a welcome centre for visitors to Expo '86. It was the only pavilion built to remain in place after the big event. The sphere representing the Earth has supplanted the tower as the quintessential symbol of these fairs since Expo '67 in Montreal. Vancouver's sphere contains an Omnimax theatre, which presents films on a giant, dome-shaped screen. The rest of the building is now occupied by a museum that explores the secrets of science from all different angles.

During the summer of 1986, the vast stretch of unused land along the north shore of False Creek was occupied by dozens of showy pavilions with visitors crowding around them. Visible on the other side of an access road, **GM Place** (*Pacific Blvd. at the corner of Abbott, ☎899-7400*) is a 20,000-seat amphitheatre which was completed in 1995 and now hosts the home games of the local hockey and basketball teams, the Vancouver Canucks and Grizzlies respectively. Its big brother, **BC Place Stadium** *(777 Pacific Blvd. N., ☎669-2300, 661-7373 or 661-2122, ⬝661-3412)* stands to the south. Its 60,000 seats are highly coveted by fans of Canadian football, who come here to cheer on the B.C. Lions. Big trade fairs and rock concerts are also held in the stadium.

Follow Pacific Boulevard under Granville Bridge, then turn left on Hornby Street and right on Beach Avenue. The False Creek ferry docks are nearby, catch a ferry for **Granville Island and its public market** ★★. You'll notice the vaguely Art Deco pillars of the Burrard Street Bridge (1930). In 1977, this artificial island, created in 1914 and once used for industrial purposes, saw its warehouses and factories transformed into a major recreational and commercial centre. The area has since come to life thanks to a revitalization project. A public market, many shops and all sorts of restaurants, plus theatres and artists' studios, are all part of Granville Island.

Van Dusen Botanical Gardens ★★ *(summer $5.50, winter $2.75; every day, summer 10am to nightfall, call for exact schedule; Apr and Sep 10am to 6pm; Oct to Mar 10am to 4pm; free guided tours every day, 1pm, 2pm and 3pm; 5251 Oak St., ☎878-9274)*. Since Vancouver is so blessed by Mother Nature, a number of lovely gardens have been planted in the area, including this one, which boasts plant species from all over the world. When the rhododendrons are in bloom (late May), the garden deserves another star. At the far end is a housing co-op that blends in so perfectly with the greenery that it looks like a gigantic ornamental sculpture (McCarter, Nairne and Associates, 1976).

Farther east on 33rd Avenue is another magnificent green space, **Queen Elizabeth Park** ★★ *(corner of 33rd Ave. and Cambie St.)*, laid out around the **Bloedel Floral Conservatory** *($3.25; Apr to Sep, Mon to Fri 9am to 8pm, Sat and Sun 10am to 9pm; Oct to Mar, every day 10am to 5pm; at the top of Queen Elizabeth Park, ☎257-8570)*. The latter, shaped like an overturned glass saucer, houses exotic plants and birds. The Bloedel company, which sponsored the conservatory, is the principal lumber company in British Columbia. This park's rhododendron bushes also merit a visit in springtime. Finally, the outdoor gardens offer spectacular views of the city, English Bay and the surrounding mountains.

The **Vanier Park** is home to three museums. The **Vancouver Museum** ★★ *($5; Jul and Aug, every day 10am to 5pm; Sep to June closed Mon; 1100 Chestnut St., in Vanier Park, ☎736-4431)* forms its centrepiece. This museum, whose dome resembles the head-dress worn by Coast Salish Indians, presents exhibitions on the history of the different peoples who have inhabited the region. At the same spot is the **Pacific Space Centre** *($6.50; presentations Tue to Sun 2:30pm and 8pm, extra shows Sat and Sun 1pm and 4pm; Ms. Dawn Charles, ☎738-7827)*, which houses the H.R. MacMillan Planetarium and relates the creation of our universe. It has a telescope through which you can admire the stars. The **Maritime Museum** *($6; May to Oct, every day 10am to 5pm; Nov to Apr closed Mon; 1905 Ogden Ave., ☎257-8300)* completes the trio of institutions in Vanier Park. Being a major seaport, it is only natural that Vancouver should have its own maritime museum. The key attraction is the **Saint-Roch**, the first boat to circle North America by navigating the Panamá Canal and the Northwest Passage.

The **University of British Columbia** ★, or UBC, was created by the provincial government in 1908, but it was not until 1925 that the campus opened its doors on this lovely site on Point Grey. An architectural contest had been organized for the site layout, but the First World War halted construction work, and it took a student demonstration denouncing government inaction in this matter to get the buildings completed. Only the library and the science building were executed according to the original plans. **Set Foot for UBC** *(May to Aug, free tours organized by students, ☎822-TOUR)*.

To this day, the UBC campus is constantly expanding, so don't be surprised by its somewhat heterogeneous appearance. There are a few gems however, including the **Museum of Anthropology** ★★★ *($6, free admission Tue 5pm to 9pm; in the summer, every day 10am to 5pm, in the winter closed Mon and on Dec 25 and 26; 6393 NW Marine Dr.; from downtown, take bus #4 UBC or bus #10 UBC; ☎822-3825)* which is not to be missed both for the quality of native artwork displayed here, including totem poles, and for the architecture of Arthur Erickson. Big concrete beams and columns imitate the shapes of traditional native houses, beneath which have been erected immense totem poles gathered from former native villages along the coast and on the islands. Wooden sculptures

BRITISH COLUMBIA

and various works of art form part of the permanent exhibition.

Whistler ★★★

Whistler has grown and become an important location not only for people who live there on a permanent basis, but also for the development of tourism. Besides the big hotels, more and more condominiums are being built and stores have multiplied. To allow visitors to get around more easily, a shuttle service around the village has been instituted. Of course, the shops are mostly geared towards tourists but many are also for residents; there are shopping centres and large grocery stores. This encourages people to buy condos as secondary residences and benefits Whistler's economy.

Whistler attracts skiers, golfers, hikers, sailors and snowboarders from all over the world. An impressive hotel complex graces the little village at the foot of Blackcomb and Whistler Mountains. Other amenities at this internationally renowned resort include restaurants, shops, sports facilities and a convention centre. Whistler is popular in summer and winter alike, and each season offers its own assortment of activities.

The Gulf Islands

Each of these islands is a different place to commune with nature and enjoy a little seclusion, far from traffic jams. Time is measured here according to the arrival and departure of the ferries. A convivial atmosphere prevails on these little havens of peace.

Salt Spring Island

Salt Spring is the most touristy of the Gulf Islands, with many art galleries, restaurants and boutiques. During the summer, artists and artisans flood the streets, exhibiting their work. Throughout the island, "Studio" signs line the streets, indicating that is it possible to visit artists in their studios. Salt Spring Island boasts over 75 bed and breakfasts, hotels and log cabins by the water. For further details, contact the **Salt Spring Island Visitor Information Centre** (☎250-537-5252).

Mayne Island

Unlike Salt Spring, Mayne does nothing to court tourists. Roadsigns are virtually non-existent. It is therefore recommended that you study the only public road map, set up near the harbour. Only a few remaining historic buildings testify to the island's past role as a prison; then it was nicknamed Little Hell. Relics confirm the island was once a colonial outpost with old trading posts and shops; the old **Mayne Inn Hotel** (☎250-539-3122), with its period architecture, remains intact. For provisions and camping or hiking gear, **Miners Trading Post** (☎250-539-2214), in the village of **Fernhill**, is a good bet. You can purchase good organic fruits and vegetables at the **Mayne Open Market** (☎250-539-5024), locally known as MOM. The **Arbutus Deer Farm** (☎250-539-2301) sells venison and beef for barbecues. **Bennett Bay Beach** is a lovely place for a stroll. Both **Hanna Air** (☎1-800-665-2359) and **Harbour Air** (☎1-800-665-0212) offer direct flights between Vancouver and Mayne Island.

Pender Islands

Linked by a wooden bridge, the two Pender Islands, much like Mayne, are very quiet and their inhabitants do not like to be disturbed. Visitors come here especially to go bike riding and stroll along the long stretch of **beaches**. Mount Normand has a good reputation among hikers. The summit offers a unique view of the San Juan Islands. The "hippie-cool" ambiance of these islands is obvious; natural food stores and organic produce farms are prevalent here. Try the **Southridge Farms Country Store** (☎250-629-2051) for organic fruits and vegetables. Sample excellent cuisine at the **Bedwell** restaurant (☎250-629-3212) or enjoy a beer at the **Port Browning Marina** pub (☎250-629-3493), where local musicians often get together for jam nights. Bed and breakfasts ensure accommodation. For further information, write to the **South Pender Island B & B** (9956 Boundary Pass Dr., R.R. 1, Pender Island, VON 2M0), or call the **Canadian Gulf Islands B & B Association** (☎250-539-5390) for free accommodation and adventure-package booking.

Galiano Island

The first thing you will notice upon arriving in Galiano is the scarcity of infrastructure and commercial development. The inhabitants' passionate protests to protect the ecological balance have attracted worldwide attention. Their efforts have enabled Galiano to preserve its vast stretches of great natural landscapes. The island also has many meditation centres and retreats for New Age enthusiasts, such as **Serenity By-the-Sea** *(☎1-800-944-2655)*.

The **Galiano Planet Revival Festival of Music** *(☎250-539-5778 for information)*, featuring indigenous dance performances and a varied repertoire of folk, jazz and funk offered by local artists, takes place in the summer. Not to be missed! Galiano also boasts many bed and breakfasts and rustic cabins for rent, as well as **campsites** in **Montague Harbour** *(☎250-539-2115)*. There is also a good selection of restaurants here, including **La Berengerie** *(☎250-539-5392)*, renowned for its Algerian food and lamb chops; it is also a bed and breakfast. Do not forget to bring bottled water as Galiano has no running water. Call **Galiano Getaways** *(☎250-539-5551 for B & B reservations)*. They also offer adventure packages; for more information, call the **Galiano Island Chamber of Commerce** *(☎250-539-2233)*.

Saturna Island

Saturna is perhaps the most isolated and least accessible of the Gulf Islands, and its inhabitants are determined to keep it that way. It has very limited facilities and only two restaurants. Nevertheless, there are many good reasons to visit the island. Nature lovers will be fascinated by its unusual fauna and flora, like the **giant mushrooms** at the base of **Mount Warburton**. On Canada Day (July 1st), a great annual lamb barbecue is organized. It is the largest local gathering of the year on the island. **Saturna Lodge** *(☎250-539-2254)* is one of the few inns here. Camping is forbidden on Saturna. For more information on accommodations, call ☎250-539-2930. To get to Saturna Island: **B.C. Ferries** *(☎1-888-223-3779)*. Reservations are essential during the summer.

OUTDOORS

Beaches

Vancouver

The Vancouver shoreline is made up in large part of easily accessible sandy beaches. All these beaches lie along English Bay, where it is possible to walk, cycle, play volleyball and, of course, take a dip in the sea to fully enjoy this environment. Stanley Park is fringed by **Third Beach** and **Second Beach**, and then, farther east, along Beach Avenue, by **First Beach** where, on January 1, hundreds of bathers brave the icy water to celebrate the new year. A little farther east, **Sunset Beach** celebrates the day's end with gorgeous sunsets. At the southern edge of English Bay are **Kitsilano Beach, Jericho Beach, Locarno Beach, Spanish Banks Beach, Tower Beach** and, finally, **Wreck Beach** at the western edge of the University of British Columbia campus.

Hiking

Vancouver

There are lots of places to go walking in the Point Grey area. Myriad trails crisscross the campus of the **University of British Columbia** (UBC). One of the best known runs across the famous **Endowment Lands, Pacific Spirit Park**, which cover an area twice as large as Stanley Park. Others lead to the **UBC Botanical Gardens** *(summer $4.50; winter free; mid-Mar to mid-Oct, every day 10am to 6pm; winter, everyday 10am to 2:30pm; 6804 SW Marine Dr., ☎822-9666)*. There is also a whole network of trails through the forest, and since UBC is located on a peninsula, all trails ultimately lead to the beach.

Biking

Vancouver

The region has a multitude of trails for mountain biking. Just head to one of the mountains north of the city. A pleasant eight-kilometre ride runs along the Seawall in Stanley

BRITISH COLUMBIA

Park. Bicycle rentals are available at **Stanley Park Rentals** *(1798 W. Georgia St., corner of Denman, ☎688-5141).*

Windsurfing

Vancouver

The pleasures afforded by the sea in Vancouver are definitely not to be taken lightly. **Howe Sound**, located alongside Highway 99 North on the way to Squamish, was slated to become a major harbour for giant freighters, but, to the great relief of local windsurfers, never did. The wind rushes into the hollow formed by the mountains on either side of the fjord, making this part of British Columbia a paradise for high-speed sailboarding. You can obtain all the necessary information about where to go at the **Squamish tourist office** *(37950 Cleveland Avenue, ☎892-9244)*. To find out about wind conditions, call the **Windtalker Windline** *(☎926-9463)*. A ten dollar fee covers insurance and potential rescue costs.

Sea Kayaking

Vancouver

Like the mountains, the water is a key part of life in Vancouver, and there is an almost unlimited number of ways to get out and enjoy the sea. One option is to tour the city by sea kayak. **False Creek** stretches all the way to Main Street and Science World, and you'll pass Granville Island along the way; by paddling around **Stanley Park**, you can reach Canada Place and the skyscrapers downtown. More courageous visitors can set out along **Indian Arm ★★★** to Deep Cove, an expedition likely to include a few encounters with seals and eagles. Kayak rentals are available at **Ecomarine Ocean Kayak Centre** *(1668 Duranleau St., Granville Island, ☎689-7575)* on **Granville Island**.

Whale-watching

Vancouver

Visitors can admire great marine mammals on the outskirts of Vancouver; including **grey whales**, **killer whales** and other **finbacks**. There

are observation boats on Vancouver Island. Here are a few places that can help you plan your outing: **Bluewater Adventures** *(☎980-3800)* and **Seaker Adventure Tours** *(☎1-800-728-0244)*. **Stubbs Island Whale Watching** *(Box 7, Dept. BCOA, Telegraph Cove, V0N 3J0, ☎250-928-3185)* specializes in the observation of killer whales. A hydrophone records the singing of whales, and you can even keep the cassette.

Cross-country Skiing

Less than a half-hour from Vancouver, three ski resorts welcome snow-lovers from morning to evening. In **Cypress Provincial Park**, on **Hollyburn Ridge ★**, Cypress Bowl Ski Areas *(☎926-5612)* offers 25 kilometres of mechanically maintained trails suitable for all categories of skiers. These trails are frequented day and evening by cross-country skiers. There are also trails at **Grouse Mountain** *(☎984-0661)* and **Mount Seymour Provincial Park** *(☎986-2261)*.

Downhill Skiing

Snowboarding is permitted at all of these resorts.

Vancouver

What makes Vancouver a truly magical place is the combination of sea and mountains. The cold season is no exception, as residents desert the beaches and seaside paths to crowd the ski hills, which are literally suspended over the city. There are four ski resorts close to the city: **Mount Seymour** *($26; 1700 Mount Seymour Rd., North Vancouver, B.C., V7G 1L3; Upper Level Hwy. heading east, Deep Cove Exit, information ☎986-2261, ski conditions ☎879-3999, ☎/≈986-2267)*, a family resort with beginner trails, situated east of North Vancouver, above Deep Cove; **Grouse Mountain** *($28, night skiing $20; 6400 Nancy Greene Way, North Vancouver, information ☎984-0661, ski conditions ☎986-6262, ski school ☎980-9311)*, a small resort accessible by cable car, which offers an unobstructed view of Vancouver that is as magnificent by day as it is by night; **Cypress Bowl** *($33, night skiing $23; from North Vancouver, take TransCanada Highway 1, heading west for*

16 km, then follow road signs. Information and ski conditions ☎926-5612), a resort for the most avid skiers, also offers magnificent views of Howe Sound and of the city. For more affordable skiing, try the village-style **Hemlock Valley Resort** (*$30, night skiing $11; Hwy. 1 heading east, Agassizou Harrisson Hot Springs Exit; information* ☎797-4411, *ski conditions* ☎520-6222, *¤797-4440, accommodation reservations* ☎797-4444). Situated at the eastern tip of Vancouver's urban area, in the heart of the Cascade Mountains, this resort boasts an abundance of snow and a spectacular view of Mount Baker in the United States. As soon as enough snow blankets the slopes, in late November or early December, these four ski resorts are open every day until late at night thanks to powerful neon lighting. It should be noted, however, that the first three resorts do not provide accommodation.

Whistler

This ski resort is considered the best in North America, with an annual snowfall of nine metres and a 1,600-metre vertical drop. There are two mountains to choose from: **Whistler Mountain** and **Blackcomb Mountain** *(hotel reservations,* ☎1-604-932-4222; *from Vancouver,* ☎685-3650; *from the US,* ☎1-800-634-9622). The skiing here is extraordinary, and the facilities ultramodern — but mind your budget! You will understand why prices are so high upon seeing hordes of Japanese and American tourists monopolize the hotels and intermediate ski runs. Whistler and Blackcomb Mountains together make up the largest skiing area in Canada. These world-class, twin ski playgrounds are blessed with heavy snowfalls and boast enough hotels to house a city's entire population. This first-rate ski metropolis also offers the possibility of gliding through pristine powder and, weather permitting, you will find yourself swooshing through an incredibly beautiful alpine landscape. **Whistler Mountain** (*$42; from Vancouver, Hwy. 99 heading north for 130 km, information* ☎932-3434, *ski conditions* ☎932-4191) is the elder of the two resorts. Experts, powderhounds and skijumpers all flock to Peak Chair, the chair lift that leads to the top of Whistler Mountain. From its summit, diehard skiers and snowboarders have access to a ski area composed of blue (intermediate) and expert (black-diamond and double-diamond) trails, covered in deep fleecy snow. **Blackcomb Mountain** (*$44; in Whistler; from Vancouver, Hwy. 99 heading north for 130 km;*

4545 Blackcomb Way, Whistler, B.C., V0N 1B4; information ☎932-3141, ski conditions ☎932-4211) is the "stalwart" skiing Mecca of ski buffs in North America. For years now, a fierce debate has been waged by skiers over which of the two mountains (Whistler or Blackcomb) is the best. One thing is certain, Blackcomb wins first place for its vertical drop of 1,609 metres. Check out the glacier at Blackcomb – it is truly magnificent!

 ## ACCOMMODATIONS

Super, Natural British Columbia (☎1-800-663-6000) can make reservations for you.

Vancouver

Downtown

Vancouver International Hostel (*$16-$20; men's and women's dormitories, some private rooms, sb, tv, cafeteria from Apr to Oct; 151 Discovery St.,* ☎224-3208, *¤224-4852*). Located in Jericho Park, this youth hostel is open day and night; take UBC bus #4 from downtown to reach it. With Locarno and Jericho beaches nearby, this is a great spot for budget travellers.

Vancouver Downtown YHA (*$19 members, $23 non-members; 114 Burnaby St., V6E 1P1,* ☎684-4565, *¤684-4540*) is a big hostel (239 beds) right downtown at the corner of Thurlow. Common kitchen and tv room; coin laundry.

The **Wedgewood Hotel** (*$240; pb, ☉, △, ≈, ℜ; 845 Hornby St., V6Z 1V2,* ☎689-7777, *1-800-663-0666, ¤608-5348*) is small enough to have retained some character and style, in particular the lovely lobby complete with shiny brass accents, cosy fireplace and distinguished art, and large enough to offer a certain measure of privacy and professionalism. This is a popular option for business trips and romantic weekend getaways.

Pan Pacific Hotel Vancouver (*$410; 506 rooms; ≈, ⊛, ☉, tv, ≈, △, ℘, ℜ; 300-999 Canada Place,* ☎662-8111, *in Canada 1-800-663-1515 or in US 1-800-937-1515, ¤685-8690*) is a very luxurious hotel located in Canada Place, on the shore of Burrard Inlet facing North Vancouver, with a good view of port activities. During their visit to Vancouver in 1993, Russian President Boris Yeltsin and his entire entourage stayed at this hotel. Its lobby, with its marble decor, 20-metre-high ceilings and panoramic view of the ocean, is magnificent.

West End

Sylvia Hotel *($100; pb, tv, K, ℜ, ✖, 𝒫; 1154 Gilford St., ☎681-9321).* Located just a few steps from English Bay, this charming old hotel, built in the early 1900s, offers unspoiled views and has 118 simple rooms. People come for the atmosphere, but also for food and drink at the end of the day. For those on lower budgets, rooms without views are offered at lower rates. The manager of this ivy-covered hotel is a Frenchman who is fully and justifiably dedicated to his establishment. Request a southwest-facing room (one facing English Bay) in order to benefit from magical sunsets over the bay.

West End Guest House Bed & Breakfast *($150 bkfst incl.; pb, 𝒫, ⊗, no children under 12; 1362 Haro St., ☎681-2889, ⇒688-8812).* This magnificent inn set in a turn-of-the-century Victorian house is well situated near a park and near Robson Street. Evan Penner is your host. A minimum two-day stay may apply, but do not hesitate: the West End Guest House has an excellent reputation. (Nearby, at 1415 Barclay Street, is Roedde House, built in Victorian-Edwardian style in 1893 and designed by none other than architect Francis Rattenbury, who also created the Vancouver Art Gallery, the legislature building in Victoria and the Empress Hotel.)

The **Landmark Hotel** *($200; tv, ⊗, ⊙, ℜ, △, ≈, ♿; 1400 Robson St., ☎687-0511 or 1-800-830-6144, ⇒687-2801)* truly is a landmark with its 40 floors and its revolving resto-bar at the top. The view is fascinating and quite an experience! The whole city unfolds before you in 90 minutes as the restaurant revolves 360°. The best time is at sunset when the sky darkens and the city seems to glow.

Pacific Palisades Hotel *($225-$290; tv, ≈, 𝒫, ℜ, ℝ, ℂ, ♿, ⊙; 1277 Robson Street, ☎688-0461 or 1-800-663-1815, ⇒688-4374)* is part of the Shangri-La hotel chain. Its two towers, totalling 233 rooms, offer superb views of the sea and the mountains. Rooms facing north on the upper floors provide especially fine mountain views. A big pool and a well-equipped gymnasium are available to guests. All services for tourists or business travellers are looked after with professionalism. The staff is friendly and efficient.

Sutton Place Hotel *($265-$415; ⊗, ⊙, ≈, △, ℝ, ℜ, ♿; 845 Burrard Street, ☎682-5511 or 1-800-961-7555, ⇒682-5513),* formerly the Meridien, offers 397 rooms and the full range of five-star services normally provided by top hotel chains. The European decor has been well maintained. If you are a chocolate lover, don't miss the chocolate buffet served on Friday.

Hotel Vancouver *($330; 508 rooms; tv, ≈, ⊗, ⊙, △, ℜ, ℝ, ✖, ♿, 𝒫; 900 West Georgia St., ☎684-3131 or 1-800-441-1414, ⇒662-1929)* belongs to the Canadian Pacific Hotel chain and was built in the 1930s in the château style characteristic of Canadian railway hotels, of which the Château Frontenac in Québec City was a precursor. In 1939 it hosted George VI, the first British monarch to visit Canada. You will find tranquillity and luxury in the heart of downtown near Robson Street and Burrard Street.

Stanley Park

Johnson House Bed & Breakfast *($75-$140 bkfst incl.; sb or pb; Nov-Feb by request only; 2278 West 34th Ave., Kerrisdale district, ☎/⇒266-4175)* occupies a magnificent, fully renovated house from the 1920s, with an extra floor added. The owners, Sandy and Ron Johnson, carried out the work; they also acquired several of the antiques that form part of the decor.

The **Best Western Abercorn Inn** *($140; tv; 9260 Bridgeport Rd., Richmond, ☎270-7576 or 1-800-663-0085, ⇒270-0001)* is relatively affordable for its category. It is located close to the airport and many shopping malls. A good choice for travellers looking for something halfway between the airport and downtown.

The **Apricot Cat Guest House** *($95-$115 bkfst incl.; pb, tv; 628 Union St., ☎215-9898, ⇒255-9271)* is a beautiful, old restored house that is just at the outer edge of downtown, not far from Stanley Park, the conference centre, GM Place and Gastown. It's well suited to business people, for whom they have set up fax machines, guest-telephone lines and desks in larger rooms. The atmosphere is cozy, the ooms are bright and airy, and you can have your meals on the terrace overlooking the garden.

The **Westin Bayshore** *($200-$300; bp, tv, ℜ, △, ≈, ℙ; 1601 W. Georgia St., ☎682-3377; ↝687-3102)* is a very classy place. Its setting is typically "Vancouver" with the surrounding mountains, the proximity of the sea and the city so close by. The 517 rooms each have their own charm, not to mention the stunning views. Staying here is like staying at a tropical resort.

Other Areas

William House *($95-$190 bkfst incl.; tv, pb, ☎; 2050 W. 18th Ave., ☎/↝731-2760)* is a beautiful, completely restored country house, in the old area of Shaughnessy, a few minutes from downtown. Luxury suites and rooms offer a pleasantly calm, comfortable environment. The large garden and yard provide havens from all the noise of the city. Well suited to business people. Prices are negotiable depending on the season and the length of your stay.

The **Pillow Porridge Guest House** *($115-$135 bkfst incl.; tv, pb, ℝ, K, ☎; 2859 Manitoba St., ☎879-8977, ↝897-8966)* is a residence dating back to 1910, and the decor and ambience attest to it. These complete apartments with kitchens are pleasant and comfortable. Close to a number of ethnically diverse restaurants.

Whistler

The **Shoestring Lodge** *($55-$100 for a room, depending on the season, $20 for a shared room; pb, tv, ℜ, shuttle, pub, ℙ; 1 km north of the village, to the right on Nancy Greene Dr., ☎932-3338, ↝932-8347)* is one of the least expensive places to stay in Whistler. Its low rates make it very popular, so reservations are imperative. The rooms include beds, televisions and small bathrooms; the decor is as neutral as can be. The youthful atmosphere will make you feel as if you're at a university summer camp where the students just want to have fun, and that's pretty much what this place is. The pub is known for its excellent evening entertainment.

The luxurious **Canadian Pacific Chateau Whistler Resort** *($175-$479; ⊙, ✕, ⅙, pb, tv, ≈, ⊚, △, ℜ; 4599 Chateau Blvd., ☎938-8000,*

1-800-606-8244 or 1-800-441-1414, ↝938-2099) lies at the foot of the slopes of Blackcomb Mountain. It resembles a smaller version of Whistler Village, fully equipped to meet all your dining and entertainment needs and to ensure that your stay is a relaxing one.

The **Listel Whistler Hotel** *($199-$269; 98 rooms, pb, ⅙, ✕, tv, heated ≈, ⊚, △, ℜ; 4121 Village Green, ☎604-932-1133, Vancouver ☎688-5634 or 1-800-663-5472, ↝932-8383)* is located in the heart of the village, so you don't have to look far to find some place to eat or entertain yourself. The simple layout of the rooms makes for a comfortable stay.

The Gulf Islands

Salt Spring

The **Summerhill Guest House** *($95-$120 bkfst incl.; pb; 209 Chu-An Dr., ☎537-2727, ↝537-4301)* has been completely renovated by its owners. The interesting combination of landings and terraces lets in the sunlight and allows for some beautiful views of the Sansum Narrows. The breakfast is unusual and absolutely delicious. You'll feel right at home here.

Galiano Island

At **La Berengerie** *($65-$80 bkfst incl.; sb or pb, ℜ; Montague Harbour Rd., Galiano, ☎539-5392)*, which has four rooms, guests enjoy a relaxing atmosphere in the woods. Huguette Benger has been running the place since 1983. Originally from the South of France, Madame Benger came to Galiano on a vacation and decided to stay. Take the time to chat with her; she'll be delighted to tell you all about the island. Breakfast is served in a large dining room. La Berengerie is closed from November to March.

Mayne Island

The **Root Seller Inn** *($80 bkfst incl.; children 6 and over, sb, no smoking; 478 Village Bay Rd., ☎539-2621, ↝539-2411)* lies hidden behind the flowers and trees lovingly planted by charming Joan Drummond, who has been welcoming guests to the island for over 30 years. It all started at the Springwater Hotel in 1960, when she and her husband, having just arrived on the island, opened a hotel. Since 1983, Joan has been receiving guests in her home and showing them the island. The big wooden Cape Cod-style house, can accommodate eight people in three large rooms. It lies near Mariners Bay, guests can thus contemplate the scenery and watch the ferries on their way through Active Pass from the blacony.

RESTAURANTS

Vancouver

Gastown

Water Street Café *($; closes at 10pm weekdays, 11pm weekends; 300 Water St., ☎689-2832).* A handsome bistro with big windows facing Gastown. Tables are decorated with pretty lanterns, and service is friendly. The menu centres around creatively prepared pastas.

Greek Characters *($$; 1 Alexander St., at Maple Tree Sq., ☎681-6581).* Authentic Greek cuisine, moussaka, roasted lamb, souvlaki as well as fish dishes, with a little room left over for French onion soup and Italian pasta dishes.

Chinatown and East Vancouver

Waa Zuu Bee Café *($; 1622 Commercial Dr., ☎253-5299)* is great and inexpensive. The innovative cuisine combined with the "natural-techno-italo-bizarre" decor are full of surprises. The pasta dishes are always interesting.

The **Sun Sui Wah Seafood Restaurant** *($$; every day; 3888 Main St., at 3rd Ave., ☎872-8822)* was chosen as the "most popular Chinese-food restaurant" in 1996. Authentic Chinese food, lobster, crayfish, crab, oysters and, of course, Peking duck.

The **Cannery Seafood Restaurant** *($$$; until 10:30pm; 2205 Commissioner St., ☎254-9606)* is one of the best places in town for seafood. It is located in the East End in a renovated century-old warehouse. The view of the sea is fantastic.

Downtown

A relaxing ambience and family-style fare are served up at the **Dining Car** *($; Mon to Fri noon to 2:30pm, Fri and Sat 5pm to 10pm; at the Railway Club, 579 Dunsmuir St., ☎681-1625),* where the clientele runs the gamut from suits to artists.

The **Arena Ristorante** *($$; 300 W. Georgia St., ☎687-5434)* serves Italian specialties. The atmosphere is livelier on Friday and Saturday nights when they present live jazz performances.

Tsunami Sushi *($$; 238-1025 Robson St., ☎687-8744)* has a revolving sushi bar, much like those in Japan, from which patrons can choose specialties at will. Excellent quality for the price; huge, sunny terrace overlooking Robson Street.

Le Crocodile *($$$-$$$$; 909 Burrard St., entry by Smithe St., ☎669-4298).* This establishment is the beacon of French cuisine in Vancouver, as much for the quality of its food as for its service, decor and wine list. Lovers of great French cuisine will be spoiled by the choice of red meats and the delicacies from the sea. The salmon tartare is a must, you *are* on the Pacific coast after all!

West End

Da Pasta Bar *($; 1232 Robson St., ☎688-1288).* This Italian restaurant, located in the most refined part of Robson Street, offers original items such as pasta with curry. Full lunches for $7.50. Pleasant decor.

Luxy Bistro *($; 1235 Davie St., ☎681-9976).* The menu of this little, dark-green-walled restaurant offers pasta dishes prepared with all sorts of ingredients and just as much imagination. Good quality and reasonable prices. People come for the atmosphere more than anything, especially on weekend evenings.

Liliget *($$; every day; 1724 Davie St., ☎681-7044)* is a First Nations restaurant. It offers authentic native food: salmon grilled on a wood fire, smoked oysters, grilled seaweed, roasted wild duck. Worth exploring.

Raku *($$; 838 Thurlow St., north of Robson, ☎685-8817)* A wealthy young Japanese clientele meets here and fits right in. It has the atmosphere of a noisy bar, but it is an ideal spot to begin a promising evening. The sushi and grilled meats are recommended.

The Italian restaurant **Romano's Macaroni Grill** *($$; until 10pm, 11pm weekends, 1523 Davie, ☎689-4334)* is located in an enormous mansion. Fine olive oil on each table is just part of the cosy atmosphere. Children (and adults too) can draw on the tables with crayons provided by the restaurant. Go on a Sunday for the all-you-can-eat pasta brunch.

C *($$$; 1600 Howe St., ☎605-8263)*. This Chinese restaurant, whose name evokes the sea, has just opened in Vancouver. It is already causing much talk, and with good reason. The chef has returned from Southeast Asia with innovative and unique recipes. Served on the stroke of twelve, the *C*-style Dim Sum is a real delight. Titbits of fish marinated in tea and a touch of caviar, vol-au-vents with chanterelles, curry shrimp with coconut milk, and the list goes on... All quite simply exquisite. Desserts are equally extraordinary. For those who dare, the crème brûlée with blue cheese is an unforgettable experience. This restaurant is an absolute must.

L'Hermitage *($$$-$$$$; every day; 115-1025 Robson St., ☎689-3237)*. The chef-owner Hervé Martin, is an artist when it comes to French cuisine and will tell you stories from his days as the chef of the Belgian Royal Court. Wines from his native region of Burgundy accompany the finest of dishes, each prepared carefully and with panache. The decor is chic and the service exemplary. The terrace, set back from Robson, is lovely in the summertime.

Stanley Park

The Prospect Point Café *($; Stanley Park, ☎669-2737)* is located at the historical observation site on the tip of Stanley Park. You can contemplate Lions Gate Bridge at sunset and sample steaks, pasta and chicken burgers.

Other Areas

The **Bridges Bistro** *($; until 11:30pm; 1696 Durenleau St., Granville Island, ☎687-4400, ⊷687-0352)* boasts one of the prettiest terraces in Vancouver, right by the water in the middle of Granville Island's pleasure-boat harbour. The food and setting are decidedly West Coast.

The Naam *($; 2724 W. 4th Ave., ☎738-7151, open 24 hours)* blends live music with vegetarian meals. This little restaurant has a warm atmosphere and friendly service. This spot is frequented by a young clientele.

Monk McQueens *($$; every day; 601 Stamps Landing, ☎877-1351)*. Specialties are fish and an oyster buffet. This restaurant overlooks the inlet and has the decor of a small sailing club. Very pleasant inside and on the terrace. Impeccable service and delicious food. A pianist accompanies your meal.

Raku Kushiyaki Restaurant *($$-$$$; 4422 W. 10th Ave., ☎222-8188)*. The young chefs of this little restaurant prepare local cuisine served with oriental aesthetic rules in mind; they will help you discover their art. Take a meal for two to appreciate the spirit of this *nouvelle cuisine*, which encourages the sharing of meals among guests. The portions may seem small, but you still come away satiated. Ingredients are chosen according to the seasons, for example wild mushrooms are served accented with garlic, green bell peppers, butter, soya sauce and lime juice. This dish may seem simple, and it is, but the taste of the food is not masked by some mediocre sauce. The meats and fish are also treated with subtlety.

Seasons in the Park *($$$-$$$$; right in Queen Elizabeth Park, 33 Cambie St., ☎874-8008)* is a pleasant restaurant with classic, elegant decor and an unhindered view of the city. Succulent cuisine. Reservations required.

Whistler

Located in the heart of the village, **Città Bistro** *($; every day 11am to 1am; Whistler Village Sq., ☎932-4177)* has an elaborate menu with selections ranging from salads to pita pizzas. This is the perfect place to sample one of the local beers. In both winter and summer, a pleasant mix of locals and tourists makes for an extremely inviting atmosphere.

If you want to be among the first to ski the slopes in the morning, head to **Pika's** *($; Dec to Apr, 7:30am to 3:30pm; at the top of the Whistler Village Gondola, ☎932-3434)* for breakfast; it is worth getting up early the day after a storm.

The **Hard Rock Cafe** *($-$$; Sun to Thu 11:30am to midnight, Fri and Sat to 1am; in* the village of Whistler, near Blackcomb Way, ☎938-9922) has a lively clientele and a menu featuring salads and hamburgers.

As may be gathered by its name, **Thai One On** *($$; every day, dinner; in the Le Chamois hotel, at the foot of the Blackcomb Mountain slopes,* ☎932-4822) serves Thai food, with its wonderful blend of coconut milk and hot peppers.

At the **Trattoria di Umberto** *($$-$$$; near Blackcomb Way, on the ground floor of the Mountainside Lodge,* ☎932-5858), you'll find pasta dishes and a homey atmosphere.

The Gulf Islands

Galiano Island

La Berengerie *($$; open only in the evening; Montague Harbour Rd.,* ☎539-5392) has a four-course menu with a choice of fish or meat. The dining room, located on the ground floor of a B&B, is furnished with antiques. Candlelight makes the atmosphere that much more inviting. Owner Huguette Benger prepares the delicious meals herself. During the day, her son's restaurant, **La Bohème**, serves vegetarian dishes on the terrace looking out onto the garden.

 ENTERTAINMENT

Vancouver

ARTS Hotline *(*☎*684-ARTS)* will inform you about all shows (dance, theatre, music, cinema and literature) in the city.

***The Georgia Straight** (*☎*730-7000).* This weekly paper is published every Thursday and distributed free at many spots in Vancouver. You will find all the necessary information on coming shows and cultural events. This paper is read religiously each week by many Vancouverites and has acquired a good reputation.

Ticketmaster: ☎280-4444

Arts Line: ☎280-3311 (for tickets only)

Sports Line: ☎280-4400

Bars and Nightclubs

Gastown

The **Blarney Stone** *(216 Carrall St.)* is the spot for authentic Irish jigs and reels. The ambience is frenetic with people dancing everywhere, on the tables, on the chairs... A must-see!

The Purple Onion Cabaret *(every day; 15 Water St., 3rd floor,* ☎602-9442) is the mecca of upbeat jazz in Vancouver, with entertainment provided by a disc-jockey or live bands. Cover charge of three dollars during the week and seven dollars on weekends. Wednesdays are dedicated to Latin jazz; on Fridays and Saturdays there's live jazz near the bar and "disco-funk" on the dance floor.

Chinatown and East Vancouver

The Hot Jazz Society *(2120 Main St.,* ☎873-4131) was one of the first places in Vancouver to offer good jazz. It's a veritable institution where many of the big names in jazz perform.

Downtown

Chameleon Urban Lounge *(every day; 801 W. Georgia St.,* ☎669-0806). This excellent little downtown club is often packed on weekends unfortunately, but it is calm during the week. Don't miss their trip-hop nights on Wednesdays, Afro-Cuban and latin music on Thursdays, and Acid Jazz on Saturdays. Warning: get there early to avoid lineups. The cover charge is five dollars on Fridays and Saturdays.

Yale Hotel *(1300 Granville St.,* ☎681-9253). The big names in blues regularly play at this, the blues Mecca of Vancouver. Great ambience on the weekends. The cover charge varies depending on the performers.

Gay and Lesbian Bars

Celebrities *(free admission; 1022 Davie St.,* ☎689-3180) is definitely the best-known gay bar in Vancouver. Straights also come here for the music. Drag queens make conspicuous appearances, especially on Wednesdays, during Female Impersonators night. Packed on weekends.

Charlie's Lounge *(455 Abbott St., ☎685-7777)* is a relaxed bar with an elegant gay clientele, located on the ground floor of an old hotel. Opens at 4pm on Mondays and Tuesdays and at 3pm from Wednesday to Saturday. Sundays, they serve brunch from 11am to 2pm. Musical improv sessions in the afternoon and retro dance music at night.

Theatres

Art's Club Theatre *(1585 Johnston, ☎687-1644)* is a steadfast institution on the Vancouver theatre scene. Located on the waterfront, on Granville Island, this theatre presents contemporary works with social themes. Audience members often get together in the theatre's bar after the plays.

The **Ford Centre for the Performing Arts** *(777 Homer St., ☎280-2222)* is an immense, big-budget theatre that presents international mega-productions like *Show Boat*, *Les Misérables* and *Phantom of the Opera*.

The **Queen Elizabeth Theatre** *(Hamilton St., at Georgia St., ☎665-3050)*, a large hall with 2,000 seats, presents musicals and variety shows, but is also the main performance space for the Vancouver Opera.

Vancouver Opera *(845 Cambie St., ☎682-2871)*. Vancouver is one of the major cities in the world that doesn't have an opera house. For this reason, all operas are presented at the Queen Elizabeth Theatre, at Hamilton and Georgia Streets. The address here is for the administration office where you can phone for program information.

Festivals and Cultural Events

The **Vancouver International Children's Festival** *(Vanier Park, ☎687-7697)* takes place the last week of May under characteristically red and white tents. Children come from all over British Columbia for this big festival in the beautiful setting of Vanier Park, where 70,000 people gather every year.

Vancouver International Jazz Festival *(☎682-0706)*. Fans can come and satisfy their hunger for jazz at this distinguished festival. Artists perform throughout the city and the surrounding area.

The **Benson & Hedges Symphony of Fire** *(English Bay, ☎738-4304)* is an international fireworks festival. A barge on English Bay, which serves as the base of operations, is the centre of attention. Dazzling show, guaranteed thrills.

The **Vancouver Folk Music Festival** *(☎602-9798)* has become a tradition in Vancouver. It takes place during the third week of August and features musicians from all over the world, from sunrise to sunset on Jericho Beach.

Molson Indy Vancouver *(BC Place Stadium, False Creek, ☎684-4639, tickets ☎280-INDY)*. In the heart of downtown, a course is set up where Indy racing cars (the North American equivalent of Formula 1) compete in front of 100,000 enthusiastic spectators.

Vancouver International Film Festival *(☎685-0260)*. Vancouver, "Hollywood North", plays host to this increasingly significant festival that offers film buffs up to 150 films from all over the world.

 SHOPPING

Vancouver

You'll surely come upon all manner of interesting shops as you explore the city. To help you discover some of the best bets in Vancouver however, read on...

Bookstores

Duthie's *(919 Robson St., ☎684-4496)* is *the* bookstore in Vancouver. With an exceptional selection of books and a friendly attentive staff, Duthie's has built itself quite a reputation. They recently opened a branch *(☎602-0610)* in the impressive new Vancouver Library. The move has been a huge success leaving people wondering why no one thought of doing it before!

Little Sisters Book and Art Emporium *(every day 10am to 11pm; 1238 Davie St., ☎669-1753 or 1-800-567-1662)* is the only gay bookshop in Western Canada and offers gay literature as well as essays on homosexuality, feminism, and on related

BRITISH COLUMBIA

subjects. It is also a vast bazaar, with products like humorous greeting cards. With the support of several Canadian literary figures, this bookshop has been fighting Canada Customs, which arbitrarily blocks the importation of certain publications. Books by recognized and respected authors such as Marcel Proust have been seized by Canada Customs, which has taken on the role of censor. Some of the same titles bound for regular bookshops have mysteriously escaped seizure by Canada Customs, leading to questions about discrimination.

Manhattan Books (1089 Robson St., ☎681-9074) sells major international magazines and newspapers as well as a respectable selection of French books.

Oscar's Art Books & Books (1533 W. Broadway, at Granville, ☎731-0533) has a large selection of fiction and books on art, cooking, nature, anatomy, travel and more. Wonderful books at low prices.

UBC Bookstore (6200 University Blvd., ☎822-BOOK) is the largest bookstore west of the Rockies with more than 100,000 titles. Allow enough time to park your car as the parking situation at UBC can be a problem.

Malls, Department Stores and Markets

The **Pacific Centre** (from Robson St. to Dunsmuir St., ☎688-7236) is the largest shopping centre in the city. Approximately 300 quality boutiques offer a complete range of everything from jewellery and clothes to top-of-the-line items. Clothing and accessories at the Hermès and Louis Vuitton boutiques in Holt Renfrew; a fitness equipment store; a Ticketmaster; The Bay and Eaton's as well as Le Château, which mainly caters to a young clientele, are all to be found here. Parking fee.

Waterfront Centre (at the base of the Waterfront Hotel, Canada Place): souvenir shops, flowers and cigars; tourist information counter; insurance company; hair salon; shoe repairs; a Starbucks coffeeshop; and a handful of small fast-food counters that feature various national cuisines.

Robson Market (Robson St. at Cardero). Vegetables; fresh fish, some of it cleaned and scaled; stands with fruit salads; meats, sausages and ham; pastries and other baked

goods; a counter for Alsatian and German specialties; flowers and plants; vitamins and natural products; natural medicine clinic; hair salon; small restaurants upstairs. The market is covered, but well lit.

Music

Highlife Records & Music (1317 Commercial Dr., ☎251-6964). This is the spot to find new wave and other types of music at good prices.

HMV (1160 Robson St.) is the mega-store for music, with great prices on new releases. The store is open late on weekends.

Native Arts and Crafts

The **Inuit Gallery of Vancouver** (345 Water St., ☎688-7323) sells some magnificent pieces of native art from Canada's far north and from the Queen Charlotte Islands.

Leona Lattimer (1590 W. 2nd Ave., west of Granville Island, ☎732-4556) is a lovely gallery where you can admire some fine native art or, if you like, purchase a piece. Quality jewellery and prints. Expensive.

The Raven and The Bear (1528 Duranleau St., Granville Island, ☎669-3990). Excellent-quality native works at reasonable prices. Lithographs, sculptures and natural stonework.

The **Silver Gallery** (126 Robson St., ☎681-6884) is the least expensive store for fine-quality jewellery and native crafts. Solid silver bracelets, necklaces and rings with gold enamelling, at competitive prices. They also sell Indonesian objects, including masks, at affordable prices.

Sports

Mountain Equipment Co-op (130 W. Broadway, ☎872-7858). This giant store offers everything for outdoor activities. You must be a member to make purchases, but membership only costs five dollars.

3 Vets (2200 Yukon St., ☎872-5475) is a local institution. For 40 years, this store has been supplying reasonably priced camping equipment to everyone from professional lumberjacks to tree planters and weekend campers.

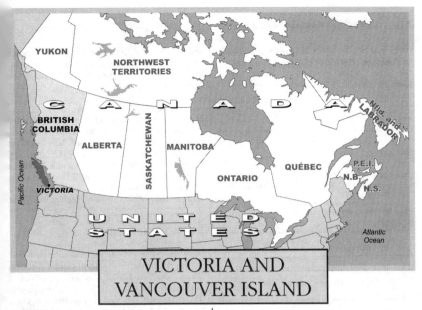

VICTORIA AND VANCOUVER ISLAND

Vast Vancouver Island stretches over 500 kilometres along the west coast, with its southern tip facing the Olympic Mountains in Washington State (U.S.A.). The island is split into two distinct regions by a chain of mountains, which divide the north from the south. The sea has sculpted the west side, creating big, deep fjords; while the shoreline on the east side is much more continuous. Most of the towns and villages on the island lie either on the east coast or along the Strait of Georgia, where the Gulf Islands are located. One of those towns is the very British and beautiful Victoria, the province's capital.

 FINDING YOUR WAY AROUND

By Plane

Victoria International Airport *(☎953-7500)* is located north of Victoria on the Saanich Peninsula, a half-hour's drive from downtown on Highway 17.

By Bus

Island Coach Lines *(700 Douglas St., Victoria, V8W 2B3, ☎250-385-4411 or 388-5248)* offer transportation from Nanaimo to Port Alberni, Ucluelet and Tofino, on the west coast of Vancouver Island.

By Train

E&N (Via Rail) *(450 Pandora Ave., Victoria, V8W 3L5, ☎1-800-561-8630)* provides transportation along the east coast of the island. The major stops on this line are Victoria, Duncan, Nanaimo, Qualicum Beach and Courtenay. The train leaves Victoria at 8:15am from Monday to Saturday and at noon on Sunday.

By Ferry

You can reach Victoria by car by taking a **BC Ferry** from Tsawwassen, located south of Vancouver on the coast. This ferry *(BC Ferry Corporation; in the summer, every day on the hour from 7am to 10pm; in the winter, every day every other hour from 7am to 9pm; ☎1-888-223-3779 in B.C. or 250-386-3431 from outside the province)* will drop you off at the Sydney terminal in Swartz Bay. From there, take Highway 17 South to Victoria.

BC Ferry also offers transportation to Victoria from the east coast of Vancouver Island. The ferry sets out from the Horseshoe Bay terminal, northwest of Vancouver, and takes passengers to Nanaimo. From there, follow the signs for the TransCanada Highway 1 South, which leads to Victoria, 113 kilometres away.

Public Transportation

Victoria

Public transportation in the greater Victoria area is provided by **BC Transit** *(☎382-6161)*.

PRACTICAL INFORMATION

Area Code: 250

Tourist Information Offices

To learn more about Vancouver Island before setting out on your trip, contact the **Tourism Association of Vancouver Island** *(302-45 Bastion Square, Victoria, V8W 1J1, ☎382-3551)*.

For any information regarding Victoria and its surroundings, contact the **Victoria Travel Information Centre** *(every day 9am to nightfall; 812 Wharf St., V8W 1T3, ☎953-2033)*.

EXPLORING

Victoria ★★

Downtown Victoria is cramped, which can make parking somewhat difficult. There are a number of public lots where you can pay to park your car, including a very inexpensive one on View Street, between Douglas and Blanshard, at the edge of Old Town (on weekdays and holidays, the cost is one dollar).

Any tour of Victoria starts at the port, which was the main point of access into the city for decades. Back in the era of tall ships, the merchant marine operating on the Pacific Ocean used to stop here to pick up goods destined for England. Once the railway reached the coast, however, the merchandise was transported across Canada by train, thus reducing the amount of time required to reach the east side of the continent. From that point on, the merchant marine only provided a sea link to Asia.

Bastion Square marks the former site of Fort Victoria, constructed by the Hudson's Bay Company in 1843, with the help of hundreds of native people. Twenty years later, the fort was demolished to make way for the city. Today, the site is occupied by public buildings like the **Maritime Museum of British Columbia** *($6; every day 9:30am to 4:30pm; 28 Bastion Sq., ☎385-4222)*, which highlights great moments in the history of sailing, from the days when tall ships sidled up alongside one another in the harbour.

Walk down Bastion Square, turn right on Wharf Street, then head up the north side of Johnson Street. Go into **Market Square ★**, which is surrounded by shops facing onto the street. This place gets very lively during the jazz, blues and theatre festivals and on the Chinese New Year.

Chinatown ★ *(west of Government St., between Fisgard and Pandora)*, is full of brightly coloured shops and its sidewalks are decorated with geometric patterns that form a Chinese character meaning "good fortune". At one time, there were over 150 businesses in Chinatown as well as three schools, five temples two churches and a hospital. On your way through this neighbourhood, you'll come across the Tong Ji Men arch, on Fisgard Street, a symbol of the spirit of cooperation between the Chinese and Canadian communities. **Fan Tan Alley ★**, which runs north-south *(south of Fisgard St.)*, is supposedly the narrowest street in Victoria. People used to come here to buy opium until 1908, when the federal government banned the sale of the drug.

Craigdarroch Castle ★ *($7.50; in the summer, every day 9am to 7pm; in winter, every day 10am to 4:30pm; 1050 Joan Cresc., ☎592-5323)* stands at the east end of the downtown area. It was built in 1890 for Robert Dunsmuir, who made a fortune in the coal-mining business. He died before it was completed, but his widow and three children went on to live here. What makes this building interesting, aside from its dimensions, is its decorative woodwork and the view from the fifth floor of the tower. This residence is indicative of the opulent lifestyle enjoyed by the wealthy around the turn of the century.

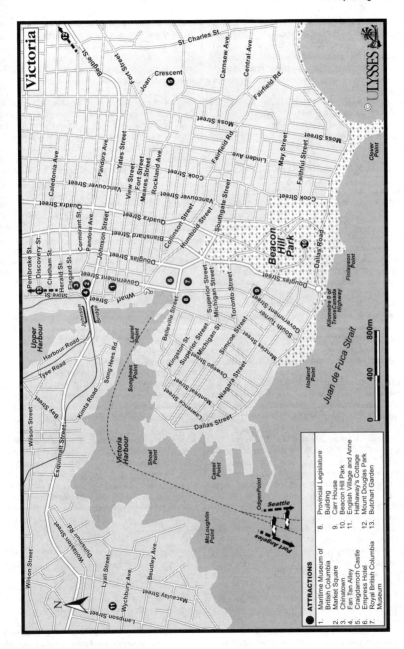

Victoria

St. Charles St.

Carnsew Ave.

Central Ave.

Crescent

Joan

Fairfield Rd.

Moss Street

Fairfield Rd.

Linden Ave.

May Street

Faithful Rd.

Fort Street

Moss Street

Cook Street

Clover
Point

Yates Street

View Street

Fort Street

Meares Street

Rockland Ave.

Vancouver Street

Cook Street

Pandora Ave.

Vancouver Street

Caledonia Ave.

Quadra Street

Collinson Street

Humbold Street

Southgate Street

Cormorant St.

Blanshard Street

Quadra Street

Pandora Ave.

Johnson Street

Douglas Street

Beacon
Hill
Park

Pembroke St.

Discovery St.

Chatham St.

Herald St.

Government Street

Superior Street

Michigan St.

Dallas Road

Finlayson
Point

Store St.

Fisgard St.

Wharf Street

Bridge

Johnson

Kilometre 0 of
TransCanada
Highway

Upper
Harbour

Harbour Road

Tyee Road

Song Hees Rd.

Laurel
Point

Belleville Street

Kingston St.

Superior Street

Michigan St.

Simcoe Street

Toronto Street

Menzies Street

Government Street

South Tunnel

Holland
Point

Juan de Fuca Strait

Songhees
Point

Kimta Road

Lawrence Street

Montreal Street

Oswego Street

Niagara Street

Dallas Street

0   400   800m

Esquimalt Street

Wilson Street

Bay Street

Victoria
Harbour

Shoal
Point

Camel
Point

Ogden Point

Seattle

Port Angeles

McLoughlin
Point

Wollaston Street

Dunsmuir Rd.

Wilson Street

Lyall Street

Wychbury Ave.

Beudley Ave.

Macaulay Street

Lampson Street

N

BRITISH COLUMBIA

● **ATTRACTIONS**

1. Maritime Museum of
   British Columbia
2. Market Square
3. Chinatown
4. Fan Tan Alley
5. Craigdarroch Castle
6. Empress Hotel
7. Royal British Columbia
   Museum
8. Provincial Legislature
   Building
9. Carr House
10. Beacon Hill Park
11. English Village and Anne
    Hathaway's Cottage
12. Mount Douglas Park
13. Butchart Garden

© ULYSSES

The **Empress Hotel** ★★ *(behind the port of Victoria, ☎384-8111)* was built in 1905 for the Canadian Pacific railway company. It was designed by Francis Rattenbury in chateau style, just like the Chateau Frontenac in Québec City, only more modern and less romantic. As you enter through the main entrance and cross the lobby let yourself be transported back to the 1920s, when influential people found their way into the guest books. Above all, make sure to stop by the Empress for afternoon tea (see p 586).

Head south on Douglas Street, then turn right on Belleville to reach the **Royal British Columbia Museum** ★★ *($7; every day 9am to 5pm; 675 Belleville St., ☎1-800-661-5411 or 387-3701, message ☎387-3014)*, where you can learn about the history of the city and the various peoples that have inhabited the province. Centrepieces of the collection are a reproduction of Captain Vancouver's ship and a Kwa-gulth Indian house. The museum also hosts some interesting temporary exhibitions.

The design for the **Provincial Legislature Buildings** ★ *(free tours)* was chosen by way of a competition. The winner was architect Francis Rattenbury, who was just 25 years old at the time and who went on to design many other public and privately owned buildings.

Take Government Street south to Simcoe Street, and you will find yourself in the Carr family's neighbourhood. Made from wood, **Carr House** ★ *($4.50; mid-May to mid-Oct, every day 10am to 5pm; 207 Government St., ☎383-5843)* was erected in 1864 for the family of Richard Carr. After the American gold rush, the Carrs, who had been living in California, returned to England then came back to North America to set up residence in Victoria. Mr. Carr made a fortune in real estate and owned many pieces of land, both developed and undeveloped, in this residential area. He died in 1888, having outlived his wife by two years. His daughter, Emily, was only 17 at the time. Shortly after, she went first to San Francisco, then London and finally Paris to study art. She returned to British Columbia around 1910 and began teaching art to the children of Vancouver. She eventually went back to Victoria and followed in her father's footsteps, entering the real-estate business. She also began travelling more along the coast in order to paint, producing her greatest works in the 1930s. A unique painter and a reclusive woman, Emily Carr is now recognized across Canada as a great artist who left her stamp on the art world. Be sure to visit the Vancouver Art Gallery to learn more about her art, since the main focus here is her private life. Carr House also distributes maps of the neighbourhood, which show where the family lived at various times.

One of these places was **Beacon Hill Park** ★ *(between Douglas and Cook Streets, facing the Juan de Fuca Strait)*, a peaceful spot where Emily Carr spent many happy days drawing. A public park laid out in 1890, it features a number of trails leading through fields of wildflowers and landscaped sections. The view of the strait and of the Olympic Mountains in the United States is positively magnificent from here. For a reminder of exactly where you are in relation to the rest of Canada, Kilometre 0 of the TransCanada Highway lies at the south end of Douglas Street.

English Village and **Anne Hathaway's Cottage** ★ *($7; summer, every day 9am to 8pm; winter, every day 10am to 6:15pm during winter; 429 Lampson St., ☎388-4353)* lie west of downtown Victoria. Cross the Johnson Street Bridge, and after the sixth traffic light, turn left on Lampson Street. The Munro Bus, which you can catch at the corner of Douglas and Yates Streets, stops at the entrance. This little bit of England is a reconstruction of the birthplace of William Shakespeare and the home of Anne Hathaway, his wife. A stroll among these buildings will take you back in time. Try to make it for afternoon tea at the Old England Inn.

At the entrance to **Mount Douglas Park** ★★, turn left on Cedar Hill Road, then right in order to reach the lookout, which offers a panoramic view of the gulf islands, the Straits of Georgia and Juan de Fuca and the snow-capped peaks along the Canadian and American coast. The colours of the sea and the mountains are most vibrant early in the morning and at the end of the day.

The **Butchart Gardens** ★★ *($15.50 high season, $6 low season; every day 9am, summer until 11:30pm, winter until 5pm; Highway 17 North, 800 Benvenuto Ave., ☎652-4422)*, which cover 26 hectares, were founded by the family of the same name in 1904. A wide array of flowers, shrubs and trees flourish in this unique space. Maps are available at the entrance. Fireworks light up the sky during July and August, and outdoor concerts are held here in the evening from June to September *(Mon to Sat)*.

From Victoria to the West Coast Trail

Head north on Government Street, which turns into Highway 1A (Old Island Highway) and follow the signs for Sooke. At Colwood, take Highway 14, which becomes Sooke Road near Port Renfrew. You'll pass through the suburbs west of town when you get to Sooke, which lies about 30 kilometres from Victoria. At the **17 Mile House** restaurant, turn left onto Gillespie Road. This will take you into **East Sooke Park ★**, where hiking trails lead through the wild vegetation by the sea. This is a perfect place for a family outing.

Head back to the 14, and turn left toward Port Renfrew. The highway runs alongside beaches and bays. The farther you get from Victoria, the more twists and turns there are in the road. The terrain is mountainous, and the views are spectacular. As you continue west on the 14, you'll notice a change in the landscape; forestry is still an important source of revenue for the province, and the large valleys in this region have been clear-cut.

Port Renfrew

Port Renfrew is a starting point for the **West Coast Trail ★★★**. This 77-kilometre trek is geared towards experienced, intrepid hikers prepared to face unstable weather conditions and widely varied terrain; in fact, it is considered one of the most difficult hiking trails in North America.

The Rest of the Island

Duncan

The **Native Heritage Centre ★★** *($9.50; May to Oct, every day 9am to 5pm; in winter, every day 9:30am to 5pm; 200 Cowichan Way, Box 20038, ☎746-8119, ☞746-9854)*, located in Duncan, was founded by the Cowichan nations in 1987. It has become a major tourist attraction over the last few years. The centre enables the Cowichan people to introduce others to their culture through interpretive activities and shows, as well as through handicraft and art exhibitions. The tour is detailed and most interesting; a beautiful, well-made film, imbued with the spirit of the community, will enthral viewers. Located near the TransCanada Highway and the Cowichan River, the centre is composed of several re-constructions of traditional structures, a restaurant, a café, a gallery and a souvenir shop, and a historical interpretive centre that offers a totem sculpture workshop. The art gallery sells only high quality, hand-made articles, such as baskets, drums, jewellery, knitwear, original or limited-edition prints, soapstone sculptures, dolls, blankets, books, as well as wood sculptures inspired by Salish, Nuu Cha Nulth (West Coast) and Kwagulth motifs.

Nanaimo

Nanaimo is an important town because of its link to the coast, where ferries pick up hundreds of tourists headed for this region. It lies 35 kilometres from Vancouver, across the Strait of Georgia, and 1 h 30 min from Victoria by way of the TransCanada. Vacationers heading for the northern part of Vancouver Island or for Long Beach to the west, pass through Nanaimo. This town is much more than just a stopover point, however; its seaport is graced with a pleasant promenade. Furthermore, visitors can easily catch a ferry to **Newcastle Island ★** and **Protection Island ★** for the outdoor facilities and to take in the view of Nanaimo. You can see all the local attractions, including old Nanaimo, on a walking tour.

Upon entering Nanaimo, Highway 1 becomes Nicol Street. Turn right on Comox Road and then immediately left on Arena Street, which will take you to Swy-A-Lana Park (you can leave your car there). Go into the park and turn right when you reach the waterfront, where you'll find **Harbourside Walkway ★★**, a pleasant promenade lined with parks, historic sites and shops.

The **Bastion ★** *(Jul and Aug, every day 9am to 5pm)* was built by the Hudson's Bay Company in 1853 in order to protect the new trading post and the local residents. Its construction was supervised by two Quebecers, Jean-Baptiste Fortier and Leon Labine, both employees of the company. The Bastion never came under attack and was abandoned when the company left in 1862. It was later used as a prison, and has served as a gathering place and a museum since 1910.

Port Alberni

Like many towns in British Columbia, Port Alberni owes its existence to the forest

BRITISH COLUMBIA

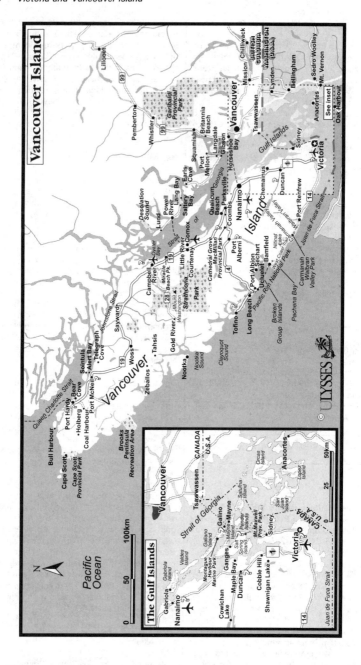

industry, fishing and trade. Its harbour is linked to the Pacific by a large canal, putting the town at an advantage as far as shipping is concerned. Port Alberni is also the gateway to the west coast of Vancouver Island. When you reach the top of the mountains surrounding Mount Arrowsmith, at an altitude of nearly 2,000 metres, you're almost at Port Alberni.

Keep left as you enter Port Alberni. Take Port Alberni Highway to Third Avenue, turn left on Argyle Street and then right toward the harbour. The **Harbour Quay** is a pleasant place to have a cup of coffee and inquire about which boats can take you to Pacific Rim National Park for the day. In the middle of the public square, you'll see a fountain adorned with granite sculptures showing the life cycle of salmon.

The *M.V. Lady Rose* *($12-40; year-round, Bamfield: Tue, Thu, Fri and Sat 8am, during summer, Tue, Thu, Sat 8am in winter; Ucluelet and Broken Group Islands: Mon, Wed, Fri 8am; Harbour Quay, ☎1-800-663-7192)* offers year-round transportation between Port Alberni and Bamfield, at the north end of the West Coast Trail. During summer, the **Frances Barkley** carries passengers to and from Ucluelet and the Broken Group Islands, south of Long Beach. All sorts of discoveries await you on these trips; make sure to bring along a camera, a pair of binoculars and a raincoat.

Ucluelet ★

Located at the south end of Long Beach, Ucluelet is a charming town whose main street is lined with old wooden houses. In the past, the only way to get here was by boat. The local economy is based on fishing and tourism. Over 200 species of birds can be found around Ucluelet. Migrating grey whales swim in the coves and near the beaches here between the months of March to May, making whale-watching one of the main attractions on the west coast.

At the south end of the village, in **He Tin Kis Park ★★**, a wooden walkway leads through a small temperate rain forest beside Terrace Beach. This short walk will help you appreciate the beauty of this type of vegetation. The **Amphitrite Point Lighthouse ★** has stood on the shore since 1908. In those days, this area was known as the "cemetery of the Pacific" because so many ships had run up onto the reefs here. The wreckage of one tall ship still

lies at the bottom of the sea near the point. The Canadian Coast Guard has a shipping checkpoint offshore *(guided tours available during summer)*.

Tofino ★

Tofino, situated at the northwest end of Long Beach, is a quiet town where visitors chat about sunsets and the outdoors. Spanish explorers Galiano and Valdes, who discovered this coast in the summer of 1792, named the place after Vincente Tofino, their hydrography professor.

This town is also an artists' colony. The local painters and sculptors draw much of their inspiration from the unspoiled landscape of the west coast. The **House of Himwitsa ★** *(at the end of the main street, near the port)* displays works by native artists.

Campbell River

Campbell River is a choice destination for salmon-fishing fans. This sport can be enjoyed here year-round, and five varieties of salmon frequent the local waters. When you get to town, take the time to go to **The Museum at Campbell River ★** *(mid-May to Sep, Mon to Sat 10am to 5pm, Sun noon to 5pm; winter, Tue to Sun noon to 5pm; 470 Island Highway, opposite Sequoia Park, Fifth Ave., ☎287-3103)*, which is interesting not only for its elegant architecture but also for its exhibits on aboriginals and pioneers. Its collection includes a number of artifacts from Campbell River's early days. Furthermore, a significant part of the museum is devoted to aboriginal engravings, sculpture and jewellery.

On your way into the centre of town, stop for a walk along **Discovery Pier ★** *(Government Wharf)*, from which you can admire the Strait of Georgia and the Coast Mountains. At the end, turn right and walk down Shoppers Row, where you can purchase souvenirs, food or basic necessities. The Travel InfoCentre is located on this street as well.

Telegraph Cove ★★

This little paradise set back from the eastern shore of Vancouver Island was once the end point of a telegraph line that ran along the coast, hence the name. Later, a wealthy family set up a sawmill on land they had purchased around the little bay. From that point on, time stopped; the little houses have been preserved, and the boardwalk alongside the bay is punctuated with commemorative plaques explaining the major stages in the village's history. Today, vacationers come here to go fishing, scuba diving and whale-watching. If you're lucky, you might catch a glimpse of a seal, an otter or even a whale from the boardwalk.

Alert Bay ★★

At the **U'mista Cultural Center** ★ *($5; year-round, Mon to Fri 9am to 5pm, noon to 5pm, and Sat and Sun during summer; Alert Bay, ☎974-5403)*, you can learn about the Potlatch ("to give") ceremony through the history of the U'mista native community. Missionaries tried to ban the ceremony; there was even a law forbidding members of the community from dancing, preparing objects for distribution or making public speeches. The ceremony was then held in secret and during bad weather, when the whites couldn't get to the island. A lovely collection of masks and jewellery adorns the walls. Don't miss the **Native Burial Grounds** and the **Memorial Totems** ★★, which testify to the richness of this art.

Port Hardy

Port Hardy, a town of fishermen and forest workers, is located at the northeast end of Vancouver Island. There is a wealth of animal life in this region, both in the water and on the land. If you aren't interested in going fishing or whale-watching, treat yourself to a walk through the forest in Cape Scott Park. Visitors en route to Prince Rupert and the Queen Charlotte Islands board the ferry in Port Hardy *($80 return)*.

The **Copper Maker** ★ *(free admission; Mon to Sat 9am to 5pm; 114 Copper Way, Fort Rupert, on the outskirts of Port Hardy, ☎949-8491)* is an native art gallery and studio, where you'll find totem poles several metres high, some in the process of being made, others waiting to be delivered to buyers. Take the time to watch the artists at work, and ask them to tell you about the symbolism behind their drawings and sculptures.

 OUTDOORS

 Parks

Victoria

The summit of **Mount Tolmie** ★★★ *(BC Parks, ☎391-2300)* offers sensational panoramic views of Victoria, Haro Strait, the ocean, and of magnificent Mount Baker and the Cascade Range in Washington State (USA).

Goldstream Provincial Park ★★★ *(20 min from Victoria by Highway 1; BC Parks, ☎391-2300)* is one of the major parks in the Victoria area. Picture 600-year-old Douglas firs lining hiking trails leading to Mount Finlayson and past magnificent waterfalls. In November, nature lovers come here to watch coho, chinook and chum salmon make their final voyage, spawn and die in Goldstream River. The fish are easy to see, as the water is crystal clear. Not to be missed.

The Rest of the Island

Pacific Rim National Park, Long Beach section ★★★ *(Long Beach information centre, Hwy 4, ☎726-4212)* This park is trimmed with kilometres of deserted beaches, running alongside temperate rain forests. The beaches, hiking trails and various facilities are clearly indicated and easy to reach. The setting is enchanting, relaxing and stimulating at once, as well as being accessible year-round. The beaches are popular with surfing buffs, and **Live to Surf** *(1180 Pacific Rim Hwy, Tofino, ☎725-4464)* rents out surfboards and wetsuits.

Exploring the Tofino area by boat will enable you to uncover the hidden treasures of the neighbouring islands and bays. If you feel like walking about, you can check out sulphur springs in the caves or bears in the forest. **Sea Trek** *(441B Campbell St., Box 627, Tofino, V0R 2Z0, ☎725-4412 or 1-800-811-9155)* can arrange an excursion for you.

Strathcona Park ★★ *(swimming, hiking, fishing and 161 campsites; 59 km west of Campbell River on Highway 28, ☎954-4600)* is the oldest provincial park in British Columbia. Its 210,000 hectares of forest and fresh water abound in natural treasures, including huge

Orca

Douglas firs over 90 metres high. The highest peak on Vancouver Island is found here, the Golden Hinde, it measures 2,220 metres.

Cape Scott Provincial Park ★★ *(67 km northwest of Port Hardy on Holberg Rd.; register at Port Hardy Chamber of Commerce, ☎949-7622; for all other information, BC Parks, ☎954-4600)* encompasses 15,070 hectares of temperate rain forest. Scott was a merchant from Bombay (India) who financed all sorts of commercial expeditions. Many ships have run aground on this coast, and a lighthouse was erected in 1960 in order to guide sailors safely along their way. Sandy beaches cover two-thirds of the 64-kilometre stretch of waterfront. On the hilly terrain farther inland, you'll find various species of giant trees, such as red cedars and pines. This remote part of Vancouver Island receives up to 500 millimetres of rainfall annually, and is frequently hit by storms. It is best to visit here during summertime.

 Beaches

There are two beaches in Victoria where families can enjoy a day of sand-castle building and swimming in calm waters. **Willows Beach** ★ *(public bathrooms, playground; in Oak Bay, at the corner of Estevan Ave. and Beach Dr.)* lies alongside a chic residential neighbourhood near a marina and Oak Bay Beach Hotel. **Cadboro Bay Beach** ★ *(public bathrooms, playground; at the corner of Sinclair Road and Beach Drive)*, a little farther east, is located in the University of Victoria neighbourhood and attracts a young crowd. It looks out onto a bay, with the Chatham Islands and Discovery Island in the distance. The ebb and flow of the tides has transformed the strand at **Beacon Hill Park** ★ (see p 578) into a pebble beach covered with pieces of driftwood.

 Scuba-Diving

The Rest of the Island

Each year, hundreds of divers flock to the eastern shore of Vancouver Island, lured by the colourful underwater scenery and rich marine life. The Nanaimo region is a wonderful place for this type of sightseeing. **Sundown Diving Charters** *(22 Esplanade, Nanaimo, V9R 4Y7, ☎753-1880, ⬦753-6445)*.

 Whale-watching

Victoria

Orca Spirit Adventures *(in the port, ☎383-8411)* offers excursions aboard the *Orca Spirit*, an elegant and extremely comfortable 15-metre ship equipped with large observation platforms. Transportation from your hotel is available.

Sea King Adventures *(950 Wharf St., ☎381-4173)* is a very professional company with an eight-metre boat that can comfortably accommodate 12 passengers. Reservations strongly recommended.

The Rest of the Island

Chinook Charters *($50; 450 Campbell St., P.O. Box 501, Tofino, VOR 2Z0,* ☎*725-3431 or 1-800-665-3646)* will take you out to sea to observe grey whales at close range. The best time to go is in March and April, when there are large numbers of these sea mammals in the area.

Robson Bight Charters *($70; Jun to Oct 9:30am; Sayward,* ☎*282-3833 or 1-800-658-0022)* arranges whale-watching tours in the Johnstone Strait. Each year, killer whales use this area as a sort of training ground for their offspring. A sight to remember.

 Fishing

Victoria

Victoria Harbour Charter *(50 Wharf St.,* ☎*381-5050)* hosts salmon-fishing excursions aboard a fully equipped nine-metre yacht. Thrills guaranteed.

The Rest of the Island

You can fish at any time, day or night, on **Discovery Pier** *($1 with valid fishing permit; rod rental 7am to 10pm, $2.50 per hour; 24 hours a day; Government Wharf, Campbell River,* ☎*286-6199)*, which stretches 150 metres. This is also a popular place to go for a stroll.

Bailey's Charters *($60 an hour; Box 124, Campbell River, V9W 5A7,* ☎*286-3474)* arranges guided salmon- and trout-fishing trips, which are terrific ways to explore the region's beautiful shoreline.

 ACCOMMODATIONS

Victoria

The **YHA Victoria Hostel** *($20; some private rooms, sb, K, laundry room; 516 Yates St.,* ☎*385-4511,* ☞*385-3232)*, a stone and brick building with 108 beds, is located in Old Town, right near the harbour. Members take precedence in youth hostels, so it can be difficult for non-members to get a bed, especially during high season.

Without question, the undeniably charming **Swans Hotel Pub & Café** *($90-$160; pb,* ℝ*,* ℜ*, tv; 506 Pandora Ave.,* ☎*361-3310 or 1-800-668-SWAN,* ☞*361-3491)* is one of the best places to stay in Victoria, especially if you're travelling as a group. The rooms are actually luxury apartments that can accommodate several people. Guests will find "real" works of art on the walls, plants, big-screen TVs and a pretty, inviting decor. The hotel, which dates back to the late 19th century, is located right in the heart of Old Town, steps away from Chinatown and the Inner Harbour. A fun pub that serves what locals claim to be the best beer in North America and an excellent restaurant known for its fresh oysters are on the ground floor.

The **Oak Bay Beach Hotel** *($174 bkfst incl.;* ℜ*, pb, tv, pub; 1175 Beach Dr.,* ☎*598-4556 or 1-800-668-7758,* ☞*598-6180)*, which has 50 comfortably laid-out rooms, caters to visitors seeking English charm and a pleasant seaside atmosphere. Located on the waterfront of a residential neighbourhood, it offers an interesting view.

The **Empress Hotel Canadian Pacific** *($375;* ✗*,* ⛵*, ≈, ◉, ☉, △, tv,* ℜ*; 721 Government St.,* ☎*384-8111 or 1-800-441-1414,* ☞*381-4334)* is located on the Inner Harbour, adjacent to the museums and the interesting public and commercial areas. Designed by architect Francis Rattenbury, this luxurious 475-room hotel offers a relaxing atmosphere and a Chateau style setting. A new wing has been added to the original quintessentially Victorian building without detracting from its legendary charm. Visitors stop here for tea or simply to admire the ivy-covered façade.

From Victoria to the West Coast Trail

The **Port Renfrew Hotel** *($25;* ✗*, sb; at the end of Highway 14, Port Renfrew,* ☎*647-5541,* ☞*647-5594)* is located on the village pier, where hikers set out for the West Coast Trail. The rustic rooms are sure to please hikers longing for a dry place to sleep. There are laundry facilities on the premises, as well as a pub that serves hot meals.

The soberly decorated **Traveller's Inn on Douglas Street** *($80 bkfst incl.; ≈, K, tv, parking; 710 Queens Avenue, Victoria,*

☎*388-6641 or 370-1000 or 1-888-753-3774,*
≈360-1190) is a renovated building with 36 rooms. Basic services are available, but there are no telephones in the rooms.

The Rest of the Island

Nanaimo

The **Best Western Northgate** *($84; ℜ, ✗, ≡, K, ⊛, △; 6450 Metral Dr.,* ☎*390-2222, ≈390-2412)* has 76 simply decorated, comfortable rooms. The layout is the same at the other Best Westerns in this region. A safe bet.

Ucluelet

The **Ucluelet Campground** *($21-$31; 100 sites, toilets, showers, ✗, ♿; 260 Seaplane Base Rd.,* ☎*726-4355)* is located within walking distance of Ucluelet. Reservations required.

The *Canadian Princess Resort ($59-$155; sb or pb; Peninsula Rd.,* ☎*726-7771 or 1-800-663-7090, ≈726-7121)* is a ship that sailed the waters along the coast for nearly 40 years, and is now permanently moored at the Ucluelet pier. It has 26 rooms, which are small and don't have a lot of extras, but offer a pleasant nautical atmosphere.

Tofino

The **Tin-Wis Best Western** *($125; tv, pb, ℜ, ♿, beach; 1119 Pacific Rim Highway,* ☎*725-4445 or 1-800-528-1234, ≈725-4447)* is a large hotel run by Tla-O-Qui-Aht First Nations people. It offers all the comforts you would expect from a Best Western. The plants and wooden decorative elements blend harmoniously with the immediate surroundings, but the place is oversized (56 rooms).

Picture a house on a beach lined with lush vegetation with the setting sun reflecting off the water; that's what awaits you at the heavenly **Chesterman's Beach Bed & Breakfast** *($160-175 bkfst incl.; pb; 1345 Chesterman's Beach Rd.,* ☎*/≈725-3726)*. A simple walk on the beach every day is all you need to enjoy a satisfying vacation here. Three rooms are available.

Qualicum Beach

The **Quatna Manor Bed & Breakfast** *($70-$85 bkfst incl.; sb or pb, no smoking; 512 Quatna Rd., Qualicum Beach,* ☎*752-6685, ≈752-8385)* is definitely a place to keep in mind. The friendly reception you will receive from hosts Bill and Betty will make your stay at their Tudor-style home all the more pleasant. A hearty breakfast is served in the dining room. Bill is retired from the air force. His job required a great deal of travelling, and his stories make for memorable breakfast conversation.

Campbell River

As its name suggests, the pretty little **Edgewater Motel** *($45-$60; ✗, K, pb, tv; 4073 South Island Highway, near Oyster Bay,* ☎*/≈923-5421)* is located on the waterfront. The rooms are decent for the price, and you can prepare meals in them — a real plus if you're on a tight budget.

Telegraph Cove

The **Telegraph Cove Resorts** *($21 for a campsite for two adults, water, electricity; $66-$149 for a cabin for 2 to 8 people, K, pb, ✗;* ☎*928-3131 or 1-800-200-4665, ≈928-3105)* welcome visitors from May to October. The campground, equipped with basic facilities, is somewhat bare, but the view of the bay makes up for that. The cabins blend into the picturesque setting. The service is friendly, and you'll feel as if you're at some sort of summer camp. If you have to spend a few days in the northern part of the island, Telegraph Cove is a thoroughly pleasant place to visit.

Port Hardy

The **Seagate Hotel** *($90-$95; tv, ℜ, pub; 8600 Granville St.,* ☎*949-6348, ≈949-6347)* is located a stone's throw from the town pier. All of the rooms are sparingly decorated, and the view makes those facing the port much more attractive.

BRITISH COLUMBIA

RESTAURANTS

Victoria

The sunny terrace at **Garrick's Head Pub** *($; Bastion Sq., on View St.)*, located on a pedestrian street, is a pleasant place to get together over a local beer. The space may be limited inside, but there is a giant-screen TV for sports fans.

The Oak Bay Beach Hotel's pub, the **Snug** *($; 1175 Beach Dr., ☎598-4556)*, serves local beer and light meals. A quiet, well-kept place, it attracts a rather mature clientele.

Spinnakers Brew Pub & Restaurant *($; every day from 7am to 11pm; 308 Catherine St., ☎386-2739)* serves beer and food in a laid-back setting, with the house specialties listed on big blackboards. The terrace is very well positioned, beckoning guests to kick back and relax. This place radiates a festive, convivial atmosphere.

Recapturing the atmosphere of the British Empire of Queen Victoria, the beautiful Empress Hotel's **Bengal Lounge** *($$; 721 Government St., Victoria, ☎384-8111)* serves a curry buffet featuring Indian specialties. The place is tastefully decorated with East Asian furniture, and guests have lots of elbow room.

Tea-lovers get together in the **Empress Hotel Canadian Pacific** *($$-$$$; behind the port, 721 Government St., ☎384-8111)* for tea with scones served with different kinds of jam. If you've got a big appetite, stop in for High Tea, which comes complete with cucumber and cream cheese sandwiches. This tradition supposedly originated during the reign of Queen Victoria, when the Duchess of Bedford, who tended to feel faint in the late afternoon, began fortifying herself with tea and little cakes and sandwiches. The old wood floors, comfortable furniture, giant teapots and courteous service make for an altogether satisfying experience.

Il Terrazzo Ristorante *($$-$$$; 555 Johnson St., ☎361-0028)* is an Italian restaurant with a menu made up mainly of pasta dishes. Creamy sauces flavoured with spices and sweet nuts make for some very interesting taste sensations. The clientele consists of young professionals and tourists. The one sour note is that the wine is kept on a mezzanine where all the heat in the room is concentrated, and is thus served at too warm a temperature.

From Victoria to the West Coast

The **17 Mile House** *($; 5126 Sooke Rd., Sooke, ☎642-5942)*, located right before the entrance of Sooke Harbour Park, serves light meals in a cozy setting. The thoroughly laid-back atmosphere here makes this just the place to quench your thirst after a day of walking along the waterfront in Sooke.

The **Sooke Harbour House** *($$$-$$$$; every day 3:30pm, dinner only, vegetarian dishes available; 1528 Whiffen Spit Rd., Sooke, ☎642-3421)* has been praised to the skies by people from all over the world. The Philips' gourmet cuisine has seduced thousands of palates. The hosts settle for nothing but the best and are masters when it comes to preparing local produce. The dining room, set up inside a country house, offers a view of Sooke Harbour. Enjoy the classic ambiance as you take your seat and look over the menu. The dishes, prepared in West Coast style, have hints of Japanese and French influences.

The Rest of the Island

Nanaimo

Dinghy Dock Pub *($; 11am to 11pm, midnight Fri and Sat; no. 8 Pirate's Plank, Protection Island, ☎753-2373)*. At this floating pub, which is attached to the Protection Island pier, you can enjoy a good local beer while observing the happenings in the Nanaimo harbour. The fish & chips are succulent. To get to the island, take the ferry from Commercial Inlet *(every hour from 9:10am to 11:10pm, midnight Fri and Sat)*.

Located on the seawall, the **Javawocky Coffee House** *($; 8-90 Front St., Pioneer Waterfront Plaza, ☎753-1688)* serves a wide assortment of coffee and light meals and offers a view of the Nanaimo port and the crowd strolling about there.

Ucluelet

People come to the **Matterson Restaurant** *($;
1682 Peninsula Rd.,* ☎*726-2200)*, located on
the main street, for lunch and tea. Don't
hesitate to order salmon here; it's very fresh.

Long Beach

Set on a big rock overlooking the beach, the
Wickaninnish Restaurant *($-$$; 11am to
9:30pm; at the bottom of Wick Rd.,*
☎*726-7706)* offers a spectacular view of the
Pacific Ocean. The menu is made up of seafood
dishes. The pasta with smoked salmon is
particularily tasty. Whatever you choose, your
meal will be that much better accompanied by
a glass of British Columbian white wine.

Tofino

Schooner Restaurant *($$$; 331 Campbell St.,*
☎*725-3444)* is a classic. It serves seafood and
British Columbian wines. An inviting place, it
has been decorated to look like a ship's hold
and deck. The soft lighting creates a relaxing
comfortable atmosphere.

Campbell River

The **Seasons Bistro** *($; 6:30am to 2pm and
5:30pm to 10pm; 261 Island Highway,*
☎*286-1131)* has an original menu featuring
seafood pasta and pheasant with passionfruit.
This place attracts both locals and tourists, and
jazz lovers in particular.

Sayward

The **Cable Cafe** *($;* ☎*282-3343)* offers simple,
quality meals at reasonable prices. This is a fun
place, with walls made of coiled cables.

Port Hardy

The **Seagate Hotel Restaurant** *($; from 6:30am
on; 8600 Granville St.,* ☎*949-6348)* has a
wide-ranging menu. While enjoying a view of
the harbour, you will dine alongside local
residents, including fishermen fresh from a day
at sea.

ENTERTAINMENT

Victoria

The **Victoria Jazz Society** *(*☎*388-4423,
⇝388-4407)* can provide you with information
on local jazz and blues shows. The Victoria
Jazz Festival takes place from late June to mid-
July.

The **Sticky Wicket Pub** *(919 Douglas St.,
Strathcona Hotel,* ☎*383-7137)* is located inside
the Strathcona Hotel, just behind the Empress.
This place attracts people of all ages and
serves good beer. In nice weather, everyone
heads up to the roof for some fun in the sun
and a game of volleyball. At **Legends Nightclub**,
also in the Strathcona, a clientele of all
different ages dances to rock, R&B and jazz.

Uforia's *(cover charge; 1208 Wharf St.,*
☎*381-2331)* attracts a fairly stylish crowd.
People come here to party and kick up their
heels on the dance floor.

SHOPPING

Victoria

It is worth stopping in at **Rogers' Chocolates**
(913 Government St., ☎*384-7021)* to see the
shop's lovely, early 20th-century decor and pair
of Art Nouveau lamps from Italy. Victoria
Creams, available in a wide variety of flavours,
are the specialty of the house.

With its stained-glass windows and eight-metre
ceilings, **Munro's** *(1108 Government St.,*
☎*382-2464)* is reputed to be the most beautiful
bookstore in Canada. Good selection of
Canadian, English and American books.

Knives and Darts *(1306 Government St.,*
☎*383-2422)* sells an assortment of, well,
knives and darts. Darts is very popular in the
local pubs, and is taken quite seriously.

BRITISH COLUMBIA

The Rest of the Island

Ucluelet

The **Du Quaii Gallery** *(1971 Peninsula Rd.,* ☎*726-7223)* exhibits native art. It is worth the trip just to see the building, which looks like a longhouse, a traditional aboriginal cedar building.

Tofino

The **House of Himwitsa** *(300 Main St.,* ☎*725-2017)* is an art gallery that displays drawings, paintings, sculptures and silver and gold jewellery. Ask about the legends referred to in these pieces and the symbolism employed by the artists.

Port Hardy

The **Copper Maker** *(every day; 112 Copper Way, Fort Rupert,* ☎*949-8491)* displays the works of a number of native artists. Masks, pottery and symbolic jewellery can all be purchased here. These articles might seem expensive, but the prices are lower than in the bigger cities.

Northern British-Columbia

The route to Northern British Columbia crosses the Rocky Mountains and leads through pleasant wooded areas strewn with lakes.

Prince George ★★

Prince George considers itself the capital of northern British Columbia. As any map will tell you, however, it actually lies in the centre of the province. Its geographic location has enabled it to become a hub not only for the railway, but also for road transport, since it lies at the intersection of Highway 16, which runs the width of the province, and Highway 97, which runs the length.

The **Fraser Fort George Regional Museum ★★** *($4.25; mid-May to mid-Sep, every day 10am to 5pm; mid-Sep to mid-May, Tue to Sun noon to 5pm; at the end of 20th Avenue,* ☎ *562-1612)* stands on the very site where Fort George was erected in 1807. The museum is an excellent place to learn about the history of Prince George, from the arrival of Alexander Mackenzie and the beginning of the fur trade to the introduction and development of the forest industry. The museum's Northwood Gallery, a sure hit with young children, presents an exhibit on the region's flora and fauna.

For a short walk or a picnic, head to the **Cottonwood Island Nature Park ★★**, which covers 33 hectares along the Nechako River, right near downtown. It has an interesting wildlife-observation area, where you can watch foxes, beavers and eagles. **Connaught Hill Park ★**, located in the centre of town, offers a 360° view of Prince George and its surroundings. To get there, take Queensway southward, then turn right on Connaught Drive and right again on Caine.

Dawson Creek ★

Dawson Creek was named after Dr. George Dawson, a geologist who, in 1879, discovered that the surrounding plains were ideal for agriculture. He might have thought that Dawson Creek would become a farming capital, but he probably never suspected that oil and natural gas would be discovered here.

The other major turning-point in Dawson Creek's history took place in 1942, when the town became kilometre/mile 0 of the Alaska Highway. Today, nearly 30,000 tourists from all over the world come to Dawson Creek to start their journey northward.

The **Station Museum ★** *(Jun to Sep, every day 8am to 7pm; winter, Tue to Sat 9am to noon and 1pm to 5pm)* traces the history of the Alaska Highway, as well as that of the area's first inhabitants. The collection on display includes the largest mammoth tusk ever found in the Canadian West, as well as a number of dinosaur bones.

BRITISH COLUMBIA

The Queen Charlotte Islands (Haida Gwaii) ★★★

However you choose to get to the islands, once there you'll discover an atmosphere and landscape that are truly beyond compare. Though the 5,000 islanders are very modest about their little piece of paradise, they actually go out of their way to attract and welcome visitors from the world over. The archipelago consists of 150 islands of various sizes. Almost all of the urban areas are located on the largest one, **Graham Island**, to the north. **Moresby Island** is the second most populous. Here, you'll find two villages, Sandspit and Alliford Bay, as well as the amazing **Gwaii Haanas National Park.**

The jagged relief of the **Queen Charlotte and San Christoval Mountains** has always protected the east coast from the westerly storms. Despite the weather, the **Haidas**, who already inhabited the archipelago, established living areas on the west coast some 10,000 years ago. The Haidas are known to this day for their high-quality handicrafts and beautiful works of art.

Skidegate

This is the first place you'll see if you take the ferry to the Queen Charlotte Islands, since the landing stage is located at the edge of the village. Skidegate is a small native community of 470 inhabitants, located on the beach in the heart of **Roonay Bay ★★★**. While you're here, make sure to visit the internationally renowned **Queen Charlotte Islands Museum ★★★** *(Tue to Fri 10am to 5pm, Sat and Sun 1pm to 5pm, closed Mon; ☎ 559-4643)*, devoted exclusively to articles made by the Haidas over the ages, up until the present day. All modes of expression are represented here: everything from totem poles, sculptures and drawings to fabrics and basketry, not to mention jewellery made with precious metals. The shop boasts an impressive but pricely selection of books and quality souvenirs.

Queen Charlotte City ★★

Located four kilometres south of Skidegate, Queen Charlotte City is a pleasant coastal village with 1,100 inhabitants. The atmosphere is very relaxed here, and the streets are filled with young people during the summer season. This is the jumping-off point for sea kayak expeditions.

As far as organized tours are concerned, the best-known company is definitely **Queen Charlotte Adventures** *(on the way into town, ☎ 559-8990 or 1-800-668-4288, ≈ 559-8983)*, which will take you to the **Gwaii Haanas National Park ★★★** *(☎ 559-8818 or 637-5362)* by motorboat, since the area cannot be reached by land. This park, located at the southern tip of the archipelago, is home to many unusual sights, each more remarkable than the last. First, there is **Hot Springs Island ★★★**, a paradise for anyone who enjoys a good soak. Then there's **Laskeek Bay ★★★**, frequented by dolphins and whales. **Ninstints ★★★**, a former Haida village on the tip of the island of Sgan Gwaii, is a UNESCO World Heritage Site. Here, you will find the largest collection of totem poles and aboriginal-built structures in the Queen Charlotte Islands. There is something unreal and mystical about the location itself. Ninstints has been declared a UNESCO World Heritage Site.

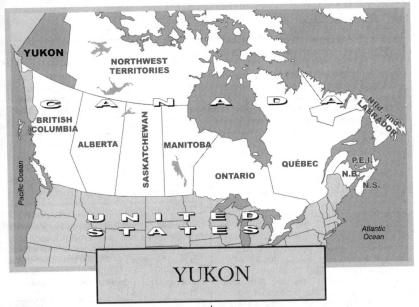

YUKON

Far to the north, above British Columbia, glaciers come and go between high peaks. Inland, Tagish Lake is the origin of a river that seems to take sly pleasure in turning its back to the sea, heading north before forking off to the west and Alaska. Enlarged by waters from many tributaries, it finally flows into Bering Strait after travelling almost 3,200 kilometres. Aboriginals called it the "great river", or *Yukon*, in their language.

Geography

This is also the name that was later given to a Canadian territory over 480,000 square kilometres in size, twice as big as the United Kingdom. It's shaped somewhat like a right-angle triangle, the sides of which are formed by the borders of Alaska on the west, The Northwest Territories to the north and east and British Columbia to the south. The northernmost tip of the triangle is on the Beaufort Sea, in the Arctic Ocean. Yukon Territory is characterized by many mountain chains, starting with the St. Elias Mountains in the southwest. This extension of the Coastal Mountains, includes Mount Logan whose peak reaches an altitude of 6,050 metres, making it the highest in Canada. To the east, the Mackenzie Mountains block off the landscape. Between the two, the land subsides to some degree, especially in the southern Yukon.

Almost 60% of the land is wooded, the density of the forest and the size of the trees diminishing towards the north.

The climate in the Yukon is very similar to the Northwest Territories. It experiences the same extreme conditions, a result of the latitude. This is also true in Dawson, where a beautiful summer day can consist of 20 hours of sunlight with temperatures reaching 35°C. Conversely, a winter night can also last 20 hours with the thermometer dropping to -50°C. During the three summer months, the average temperature is 21°C. The average winter temperature ranges from -15°C to -27°C, depending on whether you are in the southern or central area. It's worth noting that although the Yukon doesn't get the warm air currents from the Pacific, because of the barrier created by the St. Elias Mountains, it also doesn't get the heavy rain. Getting dressed for such a climate requires particular care to protect against both chilblain and sunburn. Sunglasses are required, especially in the spring when the bright sun reflecting off the snow is that much more intense.

During the spring and summer, since the nights are so short, it's difficult to see the aurora borealis. On the other hand, the sunrises and sunsets can last for many hours at this time of the year. The most striking reds fill the sky and shine sloping rays on an already imposing landscape.

Unique Lights

The Yukon's latitude doesn't only have drawbacks. In the fall and winter, the deep nights allow you to see what is perhaps the most beautiful display of lights that nature has to offer called the aurora borealis of northern lights. It's like a huge curtain of white, red, blue and green light undulating in the sky. This phenomenon occurs when solar explosions release particles that then get trapped in the earth's magnetic field.

Human Occupation

Approximately 35,500 people live in the Yukon, mostly in the southern part of the territory. The native community is comprised of about 7,000 people. English is the common language, French is spoken by only 9% of the population. Over 23,000 Yukonites live in the capital, Whitehorse. There are three other organized towns in the territory (1,500 to 3,000 residents): Dawson, Watson Lake and Faro. Some twenty towns and hamlets, sometimes more symbolic than real, bring together the rest of the population. The Yukon's political status is that of a territory under the supervision of Ottawa. Nonetheless, a local government handles most domestic affairs. Police services are provided by the Royal Canadian Mounted Police.

The modern history of the Yukon starts in 1825, when John Franklin explored its north shore. Around 1840, the Hudson's Bay Company set up fur-trading posts. In 1895, Canada affirmed its sovereignty over the territory, sending in a Mountie detachment just in time to keep the Americans from doing likewise. In 1896, gold was discovered in the Klondike. The goldrush led to a demographic boom which lasted until 1904. Subsequently, the total population fell to under 5,000, until the construction of the Alaska highway in 1942. The development of land travel soon caused a drop in river travel on the Yukon. Dawson ceased to be the capital, and Whitehorse progressively developed as services were introduced. Since the 1960s, mining towns have either been created or developed, to such a degree that the population of the Yukon is now growing twice as fast as that of Canada on the whole.

The first activity in the Yukon economy was fur trading. Trapping muskrat, lynx, marten and beaver among others, is still practised today. Except in the southeast part of the territory, there is very little in terms of forests that can be exploited for profit. Besides, the short growing season doesn't allow for any agriculture other than domestic vegetable gardens. Despite the stops and starts inherent to all mining, it's still underground exploitation that generates the most activity. Lead, zinc, silver and, of course, gold are all mined here. And finally, close to 175,000 tourists visit the Yukon every year, and leave behind, year in and year out, hundreds of millions of dollars.

Sourdough or *cheechako?*

Don't even bother checking the dictionary for the true definitions of *sourdough* or *cheechako*. To become a sourdough, a real Yukonite, there's only one way: you have to see the ice form on the rivers in the fall and stay to watch it break in the spring. *Cheechakos* are simply those unlucky souls that have never lived in the Yukon.

 FINDING YOUR WAY AROUND

By Plane

The Whitehorse Airport is served by flights from Juneau and Fairbanks, Alaska. As a rule however, visitors from the south pass through Vancouver International Airport on the way to Whitehorse. Canada's two major airline companies offer flights in Boeing 737s that take 2 hours and 20 minutes.

Almost all communities and places in the Yukon, no matter how rarely frequented by humans, have a landing strip. Various aircraft can also land on lakes, snowfields and glaciers. Four regional airlines assure regular links with

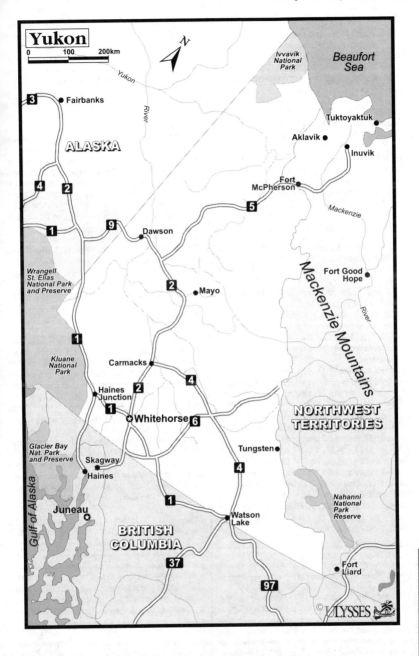

YUKON

the Yukon's main centres, and sometimes with Alaska next door. They are **Air North** *(P.O. Box 4998, Whitehorse, Y1A 4S2, ☎403-668-2228; they offer a ticket for a limited period of time valid for all their destinations)*, **Alkan Air** *(P.O. Box 4008, Whitehorse, Y1A 3S9, ☎403-668-2107)*, **NWT Air** *(Suite 02-13, Air Terminal Building, Whitehorse, Y1A 3E4, ☎1-800-661-0789)* and **Ptarmigan Airways** *(P.O. Box 100, Yellowknife, NWT, X1A 2N1, ☎403-873-4461)*.

Off the beaten path, it's also possible to charter a plane, a hydroplane or a helicopter to get to almost any part of the Yukon or to fly above a particular region. Beware, it's not cheap: a three-hour excursion flight in a bush plane can easily cost $125 per person, and a helicopter is even more expensive.

Here are a few addresses: **Air North**, **Alkan Air**, **Action Aviation** *(P.O. Box 5898, Whitehorse, Y1A 5L6)*, **Almon Landair** *(200-307 Jarvis Street, Whitehorse, Y1A 2H3, ☎403-667-7790, this company offers service in different languages and air-caravanning for one or two weeks. It's a package that allows you to travel by means of a small airplane that you rent for a certain length of time, and to camp)*, **Blacksheep Aviation** *(P.O. Box 4087, Whitehorse, Y1A 3S9, ☎403-668-7761)*, **Bonanza Aviation** *(P.O. Box 284, Dawson City, Y0B 1G0, ☎403-993-6904)*, **Capital Helicopter** *(P.O. Box 4387, Whitehorse Aerocentre, Whitehorse, Y1A 3T5, ☎403-668-6200)*, **Chilkoot Air Service** *(P.O. Box 5832, Whitehorse, Y1A 5L6, ☎403-821-4337 or 667-1055)*, **Frontier Helicopters** *(P.O. Box 10, Watson Lake, Y0A 1C0, ☎403-536-7766)*, **Heli-Dynamics** *(P.O. Box 4280, Whitehorse, Y1A 3T3, ☎403-668-3536)*, **Klondike Heli-Magic** *(P.O. Box 4730, Whitehorse, Y1A 4N6, ☎403-667-4070; they also rent canoes and kayaks)* and **Watson Lake Flying Services** *(P.O. Box 7, Watson lake, Y0A 1C0, ☎403-536-2231)*.

By Car

It is possible to get to the Yukon from the south by taking the Alaska Highway, which starts at Dawson Creek, a small town in British Columbia not far from the Alberta border. It's now a paved road with gas, food or lodgings at intervals ranging from 32 to 80 kilometres. From the west coast of Canada, Prince Rupert specifically, a second road heads inward

through the mountains. This is the Stewart Cassiar Highway, which joins the Alaska Highway just after it enters the Yukon. Before heading off on this route it's important to plan the trip carefully since there aren't many service areas along its 752 kilometres. On the other hand, the scenery can be spectacular, especially at Stikine River Valley and Dease Lake.

You can also get to the Yukon from Inuvik, a part of the Northwest Territories at the mouth of the Mackenzie River, on the Arctic Ocean. This area is linked to Dawson by Dempster Highway. Pay no mind to the name though; Dempster "Highway" is actually a 663-kilometre-long, unpaved, dirt road. And there are only two communities between Inuvik and Dawson.

There are also roads that connect the Yukon Territory to Alaska, particularly to Anchorage, Fairbanks, Shagway and Haines. The quickest access to the Yukon is from the last two towns. Skagway is where gold-seekers crossed the mountains to get to Whitehorse and then Dawson.

The two main Yukon routes, the Alaska and Klondike Highways, are paved. Some main roads aren't, but are treated to reduce the amount of dust. Most roads though are neither paved nor treated. Take note that many roads, paved and unpaved, aren't open all year so it's best to get information from the **Yukon Road Report** *(☎403-667-8215)* before heading out on a long journey. Regardless of the type of vehicle, driving on Yukon roads requires that you take precautions and that you conform to a certain etiquette. The comfort and safety of passengers depend on it. These practices are described in more detail in the chapter on the Northwest Territories (see p 612).

Many visitors decide to rent a vehicle once they've arrived, either in Alaska, British Columbia or Alberta. Those who chose to rent in the south have the advantage of choosing a rental agency that allows them to leave the vehicle in Whitehorse. Take note that Canadian residents are not allowed to enter Canada in a vehicle rented in the United States. Some agencies allow you to switch vehicles at the border.

In the Yukon, you can rent a car in Whitehorse, Watson Lake, Dawson and Faro. Other kinds of vehicles can be rented in Whitehorse; particularly vans and recreational vehicles.

These two choices are especially advantageous as they allow visitors to head out on their own for long journeys. Being able to stop wherever and whenever they want, and stay as long as they want, it's probably one of the best ways to really take advantage of the Yukon's wide open spaces. Sites set up for recreational vehicles and tents are offered by the territorial government and some private businesses.

By Bus

Buses are also an option for travellers coming from the south. Comfortable, air-conditioned vehicles can take you from Vancouver or Edmonton to Whitehorse. **Greyhound Lines of Canada** *(2191 Second Avenue, Whitehorse, Y1A 3T8, ☎403-667-2223)*; **Gold City Tours** *(in the summer; P.O. Box 960, Dawson, Y0B 1G0, ☎403-993-5175)*.

By Train

In 1898, a railway connection was established between Skagway and White Pass at the United States border. At White Pass, travellers can take a bus to Whitehorse. Contact **White Pass & Yukon Route Railway** *(P.O. Box 435, Skagway, Alaska, 99840, USA, ☎907-983-2217, or 1-800-343-7373, www.whitepassrailroad.com)* for more information. The train trip is only 45 kilometres long but goes right through the mountains, where the change in elevation is over 850 metres. Whether you take it to get to Whitehorse or just take a return trip, it's an attraction in itself.

By Boat

A ferry links Bellingham, Washington and Prince Rupert, British Columbia to Alaska's main ports. For those who want to bring a vehicle, it's undoubtedly the most pleasant way to get to the Yukon while enjoying the unique coastal scenery. Contact **Alaska Marine Highway** *(P.O. Box 25535, Juneau, Alaska, 99802-5535, USA, ☎907-465-3941 or 1-800-642-0066)* for more information.

The waterways, particularly the Yukon River, have been the main travel routes in the Yukon for over a century. There was even a time when steamships regularly fluttered the waters with their paddle wheels between Dawson and Yellowknife. Today, the Yukon River still takes many passengers between the two cities, some in canoes, some in Zodiaks and others in heavier craft. There are also a number of other rivers in the territory for water-sports enthusiasts, and it's quite easy to rent a boat. You can do so at **Klondike Recreational Rentals** *(P.O. Box 5156, Whitehorse, Y1A 2Z6, ☎403-668-6567 or 1-800-665-4755)*, **Kanoe People** *(P.O. Box 5251, Whitehorse, Y1A 4S3, ☎403-668-4899; they also rent camping equipment and mountain bikes and offer guided excursions and transportation)*, **Prospect Yukon Wilderness & Watercraft Trips** *(P.O. Box 5323, Whitehorse, Y1A 4Z2, ☎403-667-4837)*, **RRR Yukon Trail of '98 Goldrush Tours** *(P.O. Box 5254, Whitehorse, Y1A 4Z1, ☎403-633-4767)* or **Up North Boat & Canoe Rentals** *(P.O. Box 5418, Whitehorse, Y1A 5H4, ☎403-667-7905)*.

 PRACTICAL INFORMATION

Area code: 403

Tourist Information Offices

In the Yukon, there are six establishments called Visitor Reception Centres or VRCs that provide information to tourists. They are open from mid-May to mid-September. All the important general information as well as specific information on the region and particular exhibitions are offered. The centres are in **Whitehorse** *(☎667-2915)*, **Dawson** *(☎993-5566)*, **Watson Lake** *(☎536-7469)*, **Beaver Creek** *(☎862-7321)*, **Carcross** *(☎821-4431)* and **Haines Junction** *(☎634-2345)*.

The end of the century marks the hundred-year anniversary of many significant events in the Yukon, especially the goldrush in 1898. You can find out about the activities taking place throughout the territory from the **Yukon Anniversaries Commission: Bag 1898-1998** *(Whitehorse, Y1A 4K8, ☎668-1998, yukonann@mail.klondyke.com)*.

YUKON

Safety and Emergencies

In an area as scarcely populated as the Yukon, the availability of immediate medical or police services varies greatly depending on where you are. Here are a few: **Dawson** *(☎993-4444 or 993-5555)*, **Haines Junction** *(☎634-4444 or 634-5555)* and **Watson Lake** *(☎536-4444 or 536-5555)*. You can call **Whitehorse** police and health services for free from anywhere in the territory *(☎667-3333 or 667-5555)*.

 EXPLORING

Whitehorse

The capital and administrative centre of the Yukon, the little city of Whitehorse lies on the west side of the Yukon River, right at the foot of the plateau on which the airport is located and over which the Alaska Highway now runs. The city has started to spread over to the east shore of the river, which is spanned by the Robert Campbell Bridge.

Whitehorse was founded because its site is the natural upstream terminus on the Yukon River. Gold prospectors travelling to the Klondike by way of Alaska had a hard time crossing the Whitehorse and Miles Canyon rapids with loaded canoes. The most prudent way to proceed was to reach the shore and then portage the gear. Before long, a small train was shuttling back and forth alongside the rapids. Whitehorse was founded at the upstream end of the line. Once it was directly connected to the Alaskan shore by rail, the town grew quickly. Gold prospectors would stop here before transferring their merchandise onto boats or sleighs, depending on the season. Finally, in 1942, the American government decided to build the Alaska Highway. Whitehorse was clearly marked out to become one of the main bases for the Canadian portion of the construction. In 1953, it replaced Dawson as the capital of the territory.

The **Yukon Visitor Reception** *(Second Avenue and Hanson Street, ☎667-2915)* offers travellers arriving by air all sorts of general information on the entire territory and can answer questions about the capital. It presents a slide show on the national parks and historic sites.

The Yukon is celebrating the first century of its short history. The year 1995 marked the centennial of the arrival of the Royal Canadian Mounted Police; 1997 was the year of transportation and 1998, of course, commemorates the great Gold Rush. The **Anniversaries Coordinator, City of Whitehorse** *(2121 Second Avenue, Y1A 1C2, ☎668-8665)* provides all necessary information on centennial events and attractions.

Right near the bridge over the Yukon River, visitors will find the **S.S. Klondike National Historic Site** *(Room 205-300, Main Street, Y1A 2B5, ☎667-4511 during summer, or 667-3910)*. The *S.S. Klondike*, a steamer built in 1929 to travel up and down the river between Whitehorse and Dawson, sank in 1936. Rebuilt in 1937, it now houses a museum.

The best way by far to tour the city is to go on one of the guided tours offered by the **Yukon Historical & Museums Association** *(Whitehorse Heritage Buildings Walking Tours, June to Aug; Donnenworth House, 3126 Third Avenue, P.O. Box 4357, Y1A 3T5, ☎667-4704)*.

The **Yukon Gardens** *(P.O. Box 5059, Y1A 4S3, ☎668-7972)*, open from April to September, have paths, a miniature farm, a miniature golf course and a shop.

A building constructed room by room, the **McBride Museum** *(First Avenue and Woods Street, ☎667-2709)* is open from mid-May to mid-September and by appointment the rest of the year. Devoted to the history and nature of the Yukon, its collection includes objects from the Gold Rush days, trapping equipment, native artifacts and photographs. A separate collection of stuffed and mounted animals provides a clear idea of the wildlife inhabiting the Yukon. The tour continues outside the log building, where visitors will find vehicles and machines that have been used in the Yukon since whites started settling here, as well as a former telegraph office and a period cabin once owned by one Sam McGee.

The city's history is also visible in its most noteworthy buildings. At the corner of Third Avenue and Elliot Street, for example, the **Old Log Church Museum** *(☎668-2555)* houses a collection of objects related to the ancestral traditions of the native peoples and to the

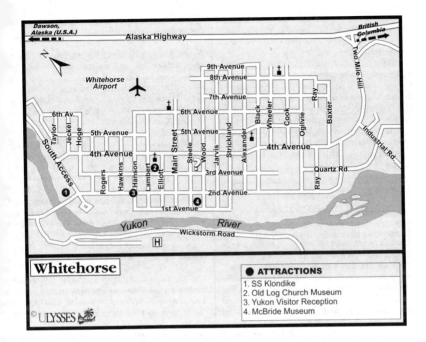

Whitehorse

© ULYSSES

● **ATTRACTIONS**
1. SS Klondike
2. Old Log Church Museum
3. Yukon Visitor Reception
4. McBride Museum

major activities carried out in the territory since Europeans started settling here. Visitors will also learn about a bishop who ate his boots, a tale that inspired a scene in Charlie Chaplin's film *The Gold Rush*.

The headquarters of the territorial government, the resolutely modern **Administration Building** *(Second Avenue)*, is equally interesting. In addition to the local government, the edifice houses a collection of native crafts and works by renowned Canadian artists, all owned by the territory.

The Administration Building isn't the only place in Whitehorse where the art world is represented. Right on Yukon Place, the **Yukon Arts Centre** *(☎667-6352)* is a magnificent building containing the largest art gallery in the territory, as well as a theatre. An outdoor amphitheatre completes the facilities.

At the **Yukon Transportation Museum** *(Km 1473, Alaska Highway, P.O. Box 5867, Y1A 5L6, ☎668-4792)* right near the airport on the Alaska Highway, visitors can discover the importance of the dogsled, relive the golden age of aviation and learn about the roads that opened up the territory.

Next to the Transportation Museum, the **Yukon Beringia Interpretive Centre** *(Km 1473, Alaska Highway, ☎667-5340, www.touryukon.com)* is an archaeology and paleontology museum devoted chiefly to the last ice age, when the Yukon and Alaska were still linked to Asia by a former land bridge called Beringia. The permanent exhibition includes a film, kiosks equipped with computers and the remains of various prehistoric animals, such as the mammoth, the giant bison, the giant beaver (weighing in at 170 kilos!), the giant bear and the sabre-toothed cat. The museum also focusses on the first waves of native peoples to migrate to the Yukon.

Though somewhat tamed by a hydroelectric dam, the waters of the Yukon River, around Miles City and the Whitehorse rapids (upstream from Whitehorse), are still a sight worth seeing. This part of the river flows, for over a kilometre, through a gorge hemmed in by strangely sculpted basalt cliffs. You can drive there, fly over the area in a helicopter *(Trans-North Helicopters, Airport Hangar "C", Y1A 3E4, ☎633-4767)* or take a guided river cruise aboard the *MV Schwatka (P.O. Box 4001, Y1A 3S9, ☎668-4716)*. Lookouts, viewpoints and a footbridge have been laid out

YUKON

for visitors on the shore. Traces of Canyon City, one of the first communities established in the area, are still visible two kilometres from the Whitehorse bridge.

Each year, from late July through August, quinnat (or Chinook) salmon swim up the Whitehorse River, nearing the end of a journey that began in the open seas, over 3,000 kilometres away. A salmon-ladder has been built to enable them to cross the dam and to return to and spawn in the exact spot where they were born. Visitors can watch this epic truggle.

Dawson

On August 16, 1896, two Tagish natives, Skookum Jim and Dawson Charlie, were prospecting in Rabbit Creek with an American friend by the name of George Carmack. Gold had already been found in the Yukon River, and this wasn't the first time the three buddies had tried their luck. What they ended up finding near the **Klondike** River, however, was beyond their wildest dreams. There was gold. Lots of gold. The prospectors renamed "their" creek Bonanza Creek. They staked their claim the next day, August 17, a date that remains in the collective memory of Yukon residents. Over the years, the bed of the Klondike and its tributaries gave forth the present-day equivalent of a billion dollars of yellow metal, making lots of people rich. It also was also the source of the last and perhaps the greatest epics of the West: the great Gold Rush. Gold fever brought tens of thousands of dreamers to the north.

Jos Ladue came up with a completely different way to make his fortune. He decided to found the town of Dawson at the confluence of the Klondike and Yukon Rivers, at the foot of the nearly-900-metre-high **Midnight Dome**. Plots of land were snatched up at astronomical sums. Dawson grew rapidly; over 30,000 people were living here before the end of the century. It was the largest town in North America west of Winnipeg and north of Seattle. The finest cuisine, best wines and most beautiful merchandise were all available here – provided you could pay the price. In those days, everything in Dawson cost a fortune. People often paid their bills with nuggets of gold. In the good-time capital of North America, whiskey flowed like water but order prevailed, as the Royal Canadian Mounted Police sent a

detachment to the town and these police officers alone were allowed to bear arms.

As of 1904, however, the surface deposits were exhausted, and the prospectors had to make room for big companies with the heavy equipment necessary to continue mining the area. The town would have died when these companies left in the 1960s if tourists hadn't started flocking here.

Today, Dawson has nearly a thousand residents in winter and many more in summer. It is a town that lives on tourism and the memory of its golden days. Most of the local attractions are only accessible during the warm weather. The place still has wooden sidewalks, unpaved roads and western façades. In preparation for the centennial of the gold rush, the federal government provided the funds necessary to restore those buildings threatening to collapse and preserve the others.

The first thing to do upon arriving in Dawson is to stop by the **Visitors Reception Centre** *(Front and King Streets, ☎993-5566)*, a reconstruction of a store from the Gold Rush era. It's the perfect introduction to Dawson, where people eat, drink, play and dance the way they did back in 1898. The centre can provide you with all the information you'll need to have a good stay in town and offers guided walking tours up to four times a day during summer.

There are several different ways to explore the town and its surroundings. **Gold City Tours** *(P.O. Box 960, YOB 1GO, ☎993-5175)* offers personalized guided bus tours. The itinerary includes the town itself, the rivers, the gold mines and a trip up the Midnight Dome (the view is splendid in clear weather). Another option is to take a steamship cruise, which includes a meal; contact **Pleasure Island Restaurant & Yukon River Cruise** *(P.O. Box 859, YOB 1GO, ☎993-5482)*.

There are a number of noteworthy buildings in town. On Third Avenue, for example, there are **Harrington's Store** *(at Princess Street)*, which houses a collection of photographs, the **Palace Grand Theatre**, a reconstruction of an earlier building dating from 1899, which visitors can tour with a guide, and the **1901 Post Office**, still in operation today.

The guided tour of **Fort Herchmer** is also worthwhile. This is where the Mounties were jarrisoned. Visitors can see the jail cells, the stables and the officers' and privates' quarters.

A town like this naturally has to have a museum. The **Dawson City Museum & Historical Society** *(5th Avenue, P.O. Box 303, Y0B 1G0, ☎993-5291)* displays objects related to the gold rush and other aspects of local history, as well as prehistoric bones. A good part of the collection is also devoted to Aboriginals of the Han nation. In addition, the museum houses a library, assorted presentations and a shop. Guided tours available.

Dawson is also the town of poet **Robert Service** (1874-1958). Wherever you go in the territory, it seems that there is always someone quoting his work. In Dawson, you can visit his cabin on 8th Avenue, where you can hear public readings of his poems. **Jack London's cabin** has been reconstructed next door (the original was 75 kilometres away). London, an American, became famous for his tales of the far north. *The Call of the Wild* and *White Fang* are among his best-known works.

Of course, anyone who visits Dawson will want to see the Klondike and its two main gold-bearing tributaries, Bonanza and Eldorado Creeks. You can take a road tour of the major sites. At Kilometre 10 of Bonanza Creek Road, visitors can try their luck at **Claim 33** *(P.O. Box 933, Y0B 1G0, ☎993-5804)*. A little farther along, on the same road, **Dredge No.4 Heritage Place** is the best possible illustration of the industrial exploitation that followed the Gold Rush. It is the largest dredge in North America.

Watson Lake

Founded by a trapper who settled here in 1898, Watson Lake is the Canadian gateway to the Yukon. The town lies just north of the British Columbia border. Its major growth period began in 1942, when it became a base camp for the construction of the Alaska Highway. Ever since, it has had all the services necessary for tourists, whether they are on their way to Whitehorse or want to enjoy one of many outdoor activities offered by the hinterland.

The **Alaska Highway Interpretive Centre** *(at the corner of Robert Campbell Street and the Alaska Highway, ☎536-7469)* is Watson Lake's Visitors Reception Centre. It presents a permanent exhibition on the huge challenges involved in laying the highway.

Another interesting attraction commemorates the construction of the Alaska Highway. In 1942, a soldier and member of the construction team, by the name of Carl K. Lindley, was feeling homesick. To help shake off the feeling, he put up a sign showing the direction and distance to Danville, Illinois. Many others followed suit, and today, there are over 30,000 signs in the **Watson Lake Signposts Forest.**

From Dawson to Inuvik

Renting an RV and road-tripping it across the Yukon is the perfect adventure for people who like to drive. You can pick up a camper in Whitehorse then take the **Klondike Highway** to Dawson, where the real journey begins on the **Dempster Highway**, which goes all the way to Inuvik, in the Northwest Territories. The trip is punctuated with panoramas, interpretive centres and native communities. And you can stop and admire the landscape or go on a hike whenever you please. If you take the trip in May or October, there is a good chance that you'll cross paths with some migrating caribou. From Inuvik, you can take a plane to **Herschel Island**, north of the Yukon. Now a territorial park, the island has long been an important stopping place for inhabitants of the far north. Traces of prehistoric native communities and the docks where American whalers used to berth can be found here.

 OUTDOORS

 Parks

The Yukon is abounding with forests, tundra, mountains, glaciers, lakes and rivers, an unspoiled and bountiful wilderness. It is no surprise, therefore, that many people – local residents and visitors alike – enjoy skiing, canoeing, rafting, snowshoeing, mountain-climbing, hiking, horseback riding, fishing, hunting and mountain biking here. Venturing into the wilderness does call for a certain amount of caution, however, as well as the utmost respect for the environment and the need to keep it clean. It is particularly

YUKON

important to bring along enough food and clothing. Carrying a firearm for protection is generally permitted. Hunting and fishing are regulated, though, so make sure that you have the required permits before setting out. To help outdoor enthusiasts take full advantage of all the territory has to offer, the **Wilderness Tourism Association of the Yukon** *(P.O. Box 3960, Whitehorse, Y1A 3M6, ☎1-800-221-3800)* provides pertinent, up-to-date information on all sorts of services.

The federal government has turned the Canadian portion of the St. Elias Mountains into one of the loveliest parks in the country, **Kluane National Park** *(P.O. Box 5495, Haines Junction, Y0B 1L0, ☎634-7201)*, which boasts the highest summit in Canada, Mount Logan, as well as the largest non-polar glaciers in the world. The park headquarters are in Haines Junction, at the local Visitors Reception Centre. Kluane National Park is laced with trails. Visitors can join a group outing or plan their trip themselves; one option is to be dropped off by a helicopter (the Visitors Centre is the best place to make the necessary arrangements). Make sure to bring along a pair of binoculars to observe the wildlife. Before entering Kluane National Park, visitors must register and pay park fees. It is also strongly recommended to make sure that your information is up to date.

Ferocious Predator Alert

In the Yukon, as almost everywhere else in the northern reaches of Canada, the most fearless, vindictive and invincible predator is not a bear, a wolf or a big cat. It's the black fly. At the end of spring and in early summer, this insect is the uncontested master of the north, chomping out little bits of hide from all mammals within reach of its jaws. You can try to protect yourself with long clothing, a hat, mosquito netting and insect repellent containing up to 95% DEET (a chrysanthemum extract that is particularly distasteful to bugs – and not all that appealing to humans either). If you want to go picnicking somewhere and the little monsters have found you, all you can do is tell yourself that you aren't the only one suffering that fate.

 Hiking

The most famous hike in the Yukon starts in Alaska and ends... in British Columbia. The **Chilkoot Trail** follows the route taken by most gold prospectors across the mountains to the inland lakes that empty into the Yukon River. In those days, the prospectors would bring along everything they'd need to survive for a year – some 800 kilos of gear, which they had to carry themselves or find someone else to carry for them. Their goal was to reach **Bennett Lake** by fall and spend the winter there. Come spring, they would follow the lake, then the river to Dawson. Many died because they fell behind schedule, had an accident or were simply unlucky. The trail starts 16 kilometres from Skagway, in Dyea, where hikers have to register. Before setting out, make sure to plan your trip well by contacting **Canadian Heritage, Parks Canada** *(300 Main Street, Room 205, Whitehorse, Y1A 2B5, ☎667-3910)*. The hike takes three to five days, leads through three former tent villages and is punctuated from one end to the other by information panels and vestiges from the Gold Rush. Bear in mind that the climate in the mountains can fluctuate drastically, even in July.

Less ambitious hikers can opt for one of the trails around the territory's major urban centres. Throughout the Yukon, moreover, it is easy to rent a horse or a bike for a short ride or a few days.

The **Yukon Conservation Association** *(302 Hawkins Street, P.O. Box 4163, Y1A 3T3, ☎668-5678)* organizes group hikes during the summer. These outings are a good opportunity to learn more about the local geology and wildlife.

  Canoeing, Kayaking and Rafting

Canoeing down the Yukon between Whitehorse and Dawson is a wonderful 10- to 14-day journey, most of which takes place on a long, quiet river. Some parts of the course are particularly interesting. At the edge of Laberge Lake, a very long canyon frames the river for about fifty kilometres. Vestiges of the Gold Rush remain on every river bank. After the village of Carmacks are the **Five Finger Rapids**, which are easily crossed by canoe. Further along, a trading post, **Fort Selkirk**, awaits canoeists. Still lower is Dawson, your final destination. Visitors should make a point of timing their arrival here with one of the many events held in town during the summer.

Other waterways also have whirlpools, running water and descents in store for fans of rafting, kayaking and even canoeing. Engaging the services of an enterprise specializing in this type of expedition is recommended, as every river holds particular difficulties. The **Alsek River** (class IV) runs through Kluane Park from Haines Junction. Its course offers the possibility of passing alongside the Lowell glacier. The 30-metre-high wall of ice accompanies peddlers for 13 kilometres. Travellers can also go down the **Tatsenshini River** (class III-IV) from Dalton Post, south of Haines Junction. Renowned for its rocky landscapes, the river runs toward British Columbia, where it meets up with the Alsek River. Finally, at the northern tip of the territory, the **Firth River** (class IV) rushes down through the tundra before flowing into the Beaufort Sea. It runs through the heart of **Ivvavik National Park**, a preserve where the Inuit still live according to ancestral ways.

Golf

Whitehorse

Outside of town, the **Mountain-View 18-hole Golf Course** *(Off Range Road, P. O. Box 5883, Y1A 5L6, ☎633-6020)* awaits golfing enthusiasts from May 1st to September 30.

Hunting and Fishing

Hunting and fishing occupy a special place in Yukon culture. Mountain goats, bears, caribou and moose are special trophies for the hunter, much like a good-sized salmon or arctic char can be to a fishing buff. There are dozens of different package deals to suit everyone's tastes and budgets, from de luxe outfitters to a riverside campsite. As a general rule, the best hunting and fishing spots are only accessible by air. Most outfitters provide transportation and invaluable information on lawful hunting and fishing.

Dogsledding

From December to March, visitors are given the unique opportunity of experiencing a dogsled ride. Whitehorse boasts a number of outfitters that can provide you with the necessary training to become true "mushers". You can then embark on a tour, generally lasting one to seven days, with rather rustic shelters along the way.

Adventure Packages

Air North flies travellers all over the Yukon and Alaska aboard its Douglas DC3s or DC4s and Piper Navajos. The crew is professional and friendly. Call ☎1-800-764-0407 free of charge or 668-2228.

Alkan Air Ltd flies to Dawson, Mayo, Inuvik, Old Crow, Faro, Ross River and Watson Lake. Reserving in advance by calling ☎1-800-661-0432 or 668-6616 is essential.

Big Bear Adventures *(Whitehorse ☎663-5642; 7- to 17-day packages offered, prices vary according to the type and length of the expedition; $1,050 to $1,595)* promises real nature lovers well managed excursions with qualified guides. Good-quality meals are provided. Excursions are particularly varied, starting with a cycling trip deep in the country, followed by a canoe or kayak ride along Snake or Yukon River and ending with a climb up the Tombstone Mountains.

Otter Wilderness School *(Whitehorse, ☎393-1212)* will teach you how to safely navigate the rushing rivers, depending on your physical capabilities, needs and desires. Lessons are offered to small groups of 8 to 10 people.

Up North Boat and Canoe Rentals *(May to Sept; Whitehorse, ☎667-7905)* not only rents boats, canoes, kayaks and waterproof travel bags, but also organizes a multitude of outings and expeditions. The enterprise provides transportation by air, sea or land, and offers one- to 19-day excursions, including fishing trips, for one person or more. Some excursions require experience. Prices are affordable compared to offered activities. Calling to find out the exact cost of the expedition you wish

YUKON

to undertake is advised, as the enterprise offers a wide variety of options.

Tatsenshini Expediting *(1062 Alder Street, Whitehorse, Y1A 3W8, ☎633-2742, ⇝633-6184)* is a highly respected adventure outfitter in the Yukon, organizing 11-day inflatable raft expeditions on the legendary waters of the Tatsenshini and Alsek Rivers. This trip is considered the "most beautiful in the world" in terms of scenery. Excursionists will go through magnificent **Kluane National Park** and end their journey in **Dry Bay**, amidst icebergs and glaciers.

Kanoe People Yukon Wilderness Outfitters *(P. O. Box 5152, Whitehorse, Y1A 4S3, ☎668-4899, ⇝668-4891)* is an excellent place from which to rent river and lake canoes and organize your own memorable excursions. Large groups can rent the Voyager Canoe, a 10-metre canoe *($160/day)* that can accommodate 8 to 16 people.

The following enterprises offer non-guided tours:

Wild & Woolly Yukon Survival Course *(P. O. Box 92, Y0A 1B0, ☎390-2682)* will teach you how to orientate yourselves on a topographical map and recognize grizzly, moose, wolf and other animal tracks. You will also learn defence tactics in case of a bear attack. Among the techniques taught here are standard ones (canoeing, recognizing edible and medicinal plants, hiking with a topographical map and compass, maintenance and sharpening of axes, using a knife, etc.), as well as ancestral aboriginal ones (starting a fire by rubbing two pieces of wood together, rope- and basket-making, using stone implements, building rudimentary shelters, etc.). This training will provide you with the means and confidence to tackle the Yukon's wild spaces.

Arctic Trails *(125 Copper Road, Whitehorse, Y1A 2Z7, ☎668-2776)* rents aluminium boats, rubber dinghies, all-terrain vehicles and snowmobiles.

 ## ACCOMMODATIONS

Whitehorse

The **Robert Service Campground** *(☎668-6678 or 668-3721, ⇝667-6334)* is located on the banks of the Yukon River, 3 minutes by car or 20 minutes walking distance from downtown Whitehorse. All 48 campsites are pleasantly wooded and equipped with a picnic table and barbecue grill (the wood is free). A small grocery store and hot showers are also at hand. A good choice.

Wild Treats Vacation Properties *(P. O. Box 9150, 29 Wann Road, Y1A 4A2, ☎633-3322)* is a firm specializing in renting apartments and houses throughout the Yukon. Offering everything from log cabins to vast residences, Wild Treats will help you find whatever you need.

The **Westmark Whitehorse** *($89 to $149; tv, ℜ, P; P. O. Box 4250, Y1A 3T3, ☎668-4700, ⇝668-2789)* is one of the most luxurious hotels in town, with 181 rooms and the biggest convention in the Yukon. A restaurant offering gastronomic cuisine is integrated into the hotel, as is a friendly bar, the Village Spring Lounge.

The **Westmark Klondike Inn** *($89 to $129; tv, ℜ, P; 2288 Second Avenue, ☎668-4747, ⇝667-7639)* comprises approximately one-hundred fully renovated and very comfortable rooms. Guests can also enjoy good American southwest cooking at the hotel's **Arizona Charlie's Restaurant**, smaller dishes in the cafeteria or a drink at the Sternwheeler Lounge.

The **Airport Chalet** *($75 to $100; tv, ℜ, parking; Mile 916 Alaska Highway, right across from the airport, ☎668-2166)* is a hotel providing all family services. Located right near museums, it offers interesting activities and spacious hotel or motel rooms. Prices are reasonable, but it is best to call ahead to inquire about seasonal rates. Full hook-up RV sites are available. The establishment also boasts a family restaurant serving fresh food.

The **Haeckel Hill Bed & Breakfast** *($60 to $85 bkfst incl.; pb, sb, ≈, △; 1501 Birch Street, Porter Creek, 5 min. by car from downtown, ☎633-5625)* is set in a quiet spot with a view of the valley. Guests will enjoy a hearty, home-made breakfast by a cozy fire in the pleasant living room. Suitable for both business people and families. Open year-round.

Located 5 minutes walking distance from downtown, the **Four Seasons Bed & Breakfast** *($65 to $85 brkfst incl.; &; 18 Tagish Road, ☎667-2161)* boasts a family atmosphere and spacious rooms with all amenities. The decor reflects the North of days gone by. Room service is provided within 15 minutes. Videos, music and books are at guests' disposal. The inn also organizes guided tours and customized excursions, according to your needs. Suitable for both families and business people. Open all year round. Prospective guests should keep in mind that the inn only accepts cash and traveller's cheques.

The **High Country Inn** *($70; ®, ☉, tv, &, ℜ, ℙ; 4051 4th Avenue, ☎667-4471)* is said to be "the best thing" in Whitehorse, with 110 rooms affording a view of the magnificent landscape and a friendly staff to greet you. The inn also provides a free shuttle service (or limo on request) from the airport. Moreover, the establishment is easily accessible to the physically handicapped and provides all comforts: pool, sauna, whirlpool baths, exercise room, free coffee in rooms and restaurant (which makes the best pancakes in the North).

Haines Junction

The **Dalton Trail Lodge** *($140 pc, $1,500 to $1,700 for the week-long adventure package; ℜ; ☎667-1099)* is owned by an adventure-tour operator. It is located near beautiful Dezadeash Lake, by superb Kluane National Park. Though situated deep in the country, the lodge offers all possible luxuries, with lovely, fully equipped rooms, a very good Swiss restaurant and a library, allowing guests to relax with a book by the fire while sipping a cocktail. During the day, you can go horseback riding or enjoy a guided tour of the park. Excursions of several days are also offered, with overnight stays in good refuges. This is also a fisher's paradise. Indeed, the lake boasts hundreds of trout weighing in at 20 kilograms; a little farther on, king, coho and sockeye salmon await you. What is more, organizers guarantee a spectacular catch only a helicopter ride away.

Mayo

The **Bedrock Motel** *(ℜ; 2 km east of Mayo, for general information or information about the Mayo Midnight Marathon, call ☎996-2730, or write to the Fly By Night Running Club at P. O. Box 152, Mayo, Y0B 1M0)*. The motel has a restaurant (see p 604).

Alaska Highway (Km 1717)

Located in Kluane National Park, the **Cottonwood Park Campground** *(Km 1717, Alaska Highway, 6 km from Sheep Mountain Visitor's Centre, ☎634-2739)* attracts those who enjoy sports of all kinds, from cyclists, walkers, fishing enthusiasts, hunters of mountain goats and other wild animals (on that note, do not forget your binoculars) to RV-travellers. Rates cover all amenities and attractions, including miniature golf. A family restaurant serves home-made dishes, and a souvenir shop offers a host of gift ideas.

Beaver Creek

The **Westmark Inn Beaver Creek** *($89 to $129; tv, ℜ, ℙ; Mile 1202, Alaska Highway, ☎862-7501, ⊸862-7902)* is a standard roadside hotel of considerable size for these northern regions. In pioneer times, transport cafés such as this one provided both meals and comfort. The Westmark Inn Beaver Creek's atmosphere manages to keep this spirit alive. The establishment boasts 174 very comfortable rooms. Don't miss the "musical dinner" at the Rendez-Vous, where a buffet is served.

Atlin Lake

Louise's Sleepy Hollow Cottage *($55; 4051 4th Avenue, two streets from Atlin Lake, ☎651-7466)* is a small, affordable establishment located in a quiet spot. Excursions are organized here. It is best to call ahead to make inquiries.

The Hitching Post *($85 to $100; Km 38 Atlin Road Mobile 2M5177 White Mountain Channel, ⊸399-4429, mailing address: R. R. 1, Site 20, Comp. 182, Whitehorse, Y1A 4Z6)*. Those who

YUKON

enjoy adventure and wild scenery will find it all at The Hitching Post, on the shores of Atlin Lake. Lovely little wood cabins await you here, as do campsites. Boats and canoes are available to fishing buffs. Horseback riding is also organized. Reservations are strongly advised.

Dawson

The **Dawson Peaks Resort** (*$35 to $80/night according to services, $8 to $14/night for RVs according to your needs; ℜ; Km 1282 Alaska Highway, 14 km from Teslin, ☎390-2310*) is set in a beautiful environment, near Teslin Lake and Morlay Bay. Guests can stay for the day or the week and benefit from amenities ideally suited to a stay in the North. Those who wish to stay here in a tent or RV should call for information about rates and services. The restaurant (see below) serves good food. Dozens of excursions, lasting anywhere from two hours to seven days, are organized: reserve in advance. The establishment will graciously send brochures upon request.

Located in the heart of Dawson, the **Westmark Inn Dawson** (*$99 to $169; tv, ℜ, ℘; P.O. Box 420, ☎993-5542, ⊷993-5623*) has been completely renovated. The 131 rooms are very comfortable and well equipped. Guests can have something to eat and drink in the Keno Lounge or savour the best steaks in town at the Klondike Barbecue (terrace in summer).

Watson Lake

The **Big Home Hotel** (*$69 to $95 according to the size of the room and the season; tv, parking; downtown, ☎536-2020*) is a family-style hotel with lovely, well-decorated rooms. The owners here do their utmost to offer guests the best possible stay at very reasonable prices. Complimentary coffee.

The **Cedar Lodge Motel** (*$70 to $90; K, tv, parking; Mile 633 Alaska Highway, P. O. Box 243, ☎536-7406*) is the only cedar-built hotel in Watson Lake. The establishment was recently renovated and extended. The rooms are most pleasant, and some are equipped with a kitchenette. A shuttle service between the airport or seaplane base and the motel is also available.

 RESTAURANTS

Whitehorse

The restaurant at the **High Country Inn** (*$-$$, 4051 4th Avenue, ☎667-4471*) makes the best pancakes in the North.

Angelo's Restaurant (*$$; 202 Strickland Street, ☎668-6266*) serves high-quality Greek and Italian cuisine. Very friendly staff and interesting choice of dishes.

The restaurant at the **Airport Chalet** (*$$; Mile 916 Alaska Highway, right across from the airport, ☎668-2166*) serves fresh and varied cuisine in a family atmosphere.

Night Club Frantic Follies is a "vaudeville" revue at the **Westmark Whitehorse Hotel** (*☎668-2042*), featuring dinner, music, magic and French cancan dancers.

Dawson

Dawson Peaks Resort (*$-$$; Km 1282 Alaska Highway, 14 km from Teslin, ☎390-2310*). This establishment's restaurant serves good food.

Haines Junction

The Raven (*$$; Oct to Apr; The Raven Haines Junction Hotel, ☎634-2804*) offers gourmets choice dishes. The restaurant was awarded *Where to Eat in Canada*'s "Silver Star".

Mayo

The restaurant of the **Bedrock Motel** (*$; 2 km east of Mayo, ☎996-2730*) has a lovely ambiance and offers a special welcome on the summer solstice, June 20, to those who run the Mayo Midnight Marathon.

ENTERTAINMENT

Whitehorse

Big events mark the passing months in Whitehorse. Setting the town astir in mid-February is the **Yukon Sourdough Rendez-vous**, a winter festival featuring myriad competitions and activities. At this same time of year, visitors can also attend a music festival, an air-balloon festival and the start of a dogsledding race, the **Annual Yukon Quest** *(mid-Feb; Yukon Quest International Association,* ☎668-4711*)*, in which the best teams journey to Fairbanks, Alaska, and vie for approximately $140,000. Another music festival as well as a folk festival are held in April. In May, the town plays host to a major meeting for all quadrille enthusiasts. A storytellers' festival takes place in June, as does a special evening celebrating the longest day of the year. In addition to the activities surrounding Canada Day, a trip down the Yukon River, a period-costume day, golf tournaments, a horse show and an authentic rodeo are held in July. Every August, Discovery Days is commemorated all across the territory, notably with a boat race? between Whitehorse and Dawson. The Laberge Lake aboriginal festivities, offering a multitude of sporting and cultural events, is also a must. In October, francophones take over with the week-long Franco-fête.

Finally, those who still have energy to spare come late evening can enjoy musical revues such as **The Canteen Show** *(103 Main Street,* ☎667-4682*)*, at the Capitol Hotel, and the Westmark Whitehorse's **Frantic Follies Vaudeville Revue** *(at Second Avenue and Wood Street,* ☎668-2042*)*.

Dawson

Dawson also hosts a number of celebrations. In 1998, the **Annual Dawson City Music Festival** *(*☎993-5584*)* celebrates its 20th anniversary under the midnight sun. The festival features Canadian and American performers, who come and organize workshops and concerts, as well as dances, meals and other fun activities. Gold was discovered in the region on August 16, 1896. Every year, the town commemorates this unique event with the **Discovery Days** *(*☎536-7445*)*. The entire population takes part in the parade, the dances, tournaments and other festivities. In September, the **Jack London Festival** *(Klondike Visitors Association,* ☎993-5575*)* honours the memory of this famous author. In 1998, the festival celebrates the 100th anniversary of the day this writer settled on the Klondike.

At night, visitors can choose between the **Palace Grand Revue—Gaslight Follies** *(reservations:* ☎993-6217*)* and an evening at **Diamond Tooth Gertie's Gambling Casino** *(every night from 7pm on)*.

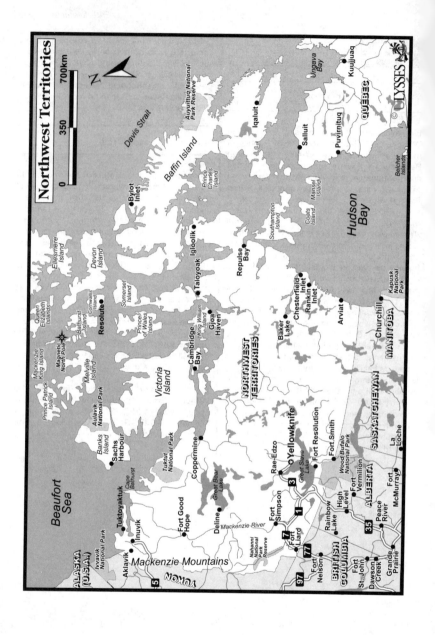

Northwest Territories

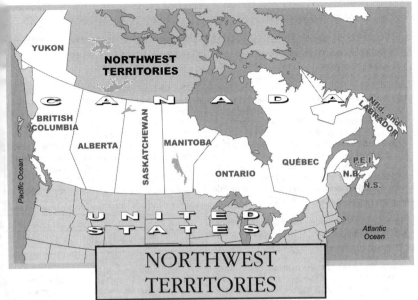

YUKON

NORTHWEST TERRITORIES

CANADA

BRITISH COLUMBIA

ALBERTA

SASKATCHEWAN

MANITOBA

ONTARIO

QUÉBEC

Nfld. and LABRADOR

P.E.I.

N.B.

N.S.

UNITED STATES

Pacific Ocean

Atlantic Ocean

NORTHWEST TERRITORIES

A ll sorts of images come to mind when one thinks of the Canadian North. Once the domain of a few aboriginal communities (mainly Dene and Inuit) struggling to survive in extremely difficult living conditions, the Northwest Territories have attracted many adventurers and missionaries over the years, followed by an entire white population from southern Canada, lured here by government jobs and the rich gold mines near Great Slave Lake.

This enormous territory, over half the size of the United States, is still very sparsely populated, with only 63,000 inhabitants, 18,000 of whom live in Yellowknife, the capital.

Over the past 30 years, living conditions have changed a lot for the indigenous peoples, who make up about 50% of the population. Even the region's most isolated communities have joined the modern world, relegating tepees, igloos and dogsleds to folklore, though aboriginals are still strongly attached to traditional culture, as evidenced by their festivities, their crafts and even their mode of government.

However, the Northwest Territories are also a land of adventure, extremes and challenges. This region has a wealth of attractions to offer anyone who loves outdoor activities and is fascinated by unspoiled wilderness and the ancestral traditions of those who make their

home there. The Northwest Territories boast two of the 10 biggest lakes in the world (Great Bear Lake and Great Slave Lake), whose icy surfaces are traversed by wide roads in winter; the majestic Virginia Falls, which are twice as high as the Niagara Falls; and the impressive 1,800-kilometre-long Mackenzie River, which flows into the Beaufort Sea a few kilometres north of Inuvik. And then there are the glaciers along Ellesmere Island, near the North Pole, which will enthrall shutterbugs in search of spectacular scenery.

Finally, the Northwest Territories are also *the* place for wildlife preservation. There are five national parks here: Auyuittuq National Park, on Baffin Island, in the northwest; Aulavik National Park, also in the northwest; Nahanni National Park in the southwest; Ellesmere Island National Park Reserve; and finally, on the Alberta border, Wood Buffalo National Park, home to the world's largest free-roaming herd of bison.

The many rich and varied attractions of this enormous region and the graciousness of its inhabitants make a visit to the Canadian North a truly unforgettable experience.

Geography

Occupying the northernmost part of the North American continent, between the 60th and the

84th parallels, the Northwest Territories cover 3,376,689 square kilometres – over a third of the area of Canada. They stretch 3,283 kilometres, from the Yukon eastward to Davis Strait, just a few kilometres from Greenland; and 3,404 kilometres from north to south. The Northwest Territories are bounded by the Arctic Ocean to the north; by Baffin Bay, Hudson Bay and Davis Strait to the east, by the provinces of Manitoba, Saskatchewan, Alberta and British Columbia to the south and by the Yukon to the west. The region is made up of a huge continental shelf and myriad islands, commonly known as the Arctic Archipelago, in the middle of which lies the north magnetic pole.

To the east, two thirds of the Canadian Shield are characterized by a hilly, rocky terrain strewn with lakes, while the western edge of the region, along the Yukon, consists of a jagged mountain range with summits about 2,000 metres high. The highest peak, as yet unnamed, rises 2,773 metres into the air. The easternmost islands of the Arctic Archipelago, for their part, are relatively mountainous, with summits ranging in altitude from 1,830 to 2,600 metres (Mount Barbeau, in Ellesmere Island National Park, is 2,616 metres high). These islands are covered with spectacular icecaps. The western islands, on the other hand, are made up of vast plains or a few plateaus and hills. The effects of the successive periods of glaciation are particularly apparent in the soil, which is usually bare or extremely poor, due to permafrost. As far as agriculture is concerned, only the land in the southernmost areas has any potential.

The glacial lakes in the Northwest Territories are too numerous to list. To the west lie two of the 10 largest lakes in the world, Great Bear Lake and Great Slave Lake. The latter was actually named after a native tribe, the Slaveys, who lived on its shores. The name Great Slave Lake is thus a corruption of Great Slavey Lake and has nothing to do with slavery; the people are now known as Slaves. The waters of the two lakes, like those of most other lakes in the west, empty into the great Mackenzie River, which stretches 1,800 kilometres and itself empties into the Beaufort Sea, a part of the Arctic Ocean. In the centre of the region, two major waterways, the Coppermine and Back Rivers, also flow into the Arctic Ocean. To the east, the Thelon River flows into Hudson Bay.

The Flag and Crest of the Northwest Territories

The vertical blue stripes on either side of the flag of the Northwest Territories symbolize the region's lakes and rivers. The white central panel, adorned with a crest, represents the snow and ice. The upper third of the crest shows a white icecap crossed by the blue waves of the Northwest Passage. The green symbolizes the forest; the red, the tree line. Finally, the gold ingots and fox's head represent the region's commercial activities.

Flora and Fauna

The tree line stretches diagonally from the mouth of the Mackenzie River northwest to Hudson Bay, on the Manitoba border. South of this limit, the vegetation is still fairly sparse, due to the rocky soil and the massif in the western part of the Northwest Territories. In fact, only 19% of this land is wooded. The vegetation consists chiefly of firs, birches and larches. North of the tree line, in the Arctic tundra, nothing grows but small, stunted shrubs, lichen and moss.

In the wooded areas, you might very well cross paths with some animals commonly found in the Canadian North – caribou, moose, black bears, the occasional grizzly, wolves, lynxes, beavers, martens, muskrats and wolverines. Wood Buffalo National Park, on the Alberta border, is home to the largest free-roaming herd of bison on earth. It is also the last nesting place for whooping cranes. Other avian species found here include rock ptarmigans, Arctic terns, gyrfalcons and ravens.

The Arctic tundra is home to huge herds of caribou, as well as musk oxen, polar bears and arctic foxes. If you take a cruise on the Arctic Ocean, with a little luck you'll get to see some whales, arguably the most impressive of the sea mammals, as well as seals, walruses, and perhaps the odd narwhal. In the past, large numbers of whales used to come here to breed in the cold, plankton-rich waters of the Arctic, but due to over-hunting there are a great deal fewer now – mostly belugas (small white whales). Fishing is a very popular activity in the Northwest Territories. The lakes are teeming with trout, whitefish (fish with non-oily, white flesh), pike, Arctic char and grayling. Whether you eat them Native-style – dried or fried in fat – or prepared according to more Western recipes, you're sure to appreciate the delicate flesh of these delicious fish.

A Brief History

The Arctic was the last large region in the world to be inhabited by human beings. About 12,000 years ago, toward the end of the last ice age, tribes from northeastern Siberia crossed the Bering Strait to present-day Alaska. They probably did this during winter, when the ice forms a dangerous and unstable bridge between Asia and America. Within several generations, these tribes of Siberian descent, had settled all over the North American Arctic, from Greenland, to the north, to Labrador, to the south. There they developed a unique way of life that enabled them to survive the intense cold. The Inuit didn't arrive for another 3,000 years; they now live mainly in the east part of the Northwest Territories, which will become Nunavut in 1999.

It appears highly probable that between the start of the millennium and the 1350s, European navigators sailed to the Canadian Arctic from Greenland and Iceland. Sir Henry Sinclair, an explorer of Scottish extraction, apparently came to Baffin Island in 1398. Officially, however, Sir Martin Frobisher, an English navigator, is recognized as the first person to explore the region. He landed on Baffin Island in 1577 and claimed it for the Crown of England. Explorers Henry Hudson, John Davis and William Baffin, to name but a few, crisscrossed the Arctic Ocean and Hudson Bay in search of the Northwest Passage, a navigable route between Europe and the Orient. Two French explorers, Médard Chouard dit Des Groseillers, and his brother-in-law, Pierre-Esprit Radisson, who had explored the Lake Superior and James Bay regions, realized that the best furs were found north of Lake Superior. Aware that the fur trade was expanding northwest on land, the two men tried to set up a commercial base on Hudson Bay, the inland sea discovered by Henry Hudson (whose life came to a tragic end when he was cast adrift on those same waters by his mutinous crew). This base would make it possible to sail into the heart of the northern regions where top-quality furs were more abundant. Unable to obtain backing from the French, Radisson and Des Groseillers went to England, where they found a sympathetic

ear at the court of King Charles II. The charter of the Hudson's Bay Company was drawn up in the spring of 1670 and signed by the King on May 2 that same year. The two Frenchmen gained a trade monopoly and permission to colonize all land that drained into Hudson Bay. This huge territory, named Rupert's Land, encompassed northern Québec and Ontario, Manitoba, a part of Saskatchewan and Alberta, as well as part of the Northwest Territories. The Hudson's Bay Company was one of England's most successful colonial enterprises in Canada, playing a major role in commerce. For Europeans, the challenge presented by North America was clear: to scout out the unknown, exploit its resources, develop trade and colonize the untamed wilderness. Tradesmen and explorers took up this challenge with zest, increasing geographical knowledge of this immense territory at lightning speed. Canadian explorer Henry Kelsey, an employee of the Hudson's Bay Company, was the first European to enter the Northwest Territories overland from Hudson Bay, in the early 18th century. The rival North West Company was also involved in the initial exploration of the Northwest Territories. In fact, an American explorer by the name of Peter Pond, who worked for that company, made the first map of the Great Slave Lake region. In 1789, Alexander Mackenzie, also employed by the North West Company, sailed down the huge river that now bears his name to the Arctic Ocean. A few years before, in 1770, Samuel Hearne had left the post at Hudson Bay to sail through the land of the Chipewyans on the Coppermine River and had reached Great Slave Lake.

The search for a northern shipping route linking the east to the west continued into the 19th century. Many explorers searched in vain, but their efforts helped us learn much about the Arctic Archipelago.

At the instigation of Prime Minister John Alexander Macdonald, the Northwest Territories were purchased by the Canadian government and joined Confederation on July 15, 1870. The region's present borders, however, were not defined until 1912. It took six months of negotiations between the Canadian government and the Hudson's Bay Company to reach a buy-back agreement. The Hudson's Bay Company was hoping to get a substantial sum for Rupert's Land, since the United States had paid Russia 7.2 million dollars for Alaska in 1867 without any knowledge of the area's possible resources.

Nevertheless, the agreement turned out to be advantageous to the Canadian government, which only had to pay one and a half million dollars for this vast region and gave a twentieth of the arable land back to the company. The newly acquired Rupert's Land was divided up into the province of Manitoba, the district of Keewatin in 1867, the districts of Franklin and Mackenzie in 1895 and the Yukon Territory in 1898. Part of the remaining land was added to the provinces of Alberta and Saskatchewan.

The Indigenous Peoples

There are eight official languages in the Northwest Territories – English and French, the two official languages of Canada, and six aboriginal languages: Chipewyan, Cree, Dogrib, Gwich'in, Inuktitut and Slave.

Eight aboriginal communities share the vast expanse of the Northwest Territories. The Inuvialuit, who number about 1,600, speak an Inuktitut dialect known as Inuvialuit. In the same region, around Aklavik, there are 1,150 Gwich'in, who speak Dene. Five thousand Métis live in the western part of the Northwest Territories. Of Cree (or Dene) and French Canadian ancestry, these natives played an important role in the fur trade, since they were bilingual. Today, they are represented politically by the Métis Nation of the Northwest Territories. The Dene who live northeast and south of Great Slave Lake, only 2,150 in all, speak Chipewyan. The Deh Cho Dene make their home in the southwestern part of the Northwest Territories, in the Fort Simpson area. Their population numbers about 2,000 and they speak Southern Slave. There are 1,025 Sahtu Dene, a Slave-speaking people who live west of Great Bear Lake, in Fort Good Hope, Norman Wells and Fort Norman. The Rae-Edzo and Rae Lakes area, north of Great Bear Lake, is home to 3,000 Dogrib. Finally, the Inuit, who number 17,500 and occupy the entire eastern part of the Northwest Territories make up the largest community. They speak Inuktitut and Inuvialuktun.

Politics

The Northwest Territories do not have provincial status in the Canadian Confederation. The region is one of the two territories that make up the Canadian North,

Woman in traditional Inuit dress

the other being the Yukon. Though the Northwest Territories have their own parliament, the federal government still exercises a great deal of influence here. The head of the government of the Northwest Territories presides over a seven-member executive cabinet and a Legislative Assembly. The interests of the federal government are represented by a commissioner, who follows the instructions of the Minister of Indian Affairs or the Governor General of Canada. The Legislative Assembly comprises 24 members elected for four-year terms. The political system is not based on negotiation between political parties but rather on decisions made by consensus. The Northwest Territories are represented at the national parliament in Ottawa by a senator designated by the Governor General of Canada, and at the House of Commons by two members elected for five-year terms.

As the result of an agreement with the federal government, reached in 1993, the Northwest Territories will be divided in two on April 1, 1999. For the first time in Canadian history, the Inuit have succeeded in obtaining extensive powers of self-government over a territory of over two million square kilometres, which will be called Nunavut, meaning "our land" in Inuktitut. While this agreement with Ottawa represents a great victory for the Inuit, they still face many challenges, such as unemployment, a very high cost of living, isolation and the population's lack of schooling.

Economics

The economy of the Northwest Territories, once based exclusively on trapping and the fur trade, got a second wind at the start of the 20th century, when a large oil field was discovered in Norman Wells in 1920. During the Second World War, the Americans helped fund the development of this oil field and the transportation of the precious liquid to refineries. In 1930, pitchblende and silver mines were discovered on the east shore of Great Slave Lake, enabling Canada to become one of the world's leading producers of radium and uranium, the main constituents of pitchblende. A few years later, more of the immense riches hidden away in the Territories' subsoil were revealed when extensive gold deposits were found on the north and south shores of Great Slave Lake, in the Yellowknife area. Zinc was also found. The 1970s saw the discovery of major oil and natural gas deposits near Tuktoyaktuk, at the mouth of the Mackenzie River. Finally, the recent discovery of what might be one of the world's largest diamond mines created a sensation and rekindled prospectors' enthusiasm. The subsoil of the Northwest Territories might very well hold even more surprises. Apart from mining resources, the region's economy is based on forestry, tourism and local crafts.

 FINDING YOUR WAY AROUND

Area Code: 403 and 819.

The Northwest Territories extend across four different time zones and are divided into eight tourist regions: **Baffin** in the northeast; **Keewatin** in the southeast, on Hudson Bay; the north central **Arctic coast**; the Yellowknife area, known as the **Northern Frontier**; **Big River**, on the Alberta border; **Nahanni River**, in the southwest; **Sahtu**, in the middle west; and finally the **Western Arctic**.

It is possible to reach the Northwest Territories by land, but due to the huge distances between the capital and the other inhabited areas, local residents usually choose to fly from one community to another.

By Plane

There is no international airport in the Northwest Territories, so you will most likely have to fly through Edmonton, Alberta, to get to the capital, Yellowknife, or through Montréal or Ottawa to reach Iqaluit, the future capital of Nunavut, located on Baffin Island.

Air Canada, through connector airline NWT Air, and Canadian North, a division of Canadian Airlines, both offer regular flights to Yellowknife and Iqaluit. As far as smaller destinations are concerned, thanks to companies like First Air, Air Inuit, Air Nunavut and Skyward Aviation, every community in the North is accessible by air. On the down side, the fares can be prohibitively high. Those wishing to visit several isolated northern communities are therefore advised to discuss their plans with the airlines, which offer more economical ticket options covering a limited number of stops in certain communities. These tickets are still fairly expensive, however. There is no regular air service to some parts of the Northwest Territories, including the Nahanni River region; the only way to get there is by air-taxi. You'll find a number of little air-taxi companies in the major towns of the Northwest Territories; all you have to do is look in the Yellow Pages and shop around for the best fare. Here is a short list: **Adlair Aviation Ltd.** *(Box 2946, Yellowknife, NT, X1A 2R3,* ☎*403-873-5161,* ⇥*403-873-8475)*, **Aero Arctic Helicopters Ltd.** *(Box 1496, Yellowknife, NT, X1A 2P1,* ☎*403-873-5230,* ⇥*403-920-4488)*, **Air Nunavut** *(Box 1239, Iqaluit, NT, X0A 0H0,* ☎*819-979-4018,* ⇥*819-979-4318)*, **Air Tindi Ltd.** *(Box 1693, Yellowknife, NT, X1A 2P3,* ☎*403-920-4177,* ⇥*403-920-2836)*, **Buffalo Airways** *(Box 1479, Hay River, NT, X0E 0R0,* ☎*403-874-3333,* ⇥*403-874-3572)*, **Keewatin Air Ltd.** *(Box 38, Rankin Inlet, NT, X0C 0G0,* ☎*819-645-2992,* ⇥*819-645-2330)*, **Kenn Borek Air** *(Iqaluit, NT, X0A 0H0,* ☎*819-979-0040,* ⇥*819-979-0132)*, **Ptarmigan Airways Ltd.** *(Box 100, Yellowknife, NT, X1A 2N1,* ☎*403-873-4461 or 800-661-0808,* ⇥*403-873-5209)* and **Skyward Aviation** *(Box 562, Rankin Inlet, NT, X0C 0G0,* ☎*819-645-3200,* ⇥*819-645-3208)*.

NORTHWEST TERRITORIES

Distances

From Yellowknife to:	Distance in kilometres
Vancouver (British Columbia)	2,595
Edmonton (Alberta)	1,513
Winnipeg (Manitoba)	2,853
Edzo (Northwest Territories)	104
Enterprise (Northwest Territories)	445
Fort Providence (Northwest Territories)	314
Fort Resolution (Northwest Territories)	628
Fort Simpson (Northwest Territories)	628
Fort Smith (Northwest Territories)	743

By Car

Generally speaking, only small sections of the major roads in the Northwest Territories, near the larger towns, are paved. The remaining parts are dirt and gravel but nonetheless in good condition. In the south, the Mackenzie Highway (Highway 1) leads into the Northwest Territories from the province of Alberta. The Liard Highway (Highway 7) links British Columbia to the Northwest Territories and then connects with the Mackenzie Highway. The latter also intersects with Highway 3, which leads to Yellowknife; Highway 2, which leads to Hay River; Highway 6, which leads to Fort Resolution; and Highway 5, which leads to Fort Smith. In the north, the Dempster Highway (Highway 8) connects the town of Dawson (Yukon) to Inuvik, located at the mouth of the Mackenzie River. Two other highways lead from the Yukon to the Northwest Territories, Canol Road (Highway 9) and Nahanni Range Road (Highway 10), but both end at the border between the two territories, in the Mackenzie Mountains.

Highways 1, 3 and 8 all cross large rivers. During summer, a free ferry service is available to motorists, while in winter the ice on the rivers is so thick that it provides a perfectly safe natural bridge over which to extend the roads. However, during the freezing and thawing periods, there are neither ferries nor ice bridges to get from one shore to the other. These periods generally last about four weeks, so if you're planning to go to the Northwest Territories at the beginning or end of winter, make sure to call the following numbers to see if river crossings are possible:

For roads in the south: ☎1-800-661-0750
For ferry service in the south: ☎1-800-661-0751
For roads and ferry service in the north: ☎1-800-661-0752

A Few Words of Advice about Driving in the North

Though the roads are kept in fairly good condition, it is wise to take a few precautions when embarking on a long car trip.

As the distances between communities can be huge, it is imperative to check how much gas you have before setting out, since you won't find a gas station along the way. Dust clouds, pebbles hitting the car, mud, and rocks obstructing the road are some of the difficulties motorists might encounter on the highways of the North. To minimize the risk of accident, it is important to:

- Make sure that your vehicle is in good condition.
- Bring along a spare tire or two (flats are common), an emergency kit, a snow shovel in winter, a towline, an axe and matches.
- Always drive with your headlights on.
- Put protectors on your lights to prevent them from being damaged by small rocks thrown up by the tires of other cars.
- Slow down when you pass another car to prepare for the dust cloud and flying rocks that this will occasion.
- Drive with your windows and air vents closed to limit the amount of dust inside the car.
- Bring along food and water in case you have to wait for help.
- Bring along some mosquito repellent in the summer and a warm change of clothing, a sleeping bag for each passenger and candles in

the winter. A lit candle can make the interior of the car several degrees warmer without wasting gas.

By Bus

The Greyhound bus company offers service between Edmonton, Alberta, and Yellowknife, with a connection to Enterprise. Though it's a long trip, this is an affordable option for travellers on a tight budget. For more information, call **Greyhound** *(☎403-256-9111)*.

This chapter covers three regions: **From Great Slave Lake to Nahanni National Park ★★★, The Western Arctic ★** and **Nunavut and Baffin Island ★★★**.

 PRACTICAL INFORMATION

The Northwest Territories are so huge that there are different area codes in the eastern and western regions. The area code for the Northwest Territories is 403, while the area code for Keewatin and Baffin Island, located in the future Nunavut, is 819. To avoid confusion, we have included the area code in each phone number.

For information on the various national parks, contact the Canadian Parks Service *(Box 1166, Yellowknife, NT, X1A 2N8)* or the Ministry of Economic Development and Tourism *(Yellowknife, NT, X1A 2L9; ☎403-873-7200 or toll-free 1-800-661-0788, ✈403-873-0294)*.

Taxes

There is no provincial sales tax in the Northwest Territories. Only a 7% federal goods and services tax, known as the GST is added.

Liquor Laws

The minimum drinking age in the territories is 19. In bars, you may be requested to show identification proving that you are of legal age. It should be noted that some communities have decided by plebiscite to curb the alcohol problem by banning all sales and consumption of alcohol within their jurisdiction. In these "dry" communities, it is absolutely forbidden to be in possession of wine, beer or spirits. To find out more about your rights, contact the local branch of the Royal Canadian Mounted Police.

 EXPLORING

From Great Slave Lake to Nahanni National Park ★★★

Yellowknife ★

The capital of the Northwest Territories since 1967, Yellowknife lies in the administrative region of Fort Smith. Located on the shores of Yellowknife Bay, at the mouth of the Yellowknife River, this town of 18,000 was founded on the north shore of Great Slave Lake.

Originally, Yellowknife was simply a small trading post established in 1789 by explorer Samuel Hearne, an employee of the Hudson's Bay Company. Hearne did not call the town Yellowknife because of the gold mines, which weren't discovered until much later, but because an aboriginal tribe that lived on the shores of the lake made knives with copper blades. The tribe was wiped out by a string of epidemics that broke out when white people arrived here, and by a fratricidal war with the Dogrib, who were trying to drive them off their land.

In 1896, miners heading for the Klondike in the Yukon discovered gold in the region. The gold proved very difficult to extract, however, and these veins were never mined. The Northwest Territories didn't attract prospectors again until 1930, when a large deposit of pitchblende was discovered in the Great Bear Lake region. Thanks to the rapid development of aviation, scores of gold miners were able to scour the Yellowknife area, and numerous concessions were granted between 1934 and 1936. Yellowknife thus rose from its ashes, becoming, here on the shores of the bay, the little town now known as the old town. Few prospectors got rich, however, and the veins were about to be exhausted when another, bigger lode was discovered at the end of the Second World War. Though extracting the gold proved very expensive, this mine is still in operation today. Hopes were so high that a new wave of miners arrived in Yellowknife.

Very soon, the little town on the shores of Yellowknife Bay had to expand, and a new, modern town was built on the other side of the hill, a little farther inland. Designated the territorial capital in 1967, the town attracted a large number of bureaucrats from the south. To this day, the territorial government is the region's primary employer, along with the gold mines. In the early 1990s, the miners, hoping to obtain better, safer working conditions, launched a major strike. The management, unwilling to give in to pressure from the workers, resorted to using scabs. Things quickly grew heated between striking and non-striking employees, and management had to post security guards at the mine entrances to protect the workers and the facilities. Nevertheless, frequent altercations broke out, both in the workplace and in the local bars. This violent situation reached its climax on the morning of September 18, 1992, when a bomb exploded in one of the mine galleries, killing nine miners. After a long investigation conducted in a climate of anger and suspicion, the bomber was finally arrested and tried. The conflict was not resolved until 18 months later.

At first glance, Yellowknife looks like a small town made up of a few skyscrapers and some small wooden houses against a huge backdrop of rocks, lakes and twisted trees. The best place to start off a tour of Yellowknife and the surrounding area is the **tourist office** *(Northern Frontier Visitors Centre, near Frame Lake, 4807 49th Street, ☎873-4262)*, where you'll find all the maps and information you need.

The **old town**, located on a peninsula in Yellowknife Bay, looks out at Latham Island. Access is gained by Franklin Avenue (50th Ave.), the main street, which runs all the way through town. The old town marks the site originally chosen by the first gold prospectors to arrive in the region, who built small houses on piles to counter the shifting of the ground during the freezing and thawing periods. A **Bush Pilot's Monument** ★ was erected on the highest rock in town to pay homage to the pilots who opened up the northern route. From atop the rock, you can take in a view of the entire old town, the Nerco-Con gold mine (the white tower with the red roof) and the skyscrapers. You'll notice that outcrops of the block of granite on which the new town was erected are visible all over, lending the town a very distinctive, desert-like atmosphere. To the northwest lies little Jolliffe Island, now a residential area accessible by car during winter, when the bay ices over, but only by boat in the

The Legend of the Sea Goddess

In the Prince of Wale Northern Heritage Centre, visitors can admire a tapestry depicting the legend of the sea goddess. According to this legend, a young girl was thrown out of a canoe into the sea. She tried to hold on to the boat and climb back in, but the other passengers hit her on the fingers with their oars over and over until her fingertips fell into the sea, where they turned into sea creatures. The young girl drowned, thus becoming the goddess of the sea. When fishermen want to make sure that the sea will be calm, they ask the shaman to contact the goddess and placate her by untangling her hair. Braided hair thus symbolizes a calm sea; tangled hair, a stormy one.

summer. Near the island, right in the middle of the bay, a few little houseboats can be seen floating on the calm waters. Although these homes are fairly rustic, at a certain time they were everywhere, due to the exorbitant housing prices in Yellowknife. With no running water and a generator for electricity, houseboats enabled their owners to save on the price of land and on local taxes.

McDonald Drive will take you all the way around the old town. Latham Island, to the northeast, is now accessible by a small bridge at the end of McDonald Drive. It, too, is residential. From the island, you can contemplate the nonstop comings and goings of the little seaplanes that land in the bay, conjuring up images of the famous bush pilots who flew in supplies for local prospecting camps. Back on the peninsula, near the Bush Pilot's Monument, you can stop by the pleasant little **Wildcat Café** (see p 627), set up inside a log house. This modest restaurant has become something of an institution over the years, and local residents often get together here during summer.

The **Prince of Wales Northern Heritage Centre** ★★ *(free admission; Jun to Aug, every day 10:30am to 5:30pm; Sep to May, Mon to Fri 10:30am to 5pm; on Frame Lake; take 50th Street, near the Ingraham Trail, ☎873-7551)* is a major ethnological research centre in this region. A well-detailed exhibition retraces the colonization of the Northwest Territories and explains the Dene and Inuit way of life. Beautiful sculptures and other indigenous crafts

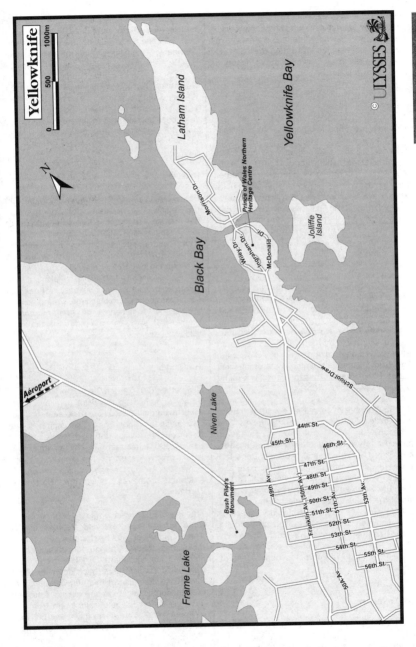

NORTHWEST
TERRITORIES

are displayed here as well. You can also ask to consult the archives, which contain pictures of the first settlers who came to the area, as well as books and manuscripts dating from that era. One room is entirely devoted to the history of aviation in the North.

Dettah

This little town on the other side of Yellowknife Bay is accessible by the Ingraham Trail during summer. Its site was originally occupied by a seasonal Dene fishing camp. Today, it is the year-round home of about a hundred aboriginals, who live in small wooden houses. They have the advantage of living close to Yellowknife, with all its services, while continuing to live on hunting and fishing, just like their ancestors. During winter, you get here by taking the road across the ice.

Rae-Edzo

These two little villages, located on either side of Marian Lake, the extension of the North Arm of Great Slave Lake, make up the largest Dene community in the Northwest Territories. Rae-Edzo is accessible by Highway 3 and lies about a hundred kilometres northwest of Yellowknife. The two villages are linked by a small road about 10 kilometres long, which skirts round Marian Lake.

In 1852, explorer John Rae set up a trading post called Fort Rae for the Hudson's Bay Company. In 1904, the trading post was moved a few kilometres to the site of present-day Rae. Over the years, the local Dene left their isolated camps to settle in Rae-Edzo and send their children to the local school. To this day, the Dene embrace the traditional way of life of their ancestors, surviving on hunting and fishing. The women still embroider pieces of cloth and hide. These local crafts may be found in the handful of stores in Rae-Edzo. The parvis of the Rae church will catch your attention, since it is made up of poles reminiscent of tepee frames.

Lac La Martre

Lac La Martre is a Dogrib community located about 250 kilometres northwest of Yellowknife, on the shores of the lake of the same name. In summer, it is only accessible by plane, but in winter you can take the ice road

that heads up to Rae Lakes. The site was chosen for a trading post in 1793 by the North West Company, a rival of the Hudson's Bay Company. Today, it is home to a picturesque cluster of little wooden houses. Like the majority of natives in small communities in the Northwest Territories, the local residents live on trapping, hunting and fishing. For a few years now, however, more and more tourists have been coming here to admire the landscape and the waterfalls and to fish in the well-stocked waters of Lac La Martre.

Rae Lakes

Rae Lakes is the northernmost community in this region. Very isolated, this Dogrib village has managed to preserve its traditional way of life. A single small motel, which also serves as a store and a restaurant, makes it possible for visitors to stay here long enough for an excursion in the area or a weekend of fishing. Rae Lakes is only accessible by plane during summer, though native residents of Rae-Edzo sometimes come here by canoe. During winter, the ice road that serves as a continuation of Highway 3 stops at the edge of the little village.

Fort Smith

Nicknamed the "Garden City of the North", Fort Smith is located on the 60th parallel, on the Alberta border, 269 kilometres southeast of Hay River by Highway 5. The capital of the Northwest Territories until 1967, this town of over 2,500 inhabitants is still an important administrative centre for the region. It is also home to Arctic College, which welcomes students from all over the Northwest Territories.

The Slave River was originally a vital canoe route for the explorers and trappers of the North. However, its extremely dangerous rapids, impassable by canoe, forced paddlers to stop and portage about 25 kilometres before they could take the river back down to Great Slave Lake. Because of this unavoidable stop, the Hudson's Bay Company set up a trading post called Fort Fitzgerald upstream from the rapids in 1872. Two years later, another fort, called Fort Smith, was built downstream from the rapids. Today, the rapids are a nesting place for white pelicans.

Though most tourists come to Fort Smith to visit **Wood Buffalo National Park** ★ (see p 622), home of the largest free-roaming herd of bison in the world and the last remaining nesting place of the endangered whooping crane, the town has other attractions as well. Start off your tour of Fort Smith at the **Tourism Information Bureau** *(Jun to Sep, every day 10am to 10pm; Portage Road)*, which distributes maps of Wood Buffalo National Park and provides information on the excursions and wildlife interpretation programs organized in the park in July and August.

In 1941, there were only 21 whooping cranes left in the world. Today, thanks to continuous efforts to preserve the species from extinction, at least 130 have been counted. Each year, these birds come to Wood Buffalo National Park to lay their eggs. Although whooping cranes lay two eggs, they only raise one chick. Over the past few years, a joint American and Canadian program has been devoted to gathering the abandoned eggs and hatching them in incubators. These chicks are raised in captivity then set free once they are fully grown.

The **Northern Life Museum and National Exhibition Centre** *(Jun to Sep, Mon to Fri 9am to 5pm, Sat and Sun 1pm to 5pm; 110 King Street; ☎872-2859)* houses a collection of objects made during the fur-trading era and gathered together by missionaries. The museum also explains the history and lifestyle of the local aboriginals, displays Inuit sculptures, dog sleds and harnesses, and presents an exhibition on bison.

If you walk downriver on Marine Drive, you'll find a lookout where you can observe the white pelicans frolicking about in the choppy waters of the Slave River through a telescope.

The **Monument to the Slave River Rapids** was erected in memory of the daring 19th-century explorers who travelled down the Slave River to open up the route to the Arctic.

Fort Fitzgerald, the first trading post established by the Hudson's Bay Company upriver from the rapids, lies 25 kilometres from Fort Smith. The old fort, once bustling with activity, is now abandoned, and all that

remains are the vestiges of a former mission and a few houses.

Lutselk'e (Snowdrift)

In 1925, the Hudson's Bay Company set up a fur trading post on the west arm of Great Slave Lake. The area Chipewyan soon settled around the trading post, forming a small village, which is only accessible by plane during summer. In Athabascan, Chipewyan means "pointed skin", a reference to their habit of leaving the tails on the pelts they used for their clothing. The area is popular with fishermen, since this part of Great Slave Lake, known as Christie Bay, is teeming with fish. In fact, it is one of the best places in the North for trout fishing. The steep cliffs that plunge into the deep, clear waters of the bay make for a wild and striking landscape.

Fort Resolution

Fort Resolution is a small Chipewyan village about 155 kilometres east of Hay River, on Highway 6. Located on the south shore of Great Slave Lake, near the mouth of the Slave River, it is one of the oldest communities in the Northwest Territories. The trading post was originally set up at the mouth of the river by the Hudson's Bay Company in 1786, then was moved to the present site of Fort Resolution in 1821. Its Chipewyan and Métis inhabitants live the same way their ancestors did, hunting and trapping animals in the Slave River delta.

Pine Point

In 1951, the Pine Point Mines company started extracting lead and zinc ore from an open-pit mine here. A small town was built to house the 2,000 people involved in the project. In 1965, a railway line reached Pine Point, and the mining company was able to increase its operations, thus attracting more miners and their families. The little town grew and built itself a hospital and a school. Unfortunately, a drop in world zinc and lead prices forced Pine Point Mines to shut down the mine. However, one of the clauses of the mining concession that had been granted to the company required the management of the mine to leave the area in its original state once all mining activities had been terminated. As a result, the town, devoted entirely to mining, was abandoned, and its buildings were taken down and reconstructed in other communities in the

Northwest Territories. Today, all that remains of Pine Point are heaps of refuse from the mine and a few vestiges of a ghost town.

Hay River

Hay River is the largest town in the Big River administrative region. Located on the south shore of Great Slave Lake, it is accessible by Highway 2 and by airplane; there are regular flights from Yellowknife and Edmonton.

Recent archeological excavations have turned up ancient vestiges indicating that the site of the Hay River was occupied by the Slavey, a nomadic people belonging to the Dene family, thousands of years ago. Though the community started appearing on maps officially in 1854, it wasn't until 1868 that the Hudson's Bay Company established a trading post on the east bank of the mouth of the Hay River. A few years later, a small mission was set up here to convert the local aboriginals to Christianity. The community gradually expanded, and a school and a small port were constructed. Starting in 1939, the northern route leading through Hay River supplanted the one that ran along the Slave River and passed through Fort Smith, thus increasing Hay River's commercial activities. The opening of the Pine Point mine and the construction of a railway line accelerated the town's development. Today, Hay River has a population of some 3,200 and is a hub for river transportation. Barges carrying supplies for other communities in the Northwest Territories set out regularly from its port. The town has a modern appearance now, complete with a few skyscrapers. The **Tourist Information Centre** *(Jul and Aug 9am to 9pm; Capital Crescent, near the post office, by the river, ☎874-3180)* has maps and books on the region.

West Channel Village was built on the west shore of Vale Island, at the mouth of the Hay River. The little community was founded when commercial fishing began on Great Slave Lake. Before long, fisheries had become the town's main employer. Today, West Channel Village is the commercial fishing headquarters on Great Slave Lake, which supplies North America with whitefish, known for its white, non-oily flesh. At the end of West Channel Road, there is a beach that is very popular with local residents on weekends.

From atop the **Mackenzie Place Apartment Building**, a 17-story tower in the middle of the

downtown area, you can take in a pretty view of West Channel Village, the surrounding boreal forest and Great Slave Lake.

The **Hay River Native Reserve** is located on the opposite shore. The native community settled on the town's former site in the 1800s. Here, you can see the old buildings of the Hudson's Bay Company's trading post and the first church built in the days of the missionaries.

Enterprise

This tiny town, located about 30 kilometres south of Hay River, is important only in that it lies at the junction of Highways 1 and 2. There is an Esso station here, and you should fill up your tank and get something to eat before continuing northward. The gas station also has a small tourist information centre.

Fort Providence

This small Slave community lies on the road to Yellowknife, just past the ferry that shuttles back and forth across the Mackenzie River in summer. To get to Fort Providence from Enterprise, take the Mackenzie Highway (1) for 85 kilometres, then turn right onto Highway 3. After 24 kilometres, you'll come to the ferry (which does not operate when the ice is forming or breaking up). Call the company (see p 612) to see if the ferry is running.

The **Mackenzie Bison Sanctuary ★**, near Fort Providence, is worth a visit (see p 622).

Fort Simpson

Located on the Mackenzie Highway, at the confluence of the Mackenzie and Liard Rivers, this little town of 1,000, originally named Fort of the Forks, was built in 1804. It was renamed in 1821 after George Simpson, the first governor of the North West and Hudson's Bay Companies, and soon became a large fur trading post. Also, its strategic location on two of the major waterways of the western Northwest Territories made it a hub for the transportation of pelts and supplies. In the 1960s, Fort Simpson became a base camp for oil prospectors working in the Mackenzie River valley. Today, these commercial activities have ceased altogether, and the little town is first and foremost the perfect place from which to explore the surrounding area, and one of the main gateways to Nahanni National Park.

The Western Arctic ★

One of the most scenic highways in the Canadian North that runs through this part of the Northwest Territories. Driving up the Dempster Highway, which starts in the Yukon and leads to the Mackenzie River delta, is a veritable feast for the eyes. Winding through mountains and then through the desert-like tundra, this road will take you across the Arctic Circle to Inuvik, the main town in the Western Arctic region.

Fort McPherson

The first town you will reach, about 75 kilometres from the Yukon border, is Fort McPherson, perched on the banks of the Peel River, between the mountains and the coastal plain that stretches out into the Arctic Ocean. For many years, the Gwich'in who lived here trading with the tribes living on the coast of British Columbia and the Inuit of the Arctic Ocean. When Alexander Mackenzie met them in 1789, this Gwich'in tribe already had iron spears and harpoon heads, as well as goods from Alaska. In the 1900s, Fort McPherson became an important base for the Royal Canadian Mounted Police. A monument to four Mounties who went to Dawson in 1910 and died on their way back stands by the Peel River.

Each summer, the community hosts a small music festival, which attracts a sizable crowd.

The little tourist information stand can provide you with information on boat rides on the Mackenzie River, as well as fishing trips.

Inuvik

Two hundred kilometres north of the Arctic Circle, at the end of the Dempster Highway, lies an amazing little town with a population of about 3,000. This modern little community was designed in 1954 to replace the little town of Aklavik, located on the west arm of the Mackenzie River delta and believed to be sinking into the water. Inuvik thus became the first community north of the Arctic Circle to be equipped with all the sanitation facilities of a modern town. This was no easy task, due to the permafrost. Visitors will find little houses built on piles and amazing overhead metal conduits, which are used to carry drinking water and liquid waste, linking homes, businesses and public buildings. During the 1970s, the town enjoyed an economic boom, thanks to the prospectors looking for oil and natural gas in the Mackenzie delta. Though oil fever has subsided somewhat and local residents now lead a peaceful existence, Inuvik is still the hub of the Arctic region.

Inuvik isn't a big place, so it won't take you long to see the town. You can start off your tour at the **tourist information office** *(every day during summer 9am to 8pm, Mackenzie Road, opposite the Mackenzie Hotel, ☎403-979-2678)*.

The best-known building in Inuvik is definitely the igloo-shaped **Church of Our Lady of Victory** *(Mackenzie Road, near the tourist information office)*. Inquire at the presbytery if you'd like to see the interior, adorned with remarkable religious scenes painted by Mona Trasher, an Inuit artist renowned in the Northwest Territories.

The **Inuvik Research Centre** *(Mon to Fri 9am to 5pm, Mackenzie Road)*, in front of the tourist information office, can provide you with information on all scientific research being carried out in the Arctic region.

For a lovely view of the Mackenzie delta, go to the top of the **Chuck Park observation tower** *(Mackenzie Road)*, south of town, toward the airport. In the same direction, you'll also find an amazing 18-hole golf course, **Lunar Links**; of course, at this latitude, there is no green! Maps of the course are available at the tourist information office.

Tuktoyaktuk

Home of the Karngmalit Inuit, Tuktoyaktuk (often shortened to "Tuk") is located in a sandpit on the shores of the Beaufort Sea. Inuvialuit traditions are still very much alive here. One of the most distinctive features of the Tuk peninsula is its small hills of ice, up to 45 metres high, known locally as *pingos*. These conical promontories, which can grow 1.5 metres in a year, generally develop in places where the permafrost is several hundred metres thick. There are no fewer than 1,400 *pingos* on the peninsula, the highest of which, **Ibyuk**, is

Church of Our Lady of Victory in Inuvik

visible from Tuktoyaktuk. There you can visit a house made of earth and grass, the Inuvialuit version of the igloo. However, the region's major tourist attractions are the low altitude flight over the peninsula, which offers a chance to take in some gorgeous views of the Mackenzie delta, and cruises that take passengers out to see the belugas and other whales swimming about peacefully offshore. For fare information, contact the **Western Arctic Tourism Association** *(Dept. EG, Box 2600, Inuvik, NT, XOE OTO, ☎403-979-4321, or toll-free ☎1-800-661-0788; ☛403-979-2434).*

Sachs Harbour

The town of Sachs Harbour, the northernmost community on this tour, is located on Banks Island. This region remained uninhabited for a very long time; it was the quest for the Northwest Passage that eventually brought an expedition here in 1918. Today, Sachs Harbour is the gateway to **Aulavik National Park ★** (see p 623).

Nunavut and Baffin Island ★★★

With an area of 507,500 square kilometres, Baffin Island is the sixth largest island in the world after Australia, Greenland, New Guinea, Borneo and Madagascar. Located on the Arctic Circle, it is a land of tundra, jagged mountains (it is sometimes referred to as "little Switzerland") glaciers and ice caps. There are many reasons to visit Baffin and Ellesmere Islands. Few places in the world offer such opportunities to gaze upon magnificent, completely untouched landscapes and embark on unforgettable adventures like those awaiting visitors to the northernmost part of Canada. To explore **Auyuittuq National Park**, on Baffin Island, or **Ellesmere National Park** is to encounter nature in its most elementary state. However, these sorts of expeditions require lots of planning, and visitors who venture into the harsh, virgin territory of the Arctic parks will have no one to count on but themselves, carrying on their back everything they'll need to cope with the sometimes abrupt changes in climate. However, those who prepare carefully and stay in top shape physically will take home some indelible memories.

Iqaluit

The future capital of Nunavut, Iqaluit is the main population centre on Baffin Island and the administrative hub for the Arctic regions. Formerly known as Frobisher Bay after Sir Martin Frobisher, a sailor who came to this region in 1576 while looking for the Northwest

Passage, it was renamed Iqaluit in 1987. During the 18th and 19th centuries, the town served as a base camp for whalers, but it wasn't until the second half of the 20th century that it became the administrative centre of the eastern Arctic. Now home to about 2,000 people, mostly Inuit, Iqaluit is preparing to face the challenges presented by its future role as the capital of the territory of Nunavut. It is also the gateway to the Arctic for anyone wishing to explore the little communities on Baffin Island.

Iqaluit is not a very big place. You can start off your tour with a stop at the **Unikkaarik tourist information office** *(Mon to Fri 10am to noon and 1pm to 7pm, Sat and Sun noon to 7pm, in the southeast part of town, on the bay; ☎819-979-4636)*, where you'll find maps of the area and a list of outfitters that offer fishing expeditions in Frobisher Bay, whose waters are teeming with fish. You can also see an audiovisual presentation on local attractions and the lifestyle in the 14 communities on Baffin Island. The **Nunatta Sunagutangit Museum** *(right next to the tourist information office)*, set up inside a restored house built by Hudson's Bay Company, displays a collection of artifacts from the oldest settlements in the region. On the other side of town, near the airport, you'll find warehouses containing Inuit sculptures from various parts of the Arctic. Unless you are lucky enough to meet one of these artists in person in the course of your travels, this is one of the best places to find magnificent serpentine and soapstone sculptures, many of which come from Cape Dorset, the cradle of new Inuit art in the 1950s, at lower prices than in southern Canada.

Twelve kilometres west of Iqaluit, there is a little island accessible only by boat, an island that was inhabited by the Thule, an Inuit people from Alaska, for a thousand years. This island is now home to the **Quammaarviit Historic Park**. Archaeological excavations have uncovered a large number of tools and bones dating back 2,600 years. As these digs have been completed, visitors can now stroll along little trails between houses made essentially of clumps of grass, the Thule equivalent of the igloo; hearths that were in the middle of the tents that once stood here, and tombs.

Pangnirtung

A small community of about 1,000 Inuit, Pangnirtung is of interest only because of its location, at the entrance of **Auyuittuq National Park ★★★** (see p 623). Perched on the shore of a magnificent fiord, this little village is built around the landing strip used by the airplanes that bring in supplies and the few hikers who come to the park. Originally, the camp was established as a base for the whalers who crisscrossed the Arctic waters of this region. When whaling started to lose speed, the Hudson's Bay Company decided to set up a fur-trading post here. You'll find maps of the area and information on the excursions that set out from Pangnirtung at the **Angmarlik tourist information office** *(every day during summer 9am to 9pm; ☎819-473-8737)*. For a **magnificent view** stretching all the way to the entrance of Auyuittuq National Park, take the seven-kilometre hiking trail from the Pisuktinu Tungavit campground, east of the village, to the top of **Mount Duval** (670 m). You'll have to exert yourself, but the panorama is ample compensation.

Resolute

Tiny Resolute's sole claim to fame, so to speak, is that it is the starting point for all expeditions in the northern Arctic, so your visit here is likely to be a quick one.

OUTDOORS

Parks

The Northwest Territories are a veritable paradise for anyone who loves nature, fresh air and vast stretches of virgin soil. Numerous wilderness parks have been established here to protect various species of plants and animals. Those who know how to appreciate a landscape shaped by the extreme conditions of a harsh climate will find some extraordinary opportunities for adventure here.

Topping the list of spectacular spots are three national parks, whose beauty could astonish even the most blasé globetrotter: Nahanni National Park, on the Yukon border; Auyuittuq National Park, on Baffin Island's Cumberland Peninsula, and finally, in the northeasternmost part of the Territories, Ellesmere Island National Park. In addition to these three major national parks, the Northwest Territories boast a number of wildlife preserves, which are home to many protected species.

From Great Slave Lake to Nahanni National Park ★

Highway 3, which leads to Yellowknife, runs alongside the **Mackenzie Bison Sanctuary ★**, located on the west shore of Great Slave Lake, for about 50 kilometres. Originally, Wood Buffalo National Park was to be the home of the last herd of northern Canadian wood buffalo, but a number of plains buffalo were also brought here, and the two species interbred. As a result, the "purebred" wood buffalo was on its way to extinction. In an effort to preserve the species, 18 wood buffalo were sent to this 10,000 square-kilometre sanctuary on the shores of Great Slave Lake in 1963. Since then, the little herd has grown considerably, numbering over 2,000 today.

Wood Buffalo National Park ★★ is accessible from the communities of Fort Chipewyan, Alberta, and Fort Smith, Northwest Territories. Fort Chipewyan can be reached by plane from Fort McMurray twice a day, Sunday through Friday; in summer motorboats travel the Athabasca and Embarras Rivers; there is a winter road open from December to March between Fort McMurray and Fort Chipewyan but this is not recommended, and finally for the really adventurous, it is possible to enter the park by canoe on the Peace and Athabasca Rivers.

The park is home to the largest, free-roaming, self-regulating herd of bison in the world; it is also the only remaining nesting ground of the whooping crane. These two facts contributed to Wood Buffalo being designated a World Heritage Site. The park was initially established to protect the last remaining herd of wood bison in northern Canada. But when plains bison were shipped to the park between 1925 and 1928, because plains in Buffalo National Park in Wainwright, Alberta, were overgrazed, the plains bison interbred with the wood bison causing the extinction of pure wood bison. Or so they thought. A herd was discovered in Elk Island National Park (see p 508), and part of it was shipped to Mackenzie Bison Sanctuary in the Northwest Territories. As a result, there are actually no pure wood buffalo in Wood Buffalo National Park.

Those who make the effort will enjoy hiking (most trails are in the vicinity of Fort Smith) excellent canoeing and camping and the chance to experience Canada's northern wilderness in the country's largest national park. Advanced planning is essential to a successful trip to this huge wilderness area and a Park Use Permit is required for all overnight stays in the park. Also remember to bring lots of insect repellent. For more information contact the park *(Box 750, Fort Smith, NWT, XOE OPO, ☎403-872-7900, or Fort Chipewyan 697-3662, ☎403-697-3560)*.

Nahanni National Park ★★★ *(Nahanni Ram Tourism Association, Dept. EG, Box 177, Fort Simpson, NT, XOE ONO, ☎403-695-3182 or 1-800-661-0788)* is probably the most beautiful park in the Northwest Territories. However, because there are no roads leading there, few people visit it. If you want to be among them, you'll have to go to the little town of Fort Simpson and rent an air-taxi, which will drop you off in the heart of the park, or take a boat. Designated a World Heritage Site by UNESCO, Nahanni National Park offers outdoor enthusiasts and adventurers some awe-inspiring landscapes. Experienced canoeists can paddle down the spectacular southern section of the Nahanni, the loveliest undammed river in Canada.. Others can go hiking along deep valleys, try whitewater rafting or admire **Virginia Falls ★★**, twice as high as Niagara Falls, as well as some magnificent still lakes. Nahanni National Park used to be called "Rivers of Myth and Mountains of Mystery". It is true that little was known about this region for a long time. The hostile wilderness, combined with the accounts of the missionaries and trappers who first scouted out the region, gave rise to numerous legends, as indicated by the uninviting names of some of the valleys – Deadmen Valley, Hell's Gate, Devils Kitchen and Death Canyon. If you aren't an adventurous soul but would still like to admire this unspoiled natural setting, you can enjoy a bird's-eye view of it aboard an air-taxi.

The 40-kilometre **Ingraham Trail** winds along the shores of several lakes (Prosperous, Madeline, Pontoon, Prelude, Hidden and Reid) east of Yellowknife. The most well laid out spot is the Prelude Lake park, which has a number of poorly marked trails and a hastily cleared picnic and camping area. Detailed maps of the Ingraham Trail are available at the tourist information office in Yellowknife. The wildlife is abundant, and it is not uncommon to see

Inukshuk

bald eagles, ospreys, grey jays, loons, bears and, in winter, caribou.

The Western Arctic

Aulavik National Park ★ (on Banks Island) is one of the best places in this part of the Territories for wildlife observation. It offers visitors the unique prospect of exploring an arctic region untouched by man. Canoeists can paddle on the peaceful waters of the Thomson River, the northernmost river in Canada that is suitable for canoeing. The abundance of arctic foxes, polar bears, wolves and musk oxen made Banks Island a favourite haunt of the Thule, who hunted here for centuries. However, it wasn't until the late 1920s that a few families became sedentary and settled in Sachs Harbour. The island is still considered one of the best places for trapping in the Arctic and is popular with photographers. In the spring, Inuvialuit guides organize dogsledding excursions for hunting and photographing polar bears and musk oxen. During summer, visitors can observe the migratory birds that stay in the park. For more information, contact the **Western Arctic Tourism Association** *(Dept. EG, Box 2600. Inuvik, NT, XOE OTO, ☎403-979-4321 or toll-free 1-800-661-0788, ▯403-979-2434).*

Nunavut and Baffin Island

Auyuittuq National Park ★★★, on Baffin Island's Cumberland Peninsula, protects the northern Davis region. The amazing arctic landscape features the Pangnirtung Pass; the Penny Icecap, which covers a large part of the park; hanging valleys, glaciers and moraines. It was the Penny Icecap that inspired the name "Auyuittuq", which means "the land of eternal ice". Visitors should bear in mind that exploring the park is no easy task. Occasionally, you'll have to cross icy torrents, since only a few primitive bridges made of cables or logs span the most dangerous streams. Getting around this harshly beautiful, virgin land, whose jagged peaks, like Mounts Thor, Asgard and Overlord, delight seasoned mountain climbers in search of extreme conditions, is not within everyone's reach, and visitors must take careful precautions, as the risk of hypothermia is great and no help is on hand. No infrastructure has been set up in the park, aside from a few shacks, which were built in case of emergency and are located a good day's walk apart. There is a single radio station, which unfortunately does not always come in. Visitors have to carry all the equipment and supplies they will need for their expedition on their backs. Anyone planning on coming to the park is required to register at the **Canada Parks office** in **Pangnirtung** *(☎819-473-8828)* or **Broughton Island** *(☎819-927-8834)* beforehand. Upon registration, you'll have to provide your itinerary and say how many days you plan to spend in the park. You are also required to check in at the end of your expedition. Maps of the park may be purchased at these offices for $10. The Overlord guard post marks the entrance to the park. Despite its name, you won't find a living soul there. It is located at the far end of the Pangnirtung fiord. Most people are brought there by boat or by snowmobile, depending on the season. You will find a list of experienced people who can take you at the park offices. The boat ride only takes about an hour and a half but costs a fortune – usually at least $300 dollars. You can always try to bargain, but make sure you're dealing with one of the guides on the list, since you'll have to make arrangements for him to pick you up on the appointed day. If the boat ride doesn't appeal to you, you can walk to the park entrance, located 32 kilometres from the village of Pangnirtung; unfortunately, this will cut your stay in the park short a few days. Little has been done to make Auyuittuq Park more accessible to visitors. The Inukshuk have marked a trail to Pangnirtung Pass. This trail leads to some of the best stream crossings, steers clear of quicksand and helps prevent hikers from damaging the tundra. Though the land looks bare and desert-like due to the unforgiving arctic climate, during the brief summer season small clusters of pastel-coloured flowers grow amidst the rocks, somehow managing to withstand the wind, cold temperatures and lack of precipitation, and lending the moraines a fragile beauty. This makes the land seem both formidable and delicate. For more information, you can write to the director of **Auyuittuq National Park** *(Auyuittuq National Park, Pangnirtung, NT, XOA ORO, ☎819-473-8828)*.

Kekertin Historic Park is accessible by boat or by snowmobile from Pangnirtung; inquire at the Angmarlik tourist information centre. Located on a small island south of Pangnirtung, this park was a whaling camp for nearly a century. Partially restored, it now has an interpretive site that examines the whalers' lifestyle and working conditions.

Ellesmere Island National Park ★★, which covers an area of 37,775 square kilometres, is literally located on top of the world, at the northern tip of Ellesmere Island. The advice we gave about preparing for an expedition in Auyuittuq National Park applies here as well. This magical place boasts spectacular glaciers and magnificent mountains, which plunge straight into the Arctic Ocean; among them is one of the highest summits in Canada, **Mount Barbeau** (2,639 metres). Most people start off their expedition at **Lake Hazen**, located right in the middle of the park. This area attracts many species of migratory birds during the brief arctic summer. Other animals commonly found here include foxes, white-furred arctic hare, musk oxen and wolves. With less than 10 centimetres of precipitation per year, this

desert-like region is one of the driest on earth. The park's main entrance is at the end of the Greely Fiord, at **Tanquary Fiord**. To get there you have to take a small plane from Resolute. Unfortunately, the exorbitant fare (over $2,000) is likely to discourage many people. For further information on the park, write to **Canada Parks** *(Ellesmere Island National Park, P.O. Box 353, Pangnirtung, NT, XOA ORO, ☎819-473-8828)*.

 ## Hiking

Hiking is obviously one of the best activities to enjoy in the parks of the Northwest Territories. The most magnificent settings are Nahanni, Auyuittuq and Ellesmere Island National Parks, but the 40-kilometre Ingraham Trail, near Yellowknife, can be a wonderful option as well.

 ## Whale-watching

The abundant plankton in the arctic waters makes this one of the best places in the world to observe certain species of whales, notably the beluga, and the narwhal near Pangnirtung. A number of naturalist guides offer sea excursions. Two good outfits to try are:

Arctic Tour Company Box 2021 E7, Inuvik, NT, XOE OTO, ☎403-979-4100, ⇰403-979-2259.

Alivaktuk Outfitting Box 3, Pangnirtung, NT, XOA ORO, ☎/⇰819-473-8721.

  ## Canoeing and River Rafting

There is no shortage of lakes and rivers in this part of Canada, but the Nahanni is without question one of the most magnificent rivers. A number of organizations specializing in outdoor adventures offer excursions on the Nahanni. The prices depend on the itinerary and the length of the trip. It's a good idea to shop around.

Adventure Canada 14 Front Street South, Misissauga, ON, L5H 2C4, ☎905-271-4000 or 1-800-363-7566, ⇰905-271-5595.

Arctic Tour Company Box 2021 E7, Inuvik, NT, XOE OTO, ☎403-979-4100, ⇰403-979-2259.

Boreal Woods and Waters Box 685 Fort Smith, NT, X0E 0P0, ☎403-872-2467, ⁓872-2126.

Nahanni River Adventures Box 4869 EX, Whitehorse, YT, Y1A 4N6, ☎403-668-3180 or 1-800-287-6827, ⁓403-668-3056.

 Fishing

The lakes and rivers of the Northwest Territories are teeming with all sorts of fish, notably the famous Arctic char, and fishing buffs can try their luck. Before setting out, make sure to inquire about the necessary fishing permits.

Arctic Safaris Box 1294-X, ,Yellowknife, NT, X1A 2N9, ☎403-873-3212, ⁓403-873-9008.

Blachford Lake Lodge Box 1568, Yellowknife, NT, X1A 2P2, ☎403-873-3303, ⁓403-920-4013.

Enodah Wilderness Travel Ltd. Box 2382, Yellowknife, NT, X1A 2P8, ☎/⁓403-873-4334.

Alivaktuk Outfitting Box 3, Pangnirtung, NT,X0A 0R0, ☎/⁓819-473-8721.

 Snowmobiling and Dogsledding

Ever dreamed of traveling across a snow-covered land with a team of dogs at your command? The Inuit still do sometimes, though most prefer the speedier snowmobile. Nowadays, visitors can enjoy this type of excursion all over the Northwest Territories.

Anderson River Nature's Best Box 240, Tuktoyaktuk, NT, X0E 1C0, ☎/⁓403-977-2415.

Great Slave Sledging Company Ltd. Moraine Point Lodge, Box 2882, Yellowknife, NT, X1A 2R2, ☎403-920-4542, ⁓403-873-4790.

Mackenzie Delta Sled Dog Tours Box 1252, Inuvik, NT, X0E 0T0, ☎403-979-3253, ⁓403-979-2434.

Alivaktuk Outfitting Box 3, Pangnirtung, NT, X0A 0R0, ☎/⁓819-473-8721.

 ACCOMMODATIONS

From Great Slave Lake to Nahanni National Park

Yellowknife

The **Blue Raven Bed and Breakfast** *($60 single, $75 double; Latham Island, 37B Otto Drive, X1A 2T9, ☎403-873-6328)*, run by Tessa Macintosh, is a big blue and white house located in the old town, atop a hill looking out onto Great Slave Lake. It has three spacious rooms, each with a lovely view of the water. Guests also enjoy access to a large terrace overlooking the lake and a pleasant common room with a fireplace. Non-smoking environment.

It would be hard to find a more dreary decor than that of the rooms at the **Igloo Inn** *($95; 42 rooms, tv, ℜ; Franklin Avenue, toward Latham Island, Box 596 X1A 2N4, ☎403-873-8511, ⁓403-873-5547)*. This motel can be noisy at times, but the rooms are clean.

The **Discovery Inn** *($100; 41 renovated rooms, tv, ℜ; on Franklin Avenue, near the Arctic Art Gallery, Box 784, X1A 2N6, ☎403-873-4151, ⁓403-920-7948)* is as modest as the Igloo Inn but has the advantage of being located closer to downtown. Some rooms have a kitchenette.

The **Yellowknife Inn** *($130; 131 rooms, tv, ℜ, bar; 5010 49th Street, Box 490, at the corner of Franklin Avenue, X1A 2N4, ☎403-873-2601 or 1-800-661-0580, ⁓403-873-2602)* is the biggest hotel in town. Its pleasant little restaurant, the Lounge Café, makes it very popular with the local civil servants, who come here for lunch. In addition to free access to a fitness centre, the hotel offers its guests a complimentary shuttle service to the airport.

The **Explorer Hotel** *($140; 128 rooms, tv, ℜ, bar, ≡; near the tourist information office, 48th Street, toward the airport, Postal Service 7000, X1A 2R3, ☎403-873-3531 or 1-800-661-0892, ⁓403-873-2789)* is definitely the most attractive hotel in Yellowknife. Its rooms are bright and spacious, with fully equipped bathrooms, as well as fax and modem jacks for business travellers. The hotel also boasts one of the finest restaurants in town and offers a complimentary shuttle service to and from the airport. Finally, there is a small souvenir shop on the ground floor.

Rae Lakes

The **Gameti Motel** *($120; 8 rooms, tv; General Delivery, NT, XOE 1RO, ☎403-997-3004, ⋯403-997-3099)*, located in town, on the northeast shore of the lake, offers modest rooms. The staff can also arrange a fishing trip for you.

Fort Smith

The only thing going for the **Pinecrest Hotel** *($60; 24 rooms, tv; 163 McDougal Road, Box 127, NT, XOE OPO, ☎403-872-2320)* is that it offers the cheapest accommodations in Fort Smith.

At the **Kana'kes Aurora Chalet** *($60; 2 rooms; Box 21, NT, XOE OPO, ☎403-872-5245, ⋯403-872-5214)*, Michael Salvisberg organizes dogsledding excursions during wintertime. No smoking is permitted at this fully equipped inn.

If you're looking for more comfortable lodgings, head to the **Pelican Rapids Inn** *($100; 50 rooms, tv, ℜ; downtown, 152 McDougal Road, Box 52, NT, XOE OPO, ☎403-872-2789, ⋯403-872-4727)*. Reservations recommended.

Snowdrift (Lutsel K'e)

The **Snowdrift Co-op Hotel** *($120; 3 rooms, K, tv, sb; General Delivery, Lutsel K'e, NT, XOE 1AO, ☎403-370-3511, ⋯403-370-3000)* is the only hotel in this tiny community.

Hay River

The **Migrator Hotel** *($75; tv, K; 912 Mackenzie Highway, NT, XOE OR8, ☎403-874-6792, ⋯403-874-6704)* has motel-style rooms, each with a kitchenette.

The **Caribou Motor Inn** *($75; 29 rooms; tv, K, ℜ, ◠; 912 Mackenzie Highway, NT, XOE OR8, ☎403-874-6706, ⋯403-874-6704)*, right next-door, is the same type of place as the Migrator.

For better accommodations, head to the **Ptarmigan Inn Hotel** *($110; 42 rooms; tv, pb, ℜ; 10 Gagnier Street, NT, XOE 1G1, ☎403-874-6591 or 1-800-661-0842,* ⋯403-874-3392)*, next to the tourist information office. A small souvenir shop, a hairdresser's and a bank are all located near by.

Fort Providence

The **Snowshoe Inn** *($80; 35 rooms, tv, K, café; on the waterfront, Box 1000, NT, XOE OLO, ☎403-699-4300)* has impersonal motel-style rooms.

Fort Simpson

The range of accommodations in Fort Simpson could hardly be called extensive; the local establishments offer basic rooms in the purest motel style. It doesn't make much difference whether you opt for the **Maroda Motel** *($110; 15 rooms; tv, K; Box 67, NT, XOE ONO, ☎403-695-2602, ⋯ 403-695-2273)* or the **Nahanni Inn** *($120; 35 rooms; tv, K, microwave, ℜ; Box 248, NT, XOE ONO, ☎403-695-2201, ⋯403-695-3000)*.

The Western Arctic

Fort McPherson

The **Tetlit Cooperative-Inns North** *($110; 9 rooms; tv; Box 27, NT; XOE 0J0, ☎403-952-2417, ⋯403-952-2602)* is the only motel in town. You'll also find a gas station there.

Inuvik

Though its rooms are impersonal, the **Eskimo Inn** *($115; 74 rooms, tv, ℜ, café; 133 Mackenzie Road, Box 1740, NT, XOE OTO, ☎403-979-2801, ⋯403-979-3234)* has the advantage of being located in town.

The most attractive rooms are at the **Mackenzie Hotel** *($120; 33 rooms, tv, ℜ, bar and café; 185 Mackenzie Road, Box 1618, NT, XOE OTO, ☎403-979-2861, ☎403-979-3317)*.

Tuktoyaktuk

The **Pingo Park Lodge Ltd.** *($130; 25 rooms, tv; 95-TDC, Box 290, NT, XOE 1C0, ☎403-977-2155, ⋯403-977-2416)* only has motel-style rooms. You'll also find a car-rental counter there.

Sachs Harbour

There are no hotels in this little native community, so you'll have to stay at **Wolkie's Bed and Breakfast** *($180 per person, fb; 3 rooms; General Delivery, NT, XOE OZO, ☎403-690-3451)*, which is open year-round. Owner Lena Wolkie will be glad to organize guided cultural and nature tours of the area for you.

Nunavut and Baffin Island

Iqaluit

The least expensive hotel in town, where the rates are nonetheless exorbitant for what you get, is the **Bayshore Inn** *($100; 21 rooms; Box 1240, NT, XOA OHO, ☎819-979-4210)*. The **Frobisher Inn** *($140; 50 renovated rooms, tv, ℜ, café; Box 610, NT, XOA OHO, ☎819-979-2222, ⊷819-979-0427)*, a bit more expensive, offers a shuttle to the airport and has a fairly good restaurant. Guests can use the fax at the front desk. Finally, the **Discovery Lodge Hotel** *($150; 52 rooms, tv, cable, radio, telephone, laundry facilities, ℜ; Box 387, NT, XOA OHO, ☎819-979-4433, ⊷819-979-6591)* also provides shuttle service to the airport.

Pangnirtung

Aside from the free campground at the edge of town, toward Auyuittuq National Park, there is only one place to stay in Pangnirtung, the **Auyuittuq Lodge** *($130; 25 rooms; restaurant with set price menu; NT, XOA ORO, ☎819-473-8955, ⊷819-473-8611)*. The rooms are very rustic, and you'll have to go down to the common room if you want to watch television. Still, after a long hike in the park, this place seems very inviting, if only because it offers the prospect of a shower and a hot meal (albeit a mediocre one). Reservations recommended during summer.

Resolute

The **International Explorers' Home** *($120 fb; 6 rooms; Box 200, NT, XOA OVO, ☎819-252-3875)* and **Narwhal Arctic Services**

($165; 48 rooms, tv, airport shuttle; NT, XOA OVO, ☎819-252-3968, ⊷819-252-3960) are the only two places to stay in town.

RESTAURANTS

From Great Slave Lake to Nahanni National Park

Yellowknife

The least expensive and most inviting place for a simple, frugal meal is definitely the **Wildcat Café** *($; in the old town, on Latham Island, 3904 Wiley Road)*. This little café, set up inside a small log house, is a favourite with local residents. It only has a few tables, and guests sit on wooden benches. Reservations are not accepted, so you have to get there early or wait outside. In the latter case, you can take the opportunity to climb up to the Bush Pilot's Monument and admire the view of the town, the lake and the little seaplanes that land near by. The café is only open during summer.

If you're looking for a family-style restaurant, try **Sam's Monkey Tree** *($; 483 Range Lake Road, ☎403-920-4914)*. The decor is a little surreal for the setting, but the food is simple and perfectly acceptable.

Our Place *($$; on the ground floor of the Franklin Avenue shopping centre, ☎403-920-2265)* is a good restaurant with a surprisingly varied menu that includes both French and Chinese dishes. The decor, in shades of pink, is unattractive, but the service is excellent and the food, tasty.

On Sunday, local residents like to get together at the **Explorer Hotel** *($$$; 47th Street, ☎403-873-3531)*, which serves a terrific brunch. The dining room, graced with picture windows, is very pleasant and the food is some of the best in town. Arctic char is one of the specialties of the house. Courteous, attentive service.

Fort Smith

The **Old Skillet** *($; in the Pinecrest Hotel, ☎403-872-3161)* is the restaurant most often recommended by local residents. You'll find delicious cakes at the **J-Bell Bakery** *(at the corner of McDougal Road and Portage Avenue)*.

Hay River

The Keys *(downtown, in the Ptarmigan Inn Hotel,* ☎*403-874-6871)* is the local favourite, while the **Board Room** *(near the Migrator Hotel, toward Vale Island,* ☎*403-874-2111)* serves reasonably priced Chinese food.

The Western Arctic

Inuvik

In this region, where prices quickly shoot through the roof, the least expensive place in town is **To Go's** *($; 69 Mackenzie Road,* ☎*403-979-3030)*, where you can sample a Northern specialty, namely the caribou or musk ox burger. Pizza also appears on the menu. The **Green Briar Dining Room** *($; in the Mackenzie Hotel, 185 Mackenzie Road,* ☎*403-979-3536)* serves dishes typical of the Canadian North. Here, too, caribou gets top billing.

Nunavut and Baffin Island

Iqaluit

Every hotel in town has a restaurant. The one in the **Navigator Inn** *($$; opposite the Discovery Lodge,* ☎*819-979-6201)* serves pizza on certain evenings. Arctic char and caribou appear on all the menus. The **Kamotiq Inn** *($$;* ☎*819-979-5937)* is the only place in town that serves Mexican food. It also has a buffet.

Pangnirtung

The only place to eat in this little village, aside from the little snack bar near the airport, is the **Auyuittuq Lodge** *($$$;* ☎*819-473-8955)*, which has a frugal, set-price menu. After days of eating camping food, a meal in a warm place can be very enjoyable.

 SHOPPING

In every community in the Canadian North, residents will try to sell you all sorts of figurines carved out of caribou antlers, whale bones or stone, or crafts made of hide or birch bark. Most of the time, you'll find items such as these on sale at the local tourist information office. In the larger communities, however, the art galleries that purchase these objects from the most renowned artists, many of whom live in remote communities, sell beautiful pieces. Like everything else in the Canadian North, they are often very expensive – but still reasonable in comparison to similar pieces sold in specialized galleries in Montréal, Toronto and Vancouver. Therefore, if you are enchanted by these splendid Inuit sculptures, don't hesitate to buy one; it will be a good investment. Aside from sculptures, you'll find leather gloves, mocassins and *mukluk*s (boots) elegantly adorned with beads. Other commonly found native crafts include birch bark boxes decorated with porcupine quills.

From Great Slave Lake to Nahanni National Park

Yellowknife

The **Arctic Art Gallery** *(Franklin Avenue, at 48th Street)* is the largest art gallery in Yellowknife. All the biggest artists in the Northwest Territories exhibit their work here. You'll find magnificent sculptures in all different price ranges, as well as engravings and paintings, including some by Mona Trasher, the Inuit artist who painted the interior of Inuvik's igloo-like church. Another, smaller art gallery is located near by, to the east, on 48th Street. It, too, has some beautiful sculptures. At the **tourist information office**, you can purchase leather goods or one of those famous birch bark boxes.

Nunavut and Baffin Island

Iqaluit

Right next to the airport, you'll see a few sculpture warehouses. The most beautiful pieces come from Pangnirtung and Cape Dorset. It is worth taking the time to browse through these places, as there are some wonderful finds to be made.

INDEX

INDEX

INDEX

INDEX

INDEX

INDEX

INDEX

INDEX

INDEX

INDEX

INDEX

ORDER FORM

■ ULYSSES TRAVEL GUIDES

☐ Affordable B&Bs in Québec $12.95 CAN
$9.95 US
☐ Atlantic Canada .... $24.95 CAN
$17.95 US
☐ Beaches of Maine ...... $12.95 CAN
$9.95 US
☐ Bahamas .... $24.95 CAN
$17.95 US
☐ Calgary .... $17.95 CAN
$12.95 US
☐ Canada .... $29.95 CAN
$21.95 US
☐ Chicago .... $19.95 CAN
$14.95 US
☐ Chile .... $27.95 CAN
$17.95 US
☐ Costa Rica .... $27.95 CAN
$19.95 US
☐ Cuba .... $24.95 CAN
$17.95 US
☐ Dominican Republic ..... $24.95 CAN
$17.95 US
☐ Ecuador Galapagos Islands $24.95 CAN
$17.95 US
☐ El Salvador .... $22.95 CAN
$14.95 US
☐ Guadeloupe .... $24.95 CAN
$17.95 US
☐ Guatemala .... $24.95 CAN
$17.95 US
☐ Honduras .... $24.95 CAN
$17.95 US
☐ Jamaica .... $24.95 CAN
$17.95 US
☐ Lisbon .... $18.95 CAN
$13.95 US
☐ Louisiana .... $29.95 CAN
$21.95 US
☐ Martinique .... $24.95 CAN
$17.95 US
☐ Montréal .... $19.95 CAN
$14.95 US
☐ New Orleans .... $17.95 CAN
$12.95 US
☐ New York City .... $19.95 CAN
$14.95 US

☐ Nicaragua .... $24.95 CAN
$16.95 US
☐ Ontario .... $24.95 CAN
$14.95US
☐ Ottawa .... $17.95 CAN
$12.95 US
☐ Panamá .... $24.95 CAN
$16.95 US
☐ Portugal .... $24.95 CAN
$16.95 US
☐ Provence - Côte d'Azur .. $29.95 CAN
$21.95US
☐ Québec .... $29.95 CAN
$21.95 US
☐ Québec and Ontario
with Via .... $9.95 CAN
$7.95 US
☐ Toronto .... $18.95 CAN
$13.95 US
☐ Vancouver .... $17.95 CAN
$12.95 US
☐ Washington D.C. ...... $18.95 CAN
$13.95 US
☐ Western Canada .... $29.95 CAN
$21.95 US

■ ULYSSES DUE SOUTH

☐ Acapulco .... $14.95 CAN
$9.95 US
☐ Belize .... $16.95 CAN
$12.95 US
☐ Cartagena (Colombia) ... $12.95 CAN
$9.95 US
☐ Cancun Cozumel .... $17.95 CAN
$12.95 US
☐ Puerto Vallarta .... $14.95 CAN
$9.95 US
☐ St. Martin and St. Barts .. $16.95 CAN
$12.95 US

■ ULYSSES TRAVEL JOURNAL

☐ Ulysses Travel Journal
(Blue, Red, Green,
Yellow, Sextant) . . . . $9.95 CAN
$7.95 US

■ ULYSSES GREEN ESCAPES

☐ Cycling in France . . . . . . $22.95 CAN
$16.95 US
☐ Hiking in the
Northeastern U.S. . . . . . . $19.95 CAN
$13.95 US
☐ Hiking in Québec . . . . . . $19.95 CAN
$13.95 US

QUANTITY	TITLES	PRICE	TOTAL

NAME:_____

ADDRESS:_____

_____

_____

Payment: ☐ Money Order ☐ Visa ☐ MasterCard

Card Number:_____Exp.:_____

Signature:_____

Sub-total	
Postage &	$8.00*
Sub-total	
G.S.T.in Canada	
TOTAL	

ULYSSES TRAVEL PUBLICATIONS
4176 St-Denis,
Montréal, Québec, H2W 2M5
(514) 843-9447 fax (514) 843-9448
www.ulysse.ca
*$15 for overseas orders

U.S. ORDERS: **GLOBE PEQUOT PRESS**
P.O. Box 833, 6 Business Park Road,
Old Saybrook, CT 06475-0833
1-800-243-0495 fax 1-800-820-2329
www.globe-pequot.com